MY THEATRE LIFE

D1379427

AUGUST BOURNONVILLE
A French lithograph after a portrait by
Edvard Lehmann from the early 1850's.
Teatermuseet, Copenhagen.

August Bournonville
MY THEATRE LIFE

Translated from the Danish
by
Patricia N. McAndrew

Foreword
by
Erik Bruhn

Introduction
by
Svend Kragh-Jacobsen

WESLEYAN UNIVERSITY PRESS
Middletown, Connecticut

FERNALD LIBRARY
COLBY-SAWYER COLLEGE
NEW LONDON, N.H. 03257

GV
1785
B64
A3313

P. Johnson 33.75 3/80

Copyright © 1979 by Wesleyan University

Library of Congress Cataloging in Publication Data

Bournonville, Auguste, 1805–1879.
    My theatre life.
    Translation of Mit theaterliv.
    Includes index.
    1. Bournonville, Auguste, 1805–1879.
2. Choreographers — Denmark — Biography.
3. Kongelige Teater og kapel. I. Title.
GV1785.B64A3313   792.8′092′4 [B] 78-27349
ISBN 0-8195-5035-3

78474

Book design by Jorgen G. Hansen
Manufactured in the United States of America

This rendering of *My Theatre Life*
is lovingly dedicated to her parents
Dr. F. J. McAndrew
and
Helen Borneman McAndrew
by the translator

CONTENTS

Foreword by Erik Bruhn   xi

Introduction by Svend Kragh-Jacobsen   xiii

Translator's Note   xvii

Acknowledgments   xix

VOLUME ONE

Preface   3

I.   The Dance   7

II.   Pantomime   12

III.   The Ballet   18

IV.   Myself   24

V.   Celebrities   35

VI.   Parallels   50

VII.   The Results of My Endeavors   59

VIII.   Ballet Compositions   66

IX.   Lyric Attempts   119

VOLUME TWO
Theatre Life and Reminiscences

Introduction   131

I.   Reflections   133

II.   The Year 1848   160

III.	Old Memories (With Notices of the Finest Members of the Ballet from 1829 to 1864)	167
IV.	Divertissements	172
V.	Ballet Compositions: Second Period	181
VI.	Danish National Festivals	235
VII.	Ballet Compositions: Third Period	264
VIII.	Three Years in Stockholm	287
IX.	Dramatic Celebrities of the Danish Stage	320
X.	A Retrospect	334

VOLUME THREE
PART I. *The Theatre Crisis and the Ballet*

	Introduction	341
I.	The Theatre Crisis	344
II.	Works Done for the Royal Danish Theatre by A.B.	407

PART II. *Memoirs and Period Pictures*

	Introduction	413
I.	Memoirs and Period Pictures	415
II.	Danish National Festivals (The Constitution Festival, 1854)	496
III.	End-Word	503

PART III. *Travel Memoirs, Reflections, and Biographical Sketches*

I.	Travel Memoirs	507
II.	Reflections	630
III.	Biographical Sketches Drawn from Memory	638
	Index	675

ILLUSTRATIONS

August Bournonville	Frontispiece
The Child Actor; The Young Man	Facing p. 34
Adolphe Nourrit; Jenny Lind	35
Paul and Virginia; Faust	70
Valdemar, "Torch Dance," costume for Astrid; *La Sylphide*, costume for James	71
Bournonville's Audience and Stage	88
The Spring of Kirsten Piil; *Napoli*, scene design, Act II	89
The Husband; The Wife	132
The Family	133
Juliette Price; Augusta Nielsen	174
Bournonville's Nordic Graces; *La Ventana*	175
Fanny Elssler; Carlotta Pochini	234
Bertel Thorvaldsen; Thorvaldsen's Arrival in Copenhagen	235
The Fair on Behalf of Distressed Jutlanders	256
The Homecoming; The Banquet for Danish Seamen	257
A Folk Tale; Far from Denmark	274
Pepita; Dolores Serral and Mariano Camprubí	275
Nicolai Peter Nielsen; Anna Nielsen	330
Johanne Luise Heiberg	331
Interior of the New Royal Theatre; *From Siberia to Moscow*	398
The Old Balletmaster with Young Students	399

Le Foyer de la Danse   Facing p. 476

Paul and Marie Taglioni   477

Augusta Bournonville   550

The Old Balletmaster (1865)   551

Lucile Grahn as the Sylphide; as Giselle   570

Marius Petipa   571

Antoine Bournonville   656

Hans Christian Andersen; Adam Oehlenschläger   657

Bournonville's Men of Music   672

The Villa Bournonville   673

FOREWORD
by
Erik Bruhn

REREADING Bournonville's memoirs, now for the first time in an English translation, I cannot help wondering what would happen if this great master of the ballet and the dance were living today. I wonder if he would have fulfilled his genius on the same international level as, say, George Balanchine, whose works are known in so many countries. Does man's fulfillment of himself depend solely on exposure to the particular time and environment within which he was born?

Certainly Bournonville fulfilled himself in Denmark. But the goal of any artist, whether he likes to admit it or not, is to reach all people. Some do not achieve this in their own time. To the artist in the living theatre, however, it is essential that he achieve it then. With the techniques presently available we can preserve theatrical events for the future. It is doubtful, though, whether we would spend the time and money to record something that did not appeal to us at the moment. The worth of the stage artist must be recognized in his lifetime.

Bournonville's ballets were preserved by the only method known in his time—they were passed on from one generation to the next. We also know that they sometimes passed through the eyes and minds of lesser talents. We still have his synopses, scripts, and notes for all the ballets in the current repertory, as well as for many we have not performed in decades. We do not, however, have detailed records of much of his actual choreography. We still have dancers who swear they remember what they learned in their early youth, yet any two of them may argue at length as to who did a step more exactly or conceived a role more correctly.

Bournonville himself went through a mass of dancers in his time. Surely lesser talents never stopped him from creating and being constructive. Through his talent and instinct, he was quick to measure a dancer's ability and therefore his limitations. Though steps and roles were interpreted by dancers, it was he who controlled body and soul as long as the idea was his. It is his idea that must live.

Today Bournonville's works have traveled widely, much against the long-time policy of our Royal Danish Ballet. Perhaps we wronged him by considering him private property—the last thing any great creative artist could wish. Bournonville's genius does not belong to Denmark alone. He is his country's pride and a national institution. Yet often we fail him when reproducing his ballets. Perhaps we take his work too much for granted. We have a passion for him, but it is not always burning.

Denmark inherited Bournonville and we have many historians with sufficient knowledge of English who could have translated his memoirs. It may seem odd that a foreigner should have given herself the immense challenge of bringing Bournonville to life for the English-speaking world. Yet I am sure he would have been pleased to know how it came about.

Young and bright, Patricia McAndrew from Bethlehem, Pennsylvania, with some ballet background of her own, saw the Royal Danish Ballet during its 1965 tour of the United States. Several Bournonville ballets were included in the repertory. Aroused and excited, her curiosity to find out more about Bournonville was frustrated by the limited material available in English. She proceeded to study the Danish language, eventually receiving a Fulbright-Hays grant to pursue her studies in Copenhagen. To master the reading of Danish is no small task, but Miss McAndrew's burning passion for the subject must have helped her during times when others would have given up. Now her passion and understanding bring Bournonville's own words to life in this translation.

The more she discovered about him as a person—with all his conflicts, doubts, contradictions, hopes, sometimes failures (whether of the stage or real life)—the more her relation to a man of the past became a happening of the present. Her intense studies took her, not only to the libraries and museums, but to all those places where Bournonville had lived and worked. She listened to and talked with Danish writers, historians, and ballet critics.

Perhaps her most lively experience has been her acquaintance with the staff of the old Court Theatre, now a museum, where Bournonville often worked and where some of his creative ideas have stayed right through to our day. It is there also that most of his theatrical belongings can be found, as well as most of his ballet manuscripts. After her daily hours of study, I am sure it was within these walls of the Court Theatre that Miss McAndrew must have felt Bournonville most alive and real.

It is this personal—and I may call it living—relationship with the past that makes her English translation so authentic for us. I feel sure that Miss McAndrew's work will bring, not only to the dance world but to the general reader, the knowledge and acquaintance of a man whose creative force and genius gave him sufficient courage to survive himself in life and work.

I feel privileged to have been asked to write this foreword. It may be argued in Denmark whether I am the most competent to introduce this work. Having read it, I was left with no choice. I thank Patricia McAndrew for her effort, conscientious study, and passion, which have made Bournonville available and so alive in a language of the world.

INTRODUCTION
by
Svend Kragh-Jacobsen, M. A.

WHEN August Bournonville died in Copenhagen on November 30, 1879, at the age of seventy-four, he had long since renounced the ambitions that had filled him upon his return to Denmark in 1829, after his years of study in Paris. He dreamed of a world-wide reputation, first for himself while he was still dancing, and later for his ballets, which he tried, during 1855–1856, to introduce at the Vienna Opera, where he served as Balletmaster for a single season.

Neither part of his dream was realized. Shortly before his death, he wrote in a spirit of resignation to his friend, the actor Frederik Høedt, "Nothing in this world lasts forever, least of all the fleeting apparitions of the stage"; and to his own daughter Charlotte—who was for many years an opera singer at the Royal Theatre—he confided, without any bitterness, that for some time to come his ballets would indeed maintain their place in the repertoire of Copenhagen's Royal Theatre but that within twenty years after he was gone they would have completely disappeared. Surely by then the next great choreographer would have emerged to provide both dancers and audience with fresh new works.

But some sort of provision would have to be made for the interim, and with this end in view, Bournonville in 1877 meticulously rehearsed a repertoire of sixteen of his most popular ballets, and in the following year published the last part of what he chose to call his "testament"—*My Theatre Life*—a book that he hoped would serve as a guideline for his successors in the Danish Ballet until such time as a new young *Compositionstalent* would appear.

He had given up the hope of seeing his dream fulfilled, but he did achieve one of his goals: in his native land he had managed to create respect for the art which his father, Antoine Bournonville, regarded as *"la carrière la plus glorieuse du monde,"* and which with its struggles, defeats, and victories had become his own. There in Denmark he succeeded in seeing ballet folk accepted as respected members of society. He himself was recognized not only by the Danish intellectual élite of his day, from Bertel Thorvaldsen to Hans Christian Andersen; he was also respected by high and low alike. Still, for him, international renown remained a vanished dream.

So he believed, and his countrymen along with him. For a long time, his pessimism appeared to be justified. In Denmark, the ballet hit a trough and for half a century experienced no new flowering, even though Hans Beck, during his tenure [1894–1915], successfully kept the "Old Master" 's works alive and "tightened" them so that the most important of the ballets could survive the many lean years.

Bournonville's great memoirs, *Mit Theaterliv*, the three volumes of which were published between 1848 and 1878, were read, to be sure, by Danish theatre historians and were of continuous "local" value because of the insight they gave into the theatre history of the time, both in Denmark and abroad. Outside Denmark, however, they were known only in individual excerpts which were, nevertheless, avidly studied in Russia. Elsewhere, people were only vaguely aware of their existence despite the fact that here was a primary source for a period of ballet history which had long been a *terra incognita* — the era before the breakthrough of the Romantic ballet in Paris — a work that in its special way reflected European ballet on the little Danish stage in Copenhagen with a balletic tradition dating back to the middle of the eighteenth century.

Because it suited his dynamic temperament, the Danish artist always set his unique stamp on whatever he did — in his ballets as well as his memoirs — even if by so doing he gave a distinctive twist to what he had learned in Paris. Thus the French artistic techniques he had learned as a youth, which were elsewhere lost, were, in a fashion, purely and personally preserved here in Denmark. In fact, his style of dancing was passed on even farther afield when his Swedish pupil, Christian Johansson, went east from his native Stockholm with Marie Taglioni in 1841, and, after his days as soloist in the theatre had ended, became the influential head of the dancing schools of the Imperial Russian Ballet. He taught for so long that among the last of his pupils were included several stars who in their later years handed down their ballet knowledge as teachers in Paris, following the 1917 revolution in their homeland.

Bournonville and his finest ballets — about a dozen of which still survive in the repertoire of Copenhagen's Royal Theatre — finally got their chance when the Danish Ballet, in the years following World War II or, more accurately, during the nineteen fifties, actually began to move out into the world, which had previously known little about them. The groundwork was laid by Harald Lander, who had been brought up in the Bournonville school since his acceptance as a pupil at the Royal Theatre in 1913. From 1932 to 1951 he was the leader of the Danish Ballet who not only — in the spirit of the "Old Master" — personally created soloists, corps, and repertoire but also, in conjunction with Hans Beck's partner, the distinguished Valborg Borchsenius, took it upon himself to shape the Bournonville repertoire into a clean, bright style. The "Old Master" 's most popular works came alive once more on the stage of the Royal Theatre. They became the most admired productions, into the bargain, when Lander's successors in the fifties and sixties had the opportunity to send the Royal Danish Ballet abroad for foreign guest appearances.

Then Bournonville came once again to France and England, where he had danced as a young man, and even farther, to the United States and a host of other countries where the ballet is cultivated and loved. Especially in the United States did his art find followers, who by dint of zealous study soon became experts. Knowledge of the Danish master became even greater when Danish soloists left home and became international stars, with Erik Bruhn and Toni Lander leading the way. They usually took *soli* and scenes from Bournonville's ballets into their repertoires or passed them on to their comrades. Bournonville's *Napoli* has been seen in various one-act excerpts on many stages, and the *pas de deux* from *The Flower Festival in Genzano* at times runs close competition with even the most famous Petipa-Ivanov bravura numbers when the great stars shine in it. Bournonville's version of Filippo Taglioni's *La Sylphide* became the norm for many productions from the United States to Australia and the Soviet Union through the agency of Harald Lander, Hans Brenaa, Kirsten Ralov, and Elsa Marianne von Rosen. *Conservatoriet* and *La Ventana* followed. A century and a half after it emerged only to disappear, Bournonville's dream of conquering the world with his art is about to be fulfilled.

But one thing August Bournonville could never have imagined: that his comprehensive memoirs would be published in a universal language— English, which he himself boasted that he learned in a short time, at least well enough to assist his French comrades during their guest appearances at the King's Theatre in London during the eighteen twenties. This linguistic ability was one of the talents of this Dane who, from his early years, in addition to Danish spoke both his father's French and his mother's Swedish, and who in his old age went out of his way to learn Russian when, in the eighteen seventies, he paid a visit to his former pupil, Christian Johansson, in St. Petersburg.

At last, here is the complete work in translation by Patricia McAndrew, who has for years studied in Copenhagen and is today one of the most learned Bournonville experts in the international ballet world. In the most worthy fashion she is, through her work, continuing the efforts her countrywoman Lillian Moore began with *Bournonville and Ballet Technique*, which she wrote together with Erik Bruhn, and the Bournonville studies Miss Moore continued with her charming little monograph about *Bournonville's London Spring*.

The fact is that if one is to know Bournonville thoroughly and to understand his position in and importance to the art of ballet, the key is to be found not only in his danced works but, to an equally high degree, in his written commentaries and reminiscences. Brilliantly worded, phenomenally recollected, and entertainingly told, they are so securely based that his writing places him among those ballet artists who have the gift of being able to enlighten as well as to say something important and original. Though Bournonville may not be the reformer Noverre was, nor a theoretician of the caliber of

Blasis, his *Theatre Life*, with its many views of the art that was his, is such an important contribution to international as well as Danish theatre and ballet history that the translation of these volumes into a universal language in the most useful fashion broadens our knowledge of an art form which the whole world now cultivates.

Bournonville's dream is thus being fulfilled far more richly than he ever dared suspect or hope. His ballets are danced for and loved by a world audience he did not have the chance to conquer in person. His fight for art, his knowledge of it, his profound insight, and his multifaceted recollections of it and its great practitioners, will now become available to an international audience. The freshness of his memoirs will conquer readers by the same vitality and joy, the liveliness and beauty, which his finest choreographic works always instill in those who see them.

TRANSLATOR'S NOTE

AUGUST Bournonville's *My Theatre Life*, the great Danish balletmaster's own account of his career and works, is unquestionably one of the most important source books in the history of the theatre and the dance. His life spanned three-quarters of the nineteenth century (1805–1879), and fifty of those years he spent as dancer, artistic "dictator," organizer, and guiding genius of Copenhagen's Royal Danish Ballet—with leaves of absence varying from six months to six years during which he worked and observed in Naples and Rome, Austria-Hungary, Sweden, England and (above all) France: and after his retirement, imperial Russia.

Like many men of his day, Bournonville was an assiduous diarist and an avid correspondent, and it was from such sources that much of *My Theatre Life* was drawn. However, his is not a conventional autobiography—a unified presentation of his life's dates and events—or a theoretical treatise and technical manual such as his friend Carlo Blasis' *Code of Terpsichore*. It is, rather, a loose collection of memories and reflections on his professional career and associations, set down at different times and published in three volumes over a thirty-year period.* Indeed, in his introduction to Volume II, Bournonville expresses the wish that his work may be regarded "not as a finished whole but, preferably, be read in piecemeal fashion," one chapter at a time.

Feeling himself called to be a kind of spiritual successor to the great eighteenth-century ballet reformer Jean-Georges Noverre (with whose written work he was thoroughly familiar), Bournonville commingles in these pages observations and thoughts on life, the arts, history, folkways, politics, personalities, and, as one critic noted in 1865, "everything between Heaven and Earth." In its pages we can see his very definite aesthetic views and the motivations behind his balletic works; here, perhaps, lies his book's greatest importance. But beyond that, he throws much light on the cultural history of western Europe and on many of the individuals who were most influential in their several spheres of activity. In fact there is hardly a person of note on the Continental political-artistic scene—from Napoleon I to Nicholas II, from Hans Christian Andersen and Jenny Lind to Marius Petipa and Richard Wagner—who does not figure somewhere in these pages.

---

*Volume I, 1848; Volume II, 1865; Volume III, in three parts, 1877–1878.

In the preparation of the present text, I have used the first—and only—published Danish edition of *Mit Theaterliv;*† but the few extant portions of Bournonville's original manuscript of Volume II and parts of Volume III, preserved in the Danish Theatre History Museum and the Royal Library, Copenhagen, have been consulted. In view of *My Theatre Life's* importance as a historic document, I have sought to remain as faithful as possible to Bournonville's nineteenth-century Danish style, though not always to his nineteenth-century spellings of the names of people and places. For the sake of clarity and consistency these have been standardized; and some of his lengthy complex sentences have been divided into more manageable units. Also, for the benefit of today's less polyglot readers, I have translated into English the sprinkling of passages—a phrase or two here, a couple of paragraphs there—which Bournonville set down in French, German, or another of the half-dozen languages he spoke. (I have, however, left in the original a scattering of familiar locutions—*en pointe, mein liebe,* and the like—to preserve something of the author's cosmopolitan flavor.)

With respect to titles of artistic works, in the original edition of *My Theatre Life* Bournonville generally gives the names of plays, operas, ballets, etc. in Danish. In many instances, however, these titles are those under which adaptations of foreign works were presented in the Danish theatre. Throughout this edition, such titles are given in English translation but are accompanied by the Danish the first time the piece is mentioned so that readers interested in a detailed study of Danish theatre history may locate the works with ease.‡ But when it is a question of a foreign work performed at a foreign theatre, the original-language title has been used wherever possible.

The present translation does not purport to be a scholarly edition of *My Theatre Life.* Upon his literary introduction to an international audience, I have thought it best to let Bournonville speak for himself. Therefore, in order to retain the intimacy of the memoir, notes have been kept to a minimum—though there are many points at which a note of analysis or explanation might easily have run to several pages.

For all errors and for whatever may have been lost in the translation, I of course hold myself responsible.

Finally, it is my hope that, to paraphrase Pascal, those who open this book expecting to find an author may close it having found also a man.

---

† In the printed Danish edition of Volume II there is, at the start of each chapter dealing with Bournonville's "Ballet Compositions," a complete libretto of the work under discussion. Due to lack of space, these twelve libretti have been omitted from the present translation. However, none of the actual text of the book has been abridged.

‡ In Aumont and Collin's *Det danske National theater, 1748–1889* (3 vols., Copenhagen, 1896) will be found a catalogue of works, performed at the Royal Theatre, together with the names of the foreign pieces from which the works were adapted.

ACKNOWLEDGEMENTS

AFTER having worked for almost ten years on a project of this magnitude, I find on looking back that I have incurred numerous debts of gratitude, many of which can never be fully repaid. However, I would be terribly remiss if I did not attempt to thank at least some of the people who—often by only so much as a few sentences spoken in passing, a newspaper article, or an old book unearthed in some attic—have helped to broaden my knowledge and understanding of Bournonville and the world he lived in.

First of all, this translation would never have seen the light of day were it not for the unflagging encouragement and support of my parents, Dr. and Mrs. F. J. McAndrew. I am equally indebted to Selma Jeanne Cohen for the interest she has shown in this undertaking from the very beginning; it was her curiosity to know just what Bournonville's memoirs contained that led to my first, rather halting, translations from *Mit Theaterliv*. A great deal of credit is due Ørnulf Valla for the countless hours he spent patiently helping me "cut my translator's teeth" on the dreadfully long, nineteenth-century Danish sentences we found in the books so kindly lent to me by Julie Jensen. I shall be eternally grateful to Erik Bruhn, Toni Lander, and Bruce Marks for their inspiration and advice, which pointed my way to Denmark.

A Fulbright Scholarship—which I would never have thought to apply for without the confident urging of Carol Dean Henn—helped to support my early research in Copenhagen, where the hospitality of Allan Fridericia and Elsa Marianne von Rosen made me feel at home during my first weeks in Denmark.

My Danish colleagues, Svend Kragh-Jacobsen, Erik Aschengreen, Karen Neiiendam, and Klaus Neiiendam, have always gone out of their way to supply answers to the countless queries with which I have bombarded them over the years. I cannot sufficiently emphasize the contributions they have made to this work.

Likewise cherished are the many happy hours I spent in the kitchen of 7V, at Otto Mønsteds Kollegium in Copenhagen, where my fellow students during the years 1968–1970 allowed themselves to be used as "living dictionaries" in my struggle to decipher Bournonville's often archaic Danish.

On a broader scale, conversations with the late Cyril W. Beaumont, John Percival, and Mr. and Mrs. Ivor Guest helped to place Bournonville's career in a European perspective, while Clement Crisp was kind enough to call my attention to an English translation of Bournonville's pamphlet *Den danske Ballet* in the collection of The Royal Academy of Dancing in London.

It also gives me great pleasure to acknowledge the generosity and interest shown by the staffs of the Danish Theatre History Museum and The Royal Library, Copenhagen; the Swedish Music History Museum, Stockholm; and the Archives Nationales, Paris. In addition, I am particularly indebted to Genevieve Oswald and her staff at The Dance Collection of The New York Public Library for their unfailing help and continual encouragement. My special thanks go to the Reverend Henry L. Williams — who has helped me more than he will ever know by allowing me to borrow a priceless, dog-eared Danish dictionary from 1863 — and the staff of Reeves Memorial Library, Moravian College, Bethlehem, Pennsylvania. As a result of their courtesy and cooperation on countless occasions, the seemingly endless business of research was a good deal less arduous than it might otherwise have been.

For her kindness in borrowing for me a copy of *Mit Theaterliv* from the Library of Congress, I most gratefully thank Carolyn Langford, as I do David Maclay for giving me a number of Danish books that had belonged to his late wife Lillian Moore; many of the notes for this translation have been lovingly drawn from their pages.

A number of people generously read all or parts of the typescript at various stages and made many welcome suggestions for its improvement: Selma Jeanne Cohen, Erik Bruhn, Svend Kragh-Jacobsen, Erik Aschengreen, Karen Neiiendam, Ivor Guest, the late Dr. J. Richard Jones, Professor Winfred Kohls, Jean Beecher, Professor Erik Rhodin, and Professor and Mrs. Franklin Reeve; in addition, Laura de la Torre Bueno kindly provided translations of Swedish quotations and play titles.

Throughout the preparation of this work, Joan Libbey provided me with much-needed information about subjects ranging from comets to composers. An excellent typist, Ida White, faithfully translated my illegible hieroglyphics into a readable manuscript, the several drafts of which were always clearly and promptly xeroxed by Clara Fistner and Anthony Zingone of the Photocopying Department of Lehigh University, Bethlehem, Pennsylvania. Still other "benefactors" must remain unnamed, but I do want to record my collective gratitude to them. I am sure they will know who they are.

Last, but by no means least, I wish to thank J. R. de la Torre Bueno: the kindest and most patient of editors.

I cannot conclude these notes, however, without paying tribute to the memory of "the Old Master" — August Bournonville himself — whose haunting wish to be remembered sustained me on many occasions when I honestly thought I had reached the quitting point.

PATRICIA N. MCANDREW

Bethlehem, Pennsylvania
November 1978

VOLUME
ONE

PREFACE

"THE theatre is the world of vanity." People often say this and realize only after more mature deliberation that the world is the theatre of vanity. But of all *transient* things here on earth, the art of the stage is one that vanishes into oblivion, leaving almost no trace behind.

The image of beauty can be retained on canvas and in stone; deeds may be preserved in writing; painters and sculptors live in their works, the composer continues to enrapture posterity, and the fortunate *skald* immortalizes his own name and those of others. But the actor, the singer, and the dancer are children of the moment: at the appointed hour the talent must stand ready, the spirits swell, the voice breathe forth the sadness of the heart, and the dance express the warmth of joy and love. Before one knows it, this talent has reached its culmination; it begins to decline, its characteristics are compared, its initial impact lessens, its luster pales; new stars arise, and the eye no longer seeks the waning one, who disappears unnoticed. "But why did you not consider this before you chose your profession? Now it is too late."

My childhood followed an irresistible call. I was born to the scenic art in general, but the dance triumphed because my abilities developed most in this direction and because of all the performing arts, this one seemed to offer the richest dividends in effectiveness and independence. I was well aware that there were other arts which left behind far more than mine; but to my mind this was compensated for by the more immediate recognition and effect the dramatic art enjoyed and compelled in inspiring moments. I felt that this excitement, though temporary, was by no means empty or without influence on one's spiritual life; and since the call to please and delight one's fellow-men is supremely alluring, I herein found compensation for all my effort.

Through trial and tribulation I have won many laurels. I have accomplished something and enjoyed my artistic career. But now, upon looking back since I have passed the halfway mark in my journey through life,* I find my footprints so faint I fear they will soon disappear. Now, for the first time, I feel the desire to be remembered: painters and poets called me brother, yet the poorest and least of them will be able to leave behind more than I will! I

---

* Bournonville was forty-one when he began to write this book in the winter of 1846–1847. (Note: Throughout this text, footnotes marked "A.B." were written by the author and appeared in the Danish original. Unmarked notes are by the translator.)

3

envy no one. I shall never regret my profession. But what a cruel thing it is to be forgotten!

People console me with these words: "If you had been nought but an outstanding dancer, you would have suffered this fate. But your compositions will live in the history of the Danish theatre." Alas! What are my ballets without a first-rate performance? The mechanical part can, if necessary, be transmitted, but the nuances fade away. Add to this the fact that in order to secure the introduction of his works before the general public, the master must sometimes yield to the demands of fashion, thereby rejecting classical purity. Finally, it is the theatre's fate that what does not win the prize at first glance fails utterly and disappears; however, that which astonishes people by virtue of its novelty and genius in a short while becomes so outworn that enthusiasm often changes into fatigue and loathing.

But of a ballet, which has addressed both the gay and the earnest, the young and the old, and brought a kind of excitement into our everyday lives, nothing remains save a libretto! Were it only so much as a sketch, an outline, a venerable ruin, or a skeleton which could give some idea of the true dimensions. But—a *libretto!* Hardly more than the scaffolding left over from exploded fireworks! The *performance,* on the other hand, is the real ballet. Let us suppose that someone else had done a similar project which was never performed at all or, if it was, then at least in a completely different manner. Surely my ballet might appear to be a plagiarism, for who, being unfamiliar with its form, could establish its originality?

And now, in stylistic respects, how vague are the demands made upon a libretto! For the intelligent it is always too detailed and drawn out; it should not exist at all, in fact, since everything is obvious to the person who is at home in art and history and whose literary and musical foundation always leads him on the right path. Those who are unversed in such matters, however, demand that everything be spelled out for them, and they are confused by any surprise. Some, and I dare say these are the chosen few, read the libretto *after* having seen the ballet; the whole thing then stands vividly before them and they need not fear that the description painted the work in all too glowing colors. If, in addition, these elect be good narrators, or writers with a feeling for the poetic, the work is crowned with success. But woe betide the man whose memory shall be perpetuated by means of ephemeral newspaper articles! A development of this proposition would lead to much scandal, and it would be a pity to awaken such critiques after several years of hibernation, not because what was good would have been rendered worthless through denigration, but because the praise which was so lavishly distributed would reduce everything to mediocrity and give posterity a poor impression of our standards of judgment.

An artist has a triple life: as a *citizen* he must complete his work; as a *Christian* he must mature to eternity; but as an *artist* he must never outlive his fame. A sculptor, who at a sovereign's command erects a hero's statue of marble and bronze, engraves his name at the base of the pedestal; here it is read on the work of his own hand and people know who and what he was. If a dramatic artist dies in the full flower of his talent, just when he has created a masterpiece, poets sing of him and he is presented to posterity in terms that far surpass reality; if he retires into rural tranquillity, there comes a time when he himself may tell how gifted he was; but if, on the contrary, he continues to plague his Muse until she turns her back on him, he enters the ranks of the wretched. In the one instance, there is too much recognition; in the other, entirely too little. I wish to be remembered. What shall I do, then, in order to be known to posterity in something of the way I really am?

Shall I collect and publish my memoirs, write about those countries I have seen and those events I have witnessed, spice the whole with character sketches and anecdotes gathered from the piquant world of the theatre? Without violating the truth, I could secure for my book a large audience and for myself a certain celebrity. But I, who have lived and worked to provide innocent pleasures, would not be content with this. No! There is something better for me to do. *Dancing and ballet as dramatic representation* is still a closed book to many people: I will attempt to open it and to awaken in them the desire to read it. I feel called to unite my experiences to Noverre's *Lettres sur les arts imitateurs.* There exist wrong opinions concerning the nature of ballet: I will combat them. People have asked me many questions: I will repeat my answers. I have gathered interesting experiences in my art and I will try to communicate them as clearly as I possibly can.

In treating dancing and ballet from the historical and aesthetic as well as from the technical side, I will strive to avoid Noverre's errors, namely, false scholarship, a patronizing tone, and bombast. I will judge all older works with caution, taking especial consideration of the times and places in which they were performed. I will, as much as possible, avoid discussing my contemporaries—aye, in this Noverre will serve me as a warning—for fear of being biased in favor of those who have delighted me and against those who have offended me. I have trouble enough making a place for myself in the Hall of Memory; my friends I *dare* not smuggle in, and my enemies I consign to oblivion. I will view the whole of the art with an open eye and acclaim it with a warm heart; and as for my own works—I shall venture to state my unreserved opinion of them. I am well aware that one cannot at the same time be both judge and defendant; self-praise is no good; but there is an artistic conscience which, given time and reflection, will not deny the truth. Therefore, I will not feel ashamed of confessing my joy over an occasionally successful undertaking. People may smile at my candor but, all the same, remember me with kindness and say: *Le style c'est l'homme!*

I

The Dance

THE idea of dancing is inseparable from music, and in her nature Terpsichore embodies both rhythm and movement. The most spontaneous in its origin and effect, the most independent and spirited, aye, the noblest of all the fine arts is music. How much, and still how little, has been written about this divine art, yet people will seldom admit that the Dance is its first-born daughter. And why? Does beauty not have the same requirements as euphony? Is the eye farther from the soul than the ear? Did not the Almighty Creator, who put harmony into the echo of the hills, into the vault of the woods, into the deep rush of the waterfall, and chose the human breast as the repository for the most beautiful sounds, also create the hovering swallow, the fleeting hind, the supple reed, and, above all, the human body, which in the calm of purity is the epitome of natural grace?

This creation called forth praise and admiration. The word was not yet formed, but the voice sounded and the paean exultantly rang out. The listeners stood round about, filled with excitement. They wished to imitate these sounds, but for one thing they lacked the gift of melody, and for another they feared to disturb the magic. Then the hand followed the eye toward the admired regions of the body. It was as if the steps wished to accompany the undulations of the sounds. The body sang . . . *they* heard the singer's music; *he* saw theirs . . . but he became their master, for he could sing without them but they could not dance without him.

The Dance, therefore, owes its existence to music. Man dances not only to express his joy but to represent excitement, aye, even gravity and sorrow. In earliest times it was a bodily declamation. There was dancing at graveside sacrifices; thus are we to understand that King David danced before the Ark of the Lord and that both heroic poems and tragedies were danced upon the stage. The sciences emerged and the fine arts flowered in their bosom: music allied itself with poetry, and dance with the plastic art; gradually they changed their forms but in their essence remained united. The fathers of civilization, the Greeks, consecrated art and science to nine virginal tutelary goddesses. The youngest and liveliest was called Terpsichore, and she was the Muse of the Dance.

We can actually form no clear idea of the manner in which the ancients danced; but the fact that this art must have been superior to the spoken drama can be ascertained from the masks, stilts, and shouting which the actors em-

ployed in their roles, whereas all plastic representations of the male and female dancers of antiquity seem to indicate the highest degree of gracefulness
and good taste. From the long draperies of the clothed statues and the small
movements of the unclothed figures, one ventures to conclude that the dancing consisted not of leaps and turns but rather of expressive attitudes and
seemly gaiety. An instrument was often played or a symbolic object swung,
referring to the god for whose glorification the dance was performed. In this
worthy form, the dance and the other fine arts (for among the Greeks beauty
was the principal requirement for all art) reached their zenith, until they became the servants of sordid passions, disgraced and decayed as the slaves of
tyranny and effeminacy. Which art was most profaned during that period of
corruption? Here the performing arts could prize their transiency: they left no
monuments, while poetry and the plastic art had to bear the whole shame. . . .
The barbarians' axes hewed a cleft between that period and the rebirth of art
in medieval Italy.

It was once again in the bosom of religion that the arts were to flourish:
the crippled gods sprang up as holy figures; vast temples rose above the martyrs' graves, and hymns resounded beneath those magnificent vaults. Here the
art of acting also emerged. Priests performed and sanctioned scenes from
Holy Writ, the so-called *mysteries*, wherein declamation, music, and dancing
were used in almost the same fashion as in present-day operas. But these
mysteries soon deteriorated, caused universal scandal, were condemned to excommunication; and it was once again the dance which, under the maternal
protection of music, survived the drama. There is dancing at children's Christmas parties, at the turn of the year, and during the merry Carnival; in Greece,
Easter morn is still hailed with dancing by the entire populace; from time immemorial, in almost every Christian country, Pentecost, Midsummer, and the
grain and wine harvests have been celebrated with dancing to hymns of
thanksgiving.

The native or so-called national dances with which we are familiar may
be divided into three types: the chaste, the voluptuous, and the martial.
Among the first ought to be classed the earlier Italian, Spanish, and French
dances which, like the Nordic, were performed to the accompaniment of romances, heroic poems, and elegies. They moved quite slowly and demanded
great dignity on the part of both the man and woman. These dances were
those of civilized nations and probably originated in the better times of the
Greeks. I would call them *classical*.

The second kind stems from Hindustan, where the female dancers are
raised in temples. They are called *Devadāsīs* (in Portugese, *balladeiras;* in
French, *bayadères*); from them come the Egyptian *almées*, the Moorish and
later Spanish and Italian dances whose central motif is the ecstasy of love and
whose performance is, for the most part, left to women. This is the *Indian*
genre.

Lastly, those dances wherein masculine grace and strength are particularly displayed, and where the female dancer is more subordinate, have their origins in northern Asia and are known throughout Russia, Poland, Hungary, and Bohemia, to Germany and the entire North, by the names of polska and waltz, and almost always move in three-four or three-eight time. These are the *Slavic* dances.

Present-day theatrical dancing is a genuine art insofar as one admits that nowadays all art contains a greater or lesser amount of technique or mechanical skill. All great masters have been outstanding practitioners, and practice has loosed the bonds of art. No talent can be acquired without innate gifts; but art has a number of directions, and natural abilities are not equally great in all of them. In dancing, for example, the person who is endowed with much lightness and elasticity generally possesses less litheness and composure, while he who overcomes the most difficulties frequently has the least grace and expression. From childhood on, these qualities and weak points should be developed and remedied by a skilled hand. The young pupil may possess desire enough, but perseverance must be found, above all, in the teacher. Before there can be any talk of genuine artistry, the apprentice must first be "placed"—that is, he must master the positions and movements of the head, torso, and arms; and secondly, be turned out, which is to say, he must obtain flexibility in the hip, knee, and foot; without this, no *aplomb* (equilibrium), lightness, or brilliance can exist. Stamina can now be developed, and here one must take care lest speed be gained at the expense of softness, or vice versa. Throughout this technical training, the various components of the dance repertoire are taught. Through toil and industry, weakness, pain, and dejection are finally overcome, and the student has now learnt his métier; that is, he can do what a dancer must be able to do before he can be said to have embarked upon an artistic career. Of course artistic principle should always prevail in the training school. Rhythmic feeling, picturesque beauty, and dramatic expression ought to be the goal; but technical difficulties must be surmounted before one may dare to trespass on the domains of *art*. Skill alone gives ease, and without it the magic is lost.

Present-day theatrical dancing according to the true French school demands far greater personal expertise than did that of former times. Forty to fifty years ago, the latter was divided into fixed classes: *sérieuse, demicaractère,* and *comique,* and the dancers were content to excel in one particular genre, wherein they also acquired considerable perfection. Now, however, it is music that determines character; the *style de perruque* has given way to the Romantic; in picturesque groupings we strive to approach antiquity; and though bravura dancing, like bravura singing, is in eternal conflict with the dramatic element, the latter has won an important victory by the acceptance of native dances as an integral part of the art.

Dancing has progressed not only in technical skill but also in effect. It is achieving hitherto unknown results: strength and inspiration in male dancing, and the intangible dreamlike quality and romantic air that characterize the *danseuse* of the modern school, are signs of unmistakable progress. "All that is beautiful is good." But is everything in modern dancing truly beautiful? A great deal, but certainly not *everything*. Here I am not referring to commonly recognized faults but simply to those which are emphasized as talents. There is a flexibility that degenerates into weak-jointedness, a bravura that transforms dancing into gymnastics and the question "How?" into "How many?" [In this respect], we are all more or less sinners; but worst of all is the audience, which seldom expresses its satisfaction at what is tasteful, but always at what is striking. The dancers are those least guilty of excess, for, on the whole, people choose to show them little forbearance, nor do they go into ecstasies over them. But what warrant can be found in the entire realm of art for a leg lifted to the height of the shoulder, nay, even to the crown of the head? Is it a pleasing impression that is produced by an entire solo *sur les pointes* and by those leaps which end in a squat? And does not this falling backward and forward into the arms of the *danseur,* which makes some coarse hands applaud with delight, cause many heads to shake and eyes to fall? "But it is the fashion! Paris fashion," people say. "We must go along with the times."— Bravo! So long as the times go forward and one does not offend good taste. Marie Taglioni and Fanny Elssler created epochs in Paris precisely because they did not follow the prevailing routine. Idolatry endowed some of their imperfections with genius; they were copied in these very faults, and defects thereby took root which obscured the dance and lowered its status and importance as an art. Happy the man who has the courage and taste to choose the beautiful! He will never regret his choice, for the true will ever know how to manifest itself.

But is everything beautiful in the dance *picturesquely* beautiful as well? The famous [Pierre] Gardel believed that drawing ought to be the touchstone of the dance. He knew dancing but had a wrong conception of the art of painting. The stage can as little become the painter's model as "studied" and overrefined nature can. A tragic or a comic scene always becomes an indifferent painting, just as a magnificent landscape with neatly divided fields and straight avenues looks abominable on canvas. The prerequisites of the dance, namely, turned-out positions and pointed feet, could never be combined with the repose that is the true life of a picture. Consequently, in addition to its musical and plastic nature, the dance also has a wholly unique one which belongs to the moment and cannot bear to be held fast; that suspended lightness, that exhilirating gaiety, cannot be transmitted to the paintbrush without modification. How would an *entrechat* or *pirouette* look as a drawing! I know of nothing lovelier in reality and more hideous on paper than groups of sylphlike creatures *sur les pointes.* The old painters and sculptors copied only what was suitable for their art (although the walls of Herculaneum do display a number of rather distorted dance poses); they understood how to express inner emotion through outward calm. Thus their busts were forceful, mild, or serious, but never tense, grinning, or angry. In the section on *Pantomime* I will touch more closely upon the affinity of the dance with the plastic art; yet here I will briefly assert its right to the name of art in its proper and noble meaning.

Like all the fine arts, the dance has its origin in nature. It comes from a warm heart, from a healthy imagination; its action expresses joy and pleasure. The body becomes eloquent and says precisely that which words cannot express. The effect is beneficial, and the mind is inclined to poetry. The simple child of nature gets tears in his eyes at the sight of lovely dancing and immediately thinks of God's angels. The desire to please has created invention, but the desire to be admired, virtuosity. This is the crossroad where the dancer so often goes astray: he wishes to astonish and arouse the dullards, to please and captivate the depraved, and then becomes as offensive as the juggler, the ropedancer, and the trick rider, who in the eyes of many are his most dangerous rivals. Standing on your head against the point of a sword, swallowing a bayonet, dancing on the back of a horse! Behold! That is an art! Can you do it? I cannot judge the difficulty of these feats, but I get the impression that they are products of a delinquent imagination: they rattle the nerves but do not touch the heart. Let beauty appear but a single time and it is soon eclipsed by daring; the laws of harmony are trodden underfoot; anxiety, not joy, is their attendant; they bend one's thoughts toward sorcery, dispose the mind to the infernal, and leave behind an indescribable emptiness. These are the sunken rocks upon which the dancer so often founders. It is not the fact that he is applauded in a real theatre or constitutes an adornment to the opera or ballet that ranks him among artists, but, rather, that he recognizes the origin and destiny of the Dance. All of the arts demand a great deal of technique. Let us, then, bring art into the craft, but never allow the craft to appear in art.

II

Pantomime

THE art of denoting characters, explaining situations, and expressing feelings and passions through gestures is identical with dance insofar as it is the form in which dancing originally appeared as dramatic representation. Dancing served to embellish festivals, but pantomime rose to the stage and was held in even greater esteem, as there were few who knew how to perform it.

It is a mistake to assume that the pantomimes which captivated the Romans under Augustus had something in common with the art form we call ballet. There is still no agreement as to whether there was scenery in the ancient theatres, where stages were not deep and where the plays were given by daylight. The famous mimes Bathyllus, Pylades, and Hylas appeared only after the death of Roscius* and played scenes from the great tragic authors. At that time the art of mime enraptured everyone to such a degree that the spoken drama was almost totally eclipsed. But whether it did indeed constitute a transition to a more natural mode of performing, since pantomime was free of the gigantic masks through whose mouthpieces the actors had to shout their tirades in order to be heard by the thousands who filled the enormous amphitheatres, or whether its picturesque beauty appealed to a people who had such great feeling for the plastic and knew the tragedies by heart, suffice it to say there was no god, no important story in history, that pantomime did not represent for enthusiastic Rome. But how, and in what form?

The action was performed, for the most part, by a single person, whose art consisted in assuming as many different characters as there were roles in the piece. On one side of the proscenium stood a flute player, who marked the rhythm and followed the shifting emotions; on the other side stood a declaimer, who related the subject matter. Contests were sometimes improvised between the most famous mimes, and the public split into violent factions. Noverre's letters contain interesting descriptions gathered from old historical writings, but I know an anecdote that Noverre has not recounted and which I will here present in order to illustrate the nature of pantomime.

Caligula, who was a passionate lover of pantomime, aye, who himself trod the stage (usually in a female role), has sentenced to death a mime who had incurred his wrath as the result of some offense. The unfortunate man begs

---

*Quintus Roscius, ca. 126 B.C.–62 B.C., Roman actor, celebrated equally for his graceful bearing, concept of character, and controlled resonance of voice.

the emperor's mercy and volunteers to act out a pantomime on a given theme, without the aid of either flute player or declaimer. If he cannot be understood or, above all, win his master's approval, he is ready to suffer death.

This takes place late at night on the eve of the execution. Caligula is astonished at this request, realizes that he is really committing himself to nothing, and curiosity triumphs. He orders that his court be assembled. With misgivings, all abandon their nocturnal rest and hasten to the tyrant, who tosses his purple about him, orders his halls illuminated, and informs the astonished assembly that it has been called hither to judge a pantomime! The artist steps forth. This time he is to act as a matter of life and death! Caligula gives him one of his peculiar looks and offers him the subject of Mars and Venus.

The mime composes himself. A toss of the cloak, a tensing of muscles, lightning in the eye, a divine smile upon the lips, heroic strides across the floor—and all have recognized the god of war. In the next instant, both facial expression and bearing have transformed the strapping youth into a langorous Aphrodite. He now expresses, in turn, the power of love over both deities and arrives at the moment when Vulcan's net ensnares the lovers. Caligula utters a cry of approbation, which is taken up by his entire court. The pledge of mercy already hovers on the lips of the bloodthirsty tyrant, but—the artist would complete his triumph. In his own person, he allows all of Olympus to parade past the captured pair. The emperor, beside himself with delight, cries out at each new apparition: "Behold! Pallas, Juno, Mercury, Jupiter, and Apollo!" He bestows life and liberty upon the mime, but imprisons him with gold and gifts.†

Pantomime is, naturally, far more comprehensible to people in countries that possess a wealth of expressive gestures, a number of which are so universally employed that they take the place of words where distance and noise prevent verbal communication, than here in the north, for example, where almost all gesticulation has disappeared. Also, mime is performed far more in places where the people are familiar with images of outstanding personages, recognize each passion or deity by its attributes, and, in a manner of speaking, study history and mythology in the streets and public squares. The common people of Rome recognize the names on ancient busts and on all of their saints wherever they see them, whereas a great number of Copenhageners still believe that a Swedish king lies beneath the Horse on Kongens Nytorv, but do not know which Christian sits upon it!‡

Therefore, how difficult it is to perform something in pantomime where there are no images to captivate the memory, where allegory is dragged down into the swamp of triviality, and where the events of the past are a sterile school lesson rather than a vigorous tree of life. Perhaps Thorvaldsen's Mu-

---

† In Lucian's *On the Dance* (cited in Lillian B. Lawler, *The Dance in Ancient Greece*, p. 141), this same story is told of a *pantomimus* named Paris, who was urged into the feat by the Cynic Demetrius in Nero's reign.
‡ Christian V, *reg.* 1670–1699, sits on the Horse.

seum is called upon to instruct the masses, who must become accustomed to lofty and noble images.* This will be beneficial for the stage as a whole, which is languishing under [the influence of] the unspiritual domestic farce. The plastic element in the production will then come to assume a worthy place, and in the most outstanding examples of art, bombast and affectation — as well as their antipodes, vulgarity and triviality — will find a counterbalance.

With respect to its use in ballet, pantomime — which in rhythm and variety is dancing, in character delineation is drama, and in its forms is virtual painting — has been viewed in various ways.

The Italians use it wholly as dialogue and chorus. They have, from olden times, certain conventional gestures, certain unchangeable forms; steps are measured exactly, gestures fall precisely on the note, and, if the musical stanza is thrice repeated, the mimed word keeps pace with it. The chorus follows the action *en masse* and marks time by a loud stamping. The size of the theatres demands such a grotesque exaggeration of facial expressions, steps, and arm movements that there can be no talk of grace or naturalness. Their strength lies in grand stage effects, such as processions, conspiracies, and festivals with horse and chariot races; but in battle scenes and crowd movements the mechanical rhythm is always discernible: the swords have the ring of tinder-steel, and the crowds move like puppets.

The dancing has no dramatic connection with the action performed by nondancing mimes. The latter can, therefore, wear costumes more in keeping with the characters they are portraying and better lend themselves to the heat of passion. On the other hand, they have the great disadvantage of being regarded as a "setting" for one or another of the pirouetting personalities who draw crowds to the theatre for the "festival act," where the principals sit idly by on a throne for three-quarters of an hour while bravura *pas*, completely foreign to the plot, are performed.

Noverre, the creator of pantomimic ballet in France, had amalgamated dancing and pantomime in the same way as singing and declamation had been combined in opera. Agamemnon returned from the war, Clytemnestra and Ægisthus conspired against him, Electra caressed her father, and Cassandra had a foreboding of the impending disaster — all this constituted a dancing quintet, with proper steps, each member of which, in his character, formed a harmonious whole. Galeotti's genre was a combination of this method and the Italian. Two lovers suffer shipwreck, are cast lifeless upon a beach, open their eyes, recognize one another, and immediately dance a little *pas de deux*. King Bluebeard sends his crown to Isaure's night table; she dances with it before the mirror; the king beholds her for the first time, and both express their passion by a *pas de deux*.

Despite Noverre's great genius, his system could not escape the mockery

*The Museum was under construction at the time of writing; it was opened to the public in September 1848.

of his own countrymen. To them, it was perfectly natural for gods, spirits, and sylphs to move about in dance; aye, Frenchmen were quite willing to allow heroes, in their perfumed pastoral life, to imitate dolls of Sèvres porcelain, but they could not bear to see the tragic figures so admirably portrayed by Baron and Lekain† express their passion in *chassés* and *pas de bourrée.* They were accustomed to hearing the heroes of Racine and Corneille meet the perils of death with roulades and long-drawn-out tones. But it is, after all, the ballet's fate that people will not tolerate as much absurdity from it as they will from opera.

The French are great actors—Talma's mime was unsurpassable—but, oddly enough, in the ballet they have had only a few outstanding mimes. As a rule there is something weak, cold, and indistinct in their pantomime, and their dancers have a great deal of trouble forgetting their "craft" for the higher demands of art.

The English, especially in their tragedies, have raised pantomime to its highest degree of picturesque perfection. What they tell of Garrick is indeed the height of mimic art ... one understood him without knowing a single word of English. I have seen Charles Kemble, Young, and Macready, as well as the actresses Kelly and Smithson, and—with the exception of a few traditional exaggerations—they fully confirmed the reputation of their school. Kean never really appealed to me; his countrymen found him truly Shakespearean, and indeed one cannot deny the genius in his acting; but to my mind he was always extremely mannered. For example, his main gesture was to scratch his chest, then clutch his heart and, as it were, violently hurl it into the faces of the audience.

Despite the independence of the English in so many other areas, in dancing and music they blindly follow what France and Italy have decreed to be the fashion: they see only Parisian ballets and listen only to Italian music. They do, indeed, have ballets of a sort, which they call "pantomimes"—an offshoot of the Italian harlequinades, but totally lacking in the splendid humor of the latter, consisting merely of artful transformations with gymnastic exercises and employing such grotesque images that the only people who can enjoy them are those who could laugh in a madhouse. On me, these farces made a disgusting impression.

I will here give an account of my own view of pantomime, and show in what direction I have cultivated this art and what demands I think it capable of fulfilling. There is music, which speaks without words; there are pictures, which tell us of an event without inscriptions, and dumb-show, which creates the deepest impression of all. If in art a symphony can conjure up a series of images that multiply before our fantasy like an animated painting, and a drama in an unfamiliar language can enrapture us, how much more, then, can

---

† Michel Baron (1653–1729) and Henri-Louis Cain *dit* Lekain (1728–1778) were outstanding interpreters of Corneille and Racine.

a thousand features of human life be expressed in a manner which the dramatic word is incapable of reproducing. Love, jealousy, devotion, joy, joviality, roguishness, surprise, dejection, weeping, anger, and despair are elements that lose rather than gain by declamation. The dramatic art demands more than exclamation, and shrieking it rejects; therefore the poet often speaks through a role, and with an order and coherence that do not exist in nature, where eloquence is a rare and highly esteemed talent.‡ Does a delightful child speak? Does a modest maid in love declaim? Is bitter sorrow poured forth in roaring tirades? Drama must often have recourse to pantomime in places where the spoken word would ruin everything, and it usually founders in children's roles, festivals, battle scenes, and *tutti* passages.

Do not misunderstand me. I am not trying to prove that pantomime is superior to spoken drama. On the contrary, both that which is achieved and will be achieved by words will ever ensure the precedence of declamation; but this does not diminish the intrinsic worth of pantomime nor limit its effect. Drama can relate the past and foretell the future; pantomime more forcefully describes the present. Drama allows but one person at a time to speak; pantomime unites whole crowds in lively harmony. Declamation requires minutes, where mime uses seconds. A drama can be understood word for word by those who are familiar with the language of the country; pantomime is presented through a group, but is intelligible to foreigners and natives alike. Drama shows us Greece with Danish speech and writing and invites the most varied nationalities to communicate fluently in the adopted tongue; pantomime leads us directly to the spot and conveys the communication without absurdity or offense. "Make believe you are deaf, and you can lend the action whatever language you wish." For the person of culture, pantomime is an animated picture to which he himself writes the words; but what about the clod? Aye, we are all badly off with him: he understands pantomime in the wrong way, but sleeps like a log during a drama.

Thus as I understand pantomime and as it has become an element in my ballets, it is not a language of dialogue fashioned from deaf-mute signs and conventional gestures. It is a harmonious and rhythmic series of picturesque poses, gathered from nature and the classical models, that must be in accord with character and costume, with nationality and emotion, with person and time. This chain of poses and movements is in itself *a dance*, but one that does not use turned-out feet; its attitudes strive only for the plastic and characteristic elements and studiously avoid anything resembling virtuosity. This dance or bodily declamation is, even in its apparent ease, the most difficult because in its every detail it must be accountable to beauty for what it represents.

In my ballets, pantomime is the medium that links the various situations,

---

‡ Cf. Jean-Georges Noverre, *Letters on Dancing and Ballets,* trans. Cyril W. Beaumont (New York, 1966), p. 15.

that is to say, the events, for these alone determine the action; the romantic or lyrical moments, especially festivals, give me occasion to blend bravura dancing with the rest of the pantomime. It is therefore only natural that I should prefer to choose such subjects as afford me the most opportunity for dancing. But it is a mistake to allege that historical material is less favorable for ballet than an idyllic theme, for example. Were I but able to overcome in antique or Oriental style—aye, even by using the Old Norse myths—the difficulties which our local conditions put in the path of every grandiose production, I would then be able to prove the truth of my assertion. Besides, pantomime cannot always be confined within the same forms; and furthermore, even if I had talent enough to compose as opera or drama the material that is stored in my imagination—it would still be only a ballet with words.

III

The Ballet

DANCING surrounded by pantomime and combined with a coherent plot, or a pantomimic drama embellished with dancing, is a spectacle that often appeared in the great festivals of the Middle Ages and dates back to the rebirth of the fine arts in Italy. It was brought to the Parisian Court by the French queens of the House of Medici and was usually performed by princely and distinguished persons. Most of Europe copied this vogue (witness Christian IV's grand celebration in honor of his son's wedding)* until Louis XIV himself ceased to dance in ballets and founded the Paris Opéra under the name of the Académie Royale de Musique et de Danse. From this moment on, the ballet underwent many changes and presently appeared in heroic or burlesque form, as *intermède* — in the comedies of Molière, for example — and finally blended with arias and choruses. The bad taste of the "peruke age," with its masks, panniers, poetic emblems, inferior music, and generally dull and immoral subjects did its share to disfigure and debase these productions.

Noverre was the man who caused a revolution in the ballet world. He introduced appropriate costumes and gave dancing and pantomime a worthy place. He drew his material from classical sources, and the immortal Gluck composed for him. Noverre encountered much opposition in the established system, and the dancers, for whom his excellent letters were especially written, were naturally the last to read them. But genius triumphed. Without himself possessing great talent as a performer, he knew how to train and inspire most outstanding pupils. His ballets were performed in Stuttgart, Mannheim, and Vienna, and from his school emerged such masters as Dauberval, the elder [Gaetan] Vestris, the younger [Pierre] Gardel, and Milon.† (My father enjoyed his [Noverre's] instruction from his ninth to his sixteenth year, so I dare say my principles are founded on good traditions.) In Paris, however, it was his disciples who reaped the fruits of his works, which were too grandiose for a frivolous and impatient public that was accustomed to ballets made from vaudevilles whose gay little ballads were entertaining because of their allusions to hidden jokes. Noverre's grand ballets were coldly received in Paris and, to some degree, indifferently performed, for the elder [Maximilien] Gardel was a wretched mime and the other *sujets* were so taken up with the per-

*The marriage of Prince Christian of Denmark to Magdalene Sibylle of Saxony in 1634.
† For details, cf. Ivor Guest, *The Romantic Ballet in Paris, passim.*

fumed "porcelain genre" that they did not understand what was required of them, but hid their stupidity beneath the mask of carelessness.

Dauberval did not become balletmaster in Paris. He gave his finest works in Bordeaux, which soon developed into a nursery for the capital. He too followed the system of adapting operettas into ballets such as *Le Déserteur, La Fille mal gardée,* and others. They were splendidly composed but all suffered from "patchwork" music. The younger Gardel was Noverre's most fortunate successor: *Télémaque, Pâris, Psyché, La Dansomanie, L'Enfant prodigue,* and *Proserpine* were original creations and marked an epoch in the higher genre of ballets. Gardel did not possess true genius but had an infinite amount of taste and experience. Never have there been more brilliant performances than those of his ballets in which Auguste Vestris, Duport, Mmes. Gardel, Chévigny, Clotilde, and Chameroy captivated the Parisians with the loveliest combination of music and dancing.

Milon had no less honorable a career in another genre: *Nina* and *Clari* were masterpieces in the more sentimental style. Gardel enchanted the eye; Milon touched the heart. When the Opéra was temporarily moved to the small Théâtre Favart (little bigger than ours), Gardel's repertoire vanished and Milon's ballets took first place. There, in the year 1820, I saw Mlle. Bigottini, the greatest female pantomimic soloist I have ever seen.

At that time, the balletmasters' monopoly excluded every foreign composer from competition at this, Europe's greatest theatre, to the irreparable injury of art, since the finest talents were thereby lost to France. The old balletmasters became worn out and idle, and when one looked about for those who were gone, they too had become old or spoiled by foreign, i.e., Italy's, bad taste.

Didelot (unquestionably the greatest choreographer after Noverre) was engaged in St. Petersburg, where he formed a *corps de ballet* which far outshone that of Paris in its ensemble. His native land, however, derived but little benefit from his rare talent, and it was only an event such as the Allied invasion and the dictate of Tsar Alexander that enabled him to present his lovely ballet, *Flore et Zéphire,* at the Grand Opéra.

Aumer was a disciple of Dauberval and followed the latter's choice of subjects, always adapting plays and *opéras-comiques.* He possessed an uncommon capacity for work but had less invention and taste. In Gallenberg, however, he had found a splendid musical composer, and this ingenious German tone-poet has given Aumer's ballets his loveliest melodies.

Under Aumer (in 1827) there occurred an unhappy turning point in the history of ballet composition; namely, with *La Somnambule.* Scribe, who had eight years earlier written his *comédie-vaudeville* of the same name, realized that this character would be highly effective in pantomime. He penned a ballet libretto and, as a joke, presented it to the director of the Opéra, who took it as a good-natured jest on the part of the vaudeville writer, who at that time was not so famous. Albert refused to compose from another's libretto, but Aumer was not so proud. He took some good music from his stock, had it arranged by Hérold, and in a short time mounted the charming ballet which our public also knows by the name of *Søvngængersken*. It created a furor, and Scribe, who up to this point had played the modest one, now had his name placed before that of Aumer, and as a matter of course took half the author's royalties for himself. Aumer, who would have had to bear the whole blame for a failure, was hardly mentioned at all in the hour of success; and since they [the management of the Opéra] naturally had the utmost confidence in Scribe's powers of invention, the next ballet was also conceived by him. This was *Manon Lescaut*, which made little or no impression. But from now on the game was up. At the Paris Opéra they will have nothing to do with libretti written by balletmasters, either because they know the ability of those concerned or because a company of vaudeville writers has established this order of things. Whatever the case may be, over every ballet one can now read the names of two or three collaborators. The singer Nourrit has written *La Sylphide;* Saint-Georges and Leuven have composed *Le Diable boiteux* and *La Gipsy;* and, as for *Giselle,* I myself have seen how Perrot taught Carlotta Grisi fragments of the main role of another ballet, while the subject, which was taken from Heine's *Die Wiles,* was conceived by Théophile Gautier, arranged and revised by Saint-Georges, and finally mounted or—if one prefers—composed by Balletmaster Coralli. Albert, who had previously rejected Scribe's offer, was a few years later forced to work with Saint-Georges, and in all the papers *La jolie Fille de Gand* was called "The charming work by Mm. Saint-Georges & Adam." What a humiliation! For if there is anything good about the new Parisian ballets it is certainly not the libretti, and when one thinks of these wretched creations being recited in a committee, with the payment of a premium for each act . . .

But I must return to the time of Noverre in order to trace the course of the ballet in Italy. Despite the revolution Noverre had effected in costume and choice of subjects, they were still treated in the characteristic Italian style. Angiolini and Canziani were very famous at that time (1770). I am only slightly acquainted with their works, but I do know that they often used singing and inscriptions to render the action intelligible. There were also a kind of "somersaulters," *grotteschi,* whose dancing consisted of marching, playing tag, and turning enormous somersaults; at their side French dancers performed their inserted *pas,* which bore no relation whatever to the plot. It is an undeniable fact that these *grotteschi* infected the more graceful dancing, for all violent movements, exaggerated poses, and wild turns stem from Italian ballet.

Little by little, the Italians picked up the French style of dancing, to which they gave an unfortunate character (masculine among the women, feminine among the men); but the *grotteschi* completely disappeared from the stage. One of them, whose muscular strength drove his *entrechats* as high as *à douze,* was named Viganò and was father to the ballet poet upon whose mausoleum his countrymen engraved the epithet: "Prince of the Art of Ballet." His *Prometheus* is unanimously recognized as an absolute masterpiece in the most grandiose style ever seen. Its greatness, however, is said to have lain not in the characters and dances but in the imposing situations; the performance was entirely according to the system of beaten time, and the action cannot have been terribly consistent, for Viganò, who worked slowly, gave a separate act in each new place (every city had its three-month season) until the ballet was completely finished.

His successor in fame was Gioja, whose reputation is still great and whose works are still given under his own name and those of his imitators. They were dependent upon grand effects produced by machinery, and also, no doubt, upon powerful roles, which were admirably performed by the mime Molinari and the renowned Pallerini, who possessed so much inner passion that she alternately flushed and paled according to the different emotions she was to portray. The subjects, however, were all cut from a certain pattern: a tyrant who continuously tramped about with dagger partly or fully drawn; a wronged and persecuted heroine who was treated in less than delicate fashion by both the tyrant and the jealous lover; a "mad scene," the storming of a burning castle, and the tyrant's fall (usually down a staircase or from a steep cliff); add to this some bandits, a prison, and lastly, the curtain calls with shouts of *"Da capo,"* together with the balletmaster, who beat time with a large stick in the wings, from which hiding place he emerged every time there was applause *per ringraziare il publico!*

Henry, a most ingenious Frenchman, had absorbed the Italian style of ballet but, by virtue of his originality, knew how to forge his own path. He employed the French style of pantomime in lyrical or idyllic subjects, and the Italian in heroic or historical ones. In this way he achieved a high degree of variety, and as he had great feeling for the picturesque, his groupings were excellent. I have learnt much from his works. Unfortunately, I am familiar with only a few of them, but his mimetic treatments of *Hamlet, Le Siège de Calais,* and *Guillaume Tell* are regarded as models. His sphere of activity was in Naples. He was admired at Italy's greatest theatres. Only at an advanced age did he come to Paris, where, at a secondary theatre and with extremely poor resources, he created a sensation by his rare genius (it was at the Théâtre Ventadour, where in 1834 I saw his *Ondines* and *Tell*). The Grand Opéra immediately sought to lay hold of this talent, and he staged his Chinese ballet *Chao-Kang,* which won the applause of many connoisseurs but did not appeal to the general public, partly because of its bizarre forms and partly because of its mechanical precision. It was not able to survive; a great amount of chicanery and intrigue, envy and stupidity, made his life a burden. He left Paris with his senses deranged and returned to Naples, where he died not long afterward of cholera morbus.

The finest living ballet composer in Italy is Salvatore Taglioni (in Naples). His *Romanov, Ettore Fieramosca,* and *Marco Visconti* are works of great merit, but circumstances which I shall later touch on hinder the flight of his genius.‡ He is already an old man and has composed, as well as arranged, a host of ballets. Europe is, by the bye, teeming with ballet-*makers* or, to put it more correctly, *venders,* who hawk each other's works from city to city while they accuse one another of thievery. Every dancer whom age has rendered stiff-legged thereby fancies himself transformed into a composer; he prods his memory (for genius is out of the question), becomes the servant and trumpeter of a popular *danseuse,* assumes all the impertinence of Noverre, arms himself with a portfolio and a large stick, makes up dances to other people's libretti, and is—lo and behold!—a balletmaster!

The oldest Danish ballet libretto I know of is an allegory concerning Caroline Mathilde's successful delivery of a prince (Frederick VI) in 1768. The ballet was by the Frenchman Martin, and consisted of a series of national dances from the various provinces and towns of the Danish state. Later came the Italian Sacco, and finally, in 1774, Vincenzo Galeotti, who was balletmaster until his death in 1816. His works, as has been said, were in the Italian-Noverrean style; the tragic ballets were entirely given up to dignity and passion; the comic ones were positively burlesque and devoid of every nuance of feeling. Actual dancing played a subordinate role and the group formation always followed the laws of symmetry. He used choruses, arias, and inscriptions, and each character appeared spontaneously, without any motivated transition. After my previously expressed opinions, the reader will not be surprised that in Galeotti's compositions I cannot discover and acknowledge the originality and taste which his surviving admirers praise so unconditionally.* In light of my position as his successor, and since I subscribe to completely different principles, I cannot be competent in the judgment of his *artistic* merits. However, I can truthfully attest to the furor his ballets created, the crowds they drew to the Theatre for a number of years, the enthusiasm and reverence with which he was mentioned, and the recognition that was bestowed upon him in so many ways by king and people alike.

My father, Antoine Bournonville, was one of the finest dancers of his day and probably the foremost mime among them; but he was the composer of only a few charming and characteristic trifles. One of the most singular things about him was that his attention was captured most by detail; consequently, he felt and performed the most masterly elements in the composition only in piecemeal fashion, but these minute details were almost always to the advantage of Galeotti's ballets. The Court Dancing Master at that time, Pierre Laurent (formerly a *danseur-comique* at the Paris Opéra and balletmaster in Mar-

---

‡ See discussion of censorship in the Neapolitan theatres, Vol. I, the chapter "Parallels."
*Galeotti's faults are not to be excused by the demands of his day, for while his ballets were indeed contemporaneous with the German *pièces à spectacle,* there flourished at the same time Oehlenschläger's tragedies, Mozart's operas, and, in France, Gardel's ballets in the French style.—A.B.

seilles) composed a number of ballets, including *Sigrid with the Veil.* He had genius but lacked taste and skill.

It is now a matter of discussing my own work and of daring to state my own merits and shortcomings! The dancer is, after all, brought up before the mirror, in a constant struggle with his defects and bad habits. He approaches his talent with his eyes open; he is seldom blind to his own weaknesses, though he might well wish others were. It is indeed difficult to know oneself, but to admit that one is fallible is even harder. In Florence there is to be found a gallery of self-portraits by several hundred painters; thus, if I view my own works at leisure, should I too not be able to judge or at least describe them? I shall, at least, attempt to do so.

IV

Myself

THERE is a kind of modesty that strongly verges on arrogance. I experienced an example of this with an actor who always arrayed himself in the garb of humility and designated his best as "the least bad," his ability as "feeble endeavor," the fruits of his labors as "modest attempts," etc. I asked him what he thought of another artist, and he heaped upon the latter the most favorable testimonials and placed him in the first rank. "But then," I was malicious enough to ask, "can this outstanding fellow equal you?" "I should certainly hope not!" replied the modest man, flushing with rage.

Noverre has done a very good thing in writing about himself, for without his *Letters* his name would by now be obliterated. But just as Mirabeau described his political ideal so remarkably like himself that Talleyrand added that it only lacked being heavily pockmarked, so too Noverre not only demands of the person he chooses to call "the balletmaster" a host of attributes but forbids him to possess certain others, such as being able to perform a role or a part. He also asserts that a beautiful voice is absolutely indicative of a bad dancer. Now, whether Noverre had truly stored in his head all the knowledge that appears in his work, I shall allow to remain unquestioned; but it is widely known that he always had a bad singing voice and was a mediocre dancer. Therefore, although I prostrate myself before the ballet's reformer, my whole nature conflicts with his demands too often for me to assume his viewpoint, which permits the light to fall upon him and the shadows upon everyone else. I therefore set forth my opinions not as dogmas but as the fruits of my experience. I offer my friends and countrymen a remembrance of the Bournonville who has from time to time provided them with happy moments, who has given the Danish theatre his best years and talents, and whom they once favored and honored with the name of artist. Should I tell them of my dancing and my ballets, the picture must be vivid; should I reveal to them the depths of my artist's soul, they shall bear witness that it must have been that way and no other. I do not intend to place myself on a pedestal but, rather, to fasten my image in the mirror of Truth.

One must distinguish self-contemplation from self-praise, just as one tells the difference between an exorbitant bill and an accurate account. I will pay my debt, but I also claim what is my due. Therefore, acknowledging that as a dancer I have never equaled Vestris' rapturous enthusiasm, Duport's perfection, Albert's correctness, Paul's brilliance, or Perrot's lightness; that the compositions of Gardel, Milon, Didelot, and Henry stand before me as unsurpassable models; that Noverre's *Letters* have given me a lofty conception of the artistic value of the dance, and my father's acting of the nobility of mime, I shall here venture to deliver a critique of myself, which no outsider *can* and no rival *will* give.

My father, Antoine Bournonville, was the youngest child of one of those alliances contracted between talent and beauty on the one hand, noble lineage and improvidence on the other. On his baptismal certificate, which I possess, it says that he was born in Lyon—with a *de* in front of his name—on May 19, 1760. However, I have reason to believe that my grandfather was not so much *noble* as *ennobled*, for after having been ruined in a theatrical venture, he deserted his wife and children, who were forced to seek refuge in the bosom of art. My aunt, Julie *de* Bournonville, was one of the most famous dancers of her day and shone at the Court Theatre in Vienna during the time of Noverre. My father entered *his* school in his ninth year, took part in all of his great master's ballets, and was present at the fantastic festivals which Hungary's magnates gave in honor of Empress Maria Theresa. He came to Paris in 1779, danced there and in London during a three-year period, and was summoned to Stockholm, where he remained until the death of Gustav III in 1791. In passing through Denmark on a journey, he made his debut in Copenhagen, married there, and was engaged as First Solodancer.

He was an extraordinarily handsome man, fiery, brave, and gallant; in short, a true *chevalier français* of the old school. Nevertheless, he became enraptured with the Revolutionary principles of Liberty and Equality, and he knew no greater hero than Lafayette. "In Virtue alone is true greatness found; in talent alone, valid claims." These lofty illusions constituted his life's fortune. He combined in his art all that he held to be noblest. He retained his ardent zeal for the dance until his last breath: I took leave of him in this life with *Polka militaire*, which I had to dance at his bedside, and he died a few days later in the firm conviction that both he and I had chosen "the most glorious career."

I was born in Copenhagen on August 21, 1805, and trod the stage for the first time as one of Lagertha's sons in October 1813. My years of apprenticeship were divided among dancing, singing, and acting. Because of the favor I won in several rather important roles, in works such as *The Little Shepherd Boy* and *The Judgment of Solomon*, for some time there was uncertainty as to which profession I should actually follow. A peculiar ease in aping people and in underscoring the comical elements in their voices and gestures even gave me a certain reputation as an actor, and many advised me to pursue the *opéra-comique*, which was so popular at that time. But my innate vocation, my father's example, the fact that this period of transition from boy to man is no good for singing and acting, together with a nervous and often quite troublesome stammer—which, as I have since learnt, was less a natural failing on my part than the result of physical exertion, and quite common among dancers and gymnasts—decided my fate, and when I accompanied my father to Paris in 1820, the die was cast. My enthusiasm was so great, in fact, that when in my twenty-first year Rossini perceived that I possessed a sonorous and flexible tenor voice and offered me instruction and engagement as a singer, I refused to abandon the Muse to whom I had offered my homage. At certain moments I have regretted this decision: as a singer I would have won more gold and greater glory with less effort, but perhaps I could not have done as much for my fellow artists as I have in my present sphere of activity. This should be a consolation to me.

Appointed Royal Dancer in 1823, the following year I traveled—at my own expense—to Paris, where I made my debut and was engaged until 1830, when I assumed the post at the Danish Royal Theatre which I am now leaving after eighteen years of completed activity.

As a dancer, I possessed a considerable measure of strength, lightness, precision, brilliance, and—when I was not carried away by the desire to display bravura—a natural grace, developed through superb training and enhanced by a sense of music. I also had a supple back, and my feet had just enough turn-out for me to be appreciated by even the severest master. The difficulties which I have worked hard to surmount, often with only partial success, were all connected with *pirouettes* and the composure necessary in slow *pas* and attitudes. My principal weaknesses were bent wrists, a swaying of the head during *pirouettes*, and a certain hardness in my elevation. (To conceal and combat these was my hardest task.) I have thrice altered the genre of my virtuosity to suit the demands of the time: in *The Sleepwalker* (1830), in *Valdemar* (1835), and in *Robert le Diable* (1841). There are dancers who possess greater *aplomb*, elevation, and ability to pirouette, who perform character dances with a greater measure of originality, but very few who have united more of the qualities of the dance or possessed greater variety than I.* I danced with a manly *joie de vivre*, and my humor and energy have made the same impression in every theatre. I delighted the audience, and before they admired me, they liked me.

My talent for ballet composition had already begun to manifest itself in my childhood. Besides the fact that all my games centered around the arrangement of tableaux and the composition of ballets or so-called *entrées*, I also wrote my first libretto when I was fourteen years old (1819). It was based on Suhm's Nordic tale, *Habor and Signe*, and was followed by a dozen more, all of which were sacrificed to the stove.†

---

*For Bournonville's enumeration and definition of these "qualities," see his *New Year's Gift for Dance Lovers* (Copenhagen, 1829), and the manuscript entitled "Explanation of Various Choreographic Symbols," now in the Museum of Musical History in Stockholm.

† Bournonville's earliest extant ballet draft dates from 1821. For a full discussion of this and other important aspects of Bournonville's works, see Erik Aschengreen, "The Beautiful Danger: Facets of the Romantic Ballet," in *Dance Perspectives* #58, Summer 1974.

I went to Paris, studied the profession of dancing for two years, and then became a soloist at the Grand Opéra, where I remained for four years. During these six years, I visited theatres and museums, studied history and languages, but never thought of composing even so much as sixteen measures of my own dance. I practiced, admired or criticized the others, contemplated the intrinsic value of ballets with the insouciance of a true Parisian, and, like my comrades, aspired to earn money and praise without any real consideration of higher art.

I finally awakened from my careless attitude when, in the year 1829, I used my three-month leave of absence to make a trip to Denmark. I had to put together a repertoire and learn a good deal of it by heart. But when I came to mount it on the stage, I was forced to supply from my own resources what my memory lacked and to make those adaptations necessitated by local conditions. Here I came to know my strengths. By teaching roles to others, I obtained a clearer impression of my own part and for the first time, in a manner of speaking, came face to face with my art. Success crowned my endeavors, the confidence of others lent me courage, and in the enthusiasm of the moment, I made my first original [choreographic] attempts, which were, in fact, nothing but portions of my own life.‡

I consequently became a composer since I wished to appear as a dancer and mime; I became a teacher because I was forced to train subjects for my compositions; and I eventually organized one of the finest *corps de ballet* in Europe because through my struggle against repeated attempts to cut down and crush the dance, I developed a strength and persistence which up till then I had never believed to be part of my character.

With Galeotti's death and my father's retirement,* there began a period during which the ballet steadily declined in the public's favor and esteem. A number of unsuccessful compositions further helped to downgrade the dance as an art. The Theatre regarded it as a troublesome burden, and it became the fashion for the audience to clear the house when the *entrée* began. Many other internal and external circumstances caused the public to consider a person who transferred from the ballet to the drama as having been saved from a fate worse than death. The ghost of a *corps de ballet* that still existed was used only as "padding" in spectacles. The humiliation reached its depth when an old *figurant*, who recoiled at the idea of being used as a footstool to a palanquin, was addressed in these words (whose tone contemporaries will surely be able to recognize): "Thank God you can be used for something!"

A great deal of hard work was needed in order to bring life back into an art which had lost its right to this name. After my first surprisingly successful attempts, people came to the conclusion that such a rapid transformation was but another proof of the unimportance of the thing. First it was said that danc-

---

‡ See Vol. I, the chapter "Acclaim to the Graces."
*Antoine Bournonville retired at the end of the 1822–1823 season.

ing was not an art, and then that I was not an artist. In the beginning, the criticism was dignified though skeptical; later, it became angry and peevish, and, finally, knowledgeable but blasé (apathetic).

My strongest argument against the troublesome opponents of the Dance was a successful production. Foot by foot, I gained ground, which, however, was not exactly defended by the most loyal weapons. I loved my *corps de ballet* as a shepherd his flock, and upon the whole we got along well with each other. They were interested in the work and were sincerely happy when it was successful. The tension under which I constantly labored often made me lose my temper with the less intelligent. My philanthropic ideas about the refinement of the heart through the influence of art were, more often than not, sorely disappointed and filled my soul with bitterness . . . nevertheless, I submit that the majority of my fellow artists learnt to appreciate my way of thinking, and I would have conquered those individuals who strayed from the fold, had they not been buttonholed by flattering backbiters *within*, and so-called "advisory protectors" *without*, the walls of the Theatre. They sowed many tares among the wheat, and often brought the harvest close to ruin. They manipulated the public and gave me coldness and contrariness instead of reward and recognition.

Twice during my career my perseverance failed. I tendered my resignation, which was turned down. I risked my future bread in order to obtain my freedom, but . . . I learnt to see things in a new and better light. Those scenes that once seemed so tragic now appeared laughable to me. I sensibly learnt to weigh advantages and disadvantages, and discovered that on the high-salaried Continent I could find just as much unpleasantness as I could here at home. If the Teatro San Carlo was more spacious, the Danish theatre gave me greater literary freedom; if it was uncertain whether my Nordic talent would please in the south, I could be sure that the store of ideas I had gathered in those southern climes would make my fortune here in the north; and finally, even though there were certain people in Copenhagen who could not tolerate me and my progress, I still had on my side writers, painters, and, above all, a whole generation of young savants who, by the letter they wrote in an effort to keep me in Denmark, gave me and my art a priceless diploma. Besides, I also had obligations to fulfill; what had been started had to be finished, and the course run out. I will soon arrive at this goal.

Whenever I read a story, the characters come alive in my imagination, with definite physiognomies, costumes, and surroundings, and make so deep an impression that if I should chance to read the same book ten years later, the same image stands before me. In this way, a whole host of *tableaux vivants* have been stored in my mind. They have become one with my art, and from the moment I took up composition, they have always been ready at hand. I may have difficulty in finding subjects that are appealing to our audience and suited to the talents of our company, but for me, nature, human life, and history will ever appear in the plastic forms of the ballet.

There are diverse opinions about the kind of material which is especially suited to the art of painting. Some people reject the historical in order to elevate the genre picture, the portrait, or the landscape. Similarly, attempts have been made to set formal boundaries for the writing of ballets and to confine them to whatever cannot be presented as drama. Even though time has weakened Noverre's assertion that tragedy is the only thing worthy of the ballet, he was perfectly right in this: everything that can, with the necessary education, be grasped from a painting can more easily be comprehended in a moving and complex picture, supported by the expressive language of music. Just as the reader can lend color and form to an artist's description, so the viewer can lend words to a mimed action, and experience has shown that it is not the choice of material but its artistic treatment that is the decisive factor.

Monotony or excessive use of the same genre is fatal to the theatrical art. If one has been successful in a certain style, one should only return to it in a roundabout way. Since I have stood completely alone, I have been forced to experiment with the most heterogeneous subjects. My proper calling is for the *Romantic,* and this is the place to state the reason why this adjective is so frequently applied to most of my ballets. First of all, my entire poetic sphere is Nordic. There may be something French in the trimmings, but the foundation is completely Danish. Oehlenschläger and Thorvaldsen have been my models, just as Shakespeare and classical antiquity were theirs. Secondly, I have often sinned against the classic unities and historical accuracy, and have considered it my duty to spice the serious with comic variety. Finally, in my productions I have often allowed my fantasy to run in nature's mystic circles and to intervene in the action, partly as dream and partly as reality personified.

The first thing that foreigners discover in my ballets—and that which they claim distinguishes them from most works of this kind—is something they have called *"une poésie toute particulière,"* and this unique quality is nothing more than a romantic air.† In my remarks concerning my own works, I will point out the places that seem to me the most successful; and, should my judgment appear suspect, I beg you to consider that I have more often had occasion to be irritated by a failure and to deplore its cause, than to see a success and rejoice at its effect. After all, I myself remember better than anyone what I have done, and in the course of time I have become so objective that often I am ashamed of my blunders but, from time to time, will also declare this or that to have been well composed, and, aye, even marvel that it was I who actually conceived and executed it.

People like to ask me how a ballet is made, with respect to its conception

---

† One of the contemporary foreigners to characterize Bournonville and his works was the English author and critic, Edmund Gosse. In his *Northern Studies* (London, 1890) he says: "If one can fancy an old Greek in whose brain the harmonious dances of a divine festival still throbbed, waking suddenly to find himself settled in this commonplace century as dancing-master at the Royal Theatre of Copenhagen, one can form some notion of the personality of Bournonville."

as well as its musical form and rehearsal. This I can answer only from my own experience. There is certainly enough material; and as for subjects of new ballets, I have many more in mind than I could possibly furnish with plots and dances.

A lovely idea, be it novel or piquant, is a gift from Heaven that comes to me only when my mind is tranquil, when I am strolling in rustic solitude, sitting quietly in a traveling carriage, or just when another *finished* work is about to be tried out. Around this idea, in itself often insignificant and having no real connection with anything, is woven a plot, an event, and whole groups of living pictures. All of this evolves in a relatively short time, and under the most varied circumstances.‡ I turn to some good sources, sit down at my writing table, and do not put down my pen until I have finished my libretto.

As I write, there are a thousand things to be taken into consideration as to *what* can be performed and *who* will perform it. I must take into account whether there is enough to satisfy the true art-lovers, and yet something to please the gallery (the crowd). Many good ideas must, of course, be rejected for lack of space and money. Luxury, however, would not be my worst stumbling block if I only had distance, lighting, good seats for the audience, and shorter intervals between the acts. Since the technical facilities of our Theatre prevent me from dazzling the eye, I must work especially hard to appeal to people's emotions and sound taste, not allowing myself to become infected by the frivolous sentimentality or the sentimental frivolity of recent times. I have had the satisfaction of seeing that while French ballet, as well as the rest of its dramatic literature, has suffered from sordidness, in my works love has been maintained in a pure and worthy form. For this I thank my Muse!

When I have completed my libretto, I set it aside for a while. Then, if I read through it again with the same interest and every picture stands clear before me, I consider it ready for composition.* I turn to the music composer, who receives a separate outline for each scene that makes up a musical number; he then comes to an agreement with me as to rhythm and character. Usually, by means of gestures and *pas*, I manage to give him a rough idea of what is to be performed; I improvise a melody to it; sometimes this melody contains a useful theme, which may be picked up, shaped, and modulated.

Now the composer works until an entire piece is finished. I get to hear it . . . it is completely different from my original conception; I need to become familiar with it, but it is lovely and good music. The length and character are

---

‡ In *August Bournonville: Spredte Minder i Anledning af Hundredaarsdagen* (Copenhagen, 1905), Charlotte Bournonville recalls one of these occasions: "Since Father had a very expressive countenance, I have a number of times been able to see the seeds of a ballet germinating in his soul. Thus, when he heard Gottschalk's 'Negro Dance'—brilliantly played by our family's talented and amiable friend, Fru Therese Henriques—the idea for *Far from Denmark* was born."

*For a discussion of the possible differences between Bournonville's original "working libretto" and the little printed book purchased by the theatre audiences, see Allan Fridericia, "Bournonville's Ballet *Napoli*: In the Light of Archive Materials and Theatrical Practice," *Theatre Research Studies* (Copenhagen, 1972), p. 53.

determined. My own working out of the ballet now assumes a new form. From the music, I get ideas for details of which the composer himself has not even the faintest notion. I become throughly acquainted with his composition, find an episode in every measure, and then, after the piece has been rehearsed, it appears as if both of the composers had agreed on every note and as if they had been of one mind. This mainly applies to original music. Arranged music, expressive melodies, and national themes I myself specify according to the needs of the ballet. I receive a violin arrangement or répétiteur's part for two violins, to assist me with the rehearsal, and only when a major portion of the music has been finished in this form does the composer begin to orchestrate it.

The system is quite different, however, for the actual transmission of roles and dancing parts. Most balletmasters think out the details only when they are surrounded by the *corps de ballet*. This method is slow and extremely tiresome. The master selects and rejects; this is a kind of improvisation that often suffers from numerous interruptions and repetitions and almost always ends up producing something highly imperfect. Gardel and Henry, on the contrary, had their material already worked out when the rehearsal began, and I follow their example. One may indeed become a bit impatient when something is not learnt quickly enough, but this is nothing compared to the agitation and irritation expressed by those who choose to arrange, aye, even await their inspiration on the spot. When ideas have been properly worked out, however, things move quickly and pleasantly, and the progress of the work inspires confidence and increases attention.

As I have progressed in my art, I have developed a "choreography" or manner of denoting the *pas*, gestures, and groupings that I wish to transmit. I write them beneath the notes of the répétiteur's part, and for this I use French technical expressions. I indicate the groupings by means of stick figures. This work takes much time and trouble, but is highly rewarding; for while in private it is quite permissible to falter and search for the proper arrangement, the balletmaster should never appear before the *corps* with anything but certainty and aplomb. Of course, if a better idea happens to strike me on the spot, I certainly make use of it; but, in any case, I have my notes to guide me, and these are a great help later on when I take a ballet back into the repertoire after a rather long period of time.

"Now, how is such a ballet rehearsed? Does each person receive his role written out? Does the balletmaster arrange the essential parts of the composition with the performers and then let them work out the details for themselves? Is the dancer permitted to follow his own inspiration?"

These questions involuntarily occur to those unversed in the dance, and to them I reply: Each member of the company must do exactly what is prescribed and generally adhere to the view that the execution [of steps or gestures] is not art but simply mechanical training. I will attempt to clarify this point:

In a ballet, gestures, *pas,* and groupings are not only the same as words, verses, and intonation in drama; they are also like notes, measures, and tempo in music. The first requirement for a good performance in all three branches of art is *correctness.* Without it, the poet is not present in his work and the audience cannot be sure it is seeing a proper interpretation. In a play, the actor takes his role home with him, delves into its spirit, grasps it, and, as early as the first rehearsal, appears with it clothed in definite form. But now, if justice is to be done to the piece, he must be prepared to modify his original interpretation in order to harmonize with his fellow actors, with the physical demands of the stage, and, above all, with the poet's idea. The character imposes many restraints on him, both in bearing and in declamation; even the costume can alter his design—and yet there is still a margin of freedom left for both talent and genius. The actor can absorb his role in such a way that in his form it becomes something new, and the author thus sees his original idea improved and surpassed. Ensemble music cannot be treated arbitrarily; yet it is the tone, feeling, and execution that determine the ingenious interpretation. It is exactly the same in ballet. Every *pas,* attitude, and movement originates with the master and is indicated by him in order to be understood, remembered, rehearsed, and performed. Since ballet is not learnt by notes and letters, the master is prompter, manuscript, and, above all, *instructeur* until the parts are fully comprehended. But we now come to the difference between art and mechanism: an ingenious performer will give the acquired form a unique stamp, and, just as grace, lightness, and brilliance animate the composed dances, so spirit and feeling enliven the role in question. One follows the poet's words but does not imitate his voice. So too the balletmaster is the teacher, not the ideal. The difference in the performance is as that between a drawing from the life and a traced copy.

There are capable people in whom the spirit is rather passive. But such persons can also be used, and often with such great success that most people cannot distinguish them from truly reflective artists. In this case the rehearsal takes on a completely different aspect, for either they possess the gift of learning quickly or they must be brought to the desired result by means of patience and mechanical exercise. Experience has taught me that *ingenious* people much more readily submit themselves to the strict demands of art and have a desire to sacrifice their personal interest for the benefit of the whole. These true artists (whom I dare not mention by name so as not to point out the false ones) have provided me with the most pleasurable hours I have spent in the theatre, and I acknowledge that I have taken the suggestions which their warm and lively feelings have given me.

One ought never to read the libretto of a ballet to the cast, for the role that is most involved with the plot is not always the most brilliant on stage, while it does lie in the composer's power to turn what is considered to be a second- or third-rate role into a veritable bravura part. A little piquant interest or an exit, even some little dances, can become high points in a ballet, and the prettiest music often motivates the best situations. After one has determined precisely which person is best suited for this or that role (for I consider it the ruination of art to arrange a role for a specific person), it is also important to make him or her acquainted *en particulier* with the plan of the ballet and to focus her attention upon the principal episodes in which she is intended to take part, without reference to what others will have to do. If one can at the same time—preferably by means of a pretty sketch—give her some idea of the costume in which she is to perform, she will immediately get a picture of what she is supposed to be. She will hereby develop a fondness for her role, and even before she has been taught a single measure, she will have so identified herself with the character that she neither can nor *will want to* covet any part other than that which was actually intended for her.

I have described this person in the feminine because this sex is the most difficult to please, not because of its higher degree of vanity (for the gentlemen certainly give them competition on this score) but because all ladies of the theatre are usually encumbered by a rear guard of mothers, advisors, protectors, troubadors, and critics, who see her as their plaything, who shall stand first, highest, and alone. From this stem all the petty scandals, into which the public is drawn, often as a collaborator; and from these, in turn, come the countless accusations that overwhelm the balletmaster who does not choose to select the prima donna of the moment as the predominant patroness of his work.

The difficulties which the balletmaster must endure even more than the playwright (who, after the play is written, has only to let it be censored, read, rehearsed, acted, and judged by others) are compensated for by great advantages: 1) the ballet, by its very nature, cannot undergo any literary censure; 2) since nobody knows the details of the ballet before it has been completely rehearsed, no one but myself can cast the roles, and the demands of the work determine my choice; 3) since I am at once director and teacher, none of the performers can object that the part does not suit him and, on these grounds, refuse to perform.

Naturally, the first requirement for a successful work is that it satisfy *me*, the man responsible for the performance. From this comes a certain assurance in the ensemble which is often lacking in the more independent spoken drama. The costumes and decorations are executed under my supervision, and until I declare a work to be "ready," no one may schedule it for performance. Thus my position becomes far better than that of the dramatic writers in this country, for of everything bestowed upon the performance—even exaggerated praise—I can, in all modesty, take my share. I acknowledge and commend those artists who perform in my ballets, delight in their glories, and admire their talented interpretations . . . but I owe them nothing.

I summarize my activity at the Danish Theatre in this way: In fifteen years I have performed in a variety of genres the most difficult, if not the most rewarding, roles in dancing and mime; but even though I have trained ex-

FERNALD LIBRARY
COLBY-SAWYER COLLEGE
NEW LONDON, N. H. 03250

cellent pupils through instruction and my own example, I have up to now defended my post as First Solodancer. I have earned for the ballet a proper place in the Kingdom of Art, and I have made it an ornament for the very stage upon which I once saw it despised and neglected. In an age when there is looseness and distortion in dramatic literature, I have forged a new path and kept myself free from the excesses of Romanticism. Deprived of all the resources that a large and wealthy theatre has to offer, and working under many hampering conditions, I have been able to extract from art, nature, and history more than one successful idea, gladdened my countrymen, and provided for the Copenhagen Ballet a justifiable renown.

THE YOUNG MAN
A miniature of August Bournonville painted in
Paris in the early 1820's by J. Turretin.
Private collection.

THE CHILD ACTOR
The twelve-year-old boy as he appeared in
The Judgment of Solomon. Oil painting signed
N. Christensen. Det kgl. Bibliotek, Copenhagen.

ADOLPHE NOURRIT
An undated print. Courtesy Music Division,
The New York Public Library at Lincoln Center,
Astor, Lenox and Tilden Foundations.
Photo by Frank Derbas.

JENNY LIND
An undated drawing by Lehmann showing the Swedish
singer as Norma. Det kgl. Bibliotek, Copenhagen.

V

Celebrities

IN writing memoirs, it is customary to adorn the pages with famous names, to give piquant portraits, and to boast of intimate relationships. I have lived during an age when a host of renowned men, both within and outside the world of art, cast about them a glory, even the farthest rays of which were not without value. I have seen and heard most of them, spoken with many, been favored by several, and worked with some, but I have been intimate with very few. I have shared the popular enthusiasm for great men and great events in Denmark, England, and especially France; but it is not for me to assume reflected glory in order to place myself in a historical light. Even though the greater world has not been without influence upon my whole artistic existence, and my bit of authorship in particular, it is mainly artists and writers who have had a bearing on my theatre life. The latter would therefore be imperfectly described were I not to mention those of my older contemporaries who have delighted me and given me a love of the stage.

Painters, poets, and composers are perpetuated in their works. One need only glance at a lexicon to discover a whole series of important men whom I have known, admired, and acclaimed. But real theatre people, my models and colleagues, will not disdain being discussed by me, and I consider it my duty to plant a tree in memory of them, whether it is I who shelter it or it that shelters me.

CHRISTIAN KNUDSEN
† 1816

Rosing and Schwartz had quitted the Danish stage, leaving behind an enormous void. A number of character roles stood vacant and the sentimental drama exerted its weakening influence. As proof of this, *Hakon Jarl*, although considered a masterpiece, did not enjoy more than eight performances in seven years. During this time, the *syngespil* or so-called *opéra-comique* flourished. Schultz, Kunzen, Du Puy, Weyse, and Schall in this country; the ever fresh Mozart and a whole host of French composers—Méhul, Cherubini, Nicolo, Dellamaria, Devienne, Dalayrac—enriched our stage with pieces which, in dramatic as well as melodic respects, were far superior to the products of the present day.

In these works, Knudsen shone with a warmth and brilliance that are unforgettable, even to those who, like myself, were children in his day. His humor and cordiality alike were irresistible. No one on our stage has possessed the charm of gaiety and sadness to the same degree that he did. His sailors, Jews, and judges have become established types, but who can ever forget him as the Watercarrier in *Two Days*, as the Shoemaker in *The Good Fairy*, or as Leporello in *Don Giovanni?* While not outstanding, his voice was most engaging; for wherever he sang, whether from the stage, at table, or on the deck of a warship, he captivated and thrilled his listeners.

Some people reproached him for too often giving in to his bubbling humor and indulging in low comedy. I was too young at the time to be able to judge his worth with a critical eye, but all older connoisseurs agree with me that even though Knudsen's talented successor, Hans Rind, had inherited a measure of his predecessor's joviality, this nuance of comic effect and communicativeness is no longer to be found in the Danish theatre. We still see striking pictures, profound studies, irony, and fine comedy; but since Knudsen's death we have found the gift of delighting people simply by the sight of a cheerful countenance, of entertaining and moving them in turn without the effort of satire or sentimentality, only in French actors; and who knows but that the Frenchmen, too, may soon lose this charming *rondeur*.

FRYDENDAHL　　　RYGE
† 1840　　　† 1842

These outstanding actors were two dramatic magnitudes as exceptional in scope as they were different in nature. Although they might not care to be discussed together, I feel that when they are appraised in relation to one another, their talents will be seen to gain in exactly the same proportion as they served to counterbalance and support each other during their lifetimes. Both of them performed a countless number of important roles; through their more or less successful imitators they have both formed "schools" and will thus reappear on our stage long after we have recovered from their loss; for only with difficulty can they be replaced in this age of ours, when originality, genius, and the desire to appear before the public take so many different roads that do not lead to the stage.

It would be extremely hard to characterize the basic nature of these two artists, for in both of them there were such contradictory elements that it is impossible to say what it was they actually respected and loved. The complexity that marked their artistic performances was also apparent in their views on life, with this difference, however: the former were almost always excellent.

If ever a master race revealed itself in a human body, then Frydendahl was a full-blooded nobleman from head to toe. His figure and his whole voice possessed an elasticity that acquired every possible nuance from a minister of state down to an ale tapster. The unique insight with which he grasped the characteristic features of every class and age gave his portrayals a classical stamp, and an innate grace deprived his caricatures of any crudeness and made even his mistakes charming.

He "filled" the stage, as it were. He not only was concerned with his own role, but also inspired his fellow actors and the audience, most notably in comedy and comic opera. In drama and tragedy he was, as a rule, forced and cold. He lacked feeling, and though he might be affected by a particular situation, it was his nerves, not his fantasy, that drove him to tears. Irony was the axis about which his talent revolved; he had hundreds of different masks, but no spontaneous individuality, as did Knudsen and Lindgreen. He provoked the most boisterous laughter but did not possess this harmless mirth himself.

Frydendahl was doubly great; for although he had never traveled, still he learnt how to acquire the perfections people admired in Molé, Fleury, and Dugazon. He was the only one of all our actors in whom I have found the same singularity that distinguished Garrick; namely, he immersed himself in his role throughout the day and, in a manner of speaking, *became* the character he was to portray that evening. The most hilarious anecdotes and the most impertinent witticisms flowed from him when he played a comic role, whereas he would be positively unbearable with self-conceit when he had to portray a cavalier. No one could abuse the nobility the way he did when he played a commoner; but no one lashed out so scornfully at the bourgeoisie as he when he put on an embroidered frock coat. One proposition, however, seemed to be deeply ingrained in him; namely, that the theatrical profession, which had provided him with bread and honor, was an occupation that ought to make one blush.

In this respect, Ryge was of a completely opposite opinion. The words of Hakon Jarl, "What a man is born for, that shall he become, and innate desire generates innate strength," were his motto. He was a born actor, and although he had been outstanding in the scientific field, he gave up that profitable career to devote himself to the theatre. There he found the one activity that answered to his fiery imagination. In spite of his great height, his appearance was by no means imposing: a small head on a short neck, weak legs for a disproportionately large body, and a rather ordinary speaking voice were the external resources with which he was equipped; but his genius knew how to remedy these defects. No one has combined greater strength, dignity, and deep emotion. No one has become more identified with the Poet's [Oehlenschläger's] creations than Ryge. Although his comic roles lacked the grace that ennobled even Frydendahl's most burlesque performances, he was usually captivating by virtue of his priceless humor and understanding of character. His Jeronimuses,* as well as the whole gamut of father and uncle parts in both high and low comedy, were genuine masterpieces. In true plastic roles,

---

*Characters in plays by Holberg.

Ryge lacked style, or, to put it more correctly, he did not have time to "get into the part" as did Frydendahl, for he was ever at the mercy of his position as Economy Supervisor—a position where the endless ups and downs were of such violence and passion that he was deprived of the classical serenity demanded by roles of high tragedy. But here again his magnificent portrayals of Nordic Viking life must prove an exception: it was sharp, rough forms that enshrouded a deeply Romantic spirit, redolent of sea fog, paganism, and sacrificial blood. He who has not seen Ryge's Hakon, Palnatoke, and Stærkodder does not really know Oehlenschläger. His words rang like sword blows on copper shields, they bored into the soul like runes cut into granite boulders. His voice resounded like the shrill tone of the *lur*† over the North Sea's breakers. . . . I fancy I can hear him still as Hakon Jarl, shouting to the gods in the sacrificial grove: "My Erling I have offered here, a mighty host of mine enemies shall follow." The curtain fell, and my hair bristled as I thought of the bloodbath that was to come.

TALMA   MLLE. MARS

Just as Ryge transported me into the heroic life of the North and enabled me to retain a picture of it that has served me as a model, so Talma brought me in turn from Jerusalem to the Capitol, from Ilion to Denmark, from the African desert to Westminster, as an ardent republican, a bloodthirsty tyrant, or an insane old man. I have seen him as the high priest Joad, as Manlius, Sulla, Nero, Orestes, Hamlet, Othello, Richard III, and finally as Charles VI. For me his performances were like strolling through the Vatican: I could do nought but take off my hat, look, and learn. Everything about him was perfect; his declamation and bearing were not "academic," but in accordance with the character, time, and place. One might follow him through fire and ice, hope and despair, but never beyond the bounds of beauty. I have seen only a single comedy role performed by Talma, namely, that of Danville in *L'Ecole des vieillards*. It was highly interesting to see this august tragedian descend to his own personality, that of a jovial, gray-haired man of sixty. Everyday life can indeed bring the mind into a tragic vein, but the external appearance ought not to put on the mask of high tragedy. He played Danville opposite his most famous rival, Mlle. Mars!

I name her as Talma's sole contender for the dramatic throne. By virtue of her own universally understandable genre, the comedy, and the advantage which her gender gives, she possibly possessed an even greater number of admirers than Talma. She was "the critics' despair." Talma was often accused of being unclassical, but with her the fact was obvious. Her acting was higher everyday life in its most amiable form: a perfectly controlled vocal organ, a

† Originally, the S-shaped battle trumpet of Bronze Age Scandinavian peoples; in later usage, a long, curved horn used to summon cattle from their pastures.

pair of eyes that had smiles, tears, aye, even lightning and sparks at their command; an appearance that instantly assumed whatever age she herself ordained; and, finally, a *sympathie* that had the effect of making the stage seem empty from the moment she made her exit into the wings. Her gay or emotional romantic heroines, coquettes, newly married women, and even soubrettes will remain alive in my soul as long as it retains a memory of "goodness and beauty." She was the antithesis of everything that could be termed "mannerism," and, in the highest sense of the word, she *argued* the principle that there ought to be a magic wall between the stage and the auditorium.

It is now nineteen years since I was among the thousands who accompanied Talma's mortal remains to the grave. At that time, the Théâtre Français still possessed Baptiste, Michelot, Armand, Monrose, and Mmes. Leverd, Mante, and Bourgoin. But this whole phalanx disappeared with Mlle. Mars, who did not retire from the stage until she was sixty [1839]. It is true that for a short while Rachel succeeded in bringing some life back into tragedy, but she lacked true genius, and with Talma and Mlle. Mars, the French drama lost its brightest stars — now twilight reigns.

POTIER   FRÉDÉRICK LEMAÎTRE

In this world, everything goes in circles; nothing perishes, but things assume new forms. In my time there was a nimble leap from the Théâtre Français to the Boulevard theatres — the same distance as that from tragedy to the so-called "melodrama," and from comedy to the *vaudeville*. But just as the classical theatre was on the decline, the Romantic, or unclassical, began to rise. What had been noble now became boring and trite, while the burlesque was ennobled by poetic invention. The Théâtre Français, which was governed by *sociétaires*, rigidly closed its doors to younger talents. These young people therefore had to turn to the smaller theatres, which, in spite of all the bonds that hampered them, gave both writers and actors the opportunity to display their talents to the public. But the moment the *vaudeville* and the farce had been transformed into *comédies à couplets* and the old "robber dramas" had assumed nobler forms, both the Gymnase and the Variétés were teeming with outstanding talents. The former had Perlet, Gontier, Fierville, Legrand, and Mmes. Jenny Vertpré and Léontine Fay; the latter Lepeintre, Odry, Vernet, Arnal, and Mmes. Pauline and Jenny Colon. But how strange it sounded when, after having ranked Talma and Mlle. Mars among the supreme dramatic delights, people were forced to give Potier a place at their side! And who gave him this place? Why, Talma himself — at the head of all those who possessed heart and feeling.

If one only names his repertoire, it appears to consist of nothing but trifles; but if one takes into account his masterly performance of these roles, it becomes something great. He was the creator of an entirely new mode of acting. He has hundreds of imitators, yet among them there is but a single genius: Bouffé! In each of his roles, Potier embodied a new idea. Without change of makeup or dialect, he moved from one character to another, from the old shopkeeper to the hundred-year-old veteran, from the recruit to the old *rentier,* and from the parasite to "the comic Englishman."

He possessed an inexhaustible fund of humor and naturalness, a unique comic force combined with profound sensibility. Even though he had a rather hoarse voice, it was easy for him to transform the mood from one of uproarious laughter to one of irresistible emotion by a single change of inflection. Here was a man who could bring poetry to the stage! How many times have I awakened in the middle of the night, laughing contentedly at something he said or did; and even today I cannot restrain my tears when I think of his last appearance at the Variétés. (Heaven knows why he left this theatre). He played *le Conscrit,* the drafted recruit who must set off into the wide world, perhaps never to see his village again. Sighing, old Brunet embraced him, and when the lovely Pauline gave him her fichu as a parting remembrance and he, doing violence to his own feelings, replied, "There's my courage for a long time," the entire audience burst into loud weeping and cries of distress.

Another remarkable phenomenon is Frédérick Lemaître, who was by nature called to be Talma's successor but who has, in fact, become a kind of "prodigal son" of higher dramatic art. Through an excess of fantasy, his talent has become so warped that he will hardly be able to return to his father's house, the Théâtre Français. His career has never progressed beyond the Porte-Saint-Martin. He has alternately shone at two neighboring theatres, the Ambigu and the Folies Dramatiques, and has not only enraptured his suburban audience but created an epoch throughout the whole of Paris and thence in the rest of the dramatic world.

He has created such roles as Kean, the Gambler, and Robert Macaire! Gifted with a magnificent appearance, he has known how to acquire the manners and pick up the customs of every class of society. He was *Les Mystères de Paris* united in one person. I had to admire him in an otherwise awful play by Victor Ducagne, *Thirty Years, or The Life of a Gambler.* In this part he went through all the stages of the gambling mania, from the victim's twentieth to his fiftieth year, falling into crime and indigence, and finally appearing as a ragged, round-shouldered beggar, retaining nothing of his former personality but the soulful eyes. Someone gave him a loaf of bread from which he was free to cut as much as he liked; he put the first piece into his pocket with a "For my family!" that made all hearts tremble with emotion. But later on, when, after having committed murder, he returned home with gold for his wife and answered her anxious query with the words: "I found it," a murmur ran through the audience as if a chasm had suddenly opened before our eyes.

His Robert Macaire, the greater part of which he wrote himself, is the most humorous portrait of a thieving rogue that has ever been produced. His appearance as sleepwalker, stock-jobber, and suiter to the general's daughter, together with the game of *écarté* in which he discovers that his father-in-law is as big a rascal as himself, are some of the most priceless moments one can imagine.

Frédérick Lemaître possesses a variety which I have seen matched only by Ryge, to whom he bears a faint resemblance. However, these slapsticks played before a less select audience have given his talent a tendency which only with difficulty can be made to conform to the stricter rules of drama. His views and character interpretations have become so unique, aye, *proverbiale* to the Boulevard, that he will hardly be able to assume a place among artists who surpass him in technique but do not possess one-tenth of his genius.

MARTIN   ADOLPHE NOURRIT

The loveliest theatrical career is certainly that of a singer—when one has a natural vocation. One ought to be an artist whether one is an actor or a dancer, but a singer can be much less of an artist and still be far more successful if Heaven has blessed him with the first requirement: a voice. There is strange magic in a beautiful singing voice; there are certain tones which are never forgotten and which become a standard for one's future judgment of singing. For example, in my early youth I heard Carl Bruun, a baritone whose voice had such a singular ring that one hardly cared what he sang, for there was something in his rendition of even the simplest melody that lifted the heart and left behind a longing to hear more. A number of years later, I went to Paris with my father and visited the Théâtre Feydeau, where I heard Martin in *Le nouveau Seigneur du village, Le petit Chaperon rouge, Les Voitures versées,* and the romance *Une Folie*—in short, in a part of his extensive repertoire. He was as good an actor as one generally expects a Frenchman to be; he possessed a natural gaiety—but what a singer! At that time I was unable to judge the excellence of his method, but his was the most delightful male voice I had ever heard. Though on a larger scale, it reminded me of Carl Bruun's, and the similarity in delivery was easily explained by the fact that Bruun was a pupil of Du Puy, who had modeled himself completely in the style of Martin. By 1824, when I returned to France, Martin had retired. But even today his roles and type of voice are known as *"les martins."* Unfortunately, I never got to hear him again.

However, I witnessed a brilliant debut at the Académie Royale de Musique: a young tenor, who was an improved edition of his father, full of life and emotion, with a handsome appearance and a rare flexibility and range in his voice. It was Adolphe Nourrit, then twenty-one years old. In a short time, using the classical repertoire of Gluck and Sacchini, he developed into the most remarkable talent the French Opéra ever possessed. New works came streaming in for him, and every role he performed was a new triumph. By rehearsing *Corinth, Moïse,* and *Comte Ory* under Rossini himself, his voice attained its peak of strength and perfection. Roles like those of Masaniello and Arnold in *Tell* put him on a par with the supreme tragic artists. His career was a frolic, a dance to the accompaniment of favor and applause. And who could help but love him! His handsome face was a faithful image of the most honest heart. Although he was praised to the skies and might have been carried away by vanity, he was winsome and modest toward his comrades, obliging to all, a loving family man, and a person with deep religious feelings. We were almost contemporaries, and though I, as a younger artist, looked up to him, "the famous one," we nevertheless became extremely good friends. He valued my friendship highly and, for myself, I recognized in him not only the great dramatic singer but also a man to whom I would have entrusted my honor, my life, and all my worldly goods.

I left the Opéra (my position as soloist at the Académie Royale) in 1830, three months before the July Revolution broke out. Nourrit, an ardent patriot, joined the National Guard and appeared in uniform to inflame his countrymen with "La Parisienne" and "La Marseillaise." Never had people heard these songs performed in such a fashion; never had his voice achieved such volume. He became the darling of the Parisians: *Robert, Gustave, La Juive*, and *Les Huguenots* became his points of culmination. Everything he undertook was successful. He wrote the libretto for *La Sylphide* and changed Don Giovanni into a tenor part—superbly. But the patriotic songs bellowed out to the people had ruined his voice and given it certain nasal tones. Furthermore, even though he fulfilled the demands of both text and music to the highest degree and knew how to electrify his audience, Nourrit certainly did not have an *Italian voice*. His pitch was unique, but even in their prime, his chest tones were of a secondary nature. Duprez, who had studied and performed successfully in Italy, returned to France and made his debut at the Opéra. He lacked everything that Nourrit possessed: a handsome appearance, imagination, falsetto, and coloratura; but he excelled in the very quality wherein Nourrit had now become deficient: his chest tones were of a power and fullness whose effects were irresistible—his reception was thunderous. No one could deny the obvious: his *voice* surpassed Nourrit's, and even the greatest art must yield to a natural phenomenon.

However, the public gave Nourrit his due. No one dreamed that his repertoire could be taken over by another. His salary was enormous, his reputation considerable, and in everyday life he possessed all that love and friendship, wealth and Parisian life could bestow. But . . . this same Adolphe, who was so amiable and modest, who had stood so long *unchallenged* in his place, could not bear to see a rival to the idolatry of which he himself had received so rich a share. He unjustly accused his countrymen of ingratitude, and was spontaneously struck with the unhappy idea that Italy would indemnify him for the loss he believed himself to have suffered. Despite all pleas and remonstrances he terminated his contract and yielded his place to Duprez, who received a salary of 100,000 francs and thrilled the public with the *fortissimo* of his voice for an entire year, and in *"Asile héréditaire!,"* the sole aria from the third act of *William Tell*. But before Duprez had sung his *"Suivez-moi"* and become an expensive luxury item for the French Opéra, Nourrit had given the artistic world a masterly example.

He immediately obtained engagement in Italy and easily familiarized himself with the compositions of Bellini and Donizetti. But, alas! His vocal organ was and remained French, and it took all the sympathy his noble features and impassioned acting could inspire to keep the sensitive Italians from letting him know how jarring they found his less sonorous tones. He compelled the Italians to like him, but at the same time, he felt that his theatrical fortune hung by a thread. The memory of his golden days, reports of his rival's triumphs, and a longing for his beloved France tormented him. There was still time for him to return and to enjoy the happiness of family life, but his insatiable desire for glory became an obsession and embittered his existence. It happened in Naples. One evening [in 1839] he had sung Edgardo in *Lucia.* The public's approval had followed him throughout the performance, but during the final aria he thought he heard an expression of displeasure, which is quite possible, for the Neapolitans are not shy about showing their disapproval, even toward their favorites. This sound haunted his imagination and prevented him from sleeping. At sunrise the next morning, he kissed his wife and children, ascended two stories, and hurled himself from the balcony of the Palazzo Barbaja onto the lava flagstones in the street below!

In the year 1841, as I walked to a restaurant each day, I had to set foot on the very spot where the fever-ridden head of my friend, the honest, God-fearing Nourrit, had been shattered. At the Campo Santo, I visited the grave that had housed his mortal remains until they could be returned to France by his wife. Friends had graven his memory in marble and planted roses on his burial mound. I plucked one of them and pressed it in a cherished book. It still reminds me of the feelings that once constricted my artist's heart, but it also teaches me that the most beautiful theatrical career is not the one that brings the most gold and triumphs, but that which leads to a peaceful old age and a natural death.

SONTAG   MALIBRÁN

There have always been controversies and factions concerning sopranos and altos, just as there have been with regard to blondes and brunettes. By altos I do not mean those female voices which, in a manner of speaking, array themselves in masculine garb, but rather those which have their intensity in low and middle notes and summon their tones from the innermost chest cavity, as if they really sang from the heart. If it were possible for these voices to move about in the high ranges with the same ease as they do in the low, they would no doubt be the finest that music produces. But nothing here upon earth is perfect; and yet in this as in everything else, we find the necessary compensations, for it is only with difficulty that the mezzo-soprano comes up into the higher registers, while the pure soprano always lacks fullness in depth. I dare say there is to be found in alto voices an indescribable expression of passion and feeling, but what heavenly clarity and supernatural revelation there are in a true soprano! I can be enraptured by both, but I am really infatuated only by angelic voices; hence my partiality for Mme. Fodor as compared with Pasta, for Sontag over Malibrán, and for Jenny Lind above all the singers I have heard.

I heard Mme. Mainvielle-Fodor (1820) as Rosina, as Zerlina in *Don Giovanni,* and as the Countess in *Figaro.* Her voice was like the clearest crystal; the notes ran like pearls upon a thread! She was no actress — I am inclined to think she did not possess any expression for passion — but one felt content in her presence, and her voice had such a pleasant ring and such power that it would have been impossible to refuse her a request.

The enthusiastic dilettanti called her *"la regina del canto."* But no rule lasts forever, and Mme. Fodor was dethroned by Mme. Pasta, who was given the title *"la diva."* She too was a goddess — a Juno. She was classically beautiful, genuinely tragic, but she looked as if she were bored until her emotions were aroused, and this moment came only as she neared the end of her role. Her voice, which was not free from hoarseness, did not discard the veil before the middle of the piece. Until then, one had to be content with her attempts, mixed with coughing, throat-clearing, and head-shaking; and thus it would have remained if the fanatics, by means of constant applause, had not given her faithful encouragement until the miracle finally happened. These moments then consisted of some passages of a shatteringly tragic effect, but, even though I confess that I might shout "Bravo!" with the crowd, my heart remained cold and I could find in her artistic character nothing more than — a *prima donna assoluta.*

One morning, Rossini came up to Vestris' dancing school and told us that "a little German, pretty as a heart" was that evening to make her debut as Rosina in *Il Barbiere.* Vestris and I got tickets for the Italian Opera, where the new attraction could not be said to have assembled many dilettanti. The little German was named Henrietta Sontag. She was, in every sense of the word, engaging: blonde curls, big blue eyes, tiny hands and feet, and a slight and supple figure. There was an amiable roguishness in her acting and a matchless self-assurance in her singing, but above all a comeliness and unpretentiousness about her whole person that made a most pleasing impression. Her success was not doubted for a moment: her boldness and perfection in passages, together with the ring of her voice, reminded one of Mme. Fodor; but she also possessed a kind of falsetto over and above the usual soprano range, which she used *pianissimo* in small cadenzas that were of a most charming effect. These were accompanied by an indescribable play of facial expression, and when her features dissolved into an *"anima"* or *"felicità,"* the whole house burst into a passionate frenzy.

From then on, the Italian Opera was positively besieged, and one had to belong to the specially favored in order to hear her as often as I did. Rosina,

Cenerentola, La Donna del Lago, Donna Anna, and Amenaide were the roles in which I admired her. Her triumph was complete, even though at that time people did not dare to "call artists before the curtain" or to "strew flowers" etc. at royal theatres. But there was no lack of acclaim. Her name resounded everywhere, and there was something extraordinary about the glory that surrounded "the virginal enchantress."

She sang one season in London and then returned to Paris. She was eagerly awaited by her many admirers, who had arranged to meet at her *rentrée*. She performed in *Donna del Lago*, but once the initial intoxication of the rendezvous had passed, one began to detect a slight change in her contour and a noticeable strain in reaching the "G" in the first cavatina. We rubbed our eyes and prodded our ears. What had happened? Could we have been mistaken before or now? We came away from the opera disappointed. There were a few more performances of a similar nature; then, suddenly, we learnt that our pretty little Sontag had sprained her foot on a peach stone. That was a hard nut to crack! It was three-quarters of a year before she recovered from it, but the hardest stone of all was a rival, who arrived from America just when the throne was vacant.

This was a daughter of a once popular singer, García, the lovely Mme. Malibrán. She was in the flower of her youth, bubbling with life and fantasy, daring in her undertakings, which often succeeded but always astonished, and, having a Spaniard's glowing expression in her full tones and abandoning herself to humor and emotion, she was certain to make an unparalleled impression on the Parisians and quickly supplant the image of Sontag with many—but not with me. I could not deny that in Malibrán genius was predominant; but I have always had a respect for perfection, and this I found to be most nearly achieved by Sontag. Furthermore, I noticed that people delighted in pitting a southern woman against a fair daughter of the North; and besides, there was an element of vengeance involved. Suffice it to say, Mme. Malibrán triumphed. Sontag, it is true, later returned, sang splendidly, and performed at the side of her rival in *Tancredi* and *Don Giovanni,* and together they formed the most beautiful ensemble in the world. But the bloom was gone. The anonymous Countess was soon taken away from the stage, and with Bellini's loveliest operas, *Norma, Straniera, Montecchi,* and *La Sonnambula,* Malibrán went to immortality and shortly afterward [1836] to eternal rest.

RUBINI   LABLACHE   GIULIA GRISI

This was a fine trefoil which for fifteen years formed the core of the finest opera company in the world, namely, that which alternated between Paris and London. They have so often been praised to the skies that my remarks will seem dull and superfluous; yet I cannot pass over them if I would mention everything that has marked an epoch in my theatre life.

I heard Rubini for the first time in 1825, in a concert, and after that in a ballet, where he came on and sang an aria from *Oreste*. It is impossible to determine whether he actually possessed an extraordinary voice, for his method consisted in loud transitions from *fortissimo* to *pianissimo,* so that there was no time for close observations. But I have never before heard such tones in any singer, and the virtuosity whereby he surmounted every difficulty bordered on the incredible. There was no wavering in his intonation, no defective opening notes or erratic trills. One could not tell whether he sang with the chest or falsetto voice. Suffice is to say, his singing was superb. But how did he behave onstage? He entered, cold and indifferent, and waited for the most effective passages, namely, the arias and duets. Then, if he felt in voice, he let himself go and now and then managed to summon up a certain amount of inspiration. In this way he performed Ottavio, Edgardo, Pollione, and Othello, wherein, as far as his acting is concerned, he was more often a supernumerary than an artist. This is what comes of shouts of *"Da capo"* and curtain calls. The artist concentrates only on details in order to bring off a *coup de théâtre.* The ensemble and the illusion disappear, and the heart remains cold.

In artistic as well as physical dimensions, Lablache is colossal. Here voice, training, taste, strength, dignity, humor, and joviality are combined. To the other singers he is like a father, but a father who can order his children about, although it is not necessary for him to do so, since they love him and do everything he wishes. The audience does likewise, for even if he is not the most honest fellow in the world, his countenance betrays nothing! His flexible talent makes him suited to lyric tragedy and the most hilarious *opérabouffe,* and his vocal range encompasses with the same ease both the clarinet and the Judgment Day trumpet. Lablache is a true artist!

Grisi is a prima donna of the first order. She is also more of an actress than female singers generally are, but . . . but . . . there is an affected languor about her, as if she were about to become indisposed. She does not blend into the piece with her fellow performers. The whole thing is like a party that has been arranged in her honor. I do not know if my judgment is completely right, but she seems to me to lack genius.

ALBERT PAUL PERROT

Wherever masculine virtuosity is outstanding, the applause granted it is all the greater an honor as it is deprived of that bewitching power that is always exerted by feminine grace, but in the dance, beauty will ever be an essential consideration. Hence it is not talent alone that is the decisive factor: no one can predict with certainty in what direction a pupil's external appearance will develop; yet when he becomes an adult with a fully developed talent, he certainly cannot forsake his career simply because he lacks a certain "type of beauty." Art must accordingly make up for what nature has denied him. Therefore, he is always lucky when dignified grace and *vigueur* are his prevailing attributes.

A *danseuse,* on the other hand, has a thousand means of embellishment. That which would render a man intolerable, she uses as bravura. Her artistic imperfections may be concealed by a charming coquetry, just as her physical ones are hidden by the ample folds of her costume. All unite to aid and protect her; triumph falls to her without reservation, while failure is attributed to her training and the part. Obviously, it would be especially *mauvais ton* to express in writing one's admiration of a *danseur's* accomplishments, but unfair criticism does not take into account that the true expression of the dance *must* be shared between man and woman, and that *danseuses* will cease to exist when male teachers vanish. If one adds to this the fact that one can, in fairness, demand that the *danseur* be a theoretician, musician, and composer in his profession, and behave like a man of the world as well, it is a wonder that the ratio of good *danseurs* to *danseuses* stands as one to ten.

Albert was an example of such a *danseur.* He was a complete gentleman, both offstage and on. Music and painting had formed his taste, and study of the classics had clarified his aesthetic views. He was a true artist, and even though he has treated me as a dear friend and comrade for many years, I have always retained the feeling of respect which his rare talent, combined with his whole manner, inspired in me during the early years of my youth. The word "gentlemanlike" fully describes Albert's demeanor as a dancer: noble, vigorous, gallant, modest, ardent, friendly, gay, but seldom inspired. He won the applause of the connoisseurs but failed to move the masses as Paul did. The difference between these two artists was as if they were both at a party, where Albert was the dignified host and Paul the jovial guest.

Paul's superiority lay in lightness, elasticity, speed, softness, and precision. He knew how to combine daring with natural grace. There was much about his "school" to be criticized, or perhaps I should say he had none at all. One could admire and envy him, but imitate almost nothing. Nature had given him more than art had, and when she took back her gift, his talent was gone; but he had enjoyed a brilliant albeit short-lived career. *"Le voilà"* resounded when he appeared. He laughed at the audience, and they at him, and there arose an interplay of delight and admiration that had a magical effect on this dancer, who was given and retained the name of *"L'aérien."*

But if Paul belonged to the air and Albert to the *salon* (so as not to say the earth), where should one allot Perrot his place? His ballet *Der Kobold* denotes his real nature: he belongs to the kingdom of the gnomes. Our mutual teacher, Vestris, characterized his ugliness by forbidding him to assume "picturesque" poses. "Jump about from place to place, turn, move around, but never give the public time to get a close look at you." With these words, the Master created *"le genre de Perrot,"* that is, Zephyr with the wings of a bat, a divinity belonging not to mythology but to cabalism, a restless creature of indescribable lightness and suppleness, with an almost phosphorescent brilliance! He truly created an epoch at the time when the diabolic was the predominant element on the French stage. He became the ideal of male dancing, and one cannot be surprised that the *danseuses* laid hold of everything that paid homage to beauty and grace.

MARIE TAGLIONI   FANNY ELSSLER   CARLOTTA GRISI

These three names, which have eclipsed everything the ballet world has produced in the last twenty years, do not owe their origins to France, much less Paris. Albert, Paul, and Perrot were born in Bordeaux, Marseilles, and Lyon, but Paris was responsible for the development of their talents. The above-named *danseuses*, on the other hand, were born in Stockholm, Vienna, and Naples respectively, and have brought their art, like ripened fruit, to the great world market, but in a roundabout way. Through them, Paris has gotten her seed-corn back refined. Burdened by established regulations and conditions of seniority, talented young dancers had abandoned the aristocratic Académie Royale de Musique and had scattered themselves about the great theatres of Europe, where they formed new schools and *corps de ballet*. In Vienna, Vestris' eldest son, Armand, had produced two outstanding pupils, Mlles. Brugnoli and Heberle, who took turns delighting the Austrian dilettanti, and both became the models which the young Marie Taglioni chose to imitate. Under her father's competent artistic direction, she learnt to combine Heberle's birdlike lightness with Brugnoli's matchless pointe work. One fine day a modest young girl came to the directors of the Paria Opéra and asked that as a special favor she be given the honor of performing a *pas de deux*. At the audition, she was judged with distinction; but when the evening came, all the stars of the Academy were eclipsed by this rising sun. It was Marie Taglioni! Here was something entirely new! But no! To be sure, she performed the very steps and attitudes that Parisian celebrities had long since rejected as "Rococo"; but now they appeared to be revived by the enlivening spirit of the Graces. No force could resist her wondrous ability to remain suspended in the air; and while fanatics tried to make people believe that this talent owed everything to nature, we connoisseurs had to admire the extraordinary technique she possessed and respectfully acknowledge her exemplary industry. I witnessed her first triumphs in 1827–1829 and danced with her a number of times. She lifted one up from this earth, and her divine dancing could make one weep; I saw Terpsichore realized in her person. The age of curtain calls then began, and Mlle. Taglioni allowed herself to be carried away by her pursuit of effect. But as she was [when I saw her] in the year 1838, I must still acknowledge her to have been the most charming Psyche, the most ethereal sylphide, I had ever seen.

It was terribly important for me to see with my own eyes whether Fanny Elssler's renown was well founded or exaggerated. I really could not conceive how she could possibly replace Taglioni, who had quitted Paris for St. Petersburg. I found the two rivals in London at the same time. There was considerable friction between their supporters, and opinions were stormily voiced.

But the truth must be told: Fanny Elssler was an outstanding talent, but as different in poetic nuance as a brunette from a blonde. Taglioni hovered high above the floor with suspended lightness, and her expression exuded gentleness mingled with poignant longing. Elssler was speed and liveliness personified. Without possessing considerable *aplomb* or elevation, she had, above all, a wealth of pretty little steps which she accompanied with a roguishness that set all hearts aflutter. But if Taglioni surpassed her in technique, she took her revenge in character dancing, and where Marie provoked enthusiastic tears, Fanny inspired joy and the laughter of contentment. I will endeavor to give a picture of her world-famous *Cachucha*. This dance began with a graceful advance, and then a few steps back. She performed the first part as if she meant to say, "Be content with a little jest"; but in the second portion a rapturous glow suffused her entire countenance, which radiated a halo of joy. This moment never failed to have its effect, and from then on the whole dance became a frolic in which she drove her audience wild with delight.

As different as these two dancers were, they resembled each other in this: they could never bear to have a *danseur* of importance at their side. Even Taglioni's repertoire was designed to show her standing alone, except in groupings, where she needed the support of a strong arm. Fanny Elssler, on the other hand, had to provide for her older sister Therese, who was so large and tall that she could never have found engagement at any theatre had she not been stipulated as Fanny's partner. I dare say Therese danced as well as the finest lad, and it often looked quite nice when she played with her smaller sister in her arms; but it was positively ludicrous when Fanny, after having played an entire role, bade her lover sit down while she danced with her tall sister, who always appeared as if she had just fallen from the clouds.

These stars are now gone from the Parisian stage, and a new meteor is attracting attention. This is Carlotta Grisi who, in addition to extraordinary precision and originality, possesses the unmistakable advantage of being a decade younger than her illustrious predecessors. She is still too much *en vogue* to be considered artistic history; but there will soon come a time when one can survey her career, like those of all celebrities who have gone before; and eventually it will come to pass that pupils at the Académie Royale de Musique will open their eyes wide with true Parisian ignorance when they hear her name, which will sound just as foreign to their egoistic ears as do those of Noverre, Ferville, Dauberval, and those goddesses of the dance, Allard, Heinel, Guimard, Chévigny, and Chameroy. What wouldn't one give to gain a theatrical name in Paris! And yet what good would that do? The public *cannot* and the artists *will not* remember that name. Even the humblest artist soon becomes convinced that since *his* age is the most modern, his place of residence the finest in Europe, and he himself supreme in his profession there, *he* must then be the most outstanding example of the culmination of progress. Still believing this, he grows old and one day takes revenge on his heedless successors by despising everything that is new.

VI

Parallels

SINCE this book is intended as a pleasant souvenir for the Danish patrons of the ballet, I will not enlarge upon the hackneyed subject of the shortcomings of the Danish Theatre, in administrative as well as architectural respects, nor will I complain about those adversities that have been so instructive for me. On the contrary, I consider it my duty to emphasize the advantages which the Danish stage, in comparison with the greatest theatres of Europe, possesses at the present time.

1. THE ROYAL PATRONAGE, WHICH MAKES THE THEATRE INTO A NATIONAL INSTITUTION FOR LITERATURE AND ART AND PROTECTS THESE THINGS FROM THE CAPRICIOUS VICISSITUDES OF THE MOMENT, FROM FANTASTIC SPECULATIONS AND SORDID COVETOUSNESS.

Before the July Revolution the French government gave 800,000 francs a year as a subsidy to the artistic institution which, under the name of "L'Opéra" or "L' Académie Royale de Musique," was obliged to present original grand operas and *ballets d'action*. There was a Royal Intendant, whose duty was mainly to ensure the dignity of the establishment, that is to say, that it actually deserved the name of *Academy* or school for good taste. The new government had enough to do with the press without getting involved with the sordid stage as well. The Opéra was handed over to an entrepreneur with an annual allowance of 750,000 francs. The State Treasury hereby saved 50,000 francs a year, but Paris lost one of its loveliest ornaments, for from this moment on the Opéra became a factory, in the most unhappy sense of the word. In addition to the director, several other jovial gentlemen had put money into this enterprise, and the banking house of Aguado vouched for the whole with a considerable sum. These gentlemen were shopkeepers, and art the merchandise; it was now a matter of the management either laying down the rules and the personnel accepting them, or vice versa. Only the talent that was supported by intrigue could come to the fore. Money had to be made, and no means was rejected; the celebrities held the knife at the management's throat, and the latter in turn exhausted itself in order to secure a profitable attendance. It was farewell to the school of art and encouragement, and pensions were discontinued for the future. Everyone thought only of today: the ensemble disappeared. But just as the entrepreneur noticed that the house could not get any fuller, the outstanding talents steadily became fewer and fewer. Certain "golden hens" therefore became the gods to whom he sacrificed, while with the lifeless gaze of a sultan he gave charity to the others or shoved the lot of them out of the way with the speed of a steam carriage. Shareholders assumed particular patronages and shared the delights of the seraglio with the master. And everywhere, the journalists swarmed about.

2. THE ATMOSPHERE AND SENSE OF DECORUM WHICH, IN COMPARISON WITH THE PAST AND FOREIGN COUNTRIES, NOW PREVAIL AT THE DANISH THEATRE.

Weakness is the lot of humanity. Bad upbringing, poverty, vanity, and eccentric temperament are causes of much immorality. But that the theatre as a whole must contain a greater measure of temptation in this direction than the rest of worldly life is a prejudice which finds its refutation in daily experience in this country and everywhere else. Gone are the days when vice was ennobled with highness and splendor; evil is recognized in and of itself as something people are ashamed of, and this is indeed a considerable step forward. All art, the picturesque as well as the dramatic, becomes in the eyes of the depraved man the source of new impurity; in his soul, the root of new corruption. But *art itself* cannot corrupt its devotees; it can ennoble the bad but certainly never scandalize the virtuous. The dramatic arts demand reflection, study, and effort. These are not the friends of frivolity; health, strength, and gaiety do not follow in the wake of dissipation.

Prejudices are the enemies of civilization; they are usually the cause of evil! People are amazed that those who could give their children a careful and religious upbringing permit them to follow their vocation for the theatre. Is it therefore among the rudest classes of society that artists are to be recruited? People are fully justified in considering it a misfortune if an outstanding university student wishes to try his voice or his speaking talent on the stage, for this attempt excludes him from certain posts, just as if he had served an infamous prison sentence. O you young liberals! Scandia's blossoms! When you decked the walls of the Ridehuus [the Royal Riding Academy at Christiansborg] with name-embellished shields, you bypassed the dramatic art and forgot that in Frydendahl, Rosing, and Hjortsberg the North has produced a trefoil that the whole world will envy. Parents wink at the son who disgraces a young actress as a result of his recklessness; but marry her! Yes, but only so long as she abandons her profession; he must first *take her out of* the theatre! And then we have the young girl who through poor circumstances and laborious work has developed a talent that is aided by a charming appearance. Many temptations have hovered about her inexperienced youth—trifling wages, lack of the necessities of life, indelicate suggestions of vulgar parents, the advice of stupid and wicked people, promises of protection and advancement, and above all, the evil spirit who whispers in her ear, "What good is your virtue? No one believes in that." She holds fast to God, for from Him alone comes strength in temptation. She repulses every attack and comes safely across the frail bridge that leads to the age in which the feminine heart feels its dignity with composure. But does she now harvest the respect and admiration she deserves? And does one not often believe himself entitled to a doubt that would be a grievous insult to even the most indiscreet lady of society? Ah! Let someone appear to defend her injured reputation: she is then disgraced beyond salvation.

But are these representations of passions, these graceful movements, not a dangerous school for the temperament and the heart? To this I reply that the most profound study of body and soul leads to the clearest recognition of the dignity and higher origin of both. The intellect is developed through *images*. The theatre is splendidly equipped to multiply these, but they ought to be ennobled by art, not dragged down into the mud of sensuality. Many are moved only by unhealthy pandering, amused only by cynicism; there is a whole sect of connoisseurs of art whose centers of attraction are a long way from art; but let these people who would elevate the false and offensive at the expense of reason and public decency choose a sphere other than the temples of art, and unfortunately dull reality will provide them with a far richer profit than the illusions of the stage can offer.

Those who have been acquainted with the internal workings of the theatre for a score of years or more will find in the atmosphere that now prevails a happy change that is all the more noticeable in the Ballet, where humble origins, little education, and wretched salaries are the lot of the majority. The relationship between past and present conditions of morality is like that between the Paris Opéra and Copenhagen's Theatre. There one can single out a few honest persons; here, on the contrary, a few bad exceptions, and public opinion will soon cause *them* to disappear. In England and France admittance into the wings is one of the subscribers' prerogatives. One must have witnessed the disorder which this bad habit causes in order to form any notion of it; it is obviously not artistic taste that brings these would-be buyers to the working side of the stage. Here the "mothers," who always accompany their daughters in order, as they say, "to watch over them," play a role that is revolting to nature. One can both laugh and cry at these caricatures, where the ludicrous figure conceals so detestable a spirit, for many of these "exchanges of love" are nothing more than "buy and sell." In France these affairs still retain a certain stamp of gallantry, but in England they resemble nothing so much as a market.

These are the seductions of gold. Now come those of ambition, which appear in the guise of an editor or journalist. He takes it upon himself to make or break a reputation and thereby procures certain favors, which he regards as legitimate compensation for the inconveniences his profession entails. —But just let love declare itself and, as so often happens, fall upon someone unworthy; before long one will espy an abyss of deep corruption. Naturally this theatrical life appears less lurid in places where external conditions bear a more or less dissolute stamp and where all sorts of liaisons are the order of society. Now where does the real corruption lie? In art? In the theatre? No, in the morals of the country, in the prejudices that allow the mask to be raised in the presence of art, in the gambling spirit of the directors, in the lack of delicacy among the great, in the notorious "mothers," and finally in the simplemindedness of people who seek oracles of praise in the newspapers.

At our Theatre, thank Heaven, things are completely different, and despite their propensity for imitation, the Danish people have too sharp an eye for *the true* and *the natural* to allow themselves to be fooled by the delusions of great nations. There is still much that can and should be improved among us, but when we sometimes complain that the public examines the private lives of theatre folk with a certain small-town curiosity, we must confidently hope that this research will lead to favorable results and that as people come to know the truth they will then render justice to the respectable.

3. FREEDOM FROM PAID AND HIRED CLAPPERS [*CLAQUEURS*], WHO BY FALSE AND FORCED APPLAUSE ROB THE TRUE AUDIENCE OF ITS VOICE.

It is a well-founded complaint that the Copenhagen public does not recognize the importance of expressing the feelings aroused by art. Applause generally occurs only for that which is astonishing or uproariously funny. Admiration may seldom generate enthusiasm, but a bit of opposition can produce ferment and put life into people; more often they clap out of pity or irony rather than true favor. This accusation cannot be made against the *genteel* public, which for the most part remains passive and allows its opinion to be determined by the applause of the majority. But this renunciation of a precious right is highly injurious to art, for it is as necessary for the actor to know what kind of an impression he has made, as it is to hear the sound when one tugs on a bellpull. Our public shows little or no reaction to something serene or pleasant in art. They are loath to clap but feel bored when no applause is heard. And so what happens? The dramatist goes to extremes, comedians fall victim to *lazzi*,* tragedians to bombast, singers to bawling, and dancers to gymnastics. Now there is excitement and the house is again filled, but feeling is exhausted and indifference spreads its dominion.

The ingenious Ryge had many curious projects (among others, his design for the introduction of a Danish national costume), but the most priceless of all was his plan for an applause machine. That is to say, he would have all expressions of opinion during the performance abolished by royal decree; how-

---

*Spontaneous jokes or bits of comic "business," ad-libbed by the actors in many comedies.

ever, after the curtain fell a kind of "wheel of fortune" was to be brought forth, upon which the actors' names would appear in turn, with graded marks—outstanding, quite good, good, rather poor, and very poor—to which the audience would give its approbation by stronger or weaker applause. . . . Just imagine such a drawing of lots at every nightly performance and, for example, the grade of *very poor* being accepted and sanctioned with thunderous acclamation! All the same, from this bizarre idea one might draw the conclusion that the public would come to realize that there must be certain degrees of expression for satisfaction and admiration—that in Holberg's *Tinker,* for example, Gedske's dog does not get the most applause, the principal role a little, and the play none at all. One has seen a new piece dwindle in the first three performances from enthusiasm to halfheartedness, and young artists who at their debuts won all the laurels of Parnassus, hardly be tolerated as supernumeraries later on. To this may even be added the phenomenon that a play which has been entertaining and interesting throughout, can be hissed when the curtain falls; and lastly, the peculiar national amusement consisting in the regulated five minutes' whistling, the end of which is marked by a gong backstage and police clubs in the pit. This contemptuous expression of displeasure is, in fact, of no importance, since it must be prepared before people are familiar with the play and, according to the regulation, cannot strike the performer but is reserved for the author alone, who is generally as uneasy as a criminal awaiting sentence. It is not my place to propose the manner in which a reform in this mode of expression might occur. But when the public one day learns to recognize its own interests, it will, no doubt, know how to give art a reward commensurate with its importance and influence.

In Germany there is great patronage and warmth for scenic performances; in Italy, people know no middle road between *fiasco* and *fanatismo;* and in England it is usually (in its double meaning) the "loaded" gallery that showers its enthusiasm on the theatre. In all these countries, however, the expression is forthright and the actor knows where he stands as far as the effect of his talent is concerned. But in France, and Paris in particular, the public is declared incapable of handling its own affairs: they are placed in the custody of *"claqueurs."*

This group has become organized in all theatres, with the exception of the Italian Opera, where every *dilettante* is also obliged to pound with his stick, stamp his feet, slam the seats, squirm and groan, shout *"Bis!"* and cry *"Fuori!,"* toss flowers onto the stage, and—if need be—act as a coach horse. But there are not to be found many more such people than the number used by the Italians, and the enthusiasm must be maintained in order that the theatre and the celebrities may not perish! This has consequently been remedied by means of *claqueurs,* who can be divided into two classes: the paying and the paid—*gants blancs* and *lustriens.*

The former are a pride of young lions of good family who perform their *premières armes* in the foyers and the wings, to which they have been granted admittance by the entrepreneur. Some old fellows join their company in order to act young, and together they form a *camaraderie* who applaud each other's mistresses and stick their white-gloved hands out of "the lions' den," which is usually in the proscenium boxes.

The second class forms a phalanx beneath the chandelier. It is, on the whole, far less elegant, looks like our salvage corps, and generally hides beer bottles under the seats. Its duties consist in receiving the actors, causing a magical murmur that changes into applause, then gradually transports those sitting roundabout into a frenzy of excitement. A story is told about a *claqueur* leader who had distributed his crew in such a way that they artificially provoked uproarious laughter by tickling people in the ribs. I cannot vouch for the truth of this, but I myself witnessed the following conversation, and it reveals the whole *claqueur* theory:

> Madame F.: Well! Why didn't you applaud my husband? Do you think he gives you his tickets so you can *take care of* Mlle. Taglioni?
> M. Auguste L.: Madame! Listen to me and see if I don't know my business. First I look around me, I see that proper dispositions are made; I hear a murmur of approval (I am not mistaken about that). I "launch an attack," my comrades dutifully follow me, and the audience joins in. We "come on strong," the house is brought down, and Taglioni is a hit. Mark you, I could do the same for Monsieur, but if the audience is listless, I risk compromising the artist. However, if you absolutely insist upon it, egad! I'm there to look after things."†

Such a *claqueur* leader is a figure who reminds me of Eugène Sue's *Mystères*. He has his quarters in a smoky café and calls on his clients at dusk. The theatre manager comes to an agreement with him about a certain number of tickets, half of which are to be sold by "scalpers" and the remainder distributed to the crew, which is divided into the paid and the volunteers. The subaltern *claqueur* can be recognized by the fact that he knows the play or opera by heart, and usually sings along during the performance; the leader always possesses considerable physical strength, and hands that have been developed by a high degree of practice. He never works for nothing, and well knows how to distinguish between his double profession of art-lover and businessman. He works cheaply for poor young debutants; they get off with giving him only twelve or sixteen complimentary tickets. But, as for pretentious artists, ladies with rich *protectors*—they must pay cash, and pay anywhere from 100 francs a month to 200 francs for a single evening. The house is rocked by thunderous applause; the piece and the prima donna are praised to the skies; and although everyone knows what it has cost, the public still falls for the illusion. The newspapers sound their trumpets, the artist has pleasure for his money, and Europe resounds with the echo of those broad fists which have promised a *réputation colossale!*

† In the original edition, this exchange is given only in French.

4.   THE LITERARY FREEDOM THAT
DRAMATIC AUTHORS IN THIS COUNTRY ENJOY
MORE THAN IN MOST OTHER PLACES.

The dramatic art has a wide range within which it can move without offense, and it takes only common sense to realize that there are extremes of sacredness and banality that have no right to be seen on the stage. It is the theatre's duty to depict passions, not to arouse them; satire ought to have a stimulating, not a dulling and depressing effect; reality must always be subordinate to the magic of art. These boundaries have never limited a truly ingenious writer; but these chosen people are few in number. Those who regard unconventionality and originality as synonymous, fancy they have found something new every time they sin against the laws of taste, and believe the latter to be only a vague notion which cannot be accounted for. They find the true only in the hideous; effect, only in what is glaring; and interest, only in scandal. Everywhere taste ought to be the only warranted theatre censorship and should be vested in the public, who would then have to punish any outrage against it. Everything bad—that is to say, affected, immoral, or banal— ought to be included under one heading: tasteless. But how is this judgment to find a suitable voice? Is it in the effect of the moment or in aesthetic treatises? Then wouldn't the theatre soon be forced to use its finest talents in an immature work, which would actually be tested only at the performance? The public's rightful demand is *art*. Everything that lies outside it ought to be rejected. Therefore, as unpleasant as the word "censorship" sounds, it can hardly be dispensed with in the theatre world. It exists under highly different forms in all the theatres of Europe, but most leniently, in my opinion, in Denmark.

In both England and France the public authorities have a stranglehold on scenic works. But in England, just dare to show something that touches upon the Britons' sensitive rivalries; just poke fun at their folkways or write something that does not reflect a certain system or for which there is no authority, and the public will exercise a right that is often as unjust as it is irrevocable. Push your way through the French *camaraderies*, buy or crush all who block the entrance to the stage, discover something new to ward off the fatal *"Connu, connu!"* of the masses—who recall everything and remember nothing—and even in fashion you will find a merciless censorship which brands as Rococo all feelings and expressions that are not in accord with the accepted *ton*.

In Germany there is a host of sensitive chords that cannot be touched. Both nature and history contain "political overtones," and reflection is deeper among the censors than among the authors themselves. In northern Germany everything is too light and frivolous for them, in southern Germany, too subtle and serious; in one place, the foreign struggles with the domestic; in the other, it is just the opposite; and everywhere the stage is subordinate to Court, State, or commercial interests.

Italy ought to be mentioned too, especially Naples, where the theatre once flourished but where the Jesuit spirit now hangs over the police, and that of the police over literature and art. One pictures a country in which nudity is the national costume and frivolity an ancestral heritage, when, in fact, Venus and the Graces are locked away in the Museum's secret rooms, to which privileged tickets alone give access, while the gods of Olympus are excluded, as being obscene, from the exhibitions of the Academy. I hate exposure of any kind, both in the theatre and in social life; attention must not be diverted from art to focus on sensual objects; but an excess of caution has precisely this unhappy result.

This is the case at the Teatro San Carlo in Naples, where the use of "flesh color" is forbidden and the regulation white tights must not show *above the knee;* at this point begins a pair of green *caleçons,* which accompany the *danseuses* through all the different ballets, from Scotland's Sylphide to Greece's Goddess of the Hunt and India's *bayadère;* and yet the skirts must be short enough to enable the officials involved to make sure of punctual compliance with the royal order without laying a hand on the dancers. *Pirouettes* do the rest, and if someone thought that by this invention modest eyes could be spared, I fear he has been sadly mistaken.

A universal wail of despair arose as a result of this momentous ordinance. The ladies nearly caused a revolt but the only concession they were granted was that these green *caleçons de bain* were also to be sewn for the men. Roman heroes had to conceal their bare arms in white knitted bed jackets. Those who disobeyed were coerced by the gendarmes, and people in the pit who were prone to laughter were thrown out by the police. The eyes of the Neapolitans gradually became accustomed to these grasshopperlike creatures, but I did not find that their morality had made any significant progress as a result of this revolution.

Uncommon weight is also placed on the combination of colors: an actor who dresses in white trousers, blue jacket, and red scarf would be "sequestered"—that is, arrested—as an animated revolutionary flag. (In gay Milan, on the contrary, there is great freedom of dress; flesh color is most predominant, and there the *danseuses* take, or more properly *give* a brilliant revenge.) Among the host of precautionary measures that distinguish the Theatre of Naples, the most striking one—apart from a very visible fireman with helmet and boathook who stands in each of the wings—is Cupid's costume; for in addition to his regulation green *caleçons,* white stockings, and sleeves, he wears butterfly wings! And why not wings made of feathers? No, that would be profanation, for then he would look like one of God's little angels.

Censorship next extends to the scenery, which may not depict anything that either inwardly or outwardly, let alone in the hazy distance, resembles a

church, a cupola, a campanile, or a temple façade. And then there is the famous regulation governing dramatic representations: holy persons, symbols,
or pictures; clerics of any kind; angels, spirits, and devils (Mephistopheles
among them); emperors, kings, princes, and dukes, together with their
spouses, are completely exempted from stage duty, which is to say they may
not be portrayed on the stage, as either good or evil. Revolution, murder, and
illicit love are alike *forbidden,* and, finally, every [opera] libretto must be
subjected beforehand to the strictest police revison, which usually aims at ob-
literating offensive words such as: *God,* read Heaven; *prince,* read regent;
prayer, read demand; *republic,* read State, etc. For example, if a ballet libretto
should happen to contain a vague allusion, it is confiscated as being a writing
with subversive tendencies, and the rehearsal of the ballet is halted. But, after
all these requirements have been fully complied with, can one feel at ease?—
By no means. In the opera *Torquato Tasso* it was noticed that the Queen of
Naples was descended from the beautiful Leonora d'Este! The names were
immediately changed and the piece was called *Sordello.* But even this was
not enough; people would surely recognize Tasso by his black clothing; an
embroidered costume quickly had to be found, and only then might the opera
be performed. But what about opposition? Two gendarmes stand by every
bench, and two grenadiers in the proscenium. But are there no newspapers?
They are being revised from Saturday to Tuesday and have no right to raise
any objections against the lessees of the Royal Theatre. But aren't any daily
newspapers published? Certainly! *Il Giornale delle due Sicilie.* But it is
printed at the police station.

VII

The Results of My Endeavors

SINCE by drawing the above-mentioned parallels I have now brought out the merits of the Danish Royal Theatre — and to these I add the considerable advantages for the Ballet of a skilled and attentive company of dancers, fine musical composers, and an audience which has an eye and feeling for the plastic — one will no doubt wonder why I do not wish to spend the rest of my days at a theatre which unites so many of the elements necessary for artistic happiness. Without going into petty detail, I will therefore state the reason for the joyous anticipation with which I await the end of my contract on

APRIL 1, 1848.

Eleven years of childhood and adolescence, together with eighteen years of manhood, spent in three laborious branches of art, constitute not only twenty-nine years of effort but also double the amount of work! For no solo-dancer at our Theatre has accomplished more than I. As balletmaster I have furnished twenty major and minor ballets, arranged five foreign works, and composed dances and groupings for nearly thirty operas and plays. Moreover, the position in which I have done the most and gained the least is that of teacher. I am really in need of rest; that is to say, freedom. I must be released from the bond that has held me in one place for so many years and from the same audience, which may very well be sick and tired of me. I must be freed from the oppressive thought of "outliving" myself and arousing pity where I once harvested admiration. Here I have no competition, save from my own works; and what comparison could be more bitter? No one cares to see an older work, but it is declared to be a masterpiece and becomes a bugbear to every new undertaking by its author. Show me a rival. Let us fight with equal weapons and, if conquered, I will acknowledge my superior. But it is unbearable to hear: "You reached your peak a long time ago. Now step down!" It is highly characteristic of Denmark that a work which in France would make an author rich and happy for the rest of his life, here kills his whole future activity.

If one now compares the obstacles that an emerging talent in a foreign country must overcome in order to achieve a celebrity equal to that of recognized men of greatness, with the eagerness with which people here at home give mediocrity a helping hand in overthrowing distinction, one must admit that a person who has forged his own path to honor and recognition abroad has achieved something far more solid than he will obtain here. Denmark loves art but not the artist: his efforts to please are received not as those of a loving child but, rather, as those of a pressing suitor. The beauty who is to be won is not the tender mother but the capricious girl; if he does not forestall her, she becomes unfaithful and repudiates him. Uncertainty, want, and absence keep the flame alive; but it is slowed by the security of comfort and completely dampened by indissoluble bonds.

One of the drawbacks of the Danish Theatre is that for their humble and often envied daily bread its members must renounce international fame — something on which the Danish public places entirely too great a value — and a brilliant memory here at home, because a pension cannot be granted until a person's growing incompetence is obvious to all. The artist is consequently supposed to wait until the Muses and Graces desert him and the public begs to be relieved of his presence! This horrifying picture haunted me as I signed my contract in 1829 and I won the advantage (which I have no intention of relinquishing) of being considered *"pensionsfähig"* — that is, to say, incompetent — after eighteen years of good service. The time is at hand, and I feel that I have done my best for the Danish Theatre. I shall strive to the utmost to fulfill my obligations; but the desire is gone, and, with it, the strength. As a composer, I have rejected nine out of ten ideas for want of space and assistance; I have played every chord that could please the Danish public. Now I am finished *here*.

I see no one among the younger dancers who possesses the proper understanding for representing the main idea of a ballet in my stead. Our stage will soon lose a measure of its excellence, and foreign delusions will also find their way to us. I therefore have good reason to wish for my freedom with all my heart. Whether I will use this freedom to attempt to make myself known on a greater stage is something that is still unclear to me. But I do know this: although I am of French extraction and filled with French sympathies, in my heart and soul I am *Danish* and wish to rest nowhere but in Denmark. There I would choose my summer residence, and should I from time to time be granted fresh opportunities to pluck some laurels, I will bind them into the wreath that shall adorn my grave.

And now, filled with good will for the coming generation — namely, those who have decided on the same career as that which I will soon have completed — and so as not to end this chapter on all too elegiac a note, I will set forth the quintessence of my experiences in the form of advice and useful suggestions:

TO PARENTS

Do not put your children into the theatre. But if both ability and desire give evidence of an irresistible calling, let them follow their inclination and experience the difficulties of art. If these do not succeed in discouraging them, if they still feel the same need to display their talents to the public, if their desire to be admired is greater than their fear of being laughed at, then they were born for the stage and in any other profession will either feel un-happy or become one of those queer souls whom people in worldly life ironi-cally refer to as "clowns."

With singing and acting, apprenticeship does not begin until the years of adolescence; with dancing, however, it starts in childhood. Eight years of age is early enough, but it is of the utmost importance that the child be able to read and write by then so as to avoid the danger—resulting from the rigors of dancing and the distractions of the theatre—of being without those requisites for a good general education. If you have your children's future at heart, see that they learn something good and useful outside the dancing school, and that they render you an account of how they pass their time.

Never speak of the Dance in dull or unseemly fashion. Do not let chil-dren relate scandalous anecdotes. Do not arouse in them pretension or envy, but show them their art not only as an occupation but as a means of winning honor and respect.

If after several years you notice that their talent is not developing, do not trouble the teachers but take your children out of the school, preferably be-fore Confirmation age. Convince them of the necessity of choosing another profession, and consider the applied physical training they have received as gymnastics beneficial to their growth and health. Furthermore, you can be thankful that they have not become doomed to idleness and dejection their whole lives through.

Beware of empty and sentimental reading, but give them a taste for his-tory and wholesome poetry. Lead them out into beautiful nature; let them ad-mire with awe the masterpieces of art and esteem the power of oratory. But, above all, give them the opportunity to learn music, not only in order to play a dance on the violin, but to open their senses to an art which is to the Dance what the soul is to the body.

Do not expect your children to obtain the highest position and salary in the Ballet, where there are only six or eight well-paid people. For one thing, such places are not always vacant; for another, advancement depends on the greatest usefulness and talent; and, finally, the justice that rewards works slowly.

Thus, as the situation now stands, no pupil can expect to earn a salary be-fore the age of fifteen, sixteen, or seventeen, and one usually starts at 40 rix-dollars a year.* One is lucky if upon coming of age one can earn the regu-lation *figurant*'s salary of 300 Rbd., supplemented by bonuses and shoe money to the amount of 100 Rbd. This position is by no means attractive, but, poor as it is, it still deserves to be taken into consideration. I am not address-ing myself to those classes where laborious work in dependent circumstances

---

*Throughout this work Bournonville uses a variety of monetary terms. Following the national bankruptcy in 1813, the Danish unit of currency became the *Rigsbankdaler* or rixdollar (abbrevi-ated "Rbd."), which was equal to 6 *Marks* of 16 *Skillings* each. One rixdollar equaled approxi-mately $1.05 at the time. A *Specie* or *Speciedaler* was the equivalent of two rixdollars, while the units of *Krone* and *Øre* referred to in later portions of the book were introduced about 1875.

brings only a meager livelihood and an old age filled with anxiety; rather, I
am speaking to those parents who, even though unable to leave behind a fortune, still find it possible to allow their sons to study for a degree and their
daughters to be taught languages and music. What prospects are there nowadays for a host of civilian and military aspirants, and as a result of this, for the
establishment of girls without private means? There are swarms of teachers
and governesses—and at what prices! See what families demand, and what
they offer! An able and well-bred *figurant* can double his annual income by
giving lessons and can live a rather comfortable domestic life with the assurance of bread for his old age and a pension for his widow. A young girl with
400 Rbd. a year and the certainty of a pension cannot exactly be called "unprovided for," and if, in addition, she be honorable and domestic, she can
easily find a good man among her peers, and her salary then makes quite a
handsome dowry. This picture is not drawn from the highest ranks of the Ballet, nor from the lowest; and yet it shows what can certainly be acquired
through industry and good conduct.

Consequently, if you put your children into the theatre because you expect an income or help from them, you are playing for high stakes and risking
their peace of mind on this wager. On the other hand, if you will be content
to secure them a modest livelihood, examining first their natural abilities and
desire, then the means of giving them a proper upbringing together with
maintenance and clothing up to a certain age, your expectations will not be
disappointed. Another thing: remember that there is a purgatory of yearning
and difficulty to be gone through. Bolster your children's morale, do not reproach them because they are unable to earn money; do not nurture their despondency or jealousy, and never doubt that their talent and uprightness will
surely be rewarded.

TO THE PUPIL

Everything that applies to the relationship between teacher and pupil in
other schools can hold true of the ballet school as well, with the single exception that the Dance includes both "the ABCs" and "the final University
examination." It is not only a branch of art but a vocational study, upon which
the apprentice's future depends. Since one must be well versed in dance
technique in order to distinguish those qualities which owe their development to the teacher, it is not easy for a person unacquainted with such matters to select the best school for his child. One must therefore adhere to the
undebatable proposition that a good teacher may certainly produce poor
scholars, but a bad teacher can never form good subjects. Consequently, if a
school turns out a number of outstanding pupils, one may be assured of its excellence, and the new student should then be advised:

Regard your teacher as the one who holds your fortune in his hands. Be
like a child to him, and he will become a second father to you. Be frank, and

he will become your friend. Learn readily, and you will become his alter ego.

Ask as many questions as you like, but never answer a reprimand.

Write down everything you learn, and you will not turn out to be ignorant. Note when, how, and from whom you learnt it, and you will prove less ungrateful.

When you have received a good lesson and your teacher praises your industry, remember that *his* exertion has been greater than *yours*.

Never think that your gifts deserve the name of talent until they have been developed, and take note that without good training, they would have been absolutely ruined.

Acquire early the habit of reflecting on your exercises, and you will save yourself needless exertion. It is not the quantity of exercises but their quality that ought to be considered, and always bear in mind that the Dance must rise to the level of *fine* art to avoid degenerating into buffoonery.

Note well that the pleasures of art are achieved only through sacrifice, and if youth is stormy, manhood will yield no harvest.

Do not regard your teacher's concern for your well-being as a dancer as irrelevant or as an attack upon your independence; for your whole spiritual and physical existence has an influence on your art. Only by combining ability with good judgment will you be able to gain independence.

Strive to improve your mind or you will never become an artist. All your life you will feel tied to schools, and you will be like the human figure which a magician molded from potter's clay and endowed with the powers of speech and movement, but which hated his master and hounded him to death because he had not been able to give him a "soul."

Do not become a copy of your teacher, but as soon as you have learnt your métier, go to him, thank him profoundly for his loving guidance, and ask to work on your own—reserving for yourself, however, his frequent advice and criticism. Practice alone, study your art through all the other fine arts, and delight your teacher with reports of your accomplishments. He will not become angry at seeing you leave the nest, even if you should rise higher in the world than he has been able to. Become an artist! But never let the flattery of others or your own vanity cause you to forget what you owe to your teacher. Remember that one day you yourself will have successors who will avenge *him* at your expense.

TO THE SOLODANCERS

Become artists! That is to say, refine your hearts and minds.

Strive to distinguish yourselves, but not outside the theatre.

Win over your comrades and superiors so that you may be mildly judged and obtain fine roles.

Do not expose your art to ridicule through blundering performances and indecent costume.

Imitate but do not duplicate. Follow the times, but only when they go forward. And remember that only the beautiful is true.

Avoid cabals. Do not seek to gain interest by arousing pity.

Value applause; do not allow yourself to be crushed by coldness, but listen to the opinions of all *cultured* people.

Should you find yourself passed over in the casting of roles, perform the smallest part with extreme care, and you will force the balletmaster to provide better for you the next time. On the other hand, if you resort to complaints, reproaches, and threats, his invention will become mixed with fear and other unpleasant elements, and even with the best will in the world, he will never again find anything good for you to perform.

Never stand in the way of a younger talent; for your opposition will have the immediate effect of turning a promising artist into an established celebrity.

Seek to earn money through all honorable means, and be wise enough to save yourself a Skilling, for no one will remember your good days if your old age is not crowned with prosperity.

Unless the desire to reproduce your talent prove all too irresistible or you, like me, are forced to do so, DO NOT GIVE LESSONS, DO NOT TRAIN ANY PUPILS, for one finds happiness in only a few rare exceptions to the general rule of ingratitude. As for honor . . . aye, it makes me think of Bajazzo,† who shouts to the jeering mob: "Look here, gentlemen, she has learnt all that from me."

TO THE TEACHER

Do not begin to teach until you yourself can no longer perform. Do not become too involved in the progress and welfare of your students.

If, like another Pygmalion, you can create a Galatea, do not become smitten with this work of your hand.

Never expect any thanks from your pupils.

Do not become angry if they should hurt you.

TO THE BALLETMASTER

If you have genius, then write ballets; but if you possess only taste and knowledge, compose and arrange. If you have nothing more than a good memory and professional experience, learn the compositions of others to perfection and conscientiously stage them; but beware of exercising your talents on the poet's libretti, for you will come to bear the responsibility and trouble, while the writer reaps the honor and profit.

Should you happen to have the dual pleasure of being both an author and

† A stock figure in German popular culture, roughly analogous to Hanswurst.

a theatre official, do not become a teacher and, even less, a performing artist; for much bad humor is carried over from the classroom to the rehearsal, and the virtuoso will always stand in the way of the composer. I have shown that it is not—as Noverre claims—impossible to combine these offices, but I have found that it can be highly disadvantageous.

If you have begun to compose only late in life, you can continue to do so until the day you die. But if you, like me, exercised your genius at an early age, you will also be finished at an early age. Do not be foolish enough to believe that physical strength, knowledge, or *esprit* can compensate for a burnt-out flame. Guard against paralyzing coldness. Retire before you have stored up bitterness for your old age! Even if it should cause you some tears to part from unfinished work and from the art that was the friend of your childhood and manhood, leave it with a feeling of affection and seek refuge in the bosom of knowledge. Study history and living languages. Live far enough away from the city so that you cannot go to the Theatre every day, but from time to time both visit and delight in the younger generation. Never become a critic, for it hardens the heart and forces one to view with coldness that which was created with warmth. Teach the young from your own experience, and one day—if you still have the courage to expose yourself to the scourge of ephemeral criticism—write about the art in which you once shone, and be glad that your genius has changed into *esprit* just as love can change into friendship.

VIII

Ballet Compositions

ACCLAIM TO THE GRACES

Divertissment with Musical Numbers by Carafa, Gallenberg, and Sor.
(September 1, 1829)

THIS little composition which upon my return to my native land afforded me the opportunity to display my progress in a solo, a graceful *pas de trois*, and a brilliant finale, contained in microcosm my whole artistic credo and a picture of my own existence as a dancer. Earlier (and often later) I let myself be carried away by my enthusiasm and the desire to exert my uncommon *vigueur;* but only by taking the hint of the Muses and following the laws of the Graces did my movements become dancing, and my dancing art. The lovely *pas de trois* was arranged for me by [Auguste] Vestris, and I herein succeeded in giving my countrymen a new and more refined idea not only of my skill but of the goal to which I aspired.

Our public has never been strong in grasping allegories, especially such as are based upon pagan mythology. Furthermore, the people with whom I had to work were somewhat deficient. As a matter of fact, *Terpsichore* had begun to attend dancing classes only a short time before, and *the Graces* were anything but virginally graceful;* consequently, my idea came under the heading of "good intentions." Apollo, the Muses, the Graces, warriors, and flower goddesses were, like old acquaintances from a lamentable age, almost laughed off the stage, and I had to be content with applause and bravos for my *entrechats* and *pirouettes* and with the flattering exclamation, "He flies!" The *divertissement* itself soon vanished amid the furor created by the ballet *The Sleepwalker.* No one asked for it again, but as an omen for my own and for the Ballet's destiny on the Danish stage, it was not without a certain importance.

---

*Bournonville started to train the Danish ballet company toward the middle of August 1829, and thus had very little time in which to fashion a *corps* before the premiere of this first original work. The role of Terpsichore was danced by Andrea Krætzmer (1811–1889), an outstanding mime who performed the leading parts in several of the balletmaster's early compositions. The three Graces were performed by Mmes. Haack and Stramboe, and Jomfru S. Møller.

SOLDIER AND PEASANT

A Pantomimic Idyll with Music by Keck and Several Numbers by Carafa, Lefebvre, and Romani.
(October 13, 1829)

I had become better acquainted with the public's taste and the Theatre's talent by the time I produced this bagatelle under the name of "pantomimic idyll." I wished to dance a *pas de trois* (partially after Albert) as well as a bravura solo that Vestris had taught me, and needing a suitable motif, I chose my own homecoming. "Cordiality" had not yet become synonymous with "sentimentality," the French soldier was not so trite a stage character as he later became, and—curiously enough—at that time France and Napoleon alluded quite nicely to Denmark and our King.

The work was highly successful. *The Sleepwalker* had already given the *corps de ballet* a certain amount of experience in performing. They were now fit to portray peasants; but higher than that we dared not go. Some danced in clogs and were called "coarse"; others wore the opposite kind of shoes and were termed "fine." I myself derived great merit from the French soldierly bearing I had so splendidly acquired, and from the peasant garb of the south, which is so suitable for dancing. Never have I danced with greater liveliness and strength. I performed brilliantly, and since I had not yet trained any pupils, I had no rivals.

To be sure, my pantomime did have many rough edges, which have since been industriously honed; but at least I had the pleasure of being understood. The sight of the ancestral home, the tenderness of the son and his parents, and, finally, the bold idea of telling a life story by means of gesture, came off quite well. From the first rehearsal on, I realized that these little true-to-life scenes were certain to make an impression. Of course they were never rewarded with the applause that I could get by five turns *à terre* and two *en l'air;* but I saw many a dry handkerchief stir, and once, when the officers from a Russian squadron that was returning after an expedition of several years came ashore in Copenhagen to attend the theatre, they were so close to their native soil that the young French soldier made their hearts melt. They burst into tears with one accord. Shortly afterward, I received a glowing offer from the Imperial Theatre in St. Petersburg. Oehlenschläger, who has so often encouraged my endeavors, said of my acting: "He speaks."

Despite the overwhelming vogue of *The Sleepwalker, Soldier and Peasant* retained a favored place in the repertoire and several years ago reached its fiftieth performance.

VICTOR'S WEDDING

An Idyllic Ballet in One Act.
Music Composed by Keck.
(April 23, 1831)

IT was an eternal question whether the Ballet should remain an independent part of the repertoire or become merely an ornament for the opera and drama. My activity was zealously opposed, and the difficulties I had to overcome with respect to the Theatre's facilities and the personnel were as nothing compared to the ill will that was vented in public, from many quarters and in many ways. The first performances were always in my favor; but no sooner had the newspapers come out and the coffeehouse criticisms been registered than the attitude of the audience would change, and the applause which had been won through the spectators' surprise would be replaced by coldness and opposition.

Thus it happened with *The Pages of the Duke of Vendôme* and *Paul and Virginia,* which I had arranged with the greatest of care after Gardel and Aumer. I dare say my own inexperience was partly to blame, for it had allowed me to overlook the fact that interest in the pages chiefly rested on the legs of twelve young female dancers dressed as pages. Men as pages! How could I be so stupid? Time has also taught me that of all sentimental pieces, those with sacrificial priests or Negroes are the most tiresome, and that blackened faces, in particular, are completely unsuitable for mime. In addition, the opera considered it a profanation that the lovely operetta by Kreutzer [*Paul et Virginie*], which had been laid to eternal rest, should be resurrected as a ballet.

As I have said, after a brilliant premiere and a dozen or so "sleepy" evenings, these two Parisian ballets completely disappeared from the stage. I thereby learnt that not all superb [foreign] works could be transplanted onto Danish soil the way *The Sleepwalker* had been. If the ballet were to succeed in this country, it would have to follow the same path as Heiberg's *vaudeville,** that is, take advantage of the mood of the moment and play well-known themes and familiar tones.

The July Revolution was completed, and the Poles fought their last fight. Sympathies were aroused, and hearts beat anxiously for the nations' fates. But here at home there was peace and prosperity, and while cholera raged everywhere else, Denmark was spared. We thanked Providence and viewed its care as a blessing on King Frederik's old age. Flag of Denmark, Dane-King, "Christian stood by lofty mast," were words that brought tears to the eye. Reviews and patriotic songs enraptured us. This period has been called the most optimistic. At that time patriotism bore a different face than it does nowadays.

---

*For a full discussion of this genre and its influence on Bournonville's ballets, see Aschengreen, "The Beautiful Danger," *op. cit.*

I shared in the general enthusiasm. I had recently won both a wife† and a home in my native land; I felt the desire and the strength to risk life and limb for that which I loved, and I expressed my feelings in *Victor's Wedding, or The Ancestral Heritage*. This was a sequel to *Soldier and Peasant*, and people sympathetically followed the little plot wherein Victor, on his wedding day, is called to the defense of the mother country. The dances, all of which were my own, were very successful, and by now the *corps* had won such favor with the public that several ensemble numbers were especially appreciated. I confess that this work owed its greatest success to the mood of the moment. I need not be ashamed of a couple of scenes and a contredanse, but the plan as well as the actual composition suffered from numerous weaknesses, and I have exercised great care not to comply with the request of several people to take this ballet back into the repertoire.

FAUST

A Romantic Ballet in Three Acts.
Music Composed in Part by Keck, with Musical
Numbers by Schneitzhoeffer, Carlini, Sor,
Spontini, Weber, and Rossini.
(April 25, 1832)

IF ever Fortune favored audacity, such was the case with my realization of the daring idea of presenting *Faust* as a ballet. If people had seen it produced as drama, opera, or a puppet show, it would not have been so strange, because through the centuries the whole Faust legend has indeed been represented on the stage in the most varied forms. But what made many a person smile was that it was *Goethe*'s *Faust* which inspired me, and that I managed to make a ballet libretto suitable for performance from a poetical work in whose metaphysical depths so many commentators have lost their way.*

Noverre says that whatever can be painted can also be represented as bal-

---

† On June 23, 1830, in the Royal Chapel of Christiansborg Palace, August Bournonville was married to Helena Fredrika Håkansson (1809–1895), a native of Landskrona, Sweden. Theirs was a purely romantic match; indeed, when shortly after his betrothal a French acquaintance asked Bournonville what dowry his bride would bring, the Danish dancer replied: "Youth, beauty, amiability, and—most important of all—love!" The marriage lasted nearly forty-seven years and produced seven children: four daughters and three sons. Two of the boys died in infancy; of the five children who reached adulthood—Augusta, Charlotte, Mathilde, Edmond, Therese—only two followed their father's footsteps by pursuing artistic careers. Augusta, for whom Bournonville's charming little *Souvenir de ton père* was written in 1846, became a dancer and an accomplished pianist, but retired at an early age to marry and raise a large family. Charlotte, on the other hand, graced the stage of the Royal Theatre for many years as an opera singer. Later she taught singing and also published several delightful memoirs of her father's artistic and family life.

*For a comparison of the various balletic treatments of the Faust legend, see Svend Kragh-Jacobsen, *"Faust på Tæerne"* ["Faust on his Toes"] in *I anledning af* [essays in honor of Hakon Stangerup] (Copenhagen, 1968).

let. Retzsch's† engravings immediately reinforced the image Goethe's master-piece had left in my soul, and the first original ballet character to appear be-fore my imagination was Mephistopheles. In her relations with her mother and brother, to which so little reference is made, Gretchen struck me as a symbol of purity and amiability. To me her temptation and seduction, her suf-fering and salvation, seemed better suited to delicate plastic treatment than to declamation and song. It still remained for me to bring Faust himself into the balletic sphere in a fairly plausible manner, for as marvelous as Faust's ti-rades are to read, I do not think they would gain by being recited on the stage. It almost seems to me that, spoken by an actor, they would hover some-where between the contemptible and the tiresome. Furthermore, as a dra-matic figure Faust is always certain to be crushed by Mephistopheles. But if I capture Faust at the moment when, weary of thinking and learning, he sum-mons the spirit world to his aid, rejects the Good Angel who offers him hope and grace, and casts himself into the arms of the Evil One who promises him knowledge and pleasure ... if I picture Faust as preferring the sensually "certain" to the spiritually "uncertain," with the Devil—that is, his pride—leading him to his own corruption and that of others, why then the learned doctor is easily transformed into a young, wealthy, pleasure-loving gentleman. Pleasure and seductions follow in his wake, and Mephistopheles assumes the guise of a servant until the fatal moment when time runs out and no power can buy Faust's release from the pact he has concluded.

From the libretto one can see how I have used Goethe's characters, what inferences I drew from his great idea and how I myself devised a plot, that is to say, a plan and intrigue that fitted the series of pictures I wished to pre-sent. The most successful moments in the first act are the scene between Faust and Mephistopheles, and the ensuing witches' sabbat. With the ex-ception of the solo dance, which is the weakest part of the ballet, I believe the second act to be one of the finest things I have ever composed; after a space of several years, I again saw the bewitching waltz followed by the scene of Gretchen's seduction, and was more than ever convinced that I could not improve on it. The third act, on the other hand, is filled with imperfec-tions. At the time the ballet was first staged, we had to use old scenery and highly Philistine properties, and there was a decided shabbiness about the whole production. The fair mentioned in the libretto was therefore reduced to several people strolling about, together with an organ grinder and a juggler. The gypsy dance was lively but lacked a definite motive. The degeneration of Faust into Mephistopheles' stable companion was only implied, while the principal scene concerned the wandering of Gretchen, now rejected by society. Herein I had created several original and moving episodes, and felt that I had depicted the wronged and repudiated woman with a masterly hand,

† Friedrich A. M. Retzsch (1779–1857), German engraver, became widely known for his series based on literary themes, especially Goethe's *Faust* and the *Gallery of Shakespeare*. He worked in a combination of Classical and Romantic tradition.

FAUST

In this sketch by Lehmann, Adolf Stramboe is Mephistopheles to the choreographer's Faust; Margaretha is either Andrea Kraetzmer or Lucile Grahn, both of whom danced the role. Teatermuseet, Copenhagen.

PAUL AND VIRGINIA

An 1835 oil painting by Lehmann showing August Bournonville and Andrea Kraetzmer in the title roles of Gardel's ballet. Teatermuseet, Copenhagen.

Above, left: *VALDEMAR*. Costume sketch for Astrid (Lucile Grahn) in the 1835 production. Right: *LA SYLPHIDE*. Costume sketch for James (Bournonville) showing Madge (Carl Fredstrup) in the background. Both by Chr. Bruun. Below: *VALDEMAR*. The "Torch Dance" from the 1866 revival. Drawing from *Illustreret Tidende*. All, Teatermuseet, Copenhagen.

when a remark by our renowned Weyse hit me like a bucket of cold water: "It is too long! There is too much misery!" I immediately began to shorten it, but the scene lost its *rondeur,* and I could never look at it again without that fatal word "misery" ringing, or rather grinding, in my ears.

The final scene, with the recognition, Gretchen's death, her return to life, and her transition to immortality while Faust sinks into the abyss, has been much praised, but, on the other hand, strongly criticized because it is Mephistopheles who calls her back to life. Can the Devil wake the dead? To this I reply: Faust's evil genius has fulfilled every one of his earthly wishes, but always by shortening the time of the pact. In his despair Faust sells his last hour to buy Gretchen's life. He also sees this wish fulfilled, but here the irony of fate appears. Her reopened eyes no longer recognize Faust. She ascends to the regions he can never enter, and the Evil One drags Faust down with him into the abyss, not because his crimes have reached the limit but because he has sold his soul, which is now the Devil's rightful possession.

Despite everything it lacked in external attractions, this ballet has been extraordinarily successful and is still viewed with interest. It made my name as a ballet poet and gave the Danish Ballet its real substance. I am well aware that later on the subject was twice treated abroad, in London by Deshayes and in Naples by Salvatore Taglioni (in the latter place it was prohibited after two performances). One can easily imagine the greater magnificence and care with which these works were mounted abroad as compared with our production, where my ballet had to rely entirely upon the imagination of the audience. And yet perhaps it is to my credit that I addressed the mind and heart through the nobler means of art and gratified the most ardent admirers of Goethe's immortal masterwork.

THE VETERAN, OR THE HOSPITABLE HOUSE

An Idyllic Ballet in One Act.
Music Composed by Zinck.
(January 29, 1833)

AFTER having satisfied the demands of the times, which tended strongly toward the diabolic, I felt the need to return to those subjects about which I was genuinely enthusiastic: rural life, children, and soldiers.

After a laborious winter I found rest in lovely Frederiksdal,* and *there* came to realize that nature contains inexhaustible sources of inspiration for my art. Dramatic characters and situations are, in a manner of speaking, exhausted; the so-called "new" is simply the "old" revitalized. Besides, there is something more or less sordid in the plots of almost all modern works, which, stripped of the subtleties of dialogue, would appear vulgar and disgusting:

*A district to the northwest of Copenhagen, near Furesø and between the suburbs of Lyngby and Holte.

pantomime is, after all, denied the wittiness of irony and intonation. Nature, on the other hand, is ever new and fresh; if landscape and genre painters cannot exhaust it, how much less ballet writers, who have so rarely made use of its riches.

I obtained an entirely new view of my art. For me, the ballet was no longer a dramatic plot to which I was to join pretty details and picturesque episodes, but a series of pictures bound together by a dramatic thread. The main thing was to find a piquant idea, which little by little could be molded into an interesting whole; for I believed that the more successful a ballet had been, the more difficult it was to relate its contents. As a result, my ballets gradually moved further away from drama and became more akin to painting and music, where the outlines melt away as the subject is being worked up.

As I fished in the millrace, where children played along the bank, I noticed that the current was strongest near the wheel, which turned with crushing speed and could only be stopped by the release of the floodgate. The farmyard there was filled with chickens and pigeons. The inn lay close by, and the idyllic domestic life alternated with the noise of the taproom. Here was material enough for me. Picture the miller as an old soldier from Napoleon's army; set the scene in my beloved Normandy (where I had spent so many wonderful holidays, comparing the country and its inhabitants with those of Denmark); make the mill the abode of hospitality; and now, at a time when Poland's exiled freedom fighters renewed the memory of Ney and Labédoyère,† let the miller's Colonel seek refuge with his brother-in-arms, who hides him in the millwork, where he will become the instrument of the child's rescue. All these images arranged themselves around my original picture, and love bestowed upon me one of its myriad rays, without which no painting can have life and a play of color.

The miller and his family were a successful group. I myself played Colin, and my alternate grief and joy were quite effective. The Drum Major created a furor. The Veteran, or Colonel Sainville, as so often happens with title roles when they constitute the noble element in the piece, was less outstanding, and I admit that this character could have been better worked out. The ballet's essential shortcoming lay in the limited size of the stage. One can easily imagine that a width of twelve ells‡ is hardly adequate space in which to depict the millpond and its wheel, together with the floodgate and bridge—all seen from the inside of the mill. Since the audience goes to the theatre to take, not to give, it would be unfair to demand that their imaginations make up for everything that is lacking in completeness; for in a bas-relief a portion of wall can denote an entire city, while an elephant need only come up to its guide's shoulder and a horse need be no taller than a lamb. Even in drama, a

† These French generals were both executed after the downfall of Napoleon for having supported the Emperor on his return from Elba in 1815.

‡ The ell (in Danish, *alen*) is an obsolete measure of length. While the length of the English ell is customarily given as forty-five inches, the Danish ell is equal to approximately two feet or roughly sixty centimeters.

few words can make a boudoir out of the humblest room; but in a ballet the eye must be satisfied and the illusion must be as complete as possible.

The Veteran was given on the same birthday evening as the *vaudeville Danes in Paris,* and scored quite a success. The faults people found in Heiberg's piece were all to the advantage of my work, which may have had a better-laid-out plan and a deeper fund of feeling. My Veteran, it was said, was an entirely different fellow than Major Jean Brun, and my Drum Major a far more elegant military man than the Jutland peasant, Mikkel.* Furthermore, my picture of France was nobler and truer. This was acknowledged as long as the works were presented together. But when they were given separately a short time later, it was *Danes in Paris* that walked off with the prize; for people responded to the witty, entertaining element and grasped the lyrical points, and the flaws evaporated amid the freshness and fragrance that are so peculiar to Heiberg's poetic works.

There could certainly be no question of a rivalry with Heiberg who was then at his height, while I myself was still a novice; but the predominant quality in my ballet was its novella-like suspense. Once this had vanished, the details were bound to appear more or less thin. I had now used soldiers in two ballets. Moreover, in those days grenadiers, emotional sergeants, and girls in uniform were to be seen in abundance every evening. Mikkel came along just in time to sweep this "ration-bread sentimentality" off the field. The melodies from my ballet did not gain popularity, but those from the *vaudeville* were sung in every nook and corner. And yet *The Veteran* survived a pleasant run of performances, and I do not regret having composed it. But unless some very special reason forces me to do so, I will never remount it on the stage.

THE TYROLEANS

An Idyllic Ballet in One Act.
Music by Frøhlich with Two Musical
Pieces by Rossini.
(March 6, 1835)

IF competition is necessary anywhere, it is surely vital where composition and invention are concerned, especially with subjects which, even if they are intended not for pleasure alone, must still aim to please, and whose favorable reception depends so much upon the mental and, yes, the physical dispositions of the audience.

From the time I first made my appearance as a choreographer, I have stood completely alone. The desire to create ballets had been lost by all those who had once had a passion for it. No foreigners visited us, and, since I

---

*Major Jean Brun and the peasant Mikkel are characters in Heiberg's *Danes in Paris.*

would not work from others' libretti, I had no competition from this quarter either. If only my course could have been judged *absolutely,* as with a horse that covers a stretch in a certain number of minutes, this isolated position of mine could have been quite pleasant. But it was always viewed in a *relative* fashion, and since the critics had no comparisons ready at hand, they pitted the deceased composers against me.

Galeotti was the champion against whom I repeatedly had to enter the lists, and he was all the more dangerous as I did not dare to expose his weaknesses without risking the charge of irreverence. Memories of the Theatre's days of prosperity, the idea that the older ballets which had been put aside could no longer be performed, and the fact that Galeotti was an Italian while I, despite my foreign origins and training, was merely Danish, greatly helped to raise his works above their true deserts. If I went through Galeotti's ballets scene by scene and group by group, I could find in them no example worthy of imitation; yet if I considered the enthusiasm they had aroused and the glorious reputation they still retained, I had to respect them.

People often asked me if they should never be given the opportunity to see these masterworks again. I was thoroughly acquainted with them, and at that time my father and Mme. Schall were still able to assist me with the rehearsal and the memorization. And by restaging these works I too was bound to gain something: either the honor of having restored these masterpieces or the advantage of playing rewarding roles.

I therefore remounted the finest of Galeotti's ballets as well as the one best suited to the abilities of our *corps: Romeo and Giulietta.* I handled it with the greatest of care, and made only minor changes which even the master's admirers deemed necessary. The ballet was superbly mounted and the performance was in no way inferior to that of its older cast. But it was no longer to the popular taste. The subject was boring, the details lacked interest, and the numerous songs with which the ballet was adorned throughout were now regarded as a ridiculous appendix, comparable to the written notes that were attached to the mouths of historical figures when the art of painting was in its infancy. We survived four lukewarm performances; then *Romeo* sank into oblivion. On one hand I received no thanks other than the assertion that I did not understand Galeotti, and on the other it was said that my invention was exhausted and that I was now forced to rehash the old. Since that experience, nothing has persuaded me to take older ballets back into the repertoire.

Among the French ballets which, from the pantomimic aspect, have had the greatest influence on my views on this art, Milon's *Nina, ou La Folle par amour* stands supreme. The subject (as usual, the mimed adaptation of an operetta) is handled with a sensitivity and charm which perfectly characterize that great master. Wherever one possesses an *artiste* with true inspiration and a speaking countenance, this ballet ought to stand as a model of this genre. At this time no one but Fru Heiberg was capable of performing the leading role. The ballet was a tremendous success and my selection [of her for the part]

was perfectly justified. But still this did not save me from a great deal of unpleasantness and a host of stupid comments. As usual, these frictions had
their effect upon our audience. The enthusiasm which attended the admirable
moments in the action at the first performances soon degenerated into the old
familiar sluggishness, and after a series of quite well-attended performances,
Fru Heiberg grew bored with playing on a silent instrument and gave up the
role. "It exhausted her," as had the part of Fenella in *The Mute Girl of Portici.* The audience often does not seem to notice how much strain one may
endure amid loud expressions of sympathy and merited applause.

After four laborious years I refreshed myself in mind and body by a trip
to Paris (1834), where I danced at the Opéra a couple of times and was received as a son of the house. I became acquainted with the ingenious Henry,
and from his talent I received an incentive which was of tremendous importance to my future career. "The gift of composing is not like soil which brings
forth wild fruit, but like ploughed sod in which a handful of choice grain
yields a rich crop." A number of my works lay finished in writing, but as a result of this trip they were reworked and greatly improved; that is to say, I had
learnt a great deal about the use of the solo.

For the rest, the ballet in Paris was not in exactly first-rate condition at
that time. From the standpoint of composition, *La Révolte au sérail, La Laitière suisse,* and *La Tentation* were beneath contempt. On the other hand, I
saw *La Sylphide* only once, but there I found that the idea and its execution
went hand in hand (more about this ballet later on).

I returned home toward autumn, used *Nina* as a prelude, and presented
The Tyroleans the following spring. To me, the myth of Anacreon had always
seemed a suitable theme for ballet,* but this time I was wise enough to
change all the external details; for to introduce Greeks onto our stage would
be the same as bringing Jews into Norway.† Emancipation is still awaited.
The popular taste for yodeling tunes and Alpine songs came along at just the
right moment for me. The idyllic scenery certainly blended well with my
idea, and as for Cupid . . . why, he belongs to all countries, times, and peoples; he assumes any form he pleases, but the rogue in him eventually peeps
out; compassion grants him an asylum, he knows how to force his way into
the heart through the senses; sometimes, he is first recognized by the pangs
of jealousy, and his mastery perceived through the confusion he causes. I derived great satisfaction from this little ballet, which has long retained the favor of the public by virtue of its lively action, varied dances, rustic atmosphere, and, last but not least, the comical village fiddler, which is one of my

*The story of *The Tyroleans* appears to have been broadly based on the third Ode of Anacreon,
which also inspired a relief by Thorvaldsen, and a story, "The Mischievous Boy," by Hans Chris-
tian Andersen.
† Even though Jews in Denmark were granted civil rights as early as 1814, in Norway—where
Henrik Wergeland so eloquently pleaded their cause in his idyllic poems "The Jew" (1842) and
"The Jewess" (1844)—they were not given freedom of the country until the early 1850's.

most successful genre pictures. The idea of using the umbrella in a storm is not of my own invention. I have simply made use of it; but since it had never before been seen on our stage, I found it especially suitable for filling the time during which the thunderstorm rages. I have always had a certain fondness for this work, which is one of the few I have had a chance to view from the audience, and which, I shamefully confess, I enjoyed as much as if I had not composed it myself.

VALDEMAR

A Romantic Ballet in Four Acts.
Music by Frøhlich.
(October 28, 1835)

FROM my earliest school years on, I pictured Svend Grathe's bloody feast at Roskilde as a vast historical painting. In my mind I saw Valdemar and Absalon leaping about on tables and benches in order to extinguish the lights; with a beating heart I followed them on their nocturnal flight and exulted when the traitor received his punishment on Grathe Heath. I naturally viewed this whole idea in terms of a ballet but with completely Galeottian forms, which were the only ones I knew at the time. Still, for a number of years I deemed it impossible that a subject wherein two kings die violent deaths could lend itself to a pantomimic treatment, complete with dancing. And then my childhood idea cropped up again. What an honor it would be for me and my art if we were able to place the ballet on an equal footing with the national drama! Love for Denmark filled my heart, and Old Norse sagas my head. I drew material from Holberg's *History of Denmark*, outlines from the *Knytlinga Saga*, tones from Ingemann's writings, and colors (I make bold to say) from my own imagination.

To my knowledge, no one else had treated this subject, and so I worked with a free hand. Moreover, the story is so highly romantic that one need not add anything in order to make it interesting and dramatic. But I did need a source of lovableness which could at once bring a bit of light into Svend's sinister character and serve as a focal point about which grace, festivity, and chivalrous gallantry could revolve. I succeeded in inventing a daughter for Svend: Astrid, who adores her father at the same time as she is animated by love for Valdemar, whose escape she encourages. Svend disowns her but, disguised as his squire, she follows him to the war and is the only one who does not abandon him in his hour of need (the saga does mention a little boy who dies in order to defend his king). She quenches the dying man's thirst, is recognized by him, and with her father's last breath is released from his malediction. She defends his corpse, and only to Valdemar himself does she surrender the standard. She is received by the cloister, and for the king her blessing inaugurates the homage that victory has granted him.

The most difficult point in this ballet is the first act and its finale, wherein the reconciliation is effected and the kingdom is divided. Danish folk life, the appearance of Valdemar and Astrid, Knud's landing, and Valdemar's mediation are elements that are merely implied but still take up so much time that, were they to be further developed, they would cease to be an exposition of the action, which does not really begin until the second act. Here events begin to unfold, and throughout the feast one can already discern Svend's treachery, until it finally erupts and the guests, with the exception of Valdemar and Axel, fall victim to it. Knud's death scene and the manner in which the lights are extinguished are considered some of the most gripping scenes ever performed on the Danish stage, and in the eyes of the connoisseurs this act is the high point of the ballet.

People are right in objecting that the dances are largely based on bravura, but this is one of the evils from which the theatre, here as everywhere else, suffers: the less cultured public demands "fireworks" and virtuosity, while the more cultured audience is bored and finds the evening cold and dull if the former does not clap and shout "Bravo!" This is the reason for Valdemar's high jumps and brilliant *pirouettes,* as well as the princess' solo on the beach, among the peasants and fishermen.

The third act depicts Valdemar in circumstances similar to those in which Gustavus Vasa found himself,* while Svend, like another Macbeth, is haunted by his own crime; but the Angel of Mercy stands by him in the figure of his daughter.

The fourth act shows us Valdemar's vision. (The fact that this is not better performed may be attributed exclusively to the limited amount of space and the imperfect *corps.*) In the battle of Grathe Heath I succeeded in solving a problem. Up till that time battle scenes were considered completely undramatic and usually aroused nought but merriment on the part of the audience. Here, on the contrary, the few but powerful moments of the battle had a shocking effect. The hosts vanished in an instant, the battlefield was strewn with the vanquished, and Svend was among them. Valdemar's triumph, his clemency, and the people's homage produced a gradually mounting fervor; the victory march brought the enthusiasm to its height, and the ballet ended with general jubilation.

No drama has enjoyed greater favor or drawn larger audiences than this ballet. It appealed to every class and every age; it was requested as a national gala performance for foreign princes and at our Theatre secured for the Ballet an esteem that aroused a great deal of envy and won me many more opponents than admirers. Until that time they [the Theatre directorate] did not

---

*In 1519, Gustavus Vasa (1496–1560) escaped from a Danish prison where he had been held hostage by the Danish king, Christjern II, perpetrator of the Stockholm Bloodbath. Continually pursued by Christjern's emissaries, he fled in disguise to Flensborg, and, after sailing to the port of Lübeck, returned to Sweden. There he raised an army of peasants, repulsed the Danes, and subsequently became king of Sweden. The first part of Act III of *Valdemar* depicts the hero's flight following the treacherous attack upon him at Roskilde.

believe that any fee whatsoever should be given for an artistic genre they
would gladly have dispensed with. But on this occasion they outdid themselves, and I received a gratuity of 300 Rbd. and the title of Balletmaster [i.e.,
head of the Ballet] *without salary* — with the clear understanding that in this
capacity I would receive in the future neither salary nor emoluments. I was
thirty years old at the time.

DON QUIXOTE AT CAMACHO'S WEDDING

An Idyllic Ballet in Three Acts.
Music Arranged by Zinck, with Musical Numbers by
Rossini, Méhul, Spontini, Schneitzhoeffer,
and Others.
(February 24, 1837)

BEFORE discussing this ballet, which survived only two performances, I
must mention as one of my most successful compositions *La Sylphide*, whose
original plan and libretto were conceived by the singer Adolphe Nourrit. It is
therefore not of my own writing, but the Danish composition of the subject is
mine, just as that of the French version is the work of Filippo Taglioni (father
of the famous Marie Taglioni). In order to mount an unfamiliar work, such as
The Sleepwalker, The Pages, Paul and Virginia, Romeo, or *Nina,* I first had to
acquire the original music, then learn the details of the ballet, and finally
adapt everything to suit our theatre's facilities. However, with *La Sylphide* it
was quite a different matter. I saw the Parisian *Sylphide* but a single time and
came away filled with nought but admiration for Mlle. Taglioni's extraordinary bravura and amazement at the splendid machinery. Both these things
were equally unattainable at our theatre and, even though I found the main
idea of the ballet most appealing, I felt that I would benefit most by drawing
from my own fund of inspiration. Besides, the score was entirely too expensive, and those who could have taught me the roles (for they had to be
taught) did not seem disposed to do so just then.

At that time there was in effect a system which was highly dangerous for
male dancers; to wit, that of using them as props for their female partners.
Hence, in *La Sylphide* James was simply a pedestal for the prima donna, and
the ingeniously poetic idea that man, in pursuing an imaginary happiness, ne-
glects the true one and loses everything just when he thinks he is about to attain the object of his desire, was completely lost amid the wondrous virtuosity
of the ballerina. I had consequently decided not to give *La Sylphide* at the
Danish Theatre. What prompted me, then, to change my mind? The desire to
present a talented pupil [Lucile Grahn] who seemed made for the title role
and whom I had trained entirely after the ideal of Taglioni, and also repeated
requests that I try a young musical talent [Løvenskjold] well suited for this
genre.

I made several changes in the plan, gave the ballet a national color that was not to be found in the Parisian version, developed the character of James, and thought up new dances and groupings. Now, since the music was completely new, the gestures and *pas* also had to be new, inasmuch as the rhythms determine the makeup of the dances. The composition and staging therefore cost me as much industry and care as if I myself had invented the plan, and I have received testimony to the fact that not only is *my* ballet completely different from Taglioni's—it even wins the prize as far as dramatic merit and precision of execution are concerned. It is still a lovely flower in our ballet repertoire and has always enjoyed favor and applause. Here I shall only hint that it has also caused me a great deal of unpleasantness, the least of which is that of being referred to in Paris as a plagiarist. I could amuse my readers with several anecdotes which at that time seemed to me as distressing as they now do laughable, but I do not wish to digress from my fixed plan. Suffice it to say that, in certain respects, the Sylphide has been for me the same as she was for James: a bad angel, whose poisonous breath has exerted its influence on every plant that sprouted in my path, and who did not tread lightly upon those leaves she would crush and ruin.

Anyone who has read Cervantes' immortal masterwork will find in the narrative about Camacho's wedding a perfect scheme for a comic ballet. It has been treated as such scores of times, and the great popularity of the subject has rendered every situation clear and made each character an old acquaintance. Neither gaiety, dancing, nor amusing complications were lacking, and it was with pleasure that I acceded to a request I received from several lovers of Spanish literature. For, you see, it is the same with Spanish poetry as with classical: it is not popular with the general public because it is not understood, and it is not understood for the simple reason that it is not known. Some individuals who attended the rehearsal rewarded my interpretation with laughter and applause and promised a favorable outcome. But when it came right down to it, to the performance, that is, my dancing was thunderously applauded, while all the things on which I had been counting most— namely, Don Quixote's adventures, Sancho's adversities, the festival and the little theatre, and the grand brawl—were hardly noticed, and I clearly perceived that people did not know what I really had in mind. I will admit that, in costume, Don Quixote and his armor-bearer were not what they had been at rehearsal. The knight was indeed most woebegone, while the scenes were somewhat overlong and the music lacked substance. A few bravura dances and a dazzling finale won me some brilliant rounds of applause after the curtain fell on the first performance. . . . It was almost a victory! But, alas! The following evening was almost a defeat, for at the end of a dreadfully cold performance there were several expressions of displeasure and a couple of flute-like sounds that did not come from the orchestra.

Some critics, who had presumably read only excerpts from *Don Quixote* and overlooked the fact that my treatment dealt with Camacho's wedding, immediately informed the public that this subject was positively unsuitable for ballet, and . . . it was not the first nor the last time that someone has, at our Theatre, gotten *prae caeteris* and *laudabilis* in every individual subject, but received *non* as a general average. However, that is exactly what happened with my work. At that time the wind was not blowing in my favor and it was impossible for me to fight against it. A very serious illness prevented me from committing the foolish act of defying the storm by means of art and industry, and when I at length returned to health and careful reflection, I unrigged the whole ship and decided to wait for better times. They came, and should my good readers still take pleasure in the nocturnal *Festival in Albano*, the Spanish character, the Melancholy Englishman in *The Toreador* as well as the merry fray in *Bellman,* they are actually greeting the old guests from *Camacho's Wedding*.

HERTHA'S OFFERING

A Divertissement.
Music After the Works of Several Composers,
Arranged by Frøhlich.
(January 29, 1838)

HEIBERG gave his *Fata Morgana* for a royal birthday celebration and, relying upon the rhythmic "dancing" of his beautiful strophes, he had rejected the assistance of the ballet in this little fairy-tale comedy. The Court insisted upon *divertissements*. I had a really good idea, but Heiberg himself, who had not found any use for it in his piece, proposed that it be performed independently and be shown before the play.

I composed and rehearsed the whole thing in less than six days. As can be seen from the libretto, it consisted solely of dances with a rather light motif: the whole thing was a bouquet (a "flower piece," as I called it) in the truest sense of the word, for about 250 Rbd. worth of flowers — garlands, baskets, cornucopias, nosegays, and wreaths — were manufactured for this occasion. The *divertissement* lasted for nearly half an hour and had a most enchanting effect.

The allegory was easy to comprehend: it signified "the Danish soil, which offers its finest gifts." People understood what I was trying to say, and the work was received with an enthusiasm that lasted through a long run of performances, until all the artificial flowers had become faded and torn. But since at our Theatre it is rare for two things to be successful at the same time, now it was Heiberg's ingenious work that suffered from the brilliant reception accorded my bagatelle.

There is a certain kind of praise that one would rather dispense with; for example, if speaking about a play: "It is very poetic or profound"; about virtuosity: "That must certainly be very difficult"; or about an opera: "That is real music." Unfortunately, these concessions do not reveal a lively sympathy [on the part of the audience]. How much better it would be to hear something like this: "The experts claim that the work is full of flaws, but we find it interesting and entertaining." It is rather annoying to have to admit it, but it is the applause of the crowd that we covet. And yet we consider ourselves lucky if, unnoticed by the crowd, we can dare to risk being true artists and smuggle in something from which the few connoisseurs can benefit.

THE ISLE OF FANTASY

A Romantic Ballet in Two Acts
and a Final Tableau.
Music for the First Act by Hartmann [with a
Musical Piece by Auber]; Music for the Second Act
by Hartmann, Bredal, Zinck, Helsted, and
Løvenskjold.
(October 28, 1838)

IT had now become a standing rule that a ballet was to be given for the royal birthdays. These occurred in October and January. But although this honor was highly flattering to me, and had the added advantage that nothing was to be spared with respect to the décor for a gala performance, there was still one drawback: the fact that I missed the initial and most important acclaim of the public, by giving my ballet for a distinguished and ceremonious audience, who according to Court etiquette denied me the first fruits of their surprise and forced me to await judgment until the critics had laid their cold, clammy hands on my newborn.

The folk comedy *Capriciosa* had earlier created an epoch on the Danish stage, and on my last trip to Paris (1838) I had become acquainted with a drama called *Victorine,* where the complications of the story are solved when the heroine awakens. The whole thing had been a dream! Captivated by some lovely moments in the Danish folk comedy, my imagination had carried me even further into the young seaman's future: he has actually set off from China, and on January 28 is fêted in Canton, while at home the festivity is mingled with longing and good wishes for him. There was an interval of nine months between the royal birthdays, the exact amount of time needed to complete a leisurely journey home.

The beloved maiden follows her dearest one, both awake and in her dreams, sharing his perils and his joys, lands with him on the enchanted isle, and sees him hurl himself, like Telemachus, from the cliffs, where temptation held him captive. She is awakened by the thundering of cannon announcing October 28, Queen Marie's birthday, and the return of the traveler from China. The entire family hastens to the Custom House to greet the seaman, who is waiting with open arms. This idea, which I had received from an outside source, allowed me to create a highly original composition which contained much for both the eye and the heart. It was also quite successful. The salient features of my composition were grasped, and the character dances received jubilant applause; but two things spoiled the overall impression: 1) the fact that a paternalistic care for my students had led me to entrust the role of the male romantic lead to a dancer in the most limited sense of the word: that is, all legs and no imagination; 2) the absence of the scene painter Christensen, which forced me to use old scenery for the enchanted isle. The set that was provided for the isle was a panorama of the charming coast of Sjælland, beginning at the old limekiln and ending at the watercrane on Nyholm—most prosaic and dull.

Next, although the ballet was only an occasional piece with special reference to two red-letter days, a number of events occurred at that time that weakened patriotic fervor and enthusiasm for the expansion of Danish power and glory. The Asiatic Company was abolished, sordid rumors about the slave trade circulated, and the running aground of a ship of the line caused much scandal to the navy. Furthermore, the public's sympathies had been pressed into service quite often and had taken a turn that in no way resembled enthusiasm. My work could not long survive. *The Isle of Fantasy* became uninhabited and unfrequented. But now, long afterward, it delights people to make a flying trip to Canton in order to see an English sailor dance his hornpipe and swing his tarpaulin hat to the great enjoyment of the Danes.

THE FESTIVAL IN ALBANO

An Idyllic Ballet in One Act.
Music by Frøhlich.
(October 28, 1839)

THORVALDSEN'S arrival in Copenhagen brought new life into all branches of art, including the dance. He was an avid theatregoer who judged works with an open eye, and his applause was all the more precious to me as I worshiped his genius. All of Denmark vied to fête him. The Theatre alone was in arrears in this respect, and it remained for me to pay this "debt of homage." It was on October 28, 1839—the last gala performance that Frederik VI lived to see. I dare say protocol found itself shortchanged by this compliment addressed to a mere "subject," but I felt that such men as Thorvaldsen were the gems of crown and country, and on a solemn day one ought to display one's finest treasures.

Few ballets have given me as much satisfaction as *The Festival in Albano*. Not only did the King declare it to be the loveliest ballet he had ever seen, but I also succeeded, using only descriptions and genre pictures, in creating so vivid an impression of life in the environs of Rome that Thorvaldsen and many other "traveled" men found themselves transported to the very spot. The appearance of the artists and the plastic dances elicited from Oeh-lenschläger a poem which shall be a rune of honor for me, and when a series of the master's most beautiful sculptures appeared, represented by real people and magically illuminated, a thunderous "Hurrah!" burst forth from Denmark's Phidias. The ballet was superbly performed and Christensen's décor was enchanting. The dance with Venus and Bacchus called forth lively applause, and an inserted tarantella (after Perrot) was most effective. *The Festival in Albano* has been performed often and always with sympathy on the part of the audience. However, the greatest joy I received from this ballet was the fact that its scenes and moods recurred to me when I visited Rome a year and a half later.

I came to Albano and recognized its costumes, fêtes, and melodies so plainly that even *after* my journey I could not have represented them more faithfully. And when on a beautiful summer's eve, in the company of a number of artists from several nations, I drove out of the Porta Pia to a vineyard, where we sat round a table (made from the enormous capital of a pillar) and enjoyed a marvelous view across the Campagna to the Sabine Hills, as if by magic one after another the scenes from my ballet appeared: the light repast, the dancing, the busy innkeeper, the game of bowls, and lastly, when darkness had fallen, the romantic homeward march, by torchlight, to the accompaniment of singing and the sound of guitars.

THE FATHERLAND'S MUSES

A Pantomimic Prologue.
Music Composed and Arranged by
Frøhlich and Gade.
(March 20, 1840)

AFTER the death of King Frederik VI the Theatre remained closed for three months, and a work suited to the occasion was requested for its reopening. I did my best and submitted my plan. It was found to be ingenious, and I executed it with the enthusiasm which always follows upon a previous successful undertaking (*The Festival in Albano*).

The allegory was as follows: Sorrow and Winter pined for the reviving warmth in whose bosom Art and Science flourish. Each of the Muses possessed a favorite in Denmark, and each garland was denoted by a *tableau vivant* alluding to the master in question. Terpsichore and Apollo decreed a celebration, and Love of the Fatherland crowned the whole.

I flattered myself with the idea that this allegory would not go unnoticed, and that the compliment addressed to those celebrities who were still living would be acknowledged with patriotic fervor. But I was completely mistaken in my reckoning. Most of the *tableaux* amazed the audience with their artistic arrangement, and the *pirouettes* and *entrechats* worked their usual magic. But the true meaning of the ballet remained my own private delight, for I do not believe a single person grasped my idea. I may have been mistaken about the feelings aroused against me, but to me it seemed as if some people had found it presumptuous that Terpsichore should erect a Pantheon for the other Muses, while others had viewed my allusions as vulgar flattery; and finally, it appeared as if those men I had acclaimed had become angry with me because this appeal to the public's enthusiasm did not catch on. Nothing is more unfortunate than to propose a toast which is a "fiasco." I swore nevermore to use allegorical figures in my ballets. Farewell, ye Muses and Graces! If you can steal in dressed in masquerade costume, by all means do—but not in the garb of Olympus. It is already asking a lot for us to tolerate Cupid and Bacchus.

THE TOREADOR

An Idyllic Ballet in Two Acts.
Music Composed and Arranged by Edvard Helsted.
(November 27, 1840)

FOR the coronation festivities, no composition was assigned to me. Instead, a Spanish dancing couple was sent for.* They were practically native dancers, and, viewed from this standpoint, were most extraordinary. There was a great deal to be learnt from their singular movements, and before my imagination there now appeared a whole new world of character dances which I had indeed suspected but had not fully understood. It was the same with their reception as it so often is: the papers complained about the lukewarmness of the audience and praised this native dancing to the skies. They openly called the school of Vestris "rope dancing," and pointed out that these *seguidillas* were nuts that our Ballet could not crack.

These dancers were granted a benefit performance and invited me to assist them in a *bolero à quatre*. I was willing and learnt the dance, and this contest contributed in no small measure to providing a full house. I imitated everything with the greatest of care and had the added advantage of possessing training and artistry. My appearance astounded the audience. All this tossing of the head and torso produced a mixture of laughter and applause, which made my usual detractors ask whether it was out of irony or seriousness that I had chosen to dance in this fashion. My answer was already prepared, but was not delivered until the premiere of *The Toreador*.

From the Spaniards' *jaleo* and *bolero* I had arranged for myself two dances that were to form a contrast to the "affected" solo which the *danseuse* Céleste performed in the ballet. The Majo costume was superbly suited to the role of a toreador. From this I created a character that owed its existence to

*The coronation was that of Christian VIII, who succeeded to the throne on the death of Frederik VI, December 13, 1839. The Spanish dancers were Dolores Serral and Mariano Camprubí; cf. Vol. II, p. 176.

pictures and verbal accounts of what a toreador looked like. I had Englishmen, in full costume, from a steamship tour. Moligne's theme, which copied the *jaleo* melody, furnished me with material for the little misunderstanding.†
To this were added some picturesque details from *Don Quixote*, and the gay, lively tone of the whole produced one of my most popular ballets and provided me with a *succès de vogue*.

At the height of this vogue there occurred an event which caused such a sensation and had so great an influence upon my destiny that I can hardly refrain from mentioning it here. Although it lay outside my duties to compose or arrange anything for drama or opera, I nevertheless made several exceptions, sometimes for state occasions, sometimes out of friendship or respect for one author or another. Thus I had composed the dance in *The Black Domino* and the stage arrangement for "The Battle of Stiklestad" and *Aladdin*. I was sought after for my taste and because I had a good eye for distributing roles on the basis of the talents of the *corps*. My school had just produced two excellent female dancers who were vying to win the favor of the public—always, however, with that rivalry becoming to sister *artistes*. The opera *Brahma and the Bayadère* furnishes the opportunity for such a competition, and, since I was well aware of their respective capabilities, I delegated the part of Zoloé to the *danseuse* who had the most fantasy and staying power, while that of Fatmé, which consisted mainly of a *pas de deux*, was reserved for the dancer who would almost be able to hold her own against Zoloé by virtue of her bravura.‡ This casting was natural and therefore justified. Both dancers seemed satisfied and agreed to put their best talents to use.

But now the tares were sown among the wheat: Fatmé's admirers, advisors, and patrons cried out that she had been slighted. Artistry and reason, arguments, the proofs at hand, the excellent performance of the work, and its brilliant success were all inadequate. After gossip, coffeehouse declamations, and impertinent private writings had been exhausted, they had recourse to the periodical press. And when they had been rejected by all the papers that still possessed some public decency, they turned to *Den Frisindede* [*The Liberal*] ! If anyone should happen to have kept this journal for the years 1840 and 1841, he will be astonished that an editor who appears under so noble a title would allow himself to become involved in such calumny.* One will also

---

† This incident occurs in Act One, when the toreador Alonzo mistakenly accuses the visiting Englishmen of having designs on his fiancée, Maria. The foreigners do not know the name of the young lady with whom they have both fallen in love. They only know that she dances the *jaleo de Xeres* with Alonzo. The latter had first danced it with Maria, but afterward taught the steps to the French ballerina Céleste—the actual object of the Englishmen's affections. It is this last performance that they had witnessed and which has led to the misunderstanding. The outraged Alonzo draws his dagger, the guard are called, and the toreador is carried off to prison.

‡ Caroline Fjeldsted was to dance the part of Zoloé, Augusta Nielsen that of Fatmé.

*For details of this complicated affair, see Svend Kragh-Jacobsen and Torben Krogh: *Den kongelige danske Ballet* (Copenhagen, 1952), pp. 232–235, and Robert Neiiendam: *En Danserinde* (Copenhagen, 1965), pp. 16–20. However, in order to understand the Balletmaster's attitude toward his critics, one should indeed take his advice and consult the Copenhagen newspapers for 1840 and 1841, including *Den Frisindede*, edited by C. M. Rosenhoff.

be surprised that in a civilized country where a sense of justice and decency prevails, a respectable *danseuse* should have been dragged through the mud in the manner in which this paper treated the interpreter of Zoloé. But what must outrage anyone who recognizes the importance of the press is that in all of Copenhagen there was not a single pen that would undertake the rebuttal of those disgraceful attacks. No criminal has been treated as I was at the very moment when the fruits of my noblest endeavor lay clear as daylight before the public eye. But "Calumniate! " says Bazile.† "There is always something in it." This is just what happened. The articles in all their ugliness were too piquant not to be widely read. I dare say people regarded the accusations as greatly exaggerated; but even if they were reduced to one-third, they would have been enough to make me out a scoundrel.

I myself ignored most of these lying articles and decided to answer them with silent contempt, for every evening I could triumphantly defend my artistic character. But the private character is one of a more sensitive nature. In our country and under our laws, it has too little protection against dirty hands. Nevertheless, my awareness and the success of my works kept me in good spirits, and I had already arrived at *The Toreador's* twelfth performance with a full house, when I was informed of the fact (which a great part of the public already knew) that on March 14 I was to be received with expressions of displeasure because I had supposedly slighted the *danseuse* who was actually performing the most rewarding role in *The Toreador!*

As usual, I faced up to the danger, scorning the wretched cabals and trusting that the true audience would surely defend me as one of its favored artists. A moment before my entrance, the Royal Family entered their box, and I now fancied that as indecent a scene as the one being prepared would be thwarted by respect for His Majesty. I therefore mounted my triumphal litter and they carried me on. I waved my hat as usual, but as I passed the lamps I was greeted by a loud hissing mixed with the sound of a couple of whistles. Even this did not upset me enough to disturb the performance of my role. It was the fact that an assembly of eleven hundred people could calmly listen to a malevolent score of troublemakers wrongfully assail a private citizen in the performance of his public duty without immediately raising a cry of indignation to bring my hidden enemies to order, and convince me that I still had friends among my countrymen, which filled my soul with a resentment that, even with the best will in the world, I have never been able to overcome. The bitterness I felt at that time cannot be described. It was not the evil deed that crushed me, but the indifference of the good people that was death to my soul.

I jumped down from the litter, advanced toward the Royal box, and asked the King in a loud voice, "What does Your Majesty command me to do?" This step was later interpreted as a *manquement* against His Majesty, but the an-

---

† A character in Beaumarchais' *Barber of Seville* and *The Marriage of Figaro,* he is the model of a smug and greedy hypocrite who delights in slander.

swer I received shows that at that moment I had been properly understood. "Continue," rang the King's word; and as a faithful and humble servant, I obeyed. I will honestly state my private feelings: in my anger, it was the audience I wanted to punish. Except for the presence of the King, I would have walked off the stage, nevermore to appear before those who had tolerated the fact that, through no fault of my own, I was trodden underfoot in their presence. It was a subject's awe and devotion that made me take the fantastic step which the exaltation of the moment produced. I am always carried away on stage, and just as I had felt inspired by the enthusiasm of the heroic king in *Valdemar,* so too I realize that a Spanish toreador would have behaved just as I did. The performance ran its course. The audience, which was actually the offended party, now made a small fuss over me, but the Court felt that its dignity had been compromised. My feelings did not change. I spent the night drafting my resignation and putting my affairs in order so as to be able to depart on the steamship at noon the following day. But I received time for reflection instead of dismissal; house arrest in place of a passport.

Only now was public indignation aroused against my jealous detractors. They pointed the finger at them, and the police laid hands on a Count, a *Skomagermester,* and two apprentices, who had to be the scapegoats for the entire clique (I shall withhold their names, for personalities recorded in the police registers have no place in the history of art), and there was scandal enough. Had I been able to travel immediately, by the Easter holiday I would have obtained engagement in either London or Vienna. But a fortnight elapsed, and the foreign newspapers, which had never before said anything about me, now broadcast my adventure to every part of Europe and thereby provided me with a renown that all of my finest works had been unable to secure. On the other hand, it did me a great deal of harm; for theatre directors came to regard me as a wild, ungovernable fellow, while I was considered by the royal courts to be a dangerous person. My decision to abandon the Danish stage was unshakable, despite the proofs of respect and affection I now received and in spite of the consoling conviction that I possessed a greater number of patrons than I had supposed.

They would not accept my resignation, even though I offered to buy my freedom by forfeiting my pension. It was proposed that I undertake a six-week journey and be given the honor of composing something new for the forthcoming nuptial festivities.‡ In this way, the whole scandal would be forgotten and the opportunity provided me for a valuable appreciation. But it was all in vain. I had to get away. My whole spiritual existence was in chaos; my invention had run dry; my imagination was focused on a single point: "my injury." This was further magnified by the fact that they qualified my refusal to present new compositions as "unwillingness" (wherefore I received further news of Royal displeasure); for my brain was filled with but a single thought, namely, that of "earning stale bread far away from Denmark."

‡ The marriage of Prince Frederik (later King Frederik VII) and Princess Mariane in June 1841.

There was a great deal involved in my decision to leave my native land, my old parents, the work I had begun, and my half-earned pension, in order— in my thirty-sixth year and with a numerous family—to begin my career all over again.

I finally received permission to travel, on condition that my whole salary was to be suspended for six months; and if milder feelings had not called me home, I would still have been recalled as a deserter, for they referred to my contract, which ran for eighteen years. It costs money to be fixed in one's pur-pose. This trip, the description of which belongs to *Napoli* and *Raphael*, de-prived me and my family of 3000 Rbd., an artist's laboriously accumulated nest egg. However, I did get to see Italy, I investigated the positions of the balletmasters at most of the major theatres, and found that things could be just as unpleasant *there* as here at home. I inquired after celebrities from the pre-vious decade: they were forgotten. I visited rich artists: they led dismal lives. Solitude and reflection restored to me my lost peace of mind, and my happi-ness returned. Familiar melodies reawakened my love for Denmark, and I set my sails for home. I was "welcomed," and did not return empty-handed. I am now completing my course and I thank God, Who has caused everything to turn out for the best.

NAPOLI, OR THE FISHERMAN AND HIS BRIDE

A Romantic Ballet in Three Acts.
Music by Paulli, Helsted, and Gade,
with a Musical Piece by Lumbye.
(March 29, 1842)

"SEE Naples, and then die," says the proverb. And indeed, when I finally came to Italy I learnt what a journey really means, for nowadays the peren-nial jaunt between Paris and Copenhagen may be regarded as simply an-other pleasure trip; one merely sees casts of once famous and accepted mod-els, a bit larger or a bit smaller, but prosaically multitudinous and totally devoid of poetry. No! I must thank my lucky star and then my adventure in *The Toreador* that I came to set foot upon a soil where the soul can at the same time find rest and work. Of course I had read something about this deli-cious clime, but found, to my good fortune, that there were still abundant sur-prises in store for me.

Even if my pen were capable of reproducing all that I saw and experi-enced during four well-spent months, amid the luxuriance of summer, I would rather spare the description and say to all those eager to travel: If you love the warmth of the sun, the sea and the clear air, flowers and lively people picturesquely posed and dressed in harmonious colors accentuated by a background of matchless landscapes, then do not waste time reading but go to Italy and study nature. If you want your schoolroom lessons to come alive, then visit those majestic relics of antiquity, where memories from the time of

BOURNONVILLE'S AUDIENCE AND STAGE

Above, left: The gallery. Lithograph by Lehmann after a drawing by
F. Westphal. Right: The genteel public. A box in the Court Theatre after a
drawing by Lehmann. Below: Interior of the Royal Theatre ca. 1830,
showing Frydendahl and Ryge in a scene from Holberg's *Jacob von Tyboe*.
This stage was the setting for most of Bournonville's ballets until its
demolition in 1874. Distemper painting by C. F. Christensen.
All, Teatermuseet, Copenhagen.

Above: THE SPRING OF KIRSTEN PIIL in Dyrehavsbakken ca. 1860.
Det kgl. Bibliotek, Copenhagen. Below: *NAPOLI*. Scene design for
Act II, the Blue Grotto, by C. F. Christensen. Reproduced by
permission of Musikmuseet, Stockholm.

the Savior of the World, of the Christian martyrs, and the romantic Middle Ages come crowding in. If you would train your eye for all that is noblest in art, then linger in those halls where perfection speaks from the walls, niches, and pedestals. Here there is much to learn, remember, and yearn to see again.

But if one should happen to be dissatisfied in political respects here at home, a new comparison will teach him to appreciate Denmark. If one is indignant, as I was, over theatrical intrigues, one ought to take a good look at those enterprises where art is dealt with like fish in the market, sought after or, as the case may be, thrust upon someone amidst pinching and quarreling, sold at third and fourth hand, served to the point of satiety, and finally tossed into the garbage. From this one can derive a serious lesson in the philosophy of life. (An example will illustrate my proposition. An entrepreneur discovers a beautiful tenor voice and engages the singer for five years at the ostensibly high salary—depending, of course, upon the singer's living conditions—of 5000, 6000, or 8000 francs a year. The young man is delighted. He gets enough to do, develops his talent, and gains a reputation. He is now a gold mine for the entrepreneur. Not only must he sing a grand opera every evening for three months, but, when this season is over, the theatre management sends him to a far-off city where, speculating on the drawing power of his talent, they pay enormous sums which accrue to the singer's entrepreneur, while the artist himself shrieks his voice away for his daily bread and after the stipulated five years is no longer of any use to anyone.)

This trip did me a tremendous amount of good. I became sound in both mind and body. I danced a couple of times at San Carlo and La Scala with my usual success, but the real purpose of my journey was to look around—and this I did, gathering ideas all the while. I actually had no intention of creating ballets from my store of impressions; it is true that I conceived *Raphael* in Rome and wrote it in Florence, but the subject matter proper fell into place only when I could survey at a distance the riches I had garnered.

Napoli came into being as I sat in the diligence between Paris and Dunkirk. That which is tiresome and monotonous often has a stimulating effect on one's power of imagination; it is not disturbed by a variety of objects, but grows like winter wheat beneath the snow. I sat and hummed something resembling a dance, and from one disjointed strophe to another I had composed the first three reprises of the "Tarantella" (D major). Around this theme, which I mechanically continued to hum for six to eight hours, the entire ballet *Napoli* began to take shape, and the following forenoon, while I awaited the steamship's departure, I wrote my libretto, which, with very few alterations, served as the outline for the one work of mine that has reaped the greatest applause here at home. Without wearying my readers with anecdotes about my traveling life, it will, nevertheless, give me great pleasure to relate the little incidents which have been revived in my ballet.

Three cheers for the speed and sturdiness of steamships, but especially for the good luck I have had in establishing interesting acquaintances aboard them! The first stop between Marseilles and Naples was Genoa. On our first evening out, under a starry sky and above a sparkling phosphorescence that shone beneath the paddlewheels and in the ship's wake, I strolled on deck, conversing with a pious monk who had taken a fancy to me, engaged me on a religious topic, and tried with all his might to convert me to Catholicism. Even though I could not comprehend the Church's unity in the same way as he, we parted as very good friends. He presented me with a little picture and gave me his blessing.

At Genoa an elderly man of unusual dignity came aboard, surrounded by a numerous staff of Sardinian officers who spoke to him with awe and departed when we weighed anchor. A slight attention on my part made a pleasing impression on the old man, who chose me to share his company, learnt my name (which he smilingly recalled having read about), and for three days provided me with the most informative and delightful conversation. He was the governor of Genoa, General Righini (well known from Wellington's Spanish Campaign). On the last evening, he promised to waken me at dawn in order to show me a sight the like of which I had never seen.

I was fast asleep when amidst my tangled dreams I heard a thunderous voice repeatedly crying: "Bournonville!" I awakened at the third call, remembered what the General had promised me, and stumbled up on deck half-dressed. The sun rose (it was May 20, 1844 [*sic;* actually, 1841] four o'clock in the morning). We were between Procida and Ischia; before us lay Naples and, to the right, Vesuvius, with its column of smoke protruding above the mist, which was just lifting. I clasped my hands and could do no more than exclaim: *"Oh mon Dieu! Oh mon Dieu!"* The General clapped me on the shoulder, and now began a geography lesson—the most delightful I have ever received. "To the left there you see Cape Miseno, Baiæ, Nisida, Posillipo, S. Elmo, and Villa Reale. And to the right you have Castellammare, Torre del Greco, dell' Annunziata, Portici, and the road down to Pompeii and Herculaneum." The morning breeze carried a balmy fragrance from the shore: it was the scent of orange. The harbor was alive with activity. I saw the half-naked fishermen in their red caps; I fancied I could already hear the sound of tambourines. We went ashore, and I became acquainted with a race of people of astonishing gaiety and originality. I jumped into the air and clapped my hands, and the beggar boys, perceiving my joy, shrieked to the skies and turned cartwheels around me by the hundred.

I chose my dwelling place on Largo di Santa Lucia, the Gammelstrand [the waterside fish market of Copenhagen] of Naples, with an expanse of water three-quarters of a mile in width extending over to Portici and Vesuvius. From my window I could, in a single hour, collect more groupings than I could use in ten ballets. Ladies and gentlemen congregated at the mineral spring, and coarse old crones, gesturing grotesquely, presented them with the sulphurous water. The church steps were covered with sitting or reclining *lazzaroni,* magnificent in their rags, heroic in their nakedness. Children swarmed about like mosquitoes; women spun on distaffs and suckled their babes; young girls sang, danced, and chatted with such lively faces that one feared they would come to blows at any moment. An enormous number of livery boats covered the beach, and the boatmen displayed the most varied temperaments; for while one of them, smoking his clay pipe, answered people only with his eyes, neck, and thumb, amongst others the desire to make money was so great that violent disputes arose, with bellowing so loud it echoed in the hills. And yet I never saw a blow struck. Amidst this moving throng, monks of every order strolled about two by two, with facial features that were more often amiably imbecilic than sternly ascetic. People paid them no special heed, whereas I was shocked to see well-dressed gentlemen kiss one another on the hand.

I swam in the bay every morning. My *marinaro*, or ferryman, was called Gennaro, and when he was absent, I looked to his brother Rafaello. I was their *padrone;* they seemed quite fond of me, were merry and good-natured souls, and all their jesting centered around *macaroni*. The Neapolitans are great swimmers, and especially divers. Often, when I had sat in the boat for several minutes without detecting the slightest movement on the surface of the water, a pair of bluish-brown men would suddenly emerge with their hands full of *frutti di mare* — that is, oysters and sea snails they had lain on the bottom to gather and which at sunset were brought ashore and offered for sale at Santa Lucia.

Here, at nightfall, there began scenes which in variety and liveliness yielded nothing to those of the daylight. The fish stalls formed an illuminated Vauxhall. The rabble camped about the numerous fires that were used to cook macaroni, or to roast corn and chestnuts; middle-class groups enjoyed their evening meal by the quay, where ready laid tables with three-branched lamps invited people to take refreshment; and the fashionable folk drove in long lines of carriages on this corso situated upon the direct road from Toledo Street to the Riviera di Chiaja, pausing in one place to eat ices, and in another stopping to regale themselves with oysters, which on large trays were handed up to them in the calèches. In addition, there was the mysterious gulf, which could in an instant become so violent that the waves lashed against the houses. Vesuvius, which was always *preparing macaroni*, sometimes furnished it in such abundance that one could feel it rumbling beneath one's feet in the streets of Naples. Finally, there were the three strong castles whose yawning throats of fire kept watch over the people's gaiety, ready to vomit death and destruction upon the motley hordes should they begin to get out of hand.

In Naples everything is intensified, above all the language. If a man has shoes on his feet and a passable hat, he is called *eccelenza;* the place in which he stays is a *palazzo;* the room in which he lodges is called a *stanza,* and the cab with its barefoot coachman and tattered beggar boys on the back a *carozza*. In these equipages, one makes excursions that are as incomparable as they are inexpensive, and if en route one should happen to pick up a fellow who rides on the back of the trap, he is called *cicerone!* And now one may drive whithersoever one pleases, certain of being able to gather treasures from nature, art, and history. Lucky is the man who has a warm heart and an impartial eye: he will spend his happiest hours here.

We came to Baiæ, that city which in the time of the emperors was the home of luxury. Here as many as 30,000 inhabitants occupied themselves solely with the pursuit of pleasure. Earthquakes, barbarians, and finally the eruption of the volcano Monte Nuovo (which in a single night, September 30, 1538, arose from the depths of Lake Lucrinus, destroyed everything around it, and since that time has stood in the middle of the landscape like an enormous ash heap), have transformed this seat of luxury into a poor fishing village with a few miserable huts and a dilapidated *osteria.* For half an hour the road leading to Baiæ passes through fields and vine-clad hills whose substrata, which form the groundwork of the highway, are made up of streets with houses, palaces, and temples overturned like the contents of a table drawer. Two ruins still stand on their foundations: the temple of Venus to the left, and, farther to the right, the vaulted hall of a bathhouse, generally assumed to be a temple of Mercury.

A group of young girls, accompanied by a haggish old woman, emerged from the first ruin and offered for sale whole platefuls of mosaic fragments, polished marble, and rusted scraps of metal, all arranged with conch shells from the beach. *"Balla pei Signori! "* the hag said to the prettiest girl, who was called Rosa. However, my traveling companions, who were in a hurry, did not wish to become involved with this improvised ballet in the heat of the sun; but as we were viewing the friezes in the beautiful rotunda of the temple of Mercury, the dancing troop suddenly burst in with a young fellow in their midst. The tambourine jangled to a kind of ballad which had the rhythm of a tarantella, but the words and melody were drowned in a piercing wail.

We settled ourselves on a gravel heap, and now the dancing began: natural, graceful, but monotonous, for each district has its conventional figures. None of my companions knew I was a dancer (name and occupation are never asked), and how great was their surprise when I threw off my coat, flourished my hat, and replaced the young fellow in the maddening tarantella, which steadily increased in tempo. I knew more than twelve different variations. Nobody wanted to relieve me; Rosa laughed and danced about, the company clapped their hands, and the villagers cried at the top of their lungs, *"Evviva,"* *"Grazioso,"* and *"Bravissimo."* That is what one calls scoring a success! My traveling companions now learnt who I was, and recorded this merry little episode in their notes. This kind of thing happened to me numerous times on the same trip, but this particular incident pertains to *Napoli.*

The feast of Pentecost was celebrated with processions and pilgrimages. The most profound devotion and the most uproarious hilarity were incessantly intermingled, but the holiday jubilation reached its height at Monte Virgine; it was our Midsummer Day multiplied by a thousand. My third act is but a feeble picture of this, and even the most theatrical effect looks dull compared with the colors that here come into play. Naples has a population of about 500,000 inhabitants, half of whom, I am certain, go barefoot and live on *cinque grán*, or eight Skillings a day. What they save on their simple entertainment is spent at the festivals, where most of them gather in splendid array (embroidered velvet jackets and fluttering silk scarves), tricked out with gold paper, feathers, flowers, and multicolored ribbons. It is the ruling passion to come in a carriage. But how? With twelve people in a two-wheeled *carriol* (the world-famous *calesso* or *cariccole*): the *signora* with a suckling babe and a couple of pretty girls with tambourines sit in the single seat; the *signore* himself drives and sits on either the frontboard or the left shaft (for it is a one-horse carriage), or he may even hang on to the back of the seat. Behind this seat stand fellows, some splendidly dressed, others half-naked, holding flags made from expensive foulard handkerchiefs which have, for the most part, been stolen from people's pockets. A couple of pedestrians have jumped up onto the carriage shafts in passing, and, finally, in the hammock which hangs in the back between the wheels, an old grandmother sits with one of her grandchildren, who is her protégé. The horse does not run, it *flies* over the slabs of lava with which the entire road is paved, and just as we see trick riders tearing along in the last thunderous gallop, held only by centrifugal force, with tensed muscles, glassy eyes, and hoarse cries, so the enthusiastic crowd returns from the festival of the Madonna with its life in its hands. Only a miracle can avert an accident, and the miracle happens: not one wagon jolts against another, not one pedestrian is injured.

All have drunk a good deal, but not a single tipsy person is to be seen. For several hours I witnessed this homeward march, while sitting on the breastwork of the Ponte della Maddalena, next to a *marinaro* with whom I shared my joy and my oranges. In the midst of these riding and running groups of Bacchantes appear whole battalions of pilgrims with cloaks and staves; banners of the saints wave, and pictures of the Madonna adorn every hat. In front and in back of this pious band skip whole rows of dancers who have promised the Holy Mother a tarantella extending from Monte Virgine straight to Santa Lucia.

It still remains for me to mention my visit to the Blue Grotto on the Isle of Capri. The weather was divine, and the swells of the sea so slight that we could venture into the low, narrow opening of the cave without danger. I had invited along two Neapolitan solodancers, Salvo and d'Arco, to whom this place was just as foreign as Rosenborg is to many Copenhageners. We passed the night in the town of Capri, and at dawn the next day visited the rock fortress of Tiberius. A bark carried us to the northern promontory of the island, where the grotto is situated.

The difference between this grotto and the hundreds of others found along this rocky coast consists in the fact that the outer wall does not extend to the bay. Consequently, the sunlight is driven down through the water, beneath the rock, and into the cave, which is illuminated like a goblet made of glass with a bluish tinge that it borrows from the peculiar color of the sea. There are two opinions about the blueness, which is so striking to us and far surpasses the color of our Sound and lakes, even when our sky is completely Italian. Some people think it is the influence of the color of the atmosphere, others that it is the components of the water, i.e., the same atoms that cause the phosphorescence of the sea; for just as the waves of the North Sea appear to be greenish regardless of the color of the sky, so too the water in the Mediterranean bays continues to look blue even when the sky is overcast. I could do nought but incline to the latter opinion, especially when I saw my pocket handkerchief and my hand take on a bluish tinge by dipping them only a couple of inches into the water. And now, inside the grotto, above which there rose no vault of blue and where the dazzling white rays of sunlight might have given the waves their original colorlessness, the blue appeared with an intensity that bordered on the phosphorescent.

It is quite a solemn moment when one rises from a recumbent position in the little vessel in which one sails through the grotto: one feels oblivious to everything else. One's whole attention is focused on the sea and its depth, and if one has learnt to swim, one cannot resist the urge to jump in. One's body glows in the water like a sulphurous flame, and each spray is a spark. To me, the vault appeared to be as high as the Ridehuus of Christiansborg Palace, and the size of the interior like that of the Slotskirke.

In one spot there is a sort of *terra piena:* an enormous column seems to support the ceiling, and in back of this a path leads up into the mountain. It is said to have gone farther, perhaps even to the tyrant's palace, but as a result of earthquakes it has collapsed, and now the imagination can have free play through the centuries during which the grotto stood forgotten and unknown, until two Swiss discovered it in the year 1826 while bathing in the vicinity. What crystalline mirrors in the sharp edges of the stone! What echoes! And how mysterious is the atmosphere, which suddenly takes away the thought of everything that has delighted—or offended—one in the outside world. In Italy, history and nature are so rich that romantic legend cannot play the strong role it does among us in the North. But there the Madonna is everywhere. She is the confidante of lovers, the seaman's guardian spirit. She reigns over all that goes on in nature, and her power can subdue its hidden forces. There is something quite miraculous in everything one experiences on this volcanic soil. I swam in and out a couple of times, from the spirit world into the sunlight, and then returned once more to reality with a horde of impressions and memories.

I accordingly wrote the rough draft of my ballet in Dunkirk and three days later arrived in Copenhagen, where I received a hearty welcome and where my absence had done some good, especially since there had been a comparison—which was all to my advantage—between the Berlin Ballet and the company of which I was the founder. A slowness in everything that should have furthered my work postponed the first performance of *Napoli* until March 29, exactly a year to the day after my departure. I take heed of omens: the first ship I hailed on my departure bore a name that was dear to me, and the first one I sighted on my return was called *The Compensation!* I was richly compensated for things I had previously had to do without. There was enthusiasm, attentiveness, discernment, and fine perception! Never has any work been so brilliantly successful. In two months there were twenty performances with packed houses, and within three years it passed its forty-ninth performance, always with a large attendance and tremendous applause.

The libretto and the historical notes related above sufficiently explain what I wished to present in this work: Naples, just as it appeared to me; Napoli, and nothing else. The little plot was but a single strand in the braided garland; the fact that the knot was tight enough to hold interest determined the result. One seldom strikes the nail on the head in that way. It became the Danes' favorite ballet. Perhaps I could have done something better, but certainly nothing more successful. My absence, Taglioni's *Laitière suisse,** the installation of the Italian opera, and the happy fact that the ballet ends in a transport of joy brought *Napoli* a renown it might not have retained to such a high degree in other places. Suffice it to say, *Napoli* became the watchword for both my friends and my opponents. The former regarded it as a bubbling wellspring, the latter as an empty vessel.

THE CHILDHOOD OF ERIK MENVED

A Romantic Ballet in Four Acts.
Music by Frøhlich (with Four Musical Numbers by Bochsa)

(January 12, 1843)

THE Danish public is unique in that it delights in seeing patriotic subjects treated dramatically—not only commonplace subjects but historic and romantic ones as well. And, contrary to the prejudice other nations have against

---

*Bournonville's departure for Italy left the Royal Theatre with no new ballet for the upcoming royal wedding in June (cf. note, p. 87) and with no one to plan and direct such a gala performance. To fill the gap, Paul Taglioni was called in from Berlin, where he was enjoying a successful career as balletmaster and leading dancer. With his wife and partner Amalia, he arrived toward the end of May. His initial plan was to present an elaborate ballet titled *The Pirates*; but, finding the Theatre's machinery inadequate, he produced instead his father's old work *Nathalie, ou La Laitière suisse*. It was not a success. The first performance, under ceremonial circumstances, was received without enthusiasm; the second was roundly hissed. The enraged Taglioni rushed offstage in mid-performance; the engagement was broken; and shortly he and his family left Copenhagen. This painful incident, however, did not interrupt the long friendship between Bournonville and Taglioni, which dated from their early years in Paris (cf. Vol. III, Part Two, p. 491) and continued via amiable correspondence and occasional meetings throughout their lives.

seeing their heroes depicted on the stage, people here become rather attached to them and even identify them with the form the artist has given
them. I am certain that in Italy *Napoli* would be hissed off the stage because
the picture was too accurate. Naked *lazzaroni*—what a scandal! Miracles of
the Madonna—what desecration! Spirits of nature—nonsense! There, they demand Greek gods, French knights, and Moorish tyrants. Nature is taboo in the
theatre, and even in an episode from the fifteenth century, the government
would see a hint of the nineteenth. Let us give thanks for our wants and our
longings, which lend poetry to that which we have and that for which we
hope (just as one can best appreciate summer in places where winter is longest), and let us also be grateful for a humane and enlightened government,
which does not hamper the spirit with oppressive bonds.

It has always been my principle, wherever possible, to alternate gaiety
and seriousness in my compositions and to transport my audiences from the
South to the North and back again. The patriotic enthusiasm with which *Valdemar* had been received caused me to contemplate a new work in the same
style, which would, after some years, be able to replace the older one.

A number of subjects occurred to me, but they were either too extravagant for our limited facilities, too difficult to stage, or too serious to tolerate
much dancing. Like so many thousands, I too love Ingemann's historical novels. While I consequently allowed myself to be carried away by the idea
which is so plastically realized in the "dancing conquest" of the Ribehuus,* it
was not a lack of other subjects that led me to choose this one, but rather a
love of the situations that were so vividly pictured in my imagination, and
also the certainty that I would find a large audience who would and could understand my composition.

Just as the libretto for *Valdemar* had had to lie in my portfolio for a number of years until the halberdiers had grown up and Astrid† had been confirmed, so I waited five years before *Erik Menved* was performed. Bochsa had
begun to work on the music but was interrupted by the death of Frederick VI,
and as if a solemn fate had extended its hand over this ballet, I danced its
premiere while people kept hidden from me the fact that my beloved father
had died at Fredensborg the day before.

During those four years, the mood of the public had changed considerably. Irony had crept into everything that had once been held sacred. If the
old patriotism had been constructive in its attitude, the new aimed at destruction and corruption. If people had formerly been too inclined to elevate Denmark at the expense of foreign nations, they now became cosmopolitan to the
detriment of their native land. The theatre is the barometer of public feeling,
and I must confess that I found it had fallen. The ballet was a great success;
at least that is what one, in Denmark, ought to call fifteen performances with
full houses during a four-month period. Even though applause decreased

---

*The twelfth-century stronghold in the town of Ribe.
† The sixteen-year-old Lucile Grahn created the role of Astrid.

sharply from the first evening to the last, there were still certain moments that never failed to have their effect. But I could no longer find the air that had so uniquely characterized *Valdemar*.

Some people claimed that *Napoli* was the only genre with which the ballet could and should have anything to do. Some were of the opinion that I had been too historical, while others felt I had been too free in my treatment of the material. And then there were those who found that both Frøhlich and I had been less successful this time than we had in *Valdemar*. I have come to the conclusion that, on the whole, *Valdemar* is actually superior to *The Childhood of Erik Menved* because the situation is the most striking our history has to offer and because I had gone to the original source. It is always a tricky business to dramatize a novel: one can condense it as much as one likes, yet demands can never be fully satisfied. Those who are well acquainted with the novel will tolerate neither abridgment nor change, while those who are unfamiliar with it will not understand the train of thought. On the whole, people are inclined to ask too much of pantomime, which for the general public can only be an easy means of tying together the events. The critics delight in dwelling on certain weak spots in the dramatization, as if they would use their swords to pierce the finest armor through its articulations. These joints can certainly be made strong and defensible, but the warrior will then be unable to move. Yet if one takes too long in making oneself understood, one runs the risk of becoming trite and boring. But, to remain faithful to the parlance of a tournament: it takes great dexterity to cover one's weak spots and overcome one's opponent. However, most people do not appreciate this sort of prowess; they would rather see the warrior fall before a well-delivered blow.

In this ballet my greatest feat was to eliminate the appearance of Erik Glipping, which could be neither dignified nor edifying. Anyone who has ever been close to a royal court will appreciate the way in which I allow the King's presence to be felt without anyone actually laying eyes on him: the audience, the hunt, and the royal mourning are perceived through the surroundings and it is the very invisibility of the principal character that heightens the suspense.

In the third act, I have used events that happened in the novel as well as things that might have happened. It is there that I have unquestionably reached the height of tragic effect. This act is the core of the ballet, the point which all the other scenes are leading up to, and it is free of the weaknesses that are to be found in the rest of the plot.

In working out the characters, I here had a great advantage over *Valdemar;* for the Queen, Lave, and above all the young Erik are roles which might appear without shame in high drama. The modest and chaste meetings between Peder and Inge, the prison scene with the Princess, Aase's somnambulism, far surpass anything I accomplished in this genre in *Valdemar*. As for the idyllic and chivalrous tone of the ballet: *The Childhood of Erik Menved* is also superior. Rane is depicted in rather conventional "traitor" style. This would be a character for the Italian ballet, and I now think *The Childhood of Erik Menved* might even create a furor in Italy. Is this something to be proud of or something to regret? Here I will state my own opinion: in *Valdemar*, the idea is far better, but the composition is far superior in the present work.

BELLMAN, OR THE POLSKA AT GRÖNA LUND

A Ballet-Vaudeville in One Act.
Music Arranged by Paulli.
(June 3, 1844)

JUST as in ancient times the songs of the *skalds* roused warriors to combat, so too have they long been the only bond among the Nordic nations that hatred and dissension have been unable to sever. The old melodies are a hereditary treasure, and the medieval ballads are marketable currency in all three kingdoms. It is a curious thing that not one defamatory song has survived its time, and, as if we were ashamed of having quarreled with our brethren, the war songs tell mostly of the struggles against the Wends, Frisians, Slavs, and Saxons. On the other hand, lyrical expressions of joy and love, sea life and patriotism, have survived both time and tempest. With them, we salute each other in brotherly fashion, and they have the power to touch our hearts by appealing to our noblest feelings.

The twilight of national hatred still hovered over the North when Holberg was known and loved in Sweden, and it is undeniable that Bellman* was a [spiritual] son of Holberg, just as the latter was of Molière. With his song, this Anacreon of the North erased all the wrinkles with which quarrels and discontent had furrowed our brows; he beckoned us to enjoy happiness, and the Furies were forced to flee before the approach of the Graces. Sweden crowned Oehlenschläger with the laurels of Parnassus; *we* adorned Bellman with the ivy and vine. Both these poets caused our tears to flow by the deep poetry in their works, which can express itself in mirth as well as gravity, and both taught us to love one another *"i nöd och låst,"* in sorrow and in joy.

For a Christmas party, the painters Sonne and Marstrand† had created a transparency showing Bellman being led by the Graces to Anacreon's vineyard, while fauns pick grapes, dwarves brew punch in their cave, and a merry little company amuses itself in the open air. I got to see this charming,

---

*Carl Michael Bellman (1740–1795) was a Swedish musical personality best known for his collections of songs, *Fredmans Epistlar och Sångar* and *Fredmans Sångar*, whose verses are set to melodies drawn from a variety of sources. Bellman's works have retained their popularity in Sweden and can also be heard in the other Scandinavian countries.

† Wilhelm Marstrand (1810–1873) and Jørgen Sonne (1801–1890) were Danish painters. The former, a pupil of Eckersberg, was known for his outstanding pictorial imagination and masterly characterization, while the latter became one of the leaders of the Romantic school of painting.

witty composition while it was still in preparation, and although I found it most appealing, I did not dream of using this group of figures for a ballet. On the other hand, for a number of years I had been able to sing one of *Fredman's Epistles,* "The Fray at Gröna Lund," which always seemed to me to be a superb episode for a comic *divertissement.*

But now came the two divergent accounts of Bellman's personality, one in Ploug's biographical sketch and the other in Heiberg's humorous discourse. And in addition to these, I recalled what my father had so often told me of his personal acquaintance with Bellman. The latter is said to have been a noble, courteous man who, although he was a much sought after and welcome guest in all merry company, never drank more than would render him capable of improvising the most delightful little verses at the end of a meal. Moreover, he possessed such a fine command of language and dramatic understanding that he played French comedy with the *beaux esprits* of the [Swedish] Court. I thereby arrived at the conclusion that one should not confuse the characters of Fredman and Bellman: the keen observer of the humorous side of tavern life cannot be the representative of drunkenness, and an avid schnapps-drinker could not possibly treat this propensity with such biting irony. For indeed, how could such a wealth of lyricism and naïve grace prevail in a poet who was himself Fredman? I therefore had to side with Ploug's opinion, and it was from this standpoint that I proceded when an occasion arose that gave me the idea of composing a little ballet about Bellman.

The ballet *Valdemar* had reached its jubilee, that is to say, its fiftieth performance. The Theatre directorate allowed me to celebrate it with a performance for my own benefit (in the summer). I dare say it is a great recommendation for a piece to have been given forty-nine times, but it is not sufficient reason to provide a full house. The ballet had been a success; there could not be many people left who would come to see it out of curiosity, and one can never rely on "respect" to secure attendance on such evenings. It was therefore vital that I provide a piquant supplement to my own performance, and after some speculation I came up with the lucky idea mentioned above. I should call it lucky because for one thing I forestalled Heiberg's *Ulla,* and for another, my work was tremendously successful and was given sixteen times the following winter. The whole life of this "peruke world" was something new. The melodies, which were an ingenious blend of pretty folk dances and motifs from *Lulu, The Sleeping Draught, The Nuns,* and *The Huntsman's Bride,* made especially lovely ballet music; and since each theme brought its own memory in words and, as it were, carried the thoughts of the pantomime, I called the whole thing a *ballet-vaudeville.*

The familiar comic figures appeared in all their drunken joviality and were greeted as old friends. Buxom, happy, dance-loving Ulla was one of the most successful characters in the ballet, for she depicted the tavern maid from a poetic angle, frivolously but without triteness. I myself portrayed the Poet, who goes to Djurgården [a pleasure park outside Stockholm] on a Sunday morning to gather sketches for his genre pictures, which crowd in upon him by the dozen. The wine refreshes and excites him, but in his eyes drunkenness is a vice that ought to be whipped with the scourge of ridicule. It is a historic fact that the real Ulla Winblad wanted to give Bellman a sound drubbing when she discovered that it was he who had written all those amorous ballads about her. I found an opportunity to depict this indignation, which is so common among simple folk, and the manner in which the poet is reconciled to the angry girl is perfectly suited to the situation and at the same time shows the sharp contrast between Fredman and Bellman. The fact that amid the bustle of this tavern life there appears a glimpse of a higher poetry, that the Genii and Graces beckon him, entwine him with fragrant garlands, and lead him to Anacreon, who hands him his lyre, while he [Bellman] reluctantly abandons the lower circles in which his Muse is wont to roam; all these are so many added facets to the poet's character, and the fact that he drains the cup of immortality while his "spiritual children" continue to gambol here upon earth is something that is deeply felt by his numerous admirers. However, this admiration must not lead us to present a series of his songs, for each one of them is a complete whole. Besides, it is only the polska I have sought to reproduce; the introduction, on the other hand, is entirely my own.

Therefore, if one were to liken my work to a glass of champagne, I should have to make Bellman himself the fermenting grape, for he must be enjoyed *by the glass,* when the festivity has reached its height, not as ordinary table wine. That is to say, he must be sung piecemeal, one poem at a time, not read as a book. My use of Marstrand's painting had the desired effect, and when I gratefully paid the great poet and the distinguished painter the credit my work owed to their invention, there still remained sufficient honor for me as the creator of this little ballet.

THE ORESTEIA

(Unperformed)

THERE are no subjects more suitable for ballet than those which are drawn from classical myths and histories. But an idea clothed in great beauty demands space and form; the grandiose is an exclusive requirement for its dramatic existence, and in this respect the realization of such an idea must fail due to our local shortcomings.

Our public may be divided into two unequal factions: "the learned" and "the unlearned." It is remarkable how much larger the latter group is; there are even those who shun any instruction designed to aid them, such as libretti, newspapers, playbills, etc. On the other hand, there are scarcely any of the former group who have any great love for those subjects with which they were plagued while in school. For myself, I confess it is with a certain reli-

gious feeling that I approach classical antiquity, whose memories are so remote that only the good and the beautiful appear distinctly before our imaginations, and whose image stands like white, translucent marble illuminated
by the warmth of the sun. There do we find models of all virtues and talents;
there is the ideal of the noblest beauty; there must the artist, be he poet or
painter, ever direct his gaze. How he longs to depict for his contemporaries
the millennium wherein his thoughts have lived and moved. But, alas! Just as
nakedness is obscene if the forms of the body are not perfectly beautiful, so
ancient life is incomprehensible if it is not depicted in suitable form. "For the
unlearned it is folly; for the learned, offense." Under our present conditions it
is, therefore, impossible to bring the classical authors to the Danish stage
with any hope of success, even in adapted translation.

Some erudite art-lovers, thinking that mime was better able to assume antique forms than any other form of art, did me the honor of inviting me to undertake an arrangement of Æschylos' trilogy, which had just been transmitted
to us in Danish by my unforgettable patron, Brøndsted.*

I immediately objected that neither our facilities nor our personnel would
permit the realization of so magnificent a project. It is true that in his day Noverre treated the death of Agamemnon, but our public has little or no sympathy for this genre. But my friends continued to urge me, and I allowed myself
to be persuaded to undertake this work which accorded so well with my love
of sublime antiquity. The result won the approval of those who had requested
me to do it, but it convinced them that if the Ballet were to present Æschylos'
trilogy in a fitting manner, it must await conditions which I myself will hardly
live to see in Denmark.

It may happen that we will get a larger theatre, but there is no indication
that we will get personnel physically and spiritually suited to such action,
who know how to make an impression on the masses while at the same time
satisfying the elect. No! It is too heavy a stone to lift. However, I believe this
libretto can find a place among my finest ballet poems, partly to show that I
have not left a higher genre untouched, and partly to give some idea of what
could be accomplished if one's hands were not tied.

A CHILDREN'S PARTY

A Divertissement, with Music by Paulli.
(Performed at the Court Theatre,
October 23, 1844)

I love children, as is clearly apparent in my works; but I am far from favoring
ballets wherein little children, like trained animals, perform miraculous feats.
Such things shock and offend my taste. But just as children have an essential

*Peter Oluf Brøndsted (1780–1842), Danish classical scholar and Greek antiquarian.

place in painting, so too are they an asset to ballet when they appear in the simplicity of childhood, with that primitive awkwardness which it would take an outstanding comedian to reproduce and which is at once so funny and yet so moving.

I had never really thought about composing a children's ballet, but a charitable purpose precipitated this little creation which, although it was performed only once, has given me indescribable pleasure. A group of noble philanthropists, whose chairman—to the honor of Denmark—holds a prominent position as a police official, has established an association for the relief of neglected children. The size of this class of unfortunate souls, its conditions, and the successful results which the efforts of the Association have had, belong to the history of civilization, and I deem it an honor for art to have had a hand in this advancement of refinement.

I was asked to make a contribution to a performance at the Court Theatre for the benefit of the Foundation. I was immediately seized with enthusiasm for this cause, and my first thought was: The fortunate must work to help the unfortunate. My Augusta is a fortunate child. She shall offer the first fruits of her talent to those poor neglected children, and thereby gather strength and blessings for her future.

Childhood is surely the most joyous time of life: Christmas and springtime rolled into one. Flora and Zephyr opened the festivities, and rushed over to the Christmas tree, which sparkled in the midst of an Elysium. Here there had to be many, many children. But to hire poor little ones whose parents might, in return for a bit of earnest money, bundle them off to the Theatre against their will, would be too bitter an irony! No! I had to have pretty, happy, well-bred children who would be eager to dance. The kindness of the public showered me with more children than I needed.

I taught them their little gallopade in a few lessons. The residents of the Palace were kind enough to allow us to use their rooms. They served tea to the charming flock, and when the signal for the ballet to begin was sounded, the little ones, dressed in their Sunday blouses and white frocks, with rose garlands on their curly heads, were taken up to the beautifully decorated Theatre. And when Flora's nymph beckoned, seventy happy children rushed forward and were greeted with transports of joy mingled with deep emotion.

They danced with a liveliness and precision that are only to be seen at children's balls. The Christmas tree was plundered, and then the merry band settled down near the lamps to eat their cakes and apples. Unseen by the children, their guardian angels hovered over them and blessed their innocent joy, while the well-known romance from *Joseph* sounded like the heavenly strains of a harp.* When the light repast was finished, the dancing began anew and ended with enthusiasm on the part of the performers as well as the

* Probably the romance "A peine au sortir de l'enfance, quatorze ans au plus je comptais," from E. H. Méhul's opera *Joseph et ses frères* (1807).

audience. The performance brought in about 1000 Rbd. and was of considerable help to the work of the Association. A selection from the ballet was later presented at a Court fête at Amalienborg.

There is a little anecdote connected with the history of *A Children's Party*. Eight days after the performance, I received from one of the Association's most zealous members a lovely poem and a bouquet of heather blossoms which were picked at Grathe Heath, close to the spot where King Svend must have fallen. It was exactly on October 23 that this gentleman had ridden across the Jutland heath, telling his peasant driver about the battlefield and Valdemar the Great, then about me and my "dancing actors," and finally, about the ballet which was to be performed that very evening for the benefit of neglected children. This so delighted the peasant that he then and there was filled with the desire to do something for this cause, and offered to take one of the unfortunate children into his own home without compensation. Such applause is certainly not to be sneezed at, and some day, when that modest heather blossom will have long since withered, my work may well have borne fruit for time and eternity.

KIRSTEN PIIL

A Romantic Ballet in Three Acts.
Music by Edvard Helsted.
(February 26, 1845)

THE legends associated with the Danish soil, strand, woods, and jagged church towers have been dealt with so frequently and so beautifully that there is not much left for someone who might wish to explore them from a new angle. The idyllic quality of such stories ought not to be wasted; yet when I consider that immediately prior to my ballet, two new plays were presented, one set at Møns Klint, the other at Rongsted Høi and Dyrehave, and that both the King of the Klint and the Brownie have been used in them, I should probably have been forewarned that the romantic portion of *Kirsten Piil* would appear less striking to the audience.

It should be noted that no actual legend concerning the Fountain of Kirsten Piil, which is so much a part of Copenhagen summer life, is to be found, although the name of the discoverer together with the date is engraved upon the stone whence the fountain springs. Many poets have sung of Kirsten Piil. Some have described her as a saint, others as a fairy, and still others as a peasant girl. Tradition preserves only one assumption: that Kirsten must have been lost in the woods; otherwise, the mysterious Midsummer Eve spreads its veil of mist over all the adventures which have through the centuries given the little woodland vale its significance. Therefore, historical accuracy did not stand in my way if I wished to invent a plot, and I needed no authority other than my own surmises.

No Catholic legend can form the foundation of the story, since the fountain was discovered in 1583, during a strongly Protestant period. Fairies are not Danish and, furthermore, belong to a much older time. And who would have taken notice of the fortunes of a peasant girl and named the spring after her? Add to this the fact that peasant girls never get lost; they know the paths in their parishes and seldom dare to venture beyond their boundaries. Finally, Kirsten had a surname, Piil. Now at that time a middle-class or peasant girl would have been called Kirsten Jensdatter or Monsdatter. Mistress Kirsten Piil must therefore have been a young noblewoman, lost on a hunt in her own forest; for who except the heiress or prospective mistress of a manor would have the right to give the spring a name?

The closing period of the Golden Age of Chivalry, the epoch of Henry IV and Daniel Rantzau, in which victorious battles and romantic love stories were the order of the day; a young nobleman who is called to take up arms one Midsummer Eve, returns in a year to the day, finds his Jomfru faithful and true, and plights his troth with her at this very spring; the hidden forces of nature embodied in the elf-maidens; Kirsten's dream, which reveals to her all the changes the spring will undergo during three centuries; and finally, the Danish Midsummer celebration itself, which diffuses its idyllic fragrance over the whole canvas—all this appeared before me in an instant, and I composed my ballet. But this work, which came into being beneath the leafy allées of Fredensborg in the middle of summer and was immediately carried into effect, did not have its premiere until eight months later.

Never had such fatal lifelessness weighed down my colleagues. Weeks and months went by while, one after another, idyllic subjects dealing with Sjælland were presented at our Theatre; and when February 26 (as it happened, the birthday of both my female soloists) was chosen as the ultimate date for its performance, the music was hardly written out by the time of the final rehearsal and the ladies' costumes were still being sewn during the intervals. It required a great deal of moral strength to keep up my spirits. "Kirsten" was completely disconcerted, and many piquant touches were lost.

The first act created a furor and the enthusiasm even lasted through the second act (the intervals took up an hour and three-quarters); but during the third act, which was intended to make *Kirsten Piil* the Danish *Napoli*, the audience remained cold and apathetic. The fatal allegory was once more my downfall. Rasmus' jest concerning the miracle of the spring was not understood, and if I had not put a couple of clever *pirouettes* into the last polska, the curtain would probably have fallen without any applause or bravos. But, alas! Close by me I heard a plaintive shriek! It was Jomfru Fjeldsted, who, just as she was going to take up her position for the final group, hit her knee against a carved wooden bush (which, like so much else, had not been finished before the final rehearsal, and she had been excused from that very rehearsal because of her birthday celebration). This contusion, which seemed so slight, had a lengthy bed of suffering as its result. The injury was not cured at home, and the Bourbons' mineral water had to accomplish what clean, clear spring water, applied immediately, would probably have done just as well.

I cannot end these reminiscences without mentioning two personalities whose great talents have marked epochs in my artistic life, and whose genius has hovered round me in unforgettable melodies: François Prume and Jenny Lind. They have both thrilled Danish hearts, giving the most brilliant concerts we and they themselves have ever witnessed, and to both of them I have always been a true friend and successful advisor.

Prume's *Concertine,* his *Rondo mélodieux, Variations militaires, Concertino héroïque,* and above all, his haunting *Mélancolie* accompanied me on my journey and consoled me in my loneliness. His silvery tone made me love the violin second only to the human voice. I sang his strophes beneath the vault of the Blue Grotto, and when all was still in Via Felice on the Monte Pincio in Rome, I sat far into the evening with my violin, improvising on the very one of his themes that I later used in *Raphael.* I could see the windows of Thorvaldsen's dwelling. That great artist was in the beloved home where I longed to be; but his spirit and that of the divine painter drifted by me in that hallowed place, appearing like the Dioscuri in the starry sky of art.

If it had been Prume's ambition to charm, to captivate, to be loved and remembered, then he achieved all that even the vainest of human beings could wish for. But just as Don Quixote was infatuated with chivalry, so, too, Prume dreamt only of badges of knighthood; and when others received the ribbons he longed to wear—his mind became deranged! I shall never forget him, even though new suns should eclipse him.

Such a sun is Jenny Lind. We still feel its warmth, and all our wishes would call it back someday, just as they do the bright orb which causes the flowers to grow and the birds to sing. But there will come a time when it will start to wane and finally go down. We must then refresh it in the bath of memory as a reward for the exquisite pleasure it has given us.

I heard her for the first time in Stockholm, in the summer of 1839. She was eighteen years old, but even then possessed such an eminent talent that her performance as Alice in *Robert le Diable* was on a par with the finest I had heard and seen in Paris; and even though her voice was not yet as highly developed as it later became, it still had the same sympathies, the same electric power, which now make it so irresistible. She was adored, the theatre subsisted solely by the *vogue* she created; but she was miserably paid. By giving concerts in small towns, she collected enough to travel to Paris at her own expense and study with García, who took her 15 francs an hour but showed so little interest in her that he never once considered letting her perform. She herself lacked the necessary confidence, and without a bit of charlatanism on either her own or her teacher's part, it was impossible to penetrate the host of privileged celebrities in order to gain access to the Parisian audience. It would certainly have known how to appreciate her!

She spent an industrious but dull year in Paris, then once again accepted a modest engagement in Stockholm, and, while on a provincial tour, chanced to come to Copenhagen in September of 1843. It was I who persuaded her to give us her incomparable Alice in *Robert*. Since I myself was quite familiar with the Swedish language, I felt that in the opera it could certainly go hand in hand with Danish, and that two such kindred nations did not require a third language to present a great talent. At our Theatre, this *artiste* met with the greatest kindness; but the worst stumbling block was Jenny's fear of appearing on a foreign stage, and since she had just seen Fru Heiberg in *Son of the Desert*, she became at once so excited and depressed that, weeping, she anxiously begged me to allow her to "escape," as she called it, from displaying the insignificance of her talent and her person on a stage that possessed such a combination of genius and beauty as that of the superb interpreter of Parthenia. My counterarguments made her so overwrought that she half-accused me of having led her into a trap! This both alarmed and affronted me. I wanted to cancel the whole thing, but now her feminine instincts came into play; for when I gave in, she stood firm. This bold experiment was crowned with success, and in Denmark Jenny Lind gained a second fatherland.

Unfortunately, the directorate of our Theatre was not wise enough to acquire this talent for our own opera. But now the ice had been broken; Jenny discovered that there was bread to be earned outside of Sweden. Furthermore, she learnt that, when all is said and done, an artist is not fated to be nurtured in his native land, but, like a bird of passage, only seek rest in it. Her name was soon known throughout Europe, gold and fame flowed in to her, royal courts and nations vied to offer her precious gems and laurels, and in winter she never wanted for flowers. Poets called her "The Nightingale of the North," and it was not her clear trills alone that made them dream, with bated breath, of a fragrant Elysium; it was, rather, her shy, modest nature, her unassuming appearance, and—just as in that little gray bird—the impossibility of suspecting her to be the queen of song. There was a timidity, a yearning, and a vague irresolution in her daily behavior that reminded one even further of this woodland favorite, and when one has been awakened on a Sunday morn by the sound of her voice—as I was in my own home (where she stayed)—which in beauteous psalm tones sent up a paean to its Creator, the resemblance was complete.

Danish theatre and art history will preserve the memory of those days when *Norma* and *The Daughter of the Regiment* caused people to stay awake all night long outside the Theatre in order to secure admission to the following evening's artistic treat, and when the Ridehuus was transformed into a temple for a nation's sincere good will and admiration. But for me there lies in her consummate acting and her charming Swedish songs a whole world of ballets. The principal motif in *Kirsten Piil* is taken from the following romance:

> The knight said to his maiden fair,
> "How long wilt thou wait should I leave thee now?"
> (Chorus) In roses ...

RAPHAEL

A Romantic Ballet in Six Tableaux (Three Acts).
Music by Frøhlich.
(May 30, 1845)

ROME! You Eternal City! Only now can I conceive how an artist who has not seen you is regarded as untraveled; for neither picture nor description can give an adequate representation of the host of things that here present themselves to the mind and eye. The time of my arrival and the length of my stay were not of my own choosing. Each season has its distinct features. Travelers generally prefer the autumn, winter, and spring; but I arrived in Rome in the middle of July, during the notorious fever season, *"l'aria cattiva,"* when the drowsy *sirocco* blows and no one save dogs and Frenchmen ventures out in the noonday sun.

I came from Naples, heard a rather recent tale of robbers, had a pretty adventurous encounter myself, and rode through the Pontine Marshes sitting beside a weak-chested devil who was going home to die in Perugia. I kept my thoughts fastened on *Corinne,** and did everything in my power to keep myself and my traveling companion awake, but he paid no heed to my warnings. "A little sooner, a little later! Let me sleep!" Ancient monuments appeared more and more majestically, sometimes surrounded by luxuriant vegetation, as at Genzano, Arricia, and Albano, and sometimes lost in a waste land, as in the scorched Campagna.

This valley (which covers the space of three Danish miles† in width) between the Sabine and the Alban Hills and the heights upon which Rome is built, once contained the most fertile fields of the Romans—the soil whose division formed the apple of discord for a number of centuries. It is now considered unfit for cultivation because the air is unhealthy, and the air is unhealthy precisely because the soil is barren.

Wild oxen lie in the morasses with their noses above the surface of the water. Whole herds of gray oxen roam the desert plain while their herdsmen, with jackets slung across their shoulders, pointed hats, leathern gaiters, and red belts, flank them on horseback with long sticks in their hands and bear a strong resemblance to Spanish picadors.

A company of Englishmen has offered to cultivate this considerable tract

* A novel by Mme. de Staël (1807).
† One Danish mile equals approximately five English miles.

of land. But how could heresy and civilization ever be combined with Papal power? And, when all is said and done, what would become of the picturesque element? Would artists exchange this Syria in the heart of Europe for level farmland with railways and smokestacks? Those solitary tombs, wherein a younger generation has taken up its abode, those unique aqueducts, two of which, having been fairly well restored, are sufficient to supply Rome with excellent water—all this give way to cabbage patches, beds of asparagus, and picket fences! Of course, it will change some day. The original Tivoli will come to resemble its namesakes. The houses will become red and the clothing dark gray, just as in the rest of Europe. But we may then consider ourselves lucky to have seen the land of the Romans in its romantic *négligé*.

The person coming from the north makes his entry into Rome via Ponte Molle and the Porta del Popolo, where the marble staircase erected by the French at the *passegiata* immediately has an imposing effect. But if one enters from the south, through the lonely Porta San Giovanni, one comes upon the mighty Lateran Church, the Holy Staircase, the Colosseum, the Forum, and a mass of pillars and obelisks, and at length drives past the majestic waterwork, the Fontana di Trevi, into the Custom House, which is an ancient temple above whose slender marble columns a frieze rises like an enormous rock that threatens to tumble down into the courtyard. But above the pinnacle of the temple, vines entwine themselves round fence and bower, and pretty matrons sit suckling their babes.

The person who visits Rome during the summer gets to see its real physiognomy. In contrast to the liveliness and frivolity of Naples, everything here bears a serious stamp. When the merriment of the Carnival has lured travelers thither and English guineas have transformed the Corso into another Regent Street, the Eternal City loses a measure of its originality. But when fear of the *terzanna* has driven "milords" back to the baths, and the summer heat has rendered one piece of clothing after another superfluous; when the working class settles down to life in the open air with its occupations and meals, and large baskets of luxuriant fruit are everywhere to be seen; when flocks of girls dressed in variegated hues gather round the fountains, and the evening bell calls people to the Ave Maria at the street corner—*then* the real life of Rome begins, *then* it can be studied and painted, *then* Rome is truly itself.

It is not my intention to describe those subjects which have already been thoroughly treated by others, nor to relate all my personal experiences. I will only describe the chain of impressions that finally became one with my art and produced a work for which I had great hopes. I have said that seriousness is the distinctive feature in the physiognomy of Rome: a mild, honest, but solemn and sorrowful gravity is imprinted on the history, the Church, and art. It is the nature of Rome and of art. Art must have a past as well as a future. The poet needs a faith and a God. The multitude sees art only as an entertainment; but if the artist discovers that he is merely a plaything, his joy is without poetry, his pleasure without thought; he admires and applauds only the low and distorted, and finally drops brush or pen, turns away, and seeks another sphere. The thinker, the poet, and the painter certainly find their richest material in Rome, so why should it appear any less vivid to me?

At four o'clock in the morning I strolled to my favorite places in ancient Rome by way of the Capitol, from whose foot the Tiber has receded so far that one can now determine only in thought the height of the cliff to which the treacherous Tarpeia gave her name, and whence Manlius hurled the attacking Gauls. Here it was that Brennus, with jeering shouts to the vanquished, cast his sword upon the golden scale, while at the same moment Furius Camillus crushed his fatherland's executioners.‡ On this spot generations of heroes offered the gods the costliest spoils of victory. Here figures by the giants of [later] art are now preserved side by side with those of antiquity, while outside the iron-fast "horse tamers" stand as a symbol of the passions which the new Rome still knows how to keep in check.* Time has turned so much upside down: the front of the Capitol now faces the modern city, while its back is turned toward the Forum. The name has been changed to *campi d'olio* — the seat of knowledge into a field of oil!

One is struck with a wondrous bewilderment upon viewing the Forum, filled with so many ruins. Did all these temples and monuments once stand upright, or did some of them lie in the dust while the masterworks of architecture surrounded them? Where did Rome's enormous populace stand when affairs of the mother city called them together or when in jubilant chorus they welcomed the victorious men who drove through triumphal arches to the Capitol? Via Latina and Via Triumphalis, whose classic stone pavements are still trodden, were but narrow streets, and even though the private dwellings are judged to have been small, it still seems as if the Forum must have lacked room in which to move about, light and distance in which to view the magnificent buildings. Yet amid this chaos the imagination can still pick out the memorable places. It depicts the road whence Coriolanus threateningly turned around and beheld his ungrateful native city; the pillar at whose foot Valerius Gracchus fell as a sacrifice for the cause of the people; and the booth from which Virginius took the fatal steel that freed his daughter from slavery and dishonor.†

To the left rises the Temple of Concord, if not the largest, at least the most impressive [site of worship] next to the Church of St. Peter. What memories this sanctuary calls to mind! Its gates were opened with the most sanguine expectations. The thankful songs of mothers and children resounded upon seeing fathers and sons return from battle and bloodshed, filled with longing for the quiet joys of home.

Here to the right, on the Palatine Hill, lies a shapeless mass of ruins that

‡ In 390 B.C. The full story is told in Livy, Plutarch, and other Classical sources.
° Presumably a reference to the statues of — in Baedeker's words — the "horse-taming *Dioscuri*" which adorn the top of the stairs that form the central approach to the Capitol.
† Cf. Livy, Book III.

seems to protrude from mounds of earth which are now covered with grape-
vines and tomato shrubs. One goes up a staircase and through a gate into a
garden where there are some round holes that resemble fishponds with pal-
ings around them. One curiously peers down into them and here, through the
gloom, one can make out apartments in the most elegant style with polished
walls, carven cornices, and fragments of gilding. No cellar this, but the main
floor of a palace. It is part of the Imperial Palace ... Livia's bath chamber!
Augustus and his successors stand before us! What giants of greatness and of
vice! Here they are still excavating to find Nero's Golden House. On this
enormous tract of land there was not room enough for those libertines, who
had only a couple of years, or even less, in which to reign. Caracalla built
himself a bath with an adjacent Circus as extensive as a whole city, and Diocletian erected for his own comfort a building so large that one corner of it
was transformed by Michelangelo into a church (Maria degli Angeli) that is
three times larger than our Frue Kirke. On these sites art reached its zenith,
but here it was also most deeply degraded.

A glance from the Imperial Palace down to the Colosseum turns our
thoughts to the Golden Age of the dramatic art under Augustus, and transports
us to the moment when jaded senses had to be excited and aroused by real
blood, shed by man against man and, finally, by wild beasts against defense-
less prisoners.

If I am to be inspired by something great, I must be alone. Company disturbs me. However, there is one companion who always accompanies me:
Music. I hum improvised melodies — wild and disjointed but which, could I
only retain them, might not be lacking in character. The games in the Circus,
the emotion of the crowd, the cruelty of the tyrants, the prayers of the priests,
the women's dancing: I *heard* all these things before I *saw* them depicted in
my mind's eye. I ran down from the hill, my feet treading the same flagstones
upon which the legions had walked. I marched along singing, and in my
mind I heard the victors' jubilation, the blaring of trumpets and the beating of
drums ... I stood beneath the arch of Titus, upon whose walls are graven
likenesses of the Jewish people in chains and the seven-branched candlestick
being carried from the Temple into the capital of the heathens as spoils of
victory! ... Then my song died away and the Colosseum (that amphitheatre
which could seat 140,000 spectators and whose stone blocks still hold together despite the fact that the barbarians wrenched out the iron staples fourteen hundred years ago) lost its charm when I thought how the people of a
fallen master had been forced to work themselves to death constructing its
arches, and how for several generations the sand of the arena had been
drenched with martyrs' blood.

In the center of the arena, upon a dais of several steps, rises a cross. I sat
down at its foot and let my gaze wander over the memorable objects. Here
were the seats of the Senators and Imperators, where people applauded the
horrors of the spectacle; there was the door through which the dead were

flung into the *spoliari.* In a corner of each of these there now stand pious chapels in memory of the resistance and suffering of the first Christians. I became lost in thought and was aroused by merry singing that rang delightfully from beneath the Arch of Constantine. It came from villagers who were bringing their fruit to market; but before proceeding on their way, they walked into the amphitheatre and offered their morning prayer in front of the cross, without noticing that I was sitting on its steps. (It was none other than Constantine, himself a convert to Christianity, who put a stop to the persecutions against the Christians, after the catacombs had received during the course of three centuries as many as 170,000 victims, most of them having been torn asunder in the Colosseum.)

I cannot describe how a Protestant traveler, enraptured by the religious spectacles, can be tempted to become Catholic. The dull routine and the all too obvious "practical" tendency that runs through the whole Catholic clergy ought to be enough to cool enthusiasm; but what involuntarily inspires awe is the historical significance of martyrs and the devotion that prevails in the churches during prayer. God's house stands open all day every day. What comfort, what fragrance and coolness! There is not lacking—as among us—a solitary corner in which a publican weary of his stall can beat his breast unseen by the crowd, and where one deeply afflicted can pour forth his pain in silence. Masses are sung every hour. Only at midday is everything silent and empty. At just such a moment, I entered the Basilica of Santa Maria Maggiore. What I felt cannot be described. No one saw me save Him whose gaze rests upon all: I fell to my knees.

The splendor and grandeur that distinguish this church as well as the Lateran, St. Peter's, and the whole of the Vatican, can be found in numerous descriptions. But what should be especially appreciated is the liberality which opens all these historic and artistic treasures to the public (either gratis or for a nominal gratuity). This liberality maintains the love of art, and it should not be forgotten that the latter was reborn in the bosom of the Church. In the Roman churches, the museums for antiquities are of enormous historical importance. One can doubt out of knowledge and out of ignorance; I like to believe in the identity of relics (though not in their miraculous powers); it satisfies my sense of the romantic, and I take comfort in the thought that, even if errors exist, antiquities are still the oldest truths we in our North possess. But art speaks for itself. Those altarpieces and statues, marble arches and bronze doors, those sky-high domes and spires, clearly and firmly speak for themselves and for the masters who created them. They assert the superiority of Rome in the Eternal Kingdom of Art. Everywhere, places are teeming with works which are admired and imitated by every nation, but only a Thorvaldsen has succeeded in creating something that can stand beside the immortal masterpieces that adorn the Vatican. Thousands of names are spoken with rapture, but one pauses when one has mentioned the name of Raphael!

When this great painter was summoned to Rome by Julius II, the people rejoiced at his coming as if he were the one who would restore to the city of Rome its lost greatness. His endearing personality captivated one and all. Only Michelangelo was reluctant to recognize him, yet it was his admiration for this master that drove Raphael to the pinnacle of art; for in Raphael one distinguishes three periods: his emergence from the Perugian school, his imitation of Leonardo da Vinci, and lastly his fresco paintings in the Vatican. From then on, he was the one and only painter. There could be no question of any rivalry. All jealousy on the part of his inferiors vanished, and Rome's leading artists gathered round their favorite as a Court and a bodyguard. Wherever he appeared, he radiated delight, and Vasari relates that everyone was forced to like him—"even the dumb animals."

Julius' successor, Leo X, raised Raphael to the height of honor and success. That is to say, Raphael was the prince of his art. He executed one masterpiece after another, lived like a prince, and died in the flower of his age and talent, mourned by a people who had adored him and by a sovereign who was his friend.

When one enters the Vatican, one seems to relive the life of a whole artistic circle. Nature and the Church have already prepared one for the momentous things one sees here. One passes through a couple of thousand years of history—not the history of battlefields and political ideas, but the quintessence of human refinement: science and art. This is not an exhibition which is to be judged, but a world of events, a selection of the select, which one must acknowledge and before which one must bow.

There is actually a sixteenth-century air about this palace. One pictures oneself as part of the retinue of artists who surrounded Raphael as he set out for Court. His most beautiful altarpieces are copied in mosaic, but the originals are kept in a couple of rooms which contain only a few choice paintings. Here the "Madonna di Foligno" and the "Transfiguration" arrest one's admiring gaze; we are approaching the artist's last moments, we already see him as too exalted for this earth, but only upon entering the well-known apartments (*stanze*) where the walls, the ceilings, and the spaces above the doors and windows are invested with the divine frescoes, do we realize that *here* Raphael reached his true height. And when we behold Peter being delivered from prison by the radiant angel, we are overwhelmed by devotion and deeply moved.—We feel ourselves uplifted with the great master and freed, as if by an angel, from the bonds of earthly life.

In these rooms there stand permanent scaffolds for those painters who have set themselves the task of imitating the inimitable. But the magic is still so powerful that one is transported back to the days when Raphael and his pupils worked there themselves. In the *stanza* of Attila,‡ I sat on the cross-girding of such a scaffold. There was activity and bustle all around me, and

‡ Commonly called the *stanza d'Eliodoro*, this room contains four Raphael frescoes: "The Repulse of Attila," "The Deliverance of St. Peter," "The Mass of Bolsena," and "The Expulsion of Heliodorus," from which it takes its name.

still there was silence. It was as if one expected the Pope to enter in order to view the soon-to-be-completed masterpiece. *Here* was the heart of the Vatican, of Rome, of the artistic world! I simply had to become inspired. I had felt dejected as an artist, but Raphael renewed my spirit. And while I could not cry with Correggio, "I too am a painter," I once again felt happy in my calling, and I summoned all my resources in order to portray this happiest of artists. Did I succeed in doing this? Is my Raphael loved by the one he adores? But must he not die in the flower of his age! Can this be called a picture of an artist's happiness?

Yes, for here upon earth all human happiness has its wants and longings. Death in the arms of Fame is the highest and the best the hero and the artist can hope to achieve.

There are very few known facts concerning Raphael's private life. He was amiable, industrious, a lover of joy, a worshiper of beauty, the favorite of Love. The people and princes bore him on their shoulders in triumph. He had the choice of a Cardinal's hat or a Cardinal's niece. He died a victim of his passions. His last, uncompleted work was the "Transfiguration," and he himself departed this life on Good Friday, exactly on his thirty-seventh birthday.

The history of his works has almost completely absorbed the anecdotal portion of his biography. His loveliest models are generally held to have been his mistresses; the one who is mentioned above all the others is "La Bella Fornarina." But what this *"amazia Rafaellis"* was really called we do not know, and there is even disagreement as to who she was. Some believe she was the wife or daughter of a townsman; others, that she was a descendant of the Fornari family. But it is by no means certain that the woman who was expelled from Raphael's house when he felt his end approaching was this famous model.

The lightness and grace that surrounded Raphael's whole personality, the festivities he adorned with his presence, and the elegant artist's life which in its depiction could avenge painters for all the triteness with which they are usually shown on the stage, the folk life (so different from that of Naples), and finally, the solemnity that always hangs over Rome, even during its Carnival, when the last *moccolo* [wax taper] is extinguished as the sound of the bells announces the beginning of Lent—all these things appeared to me to be superb elements for a ballet. Besides, an exalted ending such as that in which the artist's last masterwork is placed above his head while he, resting after having completed his task, is crowned by his august patron, must find a parallel here in Denmark, where we ourselves possessed a Prince of Art, the beloved Thorvaldsen, just as the Romans adored Raphael and bore that immortal artist to his final resting place.

To bind these episodes into a dramatic whole, to allow admirers of Raphael to rediscover his spirit and his time, and finally to be true, effective, and tasteful in the development of this theme—this was the problem I had posed for my art. There were two extremes I had to avoid: the purely material and the purely spiritual. (It was just about as fitting to have the hero die a victim of happy love as it was to portray the Ascension of Christ.) People often think that a woman's enthusiasm for an exalted artist is due to his personality, and many a girl indeed has been said to be enamored of a painter or singer when she was really only infatuated with his picture or his voice. Such an error constitutes my Raphael's greatest happiness, until his eyes are opened. He now frantically throws himself into the gaiety of the Carnival, renews old ties,* and returns home after a sleepless night, burning with fever and the emotions which assail him. Overwrought as a result of his dream, and exhausted from the completion of his "Saint Cecilia," whose attitude (in the picture she lets fall the organ in order to receive the angels who hand her the martyr's palm) resembles his own, he sinks into the arms of his friends, and the fatal bloodletting, which will put an end to his life, is prepared as the curtain falls. The Carnival merriment reappears, but it is halted by the tolling of the bells which call the people to the glorification of their favorite.

I wrote this work, which I drafted during my stay in Rome during the summer of 1841, at my Locanda al Leone bianco in Florence, close by the somber palace of the Strozzi. Here I lived right in the midst of Raphael and his contemporaries and divided my time among the Cathedral, the Palazzo Pitti, the Palazzo Vecchio, and my work, which enraptured me to such a degree that one day I suddenly jumped up from my chair and tearfully reproached myself for having taken the misery of the world so much to heart — I, who should consider myself so fortunate!

That was a Wednesday. The following morning the Boboli Gardens would be open.† I finished my ballet without reading it through, but at dawn the next day I put it in my pocket and went to the Gardens. There I chose a spot whence I could view the Arno and the beautiful city. I will confess that I was pleased with my work, and when I perceived that I had been sitting beneath a hedge of fresh laurel whose fruits lay scattered at my feet, I deemed it an omen of success.

I brought my work back to my native land. My small fortune, my nest egg, was gone; but, like a Camõens, I had rescued my poem from shipwreck,‡ and I felt no loss. However, when I had once again breathed Copenhagen air, I began to doubt whether *Raphael* could score a success at a time when people were unready for seriousness yet tired of merriment.

After the libretto had lain in my portfolio for three and a half years, I was

---

*Most likely refers to the encounter between Raphael and Paola, his former model and *"amazia,"* known as "La Bella Fornarina." See the libretto of *Raphael* (Copenhagen, 1845), Second Tableau.
† These gardens, which adjoin the Pitti Palace, were open to the public on Sundays and Thursdays.
‡ Sailing from Macao to Goa in 1559, the Portugese poet-adventurer Luis Vas de Camõens was wrecked off the Mekong and had to swim for his life. Of his personal possessions he could save only one: the unfinished manuscript of his great epic *The Lusiads*.

finally asked to present the ballet *Raphael* on the occasion of the King of Prussia's arrival in Denmark. But several circumstances combined to prevent this ceremonious representation. The ballet was, nonetheless, mounted with all the care our facilities allowed. For want of space and machinery, I had to divide the action into six tableaux instead of three acts. The music was perfectly beautiful and many things were superbly performed. But the audience was lukewarm. *Raphael,* which was to have been the crowning achievement of my whole career, was received with apathetic coldness—but the *pirouettes* were applauded! The whole thing is still too close in time for me to discover the reason for this listlessness or to judge my own work objectively. But even if this ballet is not the finest one I have ever composed, I do know this: I have never composed anything with greater industry or enthusiasm.

THE FOUR SEASONS, OR CUPID'S JOURNEY

A Ballet Cycle.

IF one could look into an artist's heart, he would discover doubt and depression more often than self-confidence and arrogance. But, oddly enough, it is precisely during times of adversity that he stands in danger of falling victim to pride. As long as I cherished the hope that the ballet *Raphael* would be extraordinarily successful, I was frequently overwhelmed by depression, but when I failed to communicate my enthusiasm to others, my pride was awakened and it seemed as if I too had painted my last picture and could not possibly produce anything better. Our Danish autumn and winter are perfect for fostering dark thoughts in an artist's mind. I wrote my testament, that is, *My Theatre Life,* and became even more firmly convinced that if I viewed our Theatre as the instrument upon which I was to play, there was no longer a single chord that could evoke a response from the public.

With spring, hope breathed forth anew. I found my last work too broad in construction, consoled myself with the thought that everywhere the genre picture was supplanting historical painting, and ventured a new attempt in a lighter, more popular style. If Raphael Sanzio could not help me delight the Danish public, then perhaps Albert Thorvaldsen* would lend me stronger support.

Who does not know his lovely bas-reliefs, *The Four Seasons?* The great master honored me with his friendship and had often encouraged me to work on the aforementioned subject. I remarked that the roguish god of Love played an important part in Thorvaldsen's creations, and, smiling as if he were old Anacreon himself, he answered me, "Aye, I am now over seventy years old, but I must confess that Cupid has always been and still is my very

---

*Thorvaldsen's given name was actually Bertel, but in Italy it was incorrectly rendered as Alberto.

good friend." Well then, I thought, perhaps in a suitable disguise Cupid will often be a welcome guest to many people and gain admittance to our unfortunately all too explicit stage. Let him, then, be the mystic thread which on an extensive journey binds the seasons of the year into a garland of four ballet poems.

He leaves his divine home during the spring festival in Greece, consoles the grieving wife, and brings her husband back from long captivity. In summer he comes to Brittany, determines the choice of the Rose-bride, and follows the troops to the field. As the faithful guardian of lovers, he attends the wine harvest on Ischia, and in winter returns to his mother after having revealed himself in the Christmas joy of the North.

THE NEW PENELOPE, OR THE SPRING FESTIVAL AT ATHENS

A Ballet in Two Acts.
Music by Herman V. Løvenskjold.

A number of original situations and a lively play of color in the dancing as well as the costumes and scenery procured for this ballet a brilliant reception. To be sure, both attendance and applause soon diminished, but I still had reason to feel encouraged to immediately embark upon my next work, which was to be in a completely opposite style. However, before moving on to this, I must discuss the mistaken impression the finale of *The Spring Festival* made upon a man whose approval, both as a writer and a Philhellene, would have meant so much to me.

He had nothing to find fault with in the first part of the finale, the "Parthenon Hymn," but he found the second, which depicted the desperate struggle of the Greeks and the sorrow of the women and orphans, to be both untrue and shocking. It was his contention that no nation, however dramatic its games might be, would renew the memory of its misfortunes and troubles at a festival. I will admit that this moment, which has always moved both myself and the rest of the company so deeply, has not particularly touched or excited the audience; so I must believe that the aforesaid opinion is shared by many. Consequently it is time for me to give my composition further explanation.

In the three segments of the finale, I had wished to denote three different periods: Antiquity, the Middle Ages, and the Present. It is not the freedom fighters of modern times who fall and above whose graves Hellas mourns; it is the heroes of antiquity and those of the fifteenth century who are awakened by the sound of the trumpet and are born again to freedom and jubilation among a younger generation. I dare to assert the right of my art to portray such features. Our main task is to lure the audience onto a field where the ballet is master. Hence, if we have reached a point in the action where a series of diversified dances is called for—all of which are to have a specific local significance—they take on the character of songs, poems, tone pictures; and, since a note of sadness is the predominant element in all national melodies, it here helps to heighten and enliven the intoxication of victory and liberation.

Since this festival is a quadruple one—that is, the celebration of springtide, Easter, Amyntas' homecoming, and the Greek insurrection (April 6 [1821])—it gives me even greater latitude; and if I have allowed myself to be carried away by an idea that was certain to encounter opposition because of its very novelty, I still believed it would triumph by virtue of its exotic charm. For just as *The Toreador* would cause a scandal in Spain and *Napoli* in Naples, so in Greece, with *The New Penelope,* I would stand in danger of suffering the same fate as the one which befell that tragic poet who was expelled from the country for having grieved the frivolous Athenians by his representation of *The Fall of the Messenians.**

THE WHITE ROSE, OR SUMMER IN BRITTANY

A Ballet in One Act.
Music by H. Paulli.

IN all the capitals of Europe, aye, even in the provincial cities, there is to be found near every theatre a coffeehouse where the personalities, pettinesses, and misfortunes of the stage serve as intellectual nourishment for a class of amateurs who are known as *"la faction des ennuyés,"* freely translated: "Brethren of Boredom." Here originates the material for a host of anecdotes, newspaper articles, and scandals. If these asylums are a haven for idle artists, they are, on the other hand, a terror to the hard-working ones, for they often bear the same relation to the theatre as the Tarpeian Rock did to the Capitol.

I dare say that with regard to external appearance neither our theatre nor our coffeehouse can compare with foreign establishments of the same sort, but as far as inner worth is concerned, both of them can hold their own. However, our coffeehouse has a unique advantage: it has created a particular tone, aye, almost a private language, which does not confine itself solely to the buffet and the smoking room but finds its way into social conversation and prevails on the benches of the Theatre, sometimes even on the stage itself.

* Thirty years later, Bournonville alluded to the same story (cf. Vol. III, Part One, p. 372), this time identifying the poet as Euripides. However, the editor has been unable to pinpoint the source of Bournonville's reference, and none of the classical scholars consulted had ever heard of *The Fall of the Messenians.* All suggested that the tragedian in question was Phrynicus, whose play *The Capture of Miletus* (produced shortly after the Persians took that Ionian city in 494 B.C.) infuriated his Athenian audience to the point that it was permanently banned and its author, though not exiled, was fined the then huge sum of 1000 drachmas. The incident is reported in Herodotus, Book VI, Chapter 21.

But what is this so-called "pothouse tone" like? Is it vile, fanatical, or Bellmanically merry? Not at all! It is, rather, dignified, empty, cold, and tiresome. In fact, it is nothing more than a vapor which robs every picture of its freshness, a mirror which reflects everything upside down. It is the sarcasm of apathy and idleness which steals in the window while working power and industry go out the door. How encouraging it was for the man who offered a spring bouquet from the sacred soil of Greece to hear his work branded, eight days before its performance, with a wrongly pronounced name that was certain to become a hit by reason of its very scurrility.*

In like manner this pothouse spirit had seized upon *The White Rose* while its scenes were still being rehearsed. They [the café's habitués] had discovered allusions of the most vulgar sort, and the single local allusion I had allowed myself—that is, the one I was counting on to immediately acquaint the audience with the motif—went as good as unnoticed. This was the rich grain harvest that had blessed Europe after a distressing year. I wished to depict summer: a full-bodied corn sheaf projecting out of the earth, whence Cupid emerged with a bouquet of cornflowers from which he bound garlands for the young girls who vied for the honor of being chosen the Rose-bride.

Country life and Breton folkways, the contrast of modern manners and customs, some comical situations, Cupid in several disguises, and love in all its noblest forms—these were the points on which I had based my expectations, not of a great success but of a lively and amicable reception. If, in addition to this, I considered some successful characters together with dances carefully composed and well performed, then I had not built my hopes on sand. And yet I met with a disappointment. My ballet was received with indifference, aye, even with displeasure and ill will. No one could tell me the reason for this, but I grasped it by myself.

The public is sick and tired of my compositions, which have occupied the Ballet for a great many years. The times demand optical illusions or farces. Our technical facilities prohibit the former, my own taste the latter. The Theatre has need of a new balletmaster, and I, perhaps, of another theatre. I feel neither the desire nor the spirit to begin working on autumn and winter, for summer was too cold for me.

---

*This allusion is explained by the following passage from Carl C. Christensen's *Fra Voldenes København* (Copenhagen, 1924): "It was mainly the tone-setting members of the literary and political fields who gathered at Mini's [café], and outsiders often felt ... offended by the critical tone that prevailed among Mini's patrons—'the *Mini*sters,' as antagonists of this circle called them—for these men had formed a kind of unofficial club where many, and usually biting criticisms, were leveled at the theatre, literature, art, and politics." Bournonville was one of those most offended by this "coffeehouse chitchat," and he had reason to feel insulted; for, says Christensen, one of the members of this clique had made a—to Bournonville's ears ghastly—pun about his Grecian ballet, *The New Penelope* [*Den nye Penelope*], calling it instead *Den pene Loppe*, which is Danish for *The Good-looking Flea*.

IX

Lyric Attempts

IF I am to mention all the fruits of my artistic endeavors, then I must certainly allow my lyric attempts to come to light. Like the songs in a *vaudeville*, these are thoughts that could not find a place in the dialogue. I am not afraid of being accused of having been overhasty in publishing them, as they have all lain unknown for a number of years; nor do I fear harsh or scornful criticism, for I do not believe anyone would have the heart to trample underfoot the flowers which during "bright moments" have sprouted along my thorny path. I say "bright moments," for though on the whole it is a plaintive tone that runs through all my poetical works—even those which have been "danced"—I have never felt luckier, happier, or more elated than at the very time I created them.

I shall spare my readers all my album and occasional verses as well as some longer poems that have nothing at all to do with my theatre life. Most of those in the series I will here present are self-explanatory and are more or less associated with moments in my professional activity.

TRANSLATOR'S NOTE:
August Bournonville, like many writers of his time, composed his poems in carefully scanned and rhymed lines, often using stanzas of unequal length and occasionally employing a refrain. The Danish edition of *My Theatre Life* contained eleven poems; but for reasons of space among others, only five are included here. Four of these are faithful to the originals in metrics as well as meaning. The fifth, "The Might of Runes," is rendered in literal, line-for-line translation. Only in this way, it turned out, could the meaning be presented without the padding, paraphrasing, or tortured grammatical structures that were entailed in attempts to keep to the original rhythmic pattern. Both this poem and "Ischia Ballad," as will be seen in Volume III, Part Three, had particular significance for their author.

THE NINETEENTH OF MAY

(1843)

The nineteenth of May's the most glorious day
Of all the days in the year.
And from my earliest childhood on,

119

I have ever held it dear.
On that day the sky was always blue,
E'en the harshest winter could ne'er endure
For spring in its glory burst triumphantly through
      The nineteenth of May.

High above fragrant meadows
Rose the forest so verdant and green.
The vast bower beautifully echoed
With the thrilling song of the birds.
And the ocean sent its cooling breeze
To drive every cloud from the weary mind,
As the heart to its heaven entered in
      The nineteenth of May.

There where the river Rhone surges,
Among the vine-clad hills,
Where the minstrel his dream can so tenderly turn
To a lover's sweet romance,
Where the olive tree grows in the blood-drenched vale
While herdsmen build in Roman halls:
My father was born in the fullness of time
      The nineteenth of May

The day was cherished; the boy was named,
And he grew in wisdom and grace.
Within her arms, Love fostered him
While the Muses happily let him tread
The path which over the toilsome way
E'er led him hovering, light and free
As a butterfly that past us flew
      The nineteenth of May.

Yet the seedling blossomed to ripened fruit,
And this fruit then scattered its seed.
No stormy autumn made the stalk to bend,
And, high above, Winter's twinkling stars
Have seen it to stand with rime-clad hair,
Surrounded by plants, honored with years,
And in festal array greet each burgeoning spring
      The nineteenth of May.

O, mem'ries from childhood's beauteous days!
When spring to our hut drew near.
Our father's birthday, so splendid and mild,
We'd never exchange for a crown.
Like birds from their prisons suddenly freed,
We flew with him beyond city walls,
And, rejoicing, cried "Welcome, Nature reborn,"
      The nineteenth of May.

Like children indeed do we wander the world;
Our souls from their cages shall soar,
Like birds of passage who on restless wing
To their family home shall be borne.
So haste we over the stormy sea,
The pilgrim his staff layeth down,
As, grieving, we stand now beside his grave
      The nineteenth of May.*

But to us spring sends its consolation
From the far-off Promised Land.
For Easter morn's celestial voice
From the Isle of the Blest resounds.
And Pentecost soon shall dazzle our eyes
With all of its solemn splendor.
O, let us then bind a memorial crown
      The nineteenth of May.

SALUTE TO NORWAY

(1840)

Norway I love, where mountain peaks
Are mirrored in the silvery fjord;
To me, her fair, proud form bespeaks
A tutelar goddess for our ancient *Nord.*
When thick clouds o'er the heavens fly,
And Earth arrays herself in mourning,
When cold and stiff the billows lie,
Norway, a veil her brow adorning,
Stands like a beauteous bride serene,
With heart so warm and face so fair,
In snowy garb, with evergreen
At hand and breast and in her hair.
From high upon the rocky verge
Her bridegroom's progress she beholds,
While Spring, below, with merry urge,
Espies the charms this maid unfolds
By North Star's torchlight from above,
For 'tis the noonday sun of Love.

A mother fair she was when I beheld her
In summer splendor green, and golden-skinned;
In morning sun her raiment glowed with rapture
And fluttered in the cooling western wind.
Her womb was filled with fruitfulness and gladness,
While from her breast flowed nectar sweet and mild;
Her children drank of strength but not of sadness,

*Antoine Bournonville had died on January 11, 1843.

For glad tears fell upon the tiny child.
The pure mountain air drove away worries deep,
And from innocent breast the *lur* sounded
While the waterfall lulled the fair creature to sleep
Where dreams of delight e'er abounded.
There, 'neath cover of branches she rested
Where the spruce tree shot forth from the stone
And with young strength made old rock, time-tested,
To yield and to grant it a home.
There Freedom to noble Reliance
As Fidelity's daughter is bound;
And wherever Faith forms such alliance,
The Lord's temple will ever be found.
There a wave can ne'er wash away sand
Nor bury the shore 'neath its crest,
For, firm and unblemished, the rocky land
Can thrust away treachery from her breast.

Hail to thee, Norway! Home of virtues old!
Saga-seat — and Freedom's hero-land!
Accept the homage my heart to thee unfolds,
I thank thee as an artist, *skald*, and man.
On mountain, in valley, 'pon field and lea,
Thy unequalled beauty before me hove,
From "Ringerike" I beheld thy glory,
And praised God in eternal love.
In the *skald*-man's teeming mind,
Many castles stand without roof or gable,
But should they e'er completion find,
Norway, I think, may well be able
This task to do, this service render.
Thy hand, Norwegian, I have pressed,
Thy heart, Norwegian, is loyal and tender.
Thy meaning thou statest without behest,
Never an issue dost thou neglect,
With thee I always know where I stand
And for this I owe thee my respect.
Thy favorite country is thy native land:
Thus can the Sons of the North be known,
For we, too, hold our green strand dear;
In this, Norwegian, thou art not alone.
"But . . ." thou sayest — Let me never hear
Those old, political refrains;
Like hellish music they torment my rest —
The clanking of old Akershus's chains.
Yet — and to this I will attest —
'Twas only on seeing this free mountain land,
With its natural beauties so rich and rare,
That I could truly understand
How highly her sons prize their Mother fair.

THE MIGHT OF RUNES

(To H. P. Holst. Written on Ischia, in 1841,
  after reading his poem "The Runes")

Deep within the heart a chord there lies
That quivers, touched by an unseen hand.
At the sound, one's eye begins to glow
As the soul slakes off its mortal bonds.
I weep with ease, but not—like child or woman—
From pain, thanks, sorrow, baffled hope;
And never has one seen my tears well up
From wounded pride, nor cry with anger fraught.
But when I'd heard of a good deed done
'Mid the strife of passions and worldly life;
When the cheers of the victor I thought I'd heard
Amid monuments of a vanished time;
When on Easter morn, 'neath the church's vaults
The trumpets proclaimed: "He hath conquered Death";
Whene'er the fierce blaze of the "Marseillaise"
and "Christian at the high mast" 's tones I heard;
When high above the southern sea
Our Dane-flag I saw waving nobly
And in distant lands, by every race,
Heard our Frederik's name with honor graced;
Then wild excitement exalted me,
My heart beat strong, my cheeks grew warm,
A forced smile played about my lips,
And tears fell from my eyes.

But the artist's holy Jerusalem
By Philistines constantly is besieged,
And cannot, as in the Psalm-king's home,
Be vanquished by simply casting a sling.
They do not carry bright copper shields;
They do not fight wildly with sword or spear,
But hide behind ramparts of haughtiness
And in ignoble meanness' mire wallow.
If they ever withstood an honest fight
They only fought with their heels, in flight,
And filled the air with a vapor vile
That killed not the body but the soul.
In gaining victory I was struck
By a venemous shaft from some dark corner.
My strength was sapped, my lips grew pale;
They lost their smile, my eyes, their sparkle.
And, dying, were muted in my breast
Tones none but the chosen can understand.
I fell, exhausted, in the lists,
By the scorn of my enemies' laugh derided.

Then heard I a deep, grave voice within
That solemnly bade me my birthplace leave
To go where my troubles could be forgot—
Where shelter from the storm would be surely found.
My wife and my children I pressed to my breast,
My old parents' blessing I received.
But, filled with the bitter pain of parting,
The mild tears did not my eyes refresh.
Yet as the city faded from view,
The heavy clouds started to disappear;
And, high up in the southern sky,
The star of Hope, so brightly shining,
New life and strength called me to find
In those places where 'tis good to be.
There I'll regain my peace of mind,
There I'll gather my family round me.
There active, happy, and gay I'll live.
For am I not still in the summer of Life?
Nor am I lacking in fruit or flowers.
But why am I frequently overwhelmed
By this dreadful feeling of self-mistrust,
Which steals upon me unawares
And seems to rob me of all volition?

Why should I lose my freedom here—
Here, where Nature engenders Art—
And fail to create a picture-world
In this beauteous home of myrtle and laurel?
What is't is lacking in my being?
My soul is happy, my mind is eager
But, like a plant that withers in heat,
My petals fade, my green leaves fall
To the ground without perfume or fragrance.

But then from thy isle thou camest, dear friend,
Where, sheltered 'neath cooling vine-branches,
With thoughts e'er directed o'er land and o'er sea,
Thy wondrous runes thou hast carven.
How well I remember that hour of sorrow
When thou strummed thy harp at Frederik's bier,†
And, grieving from sorrow deep down within thee,
Turned Grief's winter snow to a tear.
Nor were our Frode's‡ bones borne far and wide

---

† King Frederik VI; died 1839.
‡ Frode Fredegod, the Peaceful, is said to have been king of Denmark during the time of Christ. After Frode's death, in order to maintain peace in the kingdom, his body was transported from place to place for almost three years in an effort to convince people (at least from a distance) that the popular ruler was still alive. Hjarne was a poet who allegedly became king of Denmark after the legendary Frode as a reward for a poem he wrote in memory of him.

Till we'd found us a dirge and a Hjarne:
The lay that thou wrote on our lord-king's menhir
At our hearthsides shall be ever sounded.
A song I asked of thee (full well its power I knew)
And thou with love thy poet's harp brought forth
And sang of "runes" thy little child had sent thee
On the border of a letter writ from home:
Like bird song from the Sjaelland woods it echoed,
The fragrance of the fresh lay hence it bore:
Like May song sweet its stanzas gently wended
O'er Sound swells, islands, and to Ischia's shore.
At thoughts "The Runes" would conjure up before me
My heart with loneliness and longing beat;
But from my mind the bitter mem'ries vanished
And sank into Oblivion's bosom deep.
The morning sun of Hope — so bright — illumined
Those far-off shores where all my loved ones live;
While tenderly Hearth's Angel to me beckoned
And promised peace and happiness to give.
With joy I saw myself in fancy greeted:
My wife, my little ones clung to my breast;
A cry of joy resounded from my father,
And with delight my mother's days I blessed.
Then suddenly 'twas as if a paean sounded,
An elf-troop now past me began to glide;
And like the waves a cooling breeze doth ripple,
I trembled 'fore the magic of the runes.
Like rain dropt from clouds on a southern vale,
Ripe fruit to produce in its season,
My eyes were suffused with relief-bringing tears,
My health and good spirits restored.

Accept my thanks, O noble friend!
Enjoy the victory thou hast won
Through the hidden power of thy tones.
To thee I give the finest I possess:
This first-grown flower of my reborn art.
Happy am I now, for I can sing
While from its clear, clean spring the gentle tear
With its cooling waters animates the heart
And gives me strength and fortune in my work.
My airy art shalt pictures paint
Of sounds that live within me.
In dance the melody loud shall speak
And through Beauty's chain its bright way wend:
To quiet joy, then, I shall consecrate
Every moment of rest the day may give;
And the feeling that animates this breast
Shall purify me through honor and love.
And, should the *Present* bring me sorrow,

To a better *Future* I'll look instead;
If memories bitter the *Past* should send me,
My joy I shall seek in the clear, bright *Now!*
When we should happen to meet and share
Our impressions from Naples' far-off shores,
From Ischia's deep green, fertile vale
And the mountain chapel on the rocky ledge;
When, arm in arm, we shall sometimes wander
On the banks of the waters of Østersø,
As our eyes trace the path of the clouds to the South
While the bright Northern day is still long and warm;
We shall think to ourselves of the fresh drops of rain
That give fragrance to flowers and nectar to fruit.
But never shall earth, though parched, cry out in vain:
For soon 'twill be quenched with rejuvening strength —
Then the voice of the heart sayeth boldly: Fear not!
The Creator who gave thee thy passion and mettle,
Who lit deep within thee the true artist's flame,
Will never deny thee the mild, gentle tear.

ISCHIA BALLAD

The light bark skims o'er the ocean's swells
From Napoli to the isle; and there, where San Vincenzo dwells,
Guitar strains sweet in vineyards say:
"Io ti voglio ben assai, e tu non pienz' a me."

Ischia! Queen of southern isles!
How thy peace and beauty beckon, thy quiet joy beguiles!
Here a youth sings e'er at his Giovanna's knee:
"Io ti voglio ben assai, e tu non pienz' a me."

High upon the hillside grows the vineyards golden crop,
And scent of orange rises to Epomeo's top,
While 'neath myrtle cover the nightingale sighs its lay:
"Io ti voglio ben assai, e tu non pienz' a me."

Here, far from nations' tumult, our youthful poet lay,
His thoughts so swift assembled, his pen could scarce convey;
These thoughts became the accents of the southern melody:
"Io ti voglio ben assai, di me ricordati."

But homeland's Muse had beckoned: the *skald* said his good-bye
To mountain chapel, vineyards green, to vale, and sea, and sky —
Now, 'neath beech-wood shelter, his thoughts to Ischia stray:
"Io ti voglio ben assai, e sempre pienz' a te."

DAGUERREOTYPE PORTRAIT

The daguerreotype's grinning portrait
I'll not hesitate to set
In a class with an automaton — or a marionette.

It may do for architecture:
A building's cold lines to immure;
But ne'er can it hope to rival the glories of Nature.

To lend magic tone to perspective,
And make cold, dead lines to live,
This beauteous thing's not for buying: 'tis *Art*'s alone to give.

Chimie itself, aided by *méchanique*,
May only be said to approach *plastique*
To the same degree that a hurdy-gurdy can ever be called *musique*.

To the honor of Nature and artistry
There's a worldwide, sacred philosophy
That says: 'tis a different thing to *be*.

People loudly exclaim: "But can't you see
That this picture truly resembles me?
Why, it bears the stamp of *Reality*."

But truth without spirit is really Death,
And, loveless, he steadily wandereth,
Seeking to rob each thing of its breath.

Is a face made up of bones so white
On which light is thrown, too clear and bright,
Making hollows where once were our orbs of sight?

Must one's lips remain always so stern and chill?
Is there nought that a subject's mind can fill
Save the dreadful thought of "holding still"?

For the graveyard's silence and peace of mind
In a lifelike picture are two of a kind;
For the Soul in a death-mask you'll never find.

Could I discover on the glassy main
A single spot that would my face retain
I should never take to the water again.

Though Nature herself is our mother dear,
She often plays tricks both cruel and queer,
And cannot stand to be seen too near.

She gave her children hand and eye,
And light and color from on high,
Yet the painter's power she will deny.

"Try to paint me," she'll intone.
"I gave thee everything I own,
But my *Spirit* and *Love* come from God alone.

"Admire me in sea, in valley quaint,
And in the eye, which speaks without restraint,
But with nought save the *Spirit's* forces canst thou paint."

VOLUME
TWO

Theatre Life and Reminiscences

INTRODUCTION

WHEN I published *My Theatre Life* at Christmas in 1847, I little expected that my book would be received with such extraordinary sympathy or that the career which I already considered as good as finished would continue so long thereafter.

Seventeen memorable years have passed, and in both the State and its miniature image, the Theatre, much has happened and much has been lost without any prospect of compensation. However, while in politics there is but little comfort to be gained in looking back, in the realm of art and fantasy there lie rest and refreshment for the mind, even when we dwell upon the memory of what has vanished.

The first part of *My Theatre Life* was lucky enough to win approval, mainly because of its form. In this continuation I have tried to retain that form, perhaps with a little less naïveté in expression but with somewhat greater maturity of thought. Although it lies in the nature of memoirs to accord the first person "I" a prominent role, I have endeavored to withdraw into the shadows of the surroundings and events. It has not been possible to avoid delving a bit into the psychological, aye, even the political domain; and if I have touched upon some more or less famous personalities in my dramatic reflections, it has not been as a critic but as an art historian, since I hold to Voltaire's principle, which is stated in his *Histoire de Charles XII* and is especially applicable to the transient art of the stage: "The history of a king is not everything he did, but what he did that was remarkable." Nevertheless, should I have been forced to point out mistakes and blunders, particularly in administrative respects, it is for the simple reason that every effect must have its cause, every proposition its motive, and, above all, because every retrospect teaches us a lesson. I do not desire gall and wormwood to flow from my pen, but then again, pure honey would be a little too sweet. Besides, I hold to the motto of our Theatre: "Not for pleasure alone." I wish to do some good, and if one had no hope for a better future, it would not be worth while to write.

The critics neither can nor will allow this book of mine to pass unchallenged, especially since it contains propositions about which there will always be divided opinions. People have therefore advised me to publish these memoirs only after my death and thereby renounce a most uncertain pleasure in favor of avoiding a rather sure annoyance. But should Providence grant me an old age, my accounts will surely by then have lost their freshness and interest, and my counsels, should they have any value, will be considered superfluous and absolutely impractical.

Therefore, in recommending *My Theatre Life* and its vicissitudes to my benevolent contemporaries in the entire art world and reading public of Scandinavia, with the wish that the book may not be regarded as a finished whole but preferably be read *in piecemeal fashion,* I willingly submit myself to the judgment of the critics, with regard both to my views and to the manner in which I have presented them according to the best of my ability. I will only state that I am recognized for faithfulness and reliability in the presentation of facts.

AUGUST BOURNONVILLE

Fredensborg, in May, 1865.

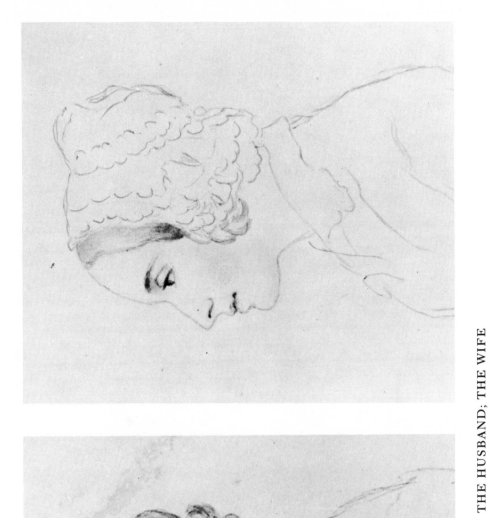

THE HUSBAND; THE WIFE
August Bournonville and Helena Fredrika Bournonville. Drawings,
probably from the 1840's, by the Swedish novelist Fredrika Bremer.
Det kgl. Bibliotek, Copenhagen.

THE FAMILY

Group portrait by Lehmann, 1852, showing (l. to r.) Wilhelmine B. (adopted daughter), Mathilde B., Edmond B., August B., Therese B., Eva Suell (Bournonville's sister-in-law), Helena B., Charlotte Håkansson (Bournonville's mother-in-law), and Charlotte B. The picture was done at the time of the marriage of the balletmaster's eldest daughter, Augusta, the only one of his children missing from the family portrait. Private collection.

I

Reflections

CHOREOGRAPHIC CREDO

THE Dance is an art because it demands vocation, knowledge, and ability.

It is a *fine* art because it strives for an ideal, not only in plastic but also in lyrical respects.

The beauty to which the Dance ought to aspire is not dependent upon taste or pleasure, but is founded on the immutable laws of *Nature*.

The art of *Mime* encompasses all the feelings of the soul. The Dance, on the other hand, is essentially an expression of joy, a desire to follow the rhythms of the music.

It is the mission of art in general, and the theatre in particular, to intensify thought, to elevate the mind, and to refresh the senses. Consequently, the Dance ought above all to beware of indulging a blasé public's fondness for impressions which are alien to true art.

Joy is a strength; *intoxication,* a weakness.

The beautiful always retains the freshness of novelty, while *the astonishing* soon grows tiresome.

The Dance can, with the aid of music, rise to the heights of *poetry*. On the other hand, through an excess of gymnastics it can also degenerate into *buffoonery*. So-called "difficult" feats can be executed by countless adepts, but the appearance of *ease* is achieved only by the chosen few.

The height of artistic skill is to know how to conceal the mechanical effort and strain beneath *harmonious calm.*

Mannerism is not *character,* and *affectation* is the avowed enemy of *grace.*

Every dancer ought to regard his laborious art as a link in the chain of beauty, as a useful ornament for the stage, and this, in turn, as an important element in the spiritual development of nations.

NATIONAL DANCING AND SOCIAL DANCING

DANCING, like singing, is at once art and recreation. One sings and dances to amuse oneself and to please others. There are Materialists and Pietists who regard art respectively as a curiosity and as a sin. For them the dance is a folly and gaiety an offense. They readily admit that a livelihood must be earned by work, but forget that the latter demands periods of rest during which one may enjoy the fruits of accomplishment and strengthen oneself for new undertakings. Even if innocent joys are not the *goal* of work, they are nevertheless one of its *rewards*, and the pleasures that lead us back to the harmless merriment of childhood must surely be the most beneficial for the mind and the healthiest for the body. I therefore dare to designate the Dance as one of the blessings that has been bestowed upon mankind to enable us to express a feeling and to tear ourselves loose from our anxieties and the triviality of daily life.*

A child moves his hands and feet, rejoicing in the sounds of music; a soldier forgets his fatigue and dangers upon hearing the inspiring music of a band; one's heart beats faster at the ring of a voice, and one thrills to the strains of an orchestra. Every glad tiding, every pleasant surprise, causes a native to hop like a bird fluttering its wings; and among all races, from the wildest to the most civilized, festive joy is expressed by dancing.

The old Frenchman still leads his lady through the measures of a sedate *Contredanse,* and both are transported back to the springtime of youth.

The stiff Englishman casts aside the bonds of etiquette in the merry *Hornpipe.* With the speed of a runner, he traverses the long rows of the *Écossais,* and sets the floor atremble beneath the thundering measures of the *Reel.*

The Hallingdaller [from Norway] and the Wermlänninger [from Sweden] test the elasticity of their feet against the rafters of the parlor.

At wedding feasts in the Faroes, where even a few years ago they had only heroic ballads to dance to, there are presented pantomimic scenes to ballads about Holger Danske and Abraham's faithful servant who secured the beauteous Rebecca for his master's son.

The Hungarian with his jingling spurs paints a picture of the horseman's life, and represents the lover who at a mad gallop carries off his stubborn bride.

The German loses himself in the whirling of the *Waltz* as if in the fog of systems, and starts as if awakened from a dream when, after such violent movement, he finds himself back at the same point from which he departed.

How often have our poets sung of the *Tarantella* to the jangling of the tambourine, and of the *Bolero* to the clacking of castanets! But not one of them has noticed the serious faces of the Italians, who know they are dancing upon volcanic soil; and few have pointed out that the Spaniards, when they bring their romantic dances to the North, season them with a sprinkling of coarseness, just as they adulterate their noble wines with distilled spirits for our fastidious palates.

---

*When I refer to the Dance as a recreation, i.e., a rebirth of strength and desire, I do not mean, of course, those excessive pleasures of the ball which cause the roses of youth to fade, any more than I do those wild and distorted gestures with which young France—perhaps without even realizing it—furnishes a picture of its own demoralization.—A.B.

Finally, I must speak of the Pole, whose nationality has been splintered among three powerful states, all equally detested. Of his proud old native heritage he now retains nothing save the language and the *elegant dances!* But it is these, above all, that make him outstanding, for whether he be a soldier on the Rhine or on the steppes of Russia, whether he be an exile in the virgin forests of America or a slave in the mines of Siberia, wherever a *Mazurka* is played, people admiringly gather round the slender, graceful Poles. They try in vain to imitate their easy, rounded movements, and, as far as dancing is concerned, even their harsh masters must confess themselves conquered by the knightly countrymen of Sobiesky.

For fear of creating a scandal, I dare not use the symbolism of the dance in reference to my beloved native land. I shall only allude to one historical fact: since the time of the Valdemars, when *the Danes danced* to the rhythm of heroic ballads and paeans of victory without the assistance of foreign musicians, Denmark has not possessed any independent national dances.

What a singularly poetic air dancing casts over certain festive occasions! Need I mention the feeling that grips young and old alike when the ballroom doors are opened, the candles gleam, and the music sounds to greet the light-hearted couples? I shall only refer to the gaiety that is diffused within a social circle when the piano is opened and the floor is set atremble, or when in a modest farmhouse the blind fiddler enters bearing his cracked viol. Both here and there a ball is improvised and lasts but an hour or two; yet it provides the climax of a happy evening.

How nice it is when a merry little group holds a dance upon the greensward beneath the shade of the trees! And then we have the stately harvest festivals; the fishermen at Sunday meeting; the artisans at the jovial guild balls; and the charming idyll when the bride and bridegroom step into the happy circle of their friends in order to modestly tread their first measure as man and wife! Here the dance is surely the interpreter not only of joy, but of love.

It is not surprising that many a time *I* have felt deeply moved by these pictures, which give me such encouraging proof that my life's endeavor has not been vain futility. But when, at a silver wedding anniversary celebration, I saw the anniversary couple open the ball with the same dance they had performed twenty-five years before, tears glistened in *everyone's* eyes.

I only hope that the world may never become so cold and sober-minded that it considers dancing to be a waste of energy. It will be a dark and sorry day when a harsh earnestness wipes the smile from our lips, steals the lightness from our feet, and forbids the young to whirl gaily about the resting old folk.

Poetry indeed holds sway over movement as well as sound. One person sings, another dances. Lucky the one who has the ability and the desire to do both!

Dancing permeates all of nature, from the flight of the birds to the billowing of the waves, and an old folk saying tells of how the whole world rejoices at the *Dance of the Sun* on Easter morn. Therefore let jesting, singing, and dancing season the hardships of life. But even our gaiety ought to be subject to the laws of taste and rhythm. In short, let us endeavor to sing *purely* and to dance *beautifully*.

ON DANCE INSTRUCTION

THE Graces, beauty's tutelary deities, are called to polish and refine our manners. Just as with its invisible, spiritual nourishment, the human body likewise deserves all the [physical] care we can give it.

Very few individuals are totally deprived of the gift of imparting lightness and grace to their movements after some training. Some are actually born with a graceful bent. In these favored persons, art merely assists in warning against exaggeration and misuse. Others, on the contrary, are like fruit trees that suffer under climatic conditions. Here the skillful gardener must use all his industry, awaken a feeling for the beautiful, graft on wholesome ideas, and bring them to maturity through practice and by reference to good models.

There are people who despite their versatile gifts have from childhood on, due to wrongful notions, imbibed such a decided contempt for anything that might be called grace and tact that later it is as difficult a task to rid them of their belief that clumsiness and rudeness are the hallmarks of genius as it is to convince them that an external "polishing" will not rob them of any of their inner worth.

Generally speaking, people have nothing against undertaking the most rudimentary exercises as long as they are necessary in order to figure at a ball with a tolerable degree of assurance. But even those who are willing to grant ballet dancing a place in the realm of art as a rule have no idea that in mastering higher social dancing they are in fact learning and cultivating a genuine art that demands both effort and a certain amount of study.

Fashion, that irresistible atmospheric pressure, has almost everywhere in the "fashionable" world reduced the social dancing to the least possible amount of technical skill. For the endless whirling in the *Polka* and the *Waltz*, little artistic preparation is needed, unless it be in a negative direction; for when one considers all the bad habits to which one can become addicted in the above-mentioned dances, special instruction could be given consisting of nothing but warnings. Even in a *Francaise* one can find the opportunity to display the results of good training, not by performing correct or difficult steps, but simply by one's carriage, rhythmical movement, and in particular the taste and dignity with which one appears before one's lady and shows consideration for one's fellow dancers. If with the rotation of time and a revival of the vogue for the Rococo, the old-fashioned *Minuets* and *Sarabandes* should, in rejuvenated form, be once again introduced at our parties, the more graceful social dancing should regain its lost esteem. But perhaps this belongs to the realm of pious wishes.

Without being passionately fond of the idea of a reaction that would take us back to the "peruke age," I do wish to ask the aristocrats of our day: "How have you profited by the knightly exercises and talents that contributed so greatly to the imposing appearance and character of your fathers?"

And to the commonalty and democrats I would say: "Pay the same heed to the outer 'polishing' as to the inner, and the merits — if there still are such things — of the upper classes will merge with yours in equality of manners."

But even apart from actual formal training, dance instruction contains so much that is beneficial to physical development and furnishes so many suggestions for broadening personal pleasure that it ought not to be omitted from any young person's education. Upon the whole, during dancing lessons a number of pertinent remarks can be made and some truths be told which, precisely because they are mounted in a framework of recreation, are accepted without offense and taken like a beneficial medicine sweetened with jam.

Such counsels, based upon natural taste and observation, have their special significance for the many and varied circumstances of life, and in one respect they are of inestimable importance; namely, one learns to observe oneself instead of constantly directing critical glances at others.

ON THE NATIONAL CUSTOM OF SALUTATION

A capital old dancing master from the middle of the previous century, M. Mereau, who served at the Court in Gotha, has written a book entitled *Thoughts about Deportment* which contains a host of valuable suggestions to the *beau monde* of that day. In particular, he teaches young gentlemen how to behave in polite society, at the same time cautioning them against a number of bad habits — for example, appearing in front of ladies with their hands in their pockets, and so forth. Manners, dress, and carriage have changed considerably since 1760, and I dare say much of what I myself have remarked in the present work will be considered "old-fashioned," not only in the next saeculum but in a very few years. I shall therefore pass over the "American" extravagance that characterizes a portion of our cigar-smoking youth, and concentrate on one (in my opinion) important expression of the civilized manners of a nation, namely, the custom of *salutation*.

There are among the different nationalities so many nuances in the concept of courtesy that it would require a lengthy travel description to emphasize the distinctive stages of civilization in this specific area. While in one country politeness is the prerogative of the upper classes, in others it is considered an obligation of the poor; and at the same time as we see civility and affability declining among nations which are considered the most cultured, we find the most exquisite attention among races where the benefits of modern civilization have been but sparingly scattered. How often do we notice that displays of courtesy gradually diminish with every step that brings us closer to the capitals!

A traveler is always—justly or unjustly—inclined to judge a country by the reception he has been given there; and I dare say it is a forgivable vanity that we inhabitants of the North usually wish to give the foreigner a favorable impression of our home. Our native land is therefore reckoned among the places where the traveler feels most "comfortable." He finds the gentle manners of the public most appealing. He encounters many who do him the pleasure of speaking his language. Families open their circles to him without distrust and without the demands of ceremony. He finds security on the streets, devotion in the churches, attentiveness at the theatre, seemly gaiety in places of amusement, and everywhere he goes, menfolk stand with hat in hand. "The Danes are a very polite people indeed!" This testimonial is heard everywhere abroad.

Bowing, dropping a curtsey, doffing one's hat or touching one's cap, waving, or shaking hands with someone are the generally accepted forms of greeting. It is impossible to set down hard and fast rules for all times, situations, or personalities; but one central principle ought to pervade every greeting—namely, *good will,* which is in fact synonymous with true courtesy. Such a concept is as far removed from gracious condescension and indifference as it is from slavish submission and obtrusiveness.

Who does not know the lovely reply which Thales—one of the seven Wise Men of antiquity—made to a person who was astonished that a passerby had paid no heed to his greeting: "Is it to *my* shame that I am more polite than he?"

The noblest philosophy is found in the behavior of the courteous man. He asserts his own dignity in recognizing that of others. He spreads happiness about him and senses it in his own inner being. He does not walk too close to majesty and never humiliates the poor. He stands on his rights but guards against conflicts. In short, he makes life happy for himself and those around him, and for the cheapest price into the bargain, for the proverb says with truth: "Courtesy does not cost money."

I have often endeavored to explain to my pupils, especially when they are offstage, the importance of a friendly greeting, and I have represented it as a benevolent disposition reflected in a mild countenance. Such an expression is not achieved by external means, but only in this way: in the many and complex circumstances of daily life one must always think of words that are filled with kindness and civility. The child who from his tender years is used to saying "Please" and "Thank you" and is in the habit of showing kindness toward servants, respect for teachers, and politeness toward his brothers and sisters, but who above all learns to treasure his parents' satisfaction as the greatest reward, is well on the way to a most satisfactory development in the direction of amiability.

There is certainly a greeting in every enthusiastic exclamation evoked by the beauty of nature. We hail the ocean, the first bird of spring, and the newly blossomed beech forest. The sailor salutes the symbol of his homeland in the waving flag, while the wanderer sets foot with awe upon his natal soil. Religious holidays are greeted with the ringing of bells and trombone chorales, and those of the native land with thundering cannonades and cries of "Hurrah!" Even the grave demands its salute. And from the little child whose first compliment consists of a kiss blown from tiny fingers, to the old man whose trembling hand extends itself in a blessing at the solemn moment of death, all certainly bear witness to the importance that lies in the custom of greeting.

A salutation is often of greater value to the giver than the receiver. There are, to be sure, displays of veneration which are given without the slightest expectation of a reply; for the Southerner who bares his head before the wayside cross, the Arab who bows in the desert sand before the rising sun, and the Frenchman who pauses with hat in hand to let the meanest funeral cortège pass by, do not think of getting anything in return. They are merely gratifying a pious impulse; and even here at home, where demonstrations are not the order of the day, I have seen a man-in-the-street lift his hat on hearing the name of an honorable deceased or upon passing one meaningful monument or another. As a peculiarly romantic case in point, I will only state that an old mechanic at the Royal Theatre, one of "Holmen's old guard,"* took off his cap every time the curtain rose for a performance, and one evening—it was the first time that *William Tell* was performed—as the last note of the overture sounded, he dropped dead at his post.

On the other hand, if we regard the greeting as a mutual sign of friendship or courtesy, there obviously can be no question of who is to greet or be greeted first. He who recognizes a person and makes himself known most quickly has the advantage of being regarded as the most gallant, while he who is afraid lest he be inferior in *courtoisie* never puts his pride on the line. It follows as a matter of course that in this respect there are duties which are incumbent upon the young, the subordinate, and the cavalier as opposed to old folk, superiors, and ladies. Nevertheless in this area it is just as wrong to insist on precedence of rank as it is to absolutely demand the right of way.

I have known great men who asserted their positions by the most exquisite politeness; their favor thereby received tenfold value, and even when they had to refuse a request, the disappointment was softened by the humane form in which it was couched. Their commands sounded like the most modest wishes, and they never received even the most dutiful service without the most affable thanks. Who indeed could deny such noble individuals the ac-

*See footnote, Vol. II., p. 173.

claim that is due them? On stepping across their thresholds, one perceives from the master himself down to the humblest servant a manner and bearing that bear witness to the deepest sense of human dignity. There Fortune's gifts have come to the right place.

It would grieve me to learn that these views belong entirely to a vanished age. And yet I am tempted to believe that what I have just stated about the special use of the greeting may seem to the younger generation an antiquated theory, founded partly upon old French and partly upon scenic principles.

To this I will only reply that the *old* France rather than the new was the school of urbanity, and that the stage remains the touchstone of everything offensive and ridiculous that fashion and the spirit of the times can beget. For that matter, the fundamental rules stated below, which have not been drawn from any textbook but are simply the result of diligent observation, might serve our successors as historical clues to the evolution of civilization.

We greet those closest to us, both at home and abroad. We salute our friends, our pastors, and our teachers, even if for obvious reasons these individuals do not immediately recognize us. We bow with proper respect to our superiors and to those in whom the dignity of our mother country is represented. But as for those with whom we are but slightly acquainted, those for whom we have no respect, and finally, those who either ignore or hate us: how are we to behave toward them?

With people in the first category, a nice greeting will always be proper. However, it must not bear the stamp of familiarity, and we must indeed guard against seeming as if we would force our closer acquaintance upon people who are half-strangers.

A person can be mistaken; he can also be misunderstood, even innocently slandered. We are not called to be judges, and even less executioners. A display of respect can perhaps raise his spirits, but a sign of our scorn might throw such a man into despair. Suppose he was guiltless: then we ourselves have certainly done him an injustice. We will therefore unconditionally greet him, not coldly, but not with artificial cordiality either. We shall only do it in the way in which we might wish to be treated were we in his place.

Is one then to salute one's enemy?

I dare say it does take quite an effort, but certainly our sacred religion exhorts us to a spirit of conciliation, and even the heathen Sages have taught us that we should make friends of our enemies. Let us see whether our kindness might not be returned with a milder disposition on his part. Hatred is like a poisonous wound upon our soul. If such a hurt could be soothed, perhaps even cured by politely lifting one's hat at a given opportunity, surely it would be worth the effort to try such an inexpensive remedy.

It is undoubtedly a nice practice in society as well as in private encounters for total or half-strangers to be introduced to one another, and thus be informed of each other's name and occupation. But from this it ought not to follow that one dares not show even common politeness to an individual with whom this ceremonial has not been duly observed. I have met people who under such circumstances have felt most unpleasantly affected by a greeting and answered it in a repellant fashion. It is for an alert observer an almost absurd comedy to see guests at the home of a close friend gape at each other with cold, staring faces, until the moment when the host performs the introduction, which is often done so quickly and indistinctly that one neither grasps nor remembers the names of those in question. In fact, it is somewhat immaterial, for people usually eat and drink and enjoy each other's company without continuing the acquaintance. Why, afterward they do not even bother to greet one another in the street! This is unfortunately "high fashion," but it can hardly be called pleasant.

The marks of respect which are accorded a royal or princely personage do not, of course, apply to his retinue. The latter therefore does not have to respond or return the greeting that is addressed exclusively to the central figure. It is quite another matter with the passivity that is shown in several nations when one is accompanied by a friend or kinsman who chances to meet an acquaintance of his who may not have been introduced to the rest of the party. I dare say that here in our inclement clime someone could think of a more convenient way of greeting people than continually baring the head. But since this has become an established custom, it is most discouraging to have one's friendly or respectful greeting, as it were, meet with protest from the person one has saluted.

Then should we also greet those whom we do not know at all?

According to the old school, it is said that at all parties every one of the invited guests is to be regarded as "known from birth," and as such he ought to go out of his way not to disturb the joy and cordial atmosphere. The stranger who enters a salon owes the company a *general* greeting, which in turn provides him with a general, albeit tacit, welcome. If one is traveling by public conveyance, if one eats at the *table d'hôte* or sits down on a bench occupied by another person in a public garden, one may offer a greeting without the benefit of a temporary introduction. The same applies at the theatre when entering a box, or in the stalls when, in passing, one must inconvenience those who are seated. Another polite custom handed down from the old days is that of stepping aside and making a salutation if one meets a lady or an elderly gentleman on a staircase. Besides, when out in the country we delight in seeing wayfarers greet one another with a "How do you do, the Lord be with you," there is something inside us that tells us we ought not to be inferior to a simple peasant in politeness.

I will now conclude this no doubt too long-winded dissertation with a friendly and respectful *greeting* to all who believe in the union of the good and the beautiful. I shall also express the wish that in all our actions, be it in work or at play—nay, even in our anger—we might submit ourselves to the gentle dominion of the Graces.

ON COMPLIMENTS AND APPLAUSE

THERE is supposed to be a passage in the Koran that says: "Speech is silver, but Silence is golden." Now whether this statement is valid in all its consequences, I shall let stand for what it is worth; nor am I able to define the full significance of Speech or Silence; and yet it seems to me that the relationship of Speech to Thought is the same as that of the Body to the Soul and must be regarded as a talent that ought not to be buried but exchanged, even carry a high rate of interest.

One says of things that are valuable and difficult to obtain that they can be had "for money and a good word." Another old proverb teaches us that "a good word always finds a good place," and when it is at once sincere and couched in the form of thanks or encouragement, it often has just as much value as a good deed, and only then does it deserve the name of compliment.

It is the same with compliments as with the grape: both can strengthen or weaken, depending on whether they are enjoyed in moderation or to the point of intoxication. Like wine, compliments can be adulterated and, especially, misused in order to flatter vanity, ridicule with folly, or ensnare the innocent. It is not so easy to array a compliment in suitable form, since every exaggeration takes on a touch of irony, while even with the greatest sincerity it is not at all difficult to say unpleasant things to people. It takes but little practice to become adept at speaking and writing nothing but impertinences, and this skill is all the more tempting as it is generally more entertaining for the onlookers than are kindness and civility. And yet we must all admit that praise, whether it be more or less deserved, positively delights us while even the mildest criticism tastes like medicine: wholesome and salubrious, but never really pleasant. I dare say there are many superfluous and highly puerile compliments to beauty, finery, and other occasional excellences, while true merit is accorded little or no attention. However, it cannot be denied that acknowledgment loudly expressed and given at the proper time works like a warming ray of sunshine. It contains mental nourishment for an industrious child and provides food for thought for a considerate housewife. For the faithful servant as for the simplest worker, an encouraging and appreciative word is often worth more than a hard-earned daily wage, for the latter certainly gives him bread but the approval teaches him to love his trade and strengthens in him the desire for new undertakings.

Even for the glories of nature a loud verbal sign of admiration must not be lacking. Just let a Dane show you his beech forest, or have a Norwegian lead you up to the view from his haughty mountains while you preserve your cold and silent *nil admirari* — then you have wounded his national feeling, deprived him of a delight, and perhaps even lowered yourself in his estimation.

"But," objects the person who either out of bashfulness, verbal poverty, or usually just plain laziness keeps silent when he is pleased but never lacks expression for his discontent, "I do not know how to say pretty things or to feign an enthusiasm which I do not feel." To this I will reply: "Do you yourself think you can do without acknowledgment, and are you actually so rich in self-confidence that you do not need the approval of others?"

It is quite interesting to explore how one may be friendly without sugary sweetness, courteous without falseness, in short, how one can give a compliment without flattery.

In order to appreciate something good and beautiful, one need not feign either astonishment or enthusiasm. As a rule there is but little excellence, and almost no perfection, in this world; but "handsome," "worthy," and "clever" are expressions that can be used for efforts which are not crowned with complete success, and we are not obliged to season this encouragement with the wormwood of criticism.

As I have earlier stated, there are people for whom words can never express joy; but just let them become really angry and they soon find enough to say! Others keep quiet because they do not have pearls of wisdom ready at hand, not to mention those who remain silent out of mischievousness, self-importance, or just plain envy. The majority of these persons think they deserve praise because they never give compliments.

It is certainly true that the word can often become "as sounding brass," but after all, what good is a bell if it does not make any noise? It is wrong to speak where one ought to keep silent, but it is even more harmful to keep silent when one ought to speak.

Good words can often overcome ill will, cheer the despondent, beautify the moment, and be preserved for the future among precious memories. Let the Arabian proverb say what it will about Silence being golden, Speech is more than both gold and silver: it is *bread!*

A compliment, as it is here understood, can be applied to any object which makes demands upon the attention and acknowledgement of *the individual.* Applause, on the other hand, is a *collective* expression of approval and, in a manner of speaking, an official mark of sympathy on the part of *more than one person.* Its purpose is partly to dispel the fright which the person appearing before the public naturally experiences, to put him in the proper mood and encourage his efforts, but chiefly to promote and reward his talent as well as sustain his desire to please a discriminating audience. This essentially applies to the art of the stage.

However, it is just as important for the writer as it is for the performer to appeal to what is best in the audience's taste. To entertain and please this personal and impersonal concept, which is made up of such unequal elements, must seem almost as impossible as the task of bringing its various sentiments into fairly conclusive agreement.

In the first volume of *My Theatre Life* as well as in a number of smaller pamphlets, I have expressed my regret at the indifference with which the more intelligent part of the public relinquishes the right to express its opinion to the often rude and ignorant masses. To be sure, one must acknowledge the attention which here at the Danish Royal Theatre, more than in many other places, is directed to the stage, and the good arrangements that prevail with respect to curtain calls and other ovations, and—above all—the banning of official *claqueurs;* but it is nevertheless an anomaly, nay, a real misfortune, that the incentive for any applause must come from the pit or the gallery, both of which, especially in our Theatre, by their total lack of comfort attune the mind to fretfulness, and by reason of their profound darkness can serve as hiding places for cabals and ambushes conceived for reasons of personal animosity.

Among the audience in the boxes and the stalls it is considered bad manners to voice approval but normal to hiss anyone who dares to violate etiquette, regardless of the fact that the performing artist might fancy that he hears in such a protest an expression of displeasure. On the contrary, they allow the oracle of public opinion to emanate from the cheaper seats, and when the occupants of these remain silent, the whole performance is considered poor and boring.

I have for many years, and not without interest, followed the various expressions of approval and disapproval on the part of our audience but have never been able to discover any fixed standard for its demands, let alone its aesthetic viewpoint. I have seen the same yardstick applied to talent, mediocrity, and absurdity. Debutantes who were greeted with thunderous cries of jubilation became unimportant and forgotten, while outstanding ability had to forge its way to recognotion only through a Purgatory of scorn and neglect. I have seen a rarely gifted artist halted in the midst of a brilliant career by a rather small coterie of personal enemies who chose to pursue him into a domain where he could not defend himself, while the very public which had followed his excellent performances with delight did not lift a finger for his rehabilitation. It would not even have taken half a score of strong arms to toss the jealous cowards out the door, as is the practice in Paris with anyone who dares to disrupt the peaceful course of the performance and defy public morality.

One must, in truth, be astonished that in a highly civilized nation and alongside a feeling for decorum and fair play there could exist such a crude means of expression as *hooting* in the theatre and that this custom is even warranted by law. Some witty fellow from the days of Absolutism declared that the Danish people were possessed of only two guaranteed rights: freedom of the pavement, and hooting.

It is a national peculiarity that in a theatre where a round of applause has never lasted for sixty seconds, five long minutes are barely sufficient for the hissing of a piece; and if a young chap gets it into his head to violate the provision forbidding him to whistle before the performance is over, he can, for a fine of five rixdollars, acquire the right to interrupt a play and inflict upon the artist a public mockery which in a sensitive temperament can destroy a whole career, nay, even produce a fatal grief!

There are few theatres in the world that would be able to show such conflicts of opinion as those which have prostituted our auditorium. Musicians like Boïeldieu, Spontini, Rossini, Bellini, and Meyerbeer have been hissed in their most celebrated works, and usually for reasons having nothing at all to do with the theatre (*vide Little Red Riding Hood, Fernando Cortez, Gazza Ladra, Straniera,* and *Robert of Normandy*).

Must one not both laugh and cry when one thinks how Kuhlau's and Weyse's superb compositions, *The Magic Harp* and *Ludlam's Cave,* were trodden in the mud and sacrificed to the fanaticism of the literary feud between the supporters of Baggesen and Oehlenschläger?

In his *Brutal Clappers* our great poet Ewald may say what he will about the warranted presence of a watchman's whistle in the theatre. I, however, cannot regard this barbaric instrument as a suitable organ of public opinion in artistic affairs: for a single whistle is in a position to make its minority voice heard above several hundred cries of "Bravo." Furthermore, at a premiere it can only have been brought about as the result of a preconceived plan. What sentiment can one then expect from a listener or spectator who carries an instrument of murder in his pocket and impatiently awaits the curtain's fall as the signal to plunge it into the actor's or writer's breast?

Thus, although one should not place too great emphasis upon noisy demonstrations, either of approval or disapproval, applause nevertheless remains a necessary sign of life in the theatre. It forms a bond between the stage and the amphitheatre and produces the interplay needed for the spiritual existence of the drama. Good humor and a bit of fantasy are the ingredients with which every artistic treat ought to be seasoned. For the artist, silence is generally a sign of coldness and discord; in any event, it cannot simultaneously express both satisfaction and indifference. It is of importance for the performer to know if he has struck the right chord; if he loses the desire to please his audience or if he becomes indifferent to its applause, he stands in danger of falling into self-idolatry, and with this the development of his talent ceases.

There are certain occasions when one can, as it were, spur the awakening of the refreshing manifestations of life which applause brings, as for example at the premieres of new works, upon the convalescence of a favorite artist, or when one internal quarrel or another has brought a bit of sensation into the theatre. *Gala performances* have always been red-letter days of boredom. But aside from this, more frequent or more sparing applause is, for the most part, aimed solely at the performer who stands apart [from the rest]: thus personal favor is the decisive factor. People applaud the *individual* but rarely *the thing*. That which is well thought out or worked out, lovely and successful, produces only quiet results, while the collective achievement of the actors — which is often the most splendid and meritorious element in the performance — goes unnoticed or is only half-perceived. People laugh at the comical and are gripped by the moving, and those expressions are, in fact, the best applause. But there are performances in which genuine artistry is predominant, and here the applause, whatever form it assumes, must be the barometer for the impression that is being produced.

It would be ungrateful of me if I were to forget the many instances in which I and my work have received honorable proofs of the favor and indulgence of the Danish public. However, I cannot deny that many a time I have felt disheartened and dejected (perhaps more on my colleagues' behalf than on my own) by a *noticeable silence* that has the same effect upon an artist's mind as drought and night frost do upon fresh vegetation, and, combined with other factors, will sooner or later lead to the decadence of the theatre.

ON THE DECLINE OF THE SCENIC ART

IN the following, I hope to prove that I am not one of those old people who, extolling only that which is past, ignore the merits of the present day; nor do I profess to belong to that sect of artists who do not credit the living, but praise only the dead; and only with reluctance would I be reckoned among those who despair of the future of art and believe that after their time will come the deluge. However, it is necessary to point out the decline in which the dramatic art finds itself at the moment, after having reached one of those zeniths which hardly any other century has known.

Voltaire, in his *Siècle de Louis XV*, refers to the elevation that had taken place during the brilliant age of Louis XIV and states that French art and literature in his own day were but pale reflections of vanished greatness. At that time it was Philosophy that suppressed Poetry; consequently, the theatre vegetated during the time of the Revolution. It picked up a bit under the Empire, but only blossomed forth with renewed vigor during the Restoration — less, I dare say, because of any measures taken by the government than because the "fullness of time" had come; for without doing an injustice to the past or present, one may with perfect truth regard the years between 1820 and 1850 as the culmination of the lyric and dramatic art, not only in France but in all of Europe.

I have previously spoken of those celebrities whom I have had occasion to admire at home as well as abroad, and I will have an opportunity to mention still more; but I must first be permitted to enumerate those creative geniuses whose productions illuminated the three decades mentioned above. I shall then ask any art lover whether one does not have reason, by way of comparison with that period, to call our present time (reflective and hypercritical indeed, but unfruitful as regards both straw and grain) "the seven lean years"?

Germany had already reached its culmination with Schiller, Goethe, and Lessing, but France had Delavigne, Lamartine, Victor Hugo, Alexandre Dumas, and Scribe! In Sweden and Norway the lyric was predominant, and only a few of their poets wrote for the stage; but in Denmark, in addition to Oehlenschläger, Ingemann, and Heiberg, we possessed Boye, Søtoft, Hauch, Hertz, and Overskou; and also among the younger authors H. C. Andersen, H. P. Holst, Arnesen, and Hostrup. In the world of music rich veins flowed from the Parnassus of composition, and many of these treasures were of benefit to the theatre. Beethoven, Mendelssohn, and Weber in the first line; Marschner, Seyfried, Reissiger, Glæser, C. Kreutzer, and Lortzing in the second maintained the precedence of Mozart's native land in the sphere of harmony, just as Spontini, Rossini, Bellini, and Donizetti triumphed in the field of song. But French dramatic music reserved for itself the right to furnish every year valuable new contributions to the lyric repertoire throughout Europe. After Cherubini, R. Kreutzer, and Berton had replaced Méhul, Grétry, and Dalayrac, there appeared Boïeldieu, Hérold, Halévy, the prosperous and prolific Auber, the light and lively Adam, and finally the magnificent Meyerbeer, whose finest works belong entirely to French opera. At this time we still possessed Weyse, Kuhlau, and Schall, and the contributions that our younger composers Hartmann, Gade, Berggreen, Bredal, Rung, and Løvenskjold have furnished for the Danish opera all fell within the above-mentioned period of time.

If one now looks to the talents which the court theatres of Vienna and Dresden possessed at that time, together with the notables who gave the greater and lesser stages of Paris such an extraordinary brilliance — if one enumerates, in addition, the outstanding personalities who at Covent Garden and Drury Lane vied to present Shakespeare's masterworks in the most worthy fashion — one will be astonished at the tremendous toll which the last twenty years, in particular, have taken.

In the year 1830, Danish drama possessed, in addition to a respectable company of second- and third-rate talents, the following outstanding artists:

Among the older actors	Frydendahl, Lindgreen, Ryge, Rosenkilde, Winsløw, Foersom, and Jfr. Jørgensen.
Among the younger ones	Nielsen, Phister, Mme. Wexschall (later Nielsen); Jfr. Pätges (later Fru Heiberg), and several years later, Jfr. Natalia Ryge.

If one now ponders the fact that of all these important stars Phister is the only one still active, and that later years have enriched the Theatre with only four *genuine* acquisitions, two of whom have already been lost, one will come to the conclusion that our dramatic stage, once so renowned, nowadays finds itself considerably weakened.

It is an undeniable fact that everywhere in the theatrical world opera has taken the upper hand, to the detriment of the spoken drama; and despite the old claim that here in Denmark the ballet has stood in the way of the latter, it must nevertheless be admitted that among us both of these arts blossomed simultaneously and that the retrogression here at home, as well as in other places, has been the signal for a decided upswing of the lyric stage.

Has opera, then, really made such rapid strides that it has had to crush the other art forms?

If one inquires as to the present state of singing in Italy, France, or Germany, one everywhere meets with the same lament over the lack of ingenious new compositions, good voices, musical understanding, and a dramatic method of singing. The whole judgment of operatic talent is now based upon the *volume* and *intensity* of the voice—that is to say, range and power—without particular concern for beauty and delivery, which results in the fact that the finest younger talents are "sung out" or, more properly speaking, "screamed out" in only a few years.

Nowhere have the great stars of the older school, whom I have discussed in the first volume of *My Theatre Life*, been compensated for; and even though here in Denmark, but particularly in Stockholm, they have bestowed the greatest care on the opera, they have still not been able to prevent it from "limping" for want of tenors or sopranos, just as on the whole voices of either extreme have rarely been able to satisfy the demands of both the music and the action. But what merits, then, make the opera so far superior to the spoken drama?

(1) The altered conception of the theatre in general. The deeper reflection, the more subtle observation, and loftier inspiration have gradually been supplanted by dazzling illusions in costumes, decorations, and machinery; loud nervous shocks, astounding accomplishments, and sensuous attractions. A large portion of the theatregoing public has no love of mental exertion, and one can go to and from the opera, particularly the Italian opera, without being troubled by reflection.

(2) A cosmopolitan repertoire which, as a consequence of its intrinsic value, is suited to every epoch and can to an even greater degree than genuine drama be revived and refreshed by a change of cast.

(3) Finally, the oft discussed materialistic view of art, which makes physical endowments the foremost qualification for assessing the worth of an opera singer or an actor. In a singer, next to a voice, a handsome appearance combined with careful instruction is enough to let him appear successfully in principal roles and even to evoke an enthusiasm which at a distance resembles that which is aroused by genius. However, one is greatly mistaken if one thinks it possible to form an actor or actress from

any pupil who happens to have a harmonious vocal organ and unconstrained emotions. Almost everywhere there are "nurseries" for growing dramatic talents, and one meets scores of lovely and very sensible young people who can not only argue about art, but by industry and careful training have even gone so far as "not to ruin any role." And yet, if one would light Diogenes' lamp in order to find among the younger generation a fairly independent—let alone original—talent, one might indeed search for a long time!

What, then, can actually be the reason for such a curious "crop failure" of outstanding actors?

I dare to offer the hypothesis that it is the equalizing process, which runs through all of modern life and manifests itself in so many other situations, that is causing *coryphées* to disappear, while over-all skill is becoming more and more common. People do not make such amusing blunders as they did in the old days, but then, striking flashes of genius are no longer the order of the day. In short, the great "types" are disappearing from the boards of the theatre as well as from the stage of the world, and even the distinguishing features of the various social classes are being wiped out by the leveling influence of education and upbringing. There are almost no "characters" who could furnish material for the preparation of the actor; and he himself from childhood on is kept within the measured bounds of daily life and has hardly had an opportunity to develop the *fantasy* and *dreams* which were so prominent among our most ingenious actors and which made great performers such as Frydendahl and Ryge into unique "types."

What applies to the performing art is even more the case with the various kinds of dramatic writing. For the moment, the latter has been driven back to a very limited terrain. Everywhere the meagreness of material, or rather its uselessness, is deplored. The stock comedy figures and *commedia dell'arte* characters that were of such great use to Molière and Holberg, Gozzi and Goldoni, are completely worn out, partly because people no longer grasp their meaning, and partly because they do not actually have any genuine authority. Mythology and allegory are completely anathema, and the classical drama has almost tempted the same fate as, for instance, historical painting, which is received with respect and piety but is bought only by the State. Parody has laid hold of the heroic element of antiquity and the sentimental quality of the Middle Ages; the bourgeois drama from the *école larmoyante* of Iffland and Kotzebue is laughed to scorn, as are costumes from the time of Clauren,* while Romanticism can assert its rights only to the extent that it permits an admixture of the comic element.

People always want something to laugh at, and if character sketches or situations are to win some interest, they must be gathered from the events of

---

*The pseudonym of K. G. S. Heun (d. 1854), a very popular German writer of novels known for their vulgarity and lasciviousness.

the day. Now although domestic life is not without its conflicts, and the present offers both complications and passions enough, these are either too Philistine or lie too close to us to be given a poetic treatment; and however much we may appreciate the talent with which the new French authors know how to put together their well-made plays, these are but seldom suited to our ideas, and even more seldom—thank Heaven!—to our situations. Our modern repertoire is therefore composed mainly of national genre pictures and photographs of everyday life which, I dare say, do not exclude a poetic interest, but give our actors too little opportunity to move in a wider sphere; and what is more, they even rob them of life and color, like those painters who occupy themselves solely with pen-and-ink drawing.

When something is threatened with ruination, it often happens that those who ought to be the most interested in preventing the destruction content themselves with blaming one another for the joint misfortune. Thus it happens in politics as well as in that miniature world, the Theatre.

Artists, authors, managers, critics, and finally the audience accuse one another, and if sentence is passed in this matter, it must, in my opinion, be based on the following premises:

The artists' egotism all too often makes them blind to their own true interests and those of art.

The authors are too much guided by the whims of fashion, and rely on certain popular personalities for the success of their pieces.

The managers at theatres supported by public subsidies regard their office as a dignity without business, and the private entrepreneurs theirs as a business without dignity. With both types of managers the words *art* and *aesthetics* are generally regarded, if not as heresy, then at least as hollow phrases.

The critics (about whose sacred mission I could go on for a whole chapter) have in certain respects misunderstood their times. It is no longer a question of *damming up* the overflowing mass of good subjects; the rich flood has *dried up* and now, more than ever, is badly in need of dissection and investigation in order to re-emerge. It is not enough to use the hoe to root out the parasitic plants; good vegetables must be coaxed forth, and we lack skilled gardeners. These people are usually a bit cross, but one must pay no heed to this so long as the garden does not become barren.

The audience, who must always take the blame whenever corrupt taste tries to gain the upper hand, has in fact made only one mistake, which, however, makes up for many others: namely, *lack of independence.* It continuously blames theatre administration, but is all the same content with anything. It allows itself to be dazzled by tinsel and all too often flatters caprice and vanity. It frequently adopts the divergent judgments of the newspapers, permits *the mob* to represent the entire *public,* and almost always forgets that the motto of our Theatre is: "Not for pleasure alone"!

bad, after all. There are almost always full houses and, even if the higher genre is in hibernation, they still give pretty good plays. If first-rate new works do not appear, they simply revive old plays, and even if we cannot pride ourselves on possessing actors as great as those who shone at an earlier time, this lack is compensated for by the *ensemble* and *stage arrangement,* two things that are making unmistakable progress." It is not my intention to interfere with my good readers' dramatic enjoyment, but since I have now touched upon *the evil* and its main source, in the following chapter I shall treat the rather interesting subject of the two aforementioned *merits* of the modern theatre.

ON STAGE DIRECTION

(With Notices of Swedish Dramatic Artists)

THE art of "mounting a piece on the stage" has two main divisions: the *ensemble* and the *arrangement.* It cannot be denied that the former has gradually triumphed with the disappearance of great celebrities from the stage; for it is a fact that the latter wished to shine completely alone, and where several actors of the same strength were present on one stage there often arose a competition which in opera and ballet might certainly have its interesting moments, but must in the spoken drama have a harmful influence on the action as a whole, where the effects are dependent mainly upon a proper distribution of light and shade, and where a measure of virtuosity must be sacrificed to the advantage of characterization.

Therefore, in the area of the *ensemble* there was at an earlier period little or no place for direction. This consisted merely of a more or less difficult compromise among the actors themselves, and was especially noticeable only when one happened to recognize the touch of a predominant talent in the *arrangement,* which generally followed certain fixed traditions, just as certain categories of roles bore the names of famous predecessors.

As far as scenery is concerned, in the old days it was downright modest in comparison with what is now demanded. By "the old days" I am not referring to Shakespeare's time, when they had no decorations to speak of and when the twenty to thirty transformations in his tragedies were denoted by a placard. I am simply talking about the era that preceded the climax in our theatre history, of which I have previously spoken. What people at that time called magnificent décor would nowadays make us laugh.

A comfortable boudoir usually consisted of a table on either side of the proscenium and, at most, four chairs. They were as little acquainted with the conception of "closed rooms" as they were with tree borders and practicable buildings. The disposition of crowds was reduced to marches, processions, and tragicomic battles. There was no question of "correct" costume, and the same furnishings and domestic utensils readily did service for ancient times, the Middle Ages, and the present.

However, with these poor external resources there were *achieved* dramatic effects far surpassing those which are at present *striven for* with the use of the greatest luxury.

Now the question is whether, between the poverty of that time and the superfluity of the present, there could not have been found a middle way that would have put stage properties in their proper place as accessory and not (as is now the case) cooperating, nay, *overwhelming* factors in the drama.

Whether scenery complete in every detail dampens the actual scenic impression or merely conceals its weaknesses, stage direction, together with the appurtenant external properties, has now become a matter of crucial importance compared with what it was formerly; for people hardly suspected its existence and, at most, regarded it as belonging to the matériel of the theatre. Nevertheless it is true that just as an orchestra would have a much greater effect if the high-throned conductor were completely invisible, so too any play whatsoever would become far more attractive if the rehearsal and arrangement were blended together with the performance to such a degree that one would never be aware of the controlling hand. With a cast of able, ingenious, and independent artists the stage director's work is either *easy* or *impossible;* for the actors in question have either at first glance struck the right note [with regard to the character] or individually created an imaginary picture that resists any alteration or moderation. However, since it often happens that a third of those with whom one has to work are recruits and the other two-thirds uninventive professionals, one may count oneself lucky if the actual core of the piece is in the hands of real artists. The task becomes all the more difficult for the director who tries to bring about a satisfactory ensemble and who responds even more to the critical eye and orderly hand; for he must function as teacher and, if possible, be a good actor himself so as to point out the various details. Here it is a matter of influencing the players in a manner which leaves no trace of imitation, but allows them to retain their individuality and make people believe that it is the actual invention of the actors themselves.

I have often performed this feat in the special field that was entrusted to my leadership, namely, *the ballet,* where the mimed portion cannot be left to the performer's own discretion or direct inspiration, but where it is nonetheless necessary that the personality appear in its most varied nuances.

In *the opera* I have also had the opportunity for interesting experiences, since singers do not generally claim dramatic independence and are, moreover, constantly being torn out of the situation by the traditional forms of the music. It was only during my three-year activity as Intendant for the Swedish stage that I succeeded in realizing some of my ideas concerning the mechanics involved in the proper rehearsal of a play.

At the Royal Theatre in Stockholm, as in a number of other places, the actors during the so-called *collation* of new plays scheduled for performance had acquired the habit of jabbering or spelling their way through the script, each taking notice only of his own role and, on the whole, neglecting the diction to the degree that the main impression—if one could imagine that such a thing could be achieved by such sloppy treatment—was certain to be destroyed and the author placed in an even worse light, as a thorough condemnation of the play is almost always the outcome of this sort of gathering.

I unconditionally demanded that the parts be read through at home so that they might be spoken with a fair amount of characterization at the collation. Next I tried to awaken an interest in the plot and poetic value of the piece by focusing the attention of those concerned on the roles of their fellow actors. And finally, with regard to the author and his work, I requested that everyone maintain the proper discretion, which is the principal requirement for the success of a piece on the stage, where the art essentially consists in concealing shortcomings and in emphasizing merits.

They came to an agreement about the time needed for studying their roles, and with my scenario already written and annotated, I arranged positions, entrances and exits, decorations, props, and processions, usually eight days before the first actual rehearsal. But at this rehearsal all speeches had to be known completely by heart so that the play would not be hindered by faulty memorization.

It had almost become a rule that the more talented an actor considered himself to be, the more carelessly he treated his rehearsals, reserving for himself the right to take his colleagues by surprise at the first performance. This bad habit had the natural consequence of either beginning the actual dress rehearsals only at the performance—or, what was even worse, long-suppressed and now unleashed humor or gushing pathos produced images all of which were rooted in the usual old forms and quickly became stereotypes. I know that almost everywhere there are artists who uphold the view that the finished working out of a character before the evening of the performance is bound to weaken the thrill that should come in that decisive moment before the audience. To this I reply that regardless of the fact that the art of acting cannot be the only one in which mastery is gained without practice, surely experience has abundantly confirmed that only when a role has been presented at many and repeated performances do its nuances properly come to light. From this it follows that if it is not done correctly *before* the public presentation, and the play runs but a few times, it will never have been satisfactorily performed.

I succeeded in convincing most of the artists involved of the advantage of my system, and I soon got them to work out their roles at serious rehearsals. Through these practice sessions the characters were quite differently evolved, new figures emerged, and far greater security was achieved, to say nothing of

how much more interesting my own duties became and also of the reas-
surance that was bestowed on the authors, who before had been close to despair. At the same time, the stage work became more comfortable and entertaining. The older actors influenced the younger; the more clever, the weaker
ones; and, what was most important in many respects, the pieces could be
given with fewer rehearsals.

I went one step further and arranged dress rehearsals with full costumes
and properties, and, despite a bit of opposition here and there, I had the satisfaction of seeing that not only did the grand opera shine with its ensemble,
but the spoken drama also came to assume a place in the public's favor which
it had never known before. Thus, during the three years that I served at the
Royal Theatre in Stockholm, I mounted nearly fifty lyric as well as dramatic
works, and among the more important productions in the latter field, I will
here mention:

Shakespeare's *Richard the Second* and *A Comedy of Errors.*
Beskow's *Torkel Knutson.*
Hedberg's *Day Waxes.*
Wijkander's *The Order of the Amaranth.**
An original Finnish play, *Daniel Hjort.*

Because of the successful experiments mentioned above, one must permit
me to undertake a small digression from my original subject in order to pay
well-deserved tribute to some of Sweden's finest dramatic acting talents,
whose presentations I will not later have the opportunity to discuss.

It is but a poor indication of the progress Scandinavism has made among
us that the artistic, and particularly the dramatic, talents of that neighboring
kingdom are so unfamiliar to us and, consequently, are even underestimated.
To be sure, we are acquainted with the names of several literary notables, but
I almost feel as though I am stating something completely new when I call to
the attention of Danish art-lovers the fact that at the Royal Theatre in Stockholm there are actors who are not at all inferior to the finest in other
countries.

Even though the Swedish dramatic stage has not known a flowering like
that which I have previously indicated at the Danish Theatre, it must, like us,
mourn the passing of many unreplaced (if not irreplaceable) talents. The
graceful and ingenious Emilie Högqvist, the witty Fru Eriksson, the humorous Fru Bock, the comedian Sevelin, the character actor Torslow, and above
all the Swedish Roscius, the incomparable Lars Hjortsberg, rightfully assume
places of honor in Thalia's pantheon.

To compare or to weigh stars of this magnitude against our Danish actors
who play the same type of roles might easily incur a charge of partiality and

---

*This was the most famous order of the eighteenth-century Swedish Court.

national arrogance. Suffice it to say, they are spoken of with awe by the younger generation and preserved in the grateful memory of all connoisseurs.

Niels Almlöf

Endowed with every physical advantage and a physiognomy that bears witness to his French origin on his mother's side, he is one of those rare actors who have known how to exchange the celebrated roles of leading men and heroes for the less rewarding but psychologically richer roles of *pères nobles,* while also being able to interpret Shakespearean drama and the most subtle nuances of high comedy with equally great natural truth. When one has seen him as King Christian in *Elves' Hill,* one must admire his grasp of historical characters; and when as Erik of Pomerania in Blanche's *Engelbrecht and his Dalecarlians* he softens the impression of this royal villain by his noble deportment, all must admit that everything he touches receives the stamp of beauty.

Edward Swartz

He is one of those actors in whom one feels uncertain whether it is nature or art, feeling or thought, spontaneous inspiration or profound study that must be considered predominant. His youthful, noble facial features actually ought to have marked him for romantic leads, and in these he has indeed won many laurels; and yet it is character portrayals that are his forte. Here, as well as upon the conception of his dramatic vocation as a whole, the masterworks of Shakespeare have brought their influence to bear. If one has come to know his multifaceted talent, for example, in his appearances as the weak and faltering King Birger, the iron-willed Gustavus Vasa, the overwrought Richard II, and finally in the role that comprises the whole of the actor's art, Hamlet, one must rank him among the finest dramatic artists of our time. He is all the more entitled to this distinction as he has had no direct models but, like all genuine talents, has forged his own path.

I cannot deny myself the pleasure of comparing his masterly performance as Hamlet with the most excellent representation I had seen of this colossal role till then, namely, that of Høedt, whose acting in my opinion was superior to that of all his Danish predecessors and even outshone those I had seen in this part abroad—that is to say, in England itself, artists such as Macready and Charles Kemble. Swartz had interpreted the character in the same manner as Høedt. Their personalities, even their accentuation of a number of essential details, were similar. Only two things were different, but in these they perhaps counterbalanced one another. That is to say, Høedt had greater force in the ironic passages, for example, in the tirade about playing on the flute; whereas Swartz's transition from sane reflection to feigned madness was more distinct, and thus more effective. But to me they are both unforgettable!

Dahlqvist and Fru Hjortsberg (Née Westerdahl)

With these two performers, each in his kind an extraordinary talent, there cannot be a moment of doubt about the question of natural gifts and the relationship of scenic instinct to reflection and study. In both these actors there is to be found such a wealth of fantasy and feeling that these qualities must in many instances silence even the sternest critic. Unfortunately, a chronic illness has all too early removed the outstanding actress from the stage, but Dahlqvist still remains as a powerful type of a character actor. His powers of transformation are so great that whether he is to portray a king or a peasant, a knight or a soldier, a virtuous martyr or a scoundrel, he always manages to find a striking picture. But what constitutes his chief merit is his genuine *Swedishness*. As Torkel Knutson, Erik XIV, and Engelbrecht he must be considered unsurpassable.

Elise Hwasser (Née Jacobsson)

This *artiste*, so rich in fantasy, is undeniably the most prominent female personality of the modern Swedish stage. The most striking thing about her is that she bears a certain resemblance to Jenny Lind, and also has the same *visionary look* with which that great singer appeared among the Druids in *Norma*. A subtle irony seems to be part of her nature, wherefore she is not perfectly suited to the genre of romantic heroines but shines especially in romantic interpretations of female "characters," those of whimiscal children of nature, eccentric young ladies (such as are to be found in Birch-Pfeifferresque† adaptations, for example), and wherever a concentrated passion eventually bursts into stormy emotion. Furthermore, there is great variety in her excellent gifts, which have not yet reached their peak, and I dare say it is with injustice that some of her less zealous admirers claim to know her *utantill*, that is to say, by heart; for from her fantastic Puck in *A Midsummer Night's Dream* and her roles in drawing room plays to her interpretation of classical antiquity, there runs through her repertoire a considerable diversity that would be all the more noteworthy could this remarkable actress only be convinced of the benefit of *thorough* rehearsals.

It would be to refuse *Beauty* and *Elegance* the praise that is their due were I to pass in silence

Fru Selma Hedin

whose services to high comedy are universally recognized.

---

† Charlotte Birch-Pfeiffer (1800–1868) was a popular German actress and playwright of her time.

Even though the comic element has always been more weakly represented in Sweden than here in Denmark, Jolin, Broman, Svensson, and Nyforss deserve to be mentioned as superb reproducers of Swedish national
types (the first of these gentlemen even being an especially prolific dramatic
author). There are in addition two outstanding figures for modern French
comedy: Svante Hedin for the good-natured bon vivant, and Knut Almlöf as a
comedian who is multifaceted, tasteful, and true to nature.

I cannot leave these dramatic precincts of my memoirs without discussing
two celebrities who, though they did indeed come from Stockholm's secondary theatres where the requirements have always been fewer and more
humble, have all the same very often been rivals for the artistic laurels of the
finest Royal actors:

Pierre Deland and Edward Stjernström

The former, of French extraction, had his main strength in portraying old
French eccentrics and Swedigh gallomaniacs. The latter has distinguished
himself in every possible kind of role and, though his sphere of activity
marked him for a lower genre, he has always shown a praiseworthy striving
for classicism. In accordance with the precept of Caesar, both have long preferred to be first in a village rather then second in Rome. They both became
managers and autocrats at their respective theatres, and often acted as such.
Deland deviated from the above-mentioned principle, saw his nimbus vanish
on the boards of the great Theatre, and died shortly after his all-too-late debut. Stjernström has retired into private life, preserving his reputation as an
outstanding actor.

As I joyously and gratefully include the names of these fine artists in this
album of mine, my readers may be completely assured of the sincerity of my
judgment. If I have not accompanied the well-merited praise I have given
them with some critical observations, it is because in this book I wish to
avoid appearing as a reviewer as much as possible: for in the dramatic sphere,
shortcomings like false declamation, hollow pathos, exaggerated comedy, and
so forth, pertain to the physiology of a play; but in the history of art, only the
best of what is achieved deserves to be preserved.

I shall now return to stage direction, and with regard to the arrangement shall
call attention to the great difference between the theatres which play for such
a numerous population, as is the case in first-class European capitals where a
successful piece may be given hundreds of times over, and those which, with
a smaller audience, must constantly renew their repertoire and therefore can
expend neither as much time nor as much money to mount a play.

It is Paris, of course, that has led the way for the enormous progress made
in the so-called *mise-en-scène*. Oddly enough, it came from the Boulevard

theatres and the Circus, where the most astounding things were performed and apparently served to fill empty spaces and conceal weaknesses. The Opéra was forced to go along with, nay, even to surpass, those spectacles, and soon displayed such magnificence in the way of scenery and costumes that it literally crushed the lyric drama. I confess that the first time I saw a performance of *Les Huguenots,* which was sung by the finest talents, I was so blinded by panoramas and magnificent processions that the music became a secondary interest, and I came away from the opera with a feeling of fatigue and disgust. On the other hand, I acquired an active appreciation of Meyerbeer's finest composition only when I heard it, sung by a much weaker cast and with a very modest décor, at the theatre in Copenhagen!

This extravagance with regard to external accessories, the abundance of which in Berlin and Petersburg has risen to an even higher degree than in Paris and London, has of late unfortunately become requisite for the progress and success of opera. And thus as they now conceive of the ballet abroad, it consists—apart from serving as a setting for the virtuosity of a certain individual—of nothing but pyrotechnic *coups de théâtre,* machines, and surprises, without the slightest trace of scenic motive, let alone a coherent plot.

It goes without saying that the demands for luxury must also have extended to the spoken drama, and since drawing room pieces are usually set amid the fashionable life of the salons, it has now become a special study for the stage director to seek out not only the most modern but also the most varied furniture, along with all its little niceties! Nobody realizes how difficult and expensive it is to carry out such a thing, or how much it contributes to creating *a distraction* rather than *an illusion,* and finally, what long intermissions are caused by having to shift it. Rarely do people care about the merits that lie in the actual rehearsal, but woe to him who has failed in this so-called *arrangement!* He is considered a bungler in his profession, and the dignity of the theatre is declared to have been imperiled.

However, one must do justice to one branch of the stage that has made real progress, namely the costuming. Nowadays it has become an actual science, and in the research as well as its application the French set us an example worth following. I dare say that what is suitable to the character still has a hard fight to wage against that which is becoming, while the correctness of a costume must combat what is merely brilliant. Ideas of what is *beautiful* are continuously dependent upon the whims of *fashion,* but the true magic of a play is realized only when the situation is supported by a faithful picture of time and place. Unfortunately, I have all too often had to recognize that only with the utmost difficulty are the demands of the ballet, and especially of modern dancing, reconciled with authentic costume. But where all theory finally breaks down is with *the prima donnas,* both in drama and in opera. As a rule, they give their imaginations such free play that they go beyond the bounds of history and geography. There is nothing to be done about this. Try to persuade them and you are laughed at. Give an order and they go into convulsions. Tell them that their talent is beneath contempt; they will let it pass. But call to their attention the extravagance of their toilette; they will never forgive you for it!

I shall conclude the present chapter with the observation that a stage director's work is the most unrewarding and, in part, the most unproductive of all as long as he does not have a voice in the acceptance of plays and the casting of roles. That this voice ought not to be the decisive one goes without saying. But since every success must be of importance to him, and since he can hardly guarantee it if the proper resources are not placed at his disposal, he must perforce be in contact with the authors and motivate the use of the finest talents.

My position as Intendant for the Stage at the Royal Theatre in Stockholm was based in part on just such an intervention into artistic affairs‡; and since many were unable to distinguish these from purely administrative matters, I was, according to the circumstances, praised, censured, or opposed as much as if I had been the theatre director himself.

‡ Cf. section "Three Years in Stockholm" later in this volume.

II

The Year 1848

WHEN I signed my contract in Copenhagen in November of 1829 and hastily returned to Paris in order to free myself from those obligations that bound me to the French Opéra, the eighteen years that were stipulated in my contract* seemed to lie before me like a boundless horizon filled with countless resolutions, plans, and expectations but with only *one* certainty: that is to say, should I manage to reach that distant goal, my career as a dancer would be finished. The years vanished, and when I looked back upon this important period of my life with a feeling of wonderment mingled with sadness, the whole thing seemed like a dream.

I was in my forty-third year, and still possessed both strength and energy. However, several pains—consequences of my strenuous vocation—which I could barely manage to forget while onstage, hampered my practicing and reminded me that I must soon cease to be a virtuoso. The prospect of appearing only as a mime did not appeal to me at all, since I was accustomed to a certain degree of bravura and was, moreover, convinced that people would not wish to see me retire into a secondary place. Therefore from the beginning of the year I busied myself with preparing a series of my ballets so that I might bid farewell to the stage and to my numerous admirers among the Danish public in my finest roles. My contract guaranteed me the privilege of spending my pension abroad, and after the cool reception my latest works had met with, it seemed as if my powers of invention could no longer live up to demands here at home. Thus I was not averse to accepting a temporary engagement at one of the larger theatres abroad, thereby rendering fruitful my past experiences.

Meanwhile, as I have already mentioned, I was most pleasantly surprised by the sympathy that greeted the publication of *My Theatre Life*. It was perhaps the last book to have been read by King Christian VIII. His Majesty was delighted with my candor, agreed with a good many of my artistic views, and ordered that the necessary steps be taken to once again attach me to the stage, if not in a performing capacity then at least in a directorial one. I was hereby afforded the opportunity to appraise the fine tact with which my superior at that time, Overhofmarskal von Levetzau, conducted the negotiations con-

---

*From April 1, 1830, to March 31, 1848.—A. B.

cerning my contract, which were interrupted by the King's illness and ensuing death.†

Denmark barely had time to mourn, much less contemplate the magnitude of the loss the fatherland had suffered with the passing of this brilliant King. It is true that he died at a rather advanced age, but his spirit was young. There were light and warmth in his presence, and our country flourished during the eight happy years of his reign. He loved beauty, whose personal representative he was, and under his peaceful scepter art enjoyed its Golden Age.

It was a true pleasure to work for such a discriminating master; for though he was a real connoisseur and was capable of giving one the most tasteful advice, he did not hold blindly to his preconceived opinions but granted the artist independence with his favorite saying: "Art is free!" Aye, his sense of justice, his versatile knowledge, his eloquence, and the patience with which he bore opposition would have made him a model for a *constitutional* monarch had motives belonging to the realm of higher politics not prevented the granter of the Eidsvold Constitution from becoming the founder of Danish freedom.

The King's good will was misunderstood; his desire to share his pleasures with the people was interpreted as a plot intended to distract their minds from more serious endeavors; his wish to spread Denmark's fame throughout other lands was represented as vanity and a preference for "the foreign." In short, an incessant stream of indecorous scoffing, which he should not have taken to heart, filled his short reign with anxiety and bitterness, and it can hardly be doubted that misunderstanding and grievances hastened his end.

What Christian VIII did for his country and what he neglected to do, perhaps through an excess of caution, history must judge in the future. But *one thing is certain:* he knew how to value art, and for this artists ought to be eternally grateful to him. For us, in his mild eye there lay feeling, encouragement, and satisfaction, and we had to admit that—even apart from his majesty—we stood before an excellent man. Let us cherish his memory!

Frederik VII ascended the throne, and in acclaiming him, the people hailed the rosy morn of freedom. This dawn came for Denmark—but shrouded in storm clouds. Hardly had the deceased monarch's body been borne to the resting place of his fathers than the February Revolution broke out in Paris. Together with his family, Louis Philippe, whom I had seen idolized by an adoring people, was driven from the very country which owed to his wise rule eighteen years of uninterrupted peace and prosperity.

As if ignited by an electric spark, flames of revolt spread across the entire European continent. Germany raged, and everyone—with the exception of the Danish government—anticipated an eruption in Holsten and Slesvig. Both from those who regarded us as the slaves of absolutism and from those who

† After having suffered several heart seizures earlier in the month, Christian VIII died on January 20, 1848, at the age of sixty-two.

sought to undermine our young freedom could we expect a violent attack; while the powers from whom we might have expected help had enough to do with their own affairs.

During this imminent danger a large crowd of zealous patriots, some of whom managed to remain cool-headed, gathered at the Casino to discuss the lawful means of getting out of this confusing situation. They decided to walk to Christiansborg in solemn procession the following day and, by means of a deputation, to ask the King for a change of government.

As an artist, I held aloof from all political demonstrations and could now be a spectator at an interesting drama. I saw people gather in most orderly fashion at the Town Hall, heard the melody "Danmark deiligst Vang og Vænge," and from a window on Gammelstrand viewed the whole procession of citizens as they marched across Højbro to the Palace Square, where they stationed themselves before the façade while an enormous crowd stood waiting behind them in almost solemn silence.

The delegation was admitted without resistance, and when its members returned from the audience, there burst forth from every side a jubilant "Long live the King!," whereupon everyone returned home. And thus occurred the event which the enemies of Denmark and freedom called a revolution.

The following morning one read in the official papers that a new and liberal ministry had been appointed, and two days later we received news of the treasonable surprise attack on Rendsborg.‡ The uprising began with Olshausen's invectives against the whole Danish nation: "An idle, lazy, irresolute people."

In the midst of this uproar my new engagement for seven years was contracted; and when on that occasion I proffered my humble thanks, His Majesty expressed his great worry about the coming times.

It was with the ballet *Valdemar* that I concluded the series of my farewell performances just as the call-to-arms sounded throughout the land, and my finest military supernumeraries, my stalwart warriors from "Grathe Heath," stood ready to march off the following day. The ballet had a strong feeling of the overwrought mood of the people; frantic bursts of applause accompanied all the patriotic situations, and when, toward the end, Valdemar burst the chains of tyranny and blessed the whole kingdom to the melody of

---

‡ On March 18, the independence of the Duchies of Schleswig and Holstein was declared at a meeting held at Rendsborg. On March 24, the fortress at Rendsborg, which contained both stores and ammunition, was seized by rebellious Holsteiners, touching off the Danish-Prussian war of 1848–1850, other events of which furnish the material for later chapters in *My Theatre Life* – e.g., "The Fair on Behalf of Distressed Jutlanders" and those immediately following it. The war itself was but one episode in the conflict over control of the Duchies – a centuries-long struggle, dating from the Middle Ages, that involved not only dynastic rivalries but also, at one time or another, the territorial or political interests of most of Europe's Great Powers. The end came in 1864 when Prussia invaded and conquered the Duchies, which in due time were annexed by the newly formed German Empire: an outcome bitterly resented by patriotic Danes like August Bournonville.

"Danmark deiligst Vang og Vænge," both the audience and the cast sang the ballad as if with one voice! I enjoyed the honor (unusual at our Theatre) of being called before the curtain, and in this way celebrated my last appearance on the Danish stage.

I was now a perfectly free man from April 1 until July 1, the date on which my new contract was to begin, and so I allowed myself to be caught up in the events of the day.

Together with eleven of my colleagues, I enlisted in the King's Corps of Volunteers, all of us convinced that the "Green Coats" from Classen's Have* were indispensible where the going was rough. I joined the Society for Order and Truth. Speech was free: I spoke; the press was free: I wrote. My tendency was the *patriotic-loyal* one; my Scandinavism was *neighborly,* not *unionistic;* the *constitutional monarchy* was my ideal of a form of government. "Life and limb for King and country! Denmark's honor and independence!" was my motto.

It is impossible to describe the mood of feverish excitement that during these fateful days animated the populace of Copenhagen, and thence spread throughout the land. Holger Danske had awakened from his long sleep! Danger was imminent, but no one could say with certainty whence the first blow would come. Copenhagen's fortifications were strengthened—perhaps in expectation of a new 1807.† The people had but one thought: "If the battle is to be forcibly waged, we must all take up arms." Wives and mothers raised no objections; adolescents armed themselves and learnt to drill at the side of sedate old bureaucrats. In a proclamation the King had called all loyal subjects to the fight, and all were ready to obey.

What emotion! What enthusiasm! Day and night the streets echoed with singing and cries of "Hurrah!" People from the most varied social classes mingled with one another, while blessings and shouts of jubilation accompanied the departing divisions of troops. Crowds were the order of the day, yet nowhere were excesses to be seen; and when a delegation of the worst agitators of the revolt drove up to the Palace to negotiate, only a few deputies from the aforementioned moderate society were needed to keep the furious mob in check.

Since I was a rather good shot with a rifle and had no difficulty mastering the manual of arms, after only six weeks of training I, together with 150 other Volunteers, was presented to General Krogh, who highly praised our speed and precision. During the course of this training, we had word of the victorious affair at Bov, and after two weeks of inactivity, which followed this initial success, we received, one after the other, reports concerning the battle at Slesvig, the alarm at Flensborg, the engagement at Oversø, and the retreat to

---

*See footnote, Vol. III, Part One, p. 368.

† In that year Denmark, trying to retain her neutrality in the Napoleonic wars, refused a proferred military alliance with Britain. As a result, the British attacked; Copenhagen was bombarded for three days before capitulating, and the entire Danish fleet was surrendered to England.

Als. "Whatever may happen, our honor has been saved," it said in the Minister of War's manifesto.

It was not uninteresting to study the impression these sad events made upon the various temperaments. In some, the irresistible urge to fight was suddenly dampened, since it was impossible to hide the fact that there was still no apparent talent for leadership in the Danish army, and it is not exactly pleasant to risk one's life and limbs without even the slightest prospect of victory. However, it must be said that most people were agreed that we had been driven back by the superiority of the enemy. The Prussian generals were not witch doctors; if we could but muster a considerable force to pit against them, luck might turn in our favor. Only now were people really filled with the desire to go to war, and from all quarters volunteers flocked to battalions formed by reserves and reinforcements. The sympathy which people had always cherished for the King's Volunteers caused them also to expect something extraordinary from the Corps on this occasion, and the belief that we would be called upon to act as sharpshooters was therefore universal.

We were only awaiting the order to set out. But no orders to march were forthcoming and, on the whole, they little understood how to make use of the enthusiasm of the moment; for when the latter had given place to more mature deliberation there was issued the chilling statement that the militia, which had formerly been considered a mobile unit, would not operate outside of Sjælland. Now, since it was increasingly thought of as a "national guard," the Corps had only to defend the ramparts of Copenhagen in the event of a possible siege. Thus it was quite certain that the Corps would never see action again, for we probably would not be involved in a series of bombardments as in 1807.

Several of the Volunteers now issued an appeal to the older and younger members of the Corps asking them to meet in order to come to a decision regarding its activity in the war, and the question was raised as to whether the Corps could mobilize three hundred volunteers, out of its present force of five hundred men, who would support the army as a special rifle brigade to be used wherever they were needed.

The discussion was dominated for the most part by the officers of the Corps, who were not particularly anxious to march since by such an expedition most of them would be jeopardizing their occupations and their whole temporal welfare, while it was consonant with the statutes that the Corps should defend the hearth in the event of an enemy attack on the capital. One old Volunteer spoke up and expressed his willingness to go, but only on the condition that the Corps was given different officers and better rifles. With respect to this last condition, one can hardly imagine anything worse than the arms which had been distributed to the Corps in accordance with the latest regulations. Rifles had suddenly been exchanged for the poorest kind of muskets, thereby depriving us of our greatest strength: the sure shot. It seemed almost a mockery of our desire to fight or, perhaps, a means of rendering us harmless in the event of a riot. A list which was presented for signatures received the names of only ninety officers and Volunteers. The proposal had therefore failed, and as a result it was decided that the Corps should await the highest orders but that any Volunteer who wished to join the battalions of the line would have the Corps' permission to do so.‡

With this my military career was finished; for even though I would have been willing to risk my life on the field of battle, aye, perhaps even to show some bravura, I was already too old to become a soldier of the line. And so I had to content myself with watch duty and participation in some small field manoeuvres. I became a member of the King's Volunteers' Benevolent Society and won a number of friends in that fine civic organization. I also joined the Four Skilling Collectors' Society and had the pleasure of raising 4000 Rbd. for the wounded and for the survivors of the fallen. I visited the lazarettos and, while bringing as much relief as I could, gained an increased respect for the Danish soldier: marvelous in adversity and suffering!

I now discovered another way in which I could serve my native land: I offered the Foreign Ministry my services as a French translator of any writings they wished to distribute as information concerning our political situation. My first work in this area was Overskou's pamphlet on "The King of Prussia and his Conduct." It was not easy to render this work into French, and I was only halfway through when the Ministry ordered me to discontinue the editing and gave me instead a very well written German dissertation by Conferentsraad Höpffner. I translated it into French with the utmost care, as I later did Wegener's pamphlet on "The Duke of Augustenborg and the Uprising." Both of these writings obtained extraordinarily wide circulation in foreign diplomatic circles; but since the former had to be completed quite rapidly and I had to work on it eight to ten hours a day for a couple of weeks, this sedentary life, coupled with my overwrought state during the events of the war, brought on a gastric typhoid fever, the several crises of which kept me bedfast in town and at Fredensborg.

I rose from my sickbed a living skeleton. But with the news of the Malmö Armistice, peace also returned to my mind. Ideas once again flowed in to my ballet portfolio, and even before I was allowed to walk about as a convalescent, I had roughly sketched the outlines for *Conservatoriet* and two other compositions, which later materialized as *Abdallah* and *The Flower Festival in Genzano* [*Blomsterfesten i Genzano*].

I began the theatre season by training younger artists in a number of my own roles, and I had the pleasure of seeing the Ballet retain the interest of the public. In early October I read in *Berlingske Tidende* that His Majesty the King had bestowed upon me knighthood in the Order of the Dannebrog. I confess that I was deeply moved by this honor, which had been recom-

‡ Many of our comrades took advantage of this and fought in all three campaigns; some fell, a number were wounded, but a good many covered themselves with glory, advanced, and graced with their presence the Corps' anniversary celebration in 1851. — A. B.

mended by the Foreign Minister, Count Knuth, as recognition of my diligent services to the Ministry. And yet I was saddened by the thought that my humble contribution should enjoy the same reward as that given to those valiant men who had risked their lives for their country. It was only when the King himself most graciously assured me that he was not conferring this honor upon me for my demonstrated patriotism alone, but mainly because of the skill and zeal I had displayed as an artist, that, with a beautiful and encouraging feeling of the full emancipation of the theatrical profession, I accepted this Cross, which had not been given to a stage artist during the last thirty-seven years, and then only on the condition that he never perform again. Now the ice had been broken and the principle firmly established that no branch of art is excepted from being honored by the citizenry.

Several extraordinary events are associated with years containing the number 48. In 1448 the Oldenborg dynasty ascended the throne of Denmark; in 1648 Christian IV died; and in 1748 Frederik V opened the Royal Danish Stage under Holberg's auspices. Unfortunately, political events had preoccupied people's minds to such a degree that the Theatre's centenary was not remembered until it was quite close at hand. December 18 took us by surprise, as it were, and if Overskou had not sounded the alarm, it would have slipped by unnoticed. Since the writers as well as the theatre directorate were unprepared, it was decided to celebrate the jubilee with Holberg's *Lying-in Room* [*Barselstue*] and, if possible, a new ballet.

I was asked to compose something to fit the occasion, and since I practically had to improvise, I naturally fell back upon my old besetting sin: the allegory. I pictured an Olympian festival where Holberg, Ewald, and—since I felt that Sweden should also be included—Bellman appear, surrounded by their genii and pictures from their poetic inspirations. Unfortunately, our excellent (except for his less than lukewarm Scandinavian sympathies) Theatre Chief, von Levetzau, could by no means accept this Norwegian-Danish-Swedish combination, and rejected my idea as completely unsuitable. I was angry, but mastered my emotions; and though my head had previously been filled with details for *Conservatoriet*, I managed to come up with a more fitting subject that met with my superior's approval, and, with only a few days of rehearsal, evolved one of my most successful presentations: *Old Memories* [*Gamle Minder*].

And thus I ended this year, which was so unforgettable to me, by embarking upon an entirely new series of my compositions, which inaugurated both the second saeculum of the Royal Theatre and the second period of my own career.

III

Old Memories

(December 18, 1848)
*(With Notices of the Finest Members of the Ballet
from 1829 to 1864)*

BEFORE raising the curtain on my reminisences of an activity that in a short while will also be reckoned among "old memories," I must pay off *an old debt* not only as a due acknowledgment but as a clarification of a passage in Volume I of *My Theatre Life* that has been misunderstood, or rather, misinterpreted; it is when I say in speaking of my association of many years with the corps de ballet:

> I acknowledge and commend those artists who perform in my ballets, delight in their glories, and admire their talented interpretations . . . *but I owe them nothing.**

This last and, I dare say, not-too-well-chosen expression must be understood in this way: when the score between my pupils and me is settled, and, on one hand, one weighs the effect that a good performance has had on the success of my ballets, but, on the other, the influence I have exerted not only upon the development and use of the respective talents but upon the whole status of the company—I do not think that I will be found in arrears. Nevertheless, I feel a deep need to accord my fine colleagues a voluntary tribute of true acknowledgment by preserving their names in this album of mine, and while I intend to spare the present as well as the future a critical representation of the imperfections of all those in question—and who has not done the same?— I will strive to place their qualities and merits in the brightest sunlight of truth. Therefore, though sincerely praising the skill and artistic participation of both the younger and older members of the *corps de ballet,* it is my intention to include in the present list only those personalities who have performed mainly in my ballets:

FREDSTRUP, SR., a veteran from Galeotti's time, the *père noble* in most of my older ballets, a good comedian and tasteful mime, from whom I have more than once received valuable advice.

ANDREA KRAËTZMER, *née* MØLLER, whose rare mimic talent, graceful

---

*See Vol. I, p. 33.

dancing, and interesting personality illuminated my earliest works for the Danish stage. Her performance as The Sleepwalker, Virginia, and Margaretha in *Faust* are unquestionably among the finest in this genre.

ADOLF STRAMBOE, SR., was a mimic actor gifted with an extraordinary dramatic instinct and an expressive physiognomy. In his particular line of work he was perhaps the finest I have ever come across. His comic humor was inexhaustible, and among a host of highly successful character parts, one must single out his masterly performance as the Jolly Englishman in *The Toreador*.

LUCILE GRAHN possessed all the qualities that distinguish a *danseuse* of the first rank. She was *my* pupil from her tenth to her seventeenth year, and fulfilled all the expectations to which her great natural gifts entitled her. It was actually she who gave our public the first idea of what female virtuosity in dancing should be, and her noble interpretations of the Sylphide and Astrid in *Valdemar* created epochs in the annals of the ballet. An irresistible hunger for fame drove her to Paris, where, after having developed her talent to a remarkable strength, she appeared to unanimous applause, and, by later dancing at the theatres of the major capitals, she acquired a European renown.†

FERDINAND HOPPE, at a time when male dancing has fallen into discredit—aye, even into degeneration—at most of the theatres abroad, has known how to uphold its merits by cultivating, without affectation and an excess of exertion, the light, graceful genre. He has also, within the sphere allotted to him, displayed a freshness and natural charm that made a stimulating impression wherever he was used as a dancer.

CAROLINE FJELDSTED, later KELLERMANN, a *danseuse* of considerable merit, which has been recognized both here at home and abroad. With no small degree of virtuosity she combined a lovely mimic talent which was

---

† Lucile Grahn, 1819–1907, is mentioned again in Vols. II and III—passing references on pp. 216 and 511, and a brief anecdote on p. 567 where Bournonville tells of meeting her in Munich in 1869 and renewing "the *best* of our common memories." Apart from these few lines, he says nothing else about this finest of his students and dancers, who is generally ranked among the half-dozen truly great Romantic ballerinas.

Although it is beyond the scope of these notes to explore those facets of Bournonville's career which he ignores or underplays, his reticence in this case—with its undertone of animosity—demands a further word. His phrase "an irresistible hunger for fame" hints that he felt betrayed by his star's disloyalty in seeking a more prestigious career than Copenhagen afforded. But a letter of 1854 from Grahn to Augusta Nielsen (quoted in Robert Neiiendam's biography of Nielsen, *En Danserinde* [n.e., Copenhagen, 1965], p. 86) depicts a quite different situation:

"My beloved parents sacrificed everything to make smooth my future path; aye, they almost starved in order to place all the costly gifts—silver tea and coffee pots and fruit dishes—at the feet of the Bournonville family. And when I was grown, my gratitude was demanded in another, far worse manner. The Master called these his 'bizarries.' I was very upset and decided to get out. . . ."

For details of Grahn's career, see Neiiendam, *op. cit., passim;* Neiiendam, *Lucile Grahn: En Skæbne i Dansen* (Copenhagen, 1963); Ivor Guest, *The Romantic Ballet in Paris,* pp. 179–184 and *passim;* Guest, *The Romantic Ballet in England,* pp. 109–112 and *passim.*

used to good effect in *Brahma and the Bayadère* and in *Napoli*, where her acting in the second act positively electrified both audience and company.

AUGUSTA NIELSEN, in her short theatrical career, has left behind her a name which is synonymous with lightness and "ladylike" elegance. These qualities have made her unforgettable as Céleste in *The Toreador.*

ANDREAS FÜSSEL is one of the personalities who have contributed essentially to the importance of my ballets as expressions of action and dramatic situations. He possessed strength, dignity, and a finely developed feeling for the plastic. His repertoire included the most diverse character parts, among which the Merman in *Napoli* and the Melancholy Englishman in *The Toreador* form two brilliant contrasts.

FERDINAND HOPPENSACH, a comedian whose full worth one can come to appreciate only by seeing what is offered in this direction at theatres abroad. Since the burlesque element has seldom been the predominant one in my works, he has actually had leading roles only in *Conservatoriet* and *The Kermesse;* but his minor parts such as the Street Singer in *Napoli*, the Fiddler in *The Crystal Palace* and the Sexton in *The Wedding Festival in Hardanger* are masterly types, performed with as much taste and moderation as originality and genuine humor.

PETRINE FREDSTRUP, the most outstanding member of a theatrical family all of whom possess talent, great zeal, and unusual intelligence. Though she has performed but rarely in the first line of the ballet's prima donnas, she still knows how, with care and correctness—aye, sometimes even with genius—to bring out the most interesting aspects of minor parts and to give every dance or role a unique character. Her superb acting as Norwegian peasant girls in *The Wedding Festival* and *The Mountain Hut* but mainly as the Troll Maiden in *A Folk Tale* mark her as a true *artiste.*

LUDVIG GADE is unquestionably one of the finest talents of the Danish Ballet. His genre is primarily strongly defined character roles, for example, those of Svend Eriksøn in *Valdemar,* the bandit Gasparo in *The Flower Festival*, Ola in *The Wedding Festival*, Svend in *The Mountain Hut,* and Bjørn in *The Valkyr.* As Ballet Director he has maintained my compositions long after my retirement, and to his taste and care I owe the fact that they still preserve a certain measure of freshness and interest.

LAURA STILLMANN, *née* STRAMBOE, an amiable personality, endowed with exceptional mimic gifts and an expression of naïveté that is both appealing and convincing. Her performance of a number of important roles, such as Nina, Fenella, and Asta in *The Mountain Hut* does honor to her powers of interpretation.

EDWARD STRAMBOE, like his sister, heir to a talent for mime, has in national dancing as well as in comic roles, particularly as Viderik in *A Folk Tale,* defended his position as an able member of our Ballet.

HARALD SCHARFF belongs to the most recent period of the ballet. He is full of life and imagination, and is unquestionably the finest leading man we have had since my own retirement. Scharff possesses many physical advantages, and by continued study he will no doubt assume a prominent place as a *mimic dancer.*

GEORG BRODERSEN has, as a performing artist, assumed only a modest place, but his activity as a *teacher* has been all the more extensive. From his school have emerged most of the younger members of the *corps de ballet,* and the insight and skill that guide his entire instruction, combined with his humanity and paternal care, can have nothing but the finest influence on his pupils' technical training and upon their whole moral character. It especially pleases me to recognize in my disciple and good friend the same striving for all that is noble and beautiful in art which has for so many years animated, and continues to stimulate, *me.*

JULIETTE PRICE is the one of all the priestesses of Terpsichore who, after Marie Taglioni and Carlotta Grisi, has come closest to *my* ideal of a *danseuse.* Though I by no means wish to place her virtuosity on a par with or above that of those celebrities whose strength lies in *quantity,* I still believe I am impartial enough to judge her talent in technical as well as aesthetic respects: and I must acknowledge that her dancing possesses not only perfection of training but is inspired by true feminine grace, which has spread a poetic air over the principal roles in most of my compositions and helped me to combat the prejudice, current among the opponents of the Ballet, that dancing is nothing but a frivolous feast for the eye.

Without wishing to diminish this dancer's merits, it must be said that her mimic as well as choreographic achievements, in contrast to most scenic phenomena, lose a measure of their effectiveness when viewed from a distance. Therefore I can hardly be mistaken when I say that, in order to fully appreciate her worth as a dancer, one must adopt a certain aesthetic viewpoint.

We therefore celebrated the Royal Theatre's centenary with a *Prologue* by H. C. Andersen, my little ballet, and, after many troublesome discussions, Holberg's *Lying-in Room.* The ballet, as is fit and proper, came at the end, and had the desired effect.

The subject was the birthday of the one-hundred-year-old Philemon, which is celebrated at a manor house in Sjælland. The old man, who was born on the very day that the Playhouse was opened on Kongens Nytorv, had been one of those ardent theatre-lovers we knew in our youth. But these types are gradually vanishing. One used to call them *amateurs* because it was love of art that had brought them to the theatre. They took notice only of that which was good and outstanding; their memories retained only what was excellent; and one therefore heard them quote nought but the most poetic tirades, hum only the loveliest melodies, and discuss "the elect" in the realm of art. It was under the influence of such men that the Danish stage experienced its flowering. Nowadays criticism plays all too prominent a part, and this at the expense of enjoyment. The word "to cultivate" has become obsolete, for reflection has taken the place of love.

The first scene shows us Philemon (so called for the significance of this name in Greek and in memory of Holberg's personal representative in *The Fortunate Shipwreck*) roused from his slumbers by Gluck's lovely sounds from Armida's magical garden — perhaps his first childhood lullaby! From several directions his relatives come, their arms filled with flowers, to bring him their congratulations. Some homelike family scenes follow, and then festive melodies call the old man into the decorated salon where he is greeted by a host of joyous friends who have prepared for him a surprise quite in keeping with his sympathies, by having transformed the background of the salon into a little theatre.

Philemon is led to the seat of honor, and as a festal gift his great-grandchildren bring him a magic lantern, which is placed so that the images which float across the stage are thought to have been produced by its prisms.

This lantern is to produce memories from the many years during which he attended the theatre, all to the accompaniment of pieces of music corresponding to the point in time and to the situations.

One sees the original Playhouse, and, in animated representation, Holberg and Ewald, surrounded by genii and several groups from their masterworks. Next come portraits of luminaries of the stage, from Rose, Schwartz, and Rosing to Frydendahl, Lindgreen, and Ryge; and, so that the ballet might not be forgotten, Galeotti and Bournonville, Sr., all surrounded by animations from their finest works.

In between each section of this series of tableaux are performed dances from the various periods, ranging from 1768 to the cessation of Philemon's theatregoing; and during an Italian *festa* his granddaughters appear as the Graces and offer him the cup of rejuvenation.

As a curiosity connected with the staging of this work, I must mention that the hundred-year-old Philemon was superbly portrayed by seventeen-year-old Axel Fredstrup, whose father (Fredstrup, Sr.) played his seventy-year-old eldest son! The second peculiarity was that we had to have the portraits copied, because the members of the drama were opposed to the "profanation" of the originals!

The ballet was given twenty times during one season and would have entered the standard repertoire had I not reminded the Theatre management that the whole thing was an "occasional piece."

IV

Divertissements

UNDER this name are included mostly the dances and pageants that are inserted into operas and ballets as festive aggregates which have no real relation to the plot. In our theatre vocabulary, however, it has also found the more independent application of denoting individual character dances as well as a succession of *pas* or so-called *entrées,* and finally as the designation of smaller *ballets* with loosely sketched motifs. Now while the real ballet (that is, the mimed representation supported by dancing, or the latter motivated by a dramatic plot) has had many and bitter opponents, people have almost always been willing to grant an unassuming bagatelle a place among theatrical works. But since I have always desired to assert the dramatic right of choreography, it is only quite by accident that my *divertissements* have appeared. Some of them were excerpts from larger compositions that had been set aside. Others owed their creation only to one festive occasion or another. But most of them were composed for benefit performances at secondary theatres and later enjoyed the honor of being danced on the stage of the Royal Theatre with more or less success.

DANES IN CHINA

A fragment from *The Isle of Fantasy* offering some comical scenes, a Russian *pas de deux,* a Chinese dance, and my own especially popular Sailor Scene and Hornpipe.

POLKA MILITAIRE

A Hungarian hussar dance for two couples. In this bagatelle I harvested more applause than in many of my most important ballet roles.

POLACCA GUERRIERA

Depicting a Polish nobleman who takes leave of his beloved, dances his last mazurka with her, and rushes off to fight for Freedom and the Fatherland. It met with a cool reception and quickly disappeared.

MARITANA

An attempt to reproduce through a carnival scene a living picture of the feeling that runs through Lumbye's masterful "Champagne Galop." It was not favorably received either.

THE PAS DES TROIS COUSINES

The first in a whole series of small compositions for the benefit of the Price family. Juliette, Amalie, and Sophie created an epoch with this dance, and were portrayed herein as a modern-day group of the Graces.

THE SAILOR'S RETURN

A scene with dancing between a young seaman and his beloved.

AN ECHO OF SUNDAY

A genre picture of Amager, portrayed by children and containing an echo of the *vaudeville*.

HOLMEN'S OLD GUARD

A little children's ballet performed by Nyboder lads and little girls. It concluded with an apotheosis for Danish navel heroes.*

LAS HERMANAS DE SEVILLA

A Spanish dance for the three [Price] cousins. The motifs were taken from the national songs "El Riqui" and "El Callessero."

---

*Bournonville had always been fascinated by naval life and was immensely proud of the exploits of the Danish fleet. Time and again in these memoirs, we encounter phrases such as "Holmen's old guard" and "Nyboder lads." It therefore seems appropriate to quote the description of these two Copenhagen "institutions" given by Jan Møller in *Borger i det gamle København* (Copenhagen, 1967), pp. 88–90: "The quarter of the city between the Royal Theatre and the harbor was built on Gammelholm, which until the 1860's housed the naval workshops. The many artificers here employed in building and repairing ships constituted, along with sailors and naval officers, 'Holmen's old guard'.... From the time of Christian IV there had been a whole town for these people and their families, Nyboder.... These long row-houses ... were at that time a world in themselves.... Children from Nyboder were, as a rule, enrolled in 'the old guard.' At eight years of age they entered school and were given uniforms: a blue jacket with anchor buttons, white trousers, and a shiny hat.... After finishing school, they often followed in their fathers' footsteps and became either sailors or naval artificers."

THE PROPHECY OF LOVE

A Tyrolean scene with a Changing Dance that takes place among three young maidens who consult the oracles of the flowers and the cards about their affairs of the heart.

THE FLOWER MAIDS OF FLORENCE

A graceful little jest. A reminiscence of my stay in Italy.

THE IRRESISTIBLES

Tempted by the success that most of the aforementioned trifles had enjoyed, and requested by private individuals as well as the Theatre management to create something that would not demand as difficult a preparation and as expensive a décor as the larger ballets, I came up with the idea of turning to account the current mood of the public to compose a *divertissement* which might have the charm of novelty at the Royal Theatre. But here I met with a defeat or, more properly speaking, got a bucket of cold water over the head because of the way in which my idea was interpreted.

The artist's life is filled with almost nothing but illusions; and yet, in spite of all his disappointments, he seldom learns from any of his experiences. In the year 1849, I was still so naïve as to imagine that the attraction which certain Hungarian and Polish dances had for the applauding occupants of the stalls—when they were performed by a single solo *danseuse*—was due to the Slavic and Magyar romanticism and characteristic melodies. For me the jingling of spurs and the rapid turns reflected the cavalry's courageous behavior, and I positively, absolutely believed that the enthusiasm which accompanied these feminine performances was produced by a knightly and martial elevation. But I was mistaken. It was not *that* at all.

For my talented Swedish pupil Charlotte Norberg I had arranged a little dance in which she was to appear upon her return to Stockholm. The music was Lumbye's *Greetings from Jutland;* the costume, the dolman and furs of a Danish hussar. It met with a brilliant reception, and in his newspaper one gallant Swedish theatre critic stated that if the King of Denmark possessed many squadrons of this sort of light cavalry, he could give this corps the same name Napoleon I had bestowed upon one of his infantry regiments: The Irresistible. The word caught on, and when at the same time I saw our handsome hussars, upon the return of the troops from the Fredericia campaign, pass through the streets on their prancing horses, bedecked with flowers amid cries of jubilation and the melody of "The Brave Soldier," it was clear to my imagination that the charge of these splendid cavalrymen must have been as irresistible to the enemy columns as their elegant uniforms were to the girls' hearts. I then pictured to myself in vivid colors the enchanting effect of a

AUGUSTA NIELSEN
Bournonville's "ladylike" ballerina is shown
as Céleste in *The Toreador*. Oil painting
by Lehmann. Teatermuseet, Copenhagen.

JULIETTE PRICE
She is seen as a young girl in this drawing
by Lehmann. Teatermuseet, Copenhagen.

BOURNONVILLE'S NORDIC GRACES

Sophie, Juliette, and Amalie Price in the *Pas des trois cousines*, 1849. Lithograph after the portrait by Lehmann. Teatermuseet, Copenhagen.

LA VENTANA

Juliette and Sophie Price in the "Mirror Dance" from 1856. Drawing by Lehmann. Teatermuseet, Copenhagen.

gliding host of modern-day *fylgjur* and *valkyries* who on the stage would re-call the memory of this inspiring moment.

With furs flying, plumes swaying, and sabers flashing, not only the young-est and prettiest but also the most excellent of the ballet's sylphides per-formed their dances with evolutions and simulated charges. At the trumpet's call they rallied round their standard, then paraded past the row of lamps while from the background the genii and tutelary deities waved to them honor and thanks. But this well-meant allusion completely failed to find its mark. The uniform, the melody, aye, even the graceful dancers and pictur-esque groupings were greeted with fashionable coolness. This was not the first time the "evil eye," like the Italian *jettatura*, followed my efforts from the dark wings and cast misfortune on my tiny brain child. But this time it struck a bit harder than usual and actively contributed to producing a wrong-ful view of the matter on the part of others.

From every side people cried out, "What is the meaning of putting skirts on hussars?" ... "It is a downright shame to allow our Army to be repre-sented by women!" ... "What boasting, to call our soldiers *irresistible*, and our *danseuses* are anything but that!" "Besides, it is humiliating to have hu-man beings perform steps that resemble a horse's gallop, etc., etc." The march past the footlights, which I had expected to be greeted with hurrahs, was made the occasion for a demonstration of dissatisfaction and scorn that was repeated at each of the nine performances which—entirely against my wishes—were granted this unfortunate product of my patriotic fervor. It was, in fact, nothing more than an "occasional poem," without any claim to mas-tery; but it was conceived with as much warmth as it was performed. I felt sorely wounded, not in my vanity, but only in my Danish heart.

LA VENTANA

It was several years before I ventured once more to "divert" my public. I sorely needed to avenge myself, and it was again at one of the Price perform-ances that I produced a little flower which was not doomed to be immedi-ately trampled underfoot.

For more than twenty years the theatres had resounded with the clacking of castanets. Fanny Elssler was the first to give Spanish dances a prominent place in the ballet by inserting her "Cachucha" in *Le Diable boiteux*, where it became the important climax. This same little dance was soon performed all over the world: it intoxicated the Yankees and even enraptured the Spaniards themselves in Havana. Marie Taglioni did not wish to take a back seat to her rival, but quickly had arranged for herself *La Gitana*, which hinted at a frivol-ity that did not seem to lie in the nature of the Sylphide.

Hundreds of *danseuses* imitated these models, but people north of the Pyrenees had not yet seen the native Spaniards' presentations in this genre. These were indeed a good deal different from what people usually called national dancing, but they did bear a certain artistic stamp, of which we received rather nice proof when Camprubí and Señora Dolores [Serral] appeared as guests in Copenhagen in 1840 and by their *jaleo* gave me occasion to compose one of my most popular ballets.† There later appeared a whole flood of Spanish *bailadores,* and since the latter tried to outdo one another in producing the kind of effects for which a certain type of audience clamored, they were not without a harmful influence on genuinely artistic dancing, which, to a more than seemly degree, seized upon the lascivious character of the *fandango.*

To combat this tendency in every branch of the stage has been one of my missions in life, and if there should be a future for my compositions, I hope they will bear witness to my efforts.

However, I was not blind to the pretty and romantic qualities to be found in the Spanish character. But here, as in everything else, it was a matter of determining what had a right to be put on the stage, of making the proper choice of material, then finding the most suitable way of using it. I wished to show how, without depriving the picture of its national physiognomy, one could idealize it and draw it into the dramatic sphere. Now in Spanish novels one always reads that the first declaration of love takes place outside the beauty's window, while she herself—hidden behind the closed jalousies—listens to her lover's sighs, which are accompanied by the mysterious strains of a guitar or a mandolin. A flower or ribbon tossed down from the balcony is a sign that this homage has been accepted, and the romance begins.

Just such a beginning provided me with the motif for a whole scene which, partly before a mirror and partly at a balcony window with closed jalousies, furnished the occasion for graceful dancing and expressive mime. The Señorita (Juliette Price) comes dancing in, fanning herself and thinking about a young man she has met at Mass or on the Alameda. She gazes at herself in the mirror, dancing before her image (Sophie Price). However, she soon tires of this, draws the curtain across the looking glass, and pensively sits down at the table. Suddenly she hears sounds outside. "It is he!" She seizes her castanets and dances to the accompaniment of his melodies. Finally she ventures over to the jalousie, pulls it aside, tosses down a topknot, and sheepishly steals away.

This bagatelle, to pretty music by Lumbye, was extraordinarily successful and was taken into the repertoire of the Royal Theatre. I later expanded it by having the Señorita's room transformed into a lovely garden with a terrace and luxuriant vegetation. The lover, enraptured by the token he has received, calls his friends together in order to celebrate his good fortune. The Señorita enters, enveloped in her mantilla. Timid and respectful, her lover approaches, repeating the refrain of his lover's lament on the guitar. She finally lifts her

† *The Toreador;* cf. Vol. I, pp. 84–88.

veil, seizes a tambourine, and her participation in the celebration is the best answer to his marriage proposal.

The final, impressive *seguidilla* was not entirely of my own composing but, rather, an imitation after Paul Taglioni. As it had a most enchanting effect and was in complete accord with my idea of character dancing, I did not hesitate to present it to the Danish audience, since I did not fail to mention its original source.

THE EARNEST MAIDEN

I have long been interested in observing the impression that theatrical dancing has on completely uninitiated children of nature, and to my edification I have found that the totally artificial left them cold and indifferent or, in the most fortunate case, made them laugh, whereas that which was genuinely *pretty* and *graceful* moved them to tears.

A biting criticism of the eccentricities of modern dancing was delivered by a man from Dalecarlia who happened to see just such a performance at the Stockholm Opera. His verdict consisted mainly of outbursts such as "Oh! Just look! Oh no!", and he finally turned his head away, crying rather loudly, "Gracious! She should be ashamed!"

I had the idea of depicting in a few short strokes the love of two young Sjælland peasants, protected by the Brownie of the place. Jørgen has an eye for Lise, but she finds him all too worldly and frivolous, for she herself is of a quiet, sedate temperament, goes about her housework, seldom laughs, and never dances. The Brownie, who has teased Jørgen on many occasions, is finally captured by the latter and must buy himself free with gifts—among others, a silken ribbon which has the power to change Lise's mind. But Jørgen has hardly tied it about her waist when she is seized with a peculiar excitement, kicks off her pattens, and displays an astonishing skill in the new kind of dancing. In his despair Jørgen wishes to flee from this enchanted spot and loads all his belongings onto a cart. But here the old fairy tale writer stands me in good stead as the Brownie pops up out of the bucket with his familiar "We're moving today!"† Jørgen regains his composure and soon realizes that home is still the best, for during the violent dance the enchanted waistband has flown off, and Lise, ashamed of her high leaps, promises to follow hereafter the smooth middle road. She becomes Jørgen's bride and just as an organ grinder comes strolling past with another merry pair of lovers, she joins him in a *Contreseire* (*Ça ira*) in true peasant style.

This little idyll or, more properly speaking, this woodcut after Chr. Winther's model, had a great deal of bravura when it was first performed at the small Court Theatre, but completely lost its effect when it appeared on the larger stage.

---

† A reference to Hans Christian Andersen's story "Moving Day." Moving Days were those on which tenants' leases customarily expired and people changed dwellings if they so desired.

POLKETTA

A *pas de deux* in a singular genre, it was the first (and I dare say the best) in a whole series of small dances I composed for a pair of interesting pupils, the sisters Agnes and Christine Healey, who had come hither from England in order to make their debut — in *Tivoli!*

They made such remarkable progress that they found engagements in Copenhagen as well as in Norway and Sweden. They eventually returned to their native land, and appeared at major theatres in Scotland and Ireland. But everywhere they went, they were a success in my "polketta," and this dance, as well as the rest of their repertoire, earned them the well-deserved praise that they did not resemble modern *danseuses* in general.

Our immortal bard Oehlenschläger, who loved me, has honored my works with the appelation of *poems*, and myself with the title of *ballet-poet*. Such an accolade is of some importance and is indeed the greatest honor that can befall a balletmaster, especially in our day, when almost everywhere choreography is being reduced to second- and third-hand copies and arrangements. However, since my activity included not only the stage but extended to a wider circle, I was also Court Balletmaster, and in this capacity had the opportunity to make interesting studies of a world with which the artist seldom comes into contact.

Thus, I have composed quadrilles, mounted tableaux, and arranged processions at Court festivities for both Frederik VI and Christian VIII, and thereby had to command, or if one would prefer, direct under conditions which were quite different from those that customarily prevail; for I did not have free disposal of the forces at hand. These were often excellent, but sometimes complete nonentities — only in choreographic respects, of course. The latter were forced to figure at the side of talented people, and though each of the participants clearly realized that something was wrong here, the evil could not be remedied, since criticism was a precarious business and alteration impossible. There were actually some poor creatures who had been raised without learning a single step, and who possessed the most perfect adroitness in everything with the exception of dancing; and while the clever souls were pleasant and gay, the clumsy ones confined themselves to stiff gentility.

But it gives me great pleasure to mention one exception to this rule. This was a most charming old French diplomat, who appeared to be the very man to figure in a musketeer quadrille. But to his own and everyone else's surprise, he discovered that he was so little acquainted with even the rudiments of dancing that he came to me in a state of despair, with the exclamation: "But I am a hindrance!" To exclude him would have caused a scandal. I therefore instructed and encouraged him to the best of his ability, and brought him to the point of at least being harmless. But he now looked at the whole thing from the humorous side, and appeared at the next rehearsal with a number of folio sheets filled with fantastic symbols and circles, and as an illustration to the whole, his own figure in the most grotesque attitudes. These caricatures and his hilarious idea were extraordinarily successful, and thus the Frenchman happily managed to extricate himself from this difficult predicament.

Unfortunately, such entertainments could not take place at the Court of Frederik VII. Therefore my duties in this area ceased completely, except for some celebrations among the princely families. Of these solemn occasions I shall single out only one, which had a rather unique character, namely:

THE GOLDEN WEDDING ANNIVERSARY OF THE LANDGRAVE WILHELM OF HESSE AND PRINCESS CHARLOTTE OF DENMARK, CELEBRATED AT THE RESIDENCE OF THE HEIR PRESUMPTIVE, FREDERIK FERDINAND, ON NOVEMBER 10, 1860.

The setting was the grand ballroom with three folding doors just opposite to the draped windows. To the left, the orchestra and an entrance door. To the right, a place for the spectators, surrounded by a barrier.

The Golden Anniversary couple was led in by the King, the Queen Dowager, and the august host and hostess. The royal guests took their seats and the brilliant company arrayed itself behind the chairs, in the doorways, in the *Coursal*, and in the space to the right.

From the entrance on the left, there now entered eight bridesmaids (young countesses and gentlewomen), who performed a *contredanse* with bouquets of flowers. With his bow and arrow, Cupid (the thirteen-year-old Princess Dagmar) joined in the dance of the bridesmaids, executed a little solo, and ended up sitting on the laps of the Anniversary couple (her grandparents). Eight elves (young ladies and little Princess Thyra), with garlands of flowers on their heads and light blue shoulder scarves, carried forth a veiled picture and, together with the bridesmaids, formed various picturesque groups. Filled with curiosity, Cupid sprang forward and unveiled the picture, which represented the Golden Bride at the age of seventeen.

One heard military music, and in marched six little drummer boys and a regimental drummer (in miniature)—all from the well-known Second Jutland, a regiment from which, in his day, the Landgrave had had great merit and which contained the fondest memories of his youth.* Elves and bridesmaids gathered round the little corps and danced to the "Rataplan March" from *The Daughter of the Regiment*. This was succeeded by the "Revue March of Frederik VI," (by DuPuy), and eight young officers, wearing red uniforms with the white facings of the Second Jutland, accompanied the same number

---

*The present brave Eleventh Regiment.—A. B.

of young ladies (among them, three of the Anniversary couple's grand-children†) into the room. In festive procession they passed by the royal and princely ladies and gentlemen, danced a minuet, and took part in the grand fi-nale whose principal features included the presentation of two golden wreaths on velvet cushions, and from the window recesses, the sudden ap-pearance of the old regimental standards, entwined with laurel wreaths.

With his torch, Cupid hovered over the end-group, which was encircled with roses and myrtle.

I dare say it will take a vivid imagination to glean from this faint outline any idea of the atmosphere that prevailed during this little performance, which blended so perfectly with the solemn character of the day, and of the impression which the whole made upon the assembly, not least upon the au-gust anniversary couple. On this occasion my art celebrated one of its love-liest triumphs, for it had exercised its magic without the help of the stage, professional training, or virtuosity! The thought had become wedded to the form, and in a circle where emotion does not usually play a principal part, I had seen tears in everyone's eyes!

It is not to be wondered at that the seriousness which I bring to Art often, before my eyes, transforms the spectacle into a spiritual reality or, at any rate, into a phenomenon of deeper significance. Here the festive element had al-most become worship; but when they asked that the performance be repeated so that those members of the crowd who had stood too far away might also get to see and delight in something, the whole work retired into the modest cate-gory of: *divertissements.*

---

†The Duke of Nassau and two princesses of Anhalt-Dessau. (It ought to be noted by way of pa-renthesis that all three spoke fluent Danish.)—A. B.

Ballet Compositions: Second Period

CONSERVATORIET, OR A PROPOSAL OF MARRIAGE THROUGH THE NEWSPAPER

A VAUDEVILLE-BALLET IN TWO ACTS.
Music Arranged and Composed by H. Paulli.
(Performed for the first time at the Royal Theatre on May 6, 1849)

If, in relating the history of my ballets, I were to limit myself to stating the number of times they have been performed, the way in which they have been received, or the circumstances under which they have been presented, this portion of my book would become rather monotonous, for there are but few variants to the fate which can befall a scenic work. But, since I have had the joy of seeing that people have found pleasure in the form in which I have placed my compositions as frames around the biographical and travel pictures which constitute my actual theatre life, I hope I shall not weary my good readers by unfolding the motives for the representations that have sprung from my fantasy and from my reflections on life and art.

Therefore, when I speak of the *Conservatoire* [in Danish, *Conservatoriet*], it is not in order to describe this magnificent French artistic institution in its entirety, but only to give a little sketch of the fresh young life that in my day went on in one corner of it, namely, in the Royal Ballet School. The headquarters of this school was in the *Hôtel des menus plaisirs*, wall-to-wall with the schools of declamation and music. However, it had its branch classes with M. Coulon in the Rue Montmartre, and at the Opéra itself with my famous teacher, Auguste Vestris.

It is an inherent tendency in the stage as well as in art to always turn the pretty side outward and to conceal as much as possible what lies on the wrong side. Among authors as well as spectators, however, there is an inexplicable urge to spy out and expose the hidden wires in the internal mechanism of the theatre, just as is the case with those children, who are not content to admire the ingenious marionettes from without but yearn to peep behind the curtain, and even wish to tear open the dolls in order to see what is inside them.

It is certain that the miniature world that exists within that extraordinary drop of water called "the theatre" yields, in every respect, a concentrated mirror image of the larger one; and that the theatre-state, like that outside, presents factions, conflicting interests, vacillating policies, and permanent dissatisfaction. It can indeed be most amusing to see all these things portrayed in novellas and in plays; but since such a physiology generally bears the same relation to the stage as the kitchen to the royal table, it is only apt to weaken illusion and rob the theatre of its magic, which is a prerequisite for aesthetic enjoyment.

I have earlier drawn parallels between theatre conditions here at home and those that exist abroad, particularly in Paris, and have shown how much we have to be grateful for in many respects. All the same, it must be said that just as the French novelists, in order to render their descriptions piquant, have lowered the moral standard of their own nation, so have people such as *feuilletonistes* and comedy writers cast an undeserved shadow upon the artistic community in general, and theatre folk in particular.

It has almost become a standing rule that every moral eccentricity is to issue from the wings, every courtesan is to be an *artiste*, and, if wantonness is to be properly personified, it must positively be in the figure of a *danseuse* from the Opéra. It would lead me too far afield were I to point out all the falseness and inhumanity that are embodied in this treatment of an entire class; but a delinquent imagination is partly to blame for the wrongful ideas that are applied to the conditions of an artist's life; and many a time it even does harm where it means to do good—for example, in *The Quaker and the Danseuse,* and in our capital Paludan-Müller's poem,* where Dione learns her art entirely *en passant,* lives the isolated life of a *grisette,* dances a solo that fills a whole evening, is seduced by a sentimental count, and ends her artistic career by jumping into the canal! It is the same case with such fantasy pictures as with fashion magazines: they are not drawn from nature, and gross imitations would only produce the most ridiculous caricatures—just suppose a talented young pupil should take Dione's story seriously!

There is something exasperating about seeing how life behind the curtain is represented in the theatre itself. It is actually like seeing a child strike out at his nurse and mistreat her. One would almost believe that a manager who accepts such a play for performance is making it his duty to prostitute his own sphere of activity—or, more properly speaking, that he is speculating on its degradation. In modern French comedies, should a husband betray his wife, it is for an actress or a prima donna; should a young gentleman or a rich financier be ruined, the poor *danseuses* must be at hand in the twinkling of an eye, as if *courtesans* were not to found by the thousand outside the theatre. And finally, should stupidity, affectation, yea, wretched cowardice, have a representative, he must be nothing less than a solo *danseur!* It is useless to cite the most respectable examples: these are regarded as exceptions to the rule, just as among misanthropes true virtues are classed as abnormalities.

---

*A reference to Paludan-Müller's 1833 poem "Dandserinden" ["The Dancing Girl"].

It is not enough that the artist should amuse people with his talents, his frailties must also serve as entertainment. If they should only happen to be of the common sort, they are magnified for the sake of effect. The worst outcome of this buffoonery is that one finally, with a certain forbearance, comes to regard such excesses as identical with the nature of the artist, and especially as the prerogative of the theatrical profession.

In the present ballet, just as in my entire activity, I have endeavored to reclaim for my fellow artists, but in particular for my French comrades of both sexes, the justice that is due them; and in some individual episodes extracted from the many I have experienced in their midst, I have attempted to describe the feelings that refined their gaiety and the joys that seasoned their strenuous work.

There was constant rivalry among the royal schools. Those of declamation and singing proudly looked down their noses at the ballet, whereas the instrumentalists were the born friends of the dance—all the more so as its pupils had free music training in the Conservatoire's classes. But they were all agreed on two things: namely, in playing practical jokes (*des farces*) and in helping the needy whenever they could. It cannot be denied that it was the dance pupils, the boys in particular, who took precedence in the so-called *espiègleries*, a word that is unquestionably derived from *Eulenspiegel* or *Uglspiel*.† In this area their invention was inexhaustible, and their usual victim was the old character who was in charge of the classrooms. To this must be added the fact that his more intimate relationships bore some resemblance to those of my Dufour.

Such mischief as drawing caricatures, tracing on the floor in chalk the outline of the largest feet, or emphasizing the lightness of an *entrechat* by dropping wooden blocks was the order of the day. But I cannot refrain from relating a couple of younger and older "*gamin* tricks," which might easily figure in a Carnival adventure and are characteristic of the Parisian youth of my day.

A lad by the name of Fauchet had acquired the fantastic habit, as he passed a cobbler's stall in the Rue Bergère every morning, of poking his head through a paper window, asking what time it was, and then darting off. At last this jest became too much for the cobbler, and he determined to capture this practical joker. To this end, he fastened his knee strap around the pane, and just as the urchin face with the usual question on its lips peeped in, he drew his snare together and gave *mein Herr Uglspiel* half a dozen good slaps in the face. Fauchet was furious and contemplated revenge. Now the cobbler's shop stood on wheels, as did our old butcher stalls, and one day when a brewer's cart, drawn by one of the well-known draught horses, happened to stop right

---

† Till Eulenspiegel ("Owl mirror") is the knavish, lying, often scatological antihero of a cycle of tales stemming from late-medieval Germany. The oldest extant version is that published in Stuttgart in 1515, which was first translated into English by Paul Oppenheimer and published by Wesleyan University Press (1972) under the title *A Pleasant Vintage of Till Eulenspiegel*.

in front of the booth in question, our *farceur* slipped in between them and with a rope tied the cart and the stall firmly together. Then he yelled "Gee-up!," and the monstrous animal charged off with both equipages, the second being overturned as if by an earthquake.

Another *farce* that was played on an eccentric Englishman by the name of Taylor can serve as proof of how far conceit and vanity can drive a person. This man, who was otherwise equipped with the character and thorough knowledge of a gentleman, had acquired such a passion for the dance that at an adult age he had had himself instructed in theatrical dancing and went so far as to publicly present his art—in a rather grotesque form, of course—in his native land.‡ The applause he enjoyed there turned his head to such a degree that he seriously fancied himself to surpass contemporary virtuosi and that the new ballets were but copies and plagiarisms of his own, in part imaginary, compositions.

In 1840 he came to Paris, and since our young madcaps had immediately "read his hand," it goes without saying that he became a rich source of amusement. *Danseurs* and *danseuses* greeted him with the utmost deference, called him their model and teacher, inflamed his enthusiasm with the most fabulous eulogies, and finally got him to perform at the Théâtre des folies dramatiques! Here they gathered *en masse* in order to applaud, call forth, and shower him with enormous wreaths. When at the end he performed a sailor dance wherein he swung the English and French flags together, there was even printed a special theatrical newspaper in which, among the most dreadful exaggerations, it was reported that the tension which had recently prevailed between England and France had now been resolved into an *entente cordiale,* and this mainly by M. Théleur's ingenious idea of mingling the national colors in the famous sailor dance.

Théleur was in seventh heaven and gave a dazzling banquet for his colleagues and admirers. These hoaxes were still going on when I visited Paris in 1841, and my jolly comrades introduced me to this strange character, whom I found to be a cultured and reasonable man until the conversation turned to dancing and ballet. He then informed me that with no difficulty at all he could execute five *tours en l'air* and rise to a height of ten and a half feet above the floor. Morever, his contract lay *in blanco* in the office of the Opéra, and the Cross of the Légion d'Honneur at his disposal in the Tuileries. We parted as old friends, for he had, of course, been my teacher and relinquished to me the subjects for several of my ballets.

As I have earlier mentioned, I received my choreographic education from Vestris in the foyer of the Opéra. Things were quite lively here, and our diligent exercises were sometimes interrupted by amusing episodes—of a more sedate kind, however, than those that took place in the *salle* at the *Menus plaisirs.*

For example, I had earned considerable renown by the rather dangerous

‡ So as to be more successful, he had *Frenchified* his name to Théleur. — A. B.

art of imitating the bad habits of a number of dancers, but especially the voices and gestures of the Opéra's principal singers — all with a touch of parody and comedy that was quite a success with those who were not themselves the subjects. This talent, which was still remembered many years after my dancing had been forgotten, served at that time as daily entertainment for the company, among whom were several *coryphées* of song.

One day his comrades laid hold of Adolphe Nourrit, [telling him that] he absolutely *must* hear an imitation of himself, and I was half-forced to display my artistry. On pressing request I then sang a colorature aria from his repertoire, and managed to strike the resemblance without caricaturing the voice. Everyone was waiting to hear what the sensitive opera hero would say to this performance, but with a charming laugh he exclaimed: "I don't know if that's like me, but it's admirably sung." The most cordial tone prevailed among most of the artists at the Académie Royale. As proof of the good will with which they accepted me, a foreign youth, I shall cite only this lovely incident: when my old father visited Paris in 1827 they everywhere came to greet him in order to bring him some compliment on his son's progress and behavior.

If it was a question of supporting some poor artist, no matter where he might be, they traveled many miles in order to raise a small sum at a provincial theatre, or they smashed the money box whose contents had been destined for celebrations or pleasure parties. If someone were to make his debut, they gathered as *claqueurs;* if ill was spoken about their teacher, they were ready to demand satisfaction with rapier in hand; and if any of our number died, generally without having the consecration of the Catholic Church, loving brothers with bared heads followed his or her coffin and delivered an edifying funeral oration at the grave.

I often returned to Paris in order to keep abreast of the times and to renew old memories. In the year 1847 I stayed there with my family, and since my daughter's health required a sojourn of several weeks in the country, we chose Saint-Germain-en-Laye. The countryside along the banks of the Seine is enchanting; we visited Marly and Bougival, where we were graciously received by Alexander Dumas, who at that time was in the process of building his fantastic villa which was to be named after his latest novel, *Monte-Cristo.* But the most glorious view was from the broad terrace outside the old château of François I, with the dense forest behind and — spread in a wide panorama — the valley of the Seine and Paris before. Here promenaders gathered in the afternoon from the little town as well as from the capital. The dragoons' band played, while young folk danced in the open air. To the right lay a pavilion in the Renaissance style. It had once belonged to the château and was named after the unforgettable Henry IV, who had once inhabited it himself. Now, however, it served as the main building of a fair-sized restaurant with adjacent garden, and was *"le rendez-vous du beau monde."* Here there appeared in my time a family of wandering entertainers. The father played the violin rather well, the mother the harp, the son the flute, while the little daughter struck the tambourine. But when the public did not pay sufficient attention to their musical presentations, the little girl received a signal, threw off her cloak, appearing in a sort of fancy Spanish costume, and to the clacking of castanets danced the *cachucha* on the lawn.

Whenever I have seen dancing or comedy abused, it has always seemed to me as if I were encountering a distant relative in misery, and I am involuntarily filled with the deepest melancholy. I offered my mite to these poor souls, struck up a conversation with the father, and discussed the little girl's dancing, which appeared to be the best support of the family. He told me that his supreme wish was to see his child accepted in a proper ballet school. They did not know they were talking to a choreographer, but every time they entered the garden their eyes sought me out, and I always received a friendly but wistful greeting.

Surely here were my Raimbaud and his little daughter standing before me in the flesh, and I was constantly reminded of the singer Garat and the violin virtuoso Boucher, who one evening, on the Boulevard Montmartre, happened to stroll past a blind musician and his wife who sought in vain to win a couple of *sols* from the passersby. The good artists paused, struck with the same idea. Boucher paid one franc to borrow the man's violin, Garat ten *sols* for the woman's guitar. Then they both performed the loveliest serenade. People flocked to the place, but immediately recognized the famous virtuosi, and their beautiful action, combined with the excellent music, had the desired effect. The plate overflowed with silver and gold, and the poor people were helped for a long time. But, alas! Who is in a position to do something like that!

My Muse was soon to grant me a favor which—not without a certain connection with these episodes—precipitated the motives for the present ballet.

But first I must return to the years 1812–1813 in order to recall to the memories of older *amateurs* a large wooden structure that stood in Vesterbro, just opposite the Royal Shooting Gallery. It was later rebuilt as a so-called Fun Theatre and eventually disappeared in order to make room for the elegant houses which now cover the old site. Here, to the great delight of both children and adults, Italian harlequinades were performed, accompanied by rope dancing and gymnastics. The Englishman Price was the head of the troupe, just as Casorti and his daughter were its principal stars: she by her extraordinary virtuosity on the rope, and he by his masterly performance of the comic roles of Pajazzo [sic] and Pierrot, wherein he was not only incomparable (since everything we have since seen in this direction is nothing but a third- or fourth-hand copy) but *unattainable,* because he was completely original.

The Price and Casorti families allied themselves with the acrobats Winther and Parent, together with the ingenious Petolettis. This troupe, which made regular guest appearances in Copenhagen every spring and summer, not only possessed the favor of a large public but—which at that time was most unusual in such circles—deserved and enjoyed the unconditional respect of the citizenry for their exemplary behavior. A new generation of Prices succeeded them, and two of the brothers married the English sisters Rosa and Flora Luin, who, as *danseuses de terre* (floor-dancers, in acrobatic jargon) captivated the Vesterbro and Nørrebro audiences. From this stalk in turn sprang forth new shoots destined for the higher genre—namely, on the floor and not on the rope.

Tired of an itinerant life, these parents, just as I returned from my trip to Paris, asked me if I would give their whole flock of children private lessons, as they could not afford to dispense with their assistance at their own performances but still wished to see them accepted at the Royal Theatre. At first I winced at the thought of undertaking such a task, since, to put it bluntly, I regarded the stepchildren of Terpsichore as completely irrelevant to my endeavors. But my eyes were soon opened to the fine gifts which needed only expert guidance to develop into real talent. It was genuinely refreshing for me to give these children lessons, and among the many good qualities I found in them I will only point out the deep affection they had for their parents. Juliette and Sophie belonged to Flora and Adolf, while Amalie and Julius were the eldest children of Rosa and James. These four were the brightest of the lot, but it was still Juliette who stood supreme as the one who was unmistakably called to fill a pre-eminent place in the ballet. For this reason I purposely held her back so that in time she would make all the more brilliant a debut. However, the war broke out. My mental stress, augmented by unusual exertions, cast me upon the sickbed, and in my feverish fantasies, which alternated between outpost skirmishes and ballet scenes, *Conservatoriet* stood complete, with little Sophie Price as Raimbaud's daughter. It was impossible for me to distinguish between her childlike expression and the picture of Goethe's Mignon! And at the rehearsal of the aforementioned work it was obvious that I had hit upon the right personality.

Since Fru Kellermann had received permission to travel abroad, the leading role, which had been destined for her from the start, had to be taken over by Juliette Price, and though the latter's first appearance at the Royal Theatre thus took place somewhat earlier than I had intended, she was received with unanimous applause. From that moment on she became our first solo *danseuse*, an ornament to the stage, an honor to her profession.

Just as the ballet was ready for performance, the sorrowful news of the Eckernförde affair struck the Copenhagen populace like a thunderbolt, and the very thought of coming forth at such a moment with a composition whose burlesque situations were intended to make people laugh seemed loathsome to me. My art seemed offensive in the midst of the deep sorrow that had gripped the whole nation. But a number of learned and sober-minded friends of art and of the homeland sought to convince me that if my work could succeed in dispelling the grief that oppressed every Danish heart, if only for an hour or so, it would be a real benefit and a triumph for the dramatic art. I therefore decided to risk it, and had no cause to regret my daring, for it appeared from the frequent and heavily attended performances that spirits had indeed been somewhat lifted.

The lively dancing school, Hoppensach's superb Dufour, the students' playfulness, and the many problems with the marriage proposal in the newspaper kept the audience's humor in play, while Raimbaud and his family appealed to their sentiments. In one of our comedies it says: "A person cannot manage to do more than laugh and cry at the same time," and, truly, as an author I could not ask more of my audience. The applause was lively, and lasted for many years through a long run of performances, until at last the ballet disappeared from the repertoire for purely economic reasons. Its equipment had cost as good as nothing, but since each member of the cast was to be compensated for the use of his own clothing, the management became uneasy about this nightly expenditure and decided to let *Conservatoriet* go.*

PSYCHE

A Ballet in One Act.
Music Composed and Arranged by Edvard Helsted.
Decorations by Messieurs Christensen and Lund.
(Performed at the Royal Theatre for
the First Time on May 7, 1850).

EVERY time I have executed a work with enthusiasm, or when I am near its completion, I am overwhelmed by a certain depression and haunted by the discouraging thought that the ballet, as some people continue to allege, might in itself actually be an absurdity and the dance might have no more significance than any other conventional exercise.

If, in addition to the call of the spirit, I had not also had that of duty, I would many a time have been deterred by the Philistinism that works to undermine every higher endeavor. But it is certainly not the ballet and the theatre alone which have become subject to the influence of materialism; it has become enmeshed with science, art, and crafts, and by a superficial consideration confuses the unintelligible with the insignificant.

When I consider what a mass of details are appurtenant to the *ensemble* of a ballet, what care they require, and how they usually go unnoticed, in moments of seriousness I liken my work to that of a gardener. But if I look at things from the humorous side, I am reminded of an old German-born regimental drummer to whose instruction I had confided two young lads who were to play drummer boys in *The Veteran*. He was filled with the importance of his calling and made it his duty to initiate my pupils into all the se-

---

*The dancing school from Act I has, however, survived in the repertoires of the Royal Danish Ballet, the Joffrey City Center Ballet of New York, and other companies.

crets of his art. I actually had to admire the variety of rhythms and the nuances that were to be found in a pair of drumsticks. But at the same time, I noticed that the drummer was also rankled by a secret feeling of distress at the neglect of his superiors and his audiences. "How many compositions have I beautifully beaten out!" he exclaimed. "They don't value me at all; for example: my march with the double slip-beat! — what have I got from that?"

I must therefore, through comparisons with the manifold and highly different appearances of art, seek consolation for the disappointments I have so often encountered in my sphere of activity and not harbor bitterness because so few people have discovered the deeper meaning that lay in my treatment of the oft-used subject *Cupid and Psyche,* taken from the writings of Apuleius. In treating a mythological subject, it was — apart from bringing a needed variety into the ballet repertoire and, if possible, viewing the work from a new angle — mainly to furnish further proof of the relationship of the dance to the fine arts. Antique beauty is and always will be the ideal of the plastic arts. To strive for this in spite of the consciousness of its unattainability is not only permissible but an absolute duty. I have earlier been forced to admit that in the dance as well as in a number of other art forms, virtuosity has developed at the expense of beauty; and since [technical] skill now seems to have reached a height that can be surpassed only by extravagance, the ballet must either be completely overwhelmed by indifference or undergo a reaction in the direction of that divine harmony which is pronounced in the masterpieces of the Greeks, the school from which our great Thorvaldsen emerged.

I confess that from the time I first came to know this eminent artist, not only in his superb works but in his own amiable person, light was shed for me upon the direction I had hitherto been following unconsciously but which I would hereafter profess with complete confidence. I had already received two honorable testimonials, one from Oehlenschläger which I have mentioned earlier, the other from Alexander von Humboldt, who had found in my compositions *"a profound meaning";* but our immortal Thorvaldsen called me *artist* when after the presentation of *Napoli* he enfolded me in his embrace, and I have striven to the best of my ability to be worthy of this name.

I decided to compose a ballet where, in the service of poetry, I would exclusively follow the demands of beauty without paying heed to virtuosity or loud applause. I hereby ventured a bold step, which did not go unnoticed by connoisseurs.

It was clear to me that if the dance were ever to find justification as the expression of a character, it would have to be mainly in the realm of fable. The *allegory,* which had not yet deserted me, deterred me all the less as I believed that in the Master's [Thorvaldsen's] superb cycle of bas-reliefs I had found an interpreter, and in Paludan-Müller's lovely poem a guide to the understanding of my pantomimic representation. I therefore steered my antique boat out upon the deep flood that had its source at the foot of Parnassus and its outlet in the Ocean of Oblivion.

I wished to portray the delights and sufferings of *the Soul*, its passage through the underworld to immortality. I had ventured to introduce but one addition by having Apollo (the Art of Poetry) lend Cupid (Love) his lyre in order by its aid to conquer Death and Sorrow and guide the beloved Psyche from the land of the Shades into the light of eternity!

Never was any work of this kind executed with greater care. The situations followed one upon the other with ease and naturalness; the dancing was completely woven into the plot, and the varying tableaux presented a series of bas-reliefs wherein I never lost sight of my goal. But if the old proverb is right when it says that "Rome was not built in a day," for my part I must admit (though it pains me to do so) that it was more than I could do to bring back through the art of mime the Golden Age of Greece, especially with the forces I had at my disposal!

The whole made a mild and favorable impression. The pantheon of Olympus produced splendid applause at the end, but my real intention came to nought—mainly because of the following circumstances:

(1) The lack of personalities capable of reproducing even approximately the perfection that antique art and myth demand;

(2) The impossibility of finding a costume that could satisfy at once the demands of the subject, the theatre, the dance, and—fashion;

(3) The lack of imagination in the décor—for example, Cupid's Magic Palace might have furnished a downright cozy *Havestue** in a country house along Strandvejen; and lastly

(4) The aversion on the part of the general public to accepting the allegory, which forms the core of the action.

The music, composed and arranged by Edvard Helsted, was lovely and characteristic throughout. The roles were performed with praiseworthy precision, and for a couple of years the ballet had a run of performances. But neither the critics nor the theatre treasury cared to retain it any longer in the repertoire, for—truth to tell—it does not seem to have been really *amusing*.

THE KERMESSE † IN BRUGES OR THE THREE GIFTS

A Romantic Ballet in Three Acts.
Music by H. Paulli.
(Performed for the First Time at the Royal
Theatre in April 1851)

AMONG the discoveries I have made with regard to the ballet as a scenic branch of art, I suppose that the happiest and most useful for me has been

---

* A room opening onto a garden, a standard feature of many Danish houses.

† Every town in the Low Countries celebrates the feast day of the patron saint of its principal church with an annual bacchanalian fair, which in Belgium is called *Kermesse*, after the German *Kirmis* or *Kirchmesse* [church fair].—A. B.

this: people have made such serious demands on motive and plot that my compositions must perforce possess a certain dramatic worth in order to merit the name of *ballets*. For this reason I have been forced to isolate myself from the new trend, which bases the whole production on individual skill surrounded by dazzling effects, as well as from the old school, with its mimetic language, symmetrical groupings, and kaleidoscopic configurations. However, it was not enough that my public and I were agreed on the necessity for this dramatic tendency, or that I used it as much as possible as the basis for the rhythmic movement that characterizes the external nature of the dance. I also had to adopt the picturesque element in order to borrow from it the images that would both render the situation lucid and also give the representation grace and vitality.

Almost always in the critical assessment of my works two opposite systems have been applied, one of which places the dancing as the focal point and motive, while the other regards it merely as "padding" for the plot. I was capable of pleasing both of them, but only one at a time; for none of the systems' advocates seemed to pay any heed to the fact that, depending upon which of the fine arts lent my Muse its assistance, I had to place greater weight sometimes on the choreographic, sometimes on the mimed part of the situation, thus producing results which bear the same relationship to each other as fruits whose pulp is to be eaten do to those in which the pip is the nutritive substance.

The difference between the picturesque in nature and the picturesque in the theatre consists essentially in the fact that *accident* is almost everywhere of use to the painter, but becomes awkward and confused on the stage; and next in the fact that pictorial art dares (but not without peril) to borrow its figures or groupings from scenic productions, whereas the latter can with absolute certainty turn to painting and the plastic art in order to find in them the forms under which the natural can best be combined with the beautiful.

Just as it impossible to imagine anything more unsuccessful than a photograph of a stage scene or a portrait figure in theatrical costume, so, too, I would consider it an artistic misfortune if even my finest groupings were to be reproduced on canvas or on paper. On the other hand, I have on many occasions used paintings as models, and it quite naturally happens that one or a number of stationary groups can furnish material for a mobile treatment which does not for a moment disavow its pictorial origin. In the present ballet I have not treated any specific subject, but sought to bring to life Netherlandish genre pictures.

The galleries of Dresden, Amsterdam, Paris, and Florence—not to mention our own collections—contain priceless treasures whose influence on taste and imagination I could not escape. The Mieris brothers, Slingeland, Van Steen, and others in their pictures of the fashionable world of their day; Wouwerman's camps, hunting parties, and fencing engagements; Gerard Dou's graceful representations of everyday life; Rembrandt's mysterious *clair-ob-*

scur, which enshrouds his guardrooms, laboratories, and council chambers; Schalken's and Honthorst's glowing effects of light; Adrian van Ostade's public houses and gaming tables; and finally, David Teniers' inimitable harvest festivals, peasant weddings, and *Kermesses* — all this seems bound to inspire a ballet composer. And then there are those matchless portraits painted by Rubens, Van Dyck, Mierevelt, and others, which look as though they are about to step out of their frames. One becomes familiar — even intimate — with them. Their shrewd eyes follow us, both awake and in dreams. If they belong to history, they tell us of interesting events; but if the persons are unknown and their names forgotten, they enter the realm of the novel and the fairy tale. They are born for the stage!

Infatuated with Raphael, I had assembled his loveliest groups in a grand ballet — it was not too successful. Enraptured with the art of antiquity, I had attempted to depict the myth of Cupid and Psyche, renouncing in advance the applause of the crowd. I now chose a direction more in keeping with the spirit of the present, for it is a fact that historical painting has been supplanted by the genre picture, just as the tragic drama has been by the drawing room play. "They want something to laugh at, gov'nor," an old theatre doorkeeper whispered in my ear after the first performance of a serious ballet. And I had to admit he was right. I did owe my public some fun after my last trip to Olympus, and I was lucky enough to find a burlesque subject in which I could envelop my impressions of art and some memories from my nursery days.

"It's settled!" I exclaimed one evening after having skimmed through the Dresden Gallery's *édition de luxe,* "I am going to compose a ballet in the Netherlandish style." And it was not long before my favorite characters had grouped themselves about a little fairy tale, for which Josias Rantzau's *sword of victory,* Tovelille's *magic ring,* and the *three gifts* that Our Lord and St. Peter bestowed upon the merry cobbler furnished me with an abundant amount of material. For me Gerard Dou's well-known *Viola da Gamba* became an instrument resembling that which in Ole Bull's hands worked real sorcery after, as he himself has told, it had hung for three hundred years in the armory at Innsbruck! The demonic power of the violin also has a beneficial effect, as it consoles the distressed, unites the lovers, and saves those who have been condemned from dying at the stake. Moreover, these three gifts contain a specific symbolism, since two of them (namely, fortune in battle and fortune in love) prove to be of no avail, while the third (a happy disposition) conquers and endures.

It was under happy and fortunate auspices that I rehearsed this work. After three honorable campaigns, Denmark had won peace and our valiant troops made their triumphal entry into the capital, where in the Ridehuus at Christiansborg Palace they were entertained by the Copenhagen citizenry at thirteen banquets in eighteen days. I had the honor of being an active member of the committee responsible for these magnificent feasts, and a number of my patrons feared that my patriotic enthusiasm might possibly prove harmful to my artistic fervor; but I had the pleasure of giving their worries a pleasant disavowal. At the same time as my heart swelled with admiration for the strength and modesty which characterized our valiant warriors, I attended to my duties at the ballet; and often, while the glasses clinked and hurrahs resounded in the festively decorated Ridehuus just opposite the Court Theatre, I calmly and attentively held my rehearsals, then once again rushed out to deliver a toast and shake hands with our faithful "Jacks."

The ballet itself benefited from this general enthusiasm and was received with jubilant applause. The performance, especially on the female side, was quite excellent; the music, lively and expressive; while the costumes and décor supported the picturesque idea very well. In short, *The Kermesse* continuously called forth the most genuine mirth, and if justice were to be done, it really ought to be celebrated at least once a year.

ZULMA OR THE CRYSTAL PALACE

A Ballet in Three Acts.
Music Composed and Arranged by Paulli.
Decorations by Messieurs Christensen and Lund.
(Performed for the First Time at the Royal
Theatre on February 14, 1852)

THIS last title, which became the name by which the present ballet was commonly known, might furnish grounds for the kind of expectations that neither our own nor any other stage could satisfy: for one who has seen this eighth wonder of the world only as it appears since its removal to Sydenham must admit that it constitutes in itself a spectacle such as no art is capable of reproducing.* It would exceed the bounds of these notes were I to attempt to describe the artistic and industrial treasures that are housed within this fairy palace; nor do I intend to go into detail about the memories I have retained from the various times at which I have visited England. I will only—and with the greatest possible brevity—account for the impressions that have given me the motives for my composition.

Even though the politics of states neither can nor ought to be blamed on the people, still it cannot be denied that the eccentricity and repellent coldness with which Englishmen—in all the degrees so strikingly depicted under Thackeray's sobriquet of "snobs"—everywhere appear is not apt to win them

---

†The glass-and-iron Crystal Palace, as designed by Sir Joseph Paxton, was 1850 feet long and 408 feet wide, its central vault 66 feet high. It was erected in Hyde Park to house the Great Exhibition of 1851, but was dismantled and re-erected (with some modifications) in 1854 at Sydenham, south of the Thames. It continued in use for exhibitions, concerts, pantomimes, and the like until its destruction by fire late in 1936. See also the author's first-hand description of the Palace, Vol. III, Part Three, pp. 560–561.

the sympathy of other nations. The traveler who lands in one of the larger cities of Great Britain encounters an intense activity and ruthlessness that immediately have a depressing effect upon him, and the first thing he notices is the enormous chasm that separates the various social classes—a chasm that can be filled up and leveled out only with gold. Yet side by side with this heathen caste system the external precepts of Christianity are pedantically observed, while love of neighbor seems to be expressed only among equals by birth, and mostly within the confines of a rather narrow circle.

"My house is my castle," says the free—i.e., well-to-do—Englishman with a certain noble self-conceit. But the doors of this fortress do not open without safe guarantees for this hospitality. On the other hand, if a well-recommended stranger is lucky enough to gain admittance to a family circle, English life appears before him in a completely different form. The cold, stiff character vanishes and gives place to cordiality and urbanity. One discovers domestic virtues and genteel manners, which thrive in an atmosphere of coziness and well-being—the English "comfort"—which is superior to anything the Continent can display in this direction. One recognizes the mild and amiable character and facial features that delight us in English novels, and art and poetry venture modestly forth from the coal-fog that enshrouds Britain's superior everyday life.

Although freedom is not matched with the equality we Danes have come to set such great store by, still every British citizen knows how to defend his rights, and his personal safety is protected to such a degree that should he happen to be molested in the most remote corner of the globe, his government can make amends and give him compensation. This is indeed a great thing, and with the patriotism of its people, the enormous resources industry, commerce, and a formidable naval power have to offer, it is no wonder that Great Britain presumes to claim first place among the nations of Europe. France alone dares to contest this pre-eminence and has always been her rival in power and influence. Both feel compelled to control the rest of the world, but their mutual jealousy prevents a threatening danger and maintains political equilibrium. But, should they one day find themselves in complete agreement, no one could resist their collective strength, either in war or in peace.

National industrial exhibitions had already been instituted in France at the beginning of this century and had brought about an astonishing improvement in the countless branches of handicrafts. They took place at fixed intervals, either at the Louvre or in temporary structures erected on the public squares of Paris.

Zealous as they are in surpassing the French, the English only recently hit upon the idea of arranging an exhibition. However, this was not to be merely national but *universal*, not only for industry but for all the visual arts; and instead of a borrowed locale, they ordered the erection of a palace of iron and glass so large and high that its arcades could be seen above the tallest trees in Hyde Park! Nations from all over the globe were invited to take part in this glorious competition, and in 1851 hundreds of thousands of contestants and sightseers converged upon London for the World Exhibition.

This moment can, perhaps, be regarded as the culmination of Great Britain's might and prestige. At that time, no one suspected that such a great revolt could ever erupt in the East Indian possessions† or that England was to play a secondary role in the Crimean War. People were far from foreseeing that the advance of French weaponry in the Italian freedom fight was to terrify Parliament, or that English policy would appear so impotent in the face of such an outrage as the dismemberment of Denmark! All of Europe was *at this time* in favor of England; all races bowed before a greatness that combined such strength and humanity and strove for such a lofty goal. France itself had to follow the tide, though always as a rival; for its industry had the upper hand in taste, and Paris exerted its force of attraction on those travelers who wished to spend as many weeks *there* as they did days in large, monotonous London.

I was not fortunate enough to attend this great congregation of peoples, but my imagination followed it in every detail and was particularly captivated by the picture of the interior of the Crystal Palace, where one read above the splendid arcades: "India! India!" Legendary Hindustan had appeared, not only with its treasures of gold and ornaments, pearls and precious gems— among them, the Kohinoor diamond—but with all the marvelous objects fashioned by female hands in mysterious temples. In spirit, I saw all the singular figures I had read about in travel descriptions, and whose tools I had inspected at ethnographic museums. I was reminded of the Indian jugglers and *bayadères* I had seen in Paris, whose dancing had consisted of a sort of floating and swaying pantomime that is said to allude to religious excitement. A host of British melodies from the most romantic period of my youth echoed in my ears and formed a little story which, always within the balletic sphere, offered both picturesque and dramatic moments.

In the company of his friends, a young lord ventures up the River Ganges, where he arranges a party that is to be enlivened by the dancing priestesses of the temple. He falls in love with one of these maidens, who hands him a lotus blossom and later warns him of the Assassins' plot. The rescued Briton returns home. Zulma remains behind, but is brought to London the following year in order to exhibit the products of the temple. Here she encounters the young man who has gratefully and loyally preserved her memory and, in spite of all prejudice, offers her his hand.

An incident which appeared in all the newspapers at the time proved most useful to me and provided my ballet with a comical and entertaining character role. This concerned a Chinaman, who during the whole time of the exhibition had caused a sensation on the promenades of Paris and London and who was later found to be an English sailor who had deserted! The first

† The reference is to the Sepoy Rebellion or Indian Mutiny (1857–1859).

two acts depicted life in the temple, the religious symbolism of the dance, the performance of the jugglers and the *bayadères* at a country hunting party, the meaning of the lotus blossom, the sect of Assassins called *thugs*, the Britons' homesickness, and a reminiscence of the Indian poem *Sakuntalā*.‡

The third act takes us to Hyde Park, where freedom in the cooler climate of the North forms a sharp contrast to slavery beneath the burning sun of the tropics. Finally, the stage is transformed and presents the colorful sight of the interior of the Crystal Palace, where the knot of the story is untied and where through the *licentia poetica* of the ballet, all nationalities join in that universally fashionable dance, the *polka*, which forms the finale.*

The first two acts were unquestionably the best, and though the last one exercised the greatest attraction by virtue of its variety and liveliness, the resolution (that is to say, the union of the lord with the pretty pagan child) is certainly a bit improbable—all the more so as the daughters of India are rather dark-complected. But for one thing, it must naturally be assumed that Zulma will be instructed in the Christian religion before she is led to the altar; and for another, it is well known that in Kashmir, for example, the women who do not move about in the sun have almost as fair coloring as European women. Finally, as far as Zulma's class and condition are concerned, one has certainly seen dancers who in talent and beauty were greatly inferior to the high-minded and virtuous *bayadères* make matches that bordered on the fabulous. Therefore, one can surely permit an Englishman, in love and eccentric to boot, to follow the call of love and gratitude.

It was, on the whole, a good idea to make use of the current enthusiasm for proud England for the benefit of my ballet. I was lucky enough to hit upon a factor which may never present itself again. The applause was strong and unanimous. If it had not been a kind of "occasional piece," this work would have remained among my better compositions, but various local matters halted its run after only a couple of seasons, and since I myself later lost interest in this ballet, it would have been unfair to demand a continued sympathy on the part of the audience.

---

‡ This Sanskrit poem-drama was first translated into English in 1789 and had an influence on the developing Romantic movement. Its plot involves, among other details, a ring given by King Dushyanta to Sakuntalā as a pledge of love—analogous to Zulma's golden lotus blossom. For an account of Théophile Gautier and Lucien Petipa's balletic treatment of the Sakuntalā theme, in 1858, see Ivor Guest, *The Ballet of the Second Empire*, pp. 116–120.

* Bournonville was not the only choreographer to be inspired by the Crystal Palace. About six months before the premiere of *Zulma*, Arthur Saint-Léon had arranged an allegorical *divertissement*, *Les Nations*, consisting of ten dances designed, as Ivor Guest notes, "to show all the great nations united by Peace before a backcloth . . . depicting the Crystal Palace in Hyde Park" (*ibid.*, pp. 56–57).

THE WEDDING FESTIVAL IN HARDANGER

A Ballet in Two Acts.
Music by H. Paulli.
Decorations by Christensen and Lund.
Costumes Designed by E. Lehmann.
(Performed for the First Time at the Royal
Theatre on March 4, 1853)

I love Norway, and this love stems from the days of my boyhood when images from *Hakon Jarl, Axel and Valborg,* together with Malling and Munthe's tales of Norwegian heroic deeds, became fused with my most sacred feelings for my Danish homeland.

I early followed the events that denoted the great Napoleon's course of victory and adversity—that transition from supreme happiness to the depths of grief; but what pained me most of all was Norway's separation from Denmark! We had shared good and bad with one another for nearly four hundred years. However, the art of administration was so infantile that only several years after the separation were our eyes opened to the blunders of our government when we saw the country Denmark had regarded as a costly appendage freely and independently blossoming forth by virtue of its natural resources and requiring not the slightest assistance from Sweden, whose king it had acknowledged as its constitutional head. We learnt, albeit too late, how things ought to have been during the time of our union. But, even if we sorrowfully had to admit that as a *country* Norway was badly governed, the Norwegians as a *people* had little or no reason to complain; for the relationship was entirely fraternal, and in many respects granted them essential advantages. Danish and Norwegian honor had hitherto constituted a joint estate; but things were to be different from now on. Danish literature, which proudly reckoned among its stars outstanding Norwegians, was to wander alone, divide the common laurels we had won, and experience the sorrow of seeing the common language, so beautifully formed by united efforts, banned by a whole Norwegian school, only to be diluted with Norwegian-Swedish dialects. The Danish monarchy lost not only a portion of its geographical area and political importance. The national character lost an additional element as well; for anyone who has had the opportunity to observe those points on which Danes and Norwegians are united or divided will acknowledge that only the most advantageous results can come from their cooperation.

Just as all of nature has a stronger character in Norway than it does here in Denmark, so too the impressions the mind receives there are far deeper and are expressed with greater force than they are among us. We can as little bring mountains and waterfalls down to Denmark as we can transport our abundant foliage and our luxuriant fields up to Norway; but spiritual forces can stand to be blended and moved. Perhaps the Norwegians possess too much of what we lack; but where each party insists on asserting its own rights, both sides are the poorer for it, whereas a joint effort produces wealth and strength. This proposition is applauded mostly by the older school, while, in spite of Scandinavism, the younger people in Norway as well as in Denmark are drifting further and further apart—in the former country because of an excessive fear of being absorbed, and in the latter out of anger at seeing a noble bond of kinship disavowed. Nonetheless, there prevail between both nations sympathies which draw them toward one another when they meet in a third country, and this affiliation lies not only in a similarity of language but in their whole intellectual outlook.

Besides the above-mentioned childhood memories, there is still a host of other circumstances that have contributed to awakening my interest in Norway. My father had many friends from this sister country and I learnt a good many Norwegian fairy tales and songs, in which I even displayed a bit of bravura. I received my first academic instruction from a Bergenite,[*] and my brother,[†] who had been a tutor in Arendal, acquainted me with several Norwegian dialects and national dances. During my several years' stay in France, it was to me as if I heard the sounds of my homeland every time I spoke with a Norwegian, especially when we sang ballads together; and when Norway obtained its own flag, in spite of the blue cross superimposed on the white, I could see no other colors than those of our old Dannebrog.[‡]

I first came to Christiania in the year 1840 and had every possible reason to be delighted with the large audience as well as the lively applause. That born friend and patron of artists, our amiable countryman Johan Dahl, had taken it upon himself to represent Norwegian hospitality, and through him I came to know young Norway's most interesting personalities: Wergeland, Schweigaard, Hansteen, Welhaven, the historian and poet Munch, Fougstad, Motzfeldt, etc. He showed us around Christiania and its delightful environs, which were not yet adorned with the magnificent buildings and villas that were later erected, but which gave us a foretaste of the beauties of nature we were to admire on a pleasure trip farther up country.

On a pilgrimage to Krogkleven, we passed by the ironworks of Bärum and stopped for the night at the farmstead of Jonsrud, where because of a torrential downpour, I had to sleep with an umbrella unfurled above the headboard of my bed. The next morning the weather was lovely, and in our stout landau we drove up the steep mountain roads which, like the highroad to Roskilde, were laid out in straight lines, without regard for the frightful inclines, which appeared most imposing when one looked back after a descent well passed; for if one did not have horses whose sure-footedness and sharp instincts defy all description, the journey would be fraught with real danger.

---

[*] See Vol. III, Part Two, p. 422.

[†] See footnote on Antoine Bournonville *fils*, Vol. III, Part Three, p. 568.

[‡] The Danish national flag—a swallow-tailed red ensign with a white cross, adopted (according to legend) by King Valdemar in 1219.

We finally reached the famous mountain gorge and found ourselves on a narrow road with a high wall of rock on one side, a deep and narrow valley to the left, and, on the other side of a torrent, an even higher mountain, covered with dense pinewoods. They had us alight from the carriage and we were told to approach the place with our faces averted. At a given signal, we turned our gaze outward through a frame of granite rock and were astounded to behold a smiling landscape of an extensiveness and variety that no brush has yet been able to reproduce. I was filled with an enthusiasm that swelled to devotion, and forgot all the petty cares of artistic life in the face of the greatness of the Almighty revealed in nature.

People often misuse the word "unequaled," but, for me, it here found its proper use; for the impression was not only indelible but unsurpassable, even though I have since traveled over the Alps, through Switzerland and Savoy. Norwegians claim that views in Telemark and Romsdal are even more glorious, but for the present I shall content myself with Ringerike.

We got horses and rode up the mountain paths to the prospect on the Dronningbjerg. From here we surveyed an area as large as the whole of Sjælland: lovely Ringerike, so full of memories from pagan and modern times! There stood a barrow from the days of Frithiof; here lay the farmstead of Steen and the parsonage of Norderhov, both historically famous because of the frank and clever Anna Colbjørnsen.* Farther off, the foaming Hønefos roared with the same hollow boom as it had for centuries! In the bosom of the valley were heights and hills that reminded me of a Norwegian who, with a smile, looked down his nose at our Himmelbjerg. Before us, like a variegated mosaic, lay meadows, fields, woods, farms, and gardens, through which the mirrorlike water flowed, sparkling like diamonds. The northern backdrop was formed by the barren mountains of Valders, and in the distance, toward the west, arose a peak resembling a crown with a flowing veil of white. It was the snow-clad Gausta which at a distance of fifteen Norwegian—i.e. twenty-two Danish—miles appeared in the sunshine before our astonished gaze.

It was a fair and solemn Sunday morning. We now turned back and during the afternoon drove past the same Jonsrud we had seen swathed in thick rain clouds the day before. The scene now lay in the most advantageous light and was animated by groups of people in variegated festive dress.

"Here you will surely get to see a *Halling!*" exclaimed Dahl, and we decided to pause in order to enrich our travel sketches with a rustic festival. But, alas! The pastor of the place had forbidden his parishioners the scandalous pleasure of dancing. Our excellent guide parleyed for a moment, and, in spite of church dicipline, succeeded to the degree that a lad by the name of Jørgen was pointed out to us as the most skillful dancer in the entire district. We finally coaxed him to come forth; but here we encountered new ob-

---

* Known in Norway as Anna Kolbjørnsdatter. The wife of the pastor of Norderhov, she managed to effect the capture of the Swedish colonel Löwen during the fighting with the Swedes in 1716.

stacles. Jørgen was not exactly available, *owing to the fact* that he had been observing the Sabbath with the schnapps glass. All the same, Dahl had a word with him and offered him a Speciedaler for a solo or a *pas de deux,* as circumstances would permit. There was no lack of objections since there was neither a fiddler nor a dancing partner present. The fiddler was fetched from a mile away, the serving maid put on lighter clothing, and before an hour had passed, Jørgen stood before us once again—but in an altered form: neat, clean, and *sober* (he had no doubt taken a shower under the nearest waterfall). He led his partner by the hand, the fiddler struck up a melody, and they now began a roundelay, the merry *springdans.*

This was actually the first time I had seen an original Norwegian dance, and this theme in all its simplicity contained material enough for me to compose endless variations. The lad had the principal part; his partner willingly allowed herself to be led by him, just as in the mazurka. He swung himself both over and under her arms, stomped, struck the floor and the soles of his shoes with his hands, fell to his knees, and lifted his *danseuse* high in the air—all with that naïve earnestness which is characteristic of all European national dances: natural, pretty, and almost moving!

Jørgen harvested well-deserved applause, got himself a tankard of beer, and caught his breath. Next he gave us a sample of the *Halling,* which is a solo wherein the man alone displays a certain dignity and strength, and in a rather slow tempo performs some violent leaps which generally aim at touching the rafters above the low room with his feet. It was, in fact, a sort of pantomime in which giant strength was the outstanding feature.

Jørgen modestly accepted his honorarium and, like other famous virtuosi, wished to give us something *extra* into the bargain. He bade us wait a moment, then he would show us his very finest dance. My expectations were keyed to the utmost, but how disappointed I was to discover that the promised masterpiece was nothing more than a *Viennese Waltz!* Thus, little by little, the original is being supplanted by the modern, just as the folk song is by the *vaudeville.* By now the polka and the lancers are probably danced at Jonsrud, if sanctity has not gained all too strong an upper hand and insobriety robbed the legs of their elasticity.

Both the maid and the fiddler likewise received a little douceur as compensation for the lecture they no doubt received because they had not resisted the temptations of the Devil. We took a friendly leave of these fine country folk, and I reaped great profit from Jørgen's worthy presentations.

Some days later, I left Norway, and it was the only time I did not feel a thrill of excitement when the lovely Danish coast hove into view. It appeared insignificant to me compared with the magnificent scenery I had recently admired, and it was a couple of weeks before I could regain my enthusiasm for the undulating contours of our backgroundless landscape. But later on I learnt to draw parallels between the beauties peculiar to each country. In Norway one is astonished by the grandeur of the picture; in Denmark it is the details one finds most appealing. In Norway the mind is filled with sublime thoughts; in Denmark one has the tranquillity in which to write them down. When in the mountain country one stands on an enchanting promontory, one always wishes oneself on the other side of the distant ridge, thinking that there he will find a better and more beautiful region; but in Denmark one can easily find a place in which to take up his abode, "for it is a nice place to be!"

Twelve years went by before I visited Christiania for a second time. Between these points in time, many events had taken place in my own little history as well as in that of the nations and the progress of art. The latter had really made remarkable strides in Norway. The New Norwegian literature had produced both fragrant blossoms and refreshing fruit. The sciences were able to display stars of the first magnitude, and Norwegian folk life had not only poets to represent it in epic and dramatic form: it had also found a painter whose superb pictures spread his own name and that of his native land throughout all of art-loving Europe.

I had dwelt with warm admiration on Tidemand's "Wedding Festival in Hardanger," the landscape portion of which was done by the talented Gude — another famous Norwegian — and I found a whole poem assembled in that one boat which glided along the glassy breast of the fjord. A number of outstanding works soon followed from the same master's hand, and the deep feeling that is expressed through his compositions transforms his delightful paintings into moving poems. All my Norwegian memories took on life and movement. I inserted a *springdans* in my *Old Memories,* and this bagatelle later became the high point of the ballet repertoire in which I presented my pupils in Norway during the summer of 1852.

The fact is that I had established a dancing course that gave me particular satisfaction both in financial respects and through the contacts I made with Christiania's most respected families, whose hospitality greatly enhanced my stay. My old friend Dahl was the same as he had always been in his cordial sympathy, and those of his friends with whom he had earlier put me in touch (most of whom had by now become notables) showed me an attention and kindness I shall never forget.

Thus matters stood when the Prices, my three Nordic Graces, together with one of their brothers and Edward Stramboe, came up to Christiania in order to confirm the good opinion that people had of my training. All their presentations were rewarded with abundant applause, but it was the *springdans* above all that produced a veritable frenzy of enthusiasm. The poet Welhaven embraced me and declared that from the raw material I had succeeded in creating a work of art, and his poetic interpretation of the lad's exultant leaps toward the four winds was so original that one of his friends very humorously added: "We Norwegians are really fond of seeing ourselves represented, especially when someone makes us look so good."

These encouragements gave me the boldness to attempt to assemble in an idyllic treatment some pictures of Norwegian folk life. Inspired by the above-mentioned factors as well as by the tales of Faye and Østgaard, filled with a host of melodies for which I was indebted to the ingenious Fru Munch and also some romances I had heard quite excellently delivered by a young lady from Tromsø, I arranged my subject and its details during my solitary wanderings through Fredensborg's shady avenues and among the statues in the Norwegian Dale, which still stand as though harkening to far-off sounds.

During my stay in Christiania, the Uppsala Students' Meeting took place and was remarkable for the fact that [students from] the very university which had the year before refused to participate in the Christiania Expedition with the other Scandinavians, now reported as guests and actually put those in charge in an awkward position with respect to both expense and enthusiasm. However, with some effort everything was arranged, and I had the chance to admire the Norwegians' tactfulness as hosts. They arranged parties and excursions, to which we Danes were also invited. But among the authorities there was an obvious tendency to promote an internal union of Swedish and Norwegian, to the exclusion of a broader Scandinavism. And they were successful for this short space of time which, because of the festive joy that was generated, came to be known as "The Swedish Holiday."

Families vied to show their guests the utmost kindness, and I was interested to hear a seventy-year-old peasant from Telemark say to a Swedish student with whom he had shaken hands at a banquet in the grove: "You know, when I was a lifeguardsman in Copenhagen, I never dreamed I would become such good friends with the Swedes." However, these two races were still very foreign to one another and, in particular, highly different in their addresses, where Danish humor was lacking to a considerable degree. A young Norwegian who was standing next to me during one of Svedelius' effusive orations said of the Swedes: "They are splendid people, but they lack irony." I am almost inclined to think we Danes possess too much of that Attic salt.

A little study trip we made to some provincial towns, in company with several of Christiania's leading actors, could provide material for a novelette with both picturesque views of nature and characteristic features of the roving life of actors, with which I here had the honor of becoming acquainted. Drammen was particularly rich in episodes, as, for instance, when at our first performance we came onstage from the blinding midsummer light outside and were completely consternated by the mysterious half-light that emanated from lamps equipped with tallow candles. We were forced to appeal to the kindness of our audience and borrow from the respective burgher families a dozen astral lamps, which we placed on some boards in the wings.

The theatre itself was very poorly equipped as far as scenery and properties were concerned. Thus for our Italian *divertissement* we had to make do with a birch forest, and when we needed an image of the Madonna, they came up with a picture which had always done service on such occasions. But since it turned out to be nothing less than a portrait of Griffenfeldt,† I was forced to renounce my idea—from artistic as well as religious and political considerations. However, we had our worst trials with the musical assistance; for even though we had in our excellent Paulli the most resourceful conductor in the world, the orchestra was in a state of total disintegration. For example, the contrabass had the misfortune of being unable to regulate or hold the beat unless it was supported by the violincello; and this last instrument, as it happened, was played by a public servant who dared not leave his office before 8:00 P.M.! Now one can imagine the difficult straits in which we found ourselves at the start of our performance. Fortunately, we had that *pièce de résistance* of all provincial orchestras, *The Caliph of Baghdad*, ready at hand; but here new problems arose. Our first French horn player was a very clever fellow—at the morning rehearsals, that is. But by afternoon he was neither disposed nor at our disposal and therefore politely sent his excuses by way of his second, who conscientiously performed *his* part—until the dancing began, at which moment he and all the other instrumentalists sat back, became happy spectators, and left it to Paulli and me to perform all the ballet music *on two first violins!*

However, this did not prevent our dancing members from creating a furor, and this in spite of Drammen's "aesthetic organ," which, a number of weeks before our arrival in the aforesaid town, had influenced public opinion to our detriment by producing some letters by Goethe, wherein this great thinker is supposed to have discussed the art of dancing in a most unfavorable manner. We did rather poor business and indemnified ourselves for the undeveloped artistic sense of this unpoetic town by strolling about its paradisically beautiful environs.

We parted company, but the talented actors Hagen and Wilhelm Wiehe accompanied us, or, more properly speaking, we accompanied them through the romantic regions of Holmestrand and Horten, via Moss, to Fredrikshald, where everything had been arranged for our reception.

At Moss, people would gladly have seen us perform, but the stage which we accidentally discovered at one end of the dining room at the inn did not appear to be suitable for our presentations, and we hurriedly passed through this town which is, by the bye, famous for its alcohol distilleries and its enormous potato fields.

At Fredrikshald we found a handsome theatre and an especially discriminating public. We gave two performances to packed houses and undertook several excursions into the surrounding countryside, which is interesting for its natural beauties and historical memories. The steamship *Gyller* carried us to Christiansand, where we enjoyed every possible advantage, on the stage as well as in society. An excursion up to the Torrisdals-Elv acquainted us

† Peder Schumacher, Count Griffenfeldt, was Chancellor of Denmark in the reign of Christian V. Overthrown by a cabal, he died at Trondheim, Norway, in 1699.

with the lovely hinterland, which one hardly suspects when one steps ashore on the barren coast. The town itself presents a remarkable contrast between the layout of the streets, which bear a perfect resemblance to Nyboder, and the language, which has the finest aristocratic accent.

We now covered by sea the distance to Arendal, where we were expected and where we enjoyed the climax of our circuit tour. This little town, remarkable for its considerable shipping and for its Venetian geographical situation, possesses one of the very smallest theatres in Europe, and our three performances were like so many family parties, the last of which ended with a banquet which was arranged in our honor on the stage itself, decorated to represent the most elegant salon. Our amiable hosts vied to show us the most exquisite politeness, and we did not say good-bye to them until midnight, when the back of the theatre was opened to reveal the roadstead, where in the glorious moonlight a decorated barge carried us out to the steamship, which was to cast off at dawn.

The last stage we played on was at Larvik, whose wonderful landscape unites the Danish with the Norwegian character in a luxuriant beech forest in the midst of mountains and waterfalls. Here I almost ended my career in this life when, an hour after my arrival, I was bathing among the rocks and while taking a dive, struck my head against a rock under the water. With a great deal of effort, I rose to the surface, bleeding. But if the stone on which I injured myself had been sharp instead of round, I would hardly have seen the blue vault of the sky again. A skilled physician's unselfish care and the Treschow family's tender ministrations were responsible for the fact that only two days after this serious occurrence I was able to attend our only performance, which was given at the town's so-called *Herregaard,* a building which housed the town hall, the grammar school, the clerical residence and—the theatre! Here everything came off well, and since at the buffet there were no other refreshments in the heat of the summer than arrack punch and Madeira, I went down to the Dean and asked for a bit of raspberry juice, which he most kindly provided from his wife's stores.

On the whole tour, which for me was something entirely new and adventurous, our petty difficulties were richly compensated for by the extraordinary hospitality with which we were everywhere received and by the interesting observations I had the opportunity of making. I was particularly struck by the rare urbanity that prevails in these small communities and manifests itself in a mutual kindness that might serve as a model for the most renowned capitals. In addition, I derived much joy from my traveling company, and among other things had to admire Hagen's *vis comica,* especially as a dramatic improvisationist—a talent which I have never come across in any scenic artist to such a high degree.

My fine pupils harvested everywhere income, applause, and flowers, but the high point of appreciation was the *springdans.* It called forth true fanaticism, and I was ever more strengthened in my intention to compose an entire Norwegian ballet. Therefore, as soon as I was settled at my beloved Fredensborg, I gathered together my abundant materials and gave my little idyll the form in which it appeared in the course of the ensuing winter. I called it *The Wedding Festival in Hardanger,* after Tidemand's excellent picture, as it was the central point about which I had built the plot of my ballet. The action was divided between two highly different pairs of lovers, and reached its climax at the end of the first act. By doing this I no doubt made an essential break with scenic rules; but I dared not disturb the actual wedding by further suspense or conflict, and I discovered that the joyous and festive atmosphere that pervades the whole second act was, despite errors in construction, the principal reason for the ballet's extraordinary and lasting success.

This work has been of special importance for my whole artistic direction because it has given me the opportunity to free myself even more from conventional pantomime and to employ a simpler and more natural gesticulation. It has thus brought me closer to the goal which I have so often had to sacrifice owing to the forms and limited means of expression peculiar to the ballet—namely, *dramatic truth.* In a truly admirable manner, the cast fell in with my views and thereby achieved heretofore unknown results. It was my intention to bring something lovely back with me from the mountains of Norway. I wanted to see whether the old love was still there and whether the brethern of former times had not become entirely alien to one another. And I believe the attempt was successful.

A FOLK TALE

A Ballet in Three Acts.
Music Composed by Gade and Hartmann.
Decorations by Messieurs Christensen and Lund.
Costumes Designed by Hr. Edv. Lehmann.
Machinery by Hr. Weden.
(Performed for the First Time in March 1854)

IN our practical and rather unpoetic times—which seem about to precipitate a period of literary and artistic crop failure on the very lands that were once the richest soil of the imagination—one ought to consider oneself lucky to possess such collections as Nyrup and Berggreen's *national melodies* and Thiele's* *folk tales.* They constitute an invaluable store of material for lyric poetry and richness of harmony that will be of particular benefit to Nordic poets and composers. These folk tales, most of which are probably remnants of old superstitions and corruptions of historical fact, are still an inexhaustible source for romantic adaptation which, with the aid of present-day reflection, endows them with allegorical meaning and, in return, gives a tinge of poetry

---

*Just Mathias Thiele (1795–1874), Danish author and art historian, chiefly known for his biography of Thorvaldsen; cf. Vol. II, pp. 237, 239.

to the hypercritical everyday life in which we all too deeply immerse ourselves, to the small advantage of that enthusiasm which may be nothing more than a result of our illusions but still provides us with our most joyous and solemn moments.

Without *enthusiasm* or *illusions,* the poet cannot work; in them he seeks and finds his spiritual nourishment, but they also cause him painful disappointments, which are, for him, like repeated shower baths: for a time they have a stimulating effect, but finally end by subduing his spirits, weakening his desire, and breaking his strength.

To me, one such disappointment was certainly the different manner in which our great poet and foremost aesthetician, J. L. Heiberg, behaved in his position of theatre administrator and—*virkelig Etatsraad.*† After the recognition my Muse had received from this literary notability, after the views he had expressed about the art of the stage in general, and—I make bold to say— in light of our mutually amicable relations, I had every reason to assume that he would regard me as the one man in my field who would be worthy of his confidence. But, far from regarding me with the same feelings as before, it became even more apparent that to this newly appointed high official the artistic reputation I had acquired through many years of successfully passed tests was a thorn in the flesh and that this power must be broken, regardless of the fact that, put to good use, it might have become his staunchest support.

What Heiberg's views were with respect to our classical authors, tragedy and its most outstanding representatives, the new foreign drama, the lyric stage, and the higher musical element as a whole, I shall submit to another court of law; but, as far as the Ballet was concerned, I will only emphasize that he agreed to financial conditions that robbed most of the younger members of the *corps* of even the poorest prospects for their future. It was obvious that Heiberg shared the widespread view that the Ballet's progress was detrimental to the spoken drama, which he felt he ought to protect by crushing the far more dangerous opera as well. Nevertheless, the Ballet could not be abolished overnight since its credit with the public still made it a vital source of income; but it was condemned to languish slowly. To this end my works were rarely scheduled in the weekly repertoire but were all the more frequently used as "emergency pieces"; small dances were employed to excess, nay, almost to the point of offense: for example, giving *Polka Militaire* after *Joseph and his Brethren* [*Joseph og hans Brødre*]. My new ballets were never pre-

---

† A title that gave him rather high social and official standing (see footnote, Vol. II, p. 208). Since it is beyond the scope of these notes to explore the complexities of the theatrical controversies that raged throughout Heiberg's tenure as Theatre Director, the reader is referred, among other works, to *Breve og Aktstykker vedrørende Johan Ludvig Heiberg,* ed. Morten Borup, 4 vols., (Copenhagen, 1946–1950), and Johanne Luise Heiberg's *Et Liv gjenoplevet i Erindringen,* ed. Aage Friis, 4 vols., (Copenhagen, 1944). With respect to Bournonville's views on Heiberg, it must be remembered that he saw his art as threatened with the possibility of extinction, and also that his remarks were published almost five years after Heiberg's death.

sented before the end of the season, at which time they were usually given together with worn-out and worthless one-act plays. Finally, as a reward for the *corp*'s persistent efforts, during Heiberg's seven-year reign its conditions remained totally unimproved.

However, these drastic measures did not have an immediate effect, for the morale of the ballet company was good and there were young talents who each year made it possible for me to furnish new compositions that attracted audiences and, in spite of all the hampering circumstances, were profitable.

At the same time, my personal position was made as unpleasant as possible. I was immediately alienated from the lyric stage, to which I had been specifically called in the capacity of stage director; and even though I did not have any independent report [to submit], but, on the contrary, had to put up with having a rather young junior clerk in charge of my activity, I—falling as I did into the category of *theatre officials*—was still excluded from all the prerogatives that accrued to so-called *stage artists* (among whom I could not be reckoned, according to Heiberg's definition).

They haggled in a shocking manner with the composers who had provided scores for my ballets, denying Hartmann and Gade the maximum salary (320 Rbd.!) for a score as ingenious as their music for *A Folk Tale*, simply because it was a few minutes shorter than the old regulation prescribed. An old custom of distributing ballet libretti to the Court and the personnel taking part in the performance was regarded as an abuse, and done away with; however, I was allowed to continue this token of esteem at my own expense. I was forbidden to summon the scene painter, the costumer, and the stage mechanic to my preliminary rehearsals in order to acquaint them with what I had in mind; according to his principles, Heiberg was forced to regard them as having nothing to do with this phase of the production.

The most inane complaints from subordinates were sympathetically listened to, while my recommendations were set aside unnoticed, and the most ridiculous appointments were made at his own discretion. When I had something to take up with my superior—which, you may be certain, rarely happened—I could stand outside in the corridor and wait for half an hour, while the youngest *figurant* had an audience. Finally—as the climax to a mischievousness that bordered on the puerile—when on a specific occasion I announced three weeks in advance that a close relative would be coming to the capital and that I should like to see two of my latest works performed, the repertoire was arranged so that for a fortnight, despite my repeated and urgent requests, *not a single ballet* was presented! Perhaps I ought to have forgotten these pinpricks, or at least omitted them from *My Theatre Life*; but just as they have, to a certain degree, awakened my powers of resistance, so too they have in the long run influenced my view of my position and caused me to look forward to my retirement as a godsend.

For myself, I was a sincere admirer of Heiberg as a poet and, upon the whole, as a writer. I felt irresistibly attracted by his intellectual intercourse in the days when he had not yet exchanged a first-class standing among the *beaux-esprits* for a third-class place in the social register.‡ However, I considered him unsuitable as a Director, first, because he himself was an artist (an author) and, as such, biased; secondly, because he always looked out for his own comfort; and, finally, because he was married to a prima donna. Still, by undauntedly lending him a hand, I hoped to win his favor for both myself and my art. Unfortunately, my zeal was construed as arrogance and viewed with distrust. Heiberg was mistaken about me, and I was disappointed in my expectations.

After the enthusiasm for Norway that had inflamed me during the production of *The Wedding Festival in Hardanger,* I received another, less drastic but quite bitter, disappointment upon noting the indifference with which this poetic effusion of mine had been received by the Norwegians, who had been jubilant over my *springdans* the year before. It is true that I did not bring my new ballet with me when in the spring of 1853 I again traveled to Christiania to complete the dancing course that had already given me such great satisfaction, but I still believed that the extraordinary sympathy with which this successful depiction of Norwegian folk life had been greeted by the Danish public would have produced some sort of echo—if not among the Norwegian mountains, at least in the hearts of this people to whom we were akin. Alas! It was as if my ballet had never existed! Only a handful of my friends said a word about it, and no one at all expressed the faintest desire to see it.

They say that the people's silence can serve as a lesson to sovereigns, but among us poor artists this silence arouses nought but doubt and dejection. I confess that this cold reserve filled me with sorrow; I had looked forward to being regarded as a poet and painter, yet they saw in me nothing but the skillful dancing master. I was reminded of Consul Fleischer in Naples, to whom I introduced myself, fully convinced that my name must be familiar to him; but he had never heard this name in his life, and when, in answer to his inquiry, I replied, "I compose ballets!," he looked at me and said with a smile, "Ah, that is very nice!" Such a dash of cold water is sometimes quite

---

‡ In nineteenth-century Copenhagen, social distinctions were much sharper than they are today and many people set great store by titles and social position. Numerous times throughout this work, Bournonville refers to people by their titles, many of which are now obsolete. Thus a list of these titles and their English equivalents may prove useful:

> *Overhofmarskal*—Chief Marshal of the Household
> *Hofmarskal*—Lord Chamberlain
> *Geheimeconferentsraad*—Titular Privy Councillor
> *Conferentsraad*—(title given to a high functionary)
> *Etatsraad*—Titular Councillor of State
> *Regjeringsraad*—Councillor of State
> *Justitsraad*—Councillor of Justice
> *Krigsraad*—Councillor of War
> *Cancelliraad*—Councillor of Chancery
> *Kammerjunker*—Gentleman of the Bedchamber
> *Kammerherre*—Chamberlain
> *Kammerassessor*—(an obsolete title)

useful in driving the devil of pride from an artist's soul, but this time it was not my vanity that had been unpleasantly affected. I had brought so much love with me and had harvested nothing more than a further confirmation of the teaching which the gypsy chieftain states so strikingly in *Preciosa:*

"Once a man has done well in a place
He ought never again to return there."

As an admirer of the sublime scenery and as the friend of a free and vigorous race of people, I still hope to see again before I die that country where I have received so many glorious impressions.

Just as I set foot on board the steamship to sail for home, I learnt that cholera morbus had broken out in Copenhagen, and by the time we reached the Swedish archipelago we were already subject to the strictest quarantine measures. I had never beheld this dreaded guest with my own eyes and believed that, like all other plagues in our beloved Denmark, it too would appear in a milder form. But immediately upon disembarking at the Custom House we could perceive that something unusual was going on. Everywhere, one heard tell of the spread of the plague and the inadequate measures being taken by the public. The topic of the day was the list of those affected and carried off by the disease, and a number of our friends succumbed to the terrible epidemic.

Many inhabitants moved away, but on the whole the Copenhageners displayed the same noble attributes they usually do in times of adversity. The doctors' zeal and self-sacrifice were beyond all praise; the priests, with a single exception, attended to their solemn business at the risk of their lives; and from the Heir Presumptive and his wife, who stayed in the capital to bolster morale by their courage and helpfulness, to the simplest workingman who was unafraid to enter the homes of the sick and drive them out to the hospitals, the conduct of the public was exemplary.

It so happened that that summer my family was not staying in the country. Every day, Death claimed its victims by the hundred, but just when the number reached its zenith, I received an urgent letter from my mother, who had managed to secure rooms for us at Fredensborg, and I must admit that the same pure air that had remained untainted by the plague in 1711 also passed the test this time.

Of all the precautionary measures that doctors prescribed, none was more effective against the infection of cholera than dauntlessness and the greatest possible mental diversion. Accordingly, one had to keep up one's spirits by one interesting occupation or another, and my thoughts were involuntarily drawn to the banks of the Arno, where, in the delightful Boboli Gardens at Florence, I had sat beneath the same cypress trees in whose shade the ten witty male and female friends had gathered during the plague in the fourteenth century in order, by means of merry short stories which they composed and recited by turn, to dispel all worries and forget the danger and misery that surrounded them.* I zealously decided to immerse myself in ballet composition and during those fateful days drafted *A Folk Tale* and *Abdallah;* but it was only beneath the age-old linden trees at Fredensborg that my ideas fell into place. There, in the most pleasant intercourse with my ingenious friend Høedt,† the picture of that Florentine group became doubly alive to me, and every time we met *en plein air* we imparted to each other new fragments of our intellectual creations.

The epidemic subsided, the summer passed for us in rural tranquillity, and the theatre season began some weeks later than usual. During this interval I kept up an active correspondence with my superior, who was unusually well-disposed toward me and accepted my ballet libretto with encouraging approbation.

The old legends about gnomes, elf-maidens, and bewitched children were of considerable use to me in this subject. A feature in Thiele's collection of stories – where one hears gnomes holding a banquet and toasting one another with "Skaal, Diderik!" "Thanks, Viderik!" – gave me a whole fantasy picture of life inside the hills, and from this a little plot quite naturally evolved with several original characters such as the Troll Maiden, the Mountain Lass, the dwarf brothers and their mother, the young and the old Junker, and others; and, finally, the most varied situations emerged from the cycle of legends as well as the manor life of the Middle Ages.

When I now, after so many years have passed, think back on the planning and execution of this composition, with its humorous and serious scenes into which both graceful and fantastic dances are woven, I must acknowledge it to be my most perfect and finest choreographic work, especially as regards its Danish character. I had every reason to be delighted with all aspects of the performance as well as with the public's sympathy, which recalled the golden days of *Valdemar* and *Napoli.*

It remains for me to mention the superb assistance I received from two famous composers, Hartmann and Gade, who did not disdain to shower upon my Muse the richness of their tones; nor did Terpsichore leave them unrewarded, for even though the ballet mainly occupies the eye, the ear soon reclaims its right. Thus Hartmann's second act, where the fairy-tale element is most strongly apparent, was of such a singular effect that it could be heard as an independent symphony. On the other hand, the first and third acts, by Gade, combined the sparkling humor of the operetta with the simplicity of the ryhthms of the dance, and in the idyllic as well as the romantic portion of the music, the composer seemed to have outdone himself. The Ring Dance of the elf-maidens and the lovely "Midsummer Song" from the finale of the ballet can still be found on every piano and will retain their freshness long

---

*The reference is to Boccaccio's well-known *Decameron.*
† Frederik Ludvig Høedt (1820–1885); see the character sketch of Høedt in the section "Dramatic Celebrities of the Danish Stage," Vol. II, pp. 327–331.

after my fleeting work has vanished from the stage, aye, maybe even from the memory of the younger generation. Then may these lines attest that it was I who furnished the opportunity for these lovely sounds to come forth, and that no one appreciated more than I the poetic life they gave to my pictures.

ABDALLAH

A Ballet in Three Acts.
Music Composed by Paulli.
Decorations by Messrs. Christensen and Lund.
Costumes Designed by Hr. Edvard Lehmann.
Machinery Arranged by Hr. Weden.
(Performed for the First Time in March 1855)

AN Arabian tale which I once encountered in an English reader provided me with material for this ballet, and the success that rewarded my stage arrangement for Oehlenschläger's *Aladdin** gave me the incentive to venture into the cycle of fairy tales that has been preserved for us mainly in *The Arabian Nights*.

On the two occasions mentioned above, the subject [on which I based my ballet] appeared, each time in somewhat different form. But when my libretto was read, it did not win the unconditional approval of my nearest and dearest arbiter of taste, who, precisely because she is the most anxious, is also the sharpest. And it is true that despite all the industry and care [expended on this ballet], no real success has attended its presentation on the stage. Therefore *Abdallah's* history would soon be told, were it not connected with an important and, I believe, not wholly uninteresting period of my career, namely, my sojourn in Vienna during part of the summer of 1854 and the entire Viennese theatre season of 1855–1856.

My seven-year engagement at the Royal Theatre expired; I felt that the idea I had fought for so long would not be realized, and that my efforts were like card houses which were repeatedly blown over, from one side by narrow-minded, from the other by methodical, dislike. I had assuredly learnt to do without lively applause and to sidestep criticism that was often highly unfair. But since I could no longer counteract the systematic undermining of the Ballet's future, and since my proposals for bettering the conditions of the personnel as well as for establishing a pension fund went unheeded, there was nothing left for me to do but avail myself of the benefits to which my contract entitled me and retire from a sphere of activity where perhaps my absence would accomplish more than my efforts. In any event, I did not wish to be present at the collapse.

Therefore, by the beginning of the seventh year (1854) I was already contemplating a change of position, and at the same time as I secured an old-age

*In April 1839.

refuge in my native land by acquiring a little house at Fredensborg, I also wrote to the outstanding [theatre] director Carl v. Holbein to offer the Imperial Opera Theatre in Vienna my services as balletmaster. But what could equal my surprise and—I must confess—my disappointment at receiving by return post an answer, not from that fine man of letters and Councillor of State but from the notorious former entrepreneur of the Hamburg State Theatre, Cornet†, one of the most unpleasant people in the world, who now, through Heaven knows what influence, had taken Holbein's place as director. I shuddered at his very name, for I knew him from earlier days when as an opera singer he had made his reputation by mad scenes which he later employed in both daily and administrative life. However, he was delighted with my plan, and in terms both short and to the point made me the most advantageous offer, bidding me come as quickly as possible and promising me the strongest support in everything that might favor a branch of art which, according to his own admission, was in radical need of reform. I cannot deny that I certainly felt tempted to at least investigate the terrain, and I obtained permission to make a flying visit to Vienna during the course of Holy Week.

The journey passed quickly and comfortably. I stopped over only for a single day in Berlin, where I visited my old comrade Paul Taglioni, with whom I had always maintained the most pleasant relations despite the bad luck he had had in Copenhagen.‡ I admired the magnificent new [Royal] Museum* with Kaulbach's frescoes, and attended a presentation of Lachner's opera *Catharina Cornaro*, which I found most appealing and the performance of which owed its high points to Johanna Wagner. The sumptuousness of the equipment, especially the décor, was beyond description. I traveled by railway train via Dresden and Prague, and arrived in the imperial city on Good Friday evening.

It was with an especially solemn feeling that I set foot in places which were already familiar to me through my father's childhood memories; at every step I was reminded of his stories. Nothing was foreign to me, not even the jovial dialect, which recalled to me a host of amusing anecdotes. It was a moonlit night, and the first remarkable object I encountered in my wanderings was *Stock am Eisen* [Iron Log], the remains of the trunk of an old oak tree which in the remote Middle Ages had stood upon the ramparts but now leaned against a niche by a gateway not far from the Stefanskirche. The famous or infamous *Stock* was closely studded with thousands of iron nails driven in by all the journeyman smiths who through the centuries had worked in Vienna. According to tradition, a poor boy had sold his soul to the Devil in order to learn from him how to make a burglar-proof lock. He could, however, be released from fulfillment of the pact if he heard a Mass in the Stefanskirche every morning. And so it was simply a matter of avoiding temp-

---

† Cf. the chapter on "Hamburg", Vol. III, Part Three, pp. 547–549.
‡ See footnote on Taglioni's Danish fiasco, Vol. I, p. 95.
* Now called the Staatliche Museen, located in East Berlin.

tations which might prevent him from carrying out this morning obligation. But one day he arrived too late. The Mass was over, and the Devil carried the poor smith away with him through a hole high up in the roof of the church.

The hole was long ago bricked up, but the legend still survives, and the venerable cathedral is still a constant refuge for the anxious souls of the populace. Its majestic towers herald the imperial city at a distance of several miles, and its golden eagle sparkles in the glow of evening while streets and market-places are already shrouded in darkness. Just as I looked up at the dizzying height—over four hundred feet—a beautiful star twinkled above the farthest spire. The church itself was dimly lit, the doors stood open, but everything was still. I walked in and immediately beheld to the right a gloriously illuminated chapel, from whose steps far down into the dark nave there knelt a numerous flock of devout people, who in prayer and fasting were awaiting the Resurrection, for the chapel represented the Holy Sepulchre. This silence is perhaps one of the most edifying things in the Catholic service and makes a profound impression, even upon a Protestant mind. I myself prayed with sincere devotion, and my heart was filled with the best hopes for the successful outcome of my journey.

Upon the whole, I really enjoyed my short stay. Everywhere people received me kindly, and even the loathsome Cornet seemed to me to have changed in the eleven years that had passed since I had last seen him. In the midst of his coarse wit and rather cynical outlook on life could be glimpsed an ostensible expression of esteem and genuine confidence. In addition, he boasted of a certain *crude* honesty that deceived me. My free admittance into both Court Theatres was a foregone conclusion, and wherever I went the Director's praise resounded as my recommendation. In short, every effort was made to lure me into a trap where later on my steadfastness was to be put to such severe trials.

The feast of the Resurrection was celebrated on Saturday afternoon with a magnificent procession. This gave me an opportunity to see at rather close range the young Emperor,† with a dazzling suite of courtiers and generals, among whom were the Field Marshals Hess, Windischgrätz, Schlick (a martial figure with a black bandage over one eye), and lastly, the eighty-year-old Radetzky.

The nuptials [of the Emperor] approached with new ceremonies. I was staying in the suburb of Mariahilf, and there had the finest opportunity to view the entry of the procession from Schönbrunn. The imperial bridegroom's impatience was highly interesting, and the populace itself seemed to have recovered from the sorrowful memories of the revolution, the siege and—even the bombardment that followed it! I found the Viennese merry and jovial, but people who had known them before they had tasted of Freedom's tree of the knowledge of good and evil claimed that the atmosphere in recent years had

† Francis Joseph (1830–1916) became Emperor on the abdication of his uncle, Ferdinand I, December 2, 1848.

diminished considerably. I was taken by a good friend to the home of a charming family who lived *am Graben,* one of the capital's inner squares, where the actual procession was to ride past on its way from the Teresianum to the Hofburg. All the bells rang to the sonorous bass of St. Stephen's *bourdon,* and since there was no music other than the snarling trumpets, there was something funereal about the whole. The picture was lightened however by a variegated and truly oriental splendor: cavalry escorts, costly equipages, with runners and Haiduks,‡ dignitaries in carriages and on horseback. But what astonished me above all were the Hungarian magnates in their national costumes of velvet studded with gold and precious stones. Their horses' caparisons were sewn with pearls, and each of these princes or feudal overlords had an entourage of richly dressed noblemen and foot pages. Last came the gilded glass coach with the imperial bride, who was dressed in pink and white. She wore a diamond crown upon her head and charmingly waved to all sides. At the sight of the lovely young princess the silence, which had prevailed throughout the whole mediaeval procession, broke. Hurrahs from the enormous crowd of people drowned out the thunder of cannon, and the excitement reached its pitch. It was an imposing scene.

I hailed the arrival of spring at the lovely Schönbrunn, whence I could still glimpse the snow-capped mountains in far-off Styria. On roaming through the thirty-four suburbs I everywhere encountered a good-natured people, spied upon and controlled by a numerous, vigilant, and armed police force. People were also kind enough to remind me that my steps too were watched, but I felt strong in my good conscience and in the support I had in our good Baron Langenau, once Austrian minister in Copenhagen and a warm friend of Denmark. He was now serving as Head of Public Safety. However, here I received thorough instruction in a noble art which in our dear homeland has always been rather neglected, namely, that of keeping one's mouth shut and not compromising oneself in either speech or writing. The Austrian's virtuosity in this area is most extraordinary. An old friend and artistic colleague, Isidore Carey, gave me several warnings in this area as well as with regard to theatre affairs, the importance of which I did not come to realize until later on.

I had an especially pleasant meeting with our Nordic goddess of song, Jenny Lind, now a wife and mother under the name of Madame Goldschmidt. She was the same cordial and unpretentious Jenny she had been at the time I had her as a guest in my humble home. I visited her family circle often, came to know and respect her husband, and attended two of her brilliant concerts. We had many a heated conversation about how wrong she was to turn her back on the stage forever, and thus bury the rich talent that had once been the delight and edification of so many; but I always received the reply that she had now learnt that the theatre was nothing but lies and delusions!

The Imperial Opera's German season does not begin until July and con-

‡ Originally, a class of mercenary foot soldiers who received privileges of nobility and independence in 1605; later, liveried (and often armed) guards or serving men in the household of a noble.

cludes at the end of March. The three spring months are used by the Italian opera, which has always had a great reputation in Vienna, and at the time of my arrival had just begun its performances. At that time the company was quite numerous but not very distinguished. I did notice the alto Borghi-Mamo and the superb coloratura-baritone Evrardi, who, like the prima donna Medori, had been born in Belgium. For the rest, the voices shrieked and trembled to a horrible degree. The repertoire was the same as we had heard from the Italian troupe in Copenhagen, but naturally supported by better talents in the chorus as well as the orchestra.

As far as the spoken drama was concerned, I had great enjoyment from two highly different stages in Vienna: the Burgtheater directed by Laube, and the Karltheater, headed by Nestroy.

At the former I noticed a rather varied repertoire, partly classical, but above all handled with the greatest care: for both newer and older authors and foreign as well as German dramatic literature were represented there in tasteful selection. One could go to the drama every evening for several weeks in succession without seeing the same piece twice; and along with the finest new works of the day, one was always certain to find Shakespeare, Göethe, and Schiller; indeed, even Lessing, Iffland, and Kotzebue emerged from time to time in order to maintain certain stock character roles, which were performed with great talent. The famous actor Korn had recently passed away, but there still shone Anschütz, Löwe, Laroche, the superb Fichtner, and the comedians Bechmann and Meisner—all of them older men, a phenomenon that manifests itself almost everywhere in the present artistic period. Even the leading tragic actor, Joseph Wagner, was well into his forties. Some younger actors, Baumeister, Gabillon, and Landvogt, although respectable, did not seem remarkable to me. On the whole, were I to find something to object to in the superb ensemble, it would have to be the fact that it was almost impossible to be *outstanding* in the midst of such artistic uniformity.

People enjoyed the drama with exceptional calm; reflection was satisfied, they were filled with respect, but real excitement was lacking. Still, one seemed to find oneself on consecrated ground, where respect for art pervaded the audience as well as the actors, who performed the smallest supporting roles with the same zeal and precision as they did the most brilliant leading parts, and the ensemble acting thereby acquired a *rondeur* that could hardly be equaled at the Théâtre-Français. The female personnel were excellent. Mmes. Rettich, Hebbel, and Haitzinger; Mlles. Louise Neümann and Marie Seebach (both unmarried at the time) maintained the large repertoire, and the talented Frau Bayer-Bürch from Dresden appeared as guest. Unfortunately, I did not get to see the famous Dawison. But even though I must fully acknowledge the rare forces of cooperation among this group of actors, I found in its midst not a single actress with Fru Heiberg's genius, no comedian with the variety of Phister, nor a leading man who combined poetry and naturalness to the same degree as Michael Wiehe.

At the secondary theatre, which was named for the deceased Karl—the unforgettable *Staberle* [the modern jack-pudding] of the Viennese—there reigned the Nestroyan *Posse,* a broader type of *vaudeville* which, like the Danish, gathered its material from minor French authors who, while people audaciously use and travesty their ideas, are repudiated and put down by their imitators. Here, in a cycle of *petites pièces* from the last four centuries, I saw an attempt to reclaim for Germany the patent for the invention of the *Posse.* I must frankly state that the very oldest, namely, *The Ordeal by Fire* by Hans Sachs, was the best. The indispensable "Hanswurst," though in rejuvenated form, runs through all these productions, and it was usually Nestroy himself who had the task of delivering the necessary *"Localwitz"* and occasional couplets. In this area he was a past master, but he could not really merit the name of actor.

To me, the very popular Treümann appeared to be an experienced virtuoso in the realm of German "smartness"; Grois cultivated caricature with a certain success, and Fräulein Zöllner was a most charming interpreter of the humorous and naïve Viennese dialect; but as a star of the first magnitude shone the superb comedian Scholz—also an older man. His makeup was unchanging but his humor *unverwüstlich*—one must forgive me this borrowed expression which seems made to denote his inimitable *vis comica.* He was the personification of South German *Gemütlichkeit* and unwitting irony; lovable from sheer awkwardness, the Sancho Panza of Austrian politics, the autocrat of laughter!

Scholz, who died shortly after my last trip home, is remembered not only by the jovial patrons of art but also by his fellow-citizens and comrades as a man who, by a noble character, versatile education, and rare humanity, had a beneficial effect upon all his associates.

But when I now come to my actual errand, namely, the investigation of the conditions of the Ballet, I involuntarily hesitate, seized by the fear that the theories I have so zealously sought to develop might possibly have prejudiced my judgment to such a degree that only that which was prepared from my own book could satisfy my demands, and that I myself might have fallen victim to the sort of egoism that so often seizes upon those who place themselves at the head of a system. Therefore I shall relate without commentary what I have seen with my own eyes.

The first ballet performance was none other than *Faust,* staged by Ronzani after Jules Perrot, who had composed it for Lucile Grahn (apparently after features she had remembered from my bold youthful attempt).* The plan was essentially the same, but the plot was completely obscured by overwhelming virtuoso dancing. Thickset old Ronzani, in a red velvet Don Juan costume embroidered in gold, played Faust. This role consisted mainly in admiring Gretchen, who in six brilliant changes of costume performed equally

---

* A failure of memory on Bournonville's part. Perrot's *Faust* was actually composed for Fanny Elssler (1848). Cf. Ivor Guest, *Fanny Elssler;* cf. also Svend Kragh-Jacobsen, *"Faust på Tæerne,"* in *I anledning af* (Copenhagen, 1968).

as many *soli* and *pas de deux* at both the diabolical Sardanapaulan banquet, to which her friends and relatives were invited, and at the ensuing Walpurgis Night celebration, where she was accompanied by a *banda militare;* that is to say, by a perfectly civilized band, with valve horns and bass drums, seated onstage amidst the swarm of devils!

Mephistopheles, who took part in all these dances, had not chosen Retzsch's engravings as the model for his costume but was dressed as a handsome circus rider, with bare arms and legs, enameled horns on his forehead, and *caleçons de bain;* the whole accompanied by an immovable countenance.

One of the trials which poor Gretchen had to endure was the influence of the Seven Deadly Sins personified. The seventh and last of these winsome apparitions was Sloth, and it cannot be denied that it left its mark on the ballet's prima donna; though I must admit that she possessed an iron strength and staying power which probably deserved to be put to better use.

I got to see yet another ballet, namely *Giselle*, with which I was familiar from its origin in Paris. But here it appeared in a somewhat distorted form. Borri, who played the young Duke, was exactly the same as he had been as Mephistopheles: in his fleshings and *caleçons* he looked as if he were ready to charge through three paper drums! Giselle's death, resurrection, and reburial did not move him any more than they would have moved a stone. At the same time, I made the sorely disturbing discovery that the audience was completely foreign to the idea of mime; in fact, they paid no attention at all to the action but simply awaited the third, fourth, or fifth *pas de deux* in order to burst into applause.

I felt that I could do nothing with a *corps* that had been trained in such a school. It would take several years' work and unlimited authority for me to have any hopes of seeing my better compositions performed on this stage with any chance of success. I therefore completely renounced my plan and went to bid the Director farewell. But indeed, the more determined I was to leave, the more eager Cornet was to keep me. He promised to provide new and better dancers, even left it to me to recruit and supplement the *corps*, and solemnly reassured me that this was the very thing for me to get my teeth into. However, I left him without making any firm commitment. But a few days after I had returned home, he sent me a letter couched in the most flattering terms, with an invitation to mount as an experiment *The Toreador* and *The Festival in Albano*! If they were successful, which he did not doubt for a moment, I might sign a contract that could be renewed on a yearly basis, starting with July 1, 1855.

It seemed as though they were going out of their way to be nice to me. They bade me engage Füssel to act his Melancholy Englishman. Frappart, a very popular comedian from Paris, was to play the jovial Mr. John; Fräulein Catharina Lanner, Céleste; and a pretty French *danseuse*, Mlle. Levasseur, Maria. Thus far the arrangements were fine, but I was unable to escape having Borri as the Toreador. I all too easily allowed myself to be persuaded of his willingness to learn and of the miracles that my instruction would be able to accomplish. To this was also added a hint of defiance against several people here at home who continued to assert that I would never be able to obtain engagement at a major theatre abroad. Suffice it to say, I went along with it, and since the fee was especially generous, I was able to give my wife and daughter the benefit of a pleasure trip.

The weather was delightful, hope smiled upon us, and on June 17 we departed by steamship for Stettin. The following evening we heard Frau Bürde-Ney in *Lucrezia Borgia* at the Berlin Opera; next evening Tichatczeck in Dresden, where we viewed all of this city's curiosities and art treasures, arriving in Vienna on June 22. The very next day I began my rehearsals, and on July 15 *The Festival in Albano* and *The Toreador* were performed onstage for the first time, with extraordinary applause.

One will no doubt be surprised that I presented two ballets in one evening. But herein lies an essential failing in the repertoire of the Vienna Opera; that is to say, they give performances consisting entirely of operas five times a week, while the other two days are allotted exclusively to the ballet, and this branch is then expected to fill an entire evening. This not only produces a most harmful satiety but also divides the theatregoing public into three parts. One goes to the Burgtheater; the second attends purely musical performances; leaving the ballet with only curious travelers and *amateurs*, for whom *tours de force* and voluptuous figures are the spectacle's *non plus ultra*. If one now compares the relationship between forty recognized operas, with a triple cast of Germany's finest singers, conducted by three *Kapellmeisters* and supported by the most superb orchestra, and the ballet, isolated from all dramatic assistance, equipped with poor talents, and based upon an ephemeral repertoire, one will concede that under such circumstances a balletmaster's position must be very difficult if not absolutely untenable.

Nevertheless I ventured to try it, lured on by the hope of evoking a favorable reaction and relying on vigorous support from above. Never in my life have I worked with greater energy, and the beginning boded well for the future. The qualities of sprightliness and simplicity in my compositions seemed to please everyone, and words like "poetry" and "coherence," which could never have been said of the Italian monstrosities, now resounded from several quarters. My speed and orderliness appealed to the practical sense of both the *corps* and the Director. There seemed to be general agreement that I was the man they needed.

Several portions of *The Festival in Albano* and *The Toreador* gave me genuine satisfaction. Frappart, in particular, danced his *tarantella* with inspiring liveliness, whereas he reduced the role of the Stout Englishman to the level of a circus farce. Fräulein Lanner was perfect as the *danseuse* and shared with old Mayseder the triumph for the grand solo to the violin "Polonaise," which was performed by the famous maestro himself. As mime, Füssel upheld the honor of the Danish ballet, and the secondary roles were performed with briskness and precision. But as for the title role—it is true that for this once Borri had to give up his favorite costume; but his dancing and gesticulation made it appear as if he were continuously swimming through an ocean of clumsiness and nonsense; it was certainly not thanks to him that the ballet escaped the same sorrowful fate that had struck so many of its predecessors on this same sordid battlefield. I emerged from my bold experiment with success and honor. I received applause and curtain calls from the audience, humane treatment from the press, sympathy on the part of the *corps,* and, as the most positive result, a contract for the following season, signed after the ballet's first performance.

Indeed, what more could one ask? However, I was not entirely at ease; for, in addition to the above-mentioned stumbling blocks, I still saw a host of difficulties arising from an extremely materialistic tendency on the part of the audience and the management and from the busy, restless confusion which gave an appearance of enterprise and breadth of outlook. Besides, there was a constantly changing *corps,* with neither training nor traditions, and both on and off stage a close-knit Italian clique led by the *régisseur* Golinelli, who was himself a bit of a ballet arranger.

I was still not aware that the exceptional kindness which the Director showed me was merely a hidden cabal against Paul Taglioni, who, together with his daughter [Marie Taglioni the younger] and some of the most outstanding members of the Berlin ballet, had been guest artists in Vienna for several years in succession under the direct patronage of the Emperor. It was therefore Cornet's intention to use *me* as a counterweight to unseat these troublesome guests. But I later learnt to my extreme displeasure what it means to come between protection and its object, and how little aesthetic efforts count for in the face of royal sympathies.

Convinced that only effort and discretion were required in order to emerge from the struggle victorious, I prepared to fulfill my obligations honestly. I came to an agreement about furnishing three ballets during the first season, namely, *Abdallah, Napoli,* and *The Kermesse,* but did not think of retaining for myself the exclusive right of providing the repertoire during my tenure. I was entirely preoccupied with the thought of being able to do something to raise my art from its dilapidated state in Vienna, as I had once succeeded in doing in Copenhagen. Moreover, my national feeling was flattered by the fact that at the same time no less than six Danes, in addition to myself, stood at the head of their respective professions within the Austrian monarchy: Dahlerup as admiral, Gamborg as shipbuilder, the brothers Christian and Theophilus Hansen as master builders for the two largest arsenals, Eriksen as head of steamship traffic on the Danube, and lastly, Dr. Mannheimer as chief rabbi for the Jewish community.

After my two ballets had assumed their place in the standard repertoire, I was a completely free man and could amuse myself by excursions into the charming environs of the city and be a spectator of both the colorful folk life and the finest performances. As has been said, the Opera offered superb productions and excellent singing talents. I will only mention the tenors Ander and Steger, the basses Drachsler and Beck, the sopranos Titjens, La Grua, and Wildauer, together with the altos Hermann-Czillag and Schwartz, in order to give my readers some idea of the ensemble, which was further heightened by the finest chorus I have ever heard.

Before my departure I was to see yet another of Perrot's ballets. This was *Esmeralda*, after Victor Hugo's *Notre Dame de Paris*, created, as *Faust* had been, to display an outstanding ballerina. Herein Mlle. Pocchini made her *rentrée* with great bravura. She was vivacity personified, more brilliant than graceful, but indescribably entertaining. The following year she was to be my prima donna, and would have been superbly suited for the part of the troll-maiden in *A Folk Tale*. However, such a role would not have been in keeping with her status as *prima donna assoluta*. I nevertheless had Pocchini in mind when casting the roles for *Abdallah* and therefore called Irma the *Gazelle* of Balsora. A trick of Fate was responsible for the fact that I did not carry out this one correct idea; for immediately upon my return to Denmark, I mounted this composition and Juliette Price gave the part of Irma such a sylphlike quality that, in a manner of speaking, the role became identified with her personality and no longer seemed to suit Pocchini. Besides, if here in Denmark all the other characters had been performed as well as that of Irma, *Abdallah* would undoubtedly have become one of my most successful ballets; for together with a warm local color, it had in performance acquired a measure of that virtuosity which one cannot deny the modern school and which, used in the proper places, can heighten the effect.

Unfortunately, the title role demanded a degree of fantasy for which I myself may once have had the mimic expressiveness that I was now unable to impart to the present player of the role. It often happens that authors who have earlier been actors picture themselves portraying the most important characters in their works. But then they remember the old French proverb: "If youth but knew, could age but do."

The music was characteristic and tuneful throughout, and also won recognition later on in Vienna. The dances and a number of original scenes were much applauded, while the over-all impression was favorable, largely owing to the brilliant décor. On the whole, I could regard the reception as honorable, and with this ballet I fancied that I had taken definite leave of the Danish Theatre, which I looked upon as inseparable from Heiberg and his system.

On June 28, 1855, I set out on the journey to my new sphere of activity, accompanied by a small household consisting of my wife, two daughters, my little son, a maid, and a foster child who had been entrusted to my care, Juliette Price.

During my first stay in Vienna, every time the conversation turned to the quality of dancing as opposed to its quantity, or to the tone and attitude I desired to instill in every *corps de ballet,* I could not avoid mentioning our talented countrywoman; and, quite *en passant,* I had expressed the wish that she might one day be granted the opportunity of making a guest appearance. To my surprise, I received a letter from Cornet, requesting that Frøken Price be offered engagement for an entire season, with a salary that amounted to four times what she had received here at home! This offer, as advantageous as it was honorable, was highly attractive to the young *artiste* but considerably embarrassing to me, since it made me responsible for her success at the same time as it placed me in an awkward position with regard to the Viennese *danseuses,* who were looking forward to my coming in order to obtain roles and leading parts. However, since they demanded a quick and definite answer, and the contract lay ready for signing, we decided that she should apply for a nine-months leave of absence, which was granted after some resistance, in return for which her humble salary was to be absorbed into the treasury of the Royal Theatre. It was not long before I noticed that my desire to bolster my theories by presenting one of my pupils had completely warped my relationship with the *corps* as well as an active part of the ballet audience.

On entering the Director's office immediately upon my arrival, I already perceived a remarkable change in his tone and character. The former confidence and cheerfulness had given place to an expression of uneasiness mixed with visible embarrassment. Actually, the officious Cornet had gotten involved in several matters, all of which were more or less harmful to my undertaking.

In the first place, he had lost a lawsuit to Borri, who, as balletmaster from the previous season, had asserted his right to present the second ballet which had been stipulated in his contract. The staging of this ballet was now carried over into my term of office and encumbered my works. Secondly, in his hotheadedness he had sent for a so-called *premier danseur* from Bordeaux, who was to play the leading roles in my ballets, but proved to be (in Cornet's own words) so *"unter dem Hund schlecht"* that in order to avoid an utter travesty, they were obliged to send him home with a quarter of a year's salary. But the third and worst element in this mess of adversity was that from the highest quarters the Director had received a severe reprimand for his malevolence toward Taglioni and had been expressly commanded to summon this balletmaster, his daughter, and her partner Carl Müller, to Vienna, where they were to give all the Emperor's favorite ballets during November and December and also mount a grand new work, *Balanda.*

These were highly unfortunate and most unexpected circumstances for me. As far as the first point was concerned, I had to put on the best face so as not to get all of the Italians at my throat. The second was less difficult, since by good fortune I had my clever Julius Price at hand; he was immediately engaged and later found a permanent place as soloist at the Vienna Opera. But as to the third, I could do nought but arm myself with resignation; for the royal enthusiasm for Taglioni was so considerable that when the news came from Trieste that the Archduke Max (the present Emperor of Mexico) hovered between life and death as the result of an accident with runaway horses, the Emperor, while rushing to his brother's side, commanded that the outcome of the new ballet be telegraphed to him!

I therefore had to watch my step and make use of the intervals granted me for rehearsals, by means of which I succeeded in bringing no small skill to light. But when Borri's arrangement of the French ballet *Jovitta* (which, with the original music and full details, passed as his own work under the altered title of *Caritta*) began to drag on and on, it seemed to Cornet that such a highly paid dancer as Frøken Price should not have to wait so long to make her debut, and it was decided that she should apppear as Hélène in the spectre scene in *Robert of Normandy*. The part was not disadvantageous, and since it is performed somewhat apart, it might be very suitable for introducing a graceful talent. But here too there were several obstacles; for example, Louise Meyer's debut that same evening as Alice, a role which must necessarily attract greater attention. On top of this, a most ridiculous quarrel had taken place some time before between the Director and the singer Steger because of the above-mentioned ballet scene, in which the latter had been laughed to scorn on account of his clumsiness. In a rage, he once again refused to perform this scene, and Cornet threatened him with the police. Steger responded by assaulting the Director with a box on the ears and even pulled his hat so far down over his eyes that help was needed to bring that pleasant countenance back to light. The dispute was now settled by mediation, but Steger had sworn that hereafter during the scene in question he would not budge from his spot. And he kept his word with a brutality that could take place only at a German theatre.

This was the partner with whom our noble Juliette was now to appear before a completely foreign audience! However, the good impression her personality had made upon the entire *corps* and the recognition her training enjoyed among all connoisseurs gave us hope of a successful outcome. Juliette pulled herself together and danced like an angel, but this was precisely the wrong thing to do, for people were used to seeing this role interpreted as a *she-devil*, with wild hair, half-naked limbs, and flesh color that exceeded even the strongest blush of the rose. Therefore, neither successful attitudes, suspended flight, nor all the grace that was lavished upon the clumsy Robert were of any use here. The disappointed audience remained cold and almost silent. I needed all my moral strength to console my poor pupil, to avoid Cornet's sarcasm, and to keep up my own spirits. But there were many, and among them the Emperor's own mother, the Archduchess Sophie, who appreciated the purer interpretation of the concept of dancing. The press itself was in agreement with all aesthetic arbiters of taste in the assertion that my method was the proper one as opposed to the excesses which are nowadays rampant; but the fact was: it did not entertain them.

The aforementioned plagiarism was now presented, but despite its brilliant décor was indifferently received. The whole thing was a sort of "robber ballet" about the well-known buccaneers, and all the more important situations were elucidated by inscriptions. For example, in the cave where these pirates kept their stores of gunpowder, it said in large letters on all the barrels: "Powder! Powder! " However, Mlle. Pocchini performed prodigies, and in an inserted *pas de trois* that I had arranged for Julius Price's debut, Juliette got the opportunity to take a lovely revenge for her first unappreciated appearance. And then, at last, I got leave to begin.

My first offense was an unfortunate idea that had been conceived by Cornet, who pretended to be practical; namely, that the action in *Abdallah* ought to be shifted to Italy; and when I pointed out that an Oriental fairy tale could not possibly be transformed into an Italian novella or idyll, he gave me a look of extreme pity and abandoned me to my fate. Since the comedian Frappart was a very handsome and intelligent young man and had also proven himself as a dancer, I preferred him above anyone else for the title role. He himself felt flattered by this, but the *corps* looked askance at this deviation from the rules, and the public was displeased at seeing its favorite "Hanswurst" transformed into a romantic lead. The supporting roles were filled by the secondary personnel, whose experienced lack of talent honestly glossed over every imaginable nuance. But the most difficult thing of all was to find a proper use for Pocchini (so jealous of her honor), who, to my misfortune, was not to be "the Gazelle" but was entrusted with a larger "dancing" part, to which she could add a grand new *pas de deux*, arranged by Borri and accompanied by that highly favored *banda,* which here at least found a more reasonable place than in the Witches' Sabbat in *Faust.* Suffice it to say, I thought that I had fairly well satisfied her ambition, and without endangering the ballet, opened for my pupil the prospect of acquiring a public by the successful performance of a leading role; but the plan did not come off.

The rehearsals were most promising despite the weakness of the supporting roles and Pocchini's cross looks. Several kind artists and dilettantes predicted a decided success for me, the music delighted everyone, and nothing was wanting with regard to costumes and decorations. But in Cornet's silence and the Italians' crouching in corners I could clearly perceive mischief. If so sharp an opposition had manifested itself in our beloved Copenhagen, a public scandal would have been unavoidable. Fortunately imperial theatres are places of sanctuary, where loyal patrons are allowed to clap and call out as much as they like but where cabals are punished as breaches of public tranquillity and disapproval is expressed only by silence. This negative expression can be crushing enough, and it must be admitted that with the exception of a few expressions of approbation the performance was quiet indeed. However, so that a noisy demonstration should not be lacking, the inserted *pas de deux* was thunderously applauded and the dancing couple was called forth several times.

Moreover, with all their intrigues and conspiracies, one must grant the

Italians this: they support one another like a single family when they meet in a foreign country, quite the opposite of the French and—the Danes; for if, when abroad, one hears unfavorable things about either of these two nationalities, one can be certain that they generally come from their own countrymen. I confess that it was a decided blunder on my part not to stick to my first choice for the role of Irma, for if it had been performed by the public's darling, the little Pocchini, by the help of the mood-dominating Italians, the ballet, despite its shortcomings, would have been praised to the skies, nay, even higher: "*alle stelle.*" As it was, it remained quite close to the earth. The curtain fell as if on a funeral; it was an honest but thorough defeat.

I can still feel the mood in which I returned home to my family circle that evening after the performance. It was obvious to me that I ought to renounce a career where my ideas on art and the theatre stood in such complete opposition to the demands of the present. Exclusively taken up with my endeavors, I had purposely closed my eyes to all the difficulties and drawbacks that surrounded my sphere of activity. Now the whole thing was clear to me. The miserable facilities, the eternal hullabaloo, the pernicious traditions, a spirit of slavery coupled with the most profound contempt for human dignity, and finally, a Director who was regarded by all others as a madman but whom I, unfortunately, had seen through only too late. I would gladly have made him happy by breaking my contract had it not been for the matter of damages, which neither he nor I had the desire to pay; but what chiefly restrained me was the strength of character I found in Juliette Price. It was too hurtful to her pride to return home to Denmark without success, and since I did not wish to put my pupil to shame, it was decided that we should stick it out and strive to triumph by remaining calm and standing firm. These qualities were certain to be needed in full measure, for only now did troubles begin in earnest. The reviews, although far from favorable, were the least offensive, but the grumblers triumphed; politeness, and especially obedience, declined to an astonishing degree, particularly among the male members of the *corps*. Everything that malice and rudeness could conjure up Cornet lavished upon me; and since I had no other weapon against his coarseness than the most ironic courtesy, he fumed with spite and bombarded me with insolent letters. In any other country and with any other individual one would have been able to demand a manly and honorable satisfaction; but here I could do nought but calmly send his epistles up to the Lord Chamberlain's office where, by the bye, I had a patron in Councillor of State Raymond. The Lord Chamberlain himself, Count Lanckoronski, who, as it happened, was factotum in higher theatrical affairs and not particularly gracious to me, was not fond of the Director either and considered it a pleasure to give him a severe reprimand. In turn, Cornet roared like a lion every time he saw me at a distance and thought up fabulous schemes for disconcerting me; but I did not allow myself to be confused.

Regardless of the cluttered facilities, new dances were to be hurriedly composed for *La Juive* and *Les Huguenots*. For the time being, my ballets were scheduled for performance without rehearsal; new roles were to be rehearsed without preparation. I found time, space, and talents to fulfill the most unreasonable demands, and everything stood finished as if by magic. Fortune seemed to favor my efforts more now, when I worked with hidden defiance and malice, than at the time I was guided by the most loving and most honest zeal. My dances won applause, *Abdallah* and the other ballets got into their stride, and I found the public more and more inclined to accept my artistic direction. The struggle now began to amuse me, for if they had lured me thither by flattering my vanity, at least I was not about to let myself be caught in the snares Cornet laid for my working ability and behavior.

Under these circumstances Paul Taglioni returned to Vienna and I found myself de facto suspended for over two months. Since there was no way to assert my injured rights, I armed myself with resignation, put the best face on the matter, and readily welcomed my colleague.

As it happened, he did not require my assistance at all, for he was armed — in the proper sense of the word — with carte blanche. Cornet groveled and obeyed every one of his suggestions. Enormous sums were spent for gorgeous effects in his ballets, and whole masses of complimentary tickets were distributed among "friends." Even so, only a partial success was achieved. The stately and genuinely talented Marie Taglioni in particular was treated with a coldness verging on affectation, while her partner was overwhelmed with thunderous applause, and one can hardly imagine anything more contemptuous than the manner in which the newspapers discussed the Berlin ballet compositions. I must, however, acknowledge Taglioni's merit in the area of detail and his great brilliance in making use of a luxury which in Prussia is actually a matter of state, because this fifth Great Power would consider it hurtful to its honor were Paris or Petersburg to equip their operas or ballets more richly or more elegantly than must be the case in Berlin. Therefore the Viennese shook their heads at seeing grand excavations undertaken in order to bring fountains into the Kärntnertor Theatre for the ballet *Satanella* and at seeing 20,000 gulden squandered on works that were to be used for only a few guest performances. Among those particularly noted was the aforementioned fantastic ballet, which was a dazzling compilation of all the *diableries* that French theatres have presented for over twenty years, and whose plot — if such a thing could be discovered — was a masterpiece of *Blödsinn*, but adorned with numberless piquant episodes. The most popular of all the ballets was unquestionably *Le Diable à quatre*, after the French, or what in the old days we called *Fanden er løs*. It was gay and lovely. Although the story is set entirely in Poland, this did not prevent the finale from being danced in Spanish costume; and here was performed the outstanding *seguidilla* whose principal features I have used at the end of *La Ventana*.

During this entire period I was reduced to supporting my two pupils, Juliette and Julius, who, to be sure, served only in the second line, but by the care and perfection with which they performed their parts elicited from the Berlin dancers the most sincere recognition and earned for themselves a solid place in the public's favor.

According to the terms of her contract, Mlle. Pocchini was exempt from taking part in the Taglioni productions, and her countrymen took up a waiting position. If I had ever allowed myself to be carried away by praise and fame to the point of imagining that I had an artistic mission, I was here forced to pay for my selfishness by this long and humiliating inactivity. My opponents gloated, my friends found no joy in me, and I myself began to believe that my so-called genius was only proportionate to the poor conditions so often mentioned at home. Here in Vienna, invention, motive, character, and above all reflection were, if not completely rejected, at least considered outmoded concepts. My ideals belonged to a vanished, gentler time, and if I could not answer to the word "sensational," my sentence was passed. My spirit was depressed, and repeatedly on passing the Augustinerkirche I crept in and sat down near Canova's masterwork (the Dowager Duchess Christina's sepulchral monument) and prayed from my innermost heart for strength to bear my trials so that bitterness and envy should not lead my thoughts astray and get the better of my soul! And indeed I got a clearer view of this vain world. What had before disgusted and grieved me now almost made me laugh. I was able to ask myself whether I might seriously wish to change places with those who were now celebrated and patronized, and the result was that in my comfortable home, surrounded by my faithful loved ones, I forgot my theatrical sorrows and thanked God for all the blessings He had bestowed upon me.

We had at the Bastei a most excellent dwelling, with a prospect of the glacis, the suburbs, and the distant mountains — a landscape which, especially at sunset, presented the most enchanting play of color. We often went to the Burgtheater, where people enjoyed the drama with as much reverence as if it had been a Beethoven symphony; while at the Karltheater the admirable Scholz made my sides ache with his priceless comedy. I diligently visited the distinguished collections, and social life, though in a narrower circle, afforded us many pleasues. We frequently had letters from our beloved Danish home, and I shall never forget how sympathetically and encouragingly my friend H. C. Andersen wrote to me. From time to time we assembled at our tea table Northerners traveling or residing in Vienna; and with no Scandinavian tendencies other than such as comprised mutual respect and friendship, we planted our national flags upon the Christmas tree and danced round it to the familiar melodies of our homelands.

As shadows in these bright domestic scenes I must certainly mention the numerous funeral processions that daily passed our windows, caused mainly by the ravages of cholera throughout the autumn of 1855. No less than nine generals were borne to their graves with full military honors and a peculiar pomp that consisted of a knight in black armor, with visor lowered, riding in front of the hearse. Mozart's *Requiem* was sung three times in the Augustinerkirche: for Carl v. Holbein, for the singer Staudigl, and for a younger brother of the singer Ander. But the most remarkable funeral of all was that of August Lanner, son of famous and likewise deceased waltz composer, Josef Lanner, and like his father conductor of an orchestra. All the suburbs of Vienna were astir; the people gathered by the thousand, and since my fine dancer Catharina Lanner was now alone in the world, she asked me to accompany her as a sort of paternal guardian in the sorrowful procession which, amid many clerical ceremonies and music from three different orchestras, went out to Döblinger-Friedhof.

As a transition to life and light, I shall mention two fêtes which took place during my stay in Vienna; namely, the one-hundredth anniversary of Mozart's birth and the grand Citizens' Ball in the *Redoutensaal*. For the former, considerable preparations were made. Since no outstanding musician was to found at the moment in the native land of Haydn, Gluck, and Mozart, Liszt was summoned from Weimar to direct the glorious music festival — which, as so often happens on such occasions, did not live up to expectations. Incidentally, it should be remarked that of all the operas given in Vienna, those by Mozart come off least well; and since just then they had revived *The Abduction from the Seraglio* and were at the same time looking for the place where the immortal master is supposed to have been buried, some witty fellow suggested that they look for a body which had turned over in the coffin — for that must surely be Mozart!

The second fête had assembled more than four thousand members of the imperial city's wealthy bourgeoisie, presided over by the entire Court and graced by all whom domestic and foreign fame could produce. To give a list of all these celebrities would be as long-winded as to estimate the value of the jewels that gleamed from the ladies' toilettes. I will mention only the uncommon order of the dances, for the quadrilles were formed in two lines instead of in squares, as is customary. But when I saw a group of princes and illustrious gentlemen gathered about a single point on the balcony, I was curious to know whom the object of this homage might be. To my surprise, I recognized the Viennese "Ninon de Lenclos," the renowned heroine of the *cachucha:* the fifty-year-old but still captivating Fanny Elssler!

Taglioni returned to Berlin at the beginning of the new year, and it was now high time for me to start thinking about the two new ballets I had to furnish before the end of March, which in addition to the revenge I expected from their favorable reception were also to provide me with a considerable additional fee. The obligation, however, was binding on me but not on the management. I once again had to have recourse to the Lord Chamberlain's office in order to get at least one of my ballets, *Napoli*, mounted onstage. Fuming, Cornet obeyed, but promised to make my work as laborious and difficult as possible.

This might be the place to give a brief description of the Opera Theatre "nächst dem Kärntnertor" as it stood for many years, awaiting a transfer and total transformation. The theatre lies jammed in between one of Vienna's dingiest streets and the southern Bastei. But since the facilities have gradually demanded expansion, some adjacent houses and floors have been bought or rented. These are connected with the theatre by means of passageways and suspended bridges and now contain offices, rehearsal rooms, and *garderobes*.

The auditorium is rather elegant, but with such cramped entrances and exits that one shudders at the very thought of a fire alarm. The stage itself is a bit wider and considerably higher than ours, but so inconveniently arranged that during the intermissions the settings and larger machinery must be taken through two large folding doors out onto the Bastei, whence the less well-to-do public can peep into the sanctuary and where in the daytime one can inspect temples and clouds, ships and flying dragons, just as at Dyrehavsbakken.† The artists' entrance by way of the above-mentioned street is anything but attractive, and the *garderobes* as well as the classrooms are filled with the mingled emanations from the pubs and courtyards.

One room, appointed for the use of two professions, bears the name of "foyer." But since it is always cluttered with an organ, a harp, an extra contrabass, and two Turkish drums, there is not much space left over for dancing exercises and even less for the rehearsal of grand ballets. One therefore had to take refuge in the facilities at the large Redoutensaal in the Hofburg. But since this latter underwent complete repairs at the very time I was to begin my rehearsals, and in both classrooms a new opera was being worked on, there was ample opportunity to harass me and, in a manner of speaking, bind my work "both hand and foot."

I now had to rehearse the roles and individual parts in either my own home or that of Mlle. Pocchini, who was to play Teresina and was now all eagerness and enthusiasm. I had to watch for the few hours when the stage was free of opera rehearsals and then try to persuade the *corps* to assemble. The gentlemen, for the most part, were to be found in the nearby coffeehouse. For although the entire theatre bore the most perfect resemblance to the picture that Häcklander gives in his *European Slave Life*, there was no trace of discipline present.

These circumstances had no small influence upon my views of the conditions under which I had earlier worked, and I promised myself that should I ever return to the Danish stage, I would regard my small troubles in a milder light.

The performance of *Napoli* was delayed, however, by two extraordinary theatrical events; namely, Meyerbeer's arrival in Vienna in order to conduct personally the rehearsals of *L'Etoile du Nord*, followed by Adelaide Ristori's guest appearances at the Opera itself.

It was extremely interesting for me to renew my acquaintance with the famous composer, whom I had met in Paris thirty years earlier. He was now

† A public amusement park on the outskirts of Copenhagen.

an old and rather feeble man, with a demeanor like that of the finest diplomat, exquisitely polite, gentle, pleasant, but unshakable in his convictions. He had the most extensive authority, and it was a pleasure to see how he crushed the teeth-gnashing Cornet to the ground with "iron hand in velvet glove." In order to speed up the work, the Director had had a series of singing rehearsals held before the maestro's arrival. But the latter immediately said with the most charming smile: "My dear ladies and gentlemen! Here it is not a question of good or bad, for it is obvious that you do not yet know my music at all." Only now began a Purgatory of rehearsals, lessons, and corrective rehearsals that often lasted far into the night. The personnel rivaled the Director in wishing "the Jew" down in the deepest abyss, and it became a saying to be doomed to "three months Meyerbeer." But "Emperor's command" kept the unruly elements under control and the maestro did not allow himself to be disconcerted.

Although often ill and miserable, he appeared every morning at the piano and at the podium, always with a smile on his face, drilled the singers and the chorus until his work was performed to the letter as it had been some months before in Paris. At the same time, he did not wish to neglect the help which a large *corps de ballet* could give the scenic effects and for this reason conferred with me, played all the dance melodies himself, indicated tempi, and denoted the places that he wanted "filled out" with dancing and military manoeuvres. A large camp scene was to be represented, with *cantinières*, infantrymen, and hussars. Of necessity, these last arms had to be represented by women! My objections were fruitless. "You are perfectly right, my dear Bournonville," said the old professional, "but the public is fond of such things and I dare not oppose the prevailing tendency." The recruiting of the above-mentioned corps was in and of itself no easy matter; for after the maestro had chosen the most voluptuous *figurantes* for the hussars and the prettiest girls from the chorus and the ballet for *cantinières*, there were no recruits left for the infantry but corpulent old matrons whom I was now to instruct in manual exercises, the execution of countermarches, etc. It was truly a Herculean task. In light of the circumstances, I succeeded in working wonders with these troops, and Meyerbeer was ecstatic over my arrangement.

Everything was done to place *L'Étoile du Nord* at the pinnacle of the firmament: every possible stage effect was employed, and in order to secure the support of the press, Meyerbeer was not the man to disdain paying his respects to the most obscure critic in the highest garret in the most remote suburb, and, if it were necessary, accompanying his affable expressions with irresistible arguments. World famous and a millionaire, he still had an inordinate desire to dazzle his contemporaries with a praise which, in the end, he might even disdain — what a doctrine!

The new opera went over brilliantly. Everybody wanted to see and hear it but no one was fully satisfied with this adaptation of *Vielka*, which they already knew from Jenny Lind's debuts at the Teater an der Wien. They found the music lovely but far less original than Meyerbeer's earlier compositions. In an agitated state of mind, he now hastened to depart for Milan, where they awaited him with splendid ovations but where his *Étoile du Nord* met with a cold reception.

Meanwhile, *Napoli* was finally—by orders from above—scheduled for performance, but under such unpleasant conditions that I would rather have seen it completely abandoned than further postponed, as has been said, by Ristori's guest appearances, which took up nearly three weeks of the remainder of the season. All the same, this interruption was to give my spirit a beneficial lift and in certain ways indemnify me for these endless troubles.

Adelaide Ristori (married to a Marchese del Grillo) was a tall and noble figure of a woman, already famous in Italy and most recently engaged at the Royal Theatre in Turin, where at the side of the great tragedian Modena she had earned her reputation, which became European only after she had appeared in Paris. She made her guest appearances surrounded by a rather humble company of actors, which was saved from being laughed to scorn solely by the powerful influence of her talent and the indescribable harmony of the Italian language.

In her genre, this great tragic *artiste* was a revelation whom I dare to compare only with Talma, Mlle. Mars, and—Jenny Lind! She made her debut in Alfieri's tragedy *Mirra*. The title role is that of a young princess who is cursed at her birth by the angry Goddess of Love and pines away from a passion which she reveals only in her hour of death: she is in love with her own father! Ristori knew how to raise this horror to tragic heights, as she ennobled her mental anguish with grace and majesty. She transported us back to the antiquity of Greece, and we thanked the gods who brought an end to our own and Mirra's troubles by the curtain's fall.

What a transition from this plastic paganism to the pure Catholic figure in Schiller's *Maria Stuart!* It was an historical portrait of an astonishing truth. The unfortunate Queen came to life before our eyes, with the same magic which until her dying day roused people to both love and hatred. Even if one did not understand a single word of Italian, Ristori's eloquence of eye and tone of voice alone would have been enough to interpret her feelings and emotions. I had seen Mlle. Rachel in the same role and shared the enthusiasm over her superb declamation; but with her I did not for a moment lose sight of the famous actress, whereas Ristori led me into the time and reality.

How naturally she prepared the unfolding of the drama by her meeting with Burleigh and by the receipt of the letter Mortimer hands her! But her portrayal reached its climax in the confrontation with Elizabeth. Kneeling before the Queen of England, she convulsively squeezes her rosary as if to allude to the fact that it is not before an earthly power that she humbles herself at this moment. A shudder runs through her when her gaze meets the icy countenance of her rival. With burning eloquence, she seeks to bend the proud woman's spirit—but in vain! Fighting her rising emotions, she begs

Heaven for strength and patience to bear the insults with which the irreconcilable woman continues to shower her. But at last she is driven to extremes.
She tries to answer, but her voice deserts her, and only after a violent inner
struggle do the words force their way through. Like a raging storm, the ven-
omous arrows of hatred and revenge are now hurled down upon *"la figlia
d'Anna Bolena."* Maria positively whips her off the stage, calling her *"mima,
bastarda,"* and calling upon eternal vengeance to see Elizabeth kneeling in
the dust and herself upon the throne of England.

The eruption of a volcano could not have shaken the air more violently
than the thunderous applause that followed upon that magnificent scene. The
action stopped for several minutes, during which Maria, overcome with emotion, stood trembling with deathly pale lips and blazing eyes, pointing after
the fleeing Queen as if to say: "That hit home! "

Now came the final speech, in which after so many years of distress and
humiliation she enjoys *"un momento di trionfo,"* and here the act ends in the
Italian adaptation. The curtain falls and the enthusiasm, which cannot mount
any higher, is now manifested among the electrified audience by a convulsive
tremor which dissolves into a flood of tears. In the fifth act she had returned
once again to amiable piety and devotion. The scene in which she takes leave
of her people was supremely moving, and her confession and the final meeting
with Leicester were no longer drama, but psychological and historical truth.
We followed her — yes, it was fortunate indeed that she received three curtain
calls so that we should not retain the tragic impression — to death beneath the
headsman's sword!

In order to substantiate her many-sided talent, she appeared several times
in *La Locandiera* by Goldoni and *I Gelosi Fortunati* after the French. But
neither her voice, mime, nor personality were suited to comedy, and despite
her unconditional admirers, I am forced to admit that she was great only in
tragedy.

Next to *Maria Stuart, Pia dei Tolomei* was her main showpiece. This play
was one of those "boulevard dramas" in which one can, with watch in hand,
calculate the oppression of virtue and its ultimate triumph. Ristori herein displayed her remarkable powers of transformation as the charming bride and
the wronged wife, who, in the final act, repudiated and pining with grief,
lives to see herself acquitted and dies of joy in the arms of her husband.

One can hardly begin to describe the weeping and wailing elicited by
this picture, the horrors of which did not for a moment belie a most sublime
beauty; and on seeing Pia/Ristori return to the stage happy and curtseying I
(who am an inveterate hater of curtain calls) was forced to cry out with relief:
"She lives! "

This refreshing shower of true artistry gave me the strength to face the
difficulties which had begun to mount up before my final and decisive work.
However, Mlle. Pocchini was a vigorous support and rehearsed her role with
all the more enjoyment as she had been provided with a considerable supple-

ment of bravura dances and all competition had been removed by Juliette Price's complete exemption from performing in *Napoli*. The part of Gennaro was very nicely performed by the Italian, Vienna. But as chance would have it, Frappart, whom I had been counting on for the lemonade-seller and the grand *tarantella*, had gotten aristocratic notions because of a rich marriage which he was then thinking of entering into. He found the role too insignificant, caused a commotion that went unpunished, and became so insolent that I was forced to renounce his assistance and condense the whole comic element into a single figure—for which, by the way, I found a superb interpreter in my indefatigable Julius Price. I had the greatest difficulty injecting a little tone into the ensemble, for the *corps de ballet* had not the slightest idea of the art of mime and could only be "kept in the mood" by continual contradancing (the *ballabile*). Things went fairly well with the female members of the *corps;* but the men presented the same phenomenon as do all uncultured people who are cast upon the stage. That is to say, they are never more serious than when gaiety is to be represented, while they take advantage of the solemn and moving moments to giggle and have fun.

Cornet, who under duress had given orders for the staging of the ballet, did everything in his power to oppose and injure me. The most skillful scene painter was assigned to another work and the settings for *Napoli* entrusted to a dauber; the costumes were neglected, and since, contrary to custom, the *corps* were not given any compensation for the use of their own clothing, all those in plain clothes (in Act One) were outfitted in caricaturish rags. Out of my own pocket I had to pay for the assistance of the chorists at rehearsals, and also reward the violinists who had played for my rehearsals outside the Theatre's facilities. In addition, the first performance of the ballet was "forced on stage" before I had managed to hold the necessary dress rehearsals, and in order to well and truly rob the ballet of the effect of its national color, the evening before the premiere they gave, as if by coincidence, *La Muette de Portici*. My Danish friends will no doubt exclaim: "But why did you tolerate all this?"; and I will simply answer: "I found myself in Austria and was more afraid of compromising my honor than of hazarding my work."

Fortune stood by me all the same. *Napoli* made the same impression as it had at its first performance in Copenhagen. At first glance, the Italians realized that I had interpreted their country, their customs, and their nationality *con amore*. They laughed and cried, shouted *"Bravissimo! "* and applauded every scene. Besides, they were no longer my opponents, for I had given their countrywoman the leading role; and I must accord the little Pocchini this praise: she did her best to bring life and warmth into the whole. She had the warmest feeling of rapport with the audience, which the latter in turn conveyed to the *corps de ballet*, who achieved something most uncommon and, for me, completely unexpected. Julius Price triumphed as the street singer and in the tarantella. This last dance was unanimously declared to be the finest composition of its kind, and "Maestro Bournonville" was called forth at the end of the second and third acts in order to receive the liveliest acclamation. Victory was mine! Congratulations poured in, and my heart was filled with humble gratitude for the successful outcome of all my adversities. There was joy in my home, and the news flew back to friends in my distant native land, where I knew there were many who were sympathetic to my good fortune.

The ballet had actually scored a success, a rare occurrence at the Vienna Opera. The Court loudly voiced its satisfaction, but the Emperor's sympathies were decidedly not in *my* direction, and the loyal Cornet, who throughout the performance had stood in the wings uttering imprecations, used this less than favorable royal feeling as a pretext for setting *Napoli* aside forever after only three brilliant evenings.

But what did the public and press say to such conduct? They did the same thing as I: they kept their own counsel and acknowledged that they were in Austria. Moreover, at that time all the newspapers had agreed to pass over in silence everything concerning Cornet's administration; because in order to satisfy a singer's sensitivity he had revoked the critics' complimentary seats and was, in addition, strongly supported by the censors and — the gendarmerie.

Holy Week interrupted the performances and ended this Opera season, which was to be my last in Vienna. The solemn Eastertide could do nought but gladden my spirit, and the successful outcome of my test piece caused me to view everything in a milder light. I had found many friends among the artists as well as in several charming families outside the theatre and, on the whole, met with a sympathy and hospitality that shall be preserved among my best impressions. I shall always remember Vienna, with its charming environs, its jovial folk life, its matchless military bands, and the majestic tower of St. Stephen's. Also, I too had in spirit driven my nail into the *Stock am Eisen*, exorcised the demon of Vanity, and more than ever learnt to control my violent temper. I had drawn strength from the spring which is never exhausted, and far from lamenting the disappointing results of this journey, I felt enriched by the experience I had gained. I would not exactly say that of all places on earth, the theatre is that in which *Nemesis divina* chiefly exercises rewarding retribution, but it is certain that nowhere is the chastisement so swift and decided as within this very sphere, where the mirror is held up to human passions and frailties. Examples would lead us too far afield, but as far as Cornet is concerned, the year after my departure he had already reached the limit of his vileness by insulting a respected *artiste*. On this occasion he once again brought upon himself a sound drubbing, was sentenced to fines and imprisonment, and was forced to relinquish the post which he had so unworthily filled.

To be sure, Cornet once more succeeded in impressing one of Berlin's smaller theatres with his feigned *practicality*, but within a short time he was also driven out of there and died a year later in Hamburg. His obituary notice appeared in all the German theatrical newspapers. But even if his earlier merits as a lyric artist should be forgotten, his memory as theatre manager will remain as a warning; for anyone who has been entrusted with a command can learn from his example how *not* to behave, while those who are to obey and serve can learn to appreciate cultured and humane administration, even if it does not possess every desirable and conceivable perfection.

I herewith conclude this section of the stories of my ballets, which now entered a new period. And if one should ask me what connection this lengthy description has with *Abdallah,* I will reply by pointing out the deep moral of the Arabian tale, which shows us the fortunate person who was not satisfied with the goods that four lighted candles had bestowed upon him but craved to see the fifth one burnt and was then beaten and almost lost everything.

While the rest of my household set out on the homeward journey via Hamburg, I accompanied my daughter Charlotte to Milan, where she was to develop her singing talent under the famous Professor Lamperti. I traveled home alone by way of Turin and Mount Cenis, through Savoy, where I hailed spring in bloom, and on to Paris, where I stayed a fortnight and once more saw the fruit trees in blossom. By Pentecost I finally arrived at the vaulted, leafy arcades of Fredensborg, where the scent of lily of the valley greeted me, the hawthorn stood in its festive splendor, and the chorus of birds chirped their paean. It was the third time in the same year that I experienced the glory of springtime. All the same, I was taken by surprise here at home, and I had to sing with our inspired poet [H. C. Andersen]: "I believe it is loveliest of all in Denmark! "

CARLOTTA POCHINI

Engraving by Battistelli, 1852. Courtesy Dance Collection, The New York Public Library at Lincoln Center, Astor, Lenox and Tilden Foundations. Photo by Frank Derbas.

FANNY ELSSLER

This engraving by Sarony, printed by Robinson of New York and Washington, shows her in *Cachucha* costume and probably dates from her American tour of 1840–1842. Courtesy Dance Collection, The New York Public Library at Lincoln Center, Astor, Lenox and Tilden Foundations. Photo by Frank Derbas.

Above: BERTEL THORVALDSEN. "Drawn from life by C. Küchler,
Rome, 1836." Det kgl. Bibliotek, Copenhagen.
Below: "THORVALDSEN'S ARRIVAL IN THE COPENHAGEN
ROADSTEAD, 17 SEPT. 1838." Oil painting by C. W. Eckersberg, 1839.
Copyright Thorvaldsens Museum, Copenhagen; reproduced by permission.

VI

Danish National Festivals

Before continuing this series of my ballet stories, which constitute the actual core of *My Theatre Life*, I must dwell for a moment upon those sentiments which have had such a vital influence on my artistic temperament; and, while I give myself a necessary rest by allowing my memories to hover a little outside the narrow sphere that was allotted my work, I hope at the same time to please my readers by describing some events in which I myself was not the focal point but only an observer or at most a supporting figure.

I shall try to depict faithfully and vividly some of the magnificent spectacles which the times and the spirit of the people authored and wherein every single citizen unconsciously played his role. The artist sat in the spectator's seat, gathered glorious impressions, and applauded with all his heart. Many of my contemporaries will recognize these gripping moments. Together with me they will relive them once more in thought, and then, perhaps, say with a wistful sigh: "We will never see such days again!" There will no doubt come a time when all these celebrations will be regarded as poetic and fantastic child's play; some will regard them as excesses, others as trivialities; but they shall all bear witness to one thing: that at one time there were *unity* and *cooperation* in Denmark!

THORVALDSEN IN COPENHAGEN

AS far as grand and glorious celebrations are concerned, in bygone days Copenhagen was second to no other capital. There have been triumphal entries, visits by foreign princes, marriages, solemn coronations, and especially, pompous funeral processions. Everything was done to amuse the people by the Court as well as the city; whole oxen were roasted, wine bubbled in the fountains, and the poor were solaced in many ways.

On such occasions the city was illuminated, and while the upper classes had their appointed places or drove around in their stately carriages, the rabble swarmed about in wild hordes, mixing hoots and whistles with their cries of joy, and were kept in check by the police wherever they broke through the barricades and ranks of soldiers or disregarded the orders of the hussars. Brawls and arrests were a normal part of these festivities. And yet, despite all the money and effort expended, one felt strongly that something was still lacking: namely, *a spirit of unity.*

The latter had received a tremendous boost through the institution of the Estates,* and parliamentary life had awakened many slumbering forces. The national consciousness found expression in free speech. People gathered outdoors during the loveliest days of spring to celebrate May 28 as a festival of rebirth; and, before purely material interests gained the upper hand and divided the nation into sharply conflicting factions, the universal motto was: "Success and glory to Denmark."

We felt that it was no longer by military exploits and external splendor that our native land was to maintain its reputation in the eyes of the rest of Europe, but above all by its high cultural level, both material and spiritual; and we therefore uttered with justifiable pride names whose sounds opened to us "a path to praise and power," which could at least afford us some compensation for vanished political importance.

At this time a great artistic name resounded throughout Europe with admiration and respect. This artist, the finest of his day—to whom the culture of ancient Greece had been revealed in its divine radiance, who through the chaste serenity of antiquity had found the transition to the Christian ideal, and who knew how to combine these elements to preserve in marble and bronze the best of his own time for future generations—was *a Dane*. Born in Copenhagen, he had through the years, though in the midst of Southern luxuriance and surrounded by the wonders of art and the world's acclaim, retained his Danish spirit, Danish tongue, and love of his native land.

The previous generation (that of our parents) could hardly envision such fame, and so it happened that when Albert Thorvaldsen† visited his natal city in 1819, after an absence of many years, he was much feted in private circles and some poets even wrote verses in his honor. However, according to the Court etiquette of *that* day, he could not be invited to the King's table without at least being the equal of a *Kammerjunker;* and so this world-famous man had first to be furnished with the very suitable title of *Etatsraad.*‡ The general public saw him only as a tall, handsome man of unassuming character, and rejoiced that he had accepted commissions for the Frue Kirke, which was at that time in the process of being rebuilt after having been destroyed by the bombardments [during the Napoleonic wars].

He left us after a brief stay, but from time to time sent us some of his works, which were shown at the Academy's exhibitions, met with general approval, and were sometimes judged with distinction. At last it was rumored throughout the art-loving world that in Thorvaldsen's *atelier* in Rome there had been created a statue of Christ, which came closer than any earlier one to capturing the concept of Savior, and that this masterpiece was destined for

---

*The Estates were provincial consultative assemblies, established in Jutland, the Islands, Slesvig, and Holstein by King Frederik VI in an ordinance of May 28, 1831.

†Cf. footnote, Vol. I, p. 115.

‡ Here Bournonville's irony is obvious; *Etatsraad* would be a third class title according to the rules governing order and precedence. Cf. footnote, Vol. II, p. 208.

Copenhagen's Cathedral. The Apostles were immediately forthcoming, and seemed identical with the heroes of the Gospel. Admiration everywhere abounded, and Europe turned an envious eye on the fortunate city that was finally to embrace these treasures.

At the same time as the first plaster casts arrived, Thiele* brought out his meritorious publication, *Thorvaldsen and His Works.* Only now did people realize exactly what Denmark possessed in her great countryman and his immortal works. One now came to understand his genius, and in following his bewitching chisel from the myth of Psyche to the altar, where the Shepherd of Souls opens his arms to us, it was Thorvaldsen's greatest achievement that one forgot his artistry in ascending to the realm of the divine. This had Denmark been vouchsafed: the possession of something which the greatest empires could not equal; and when we looked about us, lest we do our other worthy men an injustice, we discovered an abundance of riches that strengthened our spirit and imparted to us a previously unknown might.

Our warships brought home from the Mediterranean precious loads of Thorvaldsen's works in marble, and at last it was certain that the master himself would return to gaze upon his native soil again and perhaps even to remain there. The frigate *Rota* was expected home in late summer of 1838; and with it, Denmark's illustrious son. Copenhagen was in a joyous flurry of activity preparing to receive this glorious artist. He was truly a hero who had fought and triumphed, a king in the realm of genius and beauty.

This recognition spread, consciously or unconsciously, throughout the entire populace; and when the flag was hoisted atop Nicolai Tower as a signal that the ship had been sighted, they all rushed through the streets like a river, hurrying down to the shore. The Custom House and Langelinie were filled with countless numbers of people. Tree branches bowed beneath the weight of lively young folk; the vessels in the harbor were decked above with flags and streamers, and below with gaily dressed women. A whole flotilla of boats and gondolas with distinctive emblems, manned by poets, savants, and students, rowed out to meet the frigate in order to bid Thorvaldsen welcome with music and song. (However, our enthusiastic neighbors, the Swedes, were the first to accord him a jubilant welcome from a steamship in the middle of the Sound.) A thundershower marked the frigate's entry into the Sound, for a gun salute was against regulations. But just as it was approaching the capital, the sky cleared and a mighty rainbow enclosed the floating circle and the teeming coastline, as if in a frame of light, hope, and freedom. Resounding cheers could be heard from the Citadel to far up the harbor, and a many-voiced choir broke into a song of welcome to the old melody: "We sailors don't use many words."

Indeed, words cannot adequately express the feeling that came over us on seeing this stately, white-haired old man, a cloak slung over his broad

* See footnote, Vol. II, p. 205.

shoulders, setting foot upon his native soil once more and being greeted by the overwhelming enthusiasm of an entire people.

The horses were unhitched from the carriage that had been sent to fetch him, and the people triumphantly pulled it past Amalienborg to the Academy of Fine Arts, where a residence had been prepared for its most prominent honorary member. Here the whole densely packed crowd, from all classes and of both genders, had gathered to greet the new arrival, and endless cheers arose from every side when the double doors on the broad balcony opened and the celebrated guest appeared—above the very portal through which he had walked as a poor youth more than half a century before in order to study the art whose hero he had now become. There he stood, decorated with medals from all the kingdoms of the world. Behind him, like an accidental apotheosis, Praxiteles' Apollo and Canova's Perseus stretched forth their hands above his head; and when the glowing rays of the setting sun tinged the full white locks, the high forehead, and the noble features, it seemed as if Phidias' masterpiece, the bust of Jupiter, had taken on life and warmth and now gazed down from within the temple upon adoring Athens.

It was the first time such an honor had been accorded a private citizen during his own lifetime. Formerly, Denmark's great men had enjoyed this triumph only at their funerals. But not everyone viewed this fiery enthusiasm with a favorable eye. Some worshipers of the obsolete saw, even in this national homage, a revolutionary movement and a disregard for the respect which one owed the monarchic principle; and, so that the artist should not fancy himself too much, he was on this occasion named *Conferentsraad*!†

Meanwhile everyone vied to entertain this famous master. Artists' and poets' fetes were arranged in his honor, and, as a lovely example which ought to be cited, Thorvaldsen's most ardent admirer and equal, Denmark's greatest skald, Adam Oehlenschläger, led the way. These two were our earthly Dioscuri. The public celebration was continued in private circles, and I count it among my noblest memories to have united these two names in a filial and grateful cup of welcome in my home.

In truth, I owed them both a debt of filial gratitude, for *their* works pointed out to me my path and my goal: their advice and encouragement gave me the heart to begin, their approval the strength to continue—but, unfortunately, not to *complete*. As a Dane I have felt inspired by the sound of their names; as an individual, privileged to have lived in the same age and to have been loved by them.

Except for a brief interval, the remainder of Thorvaldsen's life was spent among us. It was scarcely five years in all, yet one must calculate the industry he displayed and the influence he exerted to mold those few years into a period equivalent to a whole generation.

---

† Again the irony is apparent: almost twenty years after his last visit to Denmark, the authorities of his native land were "generous" enough to award this internationally famous artist a second-class title.

By Thiele's commendable efforts, all friends of art joined together in a national undertaking that was unique in its kind; namely, the erection of a museum to house Thorvaldsen's works! The great master had donated all his artistic treasures and a considerable sum of money to his native Copenhagen. All of Denmark contributed to the building, and King Frederik VI allotted a site near Christiansborg Palace. Neither the place nor the architectural execution was a worthy one. (The completion of the Marmor Kirke on a modified scale would, for the same cost, have produced a Danish Valhalla had not petty considerations forced the high-flown idea to root itself firmly in the ground.) Now magnificence was once again obliged to clothe itself in the guise of mediocrity. Whether out of natural modesty, or perhaps because the sepulchral style appealed to him, Thorvaldsen approved the designs for the peculiar half-Egyptian, half-Etruscan shrine that was to shelter his invaluable treasures and house his earthly remains.

The theatre was Thorvaldsen's greatest pleasure. At that time we had only one, but it was good. He followed it with lively interest, and delighted in sitting next to his friend Oehlenschläger. They both enjoyed the pleasures of the stage with an open and childlike mind, and were therefore quite willing to reward artistic efforts with friendly encouragement. It was a golden time for applause, when it was led by men such as those two great artists and Denmark's art-loving King, Christian VIII!

It was a harsh winter evening in March of 1844 when Thorvaldsen hastily took leave of a friendly circle in order to attend the first performance of Halm's *Griseldis.* He entered the stalls a little short of breath, exchanged greetings, and sat down just as the overture was about to begin. But as the first chords sounded, people saw the majestic head fall and the stout shoulders slump over the seat. The poet Holst gathered him in his arms and, with the aid of some friends, carried him from the auditorium. The noble man had passed away! His illustrious soul had gone to behold God's ideal perfection face to face!

Outside the Theatre, all who heard the news of his sudden death were thunderstruck; but *inside,* the performance was resumed and another spectator occupied the vacant seat. One must indeed admit that an awareness of proper public behavior had not yet matured in Copenhagen, and it was several years before we acquired the accord with which the Christiania Theatre was abandoned upon the announcement of the defeat at Slesvig. The audience deemed it improper to allow the Danish actors to appear under such circumstances, and not a single person demanded his money back. This is an example of national tactfulness which is surely worthy of mention.

Meanwhile, it had become a truly national mourning. Thorvaldsen's burial place had already been chosen, but until his museum could be completed his body was to rest in the Frue Kirke, and his coffin was borne thither (as those of the kings had been in days of old) on the shoulders of the people. All of Copenhagen turned out for his funeral, and from distant places people gathered at his bier to pay their last respects to his mortal remains.

The young schoolchildren presented a silver chaplet in his memory; Denmark's finest lyres joined in the lament; the farewell of the Italians resounded from the picture gallery of the Academy; while his father's countrymen, the Icelanders, brought up the rear of the procession as relatives. The Court, the clergy, the armed services, the University, and various representatives of art, science, commerce, and industry formed an immense procession, which, to the sound of muffled drums and the tolling of bells from all the city's churches, passed through the main streets, where the guilds with their banners and emblems were drawn up in closed ranks. The female population was universally dressed in mourning, and sorrow could be read on every face.

Together with my colleagues, I found myself one of those bearing the coffin as it was about to be carried into the portal of the church. Here stood King Christian VIII, who, as if he were the son of the deceased, took his place at the rear of the procession. The great doors opened and Hartmann's imposing "Funeral March" swelled from the organ, accompanied by gongs and trombones. Then suddenly it seemed to me as if the black-draped floor of the church heaved beneath my feet. It was as though I were the victim of some hideous trick: the marble apostles appeared to step down from their pedestals, while the Savior himself floated toward us from the chancel! I held fast to the handle of the bier and retained my composure, but the experience had left such a strong impression that not even the long and rather dry funeral oration was able to weaken it.

The museum was later inaugurated and Thorvaldsen's coffin was lowered into the stone chamber, above which rose blossoms every year shall greet the Danish summer. But from a gravel heap outside the newly erected sanctuary, plants and flowers hitherto unknown in our clime had sprung forth: germinations of seeds that had been mixed with the packing materials of the masterpieces which had been brought home. It was the last tribute from beautiful Italy, from Rome, the Eternal City!

I shall end this description with an incident which even though it occurred several years before Thorvaldsen's death, still bears some relation to that of the flower tribute. On my way home from Naples in 1841, I visited in Florence with the witty Countess Lenzoni-Medici, to whom I had been especially recommended by our admirable Brøndsted.‡ I was invited to attend her Thursday *soirée*, where I was presented to the most prominent persons of the Court and the world of science under the title of *"Compatriota del cavaliere Brøndsted."*

They greeted me with visible sympathy and questioned me quite a bit about Denmark, but about Thorvaldsen in particular. I then summoned all the Italian I knew in order to relate, as best I could, the tale of the great artist's

‡ Cf. footnote, Vol. I, p. 101.

reception in Copenhagen, and when the subject rendered me more eloquent than even I had dared to expect, the salon suddenly became still and I saw tears in many eyes. Then Prince Corsini stepped forth and with noble impetuosity exclaimed: "Do you hear that, Signori? It is now the North alone which knows how to venerate art. Thus it was in Italy three hundred years ago, when Raphael Sanzio made his entry into Rome!"

THE SCANDINAVIAN STUDENTS' MEETING OF 1845

WHAT do we understand by Scandinavism? Does the word mean war or peace, or does it merely embody a nebulous conception? Is it the desire to play a prominent part in the world arena, or the fear of being absorbed by the Great Powers? Is it confidence in receiving mutual help in time of danger, or the hope of reconquering lost territory? Might it seriously imply a renewal of the Kalmar Union?* Or is it the consciousness of tribal kinship, the admission of past mistakes and bygone errors, the urge toward a friendly *rapprochement*, and a conviction that a sincere and peaceful cooperation in many areas would place the three Nordic sister nations at the highest level of civilization?

In fairness it should be noted that the first steps taken in this direction came from the Swedish side, with the solemn and honorable reception accorded our chosen *skald* Oehlenschläger at Lund, whereby the ingenious Tegnér earned for himself a lasting memory in Danish hearts.

Two Swedish and one Norwegian doctors brought about the first naturalists' meeting in Göteborg in 1839. A crowd of students crossed the frozen Sound and were received in a most friendly manner by the local association, and the following summer our beech groves resounded with their harmonious songs. It was these tones that melted the last ice which had stood between neighboring peoples; they promised to repeat and to return the visit. The first expedition to Uppsala took place in 1843, and, when we discovered that there was a lot to be learnt from our Nordic brethern, we began by assembling our musical forces and learning some of the lovely Lindblad Quartets.

It was most fitting and natural that Poetry, Art, and Science should cement the bond of friendship among these nations. The people, and the government too, were agreed on this, so long as it did not point to more extensive combinations. No one was better qualified than the young generation to receive and to produce favorable impressions, and the mutual knowledge acquired under such fortunate circumstances could not be anything but beneficial for future relations. The Danish Students' Society's invitation was enthusiastically accepted by the universities of Lund, Christiania, and Uppsala.

On Midsummer Eve in 1845, a squadron of three steamships, which had

---

*Established 1397 by Queen Margaret of Denmark, who sought to combine the three Scandinavian states into a single country under Danish domination. Never fully accepted by the Swedes and opposed by the powerful Hanseatic League, the system had become a dead issue by ca. 1450.

arranged to converge at Malmö, was met midway and hailed by a fourth, containing the Danish delegation. All of Copenhagen was present, as it had been for Thorvaldsen's return, at the Custom House and Langelinie, to accord the guests a jubilant welcome. It was an inspiring sight as this landing fleet steamed into the harbor. Here were the flower of Norway's and Sweden's intelligent youth, their parents' hope and delight and their homelands' future! All hearts went out to them, and it was not only a student celebration but truly a gathering of peoples. Our guests discovered not only friends and comrades but also fathers, mothers, brothers, and sisters along the Danish coast. Those from Lund were already our old acquaintances; everyone noticed the selection of lovely, stalwart youths who formed the Norwegian contingent; and those from Uppsala with their *"hvita mösser"* took a certain precedence [over the others] by their excellent singing chorus and their extraordinarily urbane character.

Songs, speeches, and cheers greeted them at the point of debarkation, and with banners flying amid a hail of flowers, they were accompanied through the city to the University. Delighted faces were everywhere to be seen, while gaiety and order reigned throughout; but happiest of all were those families who would house the strangers, who soon came to be regarded as members of their family circles.

Everyone vied to show them kindness. Retail merchants refused to accept payment from the dear guests, and from the richest to the poorest, all were animated by a sincere feeling of brotherhood during these unforgettable days. Churches, collections, and museums were open to those desirous of seeing them, and when the capital regaled them with the finest it had to offer, it was with particular satisfaction that we saw our guests bestow their approval upon the two subjects most worthy of our delight: the theatre and—the woods.

The Drama as well as the Ballet was greeted with tumultuous applause by this lively, unspoiled audience; and when a trip to the woods was arranged for the following morning, the local farmers gathered by the hundred with their best vehicles to take the students out to Dyrehave.

It was then at the height of its summer splendor, and only now did Denmark really open her rich embrace to the welcome guests. Beneath the majestic beech trees, where the large, unfurled sails from our warships formed an enormous tent with the flags of the three nations on top, the guests and hosts sat at table, presided over by the "Veterans of Science," and, at their side, the respectable Sjælland peasantfolk, whose sturdy bearing and magnificent horses bore witness to the Danish peasant's freedom and prosperity. Cordiality and sparkling humor were expressed in the numerous *skaals,* and never has the Danish strand resounded with such beautiful harmony as that which found its interpreter in the Uppsala singers' rich choir.

I had the honor of being invited to the magnificent banquet which was held in the Christiansborg Ridehuus. A number of fine speeches were delivered, some of which were the cause of complaints and legal proceedings here at home. This might well have been avoided, for with all the enthusiasm our speaker's proclamations generated, the mood was anything but revolutionary. People toasted brotherhood, embraced one another, vowed to meet often, and hailed the spirit of the present age in contrast to older, less happy times.

The happy days flew by, and soon the hour of departure struck. "*Ångbåtsången*," called those departing. "*Farväl! Farväl!*" sounded from the sea. "We shall meet again" was answered from the coast, where the sad voices were dimmed by tears. Hats and kerchiefs waved and fluttered, and the mutual cheers were lost in the ever widening distance. The ships disappeared over the horizon, and soon all that remained of this magical dream was a golden trail of smoke!

THE FAIR ON BEHALF OF DISTRESSED JUTLANDERS

(August 16, 17, 18, 1849)

THE Malmö Convention was dissolved and the sinister armistice expired. In the field, the Danes advanced against a fully equipped host of insurgents, which was commanded by Prussian officers and supported by a numerous army of allies. Then Easter week brought us another cup of woe: the Eckernförde Affair! It was such a cruel and painful blow that many Danes, whose families Death had ravaged, claimed that never had they experienced so great a sorrow.

Was the loss of goods and human life, then, so enormous that this single defeat could render our mood the same as that of the Romans after the battle of Cannae? Certainly not. But it was our splendid naval defense, the apple of our eye, that had suffered a humiliation which could be neither compensated for nor avenged. And now the wild German's shouts resounded as he pushed on toward the north. The Kongeaa [River] was crossed, Kolding and Gudsø were but bloody stages on his way. Jutland was overrun by enemies and Fredericia leveled to the dust! However, neither courage nor confidence faltered among the Danes; they did not despair of the salvation of the state, and our vigorous faith sustained us.

Everyone suddenly felt it was his duty to hasten withersoever help was needed. Hundreds of thousands of rixdollars were freely offered; silver plate was deposited as security for a state loan; grain, horses, clothing and linen, even ships, provisions, and equipment, were furnished *en masse*. It was not enough for women to scrape lint and give refreshments to the wounded; woolen articles, mattresses, blankets, and sheets also flowed from their hands in abundance. People sought out the survivors of the fallen and gathered contributions for the families of men serving in our armed forces by means of weekly house-to-house collections. Everyone wished to offer his mite, from princes and the well-to-do down to the very nooks of poverty, even to the prisons themselves! Tombolas [a form of lottery], plays, and concerts were arranged. Everywhere, people had something to spare for our brave men and for the distressed; and indeed, the more they gave, the more they had to give. It seemed as if the miracle of the loaves and fishes were being repeated in Denmark. The losses which the blockade had caused the German seaports were but poor compensation for the sore oppression our brethern on the other side of the Belts had had to suffer under enemy occupation. The tension among us was perhaps even more terrible than it was among the Jutlanders themselves, and the thought that our inability to defend the peninsula might eventually dampen the feelings of compatriotism was unbearable. And yet we had to do something to remedy the need, or at least to alleviate our own anguish. Patriotism had nearly exhausted every known means of raising contributions, when an insignificant idea evolved into an undertaking that marked an epoch in Danish folk life.

History cannot dispense with names; for just as their excessive use renders a narrative complicated and tasteless, so too anonymous deeds elicit nought but coldness and indifference. I therefore believe that I am simply fulfilling my duty by mentioning the names of several patriots who have been the agents of an active public spirit, and all the more so as my personal participation in this successful enterprise has, I dare say, been overestimated.

Just as it had been members of the Jewish community who took the initiative in the Four Skilling Subscription, first provided help and shelter for the Slesvig refugees, furnished reading matter for the soldiers, cared for our prisoners of war, and had articles sympathetic to the Danish cause inserted in German newspapers, so too Messrs. Bendix and Magnus were the first to set in motion the collection for the benefit of distressed Jutlanders. The original idea was a "Marks-Tombola" with 12,000 numbers, and I was asked to see to the external arrangements. We enlisted the aid of our friends, and for my part, I had the good fortune to secure the services of talents such as the scene painter Christensen, the art dealer M. Bing, and the poet Borgaard. The latter was chosen chairman of our committee, which had fifteen eager members.

At our first meeting, however, Bing remarked that the goal we had set ourselves was entirely too modest to require the united efforts of fifteen active men. He therefore proposed a more extensive plan, and when we began to raise our sights from the intended 3000 to a possible 10,000 Rbd., he informed us with a smile that if we could not bring this undertaking to a profit closer to 50,000 Rbd., he would have to consider our time and energy utterly wasted! We looked at him with astonishment, but to us the practical and ingenious look in Bing's eye was a guarantee of success, and his wonderful activity gave the affair its strongest incentive.

Now there could no longer be talk of a simple tombola, and Borgaard proposed that we use a form which had earlier been successful for the Students' Association; namely, a fair, with everything that could be thought of for such an occasion. The idea won general approval, and it was now a question of finding a proper site. In turn people proposed the Casino, the Court Theatre, and the Ridehuus; but it was I who designated the Rosenborg Castle Gardens as the place which, under tolerably good weather conditions, might give our Fair a touch of grandeur.

From now on the talented Christensen became our most important member; for upon him [responsibility for] the architectural arrangements came to rest. The remaining business was divided among the rest of us, and it should be mentioned that those members who had taken it upon themselves to collect, arrange, and report on the voluntary gifts had a laborious job indeed. One can have no idea of the multitude of different objects that streamed in from every quarter: gold ornaments and toys, handwork and merchandise, books and *objets d'art*, even vehicles and live animals, several thousands in cash, promises of manpower, and the loan of tools — in short, from the public as well as the private quarter people answered our request with unequaled willingness. It was truly an uplifting moment in the hour of distress.

But for Denmark, day soon dawned anew! A brilliant feat of arms freed Jutland from the burden of the enemy and gave Danish courage European renown. The July sun of Fredericia ripened the fruits of our confidence and unity. We received compensation for what we had lost, a reward for what we had endured! There was rejoicing throughout the entire country; not arrogance, but the noble sentiment of gratitude filled every heart. We could not have begun our enterprise under more favorable auspices, for now the gay and lively character of the Fair would not arouse any offense. The festive and expressive element was entrusted exclusively to my arrangement and direction. The Gardens were placed at our disposal three days before the Festival.

The carters' guild took care of all our transportation gratis. Wooden materials and several thousand ells of duck were furnished to us free of charge. At dawn on Sunday there gathered 150 journeyman carpenters and joiners, who gave up their free day and, in accordance with Christensen's instructions, erected all the fair booths and platforms. Before nightfall the woodwork stood finished, and the following day all the master upholsterers of the city appeared, with their old guildmaster in the lead, in order to cover and drape the tents and boutiques.

At the same time, in the middle of the plain I had a platform built and a fully rigged ship's mast erected. This was seen to by the men and mate of a bark lying in the harbor, and on the festal day forty signal flags were hoisted with the Dannebrog on top.

The fine armorer, Schmidt, had arranged the army emblems in the form of a shrine, which stood at the western end of the Dame Allé. All arms were tastefully represented, from mortars down to the smallest side arms, while the bust of King Frederik stood amidst a halo of gleaming blades. At the opposite end of the Allé the Navy was represented as a counterpart to this imposing group. Master Wittkow from Holmen had reproduced the quarterdeck of a warship, with the guns secured at their ports. Here anchors, a compass, and a gilded wheel surrounded the King's bust. Cutlasses and grappling irons formed rather artful ornaments, and above the whole loomed the ship's colors.

In the Cavaleer Gang, with its back against the Drill House, arose a little pillar of cornstalks that had been bound together and entwined with flower garlands. Around the base of the column on an elevated platform with steps leading up to it, stood a richly draped counter for the sale of fruits and flowers. The architect Stillmann won much credit for this lovely decoration.

The actual marketplace was in the grove surrounding the fountain, the base of which was bordered by the loveliest laurel and myrtle trees from the Orangerie. In the pumphouse was an exhibition of paintings, engravings, and lithographs, musical instruments, and elegant furniture—all donated, and all for sale. In order to attract customers to their bazaar, a concert of chamber music by our finest virtuosi had been arranged; but this precaution was soon found to be superfluous, for business became so brisk that the lyrical element was completely lost in the "practical" swarm of customers. Booths and tents were filled with the most varied kinds of gifts, and every commercial or artisans' guild saw to the stocking as well as the operation of its boutique; the tailors' display of outfits, in particular, was a model of richness and taste. Every day the market gardeners delivered fresh fruits and flowers, and supplied two shops. Here, as well as in the boutiques for handwork, perfumery, and fancy goods, a group of the capital's older and younger ladies presided, and the Graces brought their influence to bear, for on the first day of the Fair the shelves were already empty and the wares sold. But so that the business would not come to a halt, the respective merchants hit upon a means that was as ingenious as it was generous: they furnished us with the goods at cost price and allowed the profit to accrue to the charitable cause.

Our clever chairman, Carl Borgaard, had reserved for himself the direction of the singing societies, and among other means of entertainment, had discovered a most excellent one; namely, a ballad booth, amply supplied with fine and curious items. It came to play a vitally important role by its effect upon the atmosphere as well as by the fabulous business it did. It was really one of the high points of the Fair, and the inexhaustible good humor with which Chancellor Borre managed this lyrical enterprise contributed greatly to its tremendous success.

The Tivoli orchestra, under the direction of our admirable Lumbye, alternated with the bands of the militia and the Volunteers, in order to heighten this lovely harmony by the magic of music. They were stationed beneath the tall chestnut trees, between the main entrance and the Castle, close to the platform that surrounded the flag-decked ship's mast. Here a little ballet was performed by the Theatre's pupils. They danced in the open air for an audience of several thousand spectators! At a more mature age such an appearance would have been offensive to their ideas about the dignity of art and of the stage, but they would never again have an opportunity to appear under more fortunate circumstances, in more solemn surroundings, or in a purer, more benevolent atmosphere than here. Lumbye had composed a "Rosenborg

Quadrille" and I had arranged a "Hussar Dance" to his well-known polka, "Greetings from Jutland." To my delight, I heard that the peasants called my dancing children "God's little angels," and when the melody of "Holmen's Old Guard" evolved into a merry reel and a whole troop of genuine Nyboder lads* clambered up the lines and backstays in order to man the yards, this final tableau, which was enlivened by shrill cheers, had a most gripping effect.

Music and song alternated with loud reports from Delcomyn's shooting gallery, and the tombola was held beneath a colossal Christmas tree; boys clambered up the *mât de Cocagne†* and the *Markedstidende* was offered for sale as a festival souvenir. While all this was going on, a humorous auction took place in the neighborhood of the Pavilion of Hercules. Here the most hilarious sales occurred, and the gaiety was brought to a climax when the mess from the naval frigate *Freya* sent us a whole string bag full of live chickens and a big fat pig, which, despite the most desperate cackling and squealing, were sold and resold for enormous prices.

Amid this gaiety, gravity too had its claim, even its deep need; for the Fredericia victory had mingled many tears in the mead of enthusiasm, and it was not happy people alone who had come to give their mite to "the distressed Jutlanders." In addition to their sunlit plains and byways, the Rosenborg Gardens have many lonely spots where the sounds of happiness never penetrate. Here and there stands a solitary fir, a weeping ash, or a willow tree, which likewise bends the mind to rest and reflection. I thought of adorning these places with memorial plaques in honor of our fallen officers; their number had already exceeded eighty! I had their names painted upon shields arranged for this purpose, and since people had provided us with a multitude of lovely Dannebrog banners, each memorial plaque had its own. But the swallow-tailed pennant came to hang above a tabernacle, beneath which a ship's anchor rested against Marstrand's, Krieger's, and Skibsted's menhir.

In another spot was to be seen a little altar with the rod of Aesculapius and the cup of Hygeia. This was a memorial to those who had met death in the very places whither they had hastened to bring medical aid. Sheltered by the distinguished banners of the First Battalion hung the unforgettable Olaf Rye's coat of arms, with an honor guard of two disabled soldiers.

I needed flowers for all these monuments. But how was I to procure them without robbing the surprise of its freshness? I let it be known that for a worthy cause I had need of some wreaths of a specified size, and asked the ladies of Copenhagen to grant me their assistance. On the appointed day, I received three hundred wreaths, among them many of surpassing beauty! The memorial tablets were richly decorated and we still had a good many left over. These were sold in the flower stalls to private citizens who themselves wished to pay homage to the fallen. But when from time to time a family clad

---

* See footnote, Vol. II, p. 173.

† A greased pole, usually topped with a garland which entitled the winner to an award.

in mourning came and asked for such a wreath, it received one of the love-liest, without charge.

During the three days of the Fair, over 70,000 entry tickets were sold at 2 marks apiece, but the military convalescents had free admission and were truly pampered by the patriotic public. Several of them—five in number—served as honor guards in various places, and since on this occasion people literally squandered money, when the douceurs of these brave fellows were equally divided, each of them was found to have 80 Rbd. in cash!

What could be reckoned an extraordinary success in such a cold and damp summer was the fact that all three Fair days, from eleven o'clock in the morning until eight o'clock at night, were favored by clear and pleasant weather. On the last afternoon, we did have a shower, but this could not disturb the joyous atmosphere. His Majesty the King, as well as the Princes and Princesses, visited our Fair, and the various social classes mingled with one another as though the whole affair were one large family party. People sang and danced, amused and refreshed themselves, but disorder and confusion were nowhere to be seen; and when after the presentation of the final tableau, the curfew bell in the Pavilion of Hercules sounded for departure, people quickly parted, having arranged to meet again the following day.

The final evening produced three cheers for the Fair Committee, and this expression of recognition on the part of our fellow-citizens could do nought but encourage and strengthen us after the work we had brought to fruition in ten weeks. For it was not the three market days alone which had made demands upon all our efforts; the collections, preparations, and committee meetings had also been extremely tiring. It was especially hard for me to get used to the latter, since they were held according to the newly introduced parliamentary forms. These, though we were all agreed as to the principal *end*, were occasionally used by several speakers in the discussion of the *means* as a fitting occasion to voice their grievances. Here I came to know one of the shady sides of the democratic process. However, I was forced to admit that popular cooperation, even in the realm of entertainment, can lead to far more important results than official arrangements; for here at home as well as abroad, I have attended grand celebrations that were given *for* the people, but I have never experienced anything so solemn and well ordered, yet at the same time so amiable and lively, as that which was given *by* the Danish people.

The net income from this successful enterprise amounted to no less than 65,000 Rbd., exclusively intended for the relief of the distressed Jutlanders. But it soon appeared that the actual need was only immediate and passing; and if there had been losses which it would be extremely difficult to reckon, there was also a measure of profit that was incalculable. A Compensation Bill had been proposed in the Rigsdag, but until its promulgation it was decided that the above-mentioned sum should be distributed as an advance on the expected compensation; only in those cases which were not specified by the

Bill was it to be used as a gift. Within a single year 60,000 Rbd. had already been refunded to us by the Exchequer. But since Jutland was still in need, this money was given as an interest-free loan for the construction of a highway between Kolding and Hjerting.

The repayment of the money was to take place gradually during the course of eight years; and thus this charitable sum returned to its source, like Casem's slippers in the old Arabian tale,‡ and use for it was never lacking in eternal Jutland. Schools, hospitals, insane asylums, even the paving of streets which stood in need of repair in country towns, were proposed, and it almost happened that the entire amount of capital was allotted for the planting of trees on the Jutland heath, an area which more than any other in Denmark can be considered destitute. But just as, according to legend, it was the plague which five hundred years ago laid waste this region, so too the recultivation was halted this time by cholera, which, after the capital, had hit Aalborg, Aarhuus, and Frederikshavn the hardest. Here in particular there were many fatherless children to take care of, and our assistance was needed to the utmost. The interest from 50,000 Rbd. was now earmarked for the education of these young ones up to a certain age; and it is not impossible that in future years this sum may once again come to the aid of the Jutlanders. And I cannot deny that I would find the idea of the heath planted with trees, together with its resultant cultivation and population, most appealing; for if after a couple of generations delightful groves and luxuriant gardens should arise alongside the roads which now run through a wasteland, our successors would be reminded of the Rosenborg Gardens and of the spirit that animated the Copenhageners during Jutland's hour of distress.

THE RETURN OF THE TROOPS AFTER THE CAMPAIGN OF 1849

THE Rosenborg Fair had shown us what could be accomplished in a short time by a united effort, and the solemnities that marked the return of the soldiers after the Fredericia campaign gave evidence of the beneficial influence of their prototype. A committee of respected citizens, with Overpræsident Lange at its head, issued the request for public participation and organized the festivities.

As if by a stroke of magic, the entire route—from Frederiksberg Allé, into Vesterbro, through Østergade, across Kongens Nytorv, and up Gothersgade to the Rosenborg Gardens—stood adorned as if for one of the religious proces-

---

‡ A variant of this age old story may be found in Burton's supplement to the *Arabian Nights*. Known as "The story of the Kazi and his Slipper," his version recounts the adventure or, rather, misadventures of one Abu Kasim, who tried in vain to rid himself of an old slipper. He threw it away but it hit the awning of his neighbor's house. The slipper was recognized and returned to Kasim, who had to pay to have the house repaired. He then cut the slipper in half and threw away the pieces. But one half managed to block a drain, which caused a flood, thus damaging more property. The slipper was recognized and once again returned to its owner, who this time cut it into quarters. And so the story goes . . .

sions of the Middle Ages. All along the way, the inhabitants had exhausted their invention in tasteful decorations of flowers, banners, and escutcheons. Dannebrogs fluttered by the thousand, in several places together with the colors of Sweden and Norway. Clever inscriptions, especially at the Helliggeistes Kirke, everywhere contained greetings of welcome for our brave soldiers. Above Vesterport hovered the Goddess of Victory with the simple but moving banner:

"The Brave Soldier Has Kept his Promise! "

Since on this occasion I had no official duties, I could view the whole with perfect calm, and I must admit that the impression I received on seeing Copenhagen arrayed, as it were, in her wedding dress, and in meeting the stately guilds with their fluttering emblems and shiny silver cups—all this illuminated by a delicious September sun—was so thrilling that every now and then I was forced to break into loud shouts of joy.

With drums beating and banners flying, the various corps of the militia marched out to meet the troops in order to gradually line the route from Vesterport to Store Kongensgade. I too stood here as a private in the ranks of the Volunteers and enjoyed the inspiring sight of the serried squadrons who, laden with flowers, danced amid the heaving and shouting masses of people. There was a lengthy pause for a speech at the Freedom Pillar, and this halt resulted in the disruption of the lines of infantry. It so happened that this was the First Battalion, whose wives, mothers, sweethearts, and children lived in Copenhagen and its environs; these now forced their way into the platoons, destroying the military symmetry. This grand painting disintegrated into numerous genre pictures; soldiers hurried after their colors in tangled swarms and continually broke formation by picking up bouquets and shaking friendly hands. This state of disorganization was not at all in accordance with my conception of a festive entry. I was tempted to say with the eccentric painter in the drama: "Nature is beautiful, but it is not correct"; and yet there was something classical about the whole. Like a triumphant Caesar, [General] Schleppegrell appeared on horseback in the midst of a numerous staff. His countenance shone as if he had but a single remaining wish—the one that was fulfilled a year later at Isted!*

The same generosity that had been shown at the Fair the month before by gifts of money and valuables was here renewed by the donation of enormous quantities of food and drink. The supplies were arranged in the different quarters of the city, and those who had contributed them were assigned as hosts and waiters at the richly decked tables. The groups bustling about at the dinner, stacked rifles with piled-up knapsacks, and gay clusters of spectators from both town and country afforded a picture full of life and effect. The band played nothing but favorite melodies, and to the clinking of glasses sounded the refrain: "The Dane has won a victory! Hurrah! Hurrah! "

---

*Cf. the following chapter, p. 253.

But everywhere that Frederick VII rode by, they sang: "We defy the enemy, for our King is with us!"

In one place a speech was delivered from atop a tottering table, while, due to a total lack of chairs and benches, those who were weary sat on the bare ground. In another, a pair of lovers, silent but happy, strolled by hand in hand, and farther off stood the old parents, grateful to have their son back safe and sound. Some merry dispositions relaxed after the hardships of the march by performing an endless polka, while others expressed the deepest feelings of friendship by hammering one another with clenched fists—all in good fun and fervently enjoyed.

It is truly hard to imagine what high tenor voices are to be found among our "Jacks," and though they lack training in singing and especially the musical instinct of the Germans, they are unsurpassable in cheers. These rang like a shrill hurricane far into the evening, until rollcall was blown and the battalions marched in good order to their respective quarters.

The arrival of new divisions of troops soon brought people out to Vesterport, and the ladies hastened to the windows in order to transform these valiant hosts into walking flower gardens. It took all our Danish stamina and sense of fairness to maintain this festive enthusiasm for the five days which were consumed in marching in 10,000 men. None were to be stepchildren! Music, shouts of welcome, and bouquets were evenly distributed, and the last evening was the most brilliant of all. In accordance with an old custom, His Majesty had ordered that a whole ox stuffed with fowl be roasted; there were even fountains sparkling with wine. Everything was enjoyed in great moderation, but since the soldiers had many friends who wished to empty a glass with them and, moreover, encountered comrades from the first days of the return, it is not so terribly strange that at these celebrations, in addition to an incalculable amount of beer and schnapps, over forty thousand bottles of wine were consumed!

It was not only in the King's Gardens that banquets were held for our stalwart soldiers. The Jessen and Schultz batteries were served in Christianshavn, and the wounded were also to have their share of the victory celebration. I was asked to arrange the parties in the Artillery Riding School and at the lazarettos. Since we had only six hundred men to take care of in the former place, we were able to seat all of them and, on the whole, give them more complete service. The speeches were delivered with great dignity, the songs were harmoniously performed and sounded somewhat finer than they had in the open air.

At the Garrison and Naval Hospitals there were erected colossal tents, magnificently illuminated and decorated with arms and garlands, banners and standards. Here a great many convalescents were treated to a hot dinner, while the bedridden were served in their rooms. Even the wounded prisoners of war were not forgotten, and it was a pleasure to see them touch glasses with their Danish comrades, with whom they had become the best of friends during their sufferings. It was a peculiar sight to behold this banquet for the victims of war, several of whom were true wonders of hardiness. Here sat the gigantic Toftebjerggaard, whose two arms had been crushed and who six weeks after their amputation had had a pen tied to the stump of his right arm in order to write to his parents himself. Then there was the soldier Ullerup, who had been injured aboard the unfortunate *Gefion* and himself carried his shot-off arm down to the ship's doctor. And finally, there was Karlebo, the favorite of all Copenhagen, who had lost his sight after having been shot through the temple. Among the many expressions of sympathy which the latter received, I must mention the consolation that music brought him when Paulli undertook to teach him to play the violin and presented him with a fine instrument and instructed him from carefully dictated notes and signatures. But that was not enough. When Karlebo was about to return to his home after having married the girl who had remained faithful to him in adversity, Paulli taught the wife to read notes so that she might help her husband in the preparation of new music, with which the blind man still delights both himself and others.

The Student Singing Society enlivened these parties with patriotic songs. Enthusiastic speeches were delivered and attended by a receptive audience. There was gaiety as well as rejoicing and resounding hurrahs for both King and country. Toftebjerggaard's comrade, who attended him at table, also waved his cap for him to the cries of "Vivat!" This made me think of France's most famous disabled soldier, Josias Rantzau, whose portrait hangs in Versailles. He is seated on horseback, with a wooden leg, has only one eye, and has lost his left arm; but beneath the picture frame can be read a verse that tells us this younger Holger Danske sowed his limbs on the field of honor and had retained only his heart whole and unharmed. Our brave warriors too had retained sound and vigorous hearts; no complaint came from their lips, and on these festive evenings they were all happy and elated. Above all, they felt encouraged at seeing their brave general, the amiable Schleppegrell, in their midst and hearing his sonorous voice express the feelings that animated the Danish soldier.

THE HARVEST FESTIVAL

(August 29, 30, 31, 1850)

THE enthusiasm with which the whole of Denmark had seized upon the central idea of relieving the survivors of the wounded and fallen had arisen from the heartfelt compassion of the people and from the conviction that it was their simple duty. The contribution which had already been made for this purpose therefore had to be considered only the beginning of a future and more active sympathy for those who had defended the mother country and upheld its honor with their lives.

The Rigsdag's discussion of this matter, however, had not helped to maintain, much less arouse, interest in the war victims. Here *feeling* was alienated from the immediate question in a more or less ingenious fashion, while the *sober-minded, practical principle* was used to a degree that was calculated only to dampen, not to extinguish, the ember which at some future time it might be necessary to rekindle. But this did not prevent the Central Committee and its numerous assistants from continuing their undaunted efforts. There was even established a separate division whose vigorous activity extended not only to the soldiers' widows and orphans, but also to the aged parents of the fallen and to others who were unprovided for.

Since the weekly Four Skilling Subscription was not adequate and could not in the long run be continued with the same warmth, new ways of raising the necessary funds had to be found. Since the Rosenborg Fair was remembered as a high point in the folk life of a people who knew how to combine the need to help with its love of amusement, I submitted a detailed plan and promised my cooperation in a similar endeavor to be held five years in succession for the charitable cause of the aforementioned section [of the Committee]. However, they did not venture to accept my proposal. On the other hand, a Ladies' Society had been founded, with the wife of Bishop Mynster and the generals' wives, Mmes. de Meza and Schleppegrell, at its head. Its purpose was mainly to work for the widows of officers from the two previous campaigns; and when, in addition to a good-sized collection of handiwork and bazaar articles, they wished to initiate something that could equal the memorable Fair without, however, being a repetition of it, the aid of a number of gentlemen was enlisted. Of these, Pastor Bruun, Professor Holst, and Justitsraad Sally were new; August Meyer, the scene-painter Christensen, M. Bing, and myself belonged to the older committee.

While we were busy drafting plans and deliberating their execution, the second armistice expired. A third campaign was opened and crowned with the victory at Isted. "A complete, but dearly bought, victory!" Thus ran the bulletin; and indeed, the number of dead and wounded among the officers as well as the common soldiers was so great that there could no longer be any talk of a special demonstration on behalf of the officer class—the noble Schleppegrell's widow was herself one of our leaders! Our active sympathy had to be extended to all those who had bled in the cause of the Fatherland. We therefore agreed upon arranging "A Harvest Festival for the Benefit of the Survivors of the War Dead." It was to be celebrated on three consecutive evenings from four to eleven o'clock, and was to be chiefly intended for popular entertainment and some sales but was also to include more serious moments of deeper poetic significance. It appeared inevitable that Christensen, Holst, and I would be delegated the most important work; however, the remaining duties were appropriately distributed, and the price of admission set at three marks.

This time, as in previous years, both public and private willingness showed itself in the most splendid light. But since the whole thing was intended to present a festive spectacle, the expenses were of course much greater, and a portion of the work we had previously received gratis now had to be paid for. Nevertheless, contributions of money, goods and services of all kinds flowed in to our enterprise, and even members of secondary branches of art, such as acrobats, Tyrolean singers, café musicians, and organ-grinders offered to cooperate in this charitable cause.

One can scarcely begin to picture the colorful sight that the Rosenborg Gardens presented, with thousands of happy people who strolled in the shady groves and camped on the grassy plain. It was like a reflection of the Elysian Fields of the ancients, where one spirit hovered over all. Here, it was love of native land: the rescued native land! What I shall now relate is but a feeble outline; the memories of the old and the imaginations of the young must fill in the colors for themselves.

On the plain, where a year ago the ship's mast had stood, there was now erected a column adorned with harvest emblems, tastefully arranged by the castle gardener, Rothe. At either end of the Dame Allé were theatres, one for the *vaudeville*, the other for acrobatic and gymnastic *tours de force*. About the fountain stood a number of boutiques, among which the flower stalls were particularly outstanding. The whole Cavaleer Gang was filled with refreshment tents, which paid us a royalty, and in the middle of the grove a dancing platform had been built. A puppet show was given in the Pavilion of Hercules, while in various places throughout the Gardens, one could view perspectives or see wax figures on display, ride in a swing or try one's hand at target-shooting, spin the wheel of fortune or hear German lies declaimed. But, just as last year, the "Ballad Booth" maintained its precedence among the humoristic attractions, and here were presented for the first time *The New Fire Uniform* and *The Burning of Pjaltenborg*. More than twenty thousand colored lamps and paper lanterns hovered above the allés, and at the western extremity of the Cavaleer Gang was mounted a sun made of shining reflectors.

All of this splendor was vitally dependent upon good weather. Unfortunately, the season was more changeable than usual, and throughout the days of preparation our indefatigable Christensen had to fight both rain and storm. At last August 29 dawned with the loveliest sunshine. What luck! Banners fluttered in the fresh morning breeze, garlands and lanterns were strung up under the most fortunate auspices. Confectioners' booths were stocked with cakes and refreshments, and flowers were proudly displayed beside magnificent fruits in our boutiques. The ladies assembled, clad in silken dresses and inspired by the happiness that a good deed, combined with the hope of a successful outcome, always brings. Everyone had much to do, and we paused only long enough to congratulate one another on our extraordinary success.

About three o'clock, however, the sky began to turn gray; some unpleasant gusts of wind and single bolts of lightning, which shot through the thick autumn clouds, portended no good. Our minds were filled with dark forebodings that were soon changed to sad certainty, for precisely half an hour before the Gardens were to be opened, the most frightful cloudburst came pouring down upon our decorated festival site. The rain gushed down the walks in torrents and transformed the groves into ponds and marshes; tents, theatres, and booths were dripping wet, and the glasses on the buffets were filled to the brim. Paper lanterns came tumbling down in thousands, and our sorry emblems hung as limp as did the heads of our poor Festival directors. We wandered about in the mud, gave each other dark looks, and cried: "We have given our time and our efforts, and yet the harvest is lost!" But it now happened, as it so often does in times of distress, that where a man's confidence falters, a woman's courage stands firm. Our ladies were undismayed. They encouraged us to open the Festival and gave us the best hopes that the evening might still prove favorable. The weather cleared, and at the ladies' command we unlocked the entrance to the Gardens, which was already besieged by a numerous crowd who had borne the whole thundershower with stoic patience: they were our guests, convalescents from the nearby lazarettos, disabled soldiers from the battle of Fredericia, and the wounded from Isted, some on crutches and with canes, others with arm or head bandaged, three to four hundred in number, but all happy and delighted; for they had truly—one of the *Frederickssteen's* men exclaimed—"recovered from their victory."

The band played its first pieces for this special audience, and the brave fellows strolled about the Gardens as if the Festival had been arranged solely in their honor. But Copenhagen's good burgher families soon appeared with their servants and children. Little by little the walks filled and nearly twelve thousand tickets were sold. People were not discouraged by the mud underfoot. The evening grew really pleasant; the illumination was fairly well repaired, the bazaar enjoyed frequent visits from avid buyers, the restaurants had good custom, and the flower shops traded their articles for specie, bank notes, and gold coin. The ballad-maker and the liar inspired hearty laughter; the floor of the dance hall shook beneath the feet of hundreds of couples at a time; gaiety and beneficence clasped hands, while everyone's eyes shone with mildness and joy. It was truly a glorious evening.

At nine o'clock the gates from the Gardens to the Drill Grounds were opened, and here was enacted a drama as sublime as any of its kind. Only now did the Festival assume its real character. Thirty-two obelisks with flaming urns on top and transparent inscriptions on the sides formed an ellipse in the middle of the *Plads*. Beneath Rosenborg, in a magical illumination, stood a military trophy, and alongside the barracks a platform for the numerous musicians and two hundred singing voices: a choir composed of opera singers, dilettantes, and schoolboys. Finally, at the western extremity, between two colossal pyramids, there arose the Temple of Memory.

The inscriptions on the obelisks were outstanding verses by H. P. Holst and commemorated our fallen heroes as well as our unforgettable days of glory. The pyramids bore only the names "Fredericia" and "Isted."

The starry sky spread its vault above this Valhalla; the impression was both magnificent and moving.

Hartmann, Gade, Rung, and Løvenskjold had composed new music consisting of hymns, part-songs, and a victory march, all respectively suited to four tableaux I had arranged. These were presented in theatrical fashion in the Temple of Memory and showed us Peace, War, Victory, and Memory, all as genre pictures with an allegorical background. In conclusion, a brilliant display of fireworks was set off. The whole was like a solemn vision or, more properly, like a poetic revelation.

The masses of people returned once more to the merriment of the Gardens and to the covered tables in the tents. At eleven o'clock the departure bell was sounded, and by midnight all was empty and still.

This grand family celebration continued in the same way for three evenings, favored by superb weather and increasing attendance. On the last evening thirty-five thousand tickets were sold. The net proceeds from the whole Festival amounted to over 58,000 Rbd. and were placed in a separate Assistance Fund. The illumination increased the beauty, charitableness, and desire to dance to an extraordinary degree. Not a single disorder disrupted the pleasant atmosphere, and among the numerous foreigners who visited this uncommon national celebration was a corps of officers from an Austrian frigate that happened to be lying offshore at the time. The young seamen were wildly enthusiastic, not only over the whole arrangement, which appeared to them like *"ein Märchen,"* but mainly over the community spirit that animated the Danes. They all exclaimed with one voice: "With patriotism like that you had to win, and you did win!" We received this warning in the language which had so often resounded with scorn toward our native land, and in our hearts we answered: "God protect Denmark!"

THE HOMECOMING (1851)

THE victory at Isted led our army to the Dannevirke,* but once again the pens of diplomacy and not enemy bayonets halted the advance of our troops and prevented them from harvesting the fruits of victory. In the meantime, the barrier was put in order; but even then its dimensions were already considered to be so disproportionate to the strength of our army that it required the greatest vigilance and speed to protect every weak point of the line against an enemy who could neither be invaded nor pursued into the terrain of Holsten, while it could mass its entire strength against our scattered corps every time. The brilliant affair at Mysunde showed him that there was nothing he could accomplish on our left flank, and when he furiously hurled himself upon Frederikstad, he discovered that the Danes were as staunch in defense as they had been irresistible in attack.

*The ancient fortified line that from the time of King Harald Bluetooth (A.D. 940–986) had defended the southern border of Slesvig (and of Denmark) from German attack.

THE FAIR ON BEHALF OF DISTRESSED JUTLANDERS, 1849
A series of tiny watercolors by Lehmann, done on the pages of a
miniature "Drawing Book for Dolls" and capturing various scenes in the
Rosenborg Gardens. Shown here are: the book's cover, the shrine of arms
in the Dame Allé, the memorial to Olaf Rye; the dancing beneath the
ship's mast, the tombola with the spires of Rosenborg Castle in the
background, the crowd surging outside the gates; the pillar of cornstalks in
the Cavaleer Gang, the auction near the Pavilion of Hercules.
Private collection.

Above: THE HOMECOMING, 1851. H. G. F. Holm's watercolor
showing Nebelong's triumphal arch at the end of Frederiksberggade.
Below: THE BANQUET FOR DANISH SEAMEN in the Ridehuus,
1851. Watercolor by Holm. Both, Bymuseet, Copenhagen. Photos by
Ole Woldbye, Kunstindustrimuseet, Copenhagen.

Family business brought me to the city of Slesvig on the same day as the news of the repulsed assault on Frederikstad reached headquarters; and, since just then a convenient opportunity presented itself to see the bombarded city in good company, I hastened thither by way of Husum and thus obtained a perfect idea of the destruction of war.

A good third of the city lay in the dust, with the ruins still smoking; the rest was more or less damaged, and at every step one encountered scattered projectiles. Trees were splintered by balls, and on the square lay whole piles of furniture and household goods. Some soldiers were camped in the open streets, while some were billeted in stables and barns and others in the church. Most of the inhabitants had fled, and the poor devils who remained lived off the bread which our brave men gave them from their own rations.

I saw those places where the struggle had been fiercest and could now examine the "insurmountable obstacle" which, according to Willisen's report, had checked the Death Battalions' assault. It was a breastwork as tall as a man, made of mud and clay, with trenches resembling broad ditches, a rather humble palisade, and, in the middle of the highway that ran across a marshland traversed by watercourses, a so-called placement for two field guns, protected by a turf roof, presumably the "formidable" blockhouse that had been mentioned in the report. I must confess that, according to the general conception of *fortifications*, these barricades were as modest as the honest faces of their courageous defenders. It was impossible to descry the slightest trace of exaltation after the bloody scenes of the preceding days. They prepared their food beneath the same breastwork, which was completely riddled with enemy bullets, and whence they could still see the spiked helmets of their foes. The relief for the outposts marched out looking as calm, bright, and polished as if it had been at home on the drill ground. And then there were the glorious officers, Helgesen's brethren-in-arms, who, while at any moment they might expect a new assault, issued subscription plans and collected contributions for the victims of the fire — surely one must love and admire such warriors! Who would not do everything possible for them!

Autumn passed amidst sleet and rough weather, while our men suffered hardships in the barracks and in exhausting outpost duty. The enemy was still counting on the frost, and promised to surprise the Danes at their Christmas pudding just as he had two years before at Easter service. We at home were apprehensive about new encounters, not because we despaired of our force of opposition, but because the glory of war had already cost us too many victims: there had been enough fighting. At last, there was also serious talk of peace. The army of insurgents was dissolved, prisoners were exchanged, and our troops were once more given the hope of seeing their hearths again. The orders for the departure and embarkation of the battalions came in rapid succession. "They're coming!" resounded across the islands and from city to city. Nearly sixteen thousand men were to be discharged in the capital, and there were not many days to prepare for their solemn reception.

The municipality of Copenhagen issued the request that her citizens greet the returning troops and bid them welcome with festive processions. Although the season did not permit a repetition of the previous year's festivities, there had still been many individual shortcomings at the latter which could be avoided on this occasion, and the whole arrangement was thereby improved. The deputation of citizens was kind enough to send for me, but since I had various grounds for wishing myself relieved of committee meetings, this time I did not join the "hosts" but offered my services anywhere that they might be of use.

The banquet in the Ridehuus was therefore entrusted to my direction, and such excellent forces were placed at my disposal that I could immediately set to work. There was no time to lose. I had only three days in which to complete my task. The "Valhalla idea" was received with approval. The motif was the Feast of Warriors, on long benches beneath a temple vault of painted shields and gleaming swords. I had a little trouble getting those concerned to accept the idea of a "sit-down dinner," but I demonstrated so zealously and satisfactorily that my plan was carried out unaltered.

While gifts of foodstuffs and cash flowed in enormous quantities into the Town Hall, where admission tickets were also issued to the contributors, everything was set in motion in order to make the entry as pompous as possible. The spruce forests were made to yield their winter green; the hothouses and flowerpots, all the gifts that this harsh season could produce. The city adorned herself even more splendidly than she had the time before, and on an even larger scale, since the procession was to march along three different routes: namely, (a) through Østergade, past Holmens Canal, (b) across Højbroplads and Gammelstrand, (c) through Raadhuusstræde and across the Marble Bridge. And in addition, Knippelsbro was decorated in honor of the artillery, and what had been neglected the year before was this year compensated for to a plentiful degree, especially with regard to the bell-ringing and gun salutes.

The decoration of the Ridehuus was now my principal task, while architect Nebelong was in charge of the triumphal arch to be placed at the end of Frederiksberggade, between the two squares. Armorer Schmidt and his clever son covered the balustrade of the gallery with twelve hundred shining blades and hung the walls with firearms and military musical instruments. The northern portal was transformed into a little arsenal from the Middle Ages, and the western end of the hall was fitted up in military splendor with polished bronze cannon, steel armaments, army drums, and colors entwined with sprigs of laurel. The whole group, which was done from a design by Edvard Lehmann† and surrounded by a grille of bayonets and halberds, was dominated by a colossal statue made to represent "Denmark proffering the garland to her stalwart defenders." It was executed by the sculptors Thielemann and Freund, Jr. In truth, one had to admire the way in which this noble feminine figure was, so to speak, improvised in less than two days by means of iron

† The artist who designed the costumes for a majority of Bournonville's ballets.

bars, straw, cloth, and plaster, which was pasted on freehand, without casting mold or model. Standing upon a pedestal almost nine feet high, it measured twelve feet from sandal to diadem, and stood against a background of purple and ermine, which was suspended from the gallery in tasteful festoons. Opposite to this, at the eastern end of the hall, the richly decorated Royal throne rested upon a colossal coat of arms. Along the galleries were mounted gilded shields bearing the names of the memorable days in this war and its most prominent personalities. Beneath the vaulted ceiling hung hundreds of Danish banners. From this height one overlooked the banquet hall, 160 feet long and 72 feet wide, with twenty tables, each fully laid for sixty men. Among the almond cakes and groaning casks stood plaster valkyries and victory goddesses, together with *one* glass of schnapps for every man. These drams were arranged in red and white rosettes on wooden table mats intended for that purpose. Beneath the three carousel columns, which had been transformed into palm trees with golden fruit, stood the officers' table, about two feet higher than the rest so that the soldiers could see their commanders and all eyes could rest upon the King on his throne. At the foot of the centermost palm there was a raised platform for the speakers. Laurel wreaths were suspended from the ceiling by invisible threads, and a variegated array of spectators, on the floor as well as in the gallery, framed this magnificent tableau. The troops arrived in Copenhagen in battalions and regiments. We were informed in good time of the strength and number of the divisions, and our luncheon banquets generally lasted from twelve o'clock until two in the afternoon.

It was the Life Guard, on foot, who opened the joyous homecoming festivities on January 31. These stalwart "bearskins" from Dybbøl, Ullerup, and Isted had something Napoleonic about them. In majestic order they passed through the triumphal arch, greeted by thunderous shouts, and before they had reached the Royal Palace they were so covered with garlands and greenery that it seemed as if the legend of Birnam Wood in *Macbeth* had come alive anew. Here, however, it was only in a spirit of joy and welcome.

King Frederik, at the head of his staff, received them on the riding ground. He rode through the ranks of brave grenadiers and addressed them in inspiring terms. The air was vibrant with cries of joy, which burst from the chosen battalions and from the surging crowd of spectators. The Overpræsident then stepped forth and, in the name of the town, invited the brave Guard to a feast of welcome. The King and the Princes were the guests of honor. Arms were stacked and the companies filed into the hall through the south portal. Our band played "The Brave Soldier" while the Committee led the guests to the tables. The long line of men wound its way about the room like a ribbon, and when the ranks arrived at their appointed tables, they took their seats on the benches, laid their knapsacks on the floor, and the meal began. It was served by twenty-five young gentlemen, most of them students, and fifty robust artillerymen. The former were called "stewards," the latter "pages," and at the head of this phalanx stood a member of the Executive Committee of the Students' Association, the invaluable Carl Borgaard. The indefatigable zeal displayed on this occasion by the printer Klein, Town Councillor Petersen, the Weigh-master Tønnesen, Høierup (keeper of the silver plate in the Royal Household), and the Fire-master Blasius was beyond all praise, and the merchant Maag's administration of provisions was a model of organizational ability. Here everything was as plentiful as at a farmer's wedding; our waiters flocked in, passed around the different courses, and continually filled the empty glasses. The highly different grades of wine were blended into a single hot drink, which tasted superb to our "Jacks." It was brewed in the Palace kitchens, was brought in in big steaming kettles, and was served from pitchers. It generally consisted of 500 bottles of wine, 50 bottles of cognac, 300 pounds of white sugar, 100 pots of water, 8 ounces of cinnamon, and 3 ounces of cloves. On the tables, in addition, stood tankards filled with beer and, as stated, one glass of schnapps per man. At the officers' table finer wine was poured and champagne corks popped for the proposed *skaals*, which alternated with military music and choral singing, and like all the rest, were answered with hurrahs, with the natural exception of the cup that was emptied each time *in memory of the fallen.*

The feast was uniform for all the divisions, whose strength varied between 1000 and 1300 men. The Guard, with its 800 broad-shouldered warriors, filled the entire room; but for several corps which had a supplement of exchanged prisoners of war or convalescents, extra tables were arranged, just as the floor had to be cleared when the Hussars and the Sixth Battalion of the Line appeared with 1600 men. Our pages worked wonders of nimbleness. Every day, two hours after the meal had ended, the tables stood freshly laid and everything was arranged for the next feast. And thus it continued with thirteen banquets in eighteen days; each time the same solemnities took place. All this while, the city was in constant motion — without, however, the slightest trace of unruliness in the streets. It is most indicative of the prevailing spirit that during this whole time the police did not have a single occasion to intervene. The last two feasts were for the Navy and the Artillery. The King bestowed upon every corps the same cordial reception, but attended only three of the above-mentioned banquets.

The most interesting days were the entry of the advance guard (First and Second Light Battalions, Rye's and Bülow's valiant soldiers). Few of its original officers were able to enjoy the happiness of homecoming, and illness prevented the heroic Bülow from making his appearance. When they proposed a toast to the General, a lance corporal from his old battalion said to me: "He's a wonderful man! If we were brave, we have him to thank for it, for he taught us how to fight." After this came the First Corps of Chasseurs, who had the most handsome bearing and were led by the bold and brilliant Wilster. Then there was the Seventh Battalion, with its fresh memories of Frederikstad, and the Tenth Light, which in so many hard fights had borne witness to the Danish sympathies of North Slesvig. Among the speakers who distinguished themselves at the Army's banquets were the clergymen Paulli, Hammerich, and Bruun; the Corps Commanders Bülow, Irminger, Räder, and Torp; Professors Hammerich and Holst; Candidates Høedt and E. Schack, together with Instructeur Nielsen. Each time, the Overpræsident began with a *skaal* to the King, and several toasts were proposed by the members of the Committee, among whom I too had the honor of figuring. The great services rendered by the Minister of War in provisioning the Army were emphasized with appreciation by the respective commanders, and the robust appearance of the soldiers bore witness to the validity of this praise. Several speeches in the Rigsdag had created bad feeling in the Army and did not arouse public sympathies in favor of the legislative assembly. It was therefore a risky business to propose a toast in its honor. Colonel Räder, however, ventured to do so; but, though probably unintentionally, he went no further in our political system than "the Estates," wherefore the glasses were emptied in a silence as profound as that which prevailed during the *skaals* in memory of the fallen.

During these days the Danish soldier enjoyed, through the expression of the heartfelt gratitude of his fellow citizens, the reward for all his pain and peril. But how beautiful and edifying was the modesty with which he received this overflowing acclaim! In these sunburnt faces with the bushy beards, in these agile fellows with the easy movements, one might almost fancy he was viewing French chasseurs rather than our own good-natured "Jacks." But their Danish character shone in their eyes, which gazed with admiration on all the unexpected finery. Their agreeable table manners and the joy that accompanied the proposed toasts were truly moving, and many a proud mother saw her son wear the Cross of Honor on his breast, many a wife lifted her little ones up to kiss their father, and many a beloved maid greeted her returning bridegroom through tears of joy! Bouquets were tossed and kerchiefs waved from every side, and it seemed almost as if the common soldiers would steal the thunder from their brave officers; but they behaved most gallantly. When, after a polite "Thank you for the meal!" they walked about and warmly shook hands with the bystanding citizens both male and female, they also displayed the various decorations they had received, saying: "This ribbon shall go with me to Jutland. . . ." "I shall press this flower in my psalm book," etc. Not one of them had drunk too much or disturbed the pleasant atmosphere in any fashion. With a shrill "Hurrah!" they bade us farewell, fell into ranks, and marched off to their quarters, followed by the jubilant shouts of the people.

In the midst of this paean and these harmonious eulogies a discordant note was heard—the memory of Eckernförde! Naval power was Denmark's oldest and most beloved son. It preserved our history's richest legacy but had, perhaps, been preferred by its mother at the expense of her other children, and in this war it fell to the lot of the Army to reclaim its share of glory and appreciation. This was indeed no naval war, where ship could fight against ship, fire broadsides, and board a vessel in a fair fight. But our fleet tripled the Army's efficacy, partly by rapid diversionary tactics, partly by defending our flanks along the coast. The blockade alone, and the injury it inflicted upon our enemies, made up for the operations of a whole army. This was felt and acknowledged by all, but it was not enough to console our glorious Navy for the misfortune that had obscured its proud career, and which was all the more annoying as it was not—for the present, at least—in a position to be redressed.

The enthusiasm for the ground troops sounded like a reproach in our seamen's ears, and it was with heavy hearts, nay, almost with resentment that they attended the celebration in the Ridehuus. Their thoughts were filled with the injustice of being the *next to the last guests* and with loathing for the caresses which they attributed to pity. The divisions in blue, with their shiny hats, entered our decorated portal somber and silent, and the elegant officers with their gold epaulets stood soberly around the banquet table. The only ones who enjoyed themselves were the cadets—the youth, the hope of the future, the avengers of the Dannebrog!

When the seamen looked up and saw the transformed decorations with the splendid naval flag, hanging over the palm trees, and the long streamers entwined through the suspended laurel wreaths, with gilded anchors at the side of all the larger groups of weapons, the mood was lifted and visibly heightened by the influence of the music. "Holmen's Old Guard" greeted them at the door, and when the King saluted "his gallant lads," "King Christian stood by lofty mast" roared through the vaulted hall like a fresh gale.

Professor M. Hammerich was entrusted with the job of proposing the first toast to Danish naval power. He performed this task in masterly fashion but could not avoid touching upon the sorest spot, and I saw bitter tears flow down the weather-beaten cheeks, while many a full glass stood untouched. Major Bülow of the Fourth Battalion now appeared and in a glowing speech described the brotherhood which had been founded between the Army and Navy during the last war. He emphasized the heroism with which our seamen had fought, the dangers that had been averted by their help, and the competitive spirit which their fame had aroused in our ground forces: "A *skaal* to the cooperation of the Army and the Navy, and to their equal share in Denmark's glory!" It was balm for the wounded hearts. Thunderous applause rang out from every side, and it seemed as though the jubilation would never end. Commodore Steen Bille's speech likewise roused people to enthusiasm. Because of the keener perception of our sailors, as compared with our soldiers, not a single point escaped them; every pathetic or humorous phrase hit home, and even if it did happen to be Holmen's Most Reverend Dean, he was rewarded with applause of the most secular kind.

Now the seamen too began to wax eloquent. One of them delivered a song he himself had composed about the exploits of the steam schooner

Hekla, and proposed a "Hail! " to its brave Captain, Edward Suenson. This fine officer thanked them in the most humble phrases, but a dialogue soon developed between him and the men, who would tolerate no depreciation of the Captain's merits, and a mighty "Hurrah!" rang out in honor of the naval hero, who with his single ship had put to flight seven enemy gunboats.

This fete thus became the liveliest of all. There was a great difference between the physiognomies that had entered the hall and the beaming faces one encountered at their departure. There were no commands to be followed on the way home, but the women were waiting outside in order to accompany their brave men to Nyboder.

The last feast was for the Artillery and Engineer Corps. Here, too, many fine speeches were delivered—in particular, one by our great declaimer Nielsen, who had once been an artillery officer himself and really treated his subject *con amore.*

The King ended the banquet with an inspiring expression of thanks, which was answered with endless hurrahs.

Although I have cooperated in the Constitution Festival at the Hermitage (1854) and also taken part in the Two Hundredth Anniversary of the Storming of Copenhagen (1859), and most interesting things have happened on both these occasions, I still feel that I ought to limit myself to the foregoing series, which, in a manner of speaking, embraces the great events that have shaken our native land. I have found myself at the focal point of patriotism and national rejoicing, and harvested from it spiritual rewards. It has been especially flattering to my feelings as an artist that the confidence I had gained on the stage should one day be of benefit to higher Danish folk life. By writing down my memories of it I have relived these glorious celebrations in spirit. Should these sketches produce a pleasing impression among my contemporaries and, perhaps, develop into vivid pictures in the imaginations of our posterity, then I have wasted neither my own time nor that of my readers.

VII

Ballet Compositions: Third Period

IN THE CARPATHIANS

A Ballet in Three Acts.
Music by H. Paulli.
Decorations by Christensen.
Machinery by Weden.
Costumes Designed by E. Lehmann.
(Performed for the First Time in March 1857)

AS a rule, it is no more possible for memoirs to embrace the events of a whole era than for this *Theatre Life* of mine to contain a complete theatre history and description of the entire period during which my activity was of some importance to the Danish stage.

If one should always study history with a certain degree of criticism, it is most difficult of all to gather reliable data in the wings. This is not because lies thrive better there than elsewhere, but because the truth is seldom if ever regarded objectively but almost always subjectively; that is to say, from a more or less egotistical standpoint, whether it be through the flattering or the insulting spectacles of Vanity.

Should one pore over theatre archives in search of historical materials, one will find mainly dissatisfaction registered there: *complaints* and *petitions* from the personnel, *reprimands* from the management; and this for the simple reason that in the investigation and rejection of unfounded complaints as well as in the expression of thanks for rewards received or favors shown, the spoken word prevails. Rarely does it happen that a theatre director sends an artist or dramatist a written compliment, a copy of which might be preserved for posterity. And should one now rake up old letters, which were for the most part written in anger, or page through biased reviews that smack of either partiality or modish taste, one will get no further in the history of art than antiquarians do by their examination of "kitchen middens"; for just as these lead one to the almost certain conviction that in primeval times there lived a race of people who gnawed the flesh from bones and ate oysters, so here one discovers only that at all theatres in the civilized world there have existed eccentric characters, intrigues, dissatisfaction, vain artists, and unskilled administrators. Therefore, as valuable as a record of the components of a repertoire

264

may be; as important as it is to know the administrative measures that have advanced or halted the development of the scenic art; and lastly, as lovely as it is to transmit to future generations a faithful picture of all that is most excellent in an artistic activity which leaves behind such fleeting and perishable traces in spite of its deep impressions—just so it is fruitless to appeal to curiosity and the love of scandal by stripping the theatre of every illusion and imagining that one has introduced light and shade into one's drawing simply because he has turned it wrong side out.

I will therefore completely pass over the conflicts which during my absence in Vienna precipitated the departure of Etatsraad Heiberg and for a lengthy period also deprived the Theatre of its most important actress. Geheimeraad Hall was at that time Minister of Culture and in this capacity he was, for artistic institutions in general and for the Theatre in particular, a president whose insight and taste, combined with true humanity, must be recognized by every impartial person. And, what should be chiefly acknowledged, he was a zealous spokesman for the aesthetic as opposed to the prosaic and practical, which prided itself on regarding the whole of art as a curiosity. Heiberg had a falling out with Hall on a question of principle and tendered his resignation, which was accepted, apparently without anyone realizing that the angry Director, as is the custom in such cases, would take his talented wife with him and thus embarrass the incoming management to no small degree. It was so much the worse as the loss of such a personality left a thorn which was to be duly used by the daily press.

An old theatre lover and dramaturge, the learned translator of Greek tragedies, Professor Dorph, was appointed Director in Heiberg's stead. For the economic part of the administration, Secretary Christensen from the Ministry of Culture was assigned to assist the new Chief, wherefore the head clerk of the Theatre treasury (a most honorable man indeed, but one without literary or artistic education, who had been appointed by Heiberg as a sort of factotum) once again returned to his former position. The new Directory made it a duty to gather the scattered forces from its predecessor's time. Nielsen, Wiehe, and Høedt were recalled, and, since they thought they could use me for the ballet as well as for stage direction in the opera, I was offered a new five-year contract, by means of which my pension was absorbed and a better future promised to the *corps de ballet,* who had hitherto been treated so unfairly.

Now this was all very good, but Fru Heiberg's cooperation was missing; and her husband, who had been appointed Censor, stood in such an odd relationship to his successors that whatever *they* proposed as useful stage material, he was able to reject, while *they* could still override his decision. The tension was therefore mutual and soon degenerated into bitterness.

As has been stated, for the major portion of the 1856–1857 season the Theatre had to do without its dramatic prima donna, and since Fru Nielsen had died at Fredensborg during the summer of 1856, the female personnel could no longer serve as the mainstay of the repertoire. The success of the pieces had to rely, for the most part, on the talent displayed from the masculine side; and it cannot be denied that by his ingenious performances Høedt during this season contributed as much to providing the Royal Theatre with sold-out houses as he had hurt its receipts during the previous one, when, together with Michael Wiehe, he had lured the public to Lange's productions at the Court Theatre.

Amid these circumstances, I arranged *La Ventana* in its expanded form and I composed my grand ballet *In the Carpathians.*

Among the high-flown plans and resultant illusions engendered in my mind by my engagement at the Imperial Opera in Vienna was that of using the wealth of national characters, costumes, manners, and customs which the Austrian imperial city possesses, for the benefit of my future compositions either at home in Denmark or as a means of making myself popular in my new sphere of activity. In Vienna there is, unfortunately, very little to inspire writers, who consequently vegetate in intellectual respects in a city that has so much to offer in terms of material interests and physical well-being. With the exception of the outstanding dance music, with which one is regaled in all public places, the folk life and its pleasures consist mainly in eating, drinking, and smoking.

All of the newspapers had announced the wine harvest in the village of Grinzing. I hastened thither and also to nearby Klosterneuburg, but saw nothing of those motley groups or gay processions that I had pictured in my imagination. The people were quite well-behaved and picked grapes just as though they were in our currant and gooseberry patches!

On the whole there is little that is characteristic, and even less that is poetic, in the real Austrians. One must seek such things farther off, in Styria, Bohemia, Galicia, and especially Hungary; but I was not a tourist and thus did not have the opportunity to make local observations. What I had seen on the trip through Bohemia gave evidence of nought but bigotry and poverty, and in Vienna itself it was an accepted rule to include everything coarse and wretched under the name *bömisch.* The portrayal of this country's romantic folk tales would have met with only mediocre success, while the use of one episode or another from the heroic Middle Ages of Hungary or Poland would be most strictly forbidden as having political overtones.

The South Germans, above all, have little fondness for seeing their own folk life represented on the stage, and they harbor a contempt bordering on antipathy for those nationalities that populate the extensive Crown lands; nor do these latter yield anything to them. A Hungarian, upon being asked by an impertinent *Wiener-Stutzerle* the reason for his countrymen's presumed stupidity, rather drily replied: "Ach! mein Lieber! On one side we have Turks, on the other Austrians, and we get our brains from them."

Hungary is, however, a remarkable country, not only because it holds in its bosom the natural wealth of all the rest of Europe and embraces, besides, a host of different races such as the Slovaks, the Magyars, the Teutons, the Ruthenians, the gypsies, etc., but because the memories of its brilliant military exploits have preserved in the whole of the nation a spirit of chivalry, which, in the midst of relics of medieval barbarity, allows rare virtues to shine through; among them, the greatest hospitality and certain natural excellences, such as soldierly bearing and musical genius. But just as there runs through Hungarian folk ballads a feeling that is involuntarily reminiscent of our Nordic melodies (from Finland, Sweden, and Norway down to us), so there can be felt in all their legends and tales the hereditary pressure exerted by one race upon another and the sighs of the common people beneath the might of the overlord. None of these elements would suit the Viennese, partly because serious tones do not accord with their prevailing levity and partly because reference might be made to highly sensitive relations.

In this respect, my position was no worse than that of other authors, especially those who worked for the theatre. Domestic creations were worth little or nothing; everything had to come from abroad and preferably should deal with remote and fantastic subjects that left as little room as possible for thought.

Although I did not have the opportunity to make an actual observation tour of the Austrian states, I nevertheless took notice of all the interesting features I could see and collect. I read a number of Hungarian authors in German translation, learnt the characteristic dances, and, at a railway station on the Hungarian border, formed a superficial picture of the folk life by watching a peasant wedding which was distinguished by a variegated array of costumes and a crowd of handsome persons of both genders.

Whether in the borrowed spirit and form of the genre picture or historical painting, I had by now accustomed my Danish ballet audience to accompanying me on distant journeys in my compositions, preferably to the South, only at a given opportunity to lead them back to our Northern home and patriotic memories. This time, I wished to present a panorama from the valleys of the Danube and Theiss rivers, with the Carpathian mountain chain as a background. I had no difficulty at all in finding attractive details; it was simply a matter of procuring an interesting subject on which to center my characters.

Each of my three acts had its distinctive physiognomy: *the work in the mines, gypsy life in the woods,* and *the wine harvest in Tokay* were concise episodes of Hungarian folk life. But to weave them into a plot which could at once emphasize the picturesque element and appeal to an audience to whom this nationality was completely alien was no easy matter. To tell the truth, I was only half, maybe even two-thirds successful; for (if I may say so) the first act was *written* while the second was *composed,* but the third was only *concocted* with a certain amount of trouble. Here I ran into the same difficulty as those musicians who modulate into an unrelated key and must then return to the original theme by many, often unmelodious, detours. I had to wrack my brain in order to find a suitable *dénouement* for the story, and my third act thereby became inordinately long, thus spoiling the total effect of the ballet.

In spite of a superb performance, a décor that was rich according to our standards, enchantingly lovely music, and the fact that a great number of the details were warmly appreciated, the ballet did not achieve the kind of success which is essential in this positive age of ours: namely, frequently sold-out houses. Furthermore, the theatre was unable to provide the necessary support of good one-act plays. Suffice it to say, it enjoyed neither a long nor a profitable career, and when I later thought of entertaining people by gathering the most popular numbers into a *divertissement,* I was repaid with downright ingratitude for having mutilated "a wonderful ballet"! I had actually expended a great deal of energy and a measure of skill on this work, but the composition owed more to my effort and my will than it did to genuine inspiration. This time, I did not draw the winning number.

THE FLOWER FESTIVAL IN GENZANO

A Ballet in One Act.
Music by Messrs. Ed. Helsted and H. Paulli.
Decorations by Messrs. Christensen and Lund.
(Performed for the First Time in December 1858)

A journey to Italy must perforce leave in every artistic imagination impressions which will emerge in compositions, whether they be in poetry, music, painting, or scenic performances: and since the South is especially suited to the ballet, so Venice and Verona might have furnished the best material for opera had Shakespeare not already claimed them for the tragedy in his *Othello* and *Romeo and Juliet.*

If I did not have a well-founded fear of giving this book an inordinate thickness and, moreover, of repeating what has already been read in thousands of travel descriptions and *novelles,* I might be tempted to ask my good readers to accompany me on a little trip from Vienna, via the marvelous railway across the Semmering and through barren Istria, to pause for a moment on the mountain peak whence one first views the Adriatic Sea, which, like a dark blue backdrop, swells above Trieste, with its white buildings and flag-decked ships. Next, they should sail with me into the lagoons and see the palaces, cupolas, and campanili of Venice hovering like a *fata morgana* on the distant horizon; and finally, from one of those romantic gondolas, step ashore on a marble staircase leading up to a princely palace that has now been converted into a hotel. I must, albeit unwillingly, bypass the countless monuments which this fantastic city possesses in the vast realm of art as well as history. So far as vegetation is concerned, nature has but little to offer; but there is all the more to be observed among the populace, whose most prominent trait is an almost fanatic adoration of their native city, *Venezia la bella.* This love is expressed in many and often highly moving fashions, not least by an inveterate hatred of their German lords and guardians;* however, it is not without comic nuances, especially among exhibitors of the city's sights.

Among the latter, I cannot refrain from mentioning the custodian of the prisons in the Doges' Palace. This man was positively mad about his dungeons, the so-called "wells" (*pozzi*) and leaden chambers (*piombi*), as well as anything that had any connection at all with medieval justice. He was highly indignant at the novelists who had dared to portray his jails as chambers of horror, and he condemned the vandalism which in most recent revolutionary times had deprived these respectable devices of their original form. "In the good old days, how comfortably a prisoner here could be strangled from behind without suspecting even the humblest preparations for it. Then one had but to open a trapdoor in the floor and the canal would hide the whole unpleasant business!"

The custodian found it less than fitting that they had given the gallery leading across the *canaletto* to the Council Chamber of the Ten the name of the Bridge of Sighs. Nevertheless, he had to give his full admiration to the old Republic, which with a score of *sbirri* had maintained order far better than the [Austrian] Empire did nowadays with its thousands of bayonets. We made it our business to join in his praise of those beautiful, vanished times. It was a pleasure to see how his cross physiognomy brightened, and in his satisfaction at our good taste, he recommended that we visit the Arsenal, where we should have a chance to admire some most ingenious instruments of torture from this much lauded period of power.

Rather, I refer my readers to an independent contemplation of this most curious of all European cities, but I doubt that any foreigner, unless he intends to study Titian and Tintoretto or wishes to drift back to the golden age of the aristocracy, would care to take up residence for any length of time or could share the enthusiasm of the inhabitants for living there.

A mile-long railway bridge carried us across the lagoons, away from visions of the Middle Ages to fresh, green countryside with the Alps as a background. We arrived in Verona and inspected the well-preserved Roman amphitheatre, about an eighth of which is occupied by a modern theatre where dramas are given by daylight, while the audience sits in the open air on the ancient marble steps. But all the time we were vaguely haunted by the immortal works of Shakespeare. It is uncertain if the great poet ever set foot on Italian soil, but just as one expects to encounter Shylock at any moment on the Rialto bridge in Venice, and fancies he can glimpse the lamp in Desdemona's bedchamber through the dark halls of the thirteenth and fourteenth centuries, so there is in Verona's ancient churches and burial monuments, in the gigantic cypresses and moss-covered walls, even in the sinister forms which, swathed in brown cloaks, steal about beneath the arcades on the very

---

*Venice, a political football during the Napoleonic wars, came under Austrian rule in 1814 and so continued until 1866.

squares that once rang with the wild shrieks of civil wars, something reminiscent of the bloody controversies of the Guelphs and Ghibellines; and from the grim countenances, it even appears as if they might immediately begin the quarrel from the first scene of *Romeo and Juliet*.

This romantic legend, a charming parallel to the Habor and Signe of our North, hovers like an invisible spirit before the traveler's imagination; and, just as the British wanderer seeks to find Hamlet's grave in the gardens of Marienlyst and Helsingør, in like manner all Europe inquires for the palaces of the Montecchi and the Capuletti and the lovers' resting place. This yearning is a real source of income for Verona's hired coachmen, who, through a host of twists and turns, led us to a house with a hatter's signboard outside. In the place where a *capellaio* now has his shop they believe "most definitely" that the Capuletti must have lived. A bit crestfallen, one now drives a way outside the city's fortifications to the former Franciscan monastery, in whose dilapidated sacristy lies an open antique sarcophagus, probably from the time of the Romans. A woman explains that the hole in one corner at the head end had been carefully placed there to provide for Giulietta when she awakened in her coffin. However, it takes but meagre powers of observation and a grain of critical sense to recognize that this ancient relic and supposed *feretro* must for many years have served as a drinking vessel or washing trough at one watering place or another. This was indeed a cold shower on our romantic mood, and we came to realize, when presented with a most exorbitant hotel bill, that we were still living in a rather prosaic present.

Apart from its majestic cathedral and some old cloisters, Milan has but little to offer the tourist, whereas there is a great deal for music-lovers to observe. However at that time (1856) there was a special fragrance and freshness about Turin: this was the beneficial breeze of Freedom! One could feel how the atmosphere lightened after crossing the border from Austrian control, and whether it was the enlivening influence of springtime or the spirit's release from the constricting bonds that had weighed so heavily upon me in Vienna I cannot be sure, but here I rediscovered my desire to write and to compose. I drafted the libretto for a grand ballet, for which two highly different subjects presented themselves and long caused me to waver between the heroic and the romantic elements of the Venetian Middle Ages.

One subject was nothing less than Cort Adeler, who, as Admiral of the Republic, had performed brilliant exploits and, moreover, had a brother who fell in the same naval battle at Rhodes where Cort, with his own hand, cut down the Turkish *bassa*. This younger brother would provide an excellent *jeune premier* role, and the Republican festivals as well as the sailors' life — but especially the battle on deck — could provide interesting effects. The rather serious material, the expensive settings and machinery, and mainly the difficulty of finding a personality to play the title role, forced me to renounce this, my first and dearest idea.†

†But Bournonville returned to this theme several years later; cf. his discussion of the ballet *Cort Adeler in Venice*, Vol. III, Part One, pp. 362–363.

I therefore had to advance a bit further into the time of the Doges, and now I remembered having read about a *venieri* (Giovanni Baptista) who, on account of a violent conflict on the Piazza San Marco itself in the year 1712, was subjected the harshest sentence of exile, but in spite of the impending danger of death dared to return to his native city and only after many troubles was restored to his former dignity. Here I found the occasion to use some of the characters which I myself had observed in the singular courtyards and vestibules: gondoliers, prisoners, and — lest I forget — my jailer. Through a series of intrigues and spectacles such as regattas, masquerades, and finally, the wedding of the Adriatic, I arrived at an astonishing but nevertheless natural manner for my hero's acquittal, appointment, and union with his beloved, who gave the ballet its name: *Adriana.*

This composition, which had a host of musical situations, I entrusted to the talented care of Professor Gade. He had already begun the score for the first act when several serious matters halted his work and prevented its continuation.

I made a trip to Stockholm, and if I had not already made an agreement with the above-mentioned composer, the ingenious *Kapellmeister* Foroni, a native of Verona, would have readily undertaken the composition. In the meantime, Gade had received a large-scale opera subject to think about, and my enthusiasm for Venice cooled, especially when I began to have misgivings about the profitableness of the undertaking for the Theatre treasury, an anxiety which has of late increasingly gotten the upper hand. Finally, my eyes were opened to a circumstance peculiar to this as well as a number of my larger ballet libretti: the fact they would have been better suited for *opera texts;* and it is not entirely impossible that should I retain the desire to write after the publication of this book, I might try my hand in that genre with which I have become familiar through long practice and in which I would not have to combat the difficulties that have placed themselves in the way of clarity in my mimed compositions.

I hereby come to a branch of art that has been the object of my special attention, because as both musical dilettante and stage director for the opera, I have diligently endeavored to reconcile dramatic reflection and onstage activity with the demands which the music makes on lyric performers. I have not yet had it in my power to solve this problem, either in Copenhagen or at the Royal Theatre in Stockholm, and in these memoirs a considerable lacuna has resulted from the fact that I have not singled out the singing talents who adorn the opera stages of both countries. My reasons are the following. As an artist I have always placed the development of talent above natural gifts. Were I now, by praising the latter, to point out the lack of the first requirement or, by acknowledging it, to complain of the possible weakness of the [a singer's] resources and ability, I would have to adopt the standpoint of a critic, which I have resolved to avoid as much as possible. On the other hand, were I to bestow unconditional fame on some personalities and at the same time pass over names which, perhaps to a greater degree, have won public favor, I would leave myself open to reasonable objections from those in question as well as their patrons. I shall therefore limit myself to the observation that although neither the *syngestykke* nor the lyric drama has received its due on our stage in the last decade, and, while either in the acting or the singing there has been something halting and defective in our whole opera, many important compositions have still been performed in exemplary fashion; among them, Mozart's *Don Giovanni*, Marschner's *Hans Heiling*, and in lighter vein, *The White Lady*, *The Elixir of Love*, and *The Daughter of the Regiment*. However, it is greatly to be lamented that not a single musical product in operatic form by our native composers has found a permanent place in our lyric repertoire: and the slowness—not to say the indifference—that prevails in the admission of new foreign operas sets us far behind other European theatres, with the unpleasant result that the most prominent musical numbers have already been played to the saturation point at the changing of the guard, at balls, and by hurdy-gurdies before the opera itself has been· recognized by our theatre management, let alone become familiar as piano selections or as a libretto. To this may be added an all too great one-sidedness in those who set the tone in the musical world and who apparently do not want to distinguish between the problems of a *theatre* and those of a *philharmonic society*. Thus many operas which would have given our singers the finest opportunity to develop their talents and at the same time would have provided the public with a variety of enjoyments, are suppressed or completely rejected by reason of their genre, aye, often simply because of their names! Many internal reasons have until now hindered and will, for a long time to come, continue to place themselves in the way of the opera's progress at the Danish Theatre. It would in truth be very sad if the destruction of the other branches of art were the main reason for the rise of the lyric stage: but in any event, a new and better system must be found, with regard not only to the use of talents but also to their appreciation.

But to return to the ballet: I must now state that I abandoned *Adriana*, together with the whole of northern Italy, in order to once again make a little pilgrimage to the Alban Hills, and in memory I recalled the flowering pictures from Arriccia and Genzano. I borrowed a little "robber tale" from Alexandre Dumas' *Impressions de voyages*, and therein found a really characteristic motif for the consecutive action which is resolved in merry dancing and crowned by a lovely *saltarello*.

The decided advantage that can be won by a smaller work like *The Flower Festival in Genzano* is a certain perfection in detail, and in few of my compositions has it appeared in so refreshing a manner as in this work, whose style came close to that of the so-called "sentimental vaudeville." The atmosphere throughout was also excellent, among the audience as well as the performers, and precisely because the ballet appeared without claiming to be a work of art, it was *almost* allowed to be one.

THE MOUNTAIN HUT OR TWENTY YEARS

A Romantic Ballet in Three Tableaux.
Music by August Winding and Emil Hartmann.
(Performed for the First Time in May 1859)

I could not, however, regard my vocation as limited to binding bouquets and cultivating nothing but rootless plants. I had more than once produced genuinely dramatic situations and partially solved the problem of interpreting feelings and *affects*, sometimes even humor and satire, by means of a natural mime that was not bound to the conventional deaf-mute gestures of the pantomime. It was in the *The Wedding Festival in Hardanger* that I chiefly succeeded in this endeavor, and as I still had my thoughts fixed on Norwegian folk life as the most picturesque and least used source of material here in the North, I found in the superb descriptions of the ingenious writer Bjørnstjerne Bjørnson such a wealth of expression amid the taciturnity which marks the character of most of his protagonists, that I was strengthened even further in my intention of treating yet again a Norwegian subject, in order to realize an interesting plot through the medium of a primitive play of facial expression and an idealized representation of national dances.

The legend of the *huldre* [troll maiden] lies all too near the balletic domain for me not to have thought of using it in my compositions. It was merely a question of whether I should use the material in order to achieve a serious effect, as in *La Sylphide* and *A Folk Tale,* or treat it as an outright superstition having an influence on everyday life. I chose the latter and took the rather straightforward path of representing a young girl raised on the mountain by her father, who as a killer and prodigal son was forced to flee from his ancestral home. They live far from the rest of society, and he abandons this wild solitude only in order to earn a living by playing music for dances in the villages. The libretto will explain the rest and show that I have relied on an audience that is used to following me, even if it involves a leap of twenty years. I certainly had every reason to be delighted over the sympathy with which they followed the thread of the major episode as well as the performance in its entirety. The music, which was the test piece for two young composers, was outstanding in its grace and local color, though in rhythmic as well as melodic respects it was less easily understood than *The Wedding Festival in Hardanger,* so richly equipped with folk ballads. On the part of the *corps* the performance was thoroughly satisfactory, and in some roles postively masterful. Surely I dare (insofar as one can, after a lapse of several years, be both party and judge in one's own case) to claim that in this work I had brought my art a considerable step forward in the direction which I regarded as the best one, namely, in having the dancing woven into the action itself and the mimic effects clearly evolved from the situation.

However, a whole school of criticism could not agree with me on this, and it was more obvious than ever that to whatever side I inclined—whether to the kind of composition in which the dancing is the main thing, or to that in which the use of the dance is in accord with the dramatic effect one is endeavoring to achieve—I had to ward off the champions of the opposing system and in both cases displease those who positively wished to see the ballet abolished. One such harsh review simply placed my work on a par with those pantomimes with which Tivoli regales its public, and since independence in aesthetic judgment is a quality still undeveloped here at home, many felt that they did not need to buy an expensive ticket to see a spectacle they could have for as good as nothing at Tivoli. The much-sought-after full house was not forthcoming after the first six performances. Artists entitled to *feux* [star status] did not care to play good or new pieces before this ballet, and since during this same space of time the theatre management changed rather frequently, the most recently arrived members regarded that unfortunate ballet as an unsuccessful speculation and consigned it to eternal oblivion. It would not surprise me if this subject should some day arise in the form of a *syngestykke;* I will then be able to avoid showing the bear, which appears in the ballet only for the sake of clarity.

There was a time when I regarded the often unjust severity of the critics as directed against my humble person, or at least against the art I cultivated; but I have since discovered that immature judgments often arise because, like a piece of music, a ballet cannot be fully taken in at a single showing, and a first one at that. Now if the critic is also biased by the opinion that a success for the ballet is a step toward the destruction of the dramatic art, his attitude must be unfavorable beforehand, and his view must be prejudiced by an aversion which he himself regards as the purest zeal in the interest of a good cause.

However, it is not only those who hate our art who add to the injury, but far more those who have a false conception of its meaning, and love its excesses to the point of infatuation. I am alluding here to the *Pepita* frenzy that prevailed in Copenhagen at the very time I was seeking, in my *Mountain Hut,* to bring my Muse into consonance with the efforts [being made] on behalf of Nordic art.

Since this book of mine should be suitable for young people, as is the case with my ballets (which, I hope, have never yet given offense), it is not permissible to describe the tendency or the mimic expression that this famous Spaniard presented, or to paint the effect she exercised on the intoxicated *dilettanti.* I will only state that Pepita de Oliva,* who with varying success but for the most part with furor appeared at most of the secondary theatres in Europe, is the living representative of a whole trend, not only in scenic presentations but in literature and sculpture, which, as in the period of the decline

---

*For details of this dancer's vivid life, wealthy protector, and many children, see the biography *Pepita* (1937) by her granddaughter, V. Sackville-West.

Above: *A FOLK TALE*. Harald Scharff as Junker Ove beset by Elf
Maidens. Contemporary lithograph from the cover of the first published
sheet music of the ballet. Below: *FAR FROM DENMARK*. In this 1860
picture from *Illustreret Tidende* Juliette Price as Rosita lolls in a hammock
in a setting more Caribbean than Argentine, more quasi-Oriental than
either. Scharff, as Wilhelm, is seated at the writing table, while Axel
Fredstrup, as the Negro Jason, leans against the pillar. Both,
Teatermuseet, Copenhagen.

PEPITA

This pencil drawing by "Ed L" [Lehmann]
amply displays the charms that brought her
so much attention.
Teatermuseet, Copenhagen.

DOLORES SERRAL AND MARIANO CAMPRUBÍ

Their version of the *Cachucha*, in a print by Hautecoeur-
Martinet, Paris, n.d. Courtesy Dance Collection, The
New York Public Library at Lincoln Center, Astor,
Lenox and Tilden Foundations. Photo by Frank Derbas.

of the Roman Empire, denotes the corruption of taste and morals in our over-civilized age. To the honor of the Royal Theatre, it disdained to fill its coffers by such presentations; but since a noted Danish writer has sounded the alarm about crudeness and bad taste as consequences of private theatrical enterprises, I dare say the often misused word *prostitution* could not be used more properly than to describe the enthusiasm, whether it was affected or sincere, with which the choreographic horror *El Olé* was received by a very numerous public and even by the severely critical press as *"the true ideal of the Dance"*!

I dutifully attended Pepita's debut at the Casino, therefore before the enthusiasm for her had amounted to madness and before the crowds flocked thither more to observe her overexuberant admirers than to see the irresistible *Olé*. They had not yet drawn her carriage, overwhelmed her with flowers, nor amassed for her an income that exceeded everything Catalani, Prume, Ole Bull, and Jenny Lind together had reaped during their artistic appearances in Copenhagen. Therefore, while I could not envy her success, I was ashamed on behalf of the relationship. I wept over the desecration of my lovely Muse, and I was on the verge of cursing every hour, every thought, and every sport I had sacrificed to an art which I was now to see dedicated to such service!

I never saw Pepita again, except on the street, surrounded by a curious mob. My overwrought state of mind soon passed into sober bitterness, and I had almost forgotten the whole storm when, during a short stay in Paris, I overheard the following statement from a famous *danseuse* who had been engaged in Spain for several years: "Don't talk to me about the taste of your public, which could get fanatical about a poor *figurante* who at Madrid danced in the rear row" (that is to say, danced furthest back in the line of *figurantes*).

Naturally I strove to excuse my countrymen's Bacchanalian ecstasy as best I could, and now, when the intoxication is over, it might furnish the occasion for several humorous observations — all of which would, unfortunately, cause suffering to the idea or to the cause which I dared to call my art, and which I will never disown in spite of all the sorrows it has caused me.

FAR FROM DENMARK OR A COSTUME BALL ON BOARD

A Vaudeville-Ballet in Two Acts.
Music Partly by Hr. Glaeser, Jr.
Decorations by Messieurs Christensen and Lund.
Costumes Designed by Hr. Edv. Lehmann.
(Performed for the First Time in April 1860.)

IN this world it is not unusual for people to be passionately fond of that for which they have the least calling. I shall not speak of untalented poets, orators, actors, or politicians, but how often it happens that the very person whose greatest delight is to *play* soldier is neither a warrior nor a field mar-shal and that a poet to whom the heroic life is revealed in all its radiance is himself denied personal courage. For example, to me naval life has always ap-peared as something most romantic and attractive. Ships, flags, and naval ex-ploits have from my earliest childhood seemed to me to be surrounded with a poetic aura, and my heart has beat high at the report of battles at sea against the elements as well as against Denmark's enemies. But when, in my fif-teenth year, I made my first trip across the Baltic, I perceived to my great sor-row that I was not a good sailor and that far from seeing my ideas realized and my moral force lifted "upon the salty waves," to the contrary I found all my resolutions shaken and even sank into a torpor that disappeared only sev-eral hours after I had set foot upon solid ground. In the course of my eventful artistic career, I have been on the sea over a hundred times, not only across the Sound and Belts but on longer voyages on the Baltic, the North Sea, and the Mediterranean. Nevertheless, although I am neither apprehensive nor one of the very worst sailors, I have never been able to progress further in sea-worthiness than a certain composure in good weather, submission to my fate when it begins to blow up, and an intense longing to reach port.

I have always felt sorry for those unfortunate people who have not found their proper place in life, especially naval officers who lacked the necessary temperament. And yet, one has seen examples where physical weakness is compensated for by nautical knowledge and military bravura; but there is one profession in which qualifications are never inquired about, and that is *theatre management!*

Almost everybody to a greater or lesser degree longs to get his hands on this enchanting machine, and from this stem not only the many aspirants to such a vacant post, but the continuous revilement of every measure taken within the administrative sphere and, in part, the fanatical attacks of the press. Heiberg's successors in particular were afflicted with such things to an overwhelming degree, despite the success with which all difficulties were over-come under Dorph's chairmanship, and despite the aesthetic authority that accompanied the name of a poet such as Hauch; none of them endured the conflict for more than a year.

A cabal unprecedented in our dramatic annals deprived the repertoire of one of its firmest supports, and our most superb actress, the public's darling, had, like Achilles, withdrawn into her tent. Unfortunately, our art-loving and patronizing Minister of Education was not a Ulysses who could persuade the infuriated actress to return to the path of conviction. Copenhagen resembled Rome in the days of the Augusti, when on the part of Mæcenas a sacrifice had to be made for the people, who with shrill cries demanded the withdrawal of this famous mime. *Things had to change.* Geheimeraad Hall exchanged port-folios, and Bishop Monrad as Minister of Culture got Fru Heiberg to appear once again.

The Theatre lost in Hall its warmest spokesman, and the system from

1849 to 1856 set in with its old machinery and in full force—minus only J. L. Heiberg!

Geheimeconferentsraad v. Tillisch, "a most honorable gentleman," was acting as Theatre Chief and had now found a position for which, with all respect for the rest of his excellent qualities, he was as little suited as I would have been as captain of one of His Majesty's frigates. Whether His Exellency had ever been passionately fond of the theatre or of art I dare not state with certainty, or whether he might actually have desired a directorship after having honorably governed the King's realm under the most difficult circumstances; but it was clear to everyone that he regarded the whole institution as an *entailed property,* which because of poor housekeeping had fallen into disorder, and which was now to be helped out of its financial crisis by means of a neat and tight-fisted administration.

The Theatre had really gotten into a very considerable debt because of the obligation it had rashly undertaken of renovating at its own expense its antiquated and partly useless facilities. The stage, the wardrobes, and the foyers were most efficiently arranged, but had cost such large sums that better times had to be awaited before the whole thing could be given a tolerable architectural form by the rebuilding of the amphitheatre and the façade. The interest on these borrowed building sums, combined with the wages of the orchestra, now took up the entire public subsidy, so that the actual Danish stage now had to exist on its earned income. Would these means of assistance be sufficient, or, if not, what measures had to be taken to supplement them?

In any event, the building debt and the completion of the playhouse in a proper style would have to be handed over either to the State or, more correctly, to the municipality of Copenhagen; but what should have been of primary importance was to awaken artistic life in order to focus the greatest possible attention on the stage and thus outdistance and crush all competition. Instead of this, the Theatre building remained standing unfinished as a scandal to the capital and as a pitiful portent for our once celebrated Temple of the Muses. There was no regular plan for the Theatre's operations, and the needs of the repertoire were taken care of only insofar as it concerned using the recaptured dramatic prima donna and providing full houses for nonsubscription performances. A long list of those who were indisposed was always ready at hand in order to excuse the poor entertainment; but nobody knew how many good talents were idle for lack of proper use. For a number of years the lyric stage presented not a single real novelty. The influx of domestic as well as foreign subjects for the spoken drama was dreadfully poor, and the acceptance of one major work or another was dependent, for the most part, upon the wish of a debutant or a member of the cast, not brought about by artistic or financial considerations; and while the whole business was a gamble with as small stakes as possible, inside the mechanism a huckster's trade was carried on with the so-called *feux,* a kind of prize game which at our Theatre is organized according to a system which, far from stimulating

Art, is certain to saturate it with the coldness of calculation. The respective experts seemed to be employed merely to help man the pumps on the steadily sinking ship; and if there were still certain persons who sought satisfaction through the fulfillment of duty, the opportunity to work was sometimes granted—but only as a special favor!

I was one of those who *most respectfully* had to apply for permission to fulfill my contractual duties, and, just as in Heiberg's time, my zeal was viewed with suspicion. However, Heiberg had less of an excuse, since he both knew and understood my worth, whereas to Geheimeraad Tillisch I was a completely unknown entity. Small wonder, then, that a man whose only goal was to put the dilapidated finances back on their feet by economizing could see in me nothing more than a high salary and ballets with costly décors— in short, an *expenditure* that ought to be gotten rid of completely.

This tendency on the part of my high-ranking superior did not go unnoticed by certain zealous souls, and they honestly used it to make him so uneasy about my working plans that when in the heat of enthusiasm I strove to appeal to his powers of visualization by picturing the subject I intended to represent, my words were constantly lost amid such icy remarks as: "But what will the frills cost?" or "Do you think it can make a profit?" or "You are becoming an expensive man, Hr. Bournonville!" On such occasions there then appeared, from the material point of view, several grand, one might almost say forbidding, rough estimates—*within* the theatre these had usually already been increased by one-third, while *outside* they grew to threefold the amount—and for me there now began the work of reducing the demands of my helpers to show what could be procured more cheaply, and calling to light from dusty nooks anything old that could be used, etc. etc. This was far more tiresome than even the most difficult rehearsal.

And so I received permission to get on with my ballet, *Far from Denmark*. My desire to compose was, as one can gather from the above, put to just as hard a test as my devotion to my debased art was as a result of the Copenhagen Pepita frenzy. Nevertheless, my innate vocation triumphed, my desire to realize a favorite idea—naval life—and, finally, the feeling that this work, which would no doubt be my next to the last, might, as they say in stage jargon, "knock 'em dead."

I was not at all mistaken in assuming that most of the Danish public was as fascinated by naval life as I myself had always been. It was simply a matter of showing it from a new and attractive angle. A storm at sea or the boarding of a vessel required all too great a number of actors, and, precisely because it approaches the sublime, could by an unsuccessful representation easily be transformed into the ridiculous. On the other hand, a party on board ship, a ball or masked pageant, as when crossing the Equator, might furnish features of interest to the ballet. Strongly influenced by Bille's round-the-world voyage with the corvette *Galathea*, and mainly by his stop in Buenos Aires, where

President Rosas' daughter Manuelita,* the renowned Spanish beauty, brightened the festive evening by her presence on board ship, I here found a lovely focal point for the choreographic movement; and since we had recently witnessed the intoxication that can lie in a pair of Spanish eyes, it quite naturally occurred to me that a young lieutenant might become so enraptured by their luster — especially far from Denmark, beneath the blazing sun of the tropics — that when they were supported by coquetry and accompanied by the clacking of castanets, he could forget both his home and his engagement ring.

From the libretto one will be able to see that there is a vague reminiscence of Schiller's *Handschuh* in my resolution of the plot. But since I no longer, as in my younger years, brought my brain-children into the world fully armed, nor dared to let them go out into society so roughly clad, it was some time before my treatment of the material finally acquired the proper *rondeur*. But at last the subject, as the saying goes, got legs to stand on, and, as so often happens, this occurred through the magic of sound. One of the capital's most amiable and talented ladies, in whose house hospitality and art join hands, delivered with the most extraordinary virtuosity Gottschalk's *Negro Dance* for the pianoforte, and as if by magic my entire first act fell into place.†

I saw before me the singular life of our West Indian islands, the pleasant intercourse our naval officers enjoyed on the plantations, and the indescribable delight our seamen must feel upon the arrival of letters from their loved ones at home. In the imagination it is but a jump from St. Thomas to Buenos Aires. A person sailing around the world must surely touch both these points; and at a consul's villa at La Plata one could certainly find everything to make a temporary stay both piquant and romantic. A costume ball on board ship is indeed a lovely diversion, and the Negroes, who are not slaves here, would surely dare — like devoted servants when the master is away — to perform a dance in the *Havesal* where the piano is being played by the little Danish cadet.

The libretto will show how I have arranged the various episodes in succession, and one will discover that the inserted character dances denote the nations that one might expect to visit on a cruise around the world: the Eskimos, the Chinese, the Hindus, Spanish colonials, and South Sea natives.

The plot in itself is uncomplicated enough for the talents of the Ballet to render it clearly. But what I have placed particular weight on is *atmosphere*. In this respect I have received the greatest satisfaction, not only from a numerous and discriminating public but from our highly esteemed navy and a host of foreigners, several among them having recognized life on the other

*Juan Manuel de Rosas (1793–1877) was dictator of Argentina from 1835 to 1852. Overthrown by a rebellion in that year, he spent the rest of his life in England. His daughter Manuela, who inherited his aristocratic good looks and strong character, was an important member of his inner circle and accompanied him into exile.

†Cf. footnote, Vol. I, p. 30

side of the Equator—a part of the world which I have visited only in books and in my poet's dreams.

Surely I dare say that I composed this ballet from my heart, and as long as I live, I will feel moved at the thought of *two scenes:* the one in the first act, where one cadet receives a letter while the other one sadly sits down at the piano; and the moment in the finale of the second act when the crew stops dancing in order to harken to the melody "Wave proud on Codan's swells," which sounds from the Argentinian coast upon the ship's departure, while Poul, dressed as an Amager lass, hands Wilhelm the letter from his fiancée.

I notice that in my ballet histories I constantly speak of the performance as excellent and the music as lovely and characteristic, and these words might just as well be used here. I am only too glad to pass over the curious circumstance that brought seven different musicians to orchestrate and complete the score. As far as the roles and dancing parts are concerned, nothing was wanting; the only thing might have been a pair of Andalusian eyes for Rosita's interpreter. But I must make special mention of one division of the Ballet's personnel and pay them a well-merited tribute. This is the class of people who in universal theatre parlance are denoted as supernumeraries and extras, but whom I—with grateful recognition of their skill and uncommon readiness to serve—have called my *military and civilian assistants.* The fact that they are finer in Denmark than anywhere else has a deeper meaning than one might suspect at first glance. This lies in the esteem which the art of the stage and those who cultivate it enjoy in our native land more than in many other countries. Abroad, it is hardly conceivable that a citizen with any *point d'honneur* would bring himself to figure in a crowd scene on the stage, or that a soldier, without special orders, would mount the stage in a costumed parade or some such theatrical pageant. Here in Denmark, on the contrary, the finest people vie to offer their services; indeed, the more there is to perform, the happier and more eager they are to do it.

Our military assistants consisted only of subordinate officers (for the most part, gymnastics teachers), and they distinguished themselves not only by their agility and precision but by a poise and conduct combined with an attentiveness on stage which could serve as models for many an artist. This time, however, I needed a third type of assistance and was lucky enough to get *sixteen clever lads from Holmen*—peerless models!—for I wished to represent on stage actual naval manoeuvers as well as that air which is our seamen's own. They were indefatigable, whether working in the rigging during intermission or executing the manoeuvers demanded of them, both aloft and on deck. They were a tremendous success and became so fond of their respective roles that when they returned from their tours of duty, they reserved for themselves the right to appear in their old numbers. Indeed, they presented the scenes from the ballet on board ship on especially ceremonious occasions, and when they happened to hear the name of my next work, a deputation appeared to ask whether any crew might be needed on board *The Valkyr*. Certainly one can ask no more from a ballet, unless it must also be counted among its triumphs that the world-famous old naval hero, Kanaris, saw it *six times* and has taken the memory of *Far from Denmark* with him to the classical soil of Greece.‡

THE VALKYR

A Ballet in Four Acts.
Music by J. P. E. Hartmann, Sr.
Decorations Painted by C. F. Christensen.
Costumes Designed by Edv. Lehmann.

THERE has been a good deal of controversy about the propriety, nay, even the feasibility, of using the Old Norse as the subject for artistic and, especially, scenic adaptation; and despite the proofs which Ewald and Oehlenschläger have furnished in support of this direction in dramatic composition, it still has its zealous opponents. It certainly cannot be denied that this genre does present serious difficulties because our present concepts of poetry have little in common with the grandiose, often grotesque, forms of Norse mythology; and these forms, to be personified, must perforce undergo modifications that inevitably lead them back to the Greek ideal. And yet there is in our Nordic myths and fable-shrouded sagas such an endless amount of material for production that even the Ballet can gather from them motifs which could hardly be better interpreted by any other art form. However, the worst drawback of these ingenious subjects lies not in their form but in their *meaning,* which is completely allegorical and, as such, is not only incomprehensible to many, but repugnant to most of the younger generation.

I had special reason for avoiding the allegory, since I had a number of times burnt myself on this ancient, classical inclination and was not only uncomprehened but completely misunderstood. The present age is all too inclined to read political allusions into such pictures. I will not mention how often Thorvaldsen's "Ganymede" has had to pour his nectar for the eagles of France, Russia, Austria, and Prussia; even your humble servant has been exposed to such explanations, particularly with one of my tableaux for the two hundredth anniversary of the Storming of Copenhagen.*

The fact is that, in an effective battle scene, I had represented the ramparts of Copenhagen during the nocturnal attack on February 11, 1659; and since this picture was to have a companion piece, I had set up a tableau, the right foreground of which was occupied by Swedish-Norwegian, and the left by Danish villagers wearing their national costumes and grouped with their

‡ After an absence of many years, *Far from Denmark* was restored to the repertoire of the Royal Danish Ballet in the winter season of 1974.
*By Swedish-Norwegian forces under Charles X of Sweden.

respective attributes. In the center, a fair-haired woman with a crown on her head and the Dannebrog in her arms stood erect in a boat that was rowed by Youth and Strength but steered by sedate Old Age. To the right, at the foot of a cliff, sat an old *skald* from whose harp twined a rope of evergreen and flowers, which were brought to Denmark by mermaids and caught by the little genii who swarmed over the boat. At the top of the cliff, Svea [Sweden] sat enthroned with armor-clad Norway at her side. In the clouded background stood Peace, surrounded by Science, Agriculture, and Art, all of whom, with garlands and green boughs, blessed the central group.

Need I explain to my readers that this grouping was intended to signify the spiritual bond that exists in our Nordic poetry, sagas, and memories, and that the advantages of civilization are the surest stronghold of peace and friendship among the kingdoms? And yet this composition was interpreted by both the Scandinavian and the anti-Scandinavian press as a *unionistic* demonstration, and it enjoyed as much undeserved praise from one party as it did unwarranted censure from the other. As a result, I swore that I would never again have anything to do with the symbolic.

Still, I could not let go of the Nordic myths if, through my profession, I could possibly bring something beautiful and new out of them. By a quirk of fate, my last ballet libretto, like my very first, was to be in the Old Norse style. However, the idea of using Valhalla as a final effect had already passed through a good many stages before finally reaching *The Valkyr*. I had used it by turn with *Regnar Lodbrog, Rolf Krake, The Lay of Thrym*, and finally *Ægir's Wedding*. The latter I presented, in the form of a grand-scale *divertissement*, as a reverential offering to Oehlenschläger's memory at a performance which the great bard's disciples and admirers had planned at the unveiling of his statue.

This time, too, the Christiania Theatre was to put us to shame; for while they presented plays for the benefit of the above-mentioned memorial to the immortal author of *Hakon Jarl* and *Axel and Valborg*, all offers were rejected and all efforts proved fruitless at the Danish Theatre, which, next to Holberg, owed its greatest brilliance to Oehlenschläger! "It is contrary to principles," they said. "We cannot afford to give up an evening's profits, etc." Heaven knows whether Heiberg himself would have dared to offer such opposition. The continuator of his directorial system, however, was firm in his refusal, and on the same occasion I perceived that our august Chief had no love for Norse subjects.

I therefore suffered a moment of doubt as to whether I ought to choose for my last work a patriotic theme or bring to the stage once more the luxuriant colors of the South. But suppose I could unite both these elements in a picture of Viking life and its vicissitudes: a Danish sea-king and his *fylgja* [guardian spirit] who modifies his ferocity, keeps him from the snares of lust, preserves him from violence and guile, and, through a heroic death, leads him to Valaskjálf,† where the Hærfader bestows upon him the reward of combat and of love! The saga of Hjorvard lay before me, with Helge and the Valkyr, Svava; the legend of the sword Tyrfing had already been treated poetically by Hertz; but I needed to forge my own path and therefore invented a plot, which I based on the ballad of Stærkodder, retaining the names of the lovers: Helge and Svava! I had the whole theme worked out in my mind, but first I related it to the poet Paludan-Müller and later to our ingenious musician, Hartmann; then, prompted by their encouragement, I wrote my libretto.‡

I submitted it to the Theatre Chief under cover, since I did not wish to take him by surprise; nor did I myself wish to be taken by surprise. A long and ominous silence ensued, and when I finally asked, if not for an opinion, at least for an order to begin work, I received for my honest efforts the unhappy reply that the contents of the ballet were not to the liking of His Excellency, who, in a verbal report to His Majesty King Frederik VII, had even mentioned the alarming fact that at Braavallahede the Danes had been beaten—and by the Swedes into the bargain! Whether the historical investigation was carried to the point where Sigurd Ring's assumption of Harald Hildetand's power and control were explained as a suspicious tendency in the dynastic direction, I cannot tell; suffice it to say that the King is supposed to have replied: "Good Lord! Let us have nothing to do with *that!*"

Along with this report, there was one of those well-known *colossal* estimates that seemed designed to render the ballet an impossibility or, at any rate, to postpone its performance for a year or two! There was nothing for me to do now but rewrite my libretto and, together with a most humble letter, submit it to the King. In this letter I stated my reasons for clothing the subject in historical-mythical array in much the same way as they appear in the printed Foreword of the libretto, and, in consideration of the Royal Theatre's hard-pressed financial circumstances, requested a most gracious subsidy to aid in providing a worthy décor for my patriotic ballet. I received the most favorable and encouraging reply with the declaration of royal approval, accompanied by the warmest wishes for the success and prosperity of the work on the Danish stage. But, since His Majesty was not in the habit of making any financial contributions whatsoever to the Royal Theatre, my last humble request was contrary to an accepted principle!

The ballet's acceptance into the repertoire now came to depend on the prices and rough estimates of the artisans and contractors. But since this would take months, and the score for a composition such as the one Hartmann wished to create as a lyrical expression for my work could not be finished in less than half a year, I considered it my duty to begin my preparations. Considerable time had already been spent on this music when my good Professor

† One of Odin's dwellings.
‡ For a fine account of the genesis and realization of *The Valkyr,* see Sidsel Jacobsen, "Bournonville's Ballet *Valkyrien,*" in *Theatre Research Studies* (Copenhagen, 1972).

was informed that it was unlikely that my ballet would ever *be permitted* to appear on stage. As a result, total paralysis might have set in had I not assured Hartmann that *The Valkyr would* be performed, either here or elsewhere, and that in any case I was prepared to pay him [the equivalent of] the maximum fee. I now received the piano and violin arrangement of this superb music; and, while in the town as well as in the wings and theatre offices people talked about my fantastic project and whether this dreadful ballet would cost 22,000, 15,000, or merely 8000 Rbd., I spent all my spare time teaching the zealous and benevolent corps my ballet, my part of which was completely finished by the middle of March 1861.

All were agreed that *The Valkyr,* acted and danced within four bare walls, without costumes, scenery, or properties, was a work as impressive as it was original. I had with clear figures shown that very decent scenic equipment for the ballet could be provided for only 4000 to 5000 Rbd.! And yet the management doubted whether this reduced expenditure would be restored to the treasury and whether the ballet would have any appeal at all for the general public.

At length, the Chief ventured to give his permission for *The Valkyr* to be performed. But since it was already well into spring, and the accessory works were very far behind, they decided to postpone the whole thing until the start of the following season.

There were two tremendous drawbacks to this postponement: first, setting a freshly rehearsed work aside for half a year (for one must know something about the character and nature of ballet to realize just how much can be forgotten and lost in such a short space of time); secondly, my term of service expired with the month of June, and the appointment I had accepted as Intendant for the Royal Swedish stage was to begin on July 1, 1861. Thus obstacles were put in my way which might have deterred many others in my position, and as a result of all this pettiness, I had also lost my taste for my work—and this to no small degree! But I had promised my faithful colleague that *The Valkyr* would be performed, and the time he now gained was of great advantage to the rich orchestration, which had been held up because of the prevailing uncertainty. I was, however, anxious to end my choreographic career with a composition from which I could derive honor and, in addition, show suspicious and intriguing people that I was not a hotheaded crank. I managed to have my Stockholm engagement deferred until October 1, but this time it was not without financial sacrifice that I got my way.

On September 13, 1861, *The Valkyr* was performed for the first time and satisfied all my expectations. It was a totally new genre, and therefore the ballet could not be compared with my previous compositions. But the effects were so successfully calculated that the atmosphere was maintained throughout all four acts and reached a climax at precisely the right spot. It was through toil and trouble that I triumphed; yet I had also added, not my strength and inventiveness, but the last spark of desire to work in a profession which, despite the efforts of thirty-two years and some rather striking proofs, had still not brought me one tiny step further in the estimation of many who regarded the Dance as the representative of frivolity and the Ballet as an expensive and burdensome absurdity! I believe that several people were won over by seeing what could be accomplished in a genre where they had thought my attempt would least succeed. A real desire to retain me in my position as Balletmaster was even expressed, and I was flattered by the proof that I might one day be missed, even by those who had crossed me at every turn. But, truth to tell, I had had enough.

It had become impossible for me to compose with such bugbears before me as: "Can your ballet be performed, understood, equipped, please, *attract people,* and *make a profit?*

I was disgusted by the thought that within the Theatre itself there were parties who awaited with malicious pleasure the failure of ballets, i.e., unfilled houses, and who never tired of branding them as the arch enemies of acting, even though I myself adore the dramatic art and continually strive to follow its finest models.

I felt depressed by the silence and coldness that so often greeted my most enthusiastic ideas, while I could hear the costs of a work being estimated before its potential beauties were perceived.

I could no longer bear to see my indefatigable efforts treated with scorn by our political economists and regarded as an unprofitable luxury, whose expenses were always emphasized without any statistics ever having been computed to show the profits for which the Ballet had been responsible.

While I do not consider myself to have been worse treated by the critics than any other Danish author, and even though I side with those who recognize their vocation as a purifying and ennobling principle, I have never, because of their continually divided opinions about ballet in general and the value of my compositions in particular, been able to derive from their observations any other conclusion than that the best way of satisfying them must be to remain totally passive and simply refrain from presenting anything.

Finally, there is in the artist a feeling that Frenchmen call *amour-propre,* which lies somewhere between vanity and a sense of honor. It is the incentive for every undertaking born of a lively imagination and developed by a self-confidence which is easily confused with arrogance by outsiders, and, unless well founded, might imply unparalleled rashness. Of course, my self-esteem was considerably offended by the fact that, just when I thought I would reap the highest reward for so many years of effort in the service of art and the theatre, I was given as my superior a man who regarded me as a novice simply because I happened to be completely new to him, and who put my poetical work to a purely material test. Perhaps a special regard for the Rigsdag guided his steps as Theatre Chief: to him, art seemed to be a secondary consideration, and he did not like me, even though I was always ready to lend him a hand and, I am certain, never gave him any cause for dissatisfaction during the time I was under his supreme command.

As far as my last two works are concerned, no other author has been less generously treated by the management of the Royal Theatre than I. The fact of the matter is that so long as I was working [at the Theatre], an additional payment of 20 Rbd. was due me for every performance of my most recent works. On the whole, these works were given only scattered performances while they were new, and, as one has seen above, *The Valkyr* had to wait until a fortnight before my departure! Even after the great and profitable success of *The Valkyr*, they were still not certain of its future and thought they would reward me amply by granting me the lump sum of 200 Rbd. as compensation for an indefinite series of performances! Presumably free of all further obligations to the ballets' author, composer, or inventor—call him what you like—they have made use of them with frequency and at a profit. This can best be shown by the fact that *Far from Denmark* was performed sixty-four times (thus, thirty-four times after my departure) and *The Valkyr* thirty-two times (therefore, twenty-two times after I had left the Theatre).

Since I was fortunate enough to come away with the impression of an undertaking that was successful and recognized by the public, it was clear to me that *here* was the goal which had been set for my work in this specialized area, and, far from looking back upon my career with bitterness, I thank Providence for letting me withdraw from the contest before a feeble old age could transform the combat of art into the pity of defeat.

It is my hope that so long as the Theatre can retain its balletic forces with the prospect of replenishing them, *Far from Denmark* and *The Valkyr* will remain in the repertoire. They have gained national honor and should give the younger generation evidence of the spirit that has influenced Danish art in all its ramifications. There was a time when—without even suspecting it—the ballet *Valdemar* marked an epoch in our political life, and cries of jubilation burst forth when, after the victory, the great king broke the yoke of thralldom, forgave his enemies, and united the scattered parts of the country to the melody of "Danmark deiligst Vang og Vænge." This time it was the fallen warriors of Braavalla who were glorified in Odin's hall! On this occasion too it was not my intention to allude to the present moment or the immediate future; but surely there must be a good omen in the radiant light that once again breaks forth after the darkness of the battlefield, and in the war dance of the *einherjar* a symbol of that strength which is not subdued by death or destruction but arises renewed and reborn at the call of Heimdal's Gjallar-Horn!

VIII

Three Years in Stockholm

LOCALITIES

STOCKHOLM's Royal Theatre, the Opera House, or—as it is now called—Stora Theatern, is situated on one of the loveliest sites any capital in the world has to offer. One must picture to oneself a handsome open square, the northern side of which is taken up by good-sized hotels, the western portion is occupied by Prince Oscar's palace, while on the eastern side, as a counterpart to this elegant building, is the theatre, upon whose façade can be read:

GUSTAVUS III PATRIIS MUSIS

—a dedication that can provide as much food for thought as our own "Not for pleasure alone."

In the middle of the *Torg* (all open squares are thus entitled) stands the equestrian statue of Gustavus Adolphus, with medallions of his four most famous men, and before his commanding eye the southern prospect of the square opens out upon Norrbro, which joins the foot of the Brunkebjerg with the Old City of Stockholm, while beneath its arches Lake Mälaren, with its waterfalls, flows out into the Saltsjö—that is, the harbor formed by the entrance to the Baltic Archipelago. On the southern bank of the river, Stockholm's magnificent Royal Palace rises on the picturesque Lejonbacke, and from the very window of my office in the Theatre building, one has a tableau which the most vivid fancy could hardly imagine to be more delightful and, at the same time, more splendid or more varied. If one allows one's eye to describe a semicircle from the left to the extreme right, it encounters Blasieholmen, with its palaces and the new National Museum, whence an iron bridge leads over to Skeppsholmen. This island, planted with maple and chestnut trees, contains a church, shipyards, shops, and sailors' homes—the whole dominated by the old pleasure-palace of Johan III, which is now used as a depot for the navy's cannon. The background of this circular painting is formed by a ridge upon which the suburb of Södermalm stretches like an amphitheatre, with the dome of the Katarinakyrka as the high point.

To the right, the spacious harbor extends to the wing of the Palace adorned with a terraced garden, the so-called Logård, and ends at a *terra piena* embellished with flower gardens and refreshment pavilions beneath Norrbro's colossal pillars. From this *Strömparterre* steam launches constantly ply to the nearby Djurgård. The comparison of the beauty of this forest with that of our Dyrehave will be an eternal subject of dispute; and this magnificent panorama, alive with perpetual traffic, offers new variety with the different illuminations that daylight, moonlight, or the clear summer nights lend to the whole. It is attractive even as a winter landscape, when the entire surface of the water is frozen except for the waterfall, which foams and steams in the cold air like a seething cauldron. But I see that I am losing myself in reflections on nature, in the heart of the capital, and in my theatre office to boot!

It is high time that we take a closer look at this Temple of the Muses, and I will lead my good readers across the stage (which here is not so inaccessible to the uninitiated as it is, for instance, in Copenhagen) and down into the auditorium. This far surpasses ours in size, shape, and comfort, has four tiers of boxes and a fifth level at the price of twelve, eighteen, or twenty-four skillings a seat. The stalls are really marvelous, built in the form of an amphitheatre, and furnished with velvet-upholstered chairs. Behind this is to be found a separate platform with two rows of armchairs at a higher price, and the background is the large Royal box at whose foot the Court dignitaries have their tier. There is no pit at all, and though the cubic content of the room is almost double that of our Theatre, it holds three hundred fewer spectators and even with sold-out houses at raised prices can hardly bring in 1000 rixdollars in Danish currency.

The musical acoustics are superb, and singing voices sound remarkably better than they do beneath our flattened ceiling; on the other hand, it has always been less advantageous for the spoken drama. The entrances and exits leave much to be desired. However, there are arched stone stairways leading to all five levels. It is a universal complaint of the performers as well as the art-loving public that one can never peacefully enjoy the overture or the first scene of a play's several acts because of the continual coming and going of latecomers or those who wish to refresh themselves. It is likewise a disgusting nuisance that they allow women of dubious reputation but of very obvious character to choose the best and most prominent seats in the Theatre. Finally, all finales and curtain lines are interrupted by the bustle and haste with which people push their way toward the exits in order to get their hats and coats.

Since we now find ourselves in the center from which artistic opinion emanates, it might be most convenient to give a brief description of the distinctive features of the Stockholm audience.

This is divided into two distinctly pronounced factions: the stalls and the pit, with the *nedra raderna* [the first rows], who are particularly fond of lyric and foreign works; and the third, fourth, and fifth tiers, who, on the contrary, have a decided taste for dramatic and domestic productions. The fact that a fresher spirit dwells in the upper regions is unmistakable, whereas a rather blasé attitude often hovers over the more aristocratic valley.

Just as among us, actual applause is, to a striking degree, on the decline and is therefore seldom heard, except as acclaim for chosen favorites whose absence can cause the most deadly silence. Enthusiasm is mostly voiced during the opera, and is then accompanied by stomping and pounding with walking sticks. The applause is amost never for the ensemble numbers and has generally died down by eight bars' *Ritournelle.* On the other hand, if the bravura part is designed to finish with an abrupt ending or sudden exit, there can occur volleys of applause of far greater fullness and longer duration than those with which people in Denmark honor successful moments. Here, however, mention must be made of a genuine evil, which, due in part to an excessive number of foreign guest performers and in part to [Swedish singers'] frequent journeys abroad, has crept into the Swedish theatre and wages the most ruinous war against anything resembling dramatic illusion. This is the prevailing practice of "curtain calls," which conflict with nature, art, and common sense.

Whence this bad habit originates I cannot say with certainty; but it must come from countries where authors, composers, and artists are held in such low esteem that people think themselves entitled to obliterate every vestige of inspiration, action, and character simply in order to exact from the performers a humble expression of thanks. As a result of this abuse, true applause has become as good as anathema. Something that has been successfully performed is no longer recognized without ceremony; now one must either quickly draw oneself up against the backdrop or run off into the wings in order to gather the heavenly manna of art. This must, of course, inevitably give rise to the most ridiculous anomalies, and if the heart did not have to bleed at the triumph of materialism, parody would derive rich profit from the sight of a king who marches off proud and defiant only to return bowing most humbly; a disconsolate romantic heroine who dashes off bathed in tears and immediately afterward reappears before the enthusiastic audience, laughing and curtseying; a wronged innocent who lures her executioner onto the stage in order to help her pick up her bouquets; aye, even the captives who burst their chains and iron bars, and the dead who arise from their graves in long rows in order to receive and return compliments!

This climax had already been reached before my arrival (1861), and if as people claim, the growth of the *claqueur* system constitutes an improvement, this must have happened most recently—after my departure.

As a whole, the Stockholmers are fond of going to the theatre, and even though the city has four such establishments and prices at the Opera House are rather high, during my years in office we had reason to be happy with the large attendance. Nevertheless, there are certain unfortunate chance occurrences that can affect the prospective sale of tickets, and it is the countless evening parties, banquets, and magnificent *soupers,* not to mention Christmas preparations, Moving Days and the days on which servants change jobs, regular Court and civic celebrations, political banquets, fully attended meetings of at least fifteen fraternal orders, and finally, springtime—the holiday most anxiously awaited by one and all—that mock the Theatre's desperate efforts and lure the public, who are satiated with the pleasures of art, out into the fresh air.

It astonishes all foreigners that when on certain solemn occasions the national anthem is requested as a demonstration of loyalty, nobody sings along; instead, the orchestra plays two stanzas, which are feebly joined in by an invisible chorus behind the curtain. As a rule, there are neither "Vivats" nor "Hurrahs," and everyone files out in silence.

The tone of the public is, on the whole, humane. Although now and then a bit of opposition may be manifested, I have never been able to discover any organized cabal, and with the exception of some members of the editorial staff of a notorious "gutter paper," who made it their business to jeer at Jolin's comedy *The Slanderer* (which, by the bye, was a great success), I have not experienced any scandal whatever in the theatre.

Even if this good nature is great in many respects, in some it is inferior to that of the Copenhageners. In particular there are far greater demands made on the novelty and variety of the repertoire, and when one winter many years ago people found themselves badly served in this wise, it was decided to discontinue the subscription system and they have never since been able to reinstitute it.

Just as in so many other places, in Stockholm the concept of the *public* is often confused with *fashion* and *capricious whim*. Every time a higher endeavor is misunderstood or rewarded with indifference, every time the beautiful must give way to caricature, or masterpieces must be played to empty houses in contrast to hackworks which are heavily attended, there is an immediate outcry against the prevailing bad taste; but instead of redoubling their efforts in a better direction, they yield to the pressure of the moment and desist from further attempts—all out of regard for the public! Where, then, is one to seek and find this abstract idea? In the very place I have indicated: in the nation's inner consciousness of the true and the good, not in its curiosity and even less in its idle pleasure-seeking. One ought not only to respect this public consciousness, but cultivate and nuture it; and whether one is an artist or a director of an artistic institution, one ought to appreciate one's responsibility to coming generations.

Since we are now as good as finished with the *Salong,* we shall go up into the gilt chambers which were once the assembly rooms of the Court but are now used as the Theatre's foyers and classrooms. They all look out upon *Gustav Adolfs Torg* and make an attractive and pleasing impression. Upon entering the rooms, the first thing to meet the eye is the marble bust of King Oscar in the window recess directly in front of the great fireplace, above which hangs a large engraved portrait of Gustav III. Beneath this drawing a couple of years ago stood a plaster bust of Carl Johan, who, as is known, was not too fond of art in general and was no admirer of the theatre. This must have annoyed Gustav, for one night he allowed himself to fall down on the head of this strong soldier-king, and the following morning when I entered the room, I discovered the founder of the Swedish stage lying unharmed and smiling next to the shattered plaster figure. A large portrait of Jenny Lind as Norma adorns one wall and seems to have been intended as the start of a pantheon of stage celebrities. But here can be seen the dubiousness of erecting monuments to the living; for since neither requirements nor limitations have been placed on "the illustration" and they did not have the resources to execute an adequate number of oil paintings, the whole room was gradually filled with lithographs and photographs of highly different dimensions, and it now bears a perfect resemblance to a jolly album in which one can meet one's friends and acquaintances from the stage and orchestra. However, in the three window recesses hang in chronological order the retired Directors of the Theatre, some of whom (among others, Count Lagerbjelke) are said to have been especially capable, but all without exception became martyrs, and most of them did not last longer than it took to get acquainted with the job and then relinquish the position to a new dilettante.

In this foyer are exhibited in the evening all the major Swedish papers and a host of foreign literary journals. This diversion might be particularly pleasant if did not cause dangerous distractions, especially when one bitter-tasting criticism or another strikes the party concerned and lowers his morale in the middle of his performance of a role.

The largest room is intended for the rehearsal of plays, rehearsals with singing, and the dramatic school. Of the latter, it can only be said that much is done for its advancement; but here — as with us — the times are lean with respect to burgeoning scenic talents. I do not care to lead my readers across the corridor into the ballet's practice room. It is enough for me to state that it is called *Barntheatern* [Children's Theatre] in order to allude sorrowfully to the idiotic condition in which this branch of art, despite all its redeeming efforts, finds itself. But if we pass to the left through a corner room that serves the singing school for opera rehearsals, we find ourselves back in the office that was assigned to me, and which in addition to the gilt arabesques and the delightful view is historically memorable for the fact that it was the private office of Gustav III, from which he could see to the execution of his orders, and it was here that he was borne, bandaged and mortally wounded, after the fatal masked ball on March 16, 1792.*

It is for me a pleasant duty to point out some institutions that could serve as models for all theatres and the like of which I have never seen — these are the Library, the Music Archive, the Wardrobe, and the Property Storehouses.

The first contains, in addition to duplicate manuscript copies of all active pieces and roles, a collection of the most valuable works of dramatic literature in the original languages and is continuously augmented by novelties from abroad.

The Music Archive is outstanding for its abundance of classical and modern compositions as well as for its elegance and its efficient system. Both here

---

*At which the King was shot in the back by Count Anckarström, acting for a cabal of disaffected aristocrats,

and in the Library, a *catalogue raisoné* is to be found, and loans are made to the members of the orchestra and to the people connected with the stage.

The Wardrobe actually has no better items to display than ours. The Danish Theatre has an especially rich selection of old-fashioned (Rococo) Court costumes, and our supernumeraries are, on the whole, better dressed; but the system according to which everything is arranged and classified, particularly women's attire, is far superior with respect to both storage and use.

The Property Storehouse is a collection of stage props such as furniture, domestic utensils, weapons, and matériel of the most varied kinds, and arranged, like our ethnographic musuem, according to periods, countries, and races, in which connection it is especially rich in many respects. The property man is also the stage prompter, i.e., the stage director's adjutant and the one who gives the cues.

The fact that a machine as complex as a theatre administration demands no small number of officials is obvious. But in Stockholm, this class is a good deal more strongly represented than in most other places in the world; for in addition to the necessary experts and attendants in the various branches, there are even a Head Regisseur, two Vice-Regisseurs, two Instructeurs for the drama students, a Vice-Kapellmeister, and—although the principal management rests in the hands of the Theatre Director—there exists an impersonal concept without business dealings, without authority, and without responsibility, which is called the Directory. This comprises the Theatre Chancellery personnel, which varies according to the greater or lesser need for sinecures and in its divergent opinions meets in only two points: uneasiness about the deficit and fear of the newspapers.

It is more than likely that this abstract magnitude was not consulted about my being summoned as Intendant for the stage. However, without any personal conflict, I have received unmistakable proof that my activity has been a thorn in its side and that it has offered an at least passive resistance. Therefore, when in my plan for reform I happen to mention the Chancellery as my worst stumbling block, it never applies to a single individual or to the assembled corps, but only to that impersonal concept.

MY ENGAGEMENT

WHEN I realized at the end of the year 1860 that the ballet *The Valkyr* would probably be my last work for the Danish stage, and since according to the terms of my contract I was free to use my talents abroad, in a letter to the Director of the Swedish Royal Theatre, Hr. Baron von Stedingk, I expressed my desire—as I had during several of my previous sojourns in Stockholm—to augment their ballet repertoire with some of my smaller compositions. I received a courteous reply with an account of the obstacles which stood in the way of my plan. But since through my earlier scenic productions as well as my influence on the recently established dramatic school for the Theatre's pupils, and also, perhaps, by my writings, I had shown myself to be capable of more extensive employment, the Baron invited me to assume the vacant post of Intendant for the stage—an office whose dimensions one will best be able to judge from the copy of my contract below,* and which included not only making reasonable suggestions but, after the latter had been deliberated and accepted by the Director, of executing in the most detailed fashion everything connected with the running of the performances. This was truly a difficult task, but since art was the predominant element in my position—which at first glance seemed to be completely free from all economic questions—to me it was bound to appear as interesting and attractive as it was honorable.

Before I ventured to give a definite answer to this splendid offer, I paid a brief visit to Stockholm during the spring of 1861 in order to become a bit more closely acquainted with conditions there and also to test my own strengths. Of course I was bound to discover weak points, and on my own part it was mainly in literary and linguistic respects that a measure of study was required, since my duties embraced the stage as a whole. When I now realized that my knowledge of the Swedish language was highly inadequate and that its similarity to my mother tongue was a hindrance rather than a help, I chose to treat it as a completely foreign language. By diligent reading and recitation I progressed so far during the interval between May and October that when I was presented to the Theatre personnel I was able, in a lengthy address *in pure Swedish,* to develop my views about the dramatic element which ought to be the vital principle in all scenic production. I thereby won two substantial advantages: in the first place, I avoided wounding Swedish ears by a foreign command, and, secondly, I kept my own language unadulterated.

All the same, there were sure to be highly different opinions about the choice the Director had made when he engaged a man of my particular profession. People were afraid that I wished to elevate my own branch of art at the others' expense, aye, even treat both the opera and the drama *balletically.* However, their fears were unfounded, for I was well aware that in Stockholm there were no laurels for me to win in the field of ballet. Moreover, I felt that in whatever area I should display the greatest energy, I would best do it quietly and "unpretentiously."

Among the Theatre's acting officials it was an old and very cleverly calculated tactic not only to hold strongly to penalty clauses and fines but also to make the already complicated performance of one's duties as difficult as possible at every given opportunity—all in order to strike terror into the managing director and to give themselves importance as the ones who knew how to keep the personnel in check and dominate circumstances by their practical outlook. My presence put a hasty end to all their manoeuvers.

*In the original edition, the terms of this contract were printed as a long footnote, starting at this point and extending over the feet of several pages. Here, the text appears as a supplementary note at the end of this section.

By treating all artistic questions *discursively* and, as a rule, confidentially, much sensitivity was spared and the violent scenes, which so often before had disrupted the preliminary rehearsals, were avoided. By addressing myself to a sense of honor and good will, I had the great satisfaction of seeing the actual disappearance of acts of negligence and disorder and, consequently, the discontinuation of the strict fines. I gave "those important people" to understand that they were not dealing with a disconcerted dilettante, but that I knew how to counter all obstacles and had learnt how to avail myself of time and my dearly bought experience. Thus what had formerly called forth an alarm as great as if the country hung in peril was now arranged with an ease and tranquility that at first aroused astonishment mixed with vexation but later came to be regarded as normal. In short, a fresh breeze pervaded the whole and the public was immediately willing to give these striking results the honor of acknowledgement.

Although I continually acted in the Director's name and, I dare say, wholly in his spirit, I was disliked by the Chancellery for the way in which I managed to ingratiate myself with the personnel, created a chasm between them and the management—no doubt because all trafficking in slander had ceased—and severely reduced the receipts of the Pension Fund by the abolition of fines. To this I could only reply that my relationship to the stage artists was more that of an experienced colleague than that of an official, for they knew that I belonged to their own circle, not to that of the bureaucracy, and they followed my instructions not because I imposed them by virtue of my authority but because they were persuaded by my reasons. I really did everything in my power to maintain this confidence in my fine and humane superior as well as in the entire artistic community, particularly with regard to the native dramatic authors, whose interests I made it a matter of conscience to look after. I will leave to the judgment and impartial testimony of my coworkers how much and by what means I have worked to further the high purpose of the stage. As far as my worthy comrades are concerned, I shall only remark that at very few theatres have I found such heartfelt kindness and true humanity as in Stockholm, and if during these three years I felt some of the thorns of theatrical life, it has—oddly enough—been only among a few isolated individuals whose livelihood I myself had provided, and *they were not Swedish!*

Text of Bournonville's Contract

The Intendant for the stage shall, next to the Director in Chief, see to the arrangement and regulation of plays inasmuch as he must be responsible for the smooth running and even distribution of performances, the number of which is to be definitely fixed for each acting season by the Royal Government, with due alternation among the various branches of art, using the actors engaged in as equable a manner as possible and duly seeing to the duration of each performance. Every week he shall also draw up a proposal for and participate in discussions concerning the repertoire for the following week and shall furnish as well a list of plays that might be given in place of the scheduled works should the need arise. As far as a change of plays is concerned, the Intendant for the stage is primarily responsible for choosing whatever may be required to "fill in" for a canceled piece at the performance.

In artistic respects, the Intendant for the stage shall serve directly under the Director in Chief, without any mediators or collaborators except for the Kapellmeister, with whom he ought to confer in matters which, in accordance with Royal regulations, concern his duties with respect to the lyric stage. In case of differing opinions between these two gentlemen, the Director in Chief shall make the decision.

The Intendant is obliged to gather information and, at latest eight days thereafter, communicate remarks concerning the performance of the works in question.

When a piece has been accepted for performance, the Intendant, at latest fourteen days thereafter, shall have submitted to the Directory a proposal for the assignment of roles, together with the principal designs for the settings and costumes as well as for the arrangment of the necessary dances and music. The setting up and arrangement of scenery for all the plays which the Directory finds suitable for staging and, where such a thing is required, the adaptation of the *mise-en-scène* of previously given works, also concerns the Intendant for the stage, whose duty it is, in consequence thereof, to see to the necessary corrections and additions [to such materials].

After discussion with the Controller, all proposals and requisites pertaining to the *mise-en-scène* must be delivered to the Directory by the Intendant for the stage, whose duty it is, after the proposal has been examined and approved by the Directory, to take care of and supervise the mounting of the piece in accordance with it, as well as to communicate the Directory's orders to the régisseurs, balletmasters, scene-painters, and managers concerned, each of whom is entrusted with the responsibility of carrying out in his department the dictates of the Directory.

Next to the Director in Chief, the Intendant for the stage shall have highest supervision over the studies and training in the Theatre's schools [of acting, singing, and dancing], exercise no less careful supervision over the most expedient instruction of the accepted pupils, and also, insofar as possible, give advice and instructions and, with respect to the pupils' use on the stage, indicate, when time permits, the special guidance that might be considered appropriate for the achievement of this goal.

ARTISTIC CONDITIONS

IN Stockholm the theatre, if regarded as entertainment, assumes an especially prominent place; however, if we view it as a national artistic institution, it has not, despite the dedicatory words of its brilliant founder, been able to acquire any higher significance. Old prejudices, wrongful views, and misguided financial circumstances have resulted in the fact that the Swedish stage—while it has far more beautiful facilities, employs greater luxury in its productions, possesses a decided lyrical preponderance, and pays its members on a better scale — does not, like the Danish theatre, claim respect among its own public, its own press, and (surely I dare say it without indiscretion) within its own artistic and administrative sphere.

The principal reasons for this are, in my opinion, the following:

a) The frequent change of Directors, which contributes to overthrowing any vestige of a system, if such a thing can ever be said to have existed.

b) A mutually antagonistic relationship between the Stage and the Chancellery, which has more than once alienated superior talents, who have later because of ambition entered into a competition fatal to both themselves and the public institution.

c) An unauthorized insight into private or semiprivate affairs, which are being continually harmed by the following abuses:

The existence in the Theatre building itself of a large barroom, in addition to two smaller ones, where all sorts of petty scandals are communicated firsthand and are passed on with embellishments.

The admittance behind the scenes of persons having nothing to do with the performance, which custom originally seems to have been introduced for the purpose of bringing the artists into contact with the higher classes of society, but which has, on the whole, proved less than beneficial to the stage and its dignity.

Finally, the unfortunate practice of selling tickets to the gallery of the rigging loft, where there grows up an audience of several thousand individuals who for a cheap price have the highly questionable pleasure of being able to study the theatre from its wrong side, while every illusion is destroyed.

With full appreciation of the position which the theatrical profession occupies in Sweden as well as in Denmark, the following phenomena do deserve to be mentioned:

In Denmark the theatre is held in high esteem, individual talents are usually played down, and authorship is venerated.

The Swedes undervalue the importance of the theatre, love their artists personally, and neglect the authors.

It cannot be denied that there runs through Swedish art in general a certain tendency to imitate what is produced abroad and that too many even relish the idea of renouncing their more noble uniqueness in order to resemble foreign models! But although we have learnt and can still learn from some of the Southerners and must often admire their energy and virtuosity, there is still much in which our Theatre need not imitate Paris or Vienna, England or Italy, and we have every reason to preserve the sound reflection and deep poetry that are part of the Nordic character.

In Stockholm the lyric stage has always enjoyed preference in public favor above the other scenic branches of art. A philharmonic society, a musical academy which also includes a conservatory, and, in addition, a host of singing societies help to propagate a feeling for music. An outstanding Royal Orchestra has always been available to lend the opera performances admirable support; and yet, in spite of these favorable conditions, native-born or naturalized composers are less successful here than in Denmark in establishing their works in the repertoire. While all foreign productions, even of a lighter nature, have been naturalized on the Swedish stage, the Music Archive remains the burial place for all domestic subjects. These are almost without exception received with suspicion and indifference. I need only refer to *Youth and Folly,* which after having been "localized" under the name of *The Painter and the Models,* has reverted to Méhul's *Une Folie,* which neither in local color nor in genius can match Du Puy's lively music—but then he had also been Kapellmeister here in Stockholm! Indeed, it seems almost unbelievable that the patriotic Swedes, who amongst so many other excellent songs possess the most imposing national anthem in Otto Lindblad's "From the Depths of the Swedish Heart," always use as the official expression for their loyal feelings none other than England's "God Save the Queen"!

In spite of the harsh climate, the Swedish soil or, more correctly, the echo from the Swedish hills has produced a host of superb singing voices, particularly in the higher female register. Surely it gave its very best with Jenny Lind, who, with regard to the dramatic interpretation of singing, must perhaps be regarded more as a singular spiritual talent than as a genuine natural phenomenon. What this rare personality was and in many ways might have become for the Swedish Theatre was recognized only when, undervalued by a shortsighted management, she was induced to leave her native land in order to find considerable fortune and a world-famous name. To be sure, she did return to her old home from time to time as a guest, but her essential influence had been lost, or rather transformed into that irresistible wanderlust characteristic of all more or less genuine Swedish nightingales who, one after another, desert the Stockholm Opera in order to tempt Fate abroad. But none of them possessed the electrical current that this Nordic enchantress knew how to generate between herself and her listeners, and their disappointment was therefore often very painful.

However, it became necessary for the Royal Theatre to replace its losses with foreign talents, partly of a secondary quality, but possessed of all the bad habits adhered to by their models in the first rank. This in no way helped to refine taste; attention was focused—as with us—more on the intensity of the voices than on their fullness and beauty; training counted for as good as nothing, and there arose the greatest indifference toward the action and diction. The birds of passage gradually returned, some with clipped wings, others with metamorphosed voices, but most of them had acquired a certain aplomb, rather high pretensions, and—the ability to speak *gibberish!*

At the Danish Opera we are also not free from the so-called musical adaptations which can render the text completely unintelligible. I can well remember the time when all vowels were broken off by an aspirate *h* and when in order to say *vente, hente,* or *finde,* one said *vepmte, hepmte, fipmte!* The method has since undergone various changes, and they now seek to bring as many open vowels as possible into the singing parts. To recite a dialogue is termed "chatting" on stage and is said to ruin the voice; therefore they prefer to change everything to *recitative* regardless of whether the text is lyrical or not. A little dictionary for the modified Danish opera language will soon become a necessity in order to know that *Gad* means *Gud, Pæje — Pige, Jarda — Hjerte, sakke — sukke, lakke — lukke,* and, incidentially, *vam, lam, sam, jam, snarbe, darbe,* etc. etc.

Although we have several praiseworthy examples of clear pronunciation combined with musical delivery, these exceptions are but poorly appreciated, while one never reads a critical observation about this barbaric treatment of the poet's verse and the Danish words. People are therefore especially inclined to put the blame on the excessive softness of the language and to think that Swedish has an essential superiority by virtue of its sharp consonants and harmonious endings. Well, before my accession it had become a standing rule at the Swedish Opera that the text could be understood only when the whole thing was sung by foreigners in their respective tongues, and if one had not supplied oneself with the printed libretto it would be easier to follow the most intricate pantomime than the action in an opera, where the exposition and the plot are generally placed in a ballad or duet. It was thus a curiosity that a foreigner — a Dane — should be the one to fight for the view that the Swedish language, which is unquestionably one of the most lyrical in the world, must be purified from a host of parasitic syllables and vowels which at every instant crept into the text and produced the most ridiculous gibberish. For example, *min efar* instead of *min far, din evakt* for *din vakt, Ellevira* for *Elvira, Ma-ti-le-da* for *Mathilda, Ma-re-ta* for *Martha:* in other words, just as good a mess as we could cook up in Copenhagen. There also prevails a V-dialect, a companion piece to the old P-dialect, which gathered all its articulations from the underjaw: "*Vau-vau!*" Its most distinguished representative was undoubtedly the Dresden tenor Tichatschek, who even today calls *Bertha* with *Be-ve-re-ta!* and in Masaniello's *Barcarole* defies *des Meeres Tyran* with *Me-ve-res Ty-vi-ra-van!* Such examples are, I dare say, dangerous for willing and nonthinking imitators; and when, as here, they can lean upon a famous authority, every objection meets if not extravagant arguments then at least the most dogged resistance. All the same, I succeeded in convincing a number of people of the harmfulness of this debasement of the language, and they all found themselves richly rewarded by the increased sympathy with which the singing parts were followed when they were accompanied by the clarity of the text and the liveliness of the action. On the whole, people will not demand that a dramatic singer also be a perfect actor. However, it is astonishing how little study and practice are necessary to perform a lyric role fairly satisfactorily. Even so, this little is often neglected to an unforgiveable degree, and one must deeply lament that the majority of Kapellmeisters seem completely indifferent to the soul in dramatic music and almost always re-hearse *the score* before the singers in question have gotten the slightest con-ception of *the role*. Since these complaints apply to the greater part of the op-era world, they are not specifically aimed at the Swedish musical stage; but with regard to this area I leave it to my posthumous memory in Stockholm to state how much my efforts managed to reform and what difficulties I had to overcome.

In the following, one will be able to compare the Swedish Opera's exten-sive repertoire and considerable activity with that of our own lyric stage, and thereby perhaps find the opportunity for instructive reflections. All genres are represented there, and one cannot emphasize enough the care and correctness that run through the entire musical treatment.

Conductors such as Kapellmeister Norman, Court Singer Berg, and Chorus Master Söderman are as good as can be found at any theatre in Eu-rope. The same applies to the equipment, with regard to costumes and deco-rations. I have earlier stated my views on this point and still maintain that the magnificence with which people believe that *The Magic Flute* and *Don Gio-vanni*, for example, ought to be mounted has hurt rather than helped the mu-sical impression.

The same grounds that have prevented me from erecting a gallery of no-tables of the *Danish* stage here also deprive me of the pleasure of bestowing my sincere praise upon a number of distinguished talents. However, since Jenny Lind's renown resounds throughout the entire musical world without having discouraged but rather aroused the desire and spirit of her country-women, I ought, certainly, to mention her successor, whose unadulterated feeling and taste are destined to have an advantageous effect, if not by virtue of the same genius, then at least by the development of the noblest natural gifts. This excellent singer is Louise Michaeli, at the moment the prima donna of the Swedish Opera, but without the peculiarities and pretensions usually associated with this title. She is making continual progress, and what makes her virtually unique among the foremost singers of the present is her multifaceted interpretation of the most varied compositions and the virtuosity with which she performs Handel, Gluck, Mozart, Weber, Rossini, Meyerbeer, Bellini, and Verdi! In all their works she knows how, by means of the pure silvery tones of her voice, to find her way to the heart.

Criticism — whether it be verbal or printed, in the form of friendly advice or with whip in hand — is and always will be an unpleasant-tasting medicine. Small wonder, then, that it is unpopular; and yet everyone must realize the truth of Lessing's words: "A bad criticism is better than none at all." The ob-jection one might make against the Stockholm reviewers is not so much what they say as what they conceal; for one can rightly reproach them for their si-lence regarding the faults that can and ought to be corrected, as well as the beauties which deserve to be emphasized. Therefore one can reproach them with good reason for their tolerance, nay, almost *protection* of the mediocre; their lavish panegyrics of all foreign and transient things; and finally, their often unfair harshness, even plain injudiciousness, against their own good talents. I frankly admit that from the observations I had been able to gather from the Swedish newspapers, I came to Stockholm with rather poor expectations for the dramatic stage. The fact that these expectations might be surpassed was quite natural, but I also reached the conviction that this important branch of art suffered the greatest injustice, not only from the critics but even from the management itself, which once again pleaded public indifference.

The spoken drama did undeniably assume an all too modest place as compared with the opera, for which it seemed to serve merely as a foil and relief. It was generally given at "reduced prices" and seldom had the good fortune of seeing a popular piece performed more than six or eight times; and it is beyond all doubt that if the Rigsdag had not strictly insisted upon a National Swedish Stage as a prerequisite for its yearly subsidy, the Royal Theatre would long since have renounced the poor spoken dramas—and all the more willingly as Mindre Theatern, which was run with a certain degree of talent and availed itself of whatever was neglected and abused by the larger house, was supported by the liberal press which from the standpoint of industry and free trade was opposed to the privileged and subsidized theatre.

Instead of using its far superior resources in a worthy fashion, the Royal Theatre allowed its rival to give itself a certain classical and aesthetic mien, while it presented Birch-Pfeiffer adaptations from the Palais-Royal and the Porte-Saint-Martin. This misunderstood competition was further embittered by the frequent visit of touring virtuosi, who found herein an abundant source of income. "The Fatherland's Muses" often had to make tremendous sacrifices in order not to see the hall of their Temple transformed into a wasteland. Concerts, sailor dances, and castanet dances were woven into the most interesting dramas as interludes, and the Theatre chronicle shall record with black crosses those evenings when the Zouaves at Mindre Theatern overcame the combined Swedish-German opera, and when our Danish Nielsen's Scandinavian declamations had to put up with competition from the Negro Ira Allridge's [*sic*] African frenzy.*

I have already given a rather detailed description of the leading dramatic talents, and will only add that people formerly reproached Swedish actors for the habit of mounting their high horses every time they had a serious word to say, of using long, partially meaningful, but extremely tiresome pauses, of employing broad gestures—in short, of becoming addicted to the sort of pathos which is, I dare say, most incorrectly called a "sermon tone," since there is

---

*American-born Ira F. Aldridge, "the African Roscius," made his debut as Othello in London (1826) under the aegis of Edmund Kean. For forty years he was a popular figure in Shakespearean and contemporary tragic-dramatic roles on the English and Continental stage, gaining many honors and a considerable fortune. He died (1867) at Lodz while en route to an engagement in St. Petersburg. Bournonville's dim view of him was not shared by most of his contemporaries.

every reason to believe that from the excesses of the stage it has forged its path to the pulpit. I do not set myself up as a master; my remarks are generally clad in the modest form of questions. Therefore I in no way ascribe to my presence any positive influence. I will merely say it is as good as an acknowledged fact that during my term of office *the natural* gained ground on the Swedish stage.

When one speaks of the Swedish *dramatic* stage, one must not imagine it to be as richly equipped with national authors as, for example, is the Danish. On the other hand, the idea that the art of dramatic writing lies beyond the talent of the Swedes is a prejudice that has been propagated in the literary world more than is justified. Their polite literature does indeed have a preponderance of lyric and epic subjects, but if it has not yet succeeded in creating an actual Swedish dramatic literature, the reason for this is to be found in external conditions rather than in a lack of talent and subjects on the part of their authors.

First of all, from the above it can be seen how little encouragement there has been to write for the unfortunate dramatic stage. Next, it must be realized that the majority of Sweden's writers seek the priestly vocation and live far away from the capital and the theatre. This spirtual enjoyment does not constitute any point of recreation in university life, and the capital itself suffers from a lack of the higher intellectual life which the university teaches and the young students and their teachers disseminate in those circles where material interests would otherwise gain the upper hand. Finally, certain systems have periodically dominated Swedish literature and chiefly tyrannized dramatic authors. For the present, there seems to be no salvation for them outside of the Shakespearean direction. Sweden happens to possess the best translation of this immortal poet, by Hagberg, who has understood how to employ the mutual affinity of the languages in a manner that gives his work the freshness and power of the original. The fact that people have thereby developed a passion for the performance of these masterpieces on the stage is highly praiseworthy and can have nought but a beneficial effect upon the dramatic art in its entirety. But it is the same with such poetic monuments as with certain magnificent natural phenomena, which can be admired and studied but not imitated, let alone reproduced; for just as in music Mozartian composers are basically boring, so the Shakespearean tragedy or comedy writers most often give only caricatures of the master's external forms without being able to grasp his divine spirit at all.

Such imitation, even after the greatest foreign models, must in and of itself be a hindrance to the formation of a national drama. I do not see this [national drama] as the dominant feature of the repertoire, nor as isolated from the artistic past or present of other nations, but simply possessing that distinctive character which reflects the spirit and customs of the country and its people. The Swedish Middle Ages, although dark and bloody, possess just as many romantic incidents as, for example, the English; but they must be treated in an original fashion so as not to become, through sententious language, alien and completely unnatural. Besides, the Swedes are fully versed in the history of their native land and do not readily tolerate misrepresentation of facts and the embellishing which most foreign authors permit themselves in order to give the drama a regular structure. From this has arisen a strange sort of historical drama that does not belong to any fixed category and therefore almost always suffers harsh treatment from orthodox literati but still seems to wish to achieve an evolution wherein, as Oehlenschläger says, Clio and Melpomene can join hands.

To me, the two most tragic dramas in this area appear to be Børgeson's *Erik XIV* and Beskow's *Torkel Knutson*. (This last play, which had lain unacted for thirty years, was taken up at the recommendation of Baron v. Stedingk, and I had the honor of mounting it on the stage as my debut.) Next ought to be mentioned Blanche's *Engelbrecht and his Dalecarlians*, Jolin's *Young Han's Daughter* and Hedberg's *Day Waxes*. This last author, who had risen from the *vaudeville* and folk comedy to a higher sphere, is still far from having reached his peak; but I do not think I am mistaken—and it should delight me to see my prophecy fulfilled—when I consider him called to become Sweden's most patriotic dramatic writer. Among the younger promising talents, Josephsson deserves to be mentioned, and it is with deep pain that one has seen perish such outstanding talents as those the Finn Witzelius displayed in his first and last drama, *Daniel Hjort*, which despite its splendid language was still a bit too strongly influenced by *Hamlet*.

The comedy, like the comic element on the whole, has always had difficulty thriving on Swedish soil. (By this is understood *domestic* comedy, for both French drawing room pieces and German adaptations from novels are acted with virtuosity.) As long as it is a matter of representing idyllic folk life, with its singing and dancing, its petty prejudices, simple-minded characters, and strongly pronounced love of the native land, everything runs its level course and, far from becoming angry about it, they usually enjoy hearing and seeing the Swedish peasant speak, sing, and dance like a complete idiot. But if the author's power of portrayal goes ones step further and he dares to touch the other three *Rikets Stånder* [estates of the realm] or to depict the ridiculousness and possible weaknesses of upper classes, there arises a clamor, and whole corporations feel stung by the picture of an imaginary individual and the faults that satire is called upon to review amid jesting and laughter.

In Norway as well as in Sweden, people have claimed that actual comedy writing lies outside the scope of their respective national characters, and this may have some truth insofar as touchiness is acutally greater among our Scandinavian brethren than with us. All three nations have an inclination to persiflage, i.e., pleasure and skill in the dangerous area of poking fun; but in ridiculing themselves and putting on a good face at offensive jokes, aye, even bitter sarcasm, I think that the Danes are a considerable step ahead and for this reason better comedies are written in Denmark.

For that matter, several talented writers like Dahlgren, Jolin, Blanche, and Hedberg have successfully ventured into this genre, and it is not entirely impossible that, in contrast to the past, of which the Danish theatre can be so proud, a brilliant future is in store for the Swedish comedy. The soil is rich and as good as untilled.

Just as on my Vienna trip, I now come to my most sensitive spot, the ballet; and I must confess that in Stockholm my efforts to claim for it a modest, if nevertheless worthy, place among the aesthetic phenomena of the stage have not been crowned with success.

The history of the dance at the Swedish Theatre is soon told, and its sphere of activity has rarely extended further than to opera *divertissements* and to some weak attempts to reproduce French compositions, usually under the names of the *arrangeurs*. In Sweden, original pantomimic ballets have not been produced since the time of Queen Christina. During the Golden Age of the theatre under Gustav III, a number of foreign artists shone, among them my father and his older sister, and Marcadet and Casagli. Later came Filippo Taglioni (father of that most famous *danseuse*), Ambrosiani, and the Brulo company (who made guest appearances in Copenhagen in 1840); and finally, Isidore Carey and his wife, who left Stockholm in 1823. From this time on the ballet has vegetated and has been a victim of the spoken drama, just as the latter was of the opera, and as all three branches were of a weak management and the most wretched financial circumstances.

A Swedish *danseur*, Wallqvist, and a French *danseuse*, Mme. Daguin, still maintained the school, and in the year 1837 sent me a young and very promising pupil, Johansson, whose talent advantageously developed under my guidance. He returned to Stockholm as First Solodancer and prepared the way for my arrival in 1839. I went up there accompanied by my pupils Hoppe, Mlles Fjeldsted and Nielsen, and with great bravura we presented *The Tyroleans, The Sleepwalker,* and a number of fragments from *La Sylphide* and other ballets. In 1841 Marie Taglioni came and enraptured the city of her birth. She took Johansson with her to Petersburg, where he became one of the most prominent members of the Imperial Ballet. Some years later, Mme. Daguin once again sent me a talented pupil for further training: this was Charlotte Norberg, who was as femininely graceful as she was light as a bird. This *danseuse* perfectly understood my method and made such extraordinary progress that I allowed her to make her debut in Copenhagen, where she harvested much applause, and in 1847 I presented her to the Stockholm public as Céleste in *The Toreador* and as Margaretha in *Faust.*

On this occasion, together with my two skillful mimes Füssel and Stramboe, Sr., I presented *Bellman or The Polska at Gröna Lund.* The enthusiasm generated by this little work defies all description. It was as if the Swedes had seen one of their happiest and most delightful dreams come to life. People who had not attended the theatre for a whole generation now found themselves forced to go there in order to see *Fredman's 62nd Epistle* and their favorite poet in the flesh—through the personal resemblance that the costume and makeup gave me. The moment in which I pulled off my coat and grabbed my lute had such an astonishing effect that it was as if their hearts went out to me. And thus it was with all the classical figures which here, for the first time, oddly enough, had afforded the opportunity for a loftier view of this poet. But the strangest thing of all was that from now on Bellman, who before had been continuously beaten down to the burlesque, was at once raised up not only into the lyrical but even into the elegaic sphere. His portrait in shirtsleeves with lute in hand was supplanted by a teary melancholiac in winter furs—a personification of "Sorrow clad in rose color"—and when in 1858, after a rest of ten years, I had practiced up in order to give Bellman as a guest role, I encountered in one of Stockholm's literary papers a bitter opposition which found Sweden's Anacreon profaned by this mimed representation set within a framework of dancing.

In the meantime, at the request of the meritorious Theatre Director Hyltén-Cavallius, I had sent one of my finest pupils to Stockholm to head the school and, if possible, contribute to the advancement of the ballet. I went up there two years in succession, in the spring, in order to arrange a little repertoire and stage the following pieces: *The Festival in Albano, The Wedding Festival in Hardanger, Conservatoriet, The Kermesse in Bruges,* as well as the divertissements *Paul and Virginia* and *La Ventana.* They were all received with applause, but survived for only a very short time, partly due to lack of skillful mimic talents, partly by reason of the narrow-minded view that ballets were certain to harm the other branches, and finally because the newspapers never tired of repeating the old refrain that my happy art did not harmonize with "the Swedes' deep and serious temperament."

Therefore, immediately upon my entrance as Intendant I was warned about "my old flame," but as I realized that the ballet here in Stockholm must limit itself to being an ornament, I was anxious to see even that assert its importance before the judgment seat of taste. I immediately began by releasing the *corps de ballet* from its degrading drudgery and assigned it a suitable exercise. Although my position did not impose upon me the duties of Balletmaster, I myself arranged the dances in all the plays and operas that I staged, repaired several older ballets, among them *La Sylphide,* and composed among other things a magnificent tableau entitled *Mozartiana,* as the postlude to *The Marriage of Figaro.* Since the repertoire could not do without a variety of novelties, and since I could not, without causing a scandal, direct such great attention to my oft-discussed and suspicious old inclination, I felt called upon to recommend a French balletmaster whom I had known in his younger days and who had urgently requested me to procure him an engagement. In the most flattering terms, he volunteered to follow my advice and instructions in all respects. These were reduced to three points: 1) not to venture into large-scale undertakings, which neither he nor the Theatre could cope with; 2) to guard himself against offending common sense; and 3) to spare ladies from dancing in male attire. Moreover, since I was familiar with his work and technical skill, I outlined for him some motifs for *divertissements*, and, providing him with the desired appointment while as Intendant reserving for myself the aesthetic say, I placed at his disposal, in addition to a very well trained *corps*, three graceful young *danseuses*, namely, the Healey sisters and Mlle. Forsberg. (Fru Tørner, née Norberg, had already retired into family life.)

At first, everything went as desired. Three minor *divertissements* lent pleasant support to the dramatic stage, and a entirely new cloister scene in *Robert of Normandy* did much to strengthen interest in this already rather outworn opera. The management, who before had sided with those who regarded the ballet with distrust and aversion, now happily went over to the opposite extreme; and since I found myself obliged to hold back a bit on this enthusiasm, any zeal for a good cause was regarded as a jealous opposition against a celebrated colleague. Now whether it was the Balletmaster who in one way or another had submitted to the Director, or whether the latter believed himself specially called to manage a branch of art where my competence ought to come into consideration, suffice it to say that from now on the ballet department was completely emancipated from my Intendantship and my ideas about the use of dance and the nature of mime, if not positively rejected, were at least turned upside down.

I shall not weary my readers with repetition of the excesses of modern dancing. It is certainly possible that my views in such respects are completely outdated, and besides, one would be fully justified in telling me, "You made your bed, now lie in it!" I had actually made for myself a hard and most unpleasant bed, not because the triumph of my former protégé—now my adversary—prevented me from sleeping, but I had some disquieting dreams even with my eyes wide open. One must imagine a carnival ballet with the worst parade of buffoons in the first act, and next, as the second act, an opera ball consisting of eleven dance numbers, totally unrelated to the plot, a few of which were very pretty but whose main points were:

A quadrille of twenty *lorettes*† (called *Enfants de Paris*), who were dressed as stevedores (a kind of fantastic sailor costume) and first drained a bottle of champagne, then balanced on the empty bottle!

A comical meal where Harlequin, Pulcinello, and Cassander arranged a repast with knives and forks five ells long, a colossal egg with Cupid sitting inside, a pie containing General Tom Thumb, and a bottle of Cliquot that squirted fire and busied itself with running after the terrified company!

† Young ladies of elegant appearance and loose manner.

The ballet ended with a grand Chinese Latern March and a temple illuminated by countless colored lamps!

For this circus-jumble sums larger than had ever been known were expended. However, even according to the most modest estimation, these amounted to a good third more than the equipment for *The Valkyr*, which had in its day caused so much trouble.

The Stockholm press treated this work with special esteem, even though after the third performance they were already forced to omit the first act; but the criterion for a success, namely, large attendance, had failed to come off, and if the management—in spite of my protests—had sacrificed all aesthetic regard in the hope of possible receipts, they had to declare their speculation totally unsuccessful. I celebrated a poor triumph; but it was not to be the last, even though the following season they leaned upon a choreographic authority by treating a subject by the famous Saint-Léon and another of the patron saints of the ballet, Saint-Georges: *The Bees* (in Swedish, *Blommor och Bin*, after a French idea).

In Shakespeare's *A Midsummer Night's Dream* one had seen small elves travestied as all sorts of natural creatures: moths, mustard seeds, etc. Now they had hit upon the idea of presenting a swarm of bees as the motif for a pantomimic treatment! It was not as a jest, but in deadly earnest that a host of *danseuses* with fleshings and bristling crinolines were to represent the honey-pouring insects. And indeed, the white-clad nymphs were supplied with antennae of silver, bees embroidered in gold on their breasts and backs, while—for the sake of decency—the sharp stings were placed on their fingertips. It is obvious that the authors had not the slightest notion of the transition from masquerade to scenic performance.

After twenty-four minutes of dancing, whose monotony made the whole thing seem indescribably long, they roll forth an enormous beehive that separates into sections, like a melon, and is set in revolution by a hidden treadmill. From every side, the happy insects now swarm forth, and the ballet ends amid showers of applause.

To many this might certainly seem amusing, nay, even ingenious; but the fact that in the midst of this buzzing a shepherd, a living man, falls in love with the Queen Bee, and, having been thoroughly stung by the saucy horde and having also danced a strenuous *pas de deux*, celebrates his marriage to the piquant beauty, is to my mind the height of madness. On this so-called idea several thousands were once again squandered, always in the hope of securing attendance, which, to the honor of wholesome taste, this time too disappointed expectations.

The contempt that was shown the principles for which I fought, the disregard which my official position must thereby suffer, and finally, the character which lay at the bottom of the whole, could in my younger days have had an injurious effect upon my humor and upon my desire to work. Fortunately, this was not now the case. On the contrary, this unpoetic breeze from the

Chancellery only helped to dispel my illusions and to engender in my soul a doubt about the practical durability of my system. I asked myself: "Does the Dance actually have its principle of beauty in ever fresh nature, or only in the changing whims of fashion?"

Nevertheless, I have not been able to tear myself loose from my original view, and therefore think that even if fable is warranted and can allow a swain to die of love for a sylphide, an elf-maiden, or a mermaid, I still feel it is far overstepping the mark when a shawm-playing shepherd becomes happily married to an *insect!* Here, there are two alternatives: either these ridiculous situations are accepted as belonging to the nature of the ballet, wherefore the concept is weakened, or they lead to distaste on the part of the public and a drain on the theatre treasury, in which case the blame is thrown less upon a tasteless management than on the ballet as an art form. However, I claimed for myself, without demand of applause or financial compensation, the right to arrange *sensible* dances for my plays and operas. But this was also the only pleasure I had in Stockholm from *"min gamla flamma"!*

In order not to end this survey with miserable reflections on the irony of Fate, which seems to play tricks with the truth I seek in the beautiful, and with the beauty I strive for in fleeting illusion, I will direct the attention of all art-lovers to the eminent position scene-painting assumes on the Swedish stage.

One has no idea of the variety and wealth of imagination and practical skill that are displayed in this branch, especially in architectural respects. The landscape is inferior to our decorations, as far as hardwood trees, plants, and aerial perspectives are concerned. But lakes and cliffs, as well as palms and coniferous trees, are painted better in Stockholm. We, however, do not possess a room, a hall, a street, or a church, let alone a fairy palace, which can in the slightest degree be compared with the masterworks the outstanding Roberg has produced; and for the Egyptian prospects and monuments with which he illustrated Mozart's *Magic Flute,* a special antiquarian study had to be made.

Roberg died in the flower of his talent, and his loss would have been irreplaceable for the Swedish theatre, which by this time had spoiled its public with magnificent scenery, if a very young pupil had not seized the master's brush and, guided by genius, traveled forward on the road indicated by him. There is no doubt that [Fritz] Ahlgrensson, whose invention and speed in execution are most extraordinary, will, with further study, assume a prominent place in a profession in which one can truthfully say that Stockholm has kept up with the times.

THE STAGE AND ITS ECONOMY

AS Intendant for the stage, I thought I would have nothing to do with *ciphers* and therefore in the beginning I found my position especially pleasant, the

more so as economics is the shady side of all theatres. All the same, I was soon
to learn that here — as with us — the art of the stage is strongly subject to financial considerations, and in the theatre managment I encountered an uneasy
tension which continuously threatened to place aesthetics in the background,
to the advantage of trade. To reconcile these conflicting elements was therefore one of my principal tasks, and I set up as principles for a publicly supported Theatre the following dual propositions:

1) To present the finest in every genre.
2) To prefer quality to quantity.

To this end, one must, according to my opinion:

1) Make a selection of classical as well as modern domestic and foreign
   subjects, which, given with a pleasant variety, could promote taste
   among the general public, educate and train the personnel, and serve
   as models and encouragement for the younger authors as well as composers.
2) One must, without rejecting the system, avoid the puerile and not
   waste time and energies on padding.
3) Not set aside good pieces because they do not immediately provide
   full houses or meet with lively applause; for it is well known that the
   excellent, precisely because it is unusual and original, must have time
   to be recognized and that the performance itself really matures only
   by frequent repetition.
4) Be sparing with costly pageantry, superfluous choral masses, and dazzling effects, etc., which only contribute to focusing the attention on
   the unessential, cloying the power of reception, and cluttering up the
   storehouses with unnecessary matériel. The spoken drama ought to be
   maintained by outstanding acting, the opera by dramatic singing, the
   ballet by mimic expression and graceful dancing, and the whole by artistic inspiration. Where these conditions are present, a theatre which
   does not represent a Great Power of Europe can very well content itself with the *necessary* equipment, without superfluous magnificence,
   for if the former qualities are not to be found, external luxury will only
   contribute to exposing the internal emptiness.
5) Secure good and steady talents who are not able, by terminating their
   engagements just when they have become indispensible, to drive salaries up to disproportionate heights, or, knowing themselves to be in
   danger of receiving notice of discharge, always have other schemes in
   readiness. Hereby harmful changes of personnel would be prevented
   and the administrative machinery considerably simplified.
6) Finally, it must be regarded as far more reassuring for the interests of
   the Theatre Treasury that what is aimed at are *perfect* rather than *numerous* performances, and it is better to see frequent well-filled
   houses than an occasional sellout. It is possible that a single season
   will refute this theory, but a series of three or four years will demon-
   strate that the true enjoyment of art can at length rely upon a more numerous public than upon a suggestive curiosity.

These fundamental principles, which in and of themselves contain *loci communes*, were, however, found to be so strongly inconsistent with hitherto-followed practice that they were bound to saddle their adherents and advocates with the liability for a considerable loss of money.

Here is once again the place to point out an essential difference in the interpretation of economic ideas at the Swedish and Danish Theatres. While the Danes reckon everything that is not cash in hand under *liabilities* and regard acquired matériel as pure expenditure, the Swedes go to the opposite extreme and list the nominal amount of stores as *assets*. In Copenhagen they hold good pieces back for fear of the expense; in Stockholm they get involved in all sorts of things and plunge into the most hazardous ventures, only in order to increase the receipts. They are mistaken on both sides; the wrong and pernicious are passed on as a legacy from one management to another; opinions about a Royal Theatre's purpose become ever more vague, its signification increasingly synonymous with ruinous enterprises; and in spite of both the support of the State and the demands of art, the institution degenerates into a boutique.

It was obvious that the lyric portion [of the repertoire] was the source of life for the Theatre Treasury and that the indifference with which *den bättre publik* treated the spoken drama—even at reduced prices!—disheartened both the artists and the management, which was on the point of regarding this important branch as a burden.

In addition to the efforts I immediately directed to this quarter, I outlined a proposal that instantly won the Director's approval. It involved nothing less than *An Association for the Promotion of Swedish Dramatic Art and Literature* (the last in cooperation with Finland, Norway, and Denmark).

The intention was to hereby generate for the drama a sympathy such as that which music owes to "The Philharmonic Society." The advancement of the idea, the project, or whatever one wishes to call it, was, however, stranded upon two circumstances: the impossibility of getting a certain eminent literary personality to take the lead, and the impossibility of preventing harmful elements from mixing in the enterprise.

At this same time a renewed attempt to establish a box subscription, similar to the one that is an essential but not sufficiently appreciated source of help for the Danish Theatre, was discontinued. This would have assured the Theatre Treasury a more steady income and facilitated the admission of a regular and intelligent audience, for which the dramatic stage had a special need.

The economy's worst stumbling block always seemed to be the competition with the secondary theatres, of which the one "in the southern quarter" had seized upon the *vaudeville* while Mindre Theatern, in addition to the folk comedy (in which Overskou's *The Devil's Superior* [in Swedish, *Den Ondes Besegrare*] has created an epoch), translated and rehearsed new French comedies in less time than the management of the Royal Theatre took to read through and censor them. Furthermore, that private dramatic enterprise rendered the old classical plays so tedious that the larger speculators no longer dared have anything to do with them. Upon the visit of foreign virtuosi, as has already been stated, outbidding took place, seldom to the advantage of the winner, but almost always with great loss for the unfavored parties. In my time, there were only two such profitable affairs: the appearance of the ingenious violinist Wilhelmine Neruda as a genuine artistic phenomenon, and the Delepierre *Wunderkinder* as an amiable curiosity.

The task of maintaining a repertoire composed of such heterogeneous elements and at the same time giving a numerous personnel sufficient occupation became harder and harder. The large locale was found to be unsuitable for rapid diction, just as it was for the light conversational tone, and they still preserved the tradition of Dramatiska Theatern, which had burnt down in 1818 and whence all of the older celebrities originated. A number of years earlier, they had passed up the chance to buy Mindre Theatern at a low price, because they had hoped to erect a branch theatre, more convenient in every way for the spoken drama, on the grounds of the Opera House itself. And yet it seemed to be less the freer development of art than the troublesome competition that the management had on its mind, and it was not so much a matter of overcoming as eliminating the dangerous rival.

To me, the former alternative appeared to be both the most interesting and the most worth while. A number of times I suggested producing pieces in which the comparison might be to our advantage; for example, *The School for Scandal, The Power of the Coteries, Don Carlos,* and others. A misguided tactfulness, combined with the above-mentioned fear of pecuniary loss, opposed this competition. Finally, we succeeded — under cover of secrecy and by the attractive force of intrigue — in rehearsing the three-act comedy *La Papillonne* and presenting it on the stage three whole days before a work of a similar name appeared at the theatre run by our astounded and indignant neighbors.

The blow was violent and decisive; the public opened its eyes, and this time dared to pass an independent sentence in spite of the desperate efforts of the protecting powers. We held the battlefield, and from now on there was no more talk of rivalry. (A glance at our theatre statistics will convince the reader that this victory was not due to blind chance.) Mindre Theatern hoisted all its sails, both classical and romantic, but in vain; it fell further and further behind, and scarcely three months after the aforesaid defeat we learnt this establishment was to be sold or leased. Finally, it was offered to the Kungliga Theatern for the nice little sum of 300,000 Rbd. Swedish currency. This is how far we had gotten by November 1862. Strong in our own resources and favored by fortunate circumstances which we had known how to use, we now harvested the fruits of our endeavors; for never at any previous time had the Royal Theatre given such a large number of performances, offered such rich variety, or had such considerable receipts as in this season.

If we could have accepted the offer without the Theatre itself having the liability for paying the interest and amortizing the purchase price, which was now reduced to 270,000 Swedish Rbd. and was to be paid off in nineteen years with annual payments of 20,000 Rbd., the acquisition of a smaller locale would have been of real practical value. Then they would not have needed to augment the personnel at both theatres, and the greater convenience with which studies and rehearsals could be carried on would have contributed to a greater perfection. But, since the evenings that the large theatre would lose would have to be made up for by continual use of the drama, in order, if possible, to remedy the increased expenditures at the combined institutions, art might to an alarming degree have to become subordinate to speculation. And since Stora Theatern would have to give *four* opera performances a week, sometimes alternating with large-scale dramas, while Dramatiska Theatern, on the other hand, gave *five* performances a week, with a possible alternation with operettas, it became apparent that the undertaking, even according to the most sanguine calculations and in the most successful circumstances, would not yield the Theatre Treasury one *Øre* in surplus as a reward for its ceaseless efforts and as compensation for taking the most daring risks!

Besides these objections, the validity of which I demonstrated with incontrovertible figures, I was also forced to point out that large-scale drama, because of its difficult staging and poorer drawing power, would from now on be pushed into the background and eventually be crowded off the stage, all the more so as it hindered the run of playlets at the other theatre. In the next place, the ballet, which because of the change of locale could no longer serve as supplement to the drama, would hereafter become reduced to "an opera ornament."

These remarks were neither accepted nor refuted even though they were formulated in writing. But on New Year's Eve of 1862, when I attended the elegant party which Director Stjernström was in the habit of giving every year on this occasion, I learnt from his own lips that the fatal bargain had been made, with the stipulation that after a trial period of three years it could be called off in return for complete compensation for the matériel used. Truly a good deal! Now, I myself had limited the duration of my engagement in consideration of my talents, my family affairs, and the feeling which at an advanced age draws the man to his native land and hearth, the artist to rest and reflection; and therefore I had no intention of remaining in Stockholm beyond the stipulated three years, during which I intended to discharge my duties to the best of my ability. But, even if this had not been the case, under the present circumstances it would have been clear to me that the coming season must be my last at a theatre where my views were in such sharp opposition to those of the management. I felt that my ideas of progress would surely be stranded upon this latest daring speculation, and though I dutifully gathered all my forces in order to avert an artistic defeat, a financial debacle appeared to me to be so inevitable that a future effort in the direction I had already begun would be sheer madness. However, I attended to the management of both stages, inaugurated the new locale with a ballet *divertissement* of my own composition, and undertook the staging of eight new pieces for Dramatiska Theatern.* At Stora Theatern I mounted, in addition to its regular opera repertoire, two grand dramas, *Richard II* and the original Finnish work, *Daniel Hjort,* both of which were superbly performed, and I finally had the good fortune to contribute my poor mite for the three hundredth anniversary celebration of the birth of Shakespeare (April 23, 1564). This jubilee was celebrated all over Europe: in Stockholm at both theatres, respectively with *Hamlet* and *As You Like It* (in part, *Viola*). In Paris the celebration was forbidden; and in Copenhagen, if not forgotten, then at least neglected.

This was still the smooth side of the combined theatres' activities, but now comes the unfortunate circumstance that in order to give 208 performances at the smaller theatre, the larger house had to limit itself to 179 performances, therefore 63 less than the previous season. The salary scale was given an annual increase of over 50,000 Swedish Rbd., and the repertoire at the smaller theatre was forced up to 18 new and 21 older pieces, several of which were, naturally, of greatly subordinate value. In order to fill the often sparsely occupied house, they resorted to means which were as desperate as they were wrong. They thus degraded the Royal Theatre's dramatic stage by such presentations as a German adventuress, a *figurante* who under the name of the *Greek Woman Calipoliti from Athens* obliged the audience with some so-called Persian dances; and if by chance the Medical Faculty had declared the magnetist Hansen's experiments to be interesting, he, too, would have been asked to help our finances by a dozen or so entertaining interludes.

As I had estimated, and as will be seen from the statistical survey, neither the aesthetic nor the so-called practical efforts could prevent a considerable deficit, which was now added to the debts which had been contracted beforehand. I had proven myself with both words and deeds to have had the Theatre's interests at heart, even though the economy of it was not my actual province. Nevertheless, perhaps an echo of my theories will resound on the stage as well as in the Chancellary! I dare not abandon myself to sanguine expectations, but it would make me happy to see the Theatre's financial conditions one day reconciled with the true interests of art, for only in this union lies the hope of its future.

---

*All the pieces denoted by asterisks in the statistical survey were produced under my direction. — A.B.

THEATRE STATISTICS

IN order to judge the progressive activity and its financial consequences, it is necessary to look back on:

THE 1860–1861 SEASON

The total number of performances was.. 211.

Of these, there were — Regular performances .... 202.

Benefit performances...................... 1.

Concerts (two of which were for
the retiring *Kapellmeister*)................. 8.

The Lyric Stage presented:

A NEW OPERA:	*Rigoletto*.....................................	1.
A NEW PRODUCTION:	*The Master Mason*	1.
SWEDISH COMPOSITIONS:	*Gustav Vasa*, by Naumann; *The Malcontents*, by F. Lindblad	2.
OPERETTAS:	*The Nuremberg Doll, The Chalet, House for Sale*	3.
BALLAD OPERAS:	*The Daughter of the Regiment* and *The Painter and the Models*	2.

OPERAS:

MOZART—	*The Magic Flute, Don Giovanni,* and *Figaro*	3.
WEBER—	*Oberon, The Huntsman's Bride*..........	2.
ROSSINI—	*William Tell, The Barber*	2.
VERDI—	*The Troubadour, Ernani*	2.
MEYERBEER—	*The Prophet, The Huguenots*..............	2.
FLOTOW—	*Stradella*.....................................	2.

In all, 21 [sic] works, one of which was a novelty.

The Dramatic Stage presented:

NEW ORIGINAL SWEDISH WORKS:	*The Brothers' Debt* by Børgeson..............1.	
ADAPTATIONS FROM THE GERMAN:	*Struensee*	1.
NEW FRENCH PLAYLETS:	....	8.
NEW PRODUCTION:	*Seven Maids in Uniform*	1.

In all, 11 novelties.

OLDER SUBJECTS:

SHAKESPEARE—	*Hamlet, Othello*	2.
CALDERÓN—	*Life Is a Dream*	1.
SCHILLER—	*The Robbers*	1.
SHERIDAN—	*The Rivals*	1.
SCRIBE—	*The Baths at Dieppe, A Glass of Water, A Chain, Statesman and Burgher*	4.
HERTZ—	*The Billeting*	1.
ORIGINAL SWEDISH WORKS:	*The Wermlanders,* by Dahlgren	1.
	The Doctor and	
	Engelbrecht, by Blanche	2.
VARIOUS TRANSLATIONS		8.

In all, 21 older works.

A grand total of 21 lyric and 32 dramatic works.

According to the records of the Production Manager,

the receipts amounted to .... 208,356 Rbd., 60 Øre.

To this must be added a remuneration on the occasion

of the Court mourning for Queen Desideria .... 14,000 Rbd.—

222,356 Rbd., 60 Øre.

THE 1861–1862 SEASON

The total number of performances was.. 231.

Of these, there were

	Regular performances	223.
	Benefit performances	3.
	Concerts	2.
	The Harmonic Society's concerts	3.

The Lyric Stage presented:

NEW OPERAS:	A Swedish composition, *Estrella*, by F. Berwald, and *Faust*	2.
NEW OPERETTAS:	*The Prince's Trumpeter*	1.
NEW PRODUCTIONS:	*The Crown Jewels, *The Mute Girl, *The New Landlord*	3.
OLDER SUBJECTS:	*The Magic Flute, Figaro, Don Giovanni, The Huntsman's Bride, William Tell, The Barber, The Troubadour, The Malcontents, The Master Mason, Martha, Stradella, The Elixir of Love, The Painter and the Models, House for Sale,* and *The Chalet*	15.

In all, 21 works, 3 of which were novelties.

The Dramatic Stage presented:

NEW ORIGINAL SWEDISH WORKS:	*Torkel Knutson,* by Beskow, *The Slanderer,* by Jolin, *Hothouse Flowers,* by Hedberg	3.
NEW ORIGINAL DANISH WORKS:	*At Sunset,* by Carit Etlar, and *A Benefactor's Testament,* Anonymous	2.
A NEW GERMAN ADAPTATION:	*The Rich Farmer,* by Birch-Pfeiffer	1.
A SHAKESPEAREAN COMEDY:	*Comedy of Errors*	1.
NEW FRENCH PLAYLETS:	(3 of which were *directed* by me)	4.

In all, 11 novelties.

OLDER SUBJECTS:		
SHAKESPEARE—	*Hamlet, A Midsummer Night's Dream* .	2.
CALDERÓN—	*Life Is a Dream*	1.
SCHILLER—	*The Robbers*	1.
SCRIBE—	*A Glass of Water*	1.
BIRCH-PFEIFFER—	*Jane Eyre*	1.
A MUSICAL DRAMA—	*Preciosa*	1.
OLDER SWEDISH WORKS:	*Young Han's Daughter,* by Jolin	1.
	The Doctor, by Blanche	1.
	The Wermlanders, by Dahlgren	1.
VARIOUS TRANSLATIONS		14.

In all, 24 older works.

A grand total of 21 lyrical and 35 dramatic works.

The Ballet's activity was limited to the following works: *Festival in Albano,* *The Wedding Festival,* *La Sylphide,* and a *divertissement, Cupid's Jest.* In addition, there was a tableau, *Mozartiana,* for *The Marriage of Figaro,* and frequent assistance in opera and drama.

RECEIPTS.. 234,717 Rbd., 25 Øre.

THE 1862–1863 SEASON

The total number of performances was		246.
Of these, there were	Regular performances	242.
	Benefit performances	3.
	Concerts	1.

The Lyric Stage presented:

NEW BALLAD OPERAS:	*Brahma and the Bayadère* and *Villars' Dragoons*	2.

NEW OPERETTAS:	Fortunio's Song, and Borrowed Plumes, Swedish composition by Bendix.........	2.
NEW OPERA PRODUCTIONS:	*Lucia and *Robert........................	2.
OLDER SUBJECTS:	Mozart's three operas, Oberon, The Huntsman's Bride, William Tell, The Barber, The Mute Girl, The Crown Jewels, Faust, The Prophet, The Painter, The Chalet, and The Nuremberg Doll ...	15.

In all, 21 works, 4 of which were novelties.

The Dramatic Stage presented:

NEW ORIGINAL SWEDISH WORKS:	*Forward!, by Jolin; *Day Waxes by Hedberg.....................................	2.
NEW ORIGINAL DANISH WORKS:	*Rosa and Rosita, Anonymous............	1.
A NEW GERMAN ADAPTATION:	*The Swordsman from Ravenna, by Halm...	1.
FRENCH COMEDIES (trans.):	*The Providence of Love, by Marivaux, and La Papillonne [sic]	2.
NEW FRENCH PLAYLETS:	(3 of which were directed by me)	5.

In all, 11 novelties.

OLDER SUBJECTS:

SHAKESPEARE—	Hamlet and A Comedy of Errors	2.
MOLIÈRE—	*The Miser, The School for Husbands...	2.
CALDERÓN—	Life Is a Dream	1.
HEIBERG—	Elves' Hill	1.
CARIT ETLAR—	At Sunset	1.
SCRIBE—	*The Tales of Queen Marguerite, The Baths at Dieppe	2.
ORIGINAL SWEDISH WORKS:	Torkel Knutson, by Beskow	1.
	Engelbrecht, by Blanche...................	1.
	The Slanderer, by Jolin	1.
	The Wermlanders, by Dahlgren..........	1.
	Hothouse Flowers, by Hedberg..........	1.
OLDER TRANSLATIONS:		7.

In all, 21 older works.

A grand total of 21 lyrical and 32 dramatic works.

In the way of novelties, the Ballet presented *Carnival Night,* and the *divertissements La Variété* and *Bouquet de fantaisie.* In the category of older works, it presented *La Sylphide,* besides lending considerable assistance in drama and opera.

RECEIPTS... 297,860 Rbd., 50 Øre.

THE 1863–1864 SEASON

Stora Theatern and Dramatiska Theatern Combined

The total number of performances at *Stora Theatern* was.................... 188.

Of these, there were	Regular performances	179.
	Benefit performances......................	5.
	Concerts	4.

The total number of performances at *Dramatiska Theatern* was .... 208.

The Lyric Stage presented:

NEW BALLAD OPERAS:	*The Doctor in Spite of Himself,* by Gounod, and *The Saga of Queen Elvira,* by Ambroise Thomas.................	2.
NEW PRODUCTIONS:	*Fra Diavolo, *The White Lady, Tsar and Carpenter, *Leonora, *Joseph and his Brethren, *The Puritans*	6.
OLDER SUBJECTS BY:	MOZART and WEBER	5.
	ROSSINI and VERDI	4.
	DONIZETTI	2.
	Faust, Robert, Villars' Dragoons	3.
	The Chalet, The Nuremberg Doll.........	2.
	The Crown Jewels...........................	1.

In all, 25 works, 2 of which were novelties.

N. B. The reason for the small number of novelties, especially of grand operas, must be sought partly in the management's fondness for "the light genre" (*opéra-comique*) and partly in the fact that the presence of Fru Michaeli gave renewed freshness to the older operas.

The Dramatic Stage presented:

AT *Stora Theatern:*

A NEW ORIGINAL SWEDISH-FINNISH WORK:	*Daniel Hjort,* by Witzelius	
SHAKESPEARE:	*Richard II	2.
OLDER SUBJECTS:	*Hamlet, A Midsummer Night's Dream, The Swordsman from Ravenna*	3.
ORIGINAL SWEDISH WORKS:	*The Wermlanders* and *Day Waxes*........	2.

At *Dramatiska Theatern:*

NEW ORIGINAL SWEDISH
    WORKS: **Corpus Christi*, a vaudeville by Hedberg; *Doctor Mekara*, an anonymous vaudeville; **The Order of the Amaranth*, by Wijkander .... 3.

AN ORIGINAL DANISH WORK: **The Deportees*, by Hertz .... 1.

NEW SWEDISH ADAPTATIONS: *The Woman in White* by Hedberg, and also, by the same author, *Herr Hummer's 73 Öre* .... 2.

A NEW GERMAN
    ADAPTATION: *Queen Bell* by Birch-Pfeiffer .... 1.

A SHAKESPEAREAN COMEDY: *As You Like It* .... 1.

MOLIÈRE'S COMEDY: **The Roguery of Scapin* .... 1.

FRENCH DRAMAS: *Honest Folk, Richard Sheridan, *A Childless Home, *Montjoye, The Diplomat* .... 5.

FRENCH PLAYLETS: *Good Examples *The Suitor's Visit, A Cup of Tea, Equal Against Equal* .... 4.

OLDER SUBJECTS: Among the larger plays, *Siri Brahe*, an original Swedish work (*Gustav III*), and *King René's Daughter*, by Hertz .... 15.

                                      Older playlets .... 6.

In all, 46 works, 20 of which were novelties.

A grand total of 25 lyrical and 46 dramatic works.

The Ballet presented two new *divertissements, Mélange* and *Les Abeilles.* Also, of my own composition, **An Inaugural Divertissement*, the *intermezzo* for *The Order of the Amaranth,* and the **Apotheosis* for Shakespeare's Jubilee celebration.

According to the manager's records, the receipts for the combined theatres were approximately as follows:

STORA THEATERN .... for 179 performances, about 222,000 Rbd.
DRAMATISKA THEATERN .... for 208 performances, about 136,000 Rbd.

With the exception of *Order of the Amaranth* and *Les Abeilles*, no piece demanded especially luxurious décor. Royalties for authors and foreign guest stars' fees were relatively small, the subsidies larger,* and the repertoire was not disorganized by any lengthy indisposition. And yet the accounts for the

* See footnote opposite page.

theatrical year showed a considerable deficit! The future will determine whether or not I was mistaken.

In this account of my services during a period of three years at the Royal Theatre in Stockholm, I have as much as possible avoided touching upon the personal, and in serving the idea have dealt only with issues. I am fully aware that everywhere in the world of art and the theatre one will find traces of the same shortcomings as I have here implied, and will hardly find as many actual merits as I have emphasized out of a sense of obligation. Everywhere the same conflict is going on between spirit and matter; between theory and misguided practice, which feels itself to be justified because it has been divested of all poetry; and, finally, everywhere real or imagined reformers are returning from battle, downcast at having accomplished so very little.

Even though I have never thought of myself as possessing the ability to stand alone against the tide, I was still surprised that I was unable to achieve more of my anticipated goal than the results have shown. However, I must count these three years in Stockholm among the most successful and happy periods of my life. Honored by an amiable Royal House and by Sweden's leading men, and cordially received both within and without my sphere of activity, I have gained for myself indelible memories which I shall preserve with a grateful heart, not only as an artist but chiefly as *a Dane*.

In all personal relations, one could not have had a more humane and noble superior than I had in Hr. Baron von Stedingk. The fact that I found myself opposed to my chief and his practical advisers with respect to the purchase of Mindre Theatern, and thereby—from having stood closest to him in artistic matters according to the terms of my contract—found myself, during half of my tenure, with a dozen or so dilettantes etc. between him and me, is a *Chancellery affair* that shall in no way weaken my appreciation of the rest of his excellent qualities. He possessed a number of fine talents, and next to my unforgettable Levetzau I have never known a director with as pleasant a nature as Baron von Stedingk. As a result of being nominated by him, I was favored with a Knight's Cross of the Order of Vasa, which was accompanied by a diploma wherein my endeavors were emphasized in a manner which implied that they will have some influence on the future of the Swedish theatre. If only this prediction might be fulfilled, I would bless the activity of these three years.

---

*Earlier subsidies were:
    From H. M. the King .... 60,000 Sw. Rbd.
    From the State .... 75,000 Sw. Rbd.
After the union of the theatres, they were:
    From H. M. the King .... 65,000 Sw. Rbd.
    From the Royal Family .... 10,000 Sw. Rbd.
    From the State .... 75,000 Sw. Rbd.

—A.B.

IX

Dramatic Celebrities of the Danish Stage

WITH these comparisons *à la Plutarque* I have set myself a task that presents great difficulties, not only because of the reverence that is due famous persons now deceased, but even more because of the care with which the living must be treated. And to this are added the highly different nuances of their talents and the mistrust with which a portion of these descriptions will probably be viewed by a future age, which will claim that I have either judged my contemporaries from a choreographic standpoint, or that in this almost unadulterated praise I have brought my comrades a fragrant token of friendship.

Among all the nations which favor the dramatic art, one finds in members of the younger generation the same incredulous smile whenever there is mention of the glorious things that the older folk have seen and experienced, and they put their trust in those who censure rather than in those who praise. But one must not be surprised at this, for it is the same with revelations of art as it is with bygone summers: one does not so easily forget one splendid storm or another, but the small showers and changes in the weather are quickly obliterated, and only the bright and warm days are preserved in memory. It is such things alone that contain the poetry of life and are worthy of the interest of our inquisitive posterity.

Just as Noverre, in his *Lettres sur la danse*, has found the opportunity to give us the most vivid picture of the finest actors of his day, and has thereby erected everlasting monuments to a number of them—especially Garrick—surely I must be permitted to contribute my mite to a lasting commemoration of the splendid artists who, during the half-century which *My Theatre Life* embraces, have graced the Danish stage and delighted the Danish people.

From the aesthetic observations that are to be found in this book, one may deduce my views, and I in no way publish my personal impressions as "critical judgments." Therefore, even if these commemorative pages do not testify to a definite system, I do hope that one will find in them *love* and *warmth*.

LINDGREEN   FOERSOM, JR.

Those theatre-lovers who can remember Lindgreen from his artistic prime are now very old and rather few in number; while those who have seen him only in his latest period might easily be inclined to agree that Frydendahl was right when he stated that Lindgreen was great only as Jeppe and as Brother Sup. But that great actor was often most unfair in his judgments, and shared with several of his colleagues the weakness of only reluctantly acknowledging the merits of his contemporaries. [In this instance] he was wrong indeed; for from the splendid performances I myself saw Lindgreen give in my early youth, as well as from the opinion I have heard expressed by connoisseurs, and, finally, from the reflections I have made at a more mature age on the nature of drama, it is evident that he must have held an eminent place among the dramatic notabilities of that day. To be sure, the range of his talent was not nearly so extensive as, for example, that of Ryge and Frydendahl; but at a time when bravura roles, in both tragedy and comedy, tempted so many actors to excesses and affectation, Lindgreen held himself within the tasteful bounds of truth; and his performances of English, German, and older French comedy gave evidence of artistic perception and the most painstaking preparation.

It would take too long to enumerate all the characters from Molière, Picard, Duval, Iffland, and Kotzebue that he illustrated with his priceless humor. But his favorite sphere was the comedies of Holberg, for which he had collected and preserved valuable traditions. In some of these roles (the Henriks, for example) he has been surpassed by his ingenious disciple, Ludvig Phister; but in others, such as Peer in *Jacob v. Tyboe*, Jacob in *Erasmus Montanus*, the Pawned Peasant Lad, Geert Westphaler, and, finally, Jeppe, he remains irreplaceable.

What Lindgreen was to Holberg's comedies, Foersom later became to Heiberg's *vaudevilles* as well as the comedies of Hertz and Overskou. It is quite probable that Lindgreen based his characterizations heavily on the older school and because of this was, perhaps, less original than Foersom, who—though limited to an even narrower circle of comic characters—possessed the ability to create independent "types" and vivid genre pictures of national "Philistine" life. His George the Hatter, Burmann, Ledermann, the ship's chandler in *The Debate*, Skaarup in *The Savings Bank*, but above all his Kakadu in *Capriciosa*, were perfect masterpieces, worthy of the Dutch school of painting. I ought not to forget his *monks*, who, though they were born of his own imagination, appeared as true to life as if they had just stepped out of the cloisters of Rome.

Endowed with a skillful bass voice, he gave vital support to the *opéra-comique* and had real bravura parts as the cobbler in *The Amorous Artisans* and as the smith in *The Master Mason*.

Lindgreen and Foersom each represented the comic trend of a certain time; but both retained truth and moderation in their stage performances. What the former possessed through training and experience, the latter had earned by the study of nature and a lucky instinct. Neither of them spoke academic Danish; for Lindgreen's accent was that of a South Sjællander, while

Foersom had retained much of his Funen dialect. Lindgreen grew old and worn out in active service; Foersom died in the full strength of his maturity and talent.

NIELSEN　　　MICHAEL WIEHE

The void which Nielsen filled with his arrival on the Danish stage can only be compared with the emptiness he left behind at his departure; for, without doing his predecessors an injustice, one can safely say that before people had seen his Axel, they little suspected that a romantic lead from the heroic age of the North could appear to such fine advantage on the stage; nor could they have any idea of the harmony of strength and tenderness with which he knew how to infuse his tragic acting.

Through his inspired delivery and his sonorous voice, lyric as well as epic poetry obtained an interpreter who not only helped to further the propagation and appreciation of poetical works, but also encouraged our authors to create new products. It was truly a fruitful period!

Authors vied to furnish his repertoire with splendid roles. King Sigurd, Erik VII, Harald Hardrada, and Tordenskjold were written expressly for him; and his talent gave new luster to Einar Tamberskjælver, Thorvald Vidførle, and Correggio. Since he also shone in the tragedies of Schiller and, in addition, spoke German as beautifully as he did his mother tongue, he appeared in 1824—to great applause—on a number of Germany's major stages. Fortunately, he did not allow himself to become infected by Germanic bombast, but with rare taste and discrimination grasped everything good that was to be found on the Continent at that time. This was later of great use to him in high comedy.

Even though he made the transition from romantic leads to the roles of fathers and more pronounced characters with uncommon success, he never equaled Ryge in the interpretation of such figures as Macbeth, Lear, Hakon Jarl, and Palnatoke. He was not of the mold from which these giant characters were cast; even the ring of his voice bore the same relation to Ryge's as the full-bodied, but soft, French horn does to the sharp, penetrating notes of the battle *lur*.

On the other hand, in many older roles he did manage to compensate for the unforgettable Frydendahl—if not by the sparkling humor and plastic beauty that characterized that master of the old school, then, nevertheless, by dignity, truth, and a certain good-natured amiability that mollified the ridiculous and narrow-minded element which usually runs through the comical so-called *"pères nobles."*

Since Nielsen's death this category of roles stands as good as vacant, and, as I have remarked above, few actors have left behind a wider breach, a deeper void, than he. For his talent not only had tremendous scope; it also represented a direction in art, namely, that which has nobility of nature as its model. In brilliant fashion he likewise proved the melodiousness of the Danish language to our Nordic sister nations, who through him received entirely new ideas about declamation and rhetoric.

In comparing departed celebrities with those who are still active,* it is a matter of not allowing oneself to be enraptured by either memory or the impression of the moment. In particular, one ought to beware of regarding the present status [of a talent] as something final, since in the rather near future it can further develop and thereby exhibit unexpected new facets.

As I write these lines, Michael Wiehe is threatened with seeing his artistic career cut short by a chronic complaint, and the public with losing an actor who rightfully possesses, and will never abuse, the name of its "chosen darling." He is presently at a Continental spa in order, if possible, to regain his health; and, joining my wishes—for the future that seems to be implied in the enigmatical development of his abundant gifts—to those of all who love his art and his noble personality, I will briefly attempt to describe the relation between his talent and that of Nielsen.

Both have interpreted the purest feelings of love with an expression and in a style the like of which was not to be found on any other stage. At least in the genre of romantic leads, these two actors have nowhere been surpassed.

What Nielsen was as a youthful hero in the heyday of poetry and inspiration, Wiehe is, as the spokesman for Romanticism in an age when reflection has put a damper on passion and filled the stage as well as the auditorium with critical rationalists. Nielsen had both the word and the pen at his command, and his whole manner was characterized by strength of movement. Wiehe speaks little and writes even less; but the first thing one detects in his artistic preparation is depth of thought. Nielsen's eroticism was "girded with a sword"; Wiehe's "sweeps the strings of a harp." In addition to his genuine pathos, Nielsen also possessed a considerable fund of humor and joviality; but Wiehe, whether he is representing blazing passion or the flame that lies hidden beneath a monkish cowl, everywhere pays homage to the ideal of beauty.

Nielsen's transition to older character roles was marked by bravura, where as Wiehe's will, in all probability, be quiet, reflective, and throw rare but dazzling gleams from the shady place where his talent will modestly, but calculatingly, draw itself away from the heroic life of youth. Through superb recitation, both have given prominence to the flower of our Danish poetry. What the one achieved as a dramatist through the magic of his voice, the other effected by grace of movement. But—so as not to transform them into absolute gods—both actors had one shortcoming: they lacked *eloquence of the eye*.

ROSENKILDE, SR.   PHISTER

Few actors, on the other hand, possessed *eloquence of the eye* to the same degree as our excellent Rosenkilde; for wherever he fixed his clear firm gaze, it was a start or a finish to his own lines or a commentary on what his fellow actors had to say. He was one of those comic actors who set little store

*This was written in September 1864; therefore, before M. Wiehe's death.—A.B.

by dialect or makeup; what he wished to portray he *became*, through his fantasy and expressive mime. Whether he appeared as a perpetual student or a fourteen-year-old schoolboy, whether as a stiff-legged courtier or an adroit petitioner, he understood to the full how to create an illusion for his audience.

His overwhelming humor, aye, even his innate poetic talent, could sometimes entice him into going a bit beyond the *correct*, and the *vaudeville*, in particular, contained many such temptations. But he never stooped to caricature, and even in the midst of his amiable hilarity, he always allowed the true and the natural to walk off with the victory. However, he was well aware when to conserve his comic force, for example, as Ludvig Thostrup in *East Side, West Side* and as Miremont in *The Comrades*. But who would ever have thought that the same actor who had so often made us shake with beneficent laughter would be able to give us a consummate picture of Michel Perrin, that model of guilelessness combined with the most amiable, apostolic dignity? There was actually a kind of spiritual affinity between Rosenkilde and the famous Potier; for both possessed to the same extent the quality of being able, at will, to inject an elegiac note into the comic and of calling forth tears from gaiety itself.

Although Rosenkilde's progress as a comedian actually dates from the Heibergian *vaudeville* and has advanced through the whole of modern comedy (Danish as well as foreign), this superb actor has had no less success *in the comedies of Holberg*. To be sure, his Vielgeschrey and Peer Degn are inferior to his most recent predecessors' performance of these roles; but his Corfitz, Rosiflengius, Stygotius, and Montanus have hardly ever found better interpreters, and since he—rightly or wrongly—rejected anything that could be called tradition, all of his comic figures bore the unmistakable stamp of originality.

If people wish to characterize an actor's extraordinary versatility, they usually turn to the myth of Proteus, and this has more than once been applied to our talented and prolific Phister, however, without the variants of the legend having been taken into account; for the *mythical* Proteus, who guarded Neptune's sea calves, assumed all sorts of forms with the sole intention of frightening people and chasing them away. Now this version is in no way applicable to our popular comedian, who continuously calls forth mirth and joy and has a decided attraction for people. The *historical* Proteus is said to have been king of Memphis at the time when Prince Paris abducted the beautiful Helen. He distinguished himself by his taciturnity and mainly by the fact that he seldom appeared in public, and then unwillingly. This image does not seem to fit Phister either. But—there is a *third* Proteus in whom people claim to recognize one of the most excellent mimes of antiquity, who was almost accused of sorcery. Such a thing is not so far removed from our great comedian's nature; for one has indeed heard and read a good deal about a Garrick, a Devrient the Elder, and we ourselves have possessed a Ryge, who could change makeup, voice, and character to a degree that rendered recognition impossible. But the fact that, within the field of comedy, Phister has created more than three hundred comic "types" — all of which lie ready to be used at the appointed time and place — is really one of the miracles of dramatic art; and I would even count myself among the unbelievers had I not followed this whole series of roles step by step.

Now this applies only to the quantity of his achievements; but when one considers that through Phister's assistance, Molière, Holberg, Heiberg, Hertz, Overskou, and all the newer as well as older comedy writers, have obtained performances that were ingenious, correct, and thought out even to the subtlest nuances — and also that in Paris itself the roles he has delivered in our comic opera have scarcely afforded a more vivid coloring than they have on our stage, under his treatment — one must truly admire this multifaceted talent and believe in the sorcery of genius.

Should one attempt to draw a parallel between Phister and his older, now deceased, colleague, one must disregard the great multitude of qualities and concentrate only on the prevailing characteristics of both these dramatic stars. What Rosenkilde possessed in inexhaustible humor, Phister has in sustained correctness. Rosenkilde often let himself get carried away; Phister is master of himself, his role, and his audience. The variety Rosenkilde produced by means of his mimic expression, Phister achieves through his intonations and the ease with which his voice adapts itself to the most varied dialects. Rosenkilde's strength was manifested mainly in the roles of pedantic scholars, hot-tempered twaddlers, and both comic and dignified fathers.

An actor who, like Phister, has mainly shone in servants' roles, from Scapin, Sganarelle, Crispin, Oldfux, and Henrik, to the batman Mikkel and the houseboy Arv, would at a French theatre be consigned exclusively to this specialty, did not interpretations such as the Wandering Jew, Skriverhans, the election candidate Mincke, and — above all — the incomparable Klokker Link, stamp him as a character actor of the first magnitude. Both Phister and Rosenkilde have portrayed by turns everyday life and the world of the imagination. Their priceless humor and subtle irony were always combined with feeling: they have thus appealed to the intellect and touched the heart, and worked together without one having eclipsed the other. However, Phister has gotten the last word in a genre whose *coryphées* are gradually disappearing from the stage. He currently occupies perhaps the most prominent place among the comic actors of Europe. It would be a lengthy and difficult task to weigh all his artistic merits; but even if I could do it, I would not dare to, for fear of being unfair to Rosenkilde.

JFR JØRGENSEN   MADAME SØDRING

In a less fortunate position than the chosen organs of wit and comic humor are those female talents who are denied the attractive force of beauty and who must in their youth already renounce the roles which afford the opportunity to display charm and emotion but also demand certain external advantages, without which the desired effect is seldom achieved.

Henriette Jørgensen, a young lady of uncommon intelligence and breeding, early felt a special calling for the stage. She had a slender figure, a superior organ of speech, a fine singing voice—in short, all the prerequisites for becoming what one calls "a good acquisition"—but her facial features were anything but pretty! Consequently she did not qualify as a leading lady. However, an avenue of escape was found in character roles of various kinds, and her talent soon asserted itself in the tragic drama as well as in drawing room plays and, on the whole, in any part that did not positively demand a combination of youth and beauty.

Her bearing was noble and her acting gave evidence of a certain ease in moving in fashionable circles and of the subtlest observation of the manners and mannerisms of the aristocracy. In contrast to this higher genre, she also had a superb grasp of Holberg's Magdelones, and when Heiberg launched the series of national *vaudevilles,* Jfr. Jørgensen created two entirely new and highly original characters: Frøken Trumfmeier and Klister's middle-aged fiancée, the classic Malle. One of her last roles was Mme. Rust in *The Savings Bank,* in which she produced a veritable explosion of comic effect.

Here she finally had to give way to a seventeen-year-old debutante, Rosenkilde's daughter Julie, who had inherited her father's rich humor and eloquent eye; but, like him, she was not destined to score a success in the erotic genre. Jfr. Jørgensen, who was either unpleasantly affected by this competition or, perhaps, simply tired of stage life, retired a short time later, and Jfr. Rosenkilde now took over the entire portion of her predecessor's repertoire consisting of duennas and bourgeois mothers, in which category she—after some years of study—rose to the height where she is presently enthroned, recognized as a talent of the first magnitude.

On the conservative playbill of the Royal Theatre she is now called *Madame* Sødring, just as her genteel predecessor did not live to be vested with the leveling title of *Frøken,*† which has gained acceptance in our social language, which, like the French, permits only *Madame* and *Mademoiselle* for the whole female sex. How long will the Danish Theatre hold to this narrow-minded view, that places a mediocre actress, who happens to be married to a *Krigsraad* or a *Kammerassessor,* above a great artiste who has wed a burgher or a savant?‡

---

† At the Danish Theatre, it was customary to refer to married actresses as *Madame* and to those who were unmarried as *Jomfru.* Although *Jomfru* and *Frøken* both denote an unmarried woman, in the old days the title of *Frøken* had a more genteel connotation; however, by the latter part of the nineteenth century *Frøken* was being used as a general designation for unmarried women, regardless of their backgrounds.

‡ As has been said above, the word *Madame* before an actress' name on the playbill indicated that she was married, while the Danish title *Fru* reflected that she was the wife of a man of distinction. A famous example is Johanne Luise Heiberg, who, as the wife of a titular professor, was permitted by royal decree to appear on the theatre playbills as *Fru* Heiberg.

If one discounts those of Jfr. Jørgensen's roles belonging to a higher dramatic sphere, the relationship between her talent and that of Madame Sødring would be approximately the following:

Rosenkilde's legacy was unquestionably of advantage to his daughter. Jfr. Jørgensen possessed greater comic force, but Madame Sødring has more naïveté and *rondeur*. Where Jfr. Jørgensen was strikingly *witty*, Madam Sødring is pricelessly *amusing*. Both of them belonged to the natural, moderate school, and though neither has played romantic leads, they are both most winsome in their art.

WINSLØW   HØEDT

Genius and *talent* are not only conceptions, which are all too often confused, but words that are wrongly applied to gifts and natural aptitudes. I will not take it upon myself to define the former; but as far as talent is concerned, I think I have made it clear in the foregoing that by this I understand a combination of gifts and skill.

It is not enough for an actor to possess fantasy and invention. He also must have powers of observation and must acquire knowledge. For him, it is a matter of not only grasping but also of representing the character; in short, his gift must be developed through study and practice. This demand certainly ought to be made of art in general, but its validity is not fully acknowledged, and people are all too inclined to imprint the stamp of genius on a harebrained creation while disregarding that which has been carefully worked out. In acting, genius without skill can dazzle at first glance, but in the long run, errors will appear all the more sharply; whereas a combination of both is usually less striking but always retains the same freshness and permits one to discover new merits every time one encounters it.

Skill without genius can also find a place on the stage, but ceases to be art in the fullest sense of the word.

It is impossible to further develop these two elements unless one—even involuntarily—professes an often self-created and biased system. Here human vanity finds its greatest temptations; for one then readily becomes the focal point of one's own system. If it is to be made practical, one must place oneself at the head, and, in carrying it to its logical conclusion, run the risk of going astray or, at any rate, of being left in an isolated position.

It is fine to live for an idea, and to be able to render oneself an account of what has been the object of one's endeavors; but when one approaches the end of a long and arduous career, one is easily assailed by dejection and doubt and is involuntarily led to ask oneself whether one could not have used one's time and talents more fruitfully and to better advantage. I, for example—despite the seriousness of the times on the one hand, and their moral laxity on the other—have tried to claim for *the Ballet* (dancing and mime united) a place among the *fine* arts. I still do not know for certain whether I have been right or whether I have gone astray. Many have acknowledged my theory, but in practice I stand alone.

As I view Carl Winsløw, he appears to me as the one who struggled to raise nature and human idiosyncrasies to the highest degree of artistic interpretation. He himself was sparsely equipped with external means, but in his expressive countenace there lay a whole world of character sketches. His mind was constantly at work, and in his soul there was a craving for the great, which was misunderstood and misused by the injudicious, and especially by the unsympathetic.

Winsløw spent his first ten years at the Theatre ignored by the management, scorned by the critics, and underrated by his colleagues to such a degree that when he once consulted Frydendahl about a major role, he received the following encouragement: "My dear sir! You insist on playing contrabass when, in fact, you have only a piccolo violin." Another time (after a debate with a younger colleague, who was favored by the management and who had submitted a complaint about him), he received a reprimand which ran as follows: "I beg you, Herr Winsløw, to refrain from all rudeness toward Herr N. N., for he has more talent in his little finger than *you* have in your whole insolent body."

It had become the custom, both inside and outside the Theatre, to score cheap points by ridiculing Winsløw's eccentricities and his supposedly imagined artistic calling; and the injustice was all the greater as he was always willing to recognize the merits of others. Therefore, what could equal my surprise when, during my sojourn in Paris (1826), I learnt that Winsløw—as later M. Wiehe—had at a summer performance finally broken the ice and aroused universal enthusiasm as Frantz Moor in Schiller's *The Robbers*. I was still skeptical, but three years later I got to see for myself and was forced to join his most zealous admirers. The public had now opened its eyes to his extraordinary talent and acknowledged him as one of our finest actors—a designation which at that time meant a great deal.

The career that still lay before him was as brilliant as it was short; and as a result, his repertoire consisted of only a limited number of roles, but all of them were finished works of art, down to the smallest details. As evidence of the misunderstanding of the nature of talent, which I have intimated above, it must be remarked that there were still those who could not perceive this perfection; and envy, which is always ingenious, hit upon a play on words that denoted Winsløw as an illusionist [*Taskenspiller*] rather than an actor [*Skuespiller*]! But in him the magic of genius was no illusion: it was truth raised to the ideal. Frantz Moor, Georgios Maniakes, the slave Skofte, and the Jew Sheva stand as monuments among his interpretations in the serious style. Zierlig, Klister, Alderman Runge, and Joseph Goltz are comic types which even his most talented successors have not been able to avoid following stroke for stroke. The consummation of his master roles was Casimir Delavigne's Louis XI, unquestionably one of the most superb character roles ever to have been performed on the Danish stage. It was Winsløw's last strong effort! He died at an age which, in other great actors, would still be considered young.

The esteem and affection I cherish for the outstanding artist I now intend to name among the celebrities of our dramatic stage applies to an equally high degree to his talent and his personal character. As I write these lines, I am convinced that the bitterness, which has for all too long a time alienated him from the stage, must be mitigated, and that—by his own incentive as well as at the request of all true art-lovers—he must feel called upon to once more tread the stage where, among the outstanding actors, he can still be reckoned one of the younger ones.

But should this hope fail and Høedt, as an artistic figure, be forever vanished from the Danish stage, I shall tell my contemporaries and the coming generations of actors and theatre-lovers that, like Winsløw, Høedt *was* an interpreter of character and that in both of them, through industry and study, genius had developed into real talent. With regard to both humanistic education and views on the scenic art they were rather different, and their respective careers were in complete contrast to each other; for Høedt began his with true triumphs; he carried all his colleagues away with him and brought fresh new life into our whole style of acting. But he had not yet reached his culmination when, discouraged by a puerile cabal, he disappeared from the boards and retreated into his work as instructeur, in which capacity he is probably in a position to exert a beneficial influence, but one which in no way compensates for the loss of his profitable example as a performing artist.

Both Winsløw and Høedt were believers in the *true* and the *natural,* but it appears to me that just as Winsløw strove upward from nature to the ideal, so there is in Høedt an inclination in the direction of a sharply defined reality, in accordance with the opinions he has set forth in his treatise *On the Beautiful.*

This chapter would attain an unseemly breadth were I to venture into a commentary on this extraordinary book. Besides, I lack the necessary philosophical foundation for it. Nevertheless, it has struck me by its boldness, aye, in many places even opened new prospects to my artistic gaze. His belief in the importance of the theatre for the development of the spirit has both edified and encouraged me, and with all my heart I concur in his enthusiasm for the stage and especially in his admiration for Shakespeare. There is no question but that in his interpretation of this great dramatist, as well as of the art of acting as a whole, Høedt takes a unique stand. The extraordinary development he knew how to give to a soul portrait of a character such as A. Munch's Solomon de Caus (the supposed discoverer of steam power) is, therefore, of special significance, since, to some degree, Høedt too has seen his theories misunderstood and denounced.

By the bye, this role contained one of the most difficult problems that ever confronted the tragic actor; namely, that of rising to pathos without passion, at the same time as he is infatuated with and lives for an idea which, in fact, lies outside the realm of poetry. He meets with offense and persecution, is driven to madness and atheism through his conviction of the infallibility of science, regains his reason at the moment of death only to bow before the will of the Almighty, and expires with the hope of being appreciated by future generations.

The manner in which this problem was solved must have surpassed the author's boldest expectations, and Høedt's masterly interpretation made an impression that is still preserved among those who love the dramatic art. This blending of nobleman and artisan in his physical appearance, combined with a mind that is totally absorbed by a world project, and a heart which hides the tenderest feelings of a father—in short, this whole historical and psychological figure—was indescribably captivating. And so, when at last his proud castles in the air—in the colossal umbra of which he had wandered for so long—collapse, and through their ruins the eternal light streams toward him, one feels more than pity and admiration: one is seized by the awareness of a profound and instructive truth.

The fact that Høedt has found bitter opponents on the very terrain where he fought for all that is noblest and best is only one more little page to be added to the martyrology of reformers. I continue to cherish the hope that he has not said his last words to us as an actor; but so as not to miss the pleasure of giving an ingenious talent well-merited praise, I will here briefly characterize his appearance on the Danish stage.

I have already discussed his excellent performance of Hamlet in relation to the most famous interpreters of this monumental role. It was almost inevitable that an interpretation as independent and a preparation as original as was Høedt's, of a character that has been illuminated from so many angles, would call forth expressions of highly divergent opinions; and since in his entire repertoire there was not a single role that had been differently conceived by a criticism that never gets involved in the creative process in art but judges solely on the basis of what is heard, seen, read, and consequently confirmed as a rule, most of his efforts were at first bound to call forth zealous protests on the part of dramatic conservatives. However, this did not prevent the fact that wherever he performed, his acting was always attended by success, and that what had at the first performances appeared to be uncommon, nay, almost bizarre, was soon regarded as the only proper interpretation and won increased applause with each presentation.

Even though Høedt's multifaceted talent exerted its influence on comedy as well as drama, it is still to be lamented that he was not granted the opportunity to appear more frequently in Shakespearean masterworks, the study of which seems to have been his main task. What has been lost to the public in this direction can be attested to by those who have heard him recite excerpts of Shylock and Richard III. The controversy as to whether this last work was

ANNA NIELSEN
Lithograph by Bærentzen after a portrait by Lehmann.
Det kgl. Bibliotek, Copenhagen.

NICOLAI PETER NIELSEN
Lithograph by Bærentzen.
Det kgl. Bibliotek, Copenhagen.

JOHANNE LUISE HEIBERG
This portrait study by an unknown photographer, ca. 1870,
shows her as an older woman.
Det kgl. Bibliotek, Copenhagen.

suitable for performance at a Danish theatre was a partial cause of the tension and resulting friction that ended by robbing Høedt of the desire to continue an activity to which he had so obviously been called! What a shame that what began as a purely literary quarrel should degenerate to such a degree and cause the stage to suffer a loss which is not only hard on the classical repertoire but affects the whole future of the dramatic art, which can as little as the other arts live by tradition alone, but needs to be refreshed by the contemplation of nature and rejuvenated by a tasteful combination of talent and genius.

FRU NIELSEN   FRU HEIBERG

I conclude this cycle of celebrities with two stars whose personalities and whole dramatic direction are so fundamentally different that a comparison can be thought possible only insofar as they have both shared equal fame and have each had a special importance for the Danish stage. When I produce from my memory the impressions which these rare artistes have left me, I involuntarily come to dwell longest on the deceased one, because a considerable part of her career already lies a generation back in time; because the genre she represented was neglected in a heedless fashion at the very time when her talent reached its culmination; and finally because the memory of the stage's most outstanding artistic creations is so fleeting that it becomes a sacred duty for the servants of thought to perpetuate the picture of excellence and for the *written word* to preserve the life that flowed from Anna Nielsen's lips and was during an entire generation the worthiest interpreter of the art of poetry.

Her years of apprenticeship were divided between the dramatic and the lyric stage: Dyveke, Ida Münster in *Herman von Unna,* and Stephanie in Berton's opera of the same name, were her debut roles, which soon allowed us to discover in the young blonde girl a hitherto unknown Romanticism which, combined with unaffected charm and a declamation totally divergent from the traditional pathos, within a short time developed into a significant talent. As a singer she possessed a flexible and expressive soprano voice which, especially as Agatha in *The Huntsman's Bride,* had a most poetic effect. However, great dramatic roles were soon to absorb her whole attention, halt her singing studies, and partially weaken her voice, which was later only adequate for the Heibergian *vaudevilles,* whose lively lyricism she knew how to bring out in such a way that a comparable effect has since then rarely been achieved.

In her interpretations of Valborg and Signe we saw the ideal of a Nordic romantic heroine come to life. But why do we especially call this eroticism *Nordic?* Was not the Greek Maria in *The Warriors of Miklagard* a creation of the same chaste, ethereal nature? Assuredly, but we call it that because, not only in Oehlenschläger's and Boye's historical plays, but in Schiller's and Shakespeare's dramas, and even in the light French comedy, she was what we inhabitants of the North understand a romantic heroine to be — less *in love* than *loving* and *lovable!*

One might think that such a conception of the nature of love, which accords so perfectly with our national aesthetic, would form a school and find profitable imitation. But it is precisely its deep poetry that makes it so difficult to grasp; for it must first and foremost emanate from the depths of the soul in order — in the midst of its apparent calm — to diffuse rays of warmth and life. Next, its forms consist less in external perfections than in the absence of certain imperfections for which technical language has only negative appellations, namely, *sentimentality, coquetry,* and *affectation.*

The great impetus that declamation has been given by Nielsen's talented recitation of verse contributed much to the interplay which arose between the *coryphées* of the stage and the younger writers of the time, whose first lyrical fruits were brought forth at the so-called "evening entertainments," and this with an enthusiasm that inflamed the listeners and fortified the authors. Chr. Winther, H.C. Andersen, and H. P. Holst won several garlands at these Olympic Games, and Anna Nielsen plaited the loveliest and finest ones! Who, indeed, can forget her inspired rendition of Hertz's "Battle of Copenhagen"? Even today when I read this glorious poem, her voice resounds in my ears!

Heiberg did away with these recitals, together with the sometimes abused summer performances. But the only thing gained by this was that nothing could appear on the stage without the Theatre management's approval; but the freer spirit that had generated so many excellent things — and had even given Heiberg's own *vaudevilles* their first chance — was lost, and it ought not to be left unsaid that without such summer plays, we would hardly ever have discovered that Winsløw and Wiehe were great talents.

Fru Neilsen's transition from the genre of romantic heroines to the roles of young wives and strong women was as abrupt as it was successful. A number of these roles belonged to French comedy, particularly that of Scribe, in which she, with true mastery, gave us many finely delineated characters, such as Lady Marlborough in *A.Glass of Water* and Cesarine in *The Comrades.* From her tragic repertoire, we must single out Queen Margaretha and Lady Macbeth as being truly magnificent. And when she finally entered a third phase by taking over older character roles, in her we saw *maternal love* represented in all its fullness and complexity; we mention the Queen Dowager in Delavigne's *The Sons of Edward,* Fru Warberger in *The Hunters,* Palle Blok's outspoken wife in *Riff-raff,* and finally — what is unforgettable — Griffenfeldt's mother in *The Princess of Taranto.* This role, which was not meant to have any great effect, in Anna Nielsen's hands gained a totally unexpected importance; for when, dissolved in tears, she threw herself at the King's feet in order to beg mercy for her condemned son, everything around this one tragic figure vanished, and this scene became the climax of the play.

After this triumph, she celebrated no more upon this earth. Great talents always pass away too early, but still at the right moment, if they do not outlive their own fame! May Anna Nielsen's memory be preserved for the remotest art-loving posterity, not for the brilliance that can surround a name, but as an example worthy of imitation for the scenic art, in the direction that most characterizes our national poetry: *Fidelity to Nature, Feeling,* and *Purity.*

Fru Heiberg's activity has been so extensive and her influence so extraordinary that it would require a separate dramaturgical work to describe fully this eminent *artiste's* importance for the Danish stage and, even more, to enumerate her victories. Our finest authors have based the effectiveness and success of their plays on her many-sided talent, and one of Denmark's most outstanding poets, who was also her husband, both lived and wrote for her.

She rightfully maintained her position as the Danish Theatre's prima donna and outshone everyone in the other branches of art who aspired to the title. In the figurative language of art one usually calls such an individual *a star,* and it is the same with the theatre's as with the firmament's shining orbs of this name: their rank is generally determined by their greater or lesser distance from our point of view. Fru Heiberg is still in our midst, and her radiance is still so dazzling that any *ifs* or *buts* from a critical observer would sound like an attack upon her great renown. I therefore venture—in the full recognition of all the first-rate performances this ingenious actress has given in several types of roles—to advance my personal opinion that her real calling was for the *gay, witty,* and *amiable* genre. On one thing all her admirers— both the sedate and the fanatical—soon agree; namely, that on the Danish stage no star has sparkled as strongly or as long as Johanne Luise Heiberg.

If we should still have in mind a comparison between these unequal dramatic magnitudes, it must be as *conceptions* rather than as *personalities.* Both have—though with different impressions—worked in comedy and tragedy. But the august Muses will brook no divided worship. We shall, therefore, refer each of their chosen priestesses to her respective altar, and, should our capital one day feel obliged to erect to the scenic art a worthier temple than the one that is now standing, I could propose the provision of vestibule adornments which—like those of the Théâtre Français—at once afford a symbol and a memorial. If we then give Thalia Fru Heiberg's facial features, those of Anna Nielsen ought to denote Melpomene.

X

A Retrospect

I end this book in a happier and lighter frame of mind than was the case with the first volume of *My Theatre Life*, and it is with joy and gratitude that I look back upon the vanished years, although for me as for so many others they have taken away many illusions.

On July 8, 1865, it will be half a century since I was appointed as a salaried pupil by Royal decree. At that time I had already had two years of dance training and performed solo parts as well as speaking and boys' singing roles. In 1823 I was named Royal Dancer, and the following year traveled to Paris (without stipend), whence I returned after a six-year sojourn to take over the leadership of the ballet, in which I performed for eighteen years as First Solodancer and which I later headed in the capacity of composer and instructor until October 1861. On my departure from the Royal Theatre, I have left behind a repertoire whose dividends in financial respects promise to fully compensate for the pension which, according to the terms of my contract, has been granted me as a reward for long and active service, and now bestows upon me a pleasant and independent existence in my old age.

However, since I do not intend to abandon myself to idle rest, and moreover hope, even from a distance, to be of some use to *the cause* which has absorbed my most vigorous efforts, this book will give evidence of the way in which I plan to make use of my time and my experiences. Even if it is intended for an audience composed of theatre-lovers in general, it might also contain several things that could serve as lessons to people in the various theatrical professions; but I cannot conceal the fact that it will chiefly interest those of my friends and patrons who, with forbearance and good will, have followed my steps along the pathway of art. It would give me great pleasure if it might help to clarify views about subjects which really belong only to "the joyous art," but, all the same, have their profound seriousness — at least for the person who has received them as a life work.

Another less joyful consideration intrudes upon the artist when, in spite of his merry calling, he appears as a writer, and especially as *a writer of history* within the little world in which he has moved for so long. That is to say, even with the most honest intention of showing everything from the brightest side, he cannot avoid mentioning mistakes, wrong ideas, aye, even individuals who in his opinion stand in the way of the progress of art. He is also liable to share the fate of the critics who are usually blamed for having praised too much or too little, or for having passed over true merit in silence. There are bound to be complaints, and I shall be prepared to eventually correct possible errors and make up for what is lacking. However, I venture to repeat what I have said in my introduction: my opinions are not unassailable, errors can be found in my theories, but I dare to state with a clear conscience that there is *not a single untruth in my account.*

On the question as to whether this volume of *My Theatre Life* is to be the last and to end a career which I have dedicated to the art of the stage, I must reply: I think so. I will compose no more ballets, since I do not wish to take up again the fight against deep-seated prejudice, both artistic and financial, and should I one day even allow myself to be tempted by more general scenic interests, it must be under conditions which no management in our turbulent time could accept; that is to say, I would demand guarantees against *narrow-minded malice.* Since my physical strength is still unimpaired and a bit of imagination also remains in me, although the years' experience and honest endeavor have helped to cool my natural impetuosity, every vexation affects my health more harmfully than it did in my younger years, and I frankly admit that the pure air and rural tranquillity of Fredensborg appeal to me more than dusty wings and everything that goes on in them. I will preserve my love of the theatre best by strolling in the beautiful allées and philosophizing about: LIFE, NATURE, and ART.

VOLUME
THREE

PART ONE
The Theatre Crisis and the Ballet

INTRODUCTION

WHEN I published the second volume of *My Theatre Life* in 1865, I was on the verge of turning from the busy pursuit of art to the quiet activity of reflection. The springs of the imagination, which had gushed so freely in my younger days, seemed to me, if not exactly dried up, then at least so reduced that I hardly dared hope to draw from their source again. I had not actually given up the idea of future compositions, but the essential self-confidence had vanished, and with it both desire and incentive; wherefore I believed that only dire necessity would compel me to reappear as a ballet-poet. How was it, then, that life and fire sprang anew into the all but extinguished embers?

I was convinced that the conditions with which the Royal Theatre, and the Ballet in particular, were confronted during 1860–1861 must shortly lead to an upheaval which would hit hardest the branch of art that I had cultivated and encouraged through such toil and trouble. The cold calculation that greeted every one of my undertakings in the interests of art was at last bound to paralyze my powers of invention and destroy my efficacy. Therefore I did not wish to renew my contract but accepted a three-year appointment as Intendant for the Stage at the Royal Theatre in Stockholm.

People viewed my departure from the Ballet as the signal for its decline and disappearance; but they were mistaken about its own vitality as well as the public's sympathy for this branch of the theatre. They were forced to admit that as matters now stood with our drama as well as our opera, the dissolution of a fully equipped branch of art would cause a severe weakness in the repertoire and make it easier than ever for the secondary theatres to offer competition.

However, Fate willed that, after a space of four years, I should attend a performance of *The Valkyr* and be astonished at the freshness and energy that were evident throughout the entire performance; and when at the same time I discovered a considerable increase in the number of younger talents—all of them products of Brodersen's excellent school—I could no longer doubt the future of the Ballet. I therefore readily accepted the proposal to return as guest for a brief sojourn to revive some of my older works.

There was general rejoicing among the ballet company, but with mounting public sympathy the old theatre talk about "the oppression of true dramatic art, the costliness of equipment, and the burden on the little, poverty-stricken country, etc."—which was echoed in the daily press through semi-official channels and muddied the water which had been intended to at least have a refreshing effect—was certain to be renewed.

Furthermore, an unfriendly star seemed to hover over our honest efforts, for scarcely had the subscription performances of a couple of ballets been completed and *The Kermesse in Bruges* been received with thunderous applause, than at only its second presentation the public's darling, Juliette Price, twisted her foot and after several months of suffering had to be declared incapable of ever again appearing as a *danseuse*. Her misfortune was regarded by "the malicious" as the *coup de grâce* for the entire genre. And true enough, there was not to be found among the soloists a single talent who could even remotely compensate for her loss—all the more as another and younger Juliette (sister of Fru Eckardt, *née* Thorberg), who possessed the grace and lightness of Psyche, had two years earlier sailed away "on light purple wings" !*

Thus matters stood when Etatsraad Kranold, Theatre Chief at that time, thought of celebrating His Majesty's birthday (April 8, 1866) with a gala performance, in accordance with the good old custom. For this occasion he asked me to compose a new ballet or, at any rate, a suitable *divertissement*. Now I had solemnly promised my Muse that I should never plague her again; besides, the success she had granted me with *The Valkyr* was to be considered our mutual farewell. Deep within me a warning voice said: "Stop before it is too late! " and I fancied myself armed against all temptations in the theatrical area.

But weighty motives urged, nay, almost forced, me back onto the road I believed I had quitted forever; namely, the necessity of assisting my fellow artists with a novelty that might yet hold interest and also the Chief's appeal to my loyal devotion by implying that my art might possibly provide entertainment for our sorely tried monarch. It was now simply a matter of complying with this request in a dignified manner and thinking of something that might at once contain a festive element and, if possible, an expression of patriotic feeling—without, however, touching upon the wound from which our fatherland still bled after the harsh Peace of Vienna.† After a sleepless night, during which I feverishly glided from one image to another, I finally settled for "good humor," which at the moment seemed the only thing that might offer any prospect of success; and since artistic life is an area where political frictions can least find food for thought or offense, I once again decided to transport ballet-lovers to the genial clime of Italy.

Rome! The classical soil of historic memories and artistic inspiration, to which one so readily returns having once been fortunate enough to set foot upon it. Even if tragic antiquity and the romantic Middle Ages have been

---

*A reference to the untimely death of the promising young dancer Juliette Thorberg.
† By which Slesvig and Holstéin were ceded to Germany (1864).

used as dramatic material to the point of satiety, the characteristic and richly colorful folk life continues to captivate poets and painters as well as readers and viewers; and whether art is made the core of the action or merely its frame, Italian life possesses a peculiar sorcery from which no one who has felt its effect can tear himself loose. The legends and omens that are attached to certain renowned places have special significance for the traveler, who cannot accept the idea of having seen them for the last time. He tosses a parting penny into the Fontana di Trevi and drinks of its waters in the hope of standing once again at its marble basin.

The confraternity which—before political conflicts sowed the seeds of national hatred among artists from different lands—produced scenes and groupings as interesting as they were beneficial to the heart and memory, furnished the opportunity for parties of welcome and farewell, which were celebrated near the bridge across the Tiber that leads the traveler northward and owes its historical curiosity to the victory of Constantine the Great over Maxentius. In ancient times it was called the Pons Milvius, but in the course of time its original name has been changed to

PONTE MOLLE

A going-away party for a Danish artist furnished me with material for a two-act ballet. From the libretto, one will be able to see that the subject of *Ponte Molle* belongs to that genre where external trappings and atmosphere are the predominant elements. The difficulties I had to overcome were not few in number. Not only did we lack our prima donna and our only bravura *danseur* (Hoppe); our musical notabilities neither could nor would undertake the kind of slapdash work which the staging for a specific day demanded. I therefore owed Messrs. Holm and Lincke much thanks for the talent and rapidity with which they provided me with music, at once melodious and effective. In Mmes. Stillmann and Petersen I found a pair of amiable Roman ladies; the rest of the talents at my disposal vigorously supported me, and a profusion of pretty and clever pupils gave off a fragrance of spring that augured well for the future.

The humorous conclusion of the first act (an episode from the youth of Cornelius and Kaulbach) and the going-away party itself, Alfred's "Goodbye," and the French military band, had a good effect. There was much to delight the eye, and a generous measure of gaiety, mingled with a bit of emotion. Fifteen well-attended performances in two months bore witness that this time too the Ballet had managed to combine the practical with the pleasant. By provisional engagement and an annually renewed contract, I was henceforth bound to my old sphere of activity, which in addition to bringing me joyous satisfaction also gave me deeper insight into the situation we shall call the theatre crisis.

I

The Theatre Crisis

THE 1866-1867 SEASON

THIS ambivalent and exhausting state of affairs dates from 1849, when the Danish Theatre was withdrawn from direct royal patronage and, by being placed under the Ministry of Culture, became an annual topic for discussion in the legislative assembly, the Rigsdag.

While some of our political economists thought of aiding the country's finances by reducing or simply canceling the usual subsidy, others thought of benefiting the State and Art by handing the National Theatre over to private enterprise as if it were just another manufacturing operation. The most varied opinions were voiced, and while, from time to time, an eloquent defense was heard, there appeared fanatical zealots who had chosen the Theatre as the propitiatory offering for our political blunders. Others, more practical and calculating, regarded art and poetry as luxuries altogether unsuited to an agricultural and cattle-raising nation. Envy of the glories of the capital and the finer pleasures of the intelligentsia also came into play, and, finally, the old saw about "the little, poverty-stricken country" was repeated over and over again!

I found myself called upon to publish a pamphlet on "Danish Theatre Affairs" and therein discussed several aspects of the situation that certainly ought to have opened the eyes of anyone who *wanted* a clear view of the matter. Through this little publication I hoped to open a more thorough discussion of the question and, if possible, set the tone in which such a discussion might properly be carried on. But this sort of polemic did not appear to suit our opponents, who obviously preferred to remain silent and wait until our arguments had vanished into oblivion.

This silence boded no good. Because of the Rigsdag's hostile attitude toward the Theatre's fairest demand (namely, an increase of the government's subsidy to keep down the price of each seat), Etatsraad Kranold (who was the fifth Theatre Chief since Heiberg's departure) wished to be relieved of the troublesome and highly unrewarding task of running an artistic institution, with the details of which he had gradually become familiar and where he had earned well-deserved recognition. He tendered his resignation, which was reluctantly accepted. But there now arose a curious situation. No one wanted the position which at any other time a host of aspirants would have clamored to fill. They approached a number of more or less qualified people, all of whom declined the honor, and were even so gallant as to ask if I might possibly feel inclined to accept such an appointment! I answered simply by referring to my latest publication—which, I dare say, had not been without some influence on the disinclination that was expressed with regard to the filling of this position—and I added that, even if I should believe myself to possess administrative skill and even if I were given the resources needed to carry out important reforms, as an artist and a man of feeling I would still find myself incapable of calmly undertaking operations that might cause the livelihood of those involved to suffer to some extent. Besides, I was too old to stand all the agitation and vexation, which are part and parcel of such a complex management, without endangering my health. Etatsraad Linde, Department Head in the Ministry of Culture, was temporarily appointed head of the Royal Theatre. One could not have asked for a more art-loving and humane Director than this honorable man; but the well-founded timidity with which he entered this sphere, which was so new to him, made practical assistance necessary. This he obtained to excess, since Theatre Secretary Berner, as Intendant, was given the direction of all artistic and economic affairs, while the Chief's position was reduced to that of reporter to the Ministry.

These circumstances, however, did not seem very likely to strengthen weakened confidence. Therefore the Rigsdag of 1866–1867 had no sooner opened than new projects appeared in the newspapers for the guidance of the Finance Committee in the whole matter of the Theatre. *Restrictions* and *economy* were now the order of the day, without any consideration for the survival of the theatre and the various branches of art as well as a whole class of industrious individuals. Among many people it had become a cliché that "little Denmark" could not afford to maintain *a Ballet!* Without further ado, then, Denmark was to shut down a costly and unprofitable royal prerogative! Moreover, this could easily be accomplished, as most of the company were not entitled to pensions. How nice, by the mere stroke of a pen, to cast people who had from childhood on devoted themselves to a strenuous profession out into the world without bread!

To have mentioned the liveliness and brilliance, in short, the *festivity* the ballet carries with it, would have been to add fuel to the fire. I had to face in turn both *Fædrelandet* and *Flyveposten* [literary—political weeklies] and prove with figures and facts that in order to fill its evenings, hold the attention of its audience, and remedy oft recurring difficulties, the Royal Theatre could not entirely dispense with the cooperation of the Ballet. These arguments, however, were wasted on those whose opinion, once expressed, is more precious to them than all the art in the universe; and in a pamphlet which he published, Overskou did not hestitate to declare ballet to be clearly harmful to true scenic art, and even that its music must be considered potentially fatal to the existence of opera! Even a century-old claim could not ensure Terpsichore her civic right on the Danish stage. She was merely a guest there! Now she was to be driven out. Wonderful Danish hospitality!

But better than all the statements that have long since been buried beneath the daily press's tons of waste paper was the effect of the revised edition and production of the ballet

Valdemar

In the first volume of *My Theatre Life* I made no secret of the difficulties which the realization of this historical subject presented, nor of the shortcomings and errors I detected even then, but which appeared to me to be inseparably bound up with prevailing notions about the nature of the ballet. The years have considerably modified my own views as well as those of the public, and, without weakening the effect of the whole, have helped to fuse the choreographic element with the mimed action. By observing my works from the auditorium, I have been able to detect weaknesses I failed to notice when I myself was performing the leading roles; in this way several dances won lively applause at the expense of illusion and probability and found their only excuse in virtuosity. But with bravura numbers in ballet it is the same as in opera: they belong to their own times and to the personalities by whom they are performed and eventually become obsolete, whereas those which denote character retain their freshness and significance.

After a thirteen-years' "rest," the ballet *Valdemar* was revived under the following circumstances. The desire to recall to life one of Galeotti's great ballets, while at the same time granting the music-loving public the pleasure of hearing Schall's ingenious composition, was most warmly recommended. The idea immediately appealed to me — all the more as I was the sole survivor from that era and remembered perfectly the production which had won such great renown. Discussion mainly centered around *Lagertha;* but on going through the composition scene by scene, I found — on my honor — that the greatest respect one could pay Galeotti's artistic memory would be to let the works so greatly treasured in his day rest beneath the laurel tree his admiring contemporaries had planted for his glorification. I am firmly convinced that were I to ask the present generation to accept the conventions according to which tragic ballets in the Italian mode operated at the beginning of this century, and should I reproduce with painstaking accuracy the episodes and dances which in these pantomimic dramas made so deep an impression on our grandparents, my risk would be all the greater, as the end result would either produce fatal ennui or degenerate into parody.

It goes without saying that I was forced to relinquish this ambitious task, and found myself called upon more than ever to present *Valdemar*, with the emendations which I felt to be absolutely necessary in this work of my youth. With an entirely new cast, in some ways stronger and in others weaker than the original, it was of the utmost importance that I focus attention on a number of places where it had not dwelt before, and also put the bravura dancing where it would better suit the situation and the character of the roles. The three kings came to lead the Torch Dance, which I inserted after the royal banquet and the War Dance. This composition, to Frøhlich's superb "Riberhuusmarsch," had a splendid effect and gave the whole a touch of the romantic Middle Ages.

In Gade, Svend Eriksøn found a portrayer who, for tragic intensity, fully belonged to high drama, while the title role could hardly have found a more chivalrous interpreter than Valdemar Price, who combined true enthusiasm with stately figure and loyal expression.

I had two considerable difficulties to overcome. One was the Conclusion of Peace, where the division of the Danish coat-of-arms involuntarily called to mind the dismemberment that had so recently struck our unfortunate fatherland! I tried to untie this knot by having Axel Hvide hand Svend a document, which he in turn refused to sign. The other problem consisted in finding a female personality who could endow the role of Astrid with the predominant interest the ballet needed—*now* more than ever. Juliette Price had given up all hope of regaining the strength and flexibility of her foot. She was now a pensioner. Among the *danseuses* there was not a single one who could, as they say, "carry" this ballet's most difficult and also most amiable role with any prospect of success. A lucky inspiration directed my gaze and my thoughts on a rather young pupil, who, together with her lovely natural aptitude for graceful dancing, possessed a rhythmic lilt and had in her fair physiognomy that inexplicable something which so early revealed itself in Jenny Lind.

When these pages one day come to light, time will have shown how far and upon what road the genius of the stage shall bring Betty Schnell toward the goal to which she seems called. The fact that she was specially gifted was apparent even in her childhood, when she performed small parts in the drama as well as the ballet, and Høedt had even given her declamation lessons in the expectation that she might one day become an important actress or, at any rate, find on the dramatic stage a more rewarding livelihood than the one offered by a branch of art that was constantly under attack.

But each of the august Muses would hold undivided sway. It was still uncertain whether the young girl's external gifts and resources would be able to meet the requirements of the spoken drama, which, moreover, contains a host of hidden nuances that neither reading nor direction can impart. They can, as a rule, be acquired only through human experience and especially by observations made in circles that are not accessible to everyone—least of all to the poor theatre child. On the other hand, in the ballet, just as in the idealistic realm of music, innate gifts can better assert themselves: and if they be further accompanied by natural grace, the proper training can develop them into real talent which without greater effort achieves a prominent place and secures for itself a brilliant career once it has succeeded in winning sympathies.

Just such a destiny seemed to smile upon little Betty, who had recently reached the age of sixteen and just been confirmed, when she emerged from the cluster of ballet pupils to win the public's unanimous acclaim on her first appearance. Many considered it quite daring for me to entrust such an important role to a girl who, in physical development as well as artistic skill, still lacked the needed maturity. But either *Valdemar* must remain in hibernation (thereby jeopardizing the future of the Ballet) or a decided talent must be lost to this branch of art. Here, then, was no room for hesitation; and the proposition that the mind rather than the body gives life and brilliance to scenic art would have to overcome all objections. And to be sure, [in Betty's portrayal] it was not the full-grown king's daughter but an amiable princess whose youthful infatuation for Valdemar was but weakly glimpsed through the love with which she followed her father. Her dancing, though graceful and correct, was far from possessing the strength and boldness that are the mark of virtuosity; but her eyes gave off sparks of electricity that, in joy or sorrow, prayer or decision, hope or fear, found its way to the heart. She held the interest of the audience in every scene in which she appeared, and under none of her predecessors had the role of Astrid made as profound and refreshing an impression as it did in Betty Schnell's graceful rendering.

In time, may this young *artiste* fulfill the promise she showed at her successful debut, and in whatever direction her talent develops, become an ornament to the Danish stage! It is my wish that, in life as in art, she may always find the *beautiful* united with *the true* and *the good!* In my memoirs she shall one day—I hope—with honor and delight come across this paternal blessing from *the Old Master*, when she is mature enough not to accept my words as just an ordinary compliment.*

The success of this new production exceeded even the boldest expectations and was due, I dare say, to the revision and the performance but, above all, to the national feeling, which sought and found refreshment in an enthusiastic meditation upon the days of honor and heroic deeds.

I choose to believe that this success was not without a certain influence on the Rigsdag's attitude toward the national artistic institution. This ballet, which in the course of the season played twenty-two times to full houses and reached its hundredth performance (a fact which did more than the patriotic loftiness of the subject to put new heart into the management), celebrated a real triumph. Talk of the abolition of this branch of art was silenced—at least temporarily—and the handing over of the Theatre to private enterprise was no longer considered at this time.

Thus the 1866–1867 season ended under fortunate auspices. The Theatre treasury had a not inconsiderable surplus, which helped the Ministry of Culture to win a rather humble victory. That is to say, the Royal Theatre, even if only for a year, was *for the time being* permitted to retain its state subsidy un-

*But see *infra:* "The 1869–1870 Season—*Cort Adeler in Venice*"; see also "The 1871–1872 Season" and later references, *passim.*

cut—on the condition, however, that a Commission be established to draw up a new plan for the operation of the Theatre, and until the aforesaid Commission had completed its work, no permanent appointments might be made. On the contrary: as many retirements as possible were to take place—preferably without pension.

THE 1867–1868 SEASON

CURIOUSLY enough, not a single expert was asked to join the above-mentioned Commission, and the Theatre's Intendant, Justitsraad Berner, who had practical experience and was well-disposed toward the personnel, barely received permission to take a seat in an assembly which, as I have said earlier, consisted of laymen, among whom (to my horror) I descried several of the Ballet's most decided opponents. However, the interests of art were but lightly touched on, and the negotiations, which moved slowly but unsurely forward, mainly centered around economic questions such as a perennial budget, a private pension organization, and a new theatre building.

I was now gradually lured back into the world I thought I had quitted forever. The brilliant ovation I was accorded at the jubilee performance of *Valdemar* showed me that I still stood high in the favor of the Danish public, and the confidence expressed by the *corps de ballet* shook to its foundations my intention of abandoning a profession that had to combat so much narrow-mindedness—not to mention malice!

I accepted the flattering invitation to enrich the repertoire once again with a work whose magnitude and importance might serve as a "trump card" in influencing the season's subscriptions for private boxes. At my beloved Fredensborg an idea I had long been mulling over fell into place and I came up with the libretto for

The Lay of Thrym

The battle which art as a whole must wage in the face of such leveling and crushing efforts involuntarily forces upon the imagination a picture of the conflict of the Æsir and the Giants, where Loke, the representative of sensuality and falsehood, alternately serves and betrays both camps. The subject—colossal in its forms, vague and disjointed in relation to the stage, discouraging by virtue of its profound allegorical meaning—was hopeless as far as lucidity was concerned. Heretofore, each of my attempts to assemble the various elements into a scenic whole had foundered upon the inadequacy of the means which the ballet, by its very nature, can command. And yet I felt that if Norse mythology were ever to be embodied on the stage, this must be done by means of a mimed representation supported by imaginative pictures and evocative music. It was obvious to me that Loke must be the most prominent figure in the ballet. But, above all, he must be seductive, to a certain degree amusing; and—if possible—like Milton's Satan, interesting! Sigyn's loyalty, which in the Edda is depicted only in a single sublime episode, I motivated by true love on Loke's part; and this relationship came to form a dramatic thread that bound together into a pantomimic plot Thrym's proposal, the fetching of the hammer, Ægir's feast, and the fall of the gods.

In Finn Magnussen and Grundtvig as well as Petersen's Norse mythology, but mainly in Oehlenschläger's magnificent epic, *Gods of the North* [*Nordens Guder*], one will find the sources from which I have drawn my subject. To be sure, learned antiquarians may have reason to reproach me for the liberties I have taken with the material; but artistic interpretation demands at once new outlines and groupings. How often has history itself been dramatized and romanticized! Then may one not dare to give the imagination a small margin of freedom when it comes to figures and situations belonging to legend? If our Christian speakers and poets can paint for us both Paradise and Hell with living colors—nay, even people them with creatures of highly different natures—surely it must be permissible to adapt the fictions of paganism according to the demands of the stage and to presume that these characters may to a certain degree help to revive interest in the writings which contain these national treasures.

Work was begun on the music in April 1867. Hartmann was enthusiastic about the subject, which was so well suited to the whole direction of his talent, and during the course of the summer I received the first two acts which, judging from the violin score, were in no way inferior to the loveliest passages of *The Valkyr.* Therefore, on this point I could put my mind completely at ease. However, it was a different matter with the décor and machinery, for it was obvious that without the element of fantasy in pictorial effects as well as astonishing transformations, my experiment in Nordic mythology would fail.

Ægir's castle by the sea, Thrym's subterranean hall, Loke's transformation, and the collapse of the Palace of the Giants were assignments which, to some degree, lay outside the range of scenery our Theatre customarily used. I therefore sought and obtained permission to summon from Stockholm the ingenious Swedish scene-painter Ahlgrensson and stage mechanic Lindström, both of whom were engaged by provisional contract after furnishing the requisite sketches.

Unfortunately, no fixed estimate could be given, and it appeared that, what with rising prices and our craftsmen's unfamiliarity with such subjects, material expenditures for carpentry and smith's work would make the Intendant and me wish we had not gotten so deeply involved. For a moment we even considered halting these costly preparations, and the Intendant proposed that these considerable expenses be spread out over a two-year theatre budget. But since neither of us could control what might happen during these years, I hastened to mount the first two acts, and upon seeing them performed by our fine *corps,* the spirit and confidence of the Theatre administrators were revived.

Since I had also been entrusted with the stage direction of the opera, I saw to the arrangement of Overskou's and Emil Hartmann's *The Elf-Maiden* [*Elverpigen*], which had but poor success in spite of many lovely moments. This was yet another sorry proof of how unrewarding our music composers' work is, when faced with a public that—like the critics—does not wait to hear a composition several times but mercilessly condemns it simply because it cannot instantly be grasped and hummed. It is then that I praise ballet music! At least it can be played until it has had a chance to catch on: in this way *A Folk Tale* once again brought Gade's and Hartmann's lovely melodies before a discriminating audience and came into its own after the eye had wearied of the fleeting [choreographic] images.

The multitalented Høedt, who could not be prevailed upon to resume his interrupted career as a superb character actor, also gave up his position as director for the dramatic stage and from now on would serve only as declamation teacher for pupils and theatrical aspirants. This was a decided loss for the repertoire, which had gained in aesthetic importance through his taste and insight. The loss was all the more severe as they sought in vain to find someone from among the male acting personnel to replace him.

However, a curious thing now happened. In their need they were forced to turn to *a woman;* indeed, a scenic notability—Fru Heiberg! But how strange it was to see this ingenious actress, now an old woman, whose grace and amiability had been the hallmarks of her artistic demeanor, going about giving orders with the mien of an official and a voice which had none of the magic that in an earlier day had so enchanted lovers of art. Two things, however, she had retained from her days of prosperity: her love of patronage and her marked antipathies. Under her direction rich variety was achieved in the dramatic repertoire, and the personnel as well as the press showed her the deference due such a high-ranking personage. All the same, no one else would have dared to change Oehlenschläger's *Palnatoke* into a melodrama, and if anyone else had allowed himself such balletic groupings and arrangements as those that were all too frequently to be found, he would have been severely castigated by the critics.

But what further distinguished this season was a host of silver jubilees. It actually seemed as if in 1842 a number of the Theatre's finest talents had arranged this rendezvous and now foregathered as deserving veterans. But it was reserved for Phister and me to celebrate the fiftieth anniversary of our scenic activity; *he,* from the moment he entered the theatre as a ballet pupil; *I,* from my debut as Adonia in *The Judgment of Solomon* on October 29, 1817. I shall never forget this last celebration. The King honored me with the golden Medallion for Meritorious Service [*Fortjenstmedaillen*],* and the assembled theatre personnel arranged a supper where I received heartening and encouraging proofs of the sympathy of my artistic colleagues.

---

* A very rare distinction only given in exceptional cases. Bournonville was the first person from the theatre world to receive it. The medal is today in the collections of the Danish Theatre History Museum in Copenhagen.

With renewed strength I now tackled my great work, and it came rapidly from my hand. The several months needed for the orchestration of the music were used by me for thorough rehearsals and by those newspapers inimical to the Ballet to inflate the expenses to an amount that was bound to strike terror in the hearts of our political economists. To be sure, the costs had exceeded our broadest estimates; but since malice had so exaggerated matters that it was believed 30,000 Rbd. would be insufficient, the 7000 Rbd. seemed downright modest in proportion. Consequently, it became important to have not only a superior performance and appreciative applause but, above all, many heavily attended performances which could fully compensate the Theatre treasury for the considerable expenditures. And once again the result answered to the most sanguine expectations. In the course of three months, *The Lay of Thrym*, which was given for the first time on February 21, 1868, accompanied by *The Norns* (a poetic Prologue by H. P. Holst), played twenty-five performances to full houses, despite the efforts made in several quarters to minimize the artistic value of the work and emphasize its weak points; for such weaknesses could naturally be sought and found in those places where the grandiose dimensions of the Edda exceeded the capabilities of the stage.

After all, how could one represent the figure of a giant [Thrym], who in one finger of his glove could furnish living space for Aukathor and his traveling companions, and at the same time imagine this colossus proposing to the delicately built Vanadis! And if Gerda† had taken after her family, how clumsy she would look next to her chosen bridegroom, Asa-Freir. Whenever sculpture has sought to depict the battle between the gods of Valhalla and the monsters (one of whom hugged the globe while the other's jaws stretched from the vault of heaven to the depths of the abyss), it has been necessary to reduce the Midgard Serpent and Fenris-Wolf to graphic proportions. This time, as always, the ballet had followed as much as possible in the footsteps of the fine arts. If we view the myth essentially as a creation of *poetry* and as a wide field for the imagination, it is the province of art as a whole—and not least of that branch where sounds and moods appear as moving pictures.

The fight in Ida Plain, which is alluded to only superficially, and *Ragnarok* [the Twilight of the Gods] itself would have demanded greater space, a larger *corps*, and, especially, greater expenditures than our local financial conditions would permit, and, withal, might have failed to produce the desired effect. This is certainly the place to add that, just as it would be grossly unfair of us to demand in our scenic productions magnificence such as that which the spectacles staged by the Great Powers have at their disposal, so too is it unreasonable to ask that all the requisites of a drama be present in a ballet, which genre has its own merits and shortcomings. Here, where the [spoken] word is missing, the past is explained by the present, and the latter, in turn, by the future. The situations generally follow each other in such rapid succession that it takes as much attentiveness and theatregoing experience as it does

† Daughter of the Giant Gýmir, and the most beautiful of women.

imagination and willingness to understand the plot. Like the tuneful singing numbers in an opera, what makes a mimed drama into a ballet are the dances and picturesque groupings, the rich variety and proper use of which present the greatest difficulty for the composer and are generally overlooked by the critic who, pleading his unfamiliarity with choreographic technique, exclusively uses the standards of the drama in judging a ballet.

Thor, Thrym, Freia, Loke, and Sigyn were undeniably the characters who formed the core of the plot and, moreover, found superb interpreters. Valdemar Price gave a classic picture of the Ás, Thor; Gade won for the Giant, Thrym, some moments of striking comic effect; Fru Eckardt's noble figure was perfect for the Nordic Goddess of Love; Scharff's portrayal of Loke's serpentine nature was masterly; while, as the representative of pure innocence and loyal devotion, Betty Schnell played the role of Sigyn with indescribable grace from the first moment, when like a butterfly she glides into Vola's rock cave, to the solemn hour when she holds the bowl beneath the poisonous snake in order to catch the venom that drips from its jaws into Loke's eyes. Around these figures was grouped a host of supernatural beings from the race of the Æsir as well as the Giants, and the poem avoided any comparison with the earthly descendants of Asker and Embla.

Though I must frankly confess that in this chosen subject there was to be found more than one stone which I did not have the power to lift, I still feel that I made decided progress in the working out of details as well as the representation of Ægir's feast, the fetching of the hammer, and the two principal characters, Loke and Sigyn.

Upon seeing his work again after a space of several years, the poet, being no longer ensnared in the misty veil of self-interest, can judge fairly well whether it is more or less successful. Therefore, when I remember the brilliant triumph accorded *The Lay of Thrym*, I am flattered that, for me as well as for Hartmann, it was not entirely undeserved.

THE 1868-1869 SEASON

THE Theatre Crisis seemed to have taken on a chronic character. The establishment of the Danish stage as a State institution had become a recurrent theme for debate in the Rigsdag, and the selfsame declarations that were set forth, refuted, and confuted in one session were heard, unaltered and unendingly, in the next—with one slight modification, however: the abolition of the Ballet was no longer so vehemently urged.

The announced draft of a new Theatres Act was anxiously awaited, and the Theatre found itself operating under a provisional law, which could have nothing but a harmful influence, if not directly upon its temporal, then at least upon its spiritual existence. In view of the composition of the chosen Committee, little could be expected with regard to the first point, and even less with respect to the last; for the whole prolonged, lengthy, and relatively ex-

pensive task only managed to produce an economic treatise wherein the interests of art were completely ignored, while the guarantees which had heretofore numbered the Royal Theatre's personnel among civil servants were
abolished. The shaky ground on which this particular draft bill was built,
and the complicated form in which it was brought before the legislative assembly, furnished abundant opportunity for objection, in the Rigsdag as well
as the daily press, and after a long and partially unproductive debate, the bill
was denied a second reading.

It would be treasonous to disclose all the weaknesses inherent in artistic
and theatrical life in general. But when it comes to reforms in any area whatsoever, it is not simply a question of destroying existing conditions only to
create new ones, but, above all, of cautiously clearing away the obstacles that
block improvement. Such changes mainly consist in too little insight and a resultant lack of judgment on the part of the management, which, because of a
lack of real experts, listens to outside advice. To these defects must be added
the demands that are made by the public and the press. They ask for performances which in quality as well as quantity can stand on an equal footing
with those of the finest theatres abroad; but whenever recognition and compensation are mentioned, there are always outcries about our humble financial circumstances and "the little poverty-stricken country"! And yet our artists in the various métiers set greater store by an—in bourgeois respects—
humble but respected position in their native land than they do by the fame
and high salaries that foreign nations shower upon their celebrities (who in
most places form a distinct social class), for they regard themselves as performers in the service of Culture and take pride in exercising their vocation.
But in addition to the outstanding talents there are supporting performers
from whom special skill, a suitable bearing, and unlimited working hours are
demanded. These people, who make up more than two-thirds of the total
company, are rather poorly paid, having so-called nonregulation salaries, with
arbitrary notice of dismissal and without the right to a pension!

On the whole, the public only has an eye and feeling for artists of the
first water, but they hardly ever suspect that the latter have usually come up
through the ranks, where countless fine talents are stifled in the midst of their
development by dejection and financial hardship. Sometimes the sympathy
which a new talent arouses is used in one bravura part or another; but when
the first impression has faded and attention is focused on another rising star,
what has already been performed is regarded as an audition and, according to
the aforesaid Commission's draft bill, the definite appointment is dependent
on the opinion of the Rigsdag!

Is a legislative and money-granting assembly, then, to sit in judgment on
artistic matters and to administer theatre affairs? And how can these dual
functions be combined with the practical, sober-minded view of the country's
material needs? I will not for a moment mention the *Ballet* and its detail, for
should a member of the Rigsdag—no matter which side of the hall he may be-

long to—venture to declare himself to be attracted and edified by some mimed choreographic presentation, he would be laughed to scorn by the entire assembly and, perhaps, even be accused of frivolous infatuations. Let us suppose the Theatre's lyric stage was fortunate enough to obtain a prima donna who combined dramatic talent with a lovely and flexible soprano voice, an attractive appearance, personal refinement, and, above all, good health that defied the vicissitudes of the climate—in short, who possessed all the qualities we consider ourselves entitled to demand from an *artiste* who might be able to give our opera the exhiliration it has always lacked. I wonder what the Finance Committee would say to the price that a second-rate French provincial city, for example, would gladly pay for such an acquisition, namely, 30,000 francs (about 21,000 Kroner)?

Next to the parliamentary fights, the Royal Theatre's worst thorn in the flesh is the hypercritical attitude which is transmitted to the public through the newspaper reviews and which, while it does not exactly help to purify taste to any great degree, still exerts a weakening influence on the ability to "enjoy oneself." This last expression—which despite our Theatre's ingenious motto, "Not for pleasure alone," means the same thing as to abandon oneself to the poetic illusion, be it with laughter or with tears—is certainly unknown to those who must rush out the minute a play has ended, sometimes a little before, in order that same night to write a critical article which on the following morning can acquaint people with what they are permitted to enjoy.

One must not think that I, like so many other artists and writers, wish all critics would go to Hades. On the contrary, I consider them to be as necessary to art as the shadow is to the body. But when one takes into account the time and effort that are required to produce any work of art whatsoever, one certainly dares to ask those *Aristarchs,** who render unappealable judgments, to take a closer look and be a little less hasty in passing sentence.

If the Royal Theatre were not so fortunate as to possess an older, unchallenged repertoire, it would have a hard time producing a single newer work that had been shown unconditional mercy before the judgment seat of the critics or had been recommended to the public by them, whereas performances at the secondary theatres are given ample support and praised in articles an ell long. The yardstick that is applied to the aesthetic obligations of the National Theatre really aims at nothing less than the rejection of anything that does not come under the heading of "masterpiece"; and since the latter must be "Danish originals" into the bargain, they would hardly be able to present *one*, much less *seven*, acceptable performances a week—all the less as our older writers and composers wince at having to endure this "trial by water," while the younger authors turn to the secondary theatres, where parody and farce are accepted as compensation for noble pathos and true comedy. Indeed, the concept of "theatre" stands in danger of becoming so warped that

---

*This name, which has come to signify a harsh critic, is derived from that of the Greek critic and grammarian, Aristarchus (220–143 B.C.).

the Danish stage must either follow the tide or, in time, find itself deserted by the whole younger generation!

And yet, to judge from the frequent attendance, public interest seems to be on the increase, and it should be remarked that a couple of decades ago, when our famous writers furnished new pieces every year and our spoken drama, in particular, stood on a par with the Théâtre Français (which was then in full bloom) and also the Burgtheater in Vienna, the actors often played to sparsely filled houses and the average profits were considerably lower than they are nowadays.

I dare say the greatest danger to the Theatre's future lay in the provisional state in which it had been suspended for so long a time, and in the ever recurring question as to whether it should continue as a State institution or be handed over to private industry. In any case, it was well on the way to becoming an outright commercial enterprise.

Things had begun to come alive in the spoken drama. M. Goldschmidt furnished two original pieces, which were both applauded. Dingelstedt's adaptation of Shakespeare's *Winter's Tale* won but scant approval despite several interesting acting debuts; among others, a guest star, the Norwegian actress Fru Gundersen, was most effective in some brilliant moments. A couple of minor comedies provided the opportunity for some superb ensemble acting. But the season's prize was carried off by our ingenious old Hertz with *Three Days at Padua* [*Tre Dage i Padua*], which passed undismayed through a Purgatory of unfair criticism and at the same time provided true enjoyment for the public and abundant profits for the Theatre treasury.

The operatic repertoire was arranged with great circumspection; for in addition to the universally marketable subjects, *The Pasha's Daughter* [*Paschaens Datter*] by Heise, *The Magic Flute* with a text adapted from the French, and, finally, new productions of *Hans Heiling* and *The Huntsman's Bride,* were also to be staged. For variety in a lighter style, they had revived one of the many *syngestykker* that had so undeservedly been set aside; and since the order in which they intended to present the works had been disrupted by recurring obstacles, the season's lyric activity had to begin with *The Crown Jewels,* which was all the more risky as the revival of this *opéra-comique* had already been the subject of a number of bitter, almost fanatical, newspaper attacks half a year before. The music, which is unquestionably one of the loveliest of Auber's compositions, received its due as far as the performance is concerned. Viewed from a historical standpoint, the text is, no doubt, slightly absurd; but as romantic intrigue it is a little masterpiece of piquant musical situations, which has maintained its position throughout Europe. But the opposition of the press, whether it was prompted from outside or rooted in insuperable prejudice, was voiced in so vehement and unanimous a fashion that otherwise benevolent audiences did not venture to lift a finger for even the most brilliantly performed bravura spots. By only the third performance, attendance had fallen off considerably, and this lovely work, upon which so much care had been lavished from every quarter, was now laid aside or, more properly, *enshrined.*

Despite every effort, it was impossible to present the promised operas until quite late in the season. Even Heise's opera, though the score had been lying on the Theatre's shelves for three years, had to experience a year's delay, while *The Master Mason* and Du Puy's unfading *Youth and Folly* upheld the right of the *opéra-comique* in the face of those who wished to see dialogue removed from the lyric drama. However, *The Jewess* [*Jødinden*] and *The Huguenots* [*Hugenotterne*] gave a very promising debutante (Frk. Doris Pfeil) the opportunity to display her glorious vocal talents with great success, and Hartmann's lovely composition, *Little Kirsten,* once again took its place among our national treasures.

At last *The Magic Flute* appeared and, by its divine wealth of melody combined with—given our circumstances—an especially satisfactory performance, scored a genuine success. One will see from this that the operatic repertoire, although quite rich, did not offer anything really new. It was the same with the Ballet, which, in light of the expense of the décor for *The Lay of Thrym,* had to content itself with reviving older works.

Bellman and *Festival in Albano* respectively celebrated their one-hundredth performances. *La Ventana* and *The Prophecy of Love* were rejuvenated by Betty Schnell. *Far from Denmark* received new cadets. *Ponte Molle* was given only a couple of times, since the military band involved expenses that made the Theatre treasury cringe. Finally, *Valdemar* continued to run its usual victorious course with unimpaired vigor. *The Sleepwalker,* that favorite ballet from my first appearance in 1829, was restaged and beautifully performed. But, even though I had adapted the dances to meet the demands of the present, it no longer appealed to the younger generation. Wronged and eventually triumphant Innocence was a worn-out theme, and the idyllic life which forty years ago had had such a refreshing effect on people's dispositions now appeared altogether too polite and gentle for our "more worldly-wise" public.

The season's financial dividends were richer than ever. This phenomenon was accounted for in highly different ways. Some pointed to the high price of grain, others to the increasing masses of people in the capital, and still others to the influx of travelers, especially via the railroad. Finally, with a certain childish delight, people indulged in the thought that public attendance was mainly the result of an uneasy sympathy for an artistic institution that was threatened with destruction by the Rigsdag's attitude toward theatrical affairs.

The Crisis had actually reached alarming proportions, and the curious thing was that whichever way the Theatre leaned, it was bound to suffer injustice at the hands of "the uncompromising"; for if it had poor business it deserved no subsidy at all from the State, and if it took in a profit it had no need of one. Pros and cons were debated and weighed to the point of triviality, and what especially helped to rule out all artistic considerations was the

Theatre Commission's unsuccessful attempt to show how a good theatre could be established and *run* at low cost in our demanding and expensive times. In order to bring about the realization of this idea, permanent appointments would have to be dropped, pensions compensated for by annuities in return for deductions from salaries, and contracts made with the outstanding members of the company, while the supporting personnel would be left to an arbitrary fate. Finally, all existing and partially guaranteed Assistance Funds were to be absorbed into a single, so-called Support Organization under the name of *Old Age Support.* In short, the door was left wide open for the prospect of a *private enterprise!*

At the same time there also appeared a plan for a new Theatre building to replace the formless monstrosity that disfigured the loveliest quarter of the capital and elicited compassionate sneers from all travelers. And yet, one could not suppress the thought that, before this new Temple of Art could be completely erected, the supply of good talent would have ceased, and that for material considerations such talent would consider itself just as well placed in the secondary theatres or even prefer any other career to serving an establishment that rewarded its deserving members with a breadless old age.

The chairman of the Theatre Commission, Etatsraad Krieger, a parliamentary talent of the first water, would have been able to produce and carry through a better bill had he not been unsympathetic to all independent consideration of our theatre affairs. Moreover, he was obviously influenced by the Heibergian system, which, in spite of Overskou's panegyric, set personal opinion above the recognition of true ability. The government felt obliged to support the proposal, despite the opposition it met with in both the press and the Rigsdag. On the one hand, it was thought that *too little* was being demanded, while on the other it was alleged that they were asking for *too much!* Professor Høedt treated the matter in an interesting pamphlet, but posed the alternative a bit too sharply as "fix oder nix" ["all or nothing at all"]. He received small thanks for his efforts, which only produced an unedifying polemic in which the actual question was, as usual, simply overshadowed by personalities.

As I have earlier stated, the bill was denied a second reading, and, with the confidence of next year seeing the proposal appear in an improved and — if possible — abbreviated form, the usual subsidy was granted (at least for a year) on the express condition that during this interval no conclusive decisions were to be made, with regard to either appointments or other measures pertaining to the Theatre.

Thus we were thrown once again into the paralyzing uncertainty which had plagued the Theatre for a number of years. One thing was evident from the negotiations that had taken place: the pension system was our political economists' worst stumbling block, and the Theatre must either bring itself to pay much higher salaries or, from its own resources, provide for the personnel who had served their time.

The Private Pension Fund, which in 1863 had been established for the benefit of the many persons who stood on the list of nonregulation salaries, did not at present seem able to fulfill its obligations, and in the Commission's report its liquidation and dissolution were recommended, while the manner in which they later intended to meet the demands of economy and humanity remained undecided.

Whether the salaries given are large or small, with or without guarantees for old age and infirmity, one may question if there will still be enough people who, either out of improvidence or passion, vanity or the need for an additional source of income, will set forth upon the path of the theatre and art? Yes! Even if it should stand in danger of being disgraced, it will always be a source of amusement and a good means of whiling away the time! Furthermore, there will never be a lack of speculators who, even if they can foresee bankruptcy, still find an inexplicable attraction in the idea of carrying the scepter in such an imaginary realm. Under such circumstances, the institution we alternately call "The Royal Theatre," "The National Stage," and "The Danish Stage" would cease to merit these names. The Drama would lose the upper hand in its rivalry with the secondary theatres; the Opera would be forced to turn to foreign talent. And what of the Ballet? Aye, even if it were dislodged from one stage, it would reappear on another—but in what form!!

I cannot ask the friends of the Ballet, let alone its opponents, to discover the same phenomena that I do in the art to which I have seriously devoted my talents. It would be redundant to plead the *positive* aspects of the Ballet's cause with the former group of people, and futile to justify them to the latter. However, in *negative* respects, the following arguments might prove to be persuasive for both parties:

The Dance, be it as social entertainment or on the boards of the stage, reflects the taste and moral standards of a people and often furnishes a striking picture of its cultural level and social conditions. Now, since people in this country still have a certain tendency to imitate foreign customs and manners, the disgusting *cancan* might easily worm its way into our midst, confuse the notion of seemly gaiety, and bring in its wake excesses—with unpredictable results.

Though for more than a century the ballet has been fused with our national conceptions of beauty, people have wished to deny it its birthright! But, indeed, what art form has not, to a greater or a lesser degree, originated abroad? Our whole musical trend is either German or Italian; Shakespeare and Calderón are our masters for tragedy, while Molière was Holberg's model; and even though the ballet, like the comedy, is of French origin, our present productions in this branch of art are so totally divergent from everything being presented at foreign theatres in mimic-choreographic respects, that everywhere people speak of "the Danish Ballet" with laudatory recognition. And yet its hard-working and skilled *corps* was thoughtlessly overlooked in the Theatres Act! Our noble Muse, the very sister of lyric poetry and the drama, treated like a concubine's child, without the right of inheritance!

In this state of distress, I issued a call to the patrons of the Ballet in order to obtain, through their generous assistance, the establishment of a Private Pension Fund for those of my colleagues who are on the list of nonregulation salaries—and, unfortunately, they are not few in number. This undertaking made the most wonderful progress and, hopefully, will in time open more favorable prospects, not only for the *corps de ballet* but for similar organizations within the realm of the theatre.

THE 1869–1870 SEASON

JUST as it had the year before, the debate concerning the Minister of Culture's budget produced the same observations and proposals. A revised Theatres Act was submitted and a committee was appointed for its discussion, thus opening the prospect of an indefinite prolongation of the ominous crisis.

Without any great expectations of a better state of affairs, the season opened; and, since my work included both the opera and the ballet, I had a lot to do. Heise's *The Pasha's Daughter*, with a text by Henrik Hertz, was presented at the start of the season and won unanimous approval. Even though it was not likely to become a box-office play, it should be noted that it was the only opera of domestic creation in a number of years to enjoy a run of so many well-attended performances. Mozart's immortal masterwork, *Don Giovanni*, was presented in a new *mise-en-scène* on his birthday (January 27), while Richard Wagner's *Lohengrin* was readied for performance.

The attention this eccentric composer has aroused in the world of music, by both his compositions and his polemical writings, allows no lyric stage to ignore his works. Therefore, the Theatre administration, zealously urged on by our most respected musicians, decided to offer the Danish public a taste of this so-called "Music of the Future." Since *Lohengrin* seemed to be the work most suitable for introducing us to this genre, it was chosen in preference to *Tannhäuser*, which demanded greater ostentation and whose action, while as static as that of the former, had less romantic body.

In order for *Capelmester* Paulli and me to become better acquainted with the musical and scenic arrangement of this piece, we were to be sent abroad to attend rehearsals and performances. But where? I entered into a correspondence with the administrators of the Berlin Opera and with Richard Wagner himself in Lucerne. I received an especially affable letter from him, informing me that the opera in question was scheduled for performance in Munich on May 28, 1869, and that every possible courtesy would be shown us by the authorities there. The flattering reception we were given, as well as my impressions of all the things I heard and saw in artistically rich Munich, I have described in a little travel sketch. At the conclusion of this season, we shall learn how the opera was received by our public.

While the difficult rehearsal of these astonishing harmonies and dissonances went on, the Theatre undertook a little excursion into the realm of melody by reviving Boïeldieu's charming operetta, *Jean de Paris*. But whether it was because expectations were fastened on a more grandiose genre, or because the performance lacked the needed finesse; whether a little "backstage gossip" had mingled poison in the sweet drink, or a glance into Overskou's handbook had informed the critics that in its day this little *syngestykke* had survived only a short run of performances — suffice it to say that it met the same fate as *The Crown Jewels:* people stayed away, and all our work was for nought.

The marriage of the Crown Prince to the daughter of the King of Sweden-Norway, and the ceremonies that marked their festive entry, caused the liveliest stir among the capital's populace, and the mood of the public was in no way disturbed by the highly unfavorable weather. About this time, an archaeological congress was meeting in Copenhagen, and its members were invited to attend the gala performance given at the Royal Theatre in honor of the royal nuptials. A little occasional piece, *Paternal Uncle* [*Farbror*] by H. P. Holst, served as a curtain-raiser, and it was once again the Ballet that represented the Danish stage before a numerous circle of different nationalities.

The Valkyr, which had been revived after a number of years' rest, celebrated a triple triumph since it painted for the foreign antiquarians the prehistoric North, while speaking a language they could all understand. Finally, it gave them a clearer idea of this art form than they had brought with them from abroad — an acknowledgment they gave us not only verbally, but through testimonials in the reports which were later published about their unforgettable stay in Denmark.

It seemed, by the way, that during this season the Theatre treasury profited most of all from the revival of older works, especially in the dramatic sphere. Holberg's *Lying-in Room* gave striking proof of this by surviving an even longer run of heavily attended performances than it had in the heyday of his plays. Among the few interesting new works a curious thing happened: namely, two original comedies, one of them Danish, the other by a Norwegian author, emphasizing the follies and ridiculousness of their respective countries with keen and not so keen satire, met with violent opposition. Henrik Ibsen's *The League of Youth* [*De Unges Forbund*], transplanted onto Danish soil and supported by masterly ensemble acting, scored a great success, to the small delight of the sensitive Norwegians, who avenged themselves by presenting *The Comedy of a Genius* [*Geniets Comedie*] at Christiania. This piece, which had but poor success in Copenhagen, met with great sympathy from the Norwegian public; for the whiplashes fell hot and heavy on the Danish critics, and the latter, of course, had not had one good word to say about the original play. This anonymous author was the only Dane who could stand up to Norwegian writers in the year following Hertz' death; for Munch, Bjørnson, Ibsen, and Magdalene Thoresen sustained most of the dramatic repertoire.

The words of a member of the Swedish Parliament, "I thank Heaven that every day I grow wiser," uttered when someone reproached him for having diverged from his earlier principles, might not be inappropriate with respect to the inconsistency with which the resolutions I stated in the second volume of *My Theatre Life* have been carried out. I indicated, decisively and simultaneously, both my retirement from theatre activity and the element of impracticability that lay in ballet themes such as Eddaic legends and Cort Adeler.* Nevertheless, I once again took up the thread I had let fall, and revived both myself and these two subjects! Above I have stated the reason for that first important step. Danger threatened; the battle was at hand. I had to appear at the breach and not abandon my post until every hope of defense had been lost. In *The Lay of Thrym*, I have shown how the Nordic pantheon was revealed to my imagination; and, even though I must admit that I did not achieve the goal I had set for myself, I have no reason to regret my efforts in this direction.

From my tender years, Cort Adeler has appeared to me, in both dramatic and plastic respects, as a sterling figure surrounded in singularly romantic fashion by the old majestic grandeur of Venice. I dwelt, enraptured, on his daring duel with the Bassa, and nothing has been able to weaken the impression and the belief I still hold that the reputation for courage and seamanship which he earned in the most distinguished navy of his day—and which caused the King of Denmark to bestow upon him, a commoner, a rank as high as that of Admiral-General—must have been well deserved. One of the hallmarks of modern historical criticism is that it tends to excuse, nay, even justify, tyranny and deceit, while it attempts to drag the finest episodes of virtue and valor down into the realm of triviality. Great world events are, no doubt, embellished with anecdotes, and, viewed at a distance, probably surrounded with a poetic nimbus that cannot withstand microscopic investigation. But just to give an example: whether or not it can be proven physically that Tordenskjold† could not have swum with heavy sea boots on his legs and a steel blade between his teeth, he remains the same immortal hero whose name shall be remembered as long as the Danish flag waves and Danish hearts beat high for honor and our native land.

In *Far from Denmark* I had saluted the Danish navy during peacetime; but a warship ought to appear in battle against the enemy. Our fraternal sympathies for a neighboring country did not permit the recollection of our mutual conflicts, but surely a victory over the Turks could not arouse indignation; and even though I was not blind to the problems involved in the representation of a naval battle, I still hoped to provide a striking finale by showing the boarding of a vessel.

---

*This famous sailor-of-fortune, born in 1622 in Norway, served successively in the Dutch, Venetian, and Danish navies. He died in 1675 at Copenhagen on the eve of an expedition against Sweden.

† Peder Tordenskjold (1691–1720) was a naval officer noted as much for his reckless courage as for his stunning victories in the last years of the Great Northern War against Charles XII of Sweden. Entering the service as a teen-age cadet, he died (in a duel) an admiral. The incident here referred to is one of many (possibly apocryphal) stories told of him.

CORT ADELER IN VENICE

The libretto for this ballet will show how I used the historical material and to what degree the impressions Venice made upon me influenced my understanding of situations during the Golden Age of this Republic. This important work had its premiere on January 14, 1870. It was provided with excellent music by Heise and magnificent set decorations by Ahlgrensson, and scored a success that was confirmed by sixteen performances during the first season. However, its drawing power could not compare with that of *The Lay of Thrym.*

For one thing, the performance did not fully come up to my expectations; for another, it lacked the finish which the virtuosity of the dancing must perforce give the ballet. The boarding, a feature on which I had pinned my hopes, failed to have the desired effect, because the setting up of the ship took an inordinately long time, while the deck space was too limited for the action of the battle—which was also interrupted by an abortive ventilation system that drove all the gunpowder smoke out into the auditorium instead of up to the air shafts in the ceiling, as had been intended.

However, what mainly contributed to oppressing the mood in the course of the ensuing performances was a most untimely (for the Theatre's interests) historical dissertation by Professor Becker, published after his death by the Royal Librarian Bruun, which painstakingly stripped my hero of the fame he had retained for two hundred years. It was, to put it mildly, an unfortunate occurrence that this work should be published at exactly the same time as my ballet was performed; and its result was instead of concerning themselves, as usual, with the greater or lesser value of my work, the critics only expressed regret at the loss of the halo that had shed its rays upon the hero's name, his birthplace, and his illustrious position.

I felt called upon to name the sources from which I had drawn my material, and in a detailed article attempted to defend the right to retain our illustrious memories unchallenged. But the blow had been struck, and the poison of doubt, although counteracted, had left behind a weakness that partially robbed the plot of its patriotic core; and since Cort Adeler's deeds were henceforth to be considered a myth, the whole thing was reduced to nothing more than an imaginary picture. The dances in the first and second acts were applauded in lively fashion, but the color I had striven to impart to my two principal Nordic figures, in contrast to the Venetian nobility and life in the Turkish navy, went as good as unnoticed, while the finer psychological features were, as usual, appreciated by only a very small circle.

In *Cort Adeler,* too, Betty Schnell furnished an endearing picture as the young noblewoman. But, alas! Her physical powers were not sufficient to withstand, even with adaptations, the exertions that her prominent position entailed; and though I had made a special effort to stress her mimic talents at the expense of the dancing, I noticed, particularly during this last season, how her breathing—that element so vital in both dancing and singing—gave out and paralyzed her movements. Continued activity along the path she had trodden with such great expectations would have endangered her life! Her earlier dramatic training now came to her aid, and while she abandoned the ballet, she retained the qualities and the sympathy which were partly innate and partly the results of good training. Her debut in the spoken drama was in every respect a success. But even though, year after year, she has proven herself to be one of our finest actresses—principally as an ingénue—it remains a question as to whether Thalia has gained from her more than Terpsichore has lost.‡

At last, toward the season's end, Wagner's opera *Lohengrin* appeared and succeeded beyond expectations. The performance was altogether as respectable and the scenic equipment as splendid as that at any major theatre in Germany. It was therefore a genuine pleasure for me to inform Wagner of this fact, and he replied that he was delighted to know that in Denmark people had now become acquainted with German art and German music. I could not stomach this dose of arrogant ignorance, but answered—in French, of course—that while German *politics* were certainly not welcome in Denmark, we had been raised on German music; for Gluck, Mozart, Haydn, Weber, Beethoven, and Mendelssohn had taught us to love it, and these great masters were chiefly responsible for the whole direction our music had taken. With this, our correspondence ceased forever.

The Theatre treasury's considerable profits contributed significantly to the fact that the Rigsdag accepted the proposal of a five-year budget with the hitherto-received yearly subsidy (50,000 Rbd.) uncut, and an Act confirmed that a new Theatre was to be erected and completed by September 1874.

With this, one might well consider the Theatre Crisis to be over—at least for the time being. But even if it betokened external peace, the corroding effects of the Crisis continued within the sphere of the stage. The whole younger generation of artists saw themselves placed in a precarious position: for, along with the prospect of a pension, there vanished all the reassuring arrangements that were previously intended to secure the artists' services for the Royal Theatre and provided them with a respectable social position as compensation for a salary that was meager compared to wages in other countries. It is beyond question that if nowadays a Ryge or a Nielsen were tempted to give up a scientific or military career out of love for the dramatic art, they would think first before accepting such conditions.

In artistic respects, the Crisis is far from over. The spoken drama, which more than the other two branches of art is called to give the Danish stage the character of a National Theatre, and upon which special attention is focused, suffers from the lack of good productions, original Danish works as well as good translations. If to this is added the continuously decreasing taste for the serious and the fact that the comic element is, more and more, taking on the

‡ Thalia would seem to have emerged the victor, since Betty Schnell (later Betty Hennings) is remembered chiefly as the first interpreter of Nora in Ibsen's *A Doll's House* (1879).

character of farce and caricature and is therefore reclaimed by the secondary theatres, there remains but a limited field in which our actors can work, not only at presenting their talent but also at developing it. To be sure, one can rely, with a fair degree of certainty, on the frugality of our theatregoing public, which often takes pot luck with dramatic fare; but in other places this is furnished more cheaply than it is at the Royal Theatre. And yet, if a merger of both secondary theatres were to take place (which might certainly be contemplated), together with an improvement in their repertoires, the good younger talents just might be drawn to them, thereby producing a dangerous competition that might once again raise the question of the appropriate use of the annual State subsidy.

THE 1870–1871 SEASON

OLDER works newly staged and more or less interesting debuts constituted the major portion of the dramatic repertoire, where only one little *Danish* comedy, *The Happiest Children* [*De lykkeligste Børn*], modestly ventured forth, under the veil of anonymity, at the side of two Norwegian dramas, *Mother and Son* [*Moder og Søn*] by Munch, and *The Pretenders* [*Kongs-Emnerne*] by Ibsen. This latter scored a grand success, gave the young actor Emil Poulsen the opportunity for a brilliant character interpretation, and was the outstanding box-office play of the season.

The opera did its utmost to overcome the various obstacles that were placed in the way of its progress. Of the older, recognized works, such as *Fidelio, Iphigenia,* and *The Templar and the Jewess* [*Tempelherren og Jødinden*], only the first performances were able to draw people to the Theatre. Auber's ingenious *Bronze Horse* [*Broncehesten*] was totally rejected, and *Villars' Dragoons* [*Villars Dragoner*] by Maillart—the only operatic novelty—was not fortunate enough to find favor with the critics, despite lively and graceful music to an excellent text, and regardless of the fact that in this work our most popular female singer had her finest role. The public put its faith in the newspapers and showed no inclination to become better acquainted with the piece. Consequently, it was shelved among other *"non valeurs."* Nevertheless, the Theatre treasury prospered, and one was almost tempted to view the public's frequent attendance as having been produced by a desire to forget, at least for a little while, the sorrowful political or, more properly speaking, world-historical events, whose bloody drama was unfolding before us.

"But," one will ask, "what does art have to do with politics?" Yet when history rises before our eyes with colossal features, artists as well as writers are swept into the maelstrom of events, and the Muses, even if they have not taken flight, stare silently and expectantly at the doubtful conflict.

Prompted by circumstances and public opinion more than his own desire, Napoleon III declared the Prussian War. All of Europe was jolted by an electric shock; the tricolor waved high, the thrilling strains of "The Marseillaise" spread from the banks of the Seine to the far North, where the people were moved not only by confidence in the great nation but by the prospect of a victorious cooperation. A French squadron appeared in the Danish Channel and announced a transport fleet with the flower of a forty-thousand-man army under the command of Generals Montauban (Palikao) and Trochu. We already had visions of our brave little army united with the French to fulfill the Slesvig prophecy which told that in the year 1870 the "red breeches" would oust the Prussians from Denmark's old precincts.

At such moments, it is good that a cautious government does not allow itself to be carried away by eccentric public feeling, but refuses to commit itself. Alarming symptoms of confusion in the French conduct of the war were soon evident, in sharp contrast to the exemplary organization that we—with understandable reluctance—were forced to acknowledge in the Prussian army. The equipment of the French navy was highly deficient, and the announced transport fleet, as well as the landing forces, simply failed to appear!

The blockade of the Baltic harbors was highly imperfect, and a naval engagement with the enemy could not take place, since he had cleverly removed his ships out of harm's way. The first gunshots were heard on the frontier of the Rhine, but it was only a short time before the conflict pushed its way over into French territory. The Emperor's finest troops, divided into rather weak corps, were hit by superior forces. Once again it appeared that even the most chivalrous valor cannot hold out against cold calculation and iron discipline, which unquestionably gave the Prussians superiority over their opponents, who had been weakened by more than one harmful influence and had long been deficient in the vital quality of discipline, which in a soldier usually takes precedence over personal courage. The defeats that followed one another in rapid succession could not but weigh heavily on anyone who loved France and admired its illustrious past. How much more, then, on me, who am tied to that country and its sympathetic people by the bonds of blood and gratitude, and also, as a Dane, do not envy the Prussians one-tenth of the astonishing success that attends their victorious feats of arms!

The feverish tension with which one anticipated each new telegram, and the anxiety with which one estimated the possible chances for a more favorable turn of events, were gradually bound to dull both mind and body, and it took more effort than usual to loose oneself from the dark and threatening pictures that constantly hovered round one's imagination. I literally had to do violence to my own feelings so as not to collapse. And, just as I sought to imitate the Boccaccian novellas by conceiving a pair of merry ballets at the time when cholera raged in our vicinity, so too I now occupied myself with a work of a similar kind, which gradually carried my thoughts back to the sphere which Nature—yea, why not Almighty Providence?—itself allotted me. And yet I could not completely drive away from my imagination images of war;

but they appeared in milder forms and within a setting where childhood memories and musical impressions furnished me with the motif for a little plot, and colors for a lively genre picture of Danish folk life.

THE KING'S VOLUNTEERS ON AMAGER

Among the phenomena that retained a place in the Copenhageners' affections and which have now been obliterated as a result of modern militia conditions was, without a doubt, the handsome Corps of Volunteers which, like so many other lovely things, owed its existence to the enthusiasm of 1801, when it was formed by volunteers from the different classes of citizens, among whom were also to be found artists from every profession.

From the Theatre came Rosing, my father, and his ingenious friend, the singer, violin virtuoso, and composer, Edouard Du Puy—all three, though of different nationalities, fired with patriotism. Holstein, who later became head of the Royal Theatre, was the courageous leader of the Corps, and with his stalwart Volunteers plaited undying leaves in Denmark's crown of honor during the fateful siege of 1807.

In the course of time, the Corps was given a semimilitary organization. It was entrusted with the coastal watch on Amager; later on, it was placed at the head of all grand assemblies of troops and parades, and distinguished itself by its lightness and elegant air. When the first Slesvig-Holsten War broke out in the spring of 1848, all eyes were fastened on this favorite Corps. Volunteers flocked to its ranks in the expectation that it would now, as before, be called upon to perform daring feats. But it was not actively employed, except for local watch duty. The compulsory national military service that later began brought about the dissolution of the Corps, and the light troop with its green coats and its Polish *schapska* [uhlan's shako] vanished, like so much else that delighted the older generation, and its existence will soon fade from view and become a myth and a legend, whose transmission to posterity will be reserved for art and poetry.

The memories of the Corps of Volunteers and the name of Du Puy are linked to one another not only because he distinguished himself in its ranks but particularly because, at every given opportunity, he glorified its appearance by his noble art, whose melodies still survive among the people as war songs, drinking ballads, aye, even as an incomparable funeral march! Our lyric stage possesses an invaluable treasure in his *Youth and Folly*, sparkling as it does with humor and genius, which qualities, combined with his personal charm, seem to have been his principal character traits, for his frivolity had become proverbial. Such a figure would obviously be perfect for the leading role in a ballet which was to depict a Carnival episode during the stationing of the King's Volunteers on Amager in 1808.

The period picture and choice of melodies, together with a little intrigue, made up the real core of the ballet, which is only partially appreciated by the younger generation, for whom the Exnerian* life of Amager and the lively dances exercised the greatest force of attraction. But many old people were profoundly moved by these sounds and memories from their youth, and the last surviving veteran of Classen's Have,† eighty-seven-year-old Major Aaby, who had been in Du Puy's platoon, pressed my hand with deep emotion as an expression of thanks for my ballet.

Güllich's superb painting, representing a farmhouse with a prospect of a flat winter landscape and open beach, greatly helped to create a perfect illusion. Holm's tasteful musical arrangement, in which Du Puy's melodies were woven into a characteristic composition, animated both the dancers and actors. Among the former, I must mention Anna Scholl and Daniel Krum, who, as far as technical perfection is concerned, are first-rate choreographic artists capable of appearing with bravura on any of the greatest stages of Europe. Lastly, it would have been impossible to find more charming representatives for the reckless Edouard and his good-natured wife than Valdemar Price and Fru Stillmann.

The ballet, which was performed for the first time on Shrove Monday, February 19, 1871, was extraordinarily successful, and was presented sixteen times during the same season. Its domestic tone seemed to presage a popular future, similar to those of *Valdemar* and *Far from Denmark*. My sorrow over France's misfortunes had provided a beneficial diversion and, since I had this time chosen a merry subject, I also felt I had helped to brighten the mood of the public.

THE 1871–1872 SEASON

ACCORDING to law, the design and sketches for the projected new Theatre edifice were opened to public competition, to which foreign architects were also invited, and the exhibition had already been held during the summer holidays. Most of these sketches had been executed with real talent, but only a few of them revealed a familiarity with the local requirements; particularly for foreign artists, the strictly demanded estimates posed a difficult problem, since even our own building experts could not calculate the cost of either manpower or materials. The results later showed that the sums they had asked and the amount of time within which the work was to be completed were based upon optimistic assumptions and were totally inadequate.

A Judging Committee of nine members was set up, and the Ministry did me the honor of calling me in as an expert on theatre affairs. I was present at the drafting of the program and attended the meetings at which the sketches

---

* Julius Exner (1825–1910) was a well-known painter of Amager folk scenes.
† On August 31, 1807, a band of Danish troops temporarily repulsed the English forces by an attack launched in Classen's Have, a park in the northeast quarter of Copenhagen.

were to be examined critically. But when it came to the final judgment, I found myself in such a decided minority (so as not to say *isolation*) that I simply had to resign from the Committee as being totally incompetent!

The sketch which, under the mark "*T.t.*," appeared to me to be at once the most appropriate and, according to the estimate that had been worked out, the least expensive, was declared positively useless by all the others! Therefore, as willingly as I would have helped to provide a fitting theatre for the capital, this time I was forced to shirk the responsibility that lay in rejecting a work which, in spite of several easily correctable imperfections, still seemed the best in *my* opinion. However, I was not blind to the merits of the other prize-winning drawings; but experience has taught me that not everything which looks elegant in a picture answers the purpose in practical reality. That it was not regard for my own artistic endeavor which guided my views in the matter of the new theatre edifice may be judged from the fact that I was involuntarily struck by the realization that before the building could be ready for use, I would have reached the age which qualifies one for retirement. In any case, my ideas, being antiquated, would no longer correspond to new conditions.

The start of the season was as bright as could be imagined in financial respects. Partly by virtue of its many characteristic beauties and partly as a result of the highly interesting performance of the role of Imogen, Shakespeare's *Cymbeline* scored a considerable success, which, I dare say, was also due to the reverence for the great British writer's name; for a Danish author would not have escaped the scourge of the critics had he dared to base his plot on a wager as bizarre as that which the unfortunate husband enters into, and, in addition, provided his drama with episodes such as the one with Cloten's headless cadaver!

Hakon Jarl, Elves' Hill, The Critic and the Animal [*Recensenten og Dyret*], newly staged and with a cast that was far inferior to the original, always played to full houses, and the Theatre treasury's profits increased to such a degree that it even caused a commotion in the enemy camp, where they attempted to alter the Act which had guaranteed the subsidy for a five-year period. This good business involuntarily carried one's thoughts back to the time when, for a quite modest fee, our dramatic authors each year brought us fresh creations, and our dramatic personnel were at their zenith, with regard to talent as well as superb ensemble acting. In those days, sparsely filled houses were the order of the day, and receipts which would nowadays be considered poor were regarded as downright handsome! Now, what ought to be the actual duty of a national theatre? And should it not be possible to bring material interests a little closer to the idealistic?

On our lyric stage, things "limped along" as usual. A superb orchestra, a well-trained chorus, and a number of especially fine singing voices were to be found in the opera, but genuine lyrical *fluidity*, whether in the dialogue of the *syngespil* or in opera recitative, was lacking. The so-called musical audience itself is partly to blame for this, for people no longer ask for *beautiful* but only *big* voices. They care little about delivery and even less about a pure intonation, as long as it is strong, yes, extremely strong, regardless of whether it suits the character and situation or whether the language that forms the text sounds like Greek or out-and-out gibberish!

Our dilettantes may be divided into two groups. The first is the critical music lovers, who exclusively demand the kind of classicism that distinguishes the symphony and the oratorio, and will have nothing to do with the lighter melodic material which denotes the character of theatre music. The second group, which among us constitutes the majority, regards music as a pleasant bonus to a good dramatic presentation and as an interpreter of an interesting plot; here, above all, are demanded personality, expression, and distinctness.

Partly for the above-mentioned reasons and partly as a result of illness, during this season, more than ever before, the opera failed to win the sympathy of the public. We shall see whether the efforts expended on *The Mastersingers of Nuremberg* [*Mestersangerne i Nürnberg*] will produce a more favorable result. *Lohengrin* had already given us a glimpse of the system Richard Wagner wishes to introduce into opera and upon which he bases his supposed mission. One can only be astounded at his audacious harmonies and, above all, the great skill with which he handles the orchestra. But on the whole (so as not to say that he finds them burdensome and detestable), he seems to be indifferent to melody and the actual art of singing. Only as a rare exception does singing appear as more than a mere accompaniment to a brilliant orchestration, which frequently drowns out the voice and crushes the text.

In his work *Oper und Drama* Wagner has, with more or less indulgence, denounced all hitherto accepted operatic forms as *Unsinn* [nonsense] and *Blödsinn* [idiocy]. With a passion that exceeds the bounds of all *sound* criticism, he takes the field against all modern composers and lyric poets and sets himself up as the man who will show the world how a libretto should be written and set to music. But as for his own texts: they often suffer from considerable diffuseness and, despite the use of enormous stage apparatus, from a childish pursuit of effect and a scenic awkwardness that allows the leading characters to stand idle for long periods while the action drags on in endless recitatives which, *reasonable* as they might be, do not appeal to the emotions and are, on the whole, far less interesting than the arias, duets, and quintets that he scorns and rejects in his famous predecessors.

As far as Wagner's actual originality is concerned, it consists, for the most part (especially in his latest works), in a craving for eccentric effects, which his admirers unanimously call "the Music of the Future," and which, because of their difficulty in being grasped and understood, seem certain to drive both singers and listeners to despair. On the other hand, when from time to time he condescends to be melodious, he must find it remarkable that his audience follows along with him when he allows his genius to travel the old beaten path.

It is even harder for us older folk who were nursed on Mozart, Méhul, Weber, and Boïeldieu; rocked to the melodies of Weyse and Kuhlau; contemporaries of Rossini, Bellini, Meyerbeer, Spontini, Halévy, Auber, and Gounod; and, lastly, musically trained by Beethoven, Mendelssohn, Hartmann, and Gade—hard for us, I say, to be able to imagine a future like that which Wagner sets up for us and wherewith he, in his arrogance, would storm Olympus and dethrone the gods. Organized as we are, we can only go so far as to find Wagner's compositions *remarkable,* but not refreshing; *astounding* but not convincing. In short, if, in the future, poetry and music are to be clothed in such forms, or more properly speaking, formlessness, we must feel sorry for our successors.

The ballet repertoire, which had already been considerably weakened by Betty Schnell's transition to the spoken drama, during this season suffered a severe new loss as a result of the mishap that befell our talented Scharff, who, while performing a dance in a *divertissement* for *The Troubadour* ruptured one of his kneecaps, an accident which, in all my years of experience, has not happened to any dancer, either here or abroad. This tragedy was greeted with universal sympathy; for while there was certainly hope of a cure which would make it possible for him to move about unhindered in private life, and maybe even on the dramatic stage, he had to be considered lost to the Ballet.

At this time, it took a certain strength of character not only to keep up courage but to lay plans for the immediate future. To be sure, we did possess some good, aye, even superb, young talents; but it is neither easy nor rewarding to take over roles in which a popular artist, retired before his time, has shone, and upon which he has placed the stamp of his individuality. The inheritance, therefore, had to be divided among a number of dancers, and attention focused on the merits which the person in question might possibly have above those of his predecessor. The rest had to be left to the public's indulgence—and *forgetfulness!*

However, we were in no less serious a predicament with our leading female roles; for while Anna Scholl was indeed an outstanding *demi-caractère* dancer and in solo performances won great public recognition, it is the same in the ballet as it is with coloratura singers in opera: they must have more than perfect virtuosity in order to be satisfactory in the more demanding repertoire. Therefore, though with great reluctance, we were forced to look abroad; and since, during my sojourn at Stockholm's Royal Theatre, I had noticed a rather young *danseuse,* Maria Westberg—who combined an attractive appearance and outstanding, though far from developed, natural talent with those qualities we set such great store by here at home—I tried to persuade her to accept an engagement with us. Unfortunately she was bound by a one-year contract, and it was only with difficulty that she succeeded in obtaining a several months' leave of absence, during which she was to receive further training and, if possible, make her debut on the Danish stage.

In September 1871 she appeared in *La Sylphide,* as Sigyn in *The Lay of Thrym,* and finally as Zoloé in *Brahma and the Bayadère,* in which role she showed such considerable progress and won such unanimous applause that there could no longer be any doubt that she would be a valuable acquisition for our Ballet. She now received a most advantageous offer for the following season, and returned to Stockholm well pleased with her stay in Denmark.

It was important that the Ballet, at least, be able to present one new work; but circumstances rendered this task extremely difficult; for the audience usually demands that the latest composition surpass all previous ones, and added to this constant outbidding we have the press's weighing of words and the management's anxiety about the expense involved in equipping the Ballet.

It was primarily a matter of finding and choosing a subject suited both to the taste of our public and to conditions at our Theatre, yet one as different as possible from those which had already been treated. The *burlesque* borders on the harlequinade and would hardly be tolerated on our classical stage, while the *tragic* must have a happy ending; otherwise, the ballet-poet would find himself in the same boat as Euripides,* who was banished because he had grieved the theatregoers of Athens. I would not be permitted to *balleti-cize* well-known dramas and operas — a practice that made my predecessor, Galeotti, so famous. Greek myths and Roman antiquity have so greatly fallen victim to all-polluting parody that one would hardly think of approaching them seriously unless one possessed the talent and resources needed to bring off a performance of a caliber we are unable to achieve. Old Norse, Italian, and Spanish folk life had already made sufficient contributions to my ballet libretti. On the other hand, our historical memories from the romantic Middle Ages were subjects that could always count on public sympathy. However, it is dangerous to make too frequent demands on patriotic feeling, and there is nothing more depressing than an unanswered appeal to love of one's country. But there still remained the fairy tale and the fairy world, and if in their most outstanding moments one can but get the audience to take reason prisoner and follow along on the wings of fantasy, it is worth risking an attempt in the hope and, of course, the presupposition that they do not make too great demands upon the magical powers of our humble machinery.

I therefore summoned my courage and executed a long-cherished idea, namely, that of furnishing an illustration to the fairy tales and narratives of our world-famous countryman, H. C. Andersen. The motif was taken from his "Steadfast Tin Soldier" and I gave the ballet the name of *A Fairy Tale in Pictures.*

*Cf. footnote, Vol. I, p. 117.

A Fairy Tale in Pictures

With the help of a beneficent Fairy, it was essential that I transform both the Tin Soldier and the little Ballerina into living creatures, each of whom must endure several trials and tribulations before they can marry one another. The whole was enclosed in a frame of dream and reality which, in keeping with the spirit of the fairy-tale writer, was designed to amuse children and childlike souls but also to give grownups food for thought.

In and of itself, the problem was not an easy one to solve. I realized that the subject had its weaknesses and that to conceal these and, if possible, emphasize its merits must here be left to scenic effects. The Introduction, with the children and their Grandmother, undeniably had the greatest success because I had the most popular fables from the picture book reproduced on the large tableau which hung on the wall behind the performers. This scene was ingenuously interpreted through reminiscences from Schall's music for *Lagertha*, *Raoul Barbe-Bleue*, and *Mountain Peasants' Children* (memories from my own childhood).

The first part of the dream—namely, the transformation of the Grandmother into a fairy, that of the Doll and the Tin Soldier into real people, little Jenny into a winged elf and Richard into a drummer who calls the Highlanders into battle—readily blended with the composed dances and mimed episodes. On the other hand, in the second act the scene shifted to a terrain which certainly lies outside the bounds of a child's imagination; that is to say, we find ourselves in the Ballerina's domain, where, surrounded by the temptations of vanity and the desire for luxury, she is to endure her trial. However, although in the guise of dances and comic scenes—which are certainly fit entertainment for the young—this can only be understood by older people to whom the various aspects of worldly life are not unknown! But here I found myself in the same position as Hamlet when he gives the actors rules for their art. It was important for me once and for all to claim for dancing and mime a place among the ennobling spectacles and to combat the prejudices which equate *lightness* and *grace* with a frivolous treat for the eye! Even Andersen's little paper dolls with their legs lifted high in the air are not free from this frivolous implication, and it became a matter of conscience for me to give his "Steadfast Tin Soldier" a worthier object for his love. I have therefore depicted Rosalie as gentle and modest, industrious and indefatigable, talented, and unmoved by the intoxicating breeze of flattery. Misunderstood by the world, she feels strengthened by the deep inner knowledge [of the Tin Soldier's love for her,] and, placed in mortal danger, she is saved by her faithful lover and united with him, under the aegis of the beneficent Fairy.

When the children awaken, they retain in their memories only the principal details of this dream. The Grandmother returns from the fairyland of the imagination and leads the children in to festive reality. In my previous ballet, a Shrovetide festival was celebrated; this time the ballet ended with a Christmas tree, intended to awaken childhood memories and parental joys.

The first performance met with a warm reception and was inspired by the friendly mood of Christmas. At our Theatre, eleven heavily attended evenings can certainly be called a fine success; but for a ballet that fills only half an evening to be able to remain in the repertoire, a fairly interesting dramatic accompaniment is required, and this season offered extremely few. The twelfth performance drew only a poor house, and with this the *Fairy Tale*'s fate was decided. Families, who had not yet been forbidden to bring their children with them to the Theatre, had treated them to this beloved Andersen story come to life; simple souls among the older folk encountered some long-vanished impressions; and the connoisseurs of the choreographic art admired Anna Scholl, who was identified with Rosalie.

This work, upon which I had not based any great expectations for the future, nevertheless enjoyed too short a flowering time. To be sure, it was taken up a couple of times the following Christmas, but since only the first act seemed to retain interest, it was broken up into a *divertissement* which quickly disappeared from the stage.

The Mastersingers of Nuremberg, by Richard Wagner, an opera which had taken half a year of strenuous rehearsal, won only highly conditional applause. In *Lohengrin*, people had had the opportunity to acknowledge Richard Wagner's genius and outstanding skill, and also, in many places, to follow his music with unadulterated enjoyment. But in the present work the baroque was predominant, and though the subject belonged chiefly to the genre of comic opera, the instrumentation was so overwhelming that it would have been rather strong for even a cloak-and-dagger melodrama. The system whereby each of the characters was to have his own song-theme was here carried through to such a degree that the victorious knight repeated his melody at least twelve times, and the defeated mastersinger was, in both musical and dramatic respects, such a caricaturish figure that he belonged in a marionette theatre rather than in an opera.

The piece was staged with great care and there were many successful moments in the performance; but what particularly appealed to the general public were the comical apprentices, the brawl, and the guildmen's procession. The members of the orchestra found the music interesting, but—except for a glorious quintet and a few melodious spots—the singers had not a single rewarding part, while several of the principal numbers were drowned out by a mass of dissonants which frequently degenerated into downright caterwauling. This colossal composition could not hold its place in the repertoire. It was laid to rest in our "musical mausoleum," to be resurrected when the Future has matured our taste and hardened our eardrums.

In the spoken drama, new revivals assumed a prominent place. Only toward spring did there appear an original new work by a young but anonymous author: *The White Roses* [*De hvide Roser*], which was received with encouraging applause. But the event which attracted the greatest attention this season was undoubtedly Mantzius' departure from the stage. The conflicts which precipitated this major loss to our Theatre have in the past furnished the occasion for special polemics and lie outside the plan I have marked out for this book. Suffice it to say that by his popular readings this talented actor has found a source of occupation for himself and one of aesthetic enjoyment for the public.

Immediately after the season's end, the third performance for the benefit of the Ballet's Private Pension Fund was given. The ballet *Valdemar*, with a Prologue by Carl Andersen to music by Emil Hartmann, provided the Fund with considerable receipts. Schram and Frk. Doris Pfeil interpreted the lyric poem, which was of patriotic content and entitled *Dawn* [*Dæmring*]. Betty Schnell made her last appearance as Astrid, and Axel Hvide found an outstanding representative in Wilhelm Wiehe.

THE 1872–1873 SEASON

THESE notes which, especially as far as my sphere of activity is concerned, bear the name of *Theatre Crisis*, shall retain this designation inasmuch as they are a presentiment of a transition to something indefinable. If one takes into account the mounting box-office receipts, surely one must regard the present period as more productive than any previous one. But if one takes into consideration art and the opinions that guide its efforts, one will arrive at a conclusion which, even if it does not augur total dissolution, still arouses anxiety about the not too distant future.

The new Theatre edifice, which was begun in February with the demolition of the Cannon Foundry and the warehouses on Holmen and whose foundation stone was ceremoniously laid on October 18, was supposed to be ready for the start of the season in 1874. The plans promised the most elegant proportions, with internal and external ornamentation in the way of statues, busts, and paintings; illumination, ventilation, and machinery according to the latest and finest models; spacious corridors, beautiful foyers, and comfortable orchestra and box seats — all this for a sum that would astonish even the municipality and the Rigsdag by its cheapness!

But what about the stage itself? Aye, it was to be higher, wider, and deeper than the former one, with the hope of improved acoustics. But — yet another "but"! — how will our literary, dramatic, and lyric talents be affected by these external advantages? Drought and crop failure hold sway over the Parnassus from which the drama is to obtain nourishment; for our young aestheticians have taken M.A. degrees in order to devote themselves to criticism instead of themselves producing, i.e., "thinking of something." Well, then, we will make do with older works which, by means of painstaking new productions, might have a certain attraction; and such works also have the indisputable advantage of being treated reverently by the otherwise so harsh daily press. Unfortunately, when it comes to performance, the old cannot be renewed, and it is a fact that in neither the comic nor the tragic sphere can the younger generation of actors compensate for those talents which have either disappeared from the stage or are still represented by a few veterans, whose personalities have come to be identified with the kinds of roles they play.

I dare say it can be objected that in this respect we are no worse off than most of Europe's major theatres, where a lack of genius is made up for by well-rehearsed ensemble acting. But, in spite of stage direction—formerly unknown—it is only drawing room plays that are fully satisfying nowadays; and if the upheavals of time do not produce some beneficial reaction in the dramatic world, we will have no other alternative than to resort to moderation and trust in the public's frugality.

And yet, in this as well as previous seasons, happy omens for higher dramatic poetry have appeared, and our public cannot be accused of praising only that which provokes laughter. Shakespeare's *Merchant of Venice; The Warriors* and *Hakon Jarl* by Oehlenschläger; *True and Untrue* [*Sandt og Usandt*] by the authoress of *Rosa and Rosita;* and *An Evening at Giske* [*En Aften paa Giske*] by A. Munch played to full houses. But the season's most brilliant phenomena were Heiberg's *Day of the Seven Sleepers* [*Syvsoverdag*] (which after a rest of more than thirty-two years found the general public more receptive to the highly poetical beauties which, in those days, were revealed only to the reading public) and *Bertran de Born,* the first creation of twenty-four-year-old Ernst v. d. Recke, whose test-piece contains moments, aye, whole sections, that would do honor to an old master for tastefulness, lyrical richness, and tragic power. This piece, which played quite often to a numerous and discriminating public, created quite a stir and seemed to assure us that in tragic drama we would no longer allow ourselves to be outdone by Norwegian authors. At the same time, Emil Poulsen's and Agnes Dehn's performances of the leading roles gave us a sign that Melpomene was still watching over the Danish stage.

Lack of true dramatic effort, misunderstanding about the use of the voice, and careless diction are, in my opinion, the reasons why the opera has not received its due on our stage; for the public usually enjoys even the loveliest music only as it is the interpreter of an interesting plot. The fact that people, seeking to conceal the above-mentioned shortcomings and holding to the prejudice that the tone of the voice is lost through speaking, have preferred grand opera to the *syngestykke* with dialogue, has not only weakened our lyric artists' desire and eliminated their need to master the actual art of acting; it has also suppressed a genre which contains so much that is both charming and entertaining. Its right to exist cannot be denied by the assertion that it is preposterous for a piece to alternate between singing and speaking, for the recitatives can in and of themselves lay no claim to substantial naturalness. Moreover, there is a host of subjects in which situations alternate between musical and dramatic effects, where the dialogue provides breathing space and forms a connecting link that accelerates the action and also paves the way for the coming musical numbers. Need one produce examples such as *Joseph and his Brethren, Two Days, The White Lady, Fidelio, Freischütz,* and the major part of Marschner's and Auber's repertoires in order to prove how unsuitable recitative would have been in these *syngestykker?*

In spite of countless obstacles, the opera during this season offered no small amount of variety and presented partially new productions of *Robert of Normandy, Little Red Riding Hood,* and *Faust;* from the current repertoire, *The Jewess, The Marriage of Figaro, The Barber, Hans Heiling, The Master-singers, The Troubadour, The Elixir of Love,* and *The Daughter of the Regiment;* and, finally, as the single novelty, *The Corsairs [Korsarerne]* by Emil Hartmann. This work, so meritorious in a number of respects, met the same fate as most of our native compositions; namely, that of being received with coldness by the public and with fashionable indifference by the press.—Gounod's *Dove* passed over the boards unnoticed.

The Ballet repertoire, like that of the opera, consisted mainly of new productions: *Valdemar, The Flower Festival, The Valkyr,* and *Napoli,* with Maria Westberg in the leading roles; *The Kermesse in Bruges,* with Anna Scholl as Eleonore. These, as well as a number of older ballets and *divertissements,* were viewed with interest, and the two *danseuses* mentioned above won the public's sympathy to a high degree.

A number of local circumstances were responsible for the fact that smaller compositions were viewed as the most practical choreographic novelties; but it should be remarked that, at the same time as objections are raised against the considerable dimensions of historical ballets, it is these, and not the smaller works, which attract people, while the so-called ballet *divertissements* are regarded as worthless bagatelles! There are few who have any idea how hard it is to concentrate a plot or develop a theme within such narrow boundaries; and it is no easy matter to give the inserted dances a prominent place, whereas in the pantomimic ballet they serve merely as ornamentation. Consequently, while I privately prepared a larger work which was to serve as the introductory ballet at the new Theatre, I was now forced to present a useful little novelty; and, since at the moment we happened to possess an outstandingly beautiful setting from the unjustly discarded *Bronze Horse,* I decided to take my own and the Ballet's patrons along with me on an excursion to China, and composed

The Mandarin's Daughters

I had long contemplated the idea of a chess game made up of living figures, and I felt it would make a suitable focal point for a Chinese ballet. But this was not enough. I had to have a motif, the character of which would more or less describe the singular features of this remarkable people, and I found it in some French and English translations of Chinese *novelles.* I found *The Fortunate Union* especially appealing, but I must frankly admit that had I read these descriptions before I had settled on my idea, the ballet would hardly have seen the light; for these sober-minded, erudite, and skillful people, whom we know only through porcelain dolls and whom we usually find amusing, are actually the least suitable for comic representation. And, even though they themselves are terribly fond of drama, they never take part in what we would call dancing, since this physical exercise conflicts with a man's dignity and is impossible for the women because of the barbarous custom of binding their feet.

I was therefore in the same position as the French historian who was to describe a siege and answered those who brought him the official report too late: "Goodness! my siege is already finished!" I used several characteristics, created a mandarin surrounded by wives and daughters, a princely proposal, a striking wedding celebration, and used the chess game as the connecting link between the prince and his father-in-law. In short, I gave the whole thing, dancing as well as mime, a light touch of the style which we are in the habit of calling *Chinese.* But so as not to be too harshly checked by those who had recently visited the Celestial Empire, I moved the period of the action back to the sixteenth century, that is, before the Manchurian Tartars' rule in China.

Although the performance by the company was exemplary in every respect, and the scenic equipment of a perfection rarely if ever achieved at our Theatre, the work enjoyed only a lukewarm reception and increasingly strengthened me in the conviction that so-called *divertissements* are of use to the repertoire only if they can fill the stipulated three hours of performance, or be used as interludes if the same actors are to appear in two plays.

One of the season's last performances, given on May 21, 1873, was Phister's Farewell Benefit, on which occasion the public bade farewell to this superb actor, who on his departure leaves behind a void which it will be hard to fill. By a strange coincidence, I came to compose an apotheosis for our immortal Holberg at our Pension Fund performance on the third of June! Was this an omen that, with the loss of Phister as an interpreter of his priceless humor, the great dramatist would also bid us adieu?

THE 1873–1874 SEASON

WHILE during the mild winter (but under rather unfavorable conditions for the entrepreneurs) all efforts were concentrated on the new Theatre, which was to have been finished for next season's opening and in time for the transfer and rehearsals to take place beforehand, the artistic activity continued—for the most part—with new productions of older works, but with unusual public attendance, which increased the [box-office] receipts to an unheard-of degree. It was perfectly obvious to everyone that the tasteful, new, and imposing Temple of the Muses would be a good deal more expensive than the estimate had promised, because the cost of all building materials had suddenly risen by more than 50 per cent and workmen's salaries were forced up to fabulous figures; and also because the incomprehensible haste with which the old building was pulled down before the new edifice could be completed, entailed an enormous loss of money as a result of the cessation of plays and of the construction work being carried out under pressure, which, being defective in a number of respects, would soon require costly repairs. The remonstrances made by the Intendant, Justitsraad Berner, and the urgent plea to postpone the opening of the new Theatre until September 1875, met with no sympathy from the higher authorities, who in this way probably thought they could satisfy that portion of the Rigsdag which was unfavorably disposed toward the theatre. The result was left for coming years to show.

The spoken drama presented only two original new works, *Helene* and *Autumn Sun* [*Efteraarssol*]; whereas Paludan-Müller's youthful work, *Love at Court,* was received with applause after a hibernation of forty years. *Christiane,* an embarassing "drama of adultery" of the modern French school, (which, at the moment, deals only with marital conflicts, seducers, weak women, deceived husbands, and inevitable duels), unfortunately gained admittance [to our stage] with the aid of a skilled translation and excellent ensemble acting.

Phister's absence was strongly felt, and he had to be regarded as irreplaceable, especially by those who had known his many-faceted talent to its fullest extent; for at least four good actors were needed to fill the void created by his departure. Ole Poulsen* seems to have inherited just such a quarter-share. During the previous season, his refreshing humor had already given us a superb Troels in *The Lying-in Room,* and this year an outstanding Henrik in *The Political Tinker.* As Phister's finest pupil, he faithfully holds to the pictures of "types" that his master created from older traditions in our classical comedy; but this cannot be construed as slavish copying, for in his whole interpretation of the comic element there lies the seed of true originality. In him, as well as in his brother Emil, the Royal Theatre has gained a valuable acquisition, which forcefully combats the threatened decline of the dramatic art.

The lyric stage offered a rich variety of familiar works, while a century-old masterwork by Gluck, *Iphigenia in Tauris,* was the season's most important novelty and was performed with the same merits and shortcomings which are part and parcel of our opera, wherefore it, too, was able to achieve only a *succès d'estime et de piété.* Another secular festival was celebrated on March 5, in honor of our eminent composer Weyse's birthday (1774). They presented *The Sleeping Draught,* which always excites and refreshes all who thirst after melody. For this performance, I furnished a mimed Prologue:

In Memory of Weyse

In a setting that took in a major portion of Rosenborg Gardens — a place where Weyse was wont to stroll as a youth and which is the subject of one of his loveliest compositions — I depicted a series of dances and tableaux as

---

*This must be either a slip of the pen or a nickname. The actor's proper name was Olaf Poulsen.

reminiscences of his glorious compositions, which unfortunately lie buried among the musical treasures that the present does not know how to use but which the future will, perhaps, call to light. This little opus was the Ballet's single new work during this season, while Hartmann and I were zealously occupied with *Arcona*, which was intended to introduce the Ballet to the new stage. As a matter of fact, we, in a manner of speaking, exhausted both our older and newer stores; among others, *The Lay of Thrym* was given with extraordinary success, to which Krum's performance of the role of Loke especially contributed. This task was all the more difficult for him as Scharff had earlier given the part a highly individual stamp. As usual, we ended the season with our Pension Fund Performance, and, together with *A Folk Tale*, presented a mimed choreographic occasional piece which evoked a tremendous response from the audience, namely:

Farewell to the Old Theatre!

The mother of the Muses (Mnemosyne) gathered round her those of her daughters who were most closely associated with the theatre and bade them transfer their household gods from the old stage to the new. Melpomene carried Oehlenschläger's bust, Thalia, Holberg's, and, followed by illustrations to the works of both of these great writers, they sadly departed from the home that had witnessed their time of flowering. Terpsichore remained behind for a little while and was ordered to show a series of older and newer ballet scenes and dances by those who had reaped the liveliest applause. No less than fourteen of these followed in rapid succession and were greeted as beloved guests. Lastly, the picture representing the old Playhouse vanished and the new Theatre appeared in magical illumination. The audience's enthusiasm reached its height when a procession of the stage's leading artists, ladies and gentlemen from every artistic profession, in costumes depicting their favorite roles, entered the new Temple of Art, with the Muses in the lead. A few days later, hammer strokes resounded, and the last remnant of Frederik V's *Comediehuus* was leveled to the ground.

Among the trade and labor strikes which a misguided Socialism has engineered in our once so peaceful and sober-minded Copenhagen, the gasworks strike assumes a special place, since it threw the Theatre as well as the city's streets back to "the good old days" when one had to be content with one-tenth the candle power that is considered barely sufficient nowadays. Long-vanished oil lamps once again emerged from their hiding places; and, far from losing heart over this sudden reaction, Copenhageners richly enjoyed themselves and strolled out in crowds to view the illumination! Thus the demonstration was a complete fiasco, and after a couple of days of idleness the misguided workers gave in, so that we again saw ourselves moved a generation ahead, to light and tolerable brightness.

In an artistic profession which is rarely counted among the forms of poetry, I had the good fortune and the honor of being recognized as a "Danish poet," and, as such, was granted the Ancker travel stipend,† which I first used to pay a visit to Russia, and afterward to see once more the classical soil of Nature, art, and folk life—beautiful Italy! The first two elements still retain their magic; but the last, namely, the richly colorful folk life, has considerably paled during the thirty-three years that have elapsed since I first observed and gathered from it indelible impressions. To be sure, the *tarantella* is still danced in Capri and among the ruins of Baiæ and Pozzuoli; but the national costume with its vivid colors has disappeared and the characteristic head-dresses have given way to hats and caps; the barcarole and the ballad to the strains of a guitar are almost never heard; and the increasing civilization, which is in itself very respectable, has certainly brought greater order and cleanliness, but also an excess of the prosaic!

On the whole, both in Italy and in France (whose present theatre conditions I intend to discuss in a later writing), I found little that I could turn to account in my scenic activity. In Russia, on the other hand, both the folk life and the national drama offered a number of remarkable and original things which might well furnish material for interesting productions.

During this winter died the comedy writer and former actor at the Royal Theatre, Thomas Overskou, whose reminiscences, under the name of *History of the Danish Stage*, have a certain importance, inasmuch as they contain a chronological list of performances from the the oldest period of the theatre in Denmark, as well as fairly accurate information concerning how often pieces have been performed and the standard of wages at different times. Thus far one may follow this discursive work as a source book; but as for the anecdotal portion and the judgment of persons and things with which those theatre statistics are tricked out, the book is unquestionably *apocryphal*, since backstage gossip and individual feelings are highly dubious sources, whose accounts are overlong and could never deserve the name of art history.

In his autobiography, Overskou depicts himself as a self-taught man, and one can have nought but admiration for the results of his hard work. Without any profound knowledge of languages, deprived of a sense of music, and without so much as a metronome to indicate the rhythm for him, he furnished both dramatic and lyrical translations of drama and opera from the greatest foreign repertoires; and, despite the long-windedness which was a distinctive feature in both his writings and his conversations, he knew how to bring a lively, often witty dialogue into his comedies, which have long assumed a prominent place on the Danish stage.

As an actor, he was plagued by dejection over a presumed lack of recognition; for he was quite unaware of the mishaps that continually produced in his intonation, facial expression, and mannerisms an effect which was the complete opposite of what he imagined and which were responsible for the

† One of the most important travel grants that can be given a Danish artist.

fact that, from the greatest actor on the stage down to the humblest supernumerary, there was not a single person who did not smile whenever Overskou's appearance was mentioned. He therefore sought to forge other paths to
promotion, avidly applied for a number of different official posts, became the
editor of *Dagen* and collaborator in *Flyveposten*. Then, as a final attempt at
making a good bargain, he conceived the idea for a *Folketheater*, to which he
was given the concession; however, a sufficient number of shareholders failed
to materialize, wherefore the whole enterprise was dropped, to be later taken
up by others in a form that in no way corresponded to the ideas of the origi-
nator. He even ventured to mount the election platform to run as a candidate
for a seat in the Folketing; but here too an unkind fate pursued him.

At last, Heiberg agreed (in spite of or perhaps even as compensation for
an earlier violent polemic in which he had reduced Overskou to nothing with
the scourge of ridicule) to appoint him stage director for both lyric and dramatic spectacles, a position in which he was regarded—following his unpredictable patron's departure from the directorship of the Theatre—as a total incompetent, and from which he was dismissed, with a pension, by the
subsequent management. This discharge filled him with so much bitterness
that every page in the last volume of his theatre history contains attacks
against those persons he considered responsible for his removal.

For my own part, I dare not complain about the manner in which I have
been treated in his work, even though, in a number of places, he chaffs me
about the greatness of my Italian predecessor, bemoans the lack of sufficient
action in my ballets, and also unfairly lumps my original works with the obvious plagiarisms of others. However, among his records is to be found the date
of my first appearance as one of Lagertha's sons. It was October 2, 1813, and
it was commemorated with heartfelt congratulations to the activity which now
celebrated its *diamond anniversary.*

THE 1874–1875 SEASON

THIS season did not open until October 15, and only with the utmost effort
could the new Theatre be made fairly serviceable for the commencement of
plays. It is still an unsolved mystery as to why this "rush job" was expedited,
since not only were six weeks of performances and their profits lost, but a
driving force and efficiency had to be applied to the whole. This increased expenses to an enormous degree, and the work was done so imperfectly that
only a short time later it had to undergo costly repairs, in addition to the sums
that would have to be spent in the rather uncertain future.

These drawbacks prompted the Intendant, Justitsraad Berner, who had
zealously deprecated the untimely demolition of the old Theatre, to ask for a
year's leave to travel to the south in order to regain his health, which had
been impaired by all the anxieties and worries. The Theatre Chief, Confer-

entsraad Linde, was thus deprived of the valuable assistance which a businessman so knowledgeable about theatrical affairs could give him under circumstances whose difficulty one can hardly imagine.

We entered the rather crudely finished edifice with, so to speak, empty hands. The essential portion of the repertoires of all three branches of art lacked even the most rudimentary decorations; for by some remarkable want of foresight, the scene-painters had received their commissions too late, and instead of expeditiously piecing together what we had on hand in the way of side wings and backdrops, they had sold them straight away in order to make room in the warehouses! The machinery, which, according to the plan, was to be made from the latest designs, was still so incomplete that all changes had to be made by hand, and it would take only the clumsiness of a single man to endanger the performers' lives and limbs.

As I have already stated, the promise which the Minister of Culture had made to the Folketing six years before was the decisive factor in this affair; and, cost what it might, the new Theatre simply *had* to open in the autumn of 1874. And so it did—but at a price which we shall discuss later on.

In order to find out what the acoustics were like, a trial performance was arranged for October 11; dignitaries were invited and complimentary tickets were distributed to the many patrons of the Royal Theatre. The results showed that, while the singing and instrumental music for the second act of Hartmann's charming composition, *Little Kirsten,* sounded superb, the spoken drama, which was represented by Holberg's *Fortunate Shipwreck,* will henceforth demand increased distinctness of speech from most of the actors, and they must especially be warned against the bad habit of speaking their lines either off to the side or upstage.

The actual opening and inaugural celebration took place on October 15 with a *Cantata* by Ploug and Hartmann, enthusiastically recited by Wilhelm Wiehe and sung by the members of the opera. Afterward, *The Fortunate Shipwreck* was presented, and before as well as after this comedy, I furnished "apotheotic" tableaux, one in honor of Holberg, the other for Oehlenschläger, both surrounded by characters from their immortal masterworks.

To the many difficulties the management had to combat and the countless obstacles which illnesses among the most prominent members of the drama placed in the way of the repertoire's progress, there was added—as I have stated above—the eternal problem of the decorations; for even though two talented painters and their assistants were kept busy, and often furnished the last pieces—still rather wet—only minutes before the curtain rose, whatever was lacking had to be provided, at enormous expense, from Berlin, Munich, and Vienna!

In this way a number of plays were splendidly mounted; but with a major drawback. The entire system of modern scene-painting is little suited to our conditions, since it is usually intended for particular situations and is, therefore, so complex in construction that the mounting of the scenery consumes much time and produces intermissions of a length that is highly injurious to the dramatic interest.

In spite of all these difficulties, the Chief, by virtue of his subtle tact and humane conduct, managed to inspire in the personnel a spirit of cooperation and a perseverance which have seldom been the lot of any theatre director. Hardly any other season has offered so many successful new works or drawn a more numerous audience – an audience which, regardless of the increased ticket prices, flocked to the Theatre *en masse* and raised the receipts to a height which was, unfortunately, not sufficient to cover the similarly increased expenditures.

The drama presented no less than seven new plays, the stage direction of which was skillfully carried out, during Fru Heiberg's absence, by Emil Poulsen. Only one original Danish work appeared, namely, *Times Change* [*Tiderne Skifte*], a character portrait by Paludan-Müller, which was meritorious in a number of respects. Norway, on the other hand, furnished us with no less than three major dramas: *The Vikings of Helgeland* [*Hærmændene paa Helgeland*], a tragic drama by Henrik Ibsen; *A Bankruptcy* [*En Fallit*] a masterpiece in the direction of Realism by Bjørnson; and, lastly, *The Tarn* [*Fjeldsøen*], a poetic picture by Andreas Munch. This last work drew the shortest straw when compared with the extraordinary success the first two achieved; furthermore, during the final weeks of the season, it also had to compete with the lovely spring weather.

In the way of translations from the French, *Gabrielle, Life of the Working Class* [*Arbeiderliv*], and *Fire in the Cloister* [*Ildløs i Klosteret*] were presented. In the latter, Betty Schnell displayed so amiable a talent that, in this genre, nothing more perfect has been seen on the Danish stage since the days when Fru Heiberg, as a rather young girl, played *"les ingénues."*

The opera kept its current repertoire afloat partly by means of pieced-together set decorations, while all the scenery for *Tannhäuser* was obtained from Vienna. This magnificent opera, which ought to take precedence over *Lohengrin*, constitutes the actual introduction to the series of compositions with which Wagner thinks he can conquer the Future. In *Tannhäuser*, one still encounters some of the musical forms which correspond to accepted notions of lyric drama. There are many superbly thrilling moments, and in the glorious "Grand March," in particular, one finds an extraordinary wealth of melody; but at the same time, one has difficulty familiarizing oneself with the wildness that is supposed to depict the sensual pleasures of Venusberg.

As the one who was to compose dances for this fantastic scene, I could easily have arranged from this music the history of a fire, with cries for help, crowds of people, fire engines, and a salvage corps! Well, it was naiads, bacchantes, and Heaven knows what mythological creatures, that Wagner's imagination had packed into the mountain which lies quite near "die Wartburg"! The plot, which mainly revolves around the "Tournament of Song," has in singular fashion neglected this principal feature, which is rather subordinate in melodic respects; whereas the role the composer seems to have been fondest of is unquestionably that of the rejected lover, the minnesinger Wolfram.

Even though Wagner considers all other opera texts to be far inferior to his own, in many places the latter suffer from childish absurdity and scenic awkwardness. Miracles such as the transformation of the Lohengrin-swan into the little Duke of Brabant, and the departure in the shell, which is towed out of the river Scheldt with the aid of a flying dove, really seem to lie beyond the bounds of illusion. The inevitable bier at the end of each opera, and the "nonchalance" with which German kings and landgraves are treated in his texts, also give evidence of a remarkable lack of taste and historical discretion.

I have no idea how far the eccentric master has gone in his later compositions, particularly in his Bayreuthian *Ring of the Nibelung*, since I have not seen these productions; but even zealous supporters of his Muse steer clear of further explanation.

Tannhäuser was appreciatively received by our musical audience; but even though several portions of this remarkable composition will retain interest, one would hardly dare to prophesy any important future for the opera itself on our lyric stage.

In the way of lighter products, *The Postillion of Lonjumeau* was presented successfully, and two operettas, *Pathélin* and *Uncle's Wedding Present* [*Onkels Brudegave*], were rendered in *vaudeville* style by the drama company. The Ballet, which now had plenty of space in which to move, but, obviously, too small a *corps* to fill the much more capacious stage, combatted the lack of picturesque surroundings as best it could; for with the exception of *A Folk Tale*, which had been given new decorations, *The Toreador*, *Conservatoriet*, and *The Kermesse in Bruges* got along with whatever could be found useful if not exactly proper. The Amager parlor in *The King's Volunteers* underwent an adaptation, and we presented the second parts of *The Flower Festival* and *La Ventana*, due to lack of the scenery necessary for the first portions. The first act of *The Sleepwalker* was also reduced to a *divertissement*, wherein the very promising pupil, Athalia Flammé, made her debut with great success.

Arcona

By the month of January, the rehearsal of this grand ballet was already as good as finished, and even though it had previously been scheduled to introduce the mimic art to the new Theatre, it might still have been performed by the end of February or even the middle of March, had not cases of illness and our worst stumbling block—"naturalistic scene-painting"—pushed *The Vikings* and *A Bankruptcy* so far into spring that only at a very late date were the painters able to get started on the décor for *Arcona*. The orchestration of the music was also delayed, and as a result of this combination of things, the ballet did not appear on stage before *the seventh of May*—a time when attendance at Bjørnson's box-office play had not yet slackened, and the warm spring weather had lured the Ballet's finest audience out into the country.

In this account I shall not elaborate on the love and care with which I have treated this interesting subject, which mainly deals with the Danes' triumphant expedition to Venden and the capture of the Wends' chief fortress on Rügen, to which I had attached characteristic features of the heroic brothers, Absalon and Esbern Snare, as well as an imaginary picture of the worship of Svantevit. Suffice it to say that I was fortunate enough to find several new elements which concurred with the homage I have devoted to art and the proud memories of our native land.

The first performance was enthusiastically received. The conclusion of each act was hailed with thunderous approval, and the well-executed dancing numbers were rewarded with lively applause. As usual, the enthusiasm diminished considerably at subsequent performances, and what with the competition offered by Bjørnson's *Bankruptcy* and the rebirth of the beech woods in glorious spring, attendance decreased. Nonetheless, the ballet was presented seven times during the short period of the season that still remained, and was used at a gala performance for the Swedish-Norwegian royal couple, upon which occasion Hartmann, Paulli, and I were summoned to the royal box to be complimented by the august visitors. This special favor later led to honorable distinctions. Were I now to name all those who distinguished themselves in the action as well as the dances, the list would at this time be too long, while to single out some individuals might easily insult those who would not be mentioned. I will therefore save my testimonials for another occasion, and only say that the performance was worthy of the Danish stage.

The scene-painter Güllich deserves special thanks for the glorious settings with which he illustrated my work, while Hartmann's music came to assume a worthy place at the side of his ingenious compositions for *The Valkyr*, *The Lay of Thrym*, and *A Folk Tale*. Collaboration with this great artist has further attached me to his amiable personality and filled me with admiration for his spiritual gifts.

As in previous years, the Theatre's activity concluded with the benefit performance for the Ballet's Private Pension Fund.

As an introduction, I had arranged a historical hemicycle along the same lines as the artistic one by Paul Delaroche; but I had depicted a semicircle of famous men from Denmark's past, surrounded by emblems and allegorical figures. The tableau was supported by Frøhlich's overture to the ballet *Valdemar*, and met with lively sympathy on the part of the audience, which, throughout the ensuing ballet, *Arcona*, appeared to be in the best possible mood.

One must by no means think that the value of art is to be determined by clapping and bravos; but it stands to reason that anyone who has something to offer, be it from the stage or in daily life, is involuntarily influenced by the enthusiasm with which it is received, and this feeling cannot even be suspected from a silence that might signify both approval and disapproval.

Even though freedom of expression, in speech as well as in writing, is constitutionally guaranteed in the kingdom of Denmark, it seems to have been considerably limited at the "National"—honored with the designation of "Royal"—Theatre. To be sure displeasure is very seldom aired in as violent a manner as in olden days; but compared to the liveliness that prevails at the secondary theatres, especially at the often highly imperfect performances by touring—preferably Italian—opera companies, the *fashionable* silence, which among seventeen hundred spectators is only occasionally interrupted by applause from half a dozen friendly hands, must appear most peculiar.

People have vainly sought to search out the reason for this reticence, and alternately believe they have found it in the lack of a pit wherein young folk could, at a low price, enjoy a better show than that which nowadays completely warps their ideas about the scenic art. People have, and I dare say not without reason, put the blame on the—according to our conditions—all too high prices which prevent an entire class of intelligent art-lovers from attending the theatre and only on special occasions fill the house with curiosity-seekers. Discriminating and querulous criticism too has certainly had some effect on this susceptibility, and there are many who are afraid of being likened to *claqueurs de profession* if they openly express their opinions (a suspicion from which minor theatres are not entirely free). Of course, it cannot be denied that every vestige of humor is pounced upon with delight by our audience, which has a special liking for laughter and joking, and such an echo of gaiety is surely as effective and rewarding as the greatest applause. But all too often subtle dialogue, a striking speech, and the loveliest expression of true feeling go unnoticed unless they are accompanied by loud pathos, grandiose gestures, and—above all—a swift exit. In our opera singing, too, it is only the loud and the nerve-wracking that produce an effect, regardless of the fact that both intonation and delivery are completely erroneous.

It is *the Ballet,* in fact, which is in the most favorable position as far as rapport between the stage and the auditorium is concerned; for even though applause—except at premieres and on certain solemn occasions—falls but sparingly, and many a feature that depends on striking the right chord goes almost unnoticed, these marks of approval rarely fall in the wrong places, and one is almost tempted to regard choreography as the branch of art that is best understood and appreciated.

The company is—and with perfect right—forbidden to take curtain calls or to express its gratitude for applause by bowing and curtseying, which is bound to destroy any possible scenic illusion. On the other hand, it is to be wished that the "fashionable public," who sit in the numbered seats, would refrain from continually abandoning their expressions of approval to the gallery. From this would be gained unfailing encouragement for the actors and more lively entertainment for the spectators. What has chiefly contributed to preventing the members of fashionable society from applauding is, assuredly, the odious practice—as ridiculous as it is pernicious—of *claqueurs*, which has caught on at the French theatres and spread like the plague to other countries. All the same, it is a question whether the systematically organized *claque* has driven away real applause, or whether the dignified and blasé silence has lured the performing artists and directors into enlisting these robust "hired hands" so that, with their horny fists, they may prevent the audience from falling asleep.

However, financial considerations thrust artistic interests into the background. The sanguine expectations which people had cherished that the considerable proceeds would be adequate to cover all the Theatre's needs, and also yield such a profit that the Theatre could eventually renounce the public subsidy, appeared to be painfully disappointed. Not only the disproportionately high expenditures—the outcome of multifarious purchases as well as additional and more highly paid personnel—but the "rush job" and its inevitable after-effects were responsible for devouring the reserve capital which Berner had amassed during his term of administration. No doubt he had done this with the best of intentions, but had failed to consider that the money-granting Rigsdag (most of whose members did not look on the Theatre with a favorable eye) would come to the conclusion that "if an artistic institution can save money, it certainly has no need of a State subsidy."

This result was not long in coming; for *that year's* Minister of Culture—the span of the five-year budget having run out—now came forth with the proposal that, in view of the Theatre's "good business," the subsidy once again be reduced from the former 50,000 Rbd. to 80,000 Kroner. Whereupon our political economists seized the opportunity to cut it by another 20,000 Kroner; and since the enormous debt from the previous as well as the the most recent loan from the funds of the Sorø Academy remained unsettled, and the new Theatre had cost considerably more than the allotted sum, there was the prospect of a *Supreme Court action*. The Crisis now seemed to have taken on a chronic character!

THE 1875–1876 SEASON

IN former times, that is to say, thirty to forty years ago, when the demands on stage setting were not so great, when actors came to mutual agreements about their positions and the entrances and exits pertaining thereto, and the furniture in a drawing room play generally consisted of only two tables and four chairs, the stage director's job was neither as important nor as difficult as it is nowadays. It can indeed be interpreted in highly different ways. For example, Høedt in the drama and I in the opera have most closely focused our attention on the *ensemble*, and sought—when it was necessary—to influence the interpretation of roles. Others, and among them a good many theatre critics, regard new set decorations, magnificent costumes, elegant furnishings, etc. as the essentials; why, they have even gone so far in their demands upon correctness that an oil lamp in a room where the action takes place in the [eighteen-] thirties has been pointed out as an unforgiveable anachronism! Emil Poulsen soon found this work too fatiguing and also hampering to his activity as an actor. The post was therefore handed over to Etatsraad H. P. Holst, who had earlier served in this capacity.

The care that had to be expended on the Ballet and, frankly, the poor artistic dividends I derived from my efforts on behalf of the opera's progress moved me to give up my duties as stage director, except for my given promise to arrange Ivar Hallström's opera *The Bewitched* [*Den Bergtagna*], in which King Oscar cherished a very special interest. So while, out of a sense of duty and in accordance with the terms of my contract I took it on myself to compose all the dances inserted in the operas, I recommended my useful colleague Ludvig Gade for the directorial position.

In order to become more fully acquainted with the above-mentioned Swedish composition as regards the most appropriate casting of the roles and the imaginative stage setting, Paulli and I had, at the end of the previous season, been sent up to Stockholm, where we saw a successful performance with Arnoldson and Mlle. Riego in the leading roles. At the same time, we participated in the festivities that had been arranged for the Scandinavian Students Meeting, the popular character and cordial atmosphere of which remain indelibly imprinted in our memories.

Even though I had resigned from the Judging Committee from the beginning, I was nonetheless summoned to take part in the negotiations concerning the artistic embellishment [of the Theatre], and there had the opportunity to plead the cause of the lyric Muses, so that they too might have a place, at least above the projected carriage entrance if nowhere else, while Thalia and Melpomene sat enthroned next to Apollo on the Theatre's façade. Thus I was present *ex officio* at the unveiling of Stein's magnificent statue of Holberg, which forms a companion piece to that of Oehlenschläger, which has now been given a worthy place.

The inauguration took place on October 31, with an excellent address by Carl Ploug and singing by the members of the opera company. That same evening a gala performance was given, consisting of a dramatic sketch, *The Treasury Clerk* [*Renteskriveren*], by Chr. Molbech the Younger, *Pernille's Brief Ladyship* [*Pernilles korte Frøkenstand*], and an occasional ballet of my own composition, called

From the Last Century

In this work I had attempted to depict Court life at Fredensborg during the first years of the reign of Frederik V, when public entertainments were again loosed from the bonds which had oppressed them under his father of blessed memory. Holberg is portrayed as the celebrated poet and savant, and receives marks of honor from the King and his amiable Queen, who have prepared a special surprise for him by arranging an open-air spectacle and having the priceless figures from his popular comedies—from Prince Paris and the fair Helen to Peer Degn and Christoffer Eysenfresser—appear in mimed character dances.

For this fantasy-picture, I used the lovely set from the last act of *Times Change*, picturing a portion of the gardens at Fredensborg with the castle in the background. In addition, I had assembled a number of older musical pieces, which my faithful colleague, Wilhelm Holm, arranged with his usual good taste. The audience, which on this occasion was in the most pleasant mood imaginable, received Molbech's prologue and my little ballet most favorably; but what I could not expect to see perfectly understood was the characteristic reproduction of the kind of dancing which had, in the Rococo period, been considered the epitome of grace and virtuosity and which I had worked out through special study and with painstaking care. But in this, as in most artistic works, there was a host of little things that one creates for one's own enjoyment, with no claim to more widespread appreciation.

They had thought of retaining my composition as a suitable *Nachspiel* [epilogue] for several Holberg comedies; but since they are seldom performed nowadays, the interest in my occasional ballet cooled, wherefore it has now been laid aside and will soon be forgotten. Despite firmly established recognition, enthusiasm for the Holbergian Muse had diminished considerably, perhaps for the essential reason that the traditions from Lindgreen's, Frydendahl's, and Ryge's time, which were still preserved by Phister and Fru Søndring, have now been partially obliterated. The departure of these dramatic notabilities from the stage has been an irreparable loss. I have earlier spoken of Phister's great importance as an actor. But though Fru Søndring's sphere of character interpretations was certainly more limited, she brought to these portrayals a mastery that rightfully earned her a high place in the public's favor.

No previous season has displayed such a mass of adversities and obstacles of every kind. For example, lengthy illnesses, colds, mental disorders, and accidents provided us with a host of red posters, and would have caused the whole establishment extreme embarassment, had not the most indefatigable efforts on the part of the available personnel supported the management, kept the repertoire going, and brought the average proceeds up to the fixed sum. Nonetheless, an unkind press used this *Crisis* as an excuse for vehement attacks, and this led me to show matters in their true light in a little pamphlet called *Justice*.

The dramatic stage met with several misfortunes in the way of plays that would not "catch on" and others which did "catch on" but touched on overly sensitive spots. Among the former was *Imperial Festival at the Kremlin* [*Keiserfesten paa Kreml*], which, in spite of a considerable expenditure of time, energies, and money, was set aside after a few performances. In the latter category undeniably belongs the comedy *Will-o'-the-Wisps* [*Lygtemænd*], a play which, with remarkable wit and biting satire in a relatively interesting plot, described the latest movements in the direction of "freedom of thought" and eccentric "Socialism." Even before the play had come out in print and had been performed at the Theatre, a grand-scale demonstration was set in motion. *Social-Democraten* fulminated against the Theatre and the anonymous author, and the notorious trio of Pio, Brix, and Geleff,* who had recently had their terms of punishment pardoned, now appeared as the bandmasters of a violent concert of catcalls which, in spite of the standing regulation, interrupted the scenes at every pointed line. To be sure, this did result in fines and arrests, but the Socialists' fight against the applauding public continued throughout a number of performances and came to be regarded as rather indispensable, for when the conflict finally ended, the play lost a measure of its piquancy, and after seven performances this genuinely amusing and promising comedy entered into eternal rest on the shelves of the Theatre Archives.

During this winter, Fritz Holst, who had already made his appearance as a bright and popular comedy writer at the Folketheater, gave us a five-act play, *Time of Transition* [*I Overgangstiden*], wherein, just as in *Will-o'-the-Wisps*, the hysterical ideas of the present day were duly criticized. The storm of opposition had now subsided, and with uninterrupted calm, people followed the action in this character play which mainly emphasized witty and flowing dialogue that might have been more entertaining had it not lasted for four hours. The applause was unanimous, and the play survived its prescribed six or seven evenings; but since in these prosaic times "everything must be designed for utility," and the billboards in the foyer did not say "Completely sold out," it had to share the fate of other good, shelved works.

For the rest, Oehlenschläger was represented by *The Warriors of Miklagard*, Heiberg by *The Inseparables* [*De Uadskillelige*], Hertz by *The Savings Bank* and *The Poor Man's Tivoli* [*De Fattiges Dyrehave*], Hostrup by *The Neighbors* [*Gjenboerne*], and Henrik Ibsen by *The Vikings of Helgeland*. But, just as the previous year, the box-office play of the season was Bjørnson's *Bankruptcy*, which by virtue of its over-all realism not only appeals to the taste of our public but seems suited to the present talents of our dramatic stage. The French comedy, *Giboyer's Son*, also won both applause and popularity because of the same tendency and hence was superbly performed.

Except for a few interruptions, the opera presented its usual more or less classical repertoire, which won increased interest for a bit through the appearance of the Swedish singer, Fru Willman, in *The Daughter of the Regiment*. *The Two Arm-Rings* [*De to Armringe*], an adaptation of Oehlenschläger's drama to music by Axel Grandjean, enjoyed but a brief existence on our lyric stage. This talented test-piece by a younger composer was received with undeserved indifference by an audience that will never take the time to become acquainted with music that must be heard more than once in order to be fully understood.

The Doctor in Spite of Himself, another adaptation of a dramatic text to

*The first Danish Socialists.

music by Gounod, did not attract any particular attention. But finally, after lengthy preparations and unbelievable delays in the decorations and machinery, *The Bewitched* appeared *in the middle of May* and enjoyed five well-attended performances. As a result of a fatal whispering in our musical circles, this opera, which is applauded not only in Stockholm but at a number of German theatres, met with a singularly cold reception from our public. This unfavorable attitude could already be felt as early as the first choruses and ballads, which, in melody as well as characterization, contain so much that is lovely and original. The fact that Ivar Hallström is no epoch-making composer but is, on the contrary, influenced by the great masters, cannot deprive his work of its musical and dramatic worth, and he has unmistakably penetrated into the real nature of opera. As has been said, it was only with difficulty that the most poignant moments elicited from the listeners a meager applause, and—I am ashamed to say—it was only the dancing in the third act that brought a bit of life into the atmosphere. The composer, who attended one of the last performances, could do nought but admire the correct and tasteful production, and stated that in neither Stockholm nor Germany had the ballet made as effective a contribution as it had here, and that the trappings—costumes as well as set decorations—were finest at our Theatre.

The Ballet as an independent branch of art played a rather modest role during this season, partly because of a lack of the essentials needed to equip its main repertoire. To be sure, *Arcona* was still a refreshing novelty, but it had already suffered a severe blow as a result of the delay the previous spring. Attendance as well as applause had diminished considerably, and even though it was warmly appreciated in many quarters, one must concede that when an auditorium seats seventeen hundred spectators, half of whom hold complimentary tickets, the indifferent people are in the majority; and if these fail to appear, the Theatre operates at a loss.

Next to the cold and dry calculation that forces an artistic institution to weigh work and talent according to material profits, the percentage and profit-sharing system—which prevails in the form of the so-called *feux* or rewards of the game—is the thing that contributes most to subduing the spirit of the performers backstage. This last arrangement, in particular, oppresses the Ballet's performances, since the highly paid actors who are entitled to *feux* are reluctant to surrender their one-act plays to "curtain-raisers," but would rather act in several of them in one evening and, on the whole, look askance at sharing the profits with a numerous *corps de ballet* which, in the words of one man of genius, resembles a swarm of grasshoppers that devour his grain!

In Overskou's lengthy dissertation on the *feux* system, one will find my opinion to be completely divergent from the system followed, since I maintain that, as far as the rewards of the game are concerned, we ought to imitate the major theatres abroad; that is to say, we ought to fix for each prominent artist a *feu* completely independent of the greater or lesser profits of the evening. However, they tried instead to safeguard the treasury against possible risks, and chose a method which we may boast of as being unique to ourselves; in a manner of speaking, twilight fell on our auditorium.

The season was unusually rich in debuts, some of which were especially interesting; among others, the two sopranos, Julie and Augusta Schou, each of whom, in her genre, gives promise of becoming a fine acquisition for the opera.

Our Pension Fund Performance on June 1 consisted of *Youth and Folly* and the popular *King's Volunteers on Amager*. In both works it was Du Puy's melodies that "did the talking." A graceful little *divertissement*, composed by Brodersen and performed by his pupils, constituted the introduction to the evening's performance, and bore in its name a good omen for the Ballet's *Future*.

THE 1876–1877 SEASON

THE Theatre Crisis neared its climax. The attitude of the Folketing, which in previous sessions had shown itself to be particularly unfavorable toward every proposal made by the new Minister of Culture, was obviously aggravated by the considerable deficit and the enormous building debt. The reasons were ignored; the bare facts were submitted, and the numbers cried out for radical reforms. Our humane and art-loving Conferentsraad Linde was for the time being chosen as a propitiatory offering, and with the shortest possible notice received orders to relinquish his temporary appointment as Theatre Chief—an appointment that had lasted several years—and henceforth confine his activity to the post of Departmental Head in the Ministry of Culture.

It now appeared more obvious than ever that Justitsraad Berner's objections to the ill-timed demolition of the old Theatre had been perfectly justified, and he would have celebrated a less pitiful triumph if, immediately upon his return, he had given the Chief his (in many ways) valuable assistance and, especially in economic respects, striven to keep the latter's liberality and considerate indulgence within the bounds of our modest financial circumstances. Instead, he preferred to retire into an almost absolute passivity in which he acceded to demands which he would have fought against in his former position. Whether it was dissatisfaction over the use of the accumulated reserve fund or the result of a motive whose explanation he is reserving for the future, one thing is certain. This total lack of cooperation must be regarded as the essential cause of the upheaval which deprived the Theatre of a management that might have served it well, and provided us with a new Chief who, being unfamiliar with our internal affairs, assumed the position with orders to continue running the Theatre with as little expenditure and as large receipts as possible, even if it might entail the subordination of all artistic interests.

The first part of the administrative task was not so difficult after all, since the previous management had amply furnished the storehouses with the necessities, and in many areas it would be possible to introduce reasonable economies without halting the smooth operation of the Theatre. But it was a different matter with the second part, namely, the *receipts,* which were dependent not only on the makeup of the repertoire, which is so often upset by unforseen obstacles, but also on the mood of the theatregoing public. The increase in ticket prices, which was less noticeable during the first two years, since money was to be found in abundance among certain classes and the interest of novelty was also present, has to no small degree reduced the demand for the more expensive seats and has further dampened the enthusiasm at performances.

The purpose of the new Theatre, the auditorium of which was to contain three hundred more comfortable seats than before, was mainly to secure easier admittance for the general public and—if possible—thereby increase the sources of financial aid for this artistic institution. In recent years, the gross income per evening at the old Theatre was estimated at approximately 800 Rbd., subscriptions included. The new one, on the other hand, requires 2700 Kr., plus the State subsidy, to pay salaries, royalties, gas, fuel, and all other current expenses, in addition to paying the interest on the debt!

The idea that the National Theatre must be able to subsist on its own means, without the nation's help, seems to be ever more prevalent among the money-granting majority of the Rigsdag, and threatens to deprive the institution of the subsidy, which has been cut excessively, regardless of the [Theatre's] increasing needs. Thus the Danish stage, upon the façade of which *the People* are designated as builders and patrons, is open to only *the well-to-do.* But now, when the latter find themselves faced with a crisis produced by political and financial upheavals, half of the expensive seats are usually unoccupied, and, despite every effort, the prescribed gross income cannot be produced.

It would make this historical account *Overskouishly* long-winded and trivial were I to relate here the details of the economy which is presently encroaching upon the running of an artistic institution which—not entirely without reason—has been described by an honorable member of the Folketing as a *shop!* The red lantern* is the real criterion for judging the excellence of the wares displayed, and the extent to which the shop is patronized alone determines the value of the products.

The considerable sums which had been received, through voluntary gifts, for the artistic embellishment of the Theatre were now, for the most part, spent. The imposing group on the façade (after the model by the sculptor Ring) was finally put up; but an infinite number of things were missing in artistic as well as architectural respects. The projected carriage entrance with the statues of the lyric Muses was long in coming, and the vestibules and corridors were not the only parts that still stood in rough condition, for the public foyer lacked everything that could give meaning to the name. A strong,

*Indicating that the house was sold out.

new impetus was therefore needed to complete in a worthy form that which had been begun.

The brewer, Captain Jacobsen—a highly respected citizen who, out of rare patriotic devotion and great generosity, has erected for himself a lasting monument within the realm of art and science—offered, at his own expense, to have twelve marble busts and their pedestals executed in memory of famous Danish artists, musicians, and actors, on the condition that these works of art were to be set up in the public foyer as soon as it could be decorated in accordance with the accepted plan.

The offer was gratefully accepted, and the work executed by our foremost artists. But two years passed without anything having been done to give the foyer a decent appearance. The adjacent rooms were used for refreshment bars, but the serving of more substantial food and drink took place in the upper stories. However, business in the café seemed to suffer from this isolation, and it was suggested that, in return for payment of higher rent to the Theatre treasury, both the foyer and the loggia be given over to a café and the serving of food and drink, and be kept open to the public until midnight! Captain Jacobsen now sought to oppose this plan—which was completely contrary to that which had previously been decided upon—by offering 20,000 Kroner for the tasteful fitting out of the foyer, on the condition that daintier refreshments be served from the adjacent rooms. The busts were to be the principal ornaments and the whole was to correspond—as much as possible—to the high purpose of the Theatre.

In order to avoid the profanation that "pub life" involuntarily entails, the donor demanded a firm guarantee that the foyer must never be used for anything other than its original purpose, namely, that of furnishing an elegant meeting place for the audience during the intermissions. But here he ran up against the financial views of the authorities; for the rent from the food and drink concession offered an income which the Theatre treasury did not feel it ought to forego, and since the corridor separating the center of the dress circle from the foyer itself was at the same time given the name of *The Semicircular Foyer*, it was designated as the place where the busts would be mounted at some future date. In addition to this, the donor was informed that if he did not feel inclined to accept this arrangement, he was free to keep both his busts and his money!

It goes without saying that this handling of the matter did not induce other wealthy men to make further contributions to the artistic ornamentation; and those 20,000 Kroner now went to join the other considerable sums that Captain Jacobsen has spent on the restoration of Frederiksborg. Where the busts are to find their place, the future will show; in the meantime, a contract has been concluded with the confectioner, who, as temporary decoration, has had the whitewashed walls of the foyer coated with yellow distemper and given it a striking resemblance to the "second-class waiting room" in the railway station at Køge.

While the Supreme Court charge is hanging over the heads of two retired Ministers of Culture, and a majority in the Folketing urges the cessation of the running of the Theatre with the long-promised suspension of the annual State subsidy, it might be appropriate to insert here some observations on the Ballet, which, in this as in several previous critical moments, has been singled out as the Theatre's most costly and expendable luxury item.

Even though, during the current season, its activity has been hampered by obvious troubles, it has still had the good fortune not only of making the most modest demands on scenic equipment but also of being used as a relief measure whenever the repertoire found itself in dire straits. On the whole, the red billboards, which always disappoint the expectations of theatregoers, are less than favorable for the actors and most unfortunate for the ballets, which, being recorded in the cash book as the latest "poor houses," stand in danger of being set aside as worthless! Since the Ballet's opponents, both inside and outside the Rigsdag, never tire of bemoaning its costliness and advising its abolition or, at any rate, its curtailment, I must be permitted—even if I should fall victim to repetitions of what I have stated in other places and at other times—to show how it stands in relation to the rest of the Theatre's activity.

Insofar as any plan exists for the season's repertoire, the opera and the Ballet—that is, if they are not held back—will together make up *two-fifths* of the performances. But let us suppose that the Ballet, including its participation in opera and drama, fills one evening out of the seven which the theatre week usually contains; and in view of the fact that, under present conditions, the year's gross income—the public subsidy included—amounts to well over 700,000 Kroner, should not *one-seventh* rightfully be allotted to the Ballet? But since this branch of art, with salaries, scenery, teachers, *répétiteurs*, and shoe money, does not cost the Theatre 70,000 Kroner and rarely produces more than one major new ballet *every other year*, for which it not only uses older things from the drama but gladly hands over its decorations, costumes, and properties for use wherever they may be needed, where is the burden on the State and the Theatre treasury?

Were the Ballet to be abolished as an independent branch of art or be limited to an ornament in opera and drama, the repertoire would lose a vital support and scarcely be able to present the full number of performances, unless there suddenly appeared a flood of original plays, as well as good actors and singers, which would undoubtedly cost far more than the *corps de ballet*'s meager budget, and hardly less for scenic equipment.

It is so often repeated that the uninitiated might easily be influenced by the statement that "the Ballet does not pay"! If the above figures cannot persuade those prejudiced souls, it must at least be universally acknowledged that in any art there is another and higher recompense than money and more money. How much joy the pictures of folk life and the world of make-believe can arouse—pictures which the Ballet, and the Ballet alone, is capable of rendering; and who cares how large or small a contribution it has made to the evening's profits when, at the curtain's fall, the audience returns home, enlivened by the "festivity" that lies in the thrilling rhythms of the dance? It should be remarked that while the spoken drama is half and the opera almost solely made up of foreign works, *the Ballet* is a plant wholly fostered in our own soil, and has this in common with the most popular musical compositions: a successful work can retain its freshness and attraction for many years and, along with a change of cast, offer the interest of novelty even after a hundred performances. To this may be added the curious—given the nature of our national opera—circumstance that the Ballet is *the only* scenic field in which our Danish composers are able to have their works performed and appreciated!

Besides the unmistakable influence which the idealistic character of the Ballet has had on our dramatic and lyric stage, the fact remains that no small number of its most outstanding artists, male as well as female, have emerged from the Ballet. Moreover, if it be said that a branch of art, considered individually, must "pay," what are we to say about the orchestra, whose most prominent artists are miserably paid, but which in its entirety costs close to 80,000 Kroner!

The first months of the season were unusually rich in dramatic novelties, which were mounted with feverish haste, a fault one cannot blame on the opera, which succeeded in pushing its repertoire on through continual obstacles and indispositions—to be sure, with such masterworks as *Don Giovanni, The Magic Flute, The Huntsman's Bride, Youth and Folly,* and *The Barber of Seville.* But the drama did not have this kind of luck; for neither the grandiose French drama *Roland's Daughter* [*Rolands Datter*], nor *A High-Born Guest* [*En høibaaren Gjæst*] were hits, while *Between the Battles* [*Mellem Slagene*] and *The Transformed King* [*Den forvandlede Konge*] had only conditional success. Three one-act plays, *The Contest in Cremona* [*Væddekampen i Cremona*], *The Three Crispins* [*De tre Crispiner*], and H. P. Holst's *A-ing-fo-hi,* won applause and would have been able to lend fine support to the Ballet performances had the management not preferred to have them accompany operettas and comedies and—most of all—to present them on a single bill!

Lady Tartuffe, the salacious content of which had been found offensive as far back as Heiberg's Theatre directorship, was nowadays quite appealing to the public's taste and played to full houses a number of times. But those important words "Sold out" appeared on the billboards only for Scribe's interesting comedy *The Tales of Queen Marguerite,* which, in spite of a cast that is quite inferior to the one this play had at the time of its first appearance on our stage, still keeps the audience in the liveliest suspense and—like most of Scribe's dramas—leaves behind the most pleasing impression as a result of the superb development of the plot, the finely delineated characters, and the witty dialogue. If one compares this comedy writer's well-made plays with the everyday conflicts that form the core of the modern French repertoire, one must indeed admire—to a certain degree—the talent with which its authors strike the dissonant chords in modern social life and bring to light piquant episodes that belong to the crassest Realism more than to Romanticism ... but one goes home from the drama with a heavy heart and returns to Scribe, as to Mozart and Weber after having studied oneself to death on the Music of the Future.

That events in Scribe's plays often follow upon one another to the point of improbability is a natural consequence of the fact that he wishes to avoid a long and tiresome exposition of the plot; while the fact that, in the interest of the action, he frequently strikes out with vehemence against historical criticism mainly stems from the circumstance that, following Shakespeare's example, he allows history to serve as the frame for his imaginary pictures; for indeed, what saga mentions King Claudius of Denmark or Norway's stalwart ruler, the conqueror Fortinbras? Nor do we find in our chronicles any trace of the Court life that surrounds Hamlet, Prince of Denmark. And yet this tragedy is a matchless dramatic masterwork.

The opera *The Bewitched*, which, despite the care with which it was staged and performed, was received with a coldness that did not exactly give evidence of Scandinavian sympathies, barely received permission to be presented twice, while *Hans Heiling* lacked a female singer who would dare to take it upon herself to be Queen of the Spirits. On the other hand, repeated attempts were made at turning operettas into *vaudeville* song. As a result, *The Amorous Artisans*, by Gassmann, an *opera buffa* which a hundred years ago had been sung in Vienna by Italy's greatest virtuosi was presented here, abridged and adapted into a farce, with something resembling singing numbers.—It remains to be seen what the lyric stage will be permitted to present up until the end of the season.

The Ballet was apparently destined to be pushed aside; the major part of its repertoire had lost its scenery, which, instead of being augmented and adapted, was cut up and sold. However, a contract was concluded with the scene-painter whereby he agreed to furnish twenty-two new settings every year, and it seemed as though the Ballet might then be given a bit of consideration at least. But here it came up against a most original circumstance—namely, that the work was paid for by the square ell, whether it was painted or merely sketched. And, since *eleven hundred* square ells were said to constitute one setting—regardless of whether the products furnished consisted of restorations, individual set pieces, curtains to prevent anyone peeping in, carpets to lay on the floor, doors, pictures, and other movable objects—suffice it to say that it does not take long to cover eleven hundred ells, and while the Theatre treasury foots the bill for the full number, scarcely eight out of the twenty-two settings appear suitable for use on stage.

Fortunately, the set decorations for *The Valkyr* were on the account for the previous year and consequently were not included in the obligations of the contract. Thus this ballet was allowed to go on, and throughout the sub-

Above: INTERIOR OF THE NEW ROYAL THEATRE, probably depicting a scene from Bournonville's *Arcona*. Lithograph by Fritz Ahlgrensson from *Illustreret Tidende*. Below: *FROM SIBERIA TO MOSCOW*. Daniel Krum as Ivanov and Maria Westberg as Nathalia are shown in the "Mazurka" in Act I, while the Cossack leader (Ludvig Gade) delivers a toast in the foreground. Drawing from *Illustreret Tidende*, 1876. Both, Teatermuseet, Copenhagen.

THE OLD BALLETMASTER WITH YOUNG STUDENTS
As befitted Bournonville' stress on strong male dancing, boys outnumbered
girls in this undated photograph. Det kgl. Bibliotek, Copenhagen.

scription series played to particularly good houses (the red lamps were even lighted on one occasion); but because of the nightly expenses (super-numeraries, shoe money, etc.) it was once again set aside until further notice!

Far from Denmark was performed in the new Theatre for the first time, and, like *Napoli, The King's Volunteers,* and *La Ventana,* was used mostly as an emergency replacement in case of sudden changes in the scheduled reper-toire. It can almost be stated that if during this season a previous decision had not brought about the performance of a new ballet, the music for which had already been composed in the course of the summer, I would hardly have been allowed to present

From Siberia to Moscow

Among the various motifs which I have thought of as being useful for the ballet, a banishment to Siberia, with a possible escape and liberation, ap-peared to offer dramatic interest and also to provide the opportunity for char-acter dancing. Mme. Cottin's charming tale *Elisabeth* contains the description of just such an exile; and as for the escape: well, in Stockholm, at the home of Lars Hjerta, a member of the House of the Nobility and founder of [the news-paper] *Aftonbladet,* I several times met the well-known Social Democrat, Ba-kunin† — at that time an Old Russian revolutionary who, for his overwrought opinions, had been banished to one of the strictest punishment districts but had managed to escape from there in the most marvelous fashion, accom-panied by his faithful wife.

These elements had not yet sorted themselves out in my imagination, much less taken the form of a design. But when in the spring of 1874 I visited Russia's capitals and received a host of impressions (some of which I have de-scribed in a series of articles in *Illustreret Tidende*), what I had seen and ex-perienced became ever more strongly impressed upon me. Then, since my friends incessantly urged me to compose a Russian ballet, I conceived the li-bretto, and after it had won the approval of the Theatre administration, I worked out all the details with the musician C. C. Møller, whose melodious-ness has done much to give the action as well as the dancing a proper na-tional character.

Here within a condensed frame is pictured a Russian nobleman who, taken with the ideas of the first French Revolution, has incurred the disfavor of Tsar Paul and has been banished to a remote hunting district of Siberia, where he would have pined away with grief and resentment had not his young daughter striven to calm his mind and allay his pain by her filial love. Music is one of the talents with which her genteel upbringing has endowed her; from her harp she calls forth melodies that lure him back to his happier days, and by the indescribable grace with which Russian and Polish ladies

† Mikhail Bakunin (1814–1876) was the great prophet of world-revolutionary Nihilism. His major work, *God and the State,* was posthumously published in French.

perform their national dances, she momentarily succeeds in making him forget his desperate plight.

Ivanov, a young officer who as a result of a duel has been exiled to the same district, has won Nathalia's love, and when he is recalled to the army by an Imperial order, resolves to effect the escape of both father and daughter. He takes them to Moscow, where, the following year, after having brought news of the victory at the battle of Novi,‡ he receives a ring together with the Emperor's promise that whatever favor he asks shall be granted him.

At a Court fête, where in an allegorical ballet several of Europe's rivers are depicted in appropriate dances, he takes the opportunity to introduce Nathalia as the representative of the Neva. She captivates everyone with her dancing, and emboldened by the approval of the Imperial couple, dares to beg mercy for her father. But the Autocrat's forgiveness is obtained only when Ivanov reminds him of the significance of the ring and the Imperial promise. The national anthem is then played in praise of the Tsar's magnanimity.

This work, with which I hoped to conclude my series of compositions, was received with unanimous applause—a mark of approbation that might have been due to its unique character or even to the interest generated at the moment by Russia's entrance into the Oriental question. However, the ballet was undeniably successful because of the performances of the leading roles as well as the supporting parts. Frøken Westberg as Nathalia, Valdemar Price as Smirnov, Krum as Ivanov, and Carl Price as Tsar Paul were each "praiseworthy."

The Cossacks with their drunken leader (Gade) created a furor, while among the representatives of the various rivers, it was the Jockeys' Race that took the prize. The effect produced by the river Neva formed the climax, and here I will honestly state that, especially in the composition of the Slavic dances, I had allowed myself to be strongly influenced by what I had seen the superb character dancers Radina and Madayeva perform in St. Petersburg, though I neither could nor would furnish an exact copy of it.

As far as the décor for the ballet was concerned, this time the Theatre treasury got off rather cheaply, since a good part of the costumes and the magnificent hall in the second act were left over from the unsuccessful *Imperial Festival at the Kremlin.* For economy's sake the artists were asked to create the set for the Siberian log room with the raftered ceiling so that with little alteration it might be used as the room in the Norwegian farmhouse in both *The Wedding Festival* and *The Mountain Hut.* But our *naturalistic scene-painters* made this plan impossible by designing such a specialized setting that no adaptation could be made. Furthermore, there was the prospect that this ballet, which had enjoyed so favorable a reception, might be able to play often to well-filled houses; but since it took up only half an evening, it had to

‡ Fought August 15, 1799, during the French revolutionary wars in Italy. A combined Russian-Austrian force under Marshal Suvarov defeated a French army led by General Joubert, who was killed early in the battle.

be presented together with plays that ran far too long, and in this respect the combinations have not been successful, partly because of the reasons touched upon above. How this work, as well as my older ballets, will fare in the future depends upon Fate, that is to say, the Theatre administration, but above all on the public, which, not only by its applause but mainly by its large attendance, furnishes proof of the value of my work.

During this season, the problem of running of the Theatre with as large a profit and as strict an economy as possible seemed to our political economists to be solved in a fairly satisfactory manner. Part of the debt was paid off, and they hoped to persuade the majority of the Folketing to continue the annual subsidy. Thus there should be every reason to accord the new administration an unconditional vote of confidence. But where is there to be found an administration, and especially a theatre director, who dares to revel in unanimous applause! It may resound in the box office and the treasury, but the august Muses, who sit majestically enthroned at the side of Apollo on the façade of the Theatre, lead but a miserable existence within its walls. The artistic element suffers from obvious neglect, and, despite the amount of attention that is bestowed upon the spoken drama, no true satisfaction prevails within its domain, and its members wistfully look back upon the most recent past — with which they had not been at all pleased, as a matter of fact.

Truth to tell, under conditions such as those of the present, a Theatre Chief's position is anything but enviable; for whether consideration be shown for the artistic or the economic side of the administration, someone always takes offense. Artists are as little capable of engaging in financial calculations as political economists are in the proportionate evaluation of talents. It would be wonderful if one could find a way to make these interests compatible; but the present conflict is producing only apathy and dejection. We are confronting purely commercial efforts, whose sole aim is to bring about such pecuniary results as can free the State from the burden of supporting a mainly artistic institution which up to now has borne the name of "The Danish Stage" — with the sobriquet of "Royal." Whether this prolonged crisis will entail the total decline of the Theatre or give way to a sounder state of affairs, it does not seem to lie in the power of the legislature or the Theatre management to reconcile art with the practical running of the Theatre. The impetus must therefore come from writers and artists on the one hand, and from the press and the theatregoing public on the other — provided that each of the interested parties is conscious of its calling and responsibility.

For my own part, the last months of the season were taken up with rehearsals, with partly new casts, of my surviving compositions. There were sixteen of these. Among the major ones were *Valdemar, Napoli, The Kermesse, The Valkyr, A Folk Tale, The Lay of Thrym,* and *Arcona;* while the minor works included *The Toreador, The Flower Festival, Ponte Molle, The Wedding Festival, Far from Denmark, Conservatoriet, The King's Volunteers, The Mountain Hut,* and *From Siberia to Moscow.* I can expect only a small part of these works to be performed in the immediate future—partly because of the cost of the renovated décor for a number of them; partly because there is neither time nor space for the necessary rehearsals on the constantly occupied stage; and, finally, because the management does not believe these works have the power to fill the house—a view that is all the more predominant as the art of putting together a bill composed of a popular play and a good ballet is completely ignored or, I should say, avoided by the present administration. Whereas, under previous conditions, I had been *requested* to compose and present ballets, it was now a matter of *obtaining permission* to have them performed and then only on certain conditions, such as allowing the first act of *The Mountain Hut* to be set in a luxuriant Danish beech wood or seeing it laid to eternal rest! To provide four new spruce and pine wood wings in place of those that had been rashly sold from the old Theatre's storehouse was considered too costly and inexpedient. I was involuntarily reminded of our unforgettable performances in Drammen (1852), where we presented a Neapolitan *divertissement* in a setting that depicted a grove of chalk-white birch trunks. O, Bjerkebæk, my Norwegian fellow artist, what a treat that would be for you!

This year, the French author Victorien Sardou was a "goldfish" for the Danish Stage and the Folketheater, since he provided both of them with box-office plays. While *Old Bachelors* [*Gamle Ungkarle*] created a furor on Nørregade,* people came in droves to Kongens Nytorv to watch a thrilling crime story with cross-examination and a successful solution resulting from the fact that the murderer hangs himself in prison, thereby bringing the investigations to a halt. One was involuntarily transported to the *"Boulevard du Crime"* in Paris, where in my youth I had seen such melodramas as *Cartouche, Cardillac, Mandrin, Le Chiffonnier,* and others which—as far as talent in production was concerned—could fully compare with *Ferreol.* But even though this piece was superbly given by our actors, I am tempted to repeat the outcry of those French officers who saw the English cavalry under Lord Cardigan make the furious charge at Balaklava: "It's brilliant, but it's not war!" In other words, to me the piece does not seem suitable for our national stage, and I was malicious enough to fancy an exchange between the two rival theatres. Perhaps *Old Bachelors* would meet with approval at our theatre; it would, at any rate, make for good business.

Rumor has it that the staging of this play at the Folketheater is the work of Professor Høedt, whose brilliant but all too short acting career has left behind it memories and a sense of loss, mingled with disapproval of his unwavering decision to tread the stage no more. As I have previously stated, he had a number of years ago given up his post of stage director; but up until the beginning of this season he had continued to act as teacher and advisor to all those who wished to be trained for the drama. With the departure of the act-

---

*The Folketheater was located in Nørregade, while the expression *Kongens Nytorv* is synonymous with the Royal Theatre, situated on that square.

ing directors, he was asked by those in high quarters to assume the post of Theatre Chief. But whether he did not feel himself to be completely equal to this job, or whether the terms he laid down for the future existence of the Theatre were not in consonance with the accepted ideas, suffice it to say that the negotiations were broken off and the present administration appointed, with the result that Høedt definitely withdrew from every function at the Royal Theatre. It now seems as if this loss may prove to be of advantage to the secondary theatres.

Another considerable loss is approaching with the end of the current season, as the gifted and popular actor Hultmann retires, partly for reasons of health. His winning personality, combined with his refreshing humor, clear diction, and tasteful appearance, made him uncommonly excellent in the roles of elegant young "bon-vivants," in the guise of a merry student as well as in the more aloof forms of the aristocrat; and even though up to now he has retained his youthful appearance in a marvelous fashion, he still knows how to depict the character of older gentlemen with the most charming dignity mingled with deep emotion. This actor is unmistakably one of those "types" which are gradually disappearing from the stage, here as well as abroad; and his departure will leave behind a void that will be terribly difficult to fill.

We are, by the bye, approaching a period when age and infirmity will manifest themselves in a number of our most outstanding dramatic artists; and even though some fine younger talents will be able to maintain the repertoire in a single genre, there is still every reason for the management not to reject the assistance the other branches can offer.

Just as in Stockholm the lyric stage is predominant, so too will the spoken drama always remain our Theatre's principal branch, even when its creative forces are weakened, because the Danish audience is above all dramatically inclined, and because the ring and inflective character of our language exert their magic power, especially in comedy. But if one day Shakespeare and Oehlenschläger should no longer find any worthy interpreter, and should the literary currents of the nineteenth century have washed away the masterworks of Molière and Holberg, there will arise a dangerous competition with the progressive secondary theatres. Thus the Royal Theatre must assert its precedence by means of something which those other stages are unable to supply, namely, opera and ballet.

"We still actually have a Ballet!" Thus exclaims Erik Bøgh—to whom I owe special thanks for his efforts to propagate sound ideas about the art form to which I have devoted my activity—in one of his humoristic *feuilletons*. This statement of admiration is surely not unmotivated if one considers the petty, sometimes petty-minded, conditions under which the Ballet has had to fight its way forward, and, especially, the unfortunate desire to pull it down, put it down, and *shut it down*—a desire which has been constantly voiced and which has not been without a certain influence on public feeling. People delight in pointing out that even if, in the course of a season, half a dozen dramas or operas prove to be fiascoes, the prestige of these art forms remains unshaken. But just let the Ballet appear with a single unsuccessful work, and there are immediate outcries about the lack of justification for the existence of this genre and demands for its abolition or curtailment!

Like the Ballet, the opera—though to a lesser degree—suffers from indifferent treatment, and for almost the same reasons, since the latter is not allowed to present its finest repertoire. And yet it has this very year, by the appearance of Mme. Trebelli as Azucena in *The Troubadour*, given the public a rare artistic treat—a treat that was, of course, provided at the expense of the "national" idea at doubly high price, but one that was, for all that, marvelous and of great musical and dramatic interest. She was supported by the finest members of our Danish opera company and by the Swedish bass Conrad Behrens. This naturally resulted in a Babelish confusion of languages—Italian, Danish, and Swedish—the effect of which was rather like a parody and was reconciled only by Mme. Trebelli's masterly acting, subtle shading of tones, and clear rendering of the text (a useful lesson for our own opera singers).

This famous singer was less satisfactory as Rosina in *The Barber of Seville,* in which favorite opera we reluctantly encountered the farcical treatment that this lyric masterwork is currently given abroad, while here in Denmark we have always thought of the young ward as the character who is later to appear as the noble Countess Almaviva in Mozart's *Marriage of Figaro.* In Paris, in 1820, I attended one of the first performances of the aforesaid opera. Mme. Mainvielle-Fodor sang the part of Rosina in a most captivating manner, but was a bit too cold as a romantic heroine. Seven years later I heard Henrietta Sontag in the same role, which was perfectly suited to both her talent and her personality. But it was the ingenious Mme. Malibrán who gave Rosina the quality of playfulness which, through imitation, has since degenerated into vulgarity and robbed this "type" of a girl in love of its fragrance.

Even if, in this portion of the history of the Royal Theatre and the Danish Ballet, I have described the prolonged hovering between "to be and not to be" as a Crisis which has not yet been resolved but must be viewed as a transition to either disintegration or rehabilitation, I am still enough of an optimist—or more properly speaking, orthodox in my belief in the vitality of art—to always expect a successful outcome. But one cannot hide the fact that art on the whole has more and more entered the service of commerce and has thereby lost a measure of that freedom in which genius can grow. This fact cannot be argued away, but ought to be modified to the effect that commerce itself has a higher goal than that of simply "making money," although every activity is certainly dependent upon the necessary means of subsistence. When the annual State subsidy is cut back, aye, even threatened with total abolition, and there also appear motions calling for the closing of the Theatre and the temporary cessation of its operation—which would be tantamount to pensioning its permanently appointed members and casting those in a less fortunate position out into the world without bread—what will become of the

National Institution, and how will they ever manage to one day reassemble the scattered forces! May it gradually dawn on these reformers that the Theatre, as it has been understood by the nation from its origin, is not merely an entertainment establishment nor a commercial business but *a school*, which has its definite mission, of equal importance for both morals and taste.

I will not discuss the end of this season, except to wish [the Theatre] every possible success with the new works it still has in store and to recommend our good ballet company to the encouraging patronage of the public. For my own part, it would be most ungrateful of me to complain of a lack of personal recognition; but I must be permitted to remark that it is of little use to praise the master when one is continually bent on destroying his work, and such a tendency is actually present. I have faithfully fought with words, writing, and action, until I now stand at the goal, not of my efforts but of my official and artistic activity.

When in 1847 and 1865 I published the first and second volumes of *My Theatre Life,* both times I considered my career as a ballet-poet to be finished. This time it is neither dejection nor bitterness but my seventy-odd years which, more than any mental or physical weakness, convince me of my need for peace and quiet. Were I ten years younger, I would still try to defend my post; but I stand at "a turning point," and the last book by our recently deceased great lyricist† has been helpful in warning me against holding out to the bitter end. I dare say I would still be able to serve for some time as a teacher and director, but conditions are imposed on my productivity, and the ballet repertoire needs a variety of fresh new works.

Times change, taste changes; many of the strings that once resounded so delightfully are broken now or out of tune, and even if I were to succeed in working out a successful idea, in having it supported by a splendid musical score, beautifully performed and fitted out, and—in additon—well received by the public—it would not be enough nowadays, if the billboards in the vestibule did not often say "Sold out" and the red lamps did not lure the curious to the house. —Happy the man who is able to retire when he comes to grips with the fact that he does not belong here any more.

I believe I have now shown in some detail the importance of the Ballet for the Danish stage. In conclusion, I must combat the false opinion, which has often been expressed, that "with Bournonville the Ballet stands and falls." As early as during my absence in Stockholm in the years 1861–1865, it was seen that the repertoire could retain both freshness and interest. How much more now, when I am entrusting it to kind hands and have, furthermore, seen to it that those very compositions upon which the public has bestowed its favor are fully rehearsed and cast, partly with younger talents. Thus there is every reason to envisage for the Ballet a future that should

† Overskou; cf. "The 1873–1874 Season."

prove equally satisfying to both itself and its well-wishers—provided it is allowed to work.

Admittedly, this repertoire will not be able to last indefinitely; but just as only two or three works by each favorite poet and composer remain out of the whole mass of their compositions, a couple of my best ballets—as the property of the Nation—might be preserved for posterity.

At the time of Galeotti's death (1816), no one suspected that an eleven-year-old boy, "little August," was destined to become the famous master's successor. Thus there is probably no one except me who knows that as soon as I have retired—but not before—a younger man with a talent for composition will emerge and, beginning, as I did, with smaller works, commend himself to the kind indulgence of the public.

The Old Master's best wishes, good advice, and paternal blessing shall accompany this fine young artist on his future career.

I herewith conclude the first portion of the third volume of *My Theatre Life*, and as I gratefully look back upon the bygone years and confidently go to meet the coming days, I intend to prepare, at my country home, the next two sections, which shall contain *Memories from my Youth and Travels* and also *Biographical Sketches Drawn from Memory.*‡

AUGUST BOURNONVILLE

Copenhagen, April, 1877.

NOTE. Since, in the interest of truth, I have stated facts with observations that may cause objections to be raised, I must hereby declare that I shall accept any correction with a good grace.—A. B.

‡ As will be seen, these sections bore somewhat different titles when published.

II

Works Done for the Danish Royal Theatre by August Bournonville, During the Period of Time from September 1, 1829, to April 30, 1877

BALLETS ARRANGED

The Sleepwalker [*Søvngængersken*] (3 acts), after Scribe and Aumer. Music by Hérold.

The Duke of Vendôme's Pages [*Hertugen af Vendomes Pager*] (1 act), after Aumer. Music by Gyrowetz.

Paul and Virginia [*Paul og Virginie*] (3 acts), after Gardel. Music by Kreutzer.

Romeo and Giulietta [*Romeo og Giulietta*] (5 acts), after Galeotti. Music by Schall.

Nina, or The Girl Driven Mad by Love [*Nina eller den Vanvittige af Kjærlighed*] (2 acts), after Milon. Music by Persuis.

ADAPTATION FROM A FOREIGN LIBRETTO

La Sylphide [*Sylphiden*] (2 acts), after Nourrit and Taglioni. Music by Løvenskjold.

ORIGINAL WORKS

Victor's Wedding [*Victors Bryllup*] (1 act). Keck.

Faust (3 acts). Keck.

The Veteran [*Veteranen*] (1 act). Zinck.

The Tyroleans [*Tyrolerne*] (1 act). Frøhlich.

Valdemar (4 acts). Frøhlich.

Don Quixote (3 acts). Zinck.

The Isle of Fantasy [*Phantasiens Ø*] (3 acts). Hartmann and others.

Festival in Albano [*Festen i Albano*] (1 act). Frøhlich.

The Toreador [*Toreadoren*] (2 acts). E. Helsted.

Napoli (3 acts). Paulli, Helsted, Gade.

The Childhood of Erik Menved [*Erik Menveds Barndom*] (4 acts). Frøhlich.

Bellman (1 act). Paulli.

Raphael [*Rafaello*] (4 acts). Frøhlich.

Kirsten Piil (3 acts). Helsted.

The New Penelope [*Den nye Penelope*] (2 acts). Løvenskjold.

The White Rose [*Den hvide Rose*] (1 act). Paulli.

Old Memories [*Gamle Minder*] (1 act). Paulli.

Conservatoriet (2 acts). Paulli.

Psyche (2 acts). Helsted.

The Kermesse in Bruges [*Kermes-*

sen i Brügge] (3 acts). Paulli.

The Wedding Festival [Bru-defærden] (2 acts). Paulli.

The Crystal Palace [Chrystalpalad-set] (3 acts). Paulli.

A Folk Tale [Et Folkesagn] (3 acts). Gade and Hartmann.

Abdallah (3 acts). Paulli.

In the Carpathians [I Karpatherne] (3 acts). Paulli.

The Mountain Hut [Fjeldstuen] (2 acts). Winding and Hartmann, Jr.

The Flower Festival [Blomsterfes-ten] (1 act). Helsted and Paulli.

Far from Denmark [Fjernt fra Dan-mark] (2 acts). J. Glæser and others.

The Valkyr [Valkyrien] (4 acts). Hartmann.

Ponte Molle (2 Acts). Holm and Lincke.

The Lay of Thrym [Thrymsqviden] (4 acts). Hartmann.

The King's Volunteers [Livjægerne] (1 act). Holm.

Cort Adeler (4 acts). Heise.

A Fairy Tale in Pictures [Eventyr i Billeder] (3 acts). Holm.

Arcona (4 acts). Hartmann.

From Siberia to Moscow [Fra Si-berien til Moskou] (2 acts). C. C. Møller.

A TOTAL OF 36 ORIGINAL BALLETS WITH 88 ACTS.

BALLET DIVERTISSEMENTS

Acclaim to the Graces [Gratiernes Hylding]

Soldier and Peasant [Soldat og Bonde]

Hertha's Offering [Herthas Offer]

The Fatherland's Muses [Fædre-landets Muser]

The Prophecy of Love [Kjærligheds Spaadomme]

The Irresistibles [De Uimodstaael-ige]

The Sailor's Return [Matrosens Hjemkomst]

La Ventana

The Earnest Maiden [Den alvorlige Pige]

Scandinavian Quadrille [Skandi-navisk Quadrille]

In Memory of Weyse [Weyses Minde]

The Mandarin's Daughters [Man-darinens Døttre]

Farewell to the Old Theatre [Far-vel til det gamle Theater]

From the Last Century [Fra det forrige Aarhundrede]

IN ALL, 14 BALLET DIVERTISSEMENTS.

APOTHEOSES FOR

Shakespeare, Mozart, Holberg, Oehlenschläger, and a series of famous Danes.

DANCES AND ARRANGEMENTS FOR DRAMAS

Isabella

Yelva

Saint Olaf [Olaf den Hellige]

Aladdin

Gioacchino

Maskarade

DANCES AND ARRANGEMENTS FOR OPERAS BY THE FOLLOWING COMPOSERS

Adam

The Queen's Life Guard [Dronningens Livgarde]
The Postilion of Lonjumeau [Postillonen i Lonjumeau]

Auber

The Mute Girl of Portici [Den Stumme i Portici]
Brahma and the Bayadère [Brama og Bayaderen]
The Fiancée [Bruden]
The Master Mason [Muurmesteren]
The Black Domino [Den sorte Domino]
The Crown Jewels [Kronjuvelerne]
The Bronze Horse [Broncehesten]

Beethoven

Fidelio

Boïeldieu

The White Lady [Den hvide Dame]
Little Red Riding Hood [Den lille Rødhætte]
Jean de Paris [Johan fra Paris]

Bredal

The Guerilla Band [Guerillabanden]

Cimarosa

The Secret Marriage [Det hemmelige Ægteskab]

Donizetti

Lucia di Lammermoor [Lucia af Lammermoor]
Lucrezia Borgia

Glaeser

The Wedding at Lake Como [Brylluppet ved Como-Søen]
The Nix [Nøkken]

Gluck

Orpheus (Act II)
Iphigenia in Aulis [Iphigenia i Aulis]
Iphigenia in Tauris [Iphigenia paa Tauris]

Hallström

The Bewitched [Den Bjergtagne]

Hartmann the Younger

The Elf Maiden [Elverpigen]
The Corsican [Korsikaneren]

Hartmann the Elder

The Raven [Ravnen]
Little Kirsten [Liden Kirsten]

Heise

The Pasha's Daughter [Paschaens Datter]

Hérold

Zampa
Le Pré-aux-Clercs [Klerkevænget]

Lortzing

Tsar and Carpenter [Czar og Tømmermand]

Maillart

Villars' Dragoons [Villars Dragoner]

Marschner

Hans Heiling
The Templar and the Jewess [Tempelherren og Jødinden]

Méhul

Joseph and his Brethren [Joseph og hans Brødre]
Uthal

Meyerbeer

Robert of Normandy [Robert af Normandy]
The Huguenots [Huguenotterne]

Mozart

Don Giovanni [Don Juan]
The Abduction [Bortførelsen]
The Marriage of Figaro [Figaros Bryllup]
The Magic Flute [Tryllefløiten]

Nicolai

The Merry Wives of Windsor [De muntre Koner i Windsor]

Rossini

Moses
William Tell [Wilhelm Tell]

H. Rung

Federigo

Saloman

The Diamond Cross [Diamantkorset]

Verdi

The Troubadour [Troubadouren]

Wagner

Lohengrin
The Mastersingers [Mestersangerne]
Tannhäuser

IN ALL, 51 OPERAS AND *OPERAS-COMIQUES*

CHARACTER DANCES AND INDIVIDUAL *PAS* COMPOSED AND ARRANGED FOR

Mesdemoiselles:Krætzmer;Grahn; Fjeldsted; Nielsen; Fredstrup; Funck; Juliette, Sophie, and Amalie Price; the Healey sisters; Petersen; Norberg; Schnell; Scholl; Cetti; and Westberg. Messieurs: Hoppe; Brodersen; Lund; V. Price; Krum; Johansson; Funck; Julius Price; E. Hansen; and myself.

IN ALL, 32 DIFFERENT DANCES.

PART TWO

*Memoirs and
Period Pictures*

INTRODUCTION

WHEN I published the first volume of *My Theatre Life* nearly thirty years ago, I really believed I had set down *everything* I felt deeply about in artistic respects and had told *most* of what, as far as I was concerned, might be of interest to my patrons among the theatre-loving public. Strangely enough, just when I stopped performing as a dancer I became a bit of a writer and had the opportunity to develop myself stylistically through a number of small pamphlets. However when I look back on my first literary efforts—not only in my ballet libretti, where the difficulty of describing fleeting images and the inconvenience of sustaining a narrative in the present tense continually stand in the way of style, but especially in the chapter "Myself"—I am astonished at the naïveté with which I record my mistakes and shortcomings while I do justice to my good qualities. I dare say people have more than once had occasion to smile at this, but one merit cannot be denied my frank statements: they bear the unmistakable stamp of conviction.

Eighteen years later (1865) the second volume was published, and in addition to my reflections and reminiscences it contained full ballet libretti* and descriptions of national festivals from a period so memorable to all Danes. The years had considerably matured my manner of presentation as well as my opinions, but despite my use of far richer material, there were a number of people who missed my earlier naïve freshness. All the same, the former must be ascribed to the youth of my literary activity; here, on the other hand, I entered into its manhood; and now as the third volume slowly appears, with appropriate pauses, I hope it will express the mild feelings of a vigorous old age through a retrospective glance at times long past and a look ahead at what is to come.

With regard to my life's story, I will refer my good readers to Volume I of *My Theatre Life*, which contains the sum total of my earlier activity, and beg them not to be surprised that I, with good capabilities and a careful upbringing, could devote my efforts to the objective of claiming for the ballet— that is to say, the expressive art of dancing—a rightful place within the realm of "the beautiful."

Apart from the troubles and anxieties which my attempts to carry out this idea have caused me, the remainder of my career presents but an ordinary life sprinkled with episodes which, were they embellished and interwoven with a

---

*Omitted from this edition.

bit of falsehood, might make a rather interesting *novelle*. But since in my journey through the world I have been more a spectator than an actor in the life that goes on outside the gaslit stage, having been untouched by the storms that produce adventurous situations, I shall depict in all simplicity the impressions and events which appear ever more clearly before my memory now that, undisturbed by the pressures of theatrical life, I can allow reflection to hold sway.

I

Memoirs and Period Pictures

MY EARLIEST IMPRESSIONS

THE commotion following the piratical attack by the English ... the abominable destruction in the northern quarters of the city ... the leveled ruins after the burning of Copenhagen and the Palace ... the enthusiasm for the triumphant Napoleon ... the illuminations and fireworks in honor of the birth of the King of Rome* ... the Great Comet† and the festive processions on the [feast] days of the Orders of the Elephant and the Dannebrog—all these stand vividly before my memory. That amid the horrors of the bombardment I served as an amusing diversion for those families who together with my mother and my older brother and sister had sought shelter in the merchant Pechier's vaulted cellars (now the seat of the Industrial Association) and even then revealed the future theatre child has so often been told to me that I almost fancy I can remember it myself. But what I can distinctly recall is the dancing of the Spanish prisoners of war at Gammelholm on the day they were exchanged and set free.‡ For a long time thereafter the clack of imitation castanets echoed through the streets of Copenhagen.

The high points of my childhood existence were—as they generally are for children—birthdays and Christmas. Among the former the nineteenth of May reigned supreme. This day was a memorable one, not only because each year it lured us out into the greening beech woods, but also because my father, as hero of the day, did not receive presents but distributed them to us in generous fashion. Christmas Eve, on the other hand, brought us no gifts but, rather, a festive joy impossible to describe. The first time I went to church was on a Christmas morn when, in piercing frost and beneath a starry sky, I was carried to matins in Helliggeistes Kirke, where I felt solemnly uplifted by the radiant illumination, the wondrous singing, and the swelling harmonies of the organ.

The theatre early opened its magical world to me, though from the rigging loft, whence the piece itself could be seen only in fragments and melted into the busy goings-on in the wings and during the intermissions. Here it

---

*March 20, 1811.
† First seen in the south of France on March 25–26, 1811, and visible in Denmark until January 11, 1812.
‡ In August 1808.

was that I heard the operas *Zémire and Azor* by Grétry and *Alma and Elfride* by Schall; here too I saw *The Revolt in Russia, The Abandoned Daughter,* and *The Peasant as Judge.* The various *entrées,* with the *figurants* hopping along the walls and the bespangled soloists, looked considerably foreshortened from above, and to me appeared to be performed by very small creatures. Here there could be no question of picturesque illusion, since we saw only the wrong side of the wings; but my rapture was all the greater when I got to see a complete performance from the actual auditorium and entirely abandoned myself to the idea of genuine trees, clouds, and waves!

I saw my father come sailing on as an English fisherman and dance with a gilded stick that spun like a wheel between his fingers while he executed the most ingenious steps. In *Telemachus on the Isle of Calypso* he leaped from the steep rock out into the sea, followed by old Mentor, and as Æneas he left the abandoned Dido to boundless despair.

My father, whom I admired as much as I did the noble figures he portrayed so beautifully on the stage, had never thought of putting his children into the theatre. My older brother and sister displayed neither the talent nor the inclination for it, while I, from my earliest days, was the "ham actor" in the family. By the rags in which I draped myself, and most of all by the recitation of ditties and comic speeches, I revealed—often to the great annoyance of parents in the artistic community whose own children were little bunglers—an unmistakable vocation. By hopping around at the back of the dancing classes my father gave at home, my steps acquired a singular style, even though I had grasped them without special instruction. My mother,* who was Swedish by birth, serious by temperament, and deeply religious into the bargain, was little charmed by theatrical glitter. However, she could not help but notice the miniature picture I rendered of my father, and she even ventured to inform her stepchildren that it was not impossible for little August to one day become his father's successor. An outcry was raised at this presumptuous thought, but in the meantime my tiny gifts developed and my father decided to take me with him up to the Court Theatre where the dancing school and the ballet rehearsals were held at that time.

And so in my eighth year I found myself introduced into a most extraordinary world, whose nature I marveled at but did not understand. Later, however, it came home to me and might have furnished material, if not for a description of *le demi-monde* or *la vie de Bohème,* then at least for a rather jolly novel *à la* Paul de Kock. To the honor of the profession and of modern times, theatre morals, at least here at home, have changed considerably and the refining influence of art has succeeded in exerting itself.

Screaming and squabbles, aye, sometimes a few blows, seemed to be an in-

*Following the death of his first wife, Antoine Bournonville found a housekeeper to take care of his two small children. Although Lovisa Sundberg gave birth to August Bournonville in 1805, and later bore two daughters, Juliane and Frederikke, she and the dancing master were not legally married until 1816 when, after the death of Galeotti, Antoine Bournonville was to take over some of the former's official duties at the Royal Theatre.

tegral part of the classes as well as the ballet rehearsals. But this did not prevent me from seeing a whole new world of fantasy pictures conjured up before my astonished eyes, especially at the rehearsals of Galeotti's great tragic ballets. The eighty-year-old master was pleased to note my lively participation, and despite some of the older *figurantes*, who called after me: "Just look how that boy puts on airs!," he took a particular fancy to me and gave me a number of small parts.

My very first appearance was as one of Regnar Lodbrog's sons in the ballet *Lagertha* (at the side of another little boy who, due to a lack of talent for the ballet, later abandoned the dance, was apprenticed to a joiner, and went on to become one of the capital's most respected citizens). It was on October 2, 1813. Never has a day seemed so long! The hours between the stage rehearsal and the performance were like an eternity. I ran through my little part more than a score of times, performing it for anyone who had the time and the desire to watch me. I sought in vain to discover which of King Regnar's sons I was actually to portray: Sigurd Snake-eye or Ivar Beenløse? At last there arrived the important moment when the chorus within the fortress of the King of the Goths had acclaimed Thora as Regnar's bride, while outside the walls Lagertha raged over her spouse's infidelity. A tender melody replaced the stormy *furioso* and the shield-maidens led us in to our proud mother who, tender and violent by turns, first pressed us to her heart, then thrust us away from her with the intention of killing us.

When all is said and done, we princes really had nothing more to do than allow ourselves to be led back and forth by the shield-maidens, embrace our mother, and fall to our knees with our hands over our eyes. All the same, I was seized with stage fright and the scene swam before my eyes as well as those of my dumbfounded companion. The whole thing was like a dream, and I fancy I can still sense the enchanting fragrance that enveloped Mme. Schall when, as Thora, she wrapped us in her ermine cloak to defend us from the wrath of the infuriated wife, our mother.

I had now received my initiation and was allowed to appear in several more ballets. But it was in a Hungarian solo which I danced at a benefit performance at the Court Theatre in the summer of 1814 that I received my first applause, and then it was said from every quarter that I was "my father all over again." I had now become a personality esteemed by the public and envied by the older pupils, and every time *the little princess* (Vilhelmine Marie) was to attend a play, an *entrée* by *the little Bournonville* was commanded.

CHILDHOOD MEMORIES FROM AMAGER
(Set down in 1871)

THOSE fortunate people who are able to travel abroad and to inhale the balmy air of Italy will have noticed that very few of the inhabitants of Naples have ever been on the other side of the gulf to climb smoking Vesuvius or wander through the recently excavated, silent streets of Pompeii. We Copenhageners, on the other hand, make repeated excursions to the north and west, aye, even to the east across the Sound by steamship to Møn and Bornholm; but seldom if ever do we go to the nearby island of Amager—at the very most, perhaps, to its broad common when some military or criminal spectacle draws thither a curious crowd.

But what comparison can indeed be made between that Hesperidean region, filled with natural phenomena and historical memories, and the flat, treeless plain bounded by Kallebod Strand and Kongedybet! There is not even a single spot where one can lie in the shade of a tree and give oneself up to daydreams. Straight as an arrow the beaten road runs past the Sundbys, Taarnby, and Magleby, to Dragør—and everywhere the same monotony: neat little houses and farms, together with enormous cabbage patches! No tourist is tempted to make this trip. The authentic costume (which is for the most part retained only by the female population) can certainly be seen every day in the marketplaces, and, furthermore, the whole of Amager life denotes such a practical turn of mind that it hardly occurs to anyone that material for poetic inspiration might there be found.

Many people thought and spoke like this until the day when our outstanding artist, Exner,* opened our eyes to a hitherto disregarded treasure of picturesque and romantic abundance [that lay in] the manners and customs of these islanders. The almost obliterated traditions from their Dutch forbears appeared anew, and even though the inherited national character has not been able to withstand the leveling influence of time, this imaginative yet realistic painter has known how to assemble its most interesting remnants, grouped in such a way that present and future are fused, while humor and feeling together appeal to both mind and heart.

I am ashamed to say that I, too, needed this incentive to revive the memory of the happy days I spent as a child with our old vegetable- and milk-seller, Cidse Tønnesdatter, who owned a farm in Kastrup and was married to a rather young man. One can scarcely imagine the joy with which I climbed up onto the long, narrow wagon with the high, ingeniously carved backboard and the blue cushions trimmed with red woolen tassels. What a pleasure it was to sit between this Amager couple and hold the reins while the "old man" puffed on his pipe and smilingly answered the witty remarks of the passersby, who congratulated him on the new little son his aged wife had given him.

The journey progressed step by step, and at long last we arrived at the farmhouse where, according to the arrangement, I was to remain as a guest from one market day to the next. I was lifted down from the wagon by a young man in sailor's dress and was handed over to a buxom, red-cheeked lass. They were the woman's children from her first marriage, both a number

*Cf. footnote, Vol. III, Part One, p. 368.

of years older than their stepfather, but obedient and energetic farmhands. The son, Jacob, had served in the navy, and the daughter, Ane, was the treasure of the house. She had just finished painting the parlor with blue panels decorated with roses and tulips. The bed curtains and plump bolsters had been embroidered by her own hands. She knew a host of ballads and tales, danced both the *reel* and the *langengelsk* superbly, and was, moreover, the best in both the field and the cabbage patch. She was as strong as the finest farmhand, could carry a barrel of rye on her shoulders, and, if need be, toss an impertinent whippersnapper into a muddy ditch. Both she and her brother were indescribably good to me but amused themselves in true country fashion by pulling the leg of a city child; for example, by showing me one cow that gave cream and another that gave buttermilk and also by giving me a handful of salt with which to catch a sparrow, etc.

It was divine to be among these dear people. I was treated to *posegrød* [a kind of porridge] which was seasoned with saffron and filled with raisins, went with Jacob to water the horses and to the smithy, and received permission to roll in the billowing field of rye. I slept in the topmost bed, from the ceiling of which hung a splendid woolen tassel. There was nothing special about the garden but the croft was all the richer, for *there* carrots, turnips, and peas grew in abundance.

But, alas! These wonderful holidays passed all too quickly! Here I had before me the poetry of rustic life and freedom; in Copenhagen, on the other hand, the prosaic round of school and admonitions. And even though I had a loving home, I still felt strangely melancholy when we drove in through the slippery streets of Christianshavn to arrive at last at the corner of Compagnistræde and Knabrostræde, where my parents lived and where Cidse had her stall. However, I had become a favorite of these good people and was often invited to go out to them for a couple of days at a time.

I had just begun to imitate the art which was to become my livelihood but I was unable to judge the fruits of my endeavors because the mirrors in our house were hung so high that only my head reached above the consoles. At my Amager friends', on the other hand, I had admittance to the stately parlor, which stood empty and solemn with its carved oaken cupboards, large linen chests, Dutch inscriptions in the beam ceiling, shiny brass dishes with biblical bas-reliefs, and the large table with its stout, twisted legs—equally serviceable as a banquet table or a bier. Here there hung a mirror which tilted sharply forward because of the low ceiling and allowed me to view my entire little person. This was just what I needed to practice my jumping. I flung my legs rapidly out to the side and beat the soles of my feet together. It worked superbly! The inhabitants of the farm rewarded my efforts with unanimous applause, and when I showed my father these Hungarian steps, he composed a little dance in which I made my debut at the Court Theatre.

It was toward the end of the long war period from 1807 to 1815, with its hard winters, time of dearth, blockade, privateering, and—above all—the deterioration of the monetary system with its worthless issue of banknotes, of which 400 Danish rixdollars were needed to buy one pair of boots and 48 Rbd. to purchase one pound of coffee, while one gave a coachman 30 Rbd. as a tip! At that time political life was not nearly so developed as it now is. The daily papers were seldom read by country folk; in peasant circles only material pressures were felt and dealt with.

The great events which rocked and overturned Europe at that time met with little sympathy, while the older folk were still shaken by the memory of the terrible days of the bombardment of Copenhagen and lived in fear of a new enemy attack.

The memory of the encampment of the King's Corps of Volunteers in the villages along the Amager coast fell like a ray of light on this somber background. This handsome Corps, which had voluntarily assembled as early as 1801 and had distinguished itself by sorties during the siege of Copenhagen, had in its midst many fine talents from the most varied classes of society— among them a number of artists from the Royal Theatre who brought with them a superb *esprit* which not only had a stimulating effect in the heat of battle but also did much to ease the boredom of the tiresome and strenuous coastal watch.

The winter of 1808, with frequent visits of those who were related to members of the Volunteers through ties of family or friendship, actually marked an epoch in the lives of the people of Amager. One merry party succeeded another, but especially at Shrovetide people really cut loose, and the old games such as beating the cat out of the barrel, stabbing the straw man, and wringing the goose's neck, were as nothing compared with the improvised comedies and masquerades of which the ingenious Du Puy was the life and the moving spirit.

This outstanding opera singer, violin virtuoso, and composer had displayed such splendid valor as *Overjæger* that he was made Lieutenant of the Corps. But, at the same time, it was made known to him that the dignity of a *porte-épée*† did not permit him to continue to appear on the stage! However, he might play the violin wherever he pleased, and when he then accepted the appointment as *Concertmester* of the Royal Orchestra, he sacrificed his theatrical laurels to military glory and contemporary narrow-mindedness. Nonetheless, in daily life he continued to play the roles in which he had shone on the stage, and he is said to have repeated Don Juan's duet with more than one Amager Zerlina.

This poetic time was now past and the coastal watch was handed over to some companies of militia. But peace was at hand, and even though it was neither a joyful nor a favorable one, the people hailed it with delight. And now a family fête drew near among my Amager folk. It is well known that among peasants in general (just as at Court) marriages are arranged by the

† Literally, a sword-bearer—that is, a military officer.

parents or guardians of the parties concerned, with a special eye to material interests. Therefore, particularly among the farmer class, it often happens that an old widow gets a young husband while an elderly widower takes a rather young girl to wife. From this there arises, chiefly among the well-to-do, a kind of childless wedlock, whereas the poor have numerous offspring. However, this time it was a genuine love match—within the farmer class, of course, for Heaven preserve us from a misalliance!

Ane and the neighbor's son, Pe'er, had known one another well from their earliest youth, and now the time had come when he might take over his father's farm and put his feet under his own table. The wedding day was fixed, and my friend Jacob now appeared as bridesman and spokesman, rattling off an elegant formula whereby he invited my parents and me to the celebration, which was to be held for three days running at three adjacent farms.

Lodgings had been reserved in the vicinity, and they asked if they might borrow silverware and other necessities as well as some costume jewelry and gems for the bride's headdress. This was in the middle of the winter of 1815–1816, and in clear and calm frosty weather the guests arrived in sleighs from every direction. The marriage was celebrated at the altar of Taarnby Kirke, and afterward we drove back to Kastrup, drums beating and banners flying.

At all three farms tables groaned beneath the weight of roasts, hams, and cakes. Drink was furnished in abundance, and the first hours were taken up with the quiet, earnest business of eating. Only toward evening did the mood become livelier. The band struck up, and a circle was formed about the bridal couple who were now to tread their first measure as man and wife. Ane, usually so frank and robust, stood there in her shining bridal array with a solemn charm and genuine modesty which somehow transformed her into a completely different person. She danced with noble grace and fixed such a trusting gaze on her virile bridegroom that all expressed their admiration and both women and hardened men had tears in their eyes.

Now the *sextour*, the *syvspring*, the *reel*, and an endless *hospvals* were danced, while a stout innkeeper performed a "hoop dance." But most amusing of all was a little boy dressed in an old-fashioned costume with a powdered wig. He carried a large snuffbox which served as a *bonbonnière* and contained sweets for the ladies and a silver thimble for the bride. He ran from one farmhouse to another in the bright moonlight, followed by a crowd of jubilant youngsters, and performing a little comic scene with an accompanying solo dance. Even the sober parish priest had to give in to the contagious merriment, and the boy was carried home in triumph to the bridal house where, without even suspecting it, he played the part of Cupid in a costume which is still to be found in the wardrobe of the Royal Theatre and is used in the intermezzo of Holberg's *Maskerade*.

Fifty-five years have passed since that celebration. The old Amager folk are long gone to rest. Through fire and rebuilding, Kastrup has lost its distinctive character. Jacob got himself a farm and an old wife, and Ane, who was widowed early, married again—this time a healthy young man. I often met her in the city and reminded her of bygone days. After an interval of twenty-five years, during which I had traveled the major part of Europe and been in Paris half a score of times without having ventured so much as a single time outside the Amagerport, I visited Ane's farmstead and was cordially welcomed by the old woman, who, though well into her seventies, was still sharp and agile. She showed us all of her comfortable household effects and at last took forth from a hiding place a little silver thimble from 1816, which she handed me with a smile that somehow colored her features with the glow of youth. It was a memento of the little boy who had performed an improvised ballet at her wedding and who now at an advanced age presents a larger work under the title of *The King's Volunteers on Amager*.

MY FIRST YEARS OF APPRENTICESHIP

THEATRE children as a rule have difficulty in getting a regular schooling, partly because of classes and rehearsals, which are always held in the morning, and partly because their little heads are filled with the fantasies and conflicts that the acting profession embodies even in its youngest offspring. It is therefore not surprising that the ballet pupils in my boyhood and even later on (until the time when I succeeded in getting them a schoolmaster and mistress), grew up in an ignorance that left them barely able to read a Danish book or to write their names, while through the more or less scheming and emotional drama they acquired a sort of intelligence and knowledge of the world that did not always lead to the happiest results.

My formal education was therefore rudimentary, and though even at an early age I was regarded as a rather bright fellow, and might possibly have been suited to serious academic study, I was (in consideration of my theatrical destiny) enrolled in an afternoon course conducted by an assistant teacher at Helliggeistes Skole, Divinity Candidate Flindt. This worthy man, who in his modest position was instrumental in getting the poet Welhaven's father (later bishop in Bergen) to continue his studies in Copenhagen, was himself a Bergenite and an old-fashioned pedagogue who held strongly to learning by rote and enforced his authority with proper discipline and chastisement. But I soon became his favorite and, after a couple of years, top boy in the highest class. Sometimes, however, I incurred his displeasure when he discovered that I had been entertaining my comrades and his more worldly wife with dancing presentations and mimed scenes during his absence. I fancy I can hear him still, accusing me in front of my mother with his Norwegian accent: "That devil of a boy! Just as he is sitting there doing so well at his lessons, he jumps up from the bench and starts dancing all over the place." Even then I was as little lacking in ambition and the desire to perform in public as I was later on, and what the French call *amour-propre* I had received as a paternal inheritance.

Like a number of my fellow students, I would have considered it an ineffaceable disgrace to come to class unprepared. Therefore in my eleventh year I was already first in religion, geography, and history, particularly distinguishing myself in declamation and the recitation of verse. Spelling by heart and writing from dictation was actually all I ever learnt of Danish grammar, and I became so firmly attached to the orthography followed by our finest authors (both then and in the ensuing period of literary flowering) that I have been unable to accept the reform which has now been thrust upon our schools and with whose motives I intend to take issue in a detailed article in the third part of Volume III.* German grammar, on the other hand, was treated more methodically, and during singing lessons we became familiar with a number of our lyricists' loveliest poems, for example, Baggesen's "There was a time, when I was very small." In this area I also made myself conspicuous, but with this our formal education actually came to an end; for to me mathematics and the natural sciences as a whole remained a closed book which I have since peeped into and leafed through without penetrating its contents. However, I found a sufficient amount of fine literature on my father's bookshelves: Suhm's *Nordic Tales*, Malling's *Great and Good Deeds*, Rahbek's *Anthology of Danish Poets*, de luxe editions of *Peder Paars* and *Niels Klim* [both by Holberg], with illustrations by Abildgaard and Clemens; and, finally, Oehlenschläger's inspiring works, which filled my mind during all the free time that remained after my dancing and school lessons were finished. On the leaf of an album, on a given occasion, I have mentioned the influence these works had upon my future development:

In Holbergs' *Peder Paars* I found my first rhyme,
And life's philosophy I learnt from *Niels Klim;*
My first refreshing drink from *Idun's* Brage-beaker,
I, as a youth, enjoyed in *Adam Oehlenschläger.*

At the same time as I progressed in choreography's serious genre (which I did not find nearly as amusing as the lively character dances), I was trained in small speaking parts by the famous actor Michael Rosing, and appeared as little Erling at his benefit performance in *Hakon Jarl.* Here Ryge performed one of his master roles, while Peter Foersom played Olaf Trygveson. Rosing, who had been lame in both legs for a number of years, remained seated while he played the usually deleted scene in which, from his cave, the ancient Auden tempts Olaf and defends the old paganism. I fancy I can hear him still, shouting at the Christian king in his hoarse voice: "Boy! Wilt thou let my spruces stand!" I marveled that an actor with such a pronounced Thrønder accent could arouse the public's sympathy to such a degree; yet all his contemporaries agreed that both he and Schwartz were irreplaceable in the roles in which they had shone. Frydendahl, who always had a sarcastic remark ready

*Cf. the chapter "Orthography," Vol. III, Part Three.

at hand, once said of Rosing: "His speech was neither Norwegian nor Danish. We called it *Kattegatish*." Suffice it to say this artist left behind a void that was later filled by Nielsen and, curiously enough, by his grandsons, Michael and Wilhelm Wiehe.

After Rosing's death (which occurred shortly after the benefit performance), Lindgreen and Frydendahl became my instructors, and under their direction I played a number of larger or smaller children's roles, among others, Oehlenschläger's Little Shepherd Boy and the affected, bombastic hero's son in the melodrama *Johanna von Montfaucon*. Since I had quite a nice soprano voice and was musically inclined, they found me useful on the lyric stage, and in a short time I had made so much progress under the skillful chorus master Zinck that I was able to appear successfully in Kunzen's operetta *Love in the Country*, singing a ballad in which I divulged the judge's rascalish trick. You see, it was at one time a standing rule, in the *syngestykke* as well as the drama, that judges and presidents had to be fools, bunglers, or scoundrels—sometimes all three at once!

The culmination of my lyrical dramatic career was my performance of the role of Adonia in *The Judgment of Solomon*, a sentimental play with singing and dancing, adapted by N. T. Bruun to music by Kunzen. It was performed for the first time, in honor of Queen Marie's birthday, on October 29, 1817, and was splendidly fitted out, in accordance with the demands of the time. Ryge played the wise Solomon; Stage, his brother Eliphal; Jfr. Astrup, the proud Tamira; and the graceful Mme. Zinck (*née* Thomsen), the child's mother, Leila. I, who was twelve years old but rather small for my age, was to portray a child of seven, the familiar apple of discord. People found so much natural feeling in my acting and such a tender delivery in my singing that the strict etiquette of the occasion was forgotten, and from the Royal box as well as the auditorium filled with a gala audience, I was greeted with thunderous rounds of applause. The play became the season's drawing card, and for a number of years thereafter my solo, "The Mother with Drooping Wings," remained a favorite song of children and sentimental parents.

There was now serious deliberation as to which of the scenic arts I should follow; for in addition to my flexible singing voice, I possessed the singular gift of being able to imitate different dialects and also the amusing but dangerous talent of reproducing actors' and singers' recitation, delivery, and gestures—all with a slight touch of the ridiculous.

Many advised my father to encourage me in the dramatic art or at least in the *opéra-comique*, which was so popular at that time. But for one thing, my father prized *his* profession above all others, and for another, both my voice and my body were in the transitional period of the male adolescent; and finally, the impediment which has since hampered my desire to express myself in euphonious phrases had already begun to make itself felt; for while I did not actually stammer in my everyday speech, I was obliged to avoid certain consonants that threatened to cause me painful embarrassment as punishment for the parodic dexterity with which I had amused myself and others as a boy.

And yet there was something to be said for a different career; for the Ballet (which had, after Galeotti's death, lost a measure of its former brilliance and prestige, not only because its repertoire was exhausted but because the active performers had become old and the entire genre unsuited to the younger generation) was then, as now, combating the same tendency which, supported by financial and aesthetic prejudice, continuously undermines this festive branch of art. For a time it actually succeeded in forcing it down to the lowest possible level!

All the same, Terpsichore triumphed! With our sights fixed on the future and, to tell the truth, on the Continent, we continued the training that was to make a dancer of me, and the realization that my art possessed the essential advantage of being universally understandable served only to increase my energy and filled me with the brightest expectations. It also happened that on their travels to and from Sweden, a number of foreign artists passed through Copenhagen and appeared to great applause at the Royal Theatre. Among these artists, Theresa Ginetti and Filippo Taglioni (father of the later so famous Marie Taglioni) particularly distinguished themselves, and from their performances I learnt what might be accomplished within the realm of *virtuosity*. (My father's school was superior to theirs in both taste and expression.)

In rapid succession, steps were now taken to enable me to learn everything that might further my artistic development. I studied French with my brother;† for even though as a little child I had learnt to jabber some small phrases with a passable accent, at the age of twelve I was still unable to read, speak, or understand this language. I was given a drawing master, who opened my eyes to the beautiful and the picturesque. Though I had earlier studied under rather poor teachers, my musical education took a new turn with Wexschall's fruitful instruction, which in a couple of years succeeded in giving me no small amount of skill.

It was at this time that the fund *ad usos publicos* allocated rich travel stipends; and this excellent violinist was granted one of them in order to obtain further training under the great masters of France and Germany. Wexschall now advised my father to petition Frederik VI for similar support for himself and his promising son, and since we both enjoyed the favor of the Royal Family, the request was most graciously granted, and on May 2, 1820, we set out on

A JOURNEY TO PARIS

"I will never forget this journey! " Therefore, should this description suffer from a long-windedness like that of Gert the Westphaler,* it must be ascribed

---

† See footnote on Antoine Bournonville *fils*, Vol. III, Part Three, p. 658.
*The talkative hero of Holberg's comedy *Master Geert Westphaler eller Den meget talende Barbeer* (1722).

to an old man's reflections upon the impressions he received as a youth on his first excursion into a hitherto unknown world.

My father, who was approaching his sixtieth year, wished to see his native land once more after an absence of twenty-two years, during which time so many important events had occurred. I went along as his Benjamin.† After tearfully bidding adieu to my mother and sisters, we set off aboard Denmark's first and only steamship, the little *Caledonia,* which did not do many knots, but because of foul weather dropped anchor off Falster, where we passed the night. Only on the following day did we arrive at the goal of Gert's pilgrimage, Kiel, where hurrahs greeted our entrance into the harbor.

The next morning we proceeded to Hamburg by means of a so-called "post chaise." We had joined forces with an old member of the Royal Theatre Orchestra and his eccentric wife, who was a native of Bornholm. They were traveling to Erfurt, the husband's birthplace, in order to seek an heir among his relatives, since they themselves were childless. Therefore, supposing him to be knowledgeable in the various kinds of currency, which were giving my father a good deal of trouble, he was made our treasurer. Unfortunately, the tallying of Lübeck shillings and Danish national banknotes soon became too much for him, and his wife was finally forced to declare him unfit for anything but playing the contrabass. The handling of current expenditures now devolved upon me, and I rather quickly succeeded in familiarizing myself with the confusing assortment of coins: Drittler, Gute-Groschen, Neue-Groschen, Marien-Groshen, and Rhenish Gulden until at last we reached the frontier of France, with its easy reckoning in francs and centimes. To the younger generation, who are used to covering the distance from Kiel to Hamburg by rail in two and a half hours, it will no doubt seem incredible to discover the slowness with which one in those days traversed the ugliest part of Holsten, where sand, water, and marshes formed something called a "highway." We had to halt at Bramstedt, and only the following day arrived in Hamburg, where the first thing to meet our eye was the demolition of the old ramparts, which were later transformed into the loveliest promenades and gardens.

During the two days that we spent in Hamburg we visited the Stadt Theater on the Gänsemarkt—a most unimpressive edifice, but one from which had emerged the most famous German actors and, curiously enough, the first German opera. We saw a grand melodrama, *Clorinda and Tancred, or the Freeing of Jerusalem* and the following evening *Kabale und Liebe,* by Schiller. Among the players we particularly noticed Lebrun, Jacobi, Gloy, and Kühne (Lenz) (the latter had unquestionably been used by our Ryge as the model for his first representations).

Our strolls out toward Hamburgerberg led us to Altona. Even though at

---

† The Bournonvilles left Copenhagen on May 2, 1820. The son's journal of the trip has been published as Volume II, *Journal 1820,* of *August Bornonville: Lettres à la maison de son enfance,* ed. Nils Schiørring and Svend Kragh-Jacobsen (Copenhagen, 1970).

that time we had Schleswig-Holstein currency, chancellery, prelates, and knighthood, people as yet knew nothing of political Schleswig-Holsteinism, for after passing through Altona's wrought-iron gates, one read: "Now we are in Denmark," and the Hamburgers themselves, who had not forgotten our troops' cooperation with *"l'inexorable Davoust,"* ‡ harbored no bitterness against the Danes but even accorded Frederik VI the loveliest reception.

The bridge which the French had built across the islands in the Elbe estuary had been removed for extremely narrow-minded reasons, and a slow-sailing *ewert* [livery boat] took care of our crossing to Haarburg, in the Hanoverian district. From here a dreadful wheelbarrow of a diligence traversed Lüneburg and Celle, passing through a stretch of heath that is now partially tilled and planted with trees, but which at that time bore a striking resemblance to the Sahara Desert. The journey proceeded step by step. The *Schwager*, i.e., postillion, walked alongside the carriage with a pipe in his mouth, and when one asked him why the roads were in such bad repair, one usually received this answer: "The French left too soon!" At last, after a tiring two-and-a-half-day drive — during which we stopped at Lüneburg, where we had time to see the famous salt works, and in Celle, where we visited the grave of Queen Caroline Mathilde* — we reached a more fertile region and the city of Hanover.

In this capital, where the Duke of Cambridge resided as the Viceroy of Great Britain, we watched the famous Hanoverian soldiers (familiar from 1807) drill in the English manner. We strolled to the pretty pleasure palace of Herrenhausen and visited the splendid stables and the Orangerie. In the theatre we heard Mozart's *The Abduction from the Seraglio* in which Gerstäcker sang the part of Belmonte and Fraulein Campagnoli that of Constance. This singer was the daughter of a man who had in his day been a famous violinist. He was now serving as *Kapellmeister,* and with him my father renewed an old acquaintance from Stockholm.

After a couple of days' stay, we set off for Cassel, traveling on well-constructed roads and through pleasant countryside, past Göttingen and on into the wood-grown Harz Mountains. With a certain feeling of solemnity, for the first time in my life I ascended a real mountain with rock cliffs and rippling streams. We even had the opportunity to enjoy a mountain hike to relieve the horses of the weight on the upward drive. It was early morn on Ascension Day when, in the loveliest spring weather, from the heights at Münden, we could see Cassel by the Fulda, which lay glimmering in the sunlight. We

---

‡ "The implacable Davoust" (generally spelled "Davout"), Napoleonic marshal, commanded mixed Danish and French occupation forces in the Hamburg district, 1813–1814. His reputation as a mercilessly strict disciplinarian was well merited.

*Caroline Mathilde, sister of George III of England and Queen of Christian VII of Denmark, lived in Celle Castle from 1772 to 1775, following the overthrow and execution of her favorite, Struensee. Her monument stands in the French Garden there. See also note on Struensee, Vol. III. Part Three, p. 649.

heard church bells in the distance, calling people to divine service, and my father, who always felt a thrill of devotion at such moments, pressed me to his heart with an exclamation of tenderness and joy.

Cassel was dear to him from the days of his youth, for from his sixteenth to his twentieth year he, together with his sister Julie, had been engaged with the excellent ballet that was maintained during the period 1770–1780 by the old Elector—the same man who (like Denmark's fourth Frederik) furnished mercenary troops in return for the payment of a certain number of millions; with this difference, however: England honored her debt for assistance in the American War of Independence, while Spain is still in arrears with regard to both capital and interest from the balance due Denmark from the War of Succession at the beginning of the previous century.

Here, as King of Westphalia, Jérôme Bonaparte held his brilliant court, and the picturesquely situated castle of Wilhelmshöhe was still filled with souvenirs of that merry, stirring time. No one suspected that beneath these ceilings, with their allegorical paintings, a descendant of that same race was to sit half a century later as a prisoner of war, beaten, humiliated, weakened in mind and body, banished and cursed by the very nation that had chosen him Emperor by a vote eight million strong, and pitied by a Europe which for eighteen years had hearkened to his every word as to an oracle, nay, even read meaning into his silence! †

The old order had now been re-established in Hesse-Cassel. The reaction following Napoleonic control was as complete as possible, and the reinstated Elector, Wilhelm, had carried the *ancien régime* to such a degree that the army was made to don the old-fashioned equipment with a queue at the back of the neck! "Old Skinflint," as they called him, had furthermore inherited his forefathers' passion for building, and expended considerable sums not only on the little mountain fortress, "Die Löwenburg," with its collection of weapons, furnishings, and domestic utensils from the age of chivalry, but especially on the projected palace, "Die Cattenburg," which under his successors has been left standing uncompleted, rather like our Marmor Kirke.‡

Our lodging was in a large square, where the echo resounded eight times when the watchman shouted or the guard presented arms. My father revived many fond memories and even discovered several old people who had known him in his youth, among others the two Bourguignon sisters, now elderly matrons, with whom he had played when they were little girls. They greeted him with a cry of surprise mingled with sadness. They had known his mother, who had died at the beginning of this century in Cassel, which she had chosen as her place of residence and where, until the last, she had received a

† The reference is to Napoleon III, who was held at Wilhelmshöhe after his surrender at Sedan on September 2, 1870.
‡ After having lain in ruins since 1770, the Marmor Kirke or Marble Church in Copenhagen was finally completed in 1894.

yearly pension from her son. We inquired in vain as to the whereabouts of two family portraits, namely, the one of my grandfather, Amable Louis (*Employé dans les vivres de l'Armée*), and that of his elder brother, Pierre Jérôme (*Garde du Corps de la Compagnie de Luxembourg* and knight of the Order of Saint Louis). But, due to negligent handling of the estate, they were probably sold to a second-hand dealer and left his shop to adorn the walls of one Westphalian farmhouse or another.*

We remained in Cassel for four days and celebrated my father's birthday on May 19. We paid our respects to the young and pretty Princess Charlotte of Denmark (married to Prince Wilhelm of Hesse). She received her former dancing master in the most amiable fashion, and presented to us her charming little children, the youngest of whom is now our present Queen.

The theatre was not particularly flourishing, nor did it seem to be held in high esteem, as the old Elector expressed no taste for the scenic arts. However, we did attend a performance of Bürger's *The Debt* in which Zahlhas, one of Germany's most important actors, made a guest appearance in the principal role.

On the road to Frankfurt-am-Main we encountered large crowds of students from Marburg and Giesen, dressed in fantastic costumes, carrying weapons at their sides and swinging bludgeons, with the intention of marching to Mannheim to free the German Brutus, Kotzebue's murderer, Sand (but in reality to witness his execution, which took place at that very time).†

After passing Frankfurt and Mainz, we reached the French frontier at Saarbrucken, whence a diligence of the *Messageries Royales* transported us to Metz. We now felt practically at home on French soil. The dear language — though with a somewhat harsh accent — greeted us, while on the ramparts of the fortress we heard the orders and the bugle calls that had so often led Frenchmen to victory. Waterloo and the Allied invasion still weighed heavily on the soldiers' minds, but they were at least consoled by the thought that Metz had never been taken, for which reason they proudly called this fortified city *"La Pucelle."*

The journey through Lorraine and Champagne to Paris, which can nowadays be made in half a score of hours, at that time required two days and two nights of continuous driving with very brief stops at Verdun, famous for its sweets, and at Epernay, renowned for its sparkling nectar. On this trip I came to know those two unique — now almost vanished — types: the cocky, witty *conducteurs,* and the *postillons,* who in enormous jackboots rode along on

*Cf. the family history given in the biographical sketch of Antoine Bournonville *père,* Vol. III, Part Three, pp. 653 ff; see also Paul Bournonville: *Bidrag till den Bournonvilleska familiens historia," Personal historisk Tidsskrift* (Copenhagen, 1935).

†August von Kotzebue, born 1761 at Weimar, had a spectacularly varied career as lawyer, dramatist, Russian agent, poet, and opponent of the Romantic School that centered around Goethe. For this he was detested by the young German nationalists, one of whom — a theological student named Karl Ludwig Sand — stabbed him to death at Mannheim, March 23, 1819.

horseback, swearing and cracking their whips (with which they gave performances *à la Lonjumeau*‡ but also mistreated the five galloping horses in the most brutal fashion). We raced along toward the paved King's Road like Thor and Loke travelling to Jothunheim. We were almost choked by the dust and heat inside the tightly packed coach, but at last, on the third morning after our departure from Metz, we rolled into Paris (May 25) through "La Vilette" and the ugly suburb of St. Martin—a most uninviting section of that great city!—and landed in the stagecoach yard in the rue Notre-Dame-des-victoires!

PARIS IN 1820

This remarkable city, which has for centuries been the object of Europe's attention in more than one respect, and whence have emerged ideas and movements that have had an irresistible influence upon moods and conditions throughout the rest of the civilized world—this city at that time seemed to lie much farther away from us than it does nowadays, when in complete comfort one can cover the distance by rail in less than forty-eight hours, whereas in those days a letter sent by courier post took eleven days and cost a rixdollar in postage! Someone who had traveled to Paris was looked upon with a certain admiration: and when he returned to Copenhagen, people asked, just as they do in Holberg's *Jean de France;* "What does he look like?"—as if they expected a complete change of manners and dress.

Without going too far back in history, as soon as one sets foot within the walls of Paris, one must feel involuntarily moved by the memories which, in a manner of speaking, confront one at every step. While the good old "peruke days" loomed quietly and peacefully in the quarter of Le Marais (which seemed to have been totally unaffected by events), an unruly mob surged in the suburbs of St. Antoine and St. Marceau, where one might still encounter faces from the festivals of the guillotine. The Palais-Royal bespoke the first thrill of freedom, but the Place de Grève and the Place Louis XV the horrors of the Revolution; the Colonne de Vendôme, the victories of Napoleon; the Tuileries, the vicissitudes of fortune; and finally, Louis XIV's triumphal arches of St. Denis and St. Martin, France's humiliation upon the entry of the Allies [into Paris].

By strength of "legitimacy" and with the aid of 300,000 foreign bayonets, the Bourbons were restored, and Louis XVIII ascended his father's throne. The Charter which he had granted France out of wisdom and conviction was in spirit and form such a liberal constitution that the nation, which longed for peace after the upheavals of twenty-five years of revolution, war, military despotism, bloody victories, and defeats, could feel satisfied. To tell the truth,

‡ The reference is to *Le Postillon de Lonjumeau,* a three-act *opéra-comique* by Leuven and Lhérie, with music by Adolphe Adam. Its first performance took place at the Opéra-Comique on October 13, 1836.

people were weary of Napoleonic rule, and the endless sacrifice of human life had cast a pall of sorrow over many a family. It would therefore have been easy to win over the French people, had those surrounding the King (who were for the most part returning *émigrés* and inveterate supporters of the *ancien régime*) not constantly fought against his good intentions; not only the bitter memories that they preserved with indelible resentment, but also the glory France had won in their absence, was a thorn in their side. The tricolor was regarded as an ensign of revolution and exchanged for the white bunting. Troops of the line were dressed in white uniforms, and the Guard, which was partly made up of veterans from the days of the Empire, had to share watch-duty with recruited Swiss regiments. All monuments from the time of Napoleon were given different names, and the government-supported press occupied itself with denigrating everything that had truly illustrated the fallen Empire. This could not but have a harmful effect upon national feeling and produce a reaction in favor of the prisoner of St. Helena, whose martyrdom expiated his previous errors and who was privately the object of an admiration which, for the time being, was hidden beneath the mask of the Liberal Opposition.

The Duc de Berry, the King's nephew and youngest son of the Comte d'Artois, was felled by an assassin's dagger just as he was about to step into his carriage upon leaving the Grand Opéra House in the Rue de Richelieu. This dire event crushed the most profound expectations of the House of Bourbon, for though he himself did not hold the throne of France, this jovial and energetic prince had been chosen to make the dynasty secure, since the marriage of his elder brother, the Duc d'Angoulême, to the daughter of Louis XVI was childless, whereas his own union with the young Sicilian princess promised a numerous and vigorous offspring. It was this very prospect that drove a fanatical journeyman, Louvel, to commit the crime. In vain they sought to discover the source and ramification of the crime in a possible conspiracy, or to learn whether it had its root in a personal revenge called forth by the Prince's quick temper or gallant adventures. The murderer steadfastly alleged that he alone, without the aid of a conspiracy, had performed his act of hatred to the Bourbon dynasty, which he considered unworthy to rule over France. He cooly answered every other question with: "That is my system."

This grievous catastrophe almost disrupted our whole travel plan, since it was rumored that performances at the Opéra were to cease completely, and it was from this very place that we expected to harvest our real profits. But it was decided otherwise; and, curiously enough, contrary to the practice that when a holy place has been profaned in one manner or another a process of purification takes place, here they thought that since the dying man had received extreme unction in the foyer of the Opéra, this heathen temple ought to be leveled to the ground and a *monument expiatoire* erected on its site. An expiation—for whom?

Muses and Graces, demigods, nymphs, and cupids were now consigned to a smaller stage: the Théâtre Favart, and here it was that my father and I were to seek the object of our artistic endeavors.

This stage, rather limited in comparison with the previous one, did not permit the presentation of grand operas or ballets of more considerable dimensions. For this reason the repertoire was limited and we were, to a certain degree, disappointed. On the other hand, the smaller number of operas furnished the opportunity for more numerous ballet performances, of a kind that was, to be sure, less magnificent but perfectly suitable for emphasizing important mimic as well as choreographic talents, especially the *danseurs* Albert, Paul, and Ferdinand, and Mlles. Fanny Bias, Noblet, and Bigottini (so famous for her outstanding mime). At this time the ballet claimed indisputable precedence over the opera, which, although it possessed excellent dramatic singers such as Lais, the elder Derivis, the elder Nourrit, and a couple of graceful prima donnas like Mmes. Albert and Grassari, was nevertheless lacking in artistry and method. In contrast to the Italians, who *at that time* sang sweetly and pleasantly, they strained their lungs with violent vocal outpourings—a bad habit that is nowadays widespread and has almost everywhere supplanted *"il bel canto."*

On the very first evening after our arrival we went to the Théâtre de l'Opéra, which at that time was known as the Académie Royale de Musique. Here were presented Rousseau's lyric idyll *Le Devin du village, Les Prétendus* by Moline, and Gardel's charming ballet *Le Jugement de Pâris.* We had purchased our tickets and chosen our seats in the middle of the pit, without in the least suspecting the company in which we found ourselves. The dances followed one another in brilliant succession, and like an old connoisseur my father displayed his satisfaction by tasteful applause. But growling sounded to the right and left of us, and we received many an angry look, for the regulated applause had its fixed places, which were indicated by a broad-shouldered leader who did not tolerate any unwarranted initiative. We now realized that we had chosen seats in the heart of a company of *claqueurs,* and when a few days later our Minister, Count Waltersdorff, procured us free admission, we kept ourselves at a proper distance from the applause machine.

In addition to the above-mentioned works, the repertoire, which varied but little, consisted of the following one-act operas: *Aristippe* by Rodolphe Kreutzer; *Le Rossignol* by Lebrun; *Aspasie* by Dausfoigne; and also of larger works such as *Le Caravane du Caïre, Panurge,* and *Anacréon* by Grétry, and *Oedipe à Colonne* by Sacchini—all with inserted dancing *divertissements.* The evening usually ended with a ballet, and we saw *Flore et Zéphire* by Didelot; *Paul et Virginie* and *La Servante justifiée* by Gardel; *Le Carneval de Venise, L' Epreuve villageoise, Nina,* and *Clari* by Milon. This last ballet was the season's most distinguished novelty, contained a host of lovely moments, and, just as in *Nina,* gave Mlle. Bigottini the opportunity to display a mimic expressiveness that aroused enthusiasm and earned her the title of "Mlle. Mars of the Ballet."

A youngish balletmaster from Vienna, Aumer, gave *Les Pages du Duc de Vendôme,* which was superbly performed and later succeeded by a series of impressive works, among them *La Somnambule,* which first appeared in 1827. In accordance with the demands of the time, most of these ballets were adaptations from older plays and *opéras-comiques,* but gained distinction by extraordinary tastefulness and dance composition.

As far as external appearances are concerned—with the exception of the Pont d'Austerlitz and the Pont d'Jéna (which had been rechristened the Pont du Jardin des Plantes and the Pont des Invalides), of the Rue de la Paix and Rue de Rivoli, and also of the magnificent buildings begun but not completed under the Empire—my father found his old Paris almost unchanged. The notorious lanterns hung in their usual places; the same vehicles that had conveyed pleasure-seekers before the Revolution and the very tumbrils that had carried loads of victims of the Reign of Terror to the guillotine, rolled past, drawn by elephantine workhorses whose heavy trotting in the gutters—which ran through the middle of the streets—bespattered the pedestrians who had no sidewalk to turn to. Just as it had before, the Palais-Royal still housed in its uppermost stories vice and despair, and while the gamblers flourished and paid a couple of millions in contributions to the archbishopric, ladies of ambiguous appearance—but with unambiguous words and gestures—strolled in ball dress through the galleries of the Garden. From subterranean vaults which contained caverns such as the "Café des Aveugles" and the "Jardin d'Idalie" resounded the roll of drums, clarinets, and raucous singing voices— all as it had been twenty-two years ago.

As far as the dress and folkways of the people were concerned: fashion, the times, and circumstances had brought their influence to bear in a much greater way. The Carmagnol jacket and Phrygian cap had given way to the blouse and cap. "Monsieur" and "Madame" were heard again in place of the republican "Citoyen" and "Citoyenne." The clothing of fashionable people had already changed cut, color, and style a number of times, and displayed an elegance that present-day "fashion" would look upon with astonishment, nay, even with an ironic smile at the thought that in a couple of decades their modes, too, will seem ridiculous.

In front of the ancient churches—which had suffered much desecration and whose sculpture-adorned façades still bore the marks of the vandalism of a raging mob—there knelt in prayer and supplication a group of elderly men and women, whose faces, furrowed by passion, bespoke the fact that here one might find types of the "September executioners," ardent listeners at the Blood Tribunal, and industrious *"tricoteuses"* at the daily executions. While they raised their eyes to Heaven, then lowered them once more to earth, they rattled off in nasal voices a series of Pater Nosters and litanies an ell long.

God alone searches hearts: perhaps they were indeed repentant and converted sinners—and yet possibly this was nothing more than a change of scene in their eventful drama of life!

Another and more splendid change of scene took place a few days after our arrival, with the magnificent processions in honor of "*la fête Dieu*" (the Feast of Corpus Christi). My father, who had witnessed the Saturnalia of the Directoire and had heard his friends describe the consecration of the Goddess of Reason, would naturally find the contrast striking. However, the picture had retained its theatrical stamp, since the selfsame Gobelin tapestries which had at that time adorned the route from the Tuileries to the Cathedral were once again hung out and displayed features that were not exactly in accordance with the solemnity of the occasion. For example, subjects of both sacred and profane nature were intermingled: "Judith and Holofernes," "Hercules and Omphale," "Lot and his Daughters," "Perseus and Andromeda," and others. Through a double cordon of French and Swiss guards marched several detachments of troops with drums beating and banners flying, followed by whole battalions of priests and canons (most of them supernumeraries, i.e., lay people of the pallbearer and servant class, in disguise). Monks were still not to be found, but there were long rows of young girls clad in white, with wax tapers and baskets of flowers. A whole staff of courtiers and generals in dress uniform, together with a host of choir boys with censers, surrounded the splendid baldachin beneath which Archbishop Du Quelen carried the Blessed Sacrament in a monstrance heavy with diamonds.

The poles that supported the sacred banners as well as the baldachin were jointly carried by selected *émigrés* and by the very dukes and marshals who had attended the coronation ceremonies of Napoleon and both his Empresses. All of this made a tremendous impression upon me, but I was far from making those reflections that have thrust themselves upon me at a mature age. Instead, I allowed a kind neighbor to point out to me the most prominent personalities, who—in addition to the King's brother the Comte d'Artois, and his son the Duc d'Angoulême—included such names as Marshals Soult, Victor, and Suchet; and Generals Lauriston, Pajol, Molitor, and Maison. For the *émigré* leaders we cared nothing.

The procession halted at a number of places, including the church of St. Germain l'Auxerrois, before whose entrance a temporary altar had been erected. Here Mass was read and blessings were distributed, to the pealing of the very bells which had once given the signal for the St. Bartholomew's Day massacre! The procession wended its way across the Pont-Neuf to the church of Notre Dame amid the booming of cannon and the singing of hymns, which, probably in order to attract greater popularity, were set to rather well-known opera tunes. The mood that prevailed among the tightly packed crowd is not easy to explain or fathom; but their conduct was exemplary. They bared their heads and bent their knees as if they might have been in Rome itself.

A short time later, the murderer Louvel was led to the place of execution under a strong escort of cuirassiers and gendarmes. A curious mob flocked to the Place de Grève, many with as much expectation as if they were about to enjoy a play, just as they had done when Ravaillac and Damiens were executed.* But for all this revolutionary fanaticism, one blessing had been introduced: namely, "death without torture." The instrument upon which Marat and Robespierre had based their tyranny in the name of Liberty, Equality, and Fraternity, and which had claimed innocent victims by the thousand, was but seldom heard of nowadays; and this time—a single stroke, and justice was done.

The actual purpose of our trip—that is to say, the development of my dancing abilities—was not neglected. We diligently visited the various classes, where Coulon, Maze, and especially [Auguste] Vestris gave instruction. Everywhere we were received with the utmost kindness, since everyone believed it was my father's intention to enroll me in one of the schools in Paris. But this never occurred to either of us. I continued my daily practicing under my father's direction, partly on the little stage at the Conservatoire, and partly on the old stage of the Opéra, which they had not yet begun to tear down. I managed to pick up a lot by watching the outstanding soloists, and from the artistic couple M. and Mme. Baptiste Petit I learnt several lovely *pas* from the ballet *Flore et Zéphire*, which were to serve me as a debut upon my return to Copenhagen. But just at that time, Paul Funck, though almost retired as a dancer, came to Paris, hastily gathered some fragments as well as melodies from the above-mentioned ballet, and hurried home ahead of us in order to prepare a *divertissement* which he called *Zephyr and Flora* and—in accordance with the usual practice—passed off as his original composition.

I made no small progress, and since I had already acquired a certain amount of experience from my early theatrical career and possessed a psychical expression, which the French pupils lacked (though they far surpassed me in [technical] skill), I was praised by many. Marie Taglioni's mother, a daughter of the Swedish opera singer Carsten, even held *me* up as a model before her as yet undeveloped daughter, who later became world-famous and the ideal after which I, as a teacher, was one day to train my finest female pupils.

Among my father's old friends and colleagues we found a cordial reception, and even among the younger generation he won lively sympathy by his noble personality. Our Minister, Count Waltersdorff, who had in his day been Theatre Chief [in Copenhagen], was most obliging. (Unfortunately, he died during our stay in Paris.) In the Swedish ambassador, Count Løvenhjelm, my father found an old acquaintance from the happy days of Gustav III in Stockholm. The writer Desaugiers and the statesman Delamarre, both of whom had stayed in Copenhagen many years ago, the former as Secretary of the Legation, the latter as Commissary of the French Republic, greeted us with extraor-

*François Ravaillac (1578–1610) was the assassin of Henry IV, while Robert François Damiens (1715–1757) only succeeded in inflicting a slight wound on Louis XV; he was, nonetheless, condemned as a regicide and sentenced to be torn in pieces by horses on the Place de Grève.

dinary friendliness. In addition, we frequently met with old General Lenor-
mand de Bretteville, who was one of the few who did not retain the
bitterness of the emigration.

With old Heiberg† we were on the best of terms, and his son, the ingenious Johan Ludvig—who was a consummate Parisian—directed our excursions to Sèvres, St. Cloud, and Versailles. On these occasions we joined forces
with several notable Danes, for example, Dr. Phil. H. N. Clausen, Lieut.
Com. P. M. Tuxen, Kammerraad Band of Nørager, the mathematician von
Smidten, and the aesthetician Peder Hjorth. The latter, who on his travels
through Germany had been influenced by the *Frankenhasz* [hatred of France]
so prevalent there, denigrated everything that he heard and saw in France.
Since he exclusively praised the *pure* style in which our Court and State architect, Conferentsraad Hansen, had rebuilt Christiansborg and the Frue
Kirke, the magnificent buildings of neither the Renaissance nor the Rococo
period found favor in his eyes, wherefore at Versailles he had some cen-
sorious remark to make at every step. My father could not refrain from asking
him what he was doing in a country where he found everything so repul-
sive. His answer literally ran: "Yes, my good Herr Bournonville, I shall tell
you indeed. I have come hither so that when I return home I shall be able to
testify with perfect honesty that the whole thing is something—!"

Old Heiberg, who was living on a pension from the days when he had
served under Talleyrand as a secretary at the Imperial Department of Foreign
Affairs, had loyally retained his Republican ideas. He therefore could not be
reconciled with the development in a monarchical direction that was then taking place in the former demagogue Malthe Conrad Bruun, who for many
years now—under the name of Maltebrun—had been ranked among France's
most prominent savants, and as a political writer had recently published his
Traité sur la Légitimité, a book which in Royalist circles was considered a
masterpiece of sound and strict logic.

Young Heiberg, who knew how to adapt himself to the times and circumstances better than did his father, was a frequent guest at Maltebrun's and introduced us to the family, where we spent a number of pleasant evenings.
Maltebrun's wife, a native Parisienne, spoke with a soprano voice so shrill
that I have never heard it equaled, and our famous countryman, who as the
years passed found it less easy to express himself in his mother tongue, had,
in the midst of his Frenchness, retained his good old "Jutland" accent.

Through M. Baptiste *l'aîné, doyen* of the French Comédie, we often obtained complimentary tickets for the Théâtre Français, where we had the opportunity of admiring the splendid ensemble acting and Talma in his master
roles. (Mlle. Mars was absent at that time.) Desaugiers invited us to the
Théâtre du Vaudeville, and here, among other amusing and interesting *petites
pièces*, we saw *La Somnambule*, the first fruit of the young Eugène Scribe's

---

† Peter Andreas Heiberg (1758–1841), Danish author and playwright, was exiled from Denmark
in 1799 after having publicly implied that a high official was misusing his office for his personal
advantage.

later-so-prolific literary activity. We saw something similar to this at the Théâtre Feydeau, where the *opéra-comique* was enjoying its golden age at this time and where in the same year Auber opened the series of his charming compositions with *La Bergère Chatelaine*. On this lyric-dramatic stage, acting and singing were combined in the most amiable harmony, and Boïeldieu's compositions found worthy interpreters in artists like Martin, Ponchard, Gavaudan, and Lemonnier, together with Mmes. Pradher, Pallard, and Boulanger. I can hear them still. But, alas! These departed figures now live only in my memory.

The fact that we did not find the Italian opera at the Salle Louvois as appealing as we did the *opéra-comique* in no way stemmed from prejudices current among Copenhagen musical coteries, but simply from lack of the dramatic talent that distinguished the French singers; for, though Mozart's *Don Giovanni* and Rossini's new *Barbiere di Seviglia* were given with great precision and Mme. Mainvielle-Fodor sang like an angel, we nevertheless could not accustom ourselves to the total lack of dramatic art. Moreover, the famous García had most vulgar manners, while Bordogni was so icy that at a party when sparkling champagne was kept in a wine-cooler, it became a catch phrase among guests to say that it was *"frappé à la Bordogni."*

Of Danish artists who were traveling at public expense, three were to be found in Paris at that moment. Firstly, there was the engraver Heuer, who immediately gave up his engraving in order to devote himself to the newly invented lithography. Then there was Professor Schall's nephew, Peter Funck, who was to further his violin playing under Habeneck and to study composition with Reicha. Unfortunately, despite the most persistent industry and his uncle's patronage, he progressed no further than a wretched mediocrity. His first and last *Overture* was performed for the first and last time at a concert he gave on his return from abroad. Indeed, the longer he practiced on the violin, the worse his playing became — until at last it actually froze.‡

Finally, there was Benjamin Schlick, the most curious member of the trio. As a rather young man he had made a marionette theatre with a mechanism so ingenious that it attracted the attention of Court, which saw in him the future chief engineer of the Royal Theatre. For this reason he was given a travel grant and came to Paris with such glowing recommendations that through the Embassy he was immediately introduced into the most elegant society and to the foremost celebrities of the various professions. There was no longer any mention of the expectations of the post of chief engineer. On the contrary, though he had not gone through, or at any rate completed, any course at the Academy, he everywhere passed himself off as an architect and was allowed to join those in charge of the reconstruction of the recently burnt-down Théâtre de l'Odéon. His delicate facial features and dignified bearing, combined with a toilette that was always exquisite and tasteful, gave him a touch of the half-breed aristocrat, and the supposition of a mysterious origin was strengthened by the abundant resources that seemed to accrue to

‡Cf. the chapter "Claus Schall," Vol. III, Part Three, p. 644.

him with no visible work or effort on his part. Therefore, how great was people's astonishment when after a couple of years' absence he returned, bringing with him an album — gilt-clasped and velvet-bound — containing the loveliest sketches representing the design, profiles, façade, and decorative ornamentation of the Théâtre de l'Odéon. This *copy*, which he most improperly referred to as "his work," was advertised by his patron, Professor Torkel Baden, in the paper *Dagen*, which emphasized in pompous phrases that the aforementioned theatre had been executed according to Schlick's sketches and under his personal supervision.

Supported by a testimonial such as this, he submitted some color sketches to the Academy with the hope of being accepted as a member. But as bad luck would have it, these same sketches were to be found in the Academy's collection of engravings and formed part of Percier and Fontaine's work on the galleries of the Louvre. Naturally, this discovery caused quite a scandal, and the unfortunate aspirant retreated with the observation that his merit lay in having given life and color to "those dead lines."

However, this defeat did not prevent Schlick's defenders from entrusting him with the difficult task of designing the reconstruction of the Royal Theatre without demolishing the old walls. He traveled abroad once more, and after some time delivered the requested design, beautifully worked out and marked by perfect taste. The Academy rejected it as completely useless. Indignant at this, he showed it to Quatremère de Quincey, the secretary and spokesman for the French Académie des Beaux Arts, and on the latter's own recommendation was accepted as a corresponding member. Schlick had now risen to considerable heights, settled himself in Paris, and established a tasteful atelier which, to be sure, produced no results other than the fact that *"le célèbre architecte danois"* together with three other artists was mentioned in the newspapers for his cooperation in the remarkably fast renovation of the interior of the Théâtre des Variétés.

He frequently journeyed to London, whence he brought back a printed description of Brunel's colossal work, the tunnel beneath the Thames, about which he lectured at a gathering of the Académie. On another occasion he returned with a portfolio containing a new type of steel engraving, which he showed and presented to Charles X. For this he was immediately decorated with the Cross of the Légion d'Honneur.

After the July Revolution he went to Germany, where in every major or minor capital he acquired great merit, the reasons for which no one could discover. Whatever the case may be, they everywhere secured him special distinctions, including a Chamberlain's key.

The last glimpse I had of this enigmatic personality came through a letter to the secretary of our Legation in Stockholm (1863), whom he urgently enjoined to persuade King Carl XV to bestow upon him a Commander's Cross, since as the nephew of the recently deceased Austrian Field Marshal, Count Schlick, he could not in decency accept a lower Swedish decoration!

But, to return to our Parisian life in 1820: it should be noted that, after our correspondence, our Sundays were taken up by visits to museums, which we studied thoroughly—the Louvre for antiquities and the Old Masters; the Luxembourg for products of the younger school, among whom Horace Vernet had just made his debut. Without being irreverent, during our entire stay we reduced our churchgoing to one Mass in the palace chapel of the Tuileries, where an offertory by Cherubini was performed by the leading male and female singers from all three opera theatres, and where my father got the opportunity to compliment the famous maestro. We extended our wanderings to the most distant quarters and often struck up interesting conversations with men and women of the Parisian populace. We climbed down into the Catacombs at the Barrière d'Enfer, read the inscriptions on the graves in Père Lachaise Cemetery, and tossed bread to the bears in the Jardin des Plantes. With awesome devotion we entered the French Pathéon, which contains the ashes of Voltaire, Mirabeau, and Jean-Jacques Rousseau, but which by this time had been reconsecrated to St. Genevieve. There was, however, nothing which interested us more than the Hôtel des Invalides, where approximately 85,000 more or less disabled veterans from the wars of the Republic and the Empire enjoyed comfort and care after having withstood dangers, trials, and sufferings. Here they lived in the memory of bygone days of glory and cherished sympathies which were not exactly popular with the party then in power.

Strangely enough, although my father and I, as far as Denmark was concerned, were staunch Royalists and fond of the paternal government of Frederik VI, in France we adhered strongly to the Liberal Opposition. Therefore, when we secured tickets to the Chambre des Députés through the Legation, we always sided with speakers like Manuel, Benjamin Constant, Generals Foy and Gérard, all of whom belonged to the Left. At this time the debates centered mainly around the electoral law, regarding the composition of election committees and the secret ballot. The discussion, which was keen and lively but not stormy, was continued even upon leaving the session, and we then saw how the defenders of constitutional ideas, full of awe, crowded around old Lafayette.

The reactionary tendency in the majority of the Chamber could not help but arouse public unrest; and as a result of this, people gathered and ran through the streets crying: *"Vive la Charte!"* A serious incident occurred at the Porte-Saint-Denis when, armed with bludgeons and supported by *Gardes du Corps* in civilian dress, the police tore into the unarmed crowd, which was finally dispersed by the cuirassiers, leaving behind both dead and wounded. The speeches which the ultra-Royalists made in opposition to the guarantees of the Charter and the derisive manner in which they treated the nation's most sacred memories where bound to place the government of Louis XVIII in a false light and carry the people's thoughts back to a time when the lack of liberal institutions was compensated for by *"le prestige et la gloire."*

A small diversion in the midst of this political commotion was created by the scandalous lawsuit brought by Great Britain's King, George IV, against his Queen, the sorely unedifying details of which filled—nay, almost defiled—the columns of the daily papers and revealed a cynicism the like of which was not to be found. The Italian witness, who persistently answered all impudent questions with his: "I don't remember," apparently, next to Brougham's masterly defense, contributed to the complete acquittal of the sorely disgraced Queen. In the meantime, her Chamberlain (and former Queen's Messenger), Signor Bergami, had become the hero of the day and of the ladies. His portrait, with an abundance of whiskers, hung in all the bookshops next to those of Lord Byron and Walter Scott.

During the course of the summer, we were twice invited by my father's old friend and comrade, Nivelon, to visit his lovely country estate in Normandy, where he gathered about him a select circle of amusing and spirited guests, most of them older people, to be sure, but they proved the thesis that the French are at their most amiable between their fiftieth and sixtieth years. I am involuntarily reminded of a charming verse by Alexandre Dumas, which I have attempted to render thus:

> Threescore years! Now is the time
> When autumn's breeze, so fresh and mild,
> Brings forth an inner peace sublime
> To still the fire of passions wild;
> While tender-heartedness, like the star
> That glimmers through the clouded air,
> In the distance lets us see
> Hope of the dawn of Eternity!*

However, the old cousin of our good host's deceased wife, who was to do the honors in his house, presented an exception to this rule. In her youth she had figured in gallant society, had fled with the Emigration, and had returned filled with hatred for what had gone on in France during the interval. Everything went smoothly so long as politics and history did not enter the picture, but from that moment on, she spewed gall and wormwood. She regarded Lafayette as the most dastardly blackguard, and to Bonaparte, whom she time and again called Nicholas, she granted but a single virtue, namely, having put an end to mob rule: *"Il nous a délivré de la canaille!"* Later on, I shall take the opportunity to express my feelings about hospitable and comfortable "Saint Martin" in some biographical sketches.

A few days after our return from the country, we were awakened early on the morning of September 29 by the booming of guns from the Invalides. At the thirteenth shot (which was to continue up to twenty-four) all of Paris fell to its knees. *"Un garçon, un garçon!"* rang from every street corner in every quarter. For the Duchesse de Berry, who was with child at the time her con-

---

*These lines are a translation of Bournonville's Danish; it has not been possible to identify the French original.

sort was murdered, had carried the dynasty's last hope beneath her heart in the midst of her great sorrow, and had now been successfully delivered of a prince.

There was something providential in the birth of this child that with incontestable power moved even those who did not favor the Bourbons. And when the gout-ridden old King walked onto the balcony of the Tuileries holding the tiny Duc de Bordeaux out toward the people who had gathered by the thousands, the air rang with endless cries of jubilation. As foreigners, we could have no idea how the news was received in the provinces or in those circles where other dynastic combinations were contemplated. But wherever we looked, the most joyous feeling prevailed, and it was further heightened by the splendid arrangements which had been made by the public authorities to celebrate this important event.

The Champs-Elysées was adorned in its festal dress, with pyramids and garlands on the blazing lampions. On the plains were erected bandstands, *mâts de cocagne*, pantomime theatres, and wooden sheds from which wine flowed while bread, cooked chickens, and turkeys were tossed out to the lowest classes of the population, here represented by the offspring of the *Sans-culottes*. Faces which seemed to have ascended from the caves of darkness screamed, bit, and rolled in the dirt in order to catch and tear apart the victuals thrown them. In contrast to these orgies, festive banquets were arranged for the various guilds. In the covered fishmarket stood decorated tables for the market women, who, with singing and cries of "Vivat!" drank a toast to the health of the newborn child and his august mother. All public buildings were illuminated for three evenings in succession. Splendid fireworks were set off, and on every square and street corner was sung the following popular song, whose first three stanzas I remember perfectly:

> It is a son! For to my happiness
> Two dozen times I've heard the signal gun;
> All Paris is alive with joyousness
> That people with euphoria express:
> It is a son! It is a son!
>
> Berry is gone! He, who at every chance
> Made kindly deeds his life's expression!
> They struck him down, but, 'stead of vengeance,
> The final gift that he had made to France—
> It is a son! It is a son!
>
> He's a Bourbon! And if he wears a crown,
> He'll show himself deserving that grand name:
> Great soul and good deeds will cement his fame,
> He will not wish ill luck to anyone.
> He's a Bourbon! He's a Bourbon!*

*In the original edition, these stanzas are given only in French.

Even then, our thoughts were carried back to less than ten years earlier, when a similar celebration and even more brilliant fêtes had hailed the arrival of the feeble King of Rome, whose birth had crowned the great Napoleon's proudest expectations. King Louis Philippe d'Orléans later appeared on the same balcony, surrounded by his numerous flock of children, in whose midst was also to be found an heir presumptive to the throne of France; and finally, twenty years afterward, Napoleon III was also believed to hold the future in his hands when he presented his newborn son to the assembled crowd.

Alas! How inconstant are the moods of peoples and the fates of kingdoms! Of these four candidates for King and Emperor, three pretenders still remain. They have all tasted the bitterness of exile, but are always waiting for new upheavals in volcanically emotional France.

Autumn approached and our stay in Paris drew to a close. We had seen and witnessed a great deal, gathered good experiences in both scenic and choreographic respects, enjoyed much hospitality, and made highly interesting acquaintances, which were to prove vitally useful to me later on. We were to receive yet another unforgettable impression before our departure. This occurred at a dinner party at the home of our Consul, Hoppe, where a glowing French account of H. C. Ørsted's latest discovery in the field of electromagnetism was read. Few of us were sufficiently initiated into the mysteries of physics to understand the importance of the great result that had been achieved, and no one suspected the marvelous use it would lead to in time, but our Danish hearts nonetheless swelled with pride and joy and an enthusiastic cheer broke out for our highly esteemed countryman.

A homeward journey, as a rule, offers nothing remarkable. One is sick and tired of impressions and surprises and longs for the peace of the hearth and rest in the bosom of one's family. But on this occasion we were also to experience something unusual, if not exactly amusing. The aforementioned Consul General, who after Waltersdorff's death and during the absence of the Secretary of the Legation had taken over Embassy affairs, sent for my father to reveal to him in strictest confidence that rather serious information had been received: to wit, the rumor that a Danish sea captain had abducted Napoleon from St. Helena. Important dispatches were to be sent to Copenhagen, and my father was offered free conveyance if he would agree to act as courier. It was immediately settled, and we were given a shooting brake, whose forward space was hurriedly packed full of Perigordian truffle pâté addressed to Geheime-Statsminister Rosenkrantz. The post horses were ordered, the courier's passport made out, and provisional traveling money disbursed. But as far as the actual dispatches were concerned, we were to await them at the post station closest to Paris: the village of Bourget.

We lodged at the Auberge de la Rose and settled down in the expectation of promptly hearing from our diplomats. But several days went by without the arrival of our dispatches. I was sent into the city to find out what had happened, and each time returned with our subsistence allowance and assurances that everything would shortly be in order. However, the time weighed heavy on our hands, and we led the most tedious existence anyone can possibly imagine, at a rural inn which was frequented only by coachmen and carters, and on our strolls in the monotonous environs we were stopped a number of times by gendarmes who regarded us with a suspicious eye and asked to see our passports. Finally, after having waited for almost four weeks, the Secretary of the Consulate arrived with the necessary traveling money, which was, however, only enough to get us as far as Hamburg, where we were to deliver the packet containing the dispatches. Should we wish to retain the carriage for our journey through Denmark, it was at our disposal—provided that the truffle pâté accompanied us to Copenhagen.

Winter had already set in, with its alternating frost, rain, and sleet, and we continued our not too pleasant courier mission by way of Brussels, Aix-la-Chapelle, Münster, Osnabrück, and Bremen to Hamburg, where after having traveled day and night for a week we imagined ourselves to have performed prodigies of speed. We were now granted a much needed rest, and since at that time stagecoaches left much to be desired in the way of comfort, we preferred to engage post horses for the aforementioned shooting brake, and after having sped across the mainland, islands, and Belts for four days, we finally arrived at our beloved home.

I cannot state how much this blind alarm and the consequent courier expedition cost the Danish government, but as far as our so-called "free trip" was concerned, the journey by courier post through Denmark alone cost us a sum which would nowadays be sufficient to undertake a round trip to Paris and also enjoy a month's sojourn there.

AN INTERVAL

DURING our absence, Paul Funck had presented *his Zephyr and Flora*, which with himself and Mme. Jansen in the title roles was not exactly a striking picture of Didelot's poetic composition. Solo dancer Dahlén (who, though ten years younger than my father, had long since passed his prime) had, while my father was away, acted as ballet director and engaged a number of pupils, whom he was training as cupids and trolls for the grand ballet *Armida*, whose *mise-en-scène* he had prepared. Among the former were to be found Andrea Møller, who later caused a sensation as Mme. Krætzmer, and the little Johanne Pätges, whose innate grace even as a child suggested what she was one day to become for the Danish stage as the celebrated wife of Heiberg. Among the latter—that is, the trolls—no one was more conspicuous than a young lad who had recently come from Odense and whose ballet debut was to take place in the finale of the last act by tumbling headlong out of a crevice in a rock. This was none other than H. C. Andersen, to whom a marvelous destiny had pointed out this entrance as the road to world renown as a writer and to a high rung on the social scale!

People were expecting considerable results from our studies in Paris, and primarily believed that my father would bring back new ballets, either of his own invention or from the foreign repertoire. But it was the same with him as with his famous contemporary, Auguste Vestris, who modestly told anyone who asked him why he had never tried his hand at composing ballets: "I never thought I could do it." They both had decided talent for tasteful dances, pretty little episodes, and picturesque groupings; but larger dramatic combinations were outside my father's sphere. Therefore, after my home-coming, I made my debut in a serious solo he had arranged for me to the ac-companiment of a French horn and in a *pas de trois* with two of the finest *danseuses* we had at our disposal. I made but a weak impression; for though one could indeed perceive a certain development of my aptitudes, as a youth of fifteen I was still at the hobbledehoy age and completely immature in both strength and physique. Therefore it was a disappointment for us *and* for the public; and despite the fact that my father appeared with his usual bravura as Raoul Barbe-Blue, it was said in several quarters that he was too old and his son entirely too young.

Dahlén, who now more than ever fancied himself called to become Galeotti's successor, produced a host of ballet libretti which he recited to ev-eryone—except us, of course! He now continued the rehearsal of his *Armida*, which was completed only toward the end of the season. Schall had com-posed the music but had not been particularly inspired by his subject. This, incidentally, did not seem to have been influenced by Tasso's *Gerusalemme liberata*, but contained instead obscure reminiscences of Gluck's opera—how-ever, without allusion to the fact that Rinaldo and Ubaldo were Crusaders, for the gods are invoked and pagan Cupid himself presides among the magical beings in Armida's garden. The applause, which was rather lively for Ubaldo's war dance among the attacking devils in the finale of the first act, died away completely during the succeeding acts, and the ballet ended with a fiasco that was denoted not by loud expressions of displeasure but by an omi-nous giggling. The leading roles were entrusted to Mme. Schall, who was no longer young or pretty to look at, and to Paul Funck, whose nullity as a mime was established as an indisputable fact. Dahlén himself, who played the knightly Ubaldo, had long had a monopoly on arousing mirth; and if one adds to the weaknesses of his composition the extremely shoddy décor, as well as our machinery's unsuccessful attempts to produce the enchanting illusions of a magical world, one cannot wonder that this unfortunate work did its share to discredit the ballet as a scenic art form.

At this time the lyric stage was predominant and maintained itself in the public's favor by a richly varied repertoire in which both older and newer styles were tastefully represented. Along with Schultz's *The Harvest Festival* and *Peter's Wedding*, Schall's *The Travelers in China*, and Dittersdorff's *The Apothecary and the Doctor* figured Weyse, Kuhlau, Paër, C. Kreutzer, Simon Mayr, Méhul, Dalayrac, "Nicolo," Boïeldieu, Meyerbeer, and Rossini (the next to the last with his *Romilda and Constance,* which was mercilessly hissed—a fate that threatened all Italian music, against which there was an outright conspiracy, and struck Rossini's *Gazza ladra* and barely spared *Tancredi* and *Donna del Lago,* while *Il Barbiere di Seviglia* was allowed to pass only because it was regarded as "charming gibberish"). But Mozart's *Marriage of Figaro* was, then as later on, the opera's "festival piece," and so it will remain as long as melody is not ousted from the realm of art.

All of these operas were given with spoken dialogue and performed by a company of singers in whose midst were a few good actors. Rehearsals were conducted with energy and insight by the talented Chorus Master Zinck, while the actual art of singing made considerable progress through Siboni's zealous efforts. As *Orchesterchef,* Schall derived great merit from the accompaniment, which, as a result of the less noisy instrumentation of the time, did not drown out the singers' voices. Messrs. George Zinck, Cetti, Kirchheiner, C. N. Rosenkilde, and Holm, together with Mmes. Zrza, Løffler, Rind, and Winsløw, were the opera's *coryphées.* But what contributed to the constant increase in the number of outstanding novelties—apart from the musical and poetic fruitfulness of the period—was the partiality of the Court for this art form and the fixed red-letter days of January 28 and October 28, the birthdays of the Queen and King, which on the ensuing evenings were to be celebrated at the theatre with a new *syngestykke.* On such occasions there could be no objections from those who were carrying out the work, for every suggestion for a possible postponement was countered with the all-preponderant argument: "But my dear fellows, it is a *birthday!*"

The spoken drama, which possessed great talents like Frydendahl, Lindgreen, and Ryge, had in previous years lost a number of actors, some of whom were, however, irreplaceable in certain roles in which they had been outstanding "types." Among them were Rongsted as the Tinker, Heinsvig as Oldfux, Rind, Kruse, and Haack in a host of superb interpretations of comic as well as tragic characters. As Holbergian Magdelones, Mme. Clausen was unequaled by her otherwise so talented successor, Henriette Jørgensen; and even though as elegant cavaliers Stage possessed both humor and animation, he lacked the eroticism so necessary for romantic leads. Thus there were essential gaps in the ensemble acting, and the performance of subordinate roles was often below average. But then there came the fortunate appearance of a young lieutenant in the artillery, who abandoned a military career to devote his abilities to the dramatic art instead. His superb declamation, which immediately broke with the traditional manner of recitation, brought an entirely new element, so to speak, into the drama; and in a short time Nielsen became not only the public's undisputed favorite but the sincere spokesman of pure love in tragedy as well as in comedy.

In the following season, under Mme. Rosing's direction, a rather young, very blonde girl, Anna Brenøe, made her debut as Dyveke, and, since she also possessed a lovely singing voice, as Stéphanie in Berton's opera *Montano* *et Stéphanie.* Here we had found a romantic heroine with an ideality the like of which has neither before nor since appeared on the Danish stage. With a speaking voice filled with tenderness and convincing strength, she combined the most captivating femininity and knew how to give every role she played her characteristic stamp. She early abandoned the lyric stage, and the drama hereby took on an importance which in the following years developed to the point where, in dramatic respects, the Danish stage stood on an equal footing with the Théâtre Français and the Burgtheater in Vienna. (What she has meant to the theatre through the years I have endeavored to describe in Volume II of *My Theatre Life.*)*

As far as my own youthful person was concerned, I had, by my journey abroad, gained a certain degree of independence in my opinions and ideas, and felt almost like an adult, since by the time I was confirmed I had exchanged my boy's jacket for a tailcoat and overcoat. Little by little, my dancing now progressed, and I performed as a dancer of note (in light of our conditions) in my father's compositions as well as in various *divertissements* by Funck. On my own I studied history, mythology, and the classics in French translation, received instruction in figure painting (that is to say, I copied other good copies), and studied music under skillful teachers, on both the pianoforte and the violin. On this last instrument I became so proficient that I assisted as ripienist at "Harmonien's"† concerts and twice as soloist with the Society for the Propagation of Music where, together with a young student— now our highly esteemed composer J. P. E. Hartmann—I performed *Concertantes* by Kreutzer and Moralt.

Pierre Joseph Larcher, an older pupil of my father's school (son of a French artisan who had fled with the emigration, settled in Copenhagen, and was killed by a bomb during the terrifying days of 1807), had by a couple of whirlwind visits to Berlin and Paris acquired a modern flair which, combined with a measure of physical strength and stamina, appealed to the public and gave him the boldness to appear as a choreographer with several subjects borrowed from abroad. His energy and ability caught the eye of the Theatre management, and they already saw in him an acceptable—according to the humble demands of that time—balletmaster.

Despite his portfolio filled with libretti, they had renounced Dahlén with his *Armida,* and my father himself, whose mind was laden with bitter family sorrows and whose natural excitability was further inflamed by petty cabals and frequent conflicts, entertained little hope for the future of the ballet and had restricted his activity to the school and to the arrangement of dances for operas and plays—for the last time in Weber's *Preciosa.* There was thus serious contemplation of a reduction of the ballet's "veterans," female as well as male, and at the end of the 1822–1823 season, my father, together with a host

---

*See sketch of Anna Nielsen in "Dramatic Celebrities of the Danish Stage," Vol. II, p. 331.
†*Harmonien,* located in Vingaardstræde, was one of the finest clubs in Copenhagen and periodically held concerts for its members.

of his elderly colleagues, was honorably discharged from theatrical service with an especially good pension.

However, he was always passionately fond of his art and, despite his advanced age, still possessed a number of the dance's finest qualities, namely, lightness and graceful and dignified bearing. He therefore wished to bid farewell to the stage, among whose ornaments he had justly been reckoned in his day, in one of his favorite *entrées*. With due filial respect, I tried to get him to relinquish this intention—but in vain. The old man danced—and miraculously well! But I vowed to myself that if I were one day to be his successor as solo-dancer, I would retire far, far sooner.

During this interval of three and a half years, a considerable development took place in my whole character. By diligent reading of Danish and French works and by incessant preoccupation with Art in its various forms, my imagination was awakened to an extraordinary degree, while my young heart, which from my earliest days had been continuously stirred by the most tender emotions, now floated on Zephyr wings from one ideal of Beauty and Virtue to another—though always with a distant prospect of a sacred and inviolate [matrimonial] alliance. Without so much as suspecting it, at one moment I played Cherubino,‡ at another Hans Mortensen, and finally, even Cousin Charles, which role might actually have become serious had my parents not been firmly opposed to such youthful whims, which they rightly regarded as childish tricks.

I was already receiving a nice little salary and earned money by giving lessons in schools and to private families as well as to certain gentlemen who had earlier neglected to learn how to dance and now, when they were going courting, did not wish to stand and watch others dancing with their chosen ones. In spite of my seventeen years, I exercised the same authority over my pupils and demanded the same discipline during lessons as I did when I was head of the Danish Ballet; and, remarkably enough, it never seemed to have occurred to anyone, younger or older, not to obey my suggestions.

I continued my training under my father's careful supervision, and actually made some degree of progress. But my eyes had been opened to what might be achieved at the Parisian ballet, and I realized that, particularly in the gymnastics and effective use of dancing, I was still far inferior to those virtuosi I had admired in Paris. It was clear to both my father and me that under existing conditions there was no future for me at Copenhagen's Theatre. It was therefore his intention to send me abroad, but not before I had achieved in his school such perfection that I could astonish the Parisians and lead choreography back to the—in his opinion—high level at which it had stood when he was a child and had looked up to the elder Vestris and his teacher, the great Dupré.

But to me this seemed a rather distant goal, and I felt that the system un-

‡ The love-sick page in *The Marriage of Figaro,* the hero of J. L. Heiberg's *The April Fools,* and (presumably) Charles Surface in Sheridan's *School for Scandal.*

der which I had been trained was, to be sure, both tasteful and correct—but static. In his old age my beloved father became not only conservative but downright reactionary with regard to Art, and our conflicting opinions in certain areas called forth discussions whose vehemence often tempted me to replies that I would have regretted my whole life long, had they not been effectively neutralized by the wealth of French curses showered upon me for my philistine views. Thus, as deeply as my father and I loved each other, our artistic coexistence had become somewhat less than pleasant, and—though not without a struggle—I contrived to petition Frederik VI for permission to stay in Paris for fifteen months with no public support other than my salary, the five quarterly payments of which were allotted me in advance. And so I obtained the desired permission and, armed with good recommendations, accompanied by my parents' admonitions and blessings, and provided with ready money for an entire year, I left Copenhagen on April 27, 1824, in my nineteenth year, and set out alone into the wide world, to land in Paris, the home of Art and ambition, but also at the focal point of frivolity: LE FOYER DE L'OPÉRA!

SIX YEARS IN PARIS

THE goal I coveted—namely, to acquire the greatest possible skill in my profession and, after having performed successfully abroad, to assume one day a prominent place on the Danish stage—was to be attained only after much effort and persistent industry, the details of which can hardly be of interest to people other than those who cultivate this difficult but little appreciated art form. All the same, apart from this specialty, if it is more than difficult to make oneself known in this center of world movement, on the other hand the attentive spectator's dividend is all the richer, for at every step and glance, so to speak, something new presents itself, not only in the realm of art and fashion but in events and feelings whose influence extends far beyond the borders of France.

Upon my arrival in Paris, the first thing I encountered outside my limited sphere was the echo of the Spanish campaign, whose objective (hardly to the edification of the friends of freedom) was to relieve Ferdinand VII of the tiresome burden of the Constitution. By all those knowledgeable in the art of war it was regarded as a *"promenade militaire"* but was celebrated with as much pomp as if the Duc d'Angoulême, the hero of Trocadéro, had eclipsed the great Napoleon's reputation as a commanding general. One could now set one's mind at ease with regard to the latter: he rested beneath the weeping willows of St. Helena, and the young Duke of Reichstadt, whom many, though still in extreme secrecy, called Napoleon II, was rendered harmless by Metternich's care, while his august mother exchanged her position as Imperial widow for a morganatic marriage.

Several bills of a reactionary cast had aroused a zealous, albeit powerless, opposition and an episode in the Chambre des Députés—namely, the violent expulsion of Manuel—had brought the indignation of the Liberals to its climax, for in spite of the minority's protest, the gendarme brigadier's order, "Seize that man!" echoed as a menacing omen for all defenders of the Charter's guarantees.

That same year (1824) Louis XVIII died without arousing noticeable national mourning, and his brother, the Comte d'Artois, ascended the throne under the name of Charles X. His jovial nature and mild though by no means spiritual countenance made a rather pleasing impression when he appeared on horseback before the Parisians, and his word had a placating effect upon the volatile atmosphere.

The coronation at Rheims followed swiftly upon his brother's burial in St. Denis. At these solemnities an extraordinary splendor, both spiritual and temporal, was displayed. But hardly had these magnificent ceremonies brought the Roman Catholic clergy a step further into the foreground than they completely laid hold of the weak king's mind and disseminated their influence into the widest circles. While the Jesuits labored in silence, *"les Frères Ignorantins"* wandered from one parish church to another and in the most vulgar language preached that damnation and the torments of Hell would strike all who were not willing to acclaim the Holy Father in Rome. Excommunication struck not only the anti-Royalists, the Protestants, and the friends of freedom, but in particular the theatres—and this to such a degree that when actors or dancers wished to have their children confirmed, the parents' profession was most carefully concealed and only under very special circumstances might a Christian burial be granted to a member of this social class. This could do nothing but create bad blood in the enlightened element of the population. Therefore, despite strict censorship, the ministers Villèle, Corbière, and Peyronnet were subjected to the most bitter attacks, both in prose and in verse, while at the same time the Duc d'Orléans knew how to win popularity by his humane behavior and the protection he afforded those painters who glorified the memory of the Republic and the days of the Empire—pictures of which, by Horace Vernet, Bellanger, Hyppolite Lecomte, and a number of others, adorned his galleries in the Palais-Royal, which were open to the public free of charge. By his building projects he also provided the incentive for the considerable embellishments which Paris underwent at that time.

What also caused a diversion amidst the mounting dissatisfaction was the anxiety with which people followed the Greek fight for freedom, while the heroic defense of Missolonghi had an electrifying effect upon the martial spirit of the French. The opposition which the bill for the re-establishment of the right of primogeniture met with in the Chambre des Pairs produced a complete change of ministers, and a milder breeze, as it were, now entered as Martignac took over as president of the Council and introduced freer and more pleasant rules of procedure.

Sympathies were allowed to be expressed, "the cult of glory" erected its altar in all of the bookshops, and most remarkable of all: the King received permission from the bigoted people surrounding him to order and even to attend a gala performance in the theatre of the Tuileries, which had stood unused for many years. Here I had the honor of dancing at the side of Mlle. Taglioni, a circumstance which gave Count Gustav Løvenhjelm the opportunity to point us out to His Majesty as the children of Swedish mothers — the fact that I was Danish was not even mentioned.

During the Martignac ministry, General Maison was sent to Morea with a French army corps to support the Greeks, and the naval battle at Navarino was decided in favor of the united navies and to the advantage of the long-oppressed people of Greece.

Court and clerical cabals soon had the liberal Martignac ousted, and reaction appeared more threatening than ever in the person of his keenest opponent, the Prince de Polignac, who to begin with wounded the deepest feelings of the nation by placing General Bourmont, the deserter from Waterloo, in charge of the expedition against Algeria, and then by issuing the notorious ordinances, which produced a general uprising and the bloody days of July 1830.

Fortunately, I was already engaged at Copenhagen's Theatre and had celebrated my wedding when this catastrophe occurred. I later learnt with deep admiration that Martignac himself had been appointed Polignac's defense counsel in the fallen minister's trial for high treason. He managed to perform this highly responsible task with a dignity and a talent that were at once worthy of an Aristides and a Cicero.

These are, in brief, the historic moments — which have been boldly graven in my memory — from the six years in Paris during which I *aspired* and *served* at the Académie Royale de Musique. To furnish a day to day account of my "Life and Doings" during this period would be a little too tedious. But all the same, since it contains the most important part of my youth, and like all *novelles* ends with a happy marriage, I have attempted to mount its genre pictures in frames which, with my readers' permission, shall be entitled: "MY GHOSTS," "MY GARRET," "THE FIRST JOURNEY ON LEAVE OF ABSENCE," "THE THREE FOYERS," and "THE SECOND JOURNEY ON LEAVE OF ABSENCE."

My "Ghosts"

This heading might easily be interpreted as containing a hint of "Spiritualism" and as an attempt to lead my readers into one ghost story or another. But, without being one of those *esprits forts* who deny everything that cannot be demonstrated physically or mathematically (mainly because physics and mathematics played no part in my humble schooling, I no more believe in rapping spirits than I do in homeopathy and dancing furniture; neither do I understand how dreams can presage future events. But in that realm, where

Fantasy continually darts forward and Memory back in time, when both are united in dreams, images long vanished appear in rejuvenated form and the old man sees himself—albeit with a dim awareness of the number of years— transported back to the days of his youth, which emerge before him like a *fata morgana* on the distant horizon.

Only he who achieves sound sleep through bodily exertion can properly know how to appreciate its comfort and refreshment when it is accompanied by pleasant dreams. For every thinking and active person, such dreams must be to see nagging problems solved, and his hitherto fruitless endeavors crowned with success. Therefore, good reader, be not astonished when you discover that for me there was no more glorious dream than this: to be able to *soar* while dancing, without touching the ground. In my youth I was always haunted by the thought of unsuccessful performances, weak memorization, and incomplete costume, and I awakened as from a nightmare. Now, on the other hand, when as a pensioner I am enjoying my retirement far from the theatre, it often happens that as soon as I have given myself up to the arms of Morpheus, I am borne on the wings of Time back to my earlier pursuits. The journey usually carries me to Paris, where I come to a halt in the Ballet Foyer of the Opéra before the three mirrors which during the years 1824–1830 reflected my diligent exercises. To the astonishment of my onlooking comrades, I easily overcome all the difficulties that had formerly given me the worst trouble. I stand as if rooted to the spot in *attitudes*, turn with complete security in the various *pirouettes*, and need only hold my breath in order to ascend to the rafters like an aerostat, or, by stretching my feet behind me like the birds in their flight, to sail through space and soar from the stage out into the auditorium. One can hardly imagine the exhilarating feeling of excitement and satisfaction these fantastic results produce. It is the ecstasy of victory, the loosing of earthly bonds—freedom! Then I say to myself (for reflection impreceptibly creeps up on imagination): "This time it is no longer a dream! Now you have gotten it! Just make sure you do not forget the technique, and your success as a bravura dancer is assured forever!" And so I am embraced by my old father . . . together we go to compliment Vestris . . . Balletmaster Gardel renews my contract, and Nivelon, that friend of my father's youth, invites us to visit his country estate in Normandy! To be sure, I feel disappointed upon awakening, like Jeppe* after his journey to "Paradise," but I soon encounter these friendly images once more; and if in my fleeting wanderings I am not stopped by friends and well-wishers long since gone to rest, or do not find myself standing before the Royal box where Frederik VI and his family intimate their approval to me, then I am certain to land at the dancing school in Paris.

Many will no doubt be surprised that a sensible old man's thoughts can revolve around such—according to general notions—a frivolous subject as dancing. But, without repeating what I so often stated in justification of this

*The title character in Holberg's *Jeppe paa Bjerget* [*Jeppe of the Hill*].

art form and the activity to which I have devoted my talents out of love and conviction, I will consider myself fortunate if until the hour when I shall be awakened from my final nap I am visited by no visions other than those that hover about me from Terpsichore's airy regions. Among the host of deceased personalities who appear before me in dreams and, like the ghost in *Hamlet*, call to me "Remember!," the three mentioned above stand foremost as those who in real life set for me the goal to which I have until this day aspired.

PIERRE GARDEL, born at Nancy in 1758, was by his twenty-second year already an excellent *danseur sérieux* and distinguished choreographer, whom Noverre mentions in his *Lettres* with deserved recognition. As the pupil of his older brother, Philippe Gardel,† he had inherited something of the latter's rigid training and was also cold and ostensibly phlegmatic in his external appearance. But his noble figure and great correctness, combined with an uncommonly fine education (in comparison with that of his contemporary colleagues) and with musical ability, placed him foremost among the celebrities of the ballet.

However, he soon found himself overshadowed as a dancer by the younger Vestris, and early abandoned performing in order to devote himself entirely to composition. His first works in this direction appeared during the time of the Republic and were *Psyché, Télémaque,* and *Le Jugement de Pâris. La Dansomanie, Achille à Scyros, L' Enfant prodigue,* and *Paul et Virginie* were performed under the Empire; finally, *Proserpina* and *La Servante justifiée* were staged during the Restoration. All these ballets bore the stamp of perfection and, with the exception of *Paul et Virginie* and *La Servante justifiée,* were of completely original invention. Nevertheless, as far as dramatic effect is concerned, he was surpassed by Milon, who, without possessing Gardel's genius, better understood how to use the mimic talents who had nothing to do with the actual dancing.

And thus one had from this master's [Milon's] hand *Le Carnaval de Venise, Les Noces de Gamache, L'Épreuve villageoise, Nina, ou la Folle par amour,* and *Clari.* These last two ballets achieved a success that placed Gardel's classicial works somewhat in the shade, but no one was able to rival him in the scenic arrangement of grand operas, wherein dancing and magnificent pageantry played an important role. No other balletmaster, either before or since, has been able to produce *divertissements* such as those that were included in *Le Triomphe de Trajan, Les Danaïdes, Fernand Cortès,* and *La Lampe merveilleuse.* One did not know what to admire most: his inexhaustible wealth of invention or the well-calculated use of time and energies at his excellent rehearsals. It is difficult to determine just how much I have allowed myself to be influenced by this great master in the limited sphere which has been allotted me, but in accordance with his example (in direct opposition to the method of Noverre and the majority of my foreign colleagues), I have al-

†Bournonville is presemably referring to Pierre Gardel's older brother Maximilien Léopold Philippe Joseph (1741–1787), commonly known as Maximilien Gardel.

ways worked out the details of my compositions and correlated them with the violin part before I began the rehearsal, which is otherwise all too often interrupted due to a want of improvisation.

Although as good as my father's contemporary, Gardel had in his day given him instruction, and my father always looked upon him with a certain filial respect. He [Gardel] was already an old man when I became acquainted with him, and much different in appearance from those portraits that represent him as a young man in the extravagant attire of the Republic, with powdered wig and flowing shirt frills. He now wore a dark brown peruke, and in the course of time his hooked nose had become bright red, which made him look even more sarcastic. His imperturbable *sang-froid* was the same as I heard tell of from earlier days, though it did not preclude cordiality and humor in daily intercourse. But during stage duty, it was often so chilling that it could make the boldest foot quaver. He was therefore far more respected than popular with the personnel.

The radiance that surrounded him in the splendid days of Napoleon was considerably diminished under the Bourbons, who were not particularly fond of the usurper's favorite. All the same, he assumed a responsible position and took precedence over his colleagues Milon, Aumer, and Albert; but because the rich emoluments with which the Emperor had rewarded him and his talented wife were partially cut off under the present government, and partly squandered through his passion for gambling, the famous master in his old days lost a measure of his former glory; and since his genius was also in its decline, his mind was often filled with dejection and bitterness. To me he was kindness and hospitality itself. I often went to his home, where I met notables of various professions and ranks from different periods. But the treasure of the house was Mme. Gardel, who in spite of her already advanced years still retained a sylphlike lightness and grace. Just as she had once enraptured the public by her graceful and perfect dancing, so, too, she now knew how to diffuse about her a feeling of comfort and pleasure, and many a time by an encouraging word brought the young artist to risk the ultimate effort. Just such a compliment from her lips gave me, too, a strong incentive to successfully pass the examination that was required in order to attain a debut. I know of no honor which has lifted my spirits to the same degree as when the jury, "à l'unanimité," declared me worthy to perform at the Théâtre de l'Académie Royale de Musique, and when Gardel, as spokesman, in the name of the administration offered me an engagement as soloist with Europe's most renowned ballet!

I had now reached the goal of two years' continuous endeavor, and I appreciated the honor of being reckoned among *"les illustres du foyer de l'Opéra."* But what most of all appealed to my vanity (if thus one dares to call this heart's desire) was the thought of the effect my progress was sure to have in Copenhagen on my friends and colleagues, but above all on my father, whose most sanguine expectations were about to be fulfilled. In my youthful excitement I felt like Alexander the Great, when after his most glorious victories and splendid exploits he cried out: "O Athenians! What wouldn't I do in order to be praised by you!"

However, this praise was by no means unconditional, for when the Directory of the Danish Theatre (which in fact cared nothing at all about the advancement of the ballet) learnt of my engagement, it represented my arbitrary step as a veritable *desertion*, a name which it by no means deserved. In the first place, as a youth of twenty I needed to mature for the position which I might one day assume at the Royal Theatre; secondly, my debut in Paris—without which I should be returning home with my objective unaccomplished and with my entire career forfeited—entailed the signing of a two-year contract; and finally, I had offered to make compensation (to the amount of 400 Rbd.) for the two years' wages I had received during my absence—an obligation which I later had the opportunity to fulfill scrupulously.

To be engaged at the Grand Opéra, and especially with its ballet, gave one a reputation in the theatre world that was influential not only on the Continent and in the provinces, whence the most advantageous offers came, but also asserted itself when we youngsters were sent from time to time to benefit performances at the Porte-Saint-Martin or other secondary theatres to support one charitable cause or another. We were then treated as if we belonged to the aristocracy of art; they gave us the finest dressing rooms and accorded us a courtesy that bordered on awe. We were enthusiastically received by the audience, and the mayor of the *arrondissement* had a most commendatory article inserted in the *Journal des Débats*.

Although *"le jeune Bournonville"* was numbered among the brightest aspirants at the Court of Terpsichore, according to the regulations he was only in the third class in order of rank. Just as in the organization of our army, the soloists and mimes of the Opéra were divided into line, reserve, and reinforcements, with the single difference that this last division was made up of the youngest and most indefatigable forces. Thus at this time the French ballet included no less than fifteen male soloists, of differing genres and strong points, and an equal number of *danseuses*. One can well imagine that all these greater and lesser talents, two-thirds of whom had to be content with secondary roles, were not particularly satisfied with their respective positions, even though the salaries were comparatively high. But since there was usually dancing three or four times a week in the opera and grand ballets with many different *pas*, there was ample opportunity for "understudying," and it then became a matter of being up on the repertory so as to fill a vacant place without further preparation should the occasion arise. In this I had my strong point, based upon quick comprehension and a keen memory. I then danced with a zeal and pleasure that one evening caused Adolphe Nourrit to exclaim: "The little devil! Even if the house were burning above our heads, he would not leave the stage until he had finished his *pas* to the last *entrechat!*"

The same overcrowding that annoyed us youngsters was even more oppressive to the four balletmasters, whose mutual rivalry frequently led to collisions with respect to the choice of subject matter as well as superiority in execution. A pair of incidents, however, resulted in an upheaval in the entire system. The first was the appearance of Marie Taglioni, who not only put the Parisian school to shame with her hitherto unknown virtuosity, but by her extraordinary force of attraction also taught both the public and the theatre management to focus their attention on a single personality, whereby the ensemble, formerly so excellent, came to be regarded as superfluous or, at any rate, as being of no consequence for the box-office receipts. The second and most dangerous development was the libretto that Scribe submitted for *La Somnambule*. This was a new version of the subject of his popular *vaudeville*, whose plot offered a number of interesting features and, in addition, gave a popular mimic *danseuse* (Mme. Montessu) the opportunity to display great bravura. Aumer took it upon himself to stage the ballet, Hérold arranged the music, and the whole thing was carried out with as much taste as success. With this, however, the signal had been given for the transference of this kind of writing into the hands of vaudevillists, and later into a monopoly for the team of Saint-Georges and Leuven. It was now firmly established that in order to be a capable balletmaster one needed neither genius nor knowledge, only a certain measure of technical skill. In consequence of this view, men such as Gardel and Milon must be considered qualified for retirement. From this moment on, French ballet gradually declined in artistic importance; one will seek in vain to find therein a sound train of thought and fairly reasonable coherence, since the whole is, for the most part, dependent upon striking scenery and the artistry or physical superiority of a single prima donna.

When in the year 1838 I visited M. Gardel for the last time in his retreat, his dear wife had passed away, and four years later he followed her to the grave, without, however, having witnessed the later degradation of the ballet. His image still stands clearly before me, and I fancy I can hear his remarks which, uttered in the gentlest tone, remain fixed as if branded with a glowing iron. And yet he was quite fond of me and was in sincere agreement with his wife's encouragements when he predicted for me an artistic future. For my part, I admired his great talent and have, to the last, followed his principles, which have guided and strengthened me in spite of the temptations of fashion and blasé taste.

VESTRIS is a name that has become as much identified with the art of the dance as that of Garrick with drama and Mozart with music. Since it has attracted such great attention, it follows as a matter of course that in its time it was bound to arouse opposition; and though it can never be effaced from theatrical history, anecdote collectors and vaudevillists have known how to fuse *Vestris, père et fils*, into a single figure, which bears not the slightest resemblance to those conscientious artists who in their continuous striving for the ideal of Beauty gladdened and instructed their contemporaries.

For the time being, we will hold to the description which Noverre gives us of the elder Vestris, with the Christian name Gaétan, a native Florentine and endowed with such an extremely handsome appearance that at his first performance in Paris he won the epithet "L'Apollon" or "Le Dieu de la Danse." His serious dancing consisted mostly of picturesque poses, beautiful arm movements, and slow *pas*—in short, of performances which emphasized the external merits he possessed. Therefore he was sought after by all the Courts as a model of dignity and manly grace, not only on the stage but in higher circles, where his elegant toilette and tasteful coiffure became the rule for current fashion. Considerable sacrifices were made to secure his talents both for the golden halls of Versailles and for the ballet of the Théâtre de l'Opéra, where all the deities and Homeric heroes, which figured exclusively upon the French lyric stage at that time, found a worthy representative in Gaétan Vestris—who also profited by the great costume reform which Noverre brought about by banning masks, *tonnelets,* and the enormous plumes which were up to then inseparable from the shepherds and shepherdesses of Arcadia. Thus, while the famous balletmaster wrote his instructive *Lettres sur la Danse* (1760), the elder Vestris [through his appearances] defined the nature of dancing as "the art of beautifying the human form."

On reading Molière's *Bourgeois gentilhomme,* through the comical jockeying for position among the fencing, dancing, and language masters, one will be able to form some idea of the scandal such arrogance in the field of aesthetics was bound to arouse among the opponents of choreography; and with his insuperable Italian accent and his lofty feeling for the importance of his calling, Vestris was certain to become a target for the joke-hunters' arrows. There have been attributed to him a number of boasts which have become proverbs and should be preserved for their oddity alone.

For example, he is said to have designated the following as his great contemporaries: Voltaire, Himself, and the King of Prussia [Frederick the Great].

In his admiration for the handsomeness of the Duke of Devonshire, he is said to have cried: "Were I not Vestris, I would be Duke of Devonshire!"

When his son Auguste was prevented by a sudden indisposition from appearing at a gala performance given in honor of Sweden's Gustav III, and this report of his illness was taken amiss by the Court to such a degree that M. Auguste Vestris was ordered taken into custody, the old man is said to have lamented that the harmony which had always prevailed between the House of Bourbon and the House of Vestris had on this occasion been disturbed!

Finally, when General Bonaparte astonished the world by his first Italian campaign, Vestris is said to have been beside himself with enthusiasm and cried out: "The man deserves to have something striking done for him!" People crowded about him to learn what should constitute this national reward. The reply ran: "He shall see me perform again!"

Although by his many triumphs this "Grand danseur du Roi" might really have arrived at the idea that he was a great man, and as such might have looked down his nose at his colleagues more than was seemly, he is said, nevertheless, to have been a noble and good-natured character; and since he was accustomed to moving in fashionable society, he must have possessed too much tact to display such ridiculous arrogance.

We can therefore regard the above-mentioned anecdotes as fabrications invented by those envious of him, but the following incident, which has come to me through reliable tradition, denotes much that is characteristic of his position as well as the tone of the age in which he lived and worked. For a number of years he had the most brilliant engagements, and earned considerable sums of money not only in France, but especially at the German and Italian courts, and above all in England. In addition, at each place he was presented with costly gifts, which he carefully put by, and by a sensible economy had, moreover, amassed a handsome fortune which enabled him to live in a genteel fashion. Tired of being called a charlatan, he one day invited some of the worst scoffers to a splendid dinner party, and when they came to the dessert he lifted the lids of a dozen silver-gilt basins, filled partly with diamond rings and brooches, golden boxes and jeweled buckles, partly with guineas and louis d'or, and asked his guests whether they regarded *this* as charlatanism? They then unanimously acknowledged that no one knew better than their good host how to prove his solidity.

It is inevitable that in his youth such an *Apollo*, just like that deity in Ovid's *Metamorphoses*, must certainly have had several gallant adventures. Among others is mentioned the light-footed Mlle. Allard, whose *pas de deux pastoral* is found depicted in an excellent engraving; but the celebrated *danseuse* Mlle. Heinel (a German by birth) was just as *sérieuse* in character as in style, and by her our Apollo was locked in the chains of Hymen. This well-assorted marriage was not blessed with children, and the want of them had begun to feel oppressive, when one day, while inspecting the ballet school which was directed by Trancard (who was nicknamed *"Le charpentier de la Danse"*), Vestris' gaze lighted upon a nine-year-old boy with most unusual ability and an almost fully developed talent. Astonished, he asked the teacher to whom this child belonged. The answer ran: "That is the little Allard!" "But surely not a son of Mademoiselle?" "Precisely of Mlle. Allard!" "But, my God! Then he must certainly be *my* son! Do you know what, my clever lad, upon my honor, it appears that you take after your father!"

From this moment, Vestris took the little Auguste home with him, gave him a careful upbringing, and within two years brought him so far that in the year 1771, though only eleven years old, he made his debut with the greatest bravura. Just like Mozart, he was a *Wunderkind* and was shown around at the Courts, where he was kissed and regaled with sweets. In the beginning he went under his Christian name; later he was called Vestrallard, but it was not long before M. and Mme. legally adopted him as their only son and lawful heir. His artistic career was an unbroken series of triumphs and, more fortunate than that immortal composer, he saw himself richly rewarded and appreciated in his native land.

Since he was only of average height and had neither his father's fine facial features nor his classical physique, his style of dancing was *demi-caractère*, to which his astounding elasticity and speed, combined with his expressive countenance and lively spirits, made him excellently suited. Emancipated from his father's strict school, he created a completely new genre, which bore the same relation to the preceding one as a painting of brilliant hue does to a marble sculpture displaying classical perfection. In all of Gardel's ballets he developed a mimic talent that was recognized by the greatest actors of the day, and his performance of *The Prodigal Son* in particular is said to have been a true masterpiece. Even in his old age, when during classes he rehearsed some scenes from the aforesaid ballet with us, he often allowed himself to be so carried away that the illusion became complete, and we imagined that we saw before us in the flesh a youth of nineteen, with all of his follies and aberrations, with his despair and repentance.

His pure taste and sense of rhythm were superbly manifested in the composition of individual dances; but when people asked him why he did not produce more extensive works, he generally gave the modest reply which I have mentioned earlier. This limitation was especially advantageous for his younger colleagues, since, with the greatest willingness, he arranged their *pas* and knew how to place their talents in the most favorable light.

Before, during and after the great Revolution he was the most distinguished representative of the dance. He performed at the *fêtes champêtres* of the Trianon, at the inauguration of the Goddess of Reason, at the Saturnalia of the Directoire, and at the gala performances of the Empire. His talent was so identified with the rest of the glories of Paris that when he requested traveling permission from Napoleon, in order to accept a temporary engagement in Naples, he was refused with the words: "Foreigners must come to *Paris* to see Vestris dance." He received a benefit performance as compensation and on this, as well as on many other occasions, he was given ample proofs of the great Emperor's generosity.

He ought to have become, if not an extremely rich, then at least a rather wealthy man. But a high degree of improvidence, poor economy, and the desire to play a role among the *"aimable roués"* of his time were responsible for the fact that not only his rich emoluments but also his paternal inheritance slipped through his fingers. Age appeared, and with it young and talented rivals, among whom Louis Duport in particular distinguished himself by a marvelous technique. Vestris had to put up with being called "Grandfather of Zephyrs," and finally it was only his mimic talent and the direct protection of the Emperor that upheld his old renown. But with the fall of Napoleon the aura which had surrounded the great dancer's name for so many years disappeared. To be sure, the Allies inquired after him, for these foreigners too had heard him mentioned among the glories of Paris. But he avoided appearing before the arrogant enemies of France. He could look back with sadness upon the brilliant career whose material profits he had wantonly squandered, and he was now a pensioner, with the supplement to his modest income which the lessons in his *classe de perfectionnement* could earn him.

But even in this diminished state he was still *Vestris!* His gay spirit deserted him as little as his light tread and youthful bearing. With violin in hand, he inspired both himself and his pupils, and with the exception of a single sigh, in allusion to his unforgettable Emperor, one never heard him complain of the losses that time had brought him and—*mirabile dictu!*—never discuss his own talent or the triumphs he had celebrated in his prosperity.

For pupils who were already more or less trained, his instruction was invaluable; although as good as finished *artistes*, Marie Taglioni, Fanny Elssler, and Carlotta Grisi often turned to his school in order to learn something lovely or to "grind off" possible defects. Firm in his demands with regard to taste and character, he was mild in his judgment, not at all prejudiced, and furthermore willing to acknowledge any sort of ability. At the same time as he knew how to arouse the spirit of competition to a fever pitch in the rest of us, he was good nature personified and never allowed himself to be tricked into displays of temper.

From among his finest male pupils he himself singled out three: namely, his eldest son Armand (who died in Vienna in 1825), Jules Perrot, and—one must forgive me for not concealing the fact—Auguste Bournonville as the ones who have best comprehended and most successfully disseminated his choreographic principles. At the moment, unfortunately, there are on the Continent very few *danseurs* who have not been reduced to being lifting machines and props for equibrilistic groupings, while the *danseuses* outdo one another in *tours de force*. The ballet is hereby losing its importance as artistic performance and degenerating into something that ought to be relegated to the carnival tent.

For six years I enjoyed the benefit of his excellent instruction; he enjoyed teaching me. Under his aegis I presented myself for my debut, and he faithfully went through my entire youthful repertoire with me. I also became attached to him with a son's affection, and through the years, every time I visited Paris, I went to practice in his school—naturally, in return for the payment of a suitable fee, which would always be paid in advance, for the beloved master was always in financial straits, and one of his worst creditors was his former valet, who had now advanced to the position of landed proprietor and—moneylender!

The younger Vestris died the same year as my father (1843). They were the same age and reached their eighty-third year. He still appears before me in my dreams, and if one can believe it, I am then assailed by a feeling of uneasiness, as if I had forgotten to pay him the last hundred francs!

Louis Nivelon was the contemporary of Gardel and Vestris and shared with them the public's favor and applause, although he was far from their equal in artistry. But his attractive appearance and the ease and intelligence with which he grasped and peformed roles and parts of extremely different genres gave him a singular worth, which Noverre mentions with appreciation in his *Lettres.* He early abandoned his theatrical career, and we find the reason in the following passage from the aforementioned *Lettres:* "Nivelon now lives quietly and happily, cultivates his garden and his friends, which last no one knows better than he how to win and keep."

Thus it is more a figure from a *novelle* than the portrait of an artist I take it upon myself to sketch here, for no description can be more striking than the one contained in the foregoing lines. The loyalty and natural amiability I discovered in this friend of my father's youth stand before me as the ideal of what every artist must wish to achieve when he one day exchanges the active for the contemplative life.

My father had been his comrade in London in 1781. Seventeen years later he visited him in Paris, found him married to Carline, the popular actress at the Opéra-Comique, and enjoyed much hospitality in their home. Twenty-two years, without much correspondence, passed before they met again in 1820: an interval filled with remarkable events and disappointed expectations! During that time Nivelon had lost his beloved wife and his two grown daughters. He was now alone. Nevertheless, the meeting made his eyes gleam with the sparkle of youth, and though he had not retained the lightness and elasticity that my father still possessed in his sixtieth year, one could hardly imagine a lovelier figure bordering on old age. His lightly powdered silver hair, in contrast to the dark eyebrows, the mild blue eyes, the fresh complexion and well-preserved teeth, created the most pleasing impression; and as he stood there in his light summer outfit, with the gold lorgnette hanging from a wide black silk ribbon around his neck, he resembled one of those portraits by Juel, whose eternal freshness and charm always appeal to us, even if we have never known the original.

It took but a few minutes, just like an *entr'acte,* to fill the interval which now lay like a dream before the old friends, and by reminding each other of a few incidents from their merry youth, they had a hearty laugh. However, it was not without sadness that he heard my father rejoice over my talent; for though a *rentier* and a landed proprietor, he felt poor next to his old comrade. All that Love had bestowed upon him, Death had snatched away; only memory was left to him, and a heart filled with loyal friendship.

He made us promise to visit him at his country estate in Normandy, and upon a repeated written invitation we set out by diligence for the small town of Etrépagny, which lies on the road to Rouen. It took us eight hours to make a journey that now requires only two; but in return we got to see far more than one does nowadays with the tearing speed of the railway.

We passed Gisors, where a picturesque ruined castle recalled the memory of the famous tournament of "the Field of the Cloth of Gold," which took place at the meeting of Philippe Augustus and Richard Coeur-de-Lion on the occasion of their united Crusade (1190).‡ In addition, it amused us to make comparisons between this terrain—so different from the rest of French landscapes—and our beloved Denmark, whose warlike ancestors had chosen this very province, whose luxuriant pastures, quickset hedges, thatched farmhouses, and scattered patches of woods reminded them of their Nordic fatherland. Only the glistening, serpentine winding of the rivers and the fields planted with apple trees gave the present Normandy a different physiognomy.

At Etrépagny our friend's vehicle was waiting for us, and in less than a quarter of an hour it had conveyed us to his country home, "L'Ermitage de Saint-Martin-au-Bosc," where he bade us a hearty welcome and informed us of the household rule, which granted unrestricted freedom, though mealtimes had to be strictly observed. Here we lived as in *Slaraffenland* [the land of milk and honey], strolled in the delightful garden, where lanes of peach trees were placed at our disposal and where the grapes hanging in the Italian arcades had ripened by our next visit. We roamed through the surrounding countryside, rested by the water mill, visited the tenant farmer at Génétré and the country parson at Longchamps. Naturally, the woods could not display trunks such as those that constitute our national pride; but the luxuriant beech boughs greeted us, all the same, like kindred friends and invited us to dream in their shade.

After a ten days' stay, we departed early in the morning without saying good-bye, a custom which had been established by our host, who avoided touching "farewell scenes." But on the first of the month we received a new invitation when he was expecting guests to whom he wished to introduce his *"braves Danois."* (At "Saint-Martin" one generally received one nickname or another, and thus we had in the party a *Marquis*, a *Président*, a *Baronne*, and so on. My father usually went by the name of "le Général".) On this second visit the household arrangement bore a festive stamp because of the anticipated arrival of a very rich old lady. She was the cousin of the already mentioned Mme. Quincy, and whom they called "the Ninon of the Emigration."

Memoirs and *Chroniques-galantes* from the period before the Revolution of 1789 mention Rosalie Duthé as a celebrity in her genre, and her relationship with the king's youngest brother, the Comte d'Artois, placed her rather high in the elegant *demi-monde* of that time. She was now seventy-five years old, but her slender figure and her big sky-blue eyes still allowed one to catch a glimpse of how captivating this blonde Aspasia must have been in her younger days. After having stayed in England for many years, she now lived in Paris under the name Mme. Gérard, kept a hospitable house, received her distinguished old friends with the dignity of a princess, and listened to the

‡ Here, Bournonville seems to have confused several different events. The 1520 meeting of Henry VIII of England and Francis I of France on the Field of the Cloth of Gold—so called because of the magnificence there displayed—took place not at Gisors, but at a site between Guînes and Ardres. However, Gisors was the scene of other historic meetings between English and French monarchs, notably during the reigns of Henry II of England (father of Richard the Lion-Hearted) and Philip Augustus of France.

confidences of young artists with the heartfelt sympathy of a mother or an aunt. Her hand was open to the destitute, and far from resembling those penitent Magdalens who think to expiate their youthful errors by unrelenting severity against the younger generation, she was tolerance personified. Susceptible to the joys life still could offer her, she was flattered by the homage with which she was surrounded, and since the *soirées* at "Saint-Martin" always ended with dancing, she figured in the *française* with a grace that was characteristic of the old school.

On our return to Copenhagen we kept up a frequent correspondence with our friend, who resided in Paris during the winter, and, since I was contemplating a longer study trip which should lay the foundation for my future career, I relied upon Nivelon, in whom I also found a loyal supporter and fatherly advisor when in my nineteenth year I was left to my own devices in dangerous Paris.

As it happened, he was not particularly interested in my art although he himself had once been a popular dancer, for he had turned his back on the theatre forever and entertained toward the cradle of his earlier activity a bitterness which is not uncommon among retired artists. On the other hand, so far as social conduct and a knowledge of human nature were concerned, he was an advisor whom one would have to search far to equal. His principles of *honor* were completely chivalrous, and despite his age, he was prepared to defend them with rapier in hand.

Nivelon could not long endure Mme. Quincy's political fanaticism, and replaced her company with another elderly lady, Mme. Deshayes, who sheltered him in the winter while she and her family, in return, passed the summer with him in the country. A little granddaughter of hers, a five-year-old angel, had added a new *charme* to this residence, and in order to denote just how sweet she was, in the entire neighborhood she was known by the name of "Cécile la Vanille." But, alas! During the hot summer of 1825 she was stricken with typhoid fever, and within a few days she was the prey of death. The whole family, including my old patron, was plunged into the deepest grief. At exactly the same time a violent rheumatic fever cast me upon the sickbed and postponed my debut for more than half a year. Nivelon, who had accompanied his grieving guests to Paris, came to me just as I was arising from my bed a poor, emaciated convalescent. He immediately took me with him to the country and nursed me with paternal, nay, almost maternal, care for five weeks, which was sufficient for me to regain both weight and strength, while at the same time my presence seemed to serve to cheer him after such an unfortunate demise.

Little by little, something like a small artist colony had formed around "L'Ermitage de Saint-Martin": for there lived the singer Philippe (so celebrated in his day) from the Opéra-Comique; the outstanding miniaturist Vincent; Balletmaster Aumer; and the former Director of the Opéra, Courtin—all of them with wives, sisters, or aunts of a good age, for with the exception of

Clothilde Courtin, young Mainvielle (a son of the excellent singer), and myself, the company consisted for the most part of male and female "veterans." In the evening guests gathered from the small towns nearby: the doctor, M. François; the Justice of the Peace, L'Enfant; and the notary, M. Boulain, who had served as lieutenant in the Grande Armée and received the Cross of the Légion d'Honneur during the fateful Hundred Days in 1815, and as a consequence thereof had been deprived of this mark of honor by the Bourbon government. But he wore the tricolor *cocarde* on his heart. Here, too, a number of conflicting political elements were present; but they were all agreed upon one point, namely, in an irreconcilable hatred of the British, and we three youngsters were given orders by our host to cool the atmosphere with music when the discussion became too heated. Mainvielle played the piano, Clothilde delivered some lovely romances to great advantage, while I sang ballads, among others the old Nordic "Hauling Water and Hauling Wood," which became a favorite melody at the Norman estate. Dancing succeeded in reconciling tempers, and thus "the evening passed."

Here my father was to come again when in 1827 he visited France in order to rejoice at my progress and my position at the Opéra ballet. He then praised the faithful Mentor who had advised and nursed his Telemachus, but he did not suspect that the latter, who had so steadfastly resisted the sorcery on Calypso's Isle (the *Foyer de l'Opéra*), had been affected by the air in luxuriant Normandy and silently yearned for a Eucharis whose soft, silvery voice sang forth *"Je t'aimerai"* in the same romance whose melody crops up in *Ponte Molle*, when Alfred takes leave of his Roman friends. It was but a breeze from the realm of illusions! The Courtins had already long since destined Clothilde for young Mainvielle, who was the sole heir to a considerable fortune. Besides, under his famous mother's tutelage, she was to be developed into a great singer, and to this end travel with her father and mother to Naples. But they got no further than Marseilles, where a malignant fever carried off the blossoming young girl. The parents were now left disappointed in their expectations, heartbroken and childless!

Many sympathies draw my heart to France, the home of my ancestors; but I was born in Denmark, and here I was to feel the thrill of patriotism and to earn bread, honor, and success. Nevertheless, my thoughts often dwell upon those places where Gardel's mastery showed me the road to ballet-writings; where Vestris initiated me into a new sphere of the moving rhythms of the dance; finally, where Nivelon placed before my eyes the goal which should be that of every scenic artist after his career is over: namely, to be able to live, in independent circumstances, for something better than a constant hankering after capricious applause.

On my oft-repeated little trips to Paris I never neglected to visit my three old masters, but by the summer of 1838 the noble Nivelon had already gone to his rest, and in 1846, when I wished to call upon Gardel and Vestris, I found only their graves in the Cimitière Montmartre and Père-Lachaise.

I shall never forget these spirits who hover about my memory in my rural retirement, as they did earlier during my busy sojourn in the theatrical world. If only these notes may not drive them away from my dreams, for I would rather sacrifice this written monument to the flames than bid an eternal farewell to my beloved "ghosts."

My Garret

In the Rue de Provence, close to the main street of the *faubourg* of Montmartre, and not far from the "temporary" Opera House which after having stood for fifty years celebrated its jubilee by going up in flames, there still stands a *"trattoria"* [eating place] (for the word *"tracteursted"* [modest restaurant] would hardly be fitting) where for several generations masons, stonecutters, and other laborers have gathered each morning at six o'clock with their big loaves of bread under their arms to break their fast with a plate of soup—a meal which, with the addition of meat, potatoes, white beans, and a glass of wine, they enjoy year in and year out as dinner at eleven in the morning, and as supper at six in the evening—and this for such an extraordinarily low price that only the enormous crowd of customers, the modest demands of the proprietor, and the provision of wine could produce a small profit. Every evening the takings were counted, the supplies were promptly paid for, and the remaining proceeds set aside for the rent and for *"les économies."* I have mentioned these features of practical Parisian life in order to give some idea of the frugality and orderliness, but above all the energy, that distinguish the laboring and merchant classes in France and which in spite of political chaos and heavy tax burdens generally lead to a fair prosperity that astonishes the rest of Europe, whose deep prejudice takes French *mobilité* for *frivolité*.

Just about the same time that I arrived in Paris, this establishment was taken over by a young couple from Savoy, Pierre Mugnier and Véronique Grosset, who with their savings had furnished a spacious garret with (according to their circumstances) very elegant furniture. But at the sight of such magnificence, which consisted of a mahogany commode and secretary with marble tops, a large mirror over a marble fireplace, three alcoves, the middle one with a first-rate bed, they discovered that this luxury was too grand for them and decided to take a lodger, while they installed themselves in a so-called *soupente* under the eaves in the guest room.

Through private channels I came to know about this lodging and moved in with these good people, who soon became as fond of me as if I were a dear relative. Here I found comfort and rest when I came home from my strenuous training, which continued with such excessive zeal throughout the summer of 1825 that, just as I was reaching the goal of my endeavors, I was cast upon the sickbed with an inflammatory rheumatic fever. The worthy Mugniers nursed me with as much tenderness as if they had been my own parents; but what set the crowning touch upon the whole was the extraordinary skill with which the physician, Dr. Huet, who lived within the same courtyard, treated my illness, and the heart-warming manner in which he refused to accept the fifty francs I gratefully brought him as an honorarium. "Shouldn't I be proud of having put a fine young dancer back on his feet?" With these words he pressed my hand and forced me to keep my money. This splendid man later played an important role as director of the Cholera Hospital, founded in 1832, earned honorable distinctions, and—what forms an unforgettable companion piece to the commendable incident mentioned above—saved my wife's life when she was suddenly stricken with that dread disease in the summer of 1834.

I was daily attended to by the old mother-in-law, Mère Grosset, and when I began to grow and develop strength following my illness, I presented her with my discarded clothes for her two sons, who were destined for the clerical state and were studying at the seminary at Sallanches. The young men's letters of thanks were couched in the most rhetorical terms and praised my generosity to the skies to such a degree that when their old Abbé came to Paris and was housed by the Mugnier family, one of his first inquiries was for Monsieur de Bournonville (for it could be nothing less than that). I was then introduced to him and invited to the splendid dinner party that had been arranged in his honor; note well, however, with the strictest concealment of my profession, which he did not inquire after either, since he regarded me as a rich *fils de famille.*

I used the time I had left over from my choreographic studies and my rather scanty reading partly to visit my father's old and my own new friends, all of whom showed me hospitable kindness, which I was often embarrassed to accept for fear of being considered a parasite; and partly to act as guide for my countrymen. Among these I must first mention our popular actor and *instructeur,* Nielsen, with whom I attended the most excellent plays and made interesting excursions into the environs of Paris. But he did not enjoy Paris in full measure, for his mind was preoccupied and his aspirations centered on his forthcoming guest appearances at the Court Theatre in Braunschweig. During the course of the years I met with many other notable Danish savants and artists, among them Brøndsted, Eschricht, and Abrahamson; the musician Frøhlich; the painter Aumont; and the actress Henriette Jørgensen. Finally I struck up a pleasant acquaintance with the amiable old art dealer, Herman Bing, whose sons I dare to reckon among my closest friends. With Secretary Wiehe I several times strolled out to Sèvres, where at the famous factory he studied fine porcelain painting; and when Christmas Eve arrived, I generally assembled a jovial little circle of Danes in my room for a genuine Danish supper, for which occasion I taught my landlady how to make *risengrød,* a dish which was a great success in the kitchen and was later used on festive occasions as *an entremet-sucré* [a sweet side dish].

A man whose acquaintance I particularly cultivated, and with whom I visited and conversed especially on Sunday mornings, was old P. A. Heiberg, who upon my arrival dispelled, as it were, all his political bitterness and in the most congenial fashion regaled me with amusing anecdotes from old Copenhagen. He was genuinely fond of me, which I fully appreciated, and toward the end of my stay I received two proofs of his affection that I shall never forget. The one was a written invitation to learn from his own lips what an old nobleman, the Marquis N. N., had said in praise of me because of my enthusiasm for the dramatic art, which had recently been aroused by Shakespeare's masterworks, performed in Paris by the most celebrated English actors. The other was that he, who had not set foot in any theatre in seventeen years, accepted my invitation to attend, together with Frøhlich, an opera performance in which I had a brilliant dancing part, concerning which performance he the next day sent me a compliment, written in all sincerity, which I have faithfully preserved.

Meanwhile the spring of 1826 drew near, and a successful examination, which was decisive for my whole future, led to an equally successful debut on April 5. On this occasion the sympathy of my good landlord and landlady was most clearly manifested. Mugnier did not spare his fists, and *because he was my friend* was not ashamed of enthusiastically joining in the encouraging applause that greeted my first youthful appearance. From then on I also became a teacher, and transplanted the methods of Vestris onto Edouard and Gustave Carey, boys of eleven and eight years respectively. These pupils were entrusted to me by their parents who, though residing in Paris, were forced to seek employment here and there; and during the course of three years, first in my garret, later in larger facilities, I had the pleasure of seeing their outstanding abilities so well developed that it did not surprise me when, some years later, I heard them mentioned among the most popular dancers and learnt, in particular, of the important engagements they had made in the principal cities of Italy.

A beneficial diversion in my rather monotonous dancer's life was the arrival of a sixteen-year-old violinist, Carl Ebner, who together with his brother Anton had been most warmly recommended to me by Wexschall and Nielsen, with the request that I introduce them into musical circles insofar as possible. Unfortunately, Anton had died en route to Paris and Father Ebner arrived with his sole surviving son, weighed down by the deepest sorrow. Here there was really something for me to do, and I became so fondly devoted to the young virtuoso that people thought I was his brother. I had him play for Kreutzer, Baillot, and Lafont, and he astounded all of them not only by his exceptional technique and silvery intonation but also by a tone so singular that the slightest theme, regardless of "interpretation," thereby took on a peculiar charm. Oddly enough, he was the first to perform Mayseder's compositions publicly in Paris, in particular, his *Polonaise in E Major* and the *Variations* dedicated to Paganini. With these pieces, at the "Concerts Spirituels" given at the Théâtre de l'Opéra during Easter Week he harvested such enthusiastic applause that the old masters felt a bit embarrassed, while the young people allowed themselves to be influenced to a considerable degree by this new and graceful style. I too set to work again on the violin with renewed pleasure. Ebner gave me some useful suggestions, and we appeared more than once at the *quartet-soirées* which took place every week at the home of the *famille Anatole* (where the husband, formerly a skilled dancer, now applied himself to ballet composition and contemplated an engagement in London, while his wife, one of the principal *danseuses* of the Théâtre de l'Opéra, prepared to accompany him).

Here there usually gathered a select company of artists and "*hommes d'esprit,*" and these musical *soirées* were seasoned with French gaiety, which seemed to have found a worthy haven here. Carl Ebner now settled in Paris, where he associated quite a bit with his contemporary countryman Franz Liszt. But in spite of the applause he harvested for his outstanding violin playing, in order to live he was forced to give lessons on the pianoforte. His practical father advised him to put his violin on the shelf and establish a Music Institute according to Logier's system. This undertaking was crowned with success and industriously carried on for several years, until overwork laid the young musician in his grave and crushed his father's proud expectations.

My home correspondence, considering the postal conditions of the time, was rather frequent; but a lengthy absence of letters caused me small attacks of homesickness, especially on Sunday afternoons in the summer when my friends had gone out to the country and I sat alone in my garret, my reading disturbed by the neighboring grocer's boy who, in hour-long attempts, groped his way about on the flute. I then tore myself loose and sought diversion at the Théâtre des Variétés, which at that time possessed quite excellent talents. On the other hand, when a letter from home arrived, the faces of the entire Mugnier family beamed with delight. They rushed toward me holding the long-awaited object high in the air, and the house resounded with the clapping of hands at seeing me take in five bounds the three flights of stairs that led up to my room.

One such letter brought me the happy news that my father was on his way [to Paris] in order to see with his own eyes how things had gone with his beloved son after a separation of three years. The day and the hour of his arrival were most carefully estimated, and, accompanied by my persevering landlord, I hastened to the Post Yard to welcome him. As it happened, he had taken another conveyance from Brussels, and we went home a bit dejected. But an hour later there entered the courtyard a handsome old man, who inquired after a young person by the name of Bournonville. "*C'est le Papa!*" exclaimed Mugnier, with such a shrill voice that I could hear it up in my room. With a feeling that cannot be described, I flew down the stairs and in the same instant I lay in my dear father's arms. I could now be his host during his entire stay. For this brief occasion I had arranged my garret for the two of us, and the best bed was, naturally, for the old man. After our first effusions, we strolled out into Paris—at that time already considerably embellished—and the first person we chanced to meet was none other than the composer Auber, who made it his duty to delight my father with the most flattering testimonies concerning both my talent and my behavior. We met still more notable acquaintances, and Papa was proud of all the fine friends I had been fortunate enough to win. In the *stalles d'Orchestre* [the first parquet] I had further opportunity to introduce my father to a number of famous complimentary ticketholders and *abonnés* [subscribers], upon whom he made such a favorable impression by virtue of his noble appearance and urbane conversation that even many years thereafter they spoke of him with awe and sympathy. Toward autumn (1827) we parted in the hope of meeting soon again. Winter arrived with its varied artistic life, and at Christmas, in accordance with my contract, I obtained a *congé* in order to accept a three-months' engagement at the King's Theatre in London—a journey on leave of absence which I shall discuss later.

Mugnier, who had introduced a most urbane *ton* into his eating and drinking establishment, since everyone without exception was addressed as "Monsieur" and neither gambling, singing, nor tobacco smoking was permitted, was also his habitués' factotum as far as both the reception of letters and the shipment of money were concerned, for most of them came from distant provinces. Year after year he and his untiring wife had been laying shilling upon shilling and they already had purchased some annuities, whose securities they showed me in joyful confidence with the words: "We have begun together!" which was as much as to say that I had been their "good-luck child." Several small gifts from my hand had given them a taste for silver plate, and the first *couvert* had now multiplied to twelve, with accessories. During both of my *congés* they lived in my room, and after my permanent departure (1830) no stranger received permission to use the lovely furniture which I had initiated and preserved.

When I visited Paris in 1834, accompanied by my wife and the rather young Lucile Grahn, Mugnier had become a wealthy man and a sapper in the finest Legion of the National Guard (the Second). We saw him march past King Louis Philippe, who, with his brilliant staff, was stationed at the Place Vendôme, where through acquaintances we had obtained a whole mezzanine apartment for the use of ourselves and our countrymen. The 25,000 troops of the line and 80,000 of the National Guard defiled past with loud shouts of jubilation, which the King answered by lifting his hat for every single division. Carried away by enthusiasm, some sprang forward and shook the King's hands, while others lifted little children up to the pommel of his saddle. What a warm expression of popular feeling! But, alas! Scarcely fourteen years later, during which space of time no less than eight unsuccessful assassination attempts had been directed against this same adored Citizen-King, he was thrust from the French throne with violence and scorn, and his honorable family was forced to wander in exile.

Surely one cannot go from his garret down into the street and on through teeming Paris without being touched by history, and through this in turn by politics. But to return to my faithful landlords: I must only mention that the warmth with which they regarded my wife cannot be sufficiently emphasized, and their hospitable kindness extended to my pupil Hoppe (1838) and to many Danes whom I recommended to them through the years. In the early forties Mugnier sold his business to his younger brother, purchased a property at Menilmontant, and as a pastime devoted himself to gardening, at which he became so successful that he was awarded a prize medal, of which he was very proud. Here I visited him every time I came to Paris, and was received as a beloved relative; only I had to be prepared with one diplomatic, ambiguous answer or another to the ever recurring question of my financial circumstances. It usually ran thus: "Thanks to Providence and my diligent activity, I have bread for my old age," which, with meaningful nods, was taken to mean that I was a *rentier,* and fixed me even more deeply in my French friends' esteem. They would gladly have helped me had I been in need, but trade and economy had been their life work, and independence the goal which they now seemed to have attained.

When I came to Paris once again in 1856, my good Mugnier's chest was, unfortunately, sorely afflicted and his strength broken by an illness caused in part by a considerable loss of money. In an asthmatic voice he still insisted upon going over our life together in the Rue de Provence, and telling those around him about our "beginning days." He especially emphasized how highly he valued the Danes, not only because he had read about their patriotism and bravery but because in my friends and me he had studied *"le caractère du Danois."* The good qualities that his friendship had allowed him to discern in me must all be peculiar to *"cette brave nation,"* and among other character traits, he felt he ought to emphasize the following: "The Dane is lively, but he isn't rancorous."

The First Journey on Leave of Absence

The major advantage of belonging to the French Opéra ballet was that from here all the larger Court theatres recruited their personnel, if not always for permanent engagements, then at least for a single season, and often only for several months. Petersburg, Berlin, Vienna, Milan, Naples, and Madrid were supplied from the dancing schools of Paris, but London in particular presented the richest market. British "pounds" have always carried the most considerable weight, and while the demands for high fees were met, the English public, in return, demanded names that had already acquired a certain celebrity. I was a long way from being that successful, so I was surprised when M. Anatole, who was in the process of negotiating a contract with the English "menagers" [sic] for the composition of a ballet, invited me to join the company, which consisted of our most outstanding *premier danseur,* Albert, and Mme. Anatole, M. Gosselin, and Mlle. Brocard, as well as a very pretty English girl, Miss Louisa Court, who was to be my partner. They had all been engaged for the entire season, but I had only three months' leave. Therefore my salary was relatively smaller, but quite handsome nonetheless, since I was easily able to bring two-thirds of my £ 350 sterling (8750 francs) back with me to Paris.*

Even before receiving this (according to my circumstances) brilliant offer, I had become passionately fond of English drama, which throughout the autumn of 1827 had been presented, in the form of Shakespearean tragedies and original English comedies, at the Théâtre Italien. We saw Charles Kemble as Romeo and Hamlet; Edmund Kean as Othello, Shylock, and Richard the Third; and Macready as Macbeth and, outside the classical repertoire, as William Tell and Virginius. The comedian Liston and Miss Foote replaced one another, but as a constant pair of lovers we had the outstanding Mr. Abbot and Miss Smithson, whose interpretations of Juliet, Ophelia, Desdemona, Virginia, and Jane Shore bore the stamp of the most sublime tragic beauty. These superb performances, which were followed with lively enthusiasm by the audience, who in the face of such talent forgot all national antipathies, at first found me entirely ignorant of English. But, though like so many others I could follow the action and expressive mime, it nevertheless became absolutely necessary for me to learn the language, and at my urgent request, old Heiberg procured me a native teacher who, for a weekly fee, came to me every day. Without further preparation, he placed an English book before me with the words: "Read, sir!"—and when, with some help, I had managed to stammer through several pages, he laid the book aside with: "Talk, sir!" To my great surprise, he carried on with this method, since he neither spoke nor understood French, and in a very short time I actually acquired a certain measure of proficiency, especially a good pronunciation, partly by private study but mostly by our gibberish conversations, which often lasted for several hours, since Mr. Clyde had time enough at his disposal and generally accepted the bit of lunch I was able to offer him. We continued our language exercises until it was time for me to depart for London, and that eight weeks' instruction was all I could later rely on.

My new balletmaster, M. Anatole, rehearsed my partner and me repeated times so that we might learn our repertoire in time; and there could be no mistaking that it was her lovely eyes more than her mediocre talent that made an impression upon my inflammable heart. M. Anatole had already traveled on ahead in order to arrange his *corps de ballet,* but on the third day of Christmas we received orders to depart.

We filled an entire diligence. Albert, with his family, in the foremost compartment; Mme. Anatole, with her mother and two children, in the middle; and Gosselin, a Demoiselle LeClerq, Miss Louisa, and I in the rear. Mlle. Brocard rode in a comfortable traveling-carriage, together with her old mother. Her enamored friend Lord Bruce (later Marquis of Halesbury) had re-

*For a detailed account of this sojourn in England, see Lillian Moore, "Bournonville's London Spring" (New York, 1965).

served post horses, and everything was arranged for the utmost comfort. At full speed we covered the road through Picardy to Calais, but it still took twelve hours, and it was pitch dark when we arrived at the harbor jetty, which, as it happened to be flood tide, permitted us to go directly on board the English steam packet, *The Salamander.*

Amidst dreadful cries of fear from the old mothers, who had never seen, much less traveled upon, the raging sea, we cast off and commended ourselves to God; for I, at least, have never seen the like of the heavy seas that can be found in the Channel at Christmas time. At dawn we sighted the White Cliffs of Dover and shortly afterward came alongside the pier, which at ebb tide resembled a towering wooden scaffold. We were carefully set (some of us carried) ashore. But, alas; in what condition! Most of the company decided to remain in Dover for the day, but to send me, "the linguist," on ahead to announce the others' arrival. I had just gotten myself a bracing cup of tea laced with cognac at a nearby tavern and had already experienced the disappointment of not being able to understand the people's rapid speech, when "the Mailpost" [sic] with a stately coach and four pulled up outside, and without long deliberation my baggage and I were hoisted up onto the "outside" of the coach, among several well-muffled passengers.

I immediately noticed with what dignity the white-gloved coachman took the reins and whip from the deferential ostler. The guard now blew an Irish tune on his bugle, and we took off at the rate of two Danish miles an hour through the lovely county of Kent, where cattle and sheep still grazed upon the velvety green meadows. Our four-in-hand, which was changed at every fifth English mile (one Danish), consisted of horses of the finest stock, and the studdings on their harnesses glittered in the sunlight as if they belonged to a royal equipage.

When all is said and done, these observations are valuable only inasmuch as they are based upon a long-dead phase of traveling life in England, where a network of railroads now traverses the country in every direction, and where in a couple of hours one covers distances that formerly required a whole day. And yet, now one catches only a confused glimpse of the lovely countryside, while the elegant stagecoaches, with their colorful personnel and well-trained horses, have vanished.

Toward nightfall I arrived in gas-lit London, alighted at Charing Cross, and had myself taken to my reserved lodgings. I immediately carried out my errand to M. Anatole, and was most cordially welcomed by him. The following morning, the rest of the company arrived, extremely worn out from their night's journey. A gentleman of colossal stature presented himself to me, with many thanks for all the attention I had shown his daughter. It was Miss Louisa's stepfather, Mr. William Court, a taylor [sic] by profession, but genteel in his entire manner. I was obliged to accompany him to his home in Great Pultney Street, and was treated by both parents with the most exquisite politeness. This home, which was soon to prove so dangerous to my peace of mind, was arranged completely according to the "english fashion" [sic] and bespoke true middle-class comfort. What immediately captured my attention was a large oil painting showing Miss Louisa as a child in the role of Cupid, drawing a bow and ready to shoot the fatal arrow.

The performances at the King's Theatre opened on New Year's Day itself with an Italian opera in which Mme. Pasta as prima donna enjoyed a brilliant and well-deserved acclaim. M. Anatole's new ballet, *Abu Hassan*, followed immediately afterward, and was a success. The *pas de deux* of M. Albert with Mme. Anatole and M. Gosselin with Mlle. Brocard were received with thunderous applause, but who would ever have believed that we youngsters, hitherto unknown, would be greeted with such volleys of applause and our *soli* rewarded with such vigorous appreciation! To be sure, I did suspect Mr. Court of having organized a patriotic *claque* in the gallery for the benefit of "the pretty english girl" [sic], but the sparkling vivacity that animated *my* dancing, in contrast to the greater correctness of that of my predecessors, did not fail to have its effect, and, to the annoyance of the others, our *pas de deux* carried off *"les honneurs de la soirée."* Compliments on this success were like so many puffs of air on the coals that already smoldered in my breast. That Miss Louisa was a coquette, and was already noted and courted as such, was not hidden from my eyes. I therefore determined to deprive myself of her parents' hospitality and meet with her only in the theatre, but it was impossible for me to carry out this plan. I had won the family's favor once and for all. They laughed at my arguments, but, even though they acted as if they considered my infatuation a mere childish whim, it might well be that they saw in me the son-in-law who would best suit them in the future. I was drawn like a moth to the flame!

Miss Louisa, seventeen years old, was no classical beauty, possessed no domestic skills, and did not distinguish herself by her cleanliness. But her eyes had an irresistible attraction, and what exercised a special sorcery was her soft, melodious voice, for never had I suspected that the English language possessed such a tone as it acquired on her lips. All the same, it did not take many weeks for me to become convinced that my mounting passion met with no response. Rather, it seemed to me as if her parents' kindness even further alienated her mind from me and my basically honest intentions. Sometimes a ray of hope, as it were, flew past my tormented soul—for example, when at the end of one bravura performance or another I felt a warm and enthusiastic squeeze of the hand, and when on her birthday I presented her with a bouquet accompanied by a French romance to which I had written both the words and the music. I cherished the unhappy idea that my perseverance would finally end in victory, but I soon discovered, to my great sorrow, that the ideal to which she aspired was the position that Mlle. Brocard and a number of ladies of the higher *"demi-monde"* occupied, or a marriage to a rich old man which would soon leave her in a free and independent widowhood. I tried in vain to conjure up before her imagination the picture of a cozy artist's home, with the possibility of maintaining a one-horse vehicle. But she smiled scornfully, exclaiming: "No, no, I want a carriage!"

A winter spent in foggy London is not exactly designed to keep up the spirits, least of all in a rejected lover. I had recently read Walter Scott's *Kenilworth*, and fancied myself therein as Tressilian, opposite Amy Robsart. Both my mind and my body were in violent conflict with the art I practiced, but which from time to time continued to afford me satisfaction and—illusions!

On my free evenings, I visited the Covent Garden and Drury Lane theatres and found there the same great talents I had admired in Paris, but at the same time, the poor casting of subordinate roles, which was due partly to an unpardonable indifference to ensemble acting, and partly to the difficulty of filling a Shakespearean *dramatis personae* in tolerably good fashion. But what formed an inevitable appendix to all plays, both serious and comic, between Christmas and Lent was the traditional English "Pantomime," in which the most insane clowning and *"lazzi"* alternated with the dancing of Harlequin and Columbine. It is absolutely impossible for one to conceive of such an unmotivated accumulation of enormities, but one thing had to be admired: namely, the incomparable machinery that accomplished the most remarkable transformations with a speed and precision that no other country can display. The rest of London's glories—museums, churches, parks, bridges, and monuments—made little if any impression upon me in my unstable mood; nor did I occupy myself with studying the English; and though I was received in a most amiable fashion by a couple of middle-class English families, I was still unable to answer satisfactorily the usual question: "How do you like the english living?" [sic], since I dined at a private table with a French family.

On Sundays I accompanied the Court family to the nearby "Chapel" and now and then to their favorite theatre, the Adelphi, where there were to be found some excellent actors, and names such as Reeves, Mathews, Yates, and Cook. The ladies were, for the most part, insignificant, but uncommonly pretty and gifted with fine singing voices. However, my obsession had now assumed violent proportions. I tossed upon rising and falling waves of hope and despair, and if it is but a single step from the sublime to the ridiculous, I had truly reached the latter: to rend my gloves and dash outdoors belonged to the order of the day; but what no one suspected was that every morning I visited Mr. Hamon's fencing school, so as to be able to run my rapier through a supposed rival should the occasion arise!

I am not ashamed to mention these eccentricities, which denote a phase in my youthful artistic career that has, perhaps, not been without significance for my future outlook on life; for though my later activity has not precluded the fantasies conjured up by a lively imagination nor the utterances of an impetuous mind, passion has never since run away with my reason, and I must regard this trial as a storm at sea, which was to teach me to pull in my sails in time to steer to a safe harbor!

Spring drew near, and with it the end of my engagement. Miss Louisa's behavior toward me was more obliging than usual, and I was allowed to be her spokesman to Father Court to obtain permission to attend a *soirée dansante* which Lord Bruce, Lord Hereford, and Captain Brunow had arranged *in honor of* the notables of the ballet. Mr. Court was reluctant to agree to it, but finally consented, on the condition, however, that I should be his daughter's escort—a trust that filled me with joy and pride, and all the more as Miss Louisa seemed to be delighted at the prospect of my company.

The fête was brilliant. We found ourselves surrounded by the higher aristocracy—the gentlemen, that is—for the ladies all belonged to the theatrical profession. The *ton* of the occasion was thoroughly *comme il faut.* All the same, it could not escape my notice that I was being used as a blind for an intrigue that had evidently been going on for some time; and even if I had not become aware of it myself, the intimations of my comrades would soon have put me wise to the fact that a secret understanding existed between Miss Louisa and Captain Brunow. The resentment and suffering that went on inside me are not easy to describe, but I pulled myself together and managed to control myself to the extent that no one guessed the foolish role I had here been intended to play.

My castles in the air had now toppled into the dust, but the fire still raged, and the storm in my young breast threatened to destroy my health. However, a couple of days before my departure, when in the company of M. Anatole I visited the famous "London Docks" (where one of our French friends treated us to some really excellent wine), my good balletmaster took this occasion to expostulate with me on the foolhardiness of abandoning oneself, as I had done, to what was, after all, an unrequited and basically worthless passion. He succeeded in convincing me of my folly, and the following day, after I had made my farewell visits, I said good-bye to the friendly Court family and "shoke hands" [sic] in true British fashion with Miss Louisa without the slightest trace of sentimentality. I was not yet cured, but I fought valiantly.

I traveled to Dover by the usual conveyance, and here I was waiting to go on board the swift-sailing steamer *The Salamander,* when the captain of the French packet *The Henri Quatre* convinced me that it was my duty as a Frenchman to sail with him, all the more since he had half an hour's start on his English rival. All the same, *The Salamander* overtook us, passed us, and arrived at Calais before ebb tide, while we were forced to anchor outside the bar and the passengers were put ashore in boats which plowed through the breakers with as much difficulty as skill.

I was half-dead from the most dreadful seasickness, but, oh miracle! no sooner had I set foot on French soil than my soul-sickness was radically cured. The events and emotions of the past three months seemed to me like a feverish dream from which I had just awakened sound and well. My former interests now returned. I strolled about Calais, and at the Town Hall saw the busts of Eustache Saint-Pierre and his two colleagues, who, with ropes about their necks, had appeared before England's king, Edward III, as hostages and propitiatery sacrifices for the city's desperate resistance.

The diligence to Paris stopped for an hour in Amiens, where I admired the magnificent Cathedral in which three generations of Bournonvilles had served as organists and *Kapellmeisters*. (The last was Jacques B., grandson of Jean Valentin. He was over eighty years old when he died in 1758.) Toward nightfall I reached Paris, where *La Muette de Portici* was celebrating its first triumphs and where I resumed my usual duties, cultivated my faithful friends, and made my entry into the world of finance as a *rentier!*

The Three Foyers

This chapter, which a number of years ago appeared in one of our most popular weekly magazines, though in somewhat abbreviated form, presents a picture of a time that is so closely connected with my theatre life, and particularly with my six years' stay in Paris, that it must find not only a justified but an inevitable place here. Therefore, trusting that a large part of the public has long since forgotten the details in question, and that still others have never become acquainted with them, I present this section and hope that it will not be entirely without interest.

Foyer actually means the same thing as *hearth* and is generally represented by the large fireplace, about which a circle of family and friends can settle to exchange thoughts and opinions, while huge pieces of cordwood placed across andirons adorned with brass sphinxes send up crackling flames and bouquets of gushing sparks. It was into just such a fire that the singer Philippe tossed the Representative of the People, Grandmont, when the latter threatened him with the guillotine because he had refused to sing one of the blood-hymns of the Reign of Terror. Grandmont barely escaped with his life, but Philippe, who had to flee, found refuge with a coachman named Brutus, who, as an ardent patriot, was in high favor with those in power and, in addition, favored and protected the famous singer, who was from his [own] birthplace, Montpellier.

Many a time when people gathered about such a fire during the cold winter, they would meet in the circle veterans of the memorable Russian Campaign. [These former soldiers] then recalled those evenings when, exhausted from the march and continual skirmishes, they had bivouacked (even the Thirtieth) round a watchfire; and when morning reveille sounded, it was answered by only a third of the sleepers: the rest of the platoon were completely frozen! However, these foyer pictures belong only to that harsh season of the year which in France is not of long duration. The cozy name, on the other hand, suggests more the activity and movement that here in Denmark take place all year round.

In former times, all the members of the Théâtre gathered in a single foyer, to which certain magnates were also admitted to "pay their respects" to the artists, particularly the female ones. But when the theatre was later rebuilt, the facilities were expanded. The ballet obtained its own foyer, the opera its own; and, since the backstage visits of the fashionable public were found to be "inexpedient," there was established in the *bel-étage* above the vestibule a magnificent salon, which was accordingly called "The Public Foyer."

We shall begin our tour of inspection with

Le Foyer de la Danse

Since the Hôtel Choiseul (in the suburb of the Chausée d'Antin) together with its adjacent garden had been selected as the site for the new "temporary" Opéra House, the theatre itself was erected on the site of the garden while the tasteful palace was adapted to house the administrative facilities, the wardrobe, and the foyers. The salon with its fire-gilt ornaments was divided both in height and in length. The lower half was used for shops, whereas the upper story, with its vaulted ceiling and Corinthian columns, was given over to the ballet and the opera as a rendezvous and practice room.

The foyer (of which we will here give an account) had, like the stage itself, a slanting floor, and the wall that faced this slope was completely covered with mirrors. The light came from above, and in the background rose a colossal marble fireplace. A broad staircase led up to a corridor that formed the back of the stage, and from there one entered the theatre's wings. Here, from early morn, the beautiful but laborious (and, for the most part, little understood) art of Terpsichore was cultivated, partly under the direction of experienced teachers and partly by the individual practicing of the dancers themselves.

The masters of choreography were revered by the young folk, whom they encouraged by useful and pleasant suggestions. Among the foremost soloists must be mentioned Albert Decombe, who assumed an awe-inspiring position not only by virtue of his considerable artistry, but because of his elegant appearance and solid financial circumstances. After him came Antoine Paul, the public's chosen darling, whose birdlike lightness had earned him the nickname, *"L'aérien"*; and finally ought to be mentioned Ferdinand La Brunière, a dancer whose virtuosity was confined only to a limited sphere, but who had won for himself a well-deserved reputation, principally as a mime. It was really the golden age for male dancers, until they were overshadowed by Mlle. Taglioni and her foreign imitators. Mme. Gardel had abandoned the stage, Mmes. Chameroy and Gosselin had died at an early age, and Fanny Bias, despite a certain perfection in her dancing, was not pretty enough to captivate the general public. On the other hand, the graceful Bigottini enraptured all hearts by her expressive mime, and by viture of her personality and her liai-

LE FOYER DE LA DANSE, 1841

Fanny Elssler is the central figure in this well-known watercolor by
Eugène Lami, though she was touring America in the year of its date.
Photo courtesy Erik Aschengreen.

PAUL AND MARIE TAGLIONI
This undated lithograph, by F. B. and E. C. Kellogg of Hartford,
Connecticut, copies the famous painting of *La Sylphide*'s opening scene
by G. Lepaulle, 1834. Courtesy Dance Collection, The New York Public
Library at Lincoln Center, Astor, Lenox and Tilden Foundations.
Photo by Frank Derbas.

sons possessed a piquancy reminiscent of the age of Louis XIV or, more properly speaking, that of Pericles.

But, as vain and light as the chatter had been in the Foyer de la Danse during rest hours, from the moment the master's or the *répétiteur's* violin was heard, the atmosphere became one of the utmost seriousness and attention. It was now as if each person made it his business to acquire one skill or another so as to achieve, if possible, the honor of making a debut and obtaining a prominent place, if not at the Opéra itself, then at least at one of the major theatres of Europe. But yet more serious, nay, even solemn, was the situation when all that one had achieved in school was to be tested and judged before a jury composed of five professional people and four administrative officials. The foyer was then transformed into a battlefield surrounded by a semicircle of spectators more critical than sympathetic, who, as far as technique was concerned, did not allow themselves to be dazzled by tinsel.

The judges' bench stood in front of the mirrored wall. The male or female candidates stepped forward, pale, their hearts throbbing—for it was a matter of overcoming not only one's competitors but, above all, one's own emotions. As a rule, the test consisted of performing two bravura dances from the repertoire, and one pantomimic scene or another. The conscientious jury sat there, cold and stiff as at a criminal trial, and the silence was broken only by the sound of the violins and the dancers' breathing. But gradually, as talent forged its way through the difficulties, the blood rose in the candidates' cheeks, their eyes sparkled, and the hope of victory helped to redouble their efforts. In vain the judges strove to suppress smiles of satisfaction, and approval was soon voiced among the audience by thunderous applause!

Anyone who has ever passed an examination can form a clear idea of the impression that is made by a victory which is decisive for one's whole future. The jury's verdict is communicated in writing, and the debut with its obligations becomes more definitely fixed. The important day draws near, nor is it without its apprehensions; for if one had to deal only with the benevolent Parisian public, all would be settled swiftly and pleasantly. But a horde of *claqueurs* first had to be satisfied, and a host of menacing souls implored before one could with reasonable safety set foot upon the rough boards.

While censorship at that time had a stranglehold on the political press, the theatre was abandoned to the most inconsiderate, nay, even the vilest, treatment by a number of so-called "literary newspapers." The *Courier des Théâtres* was at that time the *bête-noire* of stage artists. Its editor and owner, M. Charles Maurice, had, like the Revolution's Père Duchêne, succeeded in organizing shamelessness and cynicism. To pay one's respects to this man and to have oneself enlisted as a subscriber to his paper was an unavoidable "robber tribute," to which everyone had to submit so as not to begin his career by being sullied and burdened by an epithet which, if repeated often enough, was certain to catch on. God help the one who dared to neglect or offend him!

Neither sex, age, nor reputation could protect this unfortunate creature from his attacks, which, in addition to their sordidness, were also so maliciously appropriate (and for the spectators often so entertaining) that in order to escape his venemous pen, the greatest celebrities found it necessary to negotiate with this freebooter, who proudly displayed the arm chair in which Talma had sat before him, and, framed and glazed, the five-hundred-franc banknote which the actress Mlle. Bourgoin had brought him as thanks for a commendatory article. From time to time he would get a sound drubbing from one exasperated artist or another, with whom he then fought a duel. But since he was an expert fencer and a sure shot with a pistol to boot, he was almost always lucky enough to inflict only a slight wound upon his opponent. However, when the proper attention was shown him, he could sound the trumpet of praise for the great and appear protective toward "the neophytes" (as he called the young artists), upon which occasions he laid about him with empty phrases, both aesthetic and technical. That he as well as his more or less distinguished colleagues had the right of admittance to the Foyer de la Danse was a prerogative that was modified only by the unpleasantness they sometimes had to endure from the subordinate personnel who, standing outside the range of their criticism, repayed their impudence in coin of an equal value.

On performance evenings, the Foyer de la Danse presented a rather variegated spectacle. Those who wished to appear onstage with bravura were engrossed in serious practicing, while others mustered before the mirrors to adjust their headdresses and costumes, and others still engaged in conversation and flirted with diplomats and princely persons, who were continually exposed to the pushing and kicking of pirouetting shepherds and sylphides. The most celebrated heroine of the Rococo period, Cardinal de Rohan's acknowledged mistress, the graceful Mlle. Guimard, whose bust adorned one of the niches of the room, seemed to look down with relish upon this younger generation, which promised not to degenerate from their inherited traditions!— However, the *régisseur's* bell sounds: an electric shock runs through the entire company, both the civilians and those in costume. Everyone makes for the staircase leading to the stage. The overture is finished, and the curtain rises for the ballet. . . .

Le Foyer du Chant

The corridor resounds with the shrillest cockcrow! It is the tenor, testing his *"ut de poitrine"* [high C]. A deep booming causes the windows of the staircase to vibrate. This is the bass singer, humming his paternal curse. The soprano, on the other hand, is, like the nightingale, sparing with her notes (which are equal to pieces of gold). Enveloped in her cashmere shawl and followed by her venerable mother or meek spouse, she walks in silence to the singing room, where the composer, who is basing his hopes for the success of his opera on her assistance, comes to greet her with a kiss on the hand.

For indeed, who can describe the adversities that a composer (especially if he be young and as yet unknown) and his literary collaborators must endure as opposed to the advantages of those who have received from Nature the "pound" that returns a higher interest than any other kind of capital: namely, a singing voice! As a rule, persons thus favored by Nature are dreadfully unmusical, and with a bravura repertoire hammered into their memories once and for all, and reinforced by routine, they nourish a firm hatred of all new compositions, and their rehearsal as well. Art itself excites them but rarely, and then only to the degree that it is accompanied by curtain calls and advertisements, which are usually dubious enough.

And yet in my day there were to be found in this circle several who offstage were both cultured and amiable people. But among them there was only *one* whose genius and whole understanding of the lyrical-dramatic stage gave him the right to be called artist, and a *great artist*, in the true sense of the word. This was Adolphe Nourrit!

Of a most engaging personality and endowed with a tenor voice as melodious as it was trained, he combined with the complexity of dramatic talent the finest sense of music, and was in all his relations a noble individual. For more than a decade he was the moving spirit of French opera and a strong support for the composers whose works were performed during his time. With warmth and intelligence, he rendered older classical subjects by Gluck, Sacchini, Salieri, and Spontini, and the roles he created in *Le Siège de Corinth*, *Moïse*, *Comte Ory*, and *Guillaume Tell* by Rossini; *La Muette*, *Gustave III*, *Le Dieu*, and *Le Philtre* by Auber; *Robert* and *Les Huguenots* by Meyerbeer, as well as *La Juive* by Halévy, all bore the stamp of his mastery. He even played Mozart's *Don Giovanni* with deep psychological understanding; but, transformed into a tenor part, the role lost a measure of its original feeling and timbre.

His attempt to bring to light Jean-Jacques Rousseau's lyric idyll, *Le Devin du village*, was less fortunate, for here his good intentions were ruined by a scoffer's ludicrous idea. The little opera had just reached the Round Dance in the finale when suddenly, from the topmost proscenium box, an object was lowered into the midst of the merry circle and disseminated a cloud of white dust! Olympian laughter broke out among the audience upon discovering it to be a peruke from "the good old days." This playful little joke was more than enough to forever consign this innocent score to its permanent place in the Musical Archives of the Opéra.

At this time, Hérold and Halévy were chorus masters and *répétiteurs* in conjunction with the ingenious Schneitzhoeffer, whose German name was so difficult for Frenchmen to pronounce that he always humorously added: "*Prononcez Bertrand*"! While the first two gained European renown, he, who possessed just as much talent and a wealth of harmony, progressed no further than the composition of music for ballets and melodramas. His artistic life passed away in jolly indolence and witty ideas.

The main repertoire of the Grand Opéra consisted of the classical works of the old composers I have already mentioned, in whose footsteps Grétry, Lesueur, Catel, Berton, and Kreutzer followed, though with some modification. All lighter subjects were consigned to the Opéra-Comique. Spontini"s first two compositions, *La Vestale* and *Fernand Cortès*, though their texts had a traditional form, called forth zealous opposition among the supporters of the old but nonetheless achieved colossal success. But with these, his masterpieces, his triumphal career also seemed to have reached its climax, for neither *Olympia* nor *Nurmahal* could match the brilliance that their predecessors had cast upon the name of this proud and quarrelsome maestro.

At this time, Romanticism, in music as well as in fiction and poetry, made its appearance in the name of the natural, the popular, and the interesting, as opposed to the conventional and often downright boring clad in the guise of aristocratic gentility. Certainly it cannot be denied that the new trend was guilty of a number of excesses, but it did bring with it a fresher life that was for many years thereafter to have a beneficial effect upon melody, and especially harmony. It was Weber's *Freischütz* which (under the name of *Robin des Bois*) broke the ice and played to full houses at the Théâtre de l'Odéon. Shortly afterward came Boïeldieu's *La Dame blanche* at the Feydeau, and while Auber, with his pretty *opéras-comiques*, prepared to venture into the realm of opera, Rossini arranged his *Maometto II* and his *Moïse* for the great lyric stage.

He was then thirty-four years old and in the full bloom of his talent. But though all of musical Europe had been revolutionized by his new forms, his fame met with the most fanatical opposition, and the Parisian theatrical papers were not the last to condemn this iconoclast, who was to hurl down the old operatic style from its pedestal. However, these attacks prevented neither *Le Siège de Corinth* nor the excellent opera *Moïse* from creating an epoch as Spontini's earlier works had done.

A rare commotion was caused in the Foyer du Chant when Rossini himself took over the grand piano and conducted the rehearsal with his own peculiar blend of enthusiasm and irony, by means of which (together with his thorough knowledge of the handling of voices) he produced effects one had not earlier perceived in French singers. People begged for permission to attend the piano rehearsals, and, as they gave vent to their delight by lively expressions of approval, there came a moment when the maestro was forced to hide his hands so as not to see them covered with kisses. All the same, this deeply moving effect (which in addition to the intrinsic worth of the composition was partly the result of its expressive execution) was responsible for the fact that the impact of the work was diminished to no small degree by the fullness of the instrumentation, which, as it were, stifled the melody and hurt the declamation.

Under these circumstances, it was no easy matter for Auber to gain acceptance with his first attempt in the grand style: namely, the opera *Masaniello*, which in order to escape the suspicion of containing revolutionary tendencies (but also, perhaps, to secure the patronage of an influential *danseuse*) was rechristened *La Muette de Portici*. During the rehearsal of this ingenious work, but little confidence prevailed in the talent that this modest composer and his collaborator Scribe—who was treated rather decently by the press— could display in this area. The music was treated like the catchy *"pont-neufs,"*† but in spite of these ominous portents, the results showed that the two blood brothers had struck the right note; that is to say, they had succeeded in making art interesting at the same time as its stricter demands were fully met. Prejudice still weighed a trifle heavy upon the first act, with its "Bridal Aria," its dancing, and its mimed dialogue. But hardly had the curtain risen to reveal the group of fishermen at daybreak and Nourrit entered with his "Barcarole" than the atmosphere was warmed by the glowing sun of Naples. And when in unison with Dabadie, as Pietro, he poured forth with all the fullness of his beautiful voice that echo of the forbidden "Marseillaise," "Amour sacré de la Patrie," the electrified audience uttered a cry of jubilation so wild and thunderous that it seemed to hold within its bosom the passions of one past and two future revolutions. The conspiracy, the market, the revolt, the wondrous plea, and the magnificent procession were accompanied by much enthusiasm. The mad scene set the crown upon Nourrit's mastery as a lyric actor, and the eruption of Vesuvius rained volleys of joy upon the most complete triumph.

The title role (Fenella) was the least noticed since it was, after all, lacking in dramatic nuance, moving as it did within the realm of hopelessness; and the heroine could just as easily have been burdened with an infirmity other than that of being *mute* which does not for a single moment influence the action, while the part has, I dare say, been neglected partly because Fenella did not become a singing role. However, it seems entirely probable that if it had not been developed into a mimed representation and placed in the hands of a highly influential *danseuse* [Lise Noblet], the score would still be lying among the Opéra management's papers, awaiting its acceptance. From then on, *La Muette de Portici* assumed an honorable place, not only at the French Opéra but on all the stages of Europe, and it has now retained its freshness and charm for over half a century.

Now came Rossini's turn. But in order to avoid comparison with Auber's great work, he chose a lighter subject and presented *Comte Ory*, which sparkled with humor and liveliness and, next to his peerless *Barbiere*, was his finest comic opera. And yet it could not hold its own against the ever more engaging *Muette*, with whom even Auber dared not compete, preferring to return to his customary stage, where *Fra Diavolo* headed the list of a whole series of charming *opéras-comiques* which still form the body of the repertoire of the Opéra-Comique. Only a couple of times did he permit himself to write for the Grand Opéra, but despite the applause with which *Le*

† Popular street ballads, so called because the area of the Pont-Neuf—one of the oldest bridges in Paris—was the "Tin Pan Alley" of the time.

Dieu et la Bayadère and *Gustave III* were received, they were unable to supplant Masaniello and his dumb sister, who are, perhaps, destined to survive their older and younger brothers and sisters and to render their father's name immortal.

Yet again Rossini was to delight the habitués of the Foyer du Chant with a composition, each of whose parts appeared in itself to be a masterpiece, but whose entirety formed a tiresome mass, partly due to a lack of dramatic firmness and partly because of the sentimentality of the leading role. The famous maestro had put his whole store of musical invention into his grand opus, and all true music-lovers joyfully observed that he had now taken a new road, which promised to lead to a series of works of far more sterling character than his earlier compositions. But his hopes of a magnificent success were to some degree disappointed. The enthusiasm at the premiere was far from lively enough, and Rossini, who thought that he had given his very best in *Guillaume Tell*, swore in his righteous anger never again to write for the stage. Unfortunately, he kept his promise, and in this he has, perhaps, served as an example for his successors; for the awe, nay, almost adoration, of which he became the object in his old age would hardly have attended him had he continued to plague his Muse and to court popularity.

Meyerbeer replaced him and celebrated triumphs which were of value to the master, the performers, and above all, the theatre treasury, which from now on reckoned its receipts in the millions. However, this period lies outside the scope of my six years in Paris. Suffice it to say that with Nourrit's unmotivated departure, inspiration within the walls of the Foyer du Chant vanished, and from that time on it was only a matter of giving out so much voice and taking in as large an amount of money as possible. By the artists as well as the management, Art was regarded exclusively as a business, and this viewpoint has since spread throughout the rest of Europe.

The conflict between "*le Romantique*" and "*le Classique*" continued with mounting fervor. But the curious thing about this battle was that music which had thirty years ago been classed in the Romantic school and rejected by its opponents as "wild and baroque" now seemed to be proscribed as being too *classical!*

The Opéra's *chef d'orchestre*, Habeneck, who had for a short time been named Director of the Theatre but had soon returned to his conductor's podium, was an ardent supporter of Beethoven and decided to secure his works admittance into the French musical world. At first, it was hard indeed, for the highly unusual ideas in these symphonies hurt the ears of the old professionals to such a degree that they cried "Charivari!"; while Rodolphe Kreutzer ran away from the first rehearsal of the *Symphony in D Major*, which even had to be cut and adapted so as to enjoy the honor of being performed at the *Concert Spirituel* at the Théâtre de l'Opéra.

Only very few, among them Hector Berlioz, were able to appreciate the numberless beauties of this work, but as a result of painstaking rehearsal the performance was so brilliant that on the concert evening itself the proselytes were won over *en masse* and even the most stubborn opponents were forced to admit that there was something more than just "queer" about the German "wild man's" inspirations.

At the same time there was strong agitation for the dissolution and cessation of the Conservatoire, whose achievements were underestimated by a hostile clique. Habeneck, who was a member of the Theatre administration and, in addition, professor at the violin school, was deeply hurt by such wrongful judgments and decided to refute them in a most striking fashion. He issued a proclamation to all the pupils of the Conservatoire, both young and old, and in this way mobilized from its line, reserves, and reinforcements a musical force the like of which had never been seen in Paris or, perhaps, in any other place. With the aid of forty-odd rehearsals, he succeeded in forming a repertoire in which Haydn, Mozart, and especially Beethoven assumed places of honor. One can scarcely imagine the precision that was bound to prevail in such an artistic phalanx, composed of elements reared in the same school. But what particularly contributed to the effect it produced was the fact that hardly anyone noticed the conductor, who stood shielded by his violin desk and only marked the tempo with his bow.

The concert facilities of the Conservatoire, in the form of a little theatre, were barely large enough to contain a select circle of music-lovers. The subscription seats were snatched up and handed down in every family as hereditary property, and this closed society received the name of the *Société des Concerts*. The orchestra, arranged in the form of a horseshoe on the stage, presented a most imposing sight, and the finest singing talents from the lyric theatres were joined as a chorus to the *ninety* first-rate instrumentalists, who, like the old Imperial Guard, awaited but the signal in order to determine the victory.

The individual numbers met with the liveliest sympathy, but it is impossible to describe the feelings that were evoked by Beethoven's masterworks, which were performed to the utmost degree of perfection. However, there was one moment that must remain unforgettable for anyone who witnessed these music festivals. This occurred during the first "audition" of the *Symphony in C Minor,* after the dark and mysterious three-four time—which dares to be called *Scherzo (Spøg)* only inasmuch as it contains a veritable *Spøgeri* of spirits and phantoms from a "Walpurgisnacht." Little by little, the Sabbat fades away and the string quartet slumbers, as it were, on an A flat, while the kettledrums maintain a weak thunder-roll on C. It reaches a crescendo and the violins prepare for a transition to C-major. . . . The orchestra now enters this bright, roaring mode with the full strength of the trombones, and the *"Marche triomphale"* bursts forth with an intensity as if the gates of Heaven had suddenly opened! The whole assembly arose as one body, and after a moment's breathless trembling, a storm of applause erupted, together with stomping that enveloped the hall in billows of dust. . . . The music had to stop to give the people time to regain their composure, but when the symphony had ended, it was prolonged with loud cries of *"Da capo! "* This wish could be fulfilled only by excluding the last item advertised on the bill. The entire masterwork now appeared clear and distinct to the attentive listeners, and the applause, though just as enthusiastic as it had been the first time, now held itself within the bounds of propriety.

I was involuntarily reminded of the *berserker* frenzy that Saxo describes in *Erik Eiegods Saga,* where a mysterious musician managed to evoke the most wondrous feelings, for a person sitting next to me suddenly seized me by the arm and exclaimed: "My good man! Were Beethoven himself to arise from his grave and appear before me at this moment, it would not astonish me after what I have heard here! "

Many of the less excitable patrons of music simply refuse to credit the French with such a lively sympathy for higher musical art. A number of them have even misinterpreted their enthusiasm as being the effect of the exultation of the moment, nay, have simply ascribed it to an affected "voguish" taste. But half a century of continuous sympathy, in spite of all new German antipathies and the training of a whole new school of French composers such as Berlioz, Félicien David, Gounod, etc.—all of them influenced by Beethoven's spirit—can testify to the truth and thoroughness of the impression.

The emotion that filled the Foyer du Chant was indescribable: in tears, Nourrit embraced Habeneck and confessed that only now had he realized what instrumental music could accomplish. But most enthusiastic of all was Dabadie, who in his admiration compared Beethoven to Shakespeare! This very singer was, in fact, the humorist of the foyer; but in an intimate circle he readily abandoned himself to his enthusiasm for the glorious days of the Empire. He then delivered with singular pathos songs of historical content, among others one which during the July Revolution was travestied and became known as "La Parisienne" but which as early as 1828 had celebrated Bonaparte's crossing of the Saint Bernard. It was written by Casimir Delavigne to an Austrian marching tune which Mendelssohn has since attributed to Aumer.

It may possibly be regarded as "padding " if here I rescue an excellent poem from oblivion by recording from memory the most important stanzas of:

The Crossing of Mount Saint Bernard

Forward, march! First Consul's guard:
See! Above you in the breeze
Our country's flag reflects its rays
On the white peaks of Saint Bernard.
This day, signaled by our glory,
Shall ever live in song and story.
    Set your sights
    Upon the heights;

Over the rocks, the ice, the bights,
March on to victory! . . .

Now our brilliant colors three
Fly on the mountain's highest snows.
In soaring clouds above there glows
The rainbow arch of liberty!
May it be faithful to our glory,
And centuries repeat the story.
      Set your sights, etc.

Yonder's the plain, our battleground —
There it lies, for all to see.
The Alpine torrent surging down
Shall not get there as soon as we.
Italy! Italy lies below!
Drummer, the charge! Come on, let's go!
      Forward! More fast
      Than the mountain blast,
      Surging o'er rocks and gorges vast,
      Let us fall upon Italy! ‡

LE FOYER PUBLIC

The tricolor of the Revolution and the Empire, "the rainbow arch of liberty," now waves (or did until 1875) upon the pediment of the same "temporary" Opera House which more than half a century ago received its inauguration under the white flag with the golden lilies. In this temple the Restoration, the July government, the Republic, and the reborn Empire have sacrificed to the Muses, only eight of whom, to be sure, have received places among the rows of pillars on the façade which, according to the laws of architecture, cannot support an uneven number. But if light-footed Terpsichore has found herself excluded from this lofty plane, she is fully indemnified within the walls of this sanctuary, not only on the stage itself but at the motley Carnival balls, where she has, unfortunately, gone a step further in emancipation than the Constitution of Parnassus allows.

Beneath the frieze, above which the majestic Muses sit enthroned, paying no heed to the bustling crowd below, there extends for the entire width of the building a balcony, through whose open windows one can look into a long gallery adorned with mirrors, gas chandeliers, and velvet-covered settees. From there five doors lead out into the corridor of the first tier of boxes, and in one corner of this magnificent *salle* refreshments are served while in the other is to be found a bookstall. This is the customary rendezvous for those theatregoers who have been able to salute one another only at a distance. One

‡ In the original edition, Bournonville presented six stanzas of this — in French, without any translation into Danish. Only the first, fifth, and sixth of these stanzas are presented in this English version, which follows the metrics of the French with only minor deviations.

gets a breath of fresh air, has a sherbet, and with lorgnette in hand, inspects the elegant throng.

The symbol of a *foyer,* namely, a blazing hearth, is nowhere to be found, but is compensated for in cold weather by so-called *calorifères* or heating pipes that whistle and sing from the pedestals bearing the marble busts of famous artists and composers. These venerable household gods, who have followed the Opéra's various changes of address and who will no doubt adorn the magnificent new building, have, regardless of the rivalry that once aroused their irritable dispositions, somehow managed to retain their positions, whereas the portraits of the powers-that-be have all too often been subject to change.

The boundaries of this description are confined to the period of the Restoration under Charles X, and we shall begin with an evening when the scheduled work is one that has been given so often that it is no longer of interest to the Opéra's habitués and the holders of complimentary tickets, most of whom have witnessed the interesting happenings on the great stage of the world as well as that of art. They have seen the most brightly shining stars ascend, decline, fade, and disappear, and have no lack of material for superb entertainment.

In the central embrasure, not far from Gluck's ingenious bust, sits "*L'Eremite de la Chausée d'Antin,*" the stately Jouy, who as author of *La Vestale, Cortès,* and *Guillaume Tell* has inscribed his name in the annals of French opera and has also (1824) in a verse tragedy, *Sulla,* given Talma the opportunity to present, in the guise of that Roman emperor, a *portrait vivant* of Napoleon the Great! In front of Jouy, in animated conversation, stands the co-editor of the *Courier français,* Etienne, famous for the lovely texts he has written for a host of *opéras-comiques.* About these "veterans" of a stirring time is gathered an attentive circle of younger and older fellow-partisans, for none of them cares a fig for the Bourbons.

It is a different matter with a trio who are measuring the length of the *salle* with rapid strides. The central figure is the eldest son of the Duc de Doudeauville, the Vicomte Sosthène de la Rochefoucauld, Director of Fine Arts, who has the last word in everything concerning the royal theatres. He has set himself the task of reconciling the stage to ideas of morality and dignity consistent with the aesthetic and ethical direction of the Court. Actually, it ought to be stated that in artistic respects the theatre flourished under his superintendence, but, despite his good intentions, his efforts were stranded upon a single delicate point which placed him at the mercy of the scoffers' persiflage: the ballerinas' petticoats, which he had ordered to be made a couple of inches longer! At the moment, this very issue is being raised. The virtuous reformer finds himself caught between two fires. On one side, the Director of the Opéra, Lubbert (who is influenced more than is seemly by a flighty mistress), is protesting in the name of art against a measure that is certain to put a drag on female virtuosity. On the other side he is being harangued by his seventy-year-old uncle, the ever youthful Marquis de l'Aigue, a true *voltigeur* from the golden days of Versailles but, despite his wrinkles and complete lack of teeth, still a member of the Jockey Club and the possessor of "lion's seats" in the theatres. He is most decidedly advising him against this arbitrary conflict, which might possibly provoke a reaction in the direction of "the transparent."

Another little *comité* has selected a place beneath the King's bust and seems deeply engrossed in subjects of an extremely serious nature. The physiognomies of the two spokesmen are familiar enough from the bookshops, where their portraits adorn their newly published writings. They are the poet Lamartine and the novelist the Vicomte d'Arlincourt, both ardent Royalists and infatuated with memories of the days of knights and troubadours. The third member of this group is the Vicomte's brother, who had been aide-de-camp to King Gioacchino* and only half-shares his brother's political views. A fourth man soon arrives and disrupts the serious atmosphere by his burlesque ideas, which before long cause the writers and the stern soldier to burst into irrepressible laughter. It is the Marquis de Montaigu, an elderly gentleman who possesses the gift of smoothing wrinkles and making people shake with laughter from the sovereign down to the bootblack, a privilege he has known how to maintain throughout all the changes of the throne. During the organization of the National Guard under the July Government the sixty-year-old *maréchal de camp* entered its ranks as a simple grenadier!

A little cluster has taken seats near the buffet, and several young people are gathered round two old gentlemen. One of the latter wears a dark wig, his face is thin and rather florid; the second has a scar across his nose and drags a lame foot. "Yes, gentlemen," says the former to his young listeners, "it is nothing to maintain French humor under peaceful and pleasant conditions. But when one can come up with a superb *calembourg* [pun], as I did, in the midst of the Tagus' raging current, where in the heat of battle and nearly drowning, I shouted to my troops: '*Camarades! Ne me laissez pas otage (au Taje)!,*'† and has also had several outstanding *bon mots* at hand while being driven, sorely wounded, in a sutler's cart across the groaning bridge over the Beresina, then may one permit oneself to speak of national humor and *esprit*. And yet, people have not granted me the *gloire* which I could rightfully claim for both my services and my witty ideas." This is the cavalry general, Baron de Lahoussaye, who now despite his advanced age and his wounds sought consolation for the injuries inflicted upon him in a *"liaison anacréontique"* with one of Arcadia's shepherdesses. The other old man had the advantage of

---

*Joachim Murat, b. 1767, was Marshal of France and the most brilliant cavalry officer in the armies of Napoleon, to whose sister Caroline he was married. Installed as King Gioacchino of Naples in 1808, he was ousted seven years later by the victorious Allies. Attempting to regain his throne by force, he was captured, tried for "disturbing the public peace," and executed October 13, 1815.

† Literally, "Comrades, don't leave me hostage." "Taje" (or "Tage") is the French name of the Tagus river.

still being referred to as "young" because he was the son of the long-deceased Maréchal Kellermann, the Duc de Valmy. Although the present "young" Kellermann had as early as Marengo broken through the Austrian squares and taken an honorable part in most of Napoleon's campaigns, he had not received the maréchal's baton and, like Lahoussaye, stood on the list of retired generals. He now enjoyed his retirement in the bosom of the liberal arts, into which one of the younger priestesses of Terpsichore had also initiated him. He therefore became an expert patron of us younger dancers, who readily listened to his stories and followed the advice he imparted to us with the air of a connoisseur.

One seldom saw the Barons Gros and Gérard—both of whom during the Empire had immortalized the battles of Aboukir, Austerlitz, and Eylau with their paintbrushes, and nowadays painted glowing apotheoses for the Bourbons—in the company of younger artistic colleagues, nearly all of whom held liberal views and enjoyed the protection of the Duc d'Orléans, in whose galleries their pictures found magnanimous asylum. At this time Horace Vernet, Paul Delaroche, Camille Roqueplan, Hersent, etc. stood foremost among those newer historical and genre painters. These superb artists readily gathered about the ingenious scene painter, Ciceri, who always had the battle painter Carle Vernet and the miniaturist Isabey with him in his proscenium box. Sometimes, however, he would stroll with them in the foyer, where they usually pounced upon the bookseller's corner. Here many an instructive discussion was carried on about the natural, the correct, and the beautiful in art, and more than one seeker of knowledge gathered crumbs from the rich men's table on this spot.

No one, however, was as busy as a certain Duponchel. Who this individual was, what he did, or whence he came, nobody knew. But one had to be astonished at the outspokenness with which he infiltrated all coteries, firmly attached himself to anyone who happened to bear the title of "celebrity of the moment," and laid about him with borrowed artistic words and empty aesthetic phrases. He seemed to have set himself the task of guiding ideas of Beauty back to a medieval state that was as ugly and baroque as his own unpleasant person. By some costume sketches which he succeeded in passing off as his own compositions, he talked his way into the wardrobe of the Opéra, from there into the Economy Department, and thence into the easily infatuated Administration. Since he had at the same time gained entrée into the home of the great Spanish financier, Aguado, who in difficult situations had been the Théâtre's moneyman, he was recommended by the latter for a secretarial post and, after some time, for that of absolute head of this artistic institution. There in the course of several years he amassed a considerable fortune—truly a characteristic portrait of a *parvenu* during the Orléans period.

The opening of box doors, the clattering of seats, and the nasal cries of the lorgnette sellers and newspaper hawkers announce that the opera is over and that a long intermission is needed for the setting up of the ballet. The audience streams out into the foyer, where the temperature is somewhat lower than in the poorly ventilated auditorium, which is heated by gas lamps. One takes some refreshment, strolls up and down watching for acquaintances, and tries to get a breath of fresh air on the open balcony.

It is obvious that the groups above mentioned were not all present on one and the same evening; but since these sketches from real life include pictures from an entire era, we will imagine them concentrated in this frame just as in the remotest period of our own journey through life.

Who are those two younger men who resemble each other so much they might be twins, and have such Nordic faces that one would not take them for Frenchmen? They are the brothers Casimir and Germain Delavigne, born in Normandy. They encounter a fellow-countryman of great stature, noble facial features, and grizzled, curly hair. It is Boïeldieu, who with a handshake answers a compliment on his latest work, *La Dame blanche!*

Two young fellows hasten up to join the painters' group: one of them is tall and slender, with curly mulatto hair; the other, red-and-white, like blood and milk, with flowing locks. They are both described as promising *hommes de lettres*. The former is the son of the late General Dumas, is called Monsieur Alexandre, and has already made his appearance as a dramatic author. The other, Philarète Chasles by name, is a recognized *homme d'esprit*, but more critical than productive. The coterie is soon augmented by a particularly handsome young man from whose full face a great degree of self-satisfaction radiates. His original style of writing has secured him a position as aesthetic writer for the *Journal des Débats*, where each Monday he turns out a *feuilleton* which boils over with witty thoughts in a language so packed full of intensive adjectives and piquant syntax that his style is exclusively his own and would hardly dare to be used by anyone other than—Jules Janin!

Political strong men usually have enough to do with their own public appearances and care but little for the theatre. On the other hand, one frequently encounters the writers Méry and Barthélemy, who persecuted the Minister Villèle with Juvenalian bitterness at the same time as they praised Napoleonism to the point of idolatry. The epic pamphlets "La Villéliade," "La Corbièreide," and "La Peyronnéide," together with "Rome à Paris" (a statement against Jesuitism), won extraordinarily large circulation by virtue of their spirit, strength, and perfect form. How these two talented writers worked together is still a puzzle, for though one was used to partnerships among dramatic authors, one had to be astonished at the integrity of these remarkable satires. However, when Barthélemy traveled to Vienna to present the Emperor's son, the young Duke of Reichstadt, with a copy of the grand poem *Napoléon en Egypte*, which later brought about a legal action because of an account of this fruitless journey, Méry took it upon himself to plead the cause of "*Le Fils de l'homme*"‡ in rhymed verse; and one thereby drew the conclusion that the design and bold invention were the work of Barthélemy,

‡ "The son of the Man"—i.e., Napoleon's son, the Duke of Reichstadt, d. 1832.

while the metrical treatment essentially belonged to Méry. Yet another remarkable poem was to issue from this team of writers, namely, "Waterloo!
Epitre au Général Bourmont." The faithless deserter, who the night before
that fateful battle fled to the enemy camp and betrayed his native land, was
named by the Bourbons Maréchal and Supreme Commander of the expedition
against Algeria (1830), but history had branded him, and the Muse of heroic
poetry on this occasion lashed him with scorpions. The July Revolution drove
away the Jesuits, did away with censorship, and set Napoleon's statue once
more atop the Colonne de Vendôme. . . . From this time on political poetry
lost its real zest, the collaboration between Méry and Barthélemy was broken
off, and individually they later seem to have produced nothing remarkable.

One continually notices a great many travelers, and mainly a host of
Englishmen, who are here making their first stop on their tour of the Continent. We meet Canning, the great statesman, surrounded by his numerous
family. In spite of all the harm his politics have inflicted upon France, (much
less our beloved Denmark!), he has nevertheless won popularity by his sympathy for struggling Greece. Walter Scott, on the other hand, has been received with remarkable coolness despite his excellent novels, which are read
in translation by high and low. However, upon his arrival the newspapers had
immediately called public attention to his *Edward's Letters*,"* wherein he de-
rides the defeated at Waterloo in most undignified fashion! Enemy bayonets
often wound far less deeply than a light goose quill in a relentless hand. This
was significantly shown at Queen Victoria's coronation (1838) when Maréchal
Soult appeared hand in hand with his old opponent from the battlefields of
Spain, the aged Duke of Wellington, and the British lauded them with "Hon-
nour to the Braves" [sic]!

There are several other ways of creating a sensation, which the eccentric
Briton does not slight. One turns around in order to look at the red-haired
Lord Stair, who the other evening with the utmost indifference lost 60,000
francs at "Rouge-et-Noir" in the Salon des Ambassadeurs. Farther off we see
the handsome, athletically built Lord Seymour, who is always ready to offer a
handful of sovereigns to whatever strong man will test muscles against him in
a wrestling or boxing match. He was later to be cured of this mania by a
stonecutter who, for a suitable honorarium, took it upon himself to beat the
noble lord black and blue. Another British celebrity allows herself to be seen
in the foyer, to the great indignity of her honorable countrywomen: this is the
famous courtesan, Harriette Wilson, who in her printed memoirs has placed
all her distinguished lovers in a pillory that would prostitute anyone who did
not, fortunately, belong to the English aristocracy.

Scribe and Melesville, Daguerre and Bouton, Thiers and Villemain,
Talma and Baptiste *l'aîné*, Rubini and Lablache, Rothschild and Count Apponyi stroll back and forth in pairs. The only person who through a long se-

---

*A slip of the memory. The title is *Paul's Letters to his Kinsfolk* (1816)—a novel in the form of
letters dealing with France in the late Napoleonic years, with special emphasis on Waterloo.

ries of years has gone to the theatre alone and never speaks to any Christian is the Persian ambassador, with his pointed fur cap and long caftan, his invariable costume summer and winter. With his impassive countenance and his dark gaze, he has followed political upheavals as well as scenic performances and, like the picture of "the Wandering Jew," he still goes to the foyer while generation after generation glides across the polished floor. Revolutions and dynasties have succeeded and ousted one another, and most of the personalities mounted in this frame have long since taken ship in Charon's bark and wander now beneath the shady plane trees of the Elysian Fields, while in 1873 the survivors still sit upon the same benches inspecting the younger generation and comparing it with that of the days before the July Revolution!

The Second Journey on Leave of Absence

After my return from London, my sphere of activity at the Paris Opéra seemed too limited, and though my *chefs d'emploi* occasionally afforded me the opportunity for advantageous "doubling," they frankly stated that in spite of their friendship for me they could not bring themselves to allow their places to be filled by younger dancers, since it might well occur to the management that for a lower price the latter were in a position to produce an effect that overshadowed the older talents. These circumstances contributed to the fact that more and more I lent an ear to the offers which came from every side. Thus Vienna stood open to me with 12,000 to 15,000 francs a year; Bordeaux with 10,000 francs; and Berlin with a permanent engagement and 4000 Prussian thalers. Inquiries about my terms even came in from Copenhagen; but although for the triple function of solo dancer, teacher, and director, I had adapted my price according to the humble conditions with which I was familiar, they nevertheless found it too high, and the negotiations were broken off. The contract with Berlin was ready for my signature when balletmaster Aumer called to the attention of the Opéra management the future that might be expected from my burgeoning talent, and at the same time he fired my ambition to such a degree that I immediately dropped the foreign engagement and entered into a new one whereby I would gradually work up to 11,000 francs in three years and secure *congés* [leaves] as well as a handsome repertoire of roles and bravura parts. Paul Taglioni went to Berlin in my place, where he acquired an honorable position and later gained considerable renown as a ballet composer.

My friends were always saying that I had in me the makings of a good husband, and there was no lack of hints from older ladies that here or there was a suitable match for me! Among others, I was referred to the dancer Marie Taglioni—as respectable as she was charming—who was Swedish by birth, Protestant by religion, and therefore as good as my countrywoman. I was, moreover, a welcome guest in her parents' home, sang romances for them, and entertained them with my small talents. But apart from the fact that it would have been a marriage of convenience which would have placed me in a subordinate and dependent position, Marie's heart was not free, for she was in love with a young Italian musician named Carlini, who had composed several of her loveliest dance numbers. Her parents, who had high-flown plans for their daughter, were opposed to this union, and the outcome was that the later-so-famous Sylphide became encumbered with a good-for-nothing male prima donna, M. Gilbert de Voisins. He was the son of a peer of France, but made it his duty to little by little gamble away everything his wife had earned under her maiden name, so that when a separation finally took place he left her with such considerable debts that she, thirty-some years of age, had to begin her career all over again. However, my good fortune had in store for me a happiness which I did not as yet suspect.

In accordance with the terms of my contract, my *congé* fell just toward the end of the summer of 1829, and it was now a question of where I should go to render it fruitful. Repeated attempts had been made to get me to appear as a guest in Copenhagen, but Frederik VI, to whom all theatrical matters were submitted, was still angry with me and replied: "He shall say *Pater peccavi* [Father, I have sinned] before I will have anything to do with him!" This was reported to me through official channels, and in a most humble letter I did not fail to lay my feelings of affection at the feet of my King. The result was that the negotiations concerning my guest appearances were reopened and my terms (which amounted to twenty performances at 60 *Specie*, a third of which was to serve as partial compensation for the two years' salary I had collected during my absence) were accepted—however, without a guarantee of the number of performances. I let matters take their course since I longed with all my heart to see my native home once more. And so in the beginning of August I set out and, after a rapid journey, landed in the arms of my beloved parents and was greeted and embraced by sisters, friends, and relatives! The Theatre management and the *corps de ballet* were also glad to see me again, but I still had to face a personal audience with His Majesty, and the most pleasant greeting did not await me *there!*

I walked in to the King, who, contrary to custom, did not advance to meet me from a side chamber but stood leaning on the table in the center of the room. I began with a well-prepared phrase about "a subject's affection and love of his fatherland . . ." "That is all well and good," the King interrupted, "but you stayed away!" A bit startled, I made so bold as to plead that no particular desire had been voiced to employ me at the Royal Theatre. "That's damned nonsense! Who has said that we did not want you home?" "But, Your Majesty, I was entirely too young to assume a directorial position, and in a subordinate capacity what little talent I have would have gone to ruin." "Yes, yes! I can well understand that you prefer the Paris Opéra to Copenhagen's Theatre. They certainly pay you well over there, and we cannot give such high salaries." "I pray Your Majesty to be assured that I would rather offer my talents to Your Majesty's service." "Yes, well, we will get to see what you can do. Everyone claims that you have made remarkable progress." "Then Your Majesty is no longer angry with me?" "No, of course not! We shall see you at the gala performance. God keep you! " He thereupon clicked his spurs in dismissal, and I walked out into the crowded antechamber, my face beaming with satisfaction as if I had enjoyed the greatest favor.

How I managed to give *Acclaim to the Graces, The Sleepwalker, Soldier and Peasant,* as well as several individual bravura dances, in only a couple of months and with a *corps de ballet* highly deficient in a number of respects, I have told in the first volume of *My Theatre Life;* but the fact that my dillettantish appearance as a bit of a singer and also an actor aroused an opposition as zealous as it was ridiculous one will find mentioned in Heiberg's account of the sad fate of the play *Isabella.* That is to say, the famous author had hit upon the idea of combining my singing talents with the dancing *divertissements* I had furnished for his piece; in addition, he allowed me to take part in the action by speaking a couple of lines. The whole thing came about because of the favor I had acquired as a guest artist. It was not without some reluctance that I involved myself in this *tour de force;* but it never occurred to me that this would arouse such a storm among the dramatic personnel, among whom my noble friend Nielsen made the most violent gestures and raved about the profanation and prostitution of the stage. This outstanding and celebrated artist, who in his letters mentions me as the one who by my consideration had prevented the so-called Paradise (Paris) from becoming a Hell for him, now seemed unable to tolerate the extraordinary success I had enjoyed on my return; for after only my first performances he turned his back on me and for several years actually avoided me! He now placed himself at the head of a faction which saw in the possible rise of the ballet a distinct danger for real dramatic art.

At that time the spoken drama actually stood at the highest point it has ever reached, and should the vicissitudes of time assert themselves, it must one day descend from its height without either the opera or the ballet having to bear the blame.

When we enumerate stars like Frydendahl, Ryge, Lindgreen, Nielsen, Stage, Foersom, Rosenkilde, Phister, and Holst; Mmes. Wexschall (afterward Fru Nielsen), Pätges (afterward Fru Heiberg), and Mlle. Jørgensen, together with the young beauties Heger and Lange (afterward Fru Holst and Fru Larcher), one will hardly find at any theatre—least of all at the present time— such an outstanding ensemble. And if we add to this the fact that prolific authors such as Oehlenschläger, Hauch, Boye, Heiberg, and Overskou provided the repertoire, which had earlier been maintained by the finest that France, Germany, and England had to offer at the time, one must admit that this golden age, which despite a number of deaths extended well into *the fifties,* was not in the slightest disturbed by the progress of the ballet.

However, there was violent arguing both for and against the expediency of raising the ballet from its dilapidated state, and while this narrow-minded point of view found response in a large part of the daily press, the friends of the ballet sided with the Court, which saw in this formerly so brilliant art form a festive privilege that a Royal Theatre could not dispense with. The Directory, which consisted of four members, was divided in opinion, and Collin was on the side of the actors. Holstein, who wanted to please "Royalty" but did not wish to have a falling out with the champions of the drama, cautiously placed himself in a *"juste-milieu"* and left my eventual engagement to a personal agreement between His Majesty and myself! Nowadays it sounds extremely curious to hear that such details were once referred to the monarch's discussion; nonetheless, I was summoned to Amalienborg several times to determine the conditions upon which I might possibly enter into the Theatre's service.

So as not to offend the poorly paid actors (who, by the way, knew how to indemnify themselves by gratuities, evening entertainments, and summer performances), my salary had to be divided into two parts; that is, 1000 Rbd. as First Solo Dancer, and 500 Rbd. as teacher of dancing and mime (my title of Dance Director and my ballet compositions entailed no emoluments!). I, who was used to very different figures from abroad, could not be content with this but into the bargain postulated the position of Court Dancing Master, which was as good as vacant due to old Laurent's infirmity. This point was the bone of much contention, and since I could not accept the other terms [without it], the King became really angry and informed me that I had already "carried away a good bit." "You will get no more!" sounded the Royal word, and I confessed that I deeply regretted having to go away burdened with my King's disfavor. "Not at all! I wish you a successful journey. May you earn a good deal of money—which you seem to set such great store by—but I beg you to consider how you have behaved toward your Lord and King!" It was a hard salute of dismissal from a King whose curious personality one almost always approached with a certain dread, and, moreover, an unpleasant conclusion to a triumphant run of twenty-two heavily attended performances.

I now had to regard the whole affair as abortive, and prepared for my departure. But Chamberlain Yoldi, who showed himself especially benevolent to my cause, ventured to act as intermediary and got me to tender a filial letter of submission to the King. This resulted in the fact that, in addition to my theatre salary, I was to receive 700 Rbd. and the position of Acting Court Dancing Master until Laurent's demise. And so, for the time being, I came to have 2200 Rbd.—a handsome salary for a young man of twenty-four! To be sure, these advantages could not help but arouse an outcry among many who did not seem to understand that I had on this occasion broken the ice for a better system of wages for them. I signed the contract with my foot on the carriage step, so to speak—however, with the proviso that I must first succeed in freeing myself from my three-year engagement in Paris.

I need hardly describe my parents' delight at being able to keep me at home. Nor would there enter into *My Theatre Life* the joyous event of my betrothal if in the faithful companion of my life I had not found, in addition to the comfort and peace of home, encouragement for my works, consolation in my artistic adversities, and valuable advice in many matters regarding both taste and conduct. I therefore left Copenhagen a fiancé, spent the winter in Paris, and succeeded in having my contract annulled with the forfeit of some pecuniary benefits. I then returned by way of Berlin, where I made a couple of guest appearances, and arrived in Copenhagen in time to end the 1829–1830 season.

On Midsummer Eve, June 23, my wedding took place in the Slotskirke. Confessionarius Mynster married us, and the benediction he read over us has borne fruit in a happy union which, God willing, will celebrate its fiftieth anniversary in three years!

Anything of significance that has occurred within my allotted sphere of activity from that point until my definite retirement at the end of the previous season, I have recorded in the preceding volumes of *My Theatre Life,* and I wish that it may bear witness to my love and esteem for the task that has been entrusted to me and to which I have devoted my finest talents.

II

Danish National Festivals

THE measure of cooperation that has been entrusted to me at several of the national celebrations I have earlier described can justly be reckoned among the episodes of *My Theatre Life* since, more than anything else, the confidence I have been fortunate enough to win through my scenic activity has given the authorities concerned the idea of employing my talents in the capacity of *arrangeur*—a task which I have undertaken to perform to the best of my ability and with the most loyal conception [of the events].

To such a national festival *en plein air* there are two principal challenges: the mood of the crowd, and fine weather. One can almost always count on the former among the Danish public, who bring with them a spirit and a tone one will seek in vain to equal abroad. On the other hand, in our inconstant clime, which is ruled by the winds, the latter element is so reliant on chance that only with fear and trembling does one proceed with an undertaking where both efforts and expenditures stand in danger of being rendered completely fruitless.

One such partially unsuccessful fête was that arranged in honor of the nuptials of the Crown Prince, in the Rosenborg Gardens, on August 11, 1869.* Overpræsident Bræstrup and Borgmester Gammeltoft had done me the honor of asking me to provide some ideas and suggestions for the decoration of the Gardens and the arrangement of the festivities. I presented them with a plan which was followed—but with considerable modification. In particular, no sailcloth roof was spread over the rotunda that surrounded the basin of the fountain (one of the main features of the fête, where the reception and greeting of Royal guests was to take place). Moreover, the architectural elements had been most tastefully arranged, with draped platforms and seats for the Court and dignitaries of the city; an Oriental kiosk for Lumbye's orchestra; elevated places for the singing choruses, etc.—all, however, exposed to wind and weather. In the main avenues there were festoons of gas jets, and among the trees busts of famous men from all three Nordic kingdoms, while the Drill Ground had been transformed into a circus with platforms for the different singing societies and adorned with statues in whose midst a magnificent fireworks display stood ready to be set off. All this would have yielded a roman-

*The marriage of Crown Prince Frederik (later Frederik VIII) to Louise, daughter of Charles XV of Sweden.

tic, fairy-tale evening, such as those one can read about in Italian novellas. But, alas! We do not have the Italian climate. From early morn there appeared heavy masses of clouds which upon the entry of the young Crown Princess shed their abundant blessings "like gold in the lap of the bride," while a host of umbrellas waved jubilantly to greet her.

One violent shower succeeded another, and there arose uncertainty as to the possibility of holding the appointed festivities. But after some discussion, people abandoned themselves to the hope that the weather would clear before evening. A soothing pause of several hours actually occurred. But just as the iron gates of the Gardens were unlocked to admit the rushing crowd, the sky opened its sluices and the rain pelted down upon our beautifully decorated rotunda! A momentary spell of good weather poured hope into our hearts, and we hastened to repair as best we could the damage suffered. But just as the thousand-voiced "Hurrah! " announced the arrival of the Royal Family, a new and even more violent downpour broke loose, and despair was painted upon the faces of the ladies in festive array and the gentlemen in dress uniform. Among the most disheartened were the festival's directors, though ex officio we feigned joy and agreeableness.

Two invaluable qualities seem to belong to sovereigns in general and our Royal Family in particular. The one consists in recognizing people and remembering their names and positions; the other, in being able to withstand changes of climate and to keep up heart and spirit amid all kinds of storms and vicissitudes. These outstanding virtues manifested themselves in their full splendor on this occasion and had a magical effect upon the numerous assemblage. Although the walks of the Gardens were transformed into swamps and the gas jets, for the most part, denied their services, the greetings were as gracious and the words as pleasant as if it were a Court at Christiansborg.

The address of welcome was answered by the Crown Prince with as much warmth as if the loveliest rays of sunlight had illuminated the festivities; but the music was only mediocre since the instruments bubbled with the invading water, and the young ladies, who amid all this wetness were to sing a hymn to the bride, felt the sheet music they held in their hands return to its original rag substance! Toward nine o'clock the weather grew fairly calm, and the presentations on the Drill Ground, singing as well as fireworks, foresaw no vital problems. The high point, however, of every Nordic celebration remains the food and drink—and this important element was not lacking on this occasion either. While the entire length of the Drill House was arranged for the general public, an elegant supper for the Royal Family and several hundred invited guests was served in a magnificent tent erected for the purpose. Here a toast to the august newlywed couple was proposed in a speech which was indeed so abrupt that there occurred a pause in which, with bated breath, one could hear the grass grow. . . . All the same, the finale was good and the mood superb in spite of the conditions endured. Here, once again, was reason to praise the Copenhagen public, which, with a total number of thirty thousand of the most varied classes, displayed a tact and a respect for good order that was combined in an amiable fashion with an indestructible good humor.

The mood was not nearly so pleasant at the time when there was talk of celebrating

THE CONSTITUTION FESTIVAL, 1854

A meeting was convened at the Student Association, located at that time in Boldhuusgade, to consider *whether* and *in what manner* this festival should be celebrated. In the introductory speech, as well as in various statements, no small amount of bitterness was voiced against the Ørsted ministry, which, by a number of harsh measures, had made itself suspect of harboring an unfavorable disposition toward the Constitution and toward freedom as a whole.

I was invited to attend this meeting, but because of stage duty it was necessary for me to leave before the discussion ended. That same evening I was greatly surprised to receive a request asking me to be the ninth to join the committee for the arrangement of the festival, and to meet the following day at the home of my highly esteemed fellow-citizen, the saddler Christensen.

The political horizon here at home was heavy with ominous storm clouds, and everywhere in liberal circles there prevailed a panic fear of the thunderbolts of power. My family and friends urged me to refuse the intended honor, and I did indeed hesitate for a moment. But since I rightly reflected that I had successfully influenced earlier unforgettable popular festivals, and was conscious, besides, of being able to do something to bring about a milder interpretation of this demonstration, I considered it cowardice to betray the confidence shown me; and I decided, in spite of all remonstrances, to do my best for the satisfaction of all parties.

I drafted a plan which essentially aimed at avoiding mob riots by removing us as far as possible from the turbulent capital and transferring the festivities to the beautiful site on the eastern plain at the foot of the Hermitage.† I also drew up an invitation in the form of a program which ran thus:

In the conviction that June 5 is a festival of *Memory, Hope,* and *Gratitude,* we the undersigned, in accordance with the authorization of a large part of the citizenry, do arrange a Constitution Festival to be held on the plain at the Hermitage, on the anniversary of the Constitution. We will strive to give this Festival a character that is beautiful, loyal, and consistent with the achievement of the objective. In order to accomplish this our task, we confidently rely upon the support of our fellow-citizens, which will be given mainly by the assembling of as many people as possible: men and women, high and low, rich and poor; surely all are parties

† The royal hunting lodge at Dyrehave, built in the eighteenth century and still in use.

to the blessings of our Constitution. But we also cherish the assurance that our fellow-citizens will, each according to his means, place us in a position to give this day such a solemn and festive character that it may enliven and strengthen in the people the spirit of Freedom and love of our native land.

When I appeared at the home of the saddler Christensen at the appointed time, I discovered to my surprise that no less than five of the most important men selected had resigned! Therefore only four of us remained, including Folketing member J. A. Hansen and Head Journeyman Jacobsen! For a moment we were in a great uncertainty as to whether we too should resign from the whole troublesome business; but quite unexpectedly, like a *deus ex machina*, the medallion-maker Petersen entered. He had just had his Constitution medal struck in Berlin and now presented it to us in a tasteful case containing three models: one in gold, the next in silver, and the third in bronze. We were all struck with the same idea and decided to travel the very next day to Frederiksborg, in order to secure the approval of Frederik VII and present him with the medals. I do not remember whether all four of us were present at the audience, but I stood next to our honorable chairman, Christensen, when he humbly presented the gift, which was an extraordinary success and had the instantaneous effect that His Majesty granted us his royal assistance and promised to give orders that everything that we required for the glorification of the festival should be placed at our disposal.

Overjoyed at this great kindness, we ventured to express the wish that His Majesty would grace this loyal national festival with his august presence. But suddenly the King's face became terribly grave and he emphatically replied: "I am accustomed to spend this day privately, *with my God and with my wife.*" We were herewith finished, and since no one detained us at the Castle, we enjoyed our luncheon at the inn and returned to Copenhagen fairly well pleased.

It was now a matter of drawing up our program and providing our invitation with a suitable number of notable signatures, but even here we encountered signs of the authorities' displeasure, for a high-ranking military official, who was also a member of the Rigsdag, received a peremptory order to remove his name from the list of those invited or tender his resignation! The King's orders, which were for all possible assistance, seemed to go unheeded and the prevailing terrorism did not exactly promise any significant influx of the financial means necessary for the projected arrangements. At the Stock Exchange I was positively abused by one of our most liberal merchants, who vehemently asked me if we weren't mad to hold a celebration for a Constitution that had ceased to exist!

However, time moved on, and we had to exert ourselves to procure both artistic and poetical assistance as well as promises of patriotic appearances by our most eloquent liberals. With great willingness, our excellent Bissen modeled a colossal bust of Frederik VII, and Professor Nebelong sent us his talented pupil, the architect Ove Petersen, for the erection of the column that was to form the midpoint of the festival circle, enclosed with banners and emblems. Henrik Rung was willing to compose the music for the hymn to the Constitution, but two of our best writers refused—for fear of unpleasant consequences—to write the text, which at length found a brave author in Rector H. Visby. The most difficult thing for us was to induce our patriots to speak for the Constitution and our fatherland: one after another declined, and if Pastor F. Hammerich and Instructeur Nielsen had not taken pity on the subjects mentioned, we ourselves would have had to do our humble best to furnish what was required.

In a remarkably short time, by the extraordinary energy of the architect O. Petersen, the column was raised and the festival circle tastefully decorated. The pillar, whose core was composed of the tallest and stoutest beam that was to be found in the Copenhagen lumberyards, rose 25 ells above the ground; and its base, which also served as singing and speaking platform, bore on its four sides tablets with the mottoes of Valdemar II, Christian IV, Frederik V, and Frederik VII. ("Med Lov skal man Land bygge," "Regnum firmat Pietas," "Prudentia et Constantia," and "Folkets Kjærlighed min Styrke").‡ Dannebrogs waved from atop the pillars and the King's bust on the terrace of the Castle dominated the whole.

While this arrangement was completed under Christensen's and my supervision, Jacobsen had summoned the various craft and trade guilds; and J. A. Hansen, in whom we had, with a certain fear, expected a bitter opponent to all our proposals but who to the contrary appeared the most pleasant and most agreeable colleague, was, in consideration of his presumed insight into financial affairs, entrusted with the administration of the sale of tickets and of our money matters as a whole.

Naturally the musical element could in no way be dispensed with, and besides, the Constitution hymn required a considerable orchestral accompaniment, but here we stumbled upon unforeseen hindrances because the Guards band as well as those of the Brigade and the individual battalions were strictly forbidden to participate. It is even said that by orders from above, the instruments were handed over and kept in the barracks depots! By good fortune, I cleverly managed to secure in time General Bruhn's permission to use the bands of the Civil Militia and the Volunteers, and these now performed under Rung's indefatigable direction.

The fifth of June, Whitmonday, arrived with clear skies and rather high winds, which, however, calmed down toward evening; consequently we had favorable weather conditions. All sorts of rumors were flying about concerning the consigning of troops to the barracks, the dragoons' saddled horses ready to charge against the revolutionary crowd, and orders forbidding any soldier to

‡ These four mottoes may be translated as follows:
"With law shall the land be built"; "Piety cements the rule"; "Prudence and constancy"; "My strength is the people's love."

attend the festival. The display of force, however, was reduced to only a score of policemen, who had their observation post in the topmost floor of the hunting lodge and were furnished with the necessary provisions and refreshments.

Patriots, curiosity- and pleasure-seekers of both sexes and all ages flocked to the place from the suburbs as well as the capital. The plain was filled with a surging crowd of people, but since it was a holiday it was strictly forbidden to commence any festivity before the clock struck four. The guild members had therefore gone out to Dyrehave singly and had camped in the woodlands that surrounded the Hermitage. But when the clock struck four, as if by a stroke of magic the entire body of people arose and, like a medieval procession, marched with drums beating and banners flying up toward the festival site, where it took up its stand nearest to the column.

Our honorable chairman opened the series of speeches with a cheer for the King, "the giver of the Constitution, the friend of Freedom and the people." Thereupon, Rung and Visby's solemn anthem was played. F. Hammerich now ascended the rostrum and in an inspired address emphasized the significance of the Constitution, likening its development to a child who has grown up and gotten all its teeth. In a voice whose ringing power caused the woods to echo, Nielsen spoke of our Danish homeland and vividly described its beauty in images that glowed with enthusiasm. Rimestad concluded with a warm and heartfelt appeal to the Danish people. All these speeches, which were not seasoned with any wormwood but bore the sincere stamp of loyalty, were received by the tightly packed crowd of listeners with thunderous applause. The oppressive atmosphere had vanished, and while one band assembled the choral societies for patriotic singing, those groups who wished to dance crowded around the other, which played Lumbye *gallopades* and *polkas*. The canteen-keeper's tent had plenty of custom, and peaceful gaiety everywhere prevailed.

Nevertheless, several things were lacking in the festivity, both during the day and in the evening; for the flag-decked ships that an especially liberal plutocrat had promised us as a decoration in full view on the Sound, and which were also to fire a salute, completely failed to appear; furthermore, the fireworks could not be set off for fear of disturbing Dyrehave's game animals!

On the whole, we could rejoice over the successful results; for while at Tivoli people amused themselves by spreading rumors of revolt, dragoon charges, and wagonloads of wounded, here everything went off with the greatest orderliness and the police never came into view. The only thing that did not come up to expectations was the sale of tickets to the Festival Circle, for while it was filled with a crowd of people that was estimated at nearly forty thousand, hardly three thousand tickets at *one Mark apiece* had been sold! Therefore we were threatened with a considerable deficit, and how the expenses were later met I did not learn, for a few days after the Festival I had to leave for Vienna, whither I was called to stage a number of my ballets.

I received the most flattering compliments on my assistance at this difficult Constitutional Festival, and even the thanks of certain authorities for the direction I had given a demonstration that was not peaceful in its origin. Surely they did not have to fear a riot, but a scandal could have been harmful enough. However, my noble Chief, Overhofmarskal Levetzau, advised me not to boast of this success in Vienna, but on the contrary to state my position on the constitutional affair to the Austrian minister before my departure. I followed his suggestion, and the particularly courteous Count Hartig seemed to understand me completely. But the rumor of the Freedom Festival, directed in part by me, nonetheless found its way into the German newspapers, and I needed a testimony from Baron Langenau—so kindly disposed toward the Danes—former Austrian ambassador in Copenhagen and then chief of the gendarmerie, in order not to be considered a demagogue, although I everywhere presented myself as a political nonentity and *maître des plaisirs* at the much-talked-about Festival.

III

End-Word

WITH this period picture, I conclude the present section of the third volume of *My Theatre Life,* and cherish the hope that if my book is regarded not as a *novelle* with a continuous plot, but only as a truthful description of the evolution and conclusion of an artistic career, it will not lack psychological but, perhaps, have even a certain historical interest.

The next, and presumably last section, which shall complete the third volume of *My Theatre Life,* will when it is one day published contain: TRAVEL MEMOIRS, REFLECTIONS, and BIOGRAPHICAL SKETCHES.

AUGUST BOURNONVILLE.

Fredensborg, August 3, 1877.

PART THREE

*Travel Memoirs, Reflections,
and Biographical Sketches*

I

Travel Memoirs

FOREWORD

IN glancing through these notes, which cover a long series of oft-repeated visits to foreign countries, I find myself ashamed of being so little acquainted with the most interesting regions of my own native land. Yet how often have I resolved to take a trip to Jutland and a little detour to Bornholm, to admire the natural wonders of these places which I have heard and read so much about, but which, like Møns Klint,* no description—and scarcely the finest painting—can reproduce. I have only recently visited the latter, and confess that it not only appears unique of its kind but bears comparison with the most enchanting coasts of southern Italy.

I must acknowledge the truth of our excellent Holberg's words when, in his three epistles dealing with his travels abroad, he reproaches his contemporaries for their indifference to the curiosities which their homeland offers. But just as he undertook his journeys partly in order to learn and partly in order to see his works reproduced in foreign lands, and for that reason was not a landscape but a genre and historical painter, it may also serve my humble self as a consolation and an excuse that the métier in which I was called to work did not lead me to Jutland or Bornholm. But now, when I have ceased to compose ballets, which alternately fall into one of the above-mentioned categories of pictures, the landscape must attract me with greater force, and if my advanced age does not forbid me such excursions, I hope to make up for what I have hitherto neglected.

After having led my readers through several of my study trips in the first and second parts of *My Theatre Life*, and having attempted to reproduce in my ballets a variety of pictures from reality as well as from fantasy, there now appear (since I have exchanged the stage for rural retirement) a host of episodes, personalities, and character traits which are all more or less connected with my artistic development and which, as they complete the description of my theatre life, might possibly interest not only theatre and ballet lovers but every perceptive observer of art and of the times.

BERLIN (1836)

THE success which attended my first balletic attempts in a larger and broader genre evoked a laudatory response in a number of German papers. These re-

---

*Denmark's seaside chalk cliffs.

ports came from travelers who with great delight had attended the performance of *Faust* and *Valdemar*. This caused me to contemplate the possibility
of using our summer holiday to reproduce my compositions on the larger
stages of the Continent, an undertaking that was zealously prompted by my
friends here at home. Since I was already known in Berlin, where ballet as a
scenic branch of art enjoyed universal favor and was especially patronized by
King Frederick William III, I considered it fitting to begin with this city; and
I cherished the hope of finding in my honorable colleagues, Balletmaster
Hoguet and soloist Paul Taglioni, vigorous support for my enterprise.

I was kindly and hospitably received by my fellow-artists as well as by
Chief Intendant Herr von Redern. But experience had not yet taught me that
once a terrain has been settled, occupation by a foreigner is reluctantly tolerated, be it for ever so short a time. They would have been delighted to see
me appear as dancer and actor in the ballets that were currently in their repertoire, but they would hardly make room for my original compositions without the liveliest opposition. Besides, I saw only too clearly that my whole poetic and choreographic direction was not in accordance with the Berlin
audience's ideas of mimed representations. At this time they were presenting
Hoguet's most recent composition *Der Polterabend*. This was a sort of adaptation of Scribe's *Le plus heureux Jour de ma Vie*, where, on the eve of the wedding, a number of festivities take place in the bride's house with tableaux,
dancing, and surprises of various kinds, the whole thing blended with domestic scenes and interrupted by a conflagration which brings the fire brigade
rushing to the spot to sprinkle the bridegroom, a poor fish, who in his Sunday
best becomes wet as a drowned rat!

This ballet, despite the richest variety, lacked both plot and meaning. But
it was the favorite spectacle of the moment and the old King's evening
delight, which he never neglected. Consequently, for the present and perhaps
for the future, there was nothing for me to do here, and I therefore contented
myself with enjoying Berlin *en amateur*. I saw the city's curiosities, visited
Potsdam, and attended a number of performances at the Opera as well as the
Playhouse. On the former stage, Henrietta Sontag (now Countess Rossi)
guested with great bravura as Desdemona in Rossini's *Othello*, and it was
with real delight that I saw Charlotte von Hagn, as talented as she was pretty,
in the comedy *Der Ball zu Ellerbrunnen*.

For the rest, I passed a couple of unusually pleasant weeks here and was
not at all affected by the tedium which this large, magnificent city cannot
shake off despite, or perhaps because of, its barracks and its military reviews.
I delighted in attending the latter because of the excellent regimental bands,
and had not the faintest suspicion of the bitterness which was one day to fill
my soul at the injustice Prussia has inflicted upon Denmark.

Although I had apparently failed to achieve the goal to which I had aspired, I derived one not unimportant benefit from this whirlwind tour. This
was my encounter with a troupe of French players who were engaged by

Royal patronage and performed under the direction of M. Delcour at the Schauspielhaus, alternating with the German drama. In the previous year there had been question of a guest appearance in Copenhagen, but nothing had come of it. Now the suggestion was renewed, especially since I could carry back information and a sure eyewitness account of the company's excellent composition and superb *ensemble*. I succeeded in bringing the matter to a conclusion that was as favorable for Delcour as it was delightful to that part of the Copenhagen public which was knowledgeable in French. It was also most useful for our own dramatic personnel, who received a strong incentive to imitate this masterly teamwork.

The Royal Theatre was given over to French comedy from the eleventh to the thirty-first of August, 1836. And since people had still not tired of this rare enjoyment, they played several more times at the Vesterbro Theatre. Delcour, Francisque-Lallement, together with Mmes. Brice, Deschanel, and Lancestre, are mentioned with merited praise in Overskou's *Danske Skeuplads;* but Messrs. Isidore, Marius, and Kime and the graceful Mlle. Edelin are also worthy of note, although they were not so outstanding as the former *premiers sujets.*

Two years later this same troupe appeared again, augmented by an outstanding leading man, M. Pechena, who became the ladies' darling and contributed greatly to the ever increasing applause. Unfortunately, I was unable to attend these last performances, for I was just then preparing to leave on an excursion.

LONDON AND PARIS (1838)

AN Imperial visit (namely, that of Russia's present autocrat, the Grand Duke Alexander,* then Heir Apparent, who on his first trip abroad was a guest in Copenhagen where he was festively received by Frederik VI and his Court) set the entire capital and its closest environs astir. A grand military review, with a considerably reinforced band, was held on the Slotsplads, and the gala performance which was prepared at the Royal Theatre kept the personnel busy during part of the summer holiday. The ballet *Valdemar* seemed to please the exalted guest, who had a diamond ring sent to me accompanied by a most flattering note. A brilliant Court ball was likewise promised but had to be canceled because the Grand Duke was taken ill. This kept him in Copenhagen longer than had been intended and interfered with so many well-laid plans.

The Theatre personnel, however, were given leave to disperse, and I used this opportunity to attend Queen Victoria's coronation ceremonies in London. Unfortunately, I arrived a couple of days too late and enjoyed only the echo of all the festivities which had embellished the magnificent ceremony, whose splendor is said to have surpassed all description. But oddly

*Tsar Alexander II, who ruled 1855–1881.

enough the hero of the day was the French Ambassador, the old Duke of Dalmatia, Maréchal Soult! In the beginning, when there was talk of his mission, people had almost found it offensive of King Louis Philippe to let himself be represented by this famous general, who had fought against the English auxiliaries in Spain and inflicted a defeat on Wellington at Toulouse.† But *The Times*, London's political oracle, approached the issue from the noblest side and pointed out to the public how lovely it would be to see two aged heroes like Soult and the Victor of Waterloo shaking hands as a symbol of the heartfelt understanding (*entente cordiale*) which now bound Great Britain and France to each other.

People were not slow in grasping this interpretation, and the enormous crowds who thronged the road from St. James's Palace to Westminster Abbey saluted with thunderous cries of "Marshal Soult forever!," calling out to him "How do you do?" and almost neglecting the official cheer for the crowned "Maiden Queen" who had in her retinue not only Great Britain's and the Continent's most distinguished magnates, but also a selection of young princes from among whom she could choose a consort. Our handsome Prince Christian of Glücksburg too was on the list, and might have become another Prince George to a new Queen Anne, but Providence, whose decisions still lay veiled in a fateful future, had chosen him to one day adorn Denmark's throne, and his mild and humane nature was, I dare say, better suited to our ways and customs than to rigid British Court etiquette. I received proof of this in London itself when, in his joy at meeting his dancing teacher, he took me into his carriage and drove me to his hotel to the great astonishment (aye, almost the scandalization) of his aristocratic cavaliers.

I visited my old friends from my former stay, and did not neglect the house in Great Pultney Street where I had gone through a school which, hard as it was, had given me a useful experience. Mr. Court now lived alone, abandoned by his wife who had accompanied Miss Louisa out into the theatre world on the great Continent.

On the stage where I had danced ten years earlier I now encountered the two rivals, Marie Taglioni and Fanny Elssler. The former had just finished her engagement and was replaced by the latter, who captivated her public with a piquant bagatelle, *La Cachucha*, which she infused with a charm whose characteristics I have sought to describe in *My Theatre Life*, Part I.‡

The Italian Opera was just then in its fullest bloom: Rubini, Lablache, Tamburini, and Mmes. Grisi, Persiani, and Albertazzi performed, respectively, Don Octavio, Leporello, and Don Giovanni; Donna Anna, Zerlina, and Elvira in Mozart's immortal masterwork which pleased the audience to such a

---

† Bournonville reveals his French sympathies by according Soult the victory at Toulouse. After having been attacked by Wellington's forces on April 10, 1814, Soult evacuated Toulouse on April 12 and retreated. All the same the French were later inclined to claim a victory because of the smaller number of casualities they sustained.

‡ See Vol. I, p. 49.

degree that no less than eleven numbers were "encored," i.e., demanded *da capo* — which even included the reawakening of the dead Commandant, who had to get up and sing again his dying part in the *terzetta* of the first scene of Act I. *La Prova d'un Opera seria* gave the ingenious Lablache the occasion to display his comic spirit and divert John Bull with some outbursts in broken English in the midst of the Italian recitatives. I also got to see a bit of ballet. But whether it was the weakness of the composition, or because I fancied my approach to be the only correct one, suffice it to say that my expectations were far from satisfied, and I was involuntarily seized with the fear that I would resemble actors and singers (both ladies and gentlemen) who return from their foreign travels firmly convinced that performances at home are far superior to those abroad, especially when given by themselves!

On a pleasure trip to Richmond, which is charmingly situated on the Thames, I witnessed the singular spectacle of a lay preacher, who from the opposite shore of the river delivered a sermon to Sunday guests assembled in the tea gardens and to the merry passengers on the pleasure boats. As has been said, he was one of the latter-day saints, who, with a stentorian voice that echoed from the old oak trees in the park, raged against the pleasure-seeking of the present day — which, God knows, is modest enough in England, since music, drama, and every public exhibition are strictly forbidden on Sundays and holy days. Some merry young chaps began to parody him, but now he really tasted blood and accompanied his shouts with gestures and kicks as if he would give a portrait of the Devil in his own person. It was almost a scene like that delivered by the Capuchin in *Wallenstein's Camp*.

Railroads were now to be found throughout England, the elegant stage-coaches with their stately horses and coachmen had disappeared, and one proceeded with furious speed from London to the various port cities, Dover, Brighton, and Folkestone. Nevertheless, competition between Channel steamers was so great at this time that for an extremely cheap price, one could not only come the shortest way across the Channel, but directly from London to Boulogne. Two stock companies continued to underbid each other until free passage was offered; but when one company gave lunch into the bargain, the other was forced to declare itself defeated and bankrupt.

Now the normal rates were once more in effect, and thus I traveled to Boulogne and from thence to Paris, where I planned to meet with my pupil and ward, Ferdinand Hoppe, for whom I had secured a little travel stipend and a leave of absence for a year and a half, which he had used for a temporary engagement at the Vienna Opera and to appear in Paris, without any binding obligations however. At the same time, Lucile Grahn made her debut in a graceful *pas de deux* and won much applause. For a few months she had enjoyed the guidance of the skillful teacher Barrez, who advertised her as his pupil, and it is with a queer feeling that I have since seen her identified in *Nordisk Conversations Lexicon* as being a product of Larcher's school, even though it is well known that from her tenth to her eighteenth year she enjoyed my careful teaching, and under my special direction performed her most outstanding roles at Copenhagen's Royal Theatre.

I was once again charged with being cicerone for *Instructeur* Nielsen, who was this time accompanied by his spirited wife, our unforgettable Anna Nielsen! Together we visited everything worth seeing both in and outside of Paris, but lingered most at the Théâtre Français, where Mlle. Mars, although already advanced in years, played Louise de Lignerolle and Célimène in Molière's *Misanthrope* with perfect mastery, which was fully acknowledged by our Danish *artiste*. Still, we did not neglect the minor theatres, where Nielsen and I almost caused a scandal by our irrepressible laughter at the matchless comedy with which the *vaudeville Moustache* (after Paul de Kock) was performed.

My dear countrymen were delighted over everything that their short stay had offered. But the situation was completely different with Sweden's greatest dramatic celebrity, Lars Hjortsberg. He came to Paris for the first time in his old age, and, as a veteran from the days of Gustav III, he found Frenchmen, Parisian life, and the theatre itself to be far below the ideal picture he had formed of France's widely known capital. His basically prosaic son, who had recently married the young actress Mlle. Westerdahl (an aspiring talent with innate gifts but without much formal training), fully shared the old man's opinions; and since all three were agreed in finding Paris tiresome, they spent most of their stay in their hotel rooms, playing *vira* [a card game] to while away the time.

The description I had given my countrymen of London and its glories induced them to venture a flying visit across the Channel, and I once again had to be their guide since none of them knew English. Therefore Nielsen, his wife, and Hoppe followed me to Boulogne and up the Thames, which could not but astound them with its swarm of ships, its enormous shipyards, and crowded steam vessels which with resounding cheers sailed past us by the score to land at Greenwich near the elegant tea gardens. We arrived in London only late in the evening, and since it was a rather long way to my old hotel in Leicester Square, en route I heard Nielsen repeatedly exclaim: "O, immortal London!"

Our stay lasted only a few days, which we industriously spent in seeing St. Paul's Cathedral, with the monuments to Nelson and many other famous warriors, and venerable Westminster Abbey from the time of Edward the Confessor, which was still adorned with the coronation decorations. But here we found ourselves especially pleased by Shakespeare's, Garrick's, and Mrs. Siddons' sepulchral monuments, which were all the more precious to us theatre folk, as they bore witness to the honor and esteem which the dramatic art has maintained in free England.

The major theatres had vacation in summertime, but we nevertheless had the opportunity to attend a concert which was given for a charitable purpose at the Drury Lane, where Rubini delighted us with his wonderful voice. But what made this evening especially illustrious was the entrance into a box by Wellington and Soult! They were immediately perceived and the entire audience rose, those in the stalls standing on their seats. Kerchiefs of all colors were waved and thousands of voices, accompanied by the orchestra's fanfares, joyously greeted the heroes with "Honour, Honour to the Braves!"

The historically remarkable Tower was likewise visited, and left behind mixed impressions: The Prisoners' Towers, with memories of political victims who were led to their deaths on the scaffold through the arched gateway (The Traitor's Gate)! The Crown Jewels, which twinkled like stars through the repository protected with iron latticework and, finally, the splendid Armory, where not only valuable collections of old and new weapons were symmetrically placed, but numerous victory trophies from land as well as sea battles were theatrically grouped—among others, one in memory of the Battle of Copenhagen in 1801. But here we discovered a curious thing: two six-pound bronze cannon which bore the date 1806 (consequently stemming from a campaign which the British—out of an easily understandable modesty—would prefer to have the rest of the world forget), were also included in the pyramid!* Nielsen forced me to call this ridiculous anachronism to the attention of the guard, who was dressed in the costume of a medieval halberdier; and, shrugging his shoulders, the man replied: "You will find several mistakes of that kind."

The trip now turned homeward via Hamburg, where I met with the sorrowful news that whooping cough had carried off my infant son, Theodor, and as happily as I had set out from home, as sadly I now returned.

STOCKHOLM

I have discussed my three years as Intendant for the Swedish stage at length in the second part of *My Theatre Life.* But abandoning for a moment descriptions of a scenic nature, I shall venture to give a brief sketch of the various impressions with which Sweden's old capital has left me, both as a Dane and as a worshiper of the beautiful and the memorable.

From time immemorial there has prevailed between Swedes and Danes a rivalry which has now, thanks to the spirit of the times and the evidence of common interests, been transformed into a noble contest. People have often tried to make comparisons between Stockholm and Copenhagen. But, apart from the partiality that every race has for its native land, one is confronted by the same dilemma as if one were to compare a brunette with a blonde, two beauties of highly different appearance. For the charm that Copenhagen possesses in her more regular streets and larger public squares is compensated for in Stockholm by its picturesque situation and its abundance of water, which separates the most important parts of the city. The expansion which

---

*This ironic statement seems to refer to the unprovoked British assault on Copenhagen in 1807; cf. footnote, Vol. II, p. 163.

Copenhagen has received in recent years by the destruction of the ramparts has deprived us of the few heights from whence one could enjoy a distant view; whereas Stockholm, in a number of spots, affords enchanting prospects such as few European cities are capable of offering.

It is true there is not to be found a museum of the same sort as Thorvaldsen's, nor such precious collections as those contained in the Prince's Palace and lovely Rosenborg; but in return, Stockholm has an Academy for Swedish Language and Literature and a second Academy for the art of music in its entirety. In addition, its National Museum contains invaluable treasures of art as well as historical relics.

Copenhagen has an unmistakable advantage in the presence of a University, which unconsciously affects the rest of the population by its Attic salt, without the students forming a predominant group, as is the case at Uppsala and Lund. Although the military class is numerously represented in Stockholm, one misses the stimulating element of the navy, which has its seat in Karlskrona. But as a substitute for the fleet of warships they have an enormous number of larger and smaller steamships that pass one another in every direction and produce at sea a kind of bustle like that which we find in the streets of Copenhagen. On the whole, the Stockholmers are not industrious walkers; for oddly enough, though Sweden is not lacking in granite, the streets are mostly paved with small pebbles which are a real torture for pedestrians. A trip to nearby Djurgården is therefore most frequently undertaken by water. This delightful oak forest, praised in song by the unique Bellman, offers an inevitable contrast to our Dyrehave. And indeed, one is uncertain as to which of them to give the prize; for while we Danes emphasize our leafy beech woods, our blooming hawthorn, and the numerous herds of hart stag and roe deer, the Swedes point out the fjords and creeks that cut in among the wood-clad hills and every moment provide a lively prospect of the ships sailing by.

At a crossroads, in the midst of a circle of the most varied kinds of trees, stands a granite base with the bust of Bellman cast in bronze after Byström's model; unfortunately, more like a half-drunken faun with a garland of vine leaves about his head than the singer of ironic songs in praise of Bacchus and the enthusiastic worshiper of beautiful nature. On an appointed summer day, from the splendid restaurant at Hasselbacken, where a centuries-old oak tree bears Bellman's name, a procession of merry members of a fraternal order strolls to this place of pilgrimage to pay homage to the poet's memory with banners whose emblems in no way correspond to our conception of the spirit that pervades the singular tones of those dithyrambs.

This festival, like so many others, is celebrated with grand libations; for it must be granted our Nordic brethren that every single one of them can tolerate a larger quantity of drink than three of our countrymen put together. In this connection it has struck me more than once when people complain that Sweden is a lean and poverty-stricken country unable to reward art according to its deserts, especially so far as the theatre is concerned, that if they were to reduce the yearly consumption of arrack, wine, and the customary *Svenske Sup* to one-half of the usual abundance, without causing undue privation a handsome allowance could be granted to the theatre and the other liberal arts and an armored ship built every other year from the accumulated capital. If one adds to this the numberless opportunities that are sought and furnished for parties and large banquets, it is plain to see that in such areas Sweden displays a luxury which is not to be found in any other country.

Stockholm and its closest environs contain historical memories of great importance, some of them even belonging to the darkest drama. When one steps ashore at Riddarholms Brygga, one immediately perceives a colossal edifice without any architectural character. This is *Kungshuset,* where nowadays the colleges of government have their seat, but where Charles XII resided after the burning of the old *Trekrona Slott* from whose tower Sten Sture's heroic widow Christina Gyllenstjerna defied the advancing Danes, and from whose burning stairs the body of Charles XI was carried down from his *"lit de parade"!*

At Riddarholmenstorg a statue of Birger Jarl, the founder of Stockholm, stands opposite the church which in his time belonged to the Gray Friars' cloister but which later became the shrine of the Royal graves. Here were laid the earthly remains of the great Gustavus Adolphus and the knightly Charles XII, both fallen in battle, and with the suspicion of assassination—highly unwarranted, I dare say, for only a few years ago Charles' skull was discovered and they found that the bullet which had pierced it was of a caliber that only a rampart gun and not a pistol could have fired. Here the hand of Fate was present rather than that of a traitor. It was a different matter with Gustav III, who had also heard the whistle of bullets on both land and sea, but was to fall before a fanatic assassin's blow amidst a crowd of merrymakers.

Several other famous heroic kings of the Vasa family rest here in their marble sarcophagi, and beneath the arches hang hundreds of embroidered banners and standards whose colors and emblems have been blanched and dimmed by time, but which bear witness to a brilliant martial history, rich in great exploits. Only a few years ago there stood between each of the pillars of the church a steel-clad equestrian statue with armor which was said to have once belonged to several of Sweden's kings, among them the Danish monarchs of the Kalmar Union, Christian I, Johan I, Christjern II! The most priceless of these harnesses was that of Charles IX, artfully executed by Benvenuto Cellini. These curiosities are now housed in the National Museum.

Across Munkebron, the road leads into the real city, the old Stockholm, where the eye first meets the goodly Riddarhuset, in front of which the excellent statute of Sweden's liberator Gustavus Vasa appears in an awe-inspiring attitude (a glorious composition by the French sculptor Larchevêsque, who was summoned to the North at the same time as Sally and Falconet). One now wanders through small and crooked streets, past long dark and dank alleys, and arrives at Stortorget, a comparatively small square, from whose Town Hall balcony a Danish king once ordered the Stockholm Bloodbath— which, in spite of equally numerous executions under the sons of Vasa, has never been forgotten by the inhabitants of Stockholm. Down to the tiniest child, they could show us the gutters from which the blood flowed down into the streets lying below.

We shall turn our eyes away from this nook of terror and proceed to the nearby Storkyrka, a magnificent house of worship, whose choir has been entirely cut off in order to make room for the present Palace, which disturbs the religious harmony to a considerable degree. Here are to be found several large paintings by the German artist Klöcker, who was honored by Charles XI with the name of Ehrenstrahl, and who has given us near the altar a representation of the Last Judgment, where the eye is involuntarily dazzled by a host of extraordinarily voluptuous female creatures who turn backward somersaults down into the fire and brimstone of Hell! Directly beneath the vaulting of the church hang (hardly to the edification of sensitive Norwegians) the helmet and spurs of their patron, St. Olaf—a relic of the great spoils from Trondheim Cathedral!

We now approach the Palace, which in size is inferior to our Christiansborg, but which carries off the prize as far as style and situation are concerned. From the imposing drive, the so-called Lejonbacke (where, according to legend, one lion is supposed to have lost its iron cannonball at the very moment Charles XII was killed before Frederiksteen), one overlooks the northern part of the city. This quarter, the newest and most elegant, is traversed in its whole length by Dronning and Regerings Gatorna, and is built upon the southern slope of Brunkebjerg, whose ominous name is linked to the bloody memories of a younger generation and which conjures up for us Danes memories of the battle where Christian I, after displaying the greatest personal valor, was forced to retreat before Sten Sture's victorious host. Not far from the spot where the battle raged, there now stand the noble Gustavus Adolphus' equestrian statue and the Opera House which the art-loving Gustav III consecrated to the Fatherland's Muses, *Patriis Musis*. But farther to the right, where shady allées surround the statues of Charles XII and Charles XIII with Molin's splendid fountain in their midst, there was, in olden days, a deep and open waterway that separated the hill from Blasieholmen, situated directly opposite to it. Here seven hundred Danish cavalrymen met death in the waves when the bridge, whose wooden supports had been sawn in half, gave way beneath the thundering of their horses' hooves. This chasm is now filled in and presents a pleasant promenade past the lovely Museum, across the new railway bridge out to Skeppsholmen, whence one has on the right a prospect of the busy Norrbro, beneath whose arches the waters of Lake Mälaren plunge with tearing speed into the Saltsjö that forms Stockholm's harbor. This magnificent bridge rests in the middle of the little island of Helgeandsholm, on whose outermost point, in the so-called Strömparterre, music and the clinking of glasses resound from tables occupied by the pleasure-loving public; while on the opposite side of the bridge the Royal Stables give echo of horses' neighing on the very ground where King Birger's and Merete's son, the young Prince Magnus, had to die under the headsman's axe! Directly in front of the spectator extends the harbor quay, with Logårdstrappan leading up to the Palace and the steep hill whereon stands the obelisk which Stockholm's citizenry erected in honor of Gustav III, whose statue, in an attitude imitating that of the Apollo Belvedere, stands further down at the seaside. Here a vigorous commercial life is in motion, and this whole stretch undeniably belongs to the loveliest and liveliest part of the city. To the left, the *södra* or southern city rises in the form of an amphitheatre, crowned by the dome of the *Katarinakyrka*. On the site whereon it is built the bodies of the numberless victims of the Stockholm Bloodbath were burnt.

From this tragic scene it is but a few steps to one of the most wonderful panoramas any city in the world can offer: the view from the widely known Mosebacke! Here the spirit thrills and one might even sink into a poetic—not to say "divine"—ecstasy if the bustling waiters along with the clinking of cups, glasses, and the sound of bottles being uncorked did not remind one that this enchanting spot was farmed out as a barroom. Thus the most beautiful illusion is often disturbed by prosy reality, and it cannot be denied that the life of Stockholm as well as the Swedish national character produce a number of sharp contrasts. But however that may be, one must admit that Stockholm is an especially *"trevlig"* [pleasant] city, and if the words of the ballad can truthfully be applied to the Swedes:

> This people is good to its core,
> And if you go toward them, they'll come to you,
> And then you win more than halfway.

MY ARTISTIC TRAVELS IN SWEDEN

THE reputation which the Danish Ballet School had been fortunate enough to acquire abroad gave the management of the Royal Theatre in Stockholm the idea of sending me time and again some of its finest pupils for further training.

First in the series was the young Johansson, who after one year of diligent study had progressed so far that he successfully made his debut on our stage and, provided with a small repertoire, returned to Stockholm where he immediately acquired a prominent place as soloist. The hospitable reception he had enjoyed in Copenhagen, and the friendship he had consolidated with his Danish artistic colleagues, made him desirous of working with them at Stockholm's Theatre. He therefore invited my best pupils, Ferdinand Hoppe, Caroline Fjeldsted, and Augusta Nielsen, to come up there in order to give a series of performances, under my direction, at the Opera Theatre. We took our chances and accepted his invitation without any official offer at all. He declared that we should be received with open arms, nor did he fail to keep his word.

In the last days of May 1839 we sailed for Stockholm (the young ladies accompanied by my wife). We traveled by way of Göteborg, my mother's birthplace, which I regarded with special interest; and here, in a most amiable family circle, I discovered a wonderfully beautiful soprano, who, at my urging, was sent to Paris to be trained under the famous singing teacher García and later won a certain degree of celebrity, especially as a concert singer. This young lady was named Henriette Nissen!

From thence the journey proceeded in the most agreeable company to the Göta Canal, past the Trollhättan, and through the great lakes until, after sailing for four days among the most picturesque regions, we reached the imposing entrance from Lake Mälaren to Stockholm. We stepped ashore at Riddarholmen, where Johansson, surrounded by friendly comrades, met us and led us to our previously reserved lodgings. Only an hour after arrival, I was presented to the triumvirate of the Opera—Colonel Backman, Krigsraad Forsberg, and Secretary Schyberg—and an agreement was concluded on honorable terms. To great applause, we gave several *divertissements*, fragments from *The Tyroleans*, *La Sylphide*, and *The Isle of Fantasy*, and all of *The Sleepwalker*. But the climax in this series of performances was the "Fanny Elssler *Cachucha*" in which Mlle. Fjeldsted harvested curtain calls, flowers, and a number of romantic verses.

In addition to the satisfaction we derived from our onstage achievements, offstage we encountered a kindness and cordial hospitality which, as everyone knows, are characteristic of the Swedes. Instead of paying one's respects to the journalists as in other countries, the editor and owner of *Aftonbladet*, Lars Hjerta, greeted us personally and not only sang our praises in his reviews but brought us into his family circle, where my wife and I cemented a friendship which, founded upon heartfelt sympathy, has continued to this day.

A few words of recommendation from my noble patron, Adam Oehlenschläger, to the poet Baron Beskow procured us the acquaintance of this distinguished man, and through him a most interesting visit with the sculptor Byström. This fine artist lived in Stockholm in true Roman fashion and had built himself a marble villa with a breathtaking view on one of the heights at Djurgården. Because of our activity and numerous invitations, we got to see very little of Stockholm's curiosities. But my wife heard a sermon by the great hymn writer Archbishop Wallin—one of his very last, I dare say, for at that time he was already suffering from his fatal illness. I, on the other hand, had the honor of meeting several times with the famous singer of Frithiof, Esaias Tegnér, but to little edification, unfortunately, since His Reverence carried on in extremely dissolute phrases and had apparently had a bit too much to drink. His Excellency, old Count Jakob Pontusson Delagardie, who had known my father from the happy Gustavian days, showed us most flattering attention and invited us to visit him at his estate in Skåne.

The Royal Family, including the Crown Princess Josephine's sister, the Empress of Brazil, were frequent guests at the Theatre, but King Carl Johan was not to be lured thither. He had recently returned from Norway in a rather bad humor, and, grieving over the poor appreciation he believed to exist in the Swedish nation, it sometimes happened that when he approached the balcony window which faced the northern part of the city, he stretched out his clasped hands and cried out in a tormented voice: *"Les ingrats!"*

Our ballet performances, which were as usual accompanied by a spoken drama, alternated every other evening with the opera *Robert of Normandy*, which was at that time a novelty in Stockholm's Theatre. The role of Alice was performed by nineteen-year-old Jenny Lind with an inspiration and an already developed talent which aroused general attention and earned her the public's undivided sympathy. Even then she possessed those qualities which later, enhanced by a greater technique, were to make her world-famous, especially the inexplicable ability to electrify her listeners by the power of her voice and to grasp both feeling and illusion through an extraordinary dramatic perception pervaded by psychic purity. Without suspecting the future celebrity that awaited her, she was at this time a pupil of the skillful singing teacher Berg, with a scanty beginning salary; and, in spite of the reputation which had preceded her to Göteborg, in this wealthy commercial city she was forced to reduce the highest ticket price for her concert from 48 to 32 skillings, since people had agreed to stay away if she insisted on the requested rixdollar!

Among the many proofs of kindness we received in hospitable Stockholm, I must mention first of all the comfortable haven we had in the parsonage of St. Jakob's Church with the Pastor Primarius, Abraham Pettersson, who had known my wife from her earliest days in Landskrona and had given her away at our wedding in the Christiansborg Slotskirke. We were regarded by him and his amiable wife with a warmth and sympathy which shall always remain indelible among my travel memories.

With a farewell as flattering as it was enthusiastic, on the part of the public as well as our friends, we left Stockholm to give some well-attended and well-applauded performances in Göteborg with a talented trio from the dramatic stage (Almlöf, his wife, and the outstanding actress Fru Eriksson).

On the journey from Halland down to Skåne we visited, after repeated requests and friendly invitations, at Delagardie's manor house, the delightful Löberöd, where we enjoyed a pleasant rest after the exertions of our artistic tour. Here as well as at Övedskloster, the home of Baron Ramel and his amiable wife (née Delagardie), the old Swedish aristocracy greeted us in a most urbane manner.

Eight years passed before I once again performed in Stockholm. In the meantime, we had given some performances in Malmö, and there enjoyed the same benevolent reception as in the capital. However, this time I brought with me a Swedish dancer, Mlle. Charlotte Norberg, who, like Johansson before her, had been sent down to Denmark to partake of my instruction and had developed her innate sylphlike lightness to a considerable degree of virtuosity. After having appeared with much applause in several of my compositions, and having rehearsed the role of Céleste in *The Toreador*, that of the Sylphide, and Margaretha in *Faust*, she returned to her native city, accompanied by me and two excellent assistants, our irreplaceable mimes Stramboe, Sr., and Andreas Füssel.

Our undertaking, which was this time based upon an official engagement, was crowned with the most brilliant success. Mlle. Norberg reaped lively applause, and my talented colleagues increased their renown in the roles that were entrusted to their skills. As for myself, I assisted my pupils in all the bravura dances that we performed together, acted my Toreador with the usual effect, and passed for "a thousand devils" as Mephistopheles. But what surpassed anything I have experienced on any stage was my appearance as Bellman in *The Polska at Gröna Lund*. One can hardly imagine the kind of emotion that arose in the Swedish public when I came strolling into "Djurgården" with the lute slung over my shoulder. My resemblance to their favorite poet struck all of them with astonishment, and when I pulled off my coat, and in my shirtsleeves began to strum "Hvila vid denna källa,"[*] there burst forth a storm of applause mingled with tearful bravos. Bellman had come alive before his successors' eyes, and it seemed as if the jubilation would never end. The vivacious Ulla Vinblad soon appeared, represented by the lovely Johanna Gillberg, and was received with cries of joy. Mollberg (Füssel) and Mowitz (Stramboe) were greeted as old familiars, and were followed by the whole company from *Fredman's Epistles*. The *Minuet* and the *Polska* recalled favorite melodies, and "the fray" itself was reminiscent of the motley pictures. But the allegory with Cupid, Bacchus, the Graces, the Revelation of Anacreon, and the gods of Olympus led the audience to a more idealistic view of the great lyricist than that which had prevailed in Sweden for a number of years; and I heard it said that only in Denmark did they fully understand how to interpret Bellman from the truly poetic side.

Some time later, this reversal of their conception of Bellman led to an extreme which aimed at portraying him as an elegist and discovering a deep melancholy in even his lightest dithyrambs! In place of the portrait which shows him in shirtsleeves, playing on his lute, they now brought forth another Bellman, enveloped in a traveling cloak, with his head resting on his hand! A popular writer had described his Muse as "Sorrow clad in rose color," while his contemporaries well knew that his periodic despondency arose only out of momentary financial embarrassment. Suffice it to say that when in 1858 I once again presented the ballet on the Swedish stage and from the younger generation won a lively though less enthusiastic and thunderous applause than I had

---

[*]"Rest by this Stream"—one of Bellman's most popular songs.

from the older one (upon whom I had made so strong an impression), the very critics who eleven years before thought that I had elevated the concept, now alleged that Bellman's memory had been profaned!

For me, Stockholm was the same *"trevlig"* city it had been in 1839, and I found my loyal friends and honorary brothers unchanged. Carl Johan had now gone to his adoptive fathers in the burial vaults of Riddarholms Kyrka, and the art-loving Oscar I, gentle and popular, was now King. The Theatre was under the management of an oustanding director, Baron and General Postal Director Hugo Hamilton, to whom the Fatherland's Muses had given the honor of being one of the first to strongly encourage native dramatic literature. However, the Theatre's finances were on an extremely weak footing, and among other experiments to help these miserable conditions they had hit upon the idea of arranging the salaries of the actors and singers *"på lott"*; that is to say, they were allotted shares in the eventual proceeds rather than fixed salaries! Attendance during the 1846–1847 season had been very poor. The opera had long since lost Jenny Lind, who had been denied the modest salary of 3000 Rbd. banco (6000 francs), and the shares gave only poor prospects of realization, when our dancing reinforcements arrived at the end of the season and brought one full house after another. It was not without a certain bitter feeling that the "stars" in this dramatic and lyrical "partnership" had to acknowledge that this time the ballet had been responsible for the fact that *"Lotterna"* realized not only the normal proceeds, but even a small profit.

They were most anxious to secure a return engagement for the following spring. An agreement was concluded, Mlle. Gillberg was entrusted to my further instruction, and *Napoli* was readied for performance in Stockholm. But just about the time the journey was to take place, there occurred the great events which moved all Danes and made it impossible for me, in this feverish excitement, to abandon my threatened homeland. I immediately wrote Baron Hamilton in order to be released from the obligations I had contracted the previous year. He willingly agreed to this, and, since we were in the habit of corresponding in French, he asked if I might possibly furnish him with a frank circumstantial account of Copenhagen's emotional climate and the Slesvig-Holsten revolt. I recounted my experiences for him as clearly as was possible in this tangled web of political questions, and received the reply that King Oscar had read my report and expressed his praise, saying that he did not receive such dispatches even from his diplomats.

This flattering statement was followed by a series of confidential communications on Hamilton's part, all to the effect that Sweden would consider the crossing of the Eider as a *casus belli* and furnish strong help against any aggression from the German side! What halted this *"élan"* of Royal neighborliness is not easy for lay politicians to discover, but the result limited the promised contribution to the very shabbiest. Now whether Hamilton had gone too far in his zeal or had spoken all too frankly to Oscar, who had been his childhood playmate and schoolfellow, the result was that he submitted his resigna-

tion from both the Theatre and Postal Department and retired to his activity
as owner of an ironworks and a member of the Rigsdag.

After I had once again resumed my duties at the Danish Royal Theatre in
the 1856–1857 season, and by the terms of my contract secured leaves of absence during April and May for a certain number of years, the new Director
of the Swedish Theatre, Herr Hyltén-Cavalius, came to Copenhagen to confer
with me about the establishment of a reading school for the ballet children
similar to that which I had won for our dancing pupils, and at the same time
to engage a soloist who could also serve as a kind of balletmaster. I recommended Sigurd Lund, who immediately received a favorable appointment.
There was, however, the matter of providing a ballet repertoire, and to this
end I was asked to stage several of my lighter compositions. Consequently I
went up there in April, accompanied by my wife and a new Swedish pupil,
Mlle. Jenny Hjorth.

I had but weak forces with which to secure the ballet's admittance to the
Swedish stage, for Mlles. Norberg and Gillberg, upon whom I had been
counting, were now Mmes. Tørner and Sundberg, and both were listed as
"unavailable" for stage duty at this time. Fortunately there was a young
dancer, Mlle. Arrhenius, a lovely talent, and a pair of *secondes danseuses*, who,
together with Herr Lund and a young German, Theodor Marckl (who had for
some time frequented my school in Copenhagen), constituted my main *corps*.
With them I produced *La Sylphide, The Festival in Albano,* and *Conservatoriet* – all of which, oddly enough, came off with a certain *rondeur* and *aplomb*
but survived only a few performances since the audience did not display a
feeling for this type of art and, besides, allowed itself to be influenced by a
somewhat less than benevolent press.

To this was added the fact that my *old friend* Nielsen, who the previous
year had created a furor in Stockholm as a reciter, was this year engaged to
appear in guest roles at Stora Theatern. In return for my having blown the
horn for his eminent talent, he now spread the rumor that the ballet had been
a cancer for the Danish Theatre; and such a testimony, although completely
false, was not without a harmful effect on the outcome of my endeavors. The
fact that the Danish stage had at that time lost several of its strongest pillars,
artists as well as writers, could certainly not be blamed on the ballet. But
the cancer which corroded Nielsen's whole spiritual existence, despite all
the gifts Our Lord had bestowed on him and notwithstanding the universal
recognition and temporal advantages his great talent had procured for him,
was *his jealousy*, which had degenerated into an almost ridiculous passion.
Since he had not given definite promise of his coming, Cavalius had reached
an agreement with another famous guest, namely, the Negro tragedian Ira
Allridge,† who, like a vulgar copy of Edmund Kean, gave Othello and Shylock –

---

† Cf. footnote on Ira F. Aldridge, Vol. II, p. 300.

in English, of course—while his fellow-actors spoke Swedish! But Nielsen, who to be sure had given his lovely Danish tongue a hint of a Scandinavian accent, did not find this black neighborliness fitting, and after a couple of performances of *The Castle in Poitou* broke with the management of the Opera and returned to Mindre Theatern, where he had reaped laurels and profits the previous year. Here the practical Director, Stjernström, gave him abundant opportunity to appear in his finest roles.

The nuptials of Crown Prince Oscar (the present King) and Princess Sophie of Nassau, upon the royal couple's homecoming, furnished the opportunity for a gala, at which an occasional piece by the talented actor and writer Johan Jolin was performed. Since the Rigsdag was sitting at the same time, Cavalius chose this moment to obtain from "the Estates" a more abundant subsidy for the Royal Theatre. He had a ceremonious presentation arrange d for the country's deputies, using all the facilities of the Opera: the *comptoirs*, storehouses, schools, as well as the Library and Musical Archive. In the latter place, the score of an ancient opera, *The Charitable Peasant*, lay tossed aside as if by accident! Struck by the sight, a young member of the Rigsdag from Dalecarlia, who was strong as a horse and not particularly keen on expenditures for aesthetic pleasures, exclaimed: "Well, that's easy to believe!" But when the learned political economists had been conducted to their seats in the stalls and filled the balcony, the curtain rose on a lyrical-dramatic *Apropos* that ended with an allegorical tableau depicting Svea sheltering Muses and Graces, while the four Estates of the realm were represented in the most glorious fashion. It goes without saying that here, as well as at the gala performance, I was assisted by the finest talents, and the zealous Director of the Theatre had the satisfaction of seeing the Rigsdag accept his proposal to double the annual subsidy.

Hyltén-Cavalius (the third to head the theatre since Hamilton's retirement) was a man of noble mind and firm aesthetic principles. He possessed an extensive literary education and was, moreover, Scandinavian in the best sense of the word; for during his administration not only Swedish dramatic products but also a number of the finest Danish plays were performed to great applause and staged with artistic care. Unfortunately, the Stockholm audience demanded such a constant variety that it had to be continually furnished with novelties (often of rather inferior substance) from the German as well as the French repertoire. The opera, on the other hand, remains Stockholm's favorite spectacle, and since in Sweden there is never any lack of beautiful voices, the *musical* portion usually gets its full deserts while the *dramatic* portion is usually treated with indifference.

The ballet, which had in earlier times enjoyed great favor and stood upon a respectable footing at the Swedish Theatre, now had the utmost difficulty in keeping afloat. Cavalius' efforts to regain for it an honorable place among the other scenic branches of art were greeted by both the remaining personnel and a large part of the daily press with a dislike that was aired in the most bitter attacks against his administration as a whole. Nevertheless he still wished to venture several attempts in this area, and therefore reserved for himself my cooperation for the following spring.

My daughter Charlotte, whose irrepressible desire for the art of the stage, combined with a singular musical gift and a harmonious alto voice, seemed to portend a successful and honorable future in the theatrical field, had already decided upon this career. Since I did not feel entitled to oppose such a firm vocation, and also had my reasons for preferring to see her develop her talent abroad, I took her with me to Vienna and later to Milan, where she received her further training under the guidance of the finest masters. In Paris she appeared in a number of public concerts, to great applause; but it was in Stockholm that she first set foot upon the stage in Meyerbeer's *The Prophet,* and by her performance of the important role of Fidès harvested not only thunderous applause but general recognition for her dramatic interpretation and superb rendering of the Swedish language.

She was immediately engaged for the 1857–1858 season and participated in the opera repertoire with several outstanding alto parts. Weber's glorious *Oberon,* arranged after a text adapted from the French, was just about to go into rehearsal, when in April of 1858 I learnt that I was to undertake the arrangement of various dances and groupings in the same opera. At that time I had the pleasure of experiencing with what tragic intensity my daughter represented the tender mother in *The Prophet* and also received proofs of her many-sided talent by her humorous interpretation of the role of the slave Fatima, which singing part was superbly suited to her voice. One will perhaps object that in judgments having taste and sympathy as their object, even the artistically skilled father is incompetent where it concerns his beloved child. I have therefore confined myself to quoting simple facts which cannot be brushed aside and which both deserve and need to be recorded.

Since my activity during this eleven-week season was divided between the instruction of pupils and the rehearsal of ballets, the latter did not progress as quickly as they had in the previous season. But since I once more had my prima donnas Mmes. Tørner and Sundberg at my disposal, the smaller compositions that I had presented were judged to be far better in the public's taste, and *Bellman, La Ventana,* and *The Prophecy of Love* were received with lively approbation. *The Kermesse in Bruges* was fully rehearsed, but since the season was already far advanced, the ballet's performance was postponed until the following season under Sigurd Lund's direction. Since opera performances generally continued well into the month of June, special efforts were necessary to draw the public and it had therefore become the custom to summon foreign guests. This speculation had been successful with our ballet performances, but since these too were in need of lyric variety, the opera obtained reinforcements, usually from Vienna. The outstanding singer Alois Ander had enraptured the Stockholm audience for two summers, and in addition to his own considerable honorarium, earned the box office a handsome profit. But the golden days were gone, for neither the baritone Beck nor

Frau Dustmann-Meyer was able to indemnify the management for the great expenditures these guest appearances entailed. This last lady gave Norma, Donna Anna, and Linda di Chamounix (in which role she was beautifully assisted by my daughter as Pierrotto) with much talent; but the memory of Jenny Lind stood in the way of her success, and both applause and attendance remained meager.

The same native talents that I have mentioned with deserved recognition in the second volume of *My Theatre Life* were already gracing the Swedish stage in 1857–1858. With regard to the spoken drama, Mindre Theatern, under Stjernström's direction, gained control of public opinion, though, I dare say, most unjustly and hardly to the commendation of the prevailing taste, since Overskou's *The Devil's Superior* (adapted into *The Vanquisher of the Evil One*) excited the whole public and enjoyed over a hundred performances in a short time.

A joyous celebration also took place during this springtime, heralded by the thundering of cannon. It was the first-born prince of the marriage concluded the previous year who now entered the world, and whose horoscope seemed to indicate a future king of the united kingdom of Sweden and Norway! Unfortunately, King Oscar I, whom I had seen and known in the fullness of his strength and beauty and with a look of intelligence, was now but a shadow of himself! Lethargic in both mind and body, he sat in the coach like a wax figure beside his consort, who was endowed with every feminine and royal virtue. With gentle pressure she moved his arm and head to return the greeting of his affectionate people, who bared their heads along the entire route to Djurgården, whither May Day called the Stockholmers to greet the approaching spring and "drink to put some marrow in the bones"—a ceremony conscientiously observed by high and low, each in his own way.

We did not, however, wish to leave *"trevlig"* Stockholm without having visited the lively "Leaf Market" at Munktorget in the neighborhood of Riddarholms Kyrka, on Midsummer Day. Here the newly sprouted birch tree plays a principal role, as does the fir tree at Christmas. Large and small Maypoles decorated with leaves, flowers, and gilt gewgaws are bought by the more or less well-to-do and presented to the poor, for every Swedish man and woman must have his door, his courtyard, his horse, his carriage, and his boat adorned with the fresh fronds of rebirth—the green birch boughs! On this day Stockholm resembles a large bower, and from the steamship, whose masts and yards were resplendent with the bounty of the woods, we too waved the green branches in farewell and thanks for all the kindness, friendship, and hospitality.

To those memories which my repeated visits in Stockholm's capital have left me, I think I ought to add some features that I have not touched upon in the account of my "Three Years in Stockholm" (from October 1861 to June 1864) and which will perhaps be of some interest to my good readers.

As Intendant for the stage, I had a concurrent influence upon the acceptance of pieces and the casting of roles, while the actual theatre censorship was carried on by the Director, Baron v. Stedingk, and Hofintendant Hwasser. On the other hand, as far as the judgment of the composition itself and especially the practical staging aspects of the *mise-en-scène* were concerned, my voice carried no small weight. With regard to original Swedish pieces, dramatic literature was on a significant rise, and national dramas like Beskow's *Torkel Knutson*, Børgesen's *Erik XIV*, Blanche's *Engelbrecht*, Hedberg's *Fru Märtha* and *Day Waxes*, together with Jolin's *Young Han's Daughter*, formed a repertoire that any stage would be proud to perform. In the face of such talented authors my critical opinion was out of the question, [and] the more so as these pieces had been accepted before I began my duties. All the same, Hedberg and Jolin willingly accepted my modest suggestions, and I had the great satisfaction, both as friend and experienced adviser, of contributing to the success which later attended their careers.

It was more difficult for me when, as so often happens, eccentric young characters decided to submit the first fruits of their dramatic productivity in the hope that their brain children would be accepted with acclamation. Then Messrs. Censors, to avoid the unpleasantness of passing a sentence of rejection, attempted to thrust the responsibility onto me by requesting that I dismiss the authors, either verbally or in writing.

These latter have generally treated the most bloodstained episodes of Sweden's history and painted it in such thick and glaring colors that not only the customary instruments of murder are used, but the executioner's axe set in motion to the point of excess; and in one of the submitted dramas, with such effect that by means of an ingenious machine the severed heads appeared to be rolling downstage toward the prompter's box!

The youth of Charles XII as well as his campaigns have often been the subjects of more or less unsuccessful adaptations in dramatic form; and one of these, of which I had taken special notice, portrayed Swedish soldiers with gangrenous feet marching forward on the snow-covered plains of the Ukraine! To touch upon the aesthetic side of these dramatic monstrosities would have been more than daring of me, both as a Dane and as a ballet poet. I therefore confined myself to mentioning the difficulty of making such scenes lucid and, above all, of getting the public to follow along; and, as I tried to encourage young geniuses to continue their dramatic studies in order to later undertake the necessary corrections with calm self-criticism, I sometimes succeeded in easing the pain of disappointed expectations. Most of those unsuccessful dramatists gave up the difficult work begun, and just as in other countries, developed into didactic dramaturgists.

However, I had my worst troubles with a fanatical Ritmester B——, who many years before had written a play called *The Kalabalik, or Charles XII at Bender,* which he continually submitted with every change of administration (such a thing occurred every fourth or fifth year). Each time, however, it had been returned with protest. In order to get his hero portrayed onstage he had gone in vain from one actor to another and had come at last to the comedian Sevelin, who excused himself on the ground of his genre, but offered, if it should be requested, to play Charles XIII!

In despair at all this opposition, he decided to translate his play into French, and then journeyed to Paris to get it performed. But first he turned to Scribe in order to hear his opinion. The famous playwright, in an especially polite and encouraging letter, referred him to the Opéra-Comique so that he might have the play adapted for the lyric stage. But there it was found to be better suited for the Théâtre de la Porte-Saint-Martin, which, even without the payment of royalties, would not dare to get involved in producing it. Finally, when I had been appointed Intendant for the Swedish stage, he renewed the assault, and *The Kalabalik* wended its way from the Theatre Chancellery down into my workroom. Like all the previous readers of the unfortunate manuscript, I too was forced to admit that the heroic Charles XII had been made into nothing more than a supernumerary role, surrounded by a mass of dull and tasteless episodes. One of the significant features was the burning of the headquarters at Bender, where the Swedish cavaliers ran about trying to extinguish the fire, but by mistake drew from a cask which instead of dampening augmented the fury of the blaze, whereby the act ended with the *tutti* line: "My God! it was brandy!"

Since this Ritmester, so persecuted by Fate, had written me in quite lovely French and had in his letter enclosed Scribe's flattering testimonial, it was all the easier for me to coat the bitter pill by pointing out to him in the same language that Charles XII was as little suited for scenic representation as Napoleon the Great, and that one would hardly be able to find a single actor tolerably fit to portray such an outstanding historical figure. The Ritmester was naturally furious, and had my French letter printed in one of the papers with a lot of sarcastic remarks about my aesthetic competence! At long last, however, he got his play performed at Södra Theatern, with as complete a fiasco as could have been forseen.

One peculiar feature of Swedish society as a whole is the prevailing system of fraternal orders, which, with the exception of Freemasonry (whose public activity takes the form of charity on a grand scale), comprise over half a score of societies with partially secret bylaws; their ostensible goal is to promote fraternal communication and foster the spirit of chivalry and piety, which is the basis of the Swedish national character. These associations, whose half-mystical forms are so far removed from the Danes' understanding of social and club life, nevertheless have an essential advantage and a particularly lovely side; namely, that of bringing the various social classes closer to one another than is the case in Denmark. Even though Sweden possesses an aristocracy of true historical significance, class distinction is reduced, at least in daily intercourse, to the common denominator of personal character without regard to station in life, and it was with astonishment that we discovered the use of the familiar "thou" on the most varied rungs of the social ladder. There sometimes arises confusion as to the sincerity and steadfastness of such sworn brotherhoods, since their meetings are frequently concluded with the clinking of cups. But I, together with countless others, have received satisfactory proofs of a loyalty that requires only an opportunity to be put to the most self-sacrificing test.

The fact that I found such brothers in the circle in which I traveled in my official capacity gives me pride and joy, and outside the theatrical domain I have also met with a sympathy and affection which I shall always bear in grateful memory. At the home of the well-known novelist August Blanche, who owned a house with a garden on the outskirts of the city, I often met with the writers Braun, Adlersparre (Albano), Carlén, and Bjursten, all brothers of the Order of the Society P.B., into which I was also admitted by its unforgettable president, Westerstrand. My noble patron, Baron Beskow, honored me by inviting me every year on the anniversary of the founding of the Swedish Academy to the festive dinner that he, in the capacity of spokesman, gave for its eighteen members, among whom were to be found the writers Malmström and Strandborg (*Talis Qualis*), Bishop Franzén and Archbishop Reuterdal, Minister of State Manderström and several notables, as well as some members of the diplomatic corps and our Danish Ambassador Count W. Scheel-Plessen. All these names are now stricken from the Book of Life, but not the Book of Memory; and as in these lines I dedicate a modest wreath to their memory, I shall fulfill a sacred duty by singling out Count Scheel-Plessen as a man who in the most worthy manner represented Denmark to her neighboring kingdoms. Not only was he esteemed for the richness and magnificent hospitality which gave him superior influence above all the other accredited ministers, but for his loyal Danish spirit, which, although a Holsteiner and a *Helstats* man,‡ he preserved in a time so fateful for all of us. He was popular with rich and poor alike, and only abandoned his responsible post when the weakness of old age forced him to seek rest and peace on his estate.

It now remains for me to mention the favor I enjoyed from H. M. King Charles XV, whose amiable personality captured my heart. His all too short reign, which was marked by Sweden's increasing prosperity and civilization as well as the important reform of the country's internal representation, did not give him the opportunity for the great deeds that his lively spirit craved. He was not lacking in governmental wisdom, and his many-sided talent cultivated both art and poetry; but his mind and thought were, above all, concentrated upon exploits that could secure him a name among Sweden's heroic kings, and his oft expressed wish, like that of Gustavus Adolphus, was to meet death upon a victorious battlefield! This favor was not to be granted him. He had interpreted the guarantee, which Sweden together with three Great Powers had entered into at the London Conference of 1852 for the ratification of

‡ A "whole state" man—one who believed that Slesvig and Holstein were integrally Danish.

the inviolability of the Danish monarchy, as a promise of an active defense for Denmark, which was troubled by the superior force of the enemy. His sympathy for the Danish cause was therefore both sincere and unselfish, leading him to resist the tempting suggestions for expansion made from several quarters. When in the heat of enthusiasm he promised the zealous Scandinavian, Magister Solman, to appear at the Eider with a 22,000-man Swedish army, as reinforcement for the fighting Danes, this was his firm intention, which was echoed by the greater part of the population; and at the musical soirées that were given at Court, he confided to the opera singers that "it's going to blow up next week!" — so certain was he of his cause. But "next week" came, and with it War Minister Reüthersköld's appearance in the Rigsdag with the explanation that an expeditionary army such as the one proposed required several months' preparation, for neither army nor navy was fully equipped, and the mobilization of the army would require an immediate grant of 17,000,000 Rbd. in addition to a monthly allowance of 7,000,000 for salaries and maintenance! But in the face of these crushing figures, the most magnanimous intentions had to fall to the ground, and with folded arms and bleeding heart Sweden was forced to witness the violence and injustice that were inflicted upon the sorely tried neighboring country.

During these months, so agonizing for me, I was witness to the feverish emotion that ran through the entire population. The news of the first conflict at Mysunde was received with jubilation, but the streets resounded with furious war-cries at the announcement concerning the desertion of the Dannevirke. However, in the face of the material impossibility, the most sincere volition was reduced to the fact that some courageous volunteers took up arms to participate in the Danes' hopeless but honorable struggle.

CHRISTIANA (1840)

THE mourning for Frederik VI had ended, and his paternal rule, based upon the principles of absolute monarchy, had given way to the breeze which blew in a liberal direction through the whole of Denmark upon the accession of Christian VIII. Unfortunately, the hope for a chartered constitution was disappointed, and the dissatisfaction which thereby erupted and was especially expressed in the press contributed in no small degree to embittering the King's short reign.

These eight years* were also a time of flowering for Denmark, in both material and spiritual respects. Science, Art, and Freedom itself — within certain limits — had a warm and sincere friend in King Christian. The strict Court etiquette was loosed from its obsolete bonds, and the dazzling festivals to which the various classes of society were admitted were distinguished by the most pleasant atmosphere and the most tasteful arrangements. It has been

*The reign of Christian VIII, 1839–1848.

said, not only by me but by every artist who in those days had something to
do for the King, that a more knowledgeable and discriminating patron was not
to be found.

The fact that I begin my account of an artistic journey to Norway with a
bit of Danish history is essentially founded upon an encounter I had while
sailing into Christiania Fjord with some "Ultra-Norwegian" students who,
with no provocation on my part, began to make derogatory remarks about Denmark, the Danish people, and especially about our new Danish King! I tried
to keep as cool a head as the circumstances permitted, and repudiated their
unmotivated attacks with the clearest arguments I was able to present; but
when their spokesman, a certain Candidate O——, asked me in a most naïve
fashion: "Why we had not gotten a constitution like the Norwegian one," I replied on the spur of the moment, without suspecting how dearly we ourselves
were one day to pay for our free constitution: "If we could get it as cheaply as
the Norwegians, we would have nothing against accepting it." Now they all
chimed in unison, "that they had gotten it with little or no effort," and from
now on we became *faithful* friends. Champagne was brought up on deck, and
with a hearty *skaal* we drained a glass to the success of our theatrical venture.

A few days later the above-mentioned Candidate appeared at my lodging
and offered to present me to the poet Henrik Wergeland, in whom I found a
friendly man and a loving *père de famille* instead of the fantast I had imagined. He received me with the most amiable hospitality and I spent an especially pleasant evening in his home. When leaving he pressed my hand, asking whether I really believed he was such a bear as his opponents made him
out to be.

But it is high time I came to the real purpose of the trip; namely, a series
of ballet performances at the Christiania Theatre together with the three talented pupils who the previous year had been a success in Stockholm. Some
twaddlings, which are not worth mentioning in this chapter, reduced our
quartet to a single couple—that is, Jomfru Fjeldsted and the author. We were
accompanied by Edvard Helsted as orchestra leader and by my sister-in-law
as chaperone for our young "sylphide." They were a little surprised to see the
expected company cut in half, and we had to modify our contract accordingly,
so that the number of performances depended upon the public's sympathy.

Everything, however, surpassed expectation: lively applause and packed
houses crowned our endeavors. We presented bravura and character dances,
and I undertook the venture, with the willing assistance of the dramatic personnel, of staging both *Soldier and Peasant* and *The Sleepwalker!* It went remarkably well. The choreography and dramatic art joined hands in sisterly
fashion, and, in addition, it was a pleasure to see our supernumeraries from
the Akershus chasseurs participate in the most important moments of the action with commendable zeal and precision.

The splendid impression I received during my stay of Norway's glorious scenery and characteristic folk life I have both described and extolled in the first two parts of *My Theatre Life*. But in the capital itself the old, historically curious Akershus inspires feelings of the most varied kind. Public attention at this time was focused mainly on two notorious, almost celebrated, master thieves, Ole Høiland and Jess Bårdsen, whose exploits were like something out of a Romantic novel. Every day, columns of chained convicts marched through the main streets leading from the fortress to the harbor, where among the bastions one noticed a most singular type of forced laborers, who, without irons and with regulation leather caps on their heads, wheeled pushcarts about under military guard. They were called "Crown laborers" and formed a tragicomic element amidst the misery of slavery. These were reckless chaps who in playing the Lothario had neglected to pay the necessary contribution toward the maintenance of their illegitimate children. This now had to be taken care of by means of compulsory day labor for six months at a time, during the milder seasons of the year, until the liquidation was complete.

The political and literary celebrities whose acquaintance I was fortunate enough to make through our dear countryman, the bookseller Johan Dahl, and who were at that time in the full force of their talents, have now for the most part gone to that rest where polemical rivalries no longer exist. They had not yet begun to assemble the various dialects into a so-called "national tongue," and we delighted in seeing young Norway's enthusiastic writers join the series of famous countrymen who had contributed so mightily to the development of a common language.

At that time Danish actors still formed the core of the Norwegian theatre personnel, and talents such as Jørgensen and his wife, Hagen, Mme. Schrumpf, and later on, Wilhelm Wiehe, Adolf Rosenkilde, and his wife, represented in a worthy manner both their art and the country which was once fraternally united to Norway in language and in outlook.

ITALY (1841)

FOR what reasons and with what intentions I left Copenhagen in the spring of 1841 to set out upon an extended journey abroad, I have discussed in detail in the first part of *My Theatre Life;* and in the chapters "Napoli" and "Raphael," I have attempted to describe the impressions I received at that time in Naples and Rome, where art, antiquity, and the Middle Ages confronted me at every step but where the folk life and beautiful scenery in particular captivated my imagination and restored to my mind the equilibrium I so sorely needed. There I gathered a host of living pictures that gradually unfolded in my memory and enriched my fantasy. But when I had discovered for myself that the same troubles which had hampered and embittered my work here at home would confront me at theatres abroad, on an even larger scale, I armed myself with a measure of philosophy and went home to my good Danish public, who joyously hailed my return and accorded my efforts a sympathy that convinced me that I had now entered into a new and more successful period.

I had gathered abundant material for scenic adaptation and wished to bring as much variety as possible into my compositions, but neither subjects from the history of art, from classical antiquity or its mythology would find favor with the prevailing taste; whereas *The Flower Festival in Genzano, Ponte Molle,* and especially *Napoli* became favorite ballets because they reproduced the colorful folk life, transported those who were already seasoned travelers back to unforgettable days, and awakened in others the desire to visit those Hesperidean regions.

However, considerable changes have taken place since 1841. The Italian scenery invariably remains the same; the wondrous creations of the Renaissance continue to arouse our admiration, while the mighty ruins from the time of our Redeemer emerge ever more clearly from the hiding places of the centuries; but the *folk life* has faded considerably with regard to manners and customs as well as costume. Progressing civilization, the influx of traveling foreigners, but above all the revolutions and their magnificent result, "Italian Unity," have remarkably dimmed the distinctive and characteristic element which in all its motley confusion was so extraordinarily picturesque and, to a certain degree, "poetic." But before we reach this more recent point in time, may I beg my good readers to accompany me a little of the way, via Hamburg, whose loveliest and liveliest quarters lay in ruins after the fire,* and where I embarked by night in order to sail at dawn on the English steamer. In Elbhavn, which was densely packed with ships, hymns resounded from the emigrants, while aboard our own vessel sailors in pitch darkness beat time to a merry "hornpipe" played on an invisible violin.

In the most desirable weather we crossed the unruffled North Sea on the same *Countess of Lonsdale* which had the year before carried Louis Napoléon from England to the fantastic Boulogne tour. I had myself put ashore at the delightful little city of Gravesend, whence the next forenoon I intended to take the London packet to the above-mentioned Boulogne. It happened to be Palm Sunday and spring was already in full bloom. Splashing about in a little boat on the Thames, I waited for the steamer that was to pick me up in passing but failed to turn up at the appointed time. My "waterman" grew restless and said that there must be "something wrong!" in London. He was not mistaken, for the ordinary packet had gone up in flames. Otherwise, there was "nothing amiss," for an hour later a reserve steamer appeared, called "All right!," and I and my portmanteau were hoisted up on deck, while the ship took off at tearing speed.

Late that same evening I was in Paris, where I remained for several weeks, visiting my old friends, training with Vestris, laying plans for a future

---

* Again, a lapse of memory. The fire that devastated much of old Hamburg took place May 5–8, 1842 — a year after the trip described here, a year before Bournonville's next visit to the city.

career, and studying Italian energetically. I had free admittance to performances as well as ballet rehearsals at the Opéra. Here I heard the celebrated
new tenor Duprez (who replaced the unfortunate Nourrit but could in no way
compensate for this eminent artist) and attended a rehearsal of *Giselle*,†
where Théophile Gautier and Balletmaster Coralli shared the idea and the arrangement with the dancer Perrot, whose *supposed* wife, Carlotta Grisi, performed the title role with a perfection, in choreographic respects, the like of
which was not to be found in any other ballerina; but in the area of "the poetry
of grace" she was greatly inferior to Marie Taglioni.

At the musical *soirées* of the singing teacher García, I met my Göteborg
discovery, his talented pupil Henriette Nissen, who in a year and a half of
study had made remarkable progress and acquired great skill in technical respects; but I no longer found in her voice the silvery sound that had once astounded and moved me when her talent was still like an unpolished diamond.
It had now been absorbed by a more artistic training.

At the same time, my friend and faithful colleague, Holger Paulli, arrived
from his study trip to Vienna. He had come to learn what Paris had to offer in
the area of music, and was especially pleased with the Conservatoire's excellent concerts. We agreed to celebrate Easter at a Communion Service in
the Lutheran church (Rue des Billettes). But the German sermon of preparation was so exceptionally stern and pressed so hard upon the doctrine of Original Sin, which placed all mankind in an alien and hostile relationship to
God, that the solemn feeling left us and we decided to search our souls more
thoroughly before we dared to approach the Lord's table under such discouraging requirements.

With my French colleagues I enjoyed the most pleasant intercourse, and
since I had decided to accompany my former pupil, M. Edouard, to Naples,
where he had been engaged and I intended to make a guest appearance, I
took part in a jovial farewell dinner where there unfolded a novel in the modern style. For a young *seconde danseuse* from the Opéra, Mlle. Albertine‡ by
name, who harbored a violent passion for my rather phlegmatic young friend
and had for his sake given up extremely valuable connections, was now to be
kept in the dark as to the date of his departure. She regarded me with a suspicious eye, as the one whose advice had lured her lover away from her. The
company parted after having drained numerous glasses to all the gods and
goddesses of Olympus.

The following morning found Edouard and me sitting atop the diligence
to Chalon-sur-Saône, from whence we traveled by steamship to Lyon (my father's birthplace!) and, after a brief stay, farther down the picturesque Rhone,

† This famous ballet was first performed at the Paris Opéra on June 28, 1841, with Carlotta Grisi
and Lucien Petipa in the leading roles. It has remained in the Opéra's repertoire ever since, and
is featured by other major ballet companies throughout the world.
‡ See Ivor Guest, *The Romantic Ballet in Paris*, pp. 186–191, for further details of the adventurous career of Albertine Coquilard.

past the romantic cities of Tarascon, Avignon, and Beaucaire, to Arles. There we spent the night and used the following morning to view the ancient relics from the time of the Romans: the Amphitheatre (which was first converted into a fortress by the Saracens and later filled up with houses but finally restored to its original form by Napoleon I), the Temple Ruins, and the Elysian Fields, a burial place where among other Roman epitaphs I found one for a sister of Caius Marius!

That same evening we reached Marseilles, and were to depart from the famous seaport the next day. We did everything we could hastily manage to do to see as much as possible of the city. We visited the harbor, with the colorful commercial life resulting from its multinational ships, and also enjoyed an excursion to the rocky coast. To my surprise, I read upon a theatre poster that Mlle. Louisa,* the unfortunate flame of my fair youth, was engaged at the ballet, and since I was interested in meeting her again after the vicissitudes of fourteen years, I had myself taken to her residence to pay a polite and friendly visit. She, unfortunately, was not at home, but her mother received me in the more than humble dwelling. Here there could be found no trace of the splendor she had envisioned for herself in her fantastic dreams. But a cradle with a darling little baby girl served as an explanation of all that had happened, and without expressing my thoughts in words, the old woman and I understood each other perfectly. Nineteen years later, during a short stay in London, I learnt that there was a dancing mistress by the name of Madame Louise who lived in Lincoln's Inn Street. I went there on the assumption that it might be my old dancing partner from the King's Theatre (1827). Quite right! But only by her eyes and her sonorous voice could I recognize this worldling, who now sat like an old woman in a not very comfortable sitting room. Her portrait as a child in the impish role of Cupid hung upon the wall, just as it had in her parents' home; now, however, smoky and covered with coal dust, like the rest of the surroundings. The meeting was, in fact, sad; but her face brightened when an outstandingly pretty young girl entered. It was her nineteen-year-old daughter, at the moment an aspiring actress at the Princess Theatre. We were introduced to each other, *I* as an old friend and fellow-artist, *she* with the remark that she was most proud and had firmly decided to marry a very rich man. Despite the sorrowful experiences of thirty-four years, the old illusions had cropped up again! I heaved a sigh, silently thanked God, and said good-bye forever.

But to return once more to 1841. We were just about to board the large steamship when we received the highly unwelcome news that Mlle. Albertine had arrived by post chaise and had already boarded the ship to accompany us to Naples. Edouard, who was usually so calm, flew into the most violent passion and wavered for a moment between breaking his engagement and return-

---

* Cf. the section "The First Journey on Leave of Absence," Vol. III, Part Two; cf. also Lillian Moore, "Bournonville's London Spring." Ivor Guest, *The Romantic Ballet in England*, pp. 31, 46, 128, gives further details of Louisa Court's career.

ing to Paris or behaving as a complete stranger to his ruthless pursuer. The latter course was, naturally, preferred; but the resolution scarcely lasted longer than the same evening when, in the loveliest moonlight, we glided over the Mediterranean's rippling surface where the phosphoresence flashed before the bow of the ship and beneath paddlewheels. While the reunited lovers privately (but with highly different feelings) settled their amorous accounts, I strolled up and down the deck in conversation with a young French cleric who, as vicar, was accompanying an older priest who good-naturedly and jovially remained at the richly decked table in the saloon.

The young man, on the other hand, was step by step entering the religious domain, and left no stone unturned in trying to convert me to the one saving Catholic faith, and especially to acceptance of the Pope as the rightful head of Christendom. At this time, there was still no talk of any solemn proclamation of the Virgin Mary as the Queen of Heaven nor of the infallibility of the Holy Father, although both propositions were included in the Roman Catholic creed. But Gregory XVI was a jovial old gentleman, who is said to have been fond of the juice of the grape and enjoyed reading the novels of Paul de Kock. He therefore did not bother to encumber the consciences of the faithful with reconsidered dogmas. All the same, I held valiantly to my evangelical Confirmation teachings and, while I respected the young priest's convictions, I wished to retain my own. He certainly could not deny that I was close to what he called being *"illuminé,"* but it deeply hurt him that such an apparently good man should be lost to eternal salvation as a *"hérétique"*! In spite of that we parted as good friends and turned in, each with his own convictions.

We were awakened upon entering the harbor at Genoa and were informed that the stopover would last six hours. We used the time to tour this curious city, guided by an old occasional waiter who many years before had been a *garçon* at Comestabile's café in Copenhagen and now regaled me with morsels of Danish. We visited the splendid marble palaces on the Strada Nuova and, filled with historical memories from the time of the Dorias and the Brignolis, everywhere admired the art treasures and costly furnishings. In the Cathedral dell'Annunciata, above whose portal stands a written promise of a hundred days' "indulgence" for everyone who enters the sanctuary, we were shown its golden treasure of sacred vessels and reliquaries, richly set with pearls, rubies, and diamonds. All of a sudden, I felt a light tap on my shoulder, and on turning around discovered my young tempter from the steamship. His eyes were glowing with excitement at all this magnificence and he addressed me with the following words: "What do you say now? Isn't it a wonderful religion?" I had to admit he was right as far as the outward display was concerned. But he got no further with me, and left with a sigh, abandoning me to perdition, or in the mildest case, to a severe overhauling in the cleansing flames of Purgatory.

The lower and upper city are separated by a deep rock chasm, over which a bridge or viaduct leads to the Church of the Madonna di Cavignano, whose cupola and situation are highly reminiscent of Stockholm's *Katarina-kyrka på söder*. But uppermost lies the Citadel, which, with its yawning cannon mouths, is designed to keep the revolutionary tendencies of the Genoese in check. Mlle. Albertine followed us everywhere, hanging upon her Edouard's arm, and presented such a living picture of *les inséparables* that we barely managed to get rid of her when we wished to take a swim in the salty waves of the Mediterranean.

The steamer's bell called us aboard to a well-served dinner. We put off from shore and stood out beyond the little Sardinian fleet and nearby sea forts. We stayed in sight of the coast until darkness fell, and after a gentle night's sailing, early in the morning reached Livorno, where everything in the harbor bespoke the busiest commercial activity. In this quite pretty and populous city there did not appear to be any special dividends for tourists with an appetite for art and poetry. But since we had eight hours' shore leave, we seized this opportunity to visit ancient and famous Pisa.

Albertine, who was not exactly mad about antiquities, stayed behind in Livorno together with her *"ami enchaîné,"* who consoled himself by practicing and putting himself *en train* for his debut in Naples. I joined several of the steamer's passengers in hiring a *veturin*, and through a countryside that resembled a series of fruitful gardens we drove to the old city, which lies about a [Danish] mile and a half from Livorno and is traversed by the River Arno, which for twelve centuries was navigable all the way to the sea. By this route the Pisan fleet guided the Crusaders' army to the coast of Syria. This was in Pisa's prime, when as an independent republic it rivaled Genoa's might. Now it is quiet and, in relation to the city's size, rather empty. Of the proud memories of the past only the University, with Galileo's renown, and the splendid marble buildings of the churches and palaces remain. Among these, it is chiefly the Cathedral's quadruple complex that arrests the traveler's attention, together with a little jewel: the Church of the Madonna della Spina, by the banks of the Arno.

Innumerable travel descriptions have discussed in detail the Cathedral, with its splendid chapels adorned with pictures and its roof beams made of cedar trees from Lebanon; the Baptistry with its marble font, wherein baptism was formerly given by immersion; the Campo Santo, the curious burial place surrounded by arcades in which are to be found frescoes by the famous masters of the Renaissance (the soil in this Garden of the Dead is said to have been brought as ballast in the transport ships returning from the Holy Land in the time of the Crusaders); and finally, the Leaning Tower, familiar from all pictorial works, which is thirty ells higher than our Round Tower and tilts about fifteen feet from southwest to northeast!

It is still uncertain whether the master builders of the twelfth century might actually have had the bizarre idea of erecting such a splendid monument in so unfortunate and threatening a position, reckoning its midpoint and center of gravity so accurately that it could defy the stress of time and tempest; or if the soil has gradually yielded to the enormous mass of stone, which had probably not been reinforced with pilework or built with any more solid a foundation than that, for example, of the Asinelli and Garisendi towers in Bologna and La Ghirlendaja in Modena, all of which tilt to a certain degree. Suffice it to say that on ascending to the observation platform, I found the Tower's core and gangway or spiral staircase so lopsided that I was seized with an unpleasant vertigo. For the rest, I will refer my good readers to the aforementioned travel descriptions to obtain a fuller account of Pisa than the one which I, by such a fleeting visit, have been able to present.

We steamed out of port that evening to moor at the quay of Civitavecchia. I simply had to go ashore in order to discover, if possible, the ruins of a Roman aqueduct from the time of Trajan, but I failed to ask how long our stay in this port was to last. I therefore took my time, just as in Genoa and Livorno, and strolled out to the fortifications where I chatted a bit with the Papal soldiers. . . . All of a sudden, I heard the cry *"Il vapore! Il vapore! "* and saw the smoke from the departing steamer! I rushed down to the harbor, where I was met with terrified shrieking and gesticulation! Several crazy *marinari*, with eyes flashing beneath their Phrygian caps, offered to row me out to overtake the ship. I had my doubts, but they forced me down into the boat and *"a Brio! "* they pulled out with violent strokes.

I had no idea how they could possibly achieve any results, but I soon perceived that we were taking a shortcut over the ground that the steamer, because of a longer turn, had to avoid. Hope dawned anew. But about halfway out to the ship my guides suddenly demanded their pay. I readily produced a five-franc piece . . . "Aah! " But with long faces they dropped their oars. "Ten francs, or back to Civitavecchia! " It was now truly a case of "out that way or out the window." A louis d'or changed hands on the thwart, and they set off again with chanties and vigorous strokes. In the meantime, the Captain had discovered us and ordered the engine stopped. We reached the ship to the great delight of my traveling companions, and as I received a gentle but well-deserved reprimand from the Captain, he ironically remarked that I was the first traveler to linger behind in wretched Civitavecchia!

In the first part of *My Theatre Life* I have spoken with all the life and warmth that flowed from my pen of the wondrously beautiful entry into Naples and of the impressions I received from the folk life and everything that this city and its environs have to offer. Therefore I now have only to relate those minor episodes attached to my guest appearance at the Teatro San Carlo and to the pleasant intercourse I enjoyed with my fellow-artists and countrymen during my six weeks' stay.

The San Carlo is considered the largest theatre in Europe. But although it is a regal edifice and, like our Theatre, bears the title of "Royal," it has been handed over to private enterprise and engages its personnel on a seasonal basis. Despite the fact that the drama certainly labored under oppressive clerical censorship, at this time both opera and ballet shone on the aforesaid stage; and while Mercadante elevated music to an honorable place by his magnificent compositions, choreography and the mimed drama possessed an outstanding master in Salvatore Taglioni, successor to the worthy Gioja.

Almost every evening during May and June they gave the opera *Belisario*, in which Fraschini and Tamburlick (Danieli), together with the bass, Collini, performed the principal roles. The ballet *Marco Visconti* offered much excellence and gave the nondancing mimes Démathia and Bolognetti, as well as Signora Brioli, the opportunity to display their expressive acting. This was, to be sure, according to the same conventional gesticulation that my Italian predecessor, Galeotti, had used in his ballets but with a singular rhythmic effect that formed a method quite far removed from the natural.

The dances were in part performed by foreign artists, among them my friend Edouard and Mme. Saint-Roman. With both this lady and the balletmaster's daughter, Mlle. Louise Taglioni, I danced my *grand pas de deux* from *Valdemar* and the *bolero* from *The Toreador*, both of which won lively applause with curtain calls, and great recognition on the part of my comrades. But since the Director had his complement of dancers he could not offer me an engagement for this season, though he did wish to make a deal for Carnival season next year. I could not give him a firm commitment and thus had to limit myself to these few guest appearances, at the end of which I completely gave myself up to the life of a tourist and the pleasantries of social intercourse.

Our former Ambassador, Conferentsraad Voght, showed me the greatest kindness, and I passed many a happy evening at his villa in the neighborhood of Capo di Monte. There I often met an eighty-year-old Kammerjunker, Brockenhuus, who had lived in Naples since the days of Christian VII. What was a genuine treat for me, however, and an elevation in my oppressed state of mind, was my meeting with the poet H. P. Holst, who had taken up his abode on the isle of Ischia so as to be able to write his loveliest odes and stanzas in peace. He came to visit me in Naples, recited for me his poem "The Runes," and invited me to share the delights of his *locanda*, run by the winegrower Vincenzo, in delightful Casamicciola. I accepted his invitation and spent eight unforgettable days in the most picturesque surroundings and in the midst of a family whose patriarchal naïveté and good nature reminded one of the long-gone golden age. Here the painter Marstrand and the musician Rung had once lived; the latter was remembered by the name of Don Enrico, just as Holst was called Don Giovanni, an ominous name of whose significance the good people had not the slightest idea, since they had never heard of either Mozart or his masterwork.

In my "Ischia Ballad" I have sung of how I traveled round the island with my excellent countryman and climbed the old extinct volcano, Epomeo, which has been renamed *San Nicolo;* and my poem "The Might of Runes" I improvised while riding up the mountain, penning the strophes on the pommel of my long-eared Pegasus.† But never has my vanity as a dancer been given such a jolt as on the day when our host's pretty daughter Carolina and her brother Francesco played and sang a *tarantella* (for they did not dare to dance it out of fear of the priests' anger). They had learnt from Holst that I was a famous *ballerino* and wished to see a proof of my art; but since neither the locale nor the costume allowed of any real performance, I engaged Holst in a *gallopade* which was done to the beat of the *tarantella*. We danced gaily about to the family's great delight, and it was now asked how much a *Maëstro di Ballo* such as I could earn as a yearly salary. When the reply was "About one thousand *scudi*," Carolina clapped her hands together and called out to my honorable countryman: "Then how much shall *you* get?" In her eyes, Holst was evidently my choreographic superior!

On Ischia I had the patriotic pleasure of hearing our former Ambassador Voght's name mentioned with blessings because of the help he had given the residents of Casamicciola when an earthquake had overthrown their houses. He just happened to own the lovely villa "La Sentinella," which had remained unharmed. In Castellamare I had yet another delight in seeing the bathhouse *"all'uso di Danimarca,"* a memory from the time (which the old fishermen remembered very well) when as Prince, Christian VIII had stayed there with his beautiful consort.

Letters recalled me to the bosom of my family and my old sphere of activity, which, compared to what I had seen on this trip, no longer appeared to me as thorny and thankless as it earlier had. I now bade a fond farewell to Ischia and Naples, to friends and well-wishers, to artistic brothers and sisters — and, lest I forget, Edouard and Albertine. The scenes that were continually called forth by her impetuosity and his coolness had gradually alienated me from their company. Her sudden departure from her duties with the ballet in Paris had led to a public inquiry and threats of a considerable fine. The police had demanded identification, which Edouard was forced to furnish. She was dreadfully bored and plagued her poor lover to the point where he had to procure her an engagement at the San Carlo, where she cut but a mediocre figure. Shortly afterward she fell into a painful illness and died, like "La Dame aux Camélias," a victim of her passions.

The journey now proceeded northward in eager expectation of all I was to see and discover in Rome. What I experienced on the road and during my four weeks' stay I described thirty years ago in the first volume of *My Theatre Life* (in the chapter "Raphael"). It was truly a period of initiation into the sanctuary of both art and history, and were I to go into detail about the glories and magnificent impressions that kept me in a continual state of ecstasy, this would become a long-winded book that might in fact come to resemble hundreds of others authored by inspired travelers. I will only tell of my pleasant meetings with Danish artists: Küchler, who had not yet converted to Papism

† See these poems in the section "Lyric Attempts," Vol. I.

and the cloistered life; Constantin Hansen, who besides the art of painting also cultivated the lyric and wrote superb ballads; Roed, with whom I made an interesting excursion to the Sabine mountains; and the sculptor Holbeck, who accompanied me on a delightful tour, by way of Frascati and through the wooded countryside which runs past Monte Cavo and Rocca di Papa, to Albano.

We paused at Tusculum, where amid the ruins of the theatre we declaimed stanzas from our Danish poets, to the astonishment of our muleteer who, I dare say, took us to be conjurers calling forth the shades of the heroes of antiquity. The rather young and talented Jerichau lived a more secluded life, but the historical painter Eddelin happily and gaily joined in our gatherings at the *trattoria all Lepre,* at the Café Greco, and beneath the vine-covered huts outside the Porta Pia.

The weeks passed like days, and, after having tossed some *baiocchi* into the Fontana di Trevi on the Piazza Navona and drunk of its water, which I had scooped in my hand, as an omen of a future return, I reserved my seat in a carriage whose owner, to my surprise, pressed a *scudo* into my hand as *caparra,* or security that we would meet again according to our agreement, which was formally concluded by my signature and his mark and contained the conditions for meals and lodgings for two nights and three days from here to Florence.

The following morning the carriage arrived at the appointed hour, and inside it sat a Benedictine monk, a gentleman, and a common woman. But to my disappointment it was not the coachman with whom I had settled the agreement who was to drive us to Florence but, on the contrary, a chap with a base and drunken physiognomy, who pretended to be the other man's "highly trusted" *fratello.* We now had to make do as best we could. My portmanteau was lashed to the back of the carriage, and with a touching *arrivederla* to the Eternal City, we drove out of the Porta del Popolo, across Ponte Molle, and onward to the north.

I soon made the acquaintance of my traveling company, which besides the woman consisted of a singer, who was to go to a minor provincial theatre, and of the aforesaid monk, who had quite recently been appointed Friar General of the Benedictine Order and was journeying to the cloister of Montolivetto in Florence to hold inspection there.

He was a singularly handsome man, with a Bonapartian countenance and fine white hands. He might have been about forty years old and had the most urbane manners. He carried on an animated conversation and revealed an insight into many things, especially music, which he cultivated, and he is said to have composed a number of motets and offertories. Of particular interest was his account of the terrible cholera epidemic in Palermo, of which he was a native, where the monks had aided the suffering and dying without a single one of them contracting the disease! I regarded this success as a direct dispensation of Divine Providence, but was refuted with a serious, *"Miracolo della Madonna!* " After a pause that lasted for a couple of minutes, he mildly and politely addressed me with the following words: "You are most likely Protestant." I affirmed this and added, without touching upon the matter of either Papal control or worship of the Madonna, that I cherished the greatest respect for the Catholic religion, whose ceremonies were particularly impressive, but that our evangelical teaching did not say a word about the fires of Purgatory. Upon hearing this, the singer, who was sitting next to me, moved away with a cry of indignation. But the Abbot calmed him and admitted that the dogma of the purifying flames of Purgatory had only been proclaimed by the assembled councils three hundred years after the time of the Evangelists, when the fear of eternal damnation had prevented the expansion of Christianity and they were forced to discover this *"mezzo termine"* in order to set minds at ease. Herewith all religious discussion ceased and the conversation now turned to all kinds of subjects, among others Denmark, about which the Abbot was very well informed. He wished especially to dwell upon the story of Struensee and Caroline Mathilde.‡

Our *veturin* no longer hesitated to confirm what his face already promised; for even when he had to pay the toll, he awarded the Pope the triple title of *"Ladro, Ruffiano, Galëotto"* ["Villain, ruffian, galley slave"], and at our first resting place he got, if not exactly dead drunk, then at least maliciously so and addressed both the cleric and the woman in extremely brutal fashion. It was not long before he fell asleep at the trestle table, and when I prodded him repeated times in order to waken him, he became furious and used a number of idioms that I did not understand. But when I attempted to bring him to his senses he threatened me with his knife and, prompted by my fellow-travelers, I was forced to retire silently into the carriage. The poor horse now suffered from his shrieks and whiplashes, and we drove off in a cloud of white lime dust.

Toward evening we reached Radicoffani, situated on a ridge of the Apennines, where we passed the night, and the next day we proceeded at a steady pace with the customary stop at Siena. Our coachman had, in the meantime, become more agreeable since he probably feared that we would denounce him to the more scrutinizing Tuscan police.

It was a wonderful moonlit evening, and among the city's buildings the black and white marble Cathedral shone before us with a peculiar luster. Our Abbot had the idea of celebrating Mass at one of the church's altars early the next morning before our departure, and invited us to attend, at the same time remarking that I, although Protestant, could benefit by observing a solemn morning prayer. I accepted his invitation and found myself truly edified by the dignity with which he "officiated," although the sacristan, who was to assist him, bore a striking resemblance to Phister in *The Black Domino* and, kneeling, interrupted my devotion by showing me his thick hobnailed shoes.

I rode the rest of the way to Florence alone with my Benedictine Gen-

‡ See notes on Caroline Mathilde, Vol. III, Part Two, p. 427; and on Struensee, *infra.*, p. 649.

eral, who was kindness itself and invited me, if I should one day come to Sicily, to visit him in Palermo, where he would afford me all the comforts his position could provide for me. Upon taking leave of him in Florence, where he went to his cloister and I to my hotel *all Leone bianco,* we heartily embraced, and it would make me happy if this fine man had retained as good an impression of me as I of him. (His name was Patti, like that of the famous singer.)

Of all Italy's cities, there was none that appeared more comfortable to me than Florence, especially at a time when clerical absolutism to the south and military despotism to the north had an oppressive effect on all conditions, while in Tuscany one noticed a freer air although the country was governed without a constitution by an Austrian Dowager Duchess. But here Liberalism was compensated for by a liberality that was in perfect accord with the urbane manners of the Florentines; for, coupled with a language that was certainly far inferior to that of the Romans in euphony but distinguished itself by elegance and well-chosen expressions (*"Lingua toscana in bocca romana"*), one encountered even in strangers a genuine good will and unassuming politeness. To be sure, Florence did not possess the outstandingly original stamp of Rome or Naples, nor did it contain any natural phenomena or antiquities that could equal the curiosities of those cities; but its romantic situation, its proud memories from the Middle Ages, and above all the possession of invaluable art treasures, place Florence like a costly jewel in the center of beautiful Italy.

I lodged in the vicinity of the Palazzo Strozzi and not far from the Piazza del gran Duca, where the old fortress of the Medici with its slender tower dominated the marketplace, which was swarming with fellows armed with harvesting implements. At first glance, it resembled one of those noisy assemblies from the days of the old Republic, when from the Loggia dei Lanzi the tribunes of the people addressed this turbulent democracy—but it was only a farmhands' market for farmers hiring workers for the approaching harvest. Agreements were soon concluded, and the square emptied. I could then regard and admire at my leisure the masterworks of Michelangelo, Donatello, Benvenuto Cellini, and Giovanni da Bologna that adorn the square and the vaulted hall of the Loggia. By means of the staircase leading to the Palazzo Vecchio, where the government Chancellery has its seat, one ascends to a picture gallery which is probably the richest in the world. Here I met Licentiate Kolthoff and his wife, and together with these amiable countrymen for several days I studied quite thoroughly this gallery as well as the priceless collections of the Palazzo Pitti.

In the first volume of *My Theatre Life* I have discussed my wanderings in the charming environs, how I conceived my ballet *Raphael,* and the pleasure I had as a result of "Cavaliere" Brøndsted's letter of recommendation to Countess Lenzoni-Medici. I must therefore add only the account of my visit to the opera theatre *della Pergola,* where each evening they gave Bellini's *Beatrice di Tenda*, superbly performed, especially by the tenor Roppa, whose sonorous voice and dramatic interpretation were most exciting.

After all too short a stay, but with the hope of seeing Florence once more in my lifetime, I dutifully paid my tribute to the "Flower Fairy" who, un-asked, had each day laid a fresh bouquet on my table in the café. I reserved my seat in the diligence to Bologna, and, as I turned my head in farewell outside the city's northern gate, with a genuinely patriotic feeling I discovered on the face of the portal a Latin inscription: *"Fredericus Quartus Rex Daniae & Norvegiae, etc.",* who had in the year 1709 honored Florence with his august presence.

Of particular note was the transition from well-cultivated and humanely governed Tuscany to the Papal Romagna which, as an important part of the Patrimony of Peter was now an entail of the Holy See. Whether art and science had their home here or if the famous University still maintained its ancient renown I would not be competent to judge, even if I had had the time for that purpose in hastily passing through; but during the four-and-twenty hours I spent in Bologna I took particular note of the fact that on both sides of the main streets the lowest floors of the houses were continuous ar-cades without windows. These covered passages all seemed to lead out to the large Campo Santo, for on the inner walls at nearly every twentieth step could be found a request asking passersby to pray for the soul of this or that baron or marchese now groaning in the fires of Purgatory. In one of these archways I encountered a most singular artistic phenomenon, namely, a poorly dressed youth who suddenly threw himself down and with a piece of chalk began to draw on the sidewalk, first clouds, then angels singing and playing, and finally a Madonna and Child, the whole like a perfect apotheosis. Not only did he execute this in less than a quarter of an hour but in a most beautiful manner and with a decided touch of the old Florentine school. I was quite astonished, and when the young man passed his cap to the specta-tors standing about, I gladly offered my mite for the encouragement of a talent which during Italy's more fortunate periods would have found support and further development under one of the great masters.

The churchyard at the city's extremity was Bologna's pride, and the graves amidst the cypress grove were surrounded by a wall with archways similar to those in the streets; but in every arcade there was a built-in burial vault which, for the sum of 100 *scudi,* could be obtained in perpetuity by any family that would guarantee to erect within a certain time a sculptured work in marble as a grave monument. Thus there were already several outstanding works by Marchese, by Tenerani, and by Canova and his best pupils.

The same afternoon I got to see something of an entirely different genre at the ball game (*Giuoco del Pallone*), which is carried on with a passion re-sembling the Englishmen's boxing matches and the Spaniards' bullfights. On the street corners posters had been put up telling the *noms de guerre* of the players: "Diavolo," "Diavolone," "Diavolino," and "Diavoletto." The stage was an open square surrounded by amphitheatrelike stands to which a very cheap admission was paid. The public was quite numerously represented and followed the game with feverish excitement. Considerable strength and agility were indeed displayed. The balls, which were as large as our biggest skittle balls, flew sky-high in the air and were thrown back with clenched fists. Applause and shrill bravos rewarded successful tosses, but hooting and whistling resounded every time a failure occurred. None of the Devil's brood won the prize, however. It was awarded instead to a strange pseudonym, "Diedimi," who was called forth and showered with wreaths and bouquets. I could not see what the rest of the city had to offer in the way of churches, museums, and other curiosities (I hardly had time to call upon Rossini), since the next morning I was on my way by carriage via Modena and Parma to Piacenza, where we passed the night.

In addition to two young Italians, my traveling companions consisted of a French bourgeois and his wife, two perfect types of the later so well known *famille Benoîton.** Naturally they knew no language other than their mother tongue and were so little versed in geography that we had to teach them the names of the principal cities through which we passed, not to mention the fact that for them Denmark and Dalmatia were one and the same thing. They had come from Rome and Florence and were so disgusted and bored by all the pictures of the Madonna and portraits of unknown persons that they did not bother to accompany the rest of us to admire Corregio's masterworks in the Cathedral and the picture gallery in Parma. In the same company we got to see the residential palace's large theatre, whose auditorium, due to age and neglect, was now so frail that no human foot dared enter its box seats. In the Castle Park we perceived a colossal marble bust of the Dowager Duchess Marie Louise, and with mixed emotions our thoughts flew back to her first spouse: Napoleon the Great.

Across the Po valley, with its vast rice fields and mulberry plantations traversed by numerous watercourses, the road now led to Milan, at that time the seat of the Austrian government in Lombardy and the nucleus of Italian hatred of the Germans. There I met a couple of my comrades from Vestris' school, Messrs. Lefebvre and Casati, as well as a particularly handsome merchant, Signor De Anthoni, with whom I had struck up an acquaintance in Naples. Since I intended to remain in Milan for a couple of weeks, special permission had to be obtained from the city's Austrian police, who even went so far as to remark that I did not require a fortnight in order to look about the city and its environs. Whether it was my French name or my recent adventure in *The Toreador,* known throughout Europe, that possibly caused me to be suspect as a "demagogic intriguer," suffice it to say that I needed De Anthoni's and Lefebvre's satisfactory testimonials for the necessary residence

*The archetypical middle-class family in Sardou's play of that title.

permit to be granted, though I dare say not without a secret observer on my heels to spy on my every move.

I had not yet declared my intention of appearing at the Teatro alla Scala, where another intimate friend of mine, Signor Blasis, was balletmaster. But since the leading soloist, Mérante, happened to be indisposed, this seemed to be an especially favorable occasion for a debut, and I struck an agreement with the Director, Merelli, for two appearances using the same dances I had performed at the Teatro San Carlo. It was, in fact, a fantastic idea: not wanting to return home without having appeared on the greatest stages of Europe—*enfin!*

The first evening went brilliantly. I harvested applause, curtain calls, and congratulations from all of the artists. The following day an entire band assembled outside the hotel where I was staying, and in between numbers were heard shouts whose meaning I could comprehend as little as I could the reason for this concert. However, the hotel keeper soon called my attention to the fact that it concerned *me*, my debut, and my pocket. I had to put in an appearance. A louis d'or was sent to the musicians and I expressed my thanks from the window, while the square resounded with cries of *"Evviva il reputatissimo Ballerino Augusto Bournonville! "* Now this was all very nice, but the same afternoon, on passing the Café Martini where the theatre fanciers generally congregated, I encountered dark and threatening looks such as only Italian eyes can give. I now learnt from my friends that the rumor had spread that Merelli had fired the popular dancer Mérante and engaged me in his stead. Though everything was done officially to deny this unpleasant and utterly false report, public favor had turned against me and I now stood at the crossroads (so crowded in extremist Italy) between *fanatismo* and *fiasco!* I was advised to avoid my second debut performance, but, convinced that it was my simple duty and certain of my skill, I did not allow myself to be discouraged; and while I failed to win unqualified applause in the *pas de deux sérieux*, I took a brilliant revenge in the *bolero* and walked off with *les honneurs de la soirée.*

I had now satisfied my ambition and spent the last eight days as a curious tourist and man of the world. I visited the picture gallery of the Academy of Art, where the Lombard school of painting predominated with masterworks by Leonardo da Vinci and his great pupil and emulator, Bernardino Luini. Here too I encountered Thorvaldsen's charming bas-relief, *The Graces.* In the cloister of Santa Maria delle Grazie I admired the partially damaged but still marvelous *Last Supper* by Leonardo.

On a pleasure trip to the capital of the Longobards, the nearby Monza, I had the opportunity to inspect the remarkable Cathedral and to be shown the famous Iron Crown (a circlet of gold that surrounds a nail from the True Cross) and also a collection of important relics. With a bit of imagination and simple submission, one can find oneself truly edified by the sight of such objects, despite the controversy about their authenticity. But one thing about which there can be no divided opinion is the imposing impression made by Milan's majestic Cathedral.

From its base, executed in white marble and bearing the pure Gothic stamp of the Middle Ages, rise its slender arches, which are crowned by as many lacy spires as there are days in a year and which surround the lofty central tower. In hundreds of niches and on an equal number of projecting pedestals rest statues and statuettes by the thousand, representing the heroes of both the Old and New Testaments, prophets and saints, and also prominent personages from legend and history. For generations these were executed as pious offerings by Italy's sculptors. The façade, which, like most of Italy's greatest churches, stood unfinished for centuries, was completed only during Napoleon's control, but in a more modern style that does not harmonize with the rest of the Cathedral. But when one enters the sanctuary one is seized by a solemn feeling of devotion which, in my opinion, far surpasses that inspired by the Church of St. Peter in Rome. It is, I dare say, a matter of taste, but here the difference between Catholic and Protestant is forgotten. It is truly a house of God, where every confessor of faith may offer his prayer.

Even the opera at La Scala had nothing remarkable to offer during the summer. The ballet, on the other hand, presented a major work taken from Walter Scott's *Kenilworth*. This, in accordance with the Italian method, was performed with mechanical precision, and herein the role of the traitor gave the mime, Cati, the opportunity to make some frightful faces. The *corps de ballet* was quite numerous and contained some younger talents from the school of Blasis, who were later to fill principal places at the Parisian ballet.

The inserted dances, individual as well as collective, were beautifully put together and had been superbly drilled. I especially delighted in watching Mérante, who was now fully recovered and unquestionably the finest dancer I had encountered on this journey. With him as well as my other comrades I enjoyed the most pleasant intercourse, and since Lefebvre found himself without engagement, I acquiesced in his desire to seek employment at the Danish Theatre. On my return to Copenhagen I had the opportunity of recommending him and hoped to find valuable assistance in his recognized skill. Unfortunately, his presence gave me little pleasure, since, instead of lending me a hand, he formed cabals against me and allied himself with those who most bitterly opposed my activity.

On the shore of beautiful Lake Como I said good-bye to Italy for the present, and the same evening the diligence, drawn by eight horses and mules, began the upward climb to the Hospice of St. Gotthard, where we arrived in the harshest snowy weather, although we were still in the month of August. It would be impossible to give a description of this Alpine journey, since we drove by night and were surrounded on all sides by dense clouds and snowdrifts. However, our descent was rapid. We reached smiling countryside in the cantons of Switzerland, where we were greeted by memories of Wilhelm Tell. We passed the night in Altdorf and took the steamer across the Lake of Lucerne, sailed past the chapel at Küssnacht and beneath the shadows of the trees at the foot of the mighty Righi. All this ought to be seen close at hand on a walking tour, but home beckoned and I had to hurry on.

Lucerne and Basle were scarcely noticed in passing, and I hastened on by courier post through Alsace and Champagne to Paris. Here I rested for a week's time, during which I delighted in seeing a couple of performances of *Giselle,* visited my friends and, at the Polygone de Vincennes, watched the first review of ten battalions of the *Chasseurs d'Orléans.* I also accompanied the dancer Mabille to his brother's new establishment, the Garden that later became so "notorious," where, among the spectators of the disgusting *cancan,* I saw the recently retired Minister and historian, M. Thiers, with his family. Finally, in presenting my talented young countryman Carl Helsted to the flautist Tulou, the composer Halévy, and the singing teacher García, I was unwittingly responsible for the fact that this gifted musician abandoned the flute, renounced composition, and chose the career in which he has worked so vitally for the progress of the art of singing in our native land.

I returned to Copenhagen with a lightened spirit and a hoard of impressions and experiences which were in many respects of great benefit to me, not least of all in my compositions, which now entered a new period marked by the most successful of all my works: *Napoli.*

HAMBURG (1843)

THE memories I retain of this basically prosaic city form a rather ironic contrast to those I gathered in my first journey to beautiful Italy, so rich in artistic treasures and historical curiosities. Here business life is predominant and material well-being is preferred to all aesthetic enjoyment. Therefore this chapter will be one of my shortest, though it will not lack a good number of features characteristic of the stirring life of the theatre.

At that time, the Stadt Theatre had been leased to two former actors, Mühling and Cornet,* who were not as in France given annual subsidies by the community, but, on the contrary, had to pay a high rent for the use of the facilities. Since it was impossible for them to attract and retain the Hamburgers' attention with the regular singing and acting personnel, the repertoire and the theatre treasury were supported mainly by "guest stars," who, according to whether they were major or minor celebrities and attractions, were paid with either individual fees or a share of the profits.

The fame which the Copenhagen ballet enjoyed, especially after the brilliant success of *Napoli,* gave the aforementioned Directors the idea of possibly being able to provide full houses during the difficult summer months by sending for us. On this occasion I received the most flattering request to make some guest appearances together with the élite of my *corps de ballet.* It was

*Cf. Bournonville's observations on Cornet in Vol. II, the chapter "Abdallah."

some time before I could make up my mind about this, since Hamburg was not exactly the place in which I cared to present my art. But repeated assurances of the excellence of this venture and the eager urging of my Danish colleagues finally moved me to accept the proposal, which amounted to fifteen performances with half of the theatre's net profits.

It was now a matter of organizing my company so that the most essential roles could be performed in the best fashion. I therefore *engaged* Messrs. Hoppe, Brodersen, Funck, Gade, Füssel, Stramboe (*père et fils*), Hoppensach, Fredstrup Sr. (with his son and two daughters), as well as Jfr. Larcher for the performance of older parts and as chaperone for the two young *danseuses*, Funck and Bruun. But a prima donna was lacking: Jfr. Fjeldsted was suffering from a serious knee injury and Jfr. Nielsen, upon whom I had been counting, betrayed us in order to go with M. Lefebvre! Therefore I had to find a prominent foreign talent for my major roles, and the choice fell upon Mlle. Maria,† one of the most popular dancers at the Paris Opéra and, moreover, a charming and intelligent personality. (By a peculiar chance, I found out that she was a Jewess. The prejudice I had harbored until then that the children of Israel were talented in all areas with the exception of the dance was thus most firmly dispelled, since Mlle. Maria possessed a high degree of terpsichorean virtuosity.) Nevertheless my work was as good as doubled as a result of this acquisition, since a whole new rehearsal had to be held for her sake, and while I could honorably have offered one of our own female soloists 1000 Rbd. for these six weeks, her contract cost 8000 francs. Moreover, I had concluded a written agreement for both fixed fees and traveling money for each member of my assisting corps, so that my risk was not inconsiderable.

I arrived a couple of weeks earlier than the rest of the company, in order to train the *corps de ballet* which had been granted me as a supplement. But here the trouble began, for the entire Hamburg ballet consisted of a stiff-legged old balletmaster, a rather good young *danseur*, and a lovely female pupil. The rest were recruited from partly unwilling and clumsy choristers and girls (from the street, to be honest) who could come and go as they pleased. With these forces I accomplished the impossible, but in spite of all my efforts, it was hardly a shadow of what people here at home were used to in the way of ensemble dancing. However, there were quite good new decorations and the ballets were, on the whole, properly fitted up. We gave *Napoli, The Toreador,* and *The Sleepwalker,* all with lively applause. Both I and my prima ballerina reaped applause and "curtain calls," but it was mainly the role of Zoloé in *Le Dieu et la Bayadère* that gave her the chance to display the greatest bravura, and our little Petrine Fredstrup bravely held her own in the dancing competition. With a singular feeling of satisfaction, I noticed to what a high degree our Danish company was recognized for its skill and behavior, which must have been something quite unusual in Hamburg, which ranked rather low in moral respects.

† Maria [Jacob]; see Ivor Guest, *The Romantic Ballet in Paris,* for details of her life and career.

This whole undertaking was based upon the belief that, under fairly favorable conditions, I should be able to count on a profit of about 2000 Rbd. for my strenuous work and considerable responsibility, and the first half of our series of performances actually seemed to promise such an outcome. But the strong heat of July began, and attendance declined in spite of the attention we had aroused. I duly paid out the stipulated fees and finally ended up having to contribute 1200 Rbd. every week from my own pocket!

I had to work hard to make the best of such a ruinous situation, and we even gave a final performance for the benefit of the Orchestra's Pension Fund. On this occasion Mlle. Maria displayed an uncommon degree of resolution. Mainly through catching cold, she had brought on a rheumatic pain of such a violent nature that she could hardly move without dreadful suffering, and that very evening *The Toreador* was to be given. I knew no other way out than to arrange some *divertissements* that did not require her assistance. But her sense of honor was offended by the very thought of backing out of a performance for a charitable cause. She tried all day to overcome the pain, although it caused both sighing and screaming, and she succeeded to the point that she not only danced her part superbly, but after the performance invited us all to an evening supper, at which she did the honors with exquisite grace and dignity.

In the middle of the meal we were surprised with a serenade which the members of the orchestra had arranged in our honor. The Hamburg *Liedertafel* entered and provided us with several lovely songs. The spokesman addressed a speech to me and my company, and we ordered champagne to express our thanks and a hearty farewell, with full glasses and resounding cheers, to the gallant Hamburgers. And as if we had not gotten enough dancing for one evening, this *soirée* ended with a little whirl about the floor, and with true feelings of camaraderie, we took leave of our prima donna, who returned to France the next day.

The Directors, who had gotten a good bargain, showered me with compliments and united in the general wish to see us again next year. Yes, they would even have liked to claim the Danish ballet as a permanent summer guest, but I evasively thanked them for the honor, and privately resolved not to hazard this sort of undertaking again.

MINDEN (1846)

IN the spring of 1846 I undertook a journey to Paris to broaden the training of my oldest daughter Augusta, who had just reached her fifteenth year.* She was accompanied by her aunt, and the length of her stay was temporarily estimated at a year and a half. And, inasmuch as good taste and ingenuity go hand in hand in my profession, I also intended to pay a brief visit to the

---

*For an account of this journey and Augusta Bournonville's stay in the French capital, see *August Bournonville: Souvenir de ton père*, ed. August Tuxen (Copenhagen, 1929).

theatres in order to enrich my experiences and keep abreast of the times. Everything portended a pleasant trip, and we cherished the most joyous expectations as to its results. But we had only gotten as far as Hamburg when my daughter developed a violent cough which forced us to stop for a couple of days (which I used, by the way, to hear the opera *Oberon,* in which the splendid tenor Tichatschek made a guest appearance as Huon).

We had to press on, however, and by the usual conveyance passed through Hanoverian Minden to Prussian Minden, whence we were to depart by diligence the following morning for Cologne, and travel from there, via Aix-la-Chapelle and Brussels, to Paris. But that same night symptoms of fever appeared, accompanied by an eruption consisting of small red spots; and at dawn, when I summoned a doctor, he stated that *measles* had broken out and expressed the firm opinion that we could not think of continuing our journey for at least three or four weeks. And so there was nothing to do but arm ourselves with patience, secure good Dr. Consborough's continuous supervision, and come to an agreement with the hotel owner concerning our prolonged stay. The previous evening we had reserved our seats to Cologne, and it was now a matter of getting them reserved for an unspecified day, which detail was gladly taken care of by the post office.

But just as I was standing rather dejectedly, contemplating what I should do with myself for four weeks in this city, which appeared to me to be a boring hole, the diligence from Berlin rolled into the post yard and a well-dressed gentleman greeted his adolescent daughter with signs of heartfelt joy, and asked if in Berlin she had now "learnt pretty dances." It suddenly flashed through my mind that here in Minden there might possibly be need of a dancing teacher, and that by giving some lessons I could find not only suitable employment but a means of covering our unexpectedly increased expenses. But to whom should I apply in order to carry out my plan? I was just standing there speculating upon this when an elderly man with a mild and intelligent countenance came walking by, and I did not hesitate to accost him in a courteous fashion. It happened to be the Rector of the *Gymnasium,* Dr. Immanuel, to whom I had addressed myself. I told him who I was and briefly related the story of our ill luck as well as the idea I had hit upon so as not to fall into idleness and melancholy. He kindly listened to me and took me to the city's governor, Lieutenant-General François, whose daughters might wish to take dancing lessons. I thanked the good man most obligingly, and did not waste a moment undertaking the necessary steps.

The General with the French name received me rather coldly and formally, and answered in German when I introduced myself in French. But when he observed that I was also fluent in the German language, he at once became extremely pleasant and immediately promised to impart my plan to his daughters, as well as to several other royal officials, who might possibly like their children to share in the instruction.

I now returned to the hotel and reported upon my success. But my good innkeeper, Herr Bieber, called to my attention the fact that I first had to ask

AUGUSTA BOURNONVILLE
This engraving after Lehmann's painting, 1845, shows the choreographer's
eldest child at age fifteen. Teatermuseet, Copenhagen.

THE OLD BALLETMASTER
A rare full-length photograph of 1865.
Det kgl. Bibliotek, Copenhagen.

for the Burgomaster's permission before I could begin my classes. I therefore went to the Town Hall, where I encountered this high public official sitting majestically at his green table and regarding me with a searching look. I presented to him both the aforesaid matter and its motives, and identified myself by showing my mininsterial passport, which was drawn up in French. He examined it inside and out with such a serious expression that he might have been blessed Herman von Bremenfeldt himself, and finally came to the conclusion that he could not determine from this passport whether I was really a balletmaster. However, when I took out my letters of credit for 4000 and 2000 francs respectively, he exclaimed with signs of true esteem: "You are a real balletmaster! " and excused his disbelief on the grounds that he met many traveling "riffraff," all of whom claimed to be balletmasters, so that only with the greatest caution did he dare to hand out the requested permission. I could not help but give the man his due, and left the Town Hall with a feeling of how ludicrously fantastic the whole situation was.

While my poor Augusta went through the various stages of this serious illness and her beloved aunt did not leave her bedside in the dark room with the blinds pulled down, I struggled to combat my anxiety through the activity I had taken upon myself and by seeing the curiosities which the city had to offer. But the danger was soon overcome, and it was now a matter of exercising the greatest caution and preventing uncalled-for consequences. I now continued with great pleasure the lessons I had begun, in which a number of young ladies and, later, a company of young officers took part. Most of what I taught belonged to more refined society dancing, but it was the polka-mazurka which had the greatest success as the newest choreographic figure of the day. I hereby had the opportunity of coming into contact with a highly cultured society and found among the young Prussian officers a most urbane spirit, which at that time gave no hint of the aggressive feeling which later on was to vent itself upon Denmark.

Several names like François, Arnim, Borries, and Funck have since figured in the war bulletins. At this time they shone only on the drill ground, where one certainly had to admire their outstanding precision in executing the manual of arms, as well as the soldiers' harmonious singing on the march home after the manoeuvers had ended.

On my wanderings in the city and its environs, I visited the ancient Cathedral, where, according to legend, the Saxon chieftain Wittekind was baptized in the spring which still wells up in the middle of the choir. The story cites Paderborn as the hero's christening place, but here it is no doubt the same as with the dispute about Homer's birthplace.

I also had the pleasure of meeting a former merchant, Moyer, who possessed a considerable collection of antiquities, mostly German and Nordic, and was said to be in constant correspondence with our unforgettable Thomsen. He was quite at home in Danish literature and, on the whole, an extremely fine man in whom I took a great delight.

For the rest, the city possessed little worth seeing, with the exception of its casemated fortifications, which to my eyes seemed so strong that even inside the thick walls a weak force must be able to resist a far superior siege army by shooting through the treacherous gun ports. Round about, the glacis were laid out to form the most delightful promenades, and the loveliest nightingale concert resounded from the bushes and thickets on the opposite shore of the Weser.

At this time another (according to the rules of art, more correct and serious) concert was being prepared in the Cathedral, where, under the direction of *Kapellmeister* Müller, Haydn's *Creation* was to be given by the city's musical dilettanti. Upon being invited, I joined the orchestra's first violins, and with true edification took part in this successful music festival, which resulted in a pleasure trip to the suburbs.

On the appointed afternoon, the company (which I was invited to join as a guest) assembled on the glacis outside the western gate, and in an orderly procession ladies and gentlemen marched out on the broad country highway to Porta Westphalica, a picturesque spot where the Weser channel runs between two wooded hills. Before us marched the regimental band, playing the Prussian "Brave Soldier," the centuries-old "Dessauermarsch." And whom should I see solemnly booming on the big Turkish drum but our honorable *Kapellmeister* himself, dressed in the uniform and field cap of a noncommissioned officer. We settled down beneath the beech trees and enjoyed a collation which had been tastefully arranged by Herr von Borries. *Maitrank* (Rhenish wine seasoned with aromatic herbs), mixed with four-part singing and lively musical numbers, brought forth skoals, among which there was one in improvised verse by the beloved old Rector Immanuel. There were music and singing on the trip home, and the company parted with the impression of a delightful spring celebration.

I was also invited to watch a presentation of gymnastic exercises performed by the pupils of the *Gymnasium,* and I once again had to admire the military training that Prussian youth was given in the schools. And it still did not occur to me that these very skills were in a few years to serve a policy which I certainly shy away from characterizing, as it might easily lead to my being prosecuted for injuries against a *friendly* power.

The weeks flew by, and in my letters home I could report that our beloved daughter's illness was now successfully past. After a short convalescence, we could once more set out upon our interrupted journey. At that time the express consisted of several coaches, and since we had just met the Swedish Professor Geijer† and his family, we divided ourselves so that the ladies were together in one compartment and the gentlemen in another. For

---

† Erik Gustaf Geijer (1783–1847), professor at Uppsala, was the outstanding Swedish historian of his time, giving special attention to his country's early political-social history. He also wrote and published poems, hymns, and songs—largely dealing with Sweden's legendary past—whose music he composed himself. A vivid and charming description of the meeting between the Bournonvilles and the Geijers, recounted by the professor's daughter Agnes, may be found in *August Bournonville: Souvenir de ton père,* p. 26.

me, it was a most interesting experience to travel in the company of the famous historian, whose excursions in the field of music have given such great pleasure with the outstanding songs he wrote, nearly all of which were featured by Jenny Lind. At this time he was ailing, and traveling for the good of his health to Aix-la-Chapelle, where we parted, never to meet again.

I have nothing important to relate concerning my short stay in Paris, where I installed my womenfolk, or about my flying visit to London, where I found my talented comrade Perrot as balletmaster and Lucile Grahn as his celebrated *première danseuse*. On the other hand, my wife and I both came to Paris the following year to rejoice at our daughter's progress, by then mainly in the area of the piano, which she studied under Professor Marmontel's excellent instruction.

We made several pleasant excursions into the lovely suburbs of Paris, among others to Saint-Germain-en-Laye, where I found the touching motif for my ballet *Conservatoriet,* which I have discussed in the second volume of *My Theatre Life.* On visiting the country at Marly and Bougival, we came to the villa which Alexandre Dumas *père* had built as his hermitage, and called "Monte Cristo" after his famous novel. The main building was not completely finished, but, since it was executed in the Moorish style, he had sent for Arabian painters to decorate it, and it was most fantastic to see these dark faces and half-naked figures at work on scaffolding beneath the ceilings.

In a little pool of water in the middle of the garden stood a fantastic pavilion, half Gothic and half Swiss, made of stones upon whose outer surfaces were engraved the names of the hundreds of books and poems which the owner had written. The prolific writer came out of his door and across the little drawbridge just as we had asked for permission to look at the garden. *"Vous êtes chez vous!"* he called to us with the most amiable expression, and some moments later he joined us in order to show us around the garden planted with exotic growths and inhabited by all sorts of rare animals. At this time we had already read *his* interesting *Impressions de Voyages,* and this meeting was now added to *ours* in the most pleasant fashion.

The railway now runs past Minden, which lies at some distance from the railroad station, where one stops for only a quarter of an hour to have a slap-dash meal. But every time I have seen this old city in passing through, I think of those anxious weeks when I prayed to God for my sick child, sought consolation in my work, and, strolling, listened to the nightingale's song which gave me the idea for a little souvenir poem with the refrain: *In Minden!*

PARIS — AND PARIS AGAIN (1856, 1860, AND 1865)

THE events which will remain unforgettable for those of us Danes who have lived through the years 1848 to 1851 already belong to the history of our native land. The feelings which pervaded all hearts also enraptured me, and I have described the part I played in public demonstrations, on happy as well as sad occasions, in the chapter of *My Theatre Life* dealing with "Danish National Festivals." Thus there could be no thought of journeying abroad during this entire period. My excursions to Norway in 1852–1853 were discussed under "The Wedding Festival" and "The Mountain Hut," while my stay in Vienna as well as my return via northern Italy stand with the headings "Abdallah" and "The Flower Festival." Now, so as not to weary my readers with repetition, I shall relieve them from accompanying me on my various longer and shorter visits to this world capital; rather, I will attempt to collect my impressions and reminiscences from the last of the above-mentioned years.

In the course of forty-five years, I have visited Paris eight times at irregular intervals and always found new embellishments and considerable expansion, flourishing industry and commerce, increased prosperity, greater luxury, remarkable inventions of every kind, and extraordinary facility in means of communication. At particular epochs I have been able to observe extremely interesting phenomena in the different moods which, like storms and epidemics, have swept over the populace.

The enthusiasm for the *"journées glorieuses"* of the July Revolution and the popular Citizen-King gave way to dissatisfaction and unreasonable hatred. The democratic stream was soon muddied by communistic utopias on the one hand and ambition and greed on the other. After having undergone in a few years every phase of the most unbridled freedom of speech and of the press, they had finally come to the most guarded silence in all subjects that concerned the government. Political declamations were silenced, nowhere was "La Marseillaise" heard, and patriotic songs were replaced by ballads which were to lyricism what the cancan is to decent dancing! (These ballads originated chiefly from a place of entertainment called "Alcazar," and were delivered with an original *chiqué* by a Mamsel Teresa, who, without possessing either singing skill or vocal gifts, had become famous by her emancipation and by a repertoire wherein everything was permitted, with the exception of religion and politics.)

Upon my arrival in this city, after an absence of several years, I was greeted everywhere with the exclamation: "You will hardly recognize Paris!" And there were, indeed, such great—aye, almost immense—alterations that in many places one had difficulty in orienting oneself. Whole quarters had been torn down to make room for new streets and boulevards which were lined with palaces. The markets, which had formerly been so dirty, were transformed into gigantic covered *halles*, with water fountains and vaulted cellars as storage places. All was arranged with taste and exemplary cleanliness.

On the many open squares as well as at the Louvre and on the Champs-Élysees gardens were laid out, and trees had been planted on the formerly shadeless quays.

Many new theatres were already in use, and the colossal Opera House, whose dimensions are comparable to those of the Flavian amphitheatre and for which materials almost as costly as those of St. Peter's in Rome were used, was nearing completion. (This magnificent edifice, begun during the Empire and completed under the Republic, required twelve years to be entirely finished and is said to have cost 56,000,000 francs! Its exterior as well as its stage and auditorium, together with the staircase and foyer, cannot but astonish one by their magnitude and richness. But all the same, due to an overabundance of ornamentation and gilding, it gives the impression of something heavy and oppressive. The works of sculpture, in particular, are more or less mannered, and Carpeaux's group, which is supposed to represent "The Dance," is such a disgusting picture of unrestrained shamelessness that it seems to portray the moral depravity of the Present rather than the graceful art of Terpsichore.)

The ancient churches had been completely restored and released from their disfiguring surroundings, and six magnificent new houses of worship were in the process of being built. The Louvre and the Tuileries were joined by galleries and pavilions, all in the grand style, apparently so that the Imperial Palace should not be inferior in magnificence to the Hôtel de Ville, the residence of the Prefect of the Seine; for it cannot be denied that good Monsieur Haussmann played a slightly too prominent part in the milliards-consuming drama that took place within the walls of Paris. With a certain timidity, people asked whence the money for these costly undertakings was to come, and why all this was precipitated in such haste. Was it because they feared an imminent catastrophe, or was it merely to provide work for 400,000 laborers who might possibly pose a dangerous threat to the peace of the State? However, one had to admire the guiding thought and the organizational strength that ran through these arrangements, and the foreigner received an impression which was beneficial insofar as it, at least momentarily, tore him loose from petty considerations.

Versailles, however, remains the most glorious thing of all, not only because of the splendor which Louis XIV lavished on its buildings, gardens, and fountains, but above all by reason of its historical museum where Louis Philippe has erected a meaningful monument to himself and his ungrateful fatherland by a collection of paintings, portraits, statues, and busts, all of which illustrate the martial deeds of this great nation from the most ancient times to our own day; and to this, Napoleon III has added representations of the latest campaigns in the Crimea and in Italy.

But what feelings of disgust and loathing fill the observer upon seeing the realistic perfection with which Yvon has portrayed Maréchal Ney on the retreat from Russia, and the storming of the Malakoff! Enthusiasm for heroic deeds vanishes before the horrors of reality, and far from thanking the artist for his fantasy, we censure him for having destroyed our illusions. It is then that I praise Horace Vernet, who, with poetic understanding, has in his battle scenes placed the turmoil of combat in the distance and the jubilation of victory in the foreground. And in this he is no doubt perfectly right; for not once amid the smoke and the tumult of battle is the soldier himself aware of the horror in the bloody affair.

"The Empire is peace!" These words resounded throughout Europe, but it was not very long before French troops embarked by the hundreds of thousands for the Orient to fight against the Russians for the benefit of "the Sick Man."* Hospital records give a more detailed account of what the Crimean campaign has cost in human life than the war bulletins themselves. The ensuing Italian campaign swallowed up people and money *en masse,* and in addition to what Africa annually requires, China, Cochinchina, and the Mexican Expedition have also made great demands upon the national resources. Therefore it is a high price that has been paid for those medals worn by the surviving soldiers, who, after having withstood grapeshot, cholera, and yellow fever, have returned home fairly safe and sound and as a reward are incorporated into the Imperial Guard.

What a glorious sight it was to see these voltigeurs, grenadiers, and artillerymen, true models for a military genre painting; these chasseurs, mounted on Berber stallions; these cuirassiers, who vividly reproduced the heroic images of Nansouty and Cambronne, buried on the field of Waterloo!† And now come the fantastic battalions of select daredevils in Turkish masquerade dress; destined to be thrown in where danger is greatest, these are the world-famous Zouaves, whose ranks are constantly being depleted but are filled again because fiery French youth is always ready to risk its life *"pour la gloire"!* Many think that such a race of people *must* have war so as not to fall into revolution; and yet how much energy and skill are here the spoils of death, while by a most peculiar anomaly the philanthropists of our day urge the abolition of capital punishment and take care of the worst criminals—the dregs of the human race—in prisons arranged with the utmost comfort!

A rather strange kind of warriors are the Algerian chasseurs, the so-called *Turcos,* made up of Moors, Arabs, and Negroes, well trained but disciplined only to a certain degree, whose barbarous military music seems to suggest their hereditary custom of returning from battle only with the severed heads of their dead enemies hanging from their belts. One does not keep troops like these for peace parades, and when one adds to this a standing army of 500,000 men, supported by a formidable armored fleet, one does not get any reassuring notion of the golden world peace, to the preservation of which Denmark was to be sacrificed in 1864.

Although *"la gloire"* is still the *"idole"* of the French, it has nevertheless changed its physiognomy from the days when it crowned with the laurels of immortality those chosen heroes whose exploits became the proudest property of history and the nation. Is glory now to lie in the modern system of lev-

---

*Turkey, long known as "the Sick Man of Europe."

† These generals, however, did not die on that stricken field. Cambronne, though badly wounded at Waterloo, lived until 1842, while Nansouty died at Paris in February 1815—some months before the battle of Waterloo took place.

eling or in the present conduct of war, with its enormous mass armies and the newest inventions in the art of destruction, which turn a campaign into a financial rather than a tactical or strategical question? Nowadays it depends mainly on the private soldier's endurance and contempt for death. The individual feat of arms is not singled out; people hold to *the thing* and forget *the person*. This inclination to the positivistic and the material seems to bring its influence to bear not only on the nature of war (with which, to tell the truth, I am but little acquainted) but also, unfortunately, upon art, whose various phenomena have always captured my attention.

It is most natural that art, in accordance with the necessities of life, aims at making money. But to sacrifice spirit, conviction, even conscience, to the profit of the moment is a real misfortune and an infection which threatens to spread from France into wider circles.

If one asks painters and sculptors why they have forsaken the noble, pure style and fresh, innocent Nature, in order to serve the blasé and the basest sensuality, they will most often answer with a shrug of the shoulder that they must be guided by the demands of the present. If we look at modern French literature, we find scarcely a single book that can be read aloud from cover to cover at the family hearth. At the side of an obvious talent and a lively style, one discovers the most extreme improbabilities and an urge not only to expose the weaknesses that constitute the seamy side of human nature in all countries, but to calumniate the society of their own native land. If one reproaches the author for these excesses of an unhealthy imagination, one receives the answer: "If I write a *virtuous novelle*, I find no publishers; whereas it is the very thing morality rejects that becomes a success with the public and brings in considerable sums of money to both him and me."

Everywhere, I dare say, there have been complaints about the theatres' poor productions; and yet never have these been so well attended as in recent years. The fact of the matter is: when theatre entrepreneurs only have a choice between public attendance and bankruptcy, they take refuge in *enormities,* supported by pompous advertisements. People are lured thither, are ashamed at what they see, but arouse the curiosity of others by their outcries. Now, if one estimates that at least one million people have gone there, if only a single time, one cannot be surprised that *La Belle Hélène* [by Offenbach] and *La Biche aux bois* [by Charles Foliguet] have survived a fabulous run of sold-out performances. One might be able to tolerate this as long as it concerned only the second-rate theatres. But the higher drama has allowed itself to be carried away by the new French business spirit, which runs through most of modern French art.

The Gymnase and the Vaudeville, two theatres which were formerly so wholesome, witty, and amusing in their particular genres, now show only *comédies des moeurs,* which, after having run through every phase of seduction and adultery, now nibble away at the stores of the *"demi-monde"* and camellia plants. But what is one to say when it comes to the Théâtre Français — this temple of dramatic art, where France has won its finest literary laurels! To be sure, tradition has still been maintained in Molière's excellent comedies, but the modern repertoire is unfortunately following a fatal course, and the enormous public attendance for *"Le Supplice d'une femme"* contained an unhappy omen. They ventured one step further with *Henriette Maréchal;* but despite the patronage of a high-ranking personage and Théophile Gautier's soaring praise, the piece fell before expressions of universal indignation.

I wonder if twenty-five years ago there weren't old theatre-lovers who praised a bygone era at the expense of the present? And I also wonder if we, too, could not consider ourselves a younger generation, who in another twenty-five years will look back upon the present state of art as a golden past? We old folk, who fancy ourselves to have experienced an aesthetic spring and summer, can all the same do nought but wish that the younger generation may see a new flowering emerge from the pitiable defoliation of the moment.

Fortunately, we have music to give us brighter expectations. Although not completely untouched by materialism, it nevertheless contains within itself a spiritual seed that will not be cowed; and it is both consoling and encouraging to know how large a public in Paris acclaims good and classical music.

The Conservatoire's concerts are always so heavily attended that special favor is necessary for nonsubscribers to gain admittance to them; wherefore another musical association, under the direction of M. Pasdeloup, also performs works of Haydn, Beethoven, and Mendelssohn to great applause.

The Opéra-Comique indefatigably continues to retain its old repertoire at the side of newer light and melodious subjects. Gounod and Félicien David, strongly influenced by the German school, and Hector Berlioz, in pursuit of originality, assume a prominent place among present-day composers.

Military music has likewise taken a considerable upswing, and it now possesses a Conservatory of its own under the leadership of a former *Danish* trombonist, Dieppo. And as a curiosity, I must not fail to mention a "Concert Monstre" that took place during the summer of 1856 in an open hippodrome, where eighteen hundred wind instruments worked together, in which was a *solo* performed with great precision by *one hundred and fifty trombones!*

Just as a generation ago Rossini had his ardent followers and fanatical opponents, so too Meyerbeer has in recent days been the object of completely divergent opinions. Both consolidated their renown in Paris, but when Rossini felt he had achieved his very best with *Guillaume Tell,* and, content with having left behind for our admiration and delight—out of a host of more or less successful operas—*Il Barbiere* and *Guillaume Tell,* he turned a deaf ear to all requests and temptations and retired to the seat of honor where he now (1860) sits enthroned as a hero, unconcerned by criticism. Every day I saw him stroll through the street which bears his name and, with his ironic smile, view the laurel-crowned busts of himself in the windows of all the music shops. And when I sometimes touched upon the loss that people felt with his premature retirement from the musical arena, he expressed the conviction that a continuous craving for new triumphs would have exposed his weaknesses, obscured the fame he had won, and embittered his old age.

Meyerbeer, on the other hand, strove and worked to his utmost, even sacrificing his health and peace of mind for the applause of the crowd; and although no one will justly be able to deprive him of his great merits in dramatic music, his talent nevertheless reached its culmination in *Les Huguenots,* despite the varied efforts later expended upon *Le Prophète, L'Etoile du Nord,* and *Dinorah.* With *L'Africaine,* which was performed only after his death, criticism gradually faded away and people were unanimous in admiring this work which, although less rich in melody than his earlier compositions, all the same bore witness to his superior talent.

It was with great pleasure that one took refuge from these operas, which were equipped with an enormous wealth of scenery, pageantry, and balletic effects, in the far more humble Théâtre Lyrique. Here Gounod's *Faust* was given, with the graceful Mme. Miolan-Carvalho in the role of Marguerite; and on this stage, seventy years after its creation, Mozart's *The Magic Flute* found a reception and public attendance greater than anywhere else in the world. The performance was exemplary in every respect: the duets between Pamina and Papageno (Mme. Carvalho and M. Troy) were rendered so poetically that with Mozart one was carried away in paradisical dreams. Here a young Swedish songstress, Christine Nilsson, continued her series of debut performances as Queen of the Night, with a fresh and sonorous voice, superb vocalization, and such natural acting that she won the French public's total sympathy.

And finally, at the Italian Opera I attended a performance of Donizetti's *Poliutto* (a lyrical adaptation by Scribe of Corneille's tragedy *Polyeucte,* translated into Italian). The plot describes the persecution of the Christians under Decius, who sends the Proconsul Severus to Armenia, where Felix is governor. The latter's daughter Paulina is married to Poliutto, who secretly acclaims the new Master. But when, after several conflicts, he reveals himself, throws down the images of the idols, and makes known his faith, she follows him to martyrdom.

These last two roles were masterfully performed by the tenor Fraschini and Signora Penco, known to us from her earliest debut in Copenhagen. They were both inwardly moved by the story, but at the moment when Poliutto hurls down the pagan altars and proclaims "the one true God," Fraschini unfolded a fullness of voice and tragic excitement that had an inspiring effect upon the whole audience, and the thunderous applause was only subdued by welling tears of emotion.

In artistic respects, there was something almost *prophetic* about this magnificent scene; for in the direction which art, and the theatre in particular, has taken, there is an element of paganism present. Whether the idols be called Avarice, Arousal of the Senses, or Pleasure-seeking Curiosity, they will not always prevail over taste, and their altars must eventually crumble into dust! Therefore, with the impression of the victory of *the True* and *the Beautiful,*

I left this performance and the following day set off on my journey home to Copenhagen.

As a supplement to these Parisian trips, I must mention a little detour to London. Since my previous visits, this city had increased the number of its inhabitants by a million and had received considerable embellishments, especially at the magnificent Trafalgar Square, with Nelson's statue at the pinnacle of a disproportionately tall column, which grumblers liken to a mast upon which a "midshipman" is placed for punishment and penitence. I visited the theatre in the Haymarket, where the *vaudeville* was flourishing with Buxton, Charles [James] Mathews, and Mme. Vestris, and the Queen's Theatre, with its customary Italian opera and Saint-Léon's new ballet *Lalla Rookh*,‡ portrayed by his graceful wife, *née* Fanny Cerrito.

Everyone is familiar with the English observance of the Sabbath, which transforms crowded London into a quiet and depopulated wilderness, animated only by the sound of the church bell which calls the faithful to the worship of God. I obeyed its summons, and as I was lodging in Norfolk Street, I found in nearby St. Clement Danes a church that was of historical interest to me since Harald Harefod, son of Canute the Great, lies buried there.

I used the rest of this long Sunday for an excursion into the surrounding country, and I paid a visit to my world-famous friend, Jenny Lind-Goldschmidt, at her villa in Wimbledon. She received her Danish "uncle" with such cordiality that it caused her little son to ask if it were his grandfather who had arrived; and in her cozy family circle I spent several pleasant hours, embellished by her glorious singing.

A letter from H. C. Andersen brought me into contact with the translator of his fairy tales, Mistress Bushby, in whose company I attended a large concert in St. James's Hall. But the high point of my journey's surprises was reached only at Sydenham, upon entering the remarkable Crystal Palace, which had now been moved from Hyde Park and transformed from an industrial exhibition into a museum which was to display everything great and worth seeing in the fields of art, historical memorials, and natural phenomena—most of the things only copies, but executed with astonishing precision and exquisite taste.

An enormous room, the dimensions of which I am unable to state, was divided into two zones: the northern or temperate one separated by a double glass wall from the southern or tropical clime. In both of them were to be found not only the flora and fauna peculiar to the respective regions, but also the architectural, pictorial, and sculptural phenomena which distinguished the various countries. Thus one was transported from the Arctic Ocean to the Equator, from Florence to Rome to the Alhambra, even to the pyramids, pagodas, and ancient ruins from both Nineveh and Mexico!

‡ Another lapse of memory. Actually, *Lalla Rookh* was by Jules Perrot.

A flowing brook flanked by marble banks traversed the center of the hall, with rare aquatic plants on its surface and goldfish in its ripples. Two rows of marble statues after famous ancient and modern masters (among whom was our Thorvaldsen) reflected their beauty in the shimmering waters, and the flower beds that surrounded the bubbling fountains diffused their fragrance for yards around.

Beneath the central dome extended a concert amphitheatre arranged to hold several thousand people, singers and instrumentalists as well as spectators, while in one of the side corridors was a smaller "Concert Room" where rehearsals were just then being held for Handel's *Messiah*. Here one was involuntarily transported into the realm of the marvelous!

In the basement of this enchanted palace had been established a splendid restaurant, where waiters with powdered hair, livery, kneebreeches, white silk stockings, and gloves waited at table. And here it was that the Danish merchant Simonsen, who was living in London at the time and in whose house I had enjoyed the most obliging courtesy, brought me, along with several other travelers from distant climes, and by a splendid luncheon—which, I dare say, must have cost several gold sovereigns—brought us back from the world of fantasy to the most luxurious realism of hospitality.

In the compartment of a railway train on my journey home (in the early summer of 1860) I met a French landowner, M. de Chatenay, who together with his young son intended to travel to Lapland to view the midsummer sun at midnight from Torneå and Sulitelma. These travelers stopped over in Copenhagen for several days and, in the company of a Russian Professor Grot, visited me at Fredensborg, where I had the pleasure of showing them the beautiful scenery of the place.

As it happened, the weather was lovely, and my guests were delighted with the day they spent there. The Russian, who spoke all languages, and very good Swedish into the bargain, had the greatest success among my ladies, while the Frenchman, having only his mother tongue, particularly aroused my sympathies. Both of them promised to write me, and among the family it now became a great thing to speculate as to which of them would be heard from first—wagers were laid for and against the Frenchman and the Russian!

Around New Year's a letter arrived from M. de Chatenay, who with his son had made a grand tour of Norway, Sweden, Finland, Russia, Poland, and Hungary, Austria, the Tyrol, and Italy, finally coming via Marseilles to Paris, where he had his residence in the *faubourg* St. Germain. Denmark and Fredensborg were among the high points of this lengthy trip, and praising Danish hospitality in my person (with a certain amount of exaggeration), he begged me to consider his house in Paris and his chateau of Bernicourt in northern France as open lodgings for myself and every member of my family.

I availed myself of his offer in the autumn of 1865, and passed a couple of extremely pleasant days at his country estate, where everything still bore the stamp of the old *legitimate* and *clerical* France, modified and animated by true French urbanity. Since then I have maintained a frequent exchange of letters with the old father, as well as with his son, who is now residing at Bonne-leau, another large holding in Picardy. But only *eleven* years after our farewell on the pier at Helsingør did our Russian professor realize that he owed me a letter. Oh well, better late than never! But he excused himself and made up for his negligence in the most amiable fashion by some time later sending me his brother, Councillor of State Constantin Grot, for whom I also acted as cicerone and host. In return, these good men showed me the greatest kindness in St. Petersburg, and in their family circles I was regarded as an old acquaintance and friend.

These meetings naturally lead to the reflection that when, one by one, the friends of our youth and our contemporaries begin to pass away, we old folk would run the risk of being left behind like lonely survivors in a large and densely filled churchyard, were it not that some kind Fate has granted us the good fortune to establish fine new acquaintances and to gain friends, either on the journey through life or on the railway lines through Europe.

MUNICH (1869)

THE reason for this journey has already been discussed in the first part of Volume III, under the heading "The 1869–1870 Season." Since *Lohengrin* had rightly come to be regarded as the one of Wagner's operas that would find most favor with our musical audience, the Theatre administration, to make certain of the adequacy of our forces for proper performance of this work, resolved to send Capelmester Paulli and me to Germany to observe several performances of the aforesaid opera at one of the major theatres. Through an exchange of letters with Wagner himself as well as with the theatre administrators in Berlin and Munich, I learnt that *Lohengrin,* after a lengthy rest, was scheduled for performance in Munich "by supreme command" on the twenty-eighth or thirtieth of May, 1869.

We therefore set out for Munich, traveling by way of Hamburg, Frankfurt am Main, and Hanau. Although I had traversed Germany in a number of different directions, this was the first time that I actually found myself in Bavaria, and, after a continuous and steep ascent, marveled at reaching a plain with peat moss and luxuriant watercourses two thousand feet above sea level.

After having passed Würzburg and Augsburg one enjoys no more picturesque prospects, for Munich itself is surrounded by rather monotonous scenery and only in the distance does one espy the Bavarian Alps. But as it happened, we had neither the time nor the opportunity to view the landscape because of the speed of the train, which in less than three days carried us to our journey's destination.

I had heard and read so much about this beautiful city, so rich in artistic works, and yet my expectations were in every way surpassed. What King Ludwig I has done for Munich will perpetuate his glory despite the eccentricities that tarnished the last years of his reign. His keen artistic tastes and ardent feeling for the honor of his country are evidenced in proud monuments. Magnificent buildings for public institutions, bronze statues commemorating famous men of all professions, frescoes within the Palace as well as the Arcade of the Hofgarten, and priceless treasures of older and newer art collected and tastefully arranged in the Glyptothek and in both Pinakotheks, carry the viewer back to the Golden Age of Greece. The National Museum, which he founded, now stands finished, with the inscription: "For the Honor and Example of my People." And indeed, the millions he has spent here have found a worthier object than did those which in the past were squandered on armaments and the machinery of destruction.

Within these halls of Fame and Memory Bavaria has certainly known how to assemble everything having even the remotest connection with the House of Pfalz-Wittelsbach-Zweibrücken. Thus we find the Swedish kings Charles X and XII placed among the heroes of Bavaria, not to mention Margrave Christoffer, who is receiving the homage of the three Nordic kingdoms! Several imaginary victories are likewise illustrated; for example, the Battle of Hanau, where the remnants of the French army, defeated at Leipzig, swept their faithless allies off the field like chaff before the wind, and the well-known "Erstürmung" (April 13, 1849) of the entrenchments, which were only erected and equipped with guns fourteen years later!

But I notice that I have involuntarily entered the historical-political domain, and before my departure from Copenhagen I had promised myself to refrain from all reflections, and especially from discussions, about those subjects which undeniabley constitute the German's "sore spot," upon which all grounds of reason and fairness break down. If one is fortunate enough to avoid this stumbling block, one will everywhere in Germany meet with the most amiable courtesy, and I have several times had the opportunity to appreciate the tact with which questions concerning my native land and my nationality were handled in my presence.

Therefore, on to Art! without regard to past or future conflicts. With justifiable pride we recognize the masterly hand of our great Thorvaldsen in the equestrian statue of Maximilian on Wittelsbachsplatz, in Eugène Napoleon's tomb in Michaelskirche, and in the incomparable Adonis which stands opposite to Canova's Bacchus in the Glyptothek, triumphant in the noble contest of the supreme art.

Outside this marble temple our immortal countryman's portrait stands at the side of Canova and Rauch, together with those of Phidias, Praxiteles, and Michelangelo. There he stands, carved in marble and leaning upon Hope. Even though he might have acknowledged that the ideal for which he strove was not achieved, there was no one who came closer to it than he!

Although no European capital can pride itself on possessing an architectural curiosity such as our Thorvaldsen's Museum, in Munich there is nevertheless a very remarkable collection of models and plaster casts from the works of the celebrated, all too early deceased, [Ludwig Michael] Schwanthaler [1802–1848]. The majority of these statues and groups, which have been executed in marble and in bronze, bear witness to his creative genius as well as his incredible productivity.

"Hermann's Revolt" on the pediment of the Valhalla Temple at Regensburg and the "Bavaria" at the Ruhmeshalle outside Munich are true masterpieces of composition and noble proportions. By fifty-six steps within the pedestal, one ascends to the colossal "Bavaria." Thence, by a spiral staircase consisting of a similar number of steps, one ascends to the neck of the goddess, from which one enters her lovely head where there is room for five persons standing and six sitting. Through the loopholes which are mounted in her eyes, one enjoys a broad perspective of the city and the more distant hills. Her right hand leans upon a lion couchant, and her left proffers the laurel wreath of glory. This colossus, who recalls to our imagination the gigantic figures of antiquity, is nevertheless light and harmonious in its physical proportions, and, seen at rather close range, it possesses a grace as captivating as that of the most finely formed marble statues.

The portico of the Ruhmeshalle itself, which in a semicircle surrounds the towering statue, contained at that time the busts of seventy-two famous men who lived and worked in Bavaria, among them minne- and meistersingers from the Middle Ages, such as Walther von der Vogelweide, Hans Sachs, and others. . . . For the Germans must be granted this: they are fond of the celebrities among their countrymen, and woe to him who critically attempts to hurl their heroes from the pedestal upon which national pride and recognition once placed them.

A letter from our own world-famous poet, H. C. Andersen, introduced us to the Director of the Academy of Art, Professor Kaulbach, who received us with a kindness and straightforwardness that most pleasantly reminded me of the many unforgettable hours of "initiation" I had enjoyed in Thorvaldsen's atelier. He was at that time, although sixty-four years old, still in the full strength of his talent and incontestably Germany's greatest painter. At home we had come to know his works through a host of excellent engravings and photographs; and while we admired his rich humor in the illustrations to *Reynard the Fox*, we were astonished at the almost prophetic spirit that appears in pieces like "The Tower of Babel" and "The Destruction of Jerusalem."

He showed us several new works, among others some cartoons and designs for larger paintings, several of which were commissions from America and had more of a Protestant flavor than was fitting in thoroughly Catholic Bavaria. At the side of "The Persecution of the Christians under Nero," which is to be a companion piece to the historical and allegorical pictures that adorn the main staircase in the Berlin Museum, we saw the charming love idyll

"Romeo and Juliet," as well as "Walther von der Vogelweide and his Beloved," both commissioned by the young King.

In a sequel to the Lübeck "Dance of Death" he had given his satirical humor full play, and the observations with which he accompanied this work bore witness to the spirit that had in his youth prompted him to leap through a dauber's cartoon, just as I have pictured it in the ballet *Ponte Molle*. He delighted in remembering the merry hours he had passed in the company of his old comrade, Simonsen, and earnestly prayed us to greet his dear friend Andersen, whose hovering "Angel" he has so beautifully illustrated. Their spirits have now been borne on wings of Faith and Hope to the Home of Light, but their works will long continue to gladden and refresh those living here below.

There is almost no city in Europe, with the possible exceptions of Rome and Florence, where art arrests the eye as it does in Munich. Here, as in the Age of Pericles and that of the Medici, it has literally thrust its way into life, aye, even to the resting places of the dead. I advise everyone not to leave the city without having paid a visit to the large "God's Acre" which through a majestic portal leads to gardens surrounded by brick arcades like those in Bologna. Within these cloisters are splendid marble monuments and biblical frescoes, while out in the gardens, amid luxuriant flowers, stand the more modest graves, shaded by cypress and acacia trees in which, during the very spring days of our visit, nightingales in great number warbled delightfully. Many richly furnished chapels rise above family tombs adorned with statues and busts; and almost everywhere, even at the foot of the simplest mound, there is a small stone basin with holy water and a brush for sprinkling it, in accordance with Catholic custom.

Immediately upon entering this necropolis, one's attention is fastened upon a hall with large glass doors, where the dead are placed in open coffins for several days before they are put into the ground. Here, together with children, old women, and young girls, we saw generals in full dress uniform, priests in their vestments, and public officers in the robes of some Order—all gently sleeping, surrounded by flowers and with a string in their hands. At the slightest movement, this string causes a numbered bell to ring, thereby alerting those who, being relieved at regular intervals, guard the dead both night and day. This measure is taken in case of suspended animation, but it is very seldom, I dare say, that anyone awakens in this vestibule of Eternity. On the other hand, hope smiles upon the care-laden in the delightful garden, where the evening sun gilds the marble figures and through the arches sheds its rays upon Jairus' daughter, the Son of the Widow of Nain, the Awakening of Lazarus, and the glorious Easter Morn.

The majority of the population profess the Catholic religion, without fanaticism, however, and even among the younger generation with a certain inclination to emancipate themselves from the power of the Pope. Nevertheless the magnificent church processions are still continued, and during our stay the great Memorial to the Dead was celebrated. This the King attended, accompanied by the dignitaries of the realm and the Guard of Halberdiers, in the venerable old Frauenkirche, the inside of which had been transformed into a birch wood. The glorious church singing, with full orchestra, alternated with masses chanted by priests and monks, and when the main doors were opened the air resounded with the thundering of cannon and the pealing of bells. The church was thereupon thronged with an endless column of nuns, penitents, little girls clad in white and decked with flowers, guilds of merchants and artisans with their richly embroidered banners, public officials and gentlemen of the Court in full dress uniform, several orders of monks with their silver saints, and then the Archbishop, walking beneath a baldachin, with the handsome young King behind him. The whole procession advanced with measured tread keeping time with the military band, and a division of Halberdiers brought up the rear.

We admired Ludwig II's knightly figure and perceived in his mild eye an expression of intelligence mingled with melancholy. He is said to greatly shun human company and to be especially impervious to the charms of women. Music is purported to be his avowed passion and Richard Wagner his ideal of a composer. Under the Royal patronage *Tannhäuser, Lohengrin, Der Fliegende Holländer, Die Meistersinger,* and *Tristan und Isolde* were produced and performed at the Court Opera Theatre. For *Das Rheingold,* the first act of which takes place beneath the billowing surface of the Rhine, fantastic settings were painted, while the floor of the theatre and all of the machinery underwent a magnificent transformation. All of this was but a prelude to the colossal Bayreuth performance of *Der Ring des Nibelungen,* which was some years later to astonish, if not exactly satisfy, all the lovers of "the prodigy of the music of the future."

Lohengrin, which at later performances appeared with substantial abridgements, was now, by command of the King, to be revived in its entirety, therefore demanding as good as a new production. Paulli and I arrived on the very morning that the first full rehearsal was to be held. The Theatre administrator, Herr von Perfall, who had traveled to Vienna to attend the inauguration of the new Opera, had beforehand recommended us to his secretary, Herr von Stehle, who showed us a kindness that cannot be overemphasized.

We were taken up to one of the *premières loges,* from which we could see and hear everything, unnoticed. The first impression was striking, aye, almost decisive; for we entered the loge as the first strains of the Bridal Chorus sounded at the beginning of Act III; and when this was immediately followed by the graceful duet between Elsa and Lohengrin, we were enraptured by the melodic atmosphere!

The *Kapellmeister,* Hans von Bülow, whose duties were exclusively limited to compositions by Wagner, for whom he cherishes an admiration bordering on fanaticism and self-sacrificing devotion (feelings which the Prophet has reciprocated in his own fashion), skillfully conducted the orchestra consisting of eighty well-disciplined musicians, and made a show of gymnastic agility as he sprang from his podium, across the row of footlamps, and up onto the stage to correct several unfortunate wind-players in the background. This same man, to whom we had a letter of introduction from Professor Gade, showed us great kindness. But since his wife, a daughter of Liszt, was absent (with Wagner in Lucerne) he did not keep house. Instead he treated us to a pleasure trip to Nymphenburg and dined with us at the *table d'hôte* in the Hotel Leinfelder. Here several interesting opinions were exchanged, but when I was so unfortunate as to mention Gounod as one of the modern composers who had allowed himself to be influenced by the system championed by Wagner, Bülow flew into a temper and exclaimed, "*Ach!* Don't talk to me about Gounod and his *Faust!* I rank the worst opera by Auber above it!" I attempted to defend my position, but was thrown for a loss—not of my conviction, however.

The following evening there was to be a dress rehearsal, complete with props, and His Majesty himself was to attend it, alone, without a retinue! A comfortable place was allotted us all the same. But counterorders arrived, and we had to content ourselves with a fragmentary rehearsal of the most difficult passages. However, since we were equally interested in the Theatre's other artistic offerings, we were sent complimentary tickets for the finest seats and, with the most exquisite courtesy, we were granted admission to every part of the Theatre's facilities.

The scene-painters showed us their models and designs, and the settings and machinery were set up for us. We also got to inspect the superbly arranged wardrobe magazines and had the opportunity to bestow our fullest approval on the outstanding fire-extinguishing apparatus. I paid a couple of visits to the ballet school, which was directed by one Herr Faënzel and stood under the special supervision of my former pupil, Frau Lucile Grahn-Young, who, residing in Munich, well-to-do and married to a former tenor, as temporary *Balletmeisterinn* arranges the *divertissements* in the Wagnerian operas. I renewed our acquaintance and the *best* of our common memories in the most pleasant fashion.

Munich's Hof und Nationaltheater, connected by a gallery with the smaller Residenztheater, is at once the largest and most tasteful in all of Germany. In acoustical respects, the auditorium, which contains five *étages* and has room for 2500 comfortable seats, possesses the invaluable advantage of being equally serviceable for speaking as well as singing voices and for instrumental music. On the same stage, opera and drama are presented with equal success, while the comedy in particular stands on a respectable footing and offers some superb talents among the masculine personnel. Actors like Messrs. Lang, Hertz, Possart, and Rüthling would assert their artistic rank at any theatre. The German drama, however, belongs to a direction of taste and feeling that we Danes must regard as a past phase, even when it applies to Schiller's *Kabale und Liebe,* wherein a Fraulein Hauszmann, as Louise, proved her considerable talent.

The industry and care that are lavished upon Wagner's operas seem to be at the expense of the rest of the lyric repertoire, which, from what we could judge, was treated with unforgiveable carelessness. Thus the performances of Mozart's *Figaro* and Boïeldieu's *La Dame blanche* were greatly inferior to those given here at home. I suppose that despite his advanced age the baritone Kindermann is an outstanding singer; but outside a certain genre of tyrant roles, such as Friedrich von Telramund, he is but a mediocre dramatic performer.

The long-awaited performance of *Lohengrin* took place on the appointed day and lasted for almost five hours. All the same, this did not seem long to us, partly because of our anxious attention to every detail, musical as well as scenic, and partly because the performance was altogether most exemplary. Vogel and Fraulein Mallinger were superb in the principal roles. Frau Vogel's Ortrud and, as stated, Kindermann's treacherous Friedrich formed a talented quartet with the two singers mentioned above. The chorus distinguished itself by fullness and harmony.

The scenery, all of the sketches for which were kindly turned over to me by the *regisseur*, Herr Siegel, was entirely according to Wagner's own precepts. The orchestra, which possibly plays too prominent a part in all his operas, was conducted with great skill and fine attention to detail by von Bülow, who, as already remarked, has not only devoted his entire existence to the glorification of Wagner but also shares his every opinion and speaks of Mendelssohn and Meyerbeer with pity and scorn!

This cult, however, is not universal, either in Munich or throughout greater Germany. Especially in his brochure "Das Judenthum in der Musik," Wagner succeeded in alienating the music-loving Jewish community and received an embittered response in another pamphlet entitled "Wagner der Judenfresser." However that may be, Wagner, in spite of his eccentric ideas, his contempt for the accepted forms, and his passionate and unfair judgments, must nevertheless be recognized as a musical magnitude of uncommon importance. And as for *Lohengrin*, Paulli agreed with me that, with the necessary abridgment and careful rehearsal, this opera must surely create an epoch on our lyric stage and assume a place which might be unique but, at any rate, eminent in our repertoire.

After having written Wagner and Baron Perfall to compliment them in my own name and that of my friend, and having expressed our thanks to the Theatre's artistic and administrative notabilities for their amiable kindness, we paid a final visit to the priceless collections and prepared for our departure, satisfied with the rich booty of our short stay and praising the liberality and hospitality that had been shown to us foreigners.

What especially attracted my notice in the life and manners of Bavaria were the *Gemütlichkeit* peculiar to the people of Southern Germany, and the way in which they comport themselves with pipe and tankard in the beer gardens and the characteristic *Kneiper*, where the foaming *Faszbier* is poured and drunk in pots and steins and where the tavernkeeper, his wife, and even the serving girl sit down at table and entertain the guests. That beer plays an important role in Munich, in the face of the government's disinterested efforts, is no secret. But then, what beer! All foreign imitations notwithstanding, such a drink is to be had only in Munich!

We traveled homeward via Dresden, where Paulli remained to attend a performance of *Die Meistersinger*. I, on the other hand, hurried on to Berlin to see Paul Taglioni's new ballet, *Fantasca*. In a respected newspaper, a prize-winning aesthetician once posed the question as to whether Bournonville could truly deserve the name of Balletmaster when one observed what is presented by those of his profession at the Berlin Opera? I admit that Taglioni's ballets are extremely different from mine and contain elements which I am, in some measure, denied the use of: namely, a massive *corps de ballet* and a superabundant wealth of scenery.

I admire his skill in choreographic arrangement, which, regardless of dramatic worth or poetic inspiration, must enrapture the avid spectator. Thus, when I see Fantasca, who is in love with a toreador, being carried off by a Persian wizard and dancing a solo in the golden palace of Ispahan; when I watch her unfortunate suitors endure many hard and sometimes grotesque trials, only to be dragged from the ice of the North Pole to the burning sun of the tropics; and lastly, when I everywhere perceive the beneficent influence of the fairy Aquaria, who is herself announced by German inscriptions and finally unites the faithful lovers in her magnificent Aquarium, where pike and perch swim above their heads and the bridesmaids lie picturesquely grouped in open oyster shells, surrounded by coral, polypi, and boiled lobsters! — then I feel completely alienated from this type of scenic art and share in the general rapture like a total uninitiate.

The Prussian Royal Ballet forms an integral part of this Great Power's "prestige" and cannot bear to be eclipsed, either by Russia or by France. It was with a certain amount of pride that they told me what *"barbarisches Geld"* this ballet had cost. And when, in addition to the expenditures for décor and machinery, one estimates four, five, or even more changes of costume for a *corps* of nearly two hundred persons (whereof a single Amazon Dance by forty-eight *danseuses* cost 60 Prussian thalers for costumes and fittings for each individual) a sum of 30,000 to 40,000 Prussian thalers would hardly suffice for such a magnificent outfitting.

And yet I did not think of bemoaning the limited conditions under which the Danish Theatre is forced to operate. It must even, up to a certain point, be considered beneficial that art is not overburdened with outward tinsel and that its efforts aim at satisfying the mind more than the senses. Only it would be desirable if the public would leave economic calculations to those whose proper concern they are and stop spoiling its own enjoyment by constantly mulling over what *the beautiful* costs in terms of *money*.

With such reflections, I set my course for home, sailed from Stettin, and landed at my country home in Fredensborg. There I occupied my imagination with work for the following Theatre season, while beneath the glorious beech woods I took pride and joy in a splendor that not even the mightiest prince on earth is able to call forth by royal decree.

PETERSBURG AND MOSCOW (1874)

THE great Field Marshal Condé is supposed to have said that in order to wage war three things are necessary: money, money, and more money! In these expensive times the same thing might be said of journeying abroad, if two other chief requirements were not also imposed in order to travel beneficially and comfortably: namely, good health and a cheerful disposition. The latter is to some degree dependent upon the former. But first off, allow me to say that I was well endowed in this respect, and as far as financial matters were concerned, the Ancker Foundation for *poets* gave my pocketbook as well as my self-confidence vigorous support. Therefore, in my sixty-ninth year I set out into the wide world to receive new impressions, to refresh my imagination, and, if possible, to gather material for future compositions.

As a rule, Italy and France are the places in which artists desirous of furthering their knowledge prefer to take refuge; in the first, to be revived by the stimulating warmth of Nature, the folk life, and the masterpieces of art; in the second, to be influenced by the moods and progress of the present day. Switzerland is especially suited to wealthy tourists and people who need to breathe clean and healthy air. At the moment, such a thing is not to be found in all of Germany, where an overbearing political tone has supplanted the old joviality and where we Danes, moreover, find ourselves oppressed by bitter and painful memories. Oddly enough, although rich in beautiful scenery, singular folkways, and historical treasures, Norway and Sweden are not reckoned among the countries for which travel stipends are allotted. And indeed it cannot be denied that Scandinavian hospitality, with its banquets, family fêtes, and pleasure trips, simply does not leave the foreigner traveling for artistic purposes much time for work and thorough study.

But who ever thinks of Russia when it is not a matter of traveling there to earn money or to be a representative on some solemn occasion? The distance, the climate, but above all the prejudice that this mighty kingdom lies beyond the pale of civilization frighten the tourist and prevent the art-lover from visiting it. People most often content themselves with descriptions couched either in the style of a novel or in the form of one-sided criticism. But if one has the desire to see and hear something out of the ordinary, and if one will only seek out and judge with a benevolent eye the strange and magnificent things which, especially in the Russian capitals, appear before the spectator and the thinker, the rewards of such a visit can in many respects exceed the expectations.

LUCILE GRAHN

Left: As the Sylphide. Lithograph by Chr. Vogt from about the time of the ballet's Danish premiere, 1836. Right: As Giselle. Photograph inscribed on the back to August Bournonville, dating from his 1869 visit to Munich. Both, Teatermuseet, Copenhagen.

MARIUS PETIPA
The inscription may be translated: "Respectful homage to the
wholly amiable Monsieur August Bournonville," with signature
and date. Teatermuseet, Copenhagen.

Ever since my earlier professional activities in Paris and during the years immediately following my return to Denmark, St. Petersburg had attracted my attention, partly because of the engagements that my French colleagues obtained and partly by reason of the offers which were made me many times, most recently after the present Emperor, as Heir Apparent, had visited Copenhagen in 1838 and seen the ballet *Valdemar*. A cherished and outstanding pupil of mine, the Swede Johansson, had also found a most advantageous appointment there, and my position as dancing master to several Russian diplomats had further aroused my desire to become acquainted with this interesting country. But what finally precipitated my journeying thither before age rendered such an excursion impossible were Beaulieu's* excellent articles in the *Revue des deux Mondes,* which give a clear and scholarly presentation of "La Russie et les Russes" with knowledge and great impartiality.

I had never yet visited a foreign land where I was not able to get along in the language, and I shuddered to think of finding myself like a lost sheep in the midst of words and sounds that were completely incomprehensible to me. I therefore summoned my courage and tried, old as I was, to gain at least a superficial knowledge of Russian, whose greatest difficulty lies in its total lack of similarity to prevalent European tongues. I learnt to read, write, and spell its curious alphabet, crammed my memory with a few hundred words, a bit of grammar, and several of the most useful idioms; and after working steadily for a couple of months I had progressed far enough to make myself fairly well understood. But, alas! When I myself was addressed in Russian, most often I had to repeat, shaking my head in embarrassment, *"Ne ponimayu!"* ["I don't understand"].

So as not to be too greatly disoriented, I wrote to our excellent Consul, Pallesen, and asked him to acquaint me with conditions. Fate willed that just as my letter arrived, two of my younger countrymen, the merchant Jøhnke and the outstanding violinist Hildebrand, should happen to be with the Consul, and they solved the problem on the spur of the moment by inviting me to be their guest during my entire stay. Surprised and delighted, I accepted their kind invitation, though with a certain amount of reservation. Therefore on April 16, 1874, I set out on my journey by way of Stettin and Kreutz, without touching Berlin whose victory monuments I did not care to admire, though I had to acknowledge the exemplary railroad system and the mastery with which the great bridge at Dirschau was built.

We crossed over into Russian territory at Eidkuhnen, and here, in comparison with Prussia, everything was rather shabby in appearance. The stations, the service, and the coaches were far inferior in every respect to those of the neighboring country; and although I readily admit that the season was not yet favorable for vegetation, until we reached Kovno and Vilna, where the region was lovely, the countryside presented a deplorable aspect with long,

---

*Probably Leroy-Beaulieu, who wrote an excellent three-volume history of Russia, *L'Empire des Tsars.*

uncultivated stretches, morasses, and ill-treated woods. Perhaps it got better as we neared the capital, but we covered that road by night. The following morning the cupolas of the Cathedral of St. Isaac and the gilt spire of the Admiralty appeared on the horizon, and shortly afterward we pulled into the western railway station, where my kind hosts stood waiting to receive me with a hearty Danish "Velkommen" and to convey me to the elegant lodgings they had arranged for me.

The distance between Copenhagen and St. Petersburg had been covered in less than three days. Everywhere I encountered pleasant traveling company, and since I am fortunate enough to be a sound sleeper I was unaware of any of the journey's strains. All the same, I did not feel up to complying with our Consul's kind invitation to attend a ball the same evening, but took a long stroll about the city with Hildebrand and thus got an adequate idea of its grandeur and magnificence.

The Neva still lay frozen, with black highways from one bank across to the other, but very few days later cannon salvos from the Fortress announced the imminent thaw, and from the Nikolayevsky Bridge I watched the gigantic ice floes pour out toward the Gulf of Finland with frightful crashing and at tearing speed. In order for navigation to commence, they were only awaiting the flow of ice from Lake Ladoga. It too began to thaw, but sent only the smallest part out through the Neva; for if it did not absorb its own masses of ice, such a discharge would have taken several months.

With the exception of the public's quiet joy over the approach of spring, no trace remains of the old ceremonies that used to take place at the thawing of the Neva; and on the whole St. Petersburg has the complete look of a modern capital, with splendid boutiques, cafés, and eating places. The ladies' toilette is entirely according to Parisian designs, while far into spring the gentlemen go about wrapped in furs. Now and then one meets some stock figures of Finns, Tartars, and Circassians, but the authentic national costume, especially that of the women, is worn only by wealthy people's nannies and little girls, who are resplendent with yellow braids and bright colors, preferably red, which in Russian is synonymous with beautiful, *prekrasny.*†

But what immediately strikes the eye as something peculiar are the small, open, one-horse cabs with their coachmen, *izvozchik,* dressed in long blue caftans under which they usually wear a sheepskin that gives their figures a roundness which, especially if they are young and beardless, makes them look like buxom women. They swarm about by the thousand, have neither rates nor cab stands, but scurry after one in order to offer their services. They are generally merry, good-natured, and true virtuosi at steering their horses. But one need not concern oneself with keeping out of the way of these carriages, for even at the most tearing speed they know how to steer clear of pedestrians. Besides, they know that should they be so unfortunate as to hit

† Here, Bournonville is stretching the point: *prekrasny* was not synonymous with *red; prekrasny* meant both *very red* and *very beautiful,* but now means only *very beautiful.*

someone by accident, their livelihood is forfeit! Moreover, here as on the Corso in Rome distinguished equipages drive each day through Nevsky Prospect and Great Morskaya, and one then encounters those curious vehicles called *troika,* with one horse that trots and two that gallop with their heads pulled toward the ground. This is the height of fashion for young noblemen.

Another curious thing that strikes the foreigner when he returns home late at night from the theatres or from parties is the discovery of a sleeping creature wrapped in his furs and lying crosswise between the corner posts outside the doors of large houses. This is the factotum of the house, the highly trusted *dvornik,* who serves at once as porter, deputy landlord, and watchman. He knows no other night bed, and a slanted board serves him as a mattress if he does not prefer to lie upon the bare flagstones.

This was not, in fact, the proper season to enjoy life in St. Petersburg, for the transitional period from winter to spring is not considered to be very beneficial to one's health, and the Italian Opera with its stars Adelina Patti and Christina Nilsson had already departed at the beginning of Lent. But since I was a Dane, the thaw did not bother me, and the fact that the large Theatre still gave three or four ballets a week was simply grist to my mill. The other Imperial theatres were all in full swing, and with the most engaging kindness I was granted free admittance to the French drama, the Russian and German operas, and also the Russian drama.

With rather few exceptions, the weather during my whole stay was clear and relatively mild, and I took advantage of this to make observations on foot and to study the folk life down by the river, at the marketplaces, and in the rich bazaars.

The day after my arrival happened to be the opening Sunday for the Balagan, a public amusement rather like that of Dyrehavsbakken, which begins during Carnival time and ceases for the whole of Lent, only to be resumed in the first week after Easter. It is a market camp of tents and booths, erected on the Champ de Mars in the neighborhood of the so-called Summer Garden. In both places the ground was soaked with indescribable mud, but boards and mats were spread length- and crosswise in deference to the strolling spectators. While in the garden one traveled in the highest and finest company, in the camp one encountered the most motley assortment of soldiers, sailors, and commoners of both sexes, all with the most delightful faces and a mutual courtesy that is characteristic of the Russian man-in-the-street.

Strong drink may not be served on the premises, but tea was continually being poured from the *samovars* (self-boilers), while large glass pitchers were carried about filled with the well-known favorite drink, *kvas,* which is the color of raspberry lemonade and foams like beer. However, it would hardly be fit for Danish stomachs.

There were shouts of joy from the giddy swingers, while the most varied strains of overpowering music and the stomping of hobnailed boots expressed the festive mood. But the high points were on the one hand Berg's Theatre, and on the other the comical barkers on the balconies outside the dancing pavilions and carrousel grounds. Among the latter, an old chap in a dreadfully ragged costume and with a wig and beard made of old cordage particularly distinguished himself. He could bellow his witticisms from morning to night, and made his listeners shake with laughter. I was involuntarily infected by this gaiety, and, convinced that I had understood and grasped what he had said, the man triumphantly sprang down in front of me to receive what I owed him!

Berg's Theatre was a splendid pavilion with an outside staircase and corridors leading up to the gallery, while a more imposing closed entrance led to the stalls. A mass of people were standing outside for the next performance while the seventh of twelve daily representations was still going on. The entire presentation took little more than half an hour, and the whole was very well performed. Harlequin and Columbine danced most delightfully. I left Balagan with pleasant impressions and thanked my hosts for having put my first day in St. Petersburg to such good use.

Here it would take too long to discuss my visits with high dignitaries and friends both old and new, and to give as well a faithful account of the extraordinary hospitality which was shown me wherever I went—not least in my comfortable lodgings where, despite my reservations and objections, everything was showered upon me as if I had been an older brother or some other dear relative. Here I also found exquisite musical enjoyment in the Chamber Music Society, of which the talented Hildebrand was the founder. However, I cannot overlook the reception, as cordial as it was honorable, that I found among my artistic colleagues at the great Theatre.

Led by Johansson and Balletmaster Petipa, they greeted me with an almost filial affection, showed me their accomplishments, listened to my observations, and arranged a little fête in my honor. Therefore it will come as no surprise to anyone that I saw everything, as it were, through a medium *couleur de rose;* and though I am certainly not blind to faults, especially in my own profession, my description will never come to resemble that of Custine,‡ for I neither can nor will take it upon myself to depict, after a stay of only five weeks, "Russia as it is," but only as it appeared to me.

But what Dane can come to St. Petersburg without feeling moved by the fervor and love that hover round the name of the Grand Duchess, wife of the heir to the throne—which, though it is officially Mariya Fyodorovna, echoes both in and outside of the Palace with the gentle, homely tones and precious memories of her native land? For she is called Dagmar by her spouse, by his closest circle, and by all who are touched by her amiability and natural charm. The first signboard to greet the eye upon emerging from the railroad station has as its device the "Hotel Dagmar." Therefore, both as a Dane and

‡ Astolthe, Marquis de Custine (1792–1857), was author of several novels and widely read travel books. His *Russia in 1839*, published 1843, went into many editions and is doubtless the work to which Bournonville refers here.

as her old teacher, it went without saying that I must pay my respects to Her Imperial Highness. And since I was also the bearer of letters, music, and photographs from her Royal Mother, I introduced myself for the present to the Court Marshal in the Anichkov Palace to ask when it would be convenient for the Grand Duchess to grant me an audience.

The messenger who was sent up returned immediately with word that I could come straightaway! His Excellency was kind enough to furnish me with a white tie and gloves, and with etiquette thus fulfilled, I was taken up the flower-bedecked marble staircase, through halls that gleamed with crystal, gilding, porphyry, and malachite, and now stood before the same sweet little Princess whom I had taught to dance the minuet in the presence of her parents and in the company of her older brothers and sisters.

She joyfully greeted me, shook my hand, and addressed me in her beloved mother tongue. Her darling little sons, one of whom was someday destined to become Autocrat of all the Russias,* hopped about like cherubs, and this picture of domestic happiness combined with unassuming majesty in the midst of all this golden splendor, moved me to tears. After conversing genially for half an hour, I was invited to return the following day at a time when the Grand Duke, heir to the Throne, himself would be present. I appeared, bringing with me the above-mentioned objects, which aroused much pleasure; and for my part, I had good reason to be delighted with both the lovely reception and the resemblance to our own Danish Royal Family that prevailed within this domestic circle.

I received the promise of "special patronage" for everything I might be interested in seeing or learning about. But since the public is, with the greatest liberality, given free admission to all museums and public collections, there were only a few special cases in which I might possibly require supreme assistance, for which I did not fail to ask. These reserved places included the Fortress, containing the Imperial burial monuments and the Mint, the Hospital-Clinic, and the Little House on the banks of the Neva where Tsar Peter had lived while laying out St. Petersburg.

The Grand Duke sent a carriage for me, together with an official who was to act as guide; and it goes without saying that everywhere we went we were greeted with hat in hand, as specially favored personalities. I was not surprised at the simplicity and monotony of the Imperial sepulchral monuments. This originates from the exclusion of all works of sculpture in the Greco-Russian Orthodox church, where painting alone is permitted. Therefore all the sarcophagi were only plain, quadrangular marble coffins with the names of the deceased Royal personages, their birth and death dates, and a large gilded cross printed on the center of the lid. [Before I entered the Mint] I had never seen how they managed the stamping of coins and medallions. I found it most interesting to witness the various stages of this work, which the director himself showed us, together with the rich store of precious metals.

*Her eldest son was Nicholas II, born 1868, Tsar from 1894 to 1917.

Tsar Peter's Little House is reverently maintained, and in order to preserve it from the effects of time and climate, they have built around it another house, through which one must pass before entering the little sanctuary which is protected from without by glass walls. This little house is very much in the style of northern Holland and not unlike our Amager cottages. Here everything stands as it did when Peter the Great lived and worked, and in a boathouse under a glass roof hangs the boat which he himself built and which was the first step toward a future Russian navy.

At this time it just so happened that there was an anniversary and a memorial feast for Tsar Peter. On this occasion his sleeping chamber was used for a divine service or a kind of requiem. Three priests with large beards and long, drooping hair, dressed in gold-trimmed vestments as well, chanted from a large book with Old Slavic script, and my guide (by the way, a fine man of the world who was fluent in both French and German) knelt down in deep devotion, with his head bowed to the floor. This behavior corresponded perfectly to the reverence with which he lifted his hat and made three signs of the cross on his breast each time we drove past a church or a divine emblem. These religious customs are very prevalent among Orthodox Russians, but mostly among the common people, who, in Moscow for example, where there are about four hundred churches and as many chapels, are constantly engaged in devotional exercises such as the sign of the Cross, prayer formulae, and genuflections.

One can hardly conceive of the wealth of gold, silver, pearls, and precious stones that is amassed in Russian churches, whose cupolas are most often brilliantly gilded or at least studded with golden stars. The high point in the interior is the iconostasis, or partition between humanity and the All Highest. This wall is generally fashioned of gilded silver or bronze, with five large tablets on which, besides the Savior, are depicted the four patron saints, St. Andrew, St. George, St. Nicholas, and St. Alexander Nevsky. Here the Madonna and Child theme does not occupy the same high place that it does in the Roman Catholic churches. But it does exist nonetheless, for the most part on a smaller scale and, curiously enough, with so dark a complexion that one might almost believe that the picture had been hanging in chimney smoke. The whole bears the mark of Byzantine style, with golden backgrounds on the paintings and with saints' haloes that frequently sparkle with the most precious diamonds, bequeathed by the wills of pious and penitent ladies.

The Cathedrals of St. Isaac and Kazan are familiar enough from travel descriptions and are, by virtue of their colossal size and magnificent building materials of granite and bronze, more imposing than devotion-inspiring. At the end of the Nevsky Prospect, three-quarters of a Danish mile long, lies the Monastery of St. Alexander, which should be seen so that one can get some idea of monastic life in Russia. Another splendid cloister, which resembles a palace rather in the style of Versailles, is called Smolny and has been arranged as an educational institution for the daughters of officials and officers.

Here we once again heard a devotional service with excellent singing by the young female congregation. It is also a fact that even among simple folk the singing is lovely and harmonious, usually in a slow and minor hymn tempo. In this manner I heard a chorale sung by a division of soldiers who were accompanying a deceased comrade to his grave, and I must confess that where such an ennobling element was present, there could be no mention of the word *barbarian.*

The Emperor, who was to travel abroad on May 1 (according to our calendar), held a parting review or parade the day before on the Champs de Mars. Forty thousand men-at-arms were present, and the weather was superb. The lancers' small flags waved in the light spring breeze and the gilt helmets and breast plates of the Garde des Chevaliers dazzlingly reflected the rays of the sun, while bayonets gleamed in the tight-packed infantry columns, and the brightly polished bronze cannon stood arranged *"en grande toilette."* Amid loud fanfares and military music, the troops marched by, and the fantastic squadron of Circassians rode past the Emperor and his brilliant staff at full gallop, enveloping all and sundry in clouds of dust.

It was an imposing spectacle, knightly and edifying. But . . . if one pauses to reflect upon the modern method of waging war, where it is no longer a matter of advancing with bold and noble mien, but rather of dexterously taking cover, doing harm to the enemy at as great a distance as possible, and then approaching him crawling on one's belly, the illusion is lost and in one's mind one sees this heroic band scattered by grenades fired from miles away and shattered by bullets from hidden ambushes.

Only after the Emperor's departure was the Winter Palace open to strangers. To depict its glories would take several more pages than I have reckoned upon for this description. One must have several hours to wander through its great halls and galleries. Everything that Oriental luxury combined with French taste and elegance can display is here to be found in such rich abundance that no other royal or imperial palace I have seen abroad can compare with it.

I will, however, permit myself to emphasize two high points of extremely different character. The first is the Winter Garden, where in summerlike warmth one strolls on sandy paths through a fairy-tale world of fragrant blossoms, luxuriant fruits, and tropical plants, to the sound of the songbirds' warbling mingled with the splash of fountains.

The second curiosity is the chamber in which the Crown Jewels, surrounded by trustworthy guards, are displayed for sightseers. Beneath an enormous glass dome are to be seen the crown, the sceptre, and the remaining regalia of State, which are set with precious stones to the value of 33 million rubles (88 million Kroner in our money). Round about this precious center stand "showcases" in which diamond stars, chains, brooches, bodkins with dangling tassels, and jewelry of every imaginable kind are preserved. These, according to the custodian's statement, are said to have a total value of 140 million rubles! One grows either dizzy or cold at the sight of all this splendor, but it is true that one very quickly becomes accustomed to it and regards the whole as a brilliant theatrical display.

The fact that the theatres, all of which are directly under Imperial direction, play an important role in the life of the Russian capital is sufficiently well known, and it will be a pleasure for me to relate what I have experienced within this sphere. Yet, since it is not from there that my deepest impressions stem, but rather from other artistic and historical phenomena, I must first relate my frequent visits to the Hermitage Museum, which is the Louvre of St. Petersburg and contains priceless treasures in the way of paintings, antiques, gems, and curiosities, besides a rich and well-arranged collection of coins and medallions and extremely interesting discoveries from ancient times, especially from the Kerch peninsula (homeland of the Scythians).

In the picture galleries the Italian and Spanish as well as the Netherlandish and French schools are tastefully represented; and at the side of superb portraits by Van Dyke and Velásquez are to be found splendid pictures by Rembrandt and Murillo, enchanting landscapes by Ruisdael and Claude le Lorrain. A precious fresco by Raphael from the Villa Spada is also among the treasures of this museum. In the realm of national art there are excellent paintings by the Russians Eivasovsky, Bogolyubov, Nev, Bruni, and Bryullov, and, lest we forget, the Livonian Steuben, who in part owes his training to the French school.

As far as the fine arts on the whole are concerned, Russia is making unmistakable progress; and although the formation of a special national school is not directly striven for, public exhibitions still offer much in the way of excellence, principally in the area of portrait painting, in which Van Dyke seems to serve as the model.

An ingenious genre painter had quite recently emerged in the person of a young lieutenant by the name of Vereshchagin, who had brought back with him from the campaign in China a whole series of grand pictures representing war episodes and scenes from the folk life of that country. They were displayed in a special locale illuminated as for a diorama and had a marvelously striking effect. People flocked to see them, nor did the Emperor himself fail to view them. He halted, astonished, before two curious pictures: one representing a victory pyramid of skulls and bones in the middle of a heath; the other, a soldier lying on a battlefield, dead and abandoned, and encircled by voracious ravens! Moved at this sight, His Majesty turned to the painter and asked whether these representations were reality or fantasy. When the artist replied the latter, he received from the Autocrat one of those meaningful glances which was enough for him to have the two aforementioned paintings removed. However, a host of photographs of the whole collection had already been published, and at the same time as the public admired a considerable talent, they also got some idea of the lack of enthusiasm for the military or, more properly, the reflective philosophical manner that this young officer had brought back with him from that curious campaign.

I made it my duty to see all that I could in a short time: libraries, the Mining Academy, the Naval Museum, the Arsenal, and the Tauride Palace, where memories of Potemkin and his royal mistress [Catherine the Great] speak through a threadbare and decadent splendor; the great palaces which, in accordance with Parisian models, have now been rendered less uncomfortable by enclosed "squares"; and finally, the proud monuments of bronze erected in honor of deserving individuals as well as noteworthy historical events and great sovereigns. Among these, one must especially single out the equestrian statue of Peter the Great in high-spirited gallop upon an enormous block of stone, which, with great toil and expense, was brought thither from Finland. The bold composition and masterly execution are the work of the Frenchman Falconet, who was summoned to St. Petersburg at the same time as Larchevêsque to Stockholm and Sally to Copenhagen. All three were outstanding artists, but according to the statement of competent judges, the equestrian statue of Frederik V at Amalienborg (by Sally) wins the prize, not only over his colleagues' masterworks but over all monuments of the kind in Europe.

As we have now ventured rather deeply into the realm of the beautiful, the road quite naturally leads to the theatre and everything pertaining to it, with the supposition that even if we do not always find our aesthetic sense perfectly satisfied by the products that are offered on the altar of the Muses, we ought not to cease *believing* in the high calling of the stage but to *fight* continuously for its honor and dignity.

The sums which are expended on the theatre in Russia's capitals are beyond all our notions of budget and license. Here there is no mention of the *State*. It is the *Emperor* who rewards artists from the first to the last, and pensions them—that is, if they are natives of the country or naturalized citizens—and allows everything to be fitted up with a luxury that corresponds to the concept of "a Great Power of the first magnitude." With the exception of Berg's pavilion, no private theatrical enterprise is allowed in St. Petersburg. The whole is governed by a special Imperial Chancellery whose director and intendants are all generals or excellencies! At the four Imperial theatres the activity is distributed in the following manner.

The *Mariinsky Theatre* gives opera in Russian. Here I heard Weber's *Freischütz*, in which the bass Palletschek, a Bohemian by birth, distinguished himself in the role of Caspar. On the Emperor's birthday I attended a gala performance of Glinka's famous opera, *A Life for the Tsar*, which is composed in an austere style and is not particularly melodious, except in the hymnlike numbers which seem to be the real strength of Russian music. The language appears to good effect in song, and the dramatic action is free of the usual excesses. In the finale the Russian national anthem is sung by a numberless mass of people, who are shown assembled on the Great Square beneath the walls of the Kremlin in Moscow.

The *Alexandrinsky Theatre* is chiefly given over to Russian drama and comedy, whereas the German drama gives some of its performances here and some at the Mariinsky and Mikhailovsky theatres. The Russian national stage possesses a considerable repertoire of original authors. Among these writers Van Wiesen (the Russian Holberg), the tragedian Ozerov, as well as Griboyedov, Gogol, and Ostrovsky in the lighter comic genre, have an extensive renown within their native land. Unfortunately, I did not find an opportunity to attend the performances at this theatre, but from the proofs of dramatic talent I later got to see in Moscow, I received the impression that on the whole the Russians perform well and follow the same sober direction as our finest actors here at home.

The *Mikhailovsky Theatre* presents, for the most part, French plays and has a select company of actors. Although the pieces are written with unmistakable talent and give the actors the opportunity for piquant character portrayals, the repertoire, with few exceptions, is of the sort that more or less hovers over unhealthy territory: a seducer; a weak, high-strung, and sometimes deeply fallen woman; a deceived husband; and the inevitable duel are the recurrent materials with which these modern dramatic structures are pieced together. Even if they could possibly contain a useful moral as a warning to others, one rarely comes away from these performances feeling edified, let alone encouraged.

Nevertheless I got a little taste of a purer style in a charming one-act play, *La saint François*, by Mme. Amalie Pierronet. This play dealt with a rich master-carpenter who, in spite of his wife's tears and the objections of an excellent cook, has disowned his son because the latter, instead of following his father into business, has chosen to become a playwright. Only when the carpenter reads in the papers of the success of his son's new piece is he reconciled, forgives the lad, and gives him the beloved girl in marriage. This little piece was acted with a high degree of perfection by Messrs. Luguet and Dieudonné together with Mmes. Vigne and Paul-Ernest. By the bye, this company possesses members who would be an adornment for the finest theatres in Paris, and it is with deep recognition that I mention Messrs. Dupuis, Renard, Worms, and Lagrange, as well as the foremost leading lady Mlle. Delaporte.

We now come to the *Bolshoi Theatre* (the Great Theatre), which is exclusively devoted to Italian opera and ballet. The former had already concluded its performances at the beginning of the strict Lenten season, but an echo was still to be heard in the zealous polemics that took place between the fanatical admirers of Adelina Patti and Christina Nilsson. The dilettanti of St. Petersburg were divided into two camps, each of which fought for the superiority of its chosen favorite; and although the Italian troupe had been made up of the most excellent talents, it seemed almost as if no one listened to anyone but those two nightingales from such opposite climes.

Next to the infatuation with their superb accomplishments, public attention was taken up by the fabulous salaries these *stars* had received and were even to draw the following season: 40,000 rubles for six months' very modest service! A rather nice fee, if one also takes into account the colossal bouquets filled with diamond brooches and bracelets. These garlands are not, as in other places, tossed down or up onto the stage. Rather they are presented by the conducting *Kapellmeister* to the prima donna in question in full view of the audience. I do not know if these enormous rewards could be compensated for by the income from the subscription seats that were sold out at high prices. But one thing is certain: opera singers regard Russia as their Eldorado and find in the enthusiastic and applauding public warmth enough to resist the harshness of the climate.†

The storm had abated, and a milder breeze hovered over the great stage where the ballet now reigned supreme and presented three to four performances a week of full-length compositions. I saw in turn *Le Papillon, La Fille du Pharaon, Don Quixote, Esmeralda,* and *Le Roi Candaule,* and made it my business to forget — or at least to hide — the system which for more than forty years I have followed with respect to my own works. I did justice to the richly imaginative arrangement of the settings and transformations as well as the magnificent appointments; acknowledged the considerable advantages that lay in the use of a *corps de ballet* consisting of more than *two hundred,* partly young, pretty, and clever people; and was not blind or indifferent to the superb talent that displayed itself especially among the female members, whose gymnastic virtuosity would certainly astonish anyone who did not take into account the simple truth that *Beauty* and *Grace* are the rarest and most difficult things to achieve in the art of dancing.

I sought in vain to discover plot, dramatic interest, logical consistency, or anything which might remotely resemble sanity. And even if I were fortunate enough to come upon a trace of it in Petipa's *Don Quixote,* the impression was immediately effaced by an unending and monotonous host of feats of bravura, all of which were rewarded with salvos of applause and curtain calls. For one must grant the Russians this: nowhere else in the world does there exist a livelier or more grateful audience — and this without the stimulation of an organized *claque!* In my secret heart I thought back to our beloved Temple of the Muses on Kongens Nytorv, where a *silence approbateur* is the most expedient expression of general satisfaction and where, in an assembly of seventeen hundred spectators, enthusiasm vents itself by the fact that at most *ten pairs of hands* venture an appreciative applause!

However, I could not always agree with the enraptured admirers, for the obvious lascivious tendency that pervades the whole choreographic move-

---

† That the enthusiasm for Italian virtuosi does not prevent the Russians from appreciating their own countrymen can be seen from the acclaim that their favorite bass singer, Petrov, received at his jubilee; for his benefit performance brought in 20,000 rubles, and a subscription raised by his admirers, 60,000, in addition to a golden laurel wreath set with diamonds that was also sent him (1876). — A.B.

ment—with the exception of the Slavic national dances—was of the same sort as that which a number of years ago drove the Casino's audience into a frenzy at the appearance of the Spanish dancer Pepita. The only difference was that the Russian *bayadères* had *learnt how to dance*. The feminine costume, if one dares to call it that, was just as one sees it in the most caricatured pictures, and the excessively short skirts, which might possibly be suitable for valkyries riding through the air on winged steeds, do not seem to be appropriate for a Court festival, a wedding celebration, or a society ball. However this may be, the heroines of the ballet continuously appear in the same more or less spangled costume, just as the regulation *caleçons de bain* may be regarded as an established fact for the *danseurs*. These baroque fashions are allowed at the Parisian theatres and are usually imitated with tasteless exaggeration abroad. Thus, if one can become inured to *the offensive*, that which is utterly *ridiculous* and *absurd* must strike one in the eye and gradually reduce art to nothing more than the most wretched buffoonery.

I could not possibly suppress these and similar observations during my conversations with Johansson and Balletmaster Petipa. They admitted that I was perfectly right, confessed that they privately loathed and despised this whole development, explained with a shrug of the shoulders that they were obliged to follow the current of the times, which they charged to the blasé taste of the public and the specific wishes of the high authorities.

There was no mistaking the fact that the pleasure which people sought to derive from watching the ballets was of anything but an aesthetic nature, and except for the Russian and Polish national dances that were performed by Messrs. Ivanov and Kshesinsky, and with incomparable grace by the noble Madayeva, I derived more sorrow than joy from the outstanding talents which had been put to use in a way that was so completely in conflict with my ideas about the art of Terpsichore. And yet what splendid charitable institutions are arranged for the artistic education of the *corps de ballet!* In a palace in the neighborhood of the Alexandrinsky Theatre there is an entire academy for sixty regular students (thirty-six girls and twenty-four boys) who at the Emperor's expense are housed, fed, dressed, and instructed in all school subjects as well as their principal profession—everything under the proper supervision of teachers both male and female. There are airy and comfortable dormitories, bathrooms, and even a little chapel according to the Greek Catholic rite. The whole thing bears the stamp of a distinguished finishing school where in addition to the sixty regular pupils, an equally large number of day students share in the instruction. The dancing lessons are given in three large rooms by Johansson, Petipa, and the *régisseur*, Bogdanov. Some of the ballet rehearsals are also held in these rooms, and here I was introduced to the soloists Vazem, Kemerer, Radina, Simskaya, and Sokolova, all lovely young ladies.

Almost opposite the aforesaid Ballet Academy lies the Imperial Conservatory of Music, where Rubinstein is director and where a Dane (the son of the deceased pastor Johansson of St. Peter's Church in Copenhagen) harmoniously combines the position of inspector with that of teacher. Under his guidance we had a complete tour of the facilities, and here as everywhere we were forced to acknowledge the magnificence of all public establishments in this city. Here several well-known celebrities serve as teachers, and Mme. Nissen-Salomon trains the young songstresses for the stage. Since the four Imperial theatres require five complete orchestras—the music for the Italian Opera being independent of the ballet—one will not be surprised that the number of salaried orchestra musicians, some of whom are entitled to a pension, exceeds *three hundred.* Almost half of them are foreigners, and the others, pupils of the Conservatory.

For the rest, the musical season was over, with the exception of the last chamber music *soirée*, which I attended. Here my friend Hildebrand delighted us with his masterly quartet playing and shared the laurels of the evening with the violinist Albrecht, the Danish pianist Hartvigson, and his talented brother Richard.

At a luncheon which my esteemed colleagues gave for me at the Café Borell on Great Morskaya, a distinguished, young, and dashing theatre-lover joined our party, and, after having added to our pleasure in the most amiable fashion by providing us with some "extra fine" wine, he encouraged me to visit him in Moscow, to which he would return in a few days. [He told me that] I need only ask for him in the Sloviansky Bazaar (the Slav Hotel) and he would then take pleasure in acting as my cicerone in the curious city where I was really to become acquainted with "Russia and the Russians." Since this happened to coincide perfectly with my intention of seeing Moscow and, perhaps, several other historic cities such as Kiev and Novgorod, I gratefully accepted his kind offer. And thus, with time left over for new excursions, even after having spent some weeks in St. Petersburg, I purchased a ticket for the railway sleeping car and in sixteen hours covered the eighty-eight [Danish] miles to the old capital of the Tsars.

Moscow

Upon hearing this name, there unfolds in our minds a historical drama not only from the long-gone days of Rurik, from those of Michael Romanov and his successors, but most recently from the time of Napoleon the Great and his army, which like the invincible armada of Philip II foundered upon the might of the elements and patriotism. Across endless plains the railroad train travels at tearing speed, and one has hardly had time to glimpse the church cupolas flashing past in the morning sun before the train pulls into the vaulted station and the omnibus carries one to the designated hotel.

One drives a long way through badly paved and, in comparison with those of St. Petersburg, rather small and crooked streets, where palaces and humble little dwellings stand huddled together. But their modern style bears witness to the fact that they must have been constructed after the great fire — which, however, devastated only two-thirds of the huge city. After crossing a large marketplace, where a motley crowd of peasants, fishmongers, and second-hand-clothes dealers gather beneath the high whitewashed walls that surround the inner city, where picturesque groups of women round a large fountain, washing and carrying water, lend a peculiar Oriental flavor to the whole, one enters the main street through a narrow tower gate and comes to a stop at the above-mentioned Slav Hotel, which in comfort and elegance is not inferior to the finest in Germany and Switzerland.

The whole staff wore national dress, and, since the temperature here is considerably milder than it is farther north, the costume was most summery and light. I immediately asked for my fine patron from the Café Borell [and learnt that] they were awaiting his return from a lengthy excursion. However, since I did not wish to lose a minute of my scanty time, I took a carriage and a hired servant and drove off to see the financier Zencker, to whom I had a letter of credit and in whose company I met a particularly fine countryman, Herr Louis Nägler, who had already been informed of my arrival.

From there I drove to the Imperial Ballet Theatre and produced a letter of introduction from Balletmaster Petipa to the *régisseur*, Smirnov, who received me with exquisite kindness and invited me to attend the performance that evening as well as the others that would take place during my stay. The rest of the day I drove about on my own, ate in the hotel restaurant, which resembles an enchanted garden from *The Arabian Nights*, and finally went to the theatre, where they gave the opera *Rogneda* by the recently deceased composer Sierov.

The music, which is considered a great masterpiece by connoisseurs, to me appeared so erudite and, with the exception of some religious choruses, so unmelodious that next to this composer Wagner may be regarded as a Lumbye or an Offenbach. The action, insofar as I could follow it with the help of the mime, my own meager knowledge of the language, and the *régisseur*'s kind guidance, revolved around the conversion of the heathen Vladimir to Christianity and contained a number of interesting and gripping moments. The performance was, on the whole, good; the singing voices sonorous and well trained, and the settings magnificent and splendid. In the winter Italian opera is also given here, but the ballet, which several years ago rivaled that of St. Petersburg in the number and skill of its *corps*, no longer seemed to enjoy the same high patronage as before; however, it still possessed some very fine talents.

At a benefit performance I got to see separate acts of three different ballets, namely, *Cinderella, Le Diable à quartre*, and *Koniok* (after a Russian fable). The only thing I could make of this strange assortment was an enormous number of dances of the usual wanton kind. Nevertheless in these I was forced to admire the matchless staying power and the unmistakable skill of two ballerinas with the curious names Karpakova and Slobetschanskaya.

A little Russian drama was given the same evening as an interlude and represented rural scenes in which a young girl is abandoned by her lover, who, as it happens, is a prince in disguise. The talented actress who played the role of the village girl lent it quiet sorrow which turns into madness and ends with death in the waves—a masterly piece of tragic interpretation. The remaining members of the cast distinguished themselves by naturalness and beautiful dramatic bearing. The language had a pleasant ring to my ear, and I picked up enough words to be gripped by the moving action.

So much for my observations in the Muscovite theatre world. However, the innumerable curiosities in the way of buildings, *objets d'art,* and monuments, not to mention the folk life of the city itself, presented an even more picturesque and characteristic drama.

The Slav Hotel (Slavyansky Bazaar) lies quite close to a square which is bounded on one side by a large bazaar called the *Gostiny Dvor,* and on the opposite by the majestic outer walls of the Kremlin, with its gate and bizarre towers. The extremity to the right is formed by the old fortification ditches, which had been transformed into charming promenades where trees and bushes were budding. To the left rises the fantastic edifice of the Cathedral of St. Basil, whose green cupolas resemble a host of majestically piled-up artichokes. This church was erected by command of Ivan IV (who has rightly been called "the Terrible"). Legend has it that he ordered the eyes of the architect to be put out so that the hand of the latter might never again furnish anything which might surpass this curious building in originality.

I must admit that this church, with its low nave and the spiral staircases leading up to the various chapels in the cupolas, the small vaulted corridors which unite these, and the peculiar ornamentation that surrounds the gold- and jewel-encrusted pictures of the saints, was something unique of its kind. But, since there are similar legends about the putting out of eyes connected with several works of art—for example, the altarpiece in the Cathedral of Slesvig—one can certainly imagine that the artist might well have lost his sight from overexertion, without such a revolting action having been taken. By the bye, this large and beautiful square has not been free of its own scenes of terror. In older times numberless executions were undertaken here, and it was on this spot that Peter the Great ordered the rebellious *streltsy* to bow their heads before the executioner's sword. In front of the Spassky [Savior's] Gate the condemned directed their last prayer to the saint who had delivered Smolensk from the violence of enemies.‡

‡ The *streltsy* (sometimes called "musketeers") were a class of merchants and other citizens who owed a hereditary military duty to the Tsar. In July 1698, while Peter was absent on a trip to western Europe, they staged a revolt against his "window-to-the-west" policies, and were easily subdued by loyal troops in an action that lasted hardly an hour. Nonetheless Peter, on his return, had all the captured *streltsy* put to death in a series of executions during September and October of the same year. "The saint who had delivered Smolensk" probably refers to an ancient painting of the Virgin, attributed to St. Luke and brought to Russia in 1046, which was among the treasures of the Cathedral in that city.

Through this gate all — the Emperor not excepted — pass with their heads bared, and the foreigner must follow the custom of the country. Then there is a second gate, which also faces the Great Square. This is the Nikolsky Gate, through which the Tartar Khan Toktamysch, Poland's King Sigismund III, and Napoleon the Great have made their entries. It is dedicated to St. Nicholas, whose picture hangs above the gateway, and is remarkable for the fact that when the tower together with other parts of the Kremlin was blown up at the time of the forced retreat of Napoleon, the saint's niche remained unharmed and the lamp in front of the picture continued to burn! This miracle has been commemorated by Tsar Alexander I in a bronze inscription above the arch of the gate.

Before we pass through this gate into the renowned Kremlin — which I had pictured to be a mighty fortress resembling the Tower of London rather than as a complex of palaces, churches, and State institutions that form a city in themselves about one and a half Danish miles around — we will survey length- and crosswise the long corridors that make up the quarter bearing the famous name of Gostiny Dvor, which amazes one by the variety of every possible kind of merchandise that is here offered for sale in comparatively small shops. The goldsmiths' works are especially noteworthy for their Byzantine forms and ornamentation; they are, for the most part intended for sacred use in the Orthodox church. Outside this beehive of busy sellers and haggling buyers moves a buzzing swarm of market folk in the most varied costumes and with fantastic vehicles. Amidst this human rabble rises a bronze group masterfully executed in the classical style in memory of the struggle for the fatherland in 1812.

This much I believe I have learnt about the Russian national character: attachment to religion, burning love of the fatherland, and a childlike affection for the sovereign constitute its principal features. Their hospitality toward foreigners cannot be too highly praised; but as national interests and sympathies gradually develop, the latter will also have to make its choice. For example, the Germans, who several decades ago played such an important role in Russia, have here as in many other places known how to make themselves disliked by their arrogant tone; whereas the French, despite all the blood that has flowed between them and the Russians during the Napoleonic wars as well as the Crimean campaign, are well liked by high and low. Their language and literature are universally propagated, and an offensive and defensive alliance with their country is not regarded as an impossibility. This situation, in fact, bears a certain similarity to our position with regard to Sweden, whose history, like that of Denmark, is filled with mutual accusations, bloody feuds, and — especially on our side — memories of bitter losses. All this has not, however, prevented us Danes from becoming infatuated with our sister country to such a degree that, to tie the bonds of friendship yet tighter, we have changed our system of currency, our spelling, and even our alphabet in accordance with Swedish models.

The first thing that strikes the eye when one steps inside the sacred gate of the Kremlin is a long, amphitheatrical array of bronze cannon and howitzers, 875 in number, all captured from the French during their fateful retreat—not by force of arms, however, but assembled in snowdrifts next to the brave men, thousands of whom were forced to bow beneath the winter cold and the strains of the march. About half of these field pieces are French, with pet names on the torch-hold plates; the rest belonged to the Bavarians, the Württemburgers, the Saxons, the Westphalians, the Poles, and the Italians who, all with the hope of brilliant victory, followed the eagles of Napoleon. An explanation engraved in bronze is to be found, both in Russian and in French, at the entrance to the Arsenal.

We proceed, casting a sidelong glance at the numerous divisions of recruits manouvering on the Drill Ground near the widely renowned Great Bell, which during the burning of the Ivan Tower in 1703 tumbled down, cracked, and was recast with an increase in weight from 350,000 to 440,000 pounds. It fell down once again during the fire of 1737 and sank deep into the foundation of the tower, where it lay for ninety-nine years until the Emperor Nicholas, with the aid of English engineers, had it raised from the depths and taken to the stone footing upon which it now stands. It is decorated with outstanding bas-reliefs of the Savior and the Evangelists as well as Tsar Alexis and the Empress Anna.

According to precise accounts, it measures 19 feet and 3 inches in height, 60 feet and 9 inches in circumference, and one Danish ell in thickness. An enormous clapper lies at the foot of the bell, together with a fragment which has left behind a crack through which one can enter the booming metal arch. Up in the Ivan Tower itself, from which one enjoys a captivating view, there still hang thirty-four other bells, some of which might compare with the largest ones known elsewhere. It is said to be of a singularly moving effect when on Easter morning all the bells are set in motion and the inhabitants of Moscow, awakened by the billowing clangor, rush out of their houses jubilantly shouting to friends and strangers alike, *"Khristos voskres!"* ("Christ is risen!").

To enumerate or to describe the churches that are found within as well as without the walls of the Kremlin, and to estimate the value of the precious objects that are amassed both there and, for example, in the Palace of the Patriarchs, would far exceed my capabilities and the boundaries of this travel sketch. I will only ask my readers to accompany me in spirit up to the elevated terrace that looks to the sunset, and to picture in their imaginations the radiance that blazes from several hundred fire-gilt cupolas, among which I will single out only the five new and not yet completed domes of the Church of the Savior (all of which have balustrades) for which twelve *poods*—that is, 480 pounds—of pure gold have been used.

Everything contained in the Kremlin is, in fact, so overwhelming that one must perforce distribute one's observations over a space of several days. Tickets to the Imperial Treasury are furnished with the greatest liberality, and there one wanders among historical curiosities which, even if they do not carry one far back into antiquity, nevertheless bring us by hitherto unfrequented roads into the romanticism of the Middle Ages. In a circle, beneath glass covers, stand bejeweled crowns of the old Garderik sovereigns; the thrones are of silver-gilt ornamented with several hundred precious stones. Here too can be found state coaches from older and more recent times, among them Napoleon's traveling coach and the sedan chair of Charles XII from Poltava, masses of gold and silver vessels, including some very odd wine pitchers presented to Tsar Michael Romanov by Christian IV.

The Imperial Palace in the Kremlin is perhaps in size, but certainly not in taste and richness, inferior to the Winter Palace in St. Petersburg. Like the latter, it bears witness to the way in which the demand for luxury, and particularly for spaciousness, has grown since the days of Peter the Great and his forebears. The wing of the palace that has been spared from reconstruction has only small, low rooms, and in the Romanov Palace, farther down in the city, all of the objects, which are now preserved as in a separate chronological museum, bear the stamp of a certain poverty where the furniture is concerned, while the real splendor is confined to clothing and weapons for festive occasions.

The four great halls are dedicated to the patron saints of the various Orders, but that of St. George is the most remarkable—not only because its white marble walls bear inscribed in gold the names of the regiments, generals, subordinate officers, and private soldiers who have distinguished themselves in the field of battle, but because every year these brave men, regardless of rank and station, are invited to a banquet at which the Emperor, who himself distributes the badges of the Order, may not sit down at table since Fate has not allowed him personally to see action on the battlefield.

Although I could not possibly manage to see everything worth visiting in Moscow, I nevertheless could not neglect the so-called "Cabinet of Curiosities," which is located in the northern part of the city. It houses at the same time a 200,000–volume library, a valuable collection of manuscripts, a mineralogical cabinet, an ethnographic museum, and a picture gallery of domestic works of art. I happened to go there on a day when the regulation one thousand tickets had already been taken by a large public. Thus I could not gain admittance; but the director or librarian, an especially polite man, invited me to return the following morning when he would show me around himself. I was most appreciative of his kindness, and under his thorough guidance saw all the excellent objects that were here assembled in the most beautiful order.

I was particularly struck by the richness of the manuscript and autograph collection. Just as in St. Petersburg, here too I had my eyes opened to the considerable progress the Russians have made in the fine arts, a fact of which we here at home seem to take no notice. But what must unconditionally attract the attention of the foreigner traveling for the purpose of broadening his artistic knowledge is a superb grouping of over one hundred representations of the various Russian nationalities. These models are in national costume and range from Lapps and Samoyeds to Circassians and Mingrelli—all plastically fashioned with distinctive masculine and feminine physiognomies and poses, while their dwellings, customs, domestic utensils, and work tools are represented with perfect naturalness.

I must now mention the assistance I was fortunate enough to receive from two of my fellow-countrymen living in Moscow, namely the mission bookseller, Forchhammer, and the earlier mentioned gentleman, Louis Nägler, in whose family circle I spend a most pleasant day. He arranged for us to drive to the Sparrow Hills (Vorobyovye gory) where, after traversing miry roads, we reached the point from which Napoleon gazed for the first time upon this city, which also appeared most imposing on this afternoon.

But as for my young Russian patron and guide: he was not so easy to get hold of, though he did live in the very hotel he had indicated to me. We had exchanged visiting cards several times before we were finally lucky enough to meet two days before the end of my stay. When he discovered that I had already managed to look about quite ably without his help, he proposed that after the theatre we should drive out to hear a gypsy concert—something quite unique of its kind.

I accepted his invitation and, as I mentioned before, at half past eleven his troika pulled up in front of the Opera House, and, together with *régisseur* Smirnov, we tore off at a mad clip in a heavy downpour. We drove to a faraway tavern where, in large dining rooms with private compartments, sat jovial groups of both sexes zealously occupied by their supper. This, I thought to myself, must surely be the gypsies' haunt or, in any case, the place where they serve as pleasant entertainment for the guests. But not at all! In a side room the three of us were served an elegant supper, and while my good host regaled us with the finest wines, I looked about in vain for the band of musicians. But there were none to be seen. No, only now were we to drive out to the place where the concert was being given! It was already past one o'clock and I, who was not accustomed to such night revels, had to laugh at myself, who in my old age was going on a spree with young Russia!

We now set off once more, though in God knows what direction. The horses trotted and galloped as if before Pluto's cariole, bespattering us from top to toe. We kept this pace for half an hour, and, finally leaving the gates of the city behind, we glimpsed through the darkness the park of the Petrovsky Summer Palace. We came to a stop before a splendidly illuminated pavilion, outside of which a number of light equipages were halted. After having been brushed off and smoothed a bit, we entered a sort of rotunda in the Oriental style, with divans, mirrors, and tropical plants.

Here sat a gentleman who might have been between forty and fifty years of age, carelessly leaning against the high sofa cushions, holding two quite fantastic ladies about the waist. On the table in front of this group stood champagne bottles and glasses. Round about the room strolled intimate couples, arm in arm; and although they were clad in modern ball dress, their frizzy hair, swarthy hue, and strange eyes so idelibly bore the gypsy stamp that there could be no mistaking their nationality.

Here at last we found the aforementioned virtuosi, and the gentleman on the sofa turned out to be an intimate friend of my honored host. But we now suffered a grave disappointment, for the friend, in spite of all offers, remonstrances, and pleas, was unable to share the evening's musical entertainment with anyone at all because he had engaged the company exclusively for his own pleasure in return for an honorarium of five hundred rubles for the entire night. The obstinacy with which he stuck to his refusal bore witness, to no small degree, to a half-inebriated, half-stupid condition.

I strove as much as was within my power to console my host, who was in despair over this unsuccessful expedition; and when from the adjacent concert hall we heard the horrible howls and shrieks which were to pass for singing, to the clacking of castanets and the jangling of tambourines, I burst into laughter and got my companions to look at our adventure from the comical side. We now took a separate cabinet, and the inevitable *Cliquot* appeared as compensation for the loss we had suffered. At exactly the same moment, another intimate friend arrived, accompanied by two elegant ladies who appeared to be Parisians and singing prima donnas from one of Moscow's "variety theatres." The conversation now became more interesting, the atmosphere more animated. But although Mlles. Thérèse and Corinne apparently belonged to the so-called *"demi-monde,"* I must frankly state that their deportment and entire character were in every respect *comme il faut* (as we would say in Denmark; seemly and well bred). However, it was now past three o'clock, dawn was fast approaching, and I had had enough of this "fashionable life." Smirnov, too, longed to go home, and since the young Russians wished to prolong the entertainment for several hours, the troika was placed at our disposal. I climbed out at my hotel, where the doorman, with heavy eyes, regarded me as a confirmed toper.

Several more strolls along the bank of the river, around the markets, and along the pretty boulevards; one more glance from the terraces of the Kremlin over Moscow's green-painted roofs and gleaming church cupolas; a fond and grateful farewell to my good countrymen; and I was off for St. Petersburg.

Homeward Bound

Many travelers, I dare say, make the great mistake of using the standards of home when judging the various people, places, or things they encounter abroad; so too it is harmful, and often completely ruinous for the enjoyment of the moment to make comparisons, whether they turn out to the advantage of the former or the latter. But when one has gathered a wealth of impressions and prepared oneself for acquired experience, it becomes both a consolation and a pleasure to be able to distinguish what in one's native land can counter-balance the greatness and splendor that one has been able to recognize and admire in other places.

Art and science cannot be measured according to the geographical size of countries, and in this respect little Denmark can be proud of the place it assumes among the civilized states of Europe. But what, in a material direction, occupied my thoughts throughout my return trip from Moscow to St. Petersburg and thence to the western frontier, was whether our fruitful and well-cultivated fields, our prosperous peasant farms with their enormous corn shocks, fat herds of cows, magnificent horses, fine vehicles, and abundant furnishings, might not in capitalized interest value constitute a sum as great as, or perhaps even greater than, all the dead treasure that is accumulated in all the palaces, churches, and cloisters in the Russian capitals?

Within the Empire there must of course exist more thriving provinces than those through which I passed on the railway train. But at least in those I saw agriculture seems to be neglected. The villages are scattered at distances of several miles and consist, for the most part, of wooden huts without gardens or a trace of afforestation. Russia undoubtedly has a great future, and it no longer resembles the Russia that was described half a century ago. But even if the free Russian peasant could match his Danish counterpart in enlightenment and education, it will still be many years before he equals him in prosperity.

As far as political life and the national character are concerned, I had during my short stay but a poor opportunity for thorough observation. But everywhere it appeared to me that people moved about as freely and spoke as freely as they did at home in Copenhagen. The police seem only to be for the purpose of public safety, and one hears the Knout Regiment mentioned only as a stage long past. I have found myself both amid throngs of people and in solitary places, but have never seen a single example of rudeness among the population; on the contrary, there is a courtesy and helpfulness that could serve as a model to other nations, and a natural good will that bears witness that this populace has not yet become worked up to hatred and envy of those better placed in society.

I spent several days more with my kind hosts, with whom I consolidated a bond of friendship founded upon high esteem and gratitude. During this time I witnessed the pilgrimage of the Petersburgers to the Ekateringof, and together with Hildebrand visited the magnificent Tsarskoe Selo, with its sybaritic furnishing, its delightful park and rich collection of arms. We later visited the marvelous Pavlovsk, where Kapellmeister Bisle regaled us with excellent music.

I now took leave of my friends and patrons, Danish as well as Russian, and last of all, my old colleague and pupil, the Swede Johansson. At his home I enjoyed one of the finest choreographic delights in the completely innate talent of his little four-and-a-half-year-old daughter, who, without having received any instruction at all, performed Russian and Polish national dances with a rhythm and grace whose spontaneity caused me to think of Mozart, who as a child was already inspired by his art.

Filled with the finest impressions and the most pleasant memories, I now hastened back to my home and arrived just in time to attend my highly honored friend Hartmann's fiftieth jubilee and to end the season with

FAREWELL TO THE OLD THEATRE!

THE GRAND TOUR AND A RETROSPECT (1874)

MY "Farewell" to the old Theatre, which unfortunately came to involve the décor for my ballets (no small portion of which will be set aside and disappear from the repertoire), signaled the demolition of the old building and my departure for the south. The Ancker Foundation imposes upon those who receive its grants the obligation of staying away a full six months, and because of the delay in the completion of the new Theatre, which could not be put into use before the middle of October, I was able, with minor exceptions, to reconcile this strict proviso with the duties of my job.

A most fortunate circumstance, namely the fact that my daughter Charlotte had invited her mother to accompany her on a trip to Italy, provided me with traveling companions as pleasant as they were beloved, and in the first days of June we traveled via Malmö and Stralsund to victory-drunk Berlin, whose proud memorials did not entice us into staying beyond the departure of the next railway train to Dresden.

Here we remained for a couple of days, which we used for several visits to the picture gallery, a stroll on the Brühl Terrace, an excursion to Tharand's "Sacred Hall," and to attend a grand musical Mass in the Catholic Church. The Court Theatre, which had burnt down, was under reconstruction but did not give promise of being completed very soon; nor did little Saxony seem to be as sparing with the subsidy as our national Rigsdag. Moreover, in the course of the years Dresden had grown considerably, and a host of foreigners, especially Americans, had settled in this pleasant city.

After having passed through picturesque countryside, traversing the memorable plains of Bodenbach and Wagram, we arrived at Vienna, where my good pupil Julius Price (permanent soloist with the Opera ballet) welcomed us and during our short stay showed us the most amiable kindness. He saw to it that we were allotted a box in the new Theatre, and we attended two operas and one ballet performance. The former were Verdi's highly interesting *Aïda* and Rossini's immortal *Guillaume Tell*, both cast with excellent singers (the tenor Müller, with Mmes. Materna and Dustmann-Meyer). Beck, on the other hand, was considerably past his prime. The ballet presented Taglioni's fantastic farce-pantomime *Flick und Flock*, in which the submarine world with dancing *boiled* lobsters was a prominent element. Price and Frappart danced the title roles, and the *soli* were skillfully performed by a Herr Haszreiter and Signorina Sangalli. The *corps de ballet* was expecially numerous, and the machinery superb. We inspected the magnificent new Theatre from top to bottom, and particularly admired its lighting and ventilation, whose installation had increased by millions the sum it had cost to erect this splendid edifice.

At Kärntnertor, the old Opera House with adjacent complex has now, together with this city gate, been leveled to the ground, while the glacis lying outside it has been transformed into a boulevard. The city's ring-wall (*die Bastei*) has completely disappeared, and on its site tower splendid palaces, some of which are due to our celebrated Theophilus Hansen's tasteful arrangement. Despite these radical alterations and the important events that have filled the interval since my last richly experienced stay, I still found Vienna to be the merry old *Kaiserstadt*, and on our way to the Prater as well as in the public gardens, we encountered the same jolly, good-natured faces, the same gay and lilting music as we had eighteen years ago, and Haydn's stirring national anthem greeted Franz Josef wherever he appeared before his affectionate people.

After traveling through Carinthia and Styria, across the Semmering Mountains by an ascending railway (a dizzying climb that was relieved only by the imposing views), past Mürzuschlag and Laybach, we arrived in the evening of June 11 at Adelsberg, where we alighted at an inn called "Die ungarische Krone" in order to be shown the following day the much-talked-about Stalactite Grotto.

Our most sanguine expectations were surpassed, for instead of entering a single vault of rock, as we had imagined it to be, we were to our surprise led for two and a half hours through the interior of the mountain, where subterranean watercourses formed small lakes and where stalactite formations represented pillars, natural bridges, open halls, altars, chapels with transparent draperies, sometimes figures of animals—aye, seen at a distance, even groups of devoutly kneeling and erect human beings!

This marvelous spectacle, which Nature must have been bringing into effect drop by drop for thousands of years, puts the spectator to considerable expense, inasmuch as the illumination demands at least a couple of hundred tapers which are moved in turn from one curious spot to another. But on Whitmonday the Adelsberg Grotto is open to the public free of charge and lighted at the community's expense with ten thousand tapers. These also shed their beams upon the great hall, where there is merry dancing to the strains of the rural orchestra for which subterranean forces have also formed a bandstand. On this remarkable walking tour we received indelible impressions and emerged from the mouth of the cavern into the open air feeling as if we had lived the fairy tale of *The Bewitched!*

That same evening the express train carried us to the Italian frontier at

Nabresina; toward midnight we reached Udine in the midst of a frightful thunderstorm. At dawn we passed Conegliano and Treviso (two cities which have given ducal titles to Maréchals Moncey and Mortier), and not far from there an enormous railway bridge led across the lagoons to Venice, which emerged from the surface of the sea, as it were, with the Campanile of the Piazza San Marco and the glistening dome of the Church of Santa Maria.

This remarkable city, with its canals, gondolas, marble palaces, churches, and priceless paintings by Titian, Tintoretto, and Paolo Veronese, but above all with its historic past, is thoroughly described in so many other places that here I would only be repeating what we, like hundreds of other travelers, have seen and admired. I will therefore spare my good readers superfluous details and only remark that the oppression which, at the time I passed through here in 1856, had rested upon the populace as a result of the Austrian occupation was now completely lifted. The Venetians were now themselves masters in their beloved city, *"La Bella"!* Every evening Italian military music could be heard on the Piazza San Marco, and *La bandiera d'Italia* proudly waved from the three towering flagpoles. But other than this, one could perceive nothing in the way of increased prosperity or commercial activity. From the Arsenal, hammer strokes no longer resounded as they once did when the Austrian navy had its shipyards there; but the historical collections were well worth seeing, and in front of the entryway there stood the two lions which had been carried off from Morea by the victorious admirals of the Republic and upon whose pedestals are graven Nordic runes that archeologists believe to have originated from the Varangians in the Byzantine Imperial Guard.

The weather was unsettled. There were storms and heavy seas in the Grand Canal, but this did not prevent us from visiting all the places worthy of note, lingering at the sepulchral monuments of Titian and Canova in the Church of Santa Maria Gloriosa, and witnessing a folk festival in the Giardino at the promontory of Riva degli Schiavoni.

In rough and chilly weather, though in the middle of the month of June, we tore along by rail past Padua, Verona, and Brescia, near beautiful Lake Garda, arriving at Milan the same evening. Here the very storm that had been raging in Venice brought with it destructive showers of hail that for whole stretches had whipped the leaves from the trees and, especially in Milan itself, had done great damage, crushing and splintering everything resembling a window, wounding people and animals, but mainly demolishing, so to speak, the entire Botanical Gardens. Curiously enough, the glorious Cathedral had been almost completely spared; and while everywhere people were occupied chiefly with remedying the general damage, Charlotte and I guided mother dear around those places she had so often heard us speak of from our previous stay. Our kind hostess, Signora Schock, as well as the excellent singing master Professor Lamperti, greeted us like long-lost relatives, and the days we passed in their agreeable company were infinitely pleasant.

I revived my theatrical memories from 1841 by visiting my old school-fellow Casati, who, after having composed a host of more or less successful ballets, was now a house-owner and *rentier*. Since I had announced myself as an old friend and colleague, he approached me with a rather cold and distrustful countenance, which only brightened when he learnt my position and financial circumstances. He thereupon confessed that he always received visits from former colleagues with fear and trembling, as most of them came to raise interest-free and irredeemable loans, since Milan was the central meeting place for all unemployed artists. We chatted for a while about the vanished days of our youth, and he expressed his admiration for me, who could travel thus, *en grand seigneur*, with wife and daughter.

The Teatro alla Scala was closed, and the only spectacle we observed was a secular jubilee with a magnificent procession to the Church of San Ambrosio (erected in the fifth century on the ruins of a Roman temple to Bacchus). In addition to the holy Ambrosius, the ceremonies concerned two other saints, Gervasius and Protatius, whose calcified bodies were displayed in glass coffins. A numerous public was lured thither by an excellent concert which, I dare say, bore a somewhat less than religious stamp. We were allotted outstanding places in one of the galleries of the church, and had the opportunity to admire the particularly beautiful singing.

Early the next morning, we took the train to the little city of Arona, where we boarded the steamship that sails on Lago Maggiore and set us ashore on the Borromean island bearing the name of Isola Bella. A hundred years ago this little islet was a naked rock to which a Prince Borromeo, at great expense, had soil tranported. Here he had a pleasure palace built and terraced gardens laid out, in which the loveliest fruits and flowers, mingled with rare trees and tropical plants, surround antique statues and vases. We viewed the whole accompanied by a talkative gardener who showed himself particularly attentive to my ladies, and pre-eminently honored *"La Signora Mama."* From this fairy castle we enjoyed the most glorious prospect of the lake coasts and the nearby Isola Madre. To one side we saw the hill where the huge bronze statue of Archbishop Carlo Borromeo rises like a colossus on the clear horizon, and in the distance one catches sight of the Alpine chain with Monte Rosa in the background.

The steamship fetched us back to Arona, and through the most enchanting countryside we drove back to Milan, where we made ready for our departure the following morning.

After bidding a fond farewell to our friends, we set off by train for Florence. The route now traversed almost the same places in which I had lingered and made my observations thirty-three years ago. We saw Piacenza, Parma, Reggio, Modena, and Bologna pass by as in a magic lantern. Between Pistoia and Florence the Apennines afforded the most picturesque prospects; but no less than forty-seven tunnels cut off the pleasure of our view at every turn, and when darkness fell we had to content ourselves with observing the thousands of fireflies and glowworms that sparkled on the grass on our smoke- and steam-filled track.

In Florence we had quite excellent lodgings at the Casa Rodolfo (via della Scala, N⁰ 2). This hotel is owned by a Dane, Herr Rudolph Meyer, a former opera singer, a superb host, and kindness personified. Here we settled down for a couple of weeks and promised ourselves, as our beloved H. C. Andersen put it, to imbibe the pure air of artistically rich and poetic Italy. However, we did not live by balmy currents of air alone, for our good Rodolfo did us proud, and the excellent *vino d'Asti* renewed our strength after the fatigue resulting from our visits to picture galleries, churches, and the environs. Everywhere in this abode of courtesy and urbanity we encountered amiable people; but in one friend from earlier days, Signor Paladino, we possessed an invaluable support and guide.

With far more tranquillity, and in a happier frame of mind than on my first trip, I could now in the company of my loved ones enjoy the splendors that Florence had to offer. But for all this, we did not neglect ourselves; and, sometimes by carriage and sometimes on foot, we were constantly on the move, while our evenings were usually spent with music and song in the company of notable travelers who gathered for tea at the hotel.

Like Dresden, Florence had expanded considerably, with the intention, I dare say, of becoming the capital of the United Italy—an expectation that had involved a number of disappointments. But many important changes and embellishments had taken place in recent years, and foremost among them must be mentioned the gallery which has been built over the bridge on the Arno and which extends for a long stretch on either side of the river, joining the Galleria degli Uffizi with the Palazzo Pitti and thus offering an unbroken ramble through the enchanted kingdom of art; for along the walls is mounted and hung a collection of drawings, engravings, etchings, and watercolors by famous artists; and where these end are to be seen costly tapestries and curious works in wood and ebony. One could willingly remain in these "hallowed halls" for months on end and still not finish seeing, let alone describing, their richness. Therefore I will merely emphasize the highly remarkable collection of self-portraits by famous artists. It would have been especially satisfying for me as a Dane had our excellent Juel also contributed his own, which would certainly have assumed a worthy place among the three hundred pictures chosen.

The Florentines' favorite promenade along the Arno out to the nearby Cascine had recently become a special attraction by virtue of a monument that had been erected at the expense of the English government in memory of a Hindu prince who, while journeying home from London, where he had been in the Embassy, fell ill in Florence and died there. At his express command, his body, dressed in his most expensive clothes, was burnt on the outskirts of the park and the ashes strewn in the waves of the river. On the spot where the pyre had stood a Hindu chapel had been built, in whose open niche or ogive the Rajah's bust was placed. But the marble, which was illuminated with lifelike colors, echoed his dark facial hue as well as his pearl-decked costume with a realism which, on us at least, had an uncomfortable effect.

It was then the feast of St. John (June 23), and the churches gleamed in solemn splendor. The Cathedral and the wondrously beautiful Baptistry were crowded both with the devout and with sightseers. We mingled with both classes, for the inspiring church music as well as for the works of art that met our astonished gaze at every step.

We visited our neighboring church, S. Maria Novella, with its cloister and frescoes by Giotto and Cimabue; S. Annunciata, with superb subjects by Michelangelo and Andrea del Sarto; San Michele, with the splendid tabernacle by Orcagna; San Lorenzo, where we saw the monument to the learned Benevenuti by Thorvaldsen and the beautiful sepulchral monument with the angel carrying Countess Corbelli, *née* Moltke-Huidtfeldt, to the Home of Light (a masterpiece by Dupré, probably modern Italy's greatest sculptor); and Santa Croce, whose black and white marble façade, after waiting for centuries, has finally been completed—in contrast to that of the Cathedral, which remains in a rough state even though the prize in the design competition has twice been won by our skilled countryman Wilhelm Petersen.

In Santa Croce are to be found magnificent monuments above the remains of famous men like Dante, Michelangelo, Alfieri, Machiavelli, and others. Outside on the square stands the colossal marble statue of Dante. In the Chapel of the Medici, beneath pompous mausoleums, rest the majority of this art-loving race of princes. But in the Convento di San Marco, where the painters Fra Angelico da Fiesole and Fra Bartolomeo have decorated the walls of all the cells with biblical frescoes, is kept alive the memory of Savonarola, who for his opinions which were divergent from accepted Catholic dogma was burnt alive as a heretic.

Greater tolerance nowadays prevails in young Italy. During our stay in Florence it was advertised on posters and on street corners that Signora N. N., "Freethinker," was to be borne to her grave in solemn procession by *"La società dei libri Pensatori"!* We chanced to witness this funeral procession, which passed through the streets with the red banners of the Society and a small band of musicians. The followers were few in number and the spectators, who were crowded together, regarded the whole thing with silent indifference. If the so-called "freethinking" zealots on this occasion had hoped to create a stir by their demonstration, they must have felt sorely disappointed.

Among the habitués of our hotel was the clergyman for the English community in Florence and Siena, "The Reverend Mr. Burchell of Somerset," a youngish, especially comely man, who was knowledgeable in both music and languages; he even knew and translated literally a number of our Danish writers. Since he was also a member of *"La società philologica,"* a kind of

Atheneum which in addition to its library and reading room also had a separate auditorium for classes in living languages and modern literature, he took me along with him, thereby giving me some insight into this excellent institution.

But since in the midst of all these artistic and literary interests it would not do for me to neglect my specialty, which unfortunately has nothing remarkable to offer during the summer season, especially in Italy where at this time of year most of the theatres are closed, I attended a performance at the Teatro Umberto, situated on the other side of the Arno, where excerpts from an opera unknown to me, *Contessa d'Amalfi*, were performed. These excerpts were sung by students, several of whom had particularly lovely voices. Thereupon followed one act from a grand ballet, *Armida*, the plot of which had been clipped away in order to make room for sheer dancing. On the whole, this was well executed by the *corps de ballet* as well as the soloists, Sgr. Copetti and Sgra. Galli, both of whom possessed extraordinary skill yet, to my sorrow, wore the same disgusting costume that on the entire Continent is nowadays identical for opera dancers and acrobats. As far as these last artists are concerned, I in no wise underestimate their spirit, strength, and agility. But I am reminded of our great actor Frydendahl, who in one of his aristocratic paroxysms declared in that precious tone of his: "Each of them is good in himself, and all are better than I—but with such and such a class of people I do not care to associate." I must confess that the acrobatic tendency in both dance and musical virtuosity is not in accordance with my ideas of art.

Together with our friend Signor Paladino, we undertook an excursion to ancient Fiesole, once the hostile rival of the Florentine Republic but gradually reduced to the manufacture of straw articles. With the greatest importunity, a variety of these products are offered for sale to travelers approaching this city on the heights by the steep mountain road. Nothing remains of its former splendor save for its church and a painter's famous name.* And yet it possesses a character of which neither time nor violence has been able to deprive it, especially in its enchantingly lovely prospect of the valley of the Arno, where Florence with its enormous towers and palaces, its beautiful gardens with soaring cypresses, spreads itself before the eye of the beholder in the glowing evening sun.

We took another pleasure trip to the newly laid out *chausée* which twists and turns its way between villas and public gardens leading up to the old, formerly fortified, castle of San Miniato. Only the palace chapel and the cemetery now remain. And as for the Plateau, where a bronze copy of Michelangelo's "David with his Sling" now stands in a square enclosed with an iron grill, it had already been selected as the rendezvous for the thousands of artlovers from every land who were to gather the following year to celebrate the four hundredth anniversary of the birth of Michelangelo (March 6, 1475). Here we lingered for a long while, lost in admiration of the great master, and

---

*Fra Angelico (1387–1455), also known as Giovanni da Fiesole; see above.

impressed upon our memories the magnificent panorama that extended over mountains and fertile valleys.

But we had to bid farewell to beautiful and pleasant Florence, to our good host and faithful guide, the chivalrous Paladino, who sadly accompanied us to the railway station. This time I was not to read the Latin inscription bearing the name of Frederik IV upon the northern gate of the city, for we were heading south to Rome, "the Eternal City." But just as thirty-three years ago, so too I now had to pay my tribute to Flora when a corpulent old woman handed bouquets to my ladies inside the coupé. Surely this could not be the famous Flower Fairy of so long ago! The whistle sounded and we departed, while I borrowed a phrase from those of my friends learned in Latin: "The times change and we change with them"!

My knowledge of the classical language of the Romans has never been greater than was necessary for a thorough understanding of Montanus and Stygotius, but this knowledge has also become fused with Italian, which I later studied and on this trip got an opportunity to refresh. It was a true delight to talk with this lively people and hear them set forth their naïve remarks in a language that sounded like music to our ears.

Many have deplored the Italians' greed for money and extortion. But, allowing that everywhere in the world there are people who make a living by extorting contributions from travelers, it is mainly Englishmen and persons who because of their ignorance of the language are taken to be *"Inglesi"* who must pay for everything on an exorbitant scale. And if one remembers that the influx of foreigners is generally greatest during the winter season, thereby producing a considerable *hausse* [price rise] on all articles, one will, under regular conditions, find the stay in Italy relatively cheaper than in other countries.

As far as I have been able to judge, the Italian national character is made up of lively sympathies and antipathies, both of them often to extremes with no middle ground, as with *fanatismo* and *fiasco*. If by a friendly and straightforward manner one is lucky enough to win sympathies, one can depend upon genuine good will and affection. We made efforts in this direction, and in our entire trip we met with nothing but the greatest politeness.

For anyone who can tolerate the heat of the sun, summer is certainly the best time for the trip to Italy, both because beautiful Nature then appears in all her luxuriance, the people in their picturesque *"negligé,"* and the crowds of foreigners have gone back to the North. To be sure, the thermometer does mount to 24° or 25° R. [86° or 88° F.], but the heat in Rome, and especially in Naples, is drier than here at home where the atmosphere immediately becomes oppressive and heavy with thunder. We never felt troubled by the climate which, in spite of the *sirocco* and the notorious malaria, is less dangerous in the dry heat than during the rainy season and the winter cold.

The railway route from Florence to Rome runs past Arezzo, Perugia, and

Foligno, and by express train the trip takes about ten hours. Immediately upon emerging from the railroad station in Rome the eye is greeted by the magnificent ruins of the Baths of Diocletian. There are porters and omnibuses to carry one's baggage, and with anxious expectation one seeks out the *locanda* to which one is recommended. We found ours in a French *maison garnie* on the Corso, and it was not long before we rushed up the Spanish Steps to Monte Pincio in order to gaze with solemn excitement upon *la città eterna,* which lay before us in the loveliest moonlight.

Were I, by an excerpt from my diary, to enumerate much less describe the curiosities which this world capital has to offer, it would far exceed the limits of these pages of memoirs and become nought but a repetition of what anyone can find in Baedeker's Handbook. Armed with this superb guidebook and with our indefatigable daughter as local guide, we old folk went on a pilgrimage from morning till night, driving to and visiting those places where antiquity and the Middle Ages, history and art, were encountered with overwhelming impressions. From the princely palaces and the picture galleries to the ruins of the Forum Romanum, from the enormous halls of the Palatine Hill to the Mamertine Prison beneath the Capitol (where Jugurtha and the Gallic chieftain Vercingetorix languished and whence Peter and Paul went to martyrdom); from the majestic triumphal arches, amphitheatres, and temples, we went to the Church of St. Peter, the most magnificent sanctuary in Christendom, and to the adjacent Vatican, unquestionably the most comfortable parsonage in the world.

A stroll through the vaulted arches and numerous chapels of this church as well as below and above the galleries of the cupola gives the astonished spectator an idea of *the colossal* combined with *the harmonious* in architectural design. Its wealth of artistic works and its costly materials defy all description. One must only regret that almost a quarter of the inner space has been isolated by a partition and taken up as an assembly hall for the great Council which has ratified and proclaimed the familiar dogma of Infallibility, a highly unfortunate demonstration which has influenced the desertion of many, not only from the Papacy but from the Christian faith as a whole.

Pius IX, one of the first apostles of Italian unity and the man to whom an Italian national anthem was dedicated, has now in his old days retired into his palace, where he poses as a prisoner and a martyr because the sovereign Church State, *"La barca di San Pietro"* (the fishing boat of Simon Peter), has been expropriated for the benefit of the Kingdom of Italy. In return for this expropriation the Italian kingdom has surrendered its claim to the Vatican and has also granted the Pope a yearly civil pension of three million francs, which the Holy Father has refused to accept, preferring to live off the alms which probably amount to four times as much. Although he is very well aware that his public appearance as the clergy's superior would be hailed with jubilation by high and low, by liberal and clerical alike, he holds back with affectation but gives audience to curious foreigners as he hurls impotent bolts of excommunication against those who have stubbornly disputed his secular control. Now, whether this role is his own independent conception of his office or merely a puppet show with the Jesuits pulling the strings, the whole thing has had a most harmful influence upon the feelings of the various factions.

Before attempting to give a rough sketch of the emotions and conditions which during the summer of 1874 prevailed in this capital, which has now passed from the Papal to the Royal power, whose tricolored banner flies above Hadrian's Mausoleum (the circular Castel Sant'Angelo), I will ask my readers to accompany us through the Vatican chambers, galleries, and loggias to its peerless museum, where the masterworks of sculpture appear with all the majesty of Greek and Roman antiquity, and where one comes to understand the cult which these pagan civilized nations dedicated to the beauty of forms.

Here we encounter statues of gods and goddesses, Muses and heroes, emperors and gladiators, fauns, nymphs, and symbolic figures. The majority of them were carried off from Greece and Asia Minor by victorious generals and set up in their villas and baths, only to be hurled into the dust by barbarians and buried for centuries beneath the ruins of temples and palaces. Here they were rediscovered, erected, and glorified by the care of art-loving magnates; selected pieces were brought to the Musée Napoléon in Paris, to be finally carried back and placed on the sites where they rightly draw the admiration of Europe.

At the same time, one becomes acquainted with the most famous men of the classical age through a large collection of portrait busts. From the various physiognomies, especially those of the Caesars, the French historian Beule has tried to draw conclusions about decided character traits. But if one excepts the resemblance between Augustus and Napoleon the Great, and that of Vitellius to any other greedy glutton, we could just as little determine the characteristics of Tiberius and Nero as those of Marcus Aurelius and Lucius Verus or find any more outstanding expressions than in many good-natured people now living. Thus one will not be surprised to learn that upon more closely examining the busts of Euripides, Aristides, Seneca, Cicero, and Julian the Apostate, we would agree that each of them bears some resemblance to one intelligent person or another here at home.

We paid several visits to this magnificent museum, which is open to the public every weekday; but this was hardly enough. On the other hand, we went but a single time to the picture gallery where Raphael's wondrous altarpieces hang, the same ones which have been masterfully copied in imperishable mosaics in the Church of St. Peter in Rome. In order to reach the *stanze*, one must pass through the so-called *loggias* (the arcades which, in the *belétage* of the Vatican, surround the inner palace yard). These are adorned throughout with graceful arabesques and mythological compositions from Raphael's masterly hand. Unfortunately, a portion of them have been carried off by time, and obliterated by wind and rain; but in our day they have under-

gone a painstaking restoration by an outstanding painter, Cavaliere Montavano, who with exquisite gallantry led us into his atelier and showed us his
works.

We now entered the famous Papal apartments where the wall paintings
and doorpieces evidence the culmination of Raphael's art. But here we were
astonished by two striking contrasts: the *realism* in a painting that depicted
the martyrdom of the Catholic mission in Japan or Cochinchina, where a
whole row of priests are shown hanging from the gallows; and the *idealism*
displayed in a gigantic apotheosis for the "Immaculate Conception of the
Blessed Virgin," proclaimed by Pius IX who, kneeling, hands the important
document to the Madonna who sits enthroned as Queen of Heaven, surrounded by angels and saints in episcopal vestments (the Savior of the World
is completely ignored).

An old saying reproaches the traveler "for having been to Rome and not
seen the Pope"! Many, and Protestants among them, regard it as a duty to
seek an audience with this high priest of Catholicism. We felt no such desire,
though we would have liked to hear him sing Mass before the high altar on
the feast of Sts. Peter and Paul, which had been celebrated a few days before
our arrival. We had to content ourselves with seeing a black idol which is said
to represent the apostle Peter. This statue even sat adorned with a tiara, an
episcopal cope, and crozier!

Like so much other ecclesiastical pomp, concerts in the Sistine Chapel
have in recent times fallen away, mainly because of the pretended bondage of
the Pope. The great chapel now stood like a dismal lumber room filled with
all sorts of furniture, and provided but a prosaic frame for Michelangelo's
striking "Last Judgment," which depicts with gigantic fantasy the souls of the
saved and the damned (both men and women, with limbs and muscles like
those of the Farnese Hercules). This colossal painting has certainly won
world renown, especially because of its terrifying effect; but I do not feel I
am committing any blasphemy against the immortal master by admiring him
above all as a sculptor and architect.

The sweeping reforms of most recent times have made themselves felt in
Rome more than any other place. And so with many people it is the same as
with that old Frenchman who, upon viewing the Simplon Road, exclaimed:
"You have ruined my Alps for me!" For in a number of respects the Eternal
City is vastly different from the days when legislative chambers, election campaigns, political journals, and free competition were unknown within the Papal States. Little by little the variegated folk life has faded away. The colorful
national costume has to some degree disappeared, and it is but seldom that
one encounters an example of the picturesque but loathsome monks, whose
cloisters are gradually being shut down, although the Pope has given them
asylum in his palace of Castel Gandolfo near Lake Nemi. The brown cowls as
well as the lovely peasant costumes now figure only as models in painters'
ateliers. The magnificent old-fashioned horse-drawn coaches with a Cardinal

inside and three or four lackeys outside no longer drive through the streets of Rome. A number of Papal-minded nobles have shut up their palaces, while the historically famous Villa d'Este in the neighborhood of Tivoli, which has been handed over to a Cardinal-Prince of Hohenlohe, has begun to fall into utter ruin.

There is no longer a Flower Festival at Genzano, and because of the same passive resistance on the part of the clergy the pompous church processions, which formed such an attractive spectacle for the common people, have entirely ceased. To be sure, one now and then sees groups of women and children kneeling before an image of the Madonna, or pilgrims who with hot tears kiss the cold black foot of the seated bronze statue of St. Peter, and pretty sinners who in the confessional reveal their hidden thoughts to the priest, who reflectively takes a pinch from his indispensable snuffbox. So too the divine service or, more correctly, the worship of the saints is carried on before the respective chapels whose financial circumstances permit a perpetual Mass. With regard to this, I cannot refrain from mentioning one of the numberless Maria churches, whose surname I cannot recall, but in a dark corner of which is to be found a chapel for our great Danish patron, St. Canute. It is said to have been founded by Erik Eiegod and further endorsed by rich donations from Christian I. But for many years it has stood without any Mass having been read or sung before its altarpiece. And when one asked why, the sacristan replied with a shrug of his shoulders, *"E un poveretto, questo Santo!"* — which is to say that he did not have the means to pay for the business. Several Danes, some of them artists, decided half in jest and half out of patriotic feeling to contribute for a Mass in memory of this saintly king, and it was actually performed.

It cannot be denied that while the Papacy is increasing its secular power it is losing more and more of its ecclesistical nimbus and influence; for with the removal of the dazzling cult, so appealing to the sensual masses, the crassness of superstition comes into ever sharper relief while progressive enlightenment is able to protest more strongly against dogmas that are as absurd as they are untenable, and behind which lie hidden not only political Jesuitism but ambition and covetousness as well. In hardly any other Catholic country is there such a marked hatred for the clergy as there is in Italy, and it is impossible to foresee how matters will stand when the aged Pius one day goes to his rest.

Rome is now chiefly a Royal residential city; order and cleanliness are more prevalent than in the old days. The hordes of beggars have considerably decreased; brawls and assassinations but rarely take place; bandits have been banished to Sicily, where they still ravage; and an excellent police force protects the peaceful citizenry. One is no longer molested by intrusive, whispering procurers; commerce and industry seem to be on the upswing. The railroad station's splendid waiting room and the Post Office's elegant and efficient establishment give evidence of the government's taste and care. Every evening at sunset long rows of fine equipages with the city's *"beau monde"* drive out along the Corso to the nearby Passegiata and the Villa Borghese, while a numerous public later gathers for the military concerts on the Piazza Colonna. But despite all these refinements the same busy folk life still prevails in Trastevere and in the markets. Cafés and restaurants have not made particular progress, and it is in the old *osterias* that one now, as before, drinks the best wine.

With our friendly Consul Bravo, and in the company of Danish and other Nordic artists, we assembled at the Scandinavian Club, where Charlotte brightened the evening entertainment with her singing. We were then taken to a unique wine-pub where jovial genre pictures from *The Festival in Albano* sprang to mind. Our talented countrymen, like those predecessors of theirs who had returned home, led industrious and quiet lives, though they unfortunately remained all too isolated from their fellow-artists of other nations. I was astonished to learn that the American sculptor Franklin-Simons [*sic*]† — whose atelier I had visited and where I had admired outstanding objects, amongst others a splendid monument to the fallen in the War of Secession — was completely unknown to them.

On our way to the Sabine Hills we saw the extensive ruins of Hadrian's villa, where excavations, as at Ostia and the Forum Romanum, were being carried on with scientific skill under the direction of the zealous Rosa. To give a description of the countless natural beauties that surround Tivoli would lead me too far afield. I will only say that from the colonnade of the Temple of the Sibyl, we became lost in silent rapture at the landscape which lay before us. Here frothy cascades were garlanded by motionless, hovering rainbows. The space of three miles which separates Rome from the hills, the old Agro Romano (which had for centuries remained an unhealthy and unfruitful wilderness where herds found meager grazing among the ruins of the ancient sepulchral monuments and proud aqueducts), offers striking proof of the progress of civilization and culture. This Roman campagna is now cultivated in many places, and we even passed a field where the freshly cut wheat was being threshed with steam machines! On the way home, we encountered the same reapers sitting together on a cart, singing and waving, while they jangled tambourines. It was a true genre picture *à la* Léopold Robert. Save for this, there was little of scenic value.

The Theatre of Apollo was closed, and performances given only by daylight were held in an open auditorium in the Circus, which had been excavated from the mausoleum of the emperor Augustus. Several of the artists who appeared here distinguished themselves by true dramatic talent, as I have described in Volume III, Part One. I will only remark that in one of the

---

† Franklin Simmons, born 1839 and self-taught in modeling, executed many busts of Grant, Sherman, and other Civil War leaders, as well as idealized figures and public monuments such as the one described here. He spent most of his working life in Rome, where he died in 1913. Works by him may be seen in Portland, Washington, and elsewhere.

pieces we saw, namely *Massimo d'Azeglio*, there appeared a sharp attack on bigotry, directed mainly against the Jesuits. Of dancing or ballet I got to see nothing at all, not even so much as a harmless little *saltarello!* On the other hand, side by side with pictures showing the Pope and Victor Emmanuel hand in hand as firm friends, there were to be found whole rows of photographs of counterfeit *danseuses* in such revolting costumes and poses that, had I not been conscious of having fought this indecent direction my whole life through, I would have been ashamed to be called Balletmaster!

Our sights were now set on Naples, where we had reserved lodgings with that old friend and host of the Danes, Signor Ferrari. But first we had to visit the Columbari, where urns containing the ashes of Romans from the time of the Republic are set up in small niches resembling the nests in a dovecote. Next we saw the rebuilt basilica of San Paolo fuori Muri, whose polished granite pillars are monoliths presented by the Viceroy of Egypt. Finally, in the neighborhood of this splendid church lies the Protestant cemetery, where we lingered at the graves of several Danes and Scandinavians who have found their final resting places here—among others, our amiable poet, C. Hauch!

Since Albano is mentioned as the first station on the railway line to Naples, I had thought up an itinerary which aimed at leaving Rome early in the morning, spending the day in Albano and its environs, and traveling on by night train to be in Naples the following morning. Unfortunately I had not counted on the fact that the Albano *station* lay over half a mile from the *town* itself. The road led uphill in the burning heat of the sun. There were no coaches, and we arrived tired and worn out at the place which had been so poetically and romantically depicted by me!

However, here we encountered what was perhaps the only disappointment of our whole trip. As a result of expansion, the city had entirely lost its former picturesque character, and of the lovely Alban girls, crowds of whom I had thirty-three years ago watched strolling to church in their pretty costumes with embroidered bodices, red half-sleeves, fluttering silk ribbons, and lace-trimmed headdresses, no trace remained! Everything was bourgeois, vulgar, and now there was almost no difference between the village maidens of Albano and the washerwomen at Lake Esrøm!

We tried to console ourselves by a pleasure trip to Nemi and Castel Gandolfo. Everywhere we enjoyed the lovely view, and when we drove back to the station that evening, we observed for the first time *the comet!*‡ In the wretched station we waited for the train, which arrived at midnight; and when we entered a tightly filled compartment, in spite of our three portmanteaux etc. we were greeted with an obliging courtesy that was most refreshing after the exertions of the day.

‡ First sighted at Marseilles in April 1874 by the French astronomer M. Coggia, the comet was brilliant and clearly visible over Italy during the summer of that year. It is also reputed to be the first comet examined through the spectroscope.

At dawn we reached Capua, and at seven o'clock we alighted at Naples' magnificent railroad station, where Ferrari's servants were waiting for us with a carriage and drove us to the Hotel dell'Allegria on Toledo Street. Our old host greeted us as if we were long-lost friends and relatives, and also plied us with questions about Danimarca, Marstrand, Holst, and Constantin Hansen. After having rested a bit and collected the letters from home that were waiting for us at the post office, I rushed out into the open air to see once more those places where so many years ago I had gathered both material for my most popular ballet and impressions for my whole life.

Toward evening I went down to Santa Lucia to experience once again those unforgettable scenes. But whether it was age that had cooled my ardor, or whether in the course of time changes had taken place that had disturbed the characteristic element in the picture, suffice it to say I did not rediscover my old Santa Lucia with the lively incidents and motley crowds from every walk of society. Fish, oyster, and macaroni stalls were in their usual places, naked and ragged children ran about yelling, and the rest of the conversation sounded like the most dreadful quarrel, just as in the old days. But the crush and bustle—in short, the atmosphere—were missing. On the whole, the unification of Italy does not seem to have had a beneficial effect upon the physiognomy of Naples. The *lazzaroni* life has as good as vanished with King Bomba.* Nowadays the Molo and the Marina are perfectly civilized docks, and following the fall of the rock of Pizzo-Falcone, which gave support to a whole row of houses, Santa Lucia itself has received an opening for a magnificent new street leading directly to the public gardens whose name, Villa Reale, has now been changed to Nazionale. Luckily, however, glorious Nature is conservative, and when the sun rises in the clear sky above the azure sea, Naples is still *Napoli!*

The strong July heat and several well-known inconveniences reduced our stay in the city itself to the shortest possible amount of time. We visited the great Museum, the Royal Palace, the churches of San Chiara, Trinità Maggiore, and Madonna del Carmine, whose feast was celebrated the same day with great pomp and dazzling illuminations. In the neighborhood of this church lies the Piazza del Mercato, with its memories of Masaniello! We enjoyed the delightful prospects from Capo di Monte and from the Carthusian monastery of San Martino, which had been transformed into a kind of museum. This, together with the Castel Sant'Elmo, hovers like an aerie above buzzing and roaring Naples, where the shrill voices sound like an enormous swarm of bees. After having visited a couple of my old colleagues from former times, my ladies and I betook ourselves on most interesting excursions into

*Ferdinand II (1810–1859), King of the Two Sicilies, was ruler when a Sicilian uprising signaled the start of revolutions throughout Italy and Europe. As a result of a movement in Naples, the King granted a constitution and swore to uphold it. However, following street riots in Naples the same year, Ferdinand withdrew his promise, dissolved parliament, and returned to a reactionary policy. Sicily was subjugated and its chief cities bombarded. This move won Ferdinand the nickname of "King Bomba."

the environs which I have already described in Volume I of *My Theatre Life* – though every description gives but a flat and pale idea of the singularity of the subject.

On the trip to Pozzuoli and Baiae, the Lucrine lake and Lake Avernus and the Cave of the Sibyl, the Bridge of Caligula and Caesar's Villa, we had as our guide Pietro Rocca, so highly recommended in Baedeker's handbook, who upheld his reputation in a most worthy fashion.

On the opposite side of the Bay the railroad leads to Castellammare. However, we did not climb smoking Vesuvius but set our course straight for Pompeii, where for a couple of hours we wandered through the streets which have for eighteen centuries lain beneath the ashes of the volcano and only half of which have as yet been excavated.

Anyone who has not become acquainted through the classical authors with the mores and the luxury that prevailed here during that age of refinement need only read Bulwer's novel *The Last Days of Pompeii* to get some idea of the feelings that grip one at the sight of this vanished and rediscovered city with its temples, halls, pleasure spots, and graves! Filled with these powerful impressions, we drove by carriage farther along the picturesque coast, whose cities and villas are always threatened by the destructive flow of lava, past Castellammare to our destination, charming Sorrento!

At the elegant Hotel Tramontana, which is maintained by English ladies with all the comfort of their native land, we spent several indescribably delightful days. Our rooms looked out upon a *loggia* which crowned a high cliff that dropped straight down to the sea and afforded a view the like of which we have found only at Møns Klint!

Through the mountain upon which the hotel with its luxuriant gardens is situated, a secret passage led down to the beach, where bathhouses invited a refreshing dip in the clear waves upon whose swells a saucy sailboat rolled. The city itself we found appealing only by virtue of the memory of Torquato Tasso, whose house one is shown, and the purchase of some curiously carved wooden articles. The feast of Santa Maria del Carmine was likewise celebrated here with illuminations and fireworks, and we had everything our hearts could desire.

The isles of Capri and Ischia lay invitingly on the horizon. Time and – I am ashamed to say – finances permitted us to visit only one of them. But which one? After much wavering back and forth, we chose Capri and struck an agreement with the sailboat's *padrone di barca* for a tour around this rocky island and thence directly back to Naples. With a crew of four and supplied with provisions, we put off from shore, waved a fond farewell to this earthly Paradise, and with a favorable wind glided past the promontory with the ruins of the castle of the corsair Barbarossa.

Soon we had reached *l'Arco Naturale,* a portal of rock in the middle of the sea; and while sailing along the steep coasts, we noticed a host of caves and grottoes, among which there was one with white and another with green rock. However, it was mainly the Blue Grotto that my daughter and I so ardently desired to see and with which we wanted our mother to become acquainted. But the mysterious romanticism we had hoped to inhale in this magical realm of sea sprites was to a considerable degree disturbed by the unbearable importunity of the old *marinaro* in whose little dinghy we entered the Grotto.

He positively insisted on displaying for us his prowess as a swimmer, and did not stop until we were compelled to accept his offer and demands. I came away from this marine palace in anything but a poetic mood! Toward midday we came alongside at the town of Capri and stepped ashore at a new hotel, which had borrowed the highly figurative name of Paris' "Louvre." We now prepared to ascend the heights where the ruins of the rock palace of the Tiberii seemed to stand out over the precipice. Two girls and an elderly woman appeared with two donkeys and a horse. Our *padrone di barca* came along with us and we now proceeded up the steep mountain, with jesting and merry conversation.

The girls, who recognized Charlotte from her previous trip, were soon on familiar terms with her; and after stopping several times to admire the imposing view, we reached the hut and hermit's chapel which lay among the overthrown rubble of the palace whence the bloodthirsty tyrant issued his orders. Inside the hut wine was poured and we were treated to milk fresh from the cow, after which we offered a mite to the good and courteous hermit. We then encouraged the art of dancing by rewarding a lively *tarantella* which, to the jangling of tambourines, was performed by a young chap and our little girls. But the greatest virtuosity of all was displayed by the woman who, like me, belonged to the good old school. In the meantime, evening had fallen. The moon rose and shone upon the silver-streaked sea and the picturesque mountain landscape with a brilliance peculiar to the Italian air.

We now began our descent to the sound of lovely songs. These were, curiously enough, the first folk melodies we had heard on our whole trip through Italy, which had formerly been so rich in song and sound; and with deep emotion we joined in *"Te voglio ben assai"*† and *"Dolce Napoli, suol beato."* It was an unforgettable evening!

Early the next morning, my daughter went alone by boat to the Blue Grotto, and since this time she did not wish to lose the atmosphere, she paid the old nuisance to keep still and let her enjoy the view and the impression in peace. Shortly after her return from this pilgrimage, we got under way and sailed back toward Naples, as our female guides from the previous evening waved farewell.

It was now high time I thought of heading for Paris—there to further the actual purpose of my trip: namely, the groundwork for a new ballet, *Arcona*. My ladies were to meet me there and to remain with me for only a couple of days, whereas I intended to pass three weeks in my old home, which during

† Cf. Bournonville's "Ischia Ballad," in the section "Lyric Attempts," Vol. I.

my several years' absence had undergone such dreadful shocks. They journeyed by road while I proceeded by steamer, via Marseilles. However, I did not put in at the coastal cities as I had on my previous trips, but headed directly north, past the historically curious islands of Elba, Corsica, and Capraia, espying in the distance the romantically depicted crag of Monte Cristo.

In Marseilles, whose harbor has been considerably enlarged, I encountered the same motley crowds of people of every race, especially from the Orient. At the *table d'hôte* I chanced to sit next to a Moorish chieftain who was on his way to Paris and spoke very good French. We conversed quite pleasantly with one another, and his manners were of the noblest. After a wait of only a few hours I set off by rail, traversed France at tearing speed, and the following morning (July 28) alighted at my old "Hôtel des hautes Alpes," where a couple of days later I welcomed my beloved fellow-travelers.

I shall not weary my readers with accounts of all the grand and glorious things we saw on our wanderings in Paris, but will only dwell for a moment upon the disgusting vandalism perpetrated by an unbridled mob of fanatics and criminals during a period which, short as it was, will nevertheless remain as a stigma upon both that sector of the Parisian populace which took part in these dreadful deeds and that which stood by as passive spectator of the demented behavior of the Communards.

Arson was practiced on a grand scale and intended for the major part of the capital! The Hôtel de Ville, all the seats of government together with their archives, the Palais de la Légion d'Honneur, and the historically curious Tuileries Palace presented the abomination of destruction! My noble friend, Professor Geffroy, told me that if the Government troops had forced their way into Paris but a single day later, the Louvre with its priceless art treasures and the great Bibliothèque Nationale would have gone up in flames, for the casks of petroleum had already been put in the proper places. "Then," he exclaimed, "there would have been no more France!" This sorely tried country was now once again a republic, with Radicals and Conservatives but only a few genuine patriots!

As strongly infatuated as I had been in my younger days with Napoleon I (whose genius and deeds continue to arouse my admiration), I could now feel but little sympathy for his nephew, who also played an ambiguous role in the drama that had such unhappy results for dismembered Denmark. But when I considered on the one hand the grandiose undertakings in the way of beneficial establishments and embellishments that had taken place under his *personal* regime, and on the other the infamous deeds committed in the name of the principles of liberty, equality, and humanity by a rough and demented rabble and sanctioned by the supporters of radicalism, I was involuntarily tempted to side with the Bonapartists. God alone knows what party shall walk off with the victory in years to come, but it is not inconceivable that one day, when they have tired of being the pawns of intriguers, the hundreds of thousands of workers to whom the Emperor in his time gave abundant rewards and who still live in the volatile quarters of Belleville and Menilmontant will, upon viewing the evidences of paternal care manifested in the transformation of the Buttes Chaumont from the offal heap of Paris into a delightful park and the marvelous reservoir beneath Menilmontant, look back on the Empire with a fairer judgment than that which those agitators have passed upon him and his government.

The majority of travelers in Paris focus their attention on the theatres, the museums, the magnificent boulevards and dazzling boutiques, but rarely get the opportunity to visit those remote and highly situated quarters, whither the walk is long and rather laborious. All the same, I advise anyone to devote a morning to this trip—first, to admire the splendid fashion in which the park and garden have been laid out with rock caves, waterfalls, and crystalline lakes which have artfully replaced the barren mountain slopes where night-soil was formerly spread for the preparation of fertilizer and where the carcasses of horses and other flayed domestic animals poisoned the air while the children of the servants of the establishment played with the rats, which swarmed by the thousand in this filthy element; and next, in order to descend into the vaults which, like the *piscina mirabilis* of antiquity (in two stories joined by winding iron staircases) contain enormous reservoirs where conduits lead the waters of the Marne into the upper basin, and those of the Dhuys into the lower. From here run underground pipes, through which five of the *arrondissements,* or quarters, of Paris are supplied with excellent water. This colossal work was accomplished in less than three years and is remarkable for the fact that above its covering of soil, luxuriant grain grows and cattle graze.

The great Opéra was not yet in use, but stood as good as finished. One of my recent friends from a visit at Fredensborg, the well-known skilled clockmaker and lighting engineer Henry Lepaute, guided me through the magnificent facilities, the luxury of which I have earlier discussed.

Following the burning of the old stage, the Opéra was now (1874) temporarily housed in the Salle Ventadour, where for the sake of profits the entire stalls, called *stalles d'orchestre,* and the pit with its company of claqueurs, were moved up into *the third étage!* From here I watched an opera, *L'Esclave,* with lovely and characteristic music by Membrée. The subject was Russian, and the performance by the singers Sylvia, Menu, Bataille, and Lasalle, together with Mmes. Mauduit and Geismar, was especially fine. The interpolated dances greatly pleased me and gave Mlle. Beaugrand an opportunity to distinguish herself *en pointe.*

I found *Les Huguenots* and *La Favorite,* which I later got to hear, most satisfying. Achard as Raoul and Belval as Marcel were particularly excellent, and the principal roles in *La Favorite* were sustained with true dramatic fullness by two younger talents, Mlle. Bloch and M. Bourquin. From this one may judge how large a group of singers the Opéra has at its disposal. Unfortunately, the ballet, which was once so richly staffed, is nowadays limited to one mediocre *danseur* and the aforementioned *danseuse,* together with some highly inexpressive mimes. With these weak forces, during my last stay, there was given but a single performance of Saint-Léon's ballet *Coppélia*, in which a scene with a mechanical doll [*Nürnbergerdukke*] forms the central motif. It was, on the whole, quite entertaining, without making any further intellectual demands.

At the Opéra-Comique, Ambroise Thomas' latest light opera, *Mignon*, was given. The music was both melodious and dramatic; Mlle. Chapuy was most satisfying in the title role, and Mlle. Chevalier was especially good as Philine. To me, the gentlemen appeared of lesser note; the chorus and the orchestra, on the other hand, quite excellent.

Each evening the Théâtre Français presented three pieces. I thus had the opportunity to admire the elder Coquelin as Tabarin in the drama of the same name, and also as Destournelles in *Mademoiselle de La Seiglière;* Got as the Husband in *Le Supplice d'une femme,* as Mercadet, and as Cliton in *Le Menteur;* Madeleine Brohan in *La Gageure imprévue,* and a rather young actress, Mlle. Reichenberger, in several *ingénue* roles, which she played with great naturalness, a virtue I found wanting in both M. Delaunay and Mlle. Croizette; not to mention the conventional stiltedness in the tragedy. In this genre I saw Mlle. Sarah Bernhardt as Zaire, but was unable to accept the declamation that pleads its case with bellowing and hysterical howls. However, this theatre is still, especially in comedy, a school for true dramatic art; and even though, like ours, it has through the years lost its greatest celebrities (Talma, Mlle. Mars, Mlle. Rachel, Michelot, Monrose, Samson, Provost, Bressant, etc.), it continues to uphold its reputation as the seat of good French drama.

A less noble genre, but one in which laughter robs obscenity of its sting, is cultivated at the Théâtre du Palais-Royal, where M. Hyacinthe displays priceless comic humor. Fairy-tale plays (*féeries*) were flourishing at the boulevard theatres, and the Porte-Saint-Martin delivered the 250th performance of *Le Pied de Mouton,* where magnificent scenery, dazzling pageantry, and nudity *en masse* were the main elements of the play. These same things, with the addition of lively music and very fine singing voices, distinguished Offenbach's parodies at the Théâtre de la Gaîté, where the new staging of *Orphée aux enfers* is said to have cost 200,000 francs! And everywhere there was an overabundance of female dancers—God knows where all these poor girls come from! And yet one encountered *dancing* only when the disgusting cancan was to be performed, and this was almost always used as a finale!

After my wife and daughter had departed for home, I divided my time between my friends and my work. Most of the former were from recent years, for almost none of my contemporaries remained. Only my old landlady, Mme. Mugnier, was still living at Menilmontant and welcomed me as if I were a beloved son. Also, I still had a warm friend in the superb musician, Professor

Marmontel, who twenty-seven years before had given my eldest daughter piano lessons. And finally I had an old school chum in the person of Jules Perrot, who after having amassed a fortune was now teaching privately in Paris,
although his talent as an ingenious ballet composer would have been a mainstay for this branch of art at the Grand Opéra. I had many an interesting conversation with him, both about our sojourns in Russia and about the present
decline of the art of dancing in many places. I did my best to get him to compose ballets once more, and with this in mind I wrote a memoir in the form of
a *feuilleton* article wherein I urged the rehabilitation of a genre that had once
been the gem of the Théâtre de l'Opéra. I especially attacked the distorted
concept which had been so crudely expressed in the group with which the
sculptor Carpeaux has represented "The Ballet" in front of the peristyle of
the theatre.

I showed my manuscript to Marmontel, who found the article well written and recommended it to the editor of *Le Ménestrel.* But the latter excused
himself on the grounds that his paper was devoted exclusively to music. The
editor of the *Gazette musicale* frankly confessed that he was afraid to quarrel
with the Director of the Opéra, Halanzier, and, moreover, had nothing but admiration for Carpeaux's bold composition! *Le Figaro*'s editor absolutely
refused to accept my contribution on the subject of ballet since he did not
consider it worth the trouble to get involved in a controversy over a subject
which, according to his conviction, was of so little interest to the general
public.

At last I turned to Oscar Comettant, that Danophile who edits the theatre
and music *feuilleton* in *Le Siècle.* This most agreeable man asked me if it
were really my intention to propagandize on the nature of the ballet. I could
not deny that to some degree this had indeed become my mission in life; and
yet such a reaction within the French stage would not be *my* task but rather
that of a man like Perrot. In this case, he felt that my article ought to be expanded into an actual pamphlet, the distribution of which he kindly offered to
promote by commendatory mention. I now stood at the crossroads: I could
now either hurl myself into the literary maelstrom, where my work would
soon be absorbed, or await the natural reaction that must some day inevitably
follow any extreme exaggeration. I chose the latter course, and laid my article
"ad acta."

I did, however, derive some satisfaction from my labors in the service of
Terpsichore by observing a lesson that Edouard Carey, my old pupil from
1827, gave to the female dancers who came to his school. Here pure art could
still take refuge, and his nieces Léontine and Fanny presented what was unquestionably some of the most graceful dancing I had seen on this trip. As
educated and well-bred young ladies, they were disgusted by the prevailing
mode of dancing and the wanton dress; wherefore (to the great honor of the
kind of taste for which I have continuously striven) they every summer delighted the Danish public with their appearances in Copenhagen's Tivoli—an

establishment which, it ought to be noted by way of parenthesis, excites the admiration of all foreigners by its superb organization, its outstanding artistic performances, and above all its lovely air of true *popular* enjoyment, and is denoted by French journalists as an *"institution nationale."*

The work in which I was chiefly engaged, and which I found most interesting, was becoming as familiar as possible (through French or German translations, of course) with Slavic literature and poetry, hitherto unknown to me, to be influenced thereby in drafting the ballets that were to be the fruits of this *kunstreise.*

Professor Geffroy was kind enough to provide me with an admission card for the reading room of the great Bibliothèque Nationale, and there I once again had to admire the sagacity that pervades all the improvements made during the eighteen-year reign of Napoleon III. By the complete rebuilding of the facilities, which were formerly so limited, a magnificent rotunda surrounded by galleries containing shelves full of books has been established. In the front is a desk for the librarians on duty; on the floor, in long rows, stand desks with drawers, inkhorns, chairs, and numbers for three hundred readers and people engaged in copying excerpts, while a sufficient number of *huissiers* or messengers are incessantly occupied with either fetching or returning the requested books.

As I could not state with certainty which translated poems and sagas from Slavic literature I wished to see, and as there did not seem to be an abundance of such subjects, after a rather lengthy search they furnished me with Talvj's Serbian folk songs, rendered into German. These romantic descriptions from a martial past greatly appealed to me without, however, furthering my purpose. Little did I suspect at the time that the conflict with the Turkish barbarians was so soon to be renewed with similar pictures of nobility and woe. I entered the reading room rather industriously and continued my perusal. But the contrast between the noisy bustle of Paris outside and the deadly silence within this hallowed hall of learning occasioned the fact that I was often overcome by drowsiness and rarely held out for more than an hour and a half.

One of the newest things to make its appearance in the realm of art was *Memories from the Siege of Paris*, represented as panorama and diorama, masterfully executed by the painter Philippoteaux and exhibited in a building constructed expressly for that purpose on the Champs-Elysées. The former showed us a scene during the bombardment, where a grenade explodes in a street filled with vans of furniture and with people who are milling about outside a bakery! The effect was gripping and the illusion complete. But something even more astonishing awaited me when after ascending several steps I found myself on a hill of clay and gravel in the midst of Fort Issy, with a prospect of the distant heights where the enemy batteries were positioned.

Life, and also death, within the ploughed-up breastwork and overturned gabions was reproduced with such striking veracity and all the military details so vividly portrayed that, further moved by the explanation given by an old warrior from that fateful time, I was unable to hold back my welling tears. I was involuntarily reminded of what our own brave soldiers had suffered and endured in the entrenchments at Dybbøl and at the heroic defense of Frederikstad, whose shattered houses and churches, splintered palisades, and bastions filled with fragments of shells I had seen with my own eyes the day after the assault.

From one association of ideas to another I was carried back to those ever memorable years when the Copenhageners were like one big family and had shown the hard-pressed Jutlanders, as well as the survivors of the wounded and fallen, the most devoted sympathy and a generosity unequaled by the richest nations of Europe.

In Paris at this very moment (1874) a magnificent exhibition had been arranged in the Palais Bourbon on behalf of the people of Alsace and Lorraine who, to escape Prussian might, had gone to Algeria as colonists. The most distinguished magnates of France had donated their priceless collections of art objects, antiques, and curiosities. The public thronged to see the exhibition *for four months.* The total income from the sale of admission tickets was 280,000 francs, 200,000 francs net, while we had managed to raise a like sum *in three days,* in the Rosenborg Gardens, at the Fair for the Distressed Jutlanders, and almost as much the following year (1850) for the survivors of the wounded and fallen!

The patriotic Frenchmen are industrious, frugal, and thrifty. The country is therefore remarkably fast in regaining its strength after even the most severe crises. But they are rather tight-fisted and are not so free with money as we kind-hearted Danes, who are ready with contributions for any charitable organization and with help for every need, whether it be within or without our country's borders.

On the whole, subscriptions make but little headway in France. But when it is a question of a public loan, the people gather *en masse* and frequently proffer three, four, and even five times the millions requested! At times like this one is astounded at the wealth of currency that, despite the milliards extracted, still prevails in this remarkable land, where we find gold, silver, and their equivalent in banknotes as opposed to the poor paper money that represents the miserable finances of Austria and Italy.

The time for the inauguration of the new Theatre in Copenhagen was drawing nigh, and I had to turn my thoughts to my departure, bidding a fond adieu to those places and friends I should hardly get to visit or see again. My ingenious brother artist Perrot took me with him to a dinner party at the Café Vacher (Boulevard Montmartre), where he introduced me to a group of actors and singers, most of them from the Opéra-Comique. Each month, on a certain day, they gathered in merry company—as we do here at home in our "Gode Sindelag" ["The Benevolents"]—under the club name "La Timbale," which bears the double meaning of "kettledrum" and "drinking cup," a connotation borne out by the thunderous applause that greeted the shower of witty ideas and by the clinking of brimming cups.

Although personally unacquainted with most of them, I was greeted as though I were an old comrade. A farewell toast was drunk in my honor and the names of Achard, Mocker, Ponchard, Duvernay, Bosquin, Thierry, Bernard, Nathan, Coppel, Bouhy, and Vernet were recorded as remembrances in my notebook. The company parted directly after the meal, as several of the above-mentioned gentlemen were to act that same evening. But Perrot and I stayed together, went through old memories from our student years, and strolled up and down the old Boulevard!

This much-frequented avenue which, in a semicircle about three-quarters of a mile in length, traverses the heart of Paris from the Eglise de la Madeleine to the Place de la Bastille and whose name is of Norman origin (bulwark), is different from the many other boulevards, which later decades have created, by virtue of its historical curiosity. Of the many gates which in the Middle Ages formed the exits from the fortifications of Paris, behind which the storms of the Ligue and the Fronde roared and over which the unforgettable Henry IV had bread tossed to the besieged Parisians languishing from hunger, only two triumphal arches (and modern ones at that) remain. These stand upon the foundations of the Porte-Saint-Denis and the Porte-Saint-Martin.

On the demolished and built-up terrain of the old ramparts, a restless crowd of people now moves about on business, pleasure, and idleness, often without bestowing so much as a fleeting thought upon the historical past. And indeed, where among the capitals of the world is there to be found a street that addresses the memory at every step as does this boulevard!

We need go no further back in time than to the fall of Robespierre (the 9th Thermidor), when the last tumbril with its innocent victims was led to the guillotine at the Barrière du Trône, in spite of the most violent opposition on the part of the people. The wild processions of the *sans-culottes* were soon replaced by the Saturnalia of the Directoire, and the victory fanfares from Bonaparte's Italian campaign by the triumphal marches of the Imperial Guard and the dazzling reviews of the Grand Armée.

Napoleon was cast down from his dizzying height, armed Europe hurled itself upon weakened and disunited France, and the allied sovereigns with their arrogant troops made their entries through the triumphal arches of Louis XIV! Through this very gate, draped with white banners adorned with lilies, the Bourbons returned after four-and-twenty years of exile; and although "Freedom and Constitution" was the watchword with which they greeted the French nation, this same gate and the nearby boulevard became the stage for a massacre of those who dared to cry, *"Vive la Charte!"*

Religious processions with banners of saints and baldachins appeared once more and passed among the parading troops and kneeling crowds of people. Through the Porte-Saint-Denis the body of Louis XVIII was borne in sorrowful pomp to the ancient church of King Dagobert, and shortly afterward Charles X, in a golden coronation coach, returned from Rheims via the Porte-Saint-Martin.

At Shrovetide, the grotesque *masques* wended their way from La Court-ille down to the Boulevard, with the fat ox and Grecian gods on horseback and in chariots, and were not infrequently crossed by funeral processions that silently and solemnly bore the celebrities of the Republic and the Empire to the cemetery of Père-Lachaise. The Bourbon government protected this carnival fun, but looked with a frowning eye upon the funerals, which might to a greater or lesser degree involve political demonstrations.

Just as in the time of Molière, the churches were closed to the funerals of actors. (It is worthy of note that, despite all the ideas of freedom and equality that flow through overcivilized France, and despite the prominent place the drama assumes in the pleasure life of Frenchmen, in social circles there still prevails an unfair prejudice against theatre folk in general, and even important artists when they retire make it their duty to ignore both their earlier profession and their old comrades.)

The custom of bearing famous men and patriots to the grave was forbidden by strict order of the police. Any violations, as at the burials of Larochefoucauld-Liancourt and Manuel, had as their results bayonets and the sabers of the gendarmes.

The shady old elm trees witnessed all these things and spread their branches above the various factions in a mild and friendly fashion, until one fine day in July (1830) they were felled and dragged away to the barricades. The tricolor appeared at the head of numerous crowds of people. "La Marseillaise" resounded once again after a silence of many years. The cavalry charged, the troops surged forward—but the Revolution came off with the victory. The sovereignty of the people was proclaimed, the freedom fighters who had sacrificed their lives for this ideal were buried on the site of the demolished Bastille, while the Colonne de Juillet was inaugurated together with the Orléans dynasty, which took its name from the three *"journées glorieuses"* that were every year to be celebrated with public festivities, memorial services for the fallen, and grand military parades on this very Boulevard where riots, assassinations, and infernal machines later threatened the chosen Citizen-King! Despite all his ingenuity, kindness, and good will, Louis-Philippe was forced to yield to the Socialist Republic of 1848.

This *"blouse régime"* could not long endure and was but little suited to luxury, which is the vital principle in the entire French system of labor. The capitalists withdrew, the lack of food became widespread, and the very same people who a short while ago were ready to rush to the barricades at the first cry now realized that high-flown phrases and utopian theories could not help them to get bread. The February Revolution gradually lost its "red" physiognomy, and in fact all that was left of the Republic was its name when the *coup d'état* on Austerlitz Day, December 2, 1852, swept the last riot from the Boulevard and a plebiscite with eight million "ayes" chose Napoleon III as Emperor of the French.

Here I will end my historical reflections so as not to repeat what I have already said about the fall of the Second Empire, the siege of Paris, and the mad Commune. But though in recent years the Boulevard has undergone a number of alterations and the venerable old trees have been replaced by slender runts, I was still delighted to discover the same nuances of Parisian folk life that had been there fifty years before.

It was a different matter with the theatres, which are situated on either side of the Boulevard itself or in its immediate vicinity. In the days when they were bound to particular subjects and not infrequently annoyed by petty-minded censorship, all branches of the scenic art flourished. But now, when all restrictions have been lifted, in most places it stands in danger of degenerating into profanation. However, in order to avoid tiresome senile criticism of present scenic conditions and in the hope that the future will produce something better, I will ask my readers, both those who have visited Paris in earlier years and those who are infatuated with the theatre as a whole, to accompany me on a stroll along the old Boulevard as it was some decades ago.

Upon glancing from the Boulevard des Italiens down to the Rue de Choiseul, where a portal forms the entrance to a bazaar gallery, we notice a rather small theatre which in its day was founded and run by a famous conjurer, M. Comte, who among other skills possessed that of training and directing child actors, for whom original pieces by Vanderburch and others were written.

Performances like *Rataplan, Les petits Braconniers*, and others alternated with feats of unsophisticated magic. One was superbly entertained by these miniature actors' often quite successful efforts at aping the most prominent dramatic celebrities of Paris. But this imitation, which bordered so closely on parody, gradually destroyed in these children every vestige of naïveté and charm; for just like the flowers the magician shook out of the crown of his hat, these little prodigies enjoyed but short-lived artistic careers. Some of them were scattered to provincial theatres and very few stayed behind as adults to join the "Bouffes-Parisiens," which, under Offenbach's direction and partly with his compositions, moved from the Champs-Elysées to the Théâtre de M. Comte, whose founder had by now given up his conjuring tricks.

The kind of operetta that Offenbach introduced was, in fact, only a higher form of *vaudeville*, which became all the more popular as the gay melodies could be hummed on leaving the theatre. As has been said, it was essentially Offenbach himself who furnished the repertoire, and *La Chatte metamorphosée, La Rose de Saint-Flour, La Chanson de Fortunio*, but above all *Orphée aux enfers*, consolidated his own and the little theatre's renown. All the same, when greater magnificence in production was required, these limited facilities no longer proved satisfactory, and after the popular composer had made an unsuccessful attempt at the Opéra-Comique itself, his genre found a refuge at the Théâtre des Variétés, where it completely replaced the charming popular *vaudeville* and won not only the most fanatical public attendance but European and transatlantic fame as well with subjects such as *La belle Hélène, Barbe-Bleue, La Grande-duchessa de Gérolstein,* and others.

This theatre, whence obscenity and shameless jests have driven both Comus and Momus, has a past whose memories still refresh my mind. It was founded at the beginning of the century by the popular comedian Brunet, who, as a successor of Bobeche, Gallimafré, and Volange, created figures such as Jocrisse and Cadet Roussel, true stock types of naïveté and the victims of pranks frequently improvised by the other players, while he himself (to all appearances unconsciously) evoked endless laughter. One could hardly call him an "actor" in the strictest sense of the word, but as manager, and especially as *instructeur,* he must have been quite excellent, for he knew how to assemble and make use of a larger number of outstanding comic talents than any theatre has ever been able to display at one time.

Just as the Gymnase Dramatique later (1820) gave plays whose action transpired mostly in salons and boudoirs and mainly among the distinguished and wealthy classes of society where capital and private income were absolutely necessary in order to present oneself as a lover or suitor, so the Variétés presented everyday life in country villages, on the streets of Paris, in workshops, or in the shabby homes of the laborers, most often in true-to-life genre pictures, sometimes interwoven with a little romance and moving for the most part in semi-impecunious, bourgeois circles—but always, in accordance with good French custom, with a little nest egg stored up in reserve. Sparkling gaiety spiced with fine satire, rarely if ever crossing over into lasciviousness, constituted the refreshing element of this theatre.

It might be most interesting to possess a list of the numerous authors, some younger ones among them, who by their wealth of invention and outspoken humor furnished Brunet with a repertoire that has long served the rest of Europe as a model in the *vaudeville* genre. Achille d'Artois de Bournonville was at that time one of the most productive, and after him, the whole host of Scribe's collaborators. Farces with stock figures were soon forced to move in a more wholesome and natural direction; and they discovered that as an unconscious focal point for emotion and for reaping the reward of the intriguers' toil and trouble, divine naïveté could produce a pleasing comic effect. This character no longer shared the lot of the inevitable *Hanswurst;* on the contrary, it was now the lovers who, as good as blind, were led by Cupid to the goal of their desires. Tousez the elder and Vernet especially distinguished themselves in these kinds of roles, the latter by the most charming naïveté. In particular, his representations of Tony and Vincent in the *vaudevilles* of the same name were absolute masterpieces. When he later made the transition to older parts, his *"Père de la débutante"* was considered unsurpassable. These roles, as well as the major part of his repertoire, were, to be sure, dependent upon his personality and centered mainly around everyday life. Therefore they did not require the same profound study and vivid fantasy as a historical or idealistic performance; but even within this narrow sphere, a poetic impression can by truth and naturalness compel the recognition of an inspired talent.

As a character actor, Lepeintre the elder was more versatile than Vernet and really ought to have found his proper place at the Théâtre Français. Bosquier Gavaudan possessed a superior gift for reciting couplets, while Mlle. Flore as humorous peasant girl, Mlle. Aldegonde as soubrette, Mme. Vautrin as duenna, and finally Mmes. Pauline and Jenny Colon as romantic heroines, formed the core of the female personnel.

As to Bignon, Cazot, and Lefebvre: their strength lay in the roles of soldiers and commoners, while during the years 1824–1830 Arnal, who later became the gem of the Théâtre du Vaudeville, was already the representative of elegant humor and knew how to produce the most explosive effect by carelessly tossed-off lines. Just like the priceless Odry, this superb actor had begun his career as a chorus singer; but in both instances the unmistakable talent that could be glimpsed in incidental pieces of stage business soon forged a path to actual roles, and authors vied to write for them. Odry, who in contrast to Vernet's ingenuousness and handsome face presented irony and roguish ugliness, was terribly amusing with regard to nonsense and misunderstandings (much in the style of Phister in the scene with the madman in *Soldiers' Highjinks.* But here Brunet was a match for him, and then the puns rained down to the great delight of the *calembourg* [pun] fanciers, who in turn exploited them under the name of *"odriettes"!* Neither Odry nor Arnal altered makeup or dialect in order to delineate their comic roles. And yet they possessed an inner variety which, like ever fresh Nature, always showed us a new face.

Since the Variétés wished to live up to its name, which was of course dependent upon diversity, the actor Perlet was retained to represent more refined comedy, by correctness as well as originality. However, he did not feel at home here, preferring the Gymnase Dramatique and, later on, the major provincial theatres.

But Brunet soon managed to find a brilliant replacement in Potier, who had already caused a furor at the Porte-Saint-Martin. Only now did his many-sided talent come into full flower: the Petitioner, the Parasite, the Recruit, the Burgomaster of Sardam, the Man of Sixty, the Shop-boy in *Je fais mes Farces*, the Rag-picker (Nr. 1), the Barber, and the Advocate in *La Carte à payer*, the Servant in *Les deux précepteurs*, M. Bonaventure in *Les Inconvénients de la diligence*, the Beneficiary, and finally, Lagrippe (the father to Heiberg's Hummer), were so many masterpieces not only of comedy acting but of psychological study as well. The comic strength that, combined with moderation, distinguished all his representations could serve as a model for every actor; and in having named him in the same breath as Talma in the first volume of *My Theatre Life,* I do not feel—save for the higher significance of tragedy—that I have been guilty of blasphemy. Potier has had many imitators but no worthy successors. And yet there was one who, without ever having seen or known him, was almost a match for him in several of the roles that are here recorded. This was our unforgettable C. N. Rosenkilde!

Several years after this fruitful epoch, this whole group of superb actors had vanished and a younger generation had taken their place under the direction of Brunet the Younger. Adrien, Brindeau, Lafont, Levassor, Hyacinthe, and Alcide Tousez, together with several pretty actresses whose names I do not remember, displayed great talent in plays which, though already beginning to drift into the downward path of obscenity, still upheld the old renown of the Variétés.

But one star who outshone all the rest was Bouffé, who, after having run the gamut of boulevard theatres, finally landed at the Variétés with *Le Bouffon malgré lui, Michel Perrin, L'Avare, Le Gamin de Paris, Le Père Turlututu*, and others. Every single one of these parts bore the stamp of perfection, and they were portraits which, though in another sphere of art, might be compared with the most excellent masterpieces of the Dutch school of painting.

During their leisure time these actors sat about drinking and playing dominoes at the marble tables outside the Café de Suède, which was located in the vicinity of the theatre. I often felt tempted to present myself to make their personal acquaintance, but an involuntary fear of seeing their nimbi vanish at closer range held me back. It would have pained me to see my illusions destroyed and perhaps to find dullness and coarse manners in place of the wit and nobility I had so greatly admired on the stage. However, I did risk such an attempt at the time I first saw Bouffé play Michel Perrin.

In my enthusiasm, I wrote him a rather warm letter, wherein I asked his permission to express my profound recognition in person. But—I received no answer! Perhaps the letter perished or was tossed into the wastepaper basket along with other compliments and petitions; or perhaps this famous actor was one of those people who would rather perform the labors of Hercules than sit down at a writing table. In any case, I had to console myself in my disappointment with what I learnt later on: namely, that Bouffé, who onstage was the spokesman of charming good nature, was in everyday life unfortunately filled with bitterness and scorn. He was, in short, a complete misanthrope!

All of these ingenious personalities are now either dead of exhaustion or vegetating in the provinces as *régisseurs* (some of them even as ticket collectors). Several of the more fortunate have been able to retire as *rentiers* and, as already stated, renounce their artistic past in the presence of bourgeois society!

On the pretty square by the staircase leading to the Boulevard Bonne-Nouvelle is situated the Théâtre du Gymnase Dramatique, erected in 1820 and intended for younger and hitherto untried talents. And it was actually on a mere twelve-year-old girl that the successful start of this theatre was to be based. Léontine Fay was the star who was to draw the public, and as her development progressed, this stage gradually came to rival the Théâtre Français, despite the lyrical numbers forced upon it, giving the comedies performed the name of *comédies-vaudevilles.*

It was not long before the foresighted director, M. Poirson, had acquired for his theatre the most prolific of all the younger authors, Eugène Scribe; and since its repertoire demanded constant variety, one could be nought but astonished at the rapidity with which this ingenious comedy-writer conjured up, so to speak, his frequent masterly *petites pièces à couplets.* It is still an unsolved puzzle as to how he worked in collaboration with various other authors, whose names almost always appear beside his own in his lighter pieces: that is, did he furnish the plan or work it out from their rough drafts? It is hard to imagine that he was willing to encumber himself with such literary hangers-on — all the more so as his major dramas, which have erected an imperishable monument to him at all the theatres of Europe, bear his name alone.

One must have seen these superb comedies (which are true masterpieces with regard to composition and dramatic construction, and, translated into almost every language, have given good actors the opportunity to shine) produced and performed by their original casts to get some idea of the effect they produced in their novelty. At the Gymnase they found distinguished interpreters in Ferville, Numa, Bernard-Léon, Klein, Paul, and Allan, while Perlet was lured thither from the Variétés and Gontier from the Vaudeville. This last actor had made the transition from romantic leads to character parts, and created an absolute furor as the soldier Stanislas in *Michel et Christine,* as Pierre in *Le Mariage de raison,* and, above all, in anything where priceless humor was blended with unaffected emotion.

During 1824–1830 the elite of the female personnel consisted of Jenny Vertpré, a charming miniature portrait of naïveté and roguishness; Julie Despreaux, who was Grace personified; Julienne, the nicest mother, aunt, and housekeeper imaginable; and Déjazet, superb in the bloom of her youth as soubrette, grisette, and *en travesti.* Finally, I ought to mention Léontine Fay, who, now grown up, was to Scribe and his Muse what Johanne Luise Heiberg was to Danish comedy writers. However, Léontine's fame seemed to be tied exclusively to the theatre which had been the cradle of her talent; for the prophecy uttered by Mlle. Mars when she presented the wonder child with a precious jewel (namely, that Léontine would one day bring her into oblivion) was not fulfilled when she later appeared at the Théâtre Français under the name of Mme. Volnys. She herself, as well as the public, became convinced that the Gymnase was her only proper forum and that Mlle. Mars' successor had not yet been found.

It is now almost half a century since, in the company of our long-deceased, superb actress, Henriette Jørgensen, I attended the first performance of Scribe's *Avant, pendant et après la Révolution,* which in three acts set at ten-years intervals depicted conditions during these various epochs in an interesting sequence of thrilling episodes. The dramatic art has also undergone similar changes, and I find myself in almost the same position as the old Chevalier, who was so masterfully portrayed by Ferville and who upon returning home after an absence of twenty-eight years does not recognize his beloved Paris. I myself am tempted to ask what has become of my delightful Gymnase Dramatique.

It seems almost as if Scribe's tremendous productivity had exhausted the soil, leaving behind for his successors no subjects other than the old ones turned inside out! The refreshing gaiety and the feeling of finding oneself *en bonne compagnie* gradually seem to be banished from the Gymnase as well as the Théâtre du Vaudeville, which was once so lively. *La Dame aux Camélias, Le Demi-monde,* and *Les Filles de marbre* have for a long time constituted the prevailing genre, and the spectator comes away from these plays with a heavy heart, hatred and contempt for society, and pity for the actresses, whose sensibilities must be offended at having to represent such impure and offensive characters.

Proceeding a couple of hundred steps up the Boulevard, we now come to a halt at the Théâtre de la Porte-Saint-Martin. This magnificent junk shop (where everything that was ever invented for the stage has been offered for sale, often at first hand) was erected in the year 1781, and with such remarkable speed that six weeks after the foundation stone had been laid it stood ready to receive the Opéra, whose own facilities in the Palais-Royal had been destroyed by fire. Here it was that the immortal Gluck performed his masterworks. From 1794 up to the present, melodrama, farce, *vaudeville,* the *féerie,* and the ballet have in turn dominated its repertoire.

Partly because of its size and its past, and partly because of its proximity to the Ambigu and the Gaîté, this theatre has had much to fight with and against. Here indeed there is no area within the bounds of the stage that has not been explored and, after having been tried out for some length of time, abandoned as more or less unproductive. First-rate writers and actors, balletmasters and dancers, English tragedians, mimes and clowns, even strong men and acrobats, have tried their hand here — all without having been able to prevent the fatalities of bankruptcy; and since insult is usually added to injury, in consideration of its sparsely filled benches, this theatre has on several occasions been forced to bear the epithet of *"le désert Saint-Martin."*

There have, however, been periods when this theatre was *en vogue* and attracted a public that did not employ too strict an aesthetic standard in its judgments. Thus pieces like *Le Vampire* and *Victorine, ou la nuit porte conseils* had sold-out performances by the hundred.

Later there occurred the Polichinelle frenzy, occasioned by an episode in Milon's ballet *Le Carnaval de Venise* at the Théâtre de l'Opéra. It so happened that a dancer from Bordeaux surpassed all others in suppleness of limb; and since the Porte-Saint-Martin made it a point of honor to maintain the height of fashion and art, M. Mazurier was summoned to Paris, where a piece was authored exclusively for his debut. His triumph was complete.

People came in droves to see this marvel, and as if it were not bad enough that every little child had to have a Polichinelle doll as a toy, the signs of many a boutique and millinery shop were even given the picture and name of this masquerade figure, while the small theatres vied in parodying the hero of the day. The nearby Théâtre de la Gaîté, on the other hand, took the matter seriously and acquired a rather young Polichinelle from Lyon, who, like the prophet Jonah, was swallowed by a whale. This same limber little lad later won fame as a dancer and balletmaster—he was none other than Jules Perrot!

Mazurier was, however, a genuine comic talent and useful in parts where his physical dexterity was interwoven with singing and dialogue. For a couple of years he was this theatre's glittering star. But finally, at a loss as to what surprises to hit upon, he studied the physiology of the ape and brought his imitation to such a degree of perfection that someone wrote an entire drama wherein the beast played the leading role, to which Mazurier knew how to give a most peculiar interest by his gymnastics and singular gestures. The final scene, where Jocko (who has saved the plantation owner's child from the snake) is struck by the father's bullet and, dying, drags the gathered gems to his master's feet, had a most gripping effect. A woeful sigh ran through the entire audience, and the illusion was so strong that from every side one heard the exclamation, *"Pauvre bête!"*

When all is said and done, it was really only a mediocre triumph for the stage. But Jocko won European renown, for a time superseded Polichinelle as a fashion plate, played to packed houses a couple of hundred evenings in succession, and, by the continuously repeated strain, precipitated his portrayer's all too early demise.

The melodrama now recaptured its right: the Gaîté and Ambigu theatres vied in rattling the nerves of the spectators with terrifying representations. The Gaîté had long since renounced its merry name because the working class went there to shiver and to weep, while the exaggerations made other and more critical dispositions burst into laughter, to the great indignation of the devout. The tyrant bellowed, the heroine swooned at the end of each act, and when the clock struck half-past nine one could be certain that virtue had triumphed and crime had gotten its just reward.

The Ambigu, on the other hand, seemed to gather its material from the criminal court itself: Victor Ducagne and Guilbert de Pixérécourt were first-rate talents in this area. *Les deux Forçats* and *Le Chien de Montargis* were veritable *éditions de luxe;* but they were overshadowed by *Cardillac, L'Auberge des Adrets,* and *Cartouche,* pieces wherein the ingenious Frédérick Lemaître consolidated his renown as the eager-to-rob goldsmith, the spirited rogue Robert Macaire, and that refined rascal of the old school.

The Porte-Saint-Martin had to work hard to ward off this dangerous competiton; and since in Gobert the theatre possessed a talented character actor, it attempted to outdo its enterprising rival with a splendid "robber drama." Mandrin was a subject which in addition to the romantic personality of the hero also afforded the opportunity for décor and machinery to accomplish something hitherto unseen (among other things, a transformation from a tasteful boudoir to a dense forest, beneath whose roots the robbers' hideout was to be found, while the thicket above was being searched by gendarmes).

The results answered to expectations, and opposite the lead stood Lefuret, pupil of the *great* Cartouche, played with priceless humor by Serres. The smith, who coerces Mandrin not only by the strength of his arm but by the memory of the boyhood they shared together and brings him to remorse and conversion—at the foot of the scaffold, to be sure—found a worthy interpreter in the old *régisseur* Moëssard, who after having for thirty years played *pères nobles*, doughty peasants, and loyal squires, was for his honorable private life and self-sacrificing charity awarded the prize instituted by the Marquis de Montyon, which was every year to be given to "the most virtuous man in France."

Mandrin celebrated a success that could not be topped by the incendiary Poulailler, who practiced his evil deeds at the Gaîté; but from now on the two sections of the Boulevard that bore the names of "du Temple" and "de la Porte-Saint-Martin" joined forces under the epithet of "Boulevard du Crime"!

After a number of not very successful attempts to forge a gentler path for morality, the large theatre at last decided to enter the precincts of Romanticism, and this in a form which surely deserved a better fate—*Marino Faliéro*, by Casimir Delavigne! Presented by talents like Ligier, Beauvallet, and Gobert, together with Mmes. Georges and Allan Dorval, *Angelo* and *Marion de Lorme*, by Victor Hugo, ought to have crowned this praiseworthy undertaking with success. But it had now been decided once for all that the "Boulevard style" was to be retained, and the good old days would not return before Frédérick Lemaître was lured to the Porte-Saint-Martin by advantageous offers.

I have earlier discussed this remarkable actor's appearance in *Trente ans, ou la Vie d'un joueur*, but Kean, César de Bazan, and Ruy Blas gave him further opportunity to develop his versatile talent, which would have placed him foremost among his contemporaries had his originality not sometimes spilled over into the grotesque. And indeed this was hardly to be avoided when one considers the abrupt transition from Capitaine Buridan in *La Tour de Nesle* to *Robert Macaire* and finally to *Le Chiffonier*, where from the most extreme degree of intemperance he resolved upon twenty years of total abstinence, was enticed into getting drunk once again, raged like a madman, returned to his senses, and appeared like a *deus ex machina* to expose vice and save virtue. The atmosphere he produced was indescribable; but this too could overstep the bounds of reason. I shall never forget the moment when, as the uninvited guest at the wedding celebration, he stepped forth and with his iron hook tore off the bride's veil and wreath, and with the cry *"Chiffons! à la hotte!"* tossed both pieces into the rag basket. All at once there was a commotion in the parterre behind me. Blustering with indignation, an elderly man climbed up on the bench and, stretching his arms toward the stage, shouted in a thunderous voice, *"C'est dégoûtant!"* And it was indeed as loathsome as it was revolting. Frédérick Lemaître was all the same a true genius. But his powers of imagination had demoralized him, and the passions that he was continually called upon to portray onstage had left their mark on his private character and whole external appearance.

It was a genuine blessing for the good and honest Moëssard that he was carried off by death before his old theatre was given over to the *féerie-comédie!* Through the previous criminal pieces there had usually run a moral, which, even though rather thin and insipid, still offered a coherent plot. Here, to the contrary, no such thing is to be found, and the whole would seem to have been arranged for the amusement of children and simple souls, were the sensual element not present *ad nauseam* in words, gestures, and costumes; while the unfortunate *corps de ballet,* either three-quarters naked or in the form of animals, fish, carrots, and white turnips, figures in the most outrageous cancan! *La Biche aux bois,* which played to full houses and brought in fabulous sums for three years running, also exercised a considerable attraction by virtue of its splendid décor and machinery, which are bound to make everything we in Denmark call "scenic effects" seem like toy theatre. Furthermore, one can do nought but admire the fresh spirit with which the least as well as the most important roles are performed in spite of the endless repetition tageous cooperation, like political friction, only creates parties and sects.

The Théâtre Historique, which was founded in the year 1846 by Alex. Dumas *père* and furnished with his plays, enjoyed but a short existence after having produced some dramas in fourteen tableaux and a couple of skilled actors, Mélingue and Lacressonnière. It was handed over to the entrepreneur of the newly established Théâtre Lyrique, who in turn received compensation for the expropriation for its demolition, which made room for the construction of a new boulevard, at which opportunity old Pierrot-Débureau disposed of his Théâtre des Funambules where in her day the famous Mme. Saqui had for forty years (and without balancing pole) delighted her grateful public. So too at the Théâtre des Folies Dramatiques the shadow of a former celebrity, the sixty-year-old Mlle. Déjazet, as Gentil Bernard and the Young Richelieu, and was applauded as if she were a precious heirloom! All the same, it is a commendable trait in the Parisians that they loyally stand by those artists who have outlived their day. Here too *la gloire* exercises its magical power, and a reputation once acquired is regarded as the property of the nation!

One of the old Boulevard theatres still remains to be mentioned, and is undoubtedly one of the most remarkable by virtue of its peculiar presentations as well as its influence upon the national character in its finest respects; for just as Corneille's tragedies are alleged to have contributed to kindling the heroic flame in the great army leaders of France, so it can be said that the common soldier has learned enthusiasm and daring at the Cirque Franconi!

Here there is no unhealthy toying with the passions or dissection of the seamy side of society. On the perilous race course it is simply a matter of astonishing by strength and dexterity; on the stage, however, one of leading the memory back to glorious deeds. Everything that is to be seen in the way of horsemanship and *dressage* throughout the rest of Europe has for the most part originated here; and it seems as if the people and animals have exchanged roles, for the latter possess an intelligence and grace which the former make up for in strength and daring.

After these exercises are finished and the clowns have played their tricks, the Arabs piled up their living pyramids and the contortionists wound themselves into intricate twists and turns, there is an intermission; and then the curtain rises on a spectacle which is entitled the "mimodrama," because this theatre is ordered to work as much as possible with mime and groupings.

However, this repressive servitude does not alter the fact that the recited portion of these *pièces à spectacle* provides an opportunity to present good actors who, partly because of a more or less provincial accent, have been found unsuitable for parts in the real dramatic theatres. This slight defect is as good as imperceptible to foreigners, and since these actors are not tied to any particular school, traditions, or mannerisms, one cannot be astonished that when our outstanding tragedian Nielsen saw Chery play a French officer with natural warmth and dignity on a secondary stage, he exclaimed with his usual eccentricity, "This is the only sane leading man I have encountered in all my travels!"

The grand-scale military mimodrama first made progress during the years 1828–1829, when the Martignac ministry and its more liberal system permitted the candid expression of national sympathies.

They gave *Le Vétéran* (an episode from the French campaign of 1814). A little plot connected the following episodes: the invasion, the call to arms, the Cossack camp, the foraging and plundering, the advance of the French army, and the fight and victory. Napoleon dared not be portrayed in person, but an old Marshal represented the Supreme Commander, surrounded by a numerous staff on horseback. Over a bridge, which had been laid across the orchestra, and down to the riding ground marched the troops, with a full military band and a colossal drum major in the lead. Then cavalry, artillery, and two hundred picked men ... it was the old Imperial Guard, with bearskin hats pulled far down over the grim faces and uniforms completely in accord with the familiar pattern! Thunderous applause greeted *the eagles* as visions from the spirit world, and when the torn old banners were dipped in salute, tears welled forth from every eye.

After a moment's silence, during which one could hear the beating of one's heart, the first gunshot was heard. This was answered from the enemy barricades in the background of the theatre. The chain of sharpshooters spread out along the row of lamps, while the assault columns were formed down in the arena. The firing grew more violent. The dead and wounded fell, and the stage was enveloped in vapor and smoke. The drummers beat the attack, and with booming hurrahs the whole mass stormed up onto the proscenium toward the entrenchments, where the palisades were broken down. Bayonets locked in hand-to-hand fighting, and the *tricolore* was planted on the breastwork.

For variety, a comic element was introduced in the form of a cavalry strike, where the Cossacks got some dreadful thrashings on their padded shoulders. But patriotic enthusiasm soon recaptured its right when eight trumpeters on horseback blew Grétry's well-known fanfare, "La victoire est à nous," with the whole band joining in. The curtain fell, and one went home feeling as though one had witnessed an actual event.

Another military drama, *Le Siège de Saragossa*, presented even more striking effects. Several of the proscenium boxes were taken over and transformed into houses and cloisters from which the street fighting was waged. The scene-painters had worked wonders, and as far as scenic arrangement was concerned, all the world's stage directors could go to school to Adolphe Franconi, who was a true virtuoso in this field and spared nothing to carry out his often colossal ideas. Unfortunately, even the greatest attendance could not suffice to cover the enormous expenditures, and this costly establishment would no doubt have gone bankrupt if the government had not both realized its importance and granted it a state subsidy, wherefore it has in turn borne the names of Cirque Napoléon and Cirque National.

At this theatre in the spring of 1841 I witnessed a drama whose equal has never before nor since been seen on any stage—*Les Funérailles de l'Empereur!* Louis Philippe had obtained England's consent to bring the body of Napoleon back from St. Helena. An imposing funeral procession passed through the Arc de l'Étoile, across the Champs-Élysées to the Église des Invalides. This was in the middle of February,‡ and four weeks later there had already been written, rehearsed, and staged a play which portrayed the whole magnificent ceremonial with a fidelity bordering on the miraculous. I dare say that from a purely aesthetic standpoint it was rather objectionable that personalities still living at that time, like the Prince de Joinville, Maréchal Moncey, Generals Bertrand and Montholon together with their families, were represented, if not precisely as active characters, then at least as accessories in a historical painting. But the whole thing was so well put together that one forgot both theatre and indignation in order to abandon oneself completely to the gripping illusion.

In the first act, in a wonderful setting with the ocean in the background, can be seen the lovely valley with "the weeping willow of St. Helena." An old gentleman is in the habit of visiting this spot every day, and his young daughter adorns the heroic Emperor's grave with fresh flowers as she sends gentle thoughts to distant Europe where her fiancé, a young French physi-

---

‡ Here Bournonville is once again mistaken. The body of Napoleon I was brought to the Invalides in solemn procession on December 15, 1840, two months earlier than the date given here.

cian, is serving in the French navy. At this very moment he is aboard the frigate *La Belle Poule,* which is in the offing. Its arrival and the solemn occasion are announced by gun salutes. The British troops parade past the grave, and the high-ranking messengers together with their retinue (among whom are the young doctor and his grandfather, a gray-haired grenadier of the Guard) approach with silent devotion. All grudges between the Englishmen and Frenchmen have disappeared. The good soldiers fraternally shake hands with one another and help to lift the heavy stone from the grave. The coffin is pulled up and opened to confirm the presence of the earthly remains, which appear to be in a state of perfect preservation. The faithful friends are filled with deep emotion at this sight and fall to their knees. The curtain falls.

The second act represents the gun deck of the frigate *La Belle Poule,* which has been converted into a *castrum-doloris* with religious requiem ceremonies.

The third act takes place on the deck of the royal steamship which carries the body from Le Havre to Rouen, and a moving panorama shows us both of these cities and the landscape along the banks of the Seine.

The fourth act presents the entry through the Arc de l'Étoile, with masses of soldiers and a countless host of people—partly real, partly painted figures, but so deceptively lifelike that Parisians who sat beside me claimed that the funeral procession was perfectly reproduced. Bands, standard-bearers, seamen, veterans, and soldiers of all arms seemed to number several thousands, and the pompous procession finally ended with sixteen horses (four by four) which pulled the colossal hearse with the catafalque, only half of which came into view at the curtain's fall.

Only in the fifth act did one learn what had been happening with the young lovers during all these events. Here they have arrived in France with the frigate, together with her father and the old grenadier, and here we find them in one of the rooms in the Hôtel des Invalides, with the one-hundred-year-old great-grandfather. This scene, which is apparently arranged to be mounted behind, provides the opportunity for several delightful little pieces of stage business on the part of the great-grandfather, his son (the seventy-five-year old veteran), and a *soeur de charité,* who bears the Cross of the Légion d'Honneur in memory of her assistance to the Grande Armée. The young people are united and blessed. The funeral procession draws near and the old man orders himself to be carried out so that he may fire the first gunshot which shall bid Napoleon welcome to his final resting place, close to Condé, Turenne, and Vauban, and surrounded by Lannes, Berthier, and Duroc! . . . The setting is transformed and the Église des Invalides can be seen in all its majestic splendor—a true masterpiece of the art of painting and *trompe l'oeil!* The organ and trombones join in solemn harmony, as round about the catafalque stand the great dignitaries of France, while at its foot kneel the aged generals from the Pyramids, Austerlitz, Jéna, Wagram, and— Waterloo!

The day after I had viewed this moving drama, I stood in the Église des

Invalides and peeped in through the grille of the Chapel of St. Jérôme where the Emperor's coffin was temporarily placed, surrounded by captured banners and other historical symbols. Here I spoke with several of the crippled warriors who had fought and bled on his long victorious road, and on the staircase of the Hôtel I met old General Petit, the very man who was embraced by Napoleon at the sad *adieu* at Fontainebleau.

A generation has passed between that time and my latest visit. Napoleon's magnificent burial vault now conceals his remains in a porphyry sarcophagus, and his statue on the Colonne Vendôme has twice changed its costume (from the Man in the Gray Coat to the Roman Emperor). This column, together with its base, which is entwined with memorials of honor, had to endure the most disgusting outrages of vandalism and has now been erected once more in the hope of effacing, if possible, a national disgrace! Two revolutions have thundered across France, enclosing a Second Empire which, like the First, after triumphant campaigns and brilliant measures, ended its shining course with an unsuccessful war, the siege of Paris, a humiliating peace, and the captivity and death of the conquered in exile!

The Third French Republic was introduced with the Paris Commune, whose cannibalistic thirst for blood and destructive frenzy were not inferior to those of the Reign of Terror of the *sans-culottes,* and order was established only after a desperate struggle.

The frictions that are inseparable from republican institutions do not seem to have altered the physiognomy of Paris to any special degree: trade, industry, the influx of foreigners, and public amusements run their usual course. Workers have exchanged weapons for work-tools, and everywhere industry and activity are perceivable. One can say with Mads in Wessel's *Love Without Stockings,* "A zephyr now blows since the storm is past"! How long this condition will last one cannot say. In spite of the defeats they have suffered, *la gloire* remains the *idole* of the French, and *la revanche* smoulders in the breasts of the young. Whether these abstract concepts will assert themselves in a military direction only time will tell.

In the meantime, France is preparing for a peaceful triumph at a great World Exhibition, which will presumably have opened by the time this book appears.* But since it is hardly likely that I will get to attend it, I hereby conclude my actual traveling life and its memories, which, if they are read a chapter at a time, will perhaps be of some interest to the old, who can rediscover and renew earlier impressions; to the young, whose imaginations and wanderlust are excited by the description of times and places; to friends, because of the memoirs' historical information and the artistic development of the theatre; and finally, to all those who have followed with good will the endeavors and fruits of my long theatre life.

---

*The Universal Exhibition of 1878, which attracted some 13,000,000 visitors and left a lasting memorial — the palace of the Trocadéro.

II

Reflections

UNDER this rubric, in the first two parts of *My Theatre Life* as well as in a number of independent articles, I have set forth my views on subjects which all more or less fall within the sphere of my allotted activity. Not only in periodicals but also in individual pamphlets, I have treated questions concerning our theatre affairs and the scenic art as a whole, and hereby claimed a modest place among Danish writers and, in spite of my poor philosophical foundation, thinkers. Should I have been fortunate enough to acquire recognition in this area as well as in my designated artistic milieu, surely I may dare to venture a little beyond its limits to place myself, with the warmth of conviction, on the side of those litterateurs and linguists who are opposed to the reform, as ill-timed as it is unmotivated, that is being not only recommended but forced upon our school system with regard to Danish

ORTHOGRAPHY

Surely it cannot be denied that we are all more or less "sinners and lacking in the respect we ought to have for our mother tongue." While England and France have for over a century possessed a fully developed language, whose characteristic spelling, despite its ever increasing abundance of words, has remained as good as unchanged, we Danes, whose tongue can be spoken and understood by only a few million people, fall at once into uncertainty and disunity as to how we are to spell our words, and find ourselves in the midst of an orthographic-neologistic revolution, which, far from promoting advantageous cooperation, like political frictions only creates parties and sects. Among the latter, the style of cooks and washerwomen may also claim its right; but were it to triumph, it would eventually bring us to the point where our authors, our devotion books, even the Constitution itself, would become unreadable for future generations and would have to be deciphered like the runes of antiquity.

Thus as matters stand for the moment, there is in our spelling, as in a legislative assembly, a Left, a Center, and a Right. The radicals toss out several letters of the European alphabet, all dipthongs and double vowels, use only *small* letters for nouns, employ French and Swedish accents, divide adverbs, and write exclusively in Latin script.

The Moderates, as usual, follow a middle road and accept with modification a portion of the innovations, contenting themselves with writing foreign words as they sound to the Danish ear, regardless of etymology.

Finally, the Conservatives (the faction to which I belong in linguistic respects) claim that literary evolution must take place through time and authors; for if we follow the Danish language from Anders Sørensen Vedel's translation of Saxo Grammaticus [1575] to Holberg's *Epistles* [1754] and thence up to the most flowering period of the present century, we perceive a gradual progress in the purity and richness of speech as well as orthographic correctness, without either ministerial decree or academic compulsion. Thus we possess a national treasure of writers, who—from Ewald, Baggesen, Oehlenschläger, Ingemann, Heiberg, Hertz, Paludan-Müller, Christian Winther, H. C. Andersen to the still living Holst, Richardt, Ploug, and others—have all, with almost imperceptible deviations, upheld and still do uphold an orthography which has received academic acceptance, as has been illustrated by such men of learning as Ørsted, Sibbern, Madvig, Mynster, Martensen, Scharling, and others. Even our most widely circulated periodicals and daily newspapers use the conservative spelling; and if we add to this the fact that our most outstanding novelists, Fru Gyllembourg, Carl Bernhard, Bergsøe, and Ewald, followed the same system, this must surely be regarded as a foundation upon which future progress may be built without sudden upheavals.

These arguments, like every other argument against modern trends, no doubt will be considered "a voice crying in the wilderness," but if we still stand with fertile soil behind us—should the prospect actually reveal to us a barren heath?

With regard to the basically scientific treatment of the question, I will refer to Professor Rovsing's book about its significance for literature and the people, but as far as I myself am concerned, I ask Messrs. Speech-Reformers and their disciples what is really the intention of this orthographic revolution or, more correctly, *reaction,* since it indicates a retrogression rather than a progression in written language? Is it in order to achieve a possible harmony between written and spoken language and thereby to produce a more complete phonetics?

To the answer we may hereupon expect—should they condescend to enter into any explanation at all—it may be objected in advance that just as in French and English written language there is a spelling which appears to us Danes both unnatural and baroque, so we have vowels which in the composition of words sound entirely different than when they are pronounced individually:

E has an *a* sound in Egn, Tegn, Hegn, Vej, Nei, etc.
I has an *e* sound in Kind, Sind, Vind, til, vil, etc.
O has an *aa* sound in Bog, Krog, Sprog, Klog, noget, etc.
U has an *o* sound in Flugt, Frugt, Tugt, sukke, vugge, etc.
Y has an *ø* sound in Lykke, Krykke, Smykke, brygge, trykke, etc.

Consonants often lose their point in our soft Danish, not infrequently garbled Copenhagen, accent, and D, in particular, is not heard at all at the end of words like *Aand, Baand, Haand* and rarely in *Ord, Nord, Bord,* etc. G is changed to I and J by *jeg, mig, dig, regne, blegne;* and V sounds like U in *Hav, Skov, Navn, Havn, Gavn,* etc.

Thus we come to realize that as far as correct spelling is concerned, we have nothing to throw in the teeth of the French and English written languages, and if we add to this the singular reverberant accentuation that is a distinctive feature of genuine Danish speech, we will see the impossibility of even approximating the intended result.

Moreover, if it is in order that we may embrace the Romance and to alienate ourselves from the Germanic forms of speech that Latin type and handwriting are exclusively recommended, and capital letters are to be used only for initials, place and country names, one then dares to ask why the letters C, Q, X, and Z, which are found in those civilized languages, are to be ignored? And since there is a clamor to dispense with double letters, why write our neologisms *Eksempel, Ekstra, Okse, vokse,* etc.? I dare say we have well-founded reason to complain about the great injustice German policy has inflicted upon our homeland, and, even without regard to the hostile feeling, we have a perfect right to cleanse our language of German words that have crept in. But we can just as little disavow its Germanic root and origin as elude German scholarship and German music. — If it is supposed to be a demonstration or proof of national and political independence that the Danish style of handwriting (which has been maintained among us for centuries, which we older people acquired with ease during our schooling, and which still presents the least difficulty for the writing public) should now be abolished, we are only making ourselves ridiculous and will eventually feel the same inconveniences as those that are prevalent at the moment in Sweden, where handwritten Swedish manuscripts and documents from the generation before the previous one are legible only to experts.

If the rejection of diphthongs and double vowels is intended to help ease the work of writing, then the seconds that are hereby gained are hardly to be compensated for by the minutes that are lost in reading, where, in spite of the added Swedish and French accents, the eye continually hesitates between *saa* and *saae, faa* and *faae, let* and *leet, Helt* and *heelt, Forvisning* and *Forviisning, en vis Mand* and *en viis Mand,* etc. If we admit that double vowels have belonged exclusively to our Danish written language, ought we therefore to renounce every trace of originality solely from a desire to follow other countries abroad?

Finally, if it is to draw closer to our Nordic brethren from Norway and Sweden, then it ought to be pointed out that Norwegian purism stands as a meaningful sign of a firm determination to break with our common literary past, and we can be certain that if in linguistic respects we venture one step toward young Norway, it will take two steps back from us. With regard to the Swedish language, by its sharp accentuation of vowels and by the distinction resulting from the use of double consonants, it has an essential advantage over ours, but the similarity of language which four hundred years ago could (as Oehlenschläger has his Tordenskjold say) be called the major and the minor of the same note, has in the course of time and by a continual evolution on both sides, faded out of sight to the degree that its relationship to Danish is rather like that of Italian to Spanish.

It must be recognized that Swedish grammar is basically different from Danish, and that a Swedish dictionary, in the higher style as well as in colloquial usage, contains thousands of words and expressions which are completely alien to us. Even in such glossaries as are homophonic with the Danish, there are to be found hundreds of different, even opposite, meanings, which in the course of conversation precipitate the most ridiculous, sometimes even the most dangerous, misunderstandings. — If one could imagine that the North, i.e., Scandinavia, would in time have only a common language, it would doubtless cause *our* mother tongue, so beautifully formed through its outstanding authors, to suffer.

Whether the intention of this recommended, ordered, and forced spelling reform is to carry the written language back to its primitive sources, reduce it to the level of everyday speech, and adapt it to the common man, or, perhaps, to use it as a temporary means of promoting a revival of the Kalmar Union, the whole agitation is not free from containing — consciously or unconsciously — a rather considerable measure of

AFFECTATION

This foreign word, which in our hypercritical time has been naturalized in Danish speech and writing, is often used as incorrectly as a host of other expressions borrowed from the French, which when carried back to their original meaning would hardly find favor in decent ears. This subject has been the topic of a previous dissertation, as I have always, from the scenic standpoint, regarded affectation as the avowed enemy of true grace. Here I will describe it in a general way as the expression of the untrue and artificial. One is all too inclined to call *affectation* anything which, in manner and delivery, as well as in style and external appearance, strikes one as strange and unusual, regardless of the fact that this "difference" constitutes the uniqueness of the individual. This prejudice especially applies to the meticulous, the courteous, and the emotional, but it is obvious that there is certainly an affected coarseness just as there is an assumed excess of refinement. Sham and hypocrisy can assume the masks of both friendship and piety, and affectation exists among those who play the roles of the moved and enthusiastic and in such as willfully restrain their emotions in order to pose as *esprits rudes.* — Under the same rubric are classed aristocratic bourgeois, democratic nobles, republican despots, and those politicians who fornicate with Freedom in order to divert power to their own use.

It is simply a matter of putting on the proper spectacles to distinguish clearly between the various phenomena within the sphere of this abstract concept. It might perhaps be considered a paradox and a baseless allegation when I dare to put forth the proposition that, just as a goldsmith and jeweler is not easily deceived about the genuineness of metals and precious stones, so too by a long theatrical career one acquires a most peculiar insight as to what is true and proper as opposed to what is sham. — No doubt an assumed character can become a deep-rooted habit, just as a long-cherished fancy can take root and pass from an *idée fixe* into a false conviction. But the false does not by repetition, cease to be affectation in its highest degree. Thus in the orthographic dispute discussed above, it appears to be an ill-timed desire to seek reform — in the very place where the established order guarantees a peaceful and progressive development — by tempting us with the idea of making things easy and currying political favor with our neighbors "on the other side of the Sound."

We have had several striking examples of how far political affectation can go, but uppermost stands the request to Danish men and women to contribute to the erection of a memorial column to the defeat at Lund and the loss of Skåne! I wonder if in return the Swedes would be willing to celebrate the anniversary of Niels Juel's victory at Køgebugt?

May 17 is for us as for the Norwegians a red-letter day in the annals of Freedom, and with sincere joy we can acknowledge the great progress that Norway has made by virtue of its free Constitution and its independent position. But to celebrate November 4, when Norway, which had been conquered and ceded to Sweden by Denmark in a wretched exchange of property, as compensation for Finland, might be suitable for our Scandinavian neighbors, but hardly for Denmark — a country which then, just as a few years ago, had to submit to superior force and meet the hard fate of the weak. — If the word "affectation" should not be used in this case, it must at least be recognized as an expression of highly misunderstood

SCANDINAVISM!

Here I find myself on a terrain where I need not fear suspicion of partiality and prejudice, although I do not share the views and expectations of the Scandinavists, who wish and await a future union, be it dynastic or federative. Insofar as it is a matter of sincere neighborliness, joint recognition, kindred sympathies, and exchanges of ideas in the material as well as in the spiritual sphere, I am among the warmest supporters of the idea. I especially feel myself identified with our Nordic brethren when I meet them in foreign lands, where the different nuances of nationality merge into common interests.

My love for Norway and my admiration for its glorious natural beauty have been evidenced in some of my most successful compositions; I have personally come to know its most prominent men of science, literature, and art, and the hospitality which I have enjoyed shall be forever preserved in grateful memory. To Sweden I am joined by many bonds: my mother was born in Göteborg, from Skåne I gathered my life's greatest happiness;* my father spent ten unforgettable years in Stockholm at the theatre which was founded by the art-loving Gustav III. On this same stage I have honorably presented my art and seen my daughter begin her theatrical career under the most fortunate auspices, while I myself, by a three-year engagement as Intendant, have had the opportunity to study the language and the Swedish national character—a character whose main feature, together with what is common to all mankind, presents a high degree of cordiality, piety, and a spirit of chivalry.

In view of this confession, one might perhaps be tempted to regard me as cosmopolitan, but in this one would be completely mistaken, for although my father was French and my mother Swedish, I am, despite my French name and my Franco-Swedish sympathies, *Danish* in heart and soul, through and through. Born in Copenhagen, nurtured in the love of my native land, and influenced by its whole intellectual direction, I feel doubly gladdened by every noble deed when a countryman has done it and am proud of all Danish renown. The Danish flag, in whatever harbor or channel I encounter it, causes my heart to thrill with excitement. Denmark's glorious memories fill my soul with proud awareness, and its misfortunes bind me yet closer to the beloved soil that fostered me. Therefore, I am above all *Danish,* and cannot join with those who wish to see Denmark merged in a united Scandinavia. The idea that a United Scandinavian State should be able to assume an imposing position in opposition to the Great Powers desirous of conquest is an illusion with respect not only to numbers, but also to frontiers. Sweden-Norway, whose boundaries seem to assure for their domains a lasting peace, with all its temporal advantages, would only feel weakened and threatened by a connection with *vulnerable* Denmark; and they would moreover see themselves in no better position to stand by us in time of need than we would be to help them against a superior enemy. Thus the union would be harmful for our friends and of no use to us.

One has heard and seen theories proposed to the effect that each of these countries should retain its individual government, its laws and institutions, and only be ruled by a Central Parliament in joint concerns! It is very difficult to determine in advance how fundamental principles and forms of representation, divergent in so many respects, could be harmonized. But one thing seems perfectly clear: whether these joint interests concern peaceful or martial undertakings, the stronger party would unfailingly exercise hegemony, and it would be of no use to insist upon independence. If we now consider

*I.e., his wife.

which of the three would prefer the establishment of such a federal republic, we can, *a priori*, be assured that Norway would most likely seek to retain its present position; the Danish Scandinavists would regard the union almost as a protection against Germany's arrogance; and the Swedish Friends of the Union would cherish the hope of expanded control. A poor prospect of agreement, let alone political unity.

Such a union is, moreover, completely unnecessary to advantageous cooperation in scientific, commercial, social, and economic directions. Although occasional small frictions (as, for example, the question of the Sound Dues) may engender a momentary bitterness in a not too friendly press, one soon realizes that our interests are most consistent. In any case, there are present among the three Nordic nations such striking differences in manners, customs, way of life, and character that there is little agreement, even between Norwegians and Swedes; how much less, then, when joined with us, where national feeling is at least as strong, if not as demonstrative, as among our neighbors. We will not touch upon sensitive issues that have arisen, usually from misunderstandings and lack of knowledge of the circumstances, nor will we enumerate the qualities in which one nation fancies itself superior to the other. But as far as the Swedes and the Danes are concerned, the bloody conflicts of past centuries have left traces in the consciousness of the peoples; and, in proportion to the deeper seriousness of their characters, the memory is preserved in the legends and events which history has transmitted and whose impressions are, so to speak, imbibed with mother's milk. The Dane, who has by nature a milder and more conciliatory temper, has, for example, in less than half a century nourished and then done away with three different national hatreds. He dwells with delight upon history's bright spots and the heroic deeds of his ancestors, but passes lightly over defeat and loss. When on a clear spring day he looks across to the coast of Skåne, where the shiny white churches have all been built by Danish kings, he seldom realizes that this fertile land was once one with Denmark!—It is now Sweden and nothing but, just as someday—unless the impossible happens—Slesvig, defended and lost with such great sacrifices, will be called Prussia!

This is not the case with the Swede. He knows that his military history during the last four hundred years far outshines ours—especially on land—and for over sixty years now he has enjoyed his glorious memories in complete peace and quiet; but he is always vaguely aware of the oppression which his fatherland suffered under the Danish Union; a rule that was marked by violence and deceit, by the whip and the executioner's sword. Engelbrecht, Sture, and Vasa are heroes of freedom whose names would rise up against any governmental union, of whatever sort it may be. I have no definite idea of how Swedish hegemony would be tolerated in Denmark, but it is an established fact that the mere thought of a Danish ruler in Sweden would be rejected with loathing by the entire Swedish nation.

These facts, however, have no effect upon reciprocal social intercourse;

the Danes, Norwegians, and Swedes vie to show one another the most amiable kindness. Heartfelt joy prevails at every visit, whether such visits take place singly or in whole migrations, but—*thus far and no farther!* Let the political element come into play, and the concord stands in danger of being broken. One need only imagine a Central Parliament with a discussion carried on between our numerous democracy and the proud Swedish aristocracy, founded upon the brilliant deeds of their ancestors, and emotion would soon cause historical sentiment to mount to a renewal of old grudges and bitterness. Just let us picture a cooperation of united armies in case of war. The first point of contention would concern who was to be Supreme Commander; the next, which nation's troops had contributed most to the prospective victory; and lastly, which of the parties should bear the blame for the possible defeat. Besides, there need hardly be any doubt about who would be chosen propitiatory offering at the conclusion of peace.

These reflections, which in fact do not contain anything new, will perhaps win approval among those who privately share my views, but will undoubtedly arouse vehement objections among supporters of the opposite system. And above all else, one will ask whether these reflections actually concern my theatre life. To this I will reply that as representative of a branch of art and a kind of poetry peculiar to the Danish stage (and which, in addition to the fact that it is influenced by our national taste, is also inspired by our patriotic memories), I feel obligated to combat, to the best of my abilities, the agitations that—consciously or unconsciously—have as their goal the reduction of our literary treasures to an antiquated inheritance and our beautiful language to a faltering dialect; to assert the right of the natural and true as opposed to the affected and false; and finally, to reveal the hollow and the untenable elements in those efforts that aim at causing Denmark to ascend— or, more properly, *descend*—into a Scandinavian trinity.

Would that the Danish language might blossom in writing and eloquence, while the Danish critical sense is occupied with keeping affectation and unnaturalness outside our precincts. Would that peace and concord might always prevail, not only with our neighbors and Nordic brethren, but also in our domestic relationships, and as we commend our beloved, sorely tried homeland into the hand that rules the kingdoms and peoples of the universe, let us unite in the cry: "GOD PROTECT DENMARK!"

III

Biographical Sketches Drawn From Memory

PREFACE

THESE descriptions of a number of more or less well-known contemporaries were originally intended for a *Danish Biographical Lexicon* whose publication ran into unforeseen obstacles and seems relegated to a rather uncertain future. In reality, my whole manner of presentation is better suited to the style of a memoir, since the descriptions are gathered from personal acquaintance and from information communicated by the persons themselves, with reference to no sources other than actual experience and with no guaranty other than my avowed truthfulness. Perhaps the objective form which these sketches have retained will contribute still further to giving them a certain historical-artistic interest in the sphere within which I have lived and worked; in some places it may also help to supplement and rectify several previously quoted facts.

Thus I come to discuss first of all my famous predecessor Vincenzo Galeotti, who lived at a time when criticism progressed with a certain amount of caution, especially when it dealt with artistic professions whose specialties were either outside of or remote from the critics' competence or sphere of knowledge. At this time the ballet was reckoned among such professions; it was regarded more as a festive aggregate than as a dramatic and literary product that first had to pass through the flames of Purgatory before it gained popular acceptance. Every review was therefore a panegyric rather than a critique. Here, then, would be an opportunity for me to join in the unconditional praise that was conferred upon the master's compositions and (just as on the entrance of a newly elected member into the French Academy) to deliver an outright eulogy for the deceased celebrity whose place I was called to occupy and, if possible, to fill.

But since outstanding contemporaries as well as historians of the Danish stage have furnished descriptions of those pantomimic works which aroused people to enthusiasm in their day, and since their total disappearance from the boards has been ascribed to a reprehensible lack of care, reverence, and even skill among the master's successors, I feel that in the interests of truth I ought to represent circumstances as they are and as they were, with respect both to the inner worth of the compositions and to the question of their preservation as classical works.

638

At the time of Galeotti's death (1816) his most popular ballets, *Lagertha,* *Barbe-Bleue* [*Blaaskjæg*], *Romeo, Nina,* and *The Singhalese Idol* [*Afguden paa Ceylon*] formed an active part of the Theatre's repertoire. However, most of those who held roles in them were already too old, and among the younger members of the personnel there was not a single mimic talent who could be used successfully to compensate for the loss of the older performers, who showed little desire to retire. This, and not a lack of care on the part of either the conductor or the Theatre management, gradually caused a weakening of interest in large-scale pantomimic drama, and it eventually wasted away, only to reappear with renewed strength after an interval of fourteen years, though in a completely altered form.

The memory of these magnificently tragic presentations long remained with the public as well as the ballet personnel, and the wish to see them revived to Schall's glorious music was ardently expressed on numerous occasions. I myself was most anxious to appear in some of the roles for which my father was remembered. I refreshed my memory of all the scenes and dances I had admired in my boyhood years. Then, making use of all the assistance those of the older cast still living could give me, I mounted *Romeo and Giulietta* in the full conviction that the ballet would win a judicious, if not exactly enthusiastic, reception.

The result of these honest endeavors in no way answered to expectations, for views had completely changed; that is to say, the whole form, despite the individual modifications it had undergone, seemed terribly old-fashioned; while the progressive action, so much talked about and praised, now appeared exactly the reverse, encumbered as it was with such things as arias, choruses, processions, and ecclesiastical ceremonies. Boredom got the upper hand, applause was silenced, and by the second and third performances the audiences stayed away.

The critics, who could hardly believe their eyes, reluctantly had to deny their earlier statements and now vented their wrath upon those who had rescued this masterpiece from oblivion. In return for my good will I received ingratitude, first from the older folk whose memory-pictures had lost their freshness and then from the younger people who, regarding my powers of invention as exhausted, accused me of wishing to carry the ballet back to the Rococo period.

And yet, for all this I could not forget the impressions I had received as a child when with deep emotion I saw Galeotti's works so brilliantly performed and when I myself, watched by the old master, had even played small parts in his ballets. I therefore started in turn on *Barbe-Bleue* and *Lagertha,* but reached the conviction that reverence for the great name would best be preserved by not forcing older subjects on the critical gaze of the present; for the younger generation would find occasion for the most vulgar parody in those very elements that had in their day appeared to be the most noble and moving—a defilement that even my most successful works have not escaped and one from which I would spare the memory of my august predecessor.

The conventional language of gesture, which we are getting away from more and more, created the kind of dancing which at that time was intended to express both mood and virtuosity, even the plot and its motives. There the stock types of brutal fathers, tyrants and traitors, reckless lovers and rivals, together with devoted confidantes, were surrounded, according to circumstances, by a symmetrically placed and mechanically gesticulating chorus of shepherds and knights. Today these figures would call forth either risqué hilarity or, if they were modified, dissolve into a deadly boredom.

I hereby think I have fully stated the true reasons for the unavoidable disappearance of the Galeottian ballets from the stage and for the impossibility of their maintenance in the repertoire.

VINCENZO TOMASELLI, *dit* GALEOTTI[*]

(Born in Verona, March 5, 1733; died in Copenhagen, December 16, 1816)

SINCE the only writings this famous choreographer has left behind are some business letters, one knows next to nothing about him or his theatrical career before he came to Copenhagen from London in the year 1774. He appeared as soloist and mime together with a Signorina Guidi, who later became his wife. As has been stated, there are no records concerning his youth; even the report of his birthplace varies from Verona to Vicenza to Florence. Suffice it to say, he was an Italian who took over the post of balletmaster after his countryman Sacco.

As his first productions he presented several of Angiolini's compositions. These, according to the custom of the time, were "balleticized" adaptations of French tragedies such as *Dido, Semiramis,* and *L'Orphelin de la Chine.* The music, which was brought to Copenhagen in the form of violin arrangements, was orchestrated by *Concertmester* Darbès, and the completed arrangement passed off as original—a practice much employed at the time. Even though these productions were fitted out in splendid fashion, in accordance with the demands of the day, the public seemed to feel little interest in ballet in the grand style. Just as nowadays, they would rather have had "something to laugh at." Therefore serious ballets were soon replaced by a whole string of smaller works, wherein an element of burlesque predominated. These were what people today would class as *divertissements.* Among them, *The Gypsy Camp* [Zigeunernes Leir], *The Whims of Cupid* [Amors Luner], *The Recruiting Officer* [Hververen] and *The Washerwomen and the Tinker* [Vadskepigerne og Kjedelflikkeren] won the public's unanimous applause.

[*]The origin of this curious *stage name* is unknown. In the Italian language it is most offensive, since it is both the genetive and plural of *Galeotto*—meaning *galley slave!*—A. B.

A new period entered with the *Contes moraux* of Marmontel and inspired *Annette and Lubin, Laurette, Linna and Valvais, Hermann and Dolmon,* and several others. In this whole series of major and minor ballets, the following were outstanding: *The Singhalese Idol* for its characteristic dancing and Schall's superb music, while *Mountain Peasants' Children* [*Biergbøndernes Børn*] had an idyllic charm, and the amusing mimed adaptation of the French operetta *Le Diable à quatre* (in Danish, *Fanden er løs*) was a little masterpiece of its kind. On the other hand, Galeotti's imitations of Gardel's *Télémaque, Psyché,* and *La Dansomanie* were less fortunate.

The most curious thing about Galeotti's artistic career was that he only reached his culmination as a ballet composer after twenty-six years of activity, when he was sixty-seven years old, and in precisely the same tragic style that had marked his earliest appearance. This peak in his career was signaled by *Lagertha,* which was performed for the first time on January 30, 1801, Christian VII's birthday. Schall had composed the music for it in an astonishingly short time and with an enthusiasm peculiar to that unforgettable age.

The original plot, in part a travesty of *Jason and Medea,* was drafted by the poet Pram, who had also written the text for the inserted songs and choruses, thereby giving the ballet overtones of a pantomimic opera with dancing. My father, whose performance of the legendary hero Regnar Lodbrog was most imposing, had an essential part in working out the choreography as well as the various tournaments. The rest of the principal roles, with Mme. Bjørn as Lagertha, Mlle. Birouste as Thora, and Dahlén as the King of the Goths, were ably performed. The applause was thunderous, and in this magnificent drama the national spirit found rich nourishment. Galeotti won general renown and for many years his work held a place of honor on the Danish stage.

It was a long time before a success of the same sort could supplant the brilliant triumph of *Lagertha;* Laurent strove to score a success in the same Nordic sphere with *Sigrid,* but in vain. Galeotti himself never entered it again, and both his *Nina* and *Inez de Castro* must stand in the shadow of that mighty picture of heroic antiquity.

But in 1808 he again won the prize with *Raoul Barbe-Bleue* (a mimed adaptation of the *syngestykke Barbe-Bleue*). The adventurous spirit that ran through all four acts had such an exciting, shattering effect that a number of spectators suffered nervous attacks! Under present circumstances and moods, an attempt to revive these pathetic scenes would produce a completely opposite effect; for despite the most brilliant *soli* and minuets, a monster such as this Raoul, who has his royal crown standing on his night table while the ghosts of his four murdered spouses, whose corpses are hanging in his study, hover about him in dreams wherein they are accompanied by an archbishop in full raiment together with a flaming inscription, would be laughed to scorn by our reflective contemporaries.

On April 2, 1811, *Romeo and Giulietta* was performed for the first time with great acclaim. Like *Lagertha,* it had both choruses and solo singing, and the music is unquestionably one of Schall's loveliest inspirations. The plot, which had Steibelt's opera in mind more than Shakespeare's tragedy, not only suffered from excessive breadth, as I stated earlier, but also from the fact that, strangely enough, the principal motif, the family hatred between the Montecchi and the Capuletti, was lacking. The dances, especially the anxiously awaited *pas de deux,* between the lovers at their assignation in the first act, and again in the fourth when Giulietta dances with the detested bridegroom, were very successful but could not be defended on aesthetic grounds.

In certain respects the performances might be called marvelous, for all of the principal roles were cast with artists of considerable seniority: Romeo was fifty-one years old, Giulietta about forty, Paris forty-three, and Lorenzo, who was played by Galeotti himself, seventy-eight years old! This latter role was given with apostolic dignity until the master, as a reward for his notable service, was decorated with a Knight's Cross, Order of the Dannebrog. From this moment on, his appearance on the stage was regarded as incompatible with strict decorum.

Although it was performed only four times before the season closed, in the year which followed, *Romeo and Giulietta* achieved a real *succès de vogue* and long remained a favorite ballet, comparable to *Lagertha.* And indeed it must be admitted that if the details were stripped away, there will be found scenes of true emotional effect and situations which have been treated with a masterly hand. The pantomime, according to Italian form, consisted of a complete dictionary of accepted *gestures* that had been gathered from Roman and Neapolitan folkways, and also, to lend greater clarity to the whole, of written placards, tablets, banners, and transparencies which, like the Ninevite flame-writing of old, announced fateful occurrences. In the use of these means Galeotti possessed a skill and experience such as few people had; and his public (who were through a couple of generations, in a manner of speaking, raised to understand him) followed the development of the action with confident, nay, almost devout, attention. Small wonder, then, that both poets and artists vied to give the master and his works unconditional recognition.

On the other hand, people are mistaken when they say that Galeotti was the founder of a definite trend in ballet: he was simply an imitator of the traditional Italian school, which numbers among its practitioners men like Angiolini, Canziani, Viganò, and Gioja. Their stereotyped forms of pantomimic technique have been preserved not only on Italy's major stages, but also recur in the Casorti harlequinades. In addition to a high degree of rhythmic precision and kaleidoscopic symmetry, this school is characterized by the fact that the dances bear no relation to the plot, which, as a rule, is either adapted from a well-known drama or passed around as a libretto from one writer to another—*ex professo.*

As I remember him, and as he has been represented to me by his contemporaries, Galeotti was a vigorous and handsome old man, and one of great practical ability as well, even though lacking in literary education and in taste. Nonetheless he did possess a fineness of appearance and dignity of bearing that are seldom wanting in Italians. He had a thorough grasp of musical rhythms, whereas his choreographic organization was alien to both melody and harmony. Through the years his language was transformed into the most singular dialect: he never did learn Danish, and his mother tongue was sprinkled with French and English. All the same, his pupils understood him and answered in a similar gibberish.

Galeotti's last great ballet, *Macbeth,* was an attempt (as bold, I dare say, as it was unsuccessful) to interpret Shakespeare by means of mimed acting and inscriptions. A number of the scenes were masterfully performed, but the whole was far too broad and lacking in the necessary local color. For example, the Scots were clad exactly like those who had camped in Søndermarken during the siege of 1807, while Macbeth and his wife were crowned with the same ceremonies as those for the coronation of Frederik VI and his Queen a short time before! Even though it was rather boring, one still had to admire the rare activity of the eighty-two-year-old balletmaster, whose ambition was to endure to the end of his days.

His numerous pupils, several of whom were members of the drama and opera who had begun their theatrical careers in the dancing school, arranged a celebration at the Court Theatre on the occasion of his eighty-third birthday. To this end, and unknown to him, they had had his portrait painted by the popular artist Viertel. The picture bore quite a striking resemblance to Galeotti, but the sight of it had a most depressing effect on the old man. He had refused to sit for artists a number of times because of his superstitious belief that his end would thereby be precipitated! Neither the festivity of the party nor the garlands that were presented to him by grateful and loving hands, not even the title of "Professor" which was most graciously conferred upon him on this occasion, could efface the dark impression.

A chronic complaint, which a strenuous social life had aggravated, and a cold caught during an unintentional swim, laid him on the sickbed some months after these solemnities, and shortly before Christmas of 1816, with the consolation of religion according to the Catholic rite and surrounded by his two daughters and his faithful pupil Mme. Schall, he passed away.

His daughters, Caroline and Mathilde, died a few years after their father, and since they left behind a small fortune, there was a great deal of inquiry for the rightful heirs. One of Copenhagen's most sought-after tailors, Guidi, a Neapolitan by birth, claimed to be related to Galeotti's long-deceased wife, but another very handsome Italian who (after God knows what adventures) had ended up as drum-major in one of our regiments, proved his rightful claim, and Antonio, with the family name of Tomaselli, returned to Galeotti's native land a wealthy man.

CLAUS SCHALL

(Born in Copenhagen April 28, 1760; died August 10, 1835)

HE was probably the first Danish musician to appear as a composer of any significance, and considering the circumstances under which his talent evolved, one must rightly regard him as one of the most remarkable figures in our artistic world. Self-educated to such a degree that one cannot say with certainty from whom he learnt to play the violin, acquired the rules of harmony, or even language, from the beginning he fought with incredible energy to overcome hardships and always remained unaffected by associates whose commonplaceness he himself later emphasized with priceless humor in intimate conversations.

Son of a poor shoemaker, and the eldest of a numerous flock of children, he manifested at an early age a firm desire and an innate vocation for music. He received instruction from an unknown teacher, and since his father could not stand the shrill sounds with endless repetitions, he was forced to crawl under the down quilt to continue his practicing *con Sordino.*

The father's trade, however, proved inadequate for the support of the family, and art was asked to lend a hand. Since the elder Schall had managed to have his sons accepted at the Ballet School of the Royal Theatre, and was himself not unversed in the useful society dances of the day, he established a small dancing school, such as they call in England a "Dancing Academy," which must certainly have been in very humble style as the pupils were obliged to provide for the illumination of the room by bringing candles made of wicks dipped in tallow! Here his sons assisted him, sometimes as musicians and sometimes as assistants with the instruction. But Claus was already beginning to figure in the ballets of Sacco and Galeotti. His humorous accounts of the life that went on backstage in those days could readily furnish a companion piece to the pictures in *Fredmans Epistlar;* for like the merry parties at "Krogen Wismar," they marched with a band at the head of the parade from the Playhouse to the progenitor Spendrup in "Brænde-Vingaard-stræde"!

People soon perceived a skilled violinist in young Schall, and realized that he could be of greater use as *répétiteur* than as a *figurant.* He now played indefatigably for classes and rehearsals, but used the intervals to make up for what had been neglected in his schooling. He also developed his musical talent according to the models presented by foreign virtuosi (being influenced, among other things, by Lolli's visit to Copenhagen), and studied harmony mostly by listening to the good works presented by the Royal Orchestra, especially under the direction of Naumann and Schultz. Here it was not long before he outdistanced the older *ripienists*, who evinced no greater technical skill than the ability to shout to one another "Watch out!" or "Pay attention!" every time they were required to produce, by their fingering, a C or D.

He had soon familiarized himself with the masterworks of Gluck and Haydn and was particularly attracted by the simplicity and wealth of melody that distinguished Schultz's compositions. Although conceived and created by a German, these works became so popular in Denmark that they laid the foundation for a new direction in our national song.

The fact that Schall had penetrated the surface of musical theory is apparent in his earliest attempts. These, although thin with regard to instrumentation and simple in modulation, are far superior to the Italian ballet compositions that Darbès and Lolle had furnished. Thus it was first in Galeotti's ballets that Schall began to forge the path that would lead to his renown. *Annette and Lubin, The Washerwomen and the Tinker,* as well as *The Devil Is Loose,* were the first fruits of his fresh spirit. But it was chiefly in *The Singhalese Idol* that he revealed a warmth of character and invention that brought recognition for his uncommon talent, and Chamberlain Warnstedt, the Theatre Chief at that time, nominated him for a royal travel stipend.

This stipend was used by him and his brother Peer, who was even then a skilled violoncellist. There are no notes to tell us about this no doubt interesting *kunstreise,* but judging from its results, one dares to presume that their time was well spent. This much is known, however: the heated conflict that was raging in Paris during Schall's stay between the "Gluckists" and the "Piccinists" had a considerable influence upon his understanding of dramatic music, and Mestrino's magnificent violin playing upon the style in which Schall was later to perform as virtuoso in the same instrument. This style earned him great applause when he appeared in several of Germany's capitals, especially in Prague. In this last city he had the pleasure of meeting Mozart, even before *Figaro, Don Giovanni,* and *The Magic Flute* had been recognized and, of course, only a few years before the immortal composer's all too early demise. The adoration that Schall gave to the genius of Mozart was continuously renewed and strengthened by the memory of having seen and talked with the peerless master.

Along with the merits Schall derived from the acceptance and admirable performance of the aforementioned masterworks on the Danish stage as well as from the audience he afforded Mozart's symphonies and quartets by his own inspired playing, one surely should relate a few anecdotes connected with this infatuation and the way in which it conflicted with the prosaic element in his daily life.

The fact of the matter is, he had established a lovely country seat at Lyngby, where he had a marshy terrain drained and filled in. On this site he later built a pavilion to which he gave the name of "The House of Music." All around this little sanctuary were erected menhirs in honor of the heroes of the art of music and, naturally, Mozart's was the most prominent. One day, when a Sjælland hussar had been hired to do some gardening and Schall wished to call to his attention the meaning of the inscription, the clever fellow announced that he had figured out the proper explanation for himself,

since it could be nothing more than a simple reference to the mossy ground—
that is, *"mose-art"*—a play on words which delighted the old man for years to
come.

On the other hand, what seemed to amuse him far less was his conjugal
life with a partner who was totally impervious to all higher musical enjoyment, Cathrine Salathé. In her youth she had been a beauty but only a poorly
gifted actress. This marriage endured to the golden anniversary, but in neither a loving nor fruitful fashion; and as punishment for her petty chaffing,
from morning till night she had to put up with quartets and quintets—by pupils and dilettantes as well as experienced musicians. This poor woman and
her if possible even more prosaic sister complained bitterly of the eternal music. "If they would even," they said, "play something entertaining, either by
Du Puy or by Claus himself. But day in and day out it is never anything but
that damned Mozart."

But to return to the brothers' travels abroad, from which they brought
home indelible impressions, I will only remark that of the two, Claus profited
most by the experience. He was undeniably the more ingenious and indefatigable, whereas the light-hearted and good-natured Peer limited his musical
activity to the treatment of his own instrument, both as orchestra musician
and as teacher. The insinuation that the elder brother's compositions were
due partly to Peer's cooperation must, therefore, be rejected as completely
unfounded.

The field wherein Schall enjoyed such great success, namely ballet music,
appeared a rather subordinate one to him and his admirers; and, jealous of his
honor, the musician now chose a broader genre, writing a number of large
Concertstykker and appearing as opera composer for P. A. Heiberg's *The Travelers in China* [*Kinafarerne*], which was tremendously successful and gained
unusual popularity. Notwithstanding this success, it would seem that next to
talents like Schultz and Kunzen, and even in comparison with Du Puy, whose
Youth and Folly literally bubbled over with frivolity and humor, Schall was
only of secondary importance on the lyric stage. And when Weyse and Kuhlau
later assumed first rank, his earlier works in this area were completely ignored. Terpsichore remained the Muse to whose glorification he was to offer
the finest fruits of his genius, and she, in return, provided him with his loveliest laurels.

An innumerable host of dances and mimic idylls alternated with his violin pieces; while in subjects that were gay as well as those that were rich in
feeling, he presented much that was beautiful and unique in both rhythm and
melody. But it was not until 1801 that he furnished the music for the grand
opera-ballet *Lagertha*. This immediately placed him far above all other composers who had before him tried their hand in the Nordic sphere of sound; for
this lyric-mimic drama received from Schall's excellent music a whiff of the
heathen past that had an irresistible effect upon both *the spectators* and *the*

listeners. In the various moments of this tone-poem there lay strength and passion, grace and wildness, freshness and fullness; and nothing more significant can be said of this magnificent ballet music than that it has played an essential part in inspiring those who have since treated Nordic subjects and interpreted them in sound. Laurent's ballet *Sigrid* is said to have given Schall the opportunity to produce, if possible, something even more excellent in this direction. However, the subject had but weak appeal and could not hold its place in the repertoire. Galeotti's *Inez de Castro* met with the same fate, but *Raoul Barbe-Bleue* (1810) and *Romeo and Giulietta* (1811), on the other hand, won the liveliest recognition. Like *Lagertha*, this last-named work was endowed with singing and inspired throughout by a romanticism which, though unmistakably influenced by Mozart, still bore the mark of originality and great artistic value.

That such excellent compositions lay like so much dead treasure on the dusty shelves of the Musical Archives must be ascribed to the same reasons that have withdrawn so many works by our most outstanding musicians from our lyric stage; that is to say, texts and subjects that were formerly praised and applauded are now regarded as trite and outmoded by reason of altered aesthetic views.

Of Schall's *syngestykker*, the only ones remembered are *The Canon of Milan* [*Domherren i Milano*], through some ballads that became popular with the public; *Alma and Elfride,* whose fleeting existence was cut short by the retirement of the popular singer Carl Bruun; and finally, *The Three Madmen* [*De tre Galninger*], whose first performance with C. N. Rosenkilde making his debut as tenor, was not allowed to play to the end because of the prevailing animosity toward N. T. Bruun! The last of Schall's more important works were Galeotti's *Macbeth* and Dahlén's *Armida*. Both of these works were of less value than his earlier ballet compositions. Finally, at a very advanced age, he wrote a "Cantata" in honor of the [Royal] nuptials (1828), but it was soon overshadowed by Kuhlau's masterly arrangement of the melodies for *Elves' Hill.*

After Kunzen's death, Schall, who had for many years served in the modest capacity of *Concertmester,* assumed the post of *Capelmester*—however, only with the title of *Musikdirecteur,* for people still considered it impossible for a *native-born Dane* to assume a post of such high dignity. However, he was appointed Professor, and since he was already a Knight of the Dannebrog, his triple title took up an entire line on the theatre playbill.

It was under his ingenious direction that our orchestra developed the high degree of excellence which later brought it such well-deserved renown. In the year 1818 he undertook another journey to Paris, again in the company of his brother Peer. Here he struck up an acquaintance with Cherubini, Paër, and a number of musical celebrities and was at the same time accepted as a member of the Institut de France (the *Académie des beaux Arts*).

Honored and favored as he was in so many ways, Schall had also earned for himself a considerable fortune and might have retired before his influence at Court and in fashionable circles was weakened by the popularity which the Italian singing master Siboni won by virtue of his imposing appearance and his unmistakable skill. By Siboni's efforts Italian music, with such a lively figure as Rossini at its head, assumed a predominant place in our operatic repertoire and was used especially at Royal birthdays and other solemn occasions. This music was always arranged by Siboni, and Schall was hereby reduced to *Orchesterchef*. This state of affairs frequently gave rise to friction. Factions were formed, partly out of sympathy for a wronged countryman and partly out of envy of the success of the foreigner; and we then experienced the phenomenon of seeing the most outstanding composers of the day—Paër, Simon Mayr, Spontini, Meyerbeer, and Rossini—mercilessly hissed off the stage simply because they belonged to the school that Siboni defended!

For his part, Schall was firmly opposed to this barbaric abomination, for in spite of his decided fondness for German and French music, he readily accepted everything beautiful and characteristic that modern times had to offer. However, the noisy instrumentation and undramatic "dingdong" finally became too much for him; and since his long and persevering service entitled him to retain all of his different emoluments in pension, he sought and obtained his retirement after having placed his nephew, the extremely mediocre musician Peter Funck, as his successor at the conductor's podium.

His outstanding portrait, painted by Eckersberg, which adorns the Ballet Foyer of the Royal Theatre, shows us Schall in the full strength of his manhood, with facial features that, without being regular, give evidence of intelligence and enthusiasm. To those of us older folk who have known him personally, his character was a mixture of highly different elements and had the same nuances one so often finds in ingenious people whose education has not kept pace with the development of their talent. He enjoyed his last days in jovial tranquillity, traveled about in his fine equipage, kept a hospitable house, and had his pupils play for him those quartets and sonatas which had so often delighted him and plagued his peevish spouse, who became blind shortly after the celebration of their golden wedding anniversary and died several years later. Their adopted son, Julius, who was appointed to the orchestra as a violinist, died at an early age without having answered to his father's expectations.

Like a tree which in late autumn has shed its last leaves, the old bard entered the rest of winter with the hope of a spring of rebirth, in which celestial harmonies would sound to greet him.

The Royal Theatre gave a memorial celebration in his honor, Oehlenschläger wrote a lovely poem for this occasion, and I was in charge of the scenic arrangement. His melodies still sound in my ears and carry me back to my first childhood steps on the path of art.

PIERRE JEAN LAURENT

(Born in Copenhagen March 24, 1759; died May 23, 1831)

HIS parents were both French, and his father had been summoned by Frederik V to instruct the Royal children in dancing, a part of a child's upbringing that was then considered so important that old Laurent, after having finished with the Crown Prince (Christian VII), Sophie Magdalene, later the Queen of Gustav III, as well as the Heir Presumptive Frederik, was awarded the title of *Virkelig Canceliraad.* After having given lessons to the next generation of Royal children, in accordance with the strict system of training of the day, he obtained his full Court Dancing Master's salary in pension, with permission to spend it abroad. He died in Paris at a very old age, a wealthy man.

The son, who despite his French Christian name and upbringing spoke fluent Danish and was instilled with the highest feelings of loyalty for his native land and king, did not seem by nature cut out for dancing. He was small in stature, something less than handsome, and rather bowlegged to boot. But since at that time there existed three distinct and highly different genres of dancing, namely, *sérieux, demi-caractère,* and *comique,* his father thought that a career for his son might be established in the latter métier, partly by reason of his unique gymnastic ability and partly because the son possessed a rare liveliness and gay spirit. Nothing was neglected with regard to his upbringing, and he received an uncommon musical training as well.

All that is known about his childhood is that as a small boy he often had to dance at Court for the Royal family. It so happened that on one of these occasions he was witness to a scene which in uproarious fashion characterizes the relationship between Caroline Mathilde and Struensee.* As Laurent has told the story, one evening when there was a Court ball at Christiansborg he was dozing in an armchair in an antechamber adjacent to the great hall. Suddenly the folding doors flew open and the two persons mentioned above entered, displaying violent emotions. Without suspecting the child's presence, they continued an argument that ended with the Queen turning arrogantly around to return to the ballroom, as Struensee lifted his foot as if to kick her and rushed out in the opposite direction!

In the year 1777, young Laurent was sent to Paris, there to further his training under the famous balletmaster Noverre, who allowed him to make his debut in a *Laplandish pas de deux* arranged expressly for his personality. As a result, during the twelve years that he served as comic soloist at the Grand Opéra, he was known as *"Le petit Lapon,"* and shone chiefly in parts for dev-

---

*Johan Frederick Struensee, born 1731 in Halle, was Court physician to King Christian VII, soon becoming the lover of Queen Caroline Mathilde. With this start, Struensee intrigued his way into a position of almost absolute power in Danish affairs, and thrust upon the nation a series of social-political reforms of a radical—and unpopular—nature. A countercabal caused his arrest; he was tried on charges of usurping Royal authority, found guilty, and executed April 28, 1772. See also note on Caroline Mathilde, Vol. III, Part Two, p. 427.

ils, Negroes, Chinamen, and peasants in wooden shoes. However, he was just as proud of his Danish nationality as he was of the school to which he belonged, and with some pretention he signed himself "Only Danish pupil of the celebrated Noverre."

Shortly before the outbreak of the Revolution, he married the well-to-do daughter of a bourgeois, Rose Marie Bonneau, and accepted the post of ballet-master in Marseilles. Here he composed a number of larger and smaller ballets, whose libretti I have seen and read. Among these *La Tentation de Saint Antoine* created an epoch and served later on as the prototype of a host of *diableries* which long flooded the stage in France and even spread abroad. A good number of his remaining compositions were products of the sentiments of the Reign of Terror, which poor theatre folk had to espouse so as not to be accused of *incivisme* or the even more despised *moderantisme*, with the guillotine as an ever present image of fear!

It was under such conditions that the actor Monvel, after having played the venerable Fénélon, was required to mount the pulpit in the Church of Saint Roch, and Vestris, together with Mlle. Chevigny, was forced to dance in the choir of the high altar of Notre Dame during the festival in honor of *la Déesse de la Raison!*

In Marseilles, as everyone knows, the most frightful agitation prevailed between the *sans-culottes* and the supporters of the overthrown monarchy. For a time, the latter had to bow to the superior force of the *sans-culottes;* and many a morning when Laurent opened his window after a night that had been filled with the clash of arms and wild howling, he trembled upon seeing the lamppost outside transformed into a gallows! During such outbursts of violence, he would usually flee with his family to the roadstead, where Danish ships were anchored and where he felt secure under the protecting flag of his native land.

After an absence of three-and-twenty years, Laurent finally saw his childhood home again and took over his father's former post as Court Dancing Master. He also appeared as a dancer, though without much success. However, an idyllic ballet of his own composition, *The Rose Tree [Rosentræet]*, had such an enormous success at its first performance that Galeotti, who was attending a *soirée* when the news arrived, fainted dead away! But it was not long before the crafty Italian took a brilliant revenge on his unwelcome rival; for with the production of *Lagertha* Galeotti's supremacy was established once and for all. When shortly afterward Laurent tried his hand with a similar Nordic subject in *Sigrid*, he found it impossible, despite a measure of real skill, to forge a path for himself. Popular feeling was against him to such a degree that when he later chose to present his pupils in an adaptation of Dauberval's *La Fille mal gardée*, this ballet (called *Harvest Day [Høstdagen]*) was greeted with scornful laughter and expressions of displeasure!

Herewith his career as an author was finished, for although he was certainly somewhat more knowledgeable than his successful rival, and even possessed a certain measure of *esprit* and invention, the practical skill and matchless precision that distinguished Galeotti's work lay completely outside Laurent's character, and the experienced strategist again walked off with the victory.

Laurent now devoted himself entirely to dance instruction. In addition to his official duties at Court, he took charge of the young drama students during the winter months, and, during the summer, of the princely family of Augustenborg. By virtue of an abundant income as well as a handsome inheritance, he would have been able to amass a fortune, had he not, with some of the weaknesses of a great man, displayed a one-sided talent for losing money. Still his hand was never closed to those in need, and despite the recklessness that dogged him far beyond a mature age, he possessed a good heart and a rare gift for making himself liked. Amidst the humble circumstances in which he passed his last infirm years, he retained his gay humor and witty ideas. His friends, who came to comfort and help him, never came away without having been served a good meal — laughter.

Laurent's artistic career yields but scattered and fleeting moments as a memorial. But as a Dane he has earned a name abroad and was, moreover, not without influence upon the scenic conditions of his day — partly because of his training of young actors. It is difficult to determine to what degree he deserved the name of important artist. The uninitiated remember him as an eccentric character, but to his fellow-artists he was what the French call *"un bon enfant,"* in Danish *"en god Kammerat."*

METTE MARIE ASTRUP

(Born in Copenhagen April 25, 1760; died February 16, 1834)

THE old Playhouse from 1748, which over the years was rebuilt and enlarged three times before being leveled to the ground in 1874, only to rise as a splendid edifice on the site of the neighboring Cannon Foundry, in 1820 still stood almost unchanged from what had been in Holberg's day. Although it was unimpressive in its exterior, it was a rather complete entity, with its entrance facing south and the building itself leaning up against a tiny, almost villagelike farmhouse which enclosed a yard and looked out on the canal (now filled in and built over) that surrounded Holmen's old shipyards.

There the Royal Theatre's porter had his rather comfortable abode, within whose walls three stately daughters grew up and through whose low windows and shiny panes one could at all seasons of the year admire magnificent flowers.

In this dwelling the popular actress lived, together with her two older sisters. When their parents died, by special patronage from above the position of porter was made hereditary on the distaff side, so that the eldest girl served as the Theatre's trusted *Schweitzer* and attendant. The next oldest took upon

herself the lowly duties of a dresser, and the youngest daughter, whose theatrical career we will here sketch in brief strokes, shone as a star of the first
magnitude in dignified roles and in heroine parts in both comedy and drama.

Mlle. Astrup's debut as Leonora in *The Fussbudget* [*Den Stundesløse*]
took place on June 2, 1773, which permits one to have certain reservations
about the actual date of her birth; for it seems highly unlikely that a little thirteen-year-old girl could have proved very satisfactory as a romantic lead.
However, it is obvious that her pretty appearance must quickly have attracted
attention and proved most useful to her career on the stage.

The superb (and to some degree French) school which at that time characterized Danish comedy was no doubt particularly advantageous to this
young *artiste*. But there are only scattered reports about the earliest period of
her career, and it therefore seems as if she achieved prominence in the more
important repertoire only after the departure of the two celebrated prima donnas, Mmes. Preisler and Walter.

Her principal qualities were a majestic dignity, which corresponded to
her imposing appearance—a type which at that time was much more common
in the theatre than it is nowadays, where talent is but rarely supported by
personality. Nevertheless, Mlle. Astrup could adapt or modify this attitude to
play gay and coquettish characters; but she hardly ever allowed herself to be
carried away by the warmth of emotion. The roles in which I appeared with
her as a child were Johanna von Montfaucon, and Tamira in *The Judgment of
Solomon*. These she performed with great bravura. I admired her as Cleo-
patra, as the Sultana Palmira, and as the Countess Orsini in Lessing's *Emilia
Galotti*. With a special feeling of devotion I watched her last appearance in
this role, at the benefit performance which was given on the occasion of her
jubilee on May 31, 1823. With this she ended her brilliant artistic career and
took leave of a public which had recognized in her a sublime principle of
Beauty.

It would nowadays be difficult, even for us old folk, to estimate to what
degree her performances were inspired by genius or were the result of thorough study. Ideas about dramatic diction, for which the French classical tragedies had partly served as the model, have through the years undergone considerable modification. At that time, an instinct for acting, developed by
imitation and practice, prevailed over the aesthetic education. But on the
other hand, tradition was far richer than it is now. Life off the stage, especially in fashionable society, was much more colorful with its florid mannerisms. To control this, the school had a host of rules which occasionally tightened the reins on talent, although it served as useful support and guidance to
the inexperienced or less gifted actor. Therefore, while there may be divergent opinions about Mlle. Astrup's artistic importance, one thing is indisputable: she presented a dramatic personality which we seek in vain to find
among the younger generation.

She retired at an advanced age with her full salary in pension, together with an indemnity to cover the loss of her beloved porter's lodge, which was now to be torn down to make room for facilities which a number of years later were again replaced by the vulgar mass of walls which at last had to give way in 1874 to a triumphing sense of Beauty.

The last relics of the Danish Temple of the Muses vanished from the site which had been inaugurated by our immortal Holberg, and where such great talents have flowered. O! would that this noble art had transferred its Penates to the new Playhouse, which in its elegance rises so close to the old site, where one looks out upon this magnificent quarter while one's thoughts linger on Gammelholm . . . the canal . . . and the life that once went on in that neighborhood.

ANTOINE BOURNONVILLE

(Born in Lyon May 19, 1760; died at Fredensborg January 11, 1843)

A beloved father's image, which has hovered before me my whole life through and assumes an important place in my theatrical memoirs, has certainly been mentioned in connection with my personal affairs. But since he has an obvious place in this series of biographical sketches and has left no records of his rich experiences other than those I have been able to gather from letters and verbal accounts, there is no one better qualified than myself to set them down in writing. Moreover, since the *objective* form is probably the most suitable, let us pretend that it is not a son but a foreign author who here furnishes a contribution to the history of Art.

Shortly after returning to Paris, the French writer and regular contributor to *Le Siècle*, Oscar Comettant, who during our unsuccessful war in 1864 had sojourned partly on Als and partly in Copenhagen, published a book entitled *Denmark as it Is*. In this work, besides expressing great sympathy for the Danish cause, Comettant also made pronouncements on a number of local matters with highly imperfect knowledge. Among other things, in describing our Theatre and the brilliance with which the ballet appears on the stage, he names an old *émigré*, the Marquis de Bournonville, as the founder and compositor of this branch of art. From this it is clear that, as was the case with Vestris *père* and *fils*, he has lumped the older and the younger Bournonville together and then identified this amalgamated personage with Pierre de Riel, Marquis de B., who had actually been an officer in the army of *émigrés* under the Prince de Condé and was later, at the time of the Restoration, appointed Maréchal de France (died 1821).

The name is an ancient one and stems from Picardy.[*] It is often

[*]Bournonville is not always accurate when recounting the facts of his family history. The interested reader should therefore consult the well-documented articles written by his grandson, Paul Bournonville: *"Bidrag till den Bournonvilleska familjens historia,"* Personalhistorisk Tidskrift (Copenhagen, 1935) and *"Antoine Bournonville, hans hustrur och avkomlingar,"* Personalhistorisk Tidskrift (Copenhagen, 1937).

mentioned in the history of the dukes of Burgundy and, as the result of (matrimonial) alliances, has been borne by many noble families, such as the above-mentioned Riel, Dartois, Lameth, and Esmengard. But as early as the beginning of the previous century the name the Frenchman calls *le nom patronimique* ceases to figure in Court as well as war bulletins. On the other hand, in the Cathedral of Amiens three generations of that name have served as organists and *Kapellmeisters*. Among them, Valentin and his grandson, Jacques de B., have distinguished themselves as composers of church music (*vide Biographie universelle des musiciens*). The latter died in the year 1758, at the age of eighty-one, and was the brother of Antoine's grandfather, Louis de B. (*lieutenant de vaisseau*), who was commissioned in 1735, decorated with the Order of St. Louis in 1742, and died in Brest the following year.

Louis de Bournonville had two sons: Charles Jérôme, a member of the *Garde du corps (compagnie de Luxembourg)* who was decorated in 1772 (*vide Histoire de l'ordre de St. Louis*), and Amable Louis (*Employé dans les vivres de l'Armée*), who took over the management of the large theatre in Lyon, married the popular actress Jeanne Ebrard, and, when the enterprise failed, abandoned both wife and children. They were now forced to seek employment in the theatre. Julie, the eldest of five brothers and sisters, was a superb dancer, and when she was engaged at the Court Theatre in Vienna, she brought thither her brothers Théodore and Antoine that they might enjoy the instruction of the renowned balletmaster and writer, Noverre.

Antoine was nine years old at the time, and his marked talent was noted and led to his being chosen the leading dancer in a children's ballet commissioned by the Hungarian magnate Count Palfy. This was given at Pressburg, where, under Noverre's direction and together with the Count's own children, a festive spectacle was performed in honor of Hungary's queen, the Empress Maria Theresa.

The splendor and Oriental lavishness that were here displayed bordered on the fantastic. The small pupils were dressed and treated in princely fashion, and both the magnificent arrangement and the costly gifts amounted to fabulous sums. Amidst these delights, which lasted for three weeks, several remarkable proofs of the Empress's magnanimity were revealed—among others, the following true romantic episode.

Noverre had an only son, who held a commission in the Austrian army. His colonel, a man as narrow-minded as he was brutish, had on a public occasion and in a most scornful manner thrown up to him the fact that he was *bourgeois* and the son of a *dancing master* to boot. A biting reply and a duel were the result. With a thrust of his sword, Séricourt (the Christian name under which the young Noverre served as lieutenant) dispatched the offender to the other world and was carried off in chains to the fortress of Spielberg, there to await the most severe sentence.

Maria Theresa, who had learnt the true facts of the case and had been seeking an opportunity to honor and reward the artist who had so often added luster her Court festivals, gave him proof of her appreciation by bestowing upon him a precious diamond ring, at the same time handing him a document that contained his son's pardon—with his dismissal from military service, of course.

Antoine's older brother Théodore died shortly after their return, due to overindulgence in a life of luxury—*Slaraffenliv*—at the Count's palace. But Antoine developed his gifts by studying the finest models to be found in all scenic métiers, which were then flourishing in the theatres of Vienna. At the same time, he enjoyed a comparatively good and Christian upbringing. He had reached the age of sixteen when, together with his sister, he was engaged at the Court Theatre in Cassel, where their mother came to live with them and continued to reside until her death in 1798. Here he danced for three years, leaving in 1779 to go to Paris, where he once again encountered his old teacher and, together with Gardel and the younger Vestris, appeared in his ballets. He was, however, summoned to London and thence to Stockholm (1782), where his sister Julie shortly afterward married a French physician, M. Alix de la Faye, and quitted the stage.

In Sweden's capital, favored and protected by the art-loving Gustav III, Antoine Bournonville enjoyed the ten happiest years of his life. At a time when people set such great store by "elegant dancers," he was justly reckoned among the foremost in his profession; for in addition to possessing considerable virtuosity and an expressive countenance, he was also uncommonly handsome. Onstage as well as off, he comported himself with a certain innate nobility that fully compensated for the little *de* he had voluntarily renounced for himself and his posterity, partly out of regard for his modest position and fortune, and partly out of sympathy for the [revolutionary] ideas that were already beginning to emerge.

Although he had spent very little time in his native land, he was nevertheless, in language as well as in manner, a true *chevalier français* of the old school: emotional, high-spirited, and courageous. Often hotheaded, he was easily carried away by enthusiasm but was a hater of argument and a decided opponent of criticism. Nonetheless he was a man of his word, loyal, solid in his affairs, a good and helpful comrade, and, though often embroiled in violent conflicts, he never bore anyone a grudge. Endowed with several other pleasing talents, during his sojourn in Stockholm he came into contact with Sweden's most celebrated *beaux esprits,* men like Oxenstjerna, Creutz, Leopold, Kellgren, and—lest we forget—the ingenious Bellman, who more than once improvised ballads to Bournonville's dance melodies.

He always retained his memories of those "happy days," which could furnish material for a most interesting *novelle,* and Bournonville never uttered the great Gustav's name without tears of graditude and an ardor which became a legacy to his children.

Some weeks before the horrible catastrophe at the masked ball at the Opera,† Bournonville obtained permission to undertake a *kunstreise* to London. En route, he stopped over in Copenhagen, where he made a much-applauded guest appearance. He was assisted by the *Solodandserinde* Mme. Bjørn and by the pretty Mlle. Jensen, who was employed with equal success in both drama and ballet. And here was ensnared the butterfly who up to his thirty-second year had regarded his free bachelorhood as the true ideal of life! Mariane Jensen fastened the inconstant artist to Danish soil and soon became Madame Bournonville.

The abominable assassination of the King had cast a pall of sorrow over all Sweden, and with Gustav's death his happy Temple of the Muses grew dark and empty. The Danish Theatre now made Antoine Bournonville an advantageous offer, and after a series of brilliant debut performances the contract lay ready for his signature, when a curious incident nearly ruined everything.

Upon receiving news of the recapture of Toulon, the commissaries of the French Republic in Copenhagen, Messrs. Delamarre and Castera, issued invitations to a grand ball to be held at Rauch's (the present Hôtel d'Angleterre). The invitations were stamped with the device "LIBERTÉ, ÉGALITÉ, FRATERNITÉ," and it goes without saying that Bournonville was among the guests. Everything was splendid and gay, and the quadrilles followed one another in lively succession. At length, when the orchestra struck up "Ça ira, ça ira" (an old Rococo *contredanse* which had now become the war song of the *sans-culottes*), Bournonville was asked to devise a cotillion to this melody. Since this was something brand new, he improvised that figure, now so frequently used, of passing beneath uplifted arms, and won general applause. But by the next day the cavilers (who were by no means inferior to those of our own day) had seized upon this innocent motif and spread it abroad that the aforementioned cotillion had been intended to reproduce a picture of the guillotine! This interpretation, as stupid as it was malicious, arose mainly out of the envy of the advantages that had been offered the foreign dancer and had a most discouraging influence upon the Court, which saw revolutionary tendencies therein. Count Ahlefeldt, head of the Theatre at that time, was ordered to inform B. that the suspended negotiations must now be regarded as definitely broken off. All his protests and attempts to convince the Count of his innocence were in vain. The only answer Bournonville received was a shrug of the shoulder, and he now had to resign himself to returning to Stockholm. There, to be sure, he found his old sphere of activity—but the stimulating spirit had vanished with Gustav III!

However, the unpleasant misunderstanding in Denmark was soon resolved, and since B. longed to see his wife and child, negotiations were resumed. As a result of the bonds which now held the man prisoner in his prospective home, the terms of the contract became somewhat less advantageous.

† I.e., the murder of the King by Anckarström, March 16, 1792.

ANTOINE BOURNONVILLE
Oil portrait from the 1780's by Per Krafft the Elder.
Private collection.

HANS CHRISTIAN ANDERSEN
Engraving by Borgen, n. d.
Det kgl. Bibliotek, Copenhagen.

ADAM OEHLENSCHLÄGER
Print by F. Sala & Co., n.d.
Det kgl. Bibliotek, Copenhagen.

From now on, he was a Danish citizen body and soul, and, despite his earlier Republican sympathies, he remained loyal and devoted to the Royal House until his death.

The brilliance that surrounded his theatrical career was in sharp contrast to the great misfortune in his private life. After four years of marriage he lost his beloved wife and was left a widower with three small children; his eldest son died a cripple; while two hard fires and some unsuccessful speculations devoured the small fortune he had managed to amass in Stockholm. Yet he retained uncommon efficacy and *joie de vivre,* and at the age of forty still possessed all the freshness and vigor of a young man.

Seized with the general patriotic fervor, he enrolled in 1801 in the King's Corps of Volunteers, and at the side of his friend Du Puy showed himself a fine soldier. The love he bore his art and the good taste that guided his method were truly exemplary. But his powers of invention were limited only to detail; however, these details contributed essentially to the enrichment of the Galeottian ballets. His talents were not suited to developing broad-scale subjects that called for complicated and elaborate dramatic plots. For this reason his small ballets, *The Country Miller* [*Landsbymølleren*], *The Gallant Gardener* [*Den galante Gartner*], and *The Fishermen* [*Fiskerne*] must rather be classed as *divertissements.*

What mainly distinguished his performances was his superb mime, which, influenced by the impressions he had received in his youth from men such as Garrick, Lekain, and Monvel, was independent of the universally accepted ballet gesticulation and had a decided influence upon the dramatic stage as well as on the school that later developed in the Danish Ballet. Tragic figures such as Ghengis Kahn, Æneas, Telemachus, Regnar, Othar, Don Enrico of Trastamare, Raoul Barbe-Bleue, Romeo, and Macbeth were sufficient to establish his fame as one of the most excellent mimes of his day.

After Galeotti's death in 1816, Bournonville was appointed *Dandsedirecteur,* with orders to maintain the old repertoire. This task had its difficulties, since most of those who held the leading roles were older people, and B. himself, though he had remarkable vitality and still served as *Første Solodandser,* was nevertheless far beyond the age at which such feats excite the interest of the public.

In 1820 he journeyed to Paris, whence he brought back several little novelties. But it soon appeared that in his sixty-first year he was as little fitted to move with the times as he was to breathe life into the old works. However, his school did form a lovely *corps de ballet,* even though it did not contain any dancers of outstanding ability (his son August was still an adolescent and later attended the school of Vestris). At last, when in 1823 the number of older members of the ballet was radically reduced, Bournonville retired, retaining the greater portion of his salary in pension.

He now enjoyed a pleasant and long old age, and since he still maintained a lively interest in the theatre and art in general, he divided his time between his beloved family and his favorite authors, among whom Voltaire occupied an important place. However, the theistic philosophy of the latter was incapable of supplanting the childhood faith that B. had had impressed upon him by his early Catholic upbringing. All the same, he did not believe in Papal supremacy but read his prayers from the Reformed Devotion Books. His sincere religiosity was expressed by gratitude toward Providence, reconciliation toward his enemies, and open-handed beneficence. He had a saying with regard to the faults he recognized in himself: "One can reform at any age"—and in this honest endeavor he endured well into his eighty-third year.

He spent his final days in rural tranquillity at Fredensborg Castle, where his dearly beloved King Frederik VI had allotted him a comfortable free residence. Here he properly enjoyed the evening of his life, surrounded by a faithful wife and the children of this second marriage, for his eldest daughter Gustava had died in 1831 and her brother Antoine was living as a physician in Philadelphia (died 1862).‡

His last artistic enjoyment was *Napoli,* which had such an extraordinary success in the spring of 1842. This ballet delighted the old man to such a degree that as a token of his unconditional approval he bestowed upon the author—who was none other than his own son—the same precious diamond ring he had received from the *Tjusarekungen*° himself at a performance of the opera *Gustav Vasa.* Some months later a progressive weakness set in, eventually ending in a painless death.

While with sacred trust his soul was released from its earthly bonds, his fantasies conjured up hosts of graceful little children who appeared to him to dance about his bed. Though speaking only in disjointed phrases, he addressed them in a friendly manner, as he reached out for pretty young damsels clad in white, who, to his dreaming eyes, hovered at the foot of his bed!

He lies buried in Asminderød Churchyard, where Love erected a monument in his honor.

MARGARETHE SCHALL, *neé* SCHLEÜTER

(Born in Copenhagen October 6, 1775; died November 24, 1852)

THIS *Solodandserinde,* especially popular both in her own day and for many years afterward and enthusiastically referred to by our parents, was the sort of phenomenon we read about in ancient tales and knightly romances, where a swan-shift, a ring, or some other secret amulet not only warded off danger and

‡ The odyssey of Dr. Antoine Bournonville, founder of the American branch of the Bournonville family, is a fascinating one. Born in Copenhagen in 1797, he was the oldest surviving son of the dancer Antoine Bournonville and his first wife, Mariane Jensen. While a medical student at the University of Copenhagen, he was arrested for having participated in a series of robberies and was subsequently imprisoned. Upon his release, he set sail for the United States, settled in Philadelphia, and became a prominent physician and citizen there. He died in that city in February 1863.

°The sobriquet of *"l'irrésistible,"* which the Swedes had given Gustav III.—A.B.

violence, but covered all imperfections with a magic veil and captured hearts with irresistible might. Such sorcery seemed to be present here, for a disproportionately large head with hair clipped *à la Titus,* rather commonplace facial features, in addition to short, strong legs with long feet, could hardly be called ideal beauty — least of all in one of Terpsichore's chosen daughters. But a very lovely pair of arms, a buxom figure in the Wiedeweltian mode, and a high degree of agility gave Mme. Schall's person a pleasing quality that involuntarily enraptured spectators and was beautifully to portray gay peasant girls, shepherdesses, gypsies, and other character parts with national dancing. Though her parents were poor and her education neglected (as was the case with most of her fellow-artists), she possessed, in conjunction with the humor and "mother-wit" that are so often found in the common people of Copenhagen, a rare tact and power of observation, an ease in expressing herself, and a certain ability to be in turn imposing and enchanting.

As far as the actual technique of dancing is concerned: she had acquired hardly as much as is nowadays asked of students before they may take part in a *ballabile.* Moreover, she prided herself on not having undertaken in twenty-five years a single one of the type of exercises which are deemed absolutely necessary for the maintenance of skill. All the same, every time she appeared, she brought to the stage a liveliness and fantasy which partially, at least, made up for her deficiency in lightness and aplomb. Her main strength seemed to lie in skipping up and down on the stage — a footrace that was regarded as a rather unique kind of virtuosity. Her surviving contemporaries tell "how Mme. Schall's feet moved under her like a pair of drumsticks."

To judge from this picture, one might doubt whether her personality or talent would be suitable for the portrayal of leading tragic roles. Thus she had already reached a rather mature age when she replaced Mlle. Birouste as Thora in the ballet *Lagertha* and Mlle. Lauerwaldt as Isaure in *Raoul Barbe-Bleue.* Although with regard to external excellence and choreographic skill she was considerably inferior to her predecessors, she far surpassed them in tragic forcefulness and inspiration; for at a time when a "touching" performance had not yet come into disfavor, she possessed the gift of being able to elicit tears from both her own and the spectators' eyes!

But such roles did not cause her to neglect her comic repertoire; and whether she portrayed the fisher girl or the shoemaker's wife, Nina's madness or Juliet's eternal love, she won applause, favor, and fame because she always had that "inexplicable something" which, as in the myth of the belt of Venus, exercised a magical attraction.

She remained throughout an entire generation the ballet's chosen prima donna, thereby retarding the development of younger aspirants, partly because of Galeotti's predilection for his pupil, and partly because of the right of seniority, which at that time was such a determining factor. Small wonder, then, that with the weakening of the older cast the ballet repertoire languished and disappeared from the stage!

Mme. Schall, who for some years had made only scattered appearances, retired with full pension in 1827, after forty years of service—a career which, I dare say, has neither before nor since been granted any *danseuse!* Her years of apprenticeship and her debut took place in a period which people (no doubt very improperly) still call "the good old days"—an age that had a greater wealth of original characters than original creativity, and one in which not only the theatre but the entire social life furnished rich material for quasi-romantic *novelles* which would hardly be consistent with our current ideas and least of all with our present-day theatre morals and customs.

Margarethe Schleüter was married at a very early age to Andreas Schall, a musician in the Royal Orchestra, whose insobriety precipitated a speedy divorce and soon afterward put an end to his life. The young widow now felt free and independent, and, following the tide, furnished abundant contributions to its *"Chronique galante."* Like Aspasia of antiquity, she continued to be the public's, even the ladies', darling; and until she was quite old, she, like the famous Ninon de Lenclos, continued to enjoy her pleasures at the same time as she strove to atone for her amiable little sins by extensive charity. She was the solace of the poor, saved many a fallen person from despair, and often, by her counsel and admonitions, sustained courage in tempted Virtue. To the last, she retained the liveliest interest in the theatre and a childlike reverence for her old master's memory.

FREDERIK TORKILDSON WEXSCHALL

(Born in Copenhagen April 9, 1798; died October 25, 1845)

HIS father Thorkild Wexhal, a Norwegian farmer's son, came down to Denmark as a conscript to serve in the Life Guards, where, in consideration of his self-taught playing upon the Hardanger fiddle, he was engaged as a fifer. Since he also served as officers' batman, he caused a stir by furnishing his captain (Franz v. Bülow, later renowned as Adjutant-general) with the shiniest boots in the whole Guard. This attracted the attention of the Crown Prince and he was promoted to the post of *Stadsjæger* to Frederik VI. In this capacity he accompanied the King to the Congress of Vienna, where he succeeded in finding a splendid Amati violin, which His Majesty purchased for him to give to his son, who as a boy of seven had already played at Court concerts under the direction of Professor Lehm. But it was mainly through *Concertmester* Timroth's superb training that young Wexhal's talent developed into virtuosity. And yet, despite the fact that everywhere he harvested the liveliest applause, he obtained only the modest place of younger *second violin* in the Royal Orchestra; not so much because of the current system of seniority, but because the all-powerful Claus Schall had a nephew who, though extremely mediocre, sat highest on the *Primo* side and performed all *obbligato* numbers—a tribute to the prevailing nepotism—while Wexhal's universally recognized skill was reduced to subordinate service. However, this did not hinder all concert-givers from requesting Wexhal's assistance, and moreover, he was unanimously declared the most brilliant violinist our country had produced.

In 1819 he obtained a Royal travel stipend, which he used to study his art with the greatest celebrities of the day: Spohr in Cassel and Baillot in Paris. In Vienna he met the ingenious Pechatscheck, whose playing had a great influence upon his musical interpretation.

In Paris he attracted attention and won great applause by performing Maurer's well-known *Concerto in A Major* in the "Concert Spirituel," which was given during Lent of 1820 at the Théâtre de l'Opéra. The *Journal des Débats* acclaimed the Danish virtuoso in its musical *feuilleton,* while transforming his Old Norwegian name, Wexhal, into the French Wexschall. This increase of letters was retained, perhaps not without a little play on words—to tease (*vexer*) Schall?—for he now triumphed over the man who, most unjustly, wished to place his talent in the shade.

He returned to his home a celebrated artist, gave a number of brilliant concerts, and was the first in this country to play Spohr's famous *Cantilena* (the singing scene) with great bravura. Something special now had to be done for this outstanding talent, and those responsible thought they had given him striking proof of recognition by placing him at the head of the second violins and appointing him *répétiteur* at the Dancing School—next in line to the ever conspicuous *nephew!*

He still held this humble position in 1823 when he married the gifted young actress Anna Brenøe, later so eminent as Mme. Wexschall. This outstanding artistic couple, though less suited to one another in intellectual direction and character, nevertheless for eight whole years maintained a fine and exemplary household, made a good impression, entertained a select circle of the finest minds of the day, and were blessed with a sweet little daughter. In short, it seemed to the eyes of the world that they enjoyed life's greatest happiness, when suddenly the word "divorce" sounded for all of us like a bolt out of the blue!

Although this kind of domestic event ought not to concern art and should exercise no influence on the feelings of the theatregoing public, the story nevertheless had a highly injurious effect and dimmed to no small degree the nimbus which had hitherto radiated about this outstanding *artiste.* In spite of her ever progressing gift for interpreting the most varied emotions and characters, she never again won, as Mme. Nielsen, the sympathies which had been hers in her earlier career. However, Wexschall's loss was irreparable, for he was alienated from that poetic nature which had spurred him on to higher artistic endeavors.

He had not yet realized that in addition to the skill that is required to reproduce the ingenious works of other composers, something more is demanded of the virtuoso: he must furnish something independent of them, by which his unique ability can assert itself. It is therefore to be lamented that, like our excellent violoncellist, Frederik Funck, he did not write and leave behind a single composition for his instrument. His existence as a musician would have been consigned to eternal oblivion had his contemporaries not striven to recall to the memory of the younger generation the interesting qualities that denoted his personality and his talent.

Freshness, humor, and a considerable force—which sometimes degenerated into rudeness—characterized him as a human being and violinist. It would have been desirable for him to have acquired more harmonic theory in the Realm of Sound, and some sound knowledge in the School of Life. It is also to be wished that in the area of composition he had been able to develop the same fantasy and power of invention that always seasoned his precious narratives and amusing anecdotes! Nature had richly endowed him; training would undoubtedly have produced superb results. As it was, he could win all hearts by a warmth and willingness that led him to work as readily for charitable causes as to participate in hunting or pleasure parties. He was a capital comrade, and his merits as a teacher secure him a memory among the younger generation.

The fine points that distinguished his playing were a full tone, great dexterity, and an uncommon right arm (bow). Enthusiastic and grandiose in the first *Allegro,* he could be both gentle and sad in the *Adagio.* But it was mainly in the *Scherzo* that he had his strength, and whether he executed this part in Spohr's quintets or in Pechatscheck's solo-quartets, it was impossible to resist his fresh, sparkling humor; aye, if one can imagine wittiness in the art of sound, it was to be found here.

As *Concertmester* in charge of the Orchestra String Quartet—a position which his superiority eventually earned him—he had an electrifying effect upon the whole and was an invaluable support for the *Capelmester.* He was also one of the fine and partly unreplaced talents of his time. I myself enjoyed his instruction for several years, and later took great pleasure in seeing him at the rehearsals of my ballets.

His all too early demise left an emotional gap, and from his second marriage there remained only a daughter with the woeful name of "Orpheline." But she had her father's musical talent as a legacy and was raised by her uncle—our outstanding opera singer, Schramm—who has been like a father to her and whose name she has taken by adoption.

HANS CHRISTIAN ANDERSEN

(Born in Odense April 2, 1805; died in Copenhagen August 4, 1875)

EVEN though this world-famous writer has, in the *Fairy Tale of his Life,* furnished a detailed autobiography which vividly depicts the events that led him, through struggle and adversity, to the goal he coveted and to achievements beyond his expectations, our personal relationship (which has been partly advertised in our published letters) offers a number of features that might be of some interest to those who lovingly preserve his memory.

As a boy of thirteen, his most ardent desire upon arriving in Copenhagen was to be engaged at the Theatre in any capacity at all. He was brought to my parents' home, where he was presented to my father as an aspirant for the ballet. However, his lanky figure and angular movements seemed little suited to the dance, leading my father to ask him if he might not prefer the spoken drama. The young lad thereupon asked permission to recite one of his poems. I do not remember its contents, but this much is certain: I immediately had an impression of genius; and far from finding him ridiculous, it appeared to me that he was getting the best of us rather than the other way around.

A short time later he appeared as a singing pupil of Siboni, was used by Dahlén as a Troll in the ballet *Armida,* sang in the chorus, and also figured as a Brahmin in the opera *Lanassa.* At length his industrious patrons tore him away from the tempting world of the theatre. His humanistic education was provided for, and while he divided his time and his thoughts between the classroom and the art of poesy, he became a university student and, with a certain amount of authority, presented himself as an author.

Upon returning after an absence of six years, I found Andersen fully occupied with scaling "the Danish Parnassus." His poems and tales were being read in family circles and declaimed at evening entertainments at the Royal Theatre. *A Walking Trip to Amager,* the first volume of versified tales, and, above all, the lovely poem, "The Dying Child," were universally acclaimed and aroused the highest expectations. The arresting quality to be found in these works, in the midst of the most flowering period of our poetic literature, caused the critics to emphasize with unusual harshness the shortcomings that were to be found in both the form and style of this young author, who, as a novice, had wished to be treated more leniently, and as a result was painfully affected. Nevertheless he continued his endeavors, the fruits of which all bore the unmistakable stamp of originality in spite of individual weak points. Almost as soon as he had finished drafting a new work, he had an absolute passion for reading it in those circles where he knew that people were fond of him and favored his Muse. Although he recited his creations in a highly unique fashion, it cannot be denied that many would have preferred to hear them after they had been clothed in their final dress—that is to say, upon their publication. I dare say these preliminary readings were intended more for the author to express himself than to learn the opinion of his listeners; for the suggestions and objections that might possibly be mingled with the enthusiastic applause went completely unnoticed!

Conferentsraad Collin, who was his faithful protector and whose house was Andersen's second home, secured him a stipend which enabled him to travel for several years. And while his indefatigable critics and those who envied him here at home sent him one unpleasant estimate of his work after another, under the blazing sun of the South he wrote his *Improvisatore,* which as a richly colorful picture of life in Italy assumed a worthy place at the side Mme. de Staël's *Corinne* at the same time as it assured its author an honorable place among our first novelists.

He returned home covered with praise, met with universal recognition, and produced with varying success dramas, comedies, *vaudevilles*, opera texts, and novels. He also made frequent trips to Germany, where he was fêted by princes and dignitaries alike. He had his works translated into German, and from this language into most of the European tongues, hereby winning a renown as extensive as any of our most outstanding contemporaries.

But what primarily consolidated this renown were his fairy tales and stories. As if drawn from an Aladdin's lamp, these stories flowed from his imaginative pen; and side by side with a singular naïveté in presentation, there lay hidden a core of morality and satire, aye, often a characteristic feature of his own personality. They were essentially different from other fairy tales by virtue of the fact that while they amused or entertained children, they also inclined older people to serious reflection.

The majority of these somewhat humorous fables were read, newborn, in our family circle amidst laughter, tears, and cries of approval. But what should especially be emphasized is that three of his loveliest tales, "The Ugly Duckling," "The Nightingale," and "The Angel," were inspired by Jenny Lind during her stay in our home, where Andersen was at that time a daily guest and madly in love with the great singer, whose inspired performances as Norma, Alice, Lucia, and the Daughter of the Regiment roused everyone to an enthusiasm which seemed almost supernatural. Andersen was one of the most strongly affected, and in the space of a few days brought us his delightful works, each of which had its special meaning. "The Ugly Duckling" alluded to his own nature and singular destiny; "The Nightingale," to Jenny Lind; and "The Angel"—whom he really meant by this I shall not say. But in Kaulbach's lovely picture, "The Angel" became a celestial figure who on outspread wings brought Andersen's *Fairy Tales* over land and sea, to the farthest shores of America and to Sakuntalā's homeland, the distant Hindustan.

Our relationship was at all times friendly and sincere. I saw in him a singular phenomenon, admired his genius, and understood his feverish desire for fame—a desire that so many call *vanity!* He could also be enthusiastic about the merits or rewards received by others. He delighted in my activity, that is to say, when my works were successful; for he shamefacedly avoided me if the hoped-for success had failed to appear. It was because of this that I wrote a poem of consolation for him, called "The Poet's Tree," when his little play *The Bird in the Pear Tree* had been a fiasco at the Royal Theatre.

Nemesis struck him yet another time when he visited Oehlenschläger and the latter enthusiastically greeted him, holding a book he had just been reading. Andersen believed that this happiness was occasioned by his *Ahasuerus*, but was considerably disappointed when it turned out to be none other than *My Theatre Life*, whose little eccentricities he had just been poking fun at!

The acclaim he received in his older days from high and low alike, the distinctions of every kind that were bestowed upon him, and the height of fame that he achieved, never altered his childlike, good-natured disposition. On the other hand, he was unable to soften his bitterness toward his critics or to efface the memory of earlier injuries. He was certainly envied by many, and there were those who could not accept his services to the Danish art of poesy. For all that, the critics left him in peace, and treated with reverence the weaker creations that denoted the approach of old age.

As a bachelor, he missed the joys and comforts of domestic and family life, for which his friends tried to compensate by an exemplary hospitality. In noble manor houses as well as in highly respected bourgeois homes, he was cared for, admired, aye, even indulgently spoiled as people bore with his peculiarities, which increased with old age. But foremost among these loving friends, in the last years of his life, were the Melchiors, who surrounded him with sisterly and brotherly tenderness and in whose arms he passed away.

In order to delight him on his seventieth birthday, a plan was undertaken to erect a bronze statue in his honor. A public subscription was requested, and they wished to see my name as one of his oldest friends on the list of those inviting people to subscribe. But I was sorry to admit that while I would gladly have gone along with any other mark of honor, it was against my convictions to apotheosize a man who was still living, and, feeling safe from any misunderstanding, I submitted the reason for my refusal in writing. However, the request met with the liveliest support from every class and throughout the nation. And since I too have willingly given my contribution to the cause, I shall take great pleasure in seeing the statue in the Rosenborg Gardens, surrounded by young folk who have delighted in reading *Andersen's Fairy Tales.*

JOHAN FREDERIK FRØHLICH

(Born in Copenhagen April 21, 1806; died May 21, 1860)

NEITHER during his lifetime nor after his death was this outstanding artist, whose rare skill was so brilliantly displayed on so many occasions, given the place that he deserved among our musical celebrities. Perhaps the reason for this may be ascribed to Frøhlich's modesty or to a certain peculiarity which caused him to underestimate his own compositions, only the smallest part of which passed into the music shops and thence to the public. Time and space do not permit me to enumerate these scattered works; but it is the duty of a biographer to bring to light a hitherto unnoticed treasure and to evoke a picture of an artistic career which was halted all too soon but which has left behind both precious and instructive memories.

The youngest son of a poor German musician, and christened in the Catholic Chapel, before he was old enough to read by rote he was already holding a violin so as to be able, in the course of time, to assist his father as fiddler at the dancing halls! But some kind Fate willed that his older sister should marry the Royal Orchestra musician Frederik Kittler (who was highly regarded for his military music and was the creator of both the "Banner March" and the "Tattoo"). This ingenious and practical musician looked after his little brother-in-law, gave him sound instruction in playing both piano and violin, and also trained him as a flautist, in which capacity he was heard by the Royal family at a concert in the Cannon Foundry as early as the year 1812.

Despite the applause he harvested at such a young age, his career would have been extremely humble if a noble patron, Chamberlain Berg of Nørager, had not taken an interest in the gifted lad, provided for him to be sent to a good grammar school, and also recommended him to the excellent guidance of *Concertmester* Schall. He now made such rapid progress in both places that by the time he reached his fifteenth year he was able to join the Royal Orchestra as a salaried musician, where his general education was superior to that of most of his older colleagues.

It could hardly fail that this clever young man would draw the attention of both masters and dilettantes and find himself drawn to stars of such eminent magnitude as Kuhlau and Weyse, through whose superb compositions and friendly instruction Frøhlich was gradually initiated into the mysteries of counterpoint and the use of instruments. At the same time as he acquired the thorough musicianship of these great masters, he developed independently and managed to retain his own unique style.

It was a different matter with his views on life, which were strongly influenced by Weyse's stoicism—that is, his lack of enthusiasm for and indifference to the praise of the world. Frøhlich was hardly past his youth before he had succeeded in passing himself off, if not exactly as an eccentric, then at least as a person who was very different in many respects. But just as he was involuntarily carried away by expressive virtuosity in his quartet playing, when it had been his intention to remain cold and colorless, so too in daily life, though striving to appear aloof, he nevertheless made himself beloved and sought out by all who came in contact with him.

As Chorus Master of the Royal Theatre, he brought this branch of opera to a hitherto unknown perfection. By popular request he undertook to write the music for an operetta; but it was mainly as an instrumental composer that he was to win distinction. His pieces for the flute and French horn, as well as his quartets and overtures, aroused the highest expectations; and in 1829 he obtained a travel stipend for further training in Germany, Italy, and France. We met in Paris, where he learnt of the cool reception his operetta *The Night Before the Wedding* [*Natten før Brylluppet*] had met with from the Copenhagen audience. This disappointment suddenly opened his eyes to the path he must now follow as a musician. He used his stay in this great world capital to draft a number of valuable compositions which won lively recognition from old Cherubini and young Halévy as well as the talented horn player Dauprat, with whom Frøhlich later kept up a musical correspondence.

But here let me relate a characteristic episode from Frøhlich's Parisian life. It had originally been his intention to remain in Paris for six months; but since half of his financial resources had already been consumed by the end of the first month, he determined to fight his way through the last five with the least possible expenditure, by lodging in a garret in the Latin Quarter and taking his midday meal in the Rue de Laharpe at the well-known "Flicotot" — (a classic feature of all novels concerning student life).

On his return, he once again assumed his modest position. He gave a public concert, where the new pieces he had brought with him from Paris were performed, applauded, praised, and shortly thereafter consigned to oblivion. Frøhlich, with his stoic ideal ever before him, now seemed to have given up all dazzling illusions and became completely engrossed in his official duties, his quartet playing, and teaching.

Then I came to have need of his help, and requested his collaboration with the ballets *Nina* and *The Tyroleans*. Partly by reason of his temperament, and influenced partly by the prejudices of others, he cherished but little sympathy for this type of art; consequently he undertook the work half in jest, as if to prove how far a balletmaster's absurdity could go in musical respects. But he soon discovered that my conception of the nature of the ballet offered a wide field for the kind of situations that corresponded with his particular direction. It was therefore with joyous surprise that the public perceived a wealth of melody and fullness in instrumentation which showed that here he had come into his proper sphere. Through this successful collaboration a fraternal relationship sprang up between us, which proved to be as pleasant for us as it was fruitful for art.

The ballet *Valdemar* was performed for the first time in honor of Queen Marie's birthday on October 28, 1835. The applause it received was intended as much for the music composer as it was for the ballet-poet and the excellent performance. For many years this successful work retained its freshness and popularity as a genuine national product.

The following year, Frøhlich was appointed orchestra leader with the title of *Concertmester,* since it was still not considered possible for a native-born Dane to bear the title of *Capelmester.* No sooner had he received this appointment than he suffered an accident that was to prove the fateful turning point in his career. While returning home from a church concert, he fell in the street and broke his right arm! Hardly recovered, and despite all warnings, he set out upon a lengthy foot tour of Jutland and thereby brought on a weakness which had an effect upon his whole future.

Among his outstanding characteristics was the fact that once he had taken a decision it was to be carried through no matter what stood in the way of its accomplishment. If a score had to be ready by a fixed day and time, he could not rest until he had signed his three Freemasons' crosses on the last bar of his composition just as the clock struck the hour. If there was a movement of eight, or even three, bars in an opera or some other piece of music which had pleased him, he would go only to hear the aforesaid spot; and once that portion had passed, no earthly power could keep him there a minute longer. If he undertook a long walking tour, whether to Køge or Fredensborg, and had made up his mind to lunch at a particular inn on the way, even his best friends were unable to persuade him to come to their homes to refresh himself. *Enfin*, he had promised himself that as soon as his broken arm was healed, he would visit the west coast of Jutland. But instead of choosing the most imposing point on the North Sea, and afterward starting back to the delightful region of the east coast, he gave himself over to wandering along the dunes, right up to Skagen.

This exhausting tour had the result that when on his homeward journey he stopped to visit his old friend and benefactor [Chamberlain Berg] at Nøragergaard, his bodily resources were so overtaxed that he suffered a violent fit of apoplexy. In this lamentable state he was brought back to Copenhagen, with small hope of seeing him reclaimed for art.

A year went by, and his doctors advised a journey for the sake of his health. Since the frigate *Rota* was just going to fetch Thorvaldsen and his masterworks from Italy, Frøhlich sailed with it to the Mediterranean so that the sea air and the sight of that classical soil might refresh him in body and soul. This treatment succeeded beyond all expectation, and it was a memorable occasion when we saw Frøhlich debarking at Thorvaldsen's side—he seemed to have been born anew!

He now resumed his duties as conductor for the opera, and in the autumn of 1839 composed the music for the ballet *The Festival in Albano*. It was perhaps his loveliest work, with freshness and grace diffused throughout. A number of worthy subjects followed this opus, among others *The Childhood of Erik Menved*—a ballet whose dimensions, I dare say, exceeded the strengths of our mimic and theatrical forces, but which nonetheless enjoyed a series of well-attended performances. When young Erik a short while later became a full-grown girl and a number of the leading performers had scattered, this ballet disappeared from the repertoire and nothing remained but a single number, namely Frederik VII's favorite piece, the so-called "Riberhuusmarsch." This has now found its place in the later edition of *Valdemar* as "The Torch Dance."

Frøhlich's forces were not sufficient to withstand the strains and unavoidable difficulties which his position entailed; moreover, his stoicism was not genuine enough to enable him to withstand even the mildest of critical stings. His memory failed him, and his self-confidence (which had never been strong, even in his healthiest days) was now completely broken. At the end of the 1844 season he sought and obtained his retirement, with pension; but before doing so, he helped the head of the Royal Orchestra, *Overhofmarskal* Levetzau, with its reogranization, which required that a foreign musician become *Capelmester* at a salary considerably higher than that which could be granted a native-born Dane. The Saxon Frantz Glæser was now called in and, as a practiced musician and energetic conductor, became an able support for our already excellent orchestra, though in a number of respects he was far inferior to Frøhlich. In a rather short time, he was given both a title and decoration, while our talented countryman, unnoticed and unrewarded, withdrew without uttering a single complaint—but nevertheless with a broken heart.

After his retirement he did compose the music for my ballet *Raphael*. Despite its unfortunate breadth of structure, people again found his earlier tasteful instrumentation. But when the expected success was not forthcoming, he swore a solemn oath that he would nevermore compose ballet music! "But will you then write symphonies," I asked, "or songs, or other instrumental works?" To this he repeatedly answered, "No." "Then what *will* you do, my friend?" "I shall chew my finger nails." I left him, taking along the declaration that "he loved me as a *human being*, but hated me as a *balletmaster*"!

Unfortunately for art, he kept his word for a number of years, until Heiberg enticed him into orchestrating the homemade melodies for the *vaudevilles A Sunday on Amager* [*En Søndag paa Amager*], *The Monkey* [*Abekatten*], and *A Summer Evening* [*En Sommeraften*]. Bagatelles though they were, in them one could perceive his fine sense of harmony; but these were to be the last sparks of a talent which would have needed but a pinch of charlatanism in order to pass for genius. But, when all things are considered: in time, how much is really left of artistic renown? Among the revelations of the stage, as well as in the realm of sound, only a chosen few have had their names crowned with laurels. One pages through biographical lexicons which relate the careers of hundreds of famous people of whom the present now knows nothing. How many ingenious, painstakingly worked-out scores are gathering dust on the shelves of musical archives, lucky not to appear in retail shops as wrapping paper! And while insignificant ballads or dance melodies are often transmitted to the people and preserved for centuries as popular favorites, how many masterworks of the art of music are daily supplanted by fashionable clangor and the charivari of ravings!

From now on, my highly treasured colleague led only a vegetative life. He continued his solitary wanderings on the ramparts and out onto the highroad until a progressive paralysis forced him to remain indoors. He had long since withdrawn from those family circles in which he had always been so welcome. In his quiet home he was nursed by a loving sister, and received visits from a number of sympathetic friends. Among these there was one (the now-deceased Legationsraad Schmidt-Phiseldeck) who had a most beneficial influence upon his disposition, which had been bowed by such hard trials.

As an emancipated Catholic in the manner of the French moral philosophers, Frøhlich recognized the Law, but the Gospel seemed to be completely alien to him. Honor, duty, righteousness, and loyal faithfulness constituted his religion, and although he was warm in regard for his friends, he considered it hypocrisy to conceal or to combat the burning hatred he bore toward those who had offended him in one way or another. Therefore he only partly possessed the Christian virtues of Love and Faith, and as a result was lacking in Hope — for a very long time! And from this arose the bitterness and emptiness that he felt at the loss of his illusions.

That friend of his youth, who with a distinguished education and the noblest character combined a deep and sound religiosity, visited him every day during the years when Frøhlich was confined to his sickbed. He conversed with him for several hours at a time, and, at first dwelling on light subjects, he gradually moved on to more serious reading, paving the way for the Sacred Word which alone has the power to heal the wounds of the soul and give consolation to the sorrowful heart. It had a wondrous effect upon Frøhlich; for as his physical strength declined, his spiritual vision was enhanced and clarified. He once more looked at the world from the bright side, his acquired eccentricity gave way to the most spontaneous warmth, and, seeing him bear his heavy cross, one could learn a lesson in resignation to the will of God. His vigorous nature still had a long-lasting struggle to endure. Finally, on May 21, 1860 (while I was away on a trip), he breathed his last in the arms of his sister and his friend, in the blissful consolation that even if his memory should be obliterated from the history of art, he would not be forgotten by *the All-merciful!*

HANS CHRISTIAN LUMBYE

(Born on Funen May 2, 1810; died March 20, 1874)

RICHARD Wagner, the Apostle of the Music of the Future, whose penetrating observations on the art of music in general and the lyric drama in particular carry a certain weight, has in his book about opera and drama stated the opinion that on the whole music has but two definite means of expressing itself, namely, "singing and dancing." These two principal elements frequently intertwine, and dance music has the unmistakable advantage of also being singable. We therefore dare to state that few composers of dance music offer the wealth of melody that gushes forth from Lumbye's prolific inventions. One can apply to him the same judgment that Mme. Catalani expressed with regard to Henrietta Sontag: "She is the best in her genre, but her genre is not the best."

However, Fame cares nothing for the rank of art when she marks her chosen ones. Widespread renown is often won purely by accident, and often by those works that have taken the least invention and study. Thus it is beyond question that if Hans Christian Andersen's *Fairy Tales* (like the fables of La Fontaine) had been written in verse as perfect as Christian Winther's *Woodcut* [*Træsnit*] or Paludan-Müller's *Adam Homo*, they would have been limited to a circle of readers in the Scandinavian North by virtue of their being untranslatable. Almost the same thing would have befallen Lumbye if by counterpoint training he had become a thorough musician. While Andersen's *Fairy Tales* delighted both children and old folk in every country of the world, Lumbye enraptured the young with his dance melodies, which in their pure form do not need to be translated but express happiness in every tongue.

Far be it from me to compare two such different magnitudes, who stood in relation to one another as the Councillor of War to the Councillor of State. But, as I have stated, Genius does not ask for credentials. I therefore feel that if Lumbye's name is to be preserved in grateful memory, there is no one more entitled or more obligated to give him a place in these memoirs than *I*, who have so often been influenced and aided by his talent.

About forty years ago, when Strauss and Lanner from their orchestras in the Wienerprater and Folksgarten made the whole civilized world sway to the rhythm of their music, there was heard beneath our Danish beech trees a modest echo of these enchanting tones — but one with a characteristic touch of the domestic sound-board. These attempts gradually became more daring and soon resounded from ballrooms right down to the hurdygurdies. They were played at the changing of the Guard and piped by boys in the street. But no one suspected that the inventor of these lively strophes was the same trumpeter who, on his dapple gray, rode at the head of the Horse Guard's relief when at midday it passed through the city on its way to Amalienborg; and very few people knew that his pretty dances had been inspired and drafted in his narrow army quarters, which were still large enough to contain his Muse, his love, and a growing flock of children.

Like our ingenious Schall, Lumbye was musically self-taught. But a fortunate instinct for harmony and an accurate knowledge of the nature and effect of instruments gave his light compositions a sonority which, even if they did not satisfy the strictest demands, nevertheless pleased the ear and touched the heart.

Many would find it remarkable that there can be anything moving in an art form that essentially aims at producing gaiety; but *joy* itself has its deep well of poetry, at the bottom of which one often finds the precious pearls of tears. Therefore, if Lumbye's dances are to be characterized, it must be by the childlike merriness, the unaffected enthusiasm — one might almost call it the *divine naïveté* — that pervades their wholesome melodies. His stanzas of eight measures, which always followed each other with new and piquant variations, seemed to spring from an inexhaustible source and often formed the loveliest tone-pictures. And thus there appeared a host of dances, rather like a true profusion of flowers; some of them dedicated to female tutelary spirits, and others bound into garlands to salute a country, a people, a city — even the old Balletmaster!* These compositions have traveled around the

*Lumbye's galop "Salute to August Bournonville" was first performed at the Folketheater on March 6, 1869. Thereafter, according to Charlotte Bournonville (*Scattered Reminiscences*, p. 67), it became customary for Lumbye's Tivoli Orchestra to strike up the piece whenever "the old Balletmaster" was spotted in the crowd.

world, established Lumbye's reputation, and earned him honorable distinctions. From time to time these works have been stolen from him, and in foreign lands musicians have reaped praise by using his melodies without authorization. But one can as little mistake the sound of Lumbye's works as one can a distinctive accent, and our Danish hearts are quickened when far from home we hear an echo of our native land and of the Concert Hall in Copenhagen's Tivoli.

It is one of the supreme merits of Georg Carstensen that he afforded Lumbye the encouragement and opportunity to come forth repeatedly with astonishing new works. It was principally in the *waltz* that the famous South Germans Strauss, Lanner, Gungl, and Labitsky had their strength, and in this field Lumbye was forced to let them retain first place. But when the signal was given for the *gallopade* or when the *polka* set the floor pulsating, Lumbye triumphed over all his rivals, and *there* he was on his own uncontested terrain.

While pretty and rhythmic society dancing is continuously retrogressing and a barbaric current is running through the *waltz,* which is now (though after God knows what models) danced in the modern fashion *"à deux temps"* — that is to say, with a 2/4 step in 3/8 time, a seemingly insoluble arithmetic problem, Lumbye has been both clever and successful because he has stayed with the comfortable beat that prevails under the names of *polka* and *gallopade.* We should bless these physical exercises, free as they are from demands, if for no other reason than that Lumbye's dances may become classics and may be preserved for time to come as some of the best in their genre.

"But what meaning can a piece of dance music possibly have?" This is a question that would be asked by one for whom the art of music is not only a science but also an organ of expression for the most profound and sacred feelings. To this one must reply that music is, in reality, like a flower, which uses its grace, its magnificence of color, and above all its fragrance to forge its way through the senses to the innermost soul. It is precisely by its simple, undemanding melodies that it imprints itself upon our memory and accompanies us on our wanderings, recalling to us the happiest moments of our youth.

Without forgetting the larger musical pieces that have sprung from Lumbye's imagination, or the songs he has written to the texts of *vaudevilles,* and, least of all, the military marches which presumably earned him the formidable title of Councillor of War, I cannot deny myself the pleasure of singling out some of the most beautiful expressions of homage that he offered on the altar of Terpsichore. I will therefore emphasize the mounting jubilation in the "Bacchus Galop" and the majestic strength that courses through the "Mazurka in A Minor." Now, while I certainly do not base Lumbye's whole fame on his "Champagne Galop," I must dwell for a moment upon the bubbling fermentation that fizzes in the first section of this piece; in the second, the cork pops out with a bang, and the glasses are filled; finally, the skaals are delivered and the foaming nectar drained in the third segment, while giddy transports

H. S. Løvenskjold

J. F. Frøhlich

H. S. Paulli

J. P. E. Hartmann

Edvard Helsted

Niels W. Gade

H. C. Lumbye

BOURNONVILLE'S MEN OF MUSIC

All, Det kgl. Bibliotek, Copenhagen.

THE VILLA BOURNONVILLE
The balletmaster's well-loved country home at Fredensborg.
Teatermuseet, Copenhagen.

of delight fill up the entire fourth part of the work until the welcome "da capo" brings a new bottle to the table and everyone joins in the thunderous bacchanale! I once attempted to reproduce this mood in a ballet *divertissement,* but the desired effect did not come off. On the other hand, we have worked together successfully at Court and national festivals as well as on various stages.

His superb "Telegraph Galop" is preserved in the ballet *Conservatoriet;* "Polka militaire" and "La Lithuanienne" won great popularity; and I need only mention the finale from *Napoli* in order to denote what a high degree of liveliness he had to produce after the fiery "Tarantella" so as to literally transport the spectators to the foot of smoking Vesuvius! But what delicacy and eroticism lie in the music for *La Ventana,* and what violent passion blazes through the "New Zealanders' War Dance" in *Far from Denmark!* All these superb works must never be set aside as so many outdated fashions. It would be a great tragedy if these stimulating melodies were to be lost to our successors, who would thus be forced to dance according to some confused combinations of the future.

As far as I know, Lumbye's last compositions were the "Scandinavian Quadrille" and the finale to *The King's Volunteers on Amager.* Both of these works still bubbled with freshness and humor, although his health was broken and the same infirmity that had struck Beethoven, namely deafness, had forced him to step down from the conductor's podium, where he had so gladly been seen and acclaimed by the Danish public. Only late in life was he awarded the State grant for poets and artists; and although it had not been given to him to amass a fortune, at his death he left behind no small inheritance for his children: innate genius and talent.

POSTSCRIPT

I hereby sum up the activity and reflections of "my theatre life," at the same time referring my good readers to Volumes I and II (published in 1847 and 1865, respectively) as well as to both of the foregoing parts of this *Third and Final Volume.*

In direct consideration of my age and health, together with the fact that my powers of invention no longer appear to me to answer to the demands of the times, I have finally bidden farewell to the art which I have loved and cultivated with true devotion. The battle that I have waged for nearly half a century in defense of the ballet's aesthetic rights, I have now handed over to my pupils and younger colleagues. I cherish no illusions as to the continued existence of my works in the repertoire of the Royal Theatre, but I do feel strengthened and encouraged by the confident thought that *Beauty* will never cease to maintain its place on the Danish stage.

AUGUST BOURNONVILLE.

Fredensborg, April 22, 1878.

INDEX

Aaby, Major, 368
Abbot, William, 470
Abildgaard, Nicolai, 423
Abraham, 134
Abrahamson, Joseph, 465
Absalon, Archbishop, 76, 386
Achard, 610, 615
Adam, Adolphe, 20, 147, 409, 430n.
Adam Homo (Paludan-Müller), 670
Adeler, Kurt [Cort] Sivertsen, 270, 362
Adlersparre, Count Carl August
    (Albano), 528
Adrien, 620
Æschylus, 101
Aftonbladet, 399, 518
Agamemnon, 101
Aguado, Alexandre, Marqués de las
    Marismas del Guadalquivir, 50, 488
Ahasuerus (Andersen), 664
Ahlefeldt, Count Ferdinand, 656
Ahlgrensson, Fritz, 307, 350, 363
Aigue, Marquis de l', 487
Albert (François Decombe), 19, 20, 24,
    46, 48, 67, 432, 453, 469, 470, 472,
    476
Albert, Madame, 432
Albertazzi, Emma, 510
Albertine [Coquillard], 533–536, 539
Albrecht, 583
Aldegonde, Mlle., 619
Aldridge [Allridge], Ira, 300, 522–523
Alexander I, Tsar, 19, 586
Alexander II, Tsar, 509, 571, 577, 578
Alexander III, Tsar, 575
Alexander III, the Great, 454
Alexander Nevsky, Saint, 576
Alexis, Tsar, 587

Alfieri, Vittorio, 230, 597
Allan, 621
Allan Dorval, Mme., 624
Allard, Marie, 49, 457
Almlöf, Knut, 157
Almlöf, Mme., 519
Almlöf, Niels, 155, 519
Ambrose, Saint, 595
Ambrosiani, 303
Amélie, Empress of Brazil, 519
Anacreon, 75, 98, 115, 304
Anatole, *see* Petit, Anatole
Anatole, Constance, *née* Gosselin, 467,
    469, 470, 472
Anckarström, J. J., 291n., 656
Ander, Alois, 220, 227, 524
Andersen, Carl, 375
Andersen, Hans Christian, 75, 147, 170,
    177, 226, 234, 332, 372, 443, 560, 564,
    565, 596, 631, 662–665, 670, 671
Andrea del Sarto, 597
Andrew, Saint, 576
Ane, Amager peasant, 418–419,
    421–422
Angel, The (Andersen), 664
Angelico, Fra, 597, 598
Angiolini, Gasparo, 20, 640–642
Angoulême, Duc d', 431, 434, 448
Angoulême, Duchesse d', 431
Anhalt-Dessau, Princesses of, 180
Anna, Empress of Russia, 587
Anne, Queen of Great Britain, 510
Anschütz, Heinrich, 215
Anselme, Nicolas-Baptiste, *dit l' aîné*,
    39, 436, 490
Anthology of Danish Poets (Rahbek),
    423

Anthoni, Signor de, 544
Apponyi, Count Rodolphe, 490
Apuleius, 189
Arabian Nights, The 211, 249n., 584
Aristarchus, 355n.
Aristides, 450, 601
Arlincourt, Vicomte d', 487
Armand, 39
Arnal, Benoît, 39, 619
Arnesen, Anton, 147
Arnim, 551
Arnoldson, 389
Arrhenius, Sophi Carolina, 522
Artois, Comte d', *see* Charles X, King of
    France
Aschengreen, Erik, 26n., 68n.
Aspasia, 461, 660
Astrup, Hr., 651
Astrup, Jfr. (dresser), 652
Astrup, Jfr. (theatre porter), 651
Astrup, Mette Marie, 424, 651–653
Attila, 112
Auber, Daniel-François-Esprit, 81, 147,
    356, 365, 371, 377, 409, 437, 468, 479,
    480, 481, 567
*August Bournonville: Lettres à la
    maison de son enfance*, 426n.
*August Bournonville: Spredte Minder i
    Anledning af Hundredaarsdagen*
    (Charlotte Bournonville), 30n., 671n.
Augusti, the, 276
Augustus, Emperor, 12, 110, 601, 604
Aumer, Jean, 19–20, 68, 407, 433, 452,
    455, 462, 484, 491
Aumont, Louis Auguste François, 465

Bacchus Galop (Lumbye), 672
Backman, Alexis, 518
Baden, Torkel, 438
Baedeker, 109n., 600, 607
Baggesen, Jens, 631
Baillot, Pierre-Marie-François de Sales,
    466, 661
Bakunin, Mikhail, 399
*Ballet of the Second Empire,
    1847–1858, The* (Guest), 196n.

BALLETS AND DIVERTISSEMENTS

Abdallah, 165, 210, 211–233, 408,
    547n., 554
Abeilles, Les, 318
Abu Hassan, 472
*Acclaim to the Graces / Gratiernes
    Hylding*, 27n., 66, 408, 493
Achille à Scyros, 452
Adriana (project), 271, 272
Ægir's Wedding, 282
*Annette and Lubin / Annette og
    Lubin*, 641, 645
Apotheosis for Shakespeare, 318
Arcona, 380, 385–386, 392, 401, 408,
    608
Armida, 598
Armida (Dahlén), 443, 444, 446, 647,
    663
Balanda, 221
Bees, The / Blommor och Bin, 306
*Bellman, or the Polska at Gröna
    Lund / Bellman eller Polskdandsen
    paa Grönalund*, 80, 98–100, 303,
    357, 520, 524
Bouquet de fantaisie, 317
Cachucha, 175, 510, 518
Caritta, 222–223
Carneval de Venise, Le, 432, 452, 622
Carnival Night, 317
Chao-Kang, 21
*Childhood of Erik Menved, The /
    Erik Menveds Barndom*, 95–98,
    407, 668
Children's Party, A / En Børnefest,
    101–103
Cinderella, 584
Clari, 19, 432, 452
*Conservatoriet, or A Proposal of
    Marriage Through the Newspaper /
    Conservatoriet eller Et Avisfrieri*,
    165, 166, 169, 181–188, 304, 385,
    401, 407, 522, 553, 673
Coppélia, 611
*Cort Adeler in Venice / Cort Adeler i
    Venedig*, 270, 348n., 362–363, 408

BALLETS AND DIVERTISSEMENTS (*cont.*)

Country Miller, The /
　Landsbymølleren, 657

Cupid's Jest, 315

Danes in China / *De Danske i China,*
　172

Dansomanie, La, 19, 452, 641

Déserteur, Le, 19

Devil Is Loose, The, see *Fanden er*
　løs

Diable à quatre, Le, 225, 584

Diable boiteux, Le, 20, 175

Don Quixote (Petipa), 581

Don Quixote at Camacho's Wedding
　/ *Don Quixote ved Camachos*
　Bryllup, 78–80, 85, 407

Earnest Maiden, The / *Den alvorlige*
　Pige, 177, 408

Echo of Sunday, An / *Søndags Echo,*
　173

Enfant prodigue, L', 19, 452, 458

Épreuve villageoise, L', 432, 452

Esmeralda, 220, 581

Ettore Fieramosca, 21

Fairy Tale in Pictures, A / *Et Eventyr*
　i Billeder, 372–374, 408

Fanden er løs, 225, 641, 645

Fantasca, 569

Far from Denmark, or A Costume
　Ball on Board / *Fjernt fra Danmark*
　eller Et Costumebal ombord,
　275–281, 286, 357, 362, 368, 399,
　401, 408, 673

Farewell to the Old Theatre / *Farvel*
　til det gamle Theater, 380, 408

Fatherland's Muses, The /
　Fædrelandets Muser, 83–84, 408

Faust (Bournonville), 69–71, 168,
　303, 508, 520

Faust (Perrot), 216–217, 220, 223

Festival in Albano, The / *Festen i*
　Albano, 80, 82–83, 217, 304, 315,
　357, 522, 604, 668

Fille du Pharaon, La, 581

Fille mal gardée, La, 19, 650

Fishermen, The / *Fiskerne,* 657

Flick und Flock, 592–593

Flore et Zéphire, 19, 432, 435

Flower Festival in Genzano, The /
　Blomsterfesten i Genzano, 165,
　268–272, 377, 385, 401, 408, 532,
　554

Flower Maids of Florence, The / *De*
　florentinske Blomsterpiger, 174

Folk Tale, A / *Et Folkesagn,* 169,
　205–211, 220, 273, 351, 380, 385,
　386, 401, 408

Four Seasons, or Cupid's Journey,
　The / *De fire Aarstider eller Amors*
　Reise, 115

From Siberia to Moscow / *Fra*
　Siberien til Moscou, 399–401, 408

From the Last Century / *Fra det*
　forrige Aarhundrede, 389–390, 408

Gallant Gardener, The / *Den galante*
　Gartner, 657

Gipsy, La, 20

Giselle, 20, 217, 533, 547

Gitana, La, 175

Guillaume Tell, 21

Gypsy Camp, The / *Zigeunernes Leir,*
　640

Hamlet, 21

Harvest Day/ *Høstdagen,* 650

Hermann and Dolman / *Hermman og*
　Dolman, 641

Hermanas de Sevilla, Las, 173

Hertha's Offering / *Herthas Offer,*
　80–81, 408

Holmen's Old Guard / *Holmens faste*
　Stok, 173

Hussar Dance, 247

Inaugural Divertissement, 318

In Memory of Weyse / *Weyses Minde,*
　379–380, 408

In the Carpathians / *I Karpatherne,*
　264–268, 408

Inez de Castro, 641, 647

Irresistibles, The / *De*
　Uïmodstaaelige, 174, 408

Isle of Fantasy, The / *Phantasiens Ø,*
　81–82, 172, 518

BALLETS AND DIVERTISSEMENTS *(cont.)*
Jason and Medea, 641
Jolie Fille de Gand, La, 20
Jovita [Jovitta], 222
Jugement de Pâris, Le, 19, 432, 452
Koniok, 584
*Kermesse in Bruges, The | Kermessen
i Brügge,* 169, 190–193, 219, 304,
342, 377, 385, 401, 407, 524
*King's Volunteers on Amager, The |
Livjægerne paa Amager,* 367–368,
385, 393, 399, 401, 408, 422, 673
Kirsten Piil, 103–107
Kobold, Der, 47
Lagertha, 346, 373, 417, 639, 641,
642, 646–647, 650, 659
Laitière suisse, La, see *Nathalie, ou
la Laitière suisse*
Lalla Rookh, 560
*Laurette, or The Reformed
Debaucher | Laurette eller Den
forbedrede Forfører,* 641
Lay of Thrym, The | Thrymsqviden,
282, 349–350, 352–353, 357, 362,
363, 372, 380, 386, 401, 408
*Linna and Valvais | Linna og
Valvais,* 641
Macbeth, 643, 647
*Mandarin's Daughters, The |
Mandarinens Døttre,* 377–378, 408
Manon Lescaut, 20
Marco Visconti, 21, 538
Maritana, 173
Mélange, 318
*Mountain Hut, or Twenty Years, The
| Fjeldstuen eller Tyve Aar,* 169,
273–275, 400, 401, 402, 408, 554
*Mountain Peasants' Children and the
Mirror, The | Biergbøndernes Børn
og Speilet,* 373, 641
Mozartiana, 304, 315
*Napoli, or The Fisherman and his
Bride | Napoli eller Fiskeren og
hans Brud,* 88–95, 96, 97, 104, 117,
169, 189, 210, 219, 227, 228, 230,
232–233, 377, 399, 401, 521, 531,
532, 547, 548, 658, 673

Nathalie, ou la Laitière suisse, 75, 95
Nations, Les, 196n.
*New Penelope, or The Spring Festival
in Athens, The | Den nye Penelope
eller Foraarsfesten i Athenen,*
116–117
*Nina, or The Girl Driven Mad by
Love | Nina eller den Vanvittige af
Kjærlighed* (Bournonville after
Milon), 75, 667; same (Galeotti),
639, 641
Nina, ou la Folle par Amour (Milon),
19, 74, 78, 432, 452
Noces de Gamache, Les, 452
Oresteia, The | Orestias
(unperformed), 100–101
*Old Memories, or The Magic Lantern |
Gamle Minder eller En Laterna
magica,* 166, 167–171, 201, 407
Ondines, Les, 21
Pages du Duc de Vendôme, Les, 433
*Pages of the Duke of Vendôme, The |
Hertugen af Vendomes Pager*
(Bournonville after Aumer), 68,
78
Papillon, Le, 581
Pas des trois Cousines, 173
Paul and Virginia | Paul og Virginia
(Bournonville after Gardel), 68, 78,
304
Paul et Virginie, 432, 452
Pirates, The, 95n.
Polacca Guerriera, 172
Polka militaire (Aug. Bournonville),
172, 206
Polketta, 178
Polterabend, Der, 508
Ponte Molle | Pontemolle, 343, 357,
401, 408, 463, 532, 565
Prometheus, 21
*Prophecy of Love, The | Kjærligheds
Spaadomme,* 174, 357, 408, 524
Proserpine, 19, 452
Psyche (Bournonville), 188–190, 407
Psyché (Gardel), 19, 452, 641
Raoul Bàrbe-Bleue | Rolf Blaaskjæg,
373, 639, 641, 647, 659

BALLETS AND DIVERTISSEMENTS *(cont.)*
  Raphael / Rafaello, 88, 89, 105,
    107–115, 531, 539, 542, 601, 602,
    669
  Recruiting Officer, The / Hververen,
    640
  Regnar Lodbrog, 282
  Révolte au sérail, La, 75
  Roi Candaule, Le, 581
  Rolf Krake, 282
  Romanov, 21
  *Romeo and Giulietta / Romeo og
    Giulietta* (Bournonville after
    Galeotti), 74, 407; same (Galeotti),
    78, 639, 641–642, 647
  Rose Tree, The / Rosentræet, 650
  *Sailor's Return, The / Matrosens
    Hjemkomst*, 173, 408
  Satanella, 225
  *Scandinavian Quadrille /
    Skandinavisk Quadrille*, 408
  Seguidilla (Paul Taglioni), 225
  Servante justifiée, La, 432, 452
  Siège de Calais, Le, 21
  *Sigrid with the Veil / Sigrid med
    Sløret*, 23, 641, 647, 650
  *Singhalese Idol, The / Afguden paa
    Ceylon*, 639, 641, 645
  Sleepwalker, The / Søvngængersken
    (Bournonville after Aumer), 20, 26,
    66, 67, 68, 78, 303, 357, 385, 493,
    518, 530, 548
  *Soldier and Peasant / Soldat og
    Bonde*, 67, 69, 408, 493, 530
  Somnambule, La, 19, 433, 455
  Sylphide, La / Sylphiden
    (Bournonville after Nourrit and
    Taglioni), 42, 78–79, 273, 303, 304,
    315, 317, 372, 518, 522
  Sylphide, La (F. Taglioni), 20, 42, 75,
    78–79
  Søvngængersken, see *Sleepwalker,
    The*
  *Telemachus on the Isle of Calypso /
    Telemak paa Calypsos Ø*, 416
  Télémaque, 19, 452, 641
  Tentation de Saint Antoine, La, 650

  Toreador, The / Toreadoren, 80,
    84–88, 117, 168, 169, 176n., 217,
    218–219, 303, 385, 401, 520, 538,
    544, 548, 549
  Tyroleans, The / Tyrolerne, 73–76,
    303, 518, 667
  Valdemar, 26, 76–78, 87, 96, 97, 98,
    99, 162, 168, 169, 210, 286, 346–
    348, 349, 357, 368, 375, 377, 386,
    401, 508, 509, 538, 571, 667, 668
  Valkyr, The / Valkyrien, 169,
    281–286, 292, 306, 341, 342, 350,
    361, 377, 386, 398–399, 401, 408
  Variété, La, 317
  Ventana, La, 175–177, 225, 266, 304,
    357, 385, 399, 408, 524, 673
  *Veteran, or The Hospitable House,
    The / Veteranen eller Det gjæstfrie
    Tag*, 71–73, 188, 407
  *Victor's Wedding, or The Ancestral
    Heritage / Victors Bryllup eller
    Fædrene-Arven*, 68–69, 407
  *Washerwomen and the Tinker, The /
    Vadskepigerne og Kjedelflikkeren*,
    640, 645
  *Wedding Festival in Hardanger, The /
    Brudefærden i Hardanger*, 169,
    197–205, 208, 273, 304, 315, 400,
    401, 408, 554
  *Whims of Cupid and the
    Balletmaster, The / Amors og
    Balletmesterens Luner*, 640
  *White Rose, or Summer in Brittany,
    The / Den hvide Rose eller
    Sommeren i Bretagne*, 117–118,
    407
  Zephyr and Flora / Zephyr og Flora,
    435, 443
  *Zulma, or The Crystal Palace / Zulma
    eller Chrystalpaladset*, 169, 193–
    196, 408
Bang, Chamberlain, 436
Baptiste *aîné, see* Anselme, Nicolas-
  Baptiste
Baptiste Petit, M. and Mme., 435
Barbarossa, 607
Bårdsen, Jess, 531

Baron, Michel, 15
Barrez, Jean-Baptiste, 511
Barthélemy, 489–490
Bartolomeo, Fra, 597
Bataille, Charles Amable, 610
Bathyllus, 12
Battle of Copenhagen, The (Hertz), 332
Baumeister, Bernhard, 215
Bayer-Bürch, Frau, 215
Beaugrand, Léontine, 610
Beauharnais, Eugène de, 563
Beaumarchais, Pierre Augustin Caron
　de, 86n.
Beaumont, Cyril W., 16n.
*Beautiful Danger: Facets of the
　Romantic Ballet, The* (Aschengreen),
　26n.
Beauvallet, 624
Bechmann, Friedrich, 215
Beck, Johann Nepomuk, 524, 592
Becker, Professor, 363
Beethoven, Ludwig van, 147, 364, 371,
　409, 482, 484, 558, 673
Behrens, Conrad, 404
Bella Fornarina, La, 113
Bellanger, 449
Bellini, Vincenzo, 43, 45, 145, 147, 299,
　371, 542
Bellman, Carl Michael, 98, 118, 166,
　304, 514, 520–521, 524, 655
Belval, 610
Bendix (businessman), 244
Bendix (composer), 316
Benvenuti, 597
Berg, Chamberlain, 666, 668
Berg, Court Singer, 299, 519
Bergami, Bartolomeo, 440
Berggreen, A. P., 147, 205
Bergsøe, Vilhelm, 631
Berlingske Tidende, 165
Berlioz, Hector, 482, 484, 558
Bernhard, Carl, *see* Saint-Aubain,
　Andreas Nicolai de
Bernard, 615
Bernard-Léon, 621
Bernhardt, Sarah, 611
Berner, F. J. Gottlob, 345, 349, 379,
　382, 388, 393

Berry, Charles Ferdinand, Duc de, 431
Berry, Marie Caroline, Duchesse de,
　431, 440–441
Berton, 147, 331, 445, 480
Bertrand, General, 627
Berthier, Marshal, 628
Berwald, Franz Adolf, 314
Beskow, Bernhard, Baron von, 154, 302,
　315, 316, 518, 526, 528
Beule, Charles Ernest, 601
Bias, Fanny, 432, 476
*Bidrag till den Bournonvilleska
　familiens historia* (P. Bournonville),
　429n.
Bieber, 550
Bignon, 619
Bigottini, Emilie, 19, 432, 476
Bille, Commodore Steen, 262, 278
Bing, Herman Jacob, 465
Bing, Meyer Herman, 244, 253
Birch-Pfeiffer, Charlotte, 156, 300, 315
Birger Jarl, 515
Birger, King, 517
Birouste, Juliette, 641, 659
Bisle, Kapellmeister, 591
Bissen, H. V., 499
Bjerkebæk, 402
Bjørn, Marie Christine, 641, 656
Bjørnson, Bjørnstjerne, 273, 361, 384,
　386, 391
Bjurstén, 528
Blanche, August, 155, 302, 303, 314,
　315, 316, 526, 528
Blasis, Carlo, 545, 546
Blasius, Fire-master, 260
Bloch, Mlle., 610
Bobeche, 618
Boccaccio, Giovanni, 210, 366
Bochsa, R. N. C., 95, 96
Bock, Bertha, 154
Bogdanov, Alexei, 582
Bøgh, Erik, 403
Bogolyubov, 578
Boïeldieu, François Adrien, 145, 147,
　360, 371, 409, 437, 444, 480, 489, 568
Bolognetti, 538
Bonaparte, Jérôme, 428
Bordeaux, Duc de, 441

Bordogni, 437
Borgaard, Carl, 244, 246, 260
Borger i det gamle København (Møller), 173n.
Børgeson, 302, 313, 526
Borghi-Mamo, Adelaide, 215
Borre, Chancellor, 246
Borri, Pasquale, 217, 219, 221–222, 223
Borries, 551
Borries, Hr. von, 552
Borromeo, San Carlo, 595
Borromeo, Vitaliano, 595
Borup, Morten, 206n.
Bosquin, 615
Boucher, 186
Bouffé, Hugues-Désiré, 40, 620
Bouhy, 615
Boulain, 463
Boulanger, 437
Bourbon, House of, 431, 441, 456
Bourgoin, Marie, 39, 478
Bourguignon sisters, 428
Bourmont, General, 450, 490
Bournonville, Amable Louis (grandfather), 25, 429, 654
Bournonville, Anthon [Antoine] (half-brother), 198, 415, 416, 425, 658
Bournonville, Antoine-Théodore (father), 18, 22, 25, 26, 27, 41, 74, 96, 99, 121, 125, 171, 198, 303, 367, 415, 416, 419, 423, 424, 425, 426–430, 432–437, 439–444, 446–448, 451, 453, 459, 460, 461, 462, 463, 465, 467–468, 492, 495, 518, 635, 641, 653–658, 663
Bournonville, August Antoine: birth, 25; childhood and adolescene, 3, 25–26, 415–425; training, academic, 422–423; dramatic, 423–424; in art, 425, 446; in music, 424, 425, 446; in dance, 26, 27, 416, 423, 425, 435, 446, 447–448, 453, 454–455, 459; stage debut, 25, 417; marriage, 69, 519; family, *see* entries under individual names; retirement as a dancer, 161, 163; ballet compositions, *see* entries under individual titles
Bournonville, Augusta (daughter), 69, 102, 549–553, 612
Bournonville, Charles Jérôme, 654
Bournonville, Charlotte (daughter), 30n., 69n., 234, 524, 525, 592–608, 611, 635, 671n.
Bournonville, Edmond (son), 69n., 220
Bournonville, Frederikke (sister), 416n.
Bournonville, Gustafva Adelaïde (half-sister), 415, 416n., 658
Bournonville, Helena Fredrika, *née* Håkansson (wife), 69, 211, 220, 465, 468, 495, 518–519, 611, 635
Bournonville, Jacques, 475, 654
Bournonville, Jean-Valentin, 475, 654
Bournonville, Jeanne Evrard [Ebrard] (grandmother), 25, 428, 654, 655
Bournonville, Juliane (sister), 416n.
Bournonville, Julie (aunt), *see* Fay, Léonne Julie Bournonville de la
Bournonville, Louis, 654
Bournonville, Lovisa, *née* Sundberg (mother), 125, 415, 416, 422, 492, 495, 635, 658
Bournonville, Mariane, *née* Jensen (father's first wife), 656–657, 658
Bournonville, Mathilde (daughter), 60n.
Bournonville, Paul (grandson), 429n., 653n.
Bournonville, Pierre de Riel, Marquis de, 653
Bournonville, Pierre Jérôme, 429
Bournonville, Theodor (son), 513
Bournonville, Théodore (uncle), 654–655
Bournonville, Therese (daughter), 69n.
Bournonville's Ballet Napoli: In the Light of Archive Materials and Theatrical Practice (Fridericia), 30n.
Bournonville's Ballet Valkyrien, 283n.
Bournonville's London Spring (Moore), 470n., 534n.
Bourquin, 610
Bouton, 490
Boye, Casper Johannes, 147, 331, 493
Bræstrup, Overpræsident, 496
Braun, 528
Bravo, Johan, 604
Bredal, Iver Frederik, 81, 147, 409
Brennus, 109

Bressant, 611
Bretteville, Louis-Claude Le Normand
  de, 436
*Breve og Aktstykker vedrørende Johan
  Ludvig Heiberg,* 206n.
Brice, Mlle. 509
Brignoli family, 535
Brindeau, 620
Brioli, Signora, 538
Brix, 391
Brocard, Caroline, 469, 470, 472
Brockenhuus, Kammerjunker, 538
Brodersen, Georg, 170, 341, 393, 410,
  548
Brohan, Madeleine, 611
Broman, Robert Gustaf, 157
Brøndsted, Peter Oluf, 101, 240, 465,
  542
Brosbøll, J.C.C., 315, 316
Brougham, Henry Peter, 440
Bruce, Lord, 470, 474
Brugnoli, Amalia, 48
Bruhn, General, 500
Brulo company, 303
Brunel, Isambard Kingdom, 438
Brunet, 40, 618, 619
Brunet the Younger, 620
Bruni, 578
Brunow, Captain, 474
"Brutus," coachman, 475
Bruun, Carl, 41, 647
Bruun, clergyman, 253, 261
Bruun, Jfr., 548
Bruun, librarian, 363
Bruun, Malthe Conrad, *see* Malte-Brun
Bruun, N. T., 424, 647
Bryullov, 578
Bull, Ole, 192, 275
Bulow, Corps Commander, 261
Bülow, Cosima von, 567
Bülow, Franz von, 660
Bülow, General Frederik, 260
Bülow, Hans von, 566–567, 568
Bülow, Major, 262
Bulwer-Lytton, Edward, Baron Lytton,
  607
Burchell, clergyman, 597
Bürde-Ney, Frau, 218

Bürger, 429
Burgundy, Dukes of, 654
Burton, Sir Richard, 249n.
Bushby, Mrs. Anne, 560
Buxton, 560
Byron, Lord, 440
Byström, J. N., 514, 518

Calderón de la Barca, Pedro, 314, 315,
  316, 359
Caligula, Emperor, 12–13
Calipoliti, 312
Cambridge, Duke of, 427
Camillus, Marcus Furius, 109
Camões, Luis Vas de, 114
Campagnoli, Bartolomeo, 427
Campagnoli, Giannina, 427
Camprubí, Mariano, 84, 176
Canning, George, 490
Canova, Antonio, 226, 238, 543, 563,
  594
Cantata (Hartmann), 383
Cantata (C. Schall), 647
Cantilena (Spohr), 661
Canute the Great, King of England, 560
Canute IV, Saint, King of Denmark, 603
Canziani, Giuseppe, 20, 642
Capuletti, 270
Caracalla, Emperor, 110
Carafa, Michele Enrico, 66, 67
Cardigan, Earl of, 402
Carey, André Isidore, 214, 303, 466
Carey, Edouard, 466, 533–536, 539
Carey, Fanny, 612
Carey, Gustave, 466
Carey, Josephine, *née* Sainte-Claire,
  303, 466
Carey, Léontine, 612
Carlén, 528
Carlini, 492
Carlini, Luigi, 69
Caroline Amalie, Queen of Denmark,
  179, 539
Caroline Amelia, Queen of England,
  440
Caroline Mathilde, Queen of Denmark,
  22, 427, 541, 649
Carpeaux, Jean Baptiste, 555, 612

Carstensen, Georg, 672
Casagli, 303
Casati, Giovanni, 544, 595
Casorti, Giuseppe, 186, 642; family, 186
Castera, 656
Catel, Charles-Simon, 480
Catherine II, the Great, Empress of
    Russia, 579
Catte [Cati], Efisio, 546
Cazot, Nicolas-Joseph, 619
"Cécile la Vanille," 462
Cellini, Benvenuto, 515
Cerrito, Fanny, 560
Cervantes Saavedra, Miguel de, 79
Cetti, Giovanni, 445
Cetti, Ludovica, 410
Chameroy, Louise, 19, 49, 476
Champagne Galop (Lumbye), 173, 672
Chapuy, Mlle., 611
Charles X, King of France, 431, 434,
    438, 449–450, 461, 486, 616
Charles (Carl) IX, King of Sweden, 515
Charles X, King of Sweden, 281n., 563
Charles XI, King of Sweden, 515, 516
Charles XII, King of Sweden, 362, 514,
    515, 516, 526–527
Charles XIII, King of Sweden and
    Norway, 516, 527
Charles XIV John (Carl Johan), King of
    Sweden and Norway, 290, 519, 521
Charles XV, King of Sweden and
    Norway, 438, 496, 528–529
Charlotte of Hesse, Princess, 179–180,
    429
Chasles, Philarète, 489
Chatenay, M. de, 561; the Younger,
    561–562
Chery, 626
Cherubini, Luigi, 35, 147, 439, 647, 667
Chevalier, Mlle., 611
Chevigny, Sophie-Geneviève de, 19,
    49, 650
Christensen, 498–500
Christensen, Carl C., 118n.
Christensen, Christian Ferdinand, 82,
    83, 188, 193, 197, 205, 211, 244, 245,
    253, 254, 264, 268, 275, 281
Christensen, Harald, 265

Christian, Crown Prince of Denmark,
    18
Christian I, King of Denmark and
    Norway, 515, 516, 603
Christian (Christjern) II, King of
    Denmark, Norway, and Sweden,
    77n., 515
Christian IV, King of Denmark and
    Norway, 18, 166, 173, 500, 588
Christian V, King of Denmark and
    Norway, 13, 203n.
Christian VII, King of Denmark and
    Norway, 427n., 538, 641, 649
Christian VIII, King of Denmark and
    Norway, 84n., 86–87, 160–161, 178,
    239, 240, 529–530, 539, 660
Christian IX, King of Denmark, 342,
    510
Christina, Dowager Duchess, 226
Christina, Queen of Sweden, 303
Christoffer of Bavaria, King of
    Denmark, Norway, and Sweden, 563
Ciceri, Pierre, 488
Cicero, 450, 601
Cimabue, 597
Cimarosa, Domenico, 409
Claude Lorrain, 578
Clauren, *see* Heun, K. G. S.
Clausen, Henrik Nicolai, 436
Clausen, Mme., 445
Clemens, Johan Frederik, 423
Clotilde [Malfleuroy], 19
Clyde, Mr., 470
Coggia, 605n.
Colbjørnsen, Anna, *see* Kolbjørnsdatter,
    Anna
Collin, Jonas, 494, 663
Collini, 538
Colon, Jenny, 39, 619
Comettant, Jean Pierre Oscar, 612, 653
Comte, M., 617
Concertino héroïque (Prume), 105
Concerto in A Major (Maurer), 661
Condé, Field Marshal, 570, 628
Condé, Prince Louis de, 653
Consborough, Dr., 550
Constant, Benjamin, 439
Constantine, Emperor, 111, 343

Contes moraux (Marmontel), 641
Cook, 473
Copetti, 598
Coppel, 615
Coquelin, Constant, 611
Coralli, Jean, 20, 533
Corbelli, Countess, 597
Corbière, 449
Corbièreide, La (Méry and
  Barthélemy), 489
Corinne (de Staël), 107, 664
Corinne, Mlle., 590
Coriolanus, Gaius Marcius, 109
Corneille, Pierre, 15, 625
Cornelius, Peter von, 343
Cornet, Julius, 212, 213, 217–219,
  221–225, 227, 229, 232–234, 547
Correggio, 113, 544
Corsini, Prince, 241
Cottin, Madame, 399
Coulon, Jean-François, 181, 435
Courrier [Courier] des Théâtres, 477
Courrier [Courier] français, 486
Court, Louisa, 469, 470, 471–474, 510,
  534
Court, Mrs., 510, 534
Court, William, 471, 472, 474, 510
Courtin, Clothilde, 463
Courtin, M., 462, 463
Courtin, Mme., 463
Creation, The (Haydn), 552
Creutz, Count Gustaf Philip, 655
Croizette, Mlle., 611
Custine, Astolthe, Marquis de, 574

Dabadie, Henri-Bernard, 481, 484
Dagen, 382, 438
Dagmar, Princess of Denmark, *see*
  Mariya Fyodorovna, Empress of
  Russia
Daguerre, 490
Dagobert I, Frankish King, 616
Daguin, Sophie, 303
Dahl, Johan, 198–201, 531
Dahlén, Carl, 443, 444, 446, 641, 647,
  663
Dahlerup, Admiral, 219

Dahlgren, 303, 314, 315, 316
Dahlqvist, Carl Georg, 156
Dalayrac, Nicolas-Marie, 35, 147, 444
Damiens, Robert-François, 435
Dance in Ancient Greece, The (Lawler),
  13n.
Dance Perspectives, 26n.
Dancing Girl, The (Paludan-Müller),
  182n.
Danserinde, En (Neiiendam), 85n.,
  168n.
Danske Skueplads, Den (Overskou),
  381, 509
Dante, 597
Darbès, Johannes, 640, 645
D'Arco, 93
D'Artois de Bournonville, Achille, 618
Dartois family, 654
Dauberval, Jean, 18, 19, 49, 650
Dauprat, Louis François, 667
Daussoigne [Dausfoigne], Joseph, 432
David, Félicien, 484, 558
David, King of Judah and Israel, 7
Davout [Davoust], Marshal, 427
Dawison, Bogumil, 215
Dawn (C. Andersen), 375
Débureau, Gaspard-Baptiste, 625
Decameron, The (Boccaccio), 210n.
Decius, Emperor, 559
Dehn, Agnes, 376
Déjazet, Virginie, 621, 625
Delagardie, Count Jacob Pontusson,
  518, 519
Delamarre, 435, 656
Deland, Pierre, 157
Delaporte, Mlle., 580
Delaroche, Paul, 386, 488
Delaunay, 611
Delavigne, Casimir, 147, 328, 484, 489,
  624
Delavigne, Germain, 489
Delcomyn, 247
Delcour, 509
Delepierre children, 310
Del Grillo, Marchese, 230
Della-Maria [Dellamaria], Pierre-
  Antoine-Dominique, 35

Demetrius the Cynic, 13n.
Denmark as It Is (Comettant), 653
Derivis, Henri-Etienne, 432
Desaugiers, M. A. M., 435, 436
Deschanel, Mlle., 509
Deshayes, André-Jean-Jacques, 71
Deshayes, Madame, 462
Desideria, Queen of Sweden and
  Norway, 314
Despreaux, Julie, 621
Dessauermarsch, 552
Devienne, F., 35
Devonshire, Duke of, 456
Devrient (the Elder), 324
Didelot, Charles, 19, 25, 432, 443
Dieppo, 558
Dieudonné, 580
Di Mattia [Démathia], Girolamo, 538
Dingelstedt, Franz von, 356
Diocletian, Emperor, 110, 600
Diogenes, 149
Dittersdorff, Karl Ditters von, 444
Donatello, 542
Donizetti, Gaetano, 43, 147, 317, 409
Don Quixote (Cervantes), 79
Doria family, 535
Dorph, Niels Vinding, 265, 276
Dou, Gerard, 191, 192
Doudeauville, Duc de, 486
Drachsler, 220
Ducagne, Victor, 40, 623
Dugazon, J. B. H., 37
*Duke of Augustenborg and the
  Uprising, The* (Wegener), 165
Dumas, Alexandre, *père*, 147, 185, 272,
  440, 489, 553, 625
Dumas, General Thomas-Alexandre,
  489
Duponchel, Henri, 488
Duport, Louis, 19, 24, 458
Dupré, Louis, 447
Dupré, 597
Duprez, Gilbert, 42–43, 533
Dupuis, 580
Du Puy, Jean-Baptiste-Edouard, 35, 41,
  297, 357, 367–368, 393, 420, 646, 657
Du Quelen, Archbishop, 434

Duroc, Marshal, 628
Dustmann-Meyer, Marie Louise, 525,
  592
Duthé, Marie (Cathérine-Rosalie
  Gérard), 461–462
Duval, 321
Duvernay, 615
Dying Child, The (Andersen), 663

Ebner, Anton, 466
Ebner, Carl, 466–467
Ebner, Father, 466–467
Eckardt, Josephine, *née* Thorberg, 342,
  353
Eckersberg, C. W., 98, 648
Eddelin, 540
Edelin, Mlle., 509
Edward the Confessor, 512
Edward III, King of England, 475
Ehrenstrahl, David Klöcker von, 516
Eivasovsky, 578
Elisabeth (Cottin), 399
Elssler, Fanny, 10, 48–49, 175, 216n.,
  227, 459, 510, 518
Elssler, Therese, 49
Empire des Tsars, L' (Leroy-Beaulieu),
  571n.
Enfant, M. l', 463
Engelbrekt [Engelbrecht]
  Engelbrektsson, 636
Epistles (Holberg), 631
Erik Eiegod, King of Denmark, 603
Erik Eiegods Saga (Saxo), 484
Erik Glipping, King of Denmark, 97
Eriksen, 219
Eriksson, Fru, 154, 519
Eschricht, D. F., 465
Esmengard family, 654
Este, Leonora d', 58
Etienne, 486
Etlar, Carit, *see* Brosbøll, J. C. C.
Euripides, 117n., 372, 601
European Slave Life (Häcklander), 228
Eustache Saint-Pierre, 475
Evrardi, 215
Ewald, Johannes, 145, 166, 171, 281,
  631

Exner, Julius, 368, 418
*Explanation of Various Choreographic
Symbols* (Aug. Bournonville), 26n.

Fædrelandet, 345
Faënzel, 567
Fairy Tales (Andersen), 664, 665, 670,
671
Falconet, 515, 579
Fanny Elssler (Guest), 216n.
Fauchet, 183–184
Faust (Goethe), 69
Faust (Retzsch), 70
Faust on his Toes / *Faust på Tæerne*
(Kragh-Jacobsen), 69n., 216n.
Fay [Faye], Claude Alix de la, 655
Fay, Léonne Julie Bournonville de la,
654, 655
Fay, Léontine, 39, 620–621
Faye, 202
Ferdinand I, Emperor of Austria, 213n.
Ferdinand II, King of the Two Sicilies,
606n.
Ferdinand VII, King of Spain, 448
Ferdinand [La Brunière] (Jean la
Bruyiére de Medicis), 432, 476
Ferrari, 605, 606
Ferville, 49, 621, 622
Fichtner, 215
Fierville, 39
Figaro, Le, 612
Fjeldsted, Caroline, *see* Kellermann,
Caroline
Flammé, Athalia, 385
Fleischer, Consul, 208
Fleury (Joseph-Abraham Benard), 37
Flindt, Divinity Candidate, 422
Flore, Mlle., 619
Flotow, Friedrich von, 313
Flyveposten, 345, 382
Fodor-Mainvielle, Joséphine, 44, 404,
437
Foersom, Christen, 147, 320, 322, 493
Foersom, Peter, 423
Foliquet, Charles, 557
Fontaine, Pierre-François, 438
Foote, Miss, 470
Forchhammer, 589

Fornari family, 113
Foroni, Jacopo, 271
Forsberg, Carl David, 518
Forsberg, Mlle., 305
Fortunate Union, The, 377
Fougstad, 198
Foy, General, 439
Fra Voldenes København (Christensen),
118n.
Francis I, King of France, 185, 461
Francis Joseph I, Emperor of Austria,
213, 219, 221, 222, 233, 593
Francisque-Lallement, 509
François, 551
François, Dr., 463
François, Lieutenant General, 550
Franconi, Adolphe, 625, 626, 627
Franzén, Bishop, 528
Frappart, 217, 218, 223, 232, 593
Fraschini, Gaetano, 538, 559
Frederick II, the Great, 456
Frederik, Heir Presumptive to the
Danish Throne, 649
Frederik IV, King of Denmark, 428,
543, 599
Frederik V, King of Denmark, 166, 380,
389, 500, 579, 649
Frederik VI, King of Denmark, 22, 68,
82, 83, 84, 96, 123, 124, 178, 236, 239,
425, 427, 439, 445, 448, 451, 492, 493,
494, 509, 529, 643, 658, 660
Frederik VII, King of Denmark, 87,
161–163, 165–166, 179, 245, 248, 251,
252, 259, 260, 262, 263, 283, 499–501,
668
Frederik VIII, King of Denmark, 361,
496–497
Frederik Ferdinand, Prince, Heir
Presumptive to the Danish Throne,
179, 209
Fredmans Epistlar och Sångar
(Bellman), 98–99, 520, 644
Fredmans 62nd Epistle (Bellman), 304
Fredmans Sångar (Bellman), 98n.
Fredstrup, Axel, 171, 548
Fredstrup, Carl, 167, 171, 548
Fredstrup, Julie, 548
Fredstrup, Petrine, 169, 410, 548

Freund, Georg, 258
Fridericia, Allan, 30n.
Friedrich Wilhelm III, King of Prussia, 508
Friedrich Wilhelm IV, King of Prussia, 115
Friis, Aage, 206n.
Frisindede, Den, 85
Frode, Fredegod, 124
Frøhlich, Sr., 666
Frøhlich, Johannes Frederik, 73, 76, 80, 82, 95, 97, 107, 347, 386, 407, 465, 466, 665–670
Frydendahl, Peter Jørgen, 36–38, 51, 171, 320–321, 322, 328, 390, 423, 424, 445, 493, 598
Funck, 551
Funck, Frederik, 662
Funck, Paul, 435, 443, 444, 446
Funck, Peter, 437, 648, 660, 661
Funck, Pouline Augusta, 410, 548
Funck, Wilhelm Erik, 410, 548
Füssel, Andreas, 169, 217, 218, 303, 520, 548

Gabillon, Ludwig, 215
Gade, Ludvig, 169, 347, 353, 389, 400, 548
Gade, Niels Wilhelm, 83, 88, 147, 205, 207, 210, 256, 271, 351, 371, 407, 408, 567
Galeotti, Caroline, 643
Galeotti, Mathilde, 643
Galeotti (Vincenzo Tomaselli), 14, 22, 27, 74, 76, 167, 171, 346, 372, 406, 407, 416n., 417, 425, 444, 538, 638–643, 644, 645, 647, 650, 651, 657, 659, 660
Galileo Galilei, 536
Gallenberg, Count Robert von, 19, 66
Gallery of Shakespeare (Retzsch), 70n.
Galli, Signora, 598
Gamborg, 219
Gammeltoft, Borgmester, 496
Garat, 186
García, Manuel del Popolo Vicente, 45, 105, 437, 518, 533, 547
Gardel, Marie, 19, 453, 476

Gardel, Maximilien Léopold Philippe Joseph, 18, 452
Gardel, Pierre, 10, 18, 19, 22n., 24, 31, 68, 407, 432, 451, 452–455, 458, 459, 463, 655
Garrick, David, 15, 37, 320, 324, 455, 512, 657
Gassmann, F. L., 398
Gautier, Théophile, 20, 196, 533, 558
Gavaudan, 437
Gavaudan, Bosquier, 619
Gazette musicale, 612
Geijer, Agnes, 552n.
Geijer, Erik Gustaf, 552–553
Geismar, Mme. 610
Geleff, Poul, 391
Geneviève, Saint, 439
Gennaro, Italian fisherman, 91
Geffroy, Professor A., 609, 613
George III, King of Great Britain, 427n.
George IV, King of Great Britain, 440
George [Georges], Mlle. 624
George, Prince of Denmark, 510
George, Saint, 576
Gérard, François-Pascal-Simon, Baron, 488
Gérard, General, 439
Gerstäcker, Friedrich, 427
Gerusalemme liberata (Tasso), 444
Gervasius, Saint, 595
Gilbert de Voisins, Comte, 492
Gillberg, Johanna Gustafva, *see* Sundberg, Johanna
Ginetti, Theresa, 425
Gioja, Gaetano, 21, 538, 642
Giornale del Regno delle Due Sicilie, Il [*Giornale delle due Sicilie*], 58
Giotto, 597
Giovanni da Bologna, 542
Glæser, Franz, 147, 409, 669
Glæser, Joseph, 275, 408
Glinka, Michael, 579
Gloy, Johann Christoph, 426
Gluck, Christoph Willibald von, 18, 41, 171, 227, 299, 364, 379, 409, 444, 479, 486, 622, 645
Gobert (Mongobert), 623, 624
God and the State (Bakunin), 399n.

Gods of the North (Oehlenschläger), 350

Goethe, Johann Wolfgang von, 69, 71, 147, 187, 203, 215

Gogol, Nikolai Vasilievich, 580

Goldoni, Carlo, 149, 231

Goldschmidt, Meïr Aaron, 356

Golinelli, 219

Gontier, 39, 621

Gosse, Edmund, 29n.

Gosselin, Geneviève, 476

Gosselin, Louis François, 469, 470, 472

Got, Edmond, 611

Gottschalk, Louis Moreau, 30n., 279

Gounod, Charles, 317, 371, 377, 392, 484, 558, 559, 567

Gozzi, Count Carlo, 149

Gracchus, Valerius, 109

Grahn-Young, Lucile, 78, 96, 168, 216, 410, 468, 511–512, 553, 567

Grandjean, Axel, 391

Grandmont, 475

Grant, General Ulysses, 604n.

Grassini [Grassari], Giuseppina, 432

Great and Good Deeds (Malling), 423

Greetings from Jutland (Lumbye), 174, 247

Gregory XVI, Pope, 535

Grétry, André-Ernest-Modeste, 147, 416, 432, 480, 627

Griboyedov, 580

Griffenfeldt, Peder Schumacher, Count, 203

Grisi, Carlotta, 20, 48–49, 170, 459, 533

Grisi, Giulia, 45–46, 510

Grois, 216

Gros, Antoine Jean, Baron, 488

Grosset, Mère, 465

Grot, Constantin, 562

Grot, Professor, 561

Grundtvig, Nikolai Frederik Severin, 350

Gude, Hans Frederik, 201

Guest, Ivor, 18n., 168n., 196n., 216n., 533n., 534n., 548n.

Guidi, 643

Guidi Galeotti, Antonia, 640

Guimard, Madeleine, 49, 478

Güllich, Valdemar, 368, 386

Gundersen, Laura, 356

Gungl, Joseph, 672

Gustav I (Gustav Vasa), King of Sweden, 77, 515, 636

Gustav II Adolf, King of Sweden, 287, 515, 516, 528

Gustav III, King of Sweden, 25, 287, 290, 291, 303, 435, 456, 512, 635, 649, 655, 656, 658

Gyllembourg, Thomasine, 631

Gyrowetz, Adalbert, 407

Haack, Mme., 66n.

Habaneck, François-Antoine, 437, 482–483, 484

Häcklander, 228

Hadrian, Emperor, 601, 604

Hagberg, 301

Hagen, 531

Hagen, 203

Hagn, Charlotte von, 508

Haizinger [Haitzinger], Amalie, 215

Halanzier, 612

Halévy, Jacques-François-Fromental-Élie, 147, 371, 479, 547, 667

Halm, Friedrich, 239, 316

Hall, C. C., 265, 276–277

Hallström, Ivar, 389, 392, 409

Hamilton, Hugo Adolf, Baron, 521–522

Hammerich, F., 261, 500–501

Hammerich, Professor M., 261, 262

Hamon, Mr., 473

Handel, George Frideric, 299

Handschuh, Der (Schiller), 279

Hansen, C. F., 436

Hansen, Christian, 219

Hansen, Constantin, 540, 606

Hansen, Emil, 410

Hansen, J. A., 499–500

Hansen, magnetist, 312

Hansen, Theophilus, 219, 593

Hansteen, 198

Harald Bluetooth, King of Denmark, 256

Harald Harefod, 560

Hartig, Count, 502

Hartmann, Emil, 351, 408, 409

Hartmann, Johann Peter Emilius, 81, 147, 205, 207, 210, 240, 256, 273, 281, 283–284, 350, 351, 353, 357, 371, 375, 377, 380, 383, 386, 407, 408, 409, 446, 592

Hartvigson, 583

Hartvigson, Richard, 583

Haszreiter, 593

Hauch, Johannes Carsten, 147, 276, 493, 605

Haussmann, Georges Eugène, Baron, 555

Hauszman, Fraulein, 567

Haydn, Joseph, 227, 364, 483, 558, 593, 645

Healey, Agnes Isabella, 178, 305, 410

Healey, Christine Mary, 178, 305, 410

Hebbel, Christine, 215

Heberle, Therese, 48

Hedberg, Frans Theodor, 154, 302, 303, 315, 316, 318, 526

Hedin, Selma, 156

Hedin, Svante, 157

Heiberg, Johan Ludvig, 68, 73, 80, 99, 147, 206–208, 265, 276–277, 278, 282, 316, 321, 324, 325, 326, 331, 332, 344, 358, 376, 382, 391, 397, 436, 447n., 493, 619, 631, 669

Heiberg, Johanne Luise, 74–75, 147, 206n., 215, 265, 276–277, 326n., 331–333, 351, 384, 443, 493, 621

Heiberg, Peder Andreas, 436, 465–466, 470, 646

Heinel, Anne, 49, 457

Heine, Heinrich, 20

Heinsvig, 445

Heise, Peter Arnold, 356, 357, 360, 363, 408, 409

Helgesen, 257

Heliodorus, 112

Helsted, Carl, 547

Helsted, Edvard, 81, 84, 88, 103, 188, 190, 268, 407, 408, 530

Hennings, Betty, 347–348, 353, 357, 363–364, 371, 375, 384, 410

Henriques, Therese, 30n.

Henry II, King of England, 461n.

Henry IV, King of France, 104, 185, 615

Henry VIII, King of England, 461n.

Henry, Louis, 21, 24, 31, 75

Hereford, Lord, 474

Herman-Czillag, 220

Herodotus, 117n.

Hérold, Louis-Joseph-Ferdinand, 20, 147, 407, 409, 455, 479

Hersent, 488

Hertz, 567

Hertz, Henrik, 147, 283, 314, 318, 321, 325, 332, 356, 360, 361, 391, 631

Hess, Field Marshal, 213

Heuer, Wilhelm, 437

Hildebrand, 571–572, 574

History of the Danish Stage (Overskou), *see Danske Skueplads, Den*

Histoire de Charles XII, L' (Voltaire), 131

History of Denmark (Holberg), 76

Hjarne, 124n., 125

Hjerta, Lars, 399, 518

Hjort [Hjorth], Peder, 436

Hjorth, Jenny Gustafva, 522

Hjortsberg, Jr., 512

Hjortsberg, Fru, *née* Westerdahl, 156, 512

Hjortsberg, Lars, 51, 154, 512

Høedt, Frederik Ludvig, 155, 210, 261, 265–266, 327–331, 347, 351, 358, 402–403

Högqvist, Emilie Sofia, 154

Hohenlohe, Cardinal, 603

Høierup, 260

Høiland, Ole, 531

Holbeck, 540

Holbein, Carl von, 212, 227

Holberg, Ludvig, 37n., 54, 76, 98, 149, 166, 170, 171, 282, 321, 324, 325, 326, 359, 361, 378, 380, 383, 389, 390, 403, 408, 425n., 430, 451n., 507, 631, 651, 653

Hoguet, 508

Holm, P. 445

Holm, Wilhelm, 343, 368, 390, 408

Holmen's Old Guard (Lumbye), 247, 262

Holst, Carolina, 539

Holst, Francesco, 539
Holst, Fritz, 391
Holst, Fru, *née* Heger, 493
Holst, Hans Peter, 123, 147, 239, 253, 255, 261, 332, 352, 361, 389, 397, 538, 606, 631
Holst, Wilhelm, 493
Holstein, Frederik Conrad, 367, 494
Homer, 551
Honthorst, Gerrit van, 192
Höpffner, Conferentsraad, 165
Hoppe, Ferdinand, 168, 303, 343, 410, 469, 511, 512, 517, 548
Hoppe, Johan Heinrich Christian, 442
Hoppensach, Ferdinand, 169, 188, 548
Hostrup, Jens Christian, 147, 391
Huen, K. G. S. (Clauren), 149n.
Huet, Dr., 465
Hugo, Victor, 147, 220, 624
Humboldt, Alexander von, 189
Hultmann, Fritz Wilhelm, 403
Hwasser, Elise, *née* Jacobsson, 156
Hwasser, Hofintendant, 526
Hyacinthe, 620
Hyacinthe, 611
Hylas, 12
Hyltén-Cavallius, Gunnar, 304, 522–523

I anledning af [essays in honor of Hakon Stangerup], 69n., 216n.
Ibsen, Henrik, 361, 364n., 365, 384, 391
Iffland, August Wilhelm, 149, 215, 321
Illustreret Tidende, 399
Immanuel, Dr., 550, 552
Impressions de voyages (Dumas), 272, 553
Improvisatore, The (Andersen), 663
Ingemann, Bernhard Severin, 76, 96, 147, 631
Irminger, Corps Commander, 261
Isabey, Jean-Baptiste, 488
Ischia Ballad (Aug. Bournonville), 119, 126, 538, 608n.
Isidore, 509
Isouard, Nicolo, 35, 444
Ivan IV, Tsar, 585
Ivanov, 582

Jacob, Amager farmer, 418–419, 421
Jacobsen, Head Journeyman, 499–500
Jacobsen, J. C., 394
Jacobsen, Sidsel, 283n.
Jacoby [Jacobi], 426
Janin, Jules, 489
Jansen, Karen, 443
Jensen, Mariane, *see* Bournonville, Mariane
Jerichau, Jens Adolf, 540
Jessen, 251
Jesus Christ, 192, 236
Jew, The (Wergeland), 75n.
Jewess, The (Wergeland), 75n.
Johan I, King of Denmark, Norway, and Sweden, 515
Johan III, King of Sweden, 287
Johansson, Mlle., 591–592
Johansson, Per Christian, 303, 410, 517–518, 519, 520, 571, 574, 582–583, 591
Johansson, Pastor, 583
John, Saint, 597
Jøhnke, 571–572, 574
Joinville, Prince de, 627
Jolin, Johan, 157, 290, 302, 303, 315, 316, 523, 526
Jonah, 623
Jørgen, Nor. peasant, 199–200
Jørgensen, 531
Jørgensen, Henriette, 147, 325–327, 445, 465, 493, 621
Jørgensen, Mme., 531
Joséphine, Empress of France, 434
Joséphine, Queen of Sweden, 519, 525
Josephsson, 302
Joubert, General, 400n.
Journal 1820 (Aug. Bournonville), *see August Bournonville: Lettres à la maison de son enfance*
Journal des Débats, 454, 489, 661
Jouy, 486
Judenthum in der Musik, Das, 568
Juel, Admiral Niels, 634
Juel, Jens, 460, 596
Jugurtha, 600
Julian the Apostate, 601
Julienne, Mlle., 621

Julius II, Pope, 111–112
Justice (Aug. Bournonville), 390

Kanaris, Constantine, 281
Karl, Carl, 215–216
Karlebo, 252
Karpakova, Pelageia, 584
Karsten [Carsten], Christoffer Christian, 435
Kaulbach, Wilhelm von, 212, 343, 564, 664
Kean, Edmund, 15, 300n., 470, 522
Keck, P. L., 67, 68, 69, 407
Kellermann, Caroline, 85–86, 104–105, 168–169, 187, 303, 410, 517, 530, 548
Kellermann, Marshal, 488
Kellermann (the Younger), 487–488
Kellgren, Johan Henrik, 655
Kemble, Charles, 15, 155, 470
Kemerer, Alexandra, 582
Kenilworth (Scott), 473, 546
Kime, 509
Kindermann, August, 568
King of Prussia and his Conduct, The (Overskou), 165
Kirchheiner, J. F., 445
Kittler, Frederik, 666
Kittler, Fru, 666
Klein, 621
Klein, 260
Knudsen, Hans Christian, 35–36, 37
Knuth, Count, 166
Knytlinga Saga, 76
Kock, Paul de, 416, 512, 535
Kolbjørnsdatter, Anna, 199
Koltoff, Fru, 542
Koltoff, Licentiate, 542
Kongelige danske Ballet, Den (Kragh-Jacobsen and Krogh), 85n.
Korn, Maximilian, 215
Kotzebue, August Friedrich von, 149, 215, 321, 429
Krætzmer, Andrea, *née* Møller, 66n., 167–168, 410, 443
Kragh-Jacobsen, Svend, 69n., 85n., 216n., 426n.
Kranold, Rudolph Heinrich, 342, 344
Kreutzer, C., 147, 444

Kreutzer, Rodolphe, 68, 147, 407, 432, 446, 466, 480, 482
Krieger, 247
Krieger, A. F., 358
Krogh, General, 163
Krogh, Torben, 85n.
Krum, Daniel, 368, 380, 400, 410
Kruse, Jens William, 445
Kshesinsky, 582
Küchler, Albert, 539
Kuhlau, Frederik, 145, 147, 371, 444, 646, 647, 666
Kühne, Johann Reinhold von, *see* Lenz, Johan Reinhold von
Kunzen, Friedrich Ludwig Æmilius, 35, 424, 646, 647

Labédoyère, Charles de, 72
Labitsky, Joseph, 672
Lablache, Luigi, 45–46, 490, 510, 511
Lachner, Franz, 212
Lacressonnière, 625
Lafayette, Marie-Joseph, Marquis de, 25, 439, 440
Lafont, 620
Lafont, 466
Lagerbjelke, Count, 291
Lagrange, 580
Lahoussaye, Baron de, 487–488
Lais, François, 432
Lamartine, Alphonse de, 147
Lameth family, 654
Lamperti, Francesco, 234, 594
Lancestre, Mlle., 509
Lanckoronski, Count, 224
Landvogt, 215
Lang, 567
Lange, Overpræsident, 249
Lange, Hans Wilhelm, 266
Langenau, Baron, 214, 502
Lanner, August, 227
Lanner, Catharina, 217, 218, 227
Lanner, Josef, 227, 671, 672
Lannes, Marshal, 628
Larcher, Elisabeth, 548
Larcher, Fru, *née* Lange, 493
Larcher, Pierre Joseph, 446, 511
Larchevêsque, Pierre Hubert, 515, 579

La Roche [Laroche], Karl von, 215
La Rochefoucauld-Liancourt, Duc de, 616
La Rochefoucauld, Vicomte Sosthène de, 486–487
Lasalle, Jean, 610
Last Days of Pompeii, The (Bulwer), 607
Laube, Heinrich, 215
Laurent, Pierre, 649
Laurent, Pierre Jean, 22, 494, 641, 649–651
Laurent, Rose Marie, *née* Bonneau, 650
Lauriston, General, 434
Laurwald [Lauerwaldt], Augusta, 659
Lawler, Lillian B., 13n.
Le Brun [Lebrun], Louis-Sébastien, 432
Lebrun, Carl August, 426
LeClerq, Mlle., 470
Lecomte, Hyppolite, 449
Lefebvre, 619
Lefebvre, François, 544, 546, 548
Legrand, 39
Lehmann, Edvard, 197, 205, 211, 258, 264, 275, 281
Lekain (Henri-Louis Cain), 15, 657
Lem [Lehm], Peder Mandrup, 660
Lemaître, Frédérick, 39–41, 623, 624–625
Lemmonier, 437
Lenclos, Ninon de, 227, 461, 660
Lenz, Johann Reinhold von, 426
Lenzoni-Medici, Countess, 240, 542
Leo X, Pope, 112
Leonardo da Vinci, 112, 545
Leopold, Carl Gustaf af, 655
Lepaute, Henry, 610
Lepeintre, 39, 619
Leroy-Beaulieu, Anatole, 571n.
Lessing, Gotthold Ephraim, 147, 215, 299
Lesueur, Jean-François, 480
Letters on Dancing and Ballets (Noverre), 16n.
Lettres sur les Arts Imitateurs en Général et sur la Danse en Particulier

(Noverre), 5, 24, 25, 320, 452, 456, 460
Leuven, Adolphe de, 20, 430n., 455
Levasseur, Mlle., 217
Levassor, 620
Leverd, 39
Levetzau, Joachim Godsche, 160, 166, 319, 502, 668, 669
Lewin [Luin], Flora, 187
Lewin [Luin], Rosa, 187
Lhérie, Léon, 430n.
Ligier, Pierre-Mathieu, 624
Lincke, A. F., 343, 408
Lind-Goldschmidt, Jenny, 44, 105–107, 156, 214, 229, 230, 275, 291, 297, 299, 347, 519, 521, 525, 553, 560, 664
Lindblad, A. F., 241, 313
Lindblad, Otto, 297
Linde, Andreas, 345, 383, 384, 393
Lindgreen, Ferdinand, 34, 147, 320–322, 390, 424, 445, 493
Lindström, 350
Liston, John, 470
Liszt, Franz, 227, 467, 567
Lithuanienne, La (Lumbye), 673
Liv gjenoplevet i Erindringen, Et (Johanne Luise Heiberg), 206n.
Livia, 110
Livy, 109
Løffler, Jfr., 445
Logier, Johann Bernard, 467
Lolle, Jens, 645
Lolli, Antonio, 644
Lortzing, Gustav Albert, 147, 410
Louis XIV, King of France, 18, 146, 430, 477, 555, 615
Louis XVI, King of France, 431
Louis XVIII, King of France, 430–431, 434, 439, 449, 615
Louis Philippe, King of France, 161, 442, 468, 510, 554, 555, 616, 627
Louise, Queen of Denmark, 429, 575
Louise Josephina Eugenia, Queen of Denmark, 361, 496–497
Louvel, Pierre Louis, 431, 434–435
Løvenskjold, Herman Severin, Baron, 78, 81, 116, 147, 256, 407

Löwe, Ludwig, 215
Löwen, Colonel, 19n.
Løwenhielm, Count Gustaf Carl
    Frederik, 435, 450
Lubbert, Emile, 486
Lucian of Samosata, 13n.
Lucile Grahn: En Skæbne i Dansen
    (Neiiendam), 168n.
Lucius Verus, 601
Ludwig I, King of Bavaria, 563
Ludwig II, King of Bavaria, 565–567
Luguet, 580
Luini, Bernardino, 545
Luke, Saint, 585n.
Lumbye, Hans Christian, 88, 176, 246,
    496, 501, 584, 670–673
Lund, Sigurd, 410, 522, 524
Lund, Troels, 188, 193, 197, 205, 211,
    268, 275
Lusiads, The (Camõens), 114n.

Maag, 260
Mabille, 547
Machiavelli, 597
Macready, William Charles, 15, 155,
    470
Madayeva, Matilda, 400, 582
Madvig, J. N., 631
Mæcenas, 276
Magdalene Sibylle, Princess of Saxony,
    18n.
Magnus, 244
Magnus, Prince, 244
Magnússon [Magnussen], Finn, 350
Maillart, Louis, 365, 410
Mainvielle, son of Mme. Fodor-
    Mainvielle, 463
Mainvielle-Fodor, Joséphine, *see*
    Fodor-Mainvielle, Joséphine
Maison, General, 434, 450
Malibrán, Maria, 43–45, 404
Malling, Ove, 197
Mallinger, Mathilde, 568
Malmström, 528
Malte-Brun, Conrad, 436
Malte-Brun, Mme., 436
Manderström, Minister of State, 528

Manlius, 109
Mannheimer, Dr., 219
Mante, Louise, 39
Mantzius, Kristian, 375
Manuel, Louis Pierre, 439, 449, 616
Marcadet, 303
Marckhl [Marckl], Theodor Ignaz, 522
Marcus Aurelius, 601
Margaret I, Queen of Denmark,
    Norway, and Sweden, 241n.
Maria [Jacob], 548–549
Maria Theresa, Empress, Queen of
    Hungary and Bohemia, 25, 654–655
Mariane, Princess of Mecklenburg-
    Strelitz, 87n.
Marie Louise, Empress of France, 434,
    448, 542, 544
Marie Sophie Frederikke, Queen of
    Denmark, 81, 424, 445, 643, 667
Marius, 509
Marius Gaius [Caius], 534
Marivaux, 316
Mariya Fyodorovna, Empress of Russia,
    179–180, 574–575
Marmontel, François, 641
Marmontel, Professor Antoine François,
    553, 611–612
Mars, Mlle., 38–39, 230, 433, 436, 512,
    611, 621
Marschner, Heinrich August, 147, 272,
    377, 410
Marstrand, 247
Marstrand, Wilhelm, 98, 100, 538, 606
Martensen, H. L., 631
Martignac, Jean-Baptiste, 449–450, 626
Martin, Jean-Baptiste, 22
Martin, Jean-Blaise, 41–43, 437
Masaniello, 606
Materna, Amalia, 592
Mathews, 473
Mathews, Charles James, 560
Mauduit, Mme., 610
Maurer, Ludwig Wilhelm, 661
Maurice, Charles, 477–478
Maxentius, 343
Maximilian I, Elector of Bavaria, 563
Maximilian, Emperor of Mexico, 222

Mayr, Simon, 444, 648
Mayseder, Josef, 218, 466
Maze, Georges, 435
Mazurier, Charles, 622–623
Mazurka in A Minor (Lumbye), 672
Medici, House of, 18, 565, 597
Medori, 215
Méhul, Etienne-Nicolas, 35, 78, 102n., 147, 297, 371, 410, 444
Meisner, 215
Melancholia (Prume), 105
Melchior family, 665
Melesville, 490
Mélingue, 625
Membrée, Edmond, 610
Mendelssohn-Bartholdy, Félix, 147, 364, 371, 484, 558, 568
Ménestrel, Le, 612
Menu, Pierre, 610
Mérante, 545, 546
Mercadante, 538
Mereau, 137
Merelli, Bartolomeo, 545
Merete, 517
Méry, J. P. A., 489–490
Messiah, The (Handel), 561
Mestrino, Niccolò, 645
Metamorphoses (Ovid), 457
Metternich, Prince Clemens, 448
Meyer, August, 253
Meyer, Louise, 222
Meyer, Rudolph, 596
Meyerbeer, Giacomo, 145, 147, 158, 228–230, 299, 313, 371, 410, 444, 479, 482, 524, 558–559, 568, 648
Meza, Christian Julius de, 253
Meza, Madame de, 253
Michaeli, Louise, 299, 317
Michelangelo, 110, 112, 542, 563, 597, 598–599, 602
Michelot, Théodore (Pierre-Marie-Nicolas Michelot), 39, 611
Midsummer Song (Gade), 210
Mieris brothers, 191
Mierevelt, Michiel Jansz van, 192
Might of Runes, The (Aug. Bournonville), 119, 123–126, 538

Milon, Louis, 18, 19, 25, 74, 407, 432, 452, 453, 455, 622
Milton, John, 350
Mini, Jacob, 118n.
Miolan-Carvalho, Marie, 559
Mirabeau, Honoré Gabriel Riqueti, Comte de, 24, 439
Mischievous Boy, The (Andersen), 75n.
Mocker, 615
Modena, 230
Moëssard, Simon-Pierre, 624, 625
Molbech, Christian (the Younger), 389, 390
Molé (François-René Molet), 37
Molière, 18, 98, 149, 316, 318, 321, 325, 359, 403, 456, 512, 558, 616
Moligne, 85
Molin, Johan Peter, 516
Molinari, Nicola, 21
Moline, 432
Molitor, General, 434
Møller, Carl Christian, 399, 408
Møller, Jan, 173n.
Møller, Sophie, 66n.
Moncey, Marshal, 594, 627
Monrad, Bishop D. G., 276
Monrose, Claude-Louis, 39, 611
Montaigu, Marquis de, 487
Montavano, 602
Montecchi, 270
Montessu, Pauline, 455
Montholon, General, 627
Montyon, Marquis de, 624
Monvel (Jacques-Marie Boutet), 650, 657
Moore, Lillian, 470n., 534n.
Moralt, 446
Mortier, Marshal, 594
Motzfeldt, 198
Moving Day (Andersen), 177n.
Moyer, 551
Mozart, Wolfgang Amadeus, 22, 35, 147, 227, 272, 299, 301, 307, 313, 316, 317, 360, 364, 371, 398, 408, 410, 427, 437, 445, 455, 457, 479, 483, 538, 559, 568, 592, 645–646, 647
Mugnier, Joseph, 469

Mugnier, Pierre, 464, 466, 467–469
Mugnier, Véronique, *née* Grosset, 464, 466, 468–469, 611
Mühling, 547
Müller, 592
Müller, Carl, 221, 225
Müller, Kapellmeister, 552
Munch, Andreas, 198, 329, 361, 365, 376, 384
Munch, Fru, 202
Munthe, 197
Murat, Caroline, 487n.
Murat, Joachim, 487n.
Murillo, Bartolomé Esteban, 578
My Theatre Life (Aug. Bournonville), 115, 119, 131–132, 144, 148, 160, 162, 167, 207, 235, 264, 320, 334–335, 341, 346, 362, 405, 406, 413–414, 446, 493, 495, 496, 503, 507, 510, 513, 525, 531, 537, 539, 542, 553, 554, 607, 619, 664, 673
Mynster, J. P., 495, 631
Mynster, Mme., 253
Mystères de Paris, Les (Sue), 40, 55

Nägler, Louis, 584, 589
Nansouty, General, 556
Napoléon I, Emperor of France, 72, 174, 197, 236, 259, 269n., 415, 427n., 428, 430–431, 434, 440, 442, 448, 453, 456, 458, 459, 484, 486, 487n., 488, 489, 490, 527, 534, 544, 546, 583, 586, 588, 589, 601, 609, 610, 615, 626–629
Napoléon II, King of Rome, 415, 442, 448, 489
Napoléon III, Emperor of France, 365–366, 428n., 442, 532, 555, 609, 613, 617
Napoléon en Égypte (Méry and Barthélemy), 489
Nassau, Duke of, 180n.
Nathan, 615
Naumann, Johan Gottlieb, 313, 644
Nebelong, 258, 499
Negro Dance (Gottschalk), 30n., 279
Neiiendam, Robert, 85n., 168n.
Nelson, Horatio, Lord, 512, 560

Nero, Emperor, 13n., 110, 601
Neruda, Wilhelmine, 310
Nestroy, Johann, 215–216
Neumann, Luise, 215
Nev, 578
New Year's Gift for Dance Lovers (Aug. Bournonville), 26n.
New Zealanders' War Dance (Lumbye), 673
Ney, Michel, 72, 555
Nicholas, Saint, 576, 586
Nicolai, Karl Otto, 410
Nicolas I, Tsar, 587
Nicolas II, Tsar, 575n.
Nicolo, *see* Isouard
Niels Klim (Holberg), 423
Nielsen, Anna Brenøe Wexschall, 147, 265, 331–333, 445–446, 493, 512, 661
Nielsen, Augusta, 85, 168n., 169, 303, 410, 517, 548
Nielsen, Nicolai Peter, 147, 261, 263, 300, 322–323, 364, 424, 445, 465, 466, 493, 500–501, 512–513, 522–523, 626
Nightingale, The (Andersen), 664
Nilsson, Christine, 559, 573, 580
Nineteenth of May, The (Aug. Bournonville), 119–121
Nissen, Henriette, 518, 533
Nissen-Salomon, Madame, 583
Nivelon, Louis-Marie, 440, 451, 459–463
Nivelon, Marie-Gabrielle Malagrida, *dite* Carline, 440, 460
Noblet, Lise, 432, 481
Norberg, Charlotta, *see* Törner, Maria Charlotta
Nordic Tales (Suhm), 423
Nordisk Conversations Lexicon, 511
Norman, Kapellmeister, 299
Northern Studies (Gosse), 29n.
Notre Dame de Paris (Hugo), 220
Nourrit, Adolphe, 20, 41–43, 78, 185, 407, 454, 479, 482, 484, 533
Nourrit, Louis, 41, 432
Noverre, Antoine, Baron de Séricourt, 654
Noverre, Jean-Georges, 5, 12, 14, 16n.,

Noverre, Jean-Georges *(cont.)*
18, 19, 20, 22, 24, 25, 29, 49, 65, 69,
101, 320, 452, 455, 456, 460, 649, 650,
654, 655
Numa, 621
Nyerup [Nyrup], 205
Nyforss, 157

Odry, Jacques-Charles, 39, 619
Oehlenschläger, Adam, 22n., 29, 37, 38,
83, 98, 147, 178, 189, 211, 238, 239,
241, 281, 282, 302, 331, 350, 351, 376,
380, 383, 389, 391, 403, 408, 423, 424,
493, 518, 631, 633, 648, 664
Offenbach, Jacques, 557, 584, 611, 617
Olaf, Saint, 516
Olshausen, T., 162
On the Beautiful (Høedt), 329
On the Dance (Lucian of Samosata),
13n.
Oper und Drama (Wagner), 370
OPERAS AND OPERETTAS
*Abduction from the Seraglio /
Bortførelsen fra Serailet*, 227, 410,
427
Africaine, L', 559
Aïda, 592
Alma and Elfride / Alma og Elfride,
416, 647
*Amorous Artisans, The / De forliebte
Haandværksfolk*, 321, 398
April Fools, The / Aprilsnarrene,
447n.
Anacréon, 432
*Apothecary and the Doctor, The /
Apothekeren og Doctoren*, 444
Aristippe, 432
Aspasie et Périclès, 432
Barbe-Bleue, 618
*Barber of Seville, The / Il Barbiere di
Siviglia / Barberen i Sevilla*, 44,
313, 314, 316, 377, 397, 404, 437,
445, 481, 558
Beatrice di Tenda, 542–543
Belisario, 538
Belle Hélène, La, 557, 618
Bergère Chatelaine, La, 437
Bewitched, The / Den Bjergtagne /

Den Bergtagna, 389, 392, 398, 409,
593
*Black Domino, The / Den sorte
Domino*, 85, 409, 541
Borrowed Plumes, 316
*Brahma and the Bayadère / Brama og
Bayaderen*, 85, 169, 315, 372, 409
Bronze Horse, The / Broncehesten,
365, 377, 409
Caliph of Baghdad, The, 203
*Canon of Milan, The / Domherren i
Milano*, 647
Caravane du Caïre, Le, 432
Catharina Cornaro, 212
Chalet, The, 313, 314, 316, 317
Chanson de Fortunio, La, 617
Charitable Peasant, The, 523
Chatte metamorphosée, La, 617
Comte Ory, Le, 41, 479, 481
Contessa d'Amalfi, 598
Corsairs, The / Korsarerne, 377
Corsican, The / Korsikaneren, 409
Crown Jewels, The / Kronjuvelerne,
314, 316, 317, 356, 361, 409
Dame blanche, La, 480, 489, 568
Danaïdes, Les, 452
*Daughter of the Regiment, The /
Regimentets Datter*, 106, 179, 272,
313, 377, 391
Devin du village, Le, 432, 479
Diable à quatre, Le, 641
*Diamond Cross, The /
Diamantkorset*, 410
Dieu et la Bayadère, Le, 479, 482, 548
Dinorah, 559
*Doctor in Spite of Himself / Doctoren
imod sin Villie*, 317, 391
Don Giovanni / Don Juan, 36, 44, 45,
272, 299, 313, 314, 360, 397, 410,
437, 479, 645
Donna del Lago, La, 45, 445
Dove, The / Duen, 377
Elf Maiden, The / Elverpigen, 351,
409
Elixir of Love, The / Elskovsdrikken,
272, 314, 377
Ernani, 313
Esclave, L', 610

OPERAS AND OPERETTAS (*cont.*)

Estrella di Soria, 314

Etoile du Nord, L', 228–230, 559

Faust, 314, 316, 317, 377, 559, 567

Favorite, La, 610

Federigo, 410

Fernand Cortès, [*Fernando*] 145, 452, 480, 486

Fiancée, The / Bruden, 409

Fidelio, 365, 377, 409

Fliegende Holländer, Der, 566

Folie, Une, 41, 297

Fortunio's Song, 316

Fra Diavolo, 317, 481

Freischütz, Der, 377, 480, 579

Gazza Ladra, La, 145, 445

Good Fairy, The / Dragedukken, 36

Grande Duchesse de Gérolstein, La, 618

Guerilla Band, The / Guerillabanden, 409

Guillaume Tell, 41, 42, 479, 482, 486, 558, 592

Gustave III, 42, 479, 482

Gustav Vasa, 313, 658

Hans Heiling, 272, 356, 377, 398, 410

Harvest Festival, The / Høstgildet, 444

House for Sale, 313, 314

Huguenots, The / Huguenots, Les / Huguenotterne, 42, 158, 225, 313, 357, 410, 479, 559, 610

Huntsman's Bride, The / Jægerbruden, 99, 313, 314, 316, 331, 356, 397

Iphigenia in Aulis / Iphigenia i Aulis, 365, 379, 409

Iphigenia in Tauris / Iphigenia paa Tauris, 409

Jean de Paris / Johan fra Paris, 360, 409

Jewess, The / La Juive / Jødinden, 42, 225, 357, 377, 479

Joseph and his Brethren / Joseph et ses frères / Joseph og hans Brødre, 102n., 206, 317, 377, 410

Lampe merveilleuse, La, 452

Lanassa, 663

Leonora, see *Favorite, La*

Life for the Tsar, A, 579

Little Kirsten / Liden Kirsten, 357, 383, 409

Little Red Riding Hood / Den lille Rødhætte, 145, 377, 409

Lohengrin, 360, 364, 370, 374, 384, 410, 562, 566–568

Love in the Country / Kjærlighed paa Landet, 424

Lucia di Lammermoor, 43

Lucia of Lammermoor / Lucia af Lammermoor, 316, 409

Lucrezia Borgia, 218, 409

Ludlam's Cave / Ludlams Hule, 145

Lulu, 99

Magic Flute, The / Tryllefløiten, 299, 307, 313, 314, 356, 357, 397, 410, 559, 645

Magic Harp, The / Trylleharpen, 145

Malcontents, The, 313, 314

Maometto II, 480 (*see also Siège de Corinth, Le*)

Martha, 314

Marriage of Figaro, The / Nozze di Figaro / Figaros Bryllup, 44, 304, 313, 314, 315, 377, 404, 410, 445, 447n., 568, 645

Masaniello, 480 (*see also Muette de Portici, La*)

Master Mason, The / Muurmesteren, 313, 314, 321, 357, 409

Mastersingers of Nuremburg, The / Die Meistersinger / Mestersangerne i Nürnberg, 370, 374, 377, 410, 566, 569

Merry Wives of Windsor, The / De muntre Koner i Windsor, 410

Mignon, 611

Moïse, 41, 479, 480

Montano et Stephanie, 331, 445–446

Montecchi, 45

Moses, 410

Mute Girl of Portici, The / La Muette de Portici / Den Stumme i Portici, 75, 232, 314, 316, 409, 475, 479–482

New Landlord, The, 314

OPERAS AND OPERETTAS *(cont.)*

*Night Before the Wedding, The /
Natten før Brylluppet,* 666

Nix, The / Nøkken, 409

Norma, 45, 106, 156

Nouveau Seigneur du Village, Le, 41

Nuns, The / Nonnerne, 99

Nuremburg Doll, The, 313, 316, 317

Nurmahal, 480

Oberon, 313, 316, 524, 550

Oedipe à Colonne, 432

Olympia, 480

Oreste, 46

Orphée aux enfers, 611, 617

Orpheus (Act II), 409

Othello, 508

Painter and the Models, The, 297,
313, 314, 316

Panurge, 432

*Pascha's Daughter, The / Paschaens
Datter,* 356, 360, 409

Pathelin, 385

Paul et Virginie, 68

Peter's Wedding / Peters Bryllup, 444

Petit Chaperon rouge, Le, 41

Philtre, Le, 479

Poliutto, 559

*Postilion of Lonjumeau, The /
Postillonen i Lonjumeau,* 385, 409,
430n.

Pré-aux-Clercs, Le / Klerkevænget,
409

Prétendus, Les, 432

Prince's Trumpeter, The, 314

Profète, Le, 559

Prophet, The, 313, 316, 524

Prova d'un Opera seria, La, 511

Puritani, I, 317

*Queen's Life Guard, The /
Dronningens Livgarde,* 409

Raoul Barbe-Bleue, 641

Raven, The / Ravnen, 409

Rheingold, Das, 566

Rigoletto, 313

*Ring of the Nibelung / Der Ring des
Nibelungen,* 385, 566

Robert de Diable, 26, 42, 105, 106,
479

*Robert of Normandy / Robert af
Normandiet,* 145, 222, 305, 316,
317, 377, 410, 519

Robin des Bois, see Freischütz, Der

Rogneda, 584

*Romilda and Constance / Romilda og
Constance,* 445

Rose de Saint-Flour, La, 617

Rossignol, Le, 432

Saga of Queen Elvira, The, 317

*Secret Marriage, The / Det
hemmelige ægteskab,* 409

Siège de Corinth, Le, 41, 479, 480

Sleeping Draught, The / Sovedrikken,
99, 379

Sonnambula, La, 45

Sordello, 58

Stradella, 313, 314

Straniera, 45, 145

Tancredi, 45, 445

Tannhäuser, 360, 384–385, 410, 566

*Templar and the Jewess, The /
Tempelherren og Jødinden,* 365,
410

Tentation, La, 75

*Three Madmen, The / De tre
Galninger,* 647

Torquato Tasso, see Sordello

*Travelers in China, The /
Kinafarerne,* 444, 646

Triomphe de Trajan, Le, 452

Tristan und Isolde, 566

Troubadour, The / Troubadouren,
313, 314, 371, 377, 404, 410

*Tsar and Carpenter / Czar og
Tømmermand,* 317, 410

Two Days / De to Dage, 36, 377

*Uncle's Wedding Present / Onkels
Brudegave,* 385

Uthal, 410

Vestale, La, 480, 486

Vielka, 229

Villar's Dragoons / Villars Dragoner,
315, 317, 365, 410

Voitures versées, Les, 41

*Wedding at Lake Como, The /
Brylluppet ved Como-Søen,* 409

White Lady, The / Den hvide Dame,

OPERAS AND OPERETTAS *(cont.)*
272, 317, 377, 409
William Tell | Wilhelm Tell, 139, 313,
314, 316, 410
*Youth and Folly | Ungdom og
Galskab,* 297, 357, 367, 393
Zampa, 409
Zémire and Azor | Zemire og Azor,
416
Oppenheimer, Paul, 183n.
Orcagna, 597
Orléans, Duc d', 449, 488
Ørsted, Anders Sandøe, 498
Ørsted, Hans Christian, 442, 631
Oscar I, King of Sweden and Norway,
290, 521, 525
Oscar II, King of Sweden and Norway,
287, 386, 389, 523
Ostade, Adrian van, 192
Østgaard, 202
Ostrovsky, 580
Ouverture (P. Funck), 437
Overskou, Thomas, 147, 165, 166, 309,
321, 325, 345, 351, 358, 361, 381–382,
392, 394, 405, 493, 509, 525
Ovid, 457
Oxenstjerna, Johan Gabriel, 655
Ozerov, 580

Paër, Ferdinando, 444, 647, 648
Paganini, Niccolò, 466
Pajol, General, 434
Paladino, Signor, 596, 598–599
Palfy, Count, 654, 655
Palikao, Comte Charles de, 366
Pallard, 437
Pallerini, Antonia, 21
Pallesen, Consul, 571–572
Palletschek, 579
Paludan-Müller, Frederik, 182, 189,
283, 379, 384, 631, 670
Paran [Parent], Jacques, 186
Paris, *pantomimus,* 13n.
Pasdeloup, Jules Etienne, 558
Pasta, Giuditta, 44, 472
Pätges, Hanne, *see* Heiberg, Johanne
Luise
Patti, Adelina, 573, 580

Patti, Friar General, 540–542
Paul, 621
Paul, Antoine, 24, 46–48, 432, 476
Paul-Ernest, Mme., 580
Paul, Saint, 600, 602
*Paul's Letters to his Kinsfolk [Edward's
Letters]* (Scott), 490
Pauline, Mlle., 39, 40, 619
Paulli, clergyman, 261
Paulli, Holger Simon, 88, 98, 101, 117,
190, 193, 197, 203, 211, 252, 264, 268,
360, 386, 389, 407, 408, 533, 562,
564–569
Paxton, Sir Joseph, 193n.
Pechaček [Pechatscheck], Franz, 661,
662
Pechena, 509
Pechier, 415
Peder Paars (Holberg), 423
Pe'er, Amager farmer, 421
Penco, Rosina, 559
Pepita de Oliva, 274–275, 278, 582
Percier, Charles, 438
Père Duchêne (Jacques-René Hébert),
477
Perfall, Karl von, 566, 568
Pericles, 477, 565
Perlet, 39, 619, 621
Perrot, Jules, 20, 24, 46–48, 83, 216,
220, 459, 530, 553, 560n., 612, 614,
615, 623
Persiani, Fanny, 510
Personalhistorisk Tidsskrift, 429n.
Persuis, Louis de, 407
Peter, Saint, 192, 600, 602, 603
Peter I, the Great, Tsar, 575–576, 579,
585, 588
Petersen, Johanne, 343, 410
Petersen, medallion-maker, 499–500
Petersen, N. M., 350
Petersen, Ove, 500
Petersen, town councillor, 260
Petersen, Wilhelm, 597
Petipa, Lucien, 196n., 533n.
Petipa, Marius, 574, 582–583, 584
Petit, Anatole, 467, 469, 470, 471, 472,
474
Petit, General, 629

Petoletti family, 186
Pettersson, Abraham, 519
Petrov, Ossip Afanassievich, 581n.
Peyronnéide, La (Méry and
　Barthélemy), 489
Peyronnet, Comte Pierre Denis de, 449
Pfalz-Wittelsbach-Zweibrucken, House
　of, 563
Pfeil, Doris, 357, 375
Phidias, 83, 238, 563
Philip II Augustus, King of France, 460,
　461n.
Philip II, King of Spain, 583
Philippe Cauvy, *dit* Philippe, 462, 475
Philippoteaux, 613
Phister, Ludvig, 215, 321, 323–325, 351,
　378, 379, 390, 493, 541, 619
Phrynicus, 117n.
Picard, 321
Pierronet, Mme. Amalie, 580
Pio, Louis, 391
Pius IX, Pope, 600–601, 602, 605
Pixérécourt, Guilbert de, 623

Plays, Vaudevilles, and Other
　Theatrical Spectacles
　*Abandoned Daughter, The | Den
　　forladte Datter,* 416
　A-ing-fo-hi, 397
　Aladdin, 85, 211, 408
　Angelo, Tyran de Padoue, 624
　April Fools, The | Aprilsnarrene,
　　447n.
　As You Like It, 312, 318
　At Sunset, 315, 316
　Auberge des Adrets, L', 623
　Autumn Sun | Efteraarssol, 379
　Avant, pendant et après [*la
　　Révolution*], 621
　Avare, L', 620
　Axel and Valborg | Axel og Valborg,
　　197, 282
　Ball zu Ellerbrunnen, Der, 508
　Bankruptcy, A | En Fallit, 384, 385,
　　386, 391
　Barber of Seville, The, 86n.
　Baths at Dieppe, The, 314, 316

Benefactor's Testament, A, 315
Bertran de Born, 376
*Between the Battles | Mellem
　Slagene,* 397
Biche aux bois, La, 557, 625
Billeting, The, 314
*Bird in the Pear Tree, The | Fuglen i
　Pæretræet,* 664
Bourgeois Gentilhomme, Le, 456
Brothers' Debt, The, 313
Buffon malgré lui, Le, 620
*Burning of Pjaltenborg, The |
　Pjaltenborgs Brand,* 254
Capriciosa, 81, 321
Capture of Miletus, The, 117n.
Cardillac, 402, 623
Carte à payer, La, 619
Cartouche, 402, 623
*Castle in Poitou, The | Slottet i
　Poitou,* 523
Chain, A, 314
Chien de Montargis, Le, 623
Chiffonnier, Le, 402, 624–625
Childless Home, A, 318
Christiane, 379
*Clorinda and Tancred, or The
　Freeing of Jerusalem,* 426
*Comedy of a Genius | Geniets
　Comedie,* 361
Comedy of Errors, A, 154, 315, 316
Comrades, The | Kammeraterne, 324,
　332
*Contest in Cremona, The |
　Væddekampen i Cremona,* 397
Corpus Christi, 318
*Critic and the Animal, The |
　Recensenten og Dyret,* 369
Cup of Tea, A, 318
Cymbeline, 369
Dame aux Camélias, La, 622
Danes in Paris | De Danske i Paris, 73
Daniel Hjort, 154, 302, 312, 317
*Day of the Seven Sleepers |
　Syvsoverdag,* 376
Day Waxes, 154, 302, 316, 317, 526
Debate, The | Debatten, 321
Debt, The, 429

PLAYS, VAUDEVILLES *(cont.)*

Demi-monde, Le, 622

Deportees, The, 318

Deux forçats, Les, 623

Deux précepteurs, Les, 619

Devil's Superior, The | Fandens Overmand, 309, 525

Dido, 640

Diplomat, The, 318

Doctor, The, 314, 315

Doctor Mekara, 318

Doll's House, A, 364n.

Don Carlos, 310

East Side, West Side | Østergade og Vestergade, 324

Ecole des vieillards, L', 38

Engelbrecht and his Dalecarlians, 155, 302, 314, 316, 526

Elves' Hill | Elverhøi, 155, 316, 369 647

Emilia Galotti, 652

Equal Against Equal, 318

Erasmus Montanus, 321

Erik XIV, 302, 526

Evening at Giske, An | En Aften paa Giske, 376

Fall of the Messenians, The, 117n.

Fata Morgana, 80

Ferreol, 402

Filles de Marbre, Les, 622

Fire in the Cloister | Ildløs i Klosteret, 384

Fortunate Shipwreck, The | Det lykkelige Skibbrud, 171, 383

Forward!, 316

Fru Märtha, 526

Funérailles de l'Empereur, Les, 627

Fussbudget, The | Den Stundesløse, 652

Gabrielle, 584

Gageure imprévue, La, 611

Gamin de Paris, Le, 620

Gelosi fortunati, I, 231

Giboyer's Son | Giboyers Søn, 391

Gioacchino, 408

Glass of Water, A | Et Glas Vand, 314, 315, 332

Good Examples, 318

Griseldis, 239

Gustav III, 318

Hakon Jarl, 35, 197, 282, 369, 376, 423

Hamlet, 302, 312, 314, 315, 316, 317, 452

Happiest Children, The | De lykkeligste Børn, 365

Helene, 379

Herman von Unna, 331

Henriette Maréchal, 558

Herr Hummer's 73 Ore, 318

High-Born Guest, A | En høibaaren Gjæst, 397

Honest Folk, 318

Hothouse Flowers, 315, 316

Hunters, The | Jægerne, 332

Imperial Festival at the Kremlin | Keiserfesten paa Kreml, 390, 400

Inconvénients de la diligence, Les, 619

Inseparables, The | De Uadskillelige, 391

Jacob von Tyboe, 321

Jane Eyre, 315

Jean de France, 430

Je fais mes Farces, 619

Jeppe of the Hill | Jeppe paa Bjerget, 451n.

Johanna von Montfaucon, 424

Judgment of Solomon | Salomons Dom, 25, 351, 424, 652

Kabale und Liebe, 426, 567

Kalabalik, The, 526–527

King René's Daughter, 318

Lady Tartuffe, 397

League of Youth, The | De Unges Forbund, 361

Life Is a Dream, 314, 315, 316

Life of the Working Class | Arbeiderliv, 384

Little Shepherd Boy, The | Den lille Hyrdedreng, 25

Locandiera, La, 231

Love at Court | Kjærlighed ved Hoffet, 379

PLAYS, VAUDEVILLES *(cont.)*

Love Without Stockings / *Kjærlighed uden Strømper,* 629

Lying-in Room, The / *Barselstuen,* 166, 170, 361, 379

Macbeth, 259

Mademoiselle de La Seiglière, 611

Mandrin, 402, 624

Maria Stuart, 230–231

Mariage de raison, Le, 621

Marino Faliéro, 624

Marion de Lorme, 624

Marriage of Figaro, The, 86n.

Maskarade, 408, 421

Massimo d'Azeglio, 605

Menteur, Le, 611

Merchant of Venice, The / *Kjøbmanden i Venedig,* 376

Michel et Christine, 621

Michel Perrin, 620

Midsummer Night's Dream, A, 156, 306, 315, 317

Mirra, 230

Misanthrope, Le, 512

Miser, The, 316

Monkey, The / *Abekatten,* 669

Montjoye, 318

Mother and Son / *Moder og Søn,* 365

Moustache, 512

Neighbors, The / *Gjenboerne,* 391

New Fire Uniform, The / *Den nye Branduniform,* 254

Norns, The / *Nornerne,* 352

Old Bachelors / *Gamle Ungkarle,* 402

Ordeal by Fire, The, 216

Order of the Amaranth / *Amaranther-Orden,* 154, 318

Orphelin de la Chine, L', 641

Othello, 268, 314

Palnatoke, 351

Papillonne, La, 310, 316

Paternal Uncle / *Farbror,* 361

Peasant as Judge, The / *Bonden som Dommer,* 416

Père Turlututu, Le, 620

Pernille's Brief Ladyship / *Pernilles korte Frøkenstand,* 389

Petits Braconniers, Les, 617

Pia dei Tolomei, 231

Pied de Mouton, Le, 611

Plus beau jour de la Vie, Le [*Le plus heureux jour de ma Vie*], 508

Political Tinker, The / *Den politiske Kandestøber,* 54, 379

Polyeucte, 559

Poor Man's Tivoli, The / *De Fattiges Dyrehave,* 391

Power of the Coteries, 310

Preciosa, 208, 209, 315, 446

Pretenders, The / *Kongs-Emnerne,* 365

Princess Isabella, or Three Nights at Court / *Prindsesse Isabella eller Tre Aftener ved Hoffet,* 408, 493

Princess of Taranto, The / *Prindsessen af Taranto,* 332

Prologue (Andersen), 170

Providence of Love, The / *Les jeux de l'amour et du hazard,* 316

Quaker and the Danseuse, The / *Qvækeren og Dandserinden,* 182

Queen Bell, 318

Rataplan, 617

Revolt in Russia, The / *Opstanden i Rusland,* 416

Rich Farmer, The, 315

Richard II, 154, 312, 317

Richard Sheridan, 318

Riff-raff / *Pak,* 332

Rivals, The, 314

Robbers, The, 314, 315, 328

Robert Macaire, 624

Roguery of Scapin, The, 318

Roland's Daughter / *Rolands Datter,* 397

Romeo and Juliet, 268

Rosa and Rosita / *Rosa og Rosita,* 316, 376

Saint François, La, 580

Saint Olaf / *Olaf den Hellige,* 408

Savings Bank, The / *Sparekassen,* 321, 326, 391

PLAYS, VAUDEVILLES *(cont.)*

School for Husbands, The, 316

School for Scandal, The, 310, 447n.

Sémiramis, 640

Seven Maids in Uniform, 313

Siège de Saragosse, Le, 627

Siri Brahe, 318

Slanderer, The, 290, 315, 316

Soldiers' Highjinks | Soldaterløjer, 619

Somnambule, La, 436

Son of the Desert | Ørknens Søn, 106

Sons of Edward, The | Edwards Sønner, 332

Statesman and Burgher, 314

Struensee, 313

Suitor's Visit, The, 318

Sulla, 486

Summer Evening, A | En Sommeraften, 669

Sunday on Amager, A | En Søndag paa Amager, 669

Supplice d'une femme, Le, 558, 611

Swordsman from Ravenna, The, 316, 317

Tabarin, 611

Tales of Queen Marguerite | Dronning Marguerites Noveller, 316, 397

Tarn, The | Fjeldsøen, 384

Thirty Years, or The Life of a Gambler | Trente ans, ou la Vie d'un joueur, 40, 624

Three Crispins, The | De tre Crispins, 397

Three Days at Padua | Tre Dage i Padua, 356

Time of Transition | I Overgangstiden, 391

Times Change | Tiderne Skifte, 384, 390

Tony, ou cinq années en deux heures, 618

Torkel Knutson, 154, 302, 315, 316, 526

Tour de Nesle, La, 624

Transformed King, The | Den forvandlede Konge, 397

Treasury Clerk, The | Renteskriveren, 389

True and Untrue | Sandt og Usandt, 376

Two Arm-Rings, The | De to Armringe, 391

Ulla | Ulla skal paa Bal, 99

Vampire, Le, 622

Vanquisher of the Evil One, The, 525 (see also *The Devil's Superior*)

Vétéran, Le, 626

Victorine, ou la nuit porte conseil[s], 81, 622

Vikings of Helgeland | Hærmændene paa Helgeland, 384, 385, 391

Vincent, 618

Viola, 312

Wallenstein's Camp, 511

Warriors of Miklagard, The | Væringerne, 331, 376, 391

Wermlanders, The, 314, 315, 316, 317

White Roses, The | De hvide Roser, 374

Will-o'-the-Wisps | Lygtemænd, 390–391

Winter's Tale, The | Vintereventyr, 356

Woman in White, The, 318

Yelva, 408

Young Han's Daughter, 302, 315, 526

Pleasant Vintage of Till Eulenspiegel, A (Oppenheimer), 183n.

Ploug, Carl, 99, 383, 389, 631

Plutarch, 109, 320

Pochini, Carlotta [Carolina], 220, 223–224, 226, 228, 231–232

Poet's Tree, The (Aug. Bournonville), 664

Polignac, Prince de, 450

Poirson, 621

Polka militaire (Lumbye), 673

Polonaise (Mayseder), 218

Polonaise in E Major (Mayseder), 466

Ponchard, 437, 615

Possart, 567

Potemkin, Prince Grigory, 579

Potier, Charles, 39–40, 324, 619
Poulailler, 624
Poulsen, Emil, 376, 384, 389
Poulsen, Olaf, 379
Pradher, 437
Pram, Christen, 641
Praxiteles, 238, 563
Preisler, Caroline Marie, 652
Price, Amalie, 173, 187, 201, 410
Price, Carl, 400
Price family, 173, 175, 186–187
Price, James, 186
Price, James (the Younger), 187
Price, Johan Adolf, 187
Price, Juliette, 170, 173, 176, 187, 201,
    220–221, 222–223, 224, 226, 232, 342,
    347, 410
Price, Julius, 187, 221, 223, 226, 232,
    410, 592–593
Price, Sophie, 173, 176, 187, 201, 410
Price, Valdemar, 347, 353, 368, 400
Protatius, Saint, 595
Provost, Jean-Baptiste-François, 611
Prume, François, 105, 275
Pylades, 12

Quatremère de Quincey, 438
Quincy, Madame, 440, 461, 462

Rachel [Félix], 39, 230, 611
Racine, Jean, 15
Räder, Corps Commander, 261
Radetzky, Field Marshal, 213
Radina, Lubova, 400, 582
Rafaello, Italian fisherman, 91
Ramel, Baron and Baroness, 519
Rantzau, Daniel, 104
Rantzau, Josias, 192, 252
Rataplan March, 179
Rauch, 563
Ravaillac, François, 435
Raymond, Councillor of State, 224
Rebecca, 134
Recke, Ernst von der, 376
Redern, Hr. von, 508
Reeves, 473

Reicha, Anton Joseph, 437
Reichenberger, Mlle., 611
Riel family, 654
Reissiger, Karl Gottlieb, 147
Rembrandt (Rembrandt Harmens Van
    Rijn), 191, 578
Renard, 580
Requiem (Mozart), 227
Rettich, Julie, 215
Retzsch, Friedrich, A. M., 70, 217
Reuterdal, Archbishop, 528
Reüthersköld, War Minister, 529
Revue des deux Mondes, 571
Revue March of Frederik VI (Du Puy),
    179
Reynard the Fox, 564
Riberhuusmarsch (Frøhlich), 347, 668
Richard I, King of England, 460, 461n.
Richardt, Christian, 631
Riego, Mlle., 389
Righini, General, 90
Rimestad, C. V., 501
Rind, Hans, 36, 445
Rind, Mme., 445
Ring, Ferdinand Edvard, 394
Ristori, Adelaide, 228, 230–231
Roberg, 307
Robert, Léopold, 604
Robespierre, Maximilien François, 435,
    615
Rocca, Pietro, 607
Roed, Jørgen, 540
Rohan, Cardinal de, 478
Romani, Felice, 67
Romanov, Michael, 583, 588
Romantic Ballet in England, The
    (Guest), 168n., 534n.
Romantic Ballet in Paris, The (Guest),
    18n., 168n., 533n., 548n.
Rome à Paris Méry and Barthélemy),
    489
Rome, King of, *see* Napoléon II
Rondo mélodieux (Prume), 105
Rongsted, Ole, 445
Ronzani, Domenico, 216
Roppa, 543

Roqueplan, Camille, 488

Rosa, archaeologist, 604

Rosa, Italian peasant girl, 92

Rosas, Juan Manuel de, 279

Rosas, Manuela, 279

Roscius, Quintus, 12, 154

Rose, Christoffer Pauli, 171

Rosenborg Quadrille (Lumbye), 246–247

Rosenhoff, C. M., 85n.

Rosenkilde, Adolf, 531

Rosenkilde, C. N., 147, 323–325, 326, 327, 493, 620, 647

Rosenkrantz, Geheime-Statsminister, 442

Rosing, Michael, 35, 51, 171, 367, 423–424

Rossini, Gioacchino, 26, 41, 44, 69, 73, 145, 147, 299, 313, 317, 371, 410, 437, 444, 445, 479, 480, 481–482, 508, 544, 558–559, 592, 648

Rothe, gardener, 254

Rothschild, 490

Rousseau, Jean-Jacques, 432, 439, 479

Rovsing, Professor, 631

Rubens, Peter Paul, 192

Rubenstein, 582

Rubini, Giovanni Battista, 45–46, 490, 510, 512

Ruisdael, Jacob van, 578

Runes, The (Holst), 123, 538

Rung, Henrik, 147, 256, 410, 500, 501, 538

Russia in 1839 (Custine), 574n.

Rüthling, 567

Rye, Olaf, 247, 260

Ryge, Johan Christian, 36–38, 41, 53, 147, 149, 171, 321, 322, 324, 364, 390, 423, 424, 426, 445, 493

Ryge, Nathalia, 147

Sacchini, Antonio Maria, 41, 432, 479

Sacco, Antonio, 22, 640, 644

Sachs, Hans, 216, 564

Saint-Aubain, Andreas Nicolai (Carl Bernhard), 631

Saint-Georges, Jules-Henri Vernoy de, 20, 306, 455

Saint-Léon, Arthur, 196n., 306, 560, 611

Saint-Romain, Angelica, 538

Sakuntalā, 196

Sally, 515, 579

Sally, Justitsraad, 253

Salieri, Antonio, 479

Saloman, Siegfried, 410

Salute to August Bournonville (Lumbye), 671

Salute to Norway (Aug. Bournonville), 121–122

Salvo, 93

Samson, 611

Sand, Karl Ludwig, 429

Sangalli, Signora, 593

Saqui, Madame, 625

Sanzio, Raphael, 111–114, 115, 192, 241, 578, 601, 602

Sardou, Victorien, 402, 544n.

Savonarola, 597

Saxo Grammaticus, 484, 631

Scandinavian Quadrille (Lumbye), 673

Schack, E., 261

Schalken, Godfried, 192

Schall, Andreas, 660

Schall, Anna Margrethe, *née* Schleüter, 74, 417, 444, 643, 658–660

Schall, Cathrine Salathé, 646

Schall, Claus, 35, 147, 346, 373, 407, 416, 437, 444, 445, 639, 641, 642, 644–648, 660, 661, 666, 671

Schall, Julius, 648

Schall, Peer, 645, 646, 647

Schall, shoemaker, 644

Scharff, Harald, 169, 353, 371, 380

Scharling, 631

Scheel-Plessen, Count W., 528

Schiller, Johann Christoph Friedrich von, 147, 215, 279, 314, 315, 322, 331, 426, 567

Schiørring, Nils, 426n.

Schleppegrell, Major General F. A., 250, 252

Schleppegrell, Mme., 253

Schlick, Benjamin, 437–438

Schlick, Field Marshal, 213, 438

Schmidt, 245, 258

Schmidt-Phiseldeck, Legationsraad, 669

Schmidten [Smidten], H. G. von, 436

Schneitzhoeffer, Jean-Madeleine, 69, 78, 479

Schnell, Betty, *see* Hennings, Betty

Schock, Signora, 594

Scholl, Anna, *see* Tychsen, Anna

Scholz, Wenzel, 216, 226

Schou, Augusta, 393

Schou, Julie, 393

Schram, Orpheline (Wexschall), 662

Schram, Peter, 375, 662

Schrumpf, Madame, 531

Schulenburg, Count Carl Otto v. d., 87

Schultz, 251

Schulz [Schultz], Johann Abraham Peter, 35, 444, 644, 645

Schwanthaler, Ludwig Michael, 564

Schwartz, 220

Schwarz [Schwartz], Frederik, 35, 171, 423

Schweigaard, A. M., 198

Schyberg, Svante, 518

Scott, Walter, 440, 473, 490, 546

Scribe, Eugène, 19–20, 147, 314, 315, 316, 332, 397, 398, 407, 436, 455, 481, 490, 508, 527, 559, 621, 622

Seebach, Marie, 215

Seneca, 601

Serral, Dolores, 84, 176

Serres, 624

Sevelin, Per Erik, 154, 527

Seyfried, Ignaz Xavier Ritter von, 147

Seymour, Lord, 490

Shakespeare, William, 29, 147, 154, 155, 215, 269, 300n., 301, 306, 312, 314, 315, 316, 317, 318, 329, 330, 331, 356, 359, 369, 376, 403, 408, 466, 470, 473, 484, 512, 642, 643

Sheridan, Richard Brinsley, 314, 447n.

Sherman, General William T., 604n.

Sibbern, Frederik, 631

Siboni, Giuseppe, 445, 648, 663

Siddons, Sarah, 512

Siècle, Le, 612, 653

Siècle de Louis XV (Voltaire), 146

Siegel, 568

Sierov, 584

Sigismund III, King of Poland, 586

Simmons [Simons], Franklin, 604

Simskaya, 582

Simonsen, 561

Simonsen, Niels, 565

Skibsted, 247

Slingeland, Pieter Cornelisz van, 191

Smirnov, 584, 589–590

Smithson, Henrietta, 15, 470

Sobeshchanskaya [Slobetschanskaya], Anna, 584

Sobieski, John, 135

Social-Democraten, 391

Sokolova, Yevgenia, 582

Solman, Magister, 529

Sonne, Jørgen, 98

Söderman, Chorus Master, 299

Sødring, Julie, 325–327, 390

Sontag, Henrietta (Countess Rossi), 43–45, 404, 508, 670

Sophia Wilhelmina, Queen of Sweden, 386

Sophie, Archduchess, 222

Sophie, Queen of Sweden, 523

Sophie Magdalene, Queen of Sweden, 649

Sor, Ferdinando, 66, 69

Søtoft, Nicolai, 147

Soult, Marshal, 434, 490, 510

Souvenir de ton père (Aug. Bournonville), 69n., 549n., 552n.

Spohr, Louis, 661, 662

Spontini, Gaspare Luigi Pacifico, 69, 78, 145, 147, 371, 479, 480, 648

Staël, Madame de, 107n., 664

Stage, Johan Adolf, 424, 445, 493

Stair, Lord, 490

Staudigl, Josef, 227

Steadfast Tin Soldier, The (Andersen), 372

Stedingk, Baron Eugène von, 292–294, 302, 319, 526

Steger, 220, 222
Stehle, Hr. von, 566
Steibelt, Daniel, 642
Stein, Theobald, 389
Steuben, Charles, Baron de, 578
Stillmann, 246
Stillmann, Laura, *née* Stramboe, 169, 343, 368
Stjernström, Edward, 157, 311, 523, 525
Stramboe, Adolf, 168, 303, 520, 548
Stramboe, Edward, 169, 201, 548
Stramboe, Mme., 66
Strandborg, 528
Strauss, Johan (the Elder), 671, 672
Struensee, Johan Frederick, 427n., 541, 649
Sture, Christina Gyllenstjerna, 515
Sture, Sten (the Younger), 515, 636
Suchet, Marshal, 434
Sue, Eugène, 55
Suell, Eva, 530, 551
Suenson, Edward, 263
Suhm, Peter, 423
Sundberg, Johanna Gustafva, 521, 522
Suvarov, Marshal, 400n.
Svedelius, 202
Sven Grathe, King of Denmark, 76, 103
Svensson, 157
Swartz, Edward, 155
Sylvia, 610
Symphony in C Minor (Beethoven), 483–484
Symphony in D Major (Beethoven), 482–483

Taglioni, Amalia, 95n.
Taglioni, Filippo, 78–79, 95, 303, 407, 425, 492
Taglioni, Louise, 538
Taglioni, Marie, 10, 48–49, 78, 170, 175, 303, 425, 435, 450, 455, 459, 476, 491–492, 510, 533
Taglioni, Marie (the Younger), 219, 221, 225
Taglioni, Paul, 95n., 177, 212, 219, 221, 225, 226, 491, 508, 569, 592
Taglioni, Salvatore, 21–22, 71, 538

Taglioni, Sophie, *née* Karsten, 435, 492
Talleyrand-Périgord, Charles Maurice de, 24, 436
Talma, François-Joseph, 15, 38–39, 40, 230, 436, 478, 486, 490, 611, 619
Talvj (Theresa Albertine Luise von Jacob), 613
Tamberlik [Tamburlick], Enrico, 538
Tamburini, Antonio, 510
Tarantella in D Major (Lumbye), 89, 273
Tarpeia, 109
Tasso, Torquato, 444, 607
Tegnér, Esaias, 241, 518
Telegraph Galop (Lumbye), 673
Tell, Wilhelm, 547
Teniers, David, 192
Tenerani, 543
Teresa, Mamsel, 554
Thackeray, William Makepeace, 193
Thales, 138
Theatre Research Studies, 30n., 283n.
Théleur, E. A., 184
Thérèse, Mlle., 590
Thiele, Just Mathias, 205, 210, 237, 239
Thielemann, 258
Thiers, Louis Adolphe, 490, 547
Thierry, 615
Thomas, Ambroise, 317, 611
Thomsen, Christian Jürgensen, 551
Thoresen, Magdalene, 361
Thorberg, Juliette, 342
Thorvaldsen and his Works (Thiele), 237
Thorvaldsen, Bertel, 13, 29, 75n., 82–83, 105, 113, 115, 189, 235–241, 242, 281, 514, 545, 561, 563, 564, 597, 668
Thoughts about Deportment (Mereau), 137
Thrane, shoemaker, 87
Thyra, Princess of Denmark, 179
Tiberii, the, 608
Tiberius, Emperor, 601
Tichatschek, Joseph, 218, 550
Tidemand, Adolf, 201, 205
Tiemroth [Timroth], Christian, 660

Tillisch, F. F. von, 277, 278, 282–286
Times, The, 510
Tintoretto, 594
Titian, 594
Titjens, 220
Titus, Emperor, 110
Toftebjerggaard, 252
Toktamysch, Tatar Kahn, 586
Tomaselli, Antonio, 643
Tomaselli, Vincenzo, *see* Galeotti
Tønnesdatter, Cidse, 418–421
Tønnesen, Weigh-master, 260
Tordenskjold, Peder, 362
Törner, Maria Charlotta, 174, 303, 305, 410, 519, 520, 522
Torp, Corps Commander, 261
Torslow, Olof Ulrik, 154
Toulu, 547
Tousez, Alcide, 620
Tousez (the Elder), 618
Tovelille, 192
Trancard, 457
Traité sur la Légitimité (Malte-Brun), 436
Trebelli-Bettini, Zelia, 404
Treschow family, 204
Treumann, Karl, 216
Trochu, Louis Jules, 366
Troy, 559
Turenne, 628
Tuxen, August, 549n.
Tuxen, Peter Mandrup, 436
Tychsen, Anna, 368, 371, 374, 377, 410

Ugly Duckling, The (Andersen), 664
Ullerup, 252

Valdemar I, King of Denmark, 76–77, 103
Valdemar II, King of Denmark, 198n., 500
Valdemars, the, 135
Vanderburch, E.-L., 617
Van Dyke, Sir Anthony, 192, 578
Variations (Mayseder), 466
Variations militaires (Prume), 105
Van Steen, 191

Van Wiesen, 580
Vasari, Giorgio, 112
Vauban, 628
Vautrin, Mme., 619
Vazem, Yekaterina, 582
Vedel, Anders Sørensen, 631
Velásquez, Diego Rodríguez de Silva y, 578
Vercingetorix, 600
Verdi, Giuseppe, 299, 313, 317, 410, 592
Vereshchagin, Vassili Vassilievich, 578–579
Vernet (actor), 39, 618, 619
Vernet (the younger), 615
Vernet, Carle, 488
Vernet, Horace, 439, 449, 488, 555
Veronese, Paolo, 594
Vertpré, Jenny, 39, 621
Vestris, Armand, 48, 459
Vestris, Auguste, 19, 24, 44, 47, 66, 67, 84, 181, 435, 444, 447, 451, 452, 455–459, 463, 466, 532, 544, 650, 653, 655, 657
Vestris, Gaétan, 18, 455–458, 653
Vestris, Madame, 560
Victor Emmanuel, King, 605
Victoire est à nous, La (Grétry), 627
Victor, Marshal, 434
Victoria, Queen of Great Britain, 490, 509, 510
Vienna, Lorenzo, 232
Viertel, C., 643
Viganò, Onorato, 20
Viganò, Salvatore, 20–21, 642
Vigne, Mme., 580
Vilhelmine, Princess of Denmark, 417
Villèle, Comte Joseph de, 449, 489
Villélaide, La (Méry and Barthélemy), 489
Villemain, 490
Vincent, 462
Vincenzo, winegrower, 538
Virginia, 109
Virginius, 109
Visby, Rector, 500–501
Vitellius, Emperor, 601

Vladimir, Saint, 584
Vogel, Frau, 568
Vogelweide, Walther von der, 564
Voght, Conferentsraad, 538, 539
Volange, 618
Volnys, Madame, *see* Fay, Léontine, 621
Voltaire, François Marie Arouet de, 131, 146, 439, 456, 658

Wagner der Judenfresser, 568
Wagner, Johanna, 212
Wagner, Joseph, 215
Wagner, Richard, 360, 364, 370, 371, 374, 384, 385, 410, 562, 566, 568, 584, 670
Walking Trip to Amager, A (Andersen), 663
Wallin, Archbishop Johan Olof, 518
Wallqvist, Per Erik, 303
Walter, Caroline, 652
Walterstorff [Waltersdorff], Count, 432, 435, 442
Warnstedt, Hans Wilhelm von, 645
Waterloo! Epitre au Général Bourmont (Méry and Barthélemy), 490
Weber, Carl Maria von, 69, 147, 299, 313, 364, 371, 398, 480, 524, 579
Weden, 205, 211, 264
Wegener, 165
Welhaven, Bishop, 422
Welhaven, Johann Sebastian, 198, 201, 422
Wellington, Arthur Wellesley, Duke of, 90, 490, 510
Wergeland, Henrik, 75, 198, 530
Wessel, Johan Herman, 629
Westberg, Maria Charlotta, 371, 372, 377, 400, 410
Wexhal, Thorkild, 660
Wexschall, Frederik Thorkildson, 425, 466, 660–662
Weyse, Christoph Ernst Friedrich, 35, 71, 145, 147, 371, 379, 380, 444, 646, 666
Wiedewelt, Johannes, 659
Wiehe, Carl Wilhelm, 465, 531

Wiehe, Michael, 215, 265, 266, 322, 323, 328, 332, 424
Wiehe, Wilhelm, 203, 375, 424
Wijkander, 154, 318
Wildauer, 220
Wiles, Die (Heine), 20
Wilhelm, Elector, 428, 429
Wilhelm of Hesse, Landgrave, 179, 180, 429
Willisen, 257
Willman, Fru, 391
Wilson, Harriette, 490
Wilster, 260
Winding, August, 273, 408
Windischgrätz, Field Marshal, Prince, 213
Winsløw, Carl, 147, 324–331, 332
Winsløw, Mme., 445
Winther, Christian, 177, 332, 631, 670
Winther, J. F., 186
Wittekind, 551
Wittkow, 245
Witzelius, 302, 397
Woodcut (Winther), 640
Worms, 580
Wouwerman, Philip, 191

Yates, Frederic, 473
Yoldi, Count Alphonso, 494
Young, Charles Mayne, 15
Young, Friedrich, 567
Yvon, Adolphe, 555

Zahlhass [Zahlhas], Johann Baptist von, 429
Zencker, 584
Zinck, Georg, 445
Zinck, Ludvig, 71, 78, 81, 407, 424, 445
Zöllner, Fraulein, 216
Zrza, Christine, 445

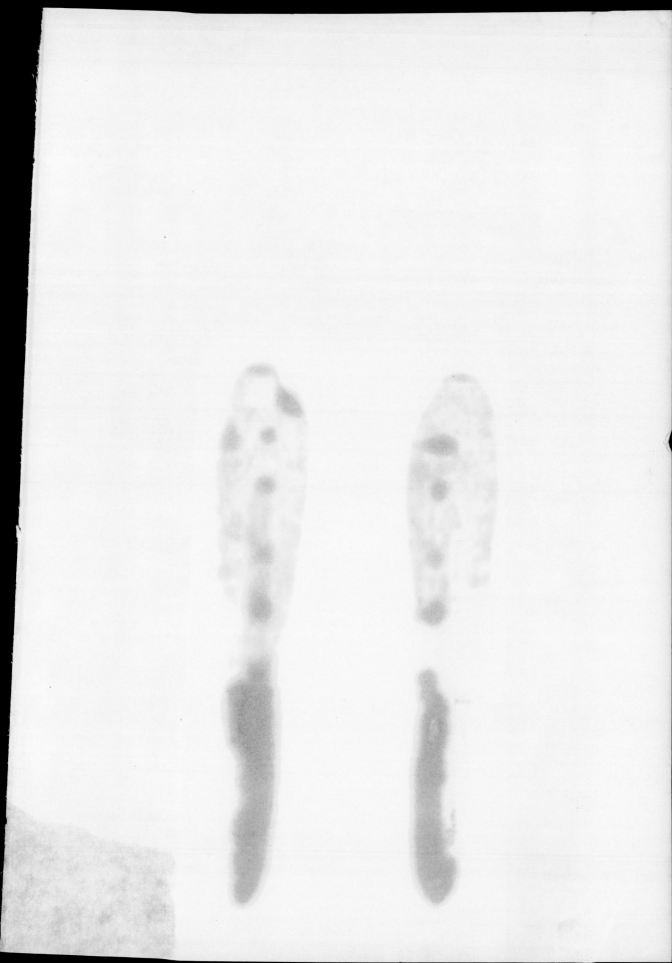

78474

GV
1785
.B64
A3313

Bournonville,
August
    My theatre
life

DATE DUE

NOV 2 0 2006	

Furnald Library
Colby-Sawyer College
New London, New Hampshire

GAYLORD   PRINTED IN U.S.A.